Praise for the Reformation Commentary on Scripture

"Protestant reformers were fundamentally exegetes as much as theologians, yet (except for figures like Luther and Calvin) their commentaries and sermons have been neglected because these writings are not available in modern editions or languages. That makes this new series of Reformation Commentary on Scripture most welcome as a way to provide access to some of the wealth of biblical exposition of the sixteenth and seventeenth centuries. The editor's introduction explains the nature of the sources and the selection process; the intended audience of modern pastors and students of the Bible has led to a focus on theological and practical comments. Although it will be of use to students of the Reformation, this series is far from being an esoteric study of largely forgotten voices; this collection of reforming comments, comprehending every verse and provided with topical headings, will serve contemporary pastors and preachers very well."

Elsie Anne McKee, *Archibald Alexander Professor of Reformation Studies and the History of Worship, Princeton Theological Seminary*

"This series provides an excellent introduction to the history of biblical exegesis in the Reformation period. The introductions are accurate, clear and informative, and the passages intelligently chosen to give the reader a good idea of methods deployed and issues at stake. It puts precritical exegesis in its context and so presents it in its correct light. Highly recommended as reference book, course book and general reading for students and all interested lay and clerical readers."

Irena Backus, *Professeure Ordinaire, Institut d'histoire de la Réformation, Université de Genève†*

"The Reformation Commentary on Scripture is a major publishing event—for those with historical interest in the founding convictions of Protestantism, but even more for those who care about understanding the Bible. As with IVP Academic's earlier Ancient Christian Commentary on Scripture, this effort brings flesh and blood to 'the communion of saints' by letting believers of our day look over the shoulders of giants from the past. By connecting the past with the present, and by doing so with the Bible at the center, the editors of this series perform a great service for the church. The series deserves the widest possible support."

Mark A. Noll, *Professor Emeritus, University of Notre Dame*

"For those who preach and teach Scripture in the church, the Reformation Commentary on Scripture is a significant publishing event. Pastors and other church leaders will find delightful surprises, challenging enigmas and edifying insights in this series, as many Reformational voices are newly translated into English. The lively conversation in these pages can ignite today's pastoral imagination for fresh and faithful expositions of Scripture."

J. Todd Billings, *Gordon H. Girod Research Professor of Reformed Theology, Western Theological Seminary*

"The reformers discerned rightly what the church desperately needed in the sixteenth century—the bold proclamation of the Word based on careful study of the sacred Scriptures. We need not only to hear that same call again for our own day but also to learn from the Reformation how to do it. This commentary series is a godsend!"

Richard J. Mouw, *President Emeritus, Fuller Theological Seminary*

"Like the Ancient Christian Commentary on Scripture, the Reformation Commentary on Scripture does a masterful job of offering excellent selections from well-known and not-so-well-known exegetes. The editor's introductory survey is, by itself, worth the price of the book. It is easy to forget that there were more hands, hearts and minds involved in the Reformation than Luther and Calvin. Furthermore, encounters even with these figures are often limited to familiar quotes on familiar topics. However, the Reformation Commentary helps us to recognize the breadth and depth of exegetical interests and skill that fueled and continue to fuel faithful meditation on God's Word. I heartily recommend this series as a tremendous resource not only for ministry but for personal edification."

Michael S. Horton, *J. G. Machen Professor of Systematic Theology and Apologetics,*
Westminster Seminary, California

"The Reformation was ignited by a fresh reading of Scripture. In this series of commentaries, we contemporary interpreters are allowed to feel some of the excitement, surprise and wonder of our spiritual forebears. Luther, Calvin and their fellow revolutionaries were masterful interpreters of the Word. Now, in this remarkable series, some of our very best Reformation scholars open up the riches of the Reformation's reading of the Scripture."

William H. Willimon, *Professor of the Practice of Christian Ministry, Duke Divinity School*

"The Reformation Scripture principle set the entirety of Christian life and thought under the governance of the divine Word, and pressed the church to renew its exegetical labors. This series promises to place before the contemporary church the fruit of those labors, and so to exemplify life under the Word."

John Webster, *Professor of Divinity, University of St. Andrews[†]*

"Since Gerhard Ebeling's pioneering work on Luther's exegesis seventy years ago, the history of biblical interpretation has occupied many Reformation scholars and become a vital part of study of the period. The Reformation Commentary on Scripture provides fresh materials for students of Reformation-era biblical interpretation and for twenty-first-century preachers to mine the rich stores of insights from leading reformers of the sixteenth century into both the text of Scripture itself and its application in sixteenth-century contexts. This series will strengthen our understanding of the period of the Reformation and enable us to apply its insights to our own days and its challenges to the church."

Robert Kolb, *Professor Emeritus, Concordia Theological Seminary*

"The multivolume Ancient Christian Commentary on Scripture is a valuable resource for those who wish to know how the Fathers interpreted a passage of Scripture but who lack the time or the opportunity to search through the many individual works. This new Reformation Commentary on Scripture will do the same for the reformers and is to be warmly welcomed. It will provide much easier access to the exegetical treasures of the Reformation and will hopefully encourage readers to go back to some of the original works themselves."

Anthony N. S. Lane, *Professor of Historical Theology and Director of Research, London School of Theology*

"This volume of the RCS project is an invaluable source for pastors and the historically/biblically interested that provides unparalleled access not only to commentaries of the leading Protestant reformers but also to a host of nowadays unknown commentaters on Galatians and Ephesians. The RCS is sure to enhance and enliven contemporary exegesis. With its wide scope, the collection will enrich our understanding of the variety of Reformation thought and biblical exegesis."

Sigrun Haude, *Associate Professor of Reformation and Early Modern European History,*
University of Cincinnati

"This grand project sets before scholars, pastors, teachers, students and growing Christians an experience that can only be likened to stumbling into a group Bible study only to discover that your fellow participants include some of the most significant Christians of the Reformation and post-Reformation (for that matter, of any) era. Here the Word of God is explained in a variety of accents: German, Swiss, French, Dutch, English, Scottish and more. Each one vibrates with a thrilling sense of the living nature of God's Word and its power to transform individuals, churches and even whole communities. Here is a series to anticipate, enjoy and treasure."

Sinclair Ferguson, *Senior Minister, First Presbyterian Church, Columbia, South Carolina*

"I strongly endorse the Reformation Commentary on Scripture. Introducing how the Bible was interpreted during the age of the Reformation, these volumes will not only renew contemporary preaching, but they will also help us understand more fully how reading and meditating on Scripture can, in fact, change our lives!"

Lois Malcolm, *Associate Professor of Systematic Theology, Luther Seminary*

"Discerning the true significance of movements in theology requires acquaintance with their biblical exegesis. This is supremely so with the Reformation, which was essentially a biblical revival. The Reformation Commentary on Scripture will fill a yawning gap, just as the Ancient Christian Commentary did before it, and the first volume gets the series off to a fine start, whetting the appetite for more. Most heartily do I welcome and commend this long overdue project."

J. I. Packer, *Board of Governors' Professor of Theology, Regent College*[†]

"There is no telling the benefits to emerge from the publication of this magnificent Reformation Commentary on Scripture series! Now exegetical and theological treasures from Reformation era commentators will be at our fingertips, providing new insights from old sources to give light for the present and future. This series is a gift to scholars and to the church; a wonderful resource to enhance our study of the written Word of God for generations to come!"

Donald K. McKim, *Executive Editor of Theology and Reference, Westminster John Knox Press*

"Why was this not done before? The publication of the Reformation Commentary on Scripture should be greeted with enthusiasm by every believing Christian—but especially by those who will preach and teach the Word of God. This commentary series brings the very best of the Reformation heritage to the task of exegesis and exposition, and each volume in this series represents a veritable feast that takes us back to the sixteenth century to enrich the preaching and teaching of God's Word in our own time."

R. Albert Mohler Jr., *President, The Southern Baptist Theological Seminary*

"Today more than ever, the Christian past is the church's future. InterVarsity Press has already brought the voice of the ancients to our ears. Now, in the Reformation Commentary on Scripture, we hear a timely word from the first Protestants as well."

Bryan Litfin, *Moody Publishers*

"I am delighted to see the Reformation Commentary on Scripture. The editors of this series have done us all a service by gleaning from these rich fields of biblical reflection. May God use this new life for these old words to give him glory and to build his church."

Mark Dever, *Senior Pastor, Capitol Hill Baptist Church, and President of 9Marks.org Ministries*

"Monumental and magisterial, the Reformation Commentary on Scripture, edited by Timothy George, is a remarkably bold and visionary undertaking. Bringing together a wealth of resources, these volumes will provide historians, theologians, biblical scholars, pastors and students with a fresh look at the exegetical insights of those who shaped and influenced the sixteenth-century Reformation. With this marvelous publication, InterVarsity Press has reached yet another plateau of excellence. We pray that this superb series will be used of God to strengthen both church and academy."

David S. Dockery, *Chancellor, Trinity International University*

"Detached from her roots, the church cannot reach the world as God intends. While every generation must steward the scriptural insights God grants it, only arrogance or ignorance causes leaders to ignore the contributions of those faithful leaders before us. The Reformation Commentary on Scripture roots our thought in great insights of faithful leaders of the Reformation to further biblical preaching and teaching in this generation."

Bryan Chapell, *Chancellor and Professor of Practical Theology, Covenant Theological Seminary*

"After reading several volumes of the Reformation Commentary on Scripture, I exclaimed, 'Hey, this is just what the doctor ordered—I mean Doctor Martinus Lutherus!' The church of today bearing his name needs a strong dose of the medicine this doctor prescribed for the ailing church of the sixteenth century. The reforming fire of Christ-centered preaching that Luther ignited is the only hope to reclaim the impact of the gospel to keep the Reformation going, not for its own sake but to further the renewal of the worldwide church of Christ today. This series of commentaries will equip preachers to step into their pulpits with confidence in the same living Word that inspired the witness of Luther and Calvin and many other lesser-known reformers."

Carl E. Braaten, *Cofounder of the Center for Catholic and Evangelical Theology*

"As a pastor, how does one cultivate a knowledge of the history of interpretation? That's where IVP's Reformation Commentary on Scripture and its forerunner, the Ancient Christian Commentary on Scripture, come in. They do an excellent job in helping pastors become more aware of the history of exegesis for the benefit of their congregations. Every pastor should have access to a set of each."

Carl R. Trueman, *Paul Woolley Chair of Church History, Westminster Theological Seminary*

REFORMATION COMMENTARY ON SCRIPTURE

NEW TESTAMENT
I

MATTHEW

EDITED BY
JASON K. LEE AND WILLIAM M. MARSH

GENERAL EDITOR
TIMOTHY GEORGE

ASSOCIATE GENERAL EDITOR
SCOTT M. MANETSCH

An imprint of InterVarsity Press
Downers Grove, Illinois

InterVarsity Press
P.O. Box 1400, Downers Grove, IL 60515-1426
ivpress.com
email@ivpress.com

InterVarsity Press® is the book-publishing division of InterVarsity Christian Fellowship/USA®, a movement of students and faculty active on campus at hundreds of universities, colleges and schools of nursing in the United States of America, and a member movement of the International Fellowship of Evangelical Students. For information about local and regional activities, visit intervarsity.org.

Design: Cindy Kiple
Images: wooden cross: iStockphoto
> *The Protestant Church in Lyon: The Protestant Church in Lyon, called "The Paradise" at Bibliotheque Publique et Universitaire, Geneva, Switzerland. Erich Lessing/Art Resource, NY.*

ISBN 978-0-8308-2964-4 (print)
ISBN 978-0-8308-8015-7 (digital)

Printed in the United States of America ∞

InterVarsity Press is committed to ecological stewardship and to the conservation of natural resources in all our operations. This book was printed using sustainably sourced paper.

Library of Congress Cataloging-in-Publication Data
A catalog record for this book is available from the Library of Congress.

| P | 27 | 26 | 25 | 24 | 23 | 22 | 21 | 20 | 19 | 18 | 17 | 16 | 15 | 14 | 13 | 12 | 11 | 10 | 9 | 8 | 7 | 6 | 5 | 4 | 3 | 2 | 1 |
| Y | 40 | 39 | 38 | 37 | 36 | 35 | 34 | 33 | 32 | 31 | 30 | 29 | 28 | 27 | 26 | 25 | 24 | 23 | 22 | 21 |

From Jason

To those who have influenced my appreciation for reading the Scriptures
and the ancient readers who proceed me—Ken and Sybil, Ronnie and Debbie,
Greg, Sid, Cecil, Scott, Steve, Peter, Paige, John (and his fellow disciples),
my friends who are and have been my colleagues.

From Billy

To Malcolm B. Yarnell III and Jason K. Lee,
two gifted teachers and scholars who were fundamental in igniting
and fanning into flame my love for the Reformation.

Reformation Commentary on Scripture
Project Staff

Project Editor
David W. McNutt

Managing Editor
Elissa Schauer

Copyeditor
Jeffrey A. Reimer

Assistant Project Editor
Scott T. Prather

Editorial and Research Assistants
David J. Hooper
Ashley Davila
April Ponto

Assistants to the General Editors
Evan Musgraves
Bryan Just
Christopher Gow

Design
Cindy Kiple

Design Assistant
Beth McGill

Content Production
Maureen G. Tobey
Daniel van Loon
Jeanna L. Wiggins

Proofreader
Travis Ables

InterVarsity Press

President and Publisher
Terumi Echols

Associate Publisher, Director of Editorial
Cindy Bunch

Editorial Director, IVP Academic
Jon Boyd

Director of Production
Benjamin M. McCoy

CONTENTS

ACKNOWLEDGMENTS

From Jason

No project of this significance happens without teamwork. I would like to acknowledge the encouragement of my coeditor, Billy, before he joined the project, and his scholarly expertise and pastoral impulse after he jumped on board. I am also grateful to Timothy George for his original conversation with me about editing a volume. Scott Manetsch and David McNutt have been indispensable to the completion of the project and to whatever quality it possesses. We are immensely grateful for the excellent service of former and current members of the IVP team who have assisted with translations (Kirk Summers, Amy Alexander, Christina Moss, David Noe, Steven Tyra) or editorial perspective (Joel Scandrett, Michael Gibson, Brannon Ellis, Andre Gazal, Todd Hains, Scott Prather). Along the way, I have been helped at length by my colleagues Ched Spellman and Randy McKinion in many unsung ways. Other friends (Scott Hildreth, Jonathan Watson) have helped with reviewing texts or working on rough spots in translations. As in all things, I am grateful to my wife, Kimberly, and my children (McKayla, Hayden, Graham, Jackson, McKenzie, and Abigail) for their patience with me and the progress of this project.

From Billy

I remain immensely humbled and grateful for the opportunity to join Jason on a project that he had already invested significant time and labor on many years before my involvement. It has been a special privilege to move from spectator to contributor to the excellent work that he had already done. Likewise, I am thankful to Timothy George and Scott Manetsch for their gracious invitation to become a part of the series as a coeditor on this volume. Much gratitude is due David McNutt and his editorial team. They have been a joy to work with, providing tremendous support, resource, and patience throughout each step of the process to bring this project to completion. I also would like to express thanks to my dear friends and colleagues Ched Spellman and Zach Bowden for their constant encouragements to me in both word and prayer while working on this volume. Another good brother for whom I am grateful and with whom I also have the privilege to be colleagues, JR Gilhooly, was a great help on some translations, providing the kind service of his skill in Latin. I would be remiss if I did not acknowledge Kelly Hellwig, my administrative assistant, who has been such a blessing not only in her warm encouragements, but also in helping to find and protect brief windows of time from slipping away in my schedule so that I could effectively turn my attention to this project. Many thanks to our students, past and present, who have shown interest in my and Jason's work on this volume and offered much encouragement. To my wife, Kim, and our children, Wyatt, Logan, and Layla, thank you for your gracious patience with me as the Reformation Commentary has been a constant companion in our home for a little while. Your loving support and sincere enthusiasm for work such as this that I get to do keeps me pressing on.

ABBREVIATIONS

ACCS   Ancient Christian Commentary on Scripture. 29 vols. Edited by Thomas C. Oden. Downers Grove, IL: InterVarsity Press, 1998–2009.

ANF   The Ante-Nicene Fathers. 10 vols. Edited by Alexander Roberts and James Donaldson. Buffalo, NY: Christian Literature, 1885–1896. Available online at www.ccel.org.

AvG   Argula von Grumbach. *Schriften*. Edited by Peter Matheson. Quellen und Forschungen zur Reformationgeschichte 83. Heidelberg: Gütersloher Verlagshaus, 2010.

CNTC   Calvin's New Testament Commentaries. 12 vols. Edited by David W. Torrance and Thomas F. Torrance. Grand Rapids, MI: Eerdmans, 1959–1972.

CO   *Ioannis Calvini Opera Quae Supersunt Omnia*. 59 vols. Corpus Reformatorum 29–88. Ed. G. Baum, E. Cunitz, E. Reuss. Brunswick and Berlin, 1863–1900.

CRR   Classics of the Radical Reformation. 12 vols. Waterloo, ON, and Scottsdale, PA: Herald Press, 1973–.

CTS   Calvin Translation Society edition of Calvin's commentaries. 46 vols. Edinburgh, 1843–1855. Several reprints, but variously bound; volume numbers (when cited) are relative to specific commentaries and not to the entire set.

CWE   *Collected Works of Erasmus*. 86 vols. planned. Toronto: University of Toronto Press, 1969–.

DHB   *The Decades of Henry Bullinger*. Translated by H. I. Edited for the Parker Society by Thomas Harding. Vols. 1–5. Cambridge: University Press, 1852.

DMBI   Donald K. McKim, ed., *Dictionary of Major Biblical Interpreters*. Downers Grove, IL: IVP Academic, 2007.

EEBO   Early English Books Online. Subscription database, eebo.chadwyck.com.

EP   Erasmus. *Paraphrase on Matthew*. Translated and annotated by Dean Simpson. Contributing editor Robert D. Sider. CWE 45. Toronto: University of Toronto Press, 2008.

FC   Fathers of the Church. 127 vols. Washington, DC: Catholic University of America Press, 1947–2013.

JBSW   Johannes Bugenhagen. *Selected Writings*. 2 vols. Edited by Kurt K. Hendel. Minneapolis: Fortress, 2015.

JMG	Juan de Maldonado. *A Commentary on the Holy Gospels: S. Matthew's Gospel.* 2 vols. Translated and edited by George J. Davie. London: John Hodges, 1888.
KSZ	Katharina Schütz Zell. *The Writings: A Critical Edition.* Edited by Elsie McKee. Studies in Medieval and Reformation Thought. Leiden: Brill, 1999.
LB	Desiderius Erasmus. *Desderii Erasmi Roterodami Opera Omnia.* 10 vols. Edited by Jean LeClerc. Leiden: Van der Aa, 1704–1706 [Lugduni Bavatorum]. Reprint, Hildesheim: Georg Olms, 1961–1962.
LCC	John Baillie et al., eds. The Library of Christian Classics. 26 vols. Philadelphia: Westminster, 1953–1966.
LCL	Loeb Classical Library. Edited by Jeffrey Henderson. Cambridge, MA: Harvard University Press, 1911–. Digital copy online at www.loebclassics.com.
LW	*Luther's Works* [= "American Edition"]. 82 vols. planned. St. Louis: Concordia; Philadelphia: Fortress, 1955–1986; 2009–.
NPNF	P. Schaff et al., eds. A Select Library of the Nicene and Post-Nicene Fathers of the Christian Church. 2 series (14 vols. each). Buffalo, NY: Christian Literature, 1887-1894; Reprint, Grand Rapids, MI: Eerdmans, 1952-1956; Reprint, Peabody, MA: Hendrickson, 1994.
MO	*Philippi Melanthonis Opera Quae Supersunt Omnia.* 28 vols. Corpus Reformatorum 1–28. Edited by C. G. Bretschneider. 1834–1860. Reprint, New York: Johnson, 1963.
RCS	The Reformation Commentary on Scripture. Edited by Timothy George and Scott M. Manetsch. 29 vols. projected. Downers Grove, IL: InterVarsity Press, 2010–.
Vg.	Vulgate
WA	*D. Martin Luthers Werke: Kritische Gesamtausgabe.* 66 vols. Weimar: Hermann Böhlaus Nachfolger, 1883–1987.
WATR	*D. Martin Luthers Werke: Kritische Gesamtausgabe: Tischreden.* 6 vols. Weimar: Hermann Böhlaus Nachfolger, 1912–1921.
WJC	*The Works of the Right Reverend Father in God John Cosin, Lord Bishop of Durham.* 5 vols. Oxford: John Henry Parker, 1843–1855.
WRS	*The Complete Works of Richard Sibbes.* 7 vols. Edited by Alexander Balloch Grosart. Edinburgh: James Nichol, 1862–1864.
WWB	*The Works of William Bridge.* 3 vols. London: For Peter Cole, Printing Press in Cornhill, 1654.

A GUIDE TO USING THIS COMMENTARY

Several features have been incorporated into the design of this commentary. The following comments are intended to assist readers in making full use of this volume.

Pericopes of Scripture

The scriptural text has been divided into pericopes, or passages, usually several verses in length. Each of these pericopes is given a heading, which appears at the beginning of the pericope. For example, the first major section in this commentary is Matthew 1:1-17, "The Genealogy of Jesus Christ." This heading is followed by the Scripture passage quoted in the English Standard Version (ESV). The Scripture passage is provided for the convenience of readers, but it is also in keeping with Reformation-era commentaries, which often followed the patristic and medieval commentary tradition, in which the citations of the reformers were arranged according to the text of Scripture.

Overviews

Following each pericope of text is an overview of the Reformation authors' comments on that pericope. The format of this overview varies among the volumes of this series, depending on the requirements of the specific book(s) of Scripture. The function of the overview is to identify succinctly the key exegetical, theological, and pastoral concerns of the Reformation writers arising from the pericope, providing the reader with an orientation to Reformation-era approaches and emphases. It tracks a reasonably cohesive thread of argument among reformers' comments, even though they are derived from diverse sources and generations. Thus, the summaries do not proceed chronologically or by verse sequence. Rather, they seek to rehearse the overall course of the reformers' comments on that pericope.

We do not assume that the commentators themselves anticipated or expressed a formally received cohesive argument but rather that the various arguments tend to flow in a plausible, recognizable pattern. Modern readers can thus glimpse aspects of continuity in the flow of diverse exegetical traditions representing various generations and geographical locations.

Topical Headings

An abundance of varied Reformation-era comment is available for each pericope. For this reason we have broken the pericopes into two levels. First is the verse with its topical heading.

The reformers' comments are then focused on aspects of each verse, with topical headings summarizing the essence of the individual comment by evoking a key phrase, metaphor, or idea. This feature provides a bridge by which modern readers can enter into the heart of the Reformation-era comment.

Identifying the Reformation Authors, Texts, and Events

Following the topical heading of each section of comment, the name of the Reformation commentator is given. An English translation (where needed) of the reformer's comment is then provided. This is immediately followed by the title of the original work.

Readers who wish to pursue a deeper investigation of the reformers' works cited in this commentary will find full bibliographic detail for each Reformation title provided in the bibliography at the back of the volume. Information on English translations (where available) and standard original-language editions and critical editions of the works cited is found in the bibliography. The Biographical Sketches section provides brief overviews of the life and work of each commentator, and each confession or collaborative work, appearing in the present volume (as well as in any previous volumes). Finally, a Timeline of the Reformation offers broader context for people, places, and events relevant to the commentators and their works.

Footnotes and Back Matter

To aid the reader in exploring the background and texts in further detail, this commentary utilizes footnotes. The use and content of footnotes may vary among the volumes in this series. Where footnotes appear, a footnote number directs the reader to a note at the bottom of the page, where one will find annotations (clarifications or biblical cross references), information on English translations (where available) or standard original-language editions of the work cited.

Where original-language texts have remained untranslated into English, we provide new translations. Where there is any serious ambiguity or textual problem in the selection, we have tried to reflect the best available textual tradition. Wherever current English translations are already well rendered, they are utilized, but where necessary they are stylistically updated. A single asterisk (*) indicates that a previous English translation has been updated to modern English or amended for easier reading. We have standardized spellings and made grammatical variables uniform so that our English references will not reflect the linguistic oddities of the older English translations. For ease of reading we have in some cases removed superfluous conjunctions.

GENERAL INTRODUCTION

The Reformation Commentary on Scripture (RCS) is a twenty-eight-volume series of exegetical comment covering the entire Bible and gathered from the writings of sixteenth-century preachers, scholars and reformers. The RCS is intended as a sequel to the highly acclaimed Ancient Christian Commentary on Scripture (ACCS), and as such its overall concept, method, format, and audience are similar to the earlier series. Both series are committed to the renewal of the church through careful study and meditative reflection on the Old and New Testaments, the charter documents of Christianity, read in the context of the worshiping, believing community of faith across the centuries. However, the patristic and Reformation eras are separated by nearly a millennium, and the challenges of reading Scripture with the reformers require special attention to their context, resources and assumptions. The purpose of this general introduction is to present an overview of the context and process of biblical interpretation in the age of the Reformation.

Goals

The Reformation Commentary on Scripture seeks to introduce its readers to the depth and richness of exegetical ferment that defined the Reformation era. The RCS has four goals: the enrichment of contemporary biblical interpretation through exposure to Reformation-era biblical exegesis; the renewal of contemporary preaching through exposure to the biblical insights of the Reformation writers; a deeper understanding of the Reformation itself and the breadth of perspectives represented within it; and a recovery of the profound integration of the life of faith and the life of the mind that should characterize Christian scholarship. Each of these goals requires a brief comment.

Renewing contemporary biblical interpretation. During the past half-century, biblical hermeneutics has become a major growth industry in the academic world. One of the consequences of the historical-critical hegemony of biblical studies has been the privileging of contemporary philosophies and ideologies at the expense of a commitment to the Christian church as the primary reading community within which and for which biblical exegesis is done. Reading Scripture with the church fathers and the reformers is a corrective to all such imperialism of the present. One of the greatest skills required for a fruitful interpretation of the Bible is the ability to listen. We rightly emphasize the importance of listening to the voices of contextual theologies today, but in doing so we often marginalize or ignore another crucial context—the community of believing Christians through the centuries. The serious study of Scripture requires more than the latest

Bible translation in one hand and the latest commentary (or niche study Bible) in the other. John L. Thompson has called on Christians today to practice the art of "reading the Bible with the dead."[1] The RCS presents carefully selected comments from the extant commentaries of the Reformation as an encouragement to more in-depth study of this important epoch in the history of biblical interpretation.

Strengthening contemporary preaching. The Protestant reformers identified the public preaching of the Word of God as an indispensible means of grace and a sure sign of the true church. Through the words of the preacher, the living voice of the gospel (*viva vox evangelii*) is heard. Luther famously said that the church is not a "pen house" but a "mouth house."[2] The Reformation in Switzerland began when Huldrych Zwingli entered the pulpit of the Grossmünster in Zurich on January 1, 1519, and began to preach a series of expositional sermons chapter by chapter from the Gospel of Matthew. In the following years he extended this homiletical approach to other books of the Old and New Testaments. Calvin followed a similar pattern in Geneva. Many of the commentaries represented in this series were either originally presented as sermons or were written to support the regular preaching ministry of local church pastors. Luther said that the preacher should be a *bonus textualis*—a good one with a text—well-versed in the Scriptures. Preachers in the Reformation traditions preached not only about the Bible but also from it, and this required more than a passing acquaintance with its contents. Those who have been charged with the office of preaching in the church today can find wisdom and insight—and fresh perspectives—in the sermons of the Reformation and the biblical commentaries read and studied by preachers of the sixteenth century.

Deepening understanding of the Reformation. Some scholars of the sixteenth century prefer to speak of the period they study in the plural, the European Reformations, to indicate that many diverse impulses for reform were at work in this turbulent age of transition from medieval to modern times.[3] While this point is well taken, the RCS follows the time-honored tradition of using *Reformation* in the singular form to indicate not only a major moment in the history of Christianity in the West but also, as Hans J. Hillerbrand has put it, "an essential cohesiveness in the heterogeneous pursuits of religious reform in the sixteenth century."[4] At the same time, in developing guidelines to assist the volume editors in making judicious selections from the vast amount of commentary material available in this period, we have stressed the multifaceted character of the Reformation across many confessions, theological orientations, and political settings.

Advancing Christian scholarship. By assembling and disseminating numerous voices from such a signal period as the Reformation, the RCS aims to make a significant contribution to the ever-growing stream of Christian scholarship. The post-Enlightenment split between the study of the Bible as an academic discipline and the reading of the Bible as spiritual nurture was foreign

---

[1] John L. Thompson, *Reading the Bible with the Dead* (Grand Rapids: Eerdmans, 2007).
[2] WA 10,2:48.
[3] See Carter Lindberg, *The European Reformations*, 2nd ed. (Malden, MA: Wiley-Blackwell, 2010).
[4] Hans J. Hillerbrand, *The Division of Christendom* (Louisville, KY: Westminster John Knox, 2007), x. Hillerbrand has also edited the standard reference work in Reformation studies, *OER*. See also Diarmaid MacCulloch, *The Reformation* (New York: Viking, 2003), and Patrick Collinson, *The Reformation: A History* (New York: Random House, 2004).

to the reformers. For them the study of the Bible was transformative at the most basic level of the human person: *coram deo*.

The reformers all repudiated the idea that the Bible could be studied and understood with dispassionate objectivity, as a cold artifact from antiquity. Luther's famous Reformation break-through triggered by his laborious study of the Psalms and Paul's letter to the Romans is well known, but the experience of Cambridge scholar Thomas Bilney was perhaps more typical. When Erasmus's critical edition of the Greek New Testament was published in 1516, it was accompanied by a new translation in elegant Latin. Attracted by the classical beauty of Erasmus's Latin, Bilney came across this statement in 1 Timothy 1:15: "Christ Jesus came into the world to save sinners." In the Greek this sentence is described as *pistos ho logos*, which the Vulgate had rendered *fidelis sermo*, "a faithful saying." Erasmus chose a different word for the Greek *pistos—certus*, "sure, cer-tain." When Bilney grasped the meaning of this word applied to the announcement of salvation in Christ, he tells us that "immediately, I felt a marvellous comfort and quietness, insomuch as 'my bruised bones leaped for joy.'"[5]

Luther described the way the Bible was meant to function in the minds and hearts of believers when he reproached himself and others for studying the nativity narrative with such cool unconcern:

> I hate myself because when I see Christ laid in the manger or in the lap of his mother and hear the angels sing, my heart does not leap into flame. With what good reason should we all despise our-selves that we remain so cold when this word is spoken to us, over which everyone should dance and leap and burn for joy! We act as though it were a frigid historical fact that does not smite our hearts, as if someone were merely relating that the sultan has a crown of gold.[6]

It was a core conviction of the Reformation that the careful study and meditative listening to the Scriptures, what the monks called *lectio divina*, could yield transformative results for *all* of life. The value of such a rich commentary, therefore, lies not only in the impressive volume of Reforma-tion-era voices that are presented throughout the course of the series but in the many particular fields for which their respective lives and ministries are relevant. The Reformation is consequential for historical studies, both church as well as secular history. Biblical and theological studies, to say nothing of pastoral and spiritual studies, also stand to benefit and progress immensely from re-newed engagement today, as mediated through the RCS, with the reformers of yesteryear.

Perspectives

In setting forth the perspectives and parameters of the RCS, the following considerations have proved helpful.

Chronology. When did the Reformation begin, and how long did it last? In some traditional accounts, the answer was clear: the Reformation began with the posting of Luther's *Ninety-five*

---

[5]John Foxe, *The Acts and Monuments of John Foxe: A New and Complete Edition*, 8 vols., ed. Stephen Reed Cattley (London: R. B. Seeley & W. Burnside, 1837), 4:635; quoting Ps 51:8; cited in A. G. Dickens, *The English Reformation*, 2nd ed. (University Park, PA: The Pennsylvannia State University Press, 1991), 102.

[6]WA 49:176-77, quoted in Roland Bainton, "The Bible in the Reformation," in *CHB*, 3:23.

Theses at Wittenberg in 1517 and ended with the death of Calvin in Geneva in 1564. Apart from reducing the Reformation to a largely German event with a side trip to Switzerland, this perspective fails to do justice to the important events that led up to Luther's break with Rome and its many reverberations throughout Europe and beyond. In choosing commentary selections for the RCS, we have adopted the concept of the long sixteenth century, say, from the late 1400s to the mid-seventeenth century. Thus we have included commentary selections from early or pre-Reformation writers such as John Colet and Jacques Lefèvre d'Étaples to seventeenth-century figures such as Henry Ainsworth and Johann Gerhard.

Confession. The RCS concentrates primarily, though not exclusively, on the exegetical writings of the Protestant reformers. While the ACCS provided a compendium of key consensual exegetes of the early Christian centuries, the Catholic/Protestant confessional divide in the sixteenth century tested the very idea of consensus, especially with reference to ecclesiology and soteriology. While many able and worthy exegetes faithful to the Roman Catholic Church were active during this period, this project has chosen to include primarily those figures that represent perspectives within the Protestant Reformation. For this reason we have not included comments on the apocryphal or deuterocanonical writings.

We recognize that "Protestant" and "Catholic" as contradistinctive labels are anachronistic terms for the early decades of the sixteenth century before the hardening of confessional identities surrounding the Council of Trent (1545–1563). Protestant figures such as Philipp Melanchthon, Johannes Oecolampadius and John Calvin were all products of the revival of sacred letters known as biblical humanism. They shared an approach to biblical interpretation that owed much to Desiderius Erasmus and other scholars who remained loyal to the Church of Rome. Careful comparative studies of Protestant and Catholic exegesis in the sixteenth century have shown surprising areas of agreement when the focus was the study of a particular biblical text rather than the standard confessional debates.

At the same time, exegetical differences among the various Protestant groups could become strident and church-dividing. The most famous example of this is the interpretive impasse between Luther and Zwingli over the meaning of "This is my body" (Mt 26:26) in the words of institution. Their disagreement at the Colloquy of Marburg in 1529 had important christological and pastoral implications, as well as social and political consequences. Luther refused fellowship with Zwingli and his party at the end of the colloquy; in no small measure this bitter division led to the separate trajectories pursued by Lutheran and Reformed Protestantism to this day. In Elizabethan England, Puritans and Anglicans agreed that "Holy Scripture containeth all things necessary to salvation: so that whatsoever is not read therein, nor may be proved thereby, is not to be required of any man" (article 6 of the Thirty-Nine Articles of Religion), yet on the basis of their differing interpretations of the Bible they fought bitterly over the structures of the church, the clothing of the clergy and the ways of worship. On the matter of infant baptism, Catholics and Protestants alike agreed on its propriety, though there were various theories as to how a practice not mentioned in the Bible could be justified biblically. The Anabaptists were outliers on this subject. They rejected infant baptism altogether. They appealed to the example of the baptism of Jesus and to his final words as recorded in the Gospel of Matthew (Mt 28:19-20): "Go therefore, and make disciples of all nations, baptizing them in the name of the Father, and of the Son, and of the Holy Spirit, teaching them to observe all that I have commanded you." New Testament Christians, they argued, are to follow not only the commands of Jesus in the Great Commission, but also the exact order in which they were given: evangelize, baptize, catechize.

These and many other differences of interpretation among the various Protestant groups are reflected in their many sermons, commentaries and public disputations. In the RCS, the volume editors' introduction to each volume is intended to help the reader understand the nature and significance of doctrinal conversations and disputes that resulted in particular, and frequently clashing, interpretations. Footnotes throughout the text will be provided to explain obscure references, unusual expressions and other matters that require special comment. Volume editors have chosen comments on the Bible across a wide range of sixteenth-century confessions and schools of interpretation: biblical humanists, Lutheran, Reformed, Anglican, Puritan, and Anabaptist. We have not pursued passages from post-Tridentine Catholic authors or from radical spiritualists and antitrinitarian writers, though sufficient material is available from these sources to justify another series.

Format. The design of the RCS is intended to offer reader-friendly access to these classic texts. The availability of digital resources has given access to a huge residual database of sixteenth-century exegetical comment hitherto available only in major research universities and rare book collections. The RCS has benefited greatly from online databases such as Alexander Street Press's Digital Library of Classical Protestant Texts (DLCPT) and Early English Books Online as well as freely accessible databases like the Post-Reformation Digital Library (prdl.org). Through the help of RCS editorial advisor Herman Selderhuis, we have also had access to the special Reformation collections of the Johannes a Lasco Bibliothek in Emden, Germany. In addition, modern critical editions and translations of Reformation sources have been published over the past generation. Original translations of Reformation sources are given unless an acceptable translation already exists.

Each volume in the RCS will include an introduction by the volume editor placing that portion of the canon within the historical context of the Protestant Reformation and presenting a summary of the theological themes, interpretive issues and reception of the particular book(s). The commentary itself consists of particular pericopes identified by a pericope heading; the biblical text in the English Standard Version (ESV), with significant textual variants registered in the footnotes; an overview of the pericope in which principal exegetical and theological concerns of the Reformation writers are succinctly noted; and excerpts from the Reformation writers identified by name according to the conventions of the *Oxford Encyclopedia of the Reformation*. Each volume will also include a bibliography of sources cited, as well as an appendix of authors and source works.

The Reformation era was a time of verbal as well as physical violence, and this fact has presented a challenge for this project. Without unduly sanitizing the texts, where they contain anti-Semitic, sexist or inordinately polemical rhetoric, we have not felt obliged to parade such comments either. We have noted the abridgement of texts with ellipses and an explanatory footnote. While this procedure would not be valid in the critical edition of such a text, we have deemed it appropriate in a series whose primary purpose is pastoral and devotional. When translating *homo* or similar terms that refer to the human race as a whole or to individual persons without reference to gender, we have used alternative English expressions to the word *man* (or derivative constructions that formerly were used generically to signify humanity at large), whenever such substitutions can be made without producing an awkward or artificial construction.

As is true in the ACCS, we have made a special effort where possible to include the voices of women, though we acknowledge the difficulty of doing so for the early modern period when for a variety of social and cultural reasons few theological and biblical works were published by women. However, recent scholarship has focused on a number of female leaders whose literary remains show us how they understood and interpreted the Bible. Women who made significant contributions to the Reformation include Marguerite d'Angoulême, sister of King Francis I, who supported French reformist evangelicals including Calvin and who published a religious poem influenced by Luther's theology, *The Mirror of the Sinful Soul*; Argula von Grumbach, a Bavarian noblewoman who defended the teachings of Luther and Melanchthon before the theologians of the University of Ingolstadt; Katharina Schütz Zell, the wife of a former priest, Matthias Zell, and a remarkable reformer in her own right—she conducted funerals, compiled hymnbooks, defended the downtrodden, and published a defense of clerical marriage as well as composing works of consolation on divine comfort and pleas for the toleration of Anabaptists and Catholics alike; and Anne Askew, a Protestant martyr put to death in 1546 after demonstrating remarkable biblical prowess in her examinations by church officials. Other echoes of faithful women in the age of the Reformation are found in their letters, translations, poems, hymns, court depositions, and martyr records.

Lay culture, learned culture. In recent decades, much attention has been given to what is called "reforming from below," that is, the expressions of religious beliefs and churchly life that characterized the popular culture of the majority of the population in the era of the Reformation. Social historians have taught us to examine the diverse pieties of townspeople and city folk, of rural religion and village life, the emergence of lay theologies, and the experiences of women in the religious tumults of Reformation Europe.[7] Formal commentaries by their nature are artifacts of learned culture. Almost all of them were written in Latin, the lingua franca of learned discourse well past the age of the Reformation. Biblical commentaries were certainly not the primary means by which the Protestant Reformation spread so rapidly across wide sectors of sixteenth-century society. Small pamphlets and broadsheets, later called *Flugschriften* ("flying writings"), with their graphic woodcuts and cartoon-like depictions of Reformation personalities and events, became the means of choice for mass communication in the early age of printing. Sermons and works of devotion were also printed with appealing visual aids. Luther's early writings were often accompanied by drawings and sketches from Lucas Cranach and other artists. This was done "above all for the sake of children and simple folk," as Luther

---

[7]See Peter Matheson, ed., *Reformation Christianity* (Minneapolis: Fortress, 2007).

put it, "who are more easily moved by pictures and images to recall divine history than through mere words or doctrines."[8]

We should be cautious, however, in drawing too sharp a distinction between learned and lay culture in this period. The phenomenon of preaching was a kind of verbal bridge between scholars at their desks and the thousands of illiterate or semiliterate listeners whose views were shaped by the results of Reformation exegesis. According to contemporary witness, more than one thousand people were crowding into Geneva to hear Calvin expound the Scriptures every day.[9] An example of how learned theological works by Reformation scholars were received across divisions of class and social status comes from Lazare Drilhon, an apothecary of Toulon. He was accused of heresy in May 1545 when a cache of prohibited books was found hidden in his garden shed. In addition to devotional works, the French New Testament and a copy of Calvin's Genevan liturgy, there was found a series of biblical commentaries, translated from the Latin into French: Martin Bucer's on Matthew, François Lambert's on the Apocalypse and one by Oecolampadius on 1 John.[10] Biblical exegesis in the sixteenth century was not limited to the kind of full-length commentaries found in Drilhon's shed. Citations from the Bible and expositions of its meaning permeate the extant literature of sermons, letters, court depositions, doctrinal treatises, records of public disputations and even last wills and testaments. While most of the selections in the RCS will be drawn from formal commentary literature, other sources of biblical reflection will also be considered.

Historical Context

The medieval legacy. On October 18, 1512, the degree *Doctor in Biblia* was conferred on Martin Luther, and he began his career as a professor in the University of Wittenberg. As is well known, Luther was also a monk who had taken solemn vows in the Augustinian Order of Hermits at Erfurt. These two settings—the university and the monastery—both deeply rooted in the Middle Ages, form the background not only for Luther's personal vocation as a reformer but also for the history of the biblical commentary in the age of the Reformation. Since the time of the Venerable Bede (d. 735), sometimes called "the last of the Fathers," serious study of the Bible had taken place primarily in the context of cloistered monasteries. The Rule of St. Benedict brought together *lectio* and *meditatio*, the knowledge of letters and the life of prayer. The liturgy was the medium through which the daily reading of the Bible, especially the Psalms, and the sayings of the church fathers came together in the spiritual formation of the monks.[11] Essential to this understanding was a belief in the unity of the people of God throughout time as well as space, and an awareness that life in this world was a preparation for the beatific vision in the next.

---

[8]Martin Luther, "Personal Prayer Book," LW 43:42-43* (WA 10,2:458); quoted in R. W. Scribner, *For the Sake of Simple Folk: Popular Propaganda for the German Reformation* (Cambridge: Cambridge University Press, 1981), xi.

[9]Letter of De Beaulieu to Guillaume Farel (1561) in *Theodor Beza nach handschriftlichen und anderen gleichzeitigen Quellen*, ed. J. W. Baum (Leipzig: Weidmann, 1851), 2:92.

[10]Francis Higman, "A Heretic's Library: The Drilhon Inventory" (1545), in Francis Higman, *Lire et Découvire: la circulation des idées au temps de la Réforme* (Geneva: Droz, 1998), 65-85.

[11]See the classic study by Jean Leclercq, *The Love of Learning and the Desire for God* (New York: Fordham University Press, 1961).

The source of theology was the study of the sacred page (*sacra pagina*); its object was the accumulation of knowledge not for its own sake but for the obtaining of eternal life. For these monks, the Bible had God for its author, salvation for its end and unadulterated truth for its matter, though they would not have expressed it in such an Aristotelian way. The medieval method of interpreting the Bible owed much to Augustine's *On Christian Doctrine*. In addition to setting forth a series of rules (drawn from an earlier work by Tyconius), Augustine stressed the importance of distinguishing the literal and spiritual or allegorical senses of Scripture. While the literal sense was not disparaged, the allegorical was valued because it enabled the believer to obtain spiritual benefit from the obscure places in the Bible, especially in the Old Testament. For Augustine, as for the monks who followed him, the goal of scriptural exegesis was freighted with eschatological meaning; its purpose was to induce faith, hope, and love and so to advance in one's pilgrimage toward that city with foundations (see Heb 11:10).

Building on the work of Augustine and other church fathers going back to Origen, medieval exegetes came to understand Scripture as possessed of four possible meanings, the famous *quadriga*. The literal meaning was retained, of course, but the spiritual meaning was now subdivided into three senses: the allegorical, the moral, and the anagogical. Medieval exegetes often referred to the four meanings of Scripture in a popular rhyme:

> The letter shows us what God and our fathers did;
> The allegory shows us where our faith is hid;
> The moral meaning gives us rules of daily life;
> The anagogy shows us where we end our strife.[12]

In this schema, the three spiritual meanings of the text correspond to the three theological virtues: faith (allegory), hope (anagogy), and love (the moral meaning). It should be noted that this way of approaching the Bible assumed a high doctrine of scriptural inspiration: the multiple meanings inherent in the text had been placed there by the Holy Spirit for the benefit of the people of God. The biblical justification for this method went back to the apostle Paul, who had used the words *allegory* and *type* when applying Old Testament events to believers in Christ (Gal 4:21-31; 1 Cor 10:1-11). The problem with this approach was knowing how to relate each of the four senses to one another and how to prevent Scripture from becoming a nose of wax turned this way and that by various interpreters. As G. R. Evans explains, "Any interpretation which could be put upon the text and was in keeping with the faith and edifying, had the warrant of God himself, for no human reader had the ingenuity to find more than God had put there."[13]

With the rise of the universities in the eleventh century, theology and the study of Scripture moved from the cloister into the classroom. Scripture and the Fathers were still important, but they came to function more as footnotes to the theological questions debated in the schools and brought together in an impressive systematic way in works such as Peter Lombard's *Books of Sentences* (the standard theology textbook of the Middle Ages) and the great scholastic *summae* of the thirteenth

---

[12]Robert M. Grant, *A Short History of the Interpretation of the Bible* (New York: Macmillan, 1963), 119. A translation of the well-known Latin quatrain: *Littera gesta docet/Quid credas allegoria/Moralis quid agas/Quo tendas anagogia.*

[13]G. R. Evans, *The Language and Logic of the Bible: The Road to Reformation* (Cambridge: Cambridge University Press, 1985), 42.

century. Indispensable to the study of the Bible in the later Middle Ages was the *Glossa ordinaria*, a collection of exegetical opinions by the church fathers and other commentators. Heiko Oberman summarized the transition from devotion to dialectic this way: "When, due to the scientific revolution of the twelfth century, Scripture became the *object* of study rather than the *subject* through which God speaks to the student, the difference between the two modes of speaking was investigated in terms of the texts themselves rather than in their relation to the recipients."[14] It was possible, of course, to be both a scholastic theologian and a master of the spiritual life. Meister Eckhart, for example, wrote commentaries on the Old Testament in Latin and works of mystical theology in German, reflecting what had come to be seen as a division of labor between the two.

An increasing focus on the text of Scripture led to a revival of interest in its literal sense. The two key figures in this development were Thomas Aquinas (d. 1274) and Nicholas of Lyra (d. 1340). Thomas is best remembered for his *Summa Theologiae*, but he was also a prolific commentator on the Bible. Thomas did not abandon the multiple senses of Scripture but declared that all the senses were founded on one—the literal—and this sense eclipsed allegory as the basis of sacred doctrine. Nicholas of Lyra was a Franciscan scholar who made use of the Hebrew text of the Old Testament and quoted liberally from works of Jewish scholars, especially the learned French rabbi Salomon Rashi (d. 1105). After Aquinas, Lyra was the strongest defender of the literal, historical meaning of Scripture as the primary basis of theological disputation. His *Postilla*, as his notes were called—the abbreviated form of *post illa verba textus*, meaning "after these words from Scripture"—were widely circulated in the late Middle Ages and became the first biblical commentary to be printed in the fifteenth century. More than any other commentator from the period of high scholasticism, Lyra and his work were greatly valued by the early reformers. According to an old Latin pun, *Nisi Lyra lyrasset, Lutherus non saltasset.* "If Lyra had not played his lyre, Luther would not have danced."[15] While Luther was never an uncritical disciple of any teacher, he did praise Lyra as a good Hebraist and quoted him more than one hundred times in his lectures on Genesis, where he declared, "I prefer him to almost all other interpreters of Scripture."[16]

Sacred philology. The sixteenth century has been called a golden age of biblical interpretation, and it is a fact that the age of the Reformation witnessed an explosion of commentary writing unparalleled in the history of the Christian church. Kenneth Hagen has cataloged forty-five commentaries on Hebrews between 1516 (Erasmus) and 1598 (Beza).[17] During the sixteenth century, more than seventy new commentaries on Romans were published, five of them by Melanchthon alone, and nearly one hundred commentaries on the Bible's prayer book, the Psalms.[18] There were two developments in the fifteenth century that presaged this development and without which it

---

[14]Heiko Oberman, *Forerunners of the Reformation* (Philadelphia: Fortress, 1966), 284.

[15]Nicholas of Lyra, *The Postilla of Nicolas of Lyra on the Song of Songs*, trans. and ed. James George Kiecker (Milwaukee: Marquette University Press, 1998), 19.

[16]LW 2:164 (WA 42:377).

[17]Kenneth Hagen, *Hebrews Commenting from Erasmus to Bèze, 1516–1598* (Tübingen: Mohr, 1981).

[18]R. Gerald Hobbs, "Biblical Commentaries," *OER* 1:167-71. See in general David C. Steinmetz, ed., *The Bible in the Sixteenth Century* (Durham: Duke University Press, 1990).

could not have taken place: the invention of printing and the rediscovery of a vast store of ancient learning hitherto unknown or unavailable to scholars in the West.

It is now commonplace to say that what the computer has become in our generation, the printing press was to the world of Erasmus, Luther, and other leaders of the Reformation. Johannes Gutenberg, a goldsmith by trade, developed a metal alloy suitable for type and a machine that would allow printed characters to be cast with relative ease, placed in even lines of composition and then manipulated again and again, making possible the mass production of an unbelievable number of texts. In 1455, the Gutenberg Bible, the masterpiece of the typographical revolution, was published at Mainz in double columns in gothic type. Forty-seven copies of the beautiful Gutenberg Bible are still extant, each consisting of more than one thousand colorfully illuminated and impeccably printed pages. What began at Gutenberg's print shop in Mainz on the Rhine River soon spread, like McDonald's or Starbucks in our day, into every nook and cranny of the known world. Printing presses sprang up in Rome (1464), Venice (1469), Paris (1470), the Netherlands (1471), Switzerland (1472), Spain (1474), England (1476), Sweden (1483), and Constantinople (1490). By 1500, these and other presses across Europe had published some twenty-seven thousand titles, most of them in Latin. Erasmus once compared himself with an obscure preacher whose sermons were heard by only a few people in one or two churches while his books were read in every country in the world. Erasmus was not known for his humility, but in this case he was simply telling the truth.[19]

The Italian humanist Lorenzo Valla (d. 1457) died in the early dawn of the age of printing, but his critical and philological studies would be taken up by others who believed that genuine reform in church and society could come about only by returning to the wellsprings of ancient learning and wisdom—*ad fontes*, "back to the sources!" Valla is best remembered for undermining a major claim made by defenders of the papacy when he proved by philological research that the so-called Donation of Constantine, which had bolstered papal assertions of temporal sovereignty, was a forgery. But it was Valla's *Collatio Novi Testamenti* of 1444 that would have such a great effect on the renewal of biblical studies in the next century. Erasmus discovered the manuscript of this work while rummaging through an old library in Belgium and published it at Paris in 1505. In the preface to his edition of Valla, Erasmus gave the rationale that would guide his own labors in textual criticism. Just as Jerome had translated the Latin Vulgate from older versions and copies of the Scriptures in his day, so now Jerome's own text must be subjected to careful scrutiny and correction. Erasmus would be *Hieronymus redivivus*, a new Jerome come back to life to advance the cause of sacred philology. The restoration of the Scriptures and the writings of the church fathers would usher in what Erasmus believed would be a golden age of peace and learning. In 1516, the Basel publisher Froben brought out Erasmus's *Novum Instrumentum*, the first published edition of the Greek New Testament. Erasmus's Greek New Testament would go through five editions in his lifetime, each one with new emendations to the text and a growing section of annotations that expanded to include not only technical notes about the text but also theological comment. The influence of Erasmus's Greek New

---

[19]E. Harris Harbison, *The Christian Scholar in the Age of the Reformation* (New York: Charles Scribner's Sons, 1956), 80.

Testament was enormous. It formed the basis for Robert Estienne's *Novum Testamentum Graece* of 1550, which in turn was used to establish the Greek *Textus Receptus* for a number of late Reformation translations including the King James Version of 1611.

For all his expertise in Greek, Erasmus was a poor student of Hebrew and only published commentaries on several of the psalms. However, the renaissance of Hebrew letters was part of the wider program of biblical humanism as reflected in the establishment of trilingual colleges devoted to the study of Hebrew, Greek and Latin (the three languages written on the *titulus* of Jesus' cross [Jn 19:20]) at Alcalá in Spain, Wittenberg in Germany, Louvain in Belgium, and Paris in France. While it is true that some medieval commentators, especially Nicholas of Lyra, had been informed by the study of Hebrew and rabbinics in their biblical work, it was the publication of Johannes Reuchlin's *De rudimentis hebraicis* (1506), a combined grammar and dictionary, that led to the recovery of *veritas Hebraica*, as Jerome had referred to the true voice of the Hebrew Scriptures. The pursuit of Hebrew studies was carried forward in the Reformation by two great scholars, Konrad Pellikan and Sebastian Münster. Pellikan was a former Franciscan friar who embraced the Protestant cause and played a major role in the Zurich reformation. He had published a Hebrew grammar even prior to Reuchlin and produced a commentary on nearly the entire Bible that appeared in seven volumes between 1532 and 1539. Münster was Pellikan's student and taught Hebrew at the University of Heidelberg before taking up a similar position in Basel. Like his mentor, Münster was a great collector of Hebraica and published a series of excellent grammars, dictionaries and rabbinic texts. Münster did for the Hebrew Old Testament what Erasmus had done for the Greek New Testament. His *Hebraica Biblia* offered a fresh Latin translation of the Old Testament with annotations from medieval rabbinic exegesis.

Luther first learned Hebrew with Reuchlin's grammar in hand but took advantage of other published resources, such as the four-volume Hebrew Bible published at Venice by Daniel Bomberg in 1516 to 1517. He also gathered his own circle of Hebrew experts, his *sanhedrin* he called it, who helped him with his German translation of the Old Testament. We do not know where William Tyndale learned Hebrew, though perhaps it was in Worms, where there was a thriving rabbinical school during his stay there. In any event, he had sufficiently mastered the language to bring out a freshly translated Pentateuch that was published at Antwerp in 1530. By the time the English separatist scholar Henry Ainsworth published his prolix commentaries on the Pentateuch in 1616, the knowledge of Hebrew, as well as Greek, was taken for granted by every serious scholar of the Bible. In the preface to his commentary on Genesis, Ainsworth explained that "the literal sense of Moses's Hebrew (which is the tongue wherein he wrote the law), is the ground of all interpretation, and that language hath figures and properties of speech, different from ours: These therefore in the first place are to be opened that the natural meaning of the Scripture, being known, the mysteries of godliness therein implied, may be better discerned."[20]

The restoration of the biblical text in the original languages made possible the revival of scriptural exposition reflected in the floodtide of sermon literature and commentary work. Of even

---

[20]Henry Ainsworth, *Annotations upon the First Book of Moses Called Genesis* (Amsterdam, 1616), preface (unpaginated).

more far-reaching import was the steady stream of vernacular Bibles in the sixteenth century. In the introduction to his 1516 edition of the New Testament, Erasmus had expressed his desire that the Scriptures be translated into all languages so that "the lowliest women" could read the Gospels and the Pauline epistles and "the farmer sing some portion of them at the plow, the weaver hum some parts of them to the movement of his shuttle, the traveler lighten the weariness of the journey with stories of this kind."[21] Like Erasmus, Tyndale wanted the Bible to be available in the language of the common people. He once said to a learned divine that if God spared his life he would cause the boy who drives the plow to know more of the Scriptures than he did![22] The project of allowing the Bible to speak in the language of the mother in the house, the children in the street and the cheesemonger in the marketplace was met with stiff opposition by certain Catholic polemicists such as Johann Eck, Luther's antagonist at the Leipzig Debate of 1519. In his *Enchiridion* (1525), Eck derided the "inky theologians" whose translations paraded the Bible before "the untutored crowd" and subjected it to the judgment of "laymen and crazy old women."[23] In fact, some fourteen German Bibles had already been published prior to Luther's September Testament of 1522, which he translated from Erasmus's Greek New Testament in less than three months' time while sequestered in the Wartburg. Luther's German New Testament became the first bestseller in the world, appearing in forty-three distinct editions between 1522 and 1525 with upward of one hundred thousand copies issued in these three years. It is estimated that 5 percent of the German population may have been literate at this time, but this rate increased as the century wore on due in no small part to the unmitigated success of vernacular Bibles.[24]

Luther's German Bible (inclusive of the Old Testament from 1534) was the most successful venture of its kind, but it was not alone in the field. Hans Denck and Ludwig Hätzer, leaders in the early Anabaptist movement, translated the prophetic books of the Old Testament from Hebrew into German in 1527. This work influenced the Swiss-German Bible of 1531 published by Leo Jud and other pastors in Zurich. Tyndale's influence on the English language rivaled that of Luther on German. At a time when English was regarded as "that obscure and remote dialect of German spoken in an off-shore island," Tyndale, with his remarkable linguistic ability (he was fluent in eight languages), "made a language for England," as his modern editor David Daniell has put it.[25] Tyndale was imprisoned and executed near Brussels in 1536, but the influence of his biblical work among the common people of England was already being felt. There is no reason to doubt the authenticity of John Foxe's recollection of how Tyndale's New Testament was received in England during the 1520s and 1530s:

---

[21]John C. Olin, *Christian Humanism and the Reformation* (New York: Fordham University Press, 1987), 101.

[22]This famous statement of Tyndale was quoted by John Foxe in his *Acts and Monuments of Matters Happening in the Church* (London, 1563). See Henry Wansbrough, "Tyndale," in *The Bible in the Renaissance*, ed. Richard Griffith (Aldershot, UK: Ashgate, 2001), 124.

[23]John Eck, *Enchiridion of Commonplaces*, trans. Ford Lewis Battles (Grand Rapids: Baker, 1979), 47-49.

[24]The effect of printing on the spread of the Reformation has been much debated. See the classic study by Elizabeth L. Eisenstein, *The Printing Press as an Agent of Change* (Cambridge: Cambridge University Press, 1979). More recent studies include Mark U. Edwards Jr., *Printing, Propaganda and Martin Luther* (Minneapolis: Fortress, 1994), and Andrew Pettegree and Matthew Hall, "The Reformation and the Book: A Reconsideration," *Historical Journal* 47 (2004): 1-24.

[25]David Daniell, *William Tyndale: A Biography* (New Haven: Yale University Press, 1994), 3.

The fervent zeal of those Christian days seemed much superior to these our days and times; as manifestly may appear by their sitting up all night in reading and hearing; also by their expenses and charges in buying of books in English, of whom some gave five marks, some more, some less, for a book: some gave a load of hay for a few chapters of St. James, or of St. Paul in English.[26]

Calvin helped to revise and contributed three prefaces to the French Bible translated by his cousin Pierre Robert Olivétan and originally published at Neuchâtel in 1535. Clément Marot and Beza provided a fresh translation of the Psalms with each psalm rendered in poetic form and accompanied by monophonic musical settings for congregational singing. The Bay Psalter, the first book printed in America, was an English adaptation of this work. Geneva also provided the provenance of the most influential Italian Bible published by Giovanni Diodati in 1607. The flowering of biblical humanism in vernacular Bibles resulted in new translations in all of the major language groups of Europe: Spanish (1569), Portuguese (1681), Dutch (New Testament, 1523; Old Testament, 1527), Danish (1550), Czech (1579–1593/94), Hungarian (New Testament, 1541; complete Bible, 1590), Polish (1563), Swedish (1541), and even Arabic (1591).[27]

Patterns of Reformation

Once the text of the Bible had been placed in the hands of the people, in cheap and easily available editions, what further need was there of published expositions such as commentaries? Given the Protestant doctrine of the priesthood of all believers, was there any longer a need for learned clergy and their bookish religion? Some radical reformers thought not. Sebastian Franck searched for the true church of the Spirit "scattered among the heathen and the weeds" but could not find it in any of the institutional structures of his time. *Veritas non potest scribi, aut exprimi*, he said, "truth can neither be spoken nor written."[28] Kaspar von Schwenckfeld so emphasized religious inwardness that he suspended external observance of the Lord's Supper and downplayed the readable, audible Scriptures in favor of the Word within. This trajectory would lead to the rise of the Quakers in the next century, but it was pursued neither by the mainline reformers nor by most of the Anabaptists. Article 7 of the Augsburg Confession (1530) declared the one holy Christian church to be "the assembly of all believers among whom the Gospel is purely preached and the holy sacraments are administered according to the Gospel."[29]

Historians of the nineteenth century referred to the material and formal principles of the Reformation. In this construal, the matter at stake was the meaning of the Christian gospel: the liberating insight that helpless sinners are graciously justified by the gift of faith alone, apart from any works or merits of their own, entirely on the basis of Christ's atoning work on the cross. For Luther especially, justification by faith alone became the criterion by which all other doctrines and

---

[26]Foxe, *Acts and Monuments*, 4:218.

[27]On vernacular translations of the Bible, see *CHB* 3:94-140 and Jaroslav Pelikan, *The Reformation of the Bible/The Bible of the Reformation* (New Haven: Yale University Press, 1996), 41-62.

[28]Sebastian Franck, *280 Paradoxes or Wondrous Sayings*, trans. E. J. Furcha (Lewiston, NY: Edwin Mellen Press, 1986), 10, 212.

[29]BoC 42 (BSLK 61).

practices of the church were to be judged. The cross proves everything, he said at the Heidelberg disputation in 1518. The distinction between law and gospel thus became the primary hermeneutical key that unlocked the true meaning of Scripture.

The formal principle of the Reformation, *sola Scriptura*, was closely bound up with proper distinctions between Scripture and tradition. "Scripture alone," said Luther, "is the true lord and master of all writings and doctrine on earth. If that is not granted, what is Scripture good for? The more we reject it, the more we become satisfied with human books and human teachers."[30] On the basis of this principle, the reformers challenged the structures and institutions of the medieval Catholic Church. Even a simple layperson, they asserted, armed with Scripture should be believed above a pope or a council without it. But, however boldly asserted, the doctrine of the primacy of Scripture did not absolve the reformers from dealing with a host of hermeneutical issues that became matters of contention both between Rome and the Reformation and within each of these two communities: the extent of the biblical canon, the validity of critical study of the Bible, the perspicuity of Scripture and its relation to preaching, and the retention of devotional and liturgical practices such as holy days, incense, the burning of candles, the sprinkling of holy water, church art, and musical instruments. Zwingli, the Puritans, and the radicals dismissed such things as a rubbish heap of ceremonials that amounted to nothing but tomfoolery, while Lutherans and Anglicans retained most of them as consonant with Scripture and valuable aids to worship.

It is important to note that while the mainline reformers differed among themselves on many matters, overwhelmingly they saw themselves as part of the ongoing Catholic tradition, indeed as the legitimate bearers of it. This was seen in numerous ways including their sense of continuity with the church of the preceding centuries; their embrace of the ecumenical orthodoxy of the early church; and their desire to read the Bible in dialogue with the exegetical tradition of the church.

In their biblical commentaries, the reformers of the sixteenth century revealed a close familiarity with the preceding exegetical tradition, and they used it respectfully as well as critically in their own expositions of the sacred text. For them, *sola Scriptura* was not *nuda Scriptura*. Rather, the Scriptures were seen as the book given to the church, gathered and guided by the Holy Spirit. In his restatement of the Vincentian canon, Calvin defined the church as "a society of all the saints, a society which, spread over the whole world, and existing in all ages, and bound together by the one doctrine and the one spirit of Christ, cultivates and observes unity of faith and brotherly concord. With this church we deny that we have any disagreement. Nay, rather, as we revere her as our mother, so we desire to remain in her bosom." Defined thus, the church has a real, albeit relative and circumscribed, authority since, as Calvin admits, "We cannot fly without wings."[31] While the reformers could not agree with the Council of Trent (though some recent Catholic theologians have challenged this interpretation) that Scripture and tradition were two separate and equal sources of divine revelation,

---

[30]LW 32:11-12* (WA 7:317).
[31]John C. Olin, ed., *John Calvin and Jacopo Sadoleto: A Reformation Debate* (New York: Harper Torchbooks, 1966), 61-62, 77.

they did believe in the coinherence of Scripture and tradition. This conviction shaped the way they read and interpreted the Bible.[32]

Schools of Exegesis

The reformers were passionate about biblical exegesis, but they showed little concern for hermeneutics as a separate field of inquiry. Niels Hemmingsen, a Lutheran theologian in Denmark, did write a treatise, *De methodis* (1555), in which he offered a philosophical and theological framework for the interpretation of Scripture. This was followed by the *Clavis Scripturae Sacrae* (1567) of Matthias Flacius Illyricus, which contains some fifty rules for studying the Bible drawn from Scripture itself.[33] However, hermeneutics as we know it came of age only in the Enlightenment and should not be backloaded into the Reformation. It is also true that the word *commentary* did not mean in the sixteenth century what it means for us today. Erasmus provided both annotations and paraphrases on the New Testament, the former a series of critical notes on the text but also containing points of doctrinal substance, the latter a theological overview and brief exposition. Most of Calvin's commentaries began as sermons or lectures presented in the course of his pastoral ministry. In the dedication to his 1519 study of Galatians, Luther declared that his work was "not so much a commentary as a testimony of my faith in Christ."[34] The exegetical work of the reformers was embodied in a wide variety of forms and genres, and the RCS has worked with this broader concept in setting the guidelines for this compendium.

The Protestant reformers shared in common a number of key interpretive principles such as the priority of the grammatical-historical sense of Scripture and the christological centeredness of the entire Bible, but they also developed a number of distinct approaches and schools of exegesis.[35] For the purposes of the RCS, we note the following key figures and families of interpretation in this period.

Biblical humanism. The key figure is Erasmus, whose importance is hard to exaggerate for Catholic and Protestant exegetes alike. His annotated Greek New Testament and fresh Latin translation challenged the hegemony of the Vulgate tradition and was doubtless a factor in the decision of the Council of Trent to establish the Vulgate edition as authentic and normative. Erasmus believed that the wide distribution of the Scriptures would contribute to personal spiritual renewal and the reform of society. In 1547, the English translation of Erasmus's *Paraphrases* was ordered to be placed in every parish church in England. John Colet first encouraged Erasmus

---

[32]See Timothy George, "An Evangelical Reflection on Scripture and Tradition," *Pro Ecclesia* 9 (2000): 184-207.

[33]See Kenneth G. Hagen, "'*De Exegetica Methodo*': Niels Hemmingsen's *De Methodis* (1555)," in *The Bible in the Sixteenth Century*, ed. David C. Steinmetz (Durham: Duke University Press, 1990), 181-96.

[34]LW 27:159 (WA 2:449). See Kenneth Hagen, "What Did the Term *Commentarius* Mean to Sixteenth-Century Theologians?" in *Théorie et pratique de l'exégèse*, eds. Irena Backus and Francis M. Higman (Geneva: Droz, 1990), 13-38.

[35]I follow here the sketch of Irena Backus, "Biblical Hermeneutics and Exegesis," *OER* 1:152-58. In this work, Backus confines herself to Continental developments, whereas we have noted the exegetical contribution of the English Reformation as well. For more comprehensive listings of sixteenth-century commentators, see Gerald Bray, *Biblical Interpretation* (Downers Grove, IL: InterVarsity Press, 1996), 165-212; and Richard A. Muller, "Biblical Interpretation in the Sixteenth and Seventeenth Centuries," *DMBI* 22-44.

to learn Greek, though he never took up the language himself. Colet's lectures on Paul's epistles at Oxford are reflected in his commentaries on Romans and 1 Corinthians.

Jacques Lefèvre d'Étaples has been called the "French Erasmus" because of his great learning and support for early reform movements in his native land. He published a major edition of the Psalter, as well as commentaries on the Pauline Epistles (1512), the Gospels (1522), and the General Epistles (1527). Guillaume Farel, the early reformer of Geneva, was a disciple of Lefèvre, and the young Calvin also came within his sphere of influence.

Among pre-Tridentine Catholic reformers, special attention should be given to Thomas de Vio, better known as Cajetan. He is best remembered for confronting Martin Luther on behalf of the pope in 1518, but his biblical commentaries (on nearly every book of the Bible) are virtually free of polemic. Like Erasmus, he dared to criticize the Vulgate on linguistic grounds. His commentary on Romans supported the doctrine of justification by grace applied by faith based on the "alien righteousness" of God in Christ. Jared Wicks sums up Cajetan's significance in this way: "Cajetan's combination of passion for pristine biblical meaning with his fully developed theological horizon of understanding indicates, in an intriguing manner, something of the breadth of possibilities open to Roman Catholics before a more restrictive settlement came to exercise its hold on many Catholic interpreters in the wake of the Council of Trent."[36] Girolamo Seripando, like Cajetan, was a cardinal in the Catholic Church, though he belonged to the Augustinian rather than the Dominican order. He was an outstanding classical scholar and published commentaries on Romans and Galatians. Also important is Jacopo Sadoleto, another cardinal, best known for his 1539 letter to the people of Geneva beseeching them to return to the Church of Rome, to which Calvin replied with a manifesto of his own. Sadoleto published a commentary on Romans in 1535. Bucer once commended Sadoleto's teaching on justification as approximating that of the reformers, while others saw him tilting away from the Augustinian tradition toward Pelagianism.[37]

Luther and the Wittenberg school. It was in the name of the Word of God, and specifically as a doctor of Scripture, that Luther challenged the church of his day and inaugurated the Reformation. Though Luther renounced his monastic vows, he never lost that sense of intimacy with *sacra pagina* he first acquired as a young monk. Luther provided three rules for reading the Bible: prayer, meditation, and struggle *(tentatio)*. His exegetical output was enormous. In the American edition of Luther's works, thirty out of the fifty-five volumes are devoted to his biblical studies, and additional translations are planned. Many of his commentaries originated as sermons or lecture notes presented to his students at the university and to his parishioners at Wittenberg's parish church of St. Mary. Luther referred to Galatians as his bride: "The Epistle to the Galatians is my dear epistle. I have betrothed myself to it. It is my Käthe von Bora."[38] He considered his 1535 commentary on Galatians his greatest exegetical work, although his massive commentary on Genesis

---

[36]Jared Wicks, "Tommaso de Vio Cajetan (1469-1534)," *DMBI* 283-87, here 286.

[37]See the discussion by Bernard Roussel, "Martin Bucer et Jacques Sadolet: la concorde possible," *Bulletin de la Société de l'histoire de protestantisme français* (1976): 525-50, and T. H. L. Parker, *Commentaries on the Epistle to the Romans, 1532–1542* (Edinburgh: T&T Clark, 1986), 25-34.

[38]WATR 1:69 no. 146; cf. LW 54:20 no. 146. I have followed Rörer's variant on Dietrich's notes.

(eight volumes in LW), which he worked on for ten years (1535–1545), must be considered his crowning work. Luther's principles of biblical interpretation are found in his *Open Letter on Translating* and in the prefaces he wrote to all the books of the Bible.

Philipp Melanchthon was brought to Wittenberg to teach Greek in 1518 and proved to be an able associate to Luther in the reform of the church. A set of his lecture notes on Romans was published without his knowledge in 1522. This was revised and expanded many times until his large commentary of 1556. Melanchthon also commented on other New Testament books including Matthew, John, Galatians, and the Petrine epistles, as well as Proverbs, Daniel, and Ecclesiastes. Though he was well trained in the humanist disciplines, Melanchthon devoted little attention to critical and textual matters in his commentaries. Rather, he followed the primary argument of the biblical writer and gathered from this exposition a series of doctrinal topics for special consideration. This method lay behind Melanchthon's *Loci communes* (1521), the first Protestant theology textbook to be published. Another Wittenberger was Johannes Bugenhagen of Pomerania, a prolific commentator on both the Old and New Testaments. His commentary on the Psalms (1524), translated into German by Bucer, applied Luther's teaching on justification to the Psalter. He also wrote a commentary on Job and annotations on many of the books in the Bible. The Lutheran exegetical tradition was shaped by many other scholar-reformers including Andreas Osiander, Johannes Brenz, Caspar Cruciger, Erasmus Sarcerius, Georg Maior, Jacob Andreae, Nikolaus Selnecker, and Johann Gerhard.

The Strasbourg-Basel tradition. Bucer, the son of a shoemaker in Alsace, became the leader of the Reformation in Strasbourg. A former Dominican, he was early on influenced by Erasmus and continued to share his passion for Christian unity. Bucer was the most ecumenical of the Protestant reformers seeking rapprochement with Catholics on justification and an armistice between Luther and Zwingli in their strife over the Lord's Supper. Bucer also had a decisive influence on Calvin, though the latter characterized his biblical commentaries as longwinded and repetitious.[39] In his exegetical work, Bucer made ample use of patristic and medieval sources, though he criticized the abuse and overuse of allegory as "the most blatant insult to the Holy Spirit."[40] He declared that the purpose of his commentaries was "to help inexperienced brethren [perhaps like the apothecary Drilhon, who owned a French translation of Bucer's *Commentary on Matthew*] to understand each of the words and actions of Christ, and in their proper order as far as possible, and to retain an explanation of them in their natural meaning, so that they will not distort God's Word through age-old aberrations or by inept interpretation, but rather with a faithful comprehension of everything as written by the Spirit of God, they may expound to all the churches in their firm upbuilding in faith and love."[41] In addition to writing commentaries on all four Gospels, Bucer published commentaries on Judges, the Psalms, Zephaniah, Romans, and Ephesians. In the early years of the Reformation, there was a great deal of back and forth between Strasbourg and Basel, and both

---

[39]CNTC 8:3 (CO 10:404).

[40]*DMBI* 249; P. Scherding and F. Wendel, eds., "Un Traité d'exégèse pratique de Bucer," *Revue d'histoire et de philosophie religieuses* 26 (1946): 32-75, here 56.

[41]Martin Bucer, *Enarrationes perpetuae in sacra quatuor evangelia*, 2nd ed. (Strasbourg: Georg Ulrich Andlanus, 1530), 10r; quoted in D. F. Wright, "Martin Bucer," *DMBI* 290.

were centers of a lively publishing trade. Wolfgang Capito, Bucer's associate at Strasbourg, was a notable Hebraist and composed commentaries on Hosea (1529) and Habakkuk (1527).

At Basel, the great Sebastian Münster defended the use of Jewish sources in the Christian study of the Old Testament and published, in addition to his famous Hebrew grammar, an annotated version of the Gospel of Matthew translated from Greek into Hebrew. Oecolampadius, Basel's chief reformer, had been a proofreader in Froben's publishing house and worked with Erasmus on his Greek New Testament and his critical edition of Jerome. From 1523 he was both a preacher and professor of Holy Scripture at Basel. He defended Zwingli's eucharistic theology at the Colloquy of Marburg and published commentaries on 1 John (1524), Romans (1525), and Haggai–Malachi (1525). Oecolampadius was succeeded by Simon Grynaeus, a classical scholar who taught Greek and supported Bucer's efforts to bring Lutherans and Zwinglians together. More in line with Erasmus was Sebastian Castellio, who came to Basel after his expulsion from Geneva in 1545. He is best remembered for questioning the canonicity of the Song of Songs and for his annotations and French translation of the Bible.

The Zurich group. Biblical exegesis in Zurich was centered on the distinctive institution of the *Prophezei*, which began on June 19, 1525. On five days a week, at seven o'clock in the morning, all of the ministers and theological students in Zurich gathered into the choir of the Grossmünster to engage in a period of intense exegesis and interpretation of Scripture. After Zwingli had opened the meeting with prayer, the text of the day was read in Latin, Greek, and Hebrew, followed by appropriate textual or exegetical comments. One of the ministers then delivered a sermon on the passage in German that was heard by many of Zurich's citizens who stopped by the cathedral on their way to work. This institute for advanced biblical studies had an enormous influence as a model for Reformed academies and seminaries throughout Europe. It was also the seedbed for sermon series in Zurich's churches and the extensive exegetical publications of Zwingli, Leo Jud, Konrad Pellikan, Heinrich Bullinger, Oswald Myconius, and Rudolf Gwalther. Zwingli had memorized in Greek all of the Pauline epistles, and this bore fruit in his powerful expository preaching and biblical exegesis. He took seriously the role of grammar, rhetoric, and historical research in explaining the biblical text. For example, he disagreed with Bucer on the value of the Septuagint, regarding it as a trustworthy witness to a proto-Hebrew version earlier than the Masoretic text.

Zwingli's work was carried forward by his successor Bullinger, one of the most formidable scholars and networkers among the reformers. He composed commentaries on Daniel (1565), the Gospels (1542–1546), the Epistles (1537), Acts (1533), and Revelation (1557). He collaborated with Calvin to produce the *Consensus Tigurinus* (1549), a Reformed accord on the nature of the Lord's Supper, and produced a series of fifty sermons on Christian doctrine, known as *Decades*, which became required reading in Elizabethan England. As the *Antistes* ("overseer") of the Zurich church for forty-four years, Bullinger faced opposition from nascent Anabaptism on the one hand and resurgent Catholicism on the other. The need for a well-trained clergy and scholarly resources, including Scripture commentaries, arose from the fact that the Bible was "difficult or obscure to the unlearned, unskillful, unexercised, and malicious or corrupted wills." While forswearing papal claims to infallibility, Bullinger and other leaders of the magisterial Reformation saw the need for a kind of Protestant magisterium as a check against the tendency to read the Bible in "such sense as everyone shall be persuaded in himself to be most convenient."[42]

Two other commentators can be treated in connection with the Zurich group, though each of them had a wide-ranging ministry across the Reformation fronts. A former Benedictine monk, Wolfgang Musculus, embraced the Reformation in the 1520s and served briefly as the secretary to Bucer in Strasbourg. He shared Bucer's desire for Protestant unity and served for seventeen years (1531–1548) as a pastor and reformer in Augsburg. After a brief time in Zurich, where he came under the influence of Bullinger, Musculus was called to Bern, where he taught the Scriptures and published commentaries on the Psalms, the Decalogue, Genesis, Romans, Isaiah, 1 and 2 Corinthians, Galatians and Ephesians, Philippians, Colossians, 1 and 2 Thessalonians, and 1 Timothy. Drawing on his exegetical writings, Musculus also produced a compendium of Protestant theology that was translated into English in 1563 as *Commonplaces of Christian Religion*.

Peter Martyr Vermigli was a Florentine-born scholar and Augustinian friar who embraced the Reformation and fled to Switzerland in 1542. Over the next twenty years, he would gain an international reputation as a prolific scholar and leading theologian within the Reformed community. He lectured on the Old Testament at Strasbourg, was made regius professor at Oxford, corresponded with the Italian refugee church in Geneva and spent the last years of his life as professor of Hebrew at Zurich. Vermigli published commentaries on 1 Corinthians, Romans, and Judges during his lifetime. His biblical lectures on Genesis, Lamentations, 1 and 2 Samuel, and 1 and 2 Kings were published posthumously. The most influential of his writings was the *Loci communes (Commonplaces)*, a theological compendium drawn from his exegetical writings.

The Genevan reformers. What Zwingli and Bullinger were to Zurich, Calvin and Beza were to Geneva. Calvin has been called "the father of modern biblical scholarship," and his exegetical work is without parallel in the Reformation. Because of the success of his *Institutes of the Christian Religion* Calvin has sometimes been thought of as a man of one book, but he always intended the *Institutes*, which went through eight editions in Latin and five in French during his lifetime, to serve as a guide to the study of the Bible, to show the reader "what he ought especially to seek in Scripture and to what end he ought to relate its contents." Jacob Arminius, who modified several principles of Calvin's theology, recommended his commentaries next to the Bible, for, as he said, Calvin "is incomparable in the interpretation of Scripture."[43] Drawing on his superb knowledge of Greek and Hebrew and his thorough training in humanist rhetoric, Calvin produced commentaries on all of the New Testament books except 2 and 3 John and Revelation. Calvin's Old Testament commentaries originated as sermon and lecture series and include Genesis, Psalms, Hosea, Isaiah, minor prophets, Daniel, Jeremiah and Lamentations, a harmony of the last four books of Moses,

---

[42]Euan Cameron, *The European Reformation* (Oxford: Oxford University Press, 1991), 120.

[43]Letter to Sebastian Egbert (May 3, 1607), in *Praestantium ac eruditorum virorum epistolae ecclesiasticae et theologicae varii argumenti*, ed. Christiaan Hartsoeker (Amsterdam: Henricus Dendrinus, 1660), 236-37. Quoted in A. M. Hunter, *The Teaching of Calvin* (London: James Clarke, 1950), 20.

kiel 1–20, and Joshua. Calvin sought for brevity and clarity in all of his exegetical work. He emphasized the illumination of the Holy Spirit as essential to a proper understanding of the text. Calvin underscored the continuity between the two Testaments (one covenant in two dispensations) and sought to apply the plain or natural sense of the text to the church of his day. In the preface to his own influential commentary on Romans, Karl Barth described how Calvin worked to recover the mind of Paul and make the apostle's message relevant to his day:

> How energetically Calvin goes to work, first scientifically establishing the text ("what stands there?"), then following along the footsteps of its thought; that is to say, he conducts a discussion with it until the wall between the first and the sixteenth centuries becomes transparent, and until there in the first century Paul speaks and here the man of the sixteenth century hears, until indeed the conversation between document and reader becomes concentrated upon the substance (which must be the same now as then).[44]

Beza was elected moderator of Geneva's Company of Pastors after Calvin's death in 1564 and guided the Genevan Reformation over the next four decades. His annotated Latin translation of the Greek New Testament (1556) and his further revisions of the Greek text established his reputation as the leading textual critic of the sixteenth century after Erasmus. Beza completed the translation of Marot's metrical Psalter, which became a centerpiece of Huguenot piety and Reformed church life. Though known for his polemical writings on grace, free will, and predestination, Beza's work is marked by a strong pastoral orientation and concern for a Scripture-based spirituality.

Robert Estienne (Stephanus) was a printer-scholar who had served the royal household in Paris. After his conversion to Protestantism, in 1550 he moved to Geneva, where he published a series of notable editions and translations of the Bible. He also produced sermons and commentaries on Job, Ecclesiastes, the Song of Songs, Romans and Hebrews, as well as dictionaries, concordances, and a thesaurus of biblical terms. He also published the first editions of the Bible with chapters divided into verses, an innovation that quickly became universally accepted.

The British Reformation. Commentary writing in England and Scotland lagged behind the continental Reformation for several reasons. In 1500, there were only three publishing houses in England compared with more than two hundred on the Continent. A 1408 statute against publishing or reading the Bible in English, stemming from the days of Lollardy, stifled the free flow of ideas, as was seen in the fate of Tyndale. Moreover, the nature of the English Reformation from Henry through Elizabeth provided little stability for the flourishing of biblical scholarship. In the sixteenth century, many "hot-gospel" Protestants in England were edified by the English translations of commentaries and theological writings by the Continental reformers. The influence of Calvin and Beza was felt especially in the Geneva Bible with its "Protestant glosses" of theological notes and references.

During the later Elizabethan and Stuart church, however, the indigenous English commentary came into its own. Both Anglicans and Puritans contributed to this outpouring of biblical studies.

---

[44]Karl Barth, *Die Römerbrief* (Zurich: TVZ, 1940), 11, translated by T. H. L. Parker as the epigraph to *Calvin's New Testament Commentaries*, 2nd ed. (Louisville, KY: Westminster John Knox, 1993).

The sermons of Lancelot Andrewes and John Donne are replete with exegetical insights based on a close study of the Greek and Hebrew texts. Among the Reformed authors in England, none was more influential than William Perkins, the greatest of the early Puritan theologians, who published commentaries on Galatians, Jude, Revelation, and the Sermon on the Mount (Mt 5–7). John Cotton, one of his students, wrote commentaries on the Song of Songs, Ecclesiastes, and Revelation before departing for New England in 1633. The separatist pastor Henry Ainsworth was an outstanding scholar of Hebrew and wrote major commentaries on the Pentateuch, the Psalms, and the Song of Songs. In Scotland, Robert Rollock, the first principal of Edinburgh University (1585), wrote numerous commentaries including those on the Psalms, Ephesians, Daniel, Romans, 1 and 2 Thessalonians, John, Colossians, and Hebrews. Joseph Mede and Thomas Brightman were leading authorities on Revelation and contributed to the apocalyptic thought of the seventeenth century. Mention should also be made of Archbishop James Ussher, whose *Annals of the Old Testament* was published in 1650. Ussher developed a keen interest in biblical chronology and calculated that the creation of the world had taken place on October 26, 4004 B.C. As late as 1945, the Scofield Reference Bible still retained this date next to Genesis 1:1, but later editions omitted it because of the lack of evidence on which to fix such dates.[45]

Anabaptism. Irena Backus has noted that there was no school of "dissident" exegesis during the Reformation, and the reasons are not hard to find. The radical Reformation was an ill-defined movement that existed on the margins of official church life in the sixteenth century. The denial of infant baptism and the refusal to swear an oath marked radicals as a seditious element in society, and they were persecuted by Protestants and Catholics alike. However, in the RCS we have made an attempt to include some voices of the radical Reformation, especially among the Anabaptists. While the Anabaptists published few commentaries in the sixteenth century, they were avid readers and quoters of the Bible. Numerous exegetical gems can be found in their letters, treatises, martyr acts (especially *The Martyrs' Mirror*), hymns, and histories. They placed a strong emphasis on the memorizing of Scripture and quoted liberally from vernacular translations of the Bible. George H. Williams has noted that "many an Anabaptist theological tract was really a beautiful mosaic of Scripture texts."[46] In general, most Anabaptists accepted the apocryphal books as canonical, contrasted outer word and inner spirit with relative degrees of strictness and saw the New Testament as normative for church life and social ethics (witness their pacifism, nonswearing, emphasis on believers' baptism and congregational discipline).

We have noted the Old Testament translation of Ludwig Hätzer, who became an antitrinitarian, and Hans Denck that they published at Worms in 1527. Denck also wrote a notable commentary on Micah. Conrad Grebel belonged to a Greek reading circle in Zurich and came to his Anabaptist convictions while poring over the text of Erasmus's New Testament. The only Anabaptist leader with university credentials was Balthasar Hubmaier, who was made a doctor of theology (Ingolstadt, 1512) in the same year as Luther. His reflections on the Bible are found in his numerous

---

[45]*The New Scofield Reference Bible* (New York: Oxford University Press, 1967), vi.
[46]George H. Williams, *The Radical Reformation*, 3rd ed. (Kirksville, MO: Sixteenth Century Journal Publishers, 1992), 1247.

writings, which include the first catechism of the Reformation (1526), a two-part treatise on the freedom of the will and a major work (*On the Sword*) setting forth positive attitudes toward the role of government and the Christian's place in society. Melchior Hoffman was an apocalyptic seer who wrote commentaries on Romans, Revelation, and Daniel 12. He predicted that Christ would return in 1533. More temperate was Pilgram Marpeck, a mining engineer who embraced Anabaptism and traveled widely throughout Switzerland and south Germany, from Strasbourg to Augsburg. His "Admonition of 1542" is the longest published defense of Anabaptist views on baptism and the Lord's Supper. He also wrote many letters that functioned as theological tracts for the congregations he had founded dealing with topics such as the fruits of repentance, the lowliness of Christ, and the unity of the church. Menno Simons, a former Catholic priest, became the most outstanding leader of the Dutch Anabaptist movement. His masterpiece was the *Foundation of Christian Doctrine* published in 1540. His other writings include *Meditation on the Twenty-fifth Psalm* (1537); *A Personal Exegesis of Psalm Twenty-five* modeled on the style of Augustine's *Confessions*; *Confession of the Triune God* (1550), directed against Adam Pastor, a former disciple of Menno who came to doubt the divinity of Christ; *Meditations and Prayers for Mealtime* (1557); and the *Cross of the Saints* (1554), an exhortation to faithfulness in the face of persecution. Like many other Anabaptists, Menno emphasized the centrality of discipleship (*Nachfolge*) as a deliberate repudiation of the old life and a radical commitment to follow Jesus as Lord.

Reading Scripture with the Reformers

In 1947, Gerhard Ebeling set forth his thesis that the history of the Christian church is the history of the interpretation of Scripture. Since that time, the place of the Bible in the story of the church has been investigated from many angles. A better understanding of the history of exegesis has been aided by new critical editions and scholarly discussions of the primary sources. The *Cambridge History of the Bible*, published in three volumes (1963–1970), remains a standard reference work in the field. The ACCS built on, and itself contributed to, the recovery of patristic biblical wisdom of both East and West. Beryl Smalley's *The Study of the Bible in the Middle Ages* (1940) and Henri de Lubac's *Medieval Exegesis: The Four Senses of Scripture* (1959) are essential reading for understanding the monastic and scholastic settings of commentary work between Augustine and Luther. The Reformation took place during what has been called "le grand siècle de la Bible."[47] Aided by the tools of Renaissance humanism and the dynamic impetus of Reformation theology (including permutations and reactions against it), the sixteenth century produced an unprecedented number of commentaries on every book in the Bible. Drawing from this vast storehouse of exegetical treasures, the RCS allows us to read Scripture along with the reformers. In doing so, it serves as a practical homiletic and devotional guide to some of the greatest masters of biblical interpretation in the history of the church.

The RCS gladly acknowledges its affinity with and dependence on recent scholarly investigations of Reformation-era exegesis. Between 1976 and 1990, three international colloquia on the

---

[47]J-R. Aarmogathe, ed., *Bible de tous les temps*, 8 vols.; vol. 6, *Le grand siècle de la Bible* (Paris: Beauchesne, 1989).

history of biblical exegesis in the sixteenth century took place in Geneva and in Durham, North Carolina.[48] Among those participating in these three gatherings were a number of scholars who have produced groundbreaking works in the study of biblical interpretation in the Reformation. These include Elsie McKee, Irena Backus, Kenneth Hagen, Scott H. Hendrix, Richard A. Muller, Guy Bedouelle, Gerald Hobbs, John B. Payne, Bernard Roussel, Pierre Fraenkel, and David C. Steinmetz (1936–2015). Among other scholars whose works are indispensible for the study of this field are Heinrich Bornkamm, Jaroslav Pelikan, Heiko A. Oberman, James S. Preus, T. H. L. Parker, David F. Wright, Tony Lane, John L. Thompson, Frank A. James, and Timothy J. Wengert.[49] Among these scholars no one has had a greater influence on the study of Reformation exegesis than David C. Steinmetz. A student of Oberman, he emphasized the importance of understanding the Reformation in medieval perspective. In addition to important studies on Luther and Staupitz, he pioneered the method of comparative exegesis showing both continuity and discontinuity between major Reformation figures and the preceding exegetical traditions (see his *Luther in Context* and *Calvin in Context*). From his base at Duke University, he spawned what might be called a Steinmetz school, a cadre of students and scholars whose work on the Bible in the Reformation era continues to shape the field. Steinmetz served on the RCS Board of Editorial Advisors, and a number of our volume editors pursued doctoral studies under his supervision.

In 1980, Steinmetz published "The Superiority of Pre-critical Exegesis," a seminal essay that not only placed Reformation exegesis in the context of the preceding fifteen centuries of the church's study of the Bible but also challenged certain assumptions underlying the hegemony of historical-critical exegesis of the post-Enlightenment academy.[50] Steinmetz helps us to approach the reformers and other precritical interpreters of the Bible on their own terms as faithful witnesses to the church's apostolic tradition. For them, a specific book or pericope had to be understood within the scope of the consensus of the canon. Thus the reformers, no less than the Fathers and the schoolmen, interpreted the hymn of the Johannine prologue about the preexistent Christ in consonance with the creation narrative of Genesis 1. In the same way, Psalm 22, Isaiah 53, and Daniel 7 are seen as part of an overarching storyline that finds ultimate fulfillment in Jesus Christ. Reading the Bible with the resources of the new learning, the reformers challenged the exegetical conclusions of their medieval predecessors at many points. However, unlike Alexander Campbell in the nineteenth century, their aim was not to "open the New Testament as if mortal man had never seen it before."[51]

---

[48]Olivier Fatio and Pierre Fraenkel, eds., *Histoire de l'exégèse au XVIe siècle: texts du colloque international tenu à Genève en 1976* (Geneva: Droz, 1978); David C. Steinmetz, ed., *The Bible in the Sixteenth Century* [Second International Colloquy on the History of Biblical Exegesis in the Sixteenth Century] (Durham: Duke University Press, 1990); Irena Backus and Francis M. Higman, eds., *Théorie et pratique de l'exégèse. Actes du troisième colloque international sur l'histoire de l'exégèse biblique au XVIe siècle, Genève, 31 août–2 septembre 1988* (Geneva: Droz, 1990); see also Guy Bedouelle and Bernard Roussel, eds., *Bible de tous les temps*, 8 vols.; vol. 5, *Le temps des Réformes et la Bible* (Paris: Beauchesne, 1989).

[49]For bibliographical references and evaluation of these and other contributors to the scholarly study of Reformation-era exegesis, see Richard A. Muller, "Biblical Interpretation in the Era of the Reformation: The View From the Middle Ages," in *Biblical Interpretation in the Era of the Reformation: Essays Presented to David C. Steinmetz in Honor of His Sixtieth Birthday*, ed. Richard A. Muller and John L. Thompson (Grand Rapids: Eerdmans, 1996), 3-22.

[50]David C. Steinmetz, "The Superiority of Pre-Critical Exegesis," *Theology Today* 37 (1980): 27-38.

[51]Alexander Campbell, *Memoirs of Alexander Campbell*, ed. Robert Richardson (Cincinnati: Standard Publishing Company, 1872), 97.

Rather, they wanted to do their biblical work as part of an interpretive conversation within the family of the people of God. In the reformers' emphatic turn to the literal sense, which prompted their many blasts against the unrestrained use of allegory, their work was an extension of a similar impulse made by Thomas Aquinas and Nicholas of Lyra.

This is not to discount the radically new insights gained by the reformers in their dynamic engagement with the text of Scripture; nor should we dismiss in a reactionary way the light shed on the meaning of the Bible by the scholarly accomplishments of the past two centuries. However, it is to acknowledge that the church's exegetical tradition is an indispensible aid for the proper interpretation of Scripture. And this means, as Richard Muller has said, that "while it is often appropriate to recognize that traditionary readings of the text are erroneous on the grounds offered by the historical-critical method, we ought also to recognize that the conclusions offered by historical-critical exegesis may themselves be quite erroneous on the grounds provided by the exegesis of the patristic, medieval, and reformation periods."[52] The RCS wishes to commend the exegetical work of the Reformation era as a program of retrieval for the sake of renewal—spiritual réssourcement for believers committed to the life of faith today.

George Herbert was an English pastor and poet who reaped the benefits of the renewal of biblical studies in the age of the Reformation. He referred to the Scriptures as a book of infinite sweetness, "a mass of strange delights," a book with secrets to make the life of anyone good. In describing the various means pastors require to be fully furnished in the work of their calling, Herbert provided a rationale for the history of exegesis and for the Reformation Commentary on Scripture:

> The fourth means are commenters and Fathers, who have handled the places controverted, which the parson by no means refuseth. As he doth not so study others as to neglect the grace of God in himself and what the Holy Spirit teacheth him, so doth he assure himself that God in all ages hath had his servants to whom he hath revealed his Truth, as well as to him; and that as one country doth not bear all things that there may be a commerce, so neither hath God opened or will open all to one, that there may be a traffic in knowledge between the servants of God for the planting both of love and humility. Wherefore he hath one comment[ary] at least upon every book of Scripture, and ploughing with this, and his own meditations, he enters into the secrets of God treasured in the holy Scripture.[53]

Timothy George
General Editor

---

[52]Richard A. Muller and John L. Thompson, "The Significance of Precritical Exegesis: Retrospect and Prospect," in *Biblical Interpretation in the Era of the Reformation: Essays Presented to David C. Steinmetz in Honor of His Sixtieth Birthday*, ed. Richard A. Muller and John L. Thompson (Grand Rapids: Eerdmans, 1996), 342.

[53]George Herbert, *The Complete English Poems* (London: Penguin, 1991), 205.

INTRODUCTION TO MATTHEW

From the earliest stages of Christian history, pastors, theologians, and apologists have produced their interpretive comments on Scripture. Even before the final formation of the Christian canon, faithful interpreters provided their audiences with published sermons, commentaries on entire books of the Bible, and treatises that grappled with a proper interpretation of the biblical text. In the Reformation era, this practice of pious efforts at biblical interpretation flourished in universities, magisterial courts, clandestine house groups, and pulpits throughout Europe.

This present commentary attempts to provide a snapshot of the abundant hermeneutical production of the time period particularly on the Gospel of Matthew. Modern interpreters of the Gospel will benefit from the exegetical competence and pastoral concerns of the Reformation authors. The reformers' thorough exegetical work and piety enable their comments to have a remarkable longevity beyond their own lifespan. Obviously, these interpreters drew on their historical context both in the theological themes that they addressed and in the hermeneutical tools that they employed to work through the interpretive issues of the biblical texts. However, the perennial nature of many of their theological questions and their use of a predominantly textual approach to interpretation will cause many modern interpreters to be struck by the timeliness and sensibility of their textual comments.[1]

Not all of the reformers' work was appreciated by their contemporaries. Some reformers were forced to be apologists as much as exegetes due to the theological and ecclesiastical upheaval of the period. This apologetic bent often affected the conclusions of their interpretive work and inevitably affected the tenor of their presentation. Other reformers labored in more humble surroundings, and their influence was constrained by their setting. However, for these lesser voices, the printed page served as a vehicle for their faithful hearers to broadcast their teachings beyond their immediate context. Together, these major and minor voices leave a literary legacy that reflects something of the excitement of their day, and yet their textual work yields a harvest for readers in many successive generations.

---

[1]See Christopher Ocker's case for the development of a "textual attitude" among late medieval and Reformation interpreters in *Biblical Poetics Before Humanism and Reformation* (Cambridge: Cambridge University Press, 2002), 214-19. Ulrich Luz makes a similar point by appealing to a christological exegesis among the patristic and Reformation exegetes. He writes, "When the biblical texts become expressions of the living Christ, the barrier between past and present that we experience is eliminated. Christ, about whom the text speaks, never is a merely past reality. There is no possibility of a 'mere' past that has nothing to do with us." Ulrich Luz, *Matthew in History: Interpretation, Influence, and Effects* (Minneapolis: Fortress, 1994), 36-37.

The Reformers, the Biblical Text, and the Grammatical Sense

The Reformation's unique contribution to the history of Christian thought is still being assessed by pastors and scholars. All agree that the time was a period of religious, intellectual, and political upheaval. However, it is also widely noted that the reformers drew heavily on their predecessors in their thought patterns, theological method, and piety. Much of the change of the Reformation period stemmed from factors that were not overtly theological in nature. The growing sense of nationalism in Europe, the expansion of a merchant (or middle) class, and the military advances of the Ottoman Turks created an environment that was ripe for revision or revolution. A Renaissance of art, literature, and architecture prompted the aspirations of poets, philosophers, priests, and princes. Within this creative atmosphere, two historical events had particular influence on the religious renewal that would eventually be known as the Reformation: the popular explosion of the printed page and the publication of Desiderius Erasmus's Greek New Testament.[2]

In the mid-fifteenth century, Johannes Gutenberg produced the Bible from his printing press using the technology of moveable type. This invention ignited an explosion of literary work. The next five centuries would see the constant growth of the production of the printed page. During the first century and a half of the printing press's history, religious literature flew from the presses and circulated throughout Europe in a manner previously unknown. Not only did professors or pastors in remote towns become widely known (e.g., Martin Luther and John Calvin), but also the rising swell of religious literature became a rich repository for future Christians to cull.

Due to the broader influences of humanism, the invention of the printing press, and a general "renaissance" of literature, the sixteenth century was characterized by a growing interest in texts, languages, and interpretation. This interest coupled with the religious upheaval of the Reformation caused Reformation theologians to become skillful advocates of the biblical text and its theological message. To mine the theological meaning of the biblical texts, the reformers renewed a textual interest in grammar and the "literal sense."[3]

Among the vast number of religious documents in the Reformation era, arguably the most influential on biblical interpretation was Erasmus' *Novum Instrumentum* (1516).[4] Erasmus's

---

[2]For significant studies on the impact of printing culture on the Reformation, see Andrew Pettegree, *The Book in the Renaissance* (New Haven, CT: Yale University Press, 2010); Pettegree, *Brand Luther: 1517, Printing, and the Making of the Reformation* (New York: Penguin, 2015); Mark U. Edwards Jr., *Printing, Propaganda, and Martin Luther* (Minneapolis: Fortress, 2005).

[3]On the relationship of the Renaissance's "literary" and "grammatical culture" to the Reformation, and the Reformation's own contribution to it, one should consult the seminal study of Brian Cummings, *The Literary Culture of the Reformation: Grammar and Grace* (Oxford: Oxford University Press, 2002), 15-26. Again, see Ocker's valuable insights on the reformers' "textual attitude," in *Biblical Poetics*, 185-213. For accounts of the reformers' understanding of the "literal sense," see Richard A. Muller, "Biblical Interpretation in the Era of the Reformation: The View from the Middle Ages," in *Biblical Interpretation in the Era of the Reformation: Essays Presented to David C. Steinmetz in Honor of His Sixtieth Birthday*, ed. Richard A. Muller and John L. Thompson (Grand Rapids: Eerdmans, 1996), 3-22, and William M. Marsh, *Martin Luther on Reading the Bible as Christian Scripture: The Messiah in Luther's Biblical Theology and Hermeneutics*, Princeton Theological Monographs (Eugene, OR: Pickwick, 2017), 4-10, 100-161.

[4]Erasmus's first edition, published in Basel in 1516, was titled *Novum Instrumentum*. Subsequent editions in 1519, 1522, 1527, and 1535 were titled *Novum Testamentum*.

work was intended to be a revision of and improvement on the Latin Vulgate with its outdated and incorrect grammatical constructions.[5] Erasmus added two other features to justify his revisions to the approved Latin text. In parallel columns with his Latin text, Erasmus provided the Greek (Byzantine) text. Later in the work, he included his annotations, which often explained why his translation revised the Latin of the Vulgate and clarified his translation's connection with the Greek text. These paratextual features were to provide the textual (the Greek text) and grammatical/theological (annotations) rationale behind Erasmus's Latin translation. Though Erasmus's intention may have been primarily to provide a better-quality Latin text, it was his secondary features of the Greek text and his annotations that would most dramatically affect the Protestant reformers, even those who rejected Erasmus's humanist program. As H. J. De Jonge notes, "That Erasmus was the first to make the Greek New Testament accessible to many in Western Europe by means of the printing press, remains a fact of evident importance."[6]

Erasmus's Greek New Testament inspired an ambition for proficiency in dealing with the biblical texts themselves, not simply the long interpretive history of these texts. His Latin-Greek text also drew attention to the textual features of the Bible such as its vocabulary, grammar, and verbal meaning. The attention to textual features caused a more prominent focus on the literal meaning (i.e., the verbal meaning) of biblical texts instead of a prevailing interest in matters outside the biblical text, whether dogmatic or historical. Through broader accessibility of the New Testament in Greek, theological discussions often focused on the meaning of Greek words. An obvious example of the effect of this "textual turn" initiated by Erasmus's Latin-Greek text is found in Luther's May 1518 letter to Johann von Staupitz. Luther writes,

> After this it happened that I learned—thanks to the work and talent of the most learned men who teach us Greek and Hebrew with such great devotion—that the word *poenitentia* means *metanoia* in Greek; it is derived from *meta* and *noun*, that is, from "afterward" and "mind." *Poenitentia* or *metanoia*, therefore, means coming to one's right mind and a comprehension of one's own evil after one has accepted the damage and recognized the error. . . . All these definitions agree so well with Pauline theology that, at least in my opinion, almost nothing could illustrate Paul's theology better than the way they do. . . . It is evident that they [medieval theologians] were misled by the Latin term, because the expression *poenitentiam agere* suggests more an action than a change in disposition; and in no way does this do justice to the Greek *metanoein*.[7]

---

[5]Henk Jan De Jonge, "*Novum Testamentum a Nobis Versum*: The Essence of Erasmus' Edition of the New Testament," *Journal of Theological Studies* 35, no. 2 (1984): 395-96. Cf. De Jonge, "Erasmus' Method of Translation in His Version of the New Testament," *The Bible Translator* 37, no. 1 (1986): 135-38.

[6]De Jonge, "Essence of Erasmus' Edition," 394. For further insight into Erasmus's impetus in his work, see Mark Vessey, "The Tongue and the Book: Erasmus' *Paraphrases on the New Testament* and the Arts of Scripture," in *Holy Scripture Speaks: The Production and Reception of Erasmus' "Paraphrases on the New Testament"* (Toronto: University of Toronto Press, 2002), 29-58. Vessey comments, "Erasmus seeks to resuscitate a literary and linguistic competence that could no longer be taken for granted, the loss of which had resulted, in his opinion, in the obscuring of gospel truths" (Vessey, "The Tongue and the Book," 30).

[7]LW 48:66-68 (WA 1:525-27). Erasmus's work on Mt 3 indicated that *poenitentiam agite* was not the preferred Latin rendering of *metanoia*.

The reformers' interest in words and the role of grammar can be seen in their comments on the biblical text. The reformers often shed the dense style and secondary discussions found in their medieval predecessors. Though some Reformation commentaries have lengthy, dogmatic discussions (e.g., Wolfgang Musculus, Heinrich Bullinger, Johannes Piscator, David Pareus, David Dickson, Christopher Blackwood), a much more typical practice can be seen in Erasmus's widely read *Annotations*, which were included in the varying editions of his *Novum Instrumentum* (*Testamentum*). These notations were not restrained to points of clarity in translation issues. As Jan Krans puts it, "The annotations were to remain the part of Erasmus' New Testament in which he pronounced himself freely, both on text-critical and translational issues and on a vast array of other subjects. They underwent several important revisions, whereas much less attention was devoted to the printed Greek and Latin texts."[8]

The Dutch humanist supplemented his *Annotations* with a more expansive set of comments in his *Paraphrase* on the Gospel of Matthew (1522). This style of producing notes on the text and providing brief insights or restatements of the text became a common way for the reformers to provide commentary on the biblical texts. This style meant that the commentary relied on the structure and vocabulary of the biblical text and served as a textually oriented reader's guide to the biblical texts rather than a distinct work to be appreciated in its own right. Subsequent reformers such as Huldrych Zwingli, William Tyndale, Luther, Johannes Oecolampadius, Philipp Melanchthon, Theodore Beza, Hugo Grotius, Jean Diodati, Johann Gerhard, and Thomas Cartwright all produced annotations on the text of Matthew. In their own ways, these notations presented insights into particular terms, phrases, or other textual features of the Gospel texts.

Furthermore, when the reformers extended their comments to the other Gospels in conjunction with Matthew, they often maintained much of the qualities of the annotations.[9] Martin Bucer, Heinrich Bullinger, Calvin, and John Lightfoot are all leading examples of those who blended some of the characteristics of the annotations with the broader desire of producing a harmony of the Gospels. Strikingly, even in their attempts at a harmony of the Gospel accounts, these authors drew heavily on textual features instead of trying to resolve supposed conflicts through historical reconstruction. Understanding the author's intention in his composition, often noted in his point of view in presenting the details of a particular event, remained a main interest of the reformers even as they attempted to present a unified Gospel presentation. Moreover, the reformers' renewed interest in preaching gave a further outlet for sharing the fruits of textual study. The literary landscape therefore became more densely

---

[8]Jan Krans, *Beyond What Is Written: Erasmus and Beza as Conjectural Critics of the New Testament*, New Testament Tools and Studies (Leiden: Brill, 2006), 22.

[9]Neither this comment nor the previous two imply that other reformers are following Erasmus slavishly or continually in content or format for their commentaries. The point is to note the paradigmatic influence of Erasmus for other Reformation exegetes. See a similar comment about Bullinger following Erasmus's general approach in W. P. Stephens, "The Interpretation of the Bible in Bullinger's Early Works," *Reformation and Renaissance Review* 11, no. 3 (2009), 328-29. Cf. John B. Payne, "Erasmus' Influence on Zwingli and Bullinger in the Exegesis of Matthew 11:28–30," in Muller and Thompson, *Biblical Interpretation in the Era of the Reformation*, 61-81.

populated with pastoral commentaries on the biblical texts, textual discussions in theological treatises, and expositional sermons that drew out meaning and implications of biblical texts for their audiences.

The Reformers and the Biblical Author's Theological Purpose

Two main interpretive issues face the readers who attempt to cull the reformers' thoughts for their own interpretive work: historical context and hermeneutical approach. Notably, there has been considerable development in the cultural, philosophical, and theological climate since the days of the reformers. Contemporary users of Reformation comments will want to garner insights in keeping with the historical milieu of the original authors. The daunting task of reconstructing the proper historical context might cause great trepidation in relying on the reformers' comments for biblical insight. There is one gleaming ray of hope in this scenario. As the Reformation exegetes demonstrate expressed attention to textual features of the biblical text, the verses in the text serve as an apt context for understanding the Reformation authors' comments. With the biblical text being a primary focus for the reformers' comments, their own historical contextual effects are minimized, though not completely expunged. Some readers will sense the need to research the historical context more fully in an attempt to situate the comments within the actual historical debate or occasion. While this historical research will surely prove useful, it may be that the reformers' careful biblical comments will communicate enough textual insight that the knowledge of the Reformation setting will only highlight the themes evident in the reformers' interpretations.

The reformers' hermeneutical emphases and their distinction from contemporary approaches can often be more difficult to negotiate than the historical distance from the Reformation era to the current one. Some of the significant hermeneutical differences come from the reformers' commitments to canonical, theological, and textual interpretations. The tendency for many contemporary approaches to Scripture is to focus on a particular section (pericope or book) in isolation from its literary context in the broader Christian canon. Occasionally, modern interpreters will appeal to the larger "Pauline corpus" or "Gospel literature" or maybe even to the Deuteronomistic History books. However, it is uncommon for modern interpreters to give extensive discussion to the role of a verse or narrative in the whole canon. Second, the reformers' confessional approach to biblical interpretation was disdained by much of the scholarly exegesis in the eighteenth through the twentieth centuries, resulting in more attention to the descriptive understanding of Scripture.[10] The close connection that the reformers affirmed between faith and valid interpretation or between

---

[10]The standard account of this transition can be found in, Hans W. Frei, *The Eclipse of Biblical Narrative: A Study in Eighteenth and Nineteenth Century Hermeneutics* (New Haven, CT: Yale University Press, 1974). For a more recent investigation into this "eclipse" oriented to the legacy of the Reformation, see Iain Provan, *The Reformation and the Right Reading of Scripture* (Waco, TX: Baylor University Press, 2017), 347-413. The movement from a confessional, theological reading of Holy Scripture to a descriptive one during this period has been addressed by Darren Sarisky in *Reading the Bible Theologically*, with special attention given to the influence of Benedict de Spinoza (seventeenth century) upon the rise of metaphysical and methodological naturalism in departure from premodern approaches to the Bible. Within Spinoza's naturalist view of reality, "Reading the Bible is about having skills to *do* certain things, not about being committed to received (theological) beliefs as starting points, which then come to be operative within the practice of exegesis." Darren Sarisky, *Reading the Bible Theologically*, Current Issues in Theology (Cambridge: Cambridge University Press, 2019), 167.

Scripture and doctrine was discouraged or abandoned by many biblical interpreters in a later period. Much of the reformers' interest in "what the text means" was gradually replaced by a pursuit of "what the text meant" by their eventual successors.[11]

In their climate of increasing literary production and revival of interest in the features of the biblical texts, many Reformation authors published their thoughts on the life and ministry of Jesus portrayed in the canonical Gospels. These authors rarely approached these Gospel texts with the scholarly detachment of their distant successors. Furthermore, their interest in Jesus as a historical figure was not distinct from their pursuit of the theological truths he taught in word and deed. Their starting point for studying Jesus was through the textual witness of the Gospel writers within the immediate context of faithful readers of those texts. This textual approach allowed the reformers to claim apostolic authority for their theology, reforms, and preaching by drawing consciously on the testimony of the apostles found in the Gospels. Particularly in the book of Matthew, the reformers heard the apostolic witness concerning Jesus' union in two natures, the necessity of repentance before entering the kingdom of God, the continuity of the Old Testament prophets and the apostolic testimony on God's purposes in Christ, and the humble submission of the Son to the will of the Father. Both in the reformers' commentaries and their sermons on Matthew, they emphasized the importance of these theological and textual features of Matthew's Gospel.

Modern exegetical concerns within the field of biblical studies deal with significantly different concerns in interpretation. A clear case in point is drawn simply from the major components of contemporary discussions of the Son of Man texts in Matthew. First, a great deal of the contemporary discussion is on the use of the Aramaic phrase of *bar nasha* in other ancient texts. The fact that this interchange focuses on Aramaic vocabulary and texts reveals that the prevailing interest of the interpreters lies in the historical occasion of Jesus' speech, rather than in the Greek text of the Gospel of Matthew.[12] Second, usually biblical scholars abbreviate any discussion of the authorial intention of the Gospel text or contrast it to Jesus' supposed consciousness in using the phrase, an implied reader's reaction, or even in the authenticity of such a saying from Jesus.[13] While modern exegetes grapple with the identity of the Son of Man by utilizing tools that enhance the historical background of the biblical texts, the reformers spent a great deal of their energies on the theological impact of the words of Matthew's texts and on the Old Testament texts lurking behind them.

Readers who are wearied by the barrage of historical data of extrabiblical details in the modern discussions will find the textual interests of the reformers to be a refreshing change. Modern interpreters interested in the grammatical, canonical, and theological meaning of biblical texts will have their interpretive skills sharpened through interacting with the reformers' interpretations. In

---

[11]Gerhard Maier, *Biblical Hermeneutics*, trans. Robert W. Yarbrough (Wheaton, IL: Crossway, 1994), 383-84.

[12]E.g., Maurice Casey, "The Jackals and the Son of Man," *Journal for the Study of the New Testament* 7, no. 23 (1985): 3-22.

[13]E.g., Ulrich Luz, "The Son of Matthew: Heavenly Judge or Human Christ," *Journal for the Study of the New Testament* 15, no. 48 (1992): 3-21. See also, David Bauer, *The Gospel of the Son of God* (Downers Grove, IL: IVP Academic, 2019), 256-58.

this manner, Stephen Fowl asserts that if biblical interpretation "is to flourish in the present, it will require contemporary believers to relearn the habits and practices that constituted a flourishing pattern of theological interpretation in the past."[14]

Of course, many aspects of the reformers' interpretive approaches remain in common practice today. Modern interpreters will appreciate the reformers' interest in subtle shifts of biblical vocabulary or the Greek verbal mood. The reformers' juxtaposition of the biblical author's viewpoint and that of the characters of the narrative provides an interesting and insightful contrast. The reformers' typical practice of homing in on the theological thrust of a particular text parallels the interests of those who are teaching or preaching the biblical texts in a church context.

For the reformers, their interest in the textual features of the Scriptures meshed well with their pursuit of the theological meaning of the author. Mickey Mattox identifies this connection in Luther's expositions. Mattox writes,

> In theological terms, this meant that Luther learned to intuit the divine mysteries inscribed into the words of the biblical texts in their original languages. Theological exegesis is focused on the biblical text itself, and the divinely intended meaning of scripture is to be found through determined struggle with the words themselves, a process that requires attention to every aspect of textual and grammatical analysis.[15]

One particular interest of the reformers that resounds with many contemporary interpreters is their interest in authorial intent. The reformers' textual interest stemmed from their perspective that authorial intention (both divine and human) was significant for textual meaning and that authorial intention could be discerned from features in the text.[16] Particularly, in the case of Matthew, the reformers are driven by two interests in their investigations of the biblical texts. First, they had a keen interest in what Jesus said and did. Second, they were interested in the unity and diversity of the Gospel accounts. Notably, they did not see these two interests as contrasting.

Luther demonstrates these interconnected interests in a sermon on Matthew 24:15-28. He writes,

> This chapter describes the termination and end of the two kingdoms: the kingdom of Judaism and the kingdom of the whole world. However, both the evangelists Matthew and Mark [chapter 13] combine the two kingdoms and do not follow the order which Luke has. They do not look further than giving and relating the words of Christ; they are unconcerned about what was said before or

---

[14]Stephen E. Fowl, *Theological Interpretation of the Bible*, Cascade Companions (Eugene: OR: Cascade, 2009), 55.

[15]Mickey L. Mattox, "Martin Luther," in *Christian Theologies of Scripture: A Comparative Introduction*, ed. Justin S. Holcomb (New York: New York University Press, 2006), 102-3.

[16]On the development of the concepts of authors and authorial intent during the Later Middle Ages that became the Reformation's inheritance, see Alastair Minnis, *Medieval Theory of Authorship: Scholastic Literary Attitudes in the Later Middle Ages*, 2nd ed. (Philadelphia: University of Pennsylvania Press, 2010), 75-103. Provan captures the reformers' understanding of reading Scripture for its "authorial intent" in this way, emphasizing their textual and/or literary outlook on the Bible: "To read Scripture 'literally,' in line with the Reformation perspectives on this topic, means to read it in accordance with its various, apparent *communicative intentions* as a collection of texts from the past now integrated into one Great Story, doing justice to such realities as literary convention, idiom, metaphor, and typology or figuration." Provan, *Reformation and the Right Reading of Scripture*, 85-86 (emphasis added). Marsh devotes special attention to Luther's interpretive vision and commitment to "authorial intent" in Marsh, *Martin Luther on Reading the Bible as Christian Scripture*, 123-40.

after. Luke, however, described it more clearly and with attention to order. He relates this discourse twice: first, briefly, in chapter 19[:41-44], where he speaks about the destruction of the Jews at Jerusalem, then in chapter 21[:5-28] he speaks about both these kingdoms successively.[17]

In this selection, Luther treats the passage as a genuine address of Jesus but also recognizes the Gospel writers' place in retelling the story. Luther also recognizes differences in the intentions of the authors demonstrated in their different presentations of the material. Where modern historical-critical scholars might note these differences and appeal to their respective source documents, the German reformer holds that the distinctions attest to authorial intentions. Luther claims that Matthew's presentation of Jesus' discourse reflects his theological intention in this passage (Mt 24–25)—namely, his concentration on the end of the world instead of the destruction of the Jews. The reformers were drawn to the theological purpose of the biblical author.

Typical Sources for Reformers' Comments on the Gospel of Matthew

Perceptive readers of the Reformation selections included in this volume will notice that there are three main types of sources used throughout this commentary. An expected and frequently used source type is the multitude of commentaries that are singularly focused on the book of Matthew. Reformation-era commentaries often included harmonies of multiple biblical books, but the Gospel of Matthew is very well represented in the extant literature.[18] Heinrich Bullinger, Franciscus Gomarus, and Wolfgang Musculus are prime examples of weighty commentary treatments on the book of Matthew. Furthermore, Zwingli, Melanchthon, and Oecolampadius are among those who produce significant "annotations" on Matthew's Gospel. Luther's published commentary on the Sermon on Mount (in Mt 5–7) is one of a multitude of full works dedicated either to the Sermon in Matthew or even just an exegetical treatment of the Lord's Prayer in Matthew 6.

The second source type from which selections are drawn is the Gospel harmonies produced by the reformers. Calvin's *Commentary on the Harmony of the Evangelists* is a well-known example of this type. In the Gospel harmonies, efforts vary as to whether attention is given to the wording of each Gospel's text (as in Calvin) or to an assimilation of all three (or four, as in Bullinger's *Sum of the Four Evangelists*). As a general rule in the harmonies, Matthean priority is observed. In so doing, the reformers are in keeping with an ancient liturgical tradition of highlighting Matthew's accounts and with a patristic exegetical tradition that often prioritized Matthew's Gospel.[19] The canonical ordering of Matthew as first among the Synoptics and the somewhat ambiguous reference to other Gospel accounts in Luke's preface allowed the reformers to utilize Matthean priority with little requisite defense.[20]

---

[17]LW 79:324.

[18]Compare the comments by Carl Beckwith in his introduction to *Ezekiel, Daniel* (RCS OT 13:xlii) and the comments by Beth Kreitzer in her introduction (xlv) to *Luke* (RCS NT 3:xlv).

[19]See Manlio Simonetti's introduction to *Matthew 1–13* (ACCS NT 1a:xxxvii-lii) for a description of the extant patristic sermons and published patristic "exegetical commentaries" on Matthew.

[20]See Kreitzer's introduction for a similarly brief discussion of Matthean priority and the comments for Lk 1:1-4 in the volume itself; RCS NT 3:xlv-xlvi.

The third source type, Reformation sermons, is used quite frequently in this volume and serves as a valuable source for textual comments. Published sermons afforded Reformation preachers the opportunity to expound on the biblical warrant of their particular program of reform. In order to make the connection between the proposed reforms (of theology or ethics) and the biblical texts, the preachers would often intersperse biblical exposition with theological or moral implications. Another regular practice of Reformation preachers was to make their textual observations toward the beginning of a sermon and then spend the remainder of the space in calling for specific applications derived from the textual meaning. Therefore, these sermons are often rich with theological exposition and vivid points of significance for their audiences.

Much Reformation preaching followed the schedule of an adopted liturgy—with notable exceptions such as Zwingli's series of sermons, beginning in 1519, from Matthew and then Acts. These common liturgies encouraged preachers to publish their sermons, knowing that they could be utilized by preachers in their tradition who would be following a similar (or identical) schedule for sermon texts. Often these sermons were collected and published in a work that covered much of the liturgical year's worth of texts (e.g., John Boys, Johannes Brenz, Niels Hemmingsen, Robert Rollock). As a literary whole, this sermon collection would cover a good number of Gospel texts, though it did result in some texts garnering more discussion than others. Due both to contemporary theological debates and to established liturgies, some Gospel texts appeared in sermonic commentaries more often than others. This disparity in sermonic commentaries could be even more exaggerated when including occasional sermons, which were sometimes the only works published by a preacher. The request to publish these occasional sermons often derived from the controversial nature of the biblical text exposited (e.g., George Close's *The Rock of Religion: Christ, Not Peter* or Ephraim Pagitt's *The Mystical Wolf*) or significance to Christian piety (e.g., Edward Reynolds's *Self-Denial* or Thomas Porter's *Spiritual Salt*). Sometimes expositional sermons of well-known reformers or preachers took several years or even decades to be collected by their successors, so that erstwhile individual sermons found a new literary context in these collections. In their latter form, the sermons provide a more comprehensive set of comments on the biblical texts (e.g., collections of the sermons of Luther, Bullinger, Cranmer, Latimer, or Donne).

Theological Themes

In any given time period of Christian history, contemporary theological debates cause certain biblical texts to garner much exegetical attention. In the Reformation era, heated discussions on particular biblical texts were a given. The Gospel of Matthew contains one of the most controversial texts of the Reformation period. In Matthew 16, the author includes an account of Peter's confession of Christ's identity. This confession and the subsequent response of Jesus, including that on "this rock" his "church" would be built, were interpreted in different ways by Roman Catholic and Protestant commentators. Indeed, this text figured into almost every debate about papal authority (as Peter's successor) and the true nature of the church (and the associated "keys"). The first issue concerned the identity of the "rock" (e.g., Peter himself, the content of his confession, or

Jesus himself as the Son of the living God). The second debate concerned the nature and identity of the "keys" (e.g., the power of absolution, the preaching of the gospel, the sacraments). As the reformers attempted to wrest the authority of the church from the grasp of the pope, a differing interpretation of this text proved crucial. Depending on one's interpretation of Matthew 16, the reformers were either usurping the provision that Christ left for his church in terms of an earthly head or they were returning to Christ's emphasis on the true confession of his identity as being foundational for the church.

Matthew 16 does not contain the only highly debated text from Matthew during the Reformation. The only other text in the canonical Gospels that makes use of the term *church* is found in Matthew 18, which also includes the idea of binding and loosing. This pivotal text played a crucial role for many reformers not only in their debates with Catholic apologists but also in the intra-Protestant debates about the nature of the true church and the significance of church discipline. Did Jesus intend to establish an orderly procedure for the church discipline in order to maintain the purity of the church? Or did he lay the groundwork for a sacramental system that would allow the church, especially its leaders, to absolve sins and grant forgiveness?

Other debates among the Protestants themselves drew heavily on texts in Matthew. The baptismal texts of Matthew 3 and Matthew 28 drew frequent comments and argumentation, especially as Anabaptist reformers insisted that these texts expected prerequisite repentance and faith from the baptismal candidate. Of course, Matthew's depiction of Jesus' last supper with his disciples figured into most of the debates about the proper understanding of the Eucharist and the presence of Christ in the elements. Matthew's important theme of the kingdom mentioned throughout the Gospel and especially in Matthew 24–25 saturated Reformation discussions on the nature of Christ's kingdom (e.g., spiritual or earthly, present or eschatological, exclusive to the church or inclusive of Jews) and the relationship of the church to the civil state. Furthermore, Christ's frequent use of Old Testament commands in his own teaching served as ample fodder for the Protestant debates on the proper use of the law for Christians (see Mt 5–7 and Mt 22). Against Roman Catholics and other Protestants, the reformers argued that their opponents' use of tradition in debate reflected the same preference for tradition over Scripture displayed by the Pharisees and religious leaders in their debates with Jesus (see Mt 15 and Mt 22).

Theological differences were not the only reasons that certain texts in Matthew drew great attention. Some texts were of particular importance because of their contribution to Christian piety either through their part in the established liturgy of the church or devotional aspects that were widely recognized in the texts. For example, a typical pattern of publishing on Matthew would be for a pastor, bishop, or lecturer to publish a sermon (or sermon series) on one section of Matthew. This focused publication is much more frequent than the more comprehensive commentaries or annotations on the entire book. Based on extant literature, the two most likely texts in Matthew for a focused publication are the Lord's Prayer and the crucifixion narrative. Both the prayer (in Mt 6) and the crucifixion (in Mt 27) receive this sermonic attention in ways that draw on church liturgy and reflect the preacher's devotional interests. The model quality of both passages becomes a frequent theme of the published sermons. Listeners are encouraged to "pray in this way" as the preacher reflects on the various features of the Lord's Prayer. Likewise, would-be disciples in the congregations are encouraged to emulate the humble sacrifice of Christ as they daily take up the cross. Furthermore, Reformation churches often maintained an orderly liturgy, including prescribed texts for given times in the Christian calendar. Certain seasons of the Christian calendar connected specifically with texts from the Gospels. Published sermons that were produced in this preaching regimen thus often focused on Gospel texts, such as the crucifixion narrative in Matthew. While these single sermons fail to provide much insight for Matthew's Gospel as a whole, taken with similar sermon efforts, these sermons provide ample insight into how Reformation preachers viewed particular texts.

Historical Reception of These Works

Some of these works were widely dispersed upon their first publication. In most cases, theological tracts or apologetic works spread more quickly than biblical commentaries. However, as the reputation of a reformer grew or the tradition to which he belonged became more established, the exegetical works had a waiting market and found quick reception. Other exegetical works had a regional or more sectarian appeal. If a work was closely tied to a particular liturgy or if it addressed the concerns of only a section of the reformers, then the readership might be much more limited. As noted previously, the type of interpretive work with the broadest readership during the Reformation was annotations, especially if they were circulated in conjunction with a translation of the Bible. If so, they would be read anywhere that particular translation circulated. The brevity of these comments does not correspond with their amount of impact.

Providing more details than the annotations, the numerous published commentaries of the Reformation period were helpful tools for the leading reformers to shape the preaching and teaching of those who belonged to their same tradition. These commentaries afforded a more comprehensive discussion of textual features or of dogmatic positions gleaned from those features. The production of such commentaries helped accomplish the consolidation of various Protestant traditions (e.g., Lutheran, Reformed) and developed the accepted interpretations of specific texts for those traditions.

This present volume on Matthew follows the trajectory of the Reformation literature itself and therefore draws significantly on published sermons or collections of sermons. Not only is this approach apt because of the frequency of published sermons in the Reformation corpus, but also because it could be argued that the "heart" of the reformers was best heard (or read) in their sermons. The Reformation ideals did not advance simply based on theological disputations, scholarly treatises, or the persuasion of the authorities. The fiery passion of the reformers comes across in their sermons as they attempt to convince peasants and princes, merchants and magistrates, the simple and the educated of the biblical veracity of their teachings.

Along with the comments from annotations and Reformation commentaries, the significant amount of sermonic material included in this commentary also benefits the contemporary preacher and teacher. Most of the textual comments included herein were chosen based on three traits. First, the most helpful comments are those that are decidedly textual in nature. The supposed "historical gap" is reduced considerably when the comments are drawn from the still current biblical texts. Second, sermonic comments of special theological importance and relevance maintain their value for contemporary readers. Many of the theological issues explained in the reformers' sermons from Matthew still interest the contemporary interpreter. Hopefully, the selections in this commentary capture the reformers' insights and not simply their ire. Most preachers and teachers will benefit from the hours (or years) of reflection by the reformers on a given biblical-theological issue.

Third, the tedium and lack of spontaneity in many modern biblical commentaries is absent from most of the comments found in the Reformation sermons. Both literary and rhetorical flair are found in the sermons of the reformers. The political upheaval, persecution, and even pending martyrdom surrounding these reformers supplied their preaching with vibrancy and urgency. This underlying enthusiasm often complemented the literary or hortatory skill of the Reformation preachers. Hopefully, reading through these comments will not be without effect on the contemporary preacher or teacher.

An Encouragement to the Reader

The use of overviews throughout this commentary intends to help the reader make the transition from one's reading of Matthew's text to the insights of the reformers. The overviews provide the main thrust of the Reformation selections to follow. The flow of thought of the succeeding selections can be anticipated with the help of the notation of this central idea. Possibly, disparate views or approaches can be more readily recognized with the help of these section overviews.

Throughout the commentary, the supplied footnotes will serve the readers who would like to explore the literary context of the comments even further. Some of the works already existed in suitable translation, and in most of those cases the existing translation was used. In other cases, a new English translation for the selection is provided with references indicating the source texts. Moreover, since some of the works were originally published in sixteenth- or seventeenth-century English or the translations into English came at an early period, many selections have been revised to remove archaisms in style, vocabulary, and grammar. In each case, great effort was given to preserve a close verbal proximity to the published form.

By drawing on commentaries, Gospel harmonies, treatises, and sermons, a good cross-section of the various confessional strands of the Reformation are represented. Furthermore, both the most familiar names of the Reformation are included along with many others who were known by their immediate contemporaries but appear as "minor" voices in contemporary assessments of the period. This variety of exegetical sources can provide a fuller picture of the Reformation conversations and might serve as catalysts for cross-denominational biblical discussions in the present day.

As readers work through the selections in this volume, our hope is that they will enjoy the creativity of the Reformation authors and, moreover, be challenged by the inherent connection they make between Christian piety and interpreting the biblical texts. By God's grace, may this study of Matthew's portrayal of the person and work of Jesus Christ, the Messiah, as interpreted by the reformers serve their purpose of proclaiming the good news about Jesus, the beloved Son and God with us (Mt 1; 3).

In his own preaching on Matthew, Luther commented that listeners should "note [something] here for the benefit of the intelligent and learned who are to discuss Scripture. Imitating or conjecturing is not right in Scripture; rather, one should and must be certain of his case."[21] Let us, then, read the Gospel According to Matthew with the men and women of the Reformation era, taking heed of Luther's reminder: Matthew "is both a terrifying and a consoling Gospel; terrifying to the great, learned, holy, and mighty, who all despise Christ; consoling to the humble and despised, to whom alone Christ is revealed."[22]

Jason K. Lee
William M. Marsh

---

[21]LW 76:303, a sermon on Mt 13:24-30, "Gospel for the Fifth Sunday After Epiphany."
[22]LW 76:71, a sermon on Mt 2:1-12, "Gospel for the Day of the Wise Men."

COMMENTARY ON MATTHEW

OVERVIEW: Reformation commentators continued the ancient and medieval practice of providing a "preface" on books of the Bible. These "prologues" aimed to orient readers to the central theological meaning or subject (i.e., *argumentum*) of a biblical book alongside establishing the distinctive contribution of the human author as an instrument through whom the Holy Spirit conveyed authoritative divine intention and truth. The Gospel of Matthew received such prefatory treatment, sometimes in prefaces submitted for all four Gospels as a whole and at other times in prologues devoted solely to Matthew's Gospel. In general, Reformation writers were concerned that the Gospel genre not be mistaken for mere historical record. Although the Gospel of Matthew certainly presented a narrative or "story," what made it "gospel" was its faithful proclamation of Jesus Christ, the Son of God and Son of David, according to the Old Testament (i.e., "the Law and the Prophets") Scriptures for the forgiveness of our sins and our salvation. In fact, Christ was to be beheld properly in the Gospel accounts as in the rest of the New Testament writings rather than sought after in venerated relics. Here in the text of holy Scripture the crucified and risen Lord Jesus would be seen more clearly and truly than if he appeared bodily before one's very eyes. The reformers are careful to indicate that it is the Spirit of Christ himself who is at work in a biblical author like Matthew, utilizing the human author's own personality, style, and rhetoric to convey under divine inspiration and power the gospel's promise of righteousness through faith in Jesus Christ. Christ is the mediator of eternal salvation—that is, God's bestowal of the truly blessed life.

Prolegomena

THE LIVING CHRIST BEHELD IN THE WRITTEN GOSPELS. DESIDERIUS ERASMUS: If someone exhibited a print made by the feet of Christ, how we Christians would prostrate ourselves, how we would adore! Why, then, do we not rather venerate his living and breathing image, preserved in these books? If someone displayed the tunic of Christ, would we not fly to the ends of the earth to kiss it? But even if you were to produce every possession he owned, there is nothing that would show Christ more clearly and more truly than the written Gospels. Through our love of Christ, we enrich a statue of wood or stone with jewels and gold. Why do we not rather adorn these books with gold and jewels and anything more precious, for they recall Christ to us more vividly than any little statue. A statue shows only the appearance of his body—if indeed it shows anything of that—but these books show you the living image of his holy mind and Christ himself, speaking, healing, dying, rising to life again. In short, they restore Christ to us so completely and so vividly that you would see him less clearly should you behold him standing before your very eyes. PARACLESIS.[1]

ONLY ONE GOSPEL. MARTIN LUTHER: The gospel is a story about Christ, God's and David's Son, who died and was raised and is established as Lord. This is the gospel in a nutshell. Just as there is no more than one Christ, so there is and may be

---

[1]CWE 41:422 (LB 5:144B-D).

no more than one gospel. Since Paul and Peter too teach nothing but Christ, in the way we have just described, so their epistles can be nothing but the gospel. Yes, even the teaching of the prophets, in those places where they speak of Christ, is nothing but the true, pure, and proper gospel—just as if Luke or Matthew had described it. For the prophets have proclaimed the gospel and spoken of Christ, as St. Paul here reports and as everyone indeed knows. Thus, when Isaiah in chapter 53 says how Christ should die for us and bear our sins, he has written the pure gospel. And I assure you, if a person fails to grasp this understanding of the gospel, they will never be able to be illuminated in the Scripture nor will they receive the right foundation. A Brief Instruction on What to Look for and Expect in the Gospels.[2]

The Gospels Are About Christ's Mediatorial Office. John Calvin: Again, the four histories, which relate how Christ discharged the office of mediator, have with great propriety received this designation. As the birth, death, and resurrection of Christ contain the whole of our salvation, and are therefore the peculiar subject of the Gospel, the name of Evangelists is justly and suitably applied to those who place before our eyes Christ who has been sent by the Father, that our faith may acknowledge him to be the Author of a blessed life. The Argument, Commentary on a Harmony on the Gospels.[3]

Matthew, from Fraud to Faith. Johannes Brenz: [He] also wanted to show in the character of the clerk[†] the greatness of the power of the gospel of Christ, as well as the extent of the efficacy and power of true faith in Christ. Matthew was for sure a wicked man and a well-known fraud. But after he was gripped with love of the gospel and believed in Christ, it became so foreign to his character to continue perpetrating crimes and deceits that he preferred to abandon all of his own interests, and

even his own life, rather than neglect Christ's calling and lead a wicked life. Therefore, the one who once had been a fraud became through faith a righteous man. He who had once been wicked became through faith holy. He who once did not refrain from engaging in every type of sin became through faith a zealous adherent of every good work. A faith that is fraudulent and merely imagined permits a man to pursue his former sins. But true faith, as it regenerates a person in Christ, so also remakes them to pursue the calling of the Holy Spirit when the lusts of the flesh have been tamed. Therefore, let us strive after this goal, in keeping with Matthew's example, to lay hold of and pursue true faith in Christ. But may we also receive and hold in mind with the greatest diligence what Matthew wrote: the verdict of the final judgment will not be rendered according to the laws of Solon, Lycurgus, Justinian, or the popes of Rome.[‡] No, it will be based upon this teaching of Matthew: he who has faith in Christ will be saved. He who does not have that faith will perish. Matthew is not the least of those of whom Christ himself testified. "Truly I say to you," he said, "that you who have followed me will also sit upon twelve thrones—when the Son of Man sits on the throne of his majesty at the renewal—judging the twelve tribes of Israel."

This is the precise point when it comes to Matthew: that we know we are to listen to his account not as we usually do when someone describes mere secular histories. Rather, we must apply our ears to him as the one who proclaim the very oracles of heaven. Preface on the Apostle and Evangelist, Matthew.[4]

Matthew's Gospel Esteemed by the Early Church. Heinrich Bullinger: The Gospel of Matthew had so much authority in the church of

---

[2]LW 35:118-19* (WA 10:1.1.10); citing Rom 1:2; Is 53.
[3]CTS 1:xxxvii (CO 45:2).

[4]Brenz, *In Scriptum Apostoli et Euangelistae Matthaei*, 10-11; citing Mt 19:28. [†]*Cancellarius*, i.e., Matthew. [‡]Solon (c. 630–c.560 BC) and Lycurgus (c. 625 BC) established the constitutions of Athens and Sparta respectively. Emperor Justinian (482–565 BC) compiled and revised Roman law into the *Codex Justinianus*. Gratian (c. 12th c.) began the codification of papal, or canon, law with the *Decretum Gratiani*.

the Lord from the time of Christ that it was always placed among the foremost documents and in the first rank, and finally it was expounded by the very apostles of the Lord. St. Athanasius[†] tells us that James, the brother of the Lord, expounded the Gospel According to Matthew to the church in Jerusalem. And he says that the histories provide evidence that the apostle Bartholomew expounded the same gospel to the Indians very faithfully. Therefore, dear readers, let us not be reluctant to apply our whole selves to it with the greatest rigor and fervent prayers, that we may understand the most holy Gospel of such an important apostle—a Gospel inspired by the Spirit of Christ our Lord and recorded with utmost scrupulousness by a most trustworthy apostle. May we understand it correctly, truly, and with devotion, and to the great benefit of our souls. The fruit that we should hope for from it is not at all typical but actually everlasting life. For the heavenly Father has offered the world life in his Son, and this Gospel proclaims that Christ is the Son of God, that whoever believes in him has everlasting life. ON THE GOSPEL OF ST. MATTHEW, THE APOSTLE AND HIS WORK.[5]

A GOSPEL FOR AFFLICTED CONSCIENCES. JOHANNES BUGENHAGEN: Matthew first writes that Christ the Son of God, promised in the Law and the Prophets, came in our flesh for both Jews and Gentiles. This means that he who saves his people from their sins was born of a virgin and the flesh of David according to God's promises. Then in the third chapter Matthew begins from John's preaching as do the other Gospel writers and shows us Christ, who reveals by his teaching of the gospel and amazing works that he is the Son of God in our flesh. But finally, he brings this God and man before us on the cross as our high priest, the sole sacrifice for our salvation, the eternal King rising from the dead, and the continual priest and mediator at the Father's right hand. Afflicted consciences will not deny that this, moreover, is a description of Christ, that it is the true gospel. THE ARGUMENT.[6]

MATTHEW, A HUMBLE INSTRUMENT OF THE SPIRIT OF CHRIST. HEINRICH BULLINGER: Now the actual construction or building of any narrative or historical account consists both in subjects and words.[†] The subject is the actual deeds and words of Jesus Christ the Son of God as they were exemplified in his particular circumstances. Specifically, it is that blessed life which—in Christ, through faith, freely—is bestowed upon those who believe. It is promised in the gospel, but it is also that truly righteous life that both Christ's words and actions exemplify and impress upon us. This is the argument of Matthew's entire work.

In addition, the subjects are related by a twofold arrangement. I mean first that natural arrangement whereby events are described in the order in which they occurred. And second, there is the arrangement dependent upon the writer's design [artificiali], whereby the natural order is not preserved in every detail, but events are explained as the writer thought fit and as the needs of his audience required. In the course of the narration and series of books, I will show that Matthew made use of both types. I have divided my commentaries on Matthew in two separate volumes for this reason especially, to make the Gospel storyline perfectly clear, to render it conspicuous, and to aid the readers' memory. Matthew uses words that are suited to history, ones that are simple, straightforward, appropriate to the subject, and not at all recondite, and the diction moves along with a certain kind of consistent gentleness. Indeed, Matthew wastes no time in his treatment of subjects on laborious descriptions of events, persons, places, and things. And he takes the same approach to the complex discussions of causes and similar practices used

---

[5]Bullinger, *In . . . Evangelium secundum Matthaeum commentariorum* (1546), 2v. [†]Athanasius, *Synopsis Scripturae Sacrae*, PG 28:431-32.

[6]Bugenhagen, *In IIII. Priora Capita Euangelii secundum Matthaeum* (1543), A5-A6.

here and there among secular histories with great pomp, as decoration for their accounts. Therefore, in the way he composes phrases Matthew does not employ rhetorical trappings and embellishments, highly colored and gaudy words. He simply offered himself as an instrument to the Spirit of Christ, and what the Spirit revealed and suggested Matthew indiscriminately set down [*profudit*]. Now the Spirit of Christ is humble, plain, untainted, undefiled, and candid. And so his style, which Matthew used, is pure and entirely distinct

from all the exaggeration and passion of human arrogance. That most divine Writer understood that it is not the polished tongue barking learnedly on the outside, but the Holy Spirit working efficaciously within that works to produce salvation. On the Gospel of St. Matthew, the Apostle and His Work.[7]

---

[7]Bullinger, *In . . . Evangelium secundum Matthaeum commentariorum* (1546), 3v. †This is a quite close adaptation of Cicero's *De Oratore* 2.15.63.

1:1-17 THE GENEALOGY OF JESUS CHRIST

The book of the genealogy of Jesus Christ, the son of David, the son of Abraham.

²Abraham was the father of Isaac, and Isaac the father of Jacob, and Jacob the father of Judah and his brothers, ³and Judah the father of Perez and Zerah by Tamar, and Perez the father of Hezron, and Hezron the father of Ram,ᵃ ⁴and Ram the father of Amminadab, and Amminadab the father of Nahshon, and Nahshon the father of Salmon, ⁵and Salmon the father of Boaz by Rahab, and Boaz the father of Obed by Ruth, and Obed the father of Jesse, ⁶and Jesse the father of David the king.

And David was the father of Solomon by the wife of Uriah, ⁷and Solomon the father of Rehoboam, and Rehoboam the father of Abijah, and Abijah the father of Asaph,ᵇ ⁸and Asaph the father of Jehoshaphat, and Jehoshaphat the father of Joram, and Joram the father of Uzziah, ⁹and Uzziah the father of Jotham, and Jotham the father of Ahaz, and Ahaz the father of Hezekiah, ¹⁰and Hezekiah the father of Manasseh,

and Manasseh the father of Amos,ᶜ and Amos the father of Josiah, ¹¹and Josiah the father of Jechoniah and his brothers, at the time of the deportation to Babylon.

¹²And after the deportation to Babylon: Jechoniah was the father of Shealtiel,ᵈ and Shealtiel the father of Zerubbabel, ¹³and Zerubbabel the father of Abiud, and Abiud the father of Eliakim, and Eliakim the father of Azor, ¹⁴and Azor the father of Zadok, and Zadok the father of Achim, and Achim the father of Eliud, ¹⁵and Eliud the father of Eleazar, and Eleazar the father of Matthan, and Matthan the father of Jacob, ¹⁶and Jacob the father of Joseph the husband of Mary, of whom Jesus was born, who is called Christ.

¹⁷So all the generations from Abraham to David were fourteen generations, and from David to the deportation to Babylon fourteen generations, and from the deportation to Babylon to the Christ fourteen generations.

a Greek *Aram*; also verse 4   b *Asaph* is probably an alternate spelling of *Asa*; some manuscripts *Asa*; also verse 8   c *Amos* is probably an alternate spelling of *Amon*; some manuscripts *Amon*; twice in this verse   d Greek *Salathiel*; twice in this verse

OVERVIEW: The Reformation commentators indicate that the primary purpose of Matthew is to identify Jesus as the Messiah seen in his being the promised seed of David and Abraham. Jesus fulfilled all the messianic expectations of the Old Testament promises, even if not those of his Jewish contemporaries. From the genealogy provided to the narratives that follow, Matthew's readers have every reason to receive Jesus as the promised Messiah. The commentators also observe a variety of intriguing features of the genealogy. For example, Thomas Cartwright notes that Matthew traces Jesus' lineage through Solomon rather than Nathan, as in Luke's Gospel, perhaps because Matthew is not interested in a detailed, natural lineage but in identifying Jesus as being in a succession of kings.

Others remark that the inclusion of "sinners" in Jesus' genealogy is to help identify him as the one who will save his people from their sins, including his progenitors.

Among the apologetic questions that the Reformation authors address are the supposed historical inaccuracies in Matthew's genealogy and why Matthew uses Joseph's instead of Mary's lineage. Potential historical inaccuracies appear when comparing Matthew's genealogy with the Old Testament narrative texts that chronicle the lives of the kings of Israel and Judah. Two common parries to this skeptical thrust are the appeals to Matthew's technique of condensing the genealogy to fit the pattern of fourteens (Mt 1:17) or to copyist errors when there are additions to the genealogy. On the issue of Joseph's lineage, many commentators assert that since both Joseph and Mary descend from David either could be used, while noting that Matthew prefers Joseph due to Jewish custom of tracing the lineage through the father.

1:1-6 *Jesus' Genealogy to David*

THE END OF GENEALOGICAL CONTROVERSIES.
MARTIN LUTHER: It is therefore enough to know from this genealogy that Christ came from the tribe of David, the son of Abraham. And if that is the case, then endless wrangling over the genera-tions of all individuals and lines is in vain. For once it has been established that Christ, the King and Priest, comes from the tribe of Judah, the Levitical priesthood is overturned at its foundation, and the boasting of the Jews about their Levitical priest-hood as if it were everlasting is false, since Christ, the King and Priest, even if he were yet to come (according to their error), would nevertheless take away their Levitical priesthood and take its place. For it is written, "You are a priest forever."

Therefore, Matthew straightaway puts forward the argument that this man, Jesus of Nazareth (who had certainly come, seeing that the Jews not only knew him but even crucified him), was the Christ, that is, the Son of David, the son of Abraham. He thereby wished to teach the Jews right at the very beginning [of his Gospel] that their worship and priesthood and kingdom had come to an end. The Jews certainly could not deny that Jesus was this man from the tribe of David, the son of Abraham. For Matthew confidently takes this as granted from their very own genealo-gies. But the point he makes is that this very Jesus is the Christ, the promised one they were awaiting. ANNOTATIONS ON MATTHEW.[1]

THE BOOK OF THE BIRTH OF JESUS CHRIST.
WOLFGANG MUSCULUS: The Evangelist intended to cover not only the history of the birth of Christ but also his life, teaching, miracles, death, and resurrection. Nevertheless, he wished to begin his history in this way because of the Hebrews, for whose sake he wrote his Gospel, so that he could declare that this Jesus was the one whom God formerly promised to their fathers. He did this to show that Christ was born by a succession of generations from Abraham to David, according to the oracles of God. The Evangelist knew that all who were required to keep the faith of the Jews shared this same beginning. With this introduction, he certainly provided no little encouragement to the minds that were not absolutely blinded when reading these commentaries, because those Jews who were godly waited with such great eagerness for the lineage and ancestry of not just anyone, but him who was promised, who was the Messiah: Christ the Lord. Therefore, the Evangelist does not say, "The book of the birth of Jesus of Nazareth or Galilee," but "The book of the begetting of Jesus Christ," that is, the Anointed One, which the Hebrews call Messiah in their own language. COMMENTARY ON MATTHEW 1:1.[2]

THE GENEALOGY AS A GUIDE FOR READERS.
HUGH BROUGHTON: The holy genealogy of Jesus Christ—which may not be reckoned in the number of those profane ones that St. Paul condemns in 1 Timothy 1:4—does not consist in a vain repetition of names, as many do think. Neither is the knowledge thereof superfluous—as some do affirm. But verily—if it be rightly understood—it is of exceedingly great use and consequence; not only to prove Christ to be the promised seed, which is a weighty point, but it also serves as a special guide to direct us in the true understanding of all the holy story. For the native judgment of all men teaches that histories cannot be learned rightly without knowledge of the person upon whom the narrations go. That being so, all who look for salvation by Scripture, which calls us unto our Savior, should have a special care to know our Lord's line. For upon it all the stories

---

[1]LW 67:8 (WA 38:448-49); citing Ps 110:4; Heb 5:6; 6:20; 7:17, 21.

[2]Musculus, *In Evangelistam Matthaeum Commentarii* (1556), 3.

principally go, either in open phrase of words, or else with some close relation. The one who will take but a serious view of our Lord's line of fathers shall soon see how all the holy story depends upon it, and from it, as from a fountain, branches itself into a most pleasant variety of all God's holy proceedings, in the wonderful preservation of his church, and in the fearful overthrow of all the enemies thereof. . . .

St. Matthew begins the story of our Lord's fathers no higher than Abraham. First, because the land of Canaan, where the kingdom should arise, was first promised to Abraham. Second, Christ was first promised to him in open, distinct, and plain words. Third, he is made father of all the heathen that should follow his belief, and the heathen were to offer first fruits at Jerusalem . . . and so for Jews and Gentiles, the beginning from him is very fit. THE HOLY GENEALOGIE OF JESUS CHRIST.[3]

JESUS AS SON OF DAVID AND SON OF ABRA-HAM. CHRISTOPHER BLACKWOOD: Here is a description of Christ's genealogy from Abraham to Christ in a direct line: Abraham begat Isaac, Isaac begat Jacob, Jacob begat Judas and his brethren— that is, Jacob begat not only Judah but the other eleven patriarchs who were in a collateral line. The Evangelist goes no higher than Abraham to derive Christ's pedigree because he counted it sufficient to show that Christ according to the flesh was the Son of Abraham and David, to whose families the promise of the Messiah was bound, "In your seed shall all the nations of the earth be blessed"; "When you shall sleep with your fathers, I will set up your seed after you, and I will establish the throne of his kingdom forever." AN EXPOSITION UPON THE GOSPEL OF MATTHEW.[4]

THE SONS OF DAVID, THE SONS OF ABRAHAM. WOLFGANG MUSCULUS: These two are distin-

guished and foremost among the fathers just as certain family heads are distinguished among the rest. Their reputation and memory had always been most sacred to all Jews, especially because of the promises made to them concerning the Christ, who would be born of their very own seed. For more about these promises, see Genesis 12 and 22; 2 Samuel 7; 1 Chronicles 17; and Psalm 89 and Psalm 132. This Evangelist knew this, and from the beginning he immediately and clearly called Jesus Christ the Son of David and Abraham, so that he would make the Jews consider with more attentive minds the list of the fathers which he drew up. COMMENTARY ON MATTHEW 1:1.[5]

JESUS AS BOTH CHRIST AND SON. CORNELIUS JANSEN: Jesus is the proper name of the incarnate Word. Christ functions as a personal title (cognomen),† not a general title of office, though in Greek it plainly signifies the same thing as the Hebrew messiah and the Latin unctus (anointed). He has been called by this personal title so that, first, he might be distinguished from others who were called "Jesus" in ancient times. Then it is signified that this [Jesus] is called "Christ" or "Anointed" in a personal and unique sense. He is the highest king, priest, and prophet, whom kings, priests, and prophets prefigured by the anointing that dedicated them to their offices. This is why this personal title (cognomen) "Christ" applies to our Jesus so uniquely that nobody except he may be understood when it is expressed without qualification. He was anointed with the oil of righteousness and the Holy Spirit in a singular way, beyond all his companions.†

"Son of David, Son of Abraham." That is, he was their descendant according to the common Hebrew usage. All the same, Matthew preferred to say "son" rather than "descendant" here because Christ was born from other parents for the sake of David and Abraham, not the reverse. He mentioned only these two because they above all received the promise that Christ would be born

---

[3]Broughton, *Holy Genealogie*, unpaginated, sections 1 and 2 including the preface "To the Christian Reader."*

[4]Blackwood, *Expositions and Sermons upon . . . Matthew* (1659), 6*; citing Gen 22:18; 2 Sam 7:12, 13.

[5]Musculus, *In Evangelistam Matthaeum Commenarii* (1556), 3.

from them. Matthew put David first because the memory of the Davidic promise was more recent, honored, celebrated, and pleasing to the Jews, as Chrysostom[5] and his followers. An everlasting kingdom was attributed to Christ as the successor of David. Therefore, he is everywhere acclaimed and called "the Son of David" by the blind, the crowd, and children, as is clear in Matthew 12:21, and elsewhere.

The word *son* in the second place in the sequence can be in reference to Christ as well, so that he is identified as the son of both David and Abraham. Or else it refers to David, so that Christ is Abraham's "son" by consequence. The latter corresponds to the Hebrew custom, which in ordered genealogies tend to refer the term "son" to the immediate predecessor. COMMENTARY ON THE GOSPEL OF MATTHEW.[6]

OUTSIDERS BROUGHT NEAR. RICHARD WARD: "Boaz of Rahab." It may here be demanded: Why in the genealogy of our blessed Savior are none of the holy women reckoned up but only those whom the Scriptures tax and reprehend as sinners? I answer: This was done first of all because Christ came into this world to save sinners and to take away their sins. Sinners are reckoned up in his genealogy, and he is said to be "descended of them," because he descended from heaven "for them." Christ, for the comfort of poor penitent sinners, assumed that nature which once was sinful that he might separate it from sin. . . . Third and last, this is done to manifest Christ's glory, in that he took not any of his holiness from his parents or progenitors, they being wicked.

"Salmon begat Boaz of Rahab: and Boaz Obed of Ruth." Here it will be questioned, to what end these are set down, for they do not seem pertinent to the matter in hand. I answer, these things are not set down in vain, but for our instruction, teaching these three things to us. First, Rahab was a harlot and yet her husband took her to himself, even though she was such. So, Christ has married himself to the Gentiles, who were spiritual fornicators through sin. Second, Ruth was a stranger and very poor, yet Boaz did not despise her for her poverty nor abhor her for the wickedness of her country. No more does Christ despise us, being most poor and beggarly, through the want of goodness and worthy to be abhorred for the wickedness of our lives. Third, to teach us that as Ruth left her country and her father's house and all her kindred, and then was ennobled by this marriage. So, we must likewise leave our old conversation so that we may be joined in marriage to Christ. THEOLOGICAL QUESTIONS.[7]

1:7-17 Jesus' Genealogy from Solomon to Jacob, Joseph's Father

MATTHEW'S GENEALOGY COMPARED TO THE PROPHET'S. FRANCISCUS GOMARUS: With respect to the kings, adversaries attack Matthew, and in their own examinations they endeavor to disagree with the prophets to demonstrate by a twofold argument (but both not of the same weight).

Indeed, the first, and trivial, is dependent on the fact that in Matthew 1:8 he writes, "Uzziah of Joram." But indeed, in contrast, the sacred history in 2 Chronicles 26:1 asserts that he was the son of Amaziah. But this is of lesser importance and explained well by men of education. Because these two, which they endeavor to combine with one another, are different but not opposed. For Amaziah—as it were his father, the closest one— begat Uzziah (also well-known as Azariah), but

---

[6]Jansen, *Commentarius in Evangelium secundum Matthaeum*, 24-25; citing 1 Kings 5:1. †A *cognomen* in ancient Rome was a "third name" or nickname, such as "Africanus," that often was passed down through a family line, effectively becoming part of the family name (or surname). Jansen's sense throughout this passage is that "Christ" does not function as a general title for Jesus as it did in the Old Testament but applies to him in a personal and unique way (*antonomastice*, meaning "to use an epithet as a personal name, surname"). †Compare the Vulgate translation of Ps 45:7 (Vg. Ps 44:8) and Heb 1:9. The echo of the latter passage especially seems intentional. §Chrysostom, *Homilies on Matthew*, NPNF[1] 10:10-11.

[7]Ward, *Theological Questions upon . . . St. Matthew* (1640), 9*; citing Ps 45:10.

indeed Joram also, as forefather, through the great grandson Amaziah, from afar off. In the same manner, in the sacred writings, posterity is called by the name not only of their own father but also of grandfathers, even of a son here and there. However, although Matthew may omit the three kings in between, nothing has made it an oratorical attack on history, but to make it suitable, helpful to the memory (to harmonize into groups of fourteen), and of profit.

But in the second, a more serious argument is seen concerning kings Josiah and Jechoniah, and with major difficulty it has thrown not a few better-known interpreters into confusion. For Matthew in verse 11 said, "And Josiah begot Jechoniah and his brothers during the deportation to Babylon." But against this, the prophet claims in 1 Chronicles 3:16 that Jechoniah was the son of Jehoiakim, from which they object that their disagreement is apparent.

With some difficulty it is attacked in two parts by ancient and later theologians. For some deny obstinately an antecedent cause of one, but others a consequence. Indeed, an antecedent cause, wherein what is put forward might not be a genuine Matthean reading, on account of those words being changed in common copies. This happens as one may be omitted by Matthew while placing descendants between Josiah and Jechoniah, following after a defect of copying. And this they regard to be demonstrated from it, because in this genealogy from the Evangelist (as v. 7 itself concludes) there are fourteen generations from David to the Babylonian transmigration, and from there to Jesus Christ, just as many are recounted and therefore just as many are maintained in a correct reading.

For neither is it still likely from anyone of sound mind to arise a writer, much less an Evangelist, who in the final bringing together of a few names of this kind (not describing process) is able to wander in mind. And, if that common reading is strong in one of two groups of fourteen (evidently second or third), a descendant may clearly be needed for a correct number. Although, with

respect to an old error of copyists, that may be rejected. On the other hand, it may not be an unimportant conjecture, or regarding a reading of codices of uncertain reliability, but restored in an earlier place by Matthew (the calculation of the number rightly withdrawn and thus, by God's providence, opposing the means of corruption) by clear evidence from sacred history. And therefore they produce another fuller and genuine reading, but they disagree, as is fitting to themselves, with a variety of names.

For some, with reference to this, with carefulness with regard to copies of this genealogy, after the words "and Josiah bore Jechoniah" recommend reading, "But Jechoniah bore Jechoniah." Because clearly, Jehoiakim himself would have the same name as his son Jechoniah. ON THE GENEALOGY OF CHRIST.[8]

THE KINGS IN JESUS' GENEALOGY. THOMAS CARTWRIGHT: The same we read to have been done of king Abijah of the posterity of David, who married in the same tribe of Benjamin. Neither ought it to trouble any, as if the stairs of Christ's natural pedigree from the Virgin Mary were thus made hazardous, unless in the tribe and family of Joseph, the tribe also and family of the virgin be concluded. For by the testimonies of the angel and the Evangelist, he is infallibly verified to be the son of David by the persecution of Herod raised against the infants of the house of David, and finally, by the constrained journey of the holy virgin to go to Bethlehem, the city of David, to be taxed. And although it is called into doubt whether our Savior came from Solomon or from Nathan, and therefore also doubted whether his natural pedigree or lineage be laid out by Matthew or Luke, yet—they both being the sons of David—there is by this doubt no question moved whether he be David's son or no. Moreover, as it is evident that the light of Solomon was quite quenched in Jechoniah, who was the last of that family, it is

---

[8]Gomarus, *Examen controversiarum de genealogia Christi*, 301-2; citing 1 Chron 3:11-12.

manifest that Matthew does not propound unto himself the natural descent of our Savior, which draws the line of his pedigree by Solomon. For the other governors of the people, which are reckoned up after Jechoniah, are not his natural posterity or succession, but only—as they are called—legal. That is to say, those whom the laws of the princes under whom the people were in bondage did appoint to succeed to him in government. Wherefore, as Luke unfolds the natural pedigree of our Savior Christ, so does Matthew set forth the kings and princes that ruled over the people of God, thereby to declare that our Savior Christ is the king and prince whom all they were the figures and shadows of. For as it is necessary to know that he was David's natural son, so it is also requisite to be understood that he succeeded him in his kingdom, to the end that the promise of the everlasting kingdom of David might be verified. The truth of which is in Christ alone, the outward scepter being utterly wrung from the hands of David's posterity. CONFUTATION OF THE RHEMISTS TRANSLATION.[9]

THE KINGS AFTER BABYLONIAN CAPTIVITY. JOHN CALVIN: That is, after the Jews were carried into captivity: for the Evangelist means that the descendants of David, from being kings, then became exiles and slaves. As that captivity was a sort of destruction, it came to be wonderfully arranged by divine providence, not only that the Jews again united in one body, but even that some vestiges of dominion remained in the family of David. For those who returned home submitted, of their own accord, to the authority of Zerubbabel. In this manner, the fragments of the royal scepter lasted till the coming of Christ was at hand, agreeably to the prediction of Jacob: "The scepter shall not depart from Judah, nor a lawgiver from between his feet, until Shiloh come." And even during that wretched and melancholy dispersion, the nation never ceased to be illuminated by some rays of the grace of God. . . .

By the name "Christ" ["Messiah"], "Anointed," Matthew points out his office to inform the readers that this was not a private person, but one divinely anointed to perform the office of Redeemer. What that anointing was, and to what it referred, I shall not now illustrate at great length. As to the word itself, it is only necessary to say that, after the royal authority was abolished, it began to be applied exclusively to him, from whom they were taught to expect a full recovery of the lost salvation. So long as any splendor of royalty continued in the family of David, the kings were typically called *christoi* (anointed). But that the fearful desolation which followed might not throw the minds of the godly into despair, it pleased God to appropriate the name of *messiah* (anointed), to the Redeemer alone: as is evident from Daniel. The evangelical history everywhere shows that this was an ordinary way of speaking at the time when the Son of God was "manifested in the flesh." COMMENTARY ON A HARMONY OF THE EVANGELISTS.[10]

MATTHEW'S REASONS FOR DESCRIBING JESUS' BIRTH. THOMAS MÜNTZER: In the Gospel before us, we must see why Matthew describes the earthly birth of Christ and why it is being dealt with today. For when Matthew was preaching that Christ had been the Messiah, it must have been objected that his works had not preceded him. For it had been predicted by David and Isaiah that the work of the Messiah would be to bring the whole world under his power. Likewise that he would gather together all the Jews who had been scattered. Likewise that there would have to be peace throughout the earth, so that weapons would be turned into plowshares and billhooks. Likewise that he would take away death, casting down death for all eternity and that God would wipe away the tears from every face and the disgrace of his people from the whole earth. . . . Likewise that Christ, who was supposed to be the Messiah, should not be born in Galilee, but of the root of David in Bethlehem in Judah. For all these

---

[9]Cartwright, *A Confutation of the Rhemists Translation . . . on the New Testament* (1618), 3*.

[10]CTS 1:92-93 (CO 45:61)*; citing Gen 49:10; Dan 9:25, 26; 1 Tim 3:16.

reasons, therefore, Matthew was constrained to describe the birth of Christ. Now in the lineage of Christ, fourteen patriarchs, fourteen kings, and fourteen priests are to be found. This accounts for the wondrous joy of the blessed virgin and the praise and adulation accorded her, for the Virgin Mary is also titled a patriarch as the daughter of Abraham; a queen, as one of the lineage of David and a priest.

Matthew could not have shown that Christ was descended from David unless he had added Mary's name in the Gospel. For by Jewish law, Gentiles were incorporated by marriage. That is how it is shown that both Christ and Mary have descended from David. TWO SERMONS FROM ZWICKAU.[11]

---

[11]Müntzer, *Works*, 384-85; citing Is 11:12, 2:4, 25:8; Jn 7:42.

1:18-25 THE BIRTH OF JESUS CHRIST

¹⁸*Now the birth of Jesus Christ*[a] *took place in this way. When his mother Mary had been betrothed*[b] *to Joseph, before they came together she was found to be with child from the Holy Spirit.* ¹⁹*And her husband Joseph, being a just man and unwilling to put her to shame, resolved to divorce her quietly.* ²⁰*But as he considered these things, behold, an angel of the Lord appeared to him in a dream, saying, "Joseph, son of David, do not fear to take Mary as your wife, for that which is conceived in her is from the Holy Spirit.* ²¹*She will bear a son, and you shall call his name Jesus, for he will save his people from their sins."* ²²*All this took place to fulfill what the Lord had spoken by the prophet:*

> ²³*"Behold, the virgin shall conceive and bear a son,*
>   *and they shall call his name Immanuel"*

(which means, God with us). ²⁴*When Joseph woke from sleep, he did as the angel of the Lord commanded him: he took his wife,* ²⁵*but knew her not until she had given birth to a son. And he called his name Jesus.*

a Some manuscripts *of the Christ*   b That is, legally pledged to be married

---

OVERVIEW: These Reformation selections grapple with the theological implications of the name of Jesus and the virgin birth as it is described to Joseph by the angel. The child is first referred to as Jesus Christ, and it is these two names or titles that frame the nature of the child's future ministry. Jesus will save his people from their sin and all evil. The title of Christ draws on the Old Testament, denoting that the child is God's anointed king. Because of his work as Jesus and Christ, Christians can call this child Lord. The uniqueness of Jesus' birth is an indication of his unique role as the Savior of the world, hence the name Jesus and his title of Christ.

Understandably, the virgin birth garners much attention from the commentators. The most significant element of the virgin birth is indicated by Matthew as the fulfilling of Isaiah 7:14. The virgin birth declares that Jesus is Immanuel, or God incarnate, and that he fulfills the expectation of the Old Testament prophets. Apologetic concerns of the reformers regarding the virgin birth include that the virgin birth reverses the effect of original sin for Jesus but does not disprove Jesus' true humanity. Instead, the virgin birth serves as the sign that was promised to the Jews in Isaiah 7.

Joseph is presented as the faithful Jew whose obedience to God's plan is exemplary for all believers.

1:18-21 *Joseph's Dream*

EVE AND MARY CONTRASTED. THOMAS JACKSON: Both Evangelists again expressly tell us that the Virgin Mary was espoused to Joseph, the son of David, before the angel Gabriel brought this message to her, hereby giving us to understand that the works the devil had wrought in our nature should in this particular—as in many others—be undone by God after the same way and method that they were done by this his enemy. The first woman we know conceived sin while she was a virgin, at least before she knew her husband Adam, who was the only man then on earth. For she was a virgin espoused from her first creation. This first woman conceived death by believing the serpent and practicing according to his counsel before she had consulted her husband. The blessed virgin conceived the Lord of life by believing the angel Gabriel's message without consent or advice of her betrothed husband, who at the first suspected her loyalty but afterward—admonished by the Holy

Ghost—admitted her as his lawful consort and permitted her to enjoy all the privileges of a wife and her son the privileges of his only son and heir without any further knowledge of her as his wife. THE KNOWLEDGE OF CHRIST JESUS.[1]

MARY'S SHAME AND HONOR AS THE MOTHER OF GOD. CATHARINA REGINA VON GREIFFEN-BERG: We ought to wonder at the fact that it was possible for the omniscient and most righteous God to permit the most innocent woman and his most holy and only child himself to be endangered by the suspicion of a dishonorable conception, [that it was possible] for him, who has all time and hours in his hands, to ordain that her pregnancy be revealed before she came together with Joseph so that piety was angered by holiness and God himself came under suspicion among the godly. . . .

How must it have pained this most innocent woman that her shame came to light before her honor did, that it was rumored that she was pregnant rather than that she was the bearer of God, that the effect was visible before the cause was known, that she could not hide her big belly and could not uncover the holy secret of salvation! How she must have shrunk from Joseph and been ashamed and hardly dared to look at him! For she knew full well that he knew nothing of her secret, which she had also not dared to confide to him. But heaven, which laid this burden upon her, also helped her to bear it. He who imposed external shame upon her gave her inner comfort. He placed a cool restorative wellspring in her heart that could cool the heat of the external shame—namely, a good conscience, which cools all fear, extinguishes all heat, sweetens all bitterness, and is a restorative and refreshment for all anguish.

It was the consolation that she was pregnant with the Holy Spirit. This sweetened all the bitterness of evil gossip, for being conscious in oneself of the work and operation of the Holy Spirit is a delight that outweighs all of the world's judgments and suspicions and is as if one sat in

heaven and from far off heard a little dog barking but nevertheless did not allow oneself to be prevented from listening to the music of the angels. MEDITATION ON THE PREGNANCY OF MARY.[2]

JESUS, THE PROMISED SAVIOR. HEINRICH BULLINGER: Now we see the words of an angel, saying, "Joseph, son of David." Indeed, by that introduction he prepared his spirit for such a great thing, while evidently he recalls David into memory, and for that reason he also recalled promises to David about the coming Messiah. As if he said, "In order that you may not be to so great an extent dejected and crushed in spirit, and may not only look at the present, maintaining a better spirit in the oracles of the prophets, examining in your mind from what origin of birth you descended, and that your promise may be greater." Then he explains it to a few whose grace the messenger venerates from God, for the mystery itself, which was being held by God, stating that he alleviates and raises all of those cares and sorrows of life: You may lay aside this fear and at the same time receive union in the fellowship of life (for this is *paralabein*, to unite) by a prescribed message from God: for the offspring which you see conceived is not adulterous, but altogether divine. For as it was not conceived from you, so neither was it born from anyone of mortal men. And so that you may know everything exactly, this offspring was conceived from the Holy Spirit and was formed in the womb of a virgin by virtue of deity without a work of a human.

Therefore, she will bring forth a son, indeed not for you—as mothers usually conceive for fathers from fathers themselves—but for the whole world. Meanwhile, because he entrusts you to him as his guardian by divine providence, in which you will be allowed of the father to perform this service, in order that you may give the name to him, not however other than what the true Father of heaven first indeed gave from eternity, namely, Jesus.

[1]Jackson, *The Knowledge of Christ Jesus* (1634), 729*.

[2]Greiffenberg, *Meditations on the Incarnation, Passion, and Death of Jesus Christ*, 253-54.

Therefore, you will call his name Jesus. For this is he who was promised by God as a Savior of your fathers and people, who will of course free the ones believing from the kingdom of darkness and the ones receiving purification by his blood into the kingdom of light and of God and eternal life. Thus, the archangel most briefly (i.e., from that name Jesus) explains to Joseph what sort of child and how great this child would be, in that his service is that of majesty and glory. In the same way also, a virgin learned about this mystery from a commission of God: "Behold, you will conceive, and you will have a son, and you will call his name Jesus. He will be great, and your son will be called the Most High. And the Lord will give to him the seed of his father David, and he will reign over the house of Jacob forever, and his reign will not have an end." From there truly he wanted the virgin to gather everything that up to this point was considered about that new conception, through all things to be most holy and pure.

But by equal sense and by end to this, he repeats this, and repeats to Joseph. As if he said, from there truly to conclude, you are able at this time to unite with nothing of deception or impurity, because he who was born from her was destined by God the Father in order to be the salvation of the world. But you are not ignorant that the unclean is not sanctified except through the most pure; therefore know from the end to which this child was destined that he might sanctify all things. COMMENTARY ON MATTHEW.[3]

JESUS THE SAVIOR. PETER MARTYR VERMIGLI: On account of which it is not in vain that in the sacred books this twofold appellation Jesus Christ is exactly depicted for us; by whose other name—namely, Jesus—they indicate nothing other than Savior, who freed the sons of God from their sins and in the same manner from all evil. For the command from the angel was that Mary's husband, Joseph, name him Jesus, who said, "He will save his

people from their sins." Truly I have further added "from all evil," although there was nothing evil in him, having not proceeded from sin. So, though he was one who was able to boast, in that an origin of wickedness was sent away from him, he is also able to prove just in order to carry away all evil. But this, if we do not judge perfectly thus far, yet at length we will experience that resurrection in eternity. Truly an older name—namely, Christ—denotes God's anointed and holy king, which fits properly for him, especially of his own Spirit. By the word's command, he would lead and bring God's sons to eternal life. Therefore, the two titles are certainly to be understood with regard to those two natures in which he existed, bringing together for him in the best way the title that is praised by us, calling him our Lord. LOCI COMMUNES.[4]

JESUS AND JOSHUA. MARTIN BUCER: It is common that after the Lord chose someone for some distinguished office he also gave them a name. In this manner, to Abram, who was appointed as the father of many nations, he gave the name Abraham, whose name expresses something about him. To that service he was allotted. In this manner, John began a declaration of grace and was first given the gospel of Christ to announce to the world. Hence was given to him a divine name, as he was called John, because it indicated favor. Therefore, when this favored son of David was sent in order that he might be the Lord's salvation all the way to the ends of the earth, and that through this one he might accomplish the redemption of the elect, appropriately a divine name was given to him that indicated this.

For the name Jesus is such because by the Hebrew yǝhôshua '—that is, it is said Jehoshua—they also indicate a Savior. For, as I stated above, the Evangelist preferred this name, as also others, to publish in like manner a received vulgar edition of the sacred books, which seems not to speak on a par with Scripture, or from a reading of a common edition, while a better one was not

[3]Bullinger, In . . . Evangelium secundum Matthaeum commentariorum (1546), 1:12.

[4]Vermigli, Loci communes (1576), 423.

possessed as though to deter the making of mistakes, by which means at the same time would have turned on the whole from a reading of Scripture. Moreover, when we were suppressing the first—which is otherwise the shortest—syllable with aspiration, which also itself emerges softened, we say Joshua for Jehoshua. The Greeks have *iēsous*—that is, Jesus—which is read for Joshua in the whole book. Therefore, it is meaningless that the Jews blaspheme having another name for our Lord, which is Jehoshua. Or because it is confirmed by the interpretation of an angel, as long as presented, for he has saved his people from their sins. . . . Therefore, nothing of any creature, or with respect to our works, is able to be qualified for this. He has made salvation for his people, that is, the elect, whom the Father draws to himself. For indeed they alone are such who know the Savior himself and also enjoy him.

And thus he has made salvation: By death he has atoned for the sins of all the elect and purchased them as a gracious father would give his spirit. Being renewed by him, they recognize this grace of God and they believe in it, whereby and in full, they at last receive it. In the meantime—and at the same time—this one is made alive, they preach this grace, they prize the nearest coming of this our Savior, in moderation of the highest life, and a ready enduring of the cross, who at that time will cleanse all the remnants of sin, and being renewed inwardly, and full of God, he restores the blessed ones in eternity. This is what Peter and John say in Acts 4: Nor is there any other name given under heaven by human beings in which we ought to be saved. Further, this deliverance thus restores abundantly in body and spirit into every condition of life, as we need nothing at all beside this. And this is that eternal life, which the Lord promises to as many who believe in him (John 3 and 6, and countless other places). Therefore, if salvation is in his own name alone and complete, as we call (not alone from spirit) on that one whom they are unwilling to crown, will it be needful for him to bend every knee? Or in like manner, will this voice of Jesus alone—how great I beseech—bring

consolation and faith to the pious and believing spirits? Therefore, the Evangelist three times, or from the beginning, proclaimed the greatest majesty and divinity of our Lord, as we have said, at the same time that he received his writing about Jesus Christ. COMMENTARY ON MATTHEW.[5]

THE SINFULNESS OF SIN. SAMUEL BOLTON: And thus, I have, in the nearest way I could, led you down to the words of the text. In which you may observe with me a grand evil expressed, a rich benefit declared, and the peculiar subjects described. First, the grand evil and grandness of this evil is described and set out to us. By its nature, it is the object of Christ's saving mercy and is laid down not only as the great, but as the universal and sole business that Christ came into the world about, to save us from sin. . . . It is set out by its nearness: their sin. That shows its nearness. It was their own, and nothing is so much a man's own as his sin.

Second, in the second branch, namely, the richness of the benefit declared, you have these three things observable: (1) The nature of this benefit is described: "Save." (2) The author of it is discovered: "He." (3) The way and means whereby he shall accomplish it is couched in this: "He shall," which points out to the way whereby Christ shall bring this about—namely, by his life, death, bloodshed, resurrection, and intercession—all of which are couched in that word as the way and means he shall accomplish this work.

Third, you have the subjects of this mercy described. More generally, they are people: It is humans, not devils, that are the subjects of Christ's saving mercy. More specially and restrictively, they are *his* people: "he shall save his people." Christ may be a Jesus to others to save them from trouble, but he is a Jesus only to his own people to save them from sin: "he shall save his people from their sins." THE SINFULNESS OF SIN.[6]

[5]Bucer, *In Sacra Quatuor Evangelia, Enarrationes Perpetuae* (1536), 12-13; citing Is 49; Phil 2.
[6]Bolton, *The Sinfulness of Sin* 1646), 4-5*.

1:22-23 *The Fulfillment of Isaiah's Prophecy*

THE VIRGIN BIRTH. JOHN HOOPER: For when the virgin heard there should be a child born of her, and she yet in the grace and perfection of her virginity, as of a thing impossible by nature to be done, wondered at the tidings and inquired of the angel the means how it may be done. Whereunto the angel, in order to satisfy the admiration of the troubled virgin, answered thus: "The Holy Ghost shall come upon you, and he shall work this wonderful work in you, although above the consent of your reason, yet not without the assistance of your nature, which shall be shadowed by the Holy Ghost." Matthew admits this interpretation of Luke in the first chapter; whereas Joseph was not less troubled to see his betrothed and promised wife to be with child, thought it had been by some sinister and forbidden means, as well as the poor virgin with reason thought it could never be without the knowledge of humankind. As from heaven her reason was confounded and made to give place to faith and the power of God; so was Joseph by night admonished for his overly hasty judgment and light suspicion, that his promised wife was not great by any man, but by the Holy Ghost. Thus the Evangelist minded to take out of Joseph the suspicion that he had of the godly virgin for her being with child, and not to prove that the child within her was not of her own substance and nature. Read the place, and mark the state and argument concerning this; then shall the text interpret itself. LESSON OF THE INCARNATION OF CHRIST.[7]

THE BIRTH OF JESUS FULFILLS ISAIAH 7. JOHANNES OECOLAMPADIUS: This prophecy was written in the seventh chapter of Isaiah. Therefore, you see another testimony about the manner and type of event the birth of Christ would be, lest you doubt about this miraculous event. It is good to know history. At the time of this prophecy, the king of Israel and the king of Damascus—also known as the king of the Assyrians—were fighting against the kingdom of Judah and its ruler Ahaz. Consequently, the house of Judah was completely surrounded. God, however, willing to deliver his own people, told Isaiah to speak to the king so that the king might ask for a sign for himself. Because that king would not give honor to God, he said, "I do not ask for a sign." Nevertheless, God demonstrated his own power for the comfort of his own people, because not only would he free them from those present enemies, but he would also do much greater deeds, and thus he promised Christ.

When the words of this prophecy are interpreted, the Jews suggest many absurd events, so that they might be able to avoid the true meaning. But since they do not wish to receive the Messiah, they do not wish anyone to recognize him as God; consequently, it is not remarkable that those Jews shrink back from this miracle. They are a most superstitious people in other ways, accepting many miraculous events from their own rabbis, but they resist this. They were sufficiently prepared in former times, and accustomed to miracles, so obviously they also ought to believe that miracle of the virgin birth. It is not a lesser miracle that Sarah bore a son, and I omit those deeds that were done by Moses, but the wretched Jews hate the word of the cross in every way, and because once they decided not to receive Christ, clearly they oppose him in all ways. . . .

And the Hebrews used this name [*'almah*] for the girls who were of a marriageable age. . . . God was not willing to perform a miracle, except by some noteworthy virgin. . . . If she had not been a virgin, would it have been necessary for the prophet to promise: "The Lord will give a sign"? It would not have been a sign if the virgin had conceived in the common manner. Christ himself will also be a sign because he willed to free his own people from the most severe adversaries—namely, from the captivity of evil spirits. Consequently, this testimony is most consistent and it cannot be ascribed to another. People ask, "How are we able to be assured from those things that are to come?" especially with respect to eternal happiness. If we receive assurance in external matters, how much

---

[7]Hooper, *Later Writings of Bishop Hooper*, 14.

more should we be assured in eternal matters which God, who cannot deceive like human beings, promises? COMMENTARY ON THE GOSPEL ACCORDING TO MATTHEW 1:23.[8]

GOD WITH US IN HIS WORD. BALTHASAR HUBMAIER: So great and mighty is the power and dignity of the prophecies of God, who has become human and been revealed through his Word, who cannot deny himself, or heaven and earth must first fall into pieces. Not that our will, word, or work are so high and valuable in themselves, but so powerful and forceful are the divine prophecies in all the believers. Therefore, God is captured, bound, and overcome with his own Word by the believers. In the Scriptures that is called "God being in our midst." FREEDOM OF THE WILL.[9]

ALL CHRISTIANS WILL CALL HIM GOD WITH US. CATHARINA REGINA VON GREIFFENBERG: "They shall," says the angel, but the prophet says, "She shall." Both can exist side by side, for first of all she, the holy mother, and then all Christians called him this. God with us in our nature. God with us in our flesh and blood. God with us on earth. God with us in our weakness. God with us! Incarnate, corporeal, with body and soul, flesh and blood, skin and bones. God with us! Naturally, substantially with nature and being. God with us, really, truly in a conceivable form.

Although his divinity is inconceivable, he will nevertheless be conceived, he who is the true God. God, the unimaginable being, the inscrutable intelligence, the unfathomable chasm, the unimaginable miracle and inexhaustible mystery, the inconceivable sea, the unreachable majesty, the vertiginous depths, and the distance that is inconceivable to all things that can be conceived, is with us human beings, that is, with weakness, vanity, wretchedness, want, and the abyss of all misery, in short: the Sum of the Universe is with nothingness in order to make it into something for the purpose of praising his glorious grace. MEDITATION ON THE PREGNANCY OF MARY.[10]

1:24-25 Joseph and Mary at the Birth of Jesus

JOSEPH'S FAITHFUL OBEDIENCE. DESIDERIUS ERASMUS: When the messenger of the supreme God had thus spoken, Joseph awoke from his sleep and cheerfully and eagerly obeyed the oracle. He set aside all plans for divorce and entered into an even closer relationship with his wife so no thought of divorce could come to anyone. And now understanding that she was wholly dedicated to the heavenly power, he venerated the divine mystery in her and did not dare touch one whom divinity had claimed for itself alone. He was there to serve her; he abstained from marital relations. In the meantime, that heavenly fetus grew in the virgin's holy womb and, coming forth in its proper time from the virgin mother, it did not take away the virginity of the parent but consecrated it. Then Joseph, just as he had been commanded by the angel, named the boy Jesus when, according to the custom of his race, he was circumcised on the eighth day, to this degree fulfilling the role of father. PARAPHRASE ON MATTHEW.[11]

JOSEPH'S GLORIOUS FAITH. CATHARINA REGINA VON GREIFFENBERG: Just consider . . . Joseph's quick pious obedience: no sooner did Joseph wake and have his senses and limbs ready to go than he did what had been bidden him. He thereby showed his glorious faith by not doubting divinely inspired matters one iota; he showed his fear of God by regretting that he had thought the holy bearer of God anything but holy; his humility by resolving henceforth to revere her as a living shrine through abstinence; his remorse for the unjust thoughts he had had, which he countered right away with his actions when he did what the angel had bidden with utmost speed. MEDITATION ON THE PREGNANCY OF MARY.[12]

---

[8]Oecolampadius, *Ennaratio in Evangelium Matthaei* (1536), 15r-16r.
[9]CRR 5:474*; citing Lk 21:33; Rom 8; Mk 9:23; Mt 18:18.
[10]Greiffenberg, *Meditations on the Incarnation, Passion, and Death of Jesus Christ*, 269*.
[11]CWE 45:45 (LB 7:7-8).
[12]Greiffenberg, *Meditations on the Incarnation, Passion, and Death of Jesus Christ*, 273*.

2:1-12 THE VISIT OF THE WISE MEN

Now after Jesus was born in Bethlehem of Judea in the days of Herod the king, behold, wise men[a] from the east came to Jerusalem, [2]saying, "Where is he who has been born king of the Jews? For we saw his star when it rose[b] and have come to worship him." [3]When Herod the king heard this, he was troubled, and all Jerusalem with him; [4]and assembling all the chief priests and scribes of the people, he inquired of them where the Christ was to be born. [5]They told him, "In Bethlehem of Judea, for so it is written by the prophet:

[6]"'And you, O Bethlehem, in the land of Judah,
    are by no means least among the rulers of
      Judah;
for from you shall come a ruler
    who will shepherd my people Israel.'"

[7]Then Herod summoned the wise men secretly and ascertained from them what time the star had appeared. [8]And he sent them to Bethlehem, saying, "Go and search diligently for the child, and when you have found him, bring me word, that I too may come and worship him." [9]After listening to the king, they went on their way. And behold, the star that they had seen when it rose went before them until it came to rest over the place where the child was. [10]When they saw the star, they rejoiced exceedingly with great joy. [11]And going into the house, they saw the child with Mary his mother, and they fell down and worshiped him. Then, opening their treasures, they offered him gifts, gold and frankincense and myrrh. [12]And being warned in a dream not to return to Herod, they departed to their own country by another way.

a Greek magi; also verses 7, 16   b Or in the east; also verse 9

OVERVIEW: The Reformation selections indicate that Herod's reign provides the vacuum of justice that was required for the Messiah's entrance as depicted in the Old Testament. Matthew's only account of guests at the nativity focuses on the magi, mysterious guests from the east. The worshipful announcement of the magi points to God opening the door of faith to the Gentiles, and the star they follow gives a brief glimpse of the greater, heavenly glory that belongs to Christ. In spite of the rejection of Jesus by Israel's leaders—Herod, in this instance—and the city of Jerusalem out of the fear of losing the status quo, many outsiders display remarkable worshipful responses to Jesus (see Mt 8:5-13; 15:21-28).

The commentators describe the royal dignity of the magi's public entrance and how their mission was announced to the king, along with the whole city. These became the occasion for an immediate interest in the Messiah's coming. Creatively, Matthew indicates the fulfillment of another Old Testament text through Jesus' birth by retelling the scribes' report to Herod. The hypocrisy and cruelty of Herod is evident in his expressed interest in worshiping the child while at the same time plotting his murder—the killing of the other male children would be a later mark of Herod's increased fury. While Herod feigns an intention to worship the Christ child, the magi follow through on their announced intentions by worshiping the child as soon as they enter his presence. Their gifts to the child are symbols of the high esteem they have for him. Many Reformation authors indicate that the worship of Christ by the magi is the model response to Christ and that worship brings to God those who were far off.

2:1-2 The Wise Men from the East

THE TIMING OF JESUS' BIRTH. JOHANN GERHARD: "In the days of Herod the king"—namely, the thirty-third year of that reign, as

Epiphanius[†] notes, in which year of his reign came the first description in Luke 2:1 of the world just before which Christ was born. Baronius[‡] believes Christ was born before the end of the twenty-ninth year of Herod's reign.

Some search for emphasis in the word *days*, as is noted briefly and confidently about earthly kingdoms, granted of which they may last a long time, nevertheless they are regarded simply as a few days if they are compared with eternity. But the noun *days* is given for a Hebrew phrase for time in kind and for years in form. Therefore, the sense is, in the days of Herod, that is, in the time of Herod, when Herod held office.

Therefore . . . this is an argument by which the Evangelist demonstrates Jesus to be the promised Messiah. For as he had so far demonstrated this from his family and place of birth, so he in truth now demonstrates from condition of time. For it was predicted that the Messiah would be born at that time when the scepter and justice of laws brought together from Judah were removed. This is why, that the time of Jesus' birth might be fulfilled, he makes clear that Herod had been a foreigner, subject to the emperor of the Romans. For this reason, Herod will have become king, and the like. Josephus[§] explains that Hyrcanus, the highest of the Judeans from the Hasmonaeans[◊] or Maccabees by birth, succeeded to king.

This Herod, brother of Antipas, named Ascalonita, was king of all the land of the twelve tribes of Israel. Therefore, the Evangelist distinctly calls him king. His command would accomplish the Bethlehemite infanticide. His brother by the same name Herod, called Antipas, who was tetrarch of Galilee and Perea, commanded in Luke 3:1 that John the Baptist be removed from his midst. ANNOTATIONS ON MATTHEW.[1]

---

[1]Gerhard, *Annotationes Posthumae in Evangelium D. Matthaei* (1663), 92-93*; citing Gen 49:10. [†]Epiphanus, *Adversus Haereses*, PG 41:275-276. [‡]Baronius, *Annales Ecclesiastici* 1:1-21. [§]Josephus, *Antiquities of the Jews* 13.8. [◊]This was the ruling dynasty of Judea after the Maccabean Revolt from about 140 BCE until 37 BCE, at which point Herod the Great began to rule as a client king of the Roman Empire.

AND THE WHOLE CITY OF JERUSALEM WITH HIM. WOLFGANG MUSCULUS: Why was the city united in anger toward Herod because of this rumor? Were they afraid of the royal authority of Herod, or did they fear his tyranny? If they feared his royal authority, then they [must have] loved him. However, it is not possible to believe that they would love a tyrant. If they did not love him, then they also did not fear his royal authority. Therefore, it follows that they feared his own affairs and wished to preserve peace with that tyrant. For such were the deeds of that tyrant that the whole city was agitated for every irritation of that man. Behold, the city, which most assuredly ought to have rejoiced and exulted at the report about the birth of the king of the Jews, was instead completely agitated. Clearly, the city was at peace at that time and loved quiet so much that it feared future riots because of Christ. Indeed, it was grieved by the very event at which it ought to have rejoiced.

The city, no less than Herod, truly had no reason to be agitated. For whatever it would have suffered because of Christ, it suffered just as much because of Herod. Christ had come as the Savior, not as the instigator of riots. The city of Jerusalem was blind and ignorant of the judgments of God, settling its own ruin because of its rejection of Christ. If it had been wise, it would have feared its denial of tribute to the Roman emperor instead. But this fear was nothing to them, so danger and ruin of every kind hung over the city.

Today there are many with this nature, who are agitated by the report of dawning truth, not because they desire it to be extinguished in themselves, but because they fear that their present tranquility would be broken. Since they themselves are blind, they do not notice the most certain future destruction that will come if the truth of God should be rejected. COMMENTARY ON MATTHEW 2:4.[2]

THE PURPOSE OF THE STAR. JOHN CALVIN: This is a very remarkable narrative. God brought magi from Chaldea to come to the land of Judea

---

[2]Musculus, *In Evangelistam Matthaeum Commenarii* (1556), 14.

for the purpose of adoring Christ in the stable where he lay amid the tokens, not of honor, but of contempt. It was a truly wonderful purpose of God that he caused the entrance of his Son into the world to be attended by deep meanness and yet bestowed upon him illustrious ornaments, both of commendation and of other outward signs, that our faith might be supplied with everything necessary to prove his divine majesty.

A beautiful instance of real harmony amid apparent contradiction is here exhibited. A star from heaven announces that he is a king, for whom a manger, intended for cattle, serves as a throne, because he is refused admittance among the lowest of the people. His majesty shines in the East, while in Judea it is so far from being acknowledged, that it is visited by many marks of dishonor. Why is this? The heavenly Father chose to appoint the star and the magi as our guides, to lead directly to his Son: while he stripped him of all earthly splendor, for the purpose of informing us that his kingdom is spiritual. This history conveys profitable instruction, not only because God brought the magi to his Son, as the first fruits of the Gentiles, but also because he appointed the kingdom of his Son to receive their commendation and that of the star, for the confirmation of our faith so that the wicked and malignant contempt of his nation might not render him less estimable in our eyes. Commentary on a Harmony of the Evangelists.[3]

The Prophecy of Micah. Niels Hemmingsen: Now let us in few words peruse the prophecy of Micah. For thus he says, "And you, Bethlehem of the land of Judah, art not the least among the princes of Judah. For out of you shall come the captain that shall feed my people Israel, and the forthcomings of him are from the beginning from the days of everlastingness." This testimony of Micah teaches many things concerning Christ. First, it points out the place of his birth. Second, it shows his office, which is to play the governor of Israel, to feed his people. Third, it

shows his incarnation, whereby he was born an actual man. For when he says, "from the beginning," he shows Christ's incarnation, who was promised from the beginning of the world, that in his time he should be born after the flesh. Fourth, when he says, "from the days of everlastingness," he signifies the nature of his divinity, whereby he was before the creation of the world. Fifth, he shows that he is one person consisting of two natures. For when he says his "forthcomings," this word of the plural number pertains to the natures both of his Godhead and of his humanity. And the word (*him*) being the singular number, covertly declares the unity of the person. And so, we see how the prophet has joined together the chief articles of our faith, which are uttered by others more at large. A Postil, or Exposition of the Gospels.[4]

2:3-8 Herod's Deceptive Scheme

Notes on the Chief Priests and Scribes. Giovanni Diodati: "The chief priest." This word is taken here and elsewhere in the Gospels at large for the heads of families and of the divisions of the priests, as 2 Chronicles 36:14. "Scribes." These were certain men well versed in holy Scriptures and who expounded them publicly in the synagogues and are called of the people because they were indifferently of all the several tribes of Israel and not of that of Levi only, to whom this office seemed properly to belong, and were also admitted into public councils, as formerly the prophets were and held the place of magistrates. Pious Annotations.[5]

The Nature of Herod's Hypocrisy. Richard Ward: It may here be questioned, why does Herod call the wise men secretly? Because he calls them for evil: he had a wicked purpose in his malicious heart toward Christ, and therefore he calls them secretly, asking their counsel but hiding his intent from them. Teaching us that it is the

---

[3]CTS 1:127-28* (CO 45:81).

[4]Hemmingsen, *A Postill, or Exposition of the Gospels* (1569), 39-40; citing Mic 5:2.
[5]Diodati, *Pious Annotations* (1643), C2r-C2v; citing 1 Chron 2:55; 2 Chron 34:13; Ezra 7:6, 11-12; Jer 26:11; 1 Macc 5:42; 7:12.

nature of wicked men to hide their counsel, that they may better hurt the religious. . . . The magi came from afar to seek Christ and from their hearts' desire to find him. Herod pretends the same outwardly, though the news touches him to the quick. Hence a question may be propounded: "How may hypocrites and the enemies of Christ be discerned from the children of God, and the true friends of Christ?" . . . They are no better than atheists, thinking that they can kill Christ—as Herod did here—or at least prevail against him and his. Thus, although many outwardly profess a love for Christ, the gospel, and true religion, yet if they are inwardly enemies, they may be discerned and unmasked, at one time or other by some one of these marks or other. THEOLOGICAL QUESTIONS.[6]

HEROD'S REASON FOR DECEPTION. MARTIN LUTHER: From this text we learn that the wise men were not kings nor princes, but common honest people, like the learned and the clergy. Herod does not treat them as belonging to royalty, but sends them to Bethlehem, tells them to attend to their mission, and, as if they were his subjects, commands them to bring him word again. He would not have done this if they had been kings or lords. He would have invited them to his palace, accompanied them on their journeys, and treated them with great honor. . . .

When he asks them about the time of the star, he does it out of the same anxiety. He was already resolved in his heart to slay the innocent children. He reasoned thus: If the new king is born the Jews will rejoice and will keep him secret for a while until he is grown up, and then will espouse his cause, put him on the throne, and banish me. I must forestall them, therefore, and carefully inquire into the time of his birth. And although he is hidden from me, I shall still find him among the people when I slay all the children, and their disguises will avail them nothing. He pursues this plan diligently so that the new king might be made known to him, commands the wise men to bring

him word again, and puts on a pious and devout face as if he wished to worship the child also. SERMON ON EPIPHANY.[7]

HE INQUIRED CAREFULLY ABOUT THE BOY. WOLFGANG MUSCULUS: See, although he had already conceived in his mind the plan of killing infants of an equal age, he still preferred to provide a pretext, so that when he had captured the one Christ, he would then be able to spare a multitude of the remaining infants. He commanded the magi clearly, so that they would diligently inquire about the boy, and when they had found him, they would return to him and report it. It is evident that the conscience of this impious man shrunk back from so great a cruelty as the killing of all infants born at the time of the star's appearing. Plainly, then, he aimed for this: if the magi could find the boy, Herod would certainly capture Christ himself, killing him alone, and then would spare the rest. Therefore, there is a certain bit of conscience even in the ungodly. It is true that ungodliness conquers in them because they are the possessions of Satan. Thus, Herod afterward did not succeed with what he had arranged by the magi and in the end gave birth to his conceived cruelty (permitted first by his shrinking conscience). COMMENTARY ON MATTHEW 2:8.[8]

REPORT TO ME. WOLFGANG MUSCULUS: Behold, the cunning king put the magi, who were seeking Christ and desiring to worship him, under pledge to himself so that he could use the acts of those imagining no such evil to extinguish Christ. He sent them to Bethlehem; he commanded them to inquire earnestly about the boy and, when he had been found, to report it to himself so that he might also come to worship him: that is, to kill him.

Herod already once had wrestled such matters with this great adroitness in a Roman court, and he pressed all of the magi who announced Christ into the service of his own power, so that he might extinguish the glory of Christ and establish and

---

[6]Ward, *Theological Questions upon . . . St. Matthew* (1640), 32-34*.

[7]Luther, *Precious and Sacred Writings*, 10:355-56.
[8]Musculus, *In Evangelistam Matthaeum Commenarii* (1556), 16.

strengthen his own power. He took power for himself, calling any ministers of Christ he pleased to himself and imposing whatever things he wished on them. Satan assumes this law for himself so that he sends all the magi of Christ for the sake of his own will and calls the sent ones back to himself so that no one may be permitted to be a preacher of Christ nor may be permitted to do anything other than in the service of his own will. Nevertheless, many are found by the grace of God, who have come out of the hall of this Herod and declared themselves for Christ, nor have they returned to Herod's hall. Commentary on Matthew 2:8.[9]

Herod Afraid to Lose Kingdom and Glory.

Menno Simons: Herod did nothing but what he was taught by the scribes. He pointed out to the wise men the town in which the King of the Jews should be born, and that with a bloodthirsty heart, as the following act shows. He sent them to Bethlehem and said, Go and search diligently for the young child, and when you have found him, bring me word again, that I may come and worship him also. Herod was afraid when he heard that their own king had been born, lest he lose his kingdom and glory. He spoke of pure hypocrisy and slyness with the wise men. He was desirous of the child's death and wished to take timely preventative action. But when he saw that his hypocrisy miscarried, he became very angry and showed his fierce, tyrannical, wicked disposition. He slew all the children—the innocent children that were in Bethlehem and in all the coasts thereof—from two years old and under, in order that he might also destroy the born king. . . . The wise men, being admonished by a heavenly inspiration, did not return to Herod. And we will by the grace of God faithfully observe the Lord's inspiration, counsel, doctrine, and admonition and turn to those who make Christ known in power and teach in the truth according to the Spirit. Foundation of Christian Doctrine.[10]

So That I Also May Come to Worship Him.

Wolfgang Musculus: This is that fox pelt; truly it is a wolf pelt. His intention is "so that I may come to kill him." . . . His words were not these, though, but "so that I also may come to worship him." It is as if he should say, "You do well, because you seek this king and worship him. For the future is great, I admit, and because of this, I myself desire to acknowledge and worship him." That is devilish hypocrisy. He hid one thing in his heart and represented another with his mouth. He understood that he was not able to extinguish Christ by a better shortcut than by a false representation of this kind. Thus Satan is accustomed to act. Where he desires to stamp out the truth, he has his own lackeys, whom he turns into angels of light, so that he may extinguish the light. He desires to harm the church, and so he feigns the advancement of the church. He desires to extinguish the glory of God, so he feigns a zeal for the glory of God. He desires to steal away the worship of God from the scene, so he feigns the promotion of the worship of God. Commentary on Matthew 2:8.[11]

2:9-12 The Magi's Joyous Worship of the Child

The Greatness of the Kings Who Worship Jesus.

John Cosin: If that place be not precisely to be understood of them, but rather of some other kings and princes that came in long after them—for if they were kings, they must be kings of some parts of the East, from whence Matthew says here they came, and not of any parts of the South, from whence it was that the queen of Sheba came, whom therefore Christ himself calls the queen of the South—and yet this hinders not but that Isaiah prophesied of them, as well as David prophesied of others; and so they might be kings still. . . .

But however it be, surely men of great rank and condition they were, for they came not to Jerusalem

[9]Musculus, *In Evangelistam Matthaeum Commenarii* (1556), 16.
[10]Simons, *Complete Writings*, 179-80*; citing Mt 2:8; 2:16.
[11]Musculus, *In Evangelistam Matthaeum Commenarii* (1556), 16.

here as men that went about their own private affairs, and nobody to regard or look after them when they came. But they made their entrance into the city after a public and a solemn manner. They are ushered in by a star from heaven. They come, if not as kings themselves, yet as the ambassadors and lieutenants of kings, at least. And they come from the whole body of the Gentiles, on the behalf of them all, to negotiate with the newborn king about their peace and alliance with him forever; a matter of greater state and more concernment than if all the kings and princes of the earth had met together at Jerusalem about their own alliance or peace, one with another. Whereupon the whole city takes notice of them, the king there, and the people, and all. And so great an embassy, so powerful a coming it was, that they were all amazed and troubled at it, Herod and all Jerusalem with him. Whether it was their great number that attended them, or whether it was their great treasures that they brought with them; or whether it was, chiefly, their business and their errand that they caused to be proclaimed and published before them; or all these together—but somewhat it was that rendered them such persons, as that the king called together his council about him for their better reception and audience, and admitted them to his own private conference with him besides, giving them their dispatch and their answer—which princes used not often to do, but to persons as great or as considerable as themselves—with his own mouth. So great persons they were. SERMON 21.[12]

THE JOY OF THE WISE MEN. JEREMY TAYLOR: When the wise men departed from Jerusalem, the star again appeared, and they rejoiced with exceeding great joy. And indeed, to new converts and persons in their first addresses to the worship of God, such spiritual and exterior comforts are often indulged, because then God judges them to be most necessary, as being invitations to duty by the entertainments of our affections with such sweetnesses which represent the glory of the reward by the appetizers and refreshments dispensed even in

the ruggedness of the way and incommodities of the journey. All other delights are the pleasures of beasts or the sports of children. These are the appetizers and foretastes of the full feasts and overflowings of eternity. When they came to Bethlehem and the star pointed them to a stable, they entered in, and being enlightened with a divine ray proceeding from the face of the holy child, and seeing through the cloud, and passing through the scandal of his mean lodging and poor condition, they bowed themselves to the earth. First giving themselves an oblation to this great king, then they made offering of their gifts, for a man's person is first accepted, then his gift. THE GREAT EXEMPLAR.[13]

THE WORSHIP OF THE WISE MEN. DESIDERIUS ERASMUS: They found the infant looking like any other; they found the mother exhibiting no sign of how extraordinary she was. All their furnishings attested to their poverty and simplicity. The magi, who had not worshiped Herod, a man who exalted himself with royal pomp as he sat on his throne, prostrated themselves at the cradle of the crying child, and bending low worshiped one who could not yet speak. Not satisfied with this act of piety, they took from their bags the gifts intended for the child, from things the region of Persia was especially rich in: gold, frankincense, and myrrh, so that the one who was soon going to flee would not be without provisions. With these firstfruits of faith the nations that were far off preceded the Jews, who seemed nearest to God, and they consecrated Christ as theirs and dedicated themselves in turn to him, offering a new sacrifice in three kinds of things, already as though through a riddle professing that ineffable Trinity—Father, Son, and Holy Ghost—and at the same time recognizing in one man mortality, priesthood, and kingship. For gold suits a king, frankincense a priest, and myrrh one who is going to die. He was born mortal, he made sacrifice on the cross, rising again he conquered, he reigns in heaven. Even after seeing so many miracles, the Jews killed a man they knew; the magi

---

[12]WJC 1:298-99.

[13]Taylor, Works, 2:95*.

saw nothing remarkable as far as their bodily eyes could perceive and they rejoiced that their journey was a success. But while they were considering whether they should return to Herod to satisfy his intent, they were advised by a divine oracle in their sleep not to go back to Herod. It was not safe either for them or for the boy, and it was not expedient for a matter of such importance that was to be made known to the world in stages, each element at just the right time. They were not slow to obey the oracle, and they returned to their own country by another way to be the new heralds of the new king among their own people. PARAPHRASES.[14]

THE FAITH OF THOSE WHO COME TO CHRIST. LANCELOT ANDREWES: What do they believe of him? Out of their own words here: (1) First that he is "born," and so he is man. His human nature. (2) And, as his nature, so his office, in "born a king." They believe that too. (3) But "of the Jews" may seem to be a bar, for then, what have they to do with "the king of the Jews"? They are Gentiles, none of his lieges, no relation to him at all. Why are they seeking or worshiping him? But, weigh it well, and it is no bar. For this they seem to believe: He is so "King of the Jews" as he is "the Gentiles to adore him." And, though born a Jew, yet whose birth concerned them though Gentiles, though born far off in the "mountains of the East." They too have some benefit by him and his birth, and for that to do him worship. A SERMON PREACHED BEFORE THE KING'S MAJESTY.[15]

---

[14]CWE 45:52–53 (LB 7:10).

[15]Andrewes, *Ninety-Six Sermons*, 1:253*.

2:13-23 THE FLIGHT TO EGYPT
AND THE RETURN TO NAZARETH

[13]*Now when they had departed, behold, an angel of the Lord appeared to Joseph in a dream and said, "Rise, take the child and his mother, and flee to Egypt, and remain there until I tell you, for Herod is about to search for the child, to destroy him." [14]And he rose and took the child and his mother by night and departed to Egypt [15]and remained there until the death of Herod. This was to fulfill what the Lord had spoken by the prophet, "Out of Egypt I called my son."*

[16]*Then Herod, when he saw that he had been tricked by the wise men, became furious, and he sent and killed all the male children in Bethlehem and in all that region who were two years old or under, according to the time that he had ascertained from the wise men. [17]Then was fulfilled what was spoken by the prophet Jeremiah:*

[18]*"A voice was heard in Ramah,*
  weeping and loud lamentation,
Rachel weeping for her children;
  she refused to be comforted, because they are
    no more."

[19]*But when Herod died, behold, an angel of the Lord appeared in a dream to Joseph in Egypt, [20]saying, "Rise, take the child and his mother and go to the land of Israel, for those who sought the child's life are dead." [21]And he rose and took the child and his mother and went to the land of Israel. [22]But when he heard that Archelaus was reigning over Judea in place of his father Herod, he was afraid to go there, and being warned in a dream he withdrew to the district of Galilee. [23]And he went and lived in a city called Nazareth, so that what was spoken by the prophets might be fulfilled, that he would be called a Nazarene.*

OVERVIEW: Just as Jacob (Israel) and his sons found refuge in Egypt during a life-threatening famine, the holy family escapes Herod's ruthless intentions there. The reformers note that Matthew highlights the flight to Egypt to set up a fulfillment of an Old Testament prophecy about Christ. Various possibilities are suggested as to how Christ fulfills prophecies including a direct fulfillment of a predicted event, the use of typological fulfillment, and a "double fulfillment." The prophet Hosea (Hos 11:1) drew on imagery from Balaam's oracles in Numbers 23–24 in declaring that God would call his son out of Egypt. The prophet Balaam provided the parallels between God's bringing Israel out of Egypt (Num 23:22) and his bringing of his future king out of Egypt (Num 24:7-9). The interweaving of these three prophetic texts allows Matthew to point to Jesus' eventual return from Egypt as the fulfillment of Hosea's prophecy.

Other comments point out that Herod's wrath cannot thwart the purposes of God and that it will be God who has the final judgment on those who oppose his reign. Herod's wrathful murders of Bethlehem's children fulfills the predicted mourning of "Rachel," the matriarch that was buried near Ephrath or Bethlehem (Gen 35:19) for her children who are no more. Ephraim's descendants grieve their slain children. It is a tragic irony that the coming of the Messiah should have prompted worship and celebration among the Jews, but instead there was weeping and mourning.

The commentators honor Joseph as he continues to evidence his faith in God's plan by following the Lord's instructions immediately. The angel's announcement contains the ironic twist that those who sought to kill the child are now dead, allowing for Jesus' return from Egypt. Jesus' exile and return from Egypt marked the beginning of his suffering for the sake of his people. In Galilee, Jesus would spend his early life in relative peace. The commentators also grapple with Matthew's comment about the fulfillment of the prophets with Christ being called a "Nazarene." While noting that Matthew provides no explicit prophecy, the reformers propose Matthew is probably drawing on multiple passages. One possibility is that he fulfills the "type" of the Nazirite vows (see Num 6:1-21; Judg 13:3-5, 13-14), which were a mark of special dedication to the Lord. Jesus fulfills the type not by abstinence from wine but by remaining pure from sinful ambitions. Another possibility is that Jesus fulfills the prophets in that the etymology of Nazareth relates to the word *branch*, and Jesus is known as the branch (Is 11:1).

2:13-15 *"Out of Egypt I Called My Son"*

BEHOLD THE ANGEL OF THE LORD. MARTIN BUCER: Besides that, which we have already observed, we must carefully consider the manner of life belonging to Christ, God's one and only, most beloved Son, directed by the Father from childhood on, filled with dangers and troubles. As he will soon indicate, this is because his kingdom is not of this world and because he wishes to encourage each one of us according to our own lot in life, so that we may not wish to rule prematurely, before the time when our Christ suffered and was crucified. His humility is also found in this, because flight was necessary to save the one who was able to reduce Herod with all his power into nothing by a word. In addition, the horrible judgment of God against the Jews is by no means to be passed by. The Jews not only considered the most powerful promised Savior, born among them and worshiped by nations from far away, to be nothing, but they were even troubled when they heard of his birth. Therefore, for this ungodly contempt and most wicked ingratitude, he gave them this punishment: when Herod, a most savage tyrant, had forsaken them, Christ himself fled into Egypt, to a people well-known for ungodliness. By this Christ also declared that the kingdom of God must be transferred from the Jews to the Gentiles and that he himself had come, so

that what he greatly desired, he sought and preserved. For there are legends, which commemorate certain miracles of Christ, performed in Egypt, and they understood that the humanity of Christ was a flitting cloud, about which Isaiah 19 speaks: "Behold, the Lord rides on a swift cloud, and he comes into Egypt, and the idols of Egypt will totter before his face." Lest the examination of this passage puff up the Egyptians, the Lord diminished Egypt with these words, saying that his own vengeance would come most swiftly to them by the Assyrians, and that every person would be completely ruined by faithfulness to idols. They themselves would be scared out of their wits and set against each other, urged on without any hope of help. Then finally, I should also note now that the Lord strengthened his own Christ with his mother and his guardian for this exile by the very beautiful offerings of the magi. Thus the Lord always tempers a trial for his own people, so that they may be able to bear it, and likewise, they have another exit and a broad path even in the distress of affliction. COMMENTARY ON MATTHEW 2:13-14.[1]

MATTHEW'S USE OF HOSEA. FRANCISCUS GOMARUS: Some respond that the same thing that happened to Israel is announced about him by the prophets, being fulfilled in Christ not exactly but in kind. Because as the Israelites were formerly brought out of Egypt by a divine work into the Promised Land, indeed this same thing happened to Christ. Because what is said to fulfill, it may be said two ways: either when the same thing that was spoken beforehand about a certain subject occurred or when the same thing by kind occurred in the same way to the other, as is indicated by the agreement of the event. Such is this place, and this they demonstrate with similar examples, such as Matthew 13:14: The prophet Isaiah is fulfilled in you: hearing you will hear and not understand. This is in agreement with the prophecy, but not of the subject itself, and the same in verse 35. . . .

---

[1]Bucer, *In Sacra Quatuor Evangelia Enarrationes* Perpetuae (1536), 26-27; citing Is 19:1.

In the same way this is similar in this place, in persons, calling Israel herself from Hosea and Exodus 4:22: "firstborn son," certainly by grace of calling, but Christ a son by nature of generation. Then in chains, led down into Egypt, and brought back; Israel from death, which famine brought about, migrating into Egypt a servant: Christ similarly set free from death that Herod set in motion, and from Egypt, carried away from that danger, at last brought back, no less than Israel into the Promised Land.

Finally, another way [to be read] is . . . as neither about Israel alone, nor about Christ alone, but it is believed that the prophet is speaking about both. Indeed, about Israel immediately and also historically, about the Israelite people thus formerly summoned again from Egypt; truly, immediately, and prophetically about Christ, whose entering and returning by a type of the people themselves was sketched by God. So, like this prophecy, it does not have two senses, historical and prophetic, as they are accustomed to speak falsely about similar places; but just one sense having two members, which gradually or by its own order, as we show, and whether it is understood. So, as if what he adapts to another such member, he lays out a certain sense, but not untouched. Because they are valued, at this place and in similar places, this is observed. ILLUSTRIOUS SELECTIONS FROM THE GOSPEL OF MATTHEW.[2]

MESSIANIC FIGURES AND PROPHECY. WOLF-GANG CAPITO: This is by no means unintelligible. The Messiah, the Son of God, is more powerful than the people, who were adopted as part of that symbolism. Nevertheless, it is uncertain by law—if it is a spiritual law whose goal is Christ—how with respect to a spiritual foreshadowing the spoken words are assumed to establish these things that affect Christ in his mortal body. . . . The whole law and all the prophets are fulfilled in Christ, in which the glory of God is contained, since he has shown it and will show it. Therefore,

let someone look closely into Scripture, examining the works of God thoroughly and becoming better trained; he will know more certainly and understand more vividly. . . .

Therefore, all figures, histories, threats, promises, rages, and favors are either the image or the truth of Christ. For whatever is spiritual and internal is smudged by flesh and external things. Therefore, all the Scriptures meet together in one person, in Christ, just as it is particularly fitting for their scope and end. . . .

Therefore, the physical setting forth into Egypt was fulfilled, which was spoken by the Lord through the prophet, "Out of Egypt I have called my Son." That is, the boy Jesus was delivered out of Egypt. . . .

Then the prophet remarks for the people of his time that he had been born once already. Nevertheless, it is also a prophecy that foreshadows Christ's flight to Egypt. The statements are histories almost at the same time that they are types and prophecies, which watch for either captivity or liberation, that is, either anger or mercy.

Therefore, the Evangelist called the prophets to witness concerning Christ in regard to his flesh, which itself truly put the finishing touches on his own body like a shadow. Christ had nothing less than a proper sense of his Spirit, besides his flesh, which he daily freed with his own Spirit. The Evangelist greatly strengthened the duplicate figures of Christ in the Old Testament by a certain repetition, lest someone think that the prophecy should not be used in another way, because it had been taken somewhere by the Evangelist in a humbler reason. For the Evangelist was referring to that age, which was greatly acknowledged by the common people, just as Christ was the end of the law. By this covenant, Christ had expressed the shadows, or what was like them, in his own flesh, and these shadows would soon be abolished in himself in the coming of his glory. COMMENTARY ON HOSEA.[3]

---

[2]Gomarus, *Illustrium Ac Selectorum Ex Evangelio Mattaei* (1644), 17; citing Is 6:9-10; Ps 78:2.

[3]Capito, *In Hoseam Prophetam* (1528), 214r-214v, 218r-219r; citing Hos 11:1.

2:16-18 *The Slaughter of the Innocents*

Herod's Reaction to Being Tricked.
Joseph Hall: Herod was subtle in mocking the
wise men, while he promised to worship him
whom he meant to kill. Now God makes the wise
men to mock him, in disappointing his expectation. It is just with God to punish those who
would beguile others with illusion. Great spirits
are so much more impatient of disgrace. How did
Herod now rage and fret, and vainly wish to have
met with those false spies and to tell with what
torments he would revenge their treachery, and to
curse himself for trusting strangers in so important a business!

The tyrant's suspicion would not let him rest
long. Before many days he sends to inquire of
them whom he sent to inquire of Christ. The
notice of their secret departure increases his
jealousy, and now his anger runs mad, and his
fear proves desperate. All the infants of Bethlehem shall bleed for this one. And, that he may
make sure work, he cuts out to himself large
measures both of time and place. It was but very
lately that the star appeared, that the wise men
reappeared not. They asked for him who was
born. They did not name when he was born.
Herod, for more security, overreaches their time,
and fetches into the slaughter all the children of
two years of age. The priests and scribes had told
him the town of Bethlehem must be the place of
the Messiah's nativity. He fetches in all the
children of the coast adjoining: yea, his own shall
for the time be a Bethlehemite. A tyrannous
guiltiness never thinks itself safe, but ever seeks
to assure itself in the excess of cruelty. Doubtless
he, who so privily inquired for Christ, did as
secretly brew this massacre. . . .

O bloody Herod, that could sacrifice so many
harmless lives to your ambition. . . . It could not
concern you, if the heat of an impotent and furious
envy had not made you thirsty of blood. It is not
long that you shall enjoy this cruelty. After a few
hateful years, your soul shall feel the weight of so
many innocents, of so many just curses.

He, for whose sake you killed so many, shall
strike you with death, and then what would you
have given to have been as one of those infants
whom you murdered? In the meantime, when your
executioners returned and told you of their
impartial dispatch, you smiled to think how you
had defeated your rival, and beguiled the star, and
deluded the prophecies; while God in heaven, and
his Son on earth, laugh you to scorn, and make
your rage an occasion of further glory to him
whom you meant to suppress. Contemplations.[4]

Matthew's Use of Jeremiah. John Lightfoot: Ramah stood not far from Bethlehem,
though they were in two tribes. And the cry that
the poor parents and children made in Bethlehem
when this matchless butchery was in hand reached
to Ramah and was plainly heard there. Now
observe the fullness of this Scripture as it is uttered
by the prophet and as it is applied by the Evangelist. It was fulfilled in one kind, in the time of
Jeremiah himself, and then was the lamentation
and weeping in Ramah itself. For to here did
Nebuzaradan bring his prisoners after he had
destroyed Jerusalem, and there did he dispose of
them to the sword or to captivity, as seemed good
to himself. And imagine what lamentation and
crying was then in that city when so many were
doomed there either to be slain in that place or to
go to Babel, never to see their own land again.
Then was the cry in Ramah, and it was heard no
doubt in Bethlehem. But now the prophecy is
fulfilled in another kind, when Herod destroys so
many children in Bethlehem and in the suburbs
and borders belonging to it. And now the cry is in
Bethlehem, and it is heard to Ramah.

Rachel's grave was between Bethlehem and
Ramah, or at least not far distant from either of
them. The Holy Ghost therefore elegantly sets
forth this lamentation by personating Rachel—
who died in the birth of her Ben-Oni, the son of
her sorrow—sorrowing for her sons and children

---

[4]Hall, *Contemplations on the Historical Passages of the Old and New
Testaments*, 1:456-61.

who were thus massacred. And this shows that the text in the prophet aims in the first place and intention at the matter of Nebuzaradan. For in Bethlehem, Rachel properly had no children at all, that city being inhabited by the children of Judah who descended from Leah. But in Ramah dwelt Rachel's children, that being a town of Ephraimites descended from Joseph. Howsoever, Rachel may be said to weep for the babes of Bethlehem as her own children, though they were not strictly and properly her seed in regard of the interest that she had in all the tribes of Israel, as being wise to their father, as Joseph is often called the father of Christ, being only husband to his mother. And see such another phrase, "Shall I and your mother come to bow down before you?" whereas Joseph's mother was dead already. THE HARMONY OF THE FOUR EVANGELISTS.[5]

THE SLAUGHTER OF THE INNOCENTS RECALLS THE PAIN OF THE BENJAMINITES. JOHN CALVIN: It is certain that Jeremiah describes the destruction of the tribe of Benjamin, which took place in his time: for he had foretold that the tribe of Judah would be cut off, to which was added the half of the tribe of Benjamin. He puts the mourning into the mouth of Rachel, who had been long dead. This is a personification (*prosōpopoiia*), which has a powerful influence in moving the affections. It was not for the mere purpose of ornamenting his style that Jeremiah employed rhetorical embellishments. There was no other way of correcting the hardness and stupidity of the living than by arousing the dead, as it were, from their graves to bewail those divine chastisements, which were commonly treated with derision. The prediction of Jeremiah having been accomplished at that time, Matthew does not mean that it foretold what Herod would do, but that the coming of Christ occasioned a renewal of that mourning, which had been experienced, many centuries before, by the tribe of Benjamin.

He intended thus to meet a prejudice that might disturb and shake pious minds. It might be supposed that no salvation could be expected from him, on whose account, as soon as he was born, infants were murdered; on the contrary, it was an unfavorable and disastrous omen that the birth of Christ kindled a stronger flame of cruelty than usually burns amid the most inveterate wars. But as Jeremiah promises a restoration, where a nation has been cut off, down to their little children, so Matthew reminds his readers that this massacre would not prevent Christ from appearing shortly afterward as the Redeemer of the whole nation; for we know that the whole chapter in Jeremiah in which those words occur is filled with the most delightful consolations. Immediately after the mournful complaint, he adds, "Refrain your voice from weeping, and your eyes from tears: for your work shall be rewarded, says the Lord, and they shall come again from the land of the enemy. And there is hope in your end, says the Lord, that your children shall come again to your own border."

Such was the resemblance between the former calamity that the tribe of Benjamin had sustained and the second calamity, which is here recorded. Both were a prelude of the salvation that was shortly to arrive. COMMENTARY ON A HARMONY OF THE EVANGELISTS.[6]

THE CAPTIVITY WAS A TYPE OF THE SLAUGHTER. JUAN DE MALDONADO: The Hebrews explain 2 Kings 24:10; 25:4 as the leading away of the two tribes Judah and Benjamin into captivity. It is not doubtful from the circumstances of Jeremiah that it ought to be so understood, and that by Rachel the whole territory of the two tribes should be understood by a double metonymy;[†] one by which a place is understood by a person, the other, by which a whole country is understood by a single city. Rachel was buried in Bethlehem, hence by Rachel, Bethlehem is to be understood. Why, then, did the prophet not simply say, "Bethlehem weeping for her children," but spoke of Rachel,

---

[5]Lightfoot, *The Harmony of the Four Evangelists* (1644), 112-13*; citing Jer 40:1; Gen 35:16-20; 1 Sam 10:2; Gen 37:10.

[6]CTS 1:160-61* (CO 45:100-101); citing Jer 31:15; 16-17.

who had long been dead, when the dead do not lament? The reason may be that Rachel was a woman, and it is the nature of women to lament calamities of this kind. . . . By this expression, the prophet most probably wished to show that the future calamity of the people would be so great that not one woman could remain who would weep, so that the mourners must call up even the dead. . . . But why, by the weeping of Rachel, is the calamity of the kingdom of Judea signified, when Rachel was the mother not of Judah but of Benjamin? Because the head of the kingdom was Jerusalem, formerly called Jebus, which was in the tribe of Benjamin.

What the prophet spoke of the captivity, St. Matthew applied to the slaughter of the infants, showing that the prophecy, though not spoken of them, could be applied to them much more properly than to the captive Jews, and because the former were men and the latter infants, the former deserving punishment, the latter innocent and underserving, the former captives, the latter cruelly slain, the former of Judah, the latter of Bethlehem. Rachel, therefore—that is, Bethlehem—should rather lament the infants than the men. A deep, profound grief is expressed by the accumulation of words, "lamentation and mourning and woe." COMMENTARY ON MATTHEW 2:18.[7]

2:19-23 *The Return to Nazareth*

THE FAITH AND FEAR OF JOSEPH. JOHN CALVIN: These words show the perseverance of Joseph's faith. He kept his feet firm in Egypt till he was recalled to his native country by a command of God. We see, at the same time, that the Lord never disappoints his own people but renders them seasonable aid. It is probable that Joseph returned from Egypt immediately after the death of Herod, before Augustus Caesar had issued his decree,

appointing Archelaus to be governor of Judea. Having been declared by his father's will to be successor to the throne, he undertook the whole charge of the government but abstained from taking the title of king, saying that this depended on the will and pleasure of Caesar. He afterward went to Rome and obtained confirmation; only the name of king was refused until he had merited it by his actions. The governor of Galilee was Philip, a man of gentle disposition and almost like a private individual. Joseph complied with the suggestion of the angel because, under a prince who had no delight in shedding blood and who treated his subjects with mildness, there was less danger.

We must always bear in mind the purpose of God in training his Son, from the commencement, under the discipline of the cross, because this was the way in which he was to redeem his church. He bore our infirmities and was exposed to dangers and to fears in order that he might deliver his church from them by his divine power and might bestow everlasting peace upon it. His danger was our safety; his fear was our confidence. Not that he ever in his life felt alarm, but as he was surrounded on every hand by the fear of Joseph and Mary, he may be justly said to have taken upon him our fears in order that he might procure for us assured confidence. COMMENTARY ON A HARMONY OF THE EVANGELISTS.[8]

JESUS AS A NAZARENE. PHILIPP MELANCHTHON: Nazarenes were those among the people taking vows, for which God had devoted a form of vow, and they did not drink wine, they did not shave their hair, and so on. This was a custom just like many other external practices in the law, as it would mark their confession, because individual ceremonies made a human noteworthy. But he was meaning a true proclamation spoken for God, not destroying doctrine by his own drunkenness, . . . not intoxicated by an ambition for glory, by human opinions. But Christ was not such a Nazarene in

---

[7]JMG 73-74*; citing Gen 35:18-19; Josh 18:28; 1 Chron 11:4.
†Metonymy is a figure of speech that substitutes a noun or nominal phrase with a word or phrase associated with an aspect or property of the original noun or phrase.

[8]CTS 1:162* (CO 45:101-2).

relation to ceremonies because he drank wine, but he was a sign of a Nazarene, that is, most pure and a proclaimer speaking for God, not intoxicated by human opinions, but preaching pure words. In like manner, without ambition for glory. ANNOTATIONS ON THE GOSPELS.[9]

JESUS AS NAZARENE FULFILLS SCRIPTURE.

THEODORE BEZA: All the Greek codices agree here. Nor is it necessary to look for further evidence from many prophets because of this, since any individual prophet is usually cited in this way and all the written prophetic books are contained in one volume, or at most two. Also, the book of Judges, from which this passage is thought to have been taken, seems to have been written by many prophets out of necessity. . . .

I consider that this particle [*hoti*] indicates that these are the words of the Evangelist, referring not so much to the very words of the prophets but to their opinion. . . . But it is certain among the Evangelists that *Nazôraion* and *Nazarênon* with a *z* is a Gentile name derived from the city of Nazareth. Although there is never a mention of this city in the Old Testament, it is necessary to understand that the author alluded to a passage from the prophet, so that clearly Jesus was called a Nazarite or Nazarene by the Jews, just as if he had been born there. But he truly was a Nazarite, whose type was Samson, although Jesus was not a Nazarite by a vow but from the most perfect holiness. . . . Other variants of this sort—whether typographical errors, interpolations, or foolish nonsense—are unlimited today and are put forth under the name of some ancient writer for the sake of profit. I prefer to say *Nazarite* rather than *Nazorite*, so that I may avoid a homonym. ANNOTATIONS ON MATTHEW 2:23.[10]

HOW JESUS FULFILLS SCRIPTURE. CHRISTOPHER BLACKWOOD: This testimony in these same words is nowhere found in Scripture. But we find it spoken in so many words of Samson in the type, "The child shall be a Nazarite unto God from the womb," which is fulfilled in Christ, who is the antitype. As Samson was exceedingly strong, so is Christ, in that he binds the strong man. As Samson slew more at his death than in his life, so Christ destroyed death by his death.

There is no witness brought out of one prophet, but there is one witness brought out of all the prophets, for all the prophets that speak of Christ set him forth to be holy. So that as in the old law they that gave themselves to some peculiar holiness above the common prescripts of the law were called Nazarites. They were to drink no wine, and to be holy, and so on. So these things were fulfilled in Christ, who did not devote himself to wine and such kinds of ceremonies but to the bloody and shameful death of the cross, so that the sense is, things were so ordered by God that Joseph and Mary being returned out of Egypt should dwell at Nazareth, that from his dwelling there the name of Nazarite might stick to him, whereby his most perfect holiness and the vow he took upon himself, which was to die for our salvation, might be signified. . . . Christ was called a Nazarite, not only in respect to his vow, but in respect to the place, alluding to the derivation of the word *Nazareth*, of the Hebrew word *neser*, that signifies a "branch," because Nazareth was situated in a place abounding with fruit trees. So Christ is often called by the prophets a tender "plant," a "rod," and a "branch." Christ is often called a "branch," the man whose name is the branch. AN EXPOSITION UPON THE GOSPEL OF MATTHEW.[11]

---

[9]MO 14:549-50.
[10]Beza, *Annotationes Majores in Novum Dn. Nostri Jesu Christi Testamentum* (1594), 16; citing Judg 13:6.

[11]Blackwood, *Expositions and Sermons upon . . . Matthew* (1659), 49-50*; citing Judg 13:5; Lk 11:22; Num 6:3, 8; Is 11:1; Zech 6:12.

3:1-12 JOHN THE BAPTIST PREPARES THE WAY

In those days John the Baptist came preaching in the wilderness of Judea, ²"Repent, for the kingdom of heaven is at hand."ᵃ ³For this is he who was spoken of by the prophet Isaiah when he said,

"The voice of one crying in the wilderness:
'Prepareᵇ the way of the Lord;
    make his paths straight.'"

⁴Now John wore a garment of camel's hair and a leather belt around his waist, and his food was locusts and wild honey. ⁵Then Jerusalem and all Judea and all the region about the Jordan were going out to him, ⁶and they were baptized by him in the river Jordan, confessing their sins.

⁷But when he saw many of the Pharisees and Sadducees coming to his baptism, he said to them,

"You brood of vipers! Who warned you to flee from the wrath to come? ⁸Bear fruit in keeping with repentance. ⁹And do not presume to say to yourselves, 'We have Abraham as our father,' for I tell you, God is able from these stones to raise up children for Abraham. ¹⁰Even now the axe is laid to the root of the trees. Every tree therefore that does not bear good fruit is cut down and thrown into the fire.

¹¹"I baptize you with water for repentance, but he who is coming after me is mightier than I, whose sandals I am not worthy to carry. He will baptize you with the Holy Spirit and fire. ¹²His winnowing fork is in his hand, and he will clear his threshing floor and gather his wheat into the barn, but the chaff he will burn with unquenchable fire."

a Or the kingdom of heaven has come near   b Or crying: Prepare in the wilderness

---

OVERVIEW: The Reformation commentators note the connections between the later sections of Isaiah (especially Is 40–55) and John the Baptist's ministry and message. Anabaptist commentators highlight that, due to the impending kingdom of heaven, both John's baptism and his preaching were focused on repentance. John proclaims God's covenant with his people and the motivation to repentance. The true fruit of that repentance would be faith in Christ and goodness toward others. The kingdom of heaven is the rule of Christ in the hearts of his people.

Though John is baptizing the crowds as they are "confessing their sins," he rebukes the Pharisees and Sadducees, who notably simply seek baptism, for their lack of repentance and prideful and self-righteous reliance on their lineage from Abraham. God will be able to keep his promises to the descendants of Abraham even as the Jews have misappropriated their Abrahamic lineage. With a proper reading of Isaiah 51, piety not patrimony would be evoked. The coming of the kingdom will climax in a period of judgment that would cut off any relying on fleshly heritage or in self-righteous piety.

The coming judgment will be fiery in its intensity and divisive in its nature, as seen in two analogies. Both the ax "already" laid at the root of the trees and the winnowing fork used to clear the threshing floor being "in his hand" illustrate that the one coming after John comes in power and judgment "with the Holy Spirit and with fire," hence the need for immediate repentance. John Eachard, citing Hosea 6:5, notes that the judgment begins by the regular preaching of the Word as a message of truth. The fire that waits the unrepentant is the wrath of God, which serves in the immediate context as a refining fire but will later be a final judgment.

3:1-9 John the Baptist Prepares the Way of the Lord

A BAPTISM OF REPENTANCE. MENNO SIMONS: The Scriptures on every hand require of us true repentance, and the sacramental signs, such as baptism and the Holy Supper, signify, represent, and teach to all true Christian believers a penitent, unblameable life. According to the Scriptures, no one can be a true Christian without true repentance, and every kind of seed brings forth fruit after its own kind, as already said; namely, lies bring forth children of lies; and truth brings forth children of truth. . . . The prophets prophesied of John. His birth was announced by an angel. Christ testified of him that he was the second Elijah, a shining light, not clothed in soft raiment and not like the waving reed: that he was the greatest of all those born of women. . . . From this it may be concluded that he was no frivolous, reckless preacher, but that he earnestly and valiantly executed his office of preaching repentance well-pleasing to God and that he rightly practiced the commanded baptism according to the ordinance. And, although his disciples were not so thoroughly instructed in all things, yet he did not baptize any but those who confessed their sins. REPLY TO GELLIUS FABER.[1]

JOHN'S MESSAGE OF REPENTANCE. PILGRAM MARPECK: Briefly, then, as the Scripture indicates, the baptism of John means repentance. John preaches repentance, teaches the people to be converted from their sins, and warns that the kingdom of God is present and available to those who are poor in spirit, that is, only to those who are repentant; they came to John, listened to his teaching, and desired to be baptized. These he baptized unto repentance—that is, he baptized them on the basis that, from henceforth, they would turn from their sins, repent of their sins, and bring forth worthy fruits of repentance. Thus, Christ, as the one healer or master of the sick, might comfort both those who were poor in spirit and those who *confessed* with their whole hearts. Christ had been sent, and he came with his gospel to comfort them, to make them whole, and to reunite them with God. In the same way John,

in his office, prepared the way for the Lord, preparing and inaugurating a perfect people for the Lord. However, he did not go beyond baptizing unto repentance in order that they might repent of their sins; he let it be at that. THE ADMONITION OF 1549.[2]

THE MOTIVE FOR REPENTANCE. WILLIAM BRIDGE: As the motive is, such is the repentance that is founded on it. The motive here is evangelical: "Repent, for the kingdom of heaven is at hand." The motive is evangelical, surely therefore, the repentance here required is not a legal but an evangelical repentance. But what is it then? What is here meant by the kingdom of heaven? And the kingdom of heaven being at hand, or approaching? In the language of the New Testament, the kingdom of heaven is sometimes put for the kingdom of glory. Sometimes it is put for the church of Christ under the New Testament. Sometimes it is put for the gospel and the preaching of the gospel. Sometimes for the whole kingdom of grace. I take it here for the whole state of the Messiah: the kingdom of grace, the preaching of the gospel, and the dispensations thereof. And he says here that the kingdom of heaven has approached; therefore, do you turn; therefore, do repent.

There are these two notes that lie before you. First, the kingdom of heaven approaches us before we come to it. Repent, or turn, because the kingdom of heaven has approached unto you. . . . Second, that the approaching or drawing near of the kingdom of heaven is the highest and the greatest motive in the world to true repentance. WORKS OF WILLIAM BRIDGE.[3]

THE MEANING OF THE KINGDOM OF HEAVEN. MARTIN BUCER: These are the briefest words, but they are the sum of all evangelical preaching. . . . The day of that salvation has shone forth, in which God wishes for people most promptly to answer

---

[1] Simons, *Complete Writings*, 632, 702*.

[2] CRR 2:174-75.
[3] WWB 2:220, 240*.

his own call, and himself to do a work, and to save them, and to bring them into the covenant of his people. By these very people, then, others may also be joined in covenant with himself, and thus they may build up the land for the kingdom of salvation and occupy the devastated inheritances of the nations, inherited by the gospel. . . . Isaiah 49 and many other passages prophesy the coming of the kingdom of heaven. If in fact the kingdom of heaven is the kingdom of Christ, then it reigns everywhere in the minds of the elect, justifying them and saving them by his own Spirit and the faith of the gospel. It had grown somewhat in the beginning among the elect, but now it is revealed openly. . . . If in fact God was known in Judea alone, the whole scattering of things turned into manifold darkness of error and ungodliness; now, however, all flesh will behold the salvation of the Lord in our deliverer Jesus Christ when the gospel is preached to every creature. Consequently, this kingdom of Christ is rightly called the kingdom of heaven, for it grows in him in the heavenly realms and incomparably exceeds every earthly thing. By its power, of which there is no doubt, we are set free from sin and death and we enjoy eternal peace and an abundance of all good things, just as we are ruled by law of the Spirit, not the letter. This law is not written on stones but on the tablets of our hearts, and we act as citizens by the faith of the soul, not by external familiarity or by seeing the King, but by faith worshiping the One reigning in the heavenly realms. Therefore, just as all spiritual and heavenly matters belong to this kingdom of Christ by heavenly law, it is also called the kingdom of heaven. COMMENTARY ON MATTHEW 3:2.[4]

BEAR FRUIT WORTHY OF REPENTANCE.

PHILIPP MELANCHTHON: The first fruit [of repentance] is to grow in faith, and John often impressed this upon them: "Behold the Lamb of God." Everyone who believes in him will have eternal life. The second fruit is the work of the second table [of the law] and it is very familiar: almsgiving. "Anyone who has two tunics, let him give to the one who does not have any." Behold, he teaches who ought to give and to what sort of person, similar to the rule of Paul: not so that the gift may be a burden for you, and so that it may be a relief to others. Let these give who have and are able to be generous with something of their own. Let them give to those who are truly in need, who are not able to work and who are honest. ANNOTATIONS ON THE GOSPELS.[5]

JOHN'S MESSAGE TO THE JEWISH LEADERS.

WOLFGANG MUSCULUS: John knew from the beginning that they were descendants of Abraham. He also knew the memory of Abraham, to which they appealed by means of Isaiah 51. If that passage was used correctly, it would be able to excite a great desire for the piety of their ancestor among the descendants of that man. If they had wished to be found in the footsteps of Abraham their father, he would never have taken this away from them. Truly, they considered in this preposterous manner that they were secure because of the divine promises to Abraham, although they themselves were ungodly. The progeny of Abraham were devoted to their sins, and they persuaded themselves that it was impossible that they would be burned up by divine vengeance, because God had made a covenant with Abraham and his descendants forever. From then on, it was the case that no threat of divine vengeance could move them to repentance. Having declared in good time that they were beyond exhortation to the fruits of penitence, John thought that their preposterous self-assurance, conceived from the privileges of Abraham their father, should be removed. It is as if he should say, "You glorify our father Abraham, and divine blessing was promised to his seed, which most certainly will give comfort to all of you. Nevertheless, it is not necessary that your ungodliness and impenitence be allowed to depart unpunished because of the promise to Abraham. As if the promises would fall

---

[4]Bucer, *In Sacra Quatuor Evangelia, Enarrationes Perpetuae* (1536), 35; citing Jer 31:33; Ezek 36:26.

[5]MO 14:551; citing Lk 3:11.

short of the truth, if they uproot you from within! The promise is not nullified. It is endowed with this power, so that when you have all completely died out, God is able to raise up genuine sons for Abraham out of these stones. The truthful God will guard those whom he promised to Abraham. For he cannot reckon the sons of Abraham by bodily descent: at any rate, both Ishmael and Esau were from Abraham."

"For I say to you, what God is able to do . . ." This is the reason joined to the warning. He took this from a consideration of divine power and what things are possible—which seem impossible to us. The Jews supposed that it was impossible, so that God did not allow his own promises to become invalid. In this way they thought rightly, for "God is truthful, and every man is a liar." However, what they supposed was false, for they thought that if they themselves were destroyed, then there would be no sons of Abraham, in whom the divine promises are fulfilled. John came to this thought by the argument of the power of God. It is as if he should say, "I assert to you that such is the power of God that he can completely wipe out all of you as you deserved, and he can take up sons for his beloved Abraham from another place, even from these stones, in whatever way he thinks is best." Christ used a very similar argument in Luke 19, saying, "Because if these [children] are silent, the stones will cry out." Abraham looked to this power of God when he was commanded to sacrifice his own son Isaac. COMMENTARY ON MATTHEW 3:9.[6]

3:10-12 The Ax and Winnowing Fork of Judgment

THE AX OF JUDGMENT AT THE ROOT OF THE TREE. JOHN EACHARD: What is meant by "the ax"? It is taken materially for an instrument, to cut down trees: So Deuteronomy 20:19: "You shall not cut down the fruit trees with an ax, when you besiege a city, for you may eat of them, for the tree

of the field is man's life," but it is taken metaphorically for God's decree and judgment, as in this place. Now the decree of God comes forth that every one who is not made a good tree by baptism into Christ is hewn down and cast into wrath. In the time of the law, there was sacrifice for wrath, but now baptism for people to get into Christ, now no more sacrifice for wrath. . . . Hew him down, is the decree of the most high. So Zephaniah 2:1-2: "Gather yourselves together, gather yourselves together, O nation not worthy to be beloved, before the decree come forth; for God's decrees are never to be recalled." The ax at the root is baptism. . . .

What is meant by "hewn down"? They are cut down before God that refuse or will not believe baptism by God's law and decree. For as Samuel hewed Agag in pieces before the Lord in Gilgal, so are all who will not receive Christ by baptism hewn down and cast into the fire of God's wrath. . . . Metaphorically it is taken for the preaching of the law by the prophets: So Hosea 6:5: "Therefore I have hewn them by my prophets, and slain them with the words of my mouth; by punishments and plagues, and curses of the law, for their sins." Therefore, the law and the prophets endured until John (hewing them, and slaying them, as in Hosea, for their sins), and since that time, the kingdom of heaven is preached, and every person presses unto it. . . .

What is meant by "fire"? By fire in this place is not meant hell fire, though they shall go afterward into hell fire that do not escape, but they are cast into the fire of God's wrath; signifying that every person who brings forth evil fruit of sin before God, that believes not by baptism their sins are all forgiven, and that in Christ they bring forth fruit of righteousness before God, they are hewn down and cast into the fire of God's wrath. THE AXE AGAINST SIN AND ERROR.[7]

CHRIST AS BAPTIZER. JOHN CALVIN: The ordinance of our Lord, viewed as a whole, includes

---

[6]Musculus, *In Evangelistam Matthaeum Commenarii* (1556), 34; citing Rom 3:4; Lk 19:40; Heb 11:17.

[7]Eachard, *The Axe Against Sin and Error . . . A Sermon on Matthew 3.10* (1646), 10-13; citing 1 Sam 15:33; Jn 3:36.

himself as its author, and the power of the Spirit, together with the figure and the minister; but where a comparison is made between our Lord and the minister, the former must have all the honor and the latter must be reduced to nothing. . . . The meaning is clear, that Christ alone bestow all the grace that is figuratively represented by outward baptism, because it is he who "sprinkles the conscience" with his blood. It is he also who mortifies the old person and bestows the Spirit of regeneration. The word "fire" is added as an epithet and is applied to the Spirit, because he takes away our pollutions, as fire purifies gold. COMMENTARY ON A HARMONY OF THE EVANGELISTS.[8]

THE LORD'S JUDGMENT ON UNFRUITFUL TREES.
SAMUEL HIERON: Let us now examine briefly the manner of his proceeding, and that is twofold: First, "hewn down." Second, "cast into the fire." This hewing down is a course performed by the ministry of the word. In the prophecy of Jeremiah, it is noted as a part of the minister's office "to destroy, to pluck up, to throw down." And in Hosea, "I have cut down (says the Lord) by my prophets." We have "ready (says the apostle) vengeance against all disobedience," so that this hewing down is a thing executed by the ordinary minister, and the meaning is this: that those who making an outward profession of religion continue still fruitless and are not reformed, at last this heavy sentence shall pass upon them, that they are past recovery, and so the Lord will even give them over to hardness of heart and leave them to their own deserved condemnation. This is the nature of the punishment; this is the reward of unprofitableness. . . .

The second part of the Lord's proceeding against unfruitful trees is casting them into the fire, which is to be performed at the last judgment and is the most certain and undoubted sequel of the hewing down by the ministry of the gospel. Those whom the ministry of the word hews down now, the justice of God at the last day shall send them to the fire. Let people imagine as they lean to one side and say of the preaching of the word that it is but a blast and the threatening thereof are by wind. Yet to their eternal woe, they shall one day find it otherwise. The sentence of the word goes before, and the fire of judgment shall surely follow after. A SERMON UPON MATTHEW 3:10.[9]

THE WINNOWING FORK AND FIERY JUDGMENT.
JOHN CALVIN: In the former verse, John preached concerning the grace of Christ in order that the Jews might yield themselves to him to be renewed; now he discourses of judgment, in order that he may strike despisers with terror. As there are always many hypocrites who proudly reject the grace of Christ offered to them, it is also necessary to denounce the judgment that awaits them. For this reason John here describes Christ as a severe judge against unbelievers. And this is an order that must be observed by us in teaching, that hypocrites may know that their rejection of Christ will not go unpunished . . . the reprobate experience, in their convictions of guilt, the heat of that fire, the actual burning of which they will feel at the last day. COMMENTARY ON A HARMONY OF THE EVANGELISTS.[10]

---

[8]CTS 1:198-99 (CO 45:122-23).

[9]Hieron, *The Discoverie of Hypocrisie in Two Sermons upon Matthew 3. Verse 10* (1609), 28-29.
[10]CTS 1:199-200 (CO 45:123-24).

3:13-17 THE BAPTISM OF JESUS

[13]*Then Jesus came from Galilee to the Jordan to John, to be baptized by him.* [14]*John would have prevented him, saying, "I need to be baptized by you, and do you come to me?"* [15]*But Jesus answered him, "Let it be so now, for thus it is fitting for us to fulfill all righteousness." Then he consented.* [16]*And when Jesus was baptized, immediately he went up from the water, and behold, the heavens were opened to him,[a] and he saw the Spirit of God descending like a dove and coming to rest on him;* [17]*and behold, a voice from heaven said, "This is my beloved Son,[b] with whom I am well pleased."*

a Some manuscripts omit *to him*   b Or *my Son, my (or the) Beloved*

OVERVIEW: During the Reformation era, the vast majority of Christians continued the medieval practice of infant baptism. Challenges to this practice, by groups such as the Anabaptists, were often made on scriptural grounds but also carried significant ecclesial, social, and civil ramifications. All Reformation commentators, though, found significance in Christ's baptism. The commentators note that Jesus is hidden among the Jews while John prepared them for him. Through baptism, John presents Jesus publicly to the Jews. Niels Hemmingsen notes that the context of the Jordan was important, because the Lord had delivered his people through the Jordan into Canaan and had later cleansed Naaman of his leprosy there as well. So, Jesus' baptism in the Jordan symbolically links the deliverance from bondage and the removal of spiritual leprosy that every believer experiences with baptism. John's humble and appropriate protests are met by Jesus' reply that because of the timing of his life and for the fulfilling of righteousness, Jesus should be baptized by John, thereby fulfilling John's particular prophetic role.

Following the endorsement of the prophet by baptism, heavenly approval comes in the form of the Holy Spirit descending on Jesus and the divine voice declaring Jesus to be the Son of God. Luther highlights the gracious "tone" of God's voice regarding his Son at the Jordan compared to the terrifying, divine voice at Sinai. Many commentators consider the theological implications of the trinitarian aspect of the baptismal narrative and the intratrinitarian divine love it reveals.

3:13-15 *Jesus Comes to John to Be Baptized*

JOHN'S BAPTISM OF JESUS. NIELS I IEM-MINGSEN: It is not for nothing that the Evangelist mentions the Jordan. For his meaning is that we should have an eye to the former miracles that were done long ago in the Jordan; that thereby we may gather how much force and effort is contained in spiritual baptism.

The first miracle therefore that comes to mind is that which happened when the people—under the conduct of Joshua—entered into the land of promise. For the river of Jordan—contrary to the nature of water—stood at one side like a wall and gave way to God's people to pass through, so as they passed dry shod, following the ark of the Lord, which the peoples of God carried before the people. By this type is signified that we are conveyed out of the kingdom of Satan into the kingdom of God by baptism, Christ going before us who is the true ark of propitiation.

Elijah divided the Jordan with his cloak, and passing the river was lifted up into heaven. Naaman the leper of Syria washing in water in the Jordan at the commandment of the prophet was made whole and sound. Now as the deed of Elijah is a shadow signified that our passage into heaven should be made by baptism, so the cleansing of Naaman the Syrian prefigured the spiritual cleansing from sins to be made by baptism. For look what baptism signifies outwardly, that the Lord works inwardly by his own power. Therefore, when we hear mention made of Jordan, let us call to mind what it signifies spiritually concerning our baptism. . . .

First concerning John's forbidding, wherein he put Christ off, both by request and with his hand. Verily, John weighed two things heedfully in this case, but the third he neglected. He weighed himself to be unworthy to loose the strap of Christ's shoes, and therefore much more to wash his naked body. And second, he weighed that Christ is free from sin, and therefore he thinks him to have no need of baptism, that he should be washed there with a token of repentance. The third thing—as I said—he neglected, namely, what belonged both to his own office and to Christ's office. For he ought to have looked upon his office, and not upon the worthiness of his person. He ought to have been resolved that Christ could not attempt anything that pertained not to the office of a mediator. And, therefore, he heard Christ say: Let be now, for so it becomes us to fulfill all righteousness. You are sent to baptize, and I come to give salvation to those who are baptized; therefore, let each of us do that which becomes him. A Postil, or Exposition of the Gospels.[1]

The Significance of Jesus' Baptism.
Heinrich Bullinger: Unto this doctrine he adds the famous and holy sacrament of baptism, whereby he might represent even visibly the mysteries of God to the worshipers of God and gather together into one body the faithful people and graft them into Christ. And then the heavenly Father calls forth also his own Son from Galilee, where he had laid hidden unto the Jews, that because the minds of the common people seemed now sufficiently prepared by the Baptist to receive Christ, he himself might come forth in open view now declaring and showing himself to the world

no longer by the testimony of others, but by his own doctrine and by his own virtues. Therefore, the Lord comes to the Jews unto Jordan, where John taught and baptized into Christ, and he also is baptized of John.

Moreover, the Baptist acknowledges forthwith the Savior of the world, and therefore witnesses in most manifest words that this very self-same is the Son of God, which should take away the sins of the world, of whom hitherto he spoke, for whom he commanded all people to wait, and now repeating the very self-same thing fervently, he sends all people to Christ only. Furthermore, the heavenly Father adds hereunto from heaven his honorable and strange witness. For after the heavens were opened, and the Holy Ghost was lighted upon the head of Christ in the visible likeness of a heavenly dove, he says, as it were pointing forth his finger toward Christ, and also adding thereunto a most clear voice: "This is my dearly beloved Son, yea and so thoroughly beloved, that for his sake only, I am now thoroughly pleased and reconciled to the world, wherewith for their sins I was most grievously offended." The Sum of the Four Evangelists.[2]

Connections Between Our Baptism and That of Christ.
Johannes Bugenhagen: The whole Trinity is present in this baptism and revealed here, the mystery that was unknown to all people, which only those who believe have recognized and confess. The Father appeared in the voice, the Son in our flesh, and the Holy Spirit in the dove—not in substance but in appearance—who also appeared as fire on the day of Pentecost. Who will doubt that that the angels were also present here out of devotion to the Lord, admiring with joy this grace that had been offered to the world?

All these things are also accomplished in our own baptism, which Christ has consecrated, instituted, and mandated for us. For when we are baptized into Christ, heaven, which was closed to us through the law, is opened to us; the Father

---

[1]Hemmingsen, *A Postill, or Exposition of the Gospels* (1569), 77*.

[2]Bullinger, *The Summe of the Foure Evangelists* (1582), A3-A4.

pronounces us to be children of God for the sake of Christ, in whom we are baptized; and the Holy Spirit regenerates us into a living hope, full assurance in our prayers, and finally a new life. Here too the angels are present who always, as Christ says, see the face of the Father in heaven and who desire, according to Peter, to look into the things that are given to us through Christ. These rejoice in heaven over a single sinner who repents, according to Christ's word.

We are not speaking foolishly or apart from God's Word, lest you should say, "These things have been done for Christ; they do not happen to us." In our baptism as well, the whole Trinity is present through the revelation of the Word. For the very thing that is revealed outwardly here is a Word concerning the presence of the Trinity—since indeed we are baptized, by Christ's institution and command, in the name of the Father, the Son, and the Holy Spirit. We confess this baptism when we say, "I believe in God the Father, in God the Son who has suffered for us, and in God the Spirit."[†] From this faith, and not from observances of the pope or others, the "holy catholic church, the communion of saints," is born and arises. There [in that church] is found the "remission of sins" through nothing but Jesus Christ alone, who has "suffered for us under Pontius Pilate." There too is the "resurrection of the flesh to eternal life." For all of this, our baptism is efficacious. I pray that the demonic doctrines of the papists and others would not drag people off to some other place! COMMENTARY ON MATTHEW 3:13-17.[3]

JESUS' BAPTISM FULFILLS RIGHTEOUSNESS.

JOHN CALVIN: For what purpose did the Son of God wish to be baptized? This may be learned, in some measure, from his answer. We have already assigned a special reason. He received the same baptism with us, in order to assure believers that they are ingrafted into his body and that they are

"buried with him in baptism," so that they may rise to "newness of life." But the end, which he here proposes, is more extensive: "for thus it became him to fulfill all righteousness." The word *righteousness* frequently signifies, in Scripture, the observation of the law, and in that sense we may explain this passage to mean that, since Christ had voluntarily subjected himself to the law, it was necessary that he should keep it in every part. But I prefer a more simple interpretation. "Say nothing for the present," said our Lord, "about my rank, for the question before us is not, which of us deserves to be placed above the other. Let us rather consider what our calling demands and what has been enjoined on us by God the Father." The general reason why Christ received baptism was so that he might render full obedience to the Father; and the special reason was that he might consecrate baptism in his own body so that we might have it in common with him.

It is certain that John acknowledged Christ to be not only a distinguished prophet, as many foolishly dream, but the Son of God, as he really was; for otherwise he would have dishonored God by lowering his holy calling to a mortal man. . . . There was, no doubt, plausibility in this ground of refusal, that Christ had no need of his baptism, but John was mistaken in not considering that it was for the sake of others that baptism was asked. And so Christ bids him consider what was suitable to the character of a servant, which he had undertaken; for a voluntary subjection takes nothing from his glory. Though the good man remained ignorant, for a time, of some part of his public duty, this particular error did not prevent him from discharging, in a proper and lawful manner, his office of "Baptist." This example shows that we do not act rashly in undertaking the commission that the Lord has given us, according to the light we enjoy, though we do not immediately comprehend all that belongs to our calling or that depends upon it. We must also observe his modesty, in giving up his opinion, and immediately obeying Christ. COMMENTARY ON A HARMONY OF THE EVANGELISTS.[4]

[3]Bugenhagen, *In IIII. Priora Capita Euangelii secundum Matthaeum* (1543), P3A- B; citing 1 Pet 1:12; Lk 15:7. [†]This and the following seem to refer to the Apostles' Creed.

[4]CTS 1:201-3* (CO 45:124-25); citing Rom 6:4; Mt 3:15; Phil. 2:7.

CHRIST'S BAPTISM WAS PERFORMATIVE, NOT NECESSARY. JUAN DE MALDONADO: The word "justice" in this passage may be taken to mean no part of the old law, nor justice placed in any positive precept, which was of necessity observation, but whatever was agreeable to the virtue and duty of a holy man, though not to do it might be without sin. All the words of John show this: "I ought to be baptized by you," as if he said "You have no need of me"; Christ answers, "Though it be not necessary, yet it becomes me to be baptized by you, that we may fulfill all justice." That is, that we may perform not only the commandments, but whatever is just and consistent with holiness. COMMENTARY ON MATTHEW 3:15.[5]

3:16-17 The Father and the Holy Spirit at Jesus' Baptism

THE DECLARATION OF THE WORD AT JESUS' BAPTISM. MARTIN LUTHER: No longer is there a barrier between God and us, since God himself descends at the Jordan. The Father lets his voice be heard, the Son sanctifies baptism with his body, and the Holy Spirit descends in the form of a dove . . . in the friendliest of forms to show that he is not wrathful toward us, but wants to help us become holy and rescue us through Christ. . . .

The Father's voice resounds. . . . But this voice is different from the voice at Mt. Sinai, where God also spoke from heaven. There his voice was so terrible that the earth quaked, the hills trembled, and the people feared for their lives. Here, however, it was all friendliness, grace, and compassion. It was as though God said, "You people, turn your eyes and open your ears in this direction. Note carefully this man who is here baptized. Do you want to know who he is? He is my beloved Son, in whom I delight with deepest pleasure. You need not fear him. He stands here stripped, like any other man, brandishing neither sword nor worldly might. Nor do you have to be afraid of me either. I do not now come with thunder and lightning . . . as at Mt Sinai. . . ."

Is there any unfriendliness here at all? The Son of God, who is without sin and guilt, stands in the Jordan and lets himself be baptized, doing more than he in any way was obliged to do. The Holy Spirit comes in the gentle form of a dove upon Jesus, right before the eyes of John. The Father speaks with us in a most kindly manner, making known to us that he does not send a prophet, an apostle, or an angel, but his own dear Son in whom he is well pleased. . . . "If you desire that I be a gracious Father, you may rest assured. Only hold fast to my Son, with whom I cannot be at enmity, and you will be beloved of me also because of him." EPIPHANY, THIRD SERMON, 1534.[6]

THE MYSTICAL WITNESS OF THE TRINITY. FRANCISCUS GOMARUS: This passage is about the first divine testimony from heaven about the excellence of Jesus, where it was declared that he himself is the Christ: namely, when the Holy Spirit descended and remained on him. The speech of the Father is another testimony. . . . Here the preface to the speech is described, then the speech itself. The preface first indicates the dignity of the speech when it says, "Behold," so that it may show that the matter must be attended to. Next, the origin must be admired, because "a voice from heaven" came; in fact, this stands out in Mark 1:11 and Luke 3:22. Truly, the speech was, "This is my Son" . . . in which the prior member or subject, about which it speaks, is indicated by the word "this." It is as if God pointed out Jesus with an outstretched finger, inasmuch as the Holy Spirit descended on him and rested on him in the form of a dove.

What is said about Jesus in the remaining words is truly attributed to his personhood, which was mentioned in an earlier passage. Next, [the Father and the Spirit] declared truly that Jesus was joined to them. Not only that, but the Father declared that he was a certain person from another nature when he said, "my Son" (*ho huioi mou*). In fact, Jesus was begotten eternally, not however by

---

[5]JMG 97*.

[6]Luther, *Complete Sermons*, 5:218-19.

creation or by the grace of adoption, but the Father's "very own" and "only-begotten" Son, so that he might baptize him by the Holy Spirit. No one is able to have this position, except the One who is true God and before the Holy Spirit in the procession of the persons. Delight and approval, simple and absolute, were truly joined to the Father's declaration. This is indicated when "beloved" is added, and more plainly, "in whom I am well-pleased" (*en hō eudokēsa*). ILLUSTRIOUS SELECTIONS FROM THE GOSPEL OF MATTHEW.[7]

THE SCRIPTURAL CONTEXT OF GOD'S WORDS TO JESUS. JOHN TRAPP: My darling, he on whom my love rests, so that I will seek no further. When the earth was founded, Christ was with his Father as his daily delight, sporting or laughing, always before him. "In whom I am well pleased." The beloved, in whom he has made us accepted. God's Hephzibah,[†] so the church is called, the dearly beloved of his soul. Yea he will rest in his love, as abundantly well pleased; he will joy therein with singing. So well thinks God of his son Christ, and of us through him. . . . God so loved his son, that he gave him all the world for his possession, but he so loved the world, as he gave his son and all for its redemption. One calls this a hyperbole, an excess of love, a miracle of mercy. A COMMENTARY OR EXPOSITION UPON THE FOUR EVANGELISTS.[8]

CAN THE SYNOPTIC DIFFERENCES BE HARMONIZED? FRANCISCUS GOMARUS: It is true that one thorny problem does occur in this passage, since at first glance, Matthew seems to disagree with Mark and Luke. If Matthew is in fact correct, the words of the Father were these: "This is my beloved Son." On the other hand, Mark 1:11, along with Luke 3:22, puts forth these words: "You are my beloved Son."

But these two statements, which seem to be contradictory, are reconciled by this: one expresses the sense [of the words], and the other expresses the very words. Whether it is said in the third person, "This is my Son," or in the first person, "You are my Son," nevertheless, in both statements, no other person is understood except Jesus Christ. It is also not an unsolvable dilemma that one account of the speech gives the sense without enumerating the individual words, nor is it particularly helpful to know whether Matthew expressed the actual words, or whether Mark and Luke did. Plainly that is not certain. At the same time, some people do conclude that Mark and Luke have expressed the actual words because they report the words similarly. Nevertheless, there is still a difference between them, because Mark agrees with Matthew by having "in whom" (*en hō*), but Luke refers to Christ in the second person, "in you" (*en soi*). If, however, Matthew reported the actual words, it would not seem strange, since the Father sometimes uses the same words elsewhere. Still, he would have been able to use a different order of words so that by repetition he could strengthen the greater meaning. ILLUSTRIOUS SELECTIONS FROM THE GOSPEL OF MATTHEW.[9]

BAPTIZED IN THE NAME OF THE FATHER, SON, AND HOLY SPIRIT. MARTIN LUTHER: Heaven is opened and the Father's voice is heard, the Son of God stands in the water, and the Holy Spirit descends in the form of a dove, and the dear angels crowd around, which happened not only at Christ's baptism, . . . but happens at every Christian's baptism. . . . Even if we do not see it with our physical eyes, which are too dull and dim to see it, we still hear the words: "I baptize you *in the name of the Father, of the Son, and of the Holy Spirit*." Do you think these are insignificant words? Even though they are simply expressed, they nonetheless convey and bring about everything that happened at Christ's baptism. Here the three persons of the

---

[7]Gomarus, *Illustrium ac selectorum ex Evangelio Mattaei*, 30; citing Rom 8:32; Jn 1:14.
[8]Trapp, *A Commentary or Exposition upon the Four Evangelists* (1647), 53-54*, citing Zeph 3:17; Prov 8:30; Eph 1:6; Is 62:4; Jer 12:7; Ps 2. [†]Hephzibah, whose name means "my delight is in her," was the wife of Hezekiah (2 Kings 21:1). In Is 62:4, she became a symbol for Judah after it was restored by God.

[9]Gomarus, *Illustrium ac Selectorum ex Evangelio Mattaei* (1644), 30; citing Mt 17:5; Mk 9:7; Lk 9:35; 2 Pet 1:17.

divine majesty, the Father, Son, and Holy Spirit, are present. Here are the hosts of the dear angels as well, who hear and see what happens. For we are not baptized into any other baptism, neither do we baptize otherwise than into the baptism of Christ. So, then, if it is a baptism, then all these things are certainly present. And because I do not see it, I must believe it nevertheless: that the Father is well pleased; that the Holy Spirit, too, is present, listening, as well as the Son of God and the dear angels. That is how beautifully and gloriously our baptism, too, is decorated, honored, and adorned. SERMON ON THE DAY OF CHRIST'S EPIPHANY (1546).[10]

KNOWING GOD BY REASON OR REVELATION. PHILIPP MELANCHTHON: There are two ways of seeking or finding a definition of what God is. One is by reason without the Word of God. For example, Plato, looking at certain laws of heavenly motions, traced their order and concluded that God is an eternal mind and that God is the cause in nature. Plato was able to add that God has impressed on human minds what he wills us to obey, according to the distinction of what is honest and what is shameful. It is no small wonder that this knowledge, whenever it shines in human minds, which would be much brighter still, if human nature had not been corrupt. But because this knowledge is already hidden in this corruption of nature, God out of his immense kindness revealed himself with his own voice and sent the Son.

There is another way of seeking what God is. Plato looked at the order of nature; we look at testimonies. As an example, I set forth to you the baptism of Christ, in which you hear the voice of the eternal Father saying, "This is my beloved Son." Our eyes see the Son standing in the Jordan, and the Holy Spirit descends in the form of a dove. Let other similar revelations and speeches be considered, in which Christ distinguishes between the persons. "My Father has been working until now in this way, and I am working." Likewise, "He will give to you another helper, the Spirit of truth."

Let us turn our mind, eyes, and ears to these testimonies. Let us set up God as he wishes to be recognized, so that he may display himself to be investigated not only by reason, but by his own testimonies, just as Christ said, "No one knows the Father, except the Son, and the one to whom the Son has willed to reveal him." . . . But God commanded us to hear his Son, "Listen to this man," and he added the testimony of the resurrection of the dead, and others, so that we may truly know that he wishes to be recognized and called upon, just as he displayed himself in this Word. ANNOTATIONS ON THE GOSPELS.[11]

---

[10]LW 58:366-67 (WA 51:115-16).

[11]MO 14:415; citing Jn 5:17; 15:26; Mt 11:27.

4:1-11 THE TEMPTATION OF JESUS

Then Jesus was led up by the Spirit into the wilderness to be tempted by the devil. ²And after fasting forty days and forty nights, he was hungry. ³And the tempter came and said to him, "If you are the Son of God, command these stones to become loaves of bread." ⁴But he answered, "It is written,

"'Man shall not live by bread alone,
    but by every word that comes from the
        mouth of God.'"

⁵Then the devil took him to the holy city and set him on the pinnacle of the temple ⁶and said to him, "If you are the Son of God, throw yourself down, for it is written,

"'He will command his angels concerning you,'

and

"'On their hands they will bear you up,
    lest you strike your foot against a stone.'"

⁷Jesus said to him, "Again it is written, 'You shall not put the Lord your God to the test.'" ⁸Again, the devil took him to a very high mountain and showed him all the kingdoms of the world and their glory. ⁹And he said to him, "All these I will give you, if you will fall down and worship me." ¹⁰Then Jesus said to him, "Be gone, Satan! For it is written,

"'You shall worship the Lord your God
    and him only shall you serve.'"

¹¹Then the devil left him, and behold, angels came and were ministering to him.

OVERVIEW: The reformers acknowledge that Jesus as the Son of God serves as the thematic connection between the introductory narratives of his baptism and his temptation by the devil. The baptism narrative ends with the heavenly voice declaring Jesus as the Son of God (cf. Mt 1:23; 2:15) and the first two temptations begin with, "If you are the Son of God . . ." So, ultimately the temptation narrative shows what type of "Son of God" Jesus is. Some commentators note that this narrative has obvious similarities with the temptations of Eve in the Garden of Eden and of Israel in the exodus in that those earlier temptations also deal with the same questions of whether God will provide, protect, and be worshiped exclusively.

Many commentators contend that the use of Old Testament quotations is a central feature of this text and a key for interpretation. Jesus draws on the imagery of Israel's temptations in the wilderness in his citation of the Deuteronomy text. His identity as the true Son of God is marked not by his exerting his divine Sonship but by his humble reliance "on every word that proceeds out of the mouth of God." Heinrich Bullinger notes

Jesus' purpose as an obedient son is shown in his willingness to serve the will of the Father, and he thereby becomes the perfect example for all of his followers in their own striving against the tempter. In so doing, Jesus' Sonship is proved, and the angels come and minister to him, the Lord's anointed (cf. Ps. 91).

A few commentators focus especially on the sinister schemes of the devil in the temptations. He boldly attacks the Son of God in a moment of perceived weakness. He twists the Scriptures to accomplish his purposes and claims for himself the worship due to God. His repeated attacks were thwarted by Jesus and should be expected by Jesus' followers.

4:1-10 Satan Tempts Jesus Three Times

TEMPTATIONS AND FASTING IN THE DESERT.
CARDINAL CAJETAN: "At that time, after being baptized, Jesus was immediately led." Perceive here the Holy Spirit at work. Jesus has not proceeded as if he were using human reason alone, but "he has been led" by the Holy Spirit who was inspiring,

directing, and conducting him. "Into the desert." In the historical sense, a place is described that is free for the works of those professing repentance, the solitary life, and the contemplative life consisting in fasts and prayers. "By the Spirit, so that he might be tempted by the devil." The conjunction "so that" is held not only to be consecutive (since the temptation was to follow in the desert) but also causal. For just as he comes for this purpose—that he might suffer—he also comes voluntarily into the desert in order to be tempted. For it is neither evil to suffer nor to be tempted, but Christ undergoes both for our sake of his own free will. And just as he chose Jerusalem as the place of his suffering, so he has chosen the desert as the place of his temptation. For a desert place is, after all, ideal for temptation, owing both to the kind of spiritual life that is conducted in the desert and from the solitude. The demon especially tries to tempt spiritual persons and lies in wait for the solitary, since with the world and the flesh subdued, their battle is against the demons alone. It is significant that after his baptism Christ seeks the desert with its fasting, prayer, and temptations. He does this not only to furnish an example to us concerning what must be done after our own profession of the Christian life but also in this way to train himself in a prelude to his preaching ministry. For this reason, the Evangelist says, "at that time." "And when he had fasted." Fasting is not a work that is in itself good, since it is the privation of nourishment. But it is good insofar as it enacts the moral virtue called "abstinence." "For forty days and forty nights." So great a quantity of fasting exceeds the scope of moral virtue so far as human reason is concerned. That someone would choose a fast that is naturally unbearable to a human being is dissonant with right human reason. But this fast was moderated by divine arrangement. For it was fitting that Christ in his fasting should be made like the most excellent prophets Moses and Elijah, both of whom had fasted in the space of forty days and nights. Also fitting was that, by this one great fast, Christ surpassed the whole abstinence (*abstinentiam*) practiced by John the Baptist. He did not extend the fast further, lest he raise a doubt whether he bore true flesh. Still, so great a fast by Christ and Moses and Elijah was beyond any doubt miraculous, and it is not presented to the world so that it may be imitated but marveled at. Gospel with Commentary.[1]

The Scope of Satan's Temptation. Christopher Blackwood: "He said unto him, 'If you are the Son of God.'" Meaning, as that voice at your baptism declared, and as John the Baptist has preached you to be, do you not suffer hunger having that by which you may assuage your hunger. Satan thought, either by the miracle or by Christ's inability to do the miracle, he might know whether he were the Son of God or no, that so he might vent his old wrath and envy against him.

It is like the devil did not come abruptly upon him, but first saluted him courteously, as, What, Sir, are you meditating on? I saw you to be baptized of John in Jordan, I heard a voice from heaven, saying, "This is my beloved Son," I would fain know whether the voice meant that you are truly the Son of God by nature, or an adopted Son by grace. I see also by your long fast of forty days that you are hungry, if therefore you are the Son of God succor your hunger and turn these stones into bread, for you can easily do it.

The scope of Satan's temptation was to tempt Christ to unbelief, as if he should say, your Father has hitherto forgotten you, and sent you no meat, now you see your God fails you, therefore necessity puts upon you to provide for yourself. The scope of Satan was to draw Christ from resting on God's word, and to follow what unbelief should suggest, and this appears by Christ his answer, "Man does not live by bread alone."

So that though I will not deny but Satan might tempt Christ to a vain boasting of his own power, yet specially he tempts Christ to unbelief, either that he should not believe that testimony that was given at his baptism, or to doubt that God would fail him of necessary livelihood: As he overcame

---

[1]Cajetan, *Evangelia cum Commentariis*, 10r-10v.

the first Adam with unbelief of the threatening, so does he endeavor to overcome the second Adam with unbelief of the promise. And seeing Satan dare call in question the sonship of Christ, no wonder if he tempts saints to call in question their sonship. AN EXPOSITION UPON THE GOSPEL OF MATTHEW.[2]

THE NATURE OF JESUS' TEMPTATION. NIELS HEMMINGSEN: In these temptations of Christ, one may see first how great the boldness of Satan is and his desire to destroy the kingdom of Christ. For he spares not even the Son of God, but approaches him, and as he invaded God's kingdom in paradise and gained the upper hand, so he practices to destroy the new paradise, the kingdom of Christ, and assails the king thereof with the darts of temptations. And second, a man may see here how much the Son of God was abased, in that he was not only afflicted with fasting, but also assaulted with the temptations of Satan. . . .

Therefore, as touching the first temptation, the occasion thereof is shown in these words of the Evangelist: "and when he had fasted forty days and forty nights, afterward he was hungry." Behold what an occasion the adversary had gotten. Christ had fasted and prepared himself to execute his office, but Satan practices another thing, and of Christ's good deed he seeks opportunity to destroy him. This has been the continual endeavor of Satan to wrest both the well-doings and the sins of the saints to their destruction. But God knows who be his and is able to deliver them out of temptation.

The manner of the temptation ensues, for the tempter says, if you are the Son of God, command these stones to become bread. The end of this temptation was to persuade Christ to make a trial whether God would by miracle confirm his Godhead or not; that if he did not, then the Lord might surmise that God cared not for him. This temptation therefore fights against God's providence, through which he provides all things for his children that are necessary to salvation and this present life.

The manner of the victory follows: To whom Jesus answering, said, "It is written, man lives not only by bread, but by every word that proceeds out of the mouth of God." Here we see how the victory against Satan consists in the Word of God. Satan would persuade Christ that he should perish if he made not bread of the stones. But Christ denies that man lives only with bread or bodily food. For meat nourishes not, unless there come with it the blessing of God, from whence bread takes his strength. For it is written, they shall eat and not be sufficed. This Scripture alleged here by Christ to this purpose, you have in the book of Deuteronomy. In which place Moses comforts the people in the desert where there was no bread, but God gave them manna from heaven and water out of the rock. This promise Christ applies to himself and to all the godly, signifying that it should come to pass that even in the midst of famine, God would succor his people and give them things needful. A POSTIL, OR EXPOSITION OF THE GOSPELS.[3]

JESUS' HAND-TO-HAND COMBAT WITH THE DEVIL. JOHN BOYS: The place where Christ was tempted is said here to be the wilderness, and that for sundry reasons, as interpreters observe. First in good correspondence to Adam overcome by the tempter in paradise: for as the first Adam was conquered of the serpent by gluttony, pride, and avarice: by gluttony, when he ate the forbidden fruit; by pride, desiring to be as God; by covetousness, in being discontent with his present estate. So the second Adam is assaulted here by the same serpent with the like temptations: With gluttony: "If you are the Son of God, command that these stones be made bread." With pride: "The devil set him on a pinnacle of the temple." With avarice: "He carried him up to the top of a high mountain, and showed him all the kingdoms of the world, and the

---

[2]Blackwood, *Expositions and Sermons upon . . . Matthew* (1659), 93-94*; citing Gen 3:3.

[3]Hemmingsen, *A Postill, or Exposition of the Gospels* (1569), 82-83; citing Hos 4:10; Ex 16:4; Deut 8:3, 16; Ex 17:6; Deut 8:15.

glory of them, and said, 'All these will I give you, if you will fall down and worship me.'" But the Savior coming into the world to gain that which Adam lost, abounding with three contrary virtues—humility, temperance, and contentment—overcame the tempter, and that in open field, because the devil had discomfited Adam in the garden.

Second, Christ was tempted and fasted in the wilderness forty days and forty nights before he executed his office publicly, that he might appear to be sent from God, rather than out of any town from men. When almighty God delivered his law to Moses, he took him up into a mountain from the sight of the people, and a cloud covered the mountain, that he might talk with Moses as in a withdrawing chamber; and after Moses had been in Mount Sinai forty days and forty nights, the Lord spoke to Moses, and afterward Moses to the people. In like manner, it was proper that Christ being far worthier a minister of a far more excellent law should forty days and forty nights abide in the wilderness, free from the tumults and troubles of the world, and then begin to teach the gospel as a God among men, at least as a man of God, and not of men.

Third, Christ was tempted in the wilderness as a most fit place for temptation, as also for dual and single combat; for men of resolution will not draw their weapons in the street, but—as we speak—challenge their adversary to go into the field. Our valiant captain therefore provoked his and our mortal enemy to fight hand to hand in a desert. AN EXPOSITION OF THE DOMINICAL EPISTLES AND GOSPELS.[4]

JESUS' PROPER USE OF SCRIPTURE. JOHN KNOX: In this answer of Christ, we may espy what weapons are to be used against our adversary the devil and how that we may confute his arguments, which craftily and of malice he makes against God's elect. Christ might have repulsed Satan with a word or thought, commanding him to silence, as

he to whom all power was given in heaven and earth, but it pleased his mercy to teach us how to use the sword of the Holy Ghost, which is the Word of God, in battle against our spiritual enemy. The Scripture that Christ brings is written in the eighth chapter of Deuteronomy. It was spoken by Moses a little before his death to establish the people in God's merciful providence. For in the same chapter and in certain others that go before, he reckons the great travail and divers dangers with the extreme necessities that they had sustained in the desert, the space of forty years, and yet, notwithstanding how constant God had been in keeping and performing his promise. For then throughout all perils had he conducted them to the sight and borders of the Promised Land. And so, this Scripture must directly answer to the temptation of Satan; for thus does Satan reason—as before is said—"You are in poverty, and have no provision to sustain your life; therefore, God takes no regard nor care over you as he does over his chosen children." Christ Jesus answers, "Your argument is false and vain; for poverty or necessity secludes not the providence or care of God which is easy to be proved by the people of God, Israel, which in the desert often lacked things necessary to the sustaining of life, and for lack of the same they grudged and murmured, yet the Lord never cast away the providence and care of them." AN EXPOSITION UPON MATTHEW 4.[5]

A HUNGER FOR THE WORD. JOHANNES OECOLAMPADIUS: "In every word," that is, in every command of God. Some people think that the Word of God is an external word, by which we are instructed for salvation. That interpretation, however, does not pertain to this passage, for the mind of God is able to feed all things by his own will. If God had commanded something, it is necessary that it be done. If he had willed to deliver him, he would also deliver him if he lacked bread, and we would still have been standing in the deepest hunger. This is how we would have

---

[4]Boys, *An Exposition of the Dominicall Epistles and Gospels* (1610), 23-25.

[5]Knox, *Works*, 4:112-13*.

thought, for we are sometimes a little more fearful, and so poor, that we seem to be abandoned by God in every way in this world. Let us think of the example of the apostles, who were themselves also hungry, and sometimes they needed many things, but they were certain of the kindness of the Lord, who desired and was able to free them.

Thus, Christ commanded with his voice and cast away the demon, lest he become the answer to his own prayer. Again, we are also warned that if we conquer the devil once, we should not exult, nor think that we are blessed and victors because of it, as if the enemy had been destroyed. For he still has a thousand other arts with which he is accustomed to attack us. Therefore, if you conquer him once and have been more holy, he will soon attack you again with a new art, and you will have to employ the highest diligence to thwart him. Likewise, there are varied characters of people: some seek more the pleasures of the body, others strive after empty glory, others desire to be made great, and so on. So also are the varied deceits and arts of Satan. See what sort of people you are, and in which part you are inferior, for he will attack you most powerfully with these things in which you are weak. He attacks our flesh with hunger, and if he does not succeed that way, he seeks another way, and so on. COMMENTARY ON THE GOSPEL OF MATTHEW 4:4.[6]

SCRIPTURE IS CHRIST'S SHIELD. JOHN CALVIN: The first thing to be observed here is that Christ uses Scripture as his shield: for this is the true way of fighting, if we wish to make ourselves sure of the victory. With good reason does Paul say, "the sword of the Spirit is the Word of God," and enjoin us to "take the shield of faith." Hence also we conclude that papists, as if they had made a bargain with Satan, cruelly give up souls to be destroyed by him at his pleasure, when they wickedly withhold the Scripture from the people of God and thus deprive them of their arms, by which alone their safety could be preserved. Those who voluntarily throw

away that armor and do not laboriously exercise themselves in the school of God deserve to be strangled at every instant by Satan, into whose hands they give themselves up unarmed. No other reason can be assigned why the fury of Satan meets with so little resistance and why so many are everywhere carried away by him, but that God punishes their carelessness and their contempt of his word.

We must now examine more closely the passage, which is quoted by Christ from Moses: "that he might make you know that man does not live by bread only, but by every word that proceeds out of the mouth of the Lord does man live." There are some who torture it to a false meaning, as referring to spiritual life; as if our Lord had said that souls are not nourished by visible bread but by the Word of God. The statement itself is, no doubt, true: but Moses had quite a different meaning. He reminds them that, when no bread could be obtained, God provided them with an extraordinary kind of nourishment in "manna, which they knew not, neither did their fathers know," and that this was intended as an evident proof, in all time coming, that human life is not confined to bread but depends on the will and good pleasure of God. The word does not mean doctrine, but the purpose that God has made known, with regard to preserving the order of nature and the lives of his creatures. Having created human beings, he does not cease to care for them: but, as "he breathed into their nostrils the breath of life," so he constantly preserves the life he has bestowed. In like manner, the apostle says, that he "upholds all things by his powerful word"—that is, the whole world is preserved, and every part of it keeps its place, by the will and decree of him whose power, above and below, is everywhere diffused. Though we live on bread, we must not ascribe the support of life to the power of bread but to the secret kindness, by which God imparts to bread the quality of nourishing our bodies.

Hence, also, follows another statement: "by every word that proceeds out of the mouth of God shall men live." God, who now employs bread for

---

[6]Oecolampadius, *Ennaratio in Evangelium Matthaei* (1536), 46v.

our support, will enable us, whenever he pleases, to live by other means. This declaration of Moses condemns the stupidity of those who reckon life to consist in luxury and abundance; while it reproves the distrust and inordinate anxiety that drives us to seek unlawful means. The precise object of Christ's reply is this: We ought to trust in God for food and for the other necessaries of the present life in such a manner that none of us may overleap the boundaries which he has prescribed. But if Christ did not consider himself to be at liberty to change stones into bread without the command of God, much less is it lawful for us to procure food by fraud, or robbery, or violence, or murder. COMMENTARY ON A HARMONY OF THE EVANGELISTS.[7]

The Devil's Use and Abuse of Scripture.

LANCELOT ANDREWES: If ever the devil came in his likeness, it was here . . . for he comes here like a white devil or like a divine, he comes with a Psalter in his hand and turns to the place, and shows our Savior the ninety-first Psalm, verse 11 and 12, wherein first we are to note that the devil reads the Psalms, as well as we, and has the words of Scripture in his mouth.

And here he uses David's words to cause presumption and to make them our bane. And not every Scripture, but if there be any Scripture more full of heavenly comfort than another, that of all other will the devil abuse, as indeed the Psalms are and of all the Psalms, this ninety-first especially. And in that part, if any one sentence be sweeter than another, that of all other will the devil abuse.

Because the wolf comes sometimes disguised in a sheep's skin, it is no reason that therefore the very sheep should lay away their fleeces. So here, because the devil uses the Word, as the slaying letter . . . or as the sword to kill with, it is no reason why Christ may not therefore use it in his own defense. Why then (will some say) one of these two inconveniences will follow: that hereby we shall think the Scripture is of the devil's side as

well as of Christ's side, and so divided as in like sort they make a division of Christ, when one holds with Paul, another of Apollos. No, it is not so, Christ alleges not this Scripture in that sort, as one nail to drive out another, but by way of harmony and exposition that the one may make plain the meaning of the other. For albeit the devil shows himself to be the devil in citing that text so as might best serve for his purpose, in that whereas the Psalm from which he takes it, has it thus, "That he might keep him in all his ways," which words he leaves out. THE WONDERFULL COMBATE BETWEENE CHRIST AND SATAN.[8]

The Many Lies of Satan.

JOHANN GERHARD: "I will give all these things to you." Satan tested him in this very matter, and nothing was so impious and wicked as this, because human beings do not risk all for the sake of reigning. Therefore, Satan tried to awaken a desire in the soul of Christ for the kingdoms of the world by this display and by an added magnificent promise, so that he could drive him to a most shameful apostasy.

Satan demanded that divine honor be shown to himself. Although he had already been thrown down from heaven because of his pride, he nevertheless remained the same, because he had already once wished to be like God. Therefore, because he had not been able to obtain worship from the angels in heaven, he hopes to be able to get it on earth from the people who follow him. . . .

[Certain errors can be avoided] if it is observed (1) that Christ was not tempted according to his divine nature, but according to his human nature. (2) That he did not always hide the rays of his own majesty but revealed himself with full light as many times as it pleased himself. (3) Consequently, it was also not enough for the devil to gaze always on the divine majesty of Christ. . . .

Truly, Satan lies in many ways. [First,] because all kingdoms are God's. God says in Job 41:11, "Everything which is under heaven is mine." Seneca[†]

---

[7]CTS 1:214-15* (CO 45:132); citing Eph 6:16-17; Deut 8:3; Gen 2:7; Heb 1:3.

[8]Andrewes, *The Wonderfull Combate Betweene Christ and Satan* (1592), 54-58; citing 1 Cor 1:13; 2 Cor 3:6.

recognizes this in his book, *Nature*, where he writes, "This is the voice of God: all things are mine." [Second,] because no monarch ever gave all his own kingdom to another. [Third,] because Satan was not able to give what he was promising. [Fourth,] because if by some great impossibility Christ would have worshiped Satan, Satan would not have stood by his own promises. ANNOTATIONS ON MATTHEW 4:9.[9]

THE PRIDE OF THE DEVIL. MARTIN CHEMNITZ: The pride of the devil . . . is ancient, because he demanded that divine honor be offered to himself and he demanded the same thing from the incarnate Son of God. It may be observed, although no one says it, that Christ wanted to prostrate himself to the devil and worship him. This observation is collected from this passage, namely, that whoever is conquered by desire, greediness, and ambition, when he puts the promises of God against the commandments of God, he becomes eager for the ungodly arts of the world. This often happens, because when he chases thus after the good things of this world, he prostrates himself to the devil in the object of his desire and worships the devil instead of God. When the one who denied God did the deed, he began to make a covenant with his adversary. For that reason, Paul calls greediness idolatry, and greedy people the worshipers of idols.

It must be observed, however, that Christ opposes such a response to this temptation. For Scripture does not only oppose this response simply—just as in the preceding passages—but it also opposes it on account of those blasphemous words: "All things are handed over to me." Because Satan had demanded to be ascribed the worship of adoration, Christ says, "What rule is employed when we turn away to a more impassioned soul because of the great unworthiness of the matter, and receive those whom we once endured with annoyance?" Thus Matthew 16:3, concerning Peter,

is employed in Matthew 20:14: "Take what is yours, and go away." Let this teaching be marked from this: blasphemous voices must not be heard with cheerful patience but rejected with serious indignation. Likewise, when the devil has excessively annoyed you with temptations of this sort that verge on blasphemy, do not begin an argument with him, but simply cast him away with indignation. Oppose him with the brief, certain, and firm opinion of Scripture, just as Christ said: "Depart, Satan! For it is written that you will worship the Lord your God." . . . The response of Christ, then, was that these things, which properly belong to the worship of God, must not be brought to any creature. Let no one allow an argument about this matter, just as Christ simply rejected the devil here. Truly, those things that belong to the worship of God should be brought to God, so that they are not shared with any creature. That is, we should not divide worship among God and the creatures, so that we either offer part to God and part to creatures, or we bring the same things to God and the creatures at the same time. For the devil does not demand that Christ stop worshiping God the Father altogether, but he only asks that some of that honor be offered to himself. Christ truly responds by this exclusive particle, "You will adore and worship God *alone*," lest someone imagine that the devil is the only one who should not be worshiped or served and that it is possible to bring those honors to angels and saints. A HARMONY OF THE GOSPELS.[10]

4:11 *The Obedience of Jesus*

THE SIGNIFICANCE OF JESUS' OBEDIENCE. JOHN FOXE: Thus Jesus, being baptized to fulfill all righteousness, revealed by his father, replenished with the Holy Ghost, and testified by John the Baptist, from thence was had immediately into the desert, as to a stage, there to try hand to hand with the devil. Where after he had fasted forty days and forty nights, to fulfill the time of Moses'

---

[9]Gerhard, *Annotationes Posthumae in Evangelium D. Matthaei* (1663), 216-17. †Seneca, *Nature* 7.3.64.

[10]Chemnitz , *Harmoniae Evangelicae*, 210-11; citing Eph 5:5.

fast, who was so long in the mount with God without meat or drink, the enemy, not ignorant what was testified of him before and yet seeing him outwardly but as a weak man and also now to wax hungry after the infirmity of flesh, was emboldened to set upon him. And as he first threw down Adam in paradise by eating, so thinking likewise to supplant this second Adam by eating, tempted him to turn stones to bread, and so after an unlawful manner to eat. When this would not be, he invaded him with other sundry and grievous assaults, but in the end he could not prevail. Innocence held by obedience, obedience held by the word, Christ overcame, man had the victory, the devil had the foil, the angels bear witness, and the poor body of Jesus was refreshed. A Sermon of Christ Crucified.[11]

The Example of Jesus' Obedience. Heinrich Bullinger: These things do exceedingly comfort the godly in temptations, who understand that nothing can happen to them without God's permission, and that he permits nothing but that which makes for our amendment and salvation, and therefore that we are always preserved by the providence and bountifulness of God. For whatsoever has hitherto been spoken concerning the power and workings of the devils pertained not hitherto to dash us out of courage and cast us down, but to make us more vigilant or watchful. The Lord that overcame the devil and shows us the way to overcome him commands us to watch. For therefore he encountered with Satan the first, second, and third time, to instruct us how we should fight against the enemy of humankind. He overcame him for us so that we should not despair of ability and power easily to overcome him, since he is already weakened and wounded. By faith, doubtless, we shall overcome him, for by faith we are knit to Christ, and by faith we draw the Spirit of Christ, by the force and virtue whereof we shall triumph. Of Evil Spirits.[12]

---

[11]Foxe, *Writings of John Fox, Bale, and Coverdale* (1831), 53-54.   [12]DHB 3:364-65.

4:12-25 JESUS' PUBLIC MINISTRY BEGINS

¹²Now when he heard that John had been arrested, he withdrew into Galilee. ¹³And leaving Nazareth he went and lived in Capernaum by the sea, in the territory of Zebulun and Naphtali, ¹⁴so that what was spoken by the prophet Isaiah might be fulfilled:

¹⁵"The land of Zebulun and the land of
    Naphtali,
    the way of the sea, beyond the Jordan,
        Galilee of the Gentiles—
¹⁶the people dwelling in darkness
    have seen a great light,
and for those dwelling in the region and shadow of
    death,
    on them a light has dawned."

¹⁷From that time Jesus began to preach, saying, "Repent, for the kingdom of heaven is at hand."ᵃ

¹⁸While walking by the Sea of Galilee, he saw two brothers, Simon (who is called Peter) and Andrew his brother, casting a net into the sea, for they were fishermen. ¹⁹And he said to them, "Follow me, and I will make you fishers of men."ᵇ ²⁰Immediately they left their nets and followed him. ²¹And going on from there he saw two other brothers, James the son of Zebedee and John his brother, in the boat with Zebedee their father, mending their nets, and he called them. ²²Immediately they left the boat and their father and followed him.

²³And he went throughout all Galilee, teaching in their synagogues and proclaiming the gospel of the kingdom and healing every disease and every affliction among the people. ²⁴So his fame spread throughout all Syria, and they brought him all the sick, those afflicted with various diseases and pains, those oppressed by demons, those having seizures, and paralytics, and he healed them. ²⁵And great crowds followed him from Galilee and the Decapolis, and from Jerusalem and Judea, and from beyond the Jordan.

a Or the kingdom of heaven has come near   b The Greek word *anthropoi* refers here to both men and women

---

OVERVIEW: Jesus' move from Nazareth to Capernaum of Galilee as his home base fulfills another of Isaiah's prophecies (Is 9:1) and provides the geographical context for much of his work. Some Reformation comments focus on a historical survey that connects the resettlement of Galilee after the Babylonian captivity with a remnant of the ten northern tribes of Israel. The remnants of Judah and Benjamin repopulated Judea, hence the differences in practices between the northern remnant in Galilee and the Judean Jews. Relatedly, most of Jesus' early disciples would then be descendants of the northern tribes. In comparing him to John, Erasmus says that Jesus' milder style is commendable, yet remains a call to repentance. By contrast, others note the similarities in Matthew's depictions of John's preaching (Mt 3:2) and Jesus' preaching (Mt 4:17), and that the rejection of Jesus' message fits with a long history of people rejecting the gracious work of God.

Jesus begins his public ministry by calling four unlikely followers, some Galilean fishermen. The reformers comment on the unlikelihood of fishermen being chosen as the first disciples. Jesus' calling of these men not only provides a protection from the growth of the gospel being attributed to the disciples' expertise, but it also makes the central qualification of their apostleship the calling of God. Jesus issues a simple call to these fishermen, which characterized both the nature ("Follow me") and the purpose ("I will make you fishers of men") of their discipleship, making preaching the gospel an essential component of the disciples' calling. These reformers comment on how the biblical text stresses sacrifice as a key characteristic of disciple-ship, seen in the response of Jesus' first disciples when they "immediately" leave their livelihoods and even families to follow him (cf. Mt 8:19-22; 9:9; 10:37-39; 16:24-25).

In Matthew 4:23, Matthew summarizes the early days of Jesus' ministry in Galilee in terms that portend his future ministry, which will be the focus of Matthew 8–20. Calvin indicates that though Matthew makes similar summaries elsewhere in his Gospel (cf. Mt 8:16; 9:35; 14:14), the repetition is appropriate to communicate how the numerous healings in Jesus' ministry were a means of estab-lishing his divine authority. Others note a close connection between Jesus' proclaiming the gospel of the kingdom and healing of every kind of disease. Jesus' ministry is unique compared to that of future generations of disciples in that he commended the "majesty and worth of the gospel" by many signs and wonders. Initially, it is Jesus' healing ministry that draws the interest of the large crowds from not only Galilee, but other regions including Jerusalem and Judea. The gathering of these crowds, presum-ably for further healings, becomes Matthew's setting for the Sermon on the Mount.

4:12-17 *Jesus Preaches the Arrival of the Kingdom of Heaven*

JESUS' PLACE OF MINISTRY. THEODORE BEZA: If Christ wished to withdraw so that he might avoid the tyrant Herod, why did he go into Galilee, which was in the jurisdiction of Herod Antipas? Or, why did he not stay instead in Judea, which had already been reduced to the status of a province? Therefore, Christ did not withdraw into Galilee, which he had left so that he might be baptized by John, from a fear of persecution. Rather, he hurried back to Galilee at once, and there began to collect his disciples. The anger of Herod meant nothing to him, even when he heard that John was killed, and Herod also threatened him. . . . Nevertheless, I do not deny that Christ had avoided persecution in his own time, as Matthew 12:15 writes, using this very word. . . .

Clearly he means lower Galilee, that is, the lake of Tiberius and Gennesaret. However, the word . . . *pros* is assumed, as Theophylactus† notes, the omission of which is naturally difficult, to the Hebrews, nevertheless, it was sufficiently familiar. But it appears that the passage from Isaiah was not cited in its entirety by the Evangelist. Therefore, it is signified in the word "seacoast"—that is, this portion of Galilee that is on the lake of Tiberius, on which are located Capernaum, Bethsaida, and Chorazin, cities very well-known in the preaching of Christ.

"The other Jordan," *peran tou Iordanou*, or "across the Jordan," which is the precise translation of the Greek word *peran*. But it is a fact because it was controlled by Judea that either Galilee was on the near side of the Jordan, so plainly *peran* corre-sponds to the Latin word *secus* in this meaning. *Latus* means the same thing to the Hebrews ('*bl*), because taken adverbially, it does not indicate the closer bank or the further bank. So also, the same phrase is frequently used in Deuteronomy about Moses, who never crossed the Jordan. Wherefore, it can be seen that Perea, that is, the Transjordan region, is not so much indicated in this passage as the shore and bank the Jordan touches. Matthew sometimes does the same thing in other passages (see below in Mt 19:1). Nevertheless, if someone wished to insist on the propriety of the Greek word *peran*—that is, "across"—I should say that it would also be more clear that the four neighboring and adjacent regions are designated here, namely, the tribe of Zebulun, the tribe of Naphtali, the furthest mouth of the lakes—that is, the further region, in which are Chorazin and Gennesaret, which regions Christ frequently visited—and finally also Galilee of the Gentiles, mentioned above. In some part, Galilee of the Gentiles includes the tribe of Naphtali, as well as the most powerful Asher, which was on the sea and close to the boundaries of Tyre, where Christ also arrived, as is told below in Matthew 15:21. ANNOTATIONS ON MATTHEW 4:12.[1]

---

[1]Beza, *Annotationes Majores in Novum Dn. Nostri Jesu Christi Testamentum* (1594), 26; citing Mt 14:13. †Theophylact, *Commentary on Matthew*, 8r.

The Biblical Context of Jesus' Ministry in Galilee. John Lightfoot: Whereas Matthew in the beginning of this section tells that Christ left Nazareth, Luke in the end of the preceding shows the reason why, namely, because he was in hazard of his life there and so the connection is made plain. In the coasts of Zebulun and Naphtali, captivity had first begun, and there Christ first begins more publicly and evidently to preach the near approach of the kingdom of heaven and redemption. In the first plantation of the land after the captivity, Galilee escaped from being Samaritan and was reserved for this happy privilege of being the first scene of Christ's preaching the gospel. And as that country was inhabited by a good part of the ten tribes before their captivity, so upon their return out of Babel in the times of Zerubbabel and Ezra, it may well be held to have been planted with some of the ten tribes again. . . . And here is the first returning of the ten tribes to be supposed and it carries fair probability that most of the twelve apostles and many of the rest of the disciples that were of Christ's most constant retinue were of the progeny of some of the ten tribes returned. The Harmony, Chronicle, and Order of the New Testament[2]

The Beginning of Jesus' Preaching. Desiderius Erasmus: Now let us hear the beginning of his preaching. As it succeeded after John so he begins with his doctrine, which was well known and familiar, lest he should have driven them away from him, which had John now in so great veneration; and he fed the weak with milk, that afterward he might bring forth strong meat to them when they were of more strength. And truly this is the order of teachers, which desire rather to profit the hearers than to set forth and magnify themselves before others. The preaching of Christ is not only more mild and gentle than John; his preaching—for he makes no mention neither of air,

nor fan, nor of fire that never shall be quenched—but also more to be commended for many benefits bestowed upon all people indifferently. Jesus therefore following John cries and says, "Change your minds, and repent your former life. For now the kingdom of heaven is at hand, which as it shall be shut unto no one, so it shall be open only unto those who be pure and clean and seek after heavenly things and cut always all worldly desires." What can be more plain and simple than this philosophy? Let every person be displeased and grieved with their own naughtiness, and heavenly things be ready for them at hand, and that freely. Paraphrases.[3]

Jesus' Call for Repentance. Wolfgang Musculus: [First,] John had called everyone to repentance, and Christ opened his preaching in the same way, so that he might strengthen John's preaching. For the preaching of repentance was fitting to the direction of the kingdom of God, and for the revealing of grace to the world, so that repentance might first be impressed upon human minds. . . .

[Second,] the most corrupt and malicious people of all are called to the kingdom of God, which Christ himself called a crooked and perverse nation. Before Christ, Moses called them a stiff-necked people; and after Christ, Stephen called them a people who always resisted the Holy Spirit. They are the people in the parable, weakened by rage, who killed the servants of God, the prophets, and would kill the heir of the vineyard, even the Son of God himself. From this, I say that the people were called to the kingdom of God, first by John, then also by the Lord himself, the Son of God. Let them consider the manner of their calling, and as Mark commands, believe the gospel. If they heed this grace, by which the kingdom of God is announced to sinners, it is such grace that it may not be stopped or held back, even by that wicked deed by which John, sent by God to this people, had been thrown by Herod into prison. Had

[2]Lightfoot, *The Harmony, Chronicle and Order of the New Testament* (1655), 16-17; citing 2 Kings 15:29.

[3]EP 16r.

Christ been able to say, "This people is unworthy, who are called to the grace of the kingdom of God. Is it not enough to them that they have sinned so greatly in so many ages, and now they even cast the crier of repentance himself and the forerunner of the kingdom of God into chains? Let them perish in their own wickedness forever." Truly such is the grace of the management of the kingdom of God, so that neither the ancient scandals nor this recent crime will be able to stop its course. COMMENTARY ON MATTHEW 4:17.[4]

4:18-22 *The Calling of the First Disciples*

JESUS CHOOSES HIS FIRST DISCIPLES.
RICHARD TAVERNER: If Christ had chosen great learned men or men of estimation, they might perhaps have said that they had deserved to be chosen because of their learning or wisdom. But our Lord Jesus Christ going about to break the neck of the proud, chose men of no learning nor reputation, which he did also for this purpose, that the glory of the gospel might not be diminished nor shadowed with worldly succors and helps. So here Christ manifestly declares to us in what kind of people he most delights, even in the humble and contempt persons of the world and in such as be simple and as it were babes in worldly wisdom, as in another place he also testifies, saying, "I confess and give thanks unto you O Father, lord of heaven and of earth, because you have hid these things from the wise and prudent persons and have disclosed them unto babes." And you shall mark that Christ calls babes here that which laying aside all worldly wisdom receive God's word without all deliberation and which prefer not their own judgment afore God's word but submit themselves unto it in all things. He called therefore two simple fishers, and when did he call them? . . . For they were casting their nets into the sea, and this fishing was a shadow of the new fishing, whereby they should not take with material nets tithes for the food of the belly, but whereby they should with the net of God's word catch men—which be drowned with earthly cares—unto the desire of the heavenly life. Wherefore whereas they were busied and toiling about their bodily living—which nevertheless was then their vocation or calling according to God's commandment that bids us that in the sweat of our face we should eat our bread—from this general calling, I say, he plucked them to a special calling, which was to preach his holy gospel. And verily his word of calling had in it a wonderful virtue, for it so brought in their hearts that they forthwith left altogether and followed him. And here we have a notable example of obedience in these apostles for us to follow. THE GOSPELS WITH BRIEF SERMONS.[5]

THE OBEDIENCE OF JESUS' DISCIPLES.
JUAN DE VALDÉS: There are here three things as it seems to me worthy of consideration. The first, that the office of an apostle, of a preacher of the gospel, is to fish for men, to drag them out of the obscurity, the darkness, and the confusion of the kingdom of the world and to bring them forth into the light, the brightness, and the peace of the kingdom of God; and the net with which these men are caught is the word of the gospel, the intimation of general indulgence and pardon by the justice of God executed upon Christ. . . .

The second, that these four apostles, when they heard Christ's voice, followed Christ without consulting human prudence nor waiting for other inducements than that, "I will make you fishers of men," which at the time they did not understand; doing as I feel sure all will do, who inwardly hear Christ's voice; they who accept the gospel and thus come forth from the kingdom of the world and enter into the kingdom of God, deliberate and go about consulting with human prudence, witness concerning themselves that they do not hear the voice of Christ, for had they heard it, they would have done what the apostles did.

---

[4]Musculus, *In Evangelistam Matthaeum Commenarii* (1556), 64; citing Deut 32:5; Mt 17:17; Phil 2:15; Ex 32:9; Acts 7:51.

[5]Taverner, *On Saynt Andrewes Day: The Gospels with Brief Sermons* (1542), fol. iii*; citing Mt 11:25.

The third, that if the sons of Zebedee had looked to the obligation of human generation (birth), they would not have left their father to follow Christ. Where it is to be understood that the man, who is called of God to be a disciple of Christ, to imitate Christ, ought to renounce the obligation of human generation (of birth), only regarding the obligation of Christian regeneration. COMMENTARY UPON THE GOSPEL OF ST. MATTHEW.[6]

THE DISCIPLES AS FISHERS OF MEN. JOHN DONNE: Those meditations and those endeavors which must bring us to heaven are removed from this world and fixed entirely upon God. And in this sea are we made fishers of men. Of men in general; not of rich men, to profit by them, nor of poor men, to pierce them the more sharply, because affliction hath opened a way into them; not of learned men, to be over-glad of their approbation of our labors, nor of ignorant men, to affect them with an astonishment, or admiration of our gifts: But we are fishers of men, of all men, of that which makes them men, their souls. And for this fishing in this sea, this gospel is our net.

Eloquence is not our net; traditions of men are not our nets; only the gospel is. The devil angles with hooks and baits, he deceives and he wounds in the catching; for every sin has his sting. The gospel of Christ Jesus is a net; It has leads and corks; it has leads, that is, the denouncing of God's judgments and a power to sink down and lay flat any stubborn and rebellious heart; and it has corks, that is, the power of absolution and application of the mercies of God that swim above all his works, means to erect a humble and contrite spirit above all the waters of tribulation and affliction. SERMON PREACHED AT WHITEHALL.[7]

4:23-25 The Crowds Follow Jesus

JESUS' MINISTRY REVEALS HIS IDENTITY. JOHN CALVIN: The same statement is again made by Matthew in another place. But though Christ was constantly employed in performing almost innumerable miracles, we ought not to think it strange that they are again mentioned, twice or three times, in a general manner. In the words of Matthew, we ought, first, to observe that Christ never remained in one place, but scattered everywhere the seed of the gospel. Again, Matthew calls it the gospel of the kingdom, by which the kingdom of God is established among humankind for their salvation. True and eternal happiness is thus distinguished from the prosperity and joys of the present life.

When Matthew says that Christ healed every disease, the meaning is that he healed every kind of disease. We know that all who were diseased were not cured; but there was no class of disease that was ever presented to him that he did not heal. An enumeration is given of particular kinds of diseases in which Christ displayed his power. "Demoniacs" is a name given in Scripture, not to all indiscriminately who are tormented by the devil, but to those who, by a secret vengeance of God, are given up to Satan so that he holds possession of their minds and of their bodily senses. "Lunatics" is the name given to those, in whom the strength of the disease increases or diminishes, according to the waxing or waning of the moon, such as those who are afflicted with epilepsy or similar diseases. As we know that diseases of this sort cannot be healed by natural means, it follows that, when Christ miraculously healed them, he proved his divinity. COMMENTARY ON A HARMONY OF THE EVANGELISTS.[8]

GREAT CROWDS COME TO HEAR JESUS. MARTIN BUCER: "And healing every disease." The Lord gave a law to those sent before and to those following like lambs for a considerable distance. He willed that this law be written to commend his own power and goodness to posterity, and to be retold carefully. For he did not wish to perform

[6]Valdés, Commentary upon the Gospel of St. Matthew, 55-56.
[7]Donne, Eighty Sermons (1640), 736*.

[8]CTS 1:244-45* (CO 45:151-52); citing Mt 9:35. Greek terms for "demoniacs" and "lunatics" were removed for fluidity.

miracles continually. Thus, from the beginning of the gospel and for a certain extent in the time after his resurrection, he commended the majesty and worth of the gospel to the world with many signs and wonders, and he was principally aided by these labors. He declared that the time had come in which humankind ought to have been healed and restored: the time in which the eyes of the blind were to gain sight, and the ears of the deaf be opened, the lame to leap like a deer, the tongue of the mute to praise, just as Isaiah had prophesied in chapter 35. In a word, it was the time in which the wounded person was returned to true health. Oppressed by the sins and diseases of the Jews and Gentiles, the people ought to have received the healing and strength of justice.

Further on with the apostles, the ability of performing these signs had either been taken back or had stopped. In the same way, prodigies very rarely came from the Hebrews after Moses. For preached signs were unable to influence this people, nor did visible signs move them. This was sufficiently apparent among the Pharisees and the remaining Jews, who more quickly attributed the miracles of Christ to Beelzebub, rather than being persuaded to believe. Faith is the work of the Holy Spirit. He is always accustomed to use preached words to work faith, and he rarely uses signs. . . .

It truly must be observed that the Evangelist wrote about the curing of every disease and every weakness by the Lord, for whom no disease was incurable, because he especially uncovered his own divinity in this healing. At the same time, the Lord showed why he came, which was certainly once to take away sins from his own people; that is, to remove the universal evils that came to all by sin. Wherefore, because the Lord had healed every disease and driven out demons from people, his deeds themselves formed a certain preaching of the gospel. For indeed, since he cast away no one who begged for his own work and there was no disease however serious or chronic which he did not heal, no demon however savage in strength which he did not remove from people with a word, he preached most clearly by these actions that he was the one who takes away the sins of the world and who was taking away the punishment which the world owed for sins. In truth, every power of Satan among humankind is from sin, and because of sins, all diseases and death itself are sent among them, as the Scripture testifies throughout.

And great crowds followed him. Doubtless the greatest part of the crowd, as has been said, followed because of the benefits of the body. Granting that these unworthy folk went after him for those things, nevertheless we are taught how eagerly they followed after Christ to greet him, even those who were quite weak in faith. Then, see that he had already become well-known in the whole region of the Hebrews: for he had followers from every part of that region, from Galilee, which was on the near side of the Jordan; from Decapolis, which was across the Jordan, about which Pliny speaks in 5.18;[†] from Jerusalem, and around the Jordan. Commentary on Matthew 4:23-25.[9]

---

[9]Bucer, *In Sacra Quatuor Evangelia Enarrationes* Perpetuae (1536), 95-96. [†]Pliny, *Naturalis Historia* 5.16(18).

5:1-12 THE BEATITUDES

Seeing the crowds, he went up on the mountain, and when he sat down, his disciples came to him.

²And he opened his mouth and taught them, saying:

³"Blessed are the poor in spirit, for theirs is the kingdom of heaven.

⁴"Blessed are those who mourn, for they shall be comforted.

⁵"Blessed are the meek, for they shall inherit the earth.

⁶"Blessed are those who hunger and thirst for righteousness, for they shall be satisfied.

⁷"Blessed are the merciful, for they shall receive mercy.

⁸"Blessed are the pure in heart, for they shall see God.

⁹"Blessed are the peacemakers, for they shall be called sons[a] of God.

¹⁰"Blessed are those who are persecuted for righteousness' sake, for theirs is the kingdom of heaven.

¹¹"Blessed are you when others revile you and persecute you and utter all kinds of evil against you falsely on my account. ¹²Rejoice and be glad, for your reward is great in heaven, for so they persecuted the prophets who were before you."

a Greek huioi

OVERVIEW: As the crowds gathered to receive his teaching, preaching, and healing ministry, Jesus ascends the hill and begins to teach. Commentators set the context for the Sermon on the Mount by saying that Jesus' chief purpose is to contend against the external righteousness of the Pharisees by addressing the hearts of the people. Many comments on the Beatitudes are embedded in Reformation sermons that focus on the Christian virtues of poverty of spirit, godly mourning, and meekness as in keeping with the gospel. In other words, the virtues extolled are kingdom virtues and all the blessings are essentially tied to the kingdom. Those desiring entrance ("hunger and thirst for righteousness") into the kingdom must be poor in spirit, mourn (penitent), gentle, and pure in heart. Having received the kingdom, their lives will reflect mercy and peace even in the midst of persecution and insults.

The reformers assert that Jesus' teaching on persecution protects believers from a version of the gospel that rejects the reality of suffering. Because of their faith in the gospel, believers will be tested as they face hardships from those who reject the gospel and would love to see it silenced. Jesus prepares his disciples to receive this persecution as a blessing of their relationship and status as children of God by faith. Calvin specifically notes that Jesus' preparation of his disciples was to result in their courage when facing persecution. To the reformers, the frequent warnings about persecution and the teachings on the blessing of it should indicate that persecution is a normal feature of the Christian experience.

5:1 The Beginning of the Sermon on the Mount

THE SERMON'S SETTING. THOMAS FULLER: In this and the two next chapters, Christ having a mountain for his pulpit and the whole law for his text, seeks to clear it from those false glosses (corrupting the text) that the priests and Pharisees have fastened upon it, and shows that God's law was not to be narrowed and confined to the outward act alone but, according to the will of the lawgiver (the surveyor that best knew the latitude thereof), is to be extended to the very thoughts of the heart and takes hold of men and women's wicked inclinations as breaches thereof, and offenses against it. We used to end our sermons with a blessing, Christ begins his with the Beatitudes. A FAST SERMON PREACHED ON INNOCENTS DAY.[1]

---

[1] Fuller, A Fast Sermon Preached on Innocents Day (1642), 3-4*.

5:2-12 *Jesus Offers Blessings*

BLESSED ARE THE POOR IN SPIRIT. THOMAS WATSON: Well then, what are we to understand by poor in spirit? The Greek word for poor, *ptōchos*, is not only taken in a strict sense for those who live upon alms, but in a larger sense for those who are destitute as well of inward as outward comfort. "Poor in spirit" then signifies those who are brought to the sense of their sins, and seeing no goodness in themselves, despair in themselves, and sue wholly to the mercy of God in Christ. . . .

Why does Christ here begin with poverty of spirit? Why is this put in the forefront? I answer, Christ does it to show that poverty of spirit is the very basis and foundation of all the other graces that follow. You may as well expect fruit to grow without a root, as the other graces without this; till a person be poor in spirit, they cannot mourn. Poverty of spirit is like the fire under the still that makes the water drop from the eyes; when a man sees his own defects and deformities and looks upon himself as undone, then he mourns after Christ. . . . Till a person be poor in spirit, they cannot hunger and thirst after righteousness; they must first be sensible of want before they can hunger; therefore, Christ begins with poverty of spirit, because this ushers in all the rest.

What is the difference between poverty of spirit and humility? . . . Chrysostom[†] by poverty of spirit understands humility, yet I think there is some difference; they differ as the cause and the effect. Tertullian[‡] says none are poor in spirit but the humble; he seems to make humility the cause of poverty of spirit; I rather think poverty of spirit is the cause of humility; for when a person sees their want of Christ and how they live on the alms of free grace, this makes them humble; those who are sensible of their own vacuity and indigence, with the violet, hang down their heads in humility; humility is the sweet spice that grows from poverty of spirit.

What is the difference between poverty of spirit and self-denial? . . . In some things they agree, for the poor in spirit are absolute self-deniers; they renounce all opinion of themselves; they acknowledge their dependence on Christ and free grace; but in some things they differ; self-deniers part with the world for Christ; the poor in spirit part with themselves for Christ, that is, their own righteousness; the poor in spirit see themselves nothing without Christ, self-deniers will leave themselves nothing for Christ. THE BEATITUDES.[2]

BLESSED ARE THOSE WHO MOURN. JOHN CARTER: In . . . verse 4, he pronounces them blessed, not who are at ease in Zion and live deliciously, but who mourn, not a thousandth part so much for their afflictions and miseries—though they be sensible of them, and bewail them also, as very bitter fruits of that bitter root of sin—but as James teaches, they are afflicted, sorrow, and weep, they turn their carnal laughter into mourning and joy into heaviness, casting down themselves for their sins before the Lord; in which respect, they grieve at the heart, that they can grieve no more. This godly sorrow for sin (wherefore it reigns) causes repentance unto salvation, not to be repented of (as was said before), and therefore cannot but make him or her blessed, in whom it is found what sorrow or anguish howsoever they meet withal in this present world; for this word of Christ must stand forever: "Blessed are those who mourn." Only let our study and care be rightly to discern this godly sorrow from the counterfeit. In godly sorrow, the mourning is for sin as it is sin and offense against the divine majesty, and not for by respects, as fear of punishment, shame of the world, loss, and crosses. Again, it is joined with hope of pardon and full purpose of an entire reformation. It is also exercised not only about our own sins and evils, but—with just Lot and those holy mourners, Ezekiel 9—it makes us to be vexed in our souls, by hearing and seeing the unlawful deeds of others. And finally, wheresoever it is, there cannot but be exceeding sorrow for the affliction of Joseph, that is,

---

[2]Watson, *The Beatitudes* (1660), 41-42*. [†]Chrysostom, *Homilies on Matthew*, NPNF[1] 10:88-89; [‡]Tertullian, *Of Patience*, ANF 3:714.

of the people of God. An Exposition of Christ's Sermon in the Mount.[3]

Blessed Are the Meek. Gervase Babington: As I say this he knew, so likewise as well did he foresee that there causes public and private of impatience and immoderate affections should arise unto his children, and therefore provided for it also. For cast your eyes about the world a little, and view the course of things, and are not the godly, harmless, and quiet men often in this world rejected and wrung and pinched at for this thing and that, when more contentious natures are let alone as shrews to deal withal? . . .

But like a wise teacher and a good God, he has done it as I say in the next verse there and commands to us the rule of our nature and the victory over our affections be the provocations never so many to the contrary, setting a crown of happiness upon the head of that glorious virtue in these words: "Blessed are the meek, for they shall inherit the earth." Now the meek, says a learned person, are those who are not easily provoked with injuries, who are not short and testy upon every offense, but are ready rather to suffer any thing than to do the things that the wicked do, men and women to conclude that resist not evil, but overcome evil with good. Or yet more fully such (as another faith) as are not of nature fierce, and desirous ever of revenge, but mild, tractable, courteous, soft, and gentle, easily forgiving a wrong, if it is done to them, hating chidings, contentions and strife, ready to give place to everybody, and choosing rather with a quiet mind to commit all to God, than with intemperate heat to pursue his own right. Blessed are these men and women, says the Lord, and happy shall they be; the earth is theirs, and the commodities in it, and they shall inherit them. And why so may you either say or think? Surely because this is not flesh and blood in them, but a heavenly alteration of crooked nature by God's renewing spirit. A Briefe Conference Betwixt Man's Frailte and Faith.[4]

Blessed Are Those Who Hunger and Thirst for Righteousness. Jeremiah Burroughs: "Blessed are those who hunger and thirst after righteousness." Thus, for first, to them is the great mystery of godliness revealed, their hearts are taken up with that which has the greatest weight in it that ever any thing had in the world. Your heart is taken with that which the thoughts and councils of the infinite God have been taken up withal from all eternity. The greatest thing that ever has taken up the heart of God, it has been this mystery of godliness in the righteousness of this Son, and the conveying of that to the children of men, whom he means to save. While others have their hearts taken up with meat, drink, play, and such kind of things, your heart is taken up in the contemplation, in the seeking after, in the longing for the most glorious thing that ever God's heart was upon. And therefore blessed are you who has had such a turn of your heart from the trifling things of this world to a matter of such infinite consequence, as this righteousness of Jesus Christ is. It is that which will be the matter of the praise of angels and saints to all eternity.

Second, blessed are you who now do hunger after it, for now it is tendered; you take God's time for the seeking after it: "You shall be satisfied." All tears, doubts, misgiving thoughts, shall be removed; all accusations shall be cast off. You shall have the good of it, as if you had satisfied and obeyed in your own persons. You shall be brought before the father, shining in this robe and garment of your elder brother. You shall have the reward of it, which is beyond expression and imagination. Now the Lord set your hearts upon this. If you perish after the making known such a mystery, the grace of God in this righteousness, you will perish with a witness. For the quickening of your appetites after this bread of life, consider. A Sermon Preached Before the Honorable House of Commons.[5]

What Kind of Righteousness? Martin Luther: "Righteousness" in this passage must not

---

[3]Carter, *A Plaine and Compendious Exposition of Christ's Sermon in the Mount* (1627), 865-66*.

[4]Babington, *A Briefe Conference Betwixt Man's Frailte and Faith . . . in the Fifth of Matthew* (1584), 35-37*.

[5]Burroughs, *A Sermon Preached Before the Honorable House of Commons* (1646), 16-17.

be taken in the sense of that principal Christian righteousness by which a person becomes pious and acceptable to God. I have said before that these eight items are nothing but instruction about the fruits and good works of a Christian. Before these must come faith, as the tree and chief part or summary of a person's righteousness and blessedness, without any work or merit of their own, out of which faith these items all must grow and follow. Therefore, take this in the sense of the outward righteousness before the world, which we maintain in our relations with each other. Thus, the short and simple meaning of these words is this: "That person is righteous and blessed who continually works and strives with all of their might to promote the general welfare and the proper behavior of everyone and who helps to maintain and support this by word and deed, by precept and example." . . .

Here you have a comforting and certain promise, with which Christ allures and attracts his Christians: "Those who hunger and thirst for righteousness shall be filled." That is, they will be recompensed for their hunger and thirst by seeing that their work was not in vain and that at last a little flock has been brought around who have been helped. Although things are not going now as they would like and they have almost despaired over it, all this will become manifest, not only here on earth, but even more in the life hereafter, when everyone will see what sort of fruit such people have brought by their diligence and perseverance. For example, a pious preacher has snatched many souls out of the jaws of the devil and brought them to heaven; or a pious, faithful ruler has helped many lands and people, who testify that he has done so and who praise him before the whole world. Sermon on the Mount.[6]

Blessed Are the Merciful. Martin Bucer: By the preceding four thoughts, Christ was teaching, as I said, that it might be suffered and believed. Now with these three he teaches what

would happen to us to whom the obligations are applied. The first duty is for kindness and beneficence, to which all Scripture exhorts with the promise of requital. In this manner, the fifth book of Moses, chapter 15, after God instructs about kindnesses toward the poor, he adds, "For therefore the Lord your God will be kind to you in all your work, and in everything to which you put your hand in pity." In the same manner, Psalm 112: "It is well with the man who has compassion and lends, he will distribute his words with justice. Who will not be moved in eternity." . . . Or then is this not the great mercy, of which this is promised to the merciful? Also Psalm 97: "You who love the Lord, have a hatred for evil, he guards the lives of his beloved, he snatches them away from the hand of the ungodly." Also Proverbs 16: "By mercy and truth iniquity is atoned." Isaiah 58 also discusses much in this sense, but these Scriptures occur everywhere. Commentary on Matthew.[7]

God Will Repay the Merciful. John Calvin: This paradox contradicts human judgment. The world reckons those people to be happy who give themselves no concern about the distresses of others but seek their own ease. Christ says that those are happy who are prepared not only to endure their own afflictions but also to take a share in the afflictions of others; who assist the wretched; who willingly take part with those who are in distress; and who clothe themselves, as it were, with the same affections, that they may be more readily disposed to render them assistance. He adds, "for they shall obtain mercy"—not only with God, but also among humankind, whose minds God will dispose to the exercise of humanity. Though the whole world may sometimes be ungrateful and may return the very worst reward to those who have done acts of kindness to them, it ought to be reckoned enough, that grace is laid up with God for the merciful and humane, so that

---

[6]LW 21:26, 28 (WA 32:318, 320).

[7]Bucer, *In Sacra Quatuor Evangelia, Enarrationes Perpetuae* (1536), 106; citing Deut 15:10; Ps 112:5-6 (Vg. Ps 111:5-6); Ps 97:10 (Vg. Ps 96:10); Prov 16:6.

they, in their turn, will find him to be gracious and merciful. COMMENTARY ON A HARMONY OF THE EVANGELISTS.[8]

BLESSED ARE THE PURE IN HEART. DESIDER-IUS ERASMUS: The common sort of person calls them unhappy that be blind and because they have lost their most pleasant sense, they say they be no longer alive, but that they abide in darkness like the dead. So pleasant a thing it seems to the eyes to look upon the light, and to behold this goodly spectacle, the light of the world. Further also seeing it is so pleasant a thing for the bodily eyes to look upon the sun. How much more pleasant a blessed thing is the eyes of the mind to behold God, the maker of the sun and of all things? You see how they leap for joy, which have been blind and do not see the sun again. Yes, they rejoice as much as if they had been delivered from hell. How much more blessed be they, who being delivered from blindness of the mind, inwardly do see God, the fountain of all joy whom to behold is high felicity and blessedness. As the sun is to clear eyes, so is God to pure and clean minds. As . . . a web is to the eyes, so are sins to the mind. Therefore, blessed are those whose hearts are pure and clean from all filthiness. For they shall have this gift, which is more to be desired than all the pleasures of the world, they shall see God. PARAPHRASES.[9]

PURITY IS THE MOTHER OF ALL VIRTUES. JOHN CALVIN: We might be apt to think that what is here stated by Christ is in accordance with the judgment of all. "Purity of heart" is universally acknowledged to be the mother of all virtues. And yet there is hardly one person in a hundred who does not put craftiness in the place of the greatest virtue. Hence those persons are commonly accounted "happy" whose ingenuity is exercised in the successful practice of deceit, who gain dexterous advantages by indirect means over those with whom they have intercourse. Christ does not at all

agree with carnal reason when he pronounces those to be "happy" who take no delight in cunning, but converse sincerely with others, and express nothing, by word or look, which they do not feel in their heart. Simple people are ridiculed for want of caution and for not looking sharply enough to themselves. But Christ directs them to higher views, and bids them consider that, if they have not sagacity to deceive in this world, they will enjoy the sight of God in heaven. COMMENTARY ON A HARMONY OF THE EVANGELISTS.[10]

BLESSED ARE THE PEACEMAKERS. THOMAS FULLER: Observe in the words the best work and the best wages; the best work, peacemakers; the best wages, they are blessed. I begin with the work that shall employ my pains and your attention this day. Now the goodness of peace will the better appear if we consider the misery of war. . . . I must confess, I ever prized peace for a pearl, but we never did or could set the true estimate and value upon it till this interruption and suspension of it. Now we know, being taught by dear experience, that peace is a beautiful blessing. . . .

Let us now come to see the means whereby private persons may and must endeavor the obtaining of peace; the first is prayer, pray for the peace of Jerusalem. Let everyone in that prayer which they use in their family or private devotions build a room and enlarge it, to pray for peace in our Israel. . . .

So, when a general deluge and inundation of God's anger seizes upon a whole kingdom, it cannot be stopped by the private endeavors of some few, but it must be an universal work, by a general repentance; all must raise banks to bound it. Till this be done, I am afraid we shall have no peace, and to speak plainly I am afraid we are not yet ripe for God's mercy, as Gideon in Judges 7:4 had too many men for God to give victory to, so we are too proud hitherto for God to give peace to. . . . Many by these wars are brought low, but few made lowly, so that we are proud in our poverty,

[8]CTS 1:263-64* (CO 45:163); citing Ps 103:8; 145:8.
[9]EP 19r.

[10]CTS 1:264* (CO 45:163-64).

and as the unjust steward said, "to beg I am ashamed," so we are too stout though half-starved on the bended knees of our souls, with true repentance, to crave pardon of God for our sins, which till it be done, we may discourse of peace and superficially desire it but never truly care for it or can comfortably receive it. A Fast Sermon Preached on Innocents Day.[11]

Blessed Are the Persecuted for Righteousness. Philipp Melanchthon: *Concerning the scandal of the cross.* First, it must be said that universal human wisdom was harshly offended, disturbed, and astonished when it looked upon this eternal species, namely, that the church appears to be burdened with miseries, scattered and despised or oppressed by a crowd. This is especially so because the leading lights and excellent members of the church are cruelly killed, just as if they had been rejected by God and offered up as accursed expiatory or purifying sacrifices—for example, Abel, Isaiah, Jeremiah, Christ, Peter, and John the Baptist. It is necessary that we be rightly forewarned against this stumbling block. In everything, let us know that the true reasons why the church is pressed more harshly and subjected to the cross in this mortal life are shown only in the word of God handed down by the fathers, prophets, Christ, and the apostles. Nevertheless, human wisdom protests the judgment of reason and argues in this way: "It is fitting for the just to fare well. We are just, therefore we ought to be without calamities. We ought to flourish and enjoy our works, glory, tranquility.". . .

Truly, though, the teaching of the gospel, which is the particular wisdom of the church, contradicts this declaration. First it responds to the major premise or the speech of the law, "The just ought to fare well." It is true only if the remnants of sin do not cling to the just and if they are already completely delivered from sin. But the voice of the gospel reveals the entire liberation. It teaches the just that as much as they are afflicted in this life,

they will have eternal goods afterward and enjoy perpetual happiness then, when they will have been delivered from the entire sin, not only by imputation and the beginning of the new work, but also by its perfection. Then the gospel teaching responds to the minor premise: "We are just," that is, through faith, by the imputation or justice imputed by God on account of the Son and by the beginning of new purity. This beginning newness still has much squalidness of infirmity, so that at the same time great filth clings to the converted. The remnants of sin, as well as sad delays, likewise many straying flames of desire, or manifold vicious inclinations, truly remain in our dirty and wretched nature until this fleshly mass, mired in sin, is completely abolished and destroyed in the mortal body.

From the beginning these things are said about the scandal of the cross, because human reason is offended by these very sad spectacles, gazing upon the pile of trouble, by which the church is annoyed and burdened. . . . Christ here speaks about both kinds of affliction, that is, testing and martyrdom, because he also wishes to acknowledge holy people and those pleasing to himself, because the remnants of sin still cling to themselves, and because this entirely corrupt nature must be destroyed because of sin. Besides these things, death and the afflictions of the saints are a testimony about the following judgment, that there is another life and another judgment after this life. Annotations on the Gospels.[12]

Be Prepared for Persecution. John Calvin: By these words Christ intended to comfort those who believe in him; that they may not lose courage, even though they see themselves to be detestable in the eyes of the world. For this was no light temptation, to be thrown out of the church as ungodly and profane. Christ knew that there is no class of people more envenomed than hypocrites, and foresaw with what furious madness the enemies of the gospel would attack his small

---

[11]Fuller, *A Fast Sermon Preached on Innocents Day* (1642), 18, 21-22*.   [12]MO 14:578-79.

and despised flock. It was therefore his will to furnish them with a sure defense, that they might not give way, though an immense mass of reproaches were ready to overwhelm them. . . .

A remedy is at hand, that we may not be overwhelmed by unjust reproaches: for, as soon as we raise our minds to heaven, we there behold vast grounds of joy, which dispel sadness. The idle reasoning of the papists, about the word *reward*, which is here used, are easily refuted: for there is not (as they dream) a mutual relation between the reward and merit, but the promise of the reward is free. Besides, if we consider the imperfections and faults of any good works that are done by the very best of people, there will be no work that God can judge to be worthy of reward. . . .

This was expressly added, so that the apostles might not expect to triumph without exertion and without a contest, and might not fail when they encountered persecutions. The restoration of all things, under the reign of Christ, being everywhere promised in Scripture, there was danger, lest they might not think of warfare, but indulge in vain and proud confidence. It is evident from other passages that they foolishly imagined the kingdom of Christ to be filled with wealth and luxuries. Christ had good reason for warning them that as soon as they succeeded to the place of the prophets, they must sustain the same contests in which the prophets were formerly engaged. The prophets . . . were [not only] before them with respect to the order of time, but . . . they were of the same class with themselves, and ought therefore to be followed as their example. COMMENTARY ON A HARMONY OF THE EVANGELISTS.[13]

HEAVEN'S MOST CHOICE NAMES. ARGULA VON GRUMBACH:

> When Christ says: You are richly blessed
> When you for me suffer duress;
> When the people against you hiss,
> Abuse you, chase you from their midst;
> Then to revile your name go on
> All for the sake of the Son of man.
> Be glad upon that day, Rejoice!
> In heaven your name will be most choice.
> Woe to you who laugh and scorn!
> For in that hour you will weep and mourn.
> Woe to you who by all are praised!
> Who blaspheme God; your foaming rage
> In the eyes of God will count for naught,
> Before God's awful judgment seat.

"JOHANNES OF LANZHUT": ATTACK AND RESPONSE.[14]

---

[13]CTS 1:266-68* (CO 45:165-66).
[14]Grumbach, *Argula von Grumbach*, 194 (AvG 150); alluding to Lk 6:22; 1 Pet 4:12-14.

5:13-48 JESUS PREACHES RIGHTEOUSNESS
TO THE CROWDS

[13]*"You are the salt of the earth, but if salt has lost its taste, how shall its saltiness be restored? It is no longer good for anything except to be thrown out and trampled under people's feet.*

[14]*"You are the light of the world. A city set on a hill cannot be hidden. *[15]*Nor do people light a lamp and put it under a basket, but on a stand, and it gives light to all in the house. *[16]*In the same way, let your light shine before others, so that[a] they may see your good works and give glory to your Father who is in heaven.*

[17]*"Do not think that I have come to abolish the Law or the Prophets; I have not come to abolish them but to fulfill them. *[18]*For truly, I say to you, until heaven and earth pass away, not an iota, not a dot, will pass from the Law until all is accomplished. *[19]*Therefore whoever relaxes one of the least of these commandments and teaches others to do the same will be called least in the kingdom of heaven, but whoever does them and teaches them will be called great in the kingdom of heaven. *[20]*For I tell you, unless your righteousness exceeds that of the scribes and Pharisees, you will never enter the kingdom of heaven.*

[21]*"You have heard that it was said to those of old, 'You shall not murder; and whoever murders will be liable to judgment.' *[22]*But I say to you that everyone who is angry with his brother[b] will be liable to judgment; whoever insults[c] his brother will be liable to the council; and whoever says, 'You fool!' will be liable to the hell[d] of fire. *[23]*So if you are offering your gift at the altar and there remember that your brother has something against you, *[24]*leave your gift there before the altar and go. First be reconciled to your brother, and then come and offer your gift. *[25]*Come to terms quickly with your accuser while you are going with him to court, lest your accuser hand you over to the judge, and the judge to the guard, and you be put in prison. *[26]*Truly, I say to you, you will never get out until you have paid the last penny.[e]*

[27]*"You have heard that it was said, 'You shall not commit adultery.' *[28]*But I say to you that everyone who looks at a woman with lustful intent has already committed adultery with her in his heart. *[29]*If your right eye causes you to sin, tear it out and throw it away. For it is better that you lose one of your members than that your whole body be thrown into hell. *[30]*And if your right hand causes you to sin, cut it off and throw it away. For it is better that you lose one of your members than that your whole body go into hell.*

[31]*"It was also said, 'Whoever divorces his wife, let him give her a certificate of divorce.' *[32]*But I say to you that everyone who divorces his wife, except on the ground of sexual immorality, makes her commit adultery, and whoever marries a divorced woman commits adultery.*

[33]*"Again you have heard that it was said to those of old, 'You shall not swear falsely, but shall perform to the Lord what you have sworn.' *[34]*But I say to you, Do not take an oath at all, either by heaven, for it is the throne of God, *[35]*or by the earth, for it is his footstool, or by Jerusalem, for it is the city of the great King. *[36]*And do not take an oath by your head, for you cannot make one hair white or black. *[37]*Let what you say be simply 'Yes' or 'No'; anything more than this comes from evil.[f]*

[38]*"You have heard that it was said, 'An eye for an eye and a tooth for a tooth.' *[39]*But I say to you, Do not resist the one who is evil. But if anyone slaps you on the right cheek, turn to him the other also. *[40]*And if anyone would sue you and take your tunic,[g] let him have your cloak as well. *[41]*And if anyone forces you to go one mile, go with him two miles. *[42]*Give to the one who begs from you, and do not refuse the one who would borrow from you.*

[43]*"You have heard that it was said, 'You shall love your neighbor and hate your enemy.' *[44]*But I say to you, Love your enemies and pray for those who persecute you, *[45]*so that you may be sons of your*

Father who is in heaven. For he makes his sun rise on the evil and on the good, and sends rain on the just and on the unjust. ⁴⁶*For if you love those who love you, what reward do you have? Do not even the tax* collectors do the same?* ⁴⁷*And if you greet only your brothers,ᵇ what more are you doing than others? Do not even the Gentiles do the same?* ⁴⁸*You therefore must be perfect, as your heavenly Father is perfect."*

a Or *house.* 16*Let your light so shine before others that*   b Some manuscripts insert *without cause*   c Greek says *Raca to* (a term of abuse)   d Greek *Gehenna;* also verses 29, 30   e Greek *kodrantes,* Roman copper coin (Latin *quadrans*) worth about 1/64 of a *denarius* (which was a day's wage for a laborer)   f Or *the evil one*   g Greek *chiton,* a long garment worn under the cloak next to the skin   h Or *brothers and sisters.* In New Testament usage, depending on the context, the plural Greek word *adelphoi* (translated "brothers") may refer either to *brothers* or to *brothers and sisters*

OVERVIEW: The theme of persecution that concludes the Beatitudes could silence the witness of a disciple or deter one from associating with the kingdom publicly. The Reformation commentators indicate that to counteract the silencing effect of religious persecution, Jesus provides two striking analogies (salt and light) to encourage not only the initial confession of the kingdom but also an ongoing public testimony to it. Grotius stresses that the full acceptance of Christ's doctrine is demonstrated in the example of the disciple's life.

In the first of a series of six examples how the righteousness required in the kingdom surpasses the legalistic righteousness of the religious leaders, Jesus quotes from the Ten Commandments. Jesus' interpretation of the fifth commandment fits perfectly with Moses' interpretation of the commandment seen in Leviticus 19:17. Martin Chemnitz contends that Jesus' full explanation of the commandment against anger as murder was therefore not a new teaching but captured that of Moses himself and served as an example that could be followed with other commands.

In the second example of dismissing a self-righteous keeping of the law, Jesus notes that the sin of adultery includes a lustful heart. Among other Reformation authors, Thomas Cranmer calls on his audience to receive the fullness of Christ's rebuke of sexual sin. An impure intention of the heart also breaks the command. Disciples, like their master, Christ, should be pure in action and thought. The biblical text uses imagery that was utilized also in Matthew 18:8-9 of losing a part of the body to save the condemnation of the whole.

Christ uses this imagery to protect a person from downplaying sin and thereby missing the true remedy for it. Jesus' end goal is not for us to put our bodies to death but to put our sin to death.

Jesus' third example of kingdom righteousness links with the second through the theme of adultery. Not only does lust equate with adultery, but marrying a divorced person does as well. The exception clause here is that if a wife has already committed adultery, then to divorce her does not make her an adulterer, since she already is. The reformers contend that Christians should value the bond of marriage in keeping with the Lord's design, though Protestants did not regard it as a sacrament like their Roman Catholic counterparts. Divorce does not help a person but instead exposes them to multiple dangers and temptations. Many reformers connect Jesus' teaching in the Sermon on Mount with his teaching in Matthew 19, saying that in both cases Jesus is correcting the sinful hearts of the husbands who had taken solace in the false interpretations on this issue by contemporary religious leaders.

In his fourth example, Jesus draws on a few Old Testament texts as he prohibits the swearing of oaths. Reflecting Anabaptist communities, Hans Denck argues that to swear an oath is presumptuous because it assumes a human ability that may or may not exist. He even cautions against an overzealous use of yes or no and recognizes that promising future actions often lacks the appropriate modesty about one's abilities or knowledge. Humility causes the disciple to note that humans have no ability to fulfill their vows.

In the Sermon on the Mount's fifth use of Old Testament sayings, Jesus presses his hearers to move from personal justice to generosity. The reformers indicate that Jesus is dealing with an inward attitude: worldly ambition. The regenerate person does not live for the goal of worldly honor. Therefore, the Christian who is uninterested in worldly ambitions can live a life reflecting regeneration and thereby not pursue revenge.

In a final example of an Old Testament saying being used as a launching point for a lesson on kingdom righteousness, Jesus exhorts his followers to love both neighbor and enemy. The commentators highlight the extreme nature of Jesus' command to love one's enemy. Every person, no matter how despicable in behavior, is to be loved as a faithful neighbor. The basis of this love is the image of God in everyone and the clear commands of God to love. On the perfection of love required of the disciple, Musculus asserts that God has revealed the perfect love of enemies in that he has loved those who were hostile to him in their sinful rebellion. All who have God as their Father are held to the same standard of "perfect love." The impossibility of perfect righteousness from self-effort would not be lost on those who had just heard Jesus speaking of the sinfulness of anger, lust, and revenge.

5:13-20 Salt and Light, Law, and True Kingdom Righteousness

ALL CHRISTIANS ARE TO BE SALT AND LIGHT. HUGO GROTIUS: If only to begin to speak, I do not see enough reason at all why these things are restricted to the apostles. For also the Beatitudes are common to all: and the address that follows after the two preceding divisions contemplates all who sustain injury for the truth. Then indeed clear it is said to those "salt of the earth" and the following division: "light of the world." But "lights of the world" is spoken not so much for the bishop, but all true Christians, as Philippians 2:15 shows. This is similar to Justin: "Whatever the spirit is in the body, this Christians are in the world."[†] Truly what is said already here about salt, in Luke 14:25, 34, is said directly "to the crowds." Therefore, the meaning is that those who receive from this Christ the true and beneficial doctrine, to seek not a living copy from others, but ought to be an example to others. But salt's excellence of strength is in contrast to rottenness. ANNOTATIONS ON MATTHEW.[1]

THE NATURE OF THE SALT IMAGERY. THOMAS PORTER: Why are they compared to salt?

(1) Because of the piercing or pinching quality. Salt (we know) bites and eats. So ministers by the doctrine of the law pinch the conscience of a sinner till they be convinced of sin. Thus did Christ himself with the woman of Samaria; thus did Peter with those hearers. Yea, they do it by the gospel too, which discreetly preached, bites the people till some of them bite their lips, and gnaw their tongues for pain. The Spirit in the gospel ministry of the apostles convinced the world of sin, of righteousness, and of judgment.

(2) Because of the purging quality. Salt (we know) scours and cleanses. Leeches are scoured with salt before the physician applies them to his patient to take away the rank humor. Glasses are rubbed and scoured with salt too. So Christ cleanses his church—by the Word. The disciples themselves were clean by the Word, which Christ spoke to them. How may a young person cleanse their way, but by the Word?

(3) Because of the preserving quality. The chiefest virtue of salt is against putrefaction. Hence the saying of Varro that nature has given to a swine a soul or life instead of salt lest it should rot above ground.[†] In former times it was an ancient rite in making a covenant to use salt, therefore called "a covenant of salt"—that is, an authentic, inviolable, and incorruptible covenant; because salt dries up the superfluous humors, which are the ground of putrefaction. . . .

---

[1]Grotius, *Annotationes in Novum Testamentum . . . ad Matth. I–XIII*, 1:90*. [†]Though Grotius attributes this quote to Justin Martyr, it comes from the anonymous second-century work *Epistle to Diognetus* 6.1.

(4) Because of the pleasing quality. Salt makes meat pleasant to the palate; it renders it savory. Thus, when Elisha threw salt into the spring, the water became savory, though I confess that proceeded not from the natural property of salt but from the supernatural power of God. A Sermon on Matthew 5:13.[2]

The Work of Proclaiming Christ. Martin Luther: Now you can draw the conclusion for yourself that Matthew does not have in mind the ordinary works that people should do for one another out of love, which he talks about in Matthew 25:35. Rather is he thinking principally about the distinctly Christian work of teaching correctly, of stressing faith, and of showing how to strengthen and preserve it; this is how we testify that we really are Christians. The other works are not such a reliable criterion, since even sham Christians can put on the adornment and cover of big, beautiful works of love. But the true teaching and confession of Christ is impossible without faith; as Paul says: "No one can say, 'Jesus is Lord,' except by the Holy Spirit." No sham Christian or schismatic spirit can understand this teaching. How much less can he truly preach it and confess it! Even though he might perceive the words and imitate them, still he does not hold to them or keep them pure. His preaching always betrays the fact that he does not have it straight. He slobbers all over it by stealing the honor from Christ and claiming it for himself.

Thus, the most reliable index to a true Christian is this: if from the way he praises and preaches Christ the people learn that they are nothing and that Christ is everything. In short, it is the kind of work that cannot be done in relation to one or two people, remaining hidden like other works. It has to shine and let itself be seen publicly, in front of the whole world. That is always why it alone is persecuted, for the world can tolerate other works.

This also entitles it to be called a work through which our Father is recognized and praised. The other and less important works are not entitled to this, since they remain purely on the human level and belong to the second table of the Decalogue.[†] The works we are talking about now deal with the first three great commandments, which pertain to God's honor, name, and word. In addition, if they are to endure, they have to be verified and purified through persecution and suffering. They also have to be slandered before the world to keep them pure of any self-esteem or presumptuousness and to make them all the more praiseworthy before God, since this is really a slander of his honor and praise. That is also why they stand so firmly and why God defends them so powerfully, leading them through despite the raging and persecution of the world. Therefore, we should also give these works a position of preeminence as the most important, followed by the others, which involve our relations with people. Thus, both will have their due. First, we should constantly teach and emphasize faith, and then we should live according to faith. In this way everything we do will be done in faith and from faith, as I have always taught. Sermon on the Mount.[3]

The Continuing Function of the Law. Heinrich Bullinger: Let everyone, therefore, be persuaded for certain that the law of God, which is the most excellent and perfect will of God, is forever eternal, and cannot be at any time dissolved, either by humans, or angels, or any other creatures. Let every person think that the law, so far as it is the rule of how to live well and happily, so far as it is the bridle by which we are kept in the fear of the Lord, so far as it is a prick that awakens the dullness of our flesh, and so far as it is given to instruct, correct, and rebuke us, that here, I say, it does remain unabrogated. And, to this day,

---

[2]Porter, *Spiritual Salt: Or, A Sermon on Matt 5:13* (1651), 5-7; citing Jn 4:18; Acts 2:37; Jn 16.8; Eph 5:26; Jn 15:3; Ps 119:9; 2 Chron 13.5; 2 Kings 2:21. [†]Varro, *De re rustica* 4.9.

[3]LW 21:66-67 (WA 32:353-54); citing Mt 25:35-46; 1 Cor 12:3. [†]Since the time of Augustine, it was common to divide the Ten Commandments into two "tables," the first containing laws related to interactions with God and the second containing laws relate to interactions with one's neighbor.

the law has its belonging in the church of God: and therefore, the abrogating of the law consists in this that follows. USE, FULFILLING, AND ABROGATION OF THE LAW.[4]

CHRIST CAME TO FULFILL THE LAW. MARTIN LUTHER: It is a sharp and intolerable salt when he attacks and condemns such people (the Pharisees) as these for not teaching or living correctly, conceding nothing good or right to them—the very best and holiest people, irreproachable, who are teaching God's commandments and performing holy acts of worship every day. In this way he gave them an opportunity for a shrill denunciation of him and for the accusation that he wanted to abolish and destroy the law that God had given. . . . He foresaw this accusation against him and this interpretation of his teaching. Hence he explains from the outset that he has no intention of abolishing the law, but had come for the very purpose of correcting and confirming the teaching of the law in opposition to those who were weakening it by their teaching. . . .

Now he says, "I have come not to destroy the law but to fulfill it." That is, "I do not intend to bring another law or a new law, but to take the very Scriptures that you have and to emphasize them, dealing with them in such a way as to teach you how to behave." What the gospel or the preaching of Christ brings is not a new doctrine to undo or change the law, but, as Paul says, the very same thing that was "promised beforehand through the prophets in the Scripture." . . . All by itself, the law is so rich and perfect that no one needs to add anything to it; for the apostles themselves had to prove the gospel and the proclamation about Christ on the basis of the Old Testament. Therefore no one, not even Christ himself, can improve upon the law. What can you make up or teach that is higher than what the first commandment teaches: "You shall love God with all your heart"? He does indeed go beyond law and doctrine when he gives his grace and Spirit to enable us to do and keep the law's demands, but that is not "supplementing" the law. And so he is not talking about that here, but about that fulfilling which takes place through teaching; similarly, by "abolishing" he does not mean acting contrary to the law, but teaching in such a way as to subtract from it.

What is said here, therefore, is not different from what Paul says: "Do we, then, overthrow the law by this faith? By no means! On the contrary, we uphold the law." He does not intend to bring another doctrine, as though the former one were no longer in force. He intends, rather, to preach it, to emphasize it, to show its real kernel and meaning, and to teach them what the law is and what it requires, in antithesis to the glosses which the Pharisees have introduced, the shells and husks which they have been preaching. . . . Thus, the Jewish teachers retained the text of the law, but they so corrupted it with their additions that neither its proper understanding nor its proper use was left. SERMON ON THE MOUNT.[5]

OUR OWN RIGHTEOUSNESS IS NOT ENOUGH. HENRY VAUGHAN: It must be then "your righteousness," yet, there was a fear, you see, in the wise virgins that there was not enough of this oil; the lamps in the sanctuary had no secret spring in the bottom, but were replenished from abroad with that which distilled from the olive branch. Our own inherent righteousness is too narrow a garment to cover nakedness; it is but . . . a clothing of fig leaves . . . like that of our first parents, which betrays the sin and shame together. When we view those that proceed from our own natural strength and arm of flesh, we find the best of them to be but the prophets' "sour grapes" and "evil figs." Yea, our most religious actions, which are crowned with an influence of grace as they issue from depraved principles and mingle with that . . . stream of brimstone that runs through the channels of the soul must needs contract if not an inherent stain and tincture thence, at leastwise much

---

[4]DHB 2:253.

[5]LW 21:67, 69-70 (WA 32:355-56); citing Rom 1:2; Deut 6:5; Rom 3:31.

imperfection. It appears by the law that the lame and blind were not to be offered in sacrifice; now if we respect our own inherent righteousness, as it proceeds from a seduced reason there, it is blind; as it is the issue of a perverted distorted will, there it is lame. This then cannot be the "sacrifice of righteousness" with which God is pleased, but rather the "sacrifice of the corrupt thing." For God who "cannot behold iniquity," requires a righteousness as untainted as his own justice, as straight as his own will without the least obliquity. To whom shall we have recourse for that? Whoever arrived at such perfection? Only the "Lamb without spot and blemish," our blessed Savior, who on the cross bore our iniquities. A SERMON PREACHED AT THE PUBLIC FAST.[6]

THE SUPERIORITY OF CHRISTIAN RIGHT-EOUSNESS. NIELS HEMMINGSEN: The righteousness of the law is a perfect obedience of a man or woman to the law of God. But the Christian or gospel righteousness is Christ's obedience imputed to the one who believes. A righteous person after the law is one who deals justly and uprightly, according to the meaning of the law; but they are righteous after the gospel, to whom God forgives their sins, and imputes Christ's righteousness, and whom he accepts to eternal life freely for Christ's sake. Justification after the law is an enabling of humankind before God for the soundness and perfection of their obedience to God's law; but Christian or gospel justification is an enabling of humankind before God for the soundness and perfection of Christ's obedience to God the Father.

Thus have we the difference between the Christian righteousness and the righteousness of the law. Now let us see how the Christian righteousness exceeds the righteousness of the Pharisees. The Christian righteousness exceeds the Pharisaical in these four things. In cause, quality, effect, and end. The cause of Christian righteousness is God, Christ's desert and faith, taking hold

of the benefit offered; but the cause of Pharisaical righteousness is mass hypocrisy, ignorance of God's righteousness, and outward observance of human traditions. The quality of Christian righteousness is the obedience and fulfilling of the law in Christ; but the quality of Pharisaical righteousness is but only an outward visor of feigned and counterfeit holiness. The effect of Christian righteousness is newness of spirit, the fear of God, true godliness, invocation, true humility, patience, and a beginning of obedience toward God's law, insomuch that a person being justified by faith desires nothing so much as to obey God. To be brief, his chief pleasure is in the law of the Lord, after he knows that damnation is taken away by Christ's merit; but the effect of Pharisaical righteousness is pride, glorying before God, superstition, disdain of one's neighbor, and (to be short) such as the tree is, such is their fruit. For an evil tree cannot bring forth good fruit. The end of Christian righteousness is to have peace with God, to have access to God, to give glory to God, and finally to obtain everlasting life freely for Christ's sake; but the end of Pharisaical righteousness is to give praise to one's own self, and to take it from God, and to vaunt among men and women; upon which at length shall ensue horrible punishment, unless there be a turning to the Lord. Let this suffice concerning the three sorts of righteousness and the differences between them, which are good and proper to bear in mind. A POSTIL, OR EXPOSITION OF THE GOSPELS.[7]

5:21-26 Anger and Murder

JESUS EXPLAINS THE FIFTH COMMANDMENT. MARTIN CHEMNITZ: The explanation of the fifth precept is plain and simple, because it has been shown and given by the Son of God himself, who shows in his explanation of the precepts of the Decalogue that there is a synecdoche to be observed—that is, that there are many more kinds of sins which are in conflict with individual commandments than are mentioned specifically in

---

[6]Vaughan, *A Sermon Preached at the Public Fast* (1644), 14-15*; citing Ps 51:19, Mal 1:14.

[7]Hemmingsen, *A Postill, or Exposition of the Gospels* (1569), 219-20.

the Decalogue. Under this heading, the Pharisees are condemned because they imagined that only external murder was in conflict with the fifth commandment and that the warnings against this precept that were added in the Scripture applied only to homicide, which is actually committed, but that anger is something much less important (for in Mt 5:19 the errors of the Pharisees are described) and certainly not worthy of God's eternal wrath. For the fact that he says, "It has been said by them of old time . . . but I say unto you," does not mean that he is opposing his doctrine to Moses and is rejecting and condemning him, as the Manichaeans[†] raved; or that he is trying to hand down commandments that are better, more perfect, or of greater importance than those of Moses, as the scholastics dream. For Moses was clearly giving the same interpretation to the fifth commandment in Leviticus 19:17: "You shall not hate your brother in your heart." Indeed, Moses clearly commands that we are to love our brother: "If you see the donkey of one who hates you. . . ." For this reason Christ condemns and rejects the errors of the Pharisees, who through the passage of a long period of time had gained a high authority, but Christ brings back to mind the oldest interpretation, which had been given by Moses and the prophets. He says for the sake of emphasis, "but I say to you." Paul affirms in 1 Corinthians 10:4 that the Lord God, who led the children of Israel out of Egypt, was Christ. He also says that he who led them out also gave the law. Therefore, Christ is asserting by this mode of speaking ("I say to you") that he who promulgated the Decalogue possesses the absolutely surest explanation of it. In this way, when the Pharisees tried to protect their long-standing errors by appealing to antiquity or the long passage of time, Christ opposed them by saying, "but I who first promulgated the Decalogue, I say to you. . . ."

Therefore, there is no need for seeking some exotic rationale or searching out the genuine meaning of the fifth commandment. For it has been clearly given by the Son of God and indeed in such a way that it is evident that he wills this example to

be applied to the interpretation of the rest of the commandments also. Loci Theologici.[8]

More Than Murder Is Forbidden. Heinrich Bullinger: The Lord does not simply forbid murder, but all things else on which murder consists. All egging on, therefore, and provoking to anger is utterly forbidden; slanderous taunts and brawling speeches are flatly prohibited; strife, wrath, and envy are plainly commanded to be suppressed. . . . You see here, therefore, that anger, slander, brawling, and all other tokens of a mind moved to utter ill words are flatly forbidden. What then must you do? You must, forsooth, come into charity again with him whom you have offended; you must lay aside all wrath and envy, unless you would rather have all the honor that you do to God be imputed for sin to you, and that, perhaps, you would choose rather utterly to be condemned. The Sixth Precept of the Ten Commandments.[9]

Many Murders Done Without Hands. Katharina Schütz Zell: To these secret sins belong many murders done without hands that may indeed happen when a person allows someone to die in their bed. There are many kinds of murder: prejudice, lack, need for food, drink, clothing, warmth, and so on: many and all bodily needs—if one snatches away all of these or omits to do them it is murder. The same is true also for spiritual things, if one fails to give to each as they have need: counsel, comfort, help, cause for gladness, and so on; each one should act according to their ability and God's law. It is the same also with opposites: It is murder to despise, afflict, mistreat, irritate, insult, abuse, revile, blame people, to make them go astray and be unhappy; it is murder to do all things by which one harms

---

[8]Chemnitz, *Loci Theologici*, 2:404-5; citing Mt 5:21; Ex 23:4; Lev 19:18; Prov. 25:21; 1 Cor 10:4-11. [†]The Manichaeans, with their leader Mani (c. 216–276), posited a dualistic cosmology in which the spiritual world of light battled against the evil material world of darkness. In their view, Christ was but one among a group of prophets who provided spiritual enlightenment. [9]DHB 1:299*.

someone's soul and makes them weak in bodily and spiritual comfort. Who can recount all these sins and murders, much less know them, without Christ the Lord who knows and teaches us to know them. THE MISERERE PSALM.[10]

5:27-32 Lust and Adultery

OBEDIENCE AT ANY COST. JOHN CALVIN: It might be thought that, considering the weakness of the flesh and of nature, Christ pressed too severely on men and therefore he anticipates all such complaints. The general meaning is that however difficult, or severe, or troublesome, or harsh, any commandment of God may be, no excuse ought to be pleaded on those grounds, because the justice of God ought to stand higher in our estimation than all that we reckon most precious and valuable. "You have no right to object to me, that you can scarcely turn your eyes in any direction without being suddenly drawn away by some temptation: for you ought rather to part with your eyes than to depart from the commandments of God." And yet Christ does not mean that we must mutilate our body in order to obey God; but as all would readily wish that they should not be restrained from the free use of their senses, Christ employs an exaggerated form of speech to show that whatever hinders us from yielding that obedience to God that he requires in his law ought to be cut off. And he does so expressly because people allow themselves too much liberty in that respect. If the mind were pure, the eyes and hands would be obedient to it; for it is certain that they have no movement of their own. But here we are deeply to blame. We are so far from being as careful as we ought to be to avoid allurements that we rather provoke our senses to wickedness by allowing them unbounded liberty. COMMENTARY ON A HARMONY OF THE EVANGELISTS.[11]

CHRIST CONDEMNS OUTER AND INNER ADULTERY. THOMAS CRANMER: Here our Savior

Christ not only confirms and establishes the law against adultery, given in the Old Testament of God the Father by his servant Moses, and makes it of full strength, continually to remain among the professors of his name in the new law; but he also—condemning the gross interpretation of the scribes and Pharisees, who taught that the aforesaid commandment only required to abstain from the outward adultery, and not from the filthy desires and impure lusts—teaches us an exact and full perfection of purity and cleanness of life, both to keep our bodies undefiled and our hearts pure and free from all evil thoughts, carnal desires, and fleshly consents. How can we then be free from this commandment, where so great [a] charge is laid upon us? May a servant do what he will in anything, having a commandment of his master to the contrary? Is not Christ our master? Are not we his servants? How then may we neglect our master's will and pleasure and follow our own will and fantasy: "You are my friends (says Christ) if you keep those things that I command you." Now has Christ our master commanded us, that we should forsake all uncleanness and lechery, both in body and spirit? This therefore must we do if we look to please God. A SERMON AGAINST WHORE-DOM AND ADULTERY.[12]

THE REASON GOD FORBIDS ADULTERY. MARTIN CHEMNITZ: We must also now consider why God has willed in the sixth commandment to speak especially by name of the sin of adultery. The Son of God himself shows the reason for this in Matthew 5:28, when he says, "He has already committed adultery in his heart," that is to say, that God in this way has willed to demonstrate the enormity of sin, because just as the Julian law recognizes that the crime of adultery is a great disgrace and worthy of severe punishment, so are the wandering flames of lust considered to be before God's judgment. And because human wickedness is accustomed to give mild and innocent names to sins of dissipation, therefore

---

[10]Zell, *Church Mother*, 146 (KSZ 327-28); citing Mt 5:21-26.
[11]CTS 1:291* (CO 45:179).

[12]Cranmer, *Certayne Sermons* (1547), T1r, T1v.

God accuses all of these practices with a harsh name, so that we are not deceived by extenuations and excuses, but rather will acknowledge our impurity and deplore it, seek forgiveness through the mediator, and put to death our acts of the flesh by the Holy Spirit, so that they do not rule over us. LOCI THEOLOGICI.[13]

ADULTERY IS MORE THAN ACTS OF THE BODY. KATHARINA SCHÜTZ ZELL: Also adultery does not consist only in acts of the body but in the heart and thoughts, as also the Lord says in Matthew chapter 5: "To look on a woman or man with lust is already to be an adulterer." Adultery also consists in much capriciousness and superfluity in many things, yes, in making occasion for each other to fall by how one eats, drinks, dresses, speaks, gestures, all the examples of that behavior cannot be enumerated, including examples among all the most spiritual people and those who fear God. THE MISERERE PSALM.[14]

JESUS FORBIDS DIVORCE AND HARDNESS OF HEART. JOHN CARTER: The remote occasion, which participates with adultery and so comes to be forbidden in the seventh commandment, is causeless divorce—now Christ allows of none to be just and warrantable, except in the case of fornication, whereby the marriage band is broken. The scribes and Pharisees taught that Moses made it lawful for men to put away their wives for every cause and that he commanded to give her a bill of divorce that made her free to marry any other; but Christ, here and elsewhere, teaches far otherwise; that for the hardness of their hearts, this was only tolerated, not allowed; and that by such putting away the hasty and furious husband occasioned both his wife and him that should marry with her to commit adultery, besides the temptations that he should put himself upon. So that by such divorces a great many transgressions of this law, both his own and of other folks, were set upon this

score. . . . This ought to be of use to Christians who, though they have no such causeless divorces tolerated, yet many times go so far as to separation of the wife from the husband, or the husband from his wife; or if not so far, yet to many brawls and much bitterness, so that though one house hold them, yet one bed will not. If this, by Christ's exposition, comes not within the compass of the breach of the seventh commandment, and add not many sins to the score of the innocent or offending party, what does? AN EXPOSITION OF CHRIST'S SERMON IN THE MOUNT.[15]

A CERTIFICATE DOES NOT ABSOLVE THE CONSCIENCE. THEODORE BEZA: Nor is this added to ridicule old men. For here the scribes were not [merely] blundering [by adding] another adjective to the words of the law; but in this they were misrepresenting the law to a certain extent by a false interpretation. As it were, the husband clearly thought that when he handed over a certificate of divorce, his conscience would be absolved before the tribunal of God. Christ denies this. For it is one thing to teach it as a right, and another to soften as much as possible what they are not able to change. For that obligation of giving a certificate of divorce was no doubt keeping back many men, who were shameless inside, from having their wives sent away, because a certificate of this sort was more of a warning about the frivolity or dishonesty of the husbands than about the dismissed woman who was sent away for a flaw. This is supported below by Matthew 19:8. From this passage, it also appears that the consciences of some had been put at rest by this false interpretation of the scribes, and that it had been disputed in the synagogues whether a certificate of divorce could be given for any cause you like. The husband had been sufficiently warned by conscience, about which Christ responded openly in this passage, and Paul in 1 Corinthians 7:10-11. . . .

[13]Chemnitz, Loci Theologici, 2:412.
[14]Zell, Church Mother, 146 (KSZ 328); citing Mt 5:28.
[15]Carter, A Plaine and Compendious Exposition of Christ's Sermon in the Mount (1627), 902-3.

Christ, however, did not allow the wife to go away from her husband, or to give a certificate of divorce to her husband, which appears from the context of the law itself, then especially from Malachi 2:16. But the husband was separating himself from his wife, so that this certificate is able to be seen not as the dismissal of the wife, but the leaving of the husband from the wife in the aspect that is called "apostasy," and in fact there is no infamy in divorce without the husband sending his wife away from himself. Although God doubtless did not approve of this sort of act of husbands, it was tolerated by the magistrate because of their hardness of heart. . . .

It appears, however, from this attached exception that the law concerning the stoning of adulterers was also negligently observed at the time among the Jews. If this law had indeed been enforced, this exception for divorce would have been superfluous, which indeed is demonstrated by the repetition of the matter itself in another clause of this verse. ANNOTATIONS ON MATTHEW 5:31-32.[16]

THREE REASONS FORNICATION IS EXCEPTED.

JUAN DE MALDONADO: Christ does not permit a bill of repudiation even for fornication, as both the words themselves and the universal custom of the church show; for he does not say, "Let him give her who is put away for fornication a writing of divorcement." This he would have said in the first place to restrain the license of repudiation if he had willed it that a woman, put away for that reason, might be married to another, as the modern heretics say, for the law, which was much more liberal in granting divorces in that very matter, put a curb on the license, as many authors of weight assert. . . .

Why, then, did Christ except fornication alone? Probably for three reasons: (1) Because for fornication alone a wife may be put away absolutely and forever so that even if she subsequently repent, the husband, unless he please, need not

receive her again. She is not put away so that she may not commit adultery but because she has committed it, and so that she may pay the penalty all the rest of her life. But when she is put away for other reasons, she is put away, not absolutely and forever, but only for a time, until she reform and repent, so that she may return to her husband if she comes to her right mind again. (2) Because, if she wishes to remain with her husband and to correct her life, the husband can still put her away, because, as we have said, she is put away for the punishment of her broken conjugal faith, not for her correction. If she be given to other vices but wishes to reform, her husband cannot put her away. . . . (3) Other reasons for separation are not peculiar to marriage but common to every condition of life; for whether wife, or friend, or relative, or sister, or mother, if she is the cause of sin to us, she must be put away. Adultery is the reason peculiar to marriage for putting away a wife, because she violates that conjugal fidelity that is the basis, as it were, of marriage, and therefore because it is a civil contract she dissolves the marriage. COMMENTARY ON MATTHEW 5:32.[17]

5:33-42 Oaths and Retaliation

THE IMPORTANCE OF SPEAKING TRUTHFULLY.

HANS DENCK: Oaths and solemn promises are not within human power to keep. Rather, whatever a friend of God knows to be right, they are to do without an oath or solemn promise, as much as is within their power. Whatever they lack in order to accomplish it, they ought to ask the Lord in prayer that they may grant it to them; but they should not vauntingly promise anything, as if it had to be granted to them. For whenever a person vows to do what they are incapable of (and they are not capable even of adding a tiny hair), it has to be either presumption without any understanding or else hypocrisy with understanding, that is, one pretends to be able to do something when in one's

---

[16]Beza, *Annotationes Majores in Novum Dn. Nostri Jesu Christi Testamentum* (1594), 35-36; citing Deut 24:1.

[17]JMG 168-70*.

heart one does not understand at all. These two explanations Scripture also gives when it says, "For you cannot turn a single hair either black or white" and, "that you may not fall into hypocrisy." . . . But no one should really be too hasty with yes and no just because this is permitted. For anyone who assures and convinces another with yes has already sworn, in that they thereby seek to anticipate the will of God. Otherwise, one would become guilty of swearing a false oath if one were incapable of keeping the promise. But this is not the case when done rightly, as for example, when Paul apologized to the Corinthians, upon finding that he could not come to them again, contrary to his earlier assurance. All this is said about the swearing of oaths concerning future events. Anyone who wishes to testify to something that has already happened, in keeping with the teaching of the Lord, should do it modestly and with as few words as possible, that is, by yes or no. Anything beyond that has to be accounted for before God. Someone who has God for a witness of what they say, that it is yes, may go with it, as Paul also did. Only they ought to be aware that God's name must not be used in vain, for this, too, is forbidden by the law as well as in the New Testament, where it is prohibited to swear by anything. CONCERNING GENUINE LOVE.[18]

THE DANGER OF MAKING OATHS. WILLIAM STRODE: To bridle the mouth and keep it from such rude sin, first ponder your words before you garnish them with oaths; weigh them like gold in the balance; consider where they tend to; understand your own meaning before you lash out with your tongue; for a birth delivered before it is conceived must needs be monstrous; and better be dumb than speak that which ought to be recalled. By thus bridling the mouth in the matter of speech, your heart and folly will be thoroughly quelled in the manner; when you take care to speak wisely, truly, and honestly, you will be quite taken off from speaking irreligiously. If opposition tempt you to sweat, do not only examine how great the matter is, how true, how well understood; but in what case and temper you are; how pure in body, how pure in soul; before what company, at what time, in what place, with what reverence, to what end you swear. If still the name of God run hastily on your tongue, mark how an oath becomes another—for some learn better by example of vice than by the rule of virtue, because it is easier to observe the faults of others than their own duties—mark how there it sounds, and then reflect on yourself. Remember also that he by whom you swear, as he is ever-present, so he is likewise omnipotent, able to turn you instantly into the curse which you utter, or into the air which you breathe in swearing.

To sum up this point, you have heard that a bare assertion or at least a double one, where there is no necessity of credence, as in common talk, is fully sufficient; that if lying were laid aside, the weightiest matters would need no swearing, and that such singleness of speech would come nearest to Christian perfection; that albeit some cases may require a toleration, yet in slight discourse, an oath is without color, nor without great prejudice; that being not absolutely but respectively good, like medicinal help referred for necessity, it proves dangerous and pernicious, if used wantonly. A SERMON CONCERNING SWEARING.[19]

THE CHRISTIAN SHOULD BE DEAD TO WORLDLY HONOR. JUAN DE VALDÉS: The scribes and Pharisees hold themselves to be righteous, provided that they live conformably to this, and hold them to be righteous who do so; while the gospel, following the obligation of regeneration, requires the regenerate person to live in the present life as dead. I admonish you to be intent upon being so mortified to ambition and to interest, that you offer no resistance to those who shall maltreat you; to such an extent that, if they shall slap your face on the one cheek, you may present no resistance in defense of the other cheek, that they

---

[18]Denck, *Selected Writings*, 280-81*; citing Mt 5:36; probably Jas 5:12; 2 Cor 1:23; Mt 5:37; Rom 1:9; Ex 20:7; Mt 5:38.

[19]Strode, *A Sermon Concerning Swearing Preached Before the King's Majesty* (1644), 18-19.

may slap your face again; should another sue you at the law to take away your coat, may your attachment to all these material things be so lost that you may hold it to be indifferent, so much so as to give him up your cloak too; and that, were a man to hire you to do one thing for him, you should be so disinterested that were it necessary, you would do two for him; and that should another ask you to give part of something that you possess, you should not take it amiss to have to give it; and that were another to ask you to lend him something, you should feel pleasure in lending it.

Thus do I understand these words of Christ. I understand his expressed intention to be the statement that it concerns the regenerate Christian to live as though dead to worldly honor; that being insulted, he should not resent it; and so disenamored of everything worldly, and so resolute as regards self that he should not resist anyone who should wish to take them from him, whether by violence or by consent. . . .

Here it appears much better than it does anywhere else, that to those who shall not have come to a resolution with the world as to ambition and with themselves as to their own satisfaction in maintaining the proprieties of Christian regeneration, it will not only not be possible, but it will be utterly impossible to reduce themselves to this Christian life, either little or much; not only practically, but even sympathetically; for this worldly honor will oppose, and then sensuality will cry out. So that it is most indispensable to the one who enters into the kingdom of heaven, by acceptance of the grace of the gospel, in order to live according to the obligation of Christian regeneration, that they very attentively consider all these words of Christ, which all contemplate this obligation. COMMENTARY UPON THE GOSPEL OF ST. MATTHEW.[20]

5:43-48 *Love Your Enemies*

LOVING YOUR ENEMIES IN DEED AND TRUTH. JOHN CARTER: He comes to the universality of

---

[20]Valdés, *Commentary upon the Gospel of St. Matthew*, 85-87.

Christian righteousness and proves it by restoring to the native sense the sum of the second table, "You shall love your neighbor," purging it from the Pharisaical dross: first, teaching that by the word "neighbor," not friends and brethren only are to be understood, but any other person, friend, enemy, or alien, who bear the image of God and participate [in] the same nature with us. In a word, those of whom we may receive or to whom we may do good any manner of way are our neighbors, as Christ makes plain in the parable or example of the Jews, falling among thieves, and cruelly handled: and relieved by a Samaritan, whom the Jews had in abomination. So Moses lays upon them the like charge of their enemies or brother's ass or ox. Second, he clears the sum of the law, teaching that our neighbor in this large sense is to be loved; not friends only, according to the lewd leaven of the scribes and Pharisees— which was, "Hate your enemy"—but even our rankest enemies, laying (after his usual manner) the weight of his own authority upon it, and urging it in many words, as knowing that this doctrine concerning the love of our enemies— which we may justly call the perfection of obedience to the second table of the law, as that of suffering persecution for righteousness sake, is of the first—would most hardly sink into our hearts. First is set down his copious proportion of the matter, then his undeniable proofs likewise: his proposition, in these words: "But I say to you, love your enemies, bless those who curse you, do good to those who hate you, and pray for those who despitefully use you, and persecute you." As if he should say, I who come as a teacher from God, and the only fulfiller of the law, declare to you that the true and natural obedience which the law calls for is to love your bitterest enemies and to love them, not teeth-forward or with mouth-love, accompanied with courtlike, or rather stage-playlike expressions of it but in deed and in truth. Blessing, that is, returning good speeches and wishes for cursing, rewarding also their heathenish usage, with Christian kindness, bounty, and prayers. This may seem a bitter pill, but a little sugar of grace and the spirit of God will make us swallow it down readily, as did Christ, Stephen, the apostle Paul, and others innumerable. AN EXPOSITION OF CHRIST'S SERMON IN THE MOUNT.[21]

THE COMMAND IS TO LOVE ALL PEOPLE. THOMAS CRANMER: These are the very words of our Savior Christ himself, touching the love of our neighbor. And for as much as the Pharisees—with their most pestilent traditions, and false interpretations and glosses—had corrupted and almost clearly stopped up this pure well of God's living word teaching that this love and charity pertained only to someone's friends and that it was sufficient for someone to love those who love them and to hate their foes. Therefore, Christ opened this well again, poured it and scoured it by giving unto his godly law of charity a true and clear interpretation, which is this: that we ought to love every person, both friend and foe, adding thereto, what benefit we shall have thereby, and what disadvantage by doing the contrary. What thing can we wish so good for us as the eternal heavenly Father to repute and take us for his children? And this shall we be sure of (says Christ) if we love everyone without exception. And if we do otherwise, he says, we are no better than the Pharisees, publicans, and heathen, and shall have our reward with them, that is, to be excluded from the number of God's elect children, and from his everlasting inheritance in heaven. A SERMON OF CHRISTIAN LOVE AND CHARITY.[22]

WHAT IT MEANS TO BE PERFECT LIKE THE FATHER. WOLFGANG MUSCULUS: He returns to the previous reference about the paternal nature referred to, and he repeats it as a conclusion instead, saying, "You will be perfect." Perfection of a thing is nothing other than the parts of it fully consummated. But it seems that we do not assume the teaching of perfection to all who are in God, but as we stand together in the matter about which it is taught. Otherwise, how would he teach to us, as we stand before God in complete perfection? It is brought closest from loving. It teaches his perfection. A pattern of that one is promised in God the heavenly Father. And this not so that we love only such as those, but that just as he loves not only those who are friends and grateful but even enemies and reprobates, so also we might fulfill not only one part of loving, which concerns friends, but also another which extends to enemies. Whoever loves only friends is imperfectly good; whoever indeed even loves his enemies, as he excludes no one from his own loving, thus insofar as he is perfect in loving just as also our heavenly Father is perfect. Those who respond this way think these teachings of Christ do not relate to all but only to those who are perfect in standing—clerics and monks. Or are only they sons of God? Is God only the Father of these? COMMENTARY ON MATTHEW.[23]

---

[21]Carter, *A Plaine and Compendious Exposition of Christ's Sermon in the Mount* (1627), 49*.

[22]Cranmer, *Certayne Sermons* (1547), K4 r.
[23]Musculus, *In Evangelistam Matthaeum Commenarii* (1556), 127.

6:1-18 GIVING, PRAYING, FASTING

"Beware of practicing your righteousness before other people in order to be seen by them, for then you will have no reward from your Father who is in heaven.

²"Thus, when you give to the needy, sound no trumpet before you, as the hypocrites do in the synagogues and in the streets, that they may be praised by others. Truly, I say to you, they have received their reward. ³But when you give to the needy, do not let your left hand know what your right hand is doing, ⁴so that your giving may be in secret. And your Father who sees in secret will reward you.

⁵"And when you pray, you must not be like the hypocrites. For they love to stand and pray in the synagogues and at the street corners, that they may be seen by others. Truly, I say to you, they have received their reward. ⁶But when you pray, go into your room and shut the door and pray to your Father who is in secret. And your Father who sees in secret will reward you.

⁷"And when you pray, do not heap up empty phrases as the Gentiles do, for they think that they will be heard for their many words. ⁸Do not be like them, for your Father knows what you need before you ask him. ⁹Pray then like this:

"Our Father in heaven,
 hallowed be your name.ᵃ
¹⁰Your kingdom come,
 your will be done,ᵇ
  on earth as it is in heaven.
¹¹Give us this day our daily bread,ᶜ
¹²and forgive us our debts,
  as we also have forgiven our debtors.
¹³And lead us not into temptation,
 but deliver us from evil.ᵈ

¹⁴For if you forgive others their trespasses, your heavenly Father will also forgive you, ¹⁵but if you do not forgive others their trespasses, neither will your Father forgive your trespasses.

¹⁶"And when you fast, do not look gloomy like the hypocrites, for they disfigure their faces that their fasting may be seen by others. Truly, I say to you, they have received their reward. ¹⁷But when you fast, anoint your head and wash your face, ¹⁸that your fasting may not be seen by others but by your Father who is in secret. And your Father who sees in secret will reward you."

a Or Let your name be kept holy, or Let your name be treated with reverence   b Or Let your kingdom come, let your will be done   c Or our bread for tomorrow
d Or the evil one; some manuscripts add For yours is the kingdom and the power and the glory, forever. Amen

---

OVERVIEW: Matthew 6 begins with a warning that Jesus' disciples must not do their righteous deeds in order to be noticed by others or they will receive no reward from their heavenly Father. The reformers recognize that like the previous chapter, Jesus is dealing with motives. The self-righteousness that had infected the Pharisees' doctrine had contaminated the motives of their piety as well. Calvin notes that Jesus' instructions here seem contradictory to Matthew 5, where Jesus encouraged public deeds that would prompt glory to the Father who is in heaven (Mt 5:16). Jesus did not prohibit any act of public giving.

Instead his intention was to remedy the selfish ambition lurking behind every public gift. Jesus warns against public piety motivated by the accolades of others.

In contrast to the displays of public prayer by the Jewish leaders (craving attention) or the Gentiles (empty repetitions), Jesus' disciples are to pray in the heartfelt manner of the model prayer. As elsewhere in the Sermon on the Mount, the motive of the one praying is crucial. Regarding the manner of prayer, Bullinger and Erasmus agree that Jesus' use of the "secret chamber" as the ideal place of prayer was figurative. A fervent prayer offered earnestly to God in humility was offered in the "chamber" regardless of location. The structure and simplicity of the prayer highlights its two most prominent themes: the glory of God and the forgiveness of sins.

The reformers explain how the opening address of the prayer draws the attention to the personal nature of God. By beginning with hallowing God's name, Jesus instructs his disciples that glorifying God should be the chief desire in prayer. Once a person has submitted to the Lord's dominion, then that disciple can desire for God's will to be done. God's mysterious will cannot be thwarted, but his revealed will comes to fruition through the obedience of his people. Bucer describes that "like it is in heaven" is praying that humans would have a mindset similar to the angels. The angels have seen the display of God's will in heaven and thereby do not hesitate to obey him in all matters.

The commentators make various observations on the order of the petitions, including the recognition of the need for sustenance from the Lord preceding the spiritual need for forgiveness. They also assert that the person who petitions for forgiveness should follow that petition with one for strength to abstain from further evil. The need for forgiveness from God and from each other connects the model prayer with the brief, concluding epilogue that follows.

In phrases that parallel his instructions on giving (Mt 6:2-4) and prayer (Mt 6:5-6), Jesus cautions against perfunctory fasts. The reformers often expand the description of fasting beyond just abstaining from food or drink. Most agree that the specific purpose of the fast is to restrain the passions of the flesh and therefore will not have a set form that works in every private or public setting. Not surprisingly, Luther indicates that fasting can cut off a person externally from lusts, but it is faith that does so inwardly.

6:1-4 *Giving to the Poor*

A RIGHTEOUS CORRECTION. MARTIN LUTHER: So far, the Lord Christ has been denouncing the false teachings and interpretations of Scripture that had led people to refrain from sinning with their fists while their hearts remained completely impure within, and he has been demonstrating and emphasizing the true interpretation of the Scriptures and the law. Now he goes on from their teaching to denounce their life as well. He attacks their good works, and he refuses to concede that they have anything good either in their teaching or in their works. This in spite of the fact that, as holy people, they taught the Scriptures every day, that they did good works, and that they had a reputation as the finest kernel of the whole Jewish people and the holiest people on earth. The whole world had to look to them as the mirror and pattern according to which they should live, just as the only place to look for true doctrine and life until now has been among our clergy, the priests, and monks. Yet now they are being rebuked by the gospel; and everyone sees that neither their teaching nor their life has been right, but that they have been misleading and deceiving both themselves and the people.

Now, a sermon is really a vexing thing if it comes into the world in order to deprive these holy people of their claims to everything right and good, and it earns the opposition and the intolerance of the world. But this does not embarrass the Holy Spirit. He goes right ahead with his denunciation of both teaching and life, in keeping with his office, wherever he may come. Both need to be denounced. It is true that where teaching is not right, there it is impossible for life to be right and good either, since life must let itself be controlled and directed by teaching. Whatever is done and accomplished on such a basis will only be a bypath and a detour, aggravated by the fact that the teaching persists in the impression and the notion that it is a true and divine teaching that points and leads to heaven, and that the works keep the title "good works," though they pay attention only to the action of the hands. Thus, they imagined that their life was satisfactory and good if only they did the works, contributed alms generously, fasted, and prayed, regardless of how their heart stood in relation to God. In addition, they were polluted by the filthy habit of doing it all only to have the people see them and give them honor and glory for it. That is why Christ here rebukes and completely rejects it. SERMON ON THE MOUNT.[1]

GIVING WITHOUT HYPOCRISY. WILLIAM BURTON: The drift of our Savior Christ both in this chapter and in the chapter following is all one with that which he had in the former. Namely, to teach his followers that if they would enter into the kingdom of heaven, it is necessary that their righteousness exceed the righteousness of the scribes and Pharisees; only with this difference. In the former he confutes the doctrine of the scribes and Pharisees, and in these two he notes and condemns their life and hypocrisy. From which observation two things are to be noted. First, that above all things the church must be purged from false doctrine. . . . Second, if the doctrine be refined and thoroughly purged, yet is it not sufficient to the true study of righteousness, unless also the life be rightly instituted, and purged too, and especially from hypocrisy. . . .

The first thing therefore to be taken heed of is all inward desire of vainglory, or worldly praise, and that is forbidden in the first verse, where our Savior says, "Give not to be seen by others," that is, with an intent, purpose, or desire that others should see you and commend you for it. Public giving is not forbidden, for Christ says, "Let your lights shine before others, that they may see. . . ." But vainglorious giving in public is forbidden, and therefore he does not simply say, "Do not give your alms before others," but adds, "to be seen by others," condemning that end which is first in heart though last in act. So in Matthew 5:16, he says not, "Let your light so shine before others, that they may see your good works, and glorify you," but "that they seeing your good works may glorify God, your heavenly Father," who works both the will and the deed. So then we see that it is not simply evil to do good works in the view of others, nay rather it is good so to do, to glorify God, and encourage others. God is much

glorified when his children walk like their Father, being merciful as their heavenly Father is merciful, though not in that degree of mercy, yet in mercy of the like nature, heavenly, free, and harmless. TEN SERMONS.[2]

THE FATHER SEES YOUR GIVING DONE IN SECRET. JOHN CALVIN: "That your alms may be in secret." This statement appears to be opposed to many passages of Scripture, in which we are commanded to edify the brethren by good examples. But if we attend to the design of Christ, we must not give a more extensive meaning to the words. He commands his disciples to devote themselves to good works purely, and without any ambition. In order to do this, he bids them turn away their eyes from the sight of others, and to reckon it enough that their duties are approved by God alone. Such simplicity of views does not at all interfere with anxiety and zeal to promote edification: and, indeed, a little before, he did not expressly forbid them to do good before others, but condemned ostentation.

"Your Father, who sees in secret." He silently glances at a kind of folly, which prevails everywhere among women and men, that they think they have lost their pains, if there have not been many spectators of their virtues. He tells them that God does not need a strong light to perceive good actions: for those things, which appear to be buried in darkness, are open to his view. We have no reason, therefore, to suppose that what escapes the notice and receives not the testimony of others is lost: for "the Lord dwells in the thick darkness." A most appropriate remedy is thus applied for curing the disease of ambition, when he reminds us to fix our eye on God: for this banishes from our minds and will utterly destroy all vainglory. In the second clause, which immediately follows, Christ reminds us that, in looking for the reward of good works, we must wait patiently till the last day, the day of resurrection. Your Father, says he, shall reward you openly. But when? It will be when the dawn of the

---

[1] LW 21:130-31 (WA 32:407-8).

[2] Burton, *Ten Sermons upon . . . the Sixth of Matthew* (1602), 1-2*.

last day shall arise, by which all that is now hidden in darkness shall be revealed. COMMENTARY ON A HARMONY OF THE EVANGELISTS.[3]

6:5-15 *Praying to Our Heavenly Father*

PRAYING TO THE FATHER IN SECRET. HEINRICH BULLINGER: As in reproving the abuse of prayer, he did not properly condemn the place, but rather spoke figuratively after this manner: The Pharisees, with their prayers that they make in the streets, hunt after praise and commendation of the people; so on the contrary part, making mention of a chamber, he [Jesus] meant not that the place of itself makes the prayer either better or worse, but he taught by a figurative speech that we ought to pray with an upright mind, and most free from hunting after the praise of others. For those who pray with a mind not troubled with affections, having regard only to God, pray in their chambers, whether they pray in the church or in the street. For otherwise, the Lord prayed with his disciples in the temple, in the city, in the field, and wheresoever occasion was offered. Also it follows, "And the Father, who sees you in secret, shall reward you openly"—that is to say, the Father, who allows the mind that is not proud but humble and free from ambition, will reward you openly. OF PRAYER.[4]

THE NATURE OF PUBLIC AND PRIVATE PRAYER. DESIDERIUS ERASMUS: It is not ill to give alms sometime before others, or to pray in a multitude and whereas as others resort, but then know not the left hand what the right hand does when the work of charity is not defiled with any affection of worldly vanity. Then you are in your secret chamber when you speak to God with such perfect clarity of mind, as though no one could see you. Those who pray in a multitude of people as earnestly, even more vehemently than if they were alone, they pray in their secret chamber. For the right hand and the left hand or the secret chamber

stand not in the things, but in the affections and desires of the heart.

This also must be considered in prayer. It is the affection and the hearty desire that moves God, not the noise of the lips. And it matters not how long and how loud the prayer is, but how fervent and sincere the affection and desire is. . . . We ought to ask of God the best things, and not all things; and we ought to pray often rather than much and vehemently rather than long; finally, with the heart rather than with voice. Neither always with prescribed and purposed words after the custom of the heathen, but so much as the fervency of the mind and the ravishment toward God does stir and provoke. PARAPHRASES.[5]

AN ORDERED PRAYER. JOHANNES PISCATOR: Further down, this formula of petition, which is customarily called the Lord's Prayer, can be separated into four parts. Of these, the first is the prologue. The second is the listing or exposition of the petitions, which are six in number. Of these, the three earlier petitions rightly consider the glory of God; the three latter petitions closely consider our necessities, first our bodily needs in the fourth petition, then our spiritual needs are treated in the remaining two petitions. In fact, the next-to-last petition is about the forgiveness of former sins and those presently committed by us, and the last petition about our preservation from future sins to which we are truly inclined by nature. The last thing that must be noted in the order of the petitions is this: that the four earlier petitions are almost like affirmations, that is, the first three seek spiritual goods and the fourth seeks bodily goods; but the remaining two are almost like negations, for they in fact pray against spiritual evils. The third part is a confirmation, whose arguments partly stem from a twofold cause: that is by the will of God, which is noted in the word *kingdom*, and by power, for God is able and willing to give those things which we ask. The arguments also stem partly from a final cause, or the effect—namely, the

---

[3]CTS 1:310-11 (CO 45:191-92); citing 2 Chron 6:1.
[4]DHB 184*.

[5]EP 27r*.

glory of God—for we ask whatever we ask from God because of his glory. His glory follows from the favorable response to our requests. The fourth and final part is the epilogue, consisting of the word *Amen*, which speaks of the assurance that God will hear and answer us. Further along, it repeats the reason joined to the fifth petition, and thus the forgiveness of recent offenses is encouraged from the effects. In fact, it is encouraged from a twofold effect: one good and saving, if we forgive recent offenses; another evil and destructive, if we do not forgive. The good effect is the divine forgiveness of our sins, on which eternal life depends. The evil effect is the divine remembrance of our sins, which no doubt follows eternal destruction. LOGICAL ANALYSIS OF MATTHEW.[6]

THE EXCEEDING VALUE OF THE LORD'S PRAYER. JOHN D'ESPAGNE: A prayer used to this present time by all the churches of God, ancient and modern, throughout all the universal world. A prayer dictated by the supreme wisdom of that great and eternal mediator, who presents our prayers to God, and who perfectly knows his Father's mind. The most complete prayer that can be made, summing up all the lawful requests that can be imagined. A prayer that is the epitome, the mirror, and the rule of all others. A prayer that in its wonderful brevity includes so great a plenty and variety of matters, as if it would cause a camel to pass through a needle's eye. A prayer that contains more histories and more mysteries than words. A prayer in sum the most methodical, the most divine that can be framed: For all the parts of this prayer cohere with an admirable symmetry. All of it is exactly made, in measure and proportion: All of it is full of torches that enlighten each other. One petition relates to another, and these same men confess that neither all the wits of the earth nor all the angels of heaven were ever capable to dictate the like. THE USE OF THE LORD'S PRAYER.[7]

INVOKING OUR GRACIOUS, HEAVENLY FATHER. BALTHASAR HUBMAIER: O gracious Father, we once again confess ourselves captive that we are in the kingdom of sin, of the devil, hell, and eternal death; but Father, we shout and call to you as to our most beloved Father, that you might soon come to us with your kingdom of grace, peace, joy, and eternal blessedness. Come to our help, O gracious Father; for without you, we are completely miserable, troubled, and forsaken. . . . "Lead us not into temptation." O heavenly Father! Behold the great anxiety, desolation, misery, persecution, and tribulation that is inflicted upon us here on earth. Consider also our human weakness. Therefore, O sweet Father, we pray to you for the sake of your fatherly love that you might not abandon us in our pain and suffering and that we might not be overcome, nor fall away from your holy Word. Let us not be tested harder than we are able to bear. We are weak and impotent, and our enemies are strong, powerful, and cruel. You know that, O merciful Father. "But deliver us from evil." From sin, from the devil, from our own body, which is our greatest enemy, and also from everything that hinders our access to you. Likewise, grant to us everything that furthers us toward you, for yours is the authority and the power and the glory in eternity. A BRIEF "OUR FATHER."[8]

A FATHER TO BELIEVERS. JUAN MALDONADO: Christ has laid his commands on us that we do not address God each as if he were his own Father alone. To effect this, he has given us not a private prayer but the public one of the whole church; so that when we pray, we pray to God as one member of the whole church. Whoever does otherwise may indeed pray to God, but he will most assuredly not obtain his prayer.

It has been observed on the passage that the words show the difference between Christ and ourselves. We do not call God "my Father," but "our Father." Christ calls him not "our Father," but "my Father." For in the sense in which he is "our Father"

---

[6]Piscator, *Analysis Logica Evangelii secundum Matthaeum* (1594), 96-97.
[7]D'Espagne, *The Use of the Lord's Prayer* (1646), 12-13*.

[8]CRR 5:242-43*.

he is the Father of all in common. For he created all, he preserves all, he supports all, and, as far as in him lies, he has redeemed all.

But in the sense in which he is the Father of Christ he is the Father of no other. For he is his Father, not as he created him, but as he begot him of his own essence, and, therefore, as St. Ambrose[†] says, Christ calls him, in a peculiar manner, his Father. We call him our Father in a general sense. He begot Christ; he created us. Another and more peculiar reason why we call God "Father" and "our Father" may be that through Christ we have been regenerated. For it is clear that they who have never been baptized and who do not believe in Christ cannot use this prayer; and yet they have been created, supported, redeemed by God. We do not, then, call God "our Father" because he has only created, supported, and redeemed us, but also because he has regenerated us through faith and the grace of baptism. . . . When, therefore, we call God "our Father," we are distinguished not only from Christ but also from unbelievers. We call God our Father, as he is the Father of those who believe and not of those who believe not. Is he not, then, the Father of all? Most assuredly he is so; but he is the Father, in a peculiar manner, of those who, through faith in Christ, are made one body with him. We are, therefore, a mean between Christ and unbelievers. Christ is the Son of God by essence; unbelievers are so, as it were, spuriously, because, though created by him, and made after his Image, they are sons by nature, and as if of the bondwoman; they are not so by grace, and as if of the free woman. They are like Ishmael by natural strength, not like Isaac by supernatural grace. We are neither sons by nature like Christ, nor spurious sons like unbelievers, but sons adopted and legitimate; otherwise, we could not be the sons of God and joint heirs of Christ. A COMMENTARY ON THE HOLY GOSPELS.[9]

[9]JMG 196-98; citing Jn 1:12; Eph 4:6; Rom 8:17. [†]Ambrose considers the relationship between the Father and the Son at length in *Exposition of the Christian Faith*, NPNF[2] 10:199-314.

OUR FATHER WHO IS IN HEAVEN. MARTIN CHEMNITZ: First, these words ["our Father"] do give us to understand that prayer ought not to be such a bare desire in a wishing manner as people are wont to say, "Would God this good might happen unto me . . . God forbid," and such like; but we must expressly name him of whom we desire to have our request granted to us. And not in general terms only, as when we say, "God grant, God forbid," but we must by name speak to and call on him, that our prayer may be directed to him [our Father] as it were in communication. . . .

Second, these words do admonish us that prayer or invocation is not to be directed to any creature, but only to the heavenly Father; so as we may not direct our prayer to them, of whom we are sure their spirits do live with God. For the name "Father" is also opposed to them. . . .

Third, those words do teach us that we must so conceive of God and speak to God in prayer as he has revealed his essence unto us in his Word. For the heathen when they go to pray, they think of a God who is eternal, the Creator, almighty, but who that God is they know not. But we are taught by these words to make a difference between our calling upon God and the prayers of the heathen; and to think that we call upon that God who has thus made known his being to us in his Word, that he is the Father, the Son, and the Holy Ghost. . . .

Fourth, the word "Father" also may very well be understood personally, or in relation for the person of the Father. . . . So by these words, that we are not commanded to call God a lord, just, great, almighty, terrible, but our Father, is stirred up in those which pray confidence that they shall be heard and obtain their requests. . . .

Fifth, whereas we do not only say ["Father," but "our Father"] this brings us to the consideration of that which Christ says, to wit, that we should conceive and think that God who is by nature the Father of Christ is for his sake by grace our Father also, not by nature but by adoption. And lest we should think that he were only the Father of some few, who are endued with great virtues and excellent gifts; therefore when we say ["our Father"] we do include the whole body of believers, wherein all the members are not alike. A SUBSTANTIAL AND GODLY EXPOSITION.[10]

HALLOWED BE THE NAME ABOVE ALL NAMES. KATHARINA SCHÜTZ ZELL: "Your name be hallowed." It will also be holy in us, that is, your (only) natural Son Jesus Christ, who is the true name, image, and being of your hidden Godhead, through whom you have revealed yourself to the world and have allowed your mercy to be seen and made your will known to us. You have also given him a name above all names, that in his name we might pray to you and the Holy Spirit would be given to us and that through faith in his name all people might benefit and become children of God. That name is holy: in it the nations hope and receive forgiveness of sins; everyone must kneel to that name, and there is no other name given to human beings by which we may be saved. O God and Father, help us to hallow this name, to magnify and honor it, set apart and distinguish it from others, to call on it, love, and confess it above all names, that name which is Jesus Christ, who saves his people from their sins. Grant also, dear Father, that we may not boast of your name without cause (in a false hypocritical folly and show of praising your grace and righteousness); grant that we may not enjoy being called by the name of your Christ while still conducting our whole like contrary to it and sinning against the other words of your commandments. If we did that, our name would be struck from the book of life. Even if we said, "Have we not done many deeds in your name?" you would answer, "I do not know you, depart from me." But grant us to acknowledge your holy name, to honor it, to call on it and confess it in truth, that we may be saved.

Grant also, O Lord and Father, that we may not swear by your holy name falsely, in lying fashion, or unnecessarily. Let us not speak or conduct ourselves in a mocking or scandalous way toward you or your name, word, and work, or also your whole kingdom, so that we may not cause anyone to be scandalized against you and your child Jesus or your name to be slandered through us. But grant that we may conduct our lives so that your name may be acknowledged and praised in us, that people may see our conduct and repent, and you, Father in heaven, may be praised by that. Grant that we may thus overcome the world with its desires, that our names may not be struck from your book of life but may stand written in heaven and also be confessed by Christ our Lord before you and your angels. THE MISERERE PSALM.[11]

HALLOWED BE YOUR NAME. RICHARD BERNARD: The first petition. This concerns God's glory and is therefore in the first place to teach that God's glory chiefly is to be preferred in our desires, "Hallowed be your name." In this petition we are taught to desire to acknowledge, ascribe, and to procure holiness to be given to the Lord in those things by which he makes himself known to us, as by a name—that is, his titles, attributes, words, and works—whence we learn first that God has made himself known to us. Second, that holiness belongs to him. Third, that such things are to be thought of, spoken, and done by us, as his name may receive glory. Fourth, that therefore such things are to be avoided, as may cause his name to be blasphemed and polluted among the wicked. Fifth, that sorrow should possess our hearts to see God dishonored; for as our desire should be to see his name glorified, so grief should arise in us to see his name abused. THE GOOD MAN'S GRACE.[12]

THE IMPORTANCE OF THE FATHER'S NAME. HENRY BULL: Your name is that by which you are known, for names serve to discern and know one thing from another. Now though you are known by your creatures, yet in this our corrupt state they serve but to make us excuseless. Therefore, most

---

[10]Chemnitz, *A Substantial and Godly Exposition of the . . . Lord's Praier,* 22-31*.

[11]Zell, *Church Mother,* 159-60 (KSZ 351-52); citing Col 1:15; Phil 2:9-10; Acts 4:12; Mt 1:21; Rev 3:5; Mt 7:22-23; Ex 20:7; Deut 5:11; Mt 18:6; Mal 1:11-12; 1 Jn 2:15-16, 4:4; Rev 3:5.
[12]Bernard, *The Good Man's Grace* (1621), B1.

properly, lively, and comfortably you are known by your holy Word, and especially by your promise of grace, and freely pardoning and receiving us into your favor for Christ Jesus' sake. For which goodness in Christ, you are praised and magnified according to your name, that is, so much as women and men know you in Christ, they magnify you and praise you, which here you call hallowing or sanctifying; not that you are the more holy in respect of yourself, but in respect of men and women who the more they know you, the more they cannot but sanctify you. . . .

By reason hereof, I see that I am far from this desire and lamentation that is in your children. I see my ignorance of the true knowledge of you and your name, for else it had not needed you so by your Word to have revealed yourself. I see also my own ignorance of the excellency of the same, for else would you not have told me that the sanctifying of your name is the chiefest thing your require of every person. Again, I see my great want of holiness, for else you need not to teach me to seek and pray for that I want not. Moreover, I see my great perversity, which would not seek at your hands for sanctification, although I see my need thereof. For that which you would not have commanded me to pray, if I seeing my want would have prayed to you for the same. Last of all, I see your wonderful goodness, which will undoubtedly give to me sanctification and holiness: for you would not that I should ask for that thing that you will not give me. Christian Prayers and Holy Meditations.[13]

Your Kingdom Come. John Smyth: This petition in order of nature goes before the third, as the cause before the effect; for God's kingdom is that only means which enables us to obey his will. First, God must erect his kingdom in our hearts, and we must be his subjects before we can yield obedience to his laws; from which order arises this instruction: That a person can never obey God's will till they have God's grace; or a person can never keep God's laws till they be God's subject, and God be their Lord and king to rule and overrule them; or (which is all one in effect) good works proceed from grace; or without faith (which is the root of grace) it is impossible to please God; or whatsoever is not of faith is sin; or the end of the commandment is love, out of a pure heart, and a good conscience and faith unstained; and the necessary consequence of this doctrine is that whatsoever a person does, wanting grace, is sin; whether they be actions natural, civil, or religious; for some preachers and prophets in the day of judgment shall be found workers of iniquity. . . .

God's kingdom is erected and set up generally and specially: Generally, when it is entertained by public consent in a country or kingdom; and that is when the magistrate by law establishes the worship of God according to the word and execution is done accordingly; and when the ministers in their ministry teach and minister the word and worship of God established. Specially, the kingdom of God is established or erected, when people by the Word of God are converted to the faith, and outwardly make profession thereof. Thus, God's kingdom is set up. A Pattern of True Prayer.[14]

The Coming of the Kingdom. Martin Luther: In the first petition we prayed about God's name and honor, that God would prevent the world from using his glory and name to dress up its lies and wickedness but would instead keep his name sacred and holy in both teaching and life so that he may be praised and exalted in us. In the same way in this petition, we ask that his kingdom may come. Just as God's name is holy in itself and yet we pray that it may be holy among us, so also his kingdom comes of itself without our prayer, and yet we pray that it may come to us, that is, that it may prevail among us and with us, so that we may be a part of those among whom his name is hallowed and his kingdom flourishes.

---

[13]Bull, *Christian Prayers and Holy Meditations* (1578), 58-60*.

[14]Smyth, *A Paterne of True Prayer* (1605), 87, 91-92.

What is the kingdom of God? Answer: Simply what we heard above in the creed, namely, that God sent his Son, Christ our Lord, into the world to redeem and deliver us from the power of the devil, to bring us to himself and to rule us as a king of righteousness, life, and salvation against sin, death, and an evil conscience. To this end he also gave his Holy Spirit to deliver this to us through his holy Word and to enlighten and strengthen us in faith by his power.

We may ask here at the outset that all this may be realized in us and that his name may be praised through God's holy Word and Christian living. This we ask, both in order that we who have accepted it may remain faithful and grow daily in it and also in order that it may find approval and gain followers among other people and advance with power throughout the world. In this way many, led by the Holy Spirit, may come into the kingdom of grace and become partakers of redemption, so that we may all remain together eternally in this kingdom that has now begun.

"The coming of God's kingdom to us" takes place in two ways: First, it comes here, in time, through the Word and faith, and second, in eternity, it comes through the final revelation. Now, we ask for both of these things: that it may come to those who are not yet in it and that, by daily growth here and in eternal life hereafter, it may come to us who have attained it. All this is nothing more than to say, "Dear Father, we ask you first to give us your Word, so that the gospel may be properly preached throughout the world and then that it may also be received in faith and may work and dwell in us, so that your kingdom may pervade among us through the Word and the power of the Holy Spirit and the devil's kingdom may be destroyed, so that he may have no right or power over us until finally his kingdom is utterly eradicated and sin, death, and hell wiped out, that we may live forever in perfect righteousness and blessedness." THE LARGE CATECHISM.[15]

MAY WE BE THE CHILDREN OF YOUR KINGDOM. KATHARINA SCHÜTZ ZELL: O dear Father, grant that all that the enemy has in us may be killed and driven out; that we may be the children of your kingdom and not cast out; that we may not fail to hear because we do not pay attention, when today we hear your voice through Jesus Christ as he says, "Repent, the kingdom of God has come near." O God, help us to recognize and flee from the kingdom of the devil, to recognize and let go of the perishable kingdom of the world, for both are enemies that oppose you. But may we seek with seriousness and not hypocrisy and find your good, enduring, imperishable kingdom and its righteousness, that we may be admitted to it and become citizens and receive wisdom and all that we need from you.

O dear God, help us: we are so far from your kingdom! Grant that we may not be so casual and stiff-necked toward you and your kingdom, so that when you come again you may not judge us to be your enemies, who would not allow you to rule over us. But grant that we may receive and obey you from the heart and be the folk of your kingdom; that through your Holy Spirit you may rule and be Lord in our hearts, souls, bodies, and consciences; that your word and commandment may live in us. For you are the King of honored lords, and Lord of the true kingdom, whom we all must acknowledge, seek, honor, fear, and love, to whom alone we should pray and to whom we should adhere as our true Lord, Ruler, and King. THE MISERERE PSALM.[16]

THE WILL OF GOD. PIERRE VIRET: You must here consider God's will, in that manner as we have considered his ruling . . . in speaking of his reign. We must consider of it then in two ways. First, we must consider of it generally, inasmuch as it concerns the universal order of all things. For, in that manner, there is nothing that does not follow his will. For, if he were not willing, nothing that is

---

[15]Kolb and Wengert, eds., *Book of Concord*, 446-47*.

[16]Zell, *Church Mother*, 160-61 (KSZ 352-53); Mt 4:17; 6:33; Lk 19:27.

done should be done, be it good or evil. For, as the apostle says, "Who shall resist his will?" But when we speak of God's will, in accordance with the holy Scriptures, we do consider it in that manner. For, if we took it in that sort, there would never be so great wickedness, neither sin so abominable, which we could not excuse and impute the fault to God. But when we speak of God's will, we speak of God's will, which is revealed to us by his Word, and which pertains to every one of our vocations, and to the first perfect order, which God has put in all his creatures. This is the will to which we must only consider because it relates to us and belongs to us. For the other, which is not revealed to us, surpasses the capacity of our understandings. Wherefore we are not directed to inquire and search too curiously, but to leave to him all that responsibility, and to content ourselves with that which he has revealed to us and commanded of us. Notwithstanding that he does nothing, but by that general and universal will of God, which respects generally the universal order of all creatures, yet nevertheless he does many things against that revealed will, which relates to us nearer, and which is revealed to us, in order to rule all our vocations and affections. . . .

When we ask of God that his will be done in earth as it is in heaven, in desiring that this perfect obedience be given to him, by which his name is sanctified and his kingdom advanced, we pray for all the estates which are among men and women, to the end that God has called them to his kingdom. [Praying] that he would direct them in the same by his Holy Spirit, that all of them may make their vocations to serve God's will, doing that for which God has ordained them, as the angels do in heaven. EXPOSITION OF THE LORD'S PRAYER.[17]

YOUR WILL BE DONE. MARTIN BUCER: "Your will be done. . . ." It is as if we should say, "O God, we prayed that your kingdom, that is, the heavenly kingdom, may come, so that when the

strong-armed man has been cast out by your Christ, we may adore and follow you, our one King. From this, our flesh most violently calls us back and holds us back. Grant, therefore, after [making us] into citizens of your kingdom, to take us into heaven, so that thus we may comply with your will on earth from our heart, just as those [angels] do in heaven. In your distinctly spiritual beings, in which you fully rule, your will is obeyed with the highest pleasure. Therefore, may the law of our members not be so powerful in us that we resist your law. The strength of foul desire has done what it does, so that the good that we wish to do, we do not do, and we do the evil thing that we hate. Give that good will [to us], so that willing and happy, we may submit ourselves in everything to your commands, which certainly Psalm 110 has foretold about your own people. . . ."

Further on after this, he joins "as it is in heaven," admonishing heavenly minds to focus on doing the will of the Father most promptly, which idea appears to have been obtained from Psalm 103, where it is sung, "Praise God all his hosts, his ministers, who carry out his pleasure." Since those angels had known nothing to be impossible so far, because God had willed to be better, thus they are eager to carry out his command with the greatest alacrity. Therefore, it is fitting to pray for the same thing, so that this eagerness may also infect us. Therefore, the prayer of spiritual beings agrees in these things, and as long as we pray for these things, the glory of the Lord is shown forth in us in our prayer. For his own name is indeed not able to be sanctified and glorified among us, unless he himself reigns among us by his own good and saving Spirit, who wherever he prevails over us, forms us thus to the will of the Father, so that we have nothing more important than to obey him and to follow him in all things, crucifying our own will continually. We have already said something in chapter 3 about why the spiritual kingdom of God, and those holy beings, obedient to God in all things, may be called heaven in the passage: "Those heavens are

---

[17]Viret, *Exposition Familière de L'oraison de Nostre Seigneur Jesus*, 318-19, 324-25.

opened" . . . following the petition for bodily needs. COMMENTARY ON MATTHEW 6:10.[18]

KNOWING AND DOING GOD'S WILL. THOMAS WATSON: We pray for two things. First, for active obedience that we may do God's will actively in what he commands. Second, for passive [obedience] that we may submit to God's will patiently in what he inflicts. We pray that we may do God's will actively, subscribe to all his commands, believe in Jesus the cardinal grace, lead holy lives. So we pray that we may actively obey God's will. This is the sum of all religion, the two tables epitomized, "The doing of God's will. Your will be done." We must know God's will before we can do it; knowledge is the eye that must direct the foot of obedience. At Athens there was an altar set up "To the unknown God." It is as bad to offer the blind to God as the dead. Knowledge is the pillar of fire to give light to practice, but though knowledge is requisite, yet the knowing of God's will is not enough without doing of his will: "Your will be done." If one had a system of divinity in his head, if he had "all knowledge," yet if obedience were wanting, his knowledge were lame and would not carry him to heaven. Knowing God's will may make a person admired, but it is doing God's will that makes them blessed; knowing God's will without doing it will not crown us with happiness. A BODY OF PRACTICAL DIVINITY.[19]

GIVE US TODAY OUR DAILY BREAD. AMANDUS POLANUS VON POLANSDORF: The fourth petition is this: Give us this day our daily bread. In it we ask the sustenance and nourishment of this temporal life. Daily bread is whatsoever is necessary for the upholding and preservation of this present life. God, indeed, has commanded us to get it with the labor of our hands, but yet we ask it of God, because neither our labor, neither those things which are gotten by our labor, do or can profit us without God's blessing, which itself also is part of daily bread. But if you are rich and abounding, yet as if you were needy, pray daily for the blessed use of your riches, think that full cellars and full storehouses or chests may be suddenly emptied, except they be kept by the Lord's hand: yea except the Lord shall season with his blessing the meat and drink that we take in, they that eat shall starve for hunger, and they that drink shall wax dry with thirst. You shall eat and not be satisfied.

Now we name it our bread indeed and yet we ask that God would give it us, because that by the gift of God it is become ours: neither can anything be ours nor become ours except God give it. We name it our bread, that so being content with that, we might not desire another man's. And we call it our bread and not mine, that so everyone might know that they ought to ask bread necessary not for themselves alone, but for their neighbor also.

Last, we ask daily bread and pray that the same may be daily given us for four causes. First, that a distrustful carefulness for tomorrow might be taken out of our minds. Second, that we might remember that for daily bread we have need of daily prayers. Third, that we might be daily admonished of the shortness of this our bodily life, as though we should live today only. Fourth, that we might not immoderately and greedily desire or covet anything besides that which God has prescribed.

The fifth petition is this: And forgive us our trespasses, as we forgive those that trespass against us. In it we ask the forgiveness of sins, or justification. And when God, in his eternal covenant, had willingly and freely promised us forgiveness of sins, he has also bound us to himself by the answering again of a good conscience to forgive our brethren. So that he is not bound to keep his promise with us, except we also continue in the obligation, covenant, or condition to be performed on our part.

Our forgiving therefore is not a cause of God's forgiving, for God first has freely promised us forgiveness, when as yet we were his enemies; and besides he has bound us to himself to pardon our

---

[18]Bucer, *In Sacra Quatuor Evangelia, Enarrationes Perpetuae* (1536), 164-65; citing Rom 7:18-19.
[19]Watson, *A Body of Practical Divinity* (1692), 483*; Acts 17:23; 1 Cor 13:2.

brethren also. The cause cannot be after his proper effect. But our forgiving of them is after God's forgiving of us. Therefore, our forgiving is not the cause of God's forgiving. The assumption is certain, for they only can pardon their brethren, to whom God has forgiven their sins; and by this testimony we feel in our hearts that our sins are pardoned us if we be fully purposed with ourselves from our hearts to pardon all those who have offended us. THE SUBSTANCE OF CHRISTIAN RELIGION.[20]

FEED US WITH SPIRITUAL AND PHYSICAL BREAD. KATHARINA SCHÜTZ ZELL: Dear Father, grant to us also wise, faithful preachers, who are faithful stewards, who will not preach to us their own inclinations but will proclaim your word, revealed from your mouth through Jesus Christ, and who at the right time will spread forth that same appropriate food. Oh, dear Father, give them also a willing spirit and strong faith so they may not become listless, dull, and tired in their work and then, because of that, their work comes to be reviled and ungratefully received on earth. Grant that they may not therefore give up and think to go away and abandon us, as if they were working to no purpose. But rather let them be like faithful servants to whom the householder earnestly commended his children and relatives, and to whom he gave command to direct the children and relatives and correct all disobedience. Let them bear abuse and suffering patiently to the end in the certain hope for holy perseverance and let them conquer in faith. . . .

Grant also, O holy Father, that as we acknowledge you and him whom you sent, Jesus Christ, and as we have received him in faith and through him have given ourselves to you in obedience as also being your children and have offered you our bodies, and as we have found our life in his death and his death truly lives in our hearts—grant then that we also may be worthy to come together to celebrate the memorial of your love and the obedience of Jesus Christ, to break the bread and to drink the cup of thanksgiving, to be fed in remembrance of him, that it may be the communion of the body and blood of Jesus Christ for the forgiveness of sins, in the communion of the saints. And so we may celebrate a living memorial of his death and proclaim it until he comes again, and in the Supper we may truly confess that his body is there given and broken for us and the record of our sins is wiped out and hung on the cross. . . .

Feed us, also, O Lord, with the daily physical bread of our body's work, according to your word. Do not feed us with excess, that our flesh, desire, and wantonness may not proudly rise up against you and you be despised and forgotten in your members. Also do not let us lack what we need, so that we fall into impatience and revile you, but supply our need like a faithful Father, as Solomon asked you. Grant that we may not defraud and strangle the poor with greed, usury, cheating, and unfair money dealings against your command or seek to abuse neighbors and bring them to the brink of ruin. If we ate our bread at their expense we would—with a curse from your wrath—eat it to our eternal destruction and punishment. Therefore, O God and Father, grant your blessing and benediction on the work of our hands, that through it we may nourish ourselves according to your command, acknowledge and praise you in it, and according to your command remember our neighbors in their need and feed them, so that they also may be protected from impatience and from denying you. And grant that we may always enjoy our food with thanks, discipline, and hallowing of your name, to the building up of your kingdom and fulfilling of your will and that we may never enjoy it to the increase of your wrath, the corruption of our souls and illness of our bodies, and the injury of neighbors—as has very often happened. May you keep that away from us and protect us henceforth as a Father. THE MISERERE PSALM.[21]

---

[20]Polansdorf, *The Substance of Christian Religion* (1595), 204-7; citing Ezek 4:14; Lev 26:26.

[21]Zell, *Church Mother*, 163-67 (KSZ 354-58); Mt 24:45; Jn 17:3; 1 Cor 11:17, 24-27; 10:16; Col 2:14; Prov 30:8-9; Ex 22:25-31; 1 Cor 11:29; Mt 6:9-10.

FORGIVE US OUR DEBTS. WILLIAM PERKINS: This is the fifth petition and the second of those that concern ourselves. In the former we craved temporal blessings; in this and the next that follows, we crave spiritual blessings. Where we may note that seeing there are two petitions that concern spiritual things, and but one for temporal; that the care for our souls must be double to the care of our bodies. In the world women and men care for their bodies, their hearts are set for wealth and promotion; they can be content to hear the word on the Sabbath, yet neither then nor in the weekday do they lay it up in their hearts and practice it, which argues that they have little or no care for their souls. . . . The order of the Holy Ghost in these petitions is wonderful; for the Lord considers the dullness and backwardness of people's natures. Therefore, he trains them up, and draws them on by little, even as a schoolmaster does his young scholars, propounding to them some elements and principles, and so carrying them to higher points. For the former petition is a step or degree to these two following. The one who will rest on God's mercy for the pardon of their sins must first of all rest on God's providence for this life, and the one who cannot put their trust in God for the provision of meat and drink, how shall they trust in God's mercy for the salvation of their soul? Here we may see the faith of the worldly: they say that God is merciful and that they believe in Christ; which how can it be true, seeing in lesser matters, as meat and drink, they distrust God, as appears by their covetousness? AN EXPOSITION OF THE LORD'S PRAYER.[22]

THE SIGNIFICANCE OF FORGIVING OTHERS. JOHN BRADFORD: By our "debts" is understood not only things we have done, but the omission and leaving undone of the good things we ought to do. By "our" is not only understood the particular sins of one, but also generally the sins of all and every one of your church. By "forgiveness" is understood free pardon and remission of sins by the merits and deserts of your dear son Jesus Christ, who gave himself a ransom for us. By our forgiving of others' offenses toward us is understood your goodwill; not only that it pleases you that we should live in love and amity but also that you would have us to be certain of your pardoning us of our sins: for as certain as we are that we pardon those who offend us, so certain should we be that you do pardon us, whereof the forgiving our trespassers is, as it were, a sacrament to us.

So that by this petition I am taught to see that your children, although by imputation they be pure from sin, yet they acknowledge sin to be and remain in them; and therefore, do they pray for the remission and forgiveness of the same. Again, I am taught hereby to see how your children consider and take to heart not only the evils they do but also the good they leave undone; and therefore, they pray to you heartily for pardon. Moreover, I am here taught to see that your children are careful for others and for their trespasses, and therefore pray that they might be pardoned, in saying "our sins," and not "my sins." Besides this I am taught here to see how your children not only forgive all that offend them but also pray for the pardoning of the offenses of their enemies and such as offend them; so far are they from maliciousness, pride, revenge, and so on. Last of all, I am taught to see how merciful you are who will have me to ask pardon: whereof you would that we should in no point doubt but be most assured that for Christ's sake you hear us and that not only for ourselves but also for many others; for you do not command us to ask for anything you will not give us. GODLY MEDITATIONS ON THE LORD'S PRAYER.[23]

FORGIVING AND BEING FORGIVEN. JOHN CALVIN: Here Christ only explains the reason why that condition was added: "Forgive us, as we forgive." The reason is that God will not be ready to hear us unless we also show ourselves ready to

---

[22]Perkins, *An Exposition of the Lord's Praier* (1593), 42-43.

[23]Bradford, *Godlie Meditations vpon the Lordes Prayer, the Beleefe, and Ten Commaundementes* (1562), 133-34.

grant forgiveness to those who have offended us. Unless we are harder than iron, this exhortation should soften us and render us disposed to forgive offenses. Except God pardon us every day many sins we know that we are ruined in innumerable ways: and on no other condition does he admit us to pardon but that we pardon our brethren whatever offenses they have committed against us. Those who refuse to forget the injuries that have been done to them devote themselves willingly and deliberately to destruction and knowingly prevent God from forgiving them. COMMENTARY ON A HARMONY OF THE EVANGELISTS.[24]

DO NOT ABANDON US IN TEMPTATIONS AND AFFLICTIONS. KATHARINA SCHÜTZ ZELL: "Lead us not into temptation." That is, do not abandon us in the affliction that comes to us in life or death on account of our sins. Even though we must once descend into hell with Christ and become faint-hearted, you want to lead us out with Christ through the gift of a living faith. But if you did not do that—though your power is able to do it—you would still deserve to be respected, even if you had led us into this for our destruction. Therefore, O dear Father, help us! In the lament and afflictions of our conscience, let us not become exhausted in battle and fall away like Judas and with him bear forever the gnawing undying worm. But with Peter and Mary Magdalene let us weep for our sins, come to repentance, and achieve much love and so be received by you through Jesus Christ, comforted and strengthened, our faith increased and our unbelief helped.

O righteous Father, also help us to be strength-ened and made sure by you to break through the afflictions of this flesh and be able to enter through the narrow gate. Grant us your Spirit of knowledge and strength, that we may not deny you because of the sin that sticks in our flesh with evil desires and unceasingly stirs it up. Therefore, the flesh struggles against the spirit and the spirit against the flesh and its evil fruits. So there is a great

conflict and struggle in us; we have the will, but we do not have the ability to fulfill it, yet both of these are yours. O holy Father, grant us help that in this affliction we may not be servants of sin but may overcome sin and be free children of your grace through Jesus Christ—who, being without sin, became sin for us that he might make us free. However, so long as there is this great struggle in us and we are weak and fleshly, strengthen us, dear Father. Grant us weapons to fight against such affliction and sins so that we may put on your yoke against the cunning assault of the devil and, with our loins girded with truth and the breastplate of righteousness and the shield of faith, we can extinguish all the arrows of the devil and our flesh. By that, dear Father, through your help we may not deny you in the afflictions and temptations of this world, even though poverty, sickness, insult, exile, prison, torment, and death come upon us. O God, we could not pass through these dangers if we were abandoned and if you did not bring us out of them; therefore, help us and grant that we may from the heart entrust ourselves to you and set ourselves willingly to obey you through the crucified Jesus. THE MISERERE PSALM.[25]

THE RELATIONSHIP BETWEEN FORGIVENESS AND TEMPTATION. ARTHUR DENT: This petition is joined with the former to teach us that as we must carefully pray for pardon of sins past, so also we must endeavor to prevent sins to come. We must not fall again into our old sins; neither must we be overtaken with new sins. Having obtained forgiveness of our sins, we desire of the Lord to be present with us that we fall not again into them. Though God forgive us our sins, yet he does not free us of natural corruption, but that still remains and is left behind as the very seed and spawn of new sins so that in respect of this, every one of God's children has his hands full, and enough to do to withstand sin after he is justified and

---

[24]CTS 1:330* (CO 45:203).

[25]Zell, *Church Mother*, 169-70 (KSZ 361-62); citing 1 Pet 3:18-19; Mt 26:47-75; Jn 18:2-27; Mk 9:24, 48; Lk 7:15, 38, 47; Mt 7:13-14; Gal 5:17; Rom 7:18, 6:17; Heb 4:15; 2 Cor 5:21; Eph 6:11-16.

sanctified. Therefore, whereas it may be objected what need he care for temptations that has the pardon of his sins. Answer: Because forgiveness of sins and grievous temptations be inseparable companions, for there is no man in this world so beaten and buffeted with temptations as the penitent sinner that cries for the pardon of his sins. . . . Temptation is nothing else but the enticement of the soul or heart, either by the corruption of human nature or the allurements of the world or the devil to any sin. A LEARNED AND FRUITFUL EXPOSITION ON THE LORD'S PRAYER.[26]

PROTECT US FROM EVIL. KATHARINA SCHÜTZ ZELL: That evil [destruction] would follow us with an everlasting gnawing worm if we did not keep ourselves as proper children in obedience to you, if we did not hallow your name, if you did not rule in us and we did not live according to your will and commandments, if you also did not feed us and forgive our sins and unite us with all people, and if you did not save us from affliction. Then all evil would follow—indeed, the everlasting evil, where there is darkness, weeping, and gnashing of teeth: protect us from that, Lord and dear Father.

Protect us also from evil that comes to our bodies, that we may not fall into the power of our enemies and they may not be able to carry out their desires against us and then say, "Where is your God?" Save us from their appetites and fury! Free us also from hunger, war, scarcity, and sickness, but yet only in such a way that in all things your name may be hallowed, your kingdom come and your will be done, as also Christ Jesus said. With him we want not our will but yours to be done, for you alone know what real evil is and what is for our harm or use. Therefore, we do not ask you to take us out of the world; that is, we do not ask you to free us from the cross—as if we did not want to suffer with our Christ, for that is why we have come to this hour. But we ask that you protect us from evil and sanctify us in the truth, that we may

not fall away from you but may remain in you and be kept in your name. THE MISERERE PSALM.[27]

6:16-18 *Fasting in Secret*

THE NATURE OF PRIVATE AND PUBLIC FASTING. NIELS HEMMINGSEN: The fast that is godly, Christian, and acceptable to God is an abstinence—not only from meat and drink whereby the body is pinched and mortified, but also from all other things that may in any wise delight the flesh—tending to this purpose, that the spirit may have full sovereignty through true patience, godly prayer, and earnest renouncing of all wrongs whereby our neighbor may be hurt. For the punishing of the body by fasting is a token of the sorrowfulness of the heart for sin and a testimony of true repentance. The ends hereof, for which also it is accepted of God, are three. Mortification of the flesh, quickening of the spirit, and a more earnest endeavor toward all godliness. Such manner a one was Paul's fast, whereof he makes mention. And surely godly people ought often to quicken by the spirit with holy fasting, lest they should yield to the lusts of the flesh.

And this holy and Christian fast is of two sorts: private and solemn. Private fast is that which everyone enjoins to themselves of their own accord, either to stir themselves to godliness—which manner of fast as I would with every Christian whose flesh has need of such chastisement to use often at other times; so would I with him chiefly to use it before he shall come to the communion—or for some new office's sake which they shall take upon them that thereby people may prepare themselves to consider their duty the more deeply and advisedly and pray to God that he of his mercy will send him a lucky entrance into his charge. Such manner of one was the fast of Moses in old time in the mountain, and of Elijah in the wilderness, and the fast of Christ also in the wilderness, whereof mention is made here.

---

[26]Dent, *A Learned and Fruitful Exposition on the Lord's Prayer* (1613), E4-E5.

[27]Zell, *Church Mother*, 163-67 (KSZ 354-58); citing Mk 9:48; Mt 8:12; Ps 42:3, 10; Mt 26:39; Jn 17:11, 15, 17; 12:27.

The solemn fast godly and Christian is that which godly magistrate or the governors of the churches enjoin, either to the intent that some present evil—as plagues, sword, sects, seditions, and such like—may by true repentance and calling upon God be taken away or mitigated; or else that the evils which seem to hang over people's heads for sins reigning over may be prevented and eschewed. Such kinds of fasts as this is have often been enjoined by holy kings and prophets, which fasts were acceptable to God for their repentance, faith, prayer, charity, minding of blessed life, and such other things, which are wont to be and must in any wise be in a Christian fast. As concerning this double fast of private and solemn, this rule is to be held that as the private fast is set freely in every person's choice, so the solemn fast binds people by the commandment of the magistrate, by the law of charity, and by the necessity of the common profit, and therefore it is very great sin to break it willfully. A Postil, or Exposition of the Gospels.[28]

What True Fasting Looks Like. Martin Luther: True fasting consists in the disciplining and restraining of your body, which pertains not only to eating, drinking, and sleeping but also to your leisure, your pleasure, and to everything that may delight your body or that you do to provide for it and take care of it. To fast means to refrain and hold back from all such things, and to do so only as a means of curbing and humbling the flesh. This is how Scripture enjoins fasting, calling it "afflicting the soul," "afflicting the body," and the like, so that it stays away from pleasure, good times, and fun. . . . You see, what I call the real fasting of Christians means that you punish your whole body and compel it, as well as all five senses, to forsake

and do without whatever makes life comfortable. This may be either voluntary or compulsory, provided that you willingly accept it. You may eat either fish or meat, but no more than your real need requires, to keep your body from being injured or incapacitated and yet to hold it in check and to keep it busy so that it does not become idle or lazy or lewd. But I will not take it upon myself to prescribe this sort of fasting, nor will I impose it upon anyone else. Here everyone has to take a look at themselves and judge their own feelings. We are not all alike, and so no one can set up a general rule. Everyone must impose or adjust the fasting in relation to their own strength and to their feelings about how much their own flesh requires. For this fasting is directed only against the lust and the passions of the flesh, not against nature itself. It is not confined to any rule or measure, to any time or place. If necessary, it should be practiced continually, to hold a tight rein on the body and to get it used to enduring discomfort, in case it should become necessary to do so.

This is as far as the general rule for all Christians goes. Everyone is commanded to live a moderate, sober, and disciplined life, not for one day or one year, but for every day and always. This is what the Scriptures call "sobriety," or sober living. . . . But above all, you must see to it that you are already pious and a true Christian and that you are not planning to render God a service by this fasting. Your service to God must be only faith in Christ and love to your neighbor, simply doing what is required of you. If this is not your situation, then you would do better to leave fasting alone. The only purpose of fasting is to discipline the body by outwardly cutting off both lust and the opportunity for lust, the same thing that faith does inwardly in the heart. Sermon on the Mount.[29]

---

[28]Hemmingsen, *A Postill, or Exposition of the Gospels* (1569), 80-81; citing 2 Cor 6.

[29]LW 21:160-62 (WA 32:432-33); citing Lev 16:29.

6:19–7:12 KINGDOM PURSUITS

[19]"Do not lay up for yourselves treasures on earth, where moth and rust[a] destroy and where thieves break in and steal, [20]but lay up for yourselves treasures in heaven, where neither moth nor rust destroys and where thieves do not break in and steal. [21]For where your treasure is, there your heart will be also.

[22]"The eye is the lamp of the body. So, if your eye is healthy, your whole body will be full of light, [23]but if your eye is bad, your whole body will be full of darkness. If then the light in you is darkness, how great is the darkness!

[24]"No one can serve two masters, for either he will hate the one and love the other, or he will be devoted to the one and despise the other. You cannot serve God and money.[b]

[25]"Therefore I tell you, do not be anxious about your life, what you will eat or what you will drink, nor about your body, what you will put on. Is not life more than food, and the body more than clothing? [26]Look at the birds of the air: they neither sow nor reap nor gather into barns, and yet your heavenly Father feeds them. Are you not of more value than they? [27]And which of you by being anxious can add a single hour to his span of life?[c] [28]And why are you anxious about clothing? Consider the lilies of the field, how they grow: they neither toil nor spin, [29]yet I tell you, even Solomon in all his glory was not arrayed like one of these. [30]But if God so clothes the grass of the field, which today is alive and tomorrow is thrown into the oven, will he not much more clothe you, O you of little faith? [31]Therefore do not be anxious, saying, 'What shall we eat?' or 'What shall we drink?' or 'What shall we wear?' [32]For the Gentiles seek after all these things, and your heavenly Father knows that you need them all. [33]But seek first the kingdom of God and his righteousness, and all these things will be added to you.

[34]"Therefore do not be anxious about tomorrow, for tomorrow will be anxious for itself. Sufficient for the day is its own trouble.

7 "Judge not, that you be not judged. [2]For with the judgment you pronounce you will be judged, and with the measure you use it will be measured to you. [3]Why do you see the speck that is in your brother's eye, but do not notice the log that is in your own eye? [4]Or how can you say to your brother, 'Let me take the speck out of your eye,' when there is the log in your own eye? [5]You hypocrite, first take the log out of your own eye, and then you will see clearly to take the speck out of your brother's eye.

[6]"Do not give dogs what is holy, and do not throw your pearls before pigs, lest they trample them underfoot and turn to attack you.

[7]"Ask, and it will be given to you; seek, and you will find; knock, and it will be opened to you. [8]For everyone who asks receives, and the one who seeks finds, and to the one who knocks it will be opened. [9]Or which one of you, if his son asks him for bread, will give him a stone? [10]Or if he asks for a fish, will give him a serpent? [11]If you then, who are evil, know how to give good gifts to your children, how much more will your Father who is in heaven give good things to those who ask him!

[12]"So whatever you wish that others would do to you, do also to them, for this is the Law and the Prophets."

a Or worm; also verse 20   b Greek mammon, a Semitic word for money or possessions   c Or a single cubit to his stature; a cubit was about 18 inches or 45 centimeters

OVERVIEW: Jesus exhorts his disciples to strive for heavenly rewards or "treasures" for two reasons. First, earthly treasures are temporary and corruptible. Second, and more importantly, "treasures" in heaven motivate the disciples to live for heavenly purposes, not earthly ones. Reformation sermons often warned the congregation that it is natural for people to set their heart on something, but that

Jesus' instructions were given to make sure that humans set their hearts on the right thing or risk the judgment of God. One common area for personal reformation was in the area of money and possessions. The one who serves money longs for things that belong to others and therefore breaks one of the Ten Commandments. The supreme ruler of the heavenly kingdom is God and of earthly pursuits is "money." The reformers warn that a disciple's life cannot be spent in pursuit of both.

God knows the needs of his people for daily sustenance. To be consumed with the pursuit of basic, daily needs can misdirect the heart just as the one seeking vast amounts of treasure. Luther contends that to fret over earthly needs or possessions betrays a lack of interest in the spiritual kingdom of God and the grace of forgiveness found therein. Living for the kingdom marks the triumph of faith over worry.

The Reformation commentators indicate how a person who tends to see themselves as having kept the commandments (Mt 5:20-48) is also likely to judge others with a less forgiving standard than by which they judge themselves, thereby furthering their inability to see their own unrighteousness. To judge others is a refusal to extend forgiveness as it has been granted by God (see Mt 6:12-15). That lack of forgiveness then appears as a "log" to God in comparison to our neighbor's "speck." The reformers also point out that self-righteous judgment can turn to violent opposition.

In keeping with his earlier instruction on prayer and especially the wisdom to seek first God's kingdom and righteousness, Jesus assures his listeners that those who are asking for the good things in the right manner will have their humble requests granted by the Father in heaven. Calvin notes that the poetic repetition of ask, seek, knock reinforces the sense of a continual petition for heavenly treasures (Mt 6:19-21) instead of a misguided desire for earthly pursuits, and the Lord listens to our prayers.

Jesus provides a masterly statement that captures both the motive and the totality of the Old Testament's teaching on relating to fellow humans. The Reformation commentators note that most people are experts in recognizing the justice due to them but are less insightful about how to show justice to others. A person would want someone else to extend love to them as well as granting them justice. The self-righteous person expects graciousness from others (including God), while only offering injustice in return.

6:19-24 *Where Your Treasure Is, Your Heart Will Be*

Your Treasure Reveals Your Heart. John Donne: Immediately before, our blessed Savior had forbidden us the laying up of treasure in this world upon this reason, that here moths and rust corrupt and thieves break in and steal. There, the reason is, because the money may be lost; but here in our text it is because the man may be lost. The phrase "for where your treasure is, there your heart will be also" is equivalent to "What profit to gain the whole world, and lose one's own soul?" . . . We bind our selves to the stake, to the stalk, to the staff, the stem of this symbolical letter, and consider in it that firmness and fixation of the heart which God requires. God requires no unnatural things from human hands. Whatsoever God requires of humankind, humankind may find imprinted in our own nature, written in our own heart. This firmness then, this fixation of the heart, is natural to humankind. Every person does set their heart upon something; and Christ in this place does not so much call upon those who would do so, set their heart upon something, as to be sure that they set it upon the right object. . . . But yet how variously soever the heart does wander and how little a while soever it stays upon one object; yet that which your heart does stay upon, Christ in this place calls your treasure. For, the words admit well that inversion, "Where your treasure is, there your heart will be also," implies that where your heart is, that is your treasure. A Lent Sermon Preached to the King at Whitehall.[1]

---

[1] Donne, *Twenty-Six Sermons* (1661), 62, 68*; citing Mt 16:25.

THE CONTRAST BETWEEN THE EARTHLY AND THE HEAVENLY. WILLIAM STRONG: There are treasures on earth; some place their happiness on the things below. Our Savior says, look not to the things that are seen, but have an eye to the things that are not seen. It was well observed by one, that that which a person loves and aims at as their end, that is their treasure. A person who has no end beyond this life has no treasure beyond this life. Let me be rich, let me be honorable and brave in this world. That is all they look at. They look not up to the treasure above; this person places their affections on the earth and makes that their portion. . . . Such are those who lay up treasure in heaven that place their happiness in the chief good, in nothing but heaven, that have aims beyond this life, the things present are but for their way, not for the end of their journey. Every person is as their chief good, and as their utmost end is; if your end be earthly, you are a person of the earth; if heavenly, you are a person of heaven. . . . Lay not up treasure on earth; that is to say, as it is contrary to a treasure in heaven, but so as it may be helpful to your treasure in heaven. Again, lay not up treasure on earth, so, as if there were an absolute necessity of it, or as if a person could not live without it, a person's life consists not in the abundance of the things that they possess. Last, lay not up treasure on earth, so as to neglect heaven. Let not this be a means to take off your hearts from higher things; if so, your treasure will be your curse, and God give you a great estate in great judgment. . . . Those who will lay up treasure in heaven must choose God for their treasure in heaven, not only the joys and delights of heaven, the happiness of heaven, but the God of heaven, that which you choose is your treasure: If a person chooses honor and riches, and pleasure, that is their treasure; what you choose first you prize most, and you shall be sure to have God for your treasure if you choose him. THE CERTAINTY OF HEAVENLY, AND THE UNCERTAINTY OF EARTHLY TREASURES.[2]

---

[2]Strong, *The Certainty of Heavenly, and the Uncertainty of Earthly Treasures* (1656), 56-69*; citing Lk 12:15.

THE SNARES OF COVETOUSNESS. NIELS HEMMINGSEN: Those who serve covetousness fall into the snares of the devil; but those who serve God bury the snares of the devil. Covetousness drowns a person into destruction and damnation; but the serving of God delivers them. Covetousness leads away from faith; but the worshiping of God keeps people in faith. Covetousness snares a person in many sorrows, but the serving of God leads a person into everlasting joy. Covetousness is the root of all evil, and the service of God is the wellspring of all good. It is no marvel therefore that Christ says, "No one can serve God and mammon." For they fight one against another and are delighted in contrary things. God commands you to seek the welfare of your brother; but covetousness counsels you to live to yourself, as we see in the rich glutton. God commands you to bestow of your goods upon the poor; but mammon bids you get other people's goods by hook or by crook. God will have you sober; but mammon bids you run to riot and take your pleasure.

Although it is here to be noted that the Lord denies not but a person may have riches and serve God both at once. For Abraham had riches; so had David; and so had Joseph in Egypt, Hezekiah, Josiah, Theodosius, Cornelius, and many others, who nevertheless served God. Why so? Because they served not their riches but made their riches servants to them. Therefore, the Lord says in express words: no one can serve God and riches. What is it to serve riches? It is to set a person's heart upon them as David says. It is to heap up riches by hook and by crook. It is to keep goods with wrong, and not to dispose them by God's commandment. It is to think from the faith, and from the fear of God, for hoarding up of riches, and to devise sundry ways to heap up riches. Although for as much as the chief cause of covetousness is heathenish carefulness for the belly; Christ endures to take away this cause. For he deals like the skillful physicians who, when they take in hand to cure any disease, show the danger of the disease, and first practice to take away the roots and causes of the disease. A POSTIL, OR EXPOSITION OF THE GOSPELS.[3]

6:25-34 Do Not Be Anxious

DO NOT BE ANXIOUS. JOHN CALVIN: Throughout the whole of this discourse, Christ reproves that *excessive* anxiety with which people torment themselves about food and clothing and, at the same time, applies a remedy for curing this disease. When he forbids them to be anxious, this is not to be taken literally, as if he intended to take away from his people all care. We know that people are born on the condition of having some care; and, indeed, this is not the least portion of the miseries which the Lord has laid upon us as a punishment, in order to humble us. But immoderate care is condemned for two reasons: either because in so doing people tease and vex themselves to no purpose, by carrying their anxiety further than is proper or than their calling demands; or because they claim more for themselves than they have a right to do, and place such a reliance on their own industry that they neglect to call upon God. We ought to remember this promise: though unbelievers shall "rise up early, and sit up late, and eat the bread of sorrows," yet believers will obtain, through the kindness of God, rest and sleep. Though the children of God are not free from toil and anxiety, yet, properly speaking, we do not say that they are anxious about life: because, through their reliance on the providence of God, they enjoy calm repose.

Hence it is easy to learn how far we ought to be anxious about food. Each of us ought to labor, as far as their calling requires and the Lord commands; and each of us ought to be led by our own wants to call upon God. Such anxiety holds an intermediate place between indolent carelessness and the unnecessary torments by which unbelievers kill themselves. But if we give proper attention to the words of Christ, we shall find that he does not forbid every kind of care, but only what arises from

distrust. Be not anxious, says he, what you shall eat, or what you shall drink. That belongs to those who tremble for fear of poverty or hunger, as if they were to be in want of food every moment. COMMENTARY ON A HARMONY OF THE EVANGELISTS.[4]

RESTING IN CHRIST'S PROMISES. JOHN CARTER: In which words also is implied an answer to a common objection, I look not for great things, my care is only for food and raiment. Yea, but (says Christ) I forbid you to have your minds distracted even about these necessary things: meat, drink, and apparel; walk with God in your callings, let all your works be done with all possible diligence, faithfulness, and forecast, and there an end, trust God with the rest. It is he alone who is able and will give such success and blessing as he knows to be most fitting. His promise is not to leave and forsake you; your part is to rest upon it with a calm mind. To do otherwise is to go about to take his work out of his hands, and to engross to yourselves; which you shall have small joy of. But for the better clearing of this point concerning covetousness—which people are extremely blind in, and are willing to be blind—we know that there are three degrees of covetousness whereby the devil fastens upon people and hooks them to himself—as the sons of Eli did the flesh out of the cauldron, with a flesh-hook of three teeth. The first is the grossest of all, carried after an unlawful object, as that of Balaam, Achan, Ahab, Judas, and such like. The second is that which Christ fights against in the former branch, which also is very foul and gross; it is carried after a lawful object—as goods gotten without oppression or fraud in any way—but excessively, consisting in heaping, hoarding, and making provision for the flesh "to fulfill the lusts thereof," as that of the fool before mentioned, rich to himself, and not to God. The third is that which is here condemned, carried after a lawful and necessary object, without any such excess, but inordinately with distress and caring instead of dependence upon God, in holy silence and security. So that the great lesson, which our Lord Christ, in this place, will have

---

[3]Hemmingsen, *A Postill, or Exposition of the Gospels* (1569), 264-65*.

[4]CTS 1:339-40* (CO 45:209); citing Ps 127:2.

us take forth is not only to be content with things necessary, such as food and raiment, but for those necessary things to look up to heaven and expect them at the hands of our heavenly Father, in rest and quietness. An Exposition of Christ's Sermon in the Mount.[5]

The Kingdom of God and the Gospel.

Martin Luther: For as much as there is often mention made in the New Testament of these words, the kingdom of heaven, the kingdom of God, the kingdom of Christ, and it is very profitable and expedient for a Christian to know these, to wit, that they are nothing else, but remission of sins, and grace preached and offered by the gospel. For in this kingdom you shall find nothing but grace and goodness, pardon and forgiveness of sins, love and gentleness; I therefore think it good to entreat somewhat at large of the state and kingdom, and of forgiveness of sins, the kingdom of God, whereby he reigns over all the faithful, and as a faithful king defends, punishes, rewards, guides, and directs them . . . they again from their heart trust in him, suffer his fatherly chastisement and correction with a patient mind, and always serve him through obedience, is not worldly or temporal, but spiritual. Neither consists in meat and drink, or in any outward thing, but only in justification, quieting and consolation of the heart and conscience of human beings. Wherefore it is nothing else but forgiveness and taking away of sins, by which consciences are defiled, troubled, and disquieted. For even as a worldly and temporal kingdom is ordained to this end that men may live quietly and peaceably one with another, so the kingdom of God gives these things spiritually and destroys the kingdom of sin, and is nothing else but an abolishing and pardoning of offenses; God reigns in the hearts, inasmuch as he works in them by his word, peace, quietness, and consolation, and even as sin works the contrary— namely, in quietness, anguish, and all kinds of evils. Herein God shows his majesty and grace in this life,

that he takes away and pardons our sins, and this is the kingdom of grace. On the Kingdom of God.[6]

7:1-6 *Judging Others*

Judging Others and Judging Ourselves.

Robert Browne: For these things we have proved before, but by judging in that place, we must understand a rash judging or condemning of any, for those deed or works they do, whereof they can give a good and probable reason. Likewise, whereas Christ says, "Judge not that you be not judged," he means that we must judge or condemn no brethren as reprobates, or rashly condemn that in them which is no fault at all, or judge every person to be worse than ourselves, but rather must judge ourselves to be the chief sinners of all. An Answer to Master Cartwright.[7]

The Log and the Speck. Martin Luther:

This warning, therefore, is highly necessary. Once we have discharged our office—be it public preaching and rebuking or brotherly admonishing, as Christ teaches it in Matthew 18:15-17—we can learn from this warning and get used to tolerating, concealing, and adorning our neighbor's transgressions. If I see something in him that does not please me very much, I should pull back and take a look at myself. There I will find many things that do not please other people either and that I want them to pardon and tolerate. This will soon relieve the itch that tickles itself and enjoys someone else's transgressions, and Master Smart Aleck will toddle along and stop passing judgment. Thus, you will be happy to square things with the other person. First you will say, "Lord, forgive me my debt"; and then you will say to your neighbor, "If you have sinned against me, or if I have sinned against you, let us forgive each other." But if you see that he is the kind of coarse person who will not stop unless you rebuke him, then go to him and tell him so by himself, as

---

[5]Carter, *A Plaine and Compendious Exposition of Christ's Sermon in the Mount* (1627), 939-40.

[6]Luther, *Complete Sermons*, 5:119.

[7]Browne, *An Answere to Master Cartwright*, 41. Browne also references Mt 7:16 in the margin of the text.

we have often pointed out on the basis of Matthew 18:15; this may cause him to improve and desist. This should not be called passing judgment on him and condemning him but admonishing him in a brotherly way to improve. Such admonition should proceed in a fine and peaceable fashion, according to God's commandment. Otherwise, if you are tickled and if you poke fun at your neighbor and ridicule him, you only make him bitter and stubborn against you. By withdrawing your love from him and finding enjoyment in his sin, you become much worse than he and twice as big a sinner. You also fall under the judgment of God by your condemnation of one whom God has not condemned. Thus, you load an even heavier judgment on yourself, as Christ warns here, and you deserve even greater condemnation from God. . . .

The grim sentence that Christ pronounces here ought to make us tremble at this vice. As I have said, the one who judges always has a log in his eye as far as God is concerned, while the one who is being judged has only a speck. Now, the log is an infinitely graver sin than the speck—that is, the kind of sin that damns altogether and leaves us no grace. However great our sins and transgressions may be otherwise, he can forgive all of these, as he shows by calling the neighbor's sin a "speck." But you spoil everything when to these sins you add the abomination and the filth of judging and condemning someone else on account of his faults and when you refuse to forgive the way you want God to forgive you. You go ahead refusing to see the log, and you imagine that you are without sin. But if you recognized yourself, as has been said, you would also refrain from judging your neighbor. Thus, your log would be called a little speck, and it would obtain the forgiveness of sins. You would also be willing to forgive and tolerate and excuse someone else's speck, in view of the fact that God forgives and pardons your log. Sermon on the Mount.[8]

Do Not Give Dogs What Is Holy. Philipp Melanchthon: Now another teaching follows

which particularly instructs and consoles the preachers and ministers of the gospel. Likewise, it reminds the listeners, so that looking at and considering themselves, they may examine themselves and think. For it makes three kinds of listeners, of whom some are dogs, others are pigs, and some are truly children of God.

The dogs are the rabid persecutors, who tear preachers apart as if with their teeth.

The pigs are foul people, dirty and filthy. They are those persevering in enormous errors and sins against their conscience. And, if these people do not want to look like persecutors at all, truly they pretend some zeal for true religion. Nevertheless, they do not truly desire to repent, nor are they eager to change their habits, but they continue in the security and filth of their wickedness, in which the unclean people continuously mire themselves as in the mud. They pollute themselves by lustful desires, they commit theft, they pillage, they lie in wait for bribes, they hold God in contempt, they do not truly fear the wrath and judgment of God, they do not pray with true faith, they attend public sermons and prayers in the temples as hypocrites, that is, with the appearance of godliness. . . .

The dogs and pigs are beasts ignorant of God, promised immortality or the life that will follow after the burial of their bodies. The light, however, has not searched for them, discerning honesty and shamefulness, likewise distinguishing a good and wise nature from a brutish and wicked nature. They live and carry with a certain blind attack, insofar as they are urged and impelled by their unmastered and bestial appetites, which accompanies consent.

The ungodly are clearly similar to those animals in this life, since they are eager for nothing. They do not care to learn or know about God, about eternal life, about the coming judgment, or about the punishment of sins, since they neither understand nor make a distinction between honest people and shameful people, or between virtues and vices, and deeds done rightly or otherwise. They neither call upon God, nor fear his anger, nor flee to him, but with a blind attack they continue to loosen the reins

---

[8]LW 21:215-16, 222 (WA 32:477-78, 483); citing Mt 18:15-17.

and to indulge their inordinate appetites and raging desires that transgress beyond the divinely appointed boundaries. The result is that tyrants are delighted by arrogance and ostentation in parades or in magnificent equipment. They burn and are enflamed with the desire for victory. Being on fire by this, they plan the bitterest combats and desire to infect others as if they were rabid dogs.

The remaining barbarian people, monsters, Cyclops, roll about as if in the mud of their wickedness. They give way to gluttony, drunkenness, and excess; they pollute themselves with lustful desires, with adulteries, with prostitutions; they commit thefts; they pillage; they lie in wait for bribes. . . . Nevertheless, after this life there will be a distinction of what is visible and a change of insignia. Then at last the dogs and pigs will learn in eternal tortures and punishments both what God is and truly that he is a judge horribly angry at sin. Before they are concealed by death, they will think to acknowledge and confess that they have lived bestially in the habit of dogs and pigs; but there, namely among the torments of hell, there is no place of help or of any hope of liberation. Those who are themselves condemned prefer much more, if it should be possible, that they themselves be completely returned to nothing. Indeed, this seems much more tolerable. They would hope to dissipate their souls into smoke, disappearing at the same time as their bodies, just as dogs, pigs and cattle are extinguished, and we see them rot. God, however, forces the ungodly to be cast away with the devil to eternal and horrific punishments, with those to whom they have joined themselves, and conspired against God. ANNOTATIONS ON THE GOSPELS.[9]

7:7-12 Prayer and the Golden Rule

THE HUMILITY REQUIRED BY PRAYER. HEINRICH BULLINGER: Unless we acknowledge our nakedness, weakness, and poverty, who, I pray you, will pray to God? "For not those who are strong, but those who are sick, have need of the physician."

And the Lord in the Gospel says, "Ask, and you shall receive; knock, and it shall be opened unto you; seek, and you shall find." Those therefore who are commanded to ask that they may receive have not as yet what they ask; those who knock, by knocking signify that they stand without doors; and those who seek have lost that for which yet they seek. We, therefore, being shut out from the joys of paradise, by prayer do seek and ask for that which we have lost and have not. Therefore, whereas David and Hezekiah and other saints of God in prayer do allege their own righteousness, for which they seem worthily to require to be heard; truly they regard not their own worthiness, but rather the truth of God. OF PRAYER.[10]

AN ENCOURAGEMENT TO PRAY. JOHN CALVIN: It is an exhortation to prayer; and as in this exercise of religion, which ought to be our first concern, we are so careless and sluggish, Christ presses the same thing upon us under three forms of expression. There is no superfluity of language when he says, "Ask, seek, knock," but lest the simple doctrine should be unimpressive, he perseveres in order to rouse us from our inactivity. Such is also the design of the promises that are added, "You shall find . . ." Nothing is better adapted to excite us to prayer than a full conviction that we shall be heard. Those who doubt can only pray in an indifferent manner; and prayer, unaccompanied by faith, is an idle and unmeaning ceremony. Accordingly, Christ, in order to excite us powerfully to this part of our duty, not only enjoins what we ought to do, but promises that our prayers shall not be fruitless. . . . First, we learn from it, that this rule of prayer is laid down and prescribed to us that we may be fully convinced that God will be gracious to us, and will listen to our requests. Again, whenever we engage in prayer, or whenever we feel that our ardor in prayer is not sufficiently strong, we ought to remember the gentle invitation by which Christ assures us of God's fatherly kindness. . . . But as we are too prone to distrust, Christ, in order to correct this fault also,

---

[9]MO 14:713-16.

[10]DHB 4:175.

repeats the promise in a variety of words. He uses the metaphor "seek" because we think that those things which our wants and necessities require are far distant from us, and "knock" because our carnal senses imagine that those things which are not immediately at hand are shut up. . . .

But as Christ here addresses disciples, he merely reminds us in what manner our heavenly Father is pleased to bestow upon us his gifts. Though he gives all things freely to us, yet in order to exercise our faith he commands us to pray, that he may grant to our requests those blessings which flow from his undeserved goodness. Commentary on a Harmony of the Evangelists.[11]

The Father Gives Good Gifts. Desiderius Erasmus: For what father is there among you so unkind that if his son requires a profitable thing as is bread, will he not give him what he requires; but for bread will he give him stone? Or if he asks him for fish to eat, will he give him a serpent instead of fish? Truly he would deny it if his son should ask him a stone, or a serpent, or some other noisome thing. You, therefore, who are naturally given to ill and also in other things ill for the most part, yet in this behalf, not by virtue, but through the instigation of nature, you keep this honest and natural affection that you can give profitable things unto your children. How much more then will your heavenly Father, being naturally good, do the same? Will not he give to you, his children, his good things if you stir and call upon his bountiful goodness with fervent and continual desires? Paraphrases.[12]

Trampling Justice and Learning Charity. John Calvin: The word "therefore" is superfluous, as we often find such particles occurring, and without any addition to the sense, in detached sentences. I have already said that Matthew does not give here a single discourse, but a summary of doctrine collected out of many sermons. We must, therefore, read this sentence by itself. It is an

exhortation to his disciples to be just and contains a short and simple definition of what justice means. We are here informed that the only reason why so many quarrels exist in the world, and why people inflict so many mutual injuries on each other, is that they knowingly and willingly trample justice under their feet, while every person rigidly demands that it shall be maintained toward themselves.

Where our own advantage is concerned, there is not one of us who cannot explain minutely and ingeniously what ought to be done. And since every person shows themselves to be a skillful teacher of justice for their own advantage, how comes it that the same knowledge does not readily occur to them when the profit or loss of another is at stake, but because we wish to be wise for ourselves only, and no one cares about their neighbors? What is more, we maliciously and purposely shut our eyes upon the rule of justice which shines in our hearts. Christ therefore shows that every person may be a rule of acting properly and justly toward their neighbors if they do to others what they require to be done to them. He thus refutes all the vain pretenses people contrive for hiding or disguising their injustice. Perfect justice would undoubtedly prevail among us if we were as faithful in learning active charity (if we may use the expression) as we are skillful in teaching passive charity.

"For this is the Law and the Prophets." Our Lord does not intend to say that this is the only point of doctrine laid down in the Law and the Prophets, but that all the precepts which they contain about charity, and all the laws and exhortations found in them about maintaining justice have a reference to this object. The meaning is that the second table of the law is fulfilled when all persons conduct themselves in the same manner toward others as they wish them to conduct themselves toward them. There is no need, he tells us, of long and involved debates, if this simplicity is preserved, and if people do not, by inordinate self-love, efface the rectitude which is engraved on their hearts. Commentary on a Harmony of the Evangelists.[13]

---

[11]CTS 1:351-53* (CO 45:217-18).
[12]EP 32v*.

[13]CTS 1:355-56* (CO 45:220).

7:13-29 TWO PATHS AND TWO FOUNDATIONS

¹³"Enter by the narrow gate. For the gate is wide and the way is easyᵃ that leads to destruction, and those who enter by it are many. ¹⁴For the gate is narrow and the way is hard that leads to life, and those who find it are few.

¹⁵"Beware of false prophets, who come to you in sheep's clothing but inwardly are ravenous wolves. ¹⁶You will recognize them by their fruits. Are grapes gathered from thornbushes, or figs from thistles? ¹⁷So, every healthy tree bears good fruit, but the diseased tree bears bad fruit. ¹⁸A healthy tree cannot bear bad fruit, nor can a diseased tree bear good fruit. ¹⁹Every tree that does not bear good fruit is cut down and thrown into the fire. ²⁰Thus you will recognize them by their fruits.

²¹"Not everyone who says to me, 'Lord, Lord,' will enter the kingdom of heaven, but the one who does the will of my Father who is in heaven. ²²On that day many will say to me, 'Lord, Lord, did we not prophesy in your name, and cast out demons in your name, and do many mighty works in your name?' ²³And then will I declare to them, 'I never knew you; depart from me, you workers of lawlessness.'

²⁴"Everyone then who hears these words of mine and does them will be like a wise man who built his house on the rock. ²⁵And the rain fell, and the floods came, and the winds blew and beat on that house, but it did not fall, because it had been founded on the rock. ²⁶And everyone who hears these words of mine and does not do them will be like a foolish man who built his house on the sand. ²⁷And the rain fell, and the floods came, and the winds blew and beat against that house, and it fell, and great was the fall of it."

²⁸And when Jesus finished these sayings, the crowds were astonished at his teaching, ²⁹for he was teaching them as one who had authority, and not as their scribes.

a Some manuscripts For the way is wide and easy

OVERVIEW: The reformers draw on the imagery of the narrow way to establish both the difficulty of discipleship and the exclusivity of salvation in Christ. Since the way to life is found only in Jesus, not many will find it. Many will witness Jesus' ministry of the kingdom, only a few will "hear" and "understand" (see Mt 11:6, 20-27; 13:10-17). Luther contends that the reason the way is so difficult is the spiritual opposition that the disciple encounters on the path.

The Reformation commentators warn that disciples trying to walk the narrow way will encounter prophets who will attempt to guide them in the way. The problem lies in the fact that not all of these prophets are true. There are wolves who masquerade as sheep. False prophets craftily infiltrate the sheep, but they can be recognized by the fruit that they produce. Theodore Beza asserts that true and false prophets cannot be distinguished by the manifestation of miracles, but only through an examination of their doctrine and their lives.

As Jesus concludes the sermon, he appeals to wisdom on the part of his hearers. The reformers note that this word-based wisdom provides a sure foundation for life. The one who hears but does not act in keeping with Jesus' words will fall as an indication of their folly.

7:13-23 The Narrow Gate and False Prophets

WHAT IT TAKES TO ENTER THE NARROW WAY.
WILLIAM TYNDALE: Enter in at the strait gate . . . The strait gate is the true knowledge and understanding of the law and of the true intent of works. Whosoever understands the same shall be driven

to Christ to fetch of his fullness and to take him for his righteousness and fulfilling of the law, altogether at the beginning, and as often as we fall afterward, and for more than the thousandth part of our fulfilling of the law and righteousness of our best works all our life long. For except the righteousness of Christ be knit to the best deed we do, it will be too short to reach to heaven.

And the narrow way is to live after this knowledge. Those who will enter in at this gate must be made anew; their head will else be too great. They must be untaught all that they have learned, to be made less for to enter in, and disused in all things to which they have been accustomed, to be made less, to walk through that narrow way, where they shall find such a heap of temptations, and so continual, that it shall be impossible to endure or to stand but by prayer of strong faith.

And note another; that few find the way. Why? For their own wisdom, their own power, and the reasons of their own sophistry blind them utterly; that is to say, the light of their own doctrine which is in them is so extreme darkness that they cannot see. EXPOSITION OF CHAPTERS 5–7 OF MATTHEW.[1]

THE TEMPTATION TO WANDER FROM THE NARROW WAY. HULDRYCH ZWINGLI: Christ, who is the only consolation and deliverance of souls, made a narrow way of salvation, as yet with respect to others in places he easily finds the inner temple through himself, saying: "Whoever believes in me will have eternal life. Indeed, we all boast faith in Christ, and yet few will find the way of salvation." In like manner he says elsewhere, "With mortals it is impossible to be saved," as here certain ones are permitted to be saved. Therefore, the meaning of Christ's words is that there are few who in reality are Christians who walk rightly in the way of God—that is, in Christ—as a fact that is frequent in Scripture is placed before a person. For there are so many enemies, so many deceptions and impediments by which they are led away even in those who walk carefully, as it is difficult for

them to escape so many traps, so many snares. Satan especially is crafty, sly, and cunning. There is the world with their enticements and vanities. There is corrupt flesh, whose affections are most vehement, carrying away and casting down people into death. Here through life, here avarice, ambition, very pleasant evil excesses, anger, envy, pleasure, and rage. In the same way, when they have these things, it is proper for men and women of God and disciples of Christ to watch carefully so as not to wander anywhere, and to speak so as not to be led into temptation, that is, so as not to yield to and fall under temptation of the enemies. Because if they are led astray, we will soon return from a distance to walk on the way, and we will not proceed in starting to wander. For those who are of Christ, they set Christ's life in view to themselves, being modeled, and if they fall or wander, soon they rise up and with respect to their wandering in a wasteland they come to their senses. ANNOTATIONS ON MATTHEW'S GOSPEL.[2]

WHY THE WAY IS SO NARROW. MARTIN LUTHER: What is it that makes the way so narrow and hard? None other than the devil himself, the world, and our own lazy flesh. It is resistant and defensive, and it refuses to go on trusting God and clinging to his Word. It cannot stand poverty, danger, and the contempt of the world. In other words, it would like to travel on the wide road. Therefore, it makes this road distasteful and hard for us. Next comes the world, with its persecution, hanging, murder, fire, and drowning, all because we refuse to travel on the wide way with it. If there is nothing else it can do, it venomously slanders and disgraces us, hounding us with sword, fire, and water. Thus it is a hard enough fight to stand there and battle against our own flesh, trusting God, loving our neighbor, living chastely, and remaining in our calling. If we manage to do all this by hard labor, then the world has to add to it by persecuting and slandering us as the worst criminals on earth, to make our life even harder. And then comes the devil

---

[1]Tyndale, *Expositions and Notes*, 120*.

[2]Zwingli, *Annotationes*, 6.1:244-45.

himself. He tortures the heart with evil thoughts of unbelief, fear, dread, and despair. Everything good that we do he turns into sin and shame. Surrounded by such enemies, we are still supposed to stand firm and to keep our goal in mind. It would be easy to get disgusted, to fall back, and to say, "I see them resting and having a good time. They move along quietly and peacefully, and they have the reputation, the glory, and the honor of being the true servants of God. Why should I be the only one to let myself be tormented, vexed, and disgraced so terribly? I want to stay where all of them stay." . . .

Think about this and guide yourself accordingly. If you want to be a Christian, then be one. It will never be any different. You will never make the way any wider, and you have to watch how few travel on it, while the great mob travels over there. But let this be your comfort: first, that God is standing next to you; and second, that after you have gone through, you will enter a beautiful and wide room. If you just cling to the Word, guiding yourself by it and not by what your eyes see, he will certainly be next to you. He will be so strong that your spirit will overcome the flesh, the world, and the devil, who will be unable to do anything with your flesh or with the world or with himself. The Word to which you cling by faith is too strong for him, though it seems tiny and we do not see it. SERMON ON THE MOUNT.[3]

BEWARE OF FALSE GUIDES. STEPHEN DENISON: This text is a main part of the narration or subject matter of the sermon itself, being the very premonition concerning false prophets, and also upon what occasion it is brought in, namely, immediately upon a direction given concerning the straight way to heaven in these two verses going before; and it is as if our Savior had said, I know my dear disciples that you hearing of the narrow way which leads to happiness will be desirous after the manner of travelers to ask all that you meet, but especially those which seem to be prophets, concerning this way for your better direction and conduction. But

let me forewarn you of all other to beware how you ask direction of false guides; for they, instead of directing you, will set you quite out of the way, as it is the manner of heresy so to do.

In the text itself we have two parts: First, our Savior's caveat given to his church concerning seducers, in these words: "Beware of false prophets." Second, his lively description of them in the rest of the text. In the first we have two things: a title, "false prophets," and a caution, "beware." In the second our Savior gives a double description of seducers; and first he describes them by their outward habit, or external shows: "They come unto you in sheep's clothing." Second, by their internal quality or disposition, but "inwardly they are ravening wolves." A SERMON PREACHED AT PAUL'S CROSS.[4]

THE WARNING OF A FRIEND. EPHRAIM PAGITT: "Beware" is the word of a friend; yea the counsel of our Lord and Savior, who is our best friend. "Beware," as if he should say, I know my dear, that you are hearing of the narrow way that leads unto life will be very desirous to inquire of every one, but especially of those who seem to be prophets concerning this way for your better direction. But let me forewarn you above all others to beware of false prophets, for they, instead of directing you, will set you out of the way. This caution he gave his disciples whom he loved: "Take heed that no one deceive you." Again, "Take heed of the leaven of the Pharisees." THE MYSTICAL WOLF.[5]

IDENTIFYING A WOLF IN SHEEP'S CLOTHING. NIELS HEMMINGSEN: In this Gospel they are called wolves, but yet masking in sheep's skins, that is to say, pretending themselves to be meek, whereas that notwithstanding, they like wolves leap privily into Christ's fold, tearing and killing Christ's sheep with false doctrine and counterfeit holiness. But what is the outward countenance of false teachers? They come (says Christ) in sheep's

---

[3]LW 21:244-46 (WA 32:502-3).

[4]Denison, *The White Wolfe, or a Sermon Preached at Paul's Crosse* (1627), 3.
[5]Pagitt, *The Mysticall Wolfe* (1645), 28-29; citing Mt 24:4.

clothing. The Lord in this place speaks not generally of all evil teachers, but only of one kind. For there are some who teach well and live amiss and some who teach amiss and live amiss, and other some who teach amiss and seem to live well. Of this third kind of prophets the Lord speaks here. For by them is greatest danger.

What is their desire? That does Christ set forth in a triune image when he terms them wolves. For as the desire of the wolf is first to scare the sheep from the fold; then to harry them into the woods; and third to devour them and destroy them. Even so the false prophets endeavor by these wiles to withdraw the sheep—that is to say, the godly and weak persons—from the true church and to drive them into the wilderness, where is no food of God's word, to the intent they may get the master of them, and the length, murder not so much their bodies, as their souls. . . .

But you say, How can I who am a rude and ignorant person discern in this variety of opinions, who are the true teachers and who the false? To the intent we may discern and judge the shepherd from the wolf, Christ shows us the marks of the wolf and he draws out the false teachers in their proper colors. They come to you (says he) in sheep's clothing. If someone looks but upon their outward visor, they would take them for most holy people or rather for angels of God. But if you pluck off their visors, you shall find them wolves; first for that their voice is not like Christ's voice; yes, rather, with a strange noise they scare away Christ's sheep from their sheepfold unto the wilderness, to the intent they may kill people's consciences and destroy their souls. And this is one mark. Besides this, he adds another when he says, "You shall know them by their fruits." Here you must be well advised that you take not the leaves for the fruit. An evil tree has now and then beautiful leaves; and again, a good tree often has plentiful fruit, but leaves not altogether so fair to see too. But what are the true fruits of prophets? They are three: worshiping, doctrine, and manners conformable to the doctrine. The true prophet has his manner of worshiping, his doctrine, and his manners according to the prescript word of God.

The false prophet has a manner of worshiping devised by humans, a doctrine of human traditions, and manners to outward show honest, but savoring altogether of hypocrisy. A Postil, or Exposition of the Gospels.[6]

Discerning Between True and False Pastors. Theodore Beza: Let this controversy therefore be first disputed before the question be made touching the form of ordination; and let these men leave off to boast of the apparel and outward show of pastors, when as inwardly they be ravening wolves. Verily Christ commands true pastors to be distinguished from false, not by laying on of hands, but by their fruits and by doctrine and manners. . . . [Moreover] miracles are not necessary to prove any holy, lawful vocation, either ordinary or extraordinary. . . . Now first it is manifest that the gift of miracles has always been free, that is, set in the power of God alone, who has given the same at certain times and to certain persons; therefore, we can make no rule of it. Next, seeing that not only Christ has foretold, but also the old and new stories witness, that this gift was common both to true and also to false prophets, what madness shall it argue to be desirous to have the false sending to be discerned from the true by miracles? A Discourse of the True and Visible Marks of the Catholic Church.[7]

The Fate of Hypocrites on the Day of the Lord. Charles Odingsells: Christ shows two things. First, what will be the vainglorying of certain hypocrites in the last day: "Many will say to me in that day, Lord, Lord." . . . Second, what censure he will give of them: "And then I will profess unto them" . . . When as the number of God's elect shall be accomplished, when this generation of Christians, which now grows old and passes away, shall have an end, then shall the

---

[6]Hemmingsen, *A Postill, or Exposition of the Gospels* (1569), 230-31*.
[7]Beza, *A Discourse of the True and Visible Markes of the Catholique Churche* (1623), n.p. Selection includes material from marginal note.

heavens being on fire be dissolved, then shall the elements melt with heat, then shall be the Day of the Lord, the day of judgment, the last day, when the Son of Man shall come in the clouds in the majesty of his Father; when all kindreds and tongues shall be gathered to him; and no one shall dare to contend in words or defend a lie or contradict the truth; when all human works shall be revealed, none shall intercede one for another, but all shall fear: "Even then," in that day, "many shall say unto Christ, 'Lord, Lord.'" . . .

The number of the righteous who are few is small in comparison to the hypocrites and unjust who are many; there is but a little wheat among a great deal of chaff; a little pure gold amid a great deal of dross. "Many are created, but few shall be saved," and our Savior says, "Many are called, but few chosen." Of six hundred and odd thousands that came out of Egypt, only two, Caleb and Joshua, entered into the land of Canaan. There are few good, few righteous, but many evil, many hypocrites; and of these Christ says, "Many will say unto me." . . . And what will they say to Christ? They will not call him by a name of love, as the elect do, who cry Abba Father, but they will call him by a name of power, by a title of fear, saying not once, but twice, "Lord, Lord." TWO SERMONS.[8]

7:24-29 Building One's House on the Rock

THE IMAGE OF THE WISE BUILDER. JOHN CARTER: His aim and scope here is to set before our eyes the image and picture of the good and evil hearer, expressed to the quick under the similitude of the "wise builder." . . . First, by his actions, truly religious, he joins practice to his hearing, turning the word into work, "Obeying from the heart" (as the apostle testifies of the Romans) "that form of doctrine, whereunto he is delivered," or whereby he is (as it were) new minted, or molded. So far forth that (as the same apostle teaches in the same epistle) he is now no more "conformed to this world, but transformed, by the renewing," not of his manners alone, but of "his very mind, that he may prove" by his own daily practice and experience (which is the best commentary of all other), "what is that good, that acceptable and perfect will of God, revealed in his Word," and more particularly in this most wise and holy sermon. This effectual hearing and doing will clearly demonstrate a person to be that good ground, commended in the parable of the sower. . . .

Second, the good hearer is described by his property which is wisdom; he likens him to a wise person. . . . Here our Lord and master (being most wise, and even wisdom itself, and coming also "to seek and save that which was lost") prescribes to us the only antidote or foreign remedy against this deadly poison, to wit, the constant hearing and doing of these his sayings. So Moses, the servant of the Lord, most divinely taught the people of Israel, "Hear (says he) and do these statutes and judgments, which the Lord my God has commanded for this is your wisdom and understanding." And David found the truth hereof by most sweet and comfortable experience (as everyone that takes his course shall) "You (says he) through your commandments have made me wiser than my enemies, for they (meaning those commandments) are ever with me. I have more understanding than all my teachers; for your testimonies are my meditation. I have understood more than the ancients because I kept your precepts." . . .

Last, the good hearer is described by the fruit, event, or success, which is his stability and perseverance in the great storms, when the devil and world have done their worst: "It fell not (says the text) for it was founded upon the rock." The good hearer is (as we heard) founded upon Christ Jesus and the promises of God (which all "in him are yea, and in him Amen") apprehended by faith and confessed with the mouth, so that the gates of hell cannot prevail against him, as we see in Matthew 16:16-18 and Romans 10:9-11. AN EXPOSITION OF CHRIST'S SERMON IN THE MOUNT.[9]

---

[8]Odingsells, *Two Sermons, Lately Preached at Langar in the Valley of Belvoir* (1620), 2-5.

[9]Carter, *A Plaine and Compendious Exposition of Christ's Sermon in the Mount* (1627), 852-57*.

THE CONTRAST BETWEEN THE WISE AND FOOLISH BUILDER. MARTIN LUTHER: This is the conclusion and the end, on which everything depends: "Whoever not only hears this sermon with their ears but also does it is a wise and clever person." The doctrine is a good and a precious thing, but it is not being preached for the sake of being heard but for the sake of action and its application to life. Particularly since we are always in danger from false prophets and miracle workers, we should think it over and accept this teaching and warning, while we still hear it and have it, both as teachers and pupils. If we want to put it off until our little hour strikes and death and the devil come storming in with their rainstorms and tempests, then we have delayed too long. Therefore, we must not only hear and be able, but actually *do* and *fight*. . . .

With this analogy he intends to give us a faithful warning to be careful that we hold tight to his teaching and do not let go of Christ in our hearts, as our only sure foundation and the cornerstone of our salvation and blessedness, as St. Paul and St. Peter call him on the basis of Isaiah 28:16. If we stand grounded and built on that, we shall remain impregnable. We can let the world and the devil and all the false teachers and schismatic spirits send rain and hail and slush on us and storm and rage around us with every kind of danger and trouble.

Those miserable and foolish people cannot have this assurance and certainty. They do not stand on the rock, that is, on the doctrine about Christ, but on the shifting sand of their own suppositions and dreams. When trouble comes and they have to battle against the devil and death, then they discover that they have put their trust in loose sand and that their stations and works cannot last. . . .

So our dear Lord has finished this beautiful sermon. Now the Evangelist concludes by saying that the whole world had to testify that this teaching was much different from any that they had been accustomed to hearing before. SERMON ON THE MOUNT.[10]

THE AUTHORITY OF CHRIST'S PREACHING. WOLFGANG MUSCULUS: Some explain this place thus, as if the Evangelist spoke Christ for that reason to teach with authority, because he would prevent by his own authority that he attended to the law and he drove away that law that he did not teach, considering the fifth chapter of his Evangelist thus to be full of law, so that he might fulfill its unfinished things and lift up indulgences. Actually correctly contemplating Christ's meaning, no one in that matter adds to law which also itself drives out all those things which are given there, if the height of the love of God is also considered closely. But he replaced the law to its own place, the law being darkened and weakened by the scribes and Pharisees, and he makes it evident.

Then they know a certain thing about the power of this certainty of perfect doctrine and also natural strength of truth that Christ's doctrine brings to the crowds standing near, nothing like this ever brought by the experts among the scribes themselves. And I might have doubted nothing such as this was done. For it is altogether true that the sermons of Christ were possessed with the highest force and the highest strength of truth. Now that stupor follows beyond when they are meanwhile loathing, and the discourses of the scribes are faint. How and from the beginning of the renewal of truth a certain man of his hearers is accustomed to bring.

Indeed, looking upon the matter deeply and weighing carefully the Greek saying, the Evangelist seems to look more greatly back to that authority of Christ that needs purposes more than reasons, just as having authority even as a king in his own kingdom. COMMENTARY ON MATTHEW.[11]

---

[10]LW 21:281-84 (WA 32:532-35); citing 1 Cor 3:11; 1 Pet 2:6.
[11]Musculus, *In Evangelistam Matthaeum Commentarii* (1556), 200.

8:1-17 JESUS REVEALS HIS POWER TO HEAL

When he came down from the mountain, great crowds followed him. ²And behold, a leper^a came to him and knelt before him, saying, "Lord, if you will, you can make me clean." ³And Jesus^b stretched out his hand and touched him, saying, "I will; be clean." And immediately his leprosy was cleansed. ⁴And Jesus said to him, "See that you say nothing to anyone, but go, show yourself to the priest and offer the gift that Moses commanded, for a proof to them."

⁵When he had entered Capernaum, a centurion came forward to him, appealing to him, ⁶"Lord, my servant is lying paralyzed at home, suffering terribly." ⁷And he said to him, "I will come and heal him." ⁸But the centurion replied, "Lord, I am not worthy to have you come under my roof, but only say the word, and my servant will be healed. ⁹For I too am a man under authority, with soldiers under me. And I say to one, 'Go,' and he goes, and to another, 'Come,' and he comes, and to my servant,^c 'Do this,' and he does it."

¹⁰When Jesus heard this, he marveled and said to those who followed him, "Truly, I tell you, with no one in Israel^d have I found such faith. ¹¹I tell you, many will come from east and west and recline at table with Abraham, Isaac, and Jacob in the kingdom of heaven, ¹²while the sons of the kingdom will be thrown into the outer darkness. In that place there will be weeping and gnashing of teeth." ¹³And to the centurion Jesus said, "Go; let it be done for you as you have believed." And the servant was healed at that very moment.

¹⁴And when Jesus entered Peter's house, he saw his mother-in-law lying sick with a fever. ¹⁵He touched her hand, and the fever left her, and she rose and began to serve him. ¹⁶That evening they brought to him many who were oppressed by demons, and he cast out the spirits with a word and healed all who were sick. ¹⁷This was to fulfill what was spoken by the prophet Isaiah: "He took our illnesses and bore our diseases."

a *Leprosy was a term for several skin diseases; see Leviticus 13*   b *Greek he*   c *Or bondservant*   d *Some manuscripts not even in Israel*

OVERVIEW: There are two things on display in this chapter: the healing power of Christ as an indicator of his identity and the faith of those receiving the healing. The reformers note that the crowds that accompanied Jesus at the conclusion of the Sermon of the Mount had diverse motives in coming to him. Heinrich Bullinger explains that just as the Sermon served as a summary of Jesus' teachings throughout his ministry, the healings and displays of power in Matthew 8–9 were also summative of Jesus' ongoing ministry. These selected miracles demonstrated both Jesus' authority and his willingness to save those who came to him.

Like the leper, the centurion recognized the power of Christ over disease. He notes that not only can Jesus heal his servant who is at home sick, but Jesus could do so at a great distance by simply saying a word. From the perspective of the reformers, this faith is exemplary. The centurion's faith begins with a humble recognition of Jesus' authority and is stirred by hearing his teaching. In a lesson that would be important to future disciples, Jesus' presence was not necessary in order to see the power of his words. He uses this occasion to show how those who are in the nations who have such faith will be able to enter the kingdom.

Jesus heals Peter's mother-in-law, who then turns and serves Jesus, reflecting her humble gratitude. The occasion gives Matthew an opportunity to reflect on the purpose of the miracles that Jesus performed. The Reformation commentators affirm how God miraculously sustains believers during persecution and that the miracles recorded in the Bible should serve as permanent "seals" to confirm God's ongoing authority and the truthfulness of Christ's doctrine.

The reformers find great significance in Matthew's quoting of Isaiah 53:4. In the prophecy of Isaiah, the suffering of the servant is tragic and horrible, but so is the hope of salvation for those for whom he intercedes (Is 53:10-12). Seeing Jesus in light of this servant serves Matthew's purpose of identifying Jesus and at the same time giving meaning to the suffering of Christ. The Reformation commentators wrestle with how the Suffering Servant imagery is intended by the Old Testament prophet in comparison to what Matthew is saying about Jesus. The theme of fulfillment reminds readers that the imagery of the Suffering Servant sounded a promissory note from the Lord about the salvation that comes through this one. The reformers emphasize that God's fulfillment of past promises encourages faith in his promises yet to be completed.

8:1-4 *Jesus Cleanses a Leper*

PHYSICAL HEALING, A SIGN OF SPIRITUAL HEALING. DESIDERIUS ERASMUS: Jesus had spoken these weighty and high things on the mount, not to everyone, but chiefly to his disciples and to such as were able to follow them with cheerfulness of spirit. Then, he does abase himself again to the humility and lowness of the common sort which had many unwieldy, weak, lame, and sick, whom he thought to allure to the desire of heavenly things through corporal benefits. And in healing them, he did the same by signification which he did by his doctrine in healing the diseases of the mind.

Either of these things gave credit and authority to the other. We believe him the more willingly, whom we love, and love is won by benefits. And his saying weighs well with us, whom we see and perceive to be so mighty in deeds. Therefore, when Jesus left the hill and came into the plain, diverse companies of men drew to him on every side, to the intent that many might bear witness of the miracles that he would do. Wherefore a great

number being gathered together, behold, there came forth a certain man giving occasion of a miracle and teaching them with a figure, from whence and by what faith, they that were diseased with the leprosy of the soul should seek remedy. For there came forth a certain man having his body infected with leprosy. PARAPHRASES.[1]

JESUS CONFIRMS HIS TEACHING BY HIS POWER. HEINRICH BULLINGER: Matthew has recited in the three chapters before, the whole sermon of Christ that he might give us a taste and as it were gather together the sum of all the doctrine of Christ, and in these two chapters following he sets forth plainly the virtue and the exceedingly great power of Christ by gathering together very many of his miraculous benefices, and proves the same power being so set forth to be diligently considered of all that thereby all the world may gather that Jesus Christ is the living, true, and almighty Son of the living and almighty God; and that he is not only almighty, but that he is also most bountiful, who came to convert, to heal, and to save sinners. This does he prove, I say, most evidently by the most divine and most strange miracles wrought by Christ. Whereof this is the sum: First he cleanses the leper who had appealed to him. Then he restores to life and perfect health a certain centurion his servant, being ready to give by the Ghost forthwith, and as it were dead. After this he heals St. Peter his wife's mother lying sick of a fever; and to be brief cures all the infirmities of all. THE SUM OF THE FOUR EVANGELISTS.[2]

JESUS HUMBLY RESPECTS THE LAW. HENRY MORLEY: Wherein it is very credible that Christ had a threefold regard: of the leper, of himself, and of the priest. First, for the leper, he would have him to show himself to the priest to the end he might perform obedience to the law, which required that every leper that was healed should present himself before the priest. For seeing the law of Moses was

---

[1]EP 35v.
[2]Bullinger, *The Summe of the Foure Evangelists* (1582), A8-B1.

not yet abrogated but did still stand in force, therefore, he would have him to perform obedience to it. Whereby he would seem to intimate that straight bond and obligatory power that is in all laws, not only in the moral law of God, but also in the judicial and political laws of human beings. For seeing the laws of humans are deduced and drawn from the law of God, or from the law of nature, if they be just and honest; hence it follows that we are in conscience to perform obedience to them, even as to the written law of God. . . .

For the reason that concerns Christ himself, he would have the leper to show himself to the priest to avoid all occasion of offense on the priests and the Pharisees' part, who reputed him as a disordered person and one who went about to pervert and violate their law; and therefore, though he needed not to have done this, as being superior both to the priest and to the law also; yet notwithstanding for the cause aforesaid, he sends him to the priest, saying, "Go and show yourself to the priest." Wherein is a singular precedent, and an example of a Christian carriage of ourselves in such sort, as none may justly be offended and grieved through any offense or default in us. . . .

Now for the reason that concerns the priest, our Savior Christ would have the leper to show himself to the priest to give the priest his due, namely, that honor and prerogative that belonged to him; who in this case was ordained as an honorable judge to discern of the leprosy and to give his sentence and his judgment of the cleansing and curing of it; and therefore, willing to give all men their duty. THE CLEANSING OF THE LEPER.[3]

THE EXAMPLE OF THE LEPER'S FAITH. HUGH LATIMER: But what brought he with him? Even his faith. He believed that Christ was able to help him, and therefore according to his faith it happened to him. Then it shall be necessary for you to bring faith with you, for without faith you can get nothing at his hands. Bring therefore, I say, faith with you; believe that he is able to help you, and that he is merciful and will help you. And when you come furnished with such a faith, surely you shall be heard; you shall find him a loving father and a faithful friend, and a redeemer of you out of all tribulation. For faith is like a hand wherewith we receive the benefits of God; and except we take his benefits with the hand of faith, we shall never have them.

Here in this Gospel, you may learn the right use of Scripture; for when you shall hear and read such stories as this is, you must not think that such stories and acts done by our Savior are but temporal; but you must consider that they are done for our sake and for our instruction and teaching. Therefore, when you hear such stories, you must consider eternal things that are set before your eyes by such stories, and so we must apply them to ourselves. As, for example, here is a leper, and he calls upon Christ with a good faith, and was healed. You will say, What is that to us? Even as he was a leper in his body, so are we lepers in our souls. He was unclean in his body, and we are unclean in our souls. He was healed by believing in Christ, so we must be healed by him, or else perish eternally. Therefore, if you will not perish, call upon him as this leper did, and you shall be helped and cleansed of your leprosy; that is, from all your sin. So I say, we must apply the Scriptures to us and take out something to strengthen our faith withal, and to edify ourselves with God's word. . . .

Now, how came it to pass that this leper had such a great faith and confidence in our Savior? Truly by hearing the word of God, for he had heard our Savior say, "Come to me, all you who are laden and oppressed with miseries, and I will refresh you." This he had heard and believed, therefore he came boldly to him, desiring help of him; and so here is verified the saying of Paul, "Faith comes by hearing." The ordinary way to get faith is through hearing the word of God: for the word of God is of such power that it enters and pierces the human heart that hears it earnestly; as well appears in this leper. THE LEPER CLEANSED.[4]

---

[3]Morley, *The Cleansing of the Leper* (1609), 181-82, 194-95, 212-13*.

[4]Latimer, *Select Sermons and Letters*, 339-40, 343*; citing Rom 10:17.

8:5-17 The Centurion's Faith and Other Healings

THE HUMILITY OF THE CENTURION. MARTIN LUTHER: "Lord, I am not worthy." Herein is the great faith of this heathen, that he knows salvation does not depend upon the bodily presence of Christ, for this does not avail but upon the Word and faith. But the apostles did not yet know this, neither perhaps did his mother, but they clung to his bodily presence and were not willing to let it go. They did not cling to his Word alone. But this heathen is so fully satisfied with his Word that he does not even desire his presence nor does he deem himself worthy of it. Moreover, he proves his strong faith by a comparison and says, I am a man and can do what I wish with mine own by a word; should not you be able to do what you wish by a word, because I am sure, and you also prove, that health and sickness, death and life are subject to you as my servants are to me? Therefore, also his servant was healed in that hour by the power of his faith. SERMON ON THIRD SUNDAY AFTER EPIPHANY.[5]

THE POWER OF CHRIST'S SIMPLE WORD. MENNO SIMONS: He acknowledged that all must bow to Christ and his word and said, I also am a man under authority, having soldiers under me, and I say to one, Go, and he goes; and to another, Come, and he comes; and to my servant, Do this, and he does it. It was as if he would say to Christ, Behold, Lord, I am but a man, and have to serve the senate at Rome. Nevertheless, I have power over my servants that they must do what I command them. But you, Lord, are such a Lord that all the mighty have to bow to you; all that is in heaven above and on earth beneath must yield to you. If you but command sickness and death, they will obey you and depart from my child. And again, if you command health and life, they will return to him. Therefore, it is not necessary that you should come into the house of your unworthy servant.

Lord, speak with a simple word and my child will be restored. When Jesus heard these words, he was amazed and said to the people that followed, Verily I say unto you, I have not found so great faith, no, not in Israel.

You see, faithful reader, here you have the centurion as a living example by which you may learn how a true Christian faith humbles itself before God and doubts not his power. Also, how kindly and graciously faith deals with poor servants, be they menservants or maidservants. TRUE CHRISTIAN FAITH.[6]

THE AUTHORITY IN CHRIST'S WORD. WOLFGANG MUSCULUS: [The centurion] says this: "So that you may come into my house to heal my boy, your kindness is great and vast, and your goodness is incomparable. True, I am not worthy that you should do this for me, namely, that you come into my house. But these things are also not hard for you, so that you can heal my slave whether you are present there or not. You are able to heal my boy with one word, I know. Therefore, only speak the word, and command that my boy be healed, and soon he will be healed without a doubt."

What else did that man attribute to Christ other than divine power? The power of great lords lies in their word, if what they say and command has its own effect. For this reason, Scripture attributes omnipotence to God, ascribing it to him by his word, as in Genesis 1 and Psalms 147 and 148.

Therefore, because the centurion said, "Only speak the word, and my boy will be healed," he clearly ascribes this [divine] power to Christ, which is greater than human [power], since he has the power of life and death in his own hand. Nor did Christ need to pray for the healing of the sick, as the prophets sometimes did, but he was able to command it. The man believed that if Christ commanded it, his boy would be healed without doubt. For he did not say, "Pray to God, and my boy will be healed," but "Speak the word," that is, "Command it." Nor did he simply say, "Speak," or

---

[5]Luther, *Precious and Sacred Writings*, 11:79; citing Jn 16:6.

[6]Simons, *Complete Writings*, 364.

"Command," or "Direct," but "Speak the word," that is, "You are able to heal with one little word," just as we are accustomed to say about those who have highest authority among themselves. . . .

For there are many things in human affairs that beautifully strengthen the soul of a believer as long as they are in faith, such as the goodness and power of God, which are confirmed from hearing the word of God. Thus, we see the centurion do this. He believes that Christ is greater than humankind, and he attributes the power of God to him. Truly, he conceived this faith by a gift of God from heaven from the hearing of the name of Christ, who is the Word, and from hearing of the deeds of Christ which testify that he is from God and clearly the Son of God. He did not conceive this faith by the inference of human reason. Besides these things, there is what he added here: "For I am a man placed under the authority of another." . . . He did not add this so that it would be the foundation of his own faith, which he has in Christ, but it is a greater declaration and a proof taken from the lesser [circumstance]. For he ought to have believed before all things that Christ was the Son of God, before he believed that he was able [to heal]. For the conclusion does not follow without pause: "I am able to do many things by ordering and commanding, therefore anyone is able to do this," but "If I, who am a man, am able to do something, how much more is God able to do this by his own Word, who is able to do all things, is subject to no one, but commands everyone?" That conclusion is valid. But what would the Son have been able to do for that man, unless the centurion had believed that Christ himself was endowed with divine strength? COMMENTARY ON MATTHEW 8:8-9.[7]

THE GENTILES AS PARTAKERS OF THE KINGDOM. RICHARD WARD: "From the east and west." Who are these who come from the east and west? The Gentiles. This is confirmed from Isaiah 49:6 and Luke 1:32.[†] Why shall many of the Gentiles be made partakers of the kingdom of God? First, because they hearkened to God; from whence we may learn that those who hearken to the word of God shall be called; read Acts 10:35; 13:26. And therefore we should highly esteem the hearing of the word of God, it being the means of our vocation, and of the opening of our heart, and of the removal of the veil of ignorance from our eyes. . . .

"Into outer darkness." What is the meaning of these words? First, "they shall be cast into outer darkness," that is, into the corporal and palpable darkness of the infernal prison, presently after their death, in regard of the soul; and at the day of judgment, both in regard of soul and body. Second, "darkness" is no other thing than a privation of light; now light is twofold, namely, spiritual, as wisdom, grace, and truth. Now the privation of this light is internal darkness and ignorance in the spirit and inward man. Also, there is a sensible and corporal light whose privation is outer darkness; and this is the darkness spoken of in this place. For although there is fire in hell, yet it is a dark and smoky fire and not clear; except only so, as the damned may see one another, for the greater increase of their misery. THEOLOGICAL QUESTIONS.[8]

THE NATURE AND FUNCTION OF CHRIST'S MIRACLES. NIELS HEMMINGSEN: So that we may have the full doctrine of miracles, more things are to be searched out that, in order to enclose within a certain number, I will put all under these five questions. What the persons are; what the ends are; what is the manner; what is the use; and why miracles are not wrought at this day.

The persons are of three sorts; first such as are opposed with diseases and with the devil's tyranny. Then the beholders of the miracles. And last Christ, who works the miracles.

The ends are many. One is that Christ might show forth his own glory; another, that he might

---

[7]Musculus, *In Evangelistam Matthaeum Commenarii* (1556), 212-13.

[8]Ward, *Theological Questions upon . . . St. Matthew* (1640), 456, 460; citing Acts 16:14; 2 Cor 3:16. [†]In the original, several references follow: Acts 9:15; 13:47; 22:21; 26:23; Rom 3:29; 9:22; and Mt 11.

seal up his doctrine; the third, that the faith of those who behold the miracles might be confirmed; the fourth, that God might be glorified by the light of his wonderful works; the fifth, that by little and little, the devil's kingdom might be destroyed. Whatever miracles are done for any other end than these are condemned as heights of the devil.

The manner is diverse; for sometimes he works a miracle by his word alone, as in this place. Another time in order to show the preciousness of his body, he lays to his hand. One while he turns himself to God with giving of thanks beforehand; and another while he works only by his power without his word, as when he turned the water into wine. To the manner also pertains the faith of him that is healed by the miracle, as is read in this Gospel.

Miracles serve three uses. That the one who is healed by miracle should sin no more; that the beholders should put their trust in the healer; and that we who read of the miracles of the Lord should be confirmed in the glory and doctrine of Christ, and therewithal conceive faith in him, that he is none otherwise affected toward us than he was toward them.

But why are no miracles wrought nowadays? They are stark blind who see no miracles at these days. The church of Christ is a little flock, which the devil, the king of darkness, and antichrist, the pope, persecute and bend all their force to this end, that they may extinguish the true religion of Christ; and yet they cannot. All the whole world persecuted that one poor man Luther, and yet they touched not one hair of his head. And yet God miraculously defended both him and also his little flock. This presence of God in his church is miraculous enough, so that we need not to seek other miracles. Moreover miracles, the power of healing human bodies, and the visible givings of the Holy Ghost were bestowed only upon the primitive church so that they might confirm Christ's glory, his doctrine, and our faith forevermore in all who should come after. The use of which for us is so that we may know they were certain seals of full authority, wherewith

God would have his doctrine confirmed and sealed forever. A POSTIL, OR EXPOSITION OF THE GOSPELS.[9]

CHRIST TAKES ON OUR SICKNESS AND SORROWS. JOHN LIGHTFOOT: Now in this allegation and application of the Evangelist out of the prophet there seems to be some hardness and impregnancy upon these considerations: First because the prophet speaks of Christ's taking human sickness "upon himself," but the Evangelist applies it of taking away diseases "from others." Second, he applies that to "bodily diseases," which the prophet seems to understand of the "diseases of the soul." And so Peter interprets it. The prophet speaks of the time of Christ's passion and what he then suffered of misery in himself; but the Evangelist applies it to the time of his actions and what he then did for benefit to others.

Answer: It is true indeed that this application will appear so harsh, if all the emphasis and stress of Isaiah's speech be laid upon the word "our" as it is most generally laid there. For it is commonly interpreted to this sense: "He was a man of sorrows and acquainted with grief, but the sicknesses and sorrows that he bore were ours," and not properly his own, for he bore them for our sakes: Which construction is most true, but not a full rendering of the prophet's meaning; for he intends also a further matter, which the Evangelist in his allegation does apparently look upon, and that is this, namely, the concernment of Christ in our sickness and sorrows and his power in reference to them or concerning them. The prophet when he says, "he bore our sickness" . . . means not only that what he bore was for our sakes, but that it concerned him and belonged to him to bear them, and he was able to bear them and to deal with them. And this sense the Evangelist follows in his quotation; when having recorded that Christ healed all the diseased that were brought to him, he produces this place of Isaiah and says that in him was fulfilled that prediction concerning the Messiah, which tells that he

---

[9]Hemmingsen, *A Postill, or Exposition of the Gospels* (1569), 51-53.

was to deal and was able to deal with our infirmities and sicknesses; for so far do the words of the prophet reach, and the application of the Evangelist so taken is smooth and facile. And howsoever the test of the prophet do refer and intend more singularly to the time of Christ's passion, in regard of our sorrows and sicknesses being then chiefly

upon him, yet is the sense given applicable also to all this time, as that he had always to deal with our sickness and sorrows. THE HARMONY OF THE FOUR EVANGELISTS.[10]

---

[10]Lightfoot, *The Harmony of the Four Evangelists* (1644), 193-94; citing 1 Pet 2:24.

8:18–9:8 JESUS REVEALS HIS AUTHORITY OVER NATURE, DEMONS, AND SIN

[18]*Now when Jesus saw a crowd around him, he gave orders to go over to the other side.* [19]*And a scribe came up and said to him, "Teacher, I will follow you wherever you go."* [20]*And Jesus said to him, "Foxes have holes, and birds of the air have nests, but the Son of Man has nowhere to lay his head."* [21]*Another of the disciples said to him, "Lord, let me first go and bury my father."* [22]*And Jesus said to him, "Follow me, and leave the dead to bury their own dead."*

[23]*And when he got into the boat, his disciples followed him.* [24]*And behold, there arose a great storm on the sea, so that the boat was being swamped by the waves; but he was asleep.* [25]*And they went and woke him, saying, "Save us, Lord; we are perishing."* [26]*And he said to them, "Why are you afraid, O you of little faith?" Then he rose and rebuked the winds and the sea, and there was a great calm.* [27]*And the men marveled, saying, "What sort of man is this, that even winds and sea obey him?"*

[28]*And when he came to the other side, to the country of the Gadarenes,[a] two demon-possessed[b] men met him, coming out of the tombs, so fierce that no one could pass that way.* [29]*And behold, they cried out, "What have you to do with us, O Son of God? Have you come here to torment us before the time?"* [30]*Now a herd of many pigs was feeding at some distance from them.* [31]*And the demons begged him, saying, "If you cast us out, send us away into the herd of pigs."* [32]*And he said to them, "Go." So they came out and went into the pigs, and behold, the whole herd rushed down the steep bank into the sea and drowned in the waters.* [33]*The herdsmen fled, and going into the city they told everything, especially what had happened to the demon-possessed men.* [34]*And behold, all the city came out to meet Jesus, and when they saw him, they begged him to leave their region.*

[9]*And getting into a boat he crossed over and came to his own city.* [2]*And behold, some people brought to him a paralytic, lying on a bed. And when Jesus saw their faith, he said to the paralytic, "Take heart, my son; your sins are forgiven."* [3]*And behold, some of the scribes said to themselves, "This man is blaspheming."* [4]*But Jesus, knowing[c] their thoughts, said, "Why do you think evil in your hearts?* [5]*For which is easier, to say, 'Your sins are forgiven,' or to say, 'Rise and walk'?* [6]*But that you may know that the Son of Man has authority on earth to forgive sins"—he then said to the paralytic—"Rise, pick up your bed and go home."* [7]*And he rose and went home.* [8]*When the crowds saw it, they were afraid, and they glorified God, who had given such authority to men.*

a Some manuscripts *Gergesenes*; some *Gerasenes*   b Greek *daimonizomai* (demonized); also verse 33; elsewhere rendered *oppressed by demons*
c Some manuscripts *perceiving*

OVERVIEW: Jesus' authority over all aspects of creation is revealed in a series of brief narratives presented by Matthew. First, Jesus challenges the statements of two would-be followers. The Reformation commentators reflect on their shortcomings. Jesus' response to the first profession shows that there was a sense of ease or perhaps even foolhardiness to the statement. Disciples who do not consider the cost of following Jesus will fall away at the first hardship. In the second statement, the procrastinating disciples' request provides an opportunity to encourage the faith required to follow Jesus. In addition, urgency and abandonment are required to follow him.

In the next episode, as the tumultuous sea rises around them, Jesus' disciples cry out desperately while Jesus sleeps and are therefore rebuked for their little faith. Their faith is minimal in comparison to the great amount of teaching that they have received from the Lord. The reformers remark that the perils facing Christians cause them to rely desperately on the Lord. The conclusion of the story serves as an example of how God's supposed indifference to believers' plight serves a stimulus to faith or despair.

The two themes of Christ's rule in the kingdom and his identity are affirmed, though from an ironic source: the demons. Johannes Oecolampadius makes the connection between Matthew's use of Isaiah in Matthew 8:17 with the healing of the soul pictured in healing those possessed with demons (Mt 8:28-34). The Reformation commentators point out further irony in that the demons recognize Jesus' authority even while recognizing their own future judgment, but the townspeople do not do so even after the healing of the demon-possessed men.

From previous healing miracles, there is little question about whether Jesus can heal the paralytic. What is in question is Jesus' authority to forgive sins. In the Reformation selections, the commentators grapple with the nature of true faith on display in this story. Moreover, they also deal with the charge of blasphemy leveled against Jesus. The scribes' contention is that only God can forgive sins (cf. Ex 34:6-7). They reason that since Jesus claims for himself a power that belongs only to God, he must be a blasphemer. Jesus' reply affirms his divine nature and his saving work of forgiving sins, thereby indicating that it is the scribes who are blaspheming. Martin Bucer and Erasmus affirm that Christ accommodates his audience by doing, in their view, the harder thing (healing the paralytic) to demonstrate his ability to do the "easier" thing (forgive sins). In reality, forgiving sin is the harder work because it is a supernatural work and demonstrates Christ's role as the one, true mediator.

8:18-22 The Cost of Discipleship

THE ILLUSION OF COSTLESS DISCIPLESHIP.
JOHN CALVIN: He wishes indeed to follow Christ but dreams of an easy and agreeable life, and of dwellings filled with every convenience; whereas the disciples of Christ must walk among thorns and march to the cross amid uninterrupted afflictions. The more eager he is, the less he is prepared. He seems as if he wished to fight in the shade and at ease, neither annoyed by sweat nor by dust, and beyond the reach of the weapons of war. There is no reason to wonder that Christ rejects such persons, for, as they rush on without consideration, they are distressed by the first uneasiness of any kind that occurs, lose courage at the first attack, give way, and basely desert their post. Besides, this scribe might have sought a place in the family of Christ in order to live at his table without expense and to feed luxuriously without toil. Let us therefore look upon ourselves as warned, in his person, not to boast lightly and at ease that we will be the disciples of Christ while we are taking no thought of the cross or of afflictions; but, on the contrary, to consider early what sort of condition awaits us. The first lesson which he gives us, on entering his school is to deny ourselves and take up his cross. . . .

"Lord, permit me to go first and bury my father." We have said that the scribe was rejected by Christ as a follower because he made his offer without consideration and imagined that he would enjoy an easy life. The person whom Christ retains had an opposite fault. He was prevented from immediately obeying the call of Christ by the weakness of thinking it a hardship to leave his father. It is probable that his father was in extreme old age, for the mode of expression "Permit me to bury" implies that he had but a short time to live. Luke says that Christ ordered him to follow; while Matthew says that he was one of his disciples. But he does not refuse the calling; he only asks leave for a time to discharge a duty which he owes to his father. The excuse bears that he looked upon himself as at liberty till his father's death. From Christ's reply we learn that children should discharge their duty to their parents in such a manner that, whenever God calls them to another employment, they should lay this aside and assign the first place to the command of God. Whatever duties we owe to men must give way when God enjoins upon us what is immediately due to himself. All ought to consider what God requires from them as individuals and what is demanded by their particular calling that earthly parents may not prevent the claims of the highest and only Father of all from remaining entire. COMMENTARY ON A HARMONY OF THE EVANGELISTS.[1]

LEAVING EVERYTHING TO FOLLOW CHRIST. MARTIN BUCER: Another from the group of his disciples said to him, "Lord permit. . . ." Luke wrote this saying by the Lord, "Follow me," and then he responded, "Lord permit me to. . . ." To whom the Lord said again, "Follow me, and let the dead bury their own dead." With Luke is added, "But you go and proclaim the kingdom of God." From here is indeed confirmed what was said in chapter 4 above about following the Lord or going after him. I have argued that without doubt it means to go after Christ and to follow him, just as he calls the apostles and he commands them to follow him and to go after him, to be on the same way and also to be his friends and to pursue him constantly. For here we see that he did not want this one to return to his house, but commands him to cleave to him and also to go preach the kingdom of God, which is a work Christ was then bringing in and to the same apostles and also disciples, especially, those whom he was leading around at that time; he wanted them to have friends and fellow workers. Indeed again this note of the Lord is used repeatedly by the versions. Are these words clear and intelligible: Let the dead bury their own dead? Who also knows that "to bury" signifies that of the dead? But who also, not contentious at least, knows Christ to call the dead, who are destitute in themselves with respect to faith? For this is life. But by no means whether this is an example or a sin, if alive, that is, believing, they should leave burying the dead to another, not called. For all ought not to depart from the other things that remain to announce the kingdom of God, but only

those who are called to it. If the pious one consecrates himself only to God and lives from charity, and does whatever his calling, whatsoever he is, does, and asks, always ready to come out with Abraham from his own land and to abandon with the apostles his parents and all things. If, therefore, he is called to the announcing of the kingdom of God, he will not be able to attend to the dead, nor to serve tables, if less, these and thus far lesser acts of charity, he will by no means refuse. COMMENTARY ON MATTHEW.[2]

8:23-27 Jesus Calms a Storm

IF ONLY WE REACH OUT TO CHRIST. MARTIN LUTHER: None are shut out from his help, no matter what devil or evil may be assailing them. That is why this kind of story is related here at this point: how those who are secure come to the depths of despair. They go out on the sea, sailing; there is a great storm; he himself is asleep; and finally, waves overwhelm the vessel, and the moment of death is at hand.

Here, in this final moment, there glimmers yet one little spark of faith, which is unaware of itself, because it says, "We are perishing!" But it perceives nothing but destruction, forgetting that it has survived up to this point and is still burning. For it would not have been aware of anything if it were not still alive and burning. But, behold, Christ does not reject this spark, this smoldering wick, this trembling reed, but he so increases it that it becomes a blaze by which all the winds and seas are calmed.

This is what he does for all of us who tremble in fear, if only we groan, sigh, and say with nothing more than a single tremor of the heart, "O Jesus Christ, bring help or there is no hope of salvation!" Soon, relief will be felt, because Christ is moved through this groaning to rebuke the winds and the sea. And thus, there is a great calm, that is, joy and peace, followed by praise and thanksgiving.

---

[1] CTS 1:388-89 (CO 45:241-42); citing Mt 16:24.

[2] Bucer, *In Sacra Quatuor Evangelia, Enarrationes Perpetuae* (1536), 230-31.

This gospel lesson could be applied to the church, the state, and the household whenever perils are thought to be so great that salvation seems impossible. Thus, in our day too, the church is considered to be on the verge of ruin because of her many enemies, the empire on the verge of destruction because of so many wars and rebellions, and the household on the verge of collapse because of poverty and other ills. But one single groan, weak as it is, will preserve and prosper everything because it rings loudly in God's ears. Therefore, let us pray; let us cry out; and let us groan against all these things, and Christ will make a great calm, to the amazement of others. Amen. ANNOTATIONS ON MATTHEW 8:23.[3]

CHRIST WAKES UP OUR SLEEPING FAITH.

SAMUEL RUTHERFURD: Why should Christ sleep when his cause requires that he should wake? Answer: Beside that this was a proof of his human nature united personally with his Godhead, that a sleeping man was God who could command the sea and the winds, it was expedient that this storm should rise when Christ was sleeping, for it might seem to arise against his will if he had been waking; or rather God of purpose will have extreme dangers to come on his church, and he will seem to sleep and to be far off, to waken up our sleeping faith. Hence the doctrine is, God will have his church and cause to be brought within a hair's breadth of losing, except the Lord arise and be only he a present help in trouble. . . . When the saints have neither hands nor feet, the Lord arises; for Christ can sail with half wind and play about and fetch a compass, yea he can sail against tide and wind, and with no wind, he never sinks his barque, nor breaks his helm, nor loses a passenger, nor misses his harbor, so how hopeless was the condition of the church, when loving Jesus Christ is couched under a cold stone in the grave? The only hope of David's throne, he who was to restore the kingdom to Israel, is gone, and what shall the people of God now do? Utter desolation is so near

that God is put to it, and the poor church's coal so cold, that they are at, Lord either now or never, either within three days restore the bread of the church or never. Then the Lord exalted the buried Christ with his right hand to be a prince and a Savior to give repentance to Israel and forgiveness of sins. A SERMON PREACHED.[4]

REASONABLE FEAR AWAKENS FAITH.

JOHN CALVIN: A pious prayer, one would think, for what else had they to do when they were lost than to implore safety from Christ? But as Christ charges them with unbelief, we must inquire in what respect they sinned. Certainly, I have no doubt that they attached too much importance to the bodily presence of their master: for, according to Mark, they do not merely pray, but expostulate with him, "Master, do you not care that we perish?" Luke describes also confusion and trembling: "Master, Master, we perish." They ought to have believed that the divinity of Christ was not oppressed by carnal sleep, and to his divinity they ought to have had recourse. But they do nothing till they are urged by extreme danger, and then they are overwhelmed with such unreasonable fear that they do not think they will be safe till Christ is awakened. This is the reason why he accuses them of unbelief for their entreaty that he would assist them was rather a proof of their faith, if, in confident reliance on his divine power, they had calmly, and without so much alarm, expected the assistance which they asked.

And here we obtain an answer to a question which might be put, and which arises out of his reproof: Is every kind of fear sinful and contrary to faith? First, he does not blame them simply because they fear, but because they are timid. Mark adds the word *houtō*—"Why are you so timid?" and by this term indicates that their alarm goes beyond proper bounds. Besides, he contrasts faith with their fear, and thus shows that he is speaking about immoderate dread, the tendency of which is not to

---

[3]LW 67:51-52* (WA 38:472); citing Is 42:3; Mt 12:20.

[4]Rutherfurd, *A Sermon Preached Before the Right Honorable House of Lords* (1645), 22-25; citing Acts 5:31.

exercise their faith but to banish it from their minds. It is not every kind of fear that is opposed to faith. This is evident from the consideration that, if we fear nothing, an indolent and carnal security steals upon us; and thus faith languishes, the desire to pray becomes sluggish, and the remembrance of God is at length extinguished. Besides, those who are not affected by a sense of calamities, so as to fear, are rather insensible than firm.

Thus, we see that fear, which awakens faith, is not in itself faulty till it goes beyond bounds. Its excess lies in disturbing or weakening the composure of faith, which ought to rest on the word of God. But as it never happens that believers exercise such restraint on themselves as to keep their faith from being injured, their fear is almost always attended by sin. Yet we ought to be aware that it is not every kind of fear which indicates a want of faith, but only that dread which disturbs the peace of the conscience in such a manner that it does not rest on the promise of God. COMMENTARY ON A HARMONY OF THE EVANGELISTS.[5]

GREATER FAITH. HULDRYCH ZWINGLI: Every action of Christ either teaches or terrifies or consoles or manifests and indicates divine power. Since, therefore, he commanded the sea and it was calm again, he did this so that human beings may acknowledge that he is God, just as they themselves testify when they have seen a miracle. Likewise, he calmed the sea to prove the smallness of their faith and to corroborate and confirm their weakness, so that he may wrench the testimony of his own divinity from unbelievers. He teaches so that we may stand firm in the waves of adversity and not despair of the help of the Lord, for he himself is the one who commands the storm and who calms the moving waves. God moves all things, he calms all things, although he himself exists unmoving and unchangeable, no less that the sun which governs all things under itself. Here it rains, there it snows, here there is an earthquake, there it is calm, and the

sun is not changed in its own course. So also, the motions which are around us do not come to pass without his providence, and God remains unmoved. Meanwhile, he truly wrenches this confession from us so that we may acknowledge and confess that he is the one who calms the storms which are impossible for human strength to calm. There are innumerable examples of this matter to be found in the ministry of the gospel today, where squalls rush in on every side and try to press the ship of the gospel, which the Lord not only calms, but makes to serve for the promotion of the gospel. Thus, Christ sleeps, but he doubtless knows what is happening. God does not sleep, but when dangers rush in with a storm, and he is not immediately present, we think that he sleeps. . . .

Next, as much as adversities and storms increase, they so much increase faith in God, and we implore with such bitter prayers that they be taken away. We run to him who alone is able to change the storm so that we may wake him from sleeping. For prayer becomes rare or scarce from us, except when evils rush in and adversities press upon us. In secondary matters we are insolent: We forget God and are given to apathy and laziness. Therefore, the Lord arouses us with afflictions and stimulates us to prayers, so that we may arouse him and seek help from him. Nor did the disciples meanwhile indulge in leisure, nor sit down in laziness, but they strained at the oars, they struggled against the crashing waves, they tried to force a way out; but all their efforts were in vain, unless God rescued them. Therefore, God trains us in the meantime and sees our labor. He considers by what diligence and industry each one carries out the task and continues his own work. The poets of the Hebrews express this time with various figures of speech. For example, they say that the Lord is absent, that he is sleeping, or that he does not regard us. Again, when he stretches out his hand and rescues, they say that he arises and looks on us. . . . Because of the frailty of our flesh, fear and cowardice and weakness of faith are often born in us. For this reason, the Lord reproaches us and gives us courage and sustains us.

---

[5]CTS 1:424-25* (CO 45:265-66); citing Mk 4:38; Lk 8:24; Mk 4:40.

Therefore, firm and constant plans are born from the firmness of faith. The Lord is with us in the ship. If we have faith in him, if we diligently pursue his business, if we promote truth and justice, then our ship is not able to be submerged, however much the storms rage and however much the waves crash. Therefore, if we direct our navigation not from faith or from the Spirit of Christ, it is not remarkable if we suffer shipwreck and sail unsuccessfully. ANNOTATIONS ON MATTHEW 8:23-28.[6]

8:28-34 Jesus' Authority over Demons

MATTHEW PROPERLY INTERPRETS THE OLD TESTAMENT IN ITS CONTEXT. JOHANNES OECOLAMPADIUS: A little before the Evangelist cited the testimony from the prophet Isaiah, that "he himself bore our infirmities." . . . This verse in the context of the prophet indicates to us that Christ redeems us from our sins. And since diseases come from sins, it follows that our sins also are removed through Christ. For we await immortality through him. Therefore, those who find fault with the Evangelist, as if he cited this passage untrue to its original context, let them know that he cited it with much more fidelity than many think, and we will understand it from this reading. For, clearly he teaches that Christ came into this world for the sake of removing sins, and that he bore the punishments which are inflicted on account of sins. At the same time, we will be able to learn why Christ came into this world, namely, on account of our weaknesses, and he removed diseases, not only of the body, but of the soul, which are greater. The person who stitches our clothes and does not care for our wounded body, if they could, would not really be looking out for our best interests. So Christ would have done little for us if, after cleansing us of our diseases, he had not cleansed our souls. COMMENTARY ON THE GOSPEL OF MATTHEW 8:34.[7]

THE NATURE AND DESTINY OF DEMONS. JUAN DE VALDÉS: We learn many things in this story. First, that demoniacs dwelt in the tombs, or great sepulchers, outside the city. Second, that demoniacs injured the public, since Matthew says that those were so terrible that no one could pass that way. Third, that there is no convention between Christ and the devil, since they themselves said to him, "What have we to do with you?" Fourth, that the demons knew Christ to be the Son of God. Where I understand two things: the one, that this knowledge is not to be called faith; for there is no faith, but where there is a promise. The demons were promised nothing good by Christ; and, therefore, although they knew that Christ was the Son of God, they had no faith, they did not believe they should have aught good through Christ. And the other, that they have not Christian faith who know Christ to be the Son of God and believe that he has reconciled humanity with God; unless they surely and firmly hold that they are comprehended in this reconciliation and thus hold themselves to be friends of God, and are sure of their resurrection and of their glorification.

Fifth, that a time is coming when demons have to be tormented by Christ. I understand that this will commence at the day of judgment; and then I understand that what God said, when he cursed the serpent that deceived Eve, saying, "she shall bruise your head," shall be fulfilled. This is to be understood as involved in that expression "before the time." Sixth, that demons have no power to injure, not even the brutes, unless God consent to their doing it; a cause of great satisfaction to Christians, for being assured that the devil cannot injure them without the will of God, they are sure that although he should assail them, in order to separate them from God, he will not ruin them. Seventh, that the devils hold it to be their province to do injury, in any way they can; and that being unable to injure human beings, they go and injure hogs. . . . Tenth, it is to be understood here that it behooves the children of God not to contend with nor set themselves in opposition to those who do not desire their society, but to depart peacefully

[6]Zwingli, *Annotationes*, 6.1:253-54.
[7]Oecolampadius, *Ennaratio in Evangelium Matthaei* (1536), 118v-19r; citing Is 53:4.

from them as did Christ from these Gergesenes. COMMENTARY UPON THE GOSPEL OF ST. MATTHEW.[8]

HOW QUICKLY WE FORGET CHRIST'S BLESS-INGS. JOHANNES OECOLAMPADIUS: "They were entreating." There are those who believe that this entreaty stemmed from modesty and because they reckoned themselves unworthy for Christ himself to live among them. But most are of the opinion that the people there were rather crass, and not appreciative of Christ, and had so little regard for him that, though provided with some small benefit that nevertheless was aiming at the salvation of their souls, they thought that he wished to destroy them completely, and therefore they were entreating him to depart when they ought rather to have given him thanks. And so, like those who are provided with great blessings, yet afterward— because of some very small thing done for their benefit—forget all the blessings that they have received, these people are worthy of the greatest hatred. If they had been wise, they would have kept Christ with them, since he is the source of life and salvation. Moreover, by this miracle the disciples were able to learn how grave a struggle awaits them. For the world has unclean people of this sort who in no way desire the truth to be taught and who do not wish to be freed from the heavy bondage to sin. In regard to this, the disciples, who were going to be sent forth, observed outstanding examples in Christ, so that amid all perils they might have confidence, specifically in him who calmed the storm, constrained the power of demons, and to whom nothing could stand in the way. COMMENTARY ON THE GOSPEL OF MATTHEW 8:34.[9]

9:1-8 Jesus Heals and Forgives

THE DANGER OF SENDING JESUS AWAY. JOHN DONNE: It was done, when Christ had dispos-

sessed those two men of furious, and raging devils, among the Gerasenes; at what time, because Christ had been an occasion of drowning their herd of swine, the whole city came out to meet him; but not with a thankful reverence and acclamation, but their procession was to beseech him to depart out of their coasts. They had rather have had their legion of devils still then have lost their hogs; and since Christ's presence was an occasion of impairing their temporal substance, they were glad to be rid of him.

We need not put on spectacles to search maps for this land of the "Gerasenes." God knows we dwell in it. . . . We love the profession of Christ only so far as that profession conduces to our temporal ends. We seek him not at the cross; there most of his friends left him; but we are content to embrace him, where the kings of the East bring him presents of gold, and myrrh, and frankincense, that we may participate in those . . . we profess not Jesus, for his, but for our own sakes. SERMON 11: ON THE PURIFICATION.[10]

CHRIST RESPONDS TO THE CHARGE OF BLASPHEMY. NIELS HEMMINGSEN: Here the grudging of the scribe and Christ's answer do show in what sort the kingdom of Christ and the kingdom of Satan meet one against another. We have here two things; of which the one is the accusation of the scribes accusing Christ and the other is Christ's most rightful defense. The accusation of the scribes was this: This man is a blasphemer. Why? Because he takes it upon himself to forgive sins, which pertains only unto God. For (according to the phrase of the Scripture) blasphemy is to attribute that thing to a creature which is proper or peculiar to God. Now to forgive sin is proper to God, which is assured by the testimony of Isaiah, where the Lord by the mouth of the prophet says: I am, I am he who wipes away your iniquities for my own sake, and I will no more remember your sins. Hereupon they think they may conclude as by an infallible consequent that Christ is a blasphemer after this

---

[8]Valdés, *Commentary upon the Gospel of St. Matthew*, 144-45.
[9]Oecolampadius, *Ennaratio in Evangelium Matthaei* (1536), 118v-19r.

[10]Donne, *Eighty Sermons* (1640), 103*.

manner. Whoever takes upon themselves that which is peculiar to God is a blasphemer. This Jesus takes upon himself that which is peculiar unto God: Ergo, this Jesus is a blasphemer. And undoubtedly it had been a true argument if Christ had been like the scribes—that is to wit, if he had been mere man, and not God also. . . .

But what says Christ to this accusation? Here Christ does three things. First, he saw the thoughts of them, which is the property of God only. Whereupon the scribes ought to have thought that Christ was more than merely human. For no human is able to see the thoughts of another human. For only the spirit of God searches the depth of the human heart. Second, he blames them: "Why do you think evil in your hearts?" As if he had said, "You sin in thinking amiss of me." By this we may note that evil thoughts are sins. Third by visible sign he confirms his hidden Godhead. As if he had said, "You say that he that takes upon himself that which is peculiar to God alone is a blasphemer: for he hurts God's name and fame. Verily, I confess this to be true. But in that you believe not me to be God, you do amiss. Wherefore you are blasphemers, and not I. And now that I may show and prove myself to be very God, I heal this palsy man with a gesture only, which surely is peculiar to the power of the Godhead. If I can do this by my divine power, why should I not also forgive sin? Who can utterly take away a disease, but he takes away the cause of the disease? Now you see with your own eyes, that I take away the disease; and why believe you not that I am able to take away the cause of the disease also, which is sin?" A POSTIL, OR EXPOSITION OF THE GOSPELS.[11]

THE NATURE OF TRUE FAITH. JOHN DONNE: But take it as our case is in a man who is come to the use of his own reason and discretion, so God never saves any man for the faith of another, otherwise then thus that the faithful man may pray for the conversion of an unfaithful who does not know, nor, if he did, would be content to be prayed for, and God, for his sake who prays, may be pleased to work upon the other; but before that man comes to the [reality] that his sins are forgiven, that man comes to have faith in himself. There is no life without faith, nor such life as constitutes righteousness without a personal faith of our own. So that this *fides illorum* in our text, this that is called "their faith," has reference to the sick man himself as well as to those who brought him.

And then, in him and in them, it was *fides visa*, faith, which, by an overt act, was declared and made evident. . . . But when all was done, when there was faith, and faith in them all, and faith declared in their outward works, yet Christ is not said to have done this miracle *because* he saw, but only *when* he saw their faith. . . . My believing that Christ will have mercy upon me is no cause of Christ's mercy; for what proportion has my temporary faith with my everlasting salvation? But yet though not as a cause, though it be not *because* he saw it, yet *when* Christ finds this faith, according to that gracious covenant and contract which he has made with us that wheresoever and whensoever he finds faith, he will enlarge his mercy, finding that in this patient, he expressed his mercy, in that which constitutes our second part, "my son be of good cheer, your sins are forgiven you." SERMON II: ON THE PURIFICATION.[12]

CHRIST'S GREAT POWER TO FORGIVE SINS. MARTIN BUCER: It is as if he were saying that from my works you should learn that I am full of the Spirit of God, and from that Spirit I do and speak all things, and in no way blaspheme. You see that by a word I restore to health those who are suffering under incurable diseases, which is certainly a work of God, so why then do you say that I am blaspheming and impiously claiming for myself the glory of God? Or do you think now that it is easier to say with effect, "Arise and walk," or "Your sins are forgiven you?" Assuredly, each word is of the same power and Spirit. But so that you might believe, behold, I demonstrate

[11]Hemmingsen, *A Postill, or Exposition of the Gospels* (1569), 287-88*.

[12]Donne, *Eighty Sermons* (1640), 106-7*.

the efficaciousness of it to you by making this paralytic whole with a word, to the point that he can take up his mat in full health and depart from us to his home. Certainly, this miracle proves that Jesus is the Christ, that is, the Savior, who saves his people from sins, which made it so that Satan prevailed over humankind and sent diseases among them. There is one mediator between God and humankind, and all of them have been chosen and given by the Father, and to whom he restored the grace of the Father through his death, then endowed them with the Spirit, so that they might have faith and partake of this grace. Thus, even the Son of Man has power of forgiving sins, even then while living on earth in the form of a servant, because even in that state of humility he retained the same mind with the Father, and by his Spirit was the purifier of souls, for he is Christ today, yesterday, and forever.

Therefore, the power to forgive sins, which Christ has, differs from that which the saints receive from him in that he, not only, as the saints, pronounces from the Spirit and the Word of God that sins are forgiven to believers, and as the ministers of Christ also forgive, but also he expiates them by his death, and the Spirit, the gift of the propitiated Father and token of the remission of sins, our highest priest and king gives. He does it in such a way that he forgives more than just past sins; he cleanses and frees from all sins forever. Let us so consider these things and draw the conclusion that we wholly depend on him, who alone will save us from sins, marveling with the crowd and glorifying God, who gave such power to human beings. And in particular he gave that power to him, who is our brother and who dearly loves us, who was tempted in all ways like his brothers and is merciful and disposed to help them in their temptation. COMMENTARY ON MATTHEW.[13]

CHRIST'S CRITICS FURTHER THE GLORY OF GOD. DESIDERIUS ERASMUS: Answering those things which they spoke within themselves in their secret thought, he says, "Why do you envy at well doing, thinking in your hearts? You suppose that because the disease of the mind is not seen with bodily eyes like physical health is that I speak untruthfully and promise something else that I cannot perform. Do you think it easier to say to him that is in sin as I said even now, 'Your sins are forgiven,' or else to say to the man diseased with the palsy, whom you see wholly bound with diseases, 'Arise and walk'?

"Therefore, I intend that by the reason of things that you can see that you may also believe the things true that you cannot see. Both are indifferently easy to the Son of Man, with a word to take away the disease and to pardon the sins. Therefore, I will give you a sign and a token manifest and open to every person's sense and understanding. With this evidence you shall see these words which I speak now not to be vain, but to have their present efficacy and strength. Doubt not but that the Son of Man has power on earth to forgive sins and that not by sacrifices . . . but by simple and plain word." . . .

But the scribes were so put to silence and they were agitated and exasperated with envy, because they sought more their own glory than the glory of God. By that glory increasing and shining forth daily through Jesus, they saw themselves to be diminished and darkened. For like as the sun darkens the candle, so the glory of God darkens and causes to vanish away the vainglory of mortals. But the envy of these men profited to no other end, but through their resistance to make the glory of Christ more manifest and notable. For God can use the malice of men to his glory and renown. PARAPHRASES.[14]

---

[13]Bucer, *In Sacra Quatuor Evangelia, Enarrationes Perpetuae* (1536), 243-44.

[14]EP 57r-57v*.

9:9-38 JESUS CALLS AND HEALS

⁹As Jesus passed on from there, he saw a man called Matthew sitting at the tax booth, and he said to him, "Follow me." And he rose and followed him.

¹⁰And as Jesus*ᵃ* reclined at table in the house, behold, many tax collectors and sinners came and were reclining with Jesus and his disciples. ¹¹And when the Pharisees saw this, they said to his disciples, "Why does your teacher eat with tax collectors and sinners?" ¹²But when he heard it, he said, "Those who are well have no need of a physician, but those who are sick. ¹³Go and learn what this means: 'I desire mercy, and not sacrifice.' For I came not to call the righteous, but sinners."

¹⁴Then the disciples of John came to him, saying, "Why do we and the Pharisees fast,*ᵇ* but your disciples do not fast?" ¹⁵And Jesus said to them, "Can the wedding guests mourn as long as the bridegroom is with them? The days will come when the bridegroom is taken away from them, and then they will fast. ¹⁶No one puts a piece of unshrunk cloth on an old garment, for the patch tears away from the garment, and a worse tear is made. ¹⁷Neither is new wine put into old wineskins. If it is, the skins burst and the wine is spilled and the skins are destroyed. But new wine is put into fresh wineskins, and so both are preserved."

¹⁸While he was saying these things to them, behold, a ruler came in and knelt before him, saying, "My daughter has just died, but come and lay your hand on her, and she will live." ¹⁹And Jesus rose and followed him, with his disciples. ²⁰And behold, a woman who had suffered from a discharge of blood for twelve years came up behind him and touched the fringe of his garment, ²¹for she said to herself, "If I only touch his garment, I will be made well." ²²Jesus turned, and seeing her he said, "Take heart, daughter; your faith has made you well." And instantly*ᶜ* the woman was made well. ²³And when Jesus came to the ruler's house and saw the flute players and the crowd making a commotion, ²⁴he said, "Go away, for the girl is not dead but sleeping." And they laughed at him. ²⁵But when the crowd had been put outside, he went in and took her by the hand, and the girl arose. ²⁶And the report of this went through all that district.

²⁷And as Jesus passed on from there, two blind men followed him, crying aloud, "Have mercy on us, Son of David." ²⁸When he entered the house, the blind men came to him, and Jesus said to them, "Do you believe that I am able to do this?" They said to him, "Yes, Lord." ²⁹Then he touched their eyes, saying, "According to your faith be it done to you." ³⁰And their eyes were opened. And Jesus sternly warned them, "See that no one knows about it." ³¹But they went away and spread his fame through all that district.

³²As they were going away, behold, a demon-oppressed man who was mute was brought to him. ³³And when the demon had been cast out, the mute man spoke. And the crowds marveled, saying, "Never was anything like this seen in Israel." ³⁴But the Pharisees said, "He casts out demons by the prince of demons."

³⁵And Jesus went throughout all the cities and villages, teaching in their synagogues and proclaiming the gospel of the kingdom and healing every disease and every affliction. ³⁶When he saw the crowds, he had compassion for them, because they were harassed and helpless, like sheep without a shepherd. ³⁷Then he said to his disciples, "The harvest is plentiful, but the laborers are few; ³⁸therefore pray earnestly to the Lord of the harvest to send out laborers into his harvest."

a Greek *he*   **b** Some manuscripts add *much*, or *often*   **c** Greek *from that hour*

OVERVIEW: The brief episode of Matthew's calling gives a further example of the call to discipleship (see Mt 1:18-22; 16:24-26) along with introducing Matthew himself to readers of his Gospel. Matthew's calling is exemplary in that it shows that Jesus extends his call to the unlikely ones and the appropriate response is immediate surrender. Thomas Cranmer warns his contemporaries not to adopt the self-righteous posture of the Pharisees in an attempt to justify themselves. That God desires mercy rather than sacrifice means that he desires those who will seek him on the basis of mercy and practice compassion rather than sacrifices committed in self-righteousness.

In response to a question about fasting, Jesus identifies himself as the bridegroom, chosen by the Father, to be wed to the Lord's chosen people (see Mt 22:1-14; 25:1-13; Is 62:5). Before that wedding is consummated, the bridegroom will be taken away through his suffering and death and ultimately his resurrection and ascension to the Father. Christ's bride, the church, will fast in his absence, noting the church's longing for his return and the establishment of his kingdom along with the great feast. The reformers note that true, Christian suffering does not come by self-inflicted austerity, but instead through God-ordained trials and persecutions that inevitably come into the disciple's life.

The desperation of his circumstances causes the synagogue official not to be aloof as the other religious leaders had been in previous narratives. He expresses his faith in Jesus to raise the dead, a great measure of faith. Similarly, the desperate state of the woman's condition is seen in both the longevity of her disease and her outsider status that being ceremonially unclean would cause. Here, the irony is that the both the synagogue insider and the outsider have desperate needs that only Jesus can meet. The Reformation commentators reflect on how the details of Matthew's account evoke faith in Jesus as the one who has power over death.

Matthew provides two more brief narratives before he concludes this section of his Gospel. Jesus' question to the blind men probes their faith. Their simple response notes their faith in his power and authority. They also demonstrate the diligence of a disciple by following him down the road and into the house even though they are blind. However, they do not follow Christ's command about not speaking publicly about the miracle. Demon-

strating that the demon has been removed, the (mute) man speaks. Calvin comments on how the amazed crowds proclaim that nothing of this magnitude has ever happened before in Israel.

Jesus' ministry is summarized as having three aspects: teaching in the synagogues, proclaiming the gospel of the kingdom, and performing healings (see Mt 4:23). The Reformation commentators assert that Matthew's presentation is driven by his doctrinal purposes, especially engendering faith, more so than a strict chronology of Jesus' ministry. Summary statements like Matthew 9:35 accomplish Matthew's doctrinal goals without providing much detail. According to Heinrich Bullinger, Matthew's theological intention drives both the selection of material presented and the order in which it is arranged.

Because of his compassion for his people, Jesus calls on the disciples to pray that the Lord of the harvest would send workers in the harvest. The needed laborers in the harvest are those who will preach the gospel and teach the Christian life. Juan de Valdés points out that God's grand plan as the Lord of the harvest is to bring people into the kingdom (see Mt 13:41-43, 49-50).

9:9-13 The Calling of Matthew

MATTHEW ANSWERS JESUS' CALL TO DISCIPLESHIP. RICHARD TAVERNER: And surely this kind of men, because they did exercise an occupation or office of filthy gains and of violent capacity, were many ways infamous, noted, and evil spoken of, and especially among the Jews. But our Savior, Jesus Christ, who had called a little before unto him Simon and Andrew, John and James from a base (though yet not unlawful) kind of living to the intent he would openly declare to the world that he abhorred no sort of person at all, so they would convert themselves to better; he calls this Matthew to him and commanded him to follow him. So Matthew, without concern for perils or at least despising all perils that might take place, forthwith and without delay, leaving his payments unfinished and leaving his gainful office, began to follow Jesus, and suddenly changed from a tax collector to a disciple. And because he forsook earthly gains, he was rightly made a steward of the Lord's talents. THE GOSPELS WITH BRIEF SERMONS.[1]

BEWARE OF THE HYPOCRISY OF THE PHARISEES. THOMAS CRANMER: He prefers the penitent publican before the proud, holy, and glorious Pharisee. He calls himself a physician, but not to those who are whole but to those who are sick and have need of his salve for their sore. He teaches us in our prayers to acknowledge ourselves sinners and to ask righteousness and deliverance from all evils at our heavenly Father's hand. He declares that the sins of our own hearts defile our own selves. He teaches that an evil word or thought deserves condemnation, affirming that we shall give an account for every idle word. He says he came not to save but the sheep that were utterly lost and cast away. Therefore, few of the proud, just, learned, wise, perfect, and holy Pharisees were saved by him because they justified themselves by their counterfeit holiness before others. A SERMON OF THE MISERY OF ALL MANKIND.[2]

CHRIST CAME TO SAVE SINNERS. WILLIAM BRIDGE: This (say I) is not to be understood of sinners only sensible of their own sins, but sinners indeed; Christ came to call sinners indeed, yea, before they are sensible of their sins. For the word (sinner) here must be understood as the word sinner before is in the tenth and eleventh verse. . . . He did eat with those who were not sensible of their sins: Sinners there are not to be meant of those only who were sensible of their sins; Christ did not only eat with those who were sensible of their sins. . . .

Again, our Savior Christ gives this account, at the twelfth verse. . . . To answer to this objection, that our Savior did eat with sinners and converse with sinners, he says, I am a physician, and

physicians are to go to those who are sick only. There is this difference between me, a physician, and other physicians: for I come unsent for; but other physicians come when sent for. I, as a physician, come to call my patients: but other physicians are called in by their patients. Now (says he) I am a physician and I come not to call the righteous, but sinners; I come to call my patients. Physicians do not only go to those who are sensible of their disease; but if a person is past sense, their friends send for the physician, and the physician goes: so does Christ here, comes to his patients when they are not sensible of their disease many times. . . .

If by the calling of the sinners we are to understand those who are sensible only, then the sense must be this: I came not to call the righteous, but people who are penitent. No, no, Christ came to call sinners, poor sinners; although they were never yet sensible of their sins. The Lord Jesus Christ came to call sinners which are so indeed. WORKS OF WILLIAM BRIDGE.[3]

GOD'S DELIGHT IN MERCY. WOLFGANG MUSCULUS: But we will investigate it in the most simple terms possible, or really, we will only touch on it, stating first with what meaning the prophet spoke these words, and second, how Christ made use of them. This passage of the prophet, although people handle it in varying ways, nevertheless seems to me simply to have this sense: The people of Israel had polluted themselves enormously through idolatry and had forsaken their own God, wherefore God was making an effort to recall them to repentance and save them from destruction. But they obstinately were consorting with idols and meanwhile were thinking that they were very pleasing to God, exceedingly because they made so many sacrifices and burnt offerings. Thus were they led astray by pseudo-prophets and priests, as if sacrifices of cattle would placate God, and in those sacrifices they were placing all their worship of God, yet they were not trusting or carrying out

---

[1] Taverner, *On Saynt Andrewes Day: The Gospels with Brief Sermons* (1542), xxxii*.
[2] Cranmer, *Certayne Sermons* (1547), C3v.

[3] WWB 2:226-27*.

acts of charity to anyone, things that God requires before all others. And in anger the Lord complains at Hosea 6, "Therefore I have hewn your prophets, and I have killed them with the words of my mouth, and judgments on you have gone forth like a light. For, I wanted compassion, and not sacrifice, and the knowledge of God more than a burnt offering." From these words the confidence that they had in oblations and burnt offerings devoid of true repentance was completely shattered. That attitude is also censured at Isaiah 1 and Jeremiah 7 and Psalms 49 and 50.

Second, let us examine now how this sentiment is used by Christ, although this is easily discerned from the preceding verses, but let us state it clearly for the sake of those who cannot figure it out. First, it will be noticed that the same disease that predominated in the time of the prophet also prevailed in this time of Christ, namely, that they were putting all the worship of God into external oblations and burnt offerings, something God was not requiring. Meanwhile, those things that God wished and that were pleasing to him, they cared not for, such as goodness and compassion. Finally, this vice particularly related to those with whom Christ here was dealing, the scribes and the Pharisees and the priests, who were seeking their own gain in this matter, as one can see also at Hosea 6 that they did.

Third, it must be observed how Christ was fulfilling that phrase, "I wish compassion and goodness," by calling to himself and caring for sinners who otherwise were going to perish, whom those self-righteous had cast off and were allowing to perish. Therefore, since the Pharisees and the scribes were neglecting compassion of that sort and were placing all the worship of God in sacrifices and burnt offerings and the rest of the external ceremonies, they were reviling and ridiculing Christ who was fulfilling the principal matter of the law when he was turning sinners to repentance and therein executing the will of the Father. Here he rightly was sending them to examine that sentiment of the prophet, saying, "But come and learn what that means, 'I desire compassion and

not a sacrifice.'" It's as if he were saying, "You are doing the same thing that your elders were doing in the time of the prophets, going astray and misleading people, yes, making a profit out of piety, when you transfer all the worship of God to sacrifices that God does not want; and you neglect goodness and compassion in helping others, which one thing he requires, and he desires more the salvation of sinners than your oblations."

Third, it must be noted that in the definition of compassion that we mentioned, that it is the sort of aching in the mind stemming from someone else's misery, which is inclined to give help. For God speaks in the holy Scriptures about true faith which by love is efficacious, and about a love which consists not in words, but in action; then too about true compassion, which has this trait, that it rushes immediately to help those in need. For just as it is characteristic of anger to be prone to revenge, and of envy to bite and detract, so it is the nature and innate propensity of compassion to ease the suffering of those in need. COMMENTARY ON MATTHEW.[4]

9:14-17 *A Question About Fasting*

FASTING AND SUFFERING. WILLIAM TYNDALE: "Mourn," that is, to suffer pain. There is pain in many ways; one way, of a person's own choice and election; as is the monks' rules, and as Baal's priests pricked themselves. Such pain does all the world, the Pharisees, yea, John's disciples, esteem great; but God despises it. Another way there is pain, and ordained of God, [is] without our election; as shame, rebuke, wrong, death: such to suffer patiently, and with goodwill, is the right cross, and pleases God well. So Christ's disciples fast not, but are merry at the marriage, while the bridegroom is yet with them; yea, and God had yet ordained no trouble for them. They fain themselves no pain; for it pleases not God. They must fast after Christ's death, and suffer pain of God's hand and ordinance.

---

[4]Musculus, *In Evangelistam Matthaeum Commentarii* (1556), 248-49, 255.

So now, whatsoever a person takes on themselves by their own election, that is reproved; yea, and where Christ shows himself friendly, as a bridegroom, there must needs be a merry heart.

With these words Christ drives them from him as them which understood not his learning, as concerning the liberty of his disciples; and says, "No one mends an old garment with new cloth, for the old holds not the stitch," as who says, "such spiritual new learning cannot be comprehended with old fleshly hearts." Preach to fleshly people, and they wax worse; as we see, when spiritual liberty is preached, the flesh draws it unto carnal lust. MARGINAL NOTES ON THE FIRST TWENTY-ONE CHAPTERS OF ST. MATTHEW'S GOSPEL.[5]

THE NEW CLOTH AND NEW WINE. THEODORE BEZA: "Can the children of the marriage chamber mourn as long as the bridegroom is with them?" Christ would spare his disciples a while, not burdening them too much, lest he should discourage them. . . . "Moreover, no one pieces an old garment with a piece of new cloth. . . . Neither do they put new wine into old vessels, for then the vessels would break." Christ compares his disciples for their infirmity to old garments and old vessels which are not able as yet to bear the perfection of his doctrine, which he means by new cloth and new wine. The mind which is infected with the dregs of superstitious ceremonies is not able to receive the pleasant wine of the gospel. THE BIBLE AND HOLY SCRIPTURES CONTAINED.[6]

THE NEW PATCH THAT TEARS THE OLD GARMENT. HULDRYCH ZWINGLI: These parables Jesus told to John's disciples and to the Pharisees in response to their complaint which they had made concerning the reason for their own observance of fasts, while his disciples fasted little. Upon this, he answered them, just before this one, by yet another parable saying that as long as the bridegroom is with his friends, they do not have any sorrow, but when the bridegroom is taken from them, they shall fast and be sorrowful knowing that where Christ is, no one needs to be concerned about how to please God. Rather, where he is, there God is pleased by everything; there is no need for sorrow but there is rejoicing as at a wedding feast. But if he should depart from them, it is solely because they have become carnal. Therefore, one would have to subordinate everything once more to the spirit through fasting and sorrow.

Soon after this he then cites the passage, mentioned earlier, in which he relates that, in the same way in which one who seeks to mend a dress, one should not take strong, new, or unpressed cloth—since the new is too strong for the old and would tear it. So also does the person err who seeks to mix the gospel—the word of the grace of God—with the law of works, thus causing both to become useless. The new patch falls off and the old dress will be torn; now the new patch falls off because the old dress is too weak to hold it in place. This is nothing other than, "Whoever is not born anew, leaving the old pieces and rags of outward works, dropping any hope in his own work and clinging freely to the grace of God—just like a child who gives up walking along benches—will become worse." For it would be better had such a one never known divine righteousness (i.e., his grace which alone justifies) than for him to turn again to the weak elements of this world, after having received the knowledge of the gospel, which is to turn again to oneself, one's wisdom, and advice, and which places so much value upon itself that it intends to attain salvation by itself. This new cloth and dress cannot bear to be sewn together with an old patch, but desires to remain pure and unmixed; this causes us to love God as he loves us. A similar meaning is intended by the other part of the parable concerning the wine containers, which also does not say anything other than that the word of the grace of God is to be preserved in new dishes which do not have the sour dough or taste of the old ones. In other words, we are not to bank on the elements of our old foolish nature which likes so much to be something; rather, we are to trust in

---

[5]Tyndale, *Expositions and Notes*, 231; citing 1 Kings 18.
[6]Beza, *The Bible and Holy Scriptures Contained* (1576), 5*.

the grace of God alone, letting him care and govern. AN EXPOSITION OF THE ARTICLES.[7]

9:18-26 A Girl Restored to Life and a Woman Healed

THE FAITH OF THE HEALED WOMAN. HUGH LATIMER: Again, by this woman you may learn that God sometimes brings some low and humbles them to that end to promote them and to bring them aloft. As in this woman, she was sick twelve years and vexed with such an irksome sickness; but at the length she was healed; and not only that, but also exalted, for Christ called her his daughter, which was the greatest promotion that could be. . . .

But mark, that Christ says not to her, "My hem has healed you," but he says, "Your faith has healed you." Perhaps, if we had this hem, we would make a great matter of it; which thing were but foolery. Let us use prayer, which has a promise; for God promises that when we pray to him we shall be heard; when we pray with a faithful heart, as this woman did who believed that Christ would help her; and for this faith's sake she was so highly commended of Christ, and all the people were edified by her example. But especially Jairus, that great man, whose daughter lay sick, he had cause to strengthen his faith by the example of this woman, who believed the word of God, and therefore came unto Christ. CHRIST THE BEST PHYSICIAN.[8]

DEATH IS ONLY SLEEP FOR THOSE IN CHRIST. URBANUS RHEGIUS: We see here of now, how great and gross blindness was in Judaism, when Christ was sent to them. He declares by mighty and marvelous works and miracles that he is the very Messiah, which Scripture promised, the Savior and deliverer of the whole world, and he does the same works which Scripture had prophesied the Messiah to do, and whereof he might be known most plainly and most easily. Nonetheless,

when he says that the girl is sleeping, that miserable and blinded people mocks their Lord and God. Yet their mocking only serves faith, for they confirm that the girl is truly dead, just as the servants of the ruler's house show their master upon meeting him that the girl is dead, that he should not offend Christ. Therefore, they might not say that the girl lay in a trance or a swoon, or collapsed naturally, but they doubted not and they confessed openly that she had verily departed from this life. And therefore, they were constrained after to acknowledge and confess that a true miracle was done here, that is to say that the girl was called again truly from death to life.

And therefore, Christ commands to give to her something, that she may eat, that they should not doubt that she was raised again truly. . . . Some suppose that that miracle which Matthew declares, where Christ only raises up again the dead girl by touching her, is a different miracle from that which Luke and Mark declare, whom they suppose to write of a girl of two years old, the daughter of a chief of the synagogue, whose name was Jairus, but I have supposed hitherto with Eusebius, Jerome, Augustine in the second book of the consent of the Evangelists the twenty sixth chapter, also with Chrysostom[†] and other of true opinion and say that these three Evangelists declare the same history and speak of the same miracle. Therefore, our Lord Jesus Christ willed to declare his divine power and ministration when he said, the girl sleeps, for as Augustine[‡] says, no one can raise up so easily from sleep a person sleeping naturally in their bed, how easily Christ raises up a dead man forth of his sepulcher. And so, Christ disinclined to speak of death, as an almighty lord, as Lord of life and death, and he calls death asleep. AN HOMILY . . . OF FAITH AND RESURRECTION.[9]

THE GIRL AND THE WOMAN PICTURE TWO KINDS OF PEOPLE. MARTIN LUTHER: There is further represented here as in a picture—both in

[7]Zwingli, *The Defense of the Reformed Faith*, 1:73-74; citing 2 Pet 2:20.
[8]Latimer, *Select Sermons and Letters*, 245-46*.

[9]Rhegius, "An Homily . . . of Faith and Resurrection, upon the Gospel of Matthew," 34-37*. [†]Augustine, *Harmony of the Gospels*, NPNF[1] 6:134-36; Chrysostom, *Homilies on Matthew*, NPNF[1] 10:200-205. [‡]Augustine, *Homilies on John*, NPNF[1] 7:273.

the woman with the flow of blood and in the girl—what happens in governing when people try to rule the conscience with the law while Christ is unknown. There are two kinds of people. One kind are the sick, poor, timid consciences, who feel secret distress from their sins and the law's verdict and curse, that is, God's wrath poured out on them. They want to be free of it; they seek help and remedy from all physicians and employ for this all their wealth, body, and life. Nevertheless, none of it helps, improves, or comforts them, but it only becomes worse, so that they finally despair and resign themselves to death, until Christ comes to them with his gospel. . . .

The second kind of people, such as the daughter of the ruler, are those who are with the law—whether Jews or Gentiles; that is, they go their way in confidence and security, do not feel the law's fright, and think that they are well off, until they are suddenly struck down and die. St. Paul says about himself that he had once lived without the law, but then through the law sin became alive and killed him. . . .

Now, for these two to be delivered from their distress and death, there is no other remedy or help than that Christ be known and his comforting, living voice of the gospel be heard. This has the power to banish sin and death and forever to give the conscience consolation, joy, and life, if it is grasped with a believing heart. This clearly shows the article that without our merit, freely, through faith alone we become righteous and saved, that is, redeemed from sin and death. The poor woman brings nothing to Christ except great unworthiness, so that she had to be ashamed, and even full of fear and fright, because she must be found out. Even less did the ruler's daughter have any of her own worthiness and merit, because she lay there dead and was completely without life and works.

In summary, we must confess that in ourselves we have nothing, nor can we live or do anything that pleases God or could bring us to grace and life. Rather, his pure grace is given to us. GOSPEL FOR TWENTY-FOURTH SUNDAY AFTER TRINITY, MT 9:18-26.[10]

---

[10]LW 79:321-22* (WA 22:403-4); citing Rom 7:9.

9:27-38 More Healings and the Harvest

THE PERSISTENT FAITH OF THE TWO BLIND MEN. DAVID DICKSON: Those who seek good from Christ must look on him as he is described in Scripture, as he is the promised Messiah, the true King of Israel. "Son of David," they say, "have mercy on us." Those who believe to get good from Christ will find a way to follow him and come to him, even if they are blind; for these blind men "follow" and "cry." More people in this sense need to join in one suit unto Christ; for these two blind men do join in one cry, saying, "Have mercy on us." The incarnation of the Son of God is a noble support to faith, "You Son of David," they say, "have mercy." Mercy is our only plea with God, and Christ. "Therefore," they say, "Have mercy on us." . . .

Christ allows them to cry on until he leads them unto his lodging. The Lord will seem not to regard the prayer which he intends to grant, and so will train the supplicant patiently to pursue his request; for no answer is given until the blind men come to his lodging and do follow him within doors. Whosoever loves to have anything from Christ ought to have a firm grasp of his power and to have their faith fixed; therefore, "Do you believe," says Christ, "that I am able to do this?" In things belonging to this life, it is sufficient to believe his power, leaving the matter of his will to himself. Therefore, here it is asked only, do you believe that I am able? And they answer, "Yea Lord," and no more. . . .

Our Lord touches their eyes and opens them. Where any faith is, the Lord will strengthen it as needed; therefore, although no touching was required, yet to strengthen their faith "he touches their eyes." Faith shall not be frustrated. Therefore, says Christ, "According to your faith be it unto you, and their eyes were opened." Our Lord loved no rash applause but that his miracles should be kept in silence awhile that women and men might take heed to his doctrine the more resolutely and praise his work the more wholly; therefore he charged them, saying, "See that no one know it," to wit, until I give you warrant. . . .

They not taking heed to the command but consulting their own wit, do contrary to the commandment, therefore is their disobedience marked: "But they spread abroad his fame." Here we learn that the most specious pretenses that can be made are not able to save a person from guiltiness if they disobey a command. A Brief Exposition.[11]

The Multitude That Wonders at Jesus.

John Calvin: It is probable that this man was not naturally dumb, but that, after he had been given up to the devil, he was deprived of the use of speech. . . . The exclamation of the multitudes, on his being cured, that nothing like it had ever been seen in Israel, appears to be hyperbolic. For God had formerly revealed his glory among that people by greater miracles. But perhaps they look to the design of the miracle, as the minds of all were at that time prepared to expect the coming of the Messiah. They intended, no doubt, to exalt this instance of the grace of God, without detracting anything from what had formerly happened. Besides, it ought to be observed that this was not a premeditated statement, but a sudden burst of admiration.

"But the Pharisees said. . . ." Hence it is evident with what rage and fury they were filled, who did not scruple to assail with wicked slander so illustrious a work of God. We ought to observe the contrast between the applause of the people and the blasphemy of those men. The saying of the people, that nothing like it ever happened in Israel, is a confession arising from a sense of the divine glory. This makes it more evident that those persons were utterly mad who ventured, as it were, to curse God to his face. We learn from it also that, when wickedness has reached the height of blindness, there is no work of God, however evident, that it will not pervert. It is, no doubt, monstrous and incredible that mortals should cry against their Creator. Commentary on a Harmony of the Evangelists.[12]

The Ordering of Matthew's Narrative.

Heinrich Bullinger: It appears also by those things that have been handled hitherto, that Matthew in the beginning used a natural order and somewhat after an artificial, that he goes forward chiefly in this order because it is most fit to teach by. For he seems to have a care not so much to set forth faithfully that which was said and done by the lord as to place everything in his own place and order, and solely to teach by fit order and chiefly to move the minds of the hearers, yea and so engraft more deeply Christ and faith in Christ. Hitherto Matthew has reported a certain abridgement of all the doctrine of Christ the Lord, whereby he plentifully instructed his worshipers in true godliness; hitherto he has joined certain of his great miracles, even divine and wonderful works, whereby he has declared that he is the mighty and gentle Lord of all things, which can make those also, who stick to him by true faith, Lord of sin, of death, of Satan, and of all things else. The Sum of the Four Evangelists.[13]

The Identity of the Laborers of the Harvest.

Juan de Valdés: Christ, in saying to his disciples "the harvest is great" . . . calls them the multitude ready for conversion, harvest crops, whom he had compared to sheep, and effectively it is so, that they who pertain to the kingdom of heaven are sheep, who follow Christ as their shepherd; and they are harvest crops, for that just as harvest crops are stored away in the farmer's barns, so they are put in possession of the kingdom of God; an occupation they continue in the life eternal. Christ, in saying, "Pray therefore to the Lord of the harvest" . . . teaches us that God will be sought in prayer even in those things on which he has determined; and even in those things wherein his own glory is illustrated; and that it is our duty to ask him for them. The laborers to gather in God's harvest I understand to be those who are sent by God to preach the gospel and to teach Christian life; and for this reason he says, "Pray that he may send." Commentary upon the Gospel of St. Matthew.[14]

---

[11]Dickson, *Brief Exposition* (1651), 103-4.
[12]CTS 1:418-19* (CO 45:261-62).

[13]Bullinger, *The Summe of the Foure Evangelists* (1582), B3.
[14]Valdés, *Commentary upon the Gospel of St. Matthew*, 162.

10:1-42 THE COST AND REWARD
OF FOLLOWING JESUS

And he called to him his twelve disciples and gave them authority over unclean spirits, to cast them out, and to heal every disease and every affliction. [2]The names of the twelve apostles are these: first, Simon, who is called Peter, and Andrew his brother; James the son of Zebedee, and John his brother; [3]Philip and Bartholomew; Thomas and Matthew the tax collector; James the son of Alphaeus, and Thaddaeus;[a] [4]Simon the Zealot,[b] and Judas Iscariot, who betrayed him.

[5]These twelve Jesus sent out, instructing them, "Go nowhere among the Gentiles and enter no town of the Samaritans, [6]but go rather to the lost sheep of the house of Israel. [7]And proclaim as you go, saying, 'The kingdom of heaven is at hand.'[c] [8]Heal the sick, raise the dead, cleanse lepers,[d] cast out demons. You received without paying; give without pay. [9]Acquire no gold or silver or copper for your belts, [10]no bag for your journey, or two tunics[e] or sandals or a staff, for the laborer deserves his food. [11]And whatever town or village you enter, find out who is worthy in it and stay there until you depart. [12]As you enter the house, greet it. [13]And if the house is worthy, let your peace come upon it, but if it is not worthy, let your peace return to you. [14]And if anyone will not receive you or listen to your words, shake off the dust from your feet when you leave that house or town. [15]Truly, I say to you, it will be more bearable on the day of judgment for the land of Sodom and Gomorrah than for that town.

[16]"Behold, I am sending you out as sheep in the midst of wolves, so be wise as serpents and innocent as doves. [17]Beware of men, for they will deliver you over to courts and flog you in their synagogues, [18]and you will be dragged before governors and kings for my sake, to bear witness before them and the Gentiles. [19]When they deliver you over, do not be anxious how you are to speak or what you are to say, for what you are to say will be given to you in that hour. [20]For it is not you who speak, but the Spirit of your Father speaking through you. [21]Brother will deliver brother over to death, and the father his child, and children will rise against parents and have them put to death, [22]and you will be hated by all for my name's sake. But the one who endures to the end will be saved. [23]When they persecute you in one town, flee to the next, for truly, I say to you, you will not have gone through all the towns of Israel before the Son of Man comes.

[24]"A disciple is not above his teacher, nor a servant[f] above his master. [25]It is enough for the disciple to be like his teacher, and the servant like his master. If they have called the master of the house Beelzebul, how much more will they malign[g] those of his household.

[26]"So have no fear of them, for nothing is covered that will not be revealed, or hidden that will not be known. [27]What I tell you in the dark, say in the light, and what you hear whispered, proclaim on the housetops. [28]And do not fear those who kill the body but cannot kill the soul. Rather fear him who can destroy both soul and body in hell.[h] [29]Are not two sparrows sold for a penny?[i] And not one of them will fall to the ground apart from your Father. [30]But even the hairs of your head are all numbered. [31]Fear not, therefore; you are of more value than many sparrows. [32]So everyone who acknowledges me before men, I also will acknowledge before my Father who is in heaven, [33]but whoever denies me before men, I also will deny before my Father who is in heaven.

[34]"Do not think that I have come to bring peace to the earth. I have not come to bring peace, but a sword. [35]For I have come to set a man against his father, and a daughter against her mother, and a daughter-in-law against her mother-in-law. [36]And a person's enemies will be those of his own household. [37]Whoever loves father or mother more than me is not worthy of me, and whoever loves son or daughter more than me is not worthy of me. [38]And whoever does not take his cross and follow me is not worthy of me. [39]Whoever finds his life will lose it, and whoever loses his life for my sake will find it.

⁴⁰"*Whoever receives you receives me, and whoever receives me receives him who sent me. ⁴¹The one who receives a prophet because he is a prophet will receive a prophet's reward, and the one who receives a righteous person because he is a*

righteous person will receive a righteous person's reward. ⁴²And whoever gives one of these little ones even a cup of cold water because he is a disciple, truly, I say to you, he will by no means lose his reward."

a Some manuscripts *Lebbaeus,* or *Lebbaeus called Thaddaeus*   b Greek *kananaios,* meaning *zealot*   c Or *The kingdom of heaven has come near*   d *Leprosy* was a term for several skin diseases; see Leviticus 13   e Greek *chiton,* a long garment worn under the cloak next to the skin   f Or *bondservant;* also verse 25   g Greek lacks *will they malign*   h Greek *Gehenna*   i Greek *assarion,* Roman copper coin (Latin *quadrans*) worth about 1/16 of a *denarius* (which was a day's wage for a laborer)

OVERVIEW: Jesus sets aside twelve of his disciples for a mission that will closely parallel his own. He grounds the disciples' ministry as "undershepherds" or workers in the field in his authority (over demons, disease, and death). The Reformation commentators provide several observations about the twelve apostles and their specific mission. The urgency of their preaching matches that of John the Baptist (Mt 3:2) and Jesus (Mt 4:17), for "the kingdom of heaven is at hand," and it probably assumes a similar message of repentance. As Valdés indicates, what these apostles are proclaiming to the "lost sheep" of Israel is entrance into the kingdom through accepting the King.

As Jesus continues his instructions to his twelve apostles, he warns them of the opposition they will face. Though his sheep will face the wolves of opposition, they are to be shrewd in recognizing the persecution as part of a spiritual opposition to the kingdom itself. Heinrich Bullinger connects the warnings of sufferings with the mission in the first section of the chapter. He also notes that Jesus' purpose in including those warnings was to prepare and to encourage his disciples concerning the coming persecutions. The persecution will be from religious leaders ("synagogues"), secular magistrates ("governors and kings"), and family relations ("brother will betray brother"). The Reformation commentators remind their readers that the comfort Jesus provides to his disciples in light of this looming persecution is the presence and power of the Spirit.

Luther is representative of the reformers by matching the warning motif of Jesus with his own

exhortation to persevere in faith. The sufferings the disciples face will cause many to fall away, especially those who affirm aspects of the gospel in their own strength only. The intensity of persecution often helps disciples to be reminded of the urgency of the mission and the humble example of Jesus.

The regular and intense suffering that Christ's followers will have to endure might lead some to fear those who are threatening them. Jesus teaches that no hidden act of persecution goes unnoticed by God. The reformers warn that God's care does not keep disciples from all injury or pain, but they assure Christians of God's abiding providence and concern, even over the little things of life.

In the final section of the discourse, Jesus drives home the costliness of following him and the required confession of a disciple. The Reformation commentators note how the divisive nature of Jesus' ministry ("sword") can be seen in the perennial conflict that can occur between the closest human relationships and the cause of Christ. To give up these human relationships captures the spirit of the disciple's need to take up one's cross. Ultimately, God rewards the sacrifices of his followers.

10:1-15 *The Twelve Apostles and Jesus' Instructions*

NOTES ON THE TWELVE DISCIPLES. GIOVANNI DIODATI: As if he had newly established twelve patriarchs, so would he in this number of twelve newly build and renew his church. "Gave them power": the right use of miracles are here seen and to what purpose they are wrought—namely, for a witness to and establishing of God's word, without which they are to be held as suspect. . . .

A Greek word that signified sent or delegated to do some business: ambassadors; as such were the Twelve called, because they were to have no certain abode of residence and that their ministry was to be about the world as in a strange country out of the church to carry the message of God's reconciliation and to gather his elect together. "The first," not only in the list as eldest, and first called with Andrew but also as it should seem, conduct and presidency over the other as an elder brother by the Lord's own disposing, for the time they lived together, for when they were separated, there is no such thing spoken of and all without any superiority in degree, much less in domination. "Is called": by a surname given him by Christ himself. . . .

"Lebbaeus," who is the same as is called Judas, the brother of James, the son of Alpheus, whose the epistle of St. Jude. It is thought that Lebbaeus the Hebrew word and Thaddeus the Syriac word are of one and the same signification, namely, a man of heart or of courage. "The Canaanite," which is according to some of the city of Cana; according to others, it is the name of a religion or sect, namely, of zealots or zealed, as it is set down. Wherewith the Hebrew word may very well agree. "Iscariot." It is not certainly known from whence this surname is taken. Some interpret it the mercenary Apostata, or the man who does or shall revolt for profit or for reward: so, Judas may be named after his treason, and in this sense might be so here named by way of anticipation, for his avarice that appeared afterward. Others hold that it signifies a man of Kerioth, which was a city of Judah. "Betrayed him." This was also spoken by way of anticipation, like that of Mary. PIOUS ANNOTATIONS.[1]

PREACHING THE KINGDOM OF HEAVEN. JUAN DE VALDÉS: Here I understand that to preach the

kingdom of heaven is nothing other than to preach the mode in which it pleases God to rule and govern not one sole nation, as he did before that Christ had reconciled humanity to God; nor by written law, as he did before that the law had been fulfilled in Christ and by Christ; but all the nations of the world, and by his Holy Spirit only; that they, who accept the grace of the gospel, enter into the kingdom of heaven, freed from personal anxiety, renouncing the government of human prudence, and casting all their care upon God, they remit themselves to his rule and to his government.

And here I seem to feel that this kingdom of God is called the kingdom of heaven because it is most divine and most perfect; just as we call things that are most perfect celestial and heavenly. So that the kingdom of heaven is the same as the celestial kingdom, most divine, most spiritual, and most perfect. Christ, having ordered his disciples as to what they should preach, gives them orders as to what works they should perform, saying, "heal the sick." . . . Where it is to be borne in mind what the works are which pertain to the preacher of the gospel, and which he does not himself perform, but the Spirit of God in him. And I hold it to be certain that this working by the Holy Spirit is annexed to the gifts of the apostolate, either conjointly upon body and mind, as was the case in the primitive church, or only upon the mind, as it has been and is from that time to the present.

That "freely you have received, freely give" tends to divest the minds of the apostles from avarice, which, possibly deceived by human prudence, might persuade them that it was right to take from the rich, whom they restored to health, in order to give to the poor, a thing that might give an evil name to the gospel. Christ, designing to remedy this, says, since you have received this gift of working these miracles from God freely, and of his grace, communicate it freely and graciously to those with whom you shall communicate, accepting no recompense for it. COMMENTARY UPON THE GOSPEL OF ST. MATTHEW.[2]

---

[1]Diodati, *Pious Annotations* (1643), D2r-D2v*; citing Mt 4:18; Jn 1:42; Lk 6:15-16; Josh 15:25; Jn 11:2.

[2]Valdés, *Commentary upon the Gospel of St. Matthew*, 165-66.

The Rich Grace of the Gospel. David Dickson: It is a worthy observation that the Lord for confirmation of faith has given power to the first preachers of his doctrine, to deliver women and men from miseries, both of soul and body; from sickness and devils; that in all time coming the power of his gospel might be believed; for "Heal the sick," says he, "Cleanse the lepers, cast out devils." To show the freedom and rich grace of the gospel—whereby, whatsoever belongs to righteousness and salvation is bestowed upon the unworthy, without money, and without price—he gave the first preachers of his grace a command to take no reward for their miraculous cures saying, "Freely have you received, freely give."

In this temporary commandment to the apostles in their first commission, our Lord teaches that such as have a calling to preach need not be solicitous for their living; and that they should not aim at the conquest of money, or means to themselves, but to bring in souls to God. Therefore, says he, "Provide neither gold, nor silver." . . . Christ esteems and declares the preachers of the gospel worthy of their sustenance, and their hearers to be obliged in equity to sustain them, saying, "The worker is worthy of their meat." When the preachers are sustained by the hearers, Christ esteems their sustenance to be no reward, neither to be anything considerable, to hinder their bestowing of the benefit of the gospel, to be esteemed a free gift. For after he says, "Freely give," he adds, "The worker is worthy of their meat." As Christ assures painful preachers that they shall not want, so he gives no order for sustenance of the idle, for there is no servant of his spoken of here, but the workers only, "The worker is worthy of their meat." A Brief Exposition.[3]

Instructions for the Apostles on Their Journey. John Trapp: Into the synagogues and other places of public meeting our Savior sends them not as yet, because they were but young beginners, and wanted boldness and other abilities;

but bids them teach privately, catechize from house to house, and not stretch the wing beyond the nest, till better fledged, and fitted for flight. . . .

The saints are the only worthies, of whom the world is not worthy. These shall walk with Christ, for they are worthy. But the heart of the wicked is of little worth. "Let your peace come upon it." Christian salutations are effectual benedictions: "We bless you in the name of the Lord." . . .

Something will come of your good wishes; if not to others, then to yourselves; you shall be paid for your pains as the physician is, though the patient dies; as the lawyer has his fee though his clients cause miscarry. God will reward his ministers though Israel be not gathered. . . .

Two sure signs of reprobate goats: (1) Not to receive Christ's ministers to house and harbor, accounting themselves happy in such an entertainment. (2) Not to hear their words. The most good is done by God's ministers commonly at first coming. Then some receive the word with admiration, others are daily more and more hardened as fish, though fearful, stir not at the great noise of the sea, whereunto they are accustomed; and as birds that build in a belfry, startle not at the tolling of the bell. . . .

In token that you sought not theirs, but them, and that you will not carry away so much as any of their accursed dust; that you will not have any communion at all with them, wait no longer upon them; that the dust of those feet (that should have been beautiful) shall be fatal and feral to them; that God shall hence forward beat them here as small as dust with his heavy judgments, as with an iron mace, and that hereafter he shall shake them off as dust, when they come to him for salvation, at the last judgment. . . .

God can better bear anything than the abuse of his free grace in the offers of mercy. Profligate professors and profane gospelers shall one day wish, "Oh that I had been from Sodom, that I had never heard a sermon! Or, Oh that I might hear but one sermon more." . . . Should Solomon forsake that God that had appeared to him twice? Good turns aggravate unkindness; and nothing more torments

---

[3]Dickson, *Brief Exposition* (1651), 109-10*.

those in hell than to think that they might have been happy, had they been worthy their years, as they say. COMMENTARY OR EXPOSITION UPON THE FOUR EVANGELISTS.[4]

WHY THE APOSTLES SHOULD SHAKE OFF THE DUST. JOHANN GERHARD: The reason Christ commanded, "Shake off the dust," which is a sign of transgression against the apostles, was in order that they not even carry off the small dust from the ungodly. Then the magnitude of the punishment, which would be so great, was in order that the godly may not even be willing to have communion of dust with the ungodly. Third is the testimony of contemptuous grace, that those who cast off the offered salvation might be cursed. It was also a prelude that his own anger might be shaken off or poured out on them.

It was customary with Jews to connect external symbols with words for a greater effect. It is not unlike what Nehemiah 5:13 says, that Nehemiah shook out the fold of his garment in testimony against those who would dishonor the given faith. But among other things it may be comprehended from this teaching of Christ that by the raging of enemies or even of those who refuse to hear the word, he by choice might go at once, as in the example of Elijah, which is seen in 1 Kings 19:3-4. ANNOTATIONS ON MATTHEW.[5]

10:16-23 Disciples Must Endure Persecution

JESUS PREPARES HIS DISCIPLES TO SUFFER. HEINRICH BULLINGER: In this business he had chosen to himself witnesses, whom hitherto he made both be holders and hearers of all his matters, as well as his sayings, as of his doings; to this end verily, that they might afterward bring forth into all the world the charge of common salvation, now conceived and laid up in their minds. And now they seemed sufficiently instructed in the rudi-

ments and principles of faith and of Christian religion, therefore it was convenient that they should be further exercised therein, and by the means therefore prepared to greater matters; and therefore, they are sent forth by the Lord himself to preach the gospel now to the people of Israel only and are instructed in certain commandments. For the Lord does diligently prescribe what they ought to do and what their office is; and he shows them also what they shall suffer, yea how perilous a thing it is to be a minister of the word in a corrupt and unthankful age. Therefore, he comforts his disciples worthily and surely with furnished talk, teaching them how they ought to continue constantly in all adversities in true godliness, and to overcome all evils. THE SUM OF THE FOUR EVANGELISTS.[6]

THE DISCIPLES ALSO FIGHT THE TYRANNY OF SATAN. AUGUSTIN MARLORAT: By these words Christ admonished the disciples that they must not only fight in Judaism, but in places of farther distance, that by long preparation, they might arm themselves to war. By this place also we see that Christ has an evil opinion of all the potentates of the world, and not without cause. For look how much more dignity they are of in this world, and the more power and authority they have, so much the more are they given to persecute Christ and his doctrine, whether they be counsels, common assemblies, magistrates, or kinds; that is, the whole seat of judgment, all the power of the world, which was ordained of God to the punishment of the wicked, and to the praise and maintenance of the good and godly. Whereby it appears that Satan, the prince of this world, has obtained tyranny in this world to fire up all the force of the world, against Christ the son of God, and that in so perverse a manner, that he has made that power, rule, and authority, which by God was appointed to punish the wicked, and to suppress all impiety, to defend his own kingdom, and to impugn and resist the kingdom of Christ. And that which is most subtle and crafty of all others is this: he does so handle

---

[4]Trapp, A Commentary or Exposition upon the Four Evangelists (1647), 329-30*; citing Prov 10:20.
[5]Gerhard, Annotationes Posthumae in Evangelium D. Matthaei (1663), 554.

[6]Bullinger, The Summe of the Foure Evangelists (1582), B3-B4*.

and use the matter that he makes the magistrates, princes, and kings believe that they do good service to God, when as in deeds they do the contrary and are such, of whom Christ speaks, saying: "The hour will come in which, whoever kills you will think that they do God good service."

The sense and meaning of this place is this: that the disciples must witness the will of God to foreign princes, far countries, to the end they might be inexcusable. Hereby let the ministers of the world learn that their labor is not in vain, although they be rejected by the wicked, because the word that they preach shall be a testimony in the day of judgment against them. EXPOSITION OF THE HOLY GOSPEL OF MATTHEW.[7]

THE HOLY SPIRIT EMPOWERS THE PERSE-CUTED. JOHANNES OECOLAMPADIUS: When they have delivered you over, even in that moment when you are forsaken by all, you should not consider yourself forsaken by God, as if you did not have him helping you; the Holy Spirit will give you a mouth and wisdom to withstand all things. We ourselves are unlearned, but truth in itself is praiseworthy and always anointed. Even if all do not believe that which they hear, yet nevertheless, it remains anointed. Yes, there are even many, who by cut off tongues do not cease to proclaim fine words to God, certainly to such an extent are assured by God in a faithful conscience. Therefore, it is not the mind of Christ, in order that now by our time we may be free from readings of divine literature and may put books altogether to the side. By much reading a work is for exhortation, so that we may be able to oppose our adversaries. COMMENTARY ON THE GOSPEL OF MATTHEW 10:19.[8]

THE FATHER'S PROMISE OF THE SPIRIT'S SPEECH. ARGULA VON GRUMBACH:

For Christ gives me assurance clear
I never need have any fear.

For even if summoned straight away.
His Father tells us what to say.
He puts his Spirit in our mouths
And speaks for us in such an hour
"You're not the ones who have to speak";
This promise makes my heart to leap.

"JOHANNES OF LANZHUT": ATTACK AND RESPONSE.[9]

NOT EVERYONE WILL RECEIVE THE GOSPEL. MARTIN LUTHER: He concludes that the spirit may be strengthened to persevere in such temptations, continual tribulations. Because at first the teaching of the gospel is seen even by flesh as lovely, and many, who consider godliness to be gain, will receive it as the hope of glory, riches, and favor. But when they feel nothing but hatred, persecutions, and tribulations by loss of wages, they forsake it and are often even made enemies. Therefore, Christ chose to say, many will begin, but few will persevere. For they will begin by a feeling of the flesh— that is, they will seek what they are themselves, not what they are in God. Therefore, when they do not succeed, they are removed and do not persevere. Wherefore, blessed are those who persevere, because they alone will be saved. Here is able to be brought together by the parable about the seed sown among rocks and strangled among thorns. For they begin with cheerfulness, but they are strangled among thorns. Whence it is said in a proverb: First it glitters, in the middle it is lukewarm, in the end, it abhors. Thus it is in every kind of life. NOTES ON SELECT CHAPTERS OF MATTHEW.[10]

THE GOSPEL WILL SPREAD IN SPITE OF ADVERSITY. DESIDERIUS ERASMUS: I grant you liberty to avoid danger and peril by fleeing and running away, not only that you may be in safety yourself, but also if by this occasion the fame of the gospel may be spread the further abroad. Therefore, if they persecute you in one city, give

---

[7]Marlorat, ed., *A Catholike and Ecclesiasticall Exposition of the Holy Gospell After S. Mathewe*, 212*.
[8]Oecolampadius, *Enarratio in Evangelium Matthae* (1536), 137v.

[9]Grumbach, *Argula von Grumbach*, 175 (AvG 136).
[10]Luther, *Annotationes in Aliquot Capita Matthei*, 21.

place to their madness and flee into another, so if in no wise at a little iniquity of persecution, cease not from your labor in the gospel. This only is to be done now that the fame of the gospel may be spread throughout all Palestine. And in this persecution shall you do good, because he shall not suffer you to tarry long in one place. The time shall come when you shall avoid persecution with flight. Now the time is short, and haste must be made. For the kingdom of God is at hand. This I assure you, before that you have gone out over all the cities of Jews, the Son of Man will show himself and will help you being in danger. An example shall be shown you in him how great adversities the preachers of the gospel must suffer. The which all ought to seem to you the more tolerable for this that you see that I have suffered all manner of reproaches and afflictions. The student is not better than the master, nor the servant better than the lord. This suffices to the student if they be equal with their master. This ought to suffice the servant, if they be equal with their lord. If they have so unworthily checked me, the father of the house, in so much that in most vile reproach they called me Beelzebub and named the Son of God by the name of the unclean devil, then what marvel is it if they be bold upon the servants of the house? I know that infamy seems a great ill and almost more grievous than death, but it is a praise and no infamy which comes of wicked people for the gospel's sake. They will say that you are witches, ill doers, and seditious, but this ignominy and shame afterward shall be turned into glory. Your sincerity and innocence shall appear unto the world, which sincerity all people shall praise, curse those which have defamed you with false report. . . .

There is nothing therefore why you should be troubled with fear of infamy and not freely preach the gospel of the kingdom. It has no dishonest thing, nor nothing to be kept close. Yes, if you hear anything of people in darkness, preach you it in the clear light. And if I have told you anything secretly, preach it openly. Our doctrine is without any coloring. It desires to come forth before all people and it is afraid to be known of no one. PARAPHRASES.[11]

10:24-39 *Disciples Must Fear Only God*

DISCIPLES OF JESUS NEED NOT FEAR DEATH. HEINRICH BULLINGER: The Lord Jesus, the true and very Son of God, the life and resurrection of the faithful, says plainly in the gospel, "Fear not those who kill the body, but are not able to kill the soul; but rather fear those who are able to destroy both body and soul in hell." If when the body being slain by tyrants the soul is not killed, then it remains alive after the body is destroyed; and so assuredly it remains that, having put off the body, it should be cast by the most just God into hell, there everlastingly to burn for his unfaithfulness. For in the same gospel the Lord says again, "Whosoever will save their life shall lose it"; again, "Whosoever will lose their life for my sake shall find it." For they not only lose their life or soul, which bridles it from the pleasures of the world and lives most temperately, but they also who offer themselves into the bloody hands of tyrants to be slain for the confession of Christian faith. And they find their life or soul which they lost. OF THE REASONABLE SOUL OF MAN.[12]

FEARING GOD, NOT MEN, BY THE INDWELLING SPIRIT. ARGULA VON GRUMBACH:

Although book learning I have not
I'm not afraid—no, not one jot!
I'll come to you without complaint
To praise and honor God's great name
Whom now so coarsely you defile
Making idols, that's your style.
In my weakness God will be
My spirit's strength, to his glory.
As Christ commands me, Matthew Ten,
Do not fear at all those men
Who take your body, naught else harm.
Fear rather God, of him I warn

---

[11]EP 46r-46v*.
[12]DHB 3:383.

With power over body and soul
To drag both down to hell.
Our flesh cannot accomplish this
Unless God's Spirit dwells within.

"Johannes of Lanzhut": Attack and Response.[13]

The Precepts and the Providence of God.

Huldrych Zwingli: In these words of Christ, we perceive that everything takes place under the precepts and the providence of God. Had he said, "The sparrows shall not be sold without the heavenly Father," one might have been able to surmise, "Yes, indeed, God sends some things and some things he does not send." But he does say, "Not one of the sparrows falls to the ground without the directive of the Father." We cannot but admit that not even the least thing takes place unless it is ordered by God. For who has ever been so concerned and curious as to find out how much hair he has on his head? There is no one. God, however, knows the number. Indeed, nothing is too small in us or in any other creature, not to be ordered by the all-knowing and all-powerful providence of God. How much more then are all our works ordered by divine decrees? Since this is so, we cannot ascribe any credit to ourselves. Rather, we should know that everything happens by the decree of God to whom alone all things ought to be credited. An Exposition of the Articles.[14]

The Particular Care of God's Providence.

Martin Chemnitz: We must note also the emphasis of the words, that in undertaking to describe the providence of God he uses the most lowly birds. For in Pliny's *Natural History*,[†] it says, "Sparrows are very short-lived. The males do not live more than a year because of their great sexual activity." Other people say that sparrows often bring leprosy or some other fatal disease. Therefore, he is saying that God's providence extends even to so vile and contemptible a bird as the sparrow, which is valued at the lowest and cheapest price (for the penny was the smallest coin made), and two can be bought for the price of one penny, if a person wants to buy them. In Luke 12:6 the number of sparrows per penny increases, for no one is willing to pay a penny, the smallest coin, even if the bird seller is willing to give two sparrows for one penny, but rather he must throw one more into the bargain. This is what the text says, "Five sparrows are sold for two pennies," that is, two *assaria*, "and yet not one of them," which are so contemptible and worthless in the eyes of humans, "falls to the ground without your Father." For because they inhabit the higher regions, they are said to "fall to the earth" when they are caught and die. Luke 12:6 makes an even clearer reference to providence: "None is forgotten before God." Matthew 10:30 adds to this idea; not only your soul, which is immortal is under God's care, not only the principal members of your body, which are called the vital parts or organs, but the very hairs, which are produced out of unnecessary fluids of the body and seem to fall off in a purely accidental manner, not only are they a matter of concern to God, but have been numbered. For we number those things that we are very anxious to keep with particular care. Loci Theologici.[15]

The Ban Is the Sword of the Church.

Balthasar Hubmaier: The ban and punishing with the sword are two different commands given by God. The first is promised and given to the church by Christ to be used according to his will for the purpose of admitting the godly into her holy communion and in the exclusion of the unworthy. Thus, whomever's sins the Christian church forgives on earth, the same are also forgiven in the heavens, and whomever's sins she does not forgive here on earth, the same are also not remitted in the heavens. . . . The second command concerns the outward temporal authority and

[13]Grumbach, *Argula von Grumbach*, 175-76 (AvG 136).
[14]Zwingli, *The Defense of the Reformed Faith*, 1:144-45.

[15]Chemnitz, *Loci Theologici*, 1:168. †Pliny the Elder, *Natural History* 10.36 (10.26.107).

government which originally was given by God to Adam after the fall. ON THE SWORD.[16]

THE GREATER DANGER OF DENYING CHRIST.

CHRISTOPHER BLACKWOOD: There is a habitual denial of Christ, when a man in the bent and frame of his heart has an intention in himself that, rather than he will leave such a dwelling, or estate, or friend, or credit, or suffer such an imprisonment, banishment, dismembering, or death, he will (if he cannot evade by distinction, and so craftily come off, which is no less guilt in the sight of God, though less reproach in human sight) flatly deny that which in his heart he acknowledges to be the eternal truth of God. Many must needs acknowledge this a horrible sin, but few think themselves to live in this sin; and yet give me leave to tell you, that most people, where the sound of the gospel is, live in this sin, though not explicitly to have such an intention expressed in the mind, yet implicitly, because they have not a habitual intention to leave all that is dear unto them for the Lord. They do not say in their hearts: they will not leave all rather than deny the truth. Neither do they say in their hearts, they will leave all rather than deny the truth, but embrace the truth at certain points, without any determination at all what to do in point of confession; the former, I mean actual denial of Christ, though it may, and commonly does fill the conscience of the person who falls into it with horror and anguish; yet does it not exclude a man out of heaven, but this habitual denial which remains in most souls with little or no anguish, and may (and too often does) remain in persons that have made a large and long profession, excludes out of heaven; and this is the denial I take to be meant here in the text. . . .

Because those who do habitually deny Christ go on in a purpose of sin, they live and die in a purpose of sin. Now a purpose of sin is punished with rejection from Christ. . . . And assuredly Christ will deny you, and in this soul-damning purpose to deny Christ for the escaping of crosses

and for the holding of earthly enjoyments, the most men in the world live. A TREATISE CONCERNING DENIAL OF CHRIST.[17]

WHAT IT MEANS TO TAKE UP THE CROSS.

JOHN MAYER: The Lord having shown what the effect of the preaching of the gospel would be through the corruption of humankind, namely, that the son would be against the father embracing it, and his nearest friends would become his deadly foes, he now . . . seeks to make them resolute that should be thus tempted; for they must either endure father and mother and any of their nearest kindred to be their enemies for Christ's sake, or else at the last be rejected as unworthy of Christ. Yea he adds that not only these things ought not to move them, but if they should with him be put to a most shameful death upon the cross; for as in suffering thus for him, they should save their souls, so in refusing to suffer they should lose them. For thus with Chrysostom[†] I understand the taking up of the cross, this sense being confirmed in the next words, which are of losing the life. And therefore, that of Hilary[‡] and of Gregory[§] is but an allegorical conceit, and not to be followed. For the phrase of taking up the cross does not argue that they should offer themselves to death . . . as the Donatists[◊] gathered; but as was their manner there toward persons condemned to be crucified, to bear each their own cross, as we see afterward, that our Lord was compelled to do. That which Luke has, "He that hates not father and mother" . . . may seem to be too harsh, but the sense is the same with this in Matthew, not to love being in the Scripture phrase to hate, as appears in many places, especially when God and anything in this world are spoken of, as being in competition one with the other. A COMMENTARY UPON THE NEW TESTAMENT.[18]

---

[16]CRR 5:504-5*; citing Mt 18:15; Jn 20:23; Gen 3:16.

[17]Blackwood, *A Treatise Concerning Denial of Christ* (1648), 3-8*.
[18]Mayer, *A Commentarie upon the New Testament* (1631), 1:161-62. [†]Chrysostom, *Homilies on Matthew*, NPNF[1] 10:228. [‡]Hilary of Poitiers, De Trinitate, NPNF[2] 9:185-86. [§]Gregory the Great, Sermon LIX, NPNF[2] 12:172. [◊]The Donatists were a North

10:40-42 *Reward for the Righteous*

TEMPORARY LOSS AND ETERNAL REWARD.
HENRY HAMMOND: This comfort means while
you have that as those who use any way of
compliance with the persecutors, and so escape
their malice and save their life shall gain little by
this, but be involved in the destruction that awaits
them. So, on the other side, those who shall hazard
the utmost, that they may stick close to me, shall
be likely to fare best even in this world. For thus I
foretell you it will be. Some, to comply with the
persecuting Jews and to escape their persecution,
will renounce Christianity and feign themselves
zealous Jews, and so when the destruction falls
upon the Jews as it certainly shall most heavily,
they shall be involved in that destruction. And that
is all they shall get by that compliance and pusilla-
nimity; whereas at the same time they that comply
not and so venture all that the Jews malice can do
against them shall by the destruction of their
persecutors be rescued from that danger and live to
see a peaceable profession of Christianity; or, if
they do not, have the loss of a short temporary life
rewarded with an eternal [one]. PARAPHRASE
AND ANNOTATIONS.[19]

CHRIST IDENTIFIES WITH HIS DISCIPLES.
JOHN CALVIN: A considerable portion of the world
may be opposed to the disciples of Christ, and the
confession of their faith may draw upon them
universal hatred. Yet here is another consolation
tending to excite a very great number of persons to
treat them with kindness. Whatever is done to
them Christ does not hesitate to reckon as done to
himself. This shows how dearly he loves them,
when he places to his own account the kind offices
which they have received. He is not speaking here
about receiving the doctrine, but about receiving

the people. The latter meaning, I admit, arises out
of the former, but we must attend to the design of
Christ. Perceiving that this was exceedingly
adapted to support their weakness, he intended to
assure them that, if anyone would receive them in a
friendly manner and do them kind offices, he
would be as highly pleased as if their benevolence
had been exercised toward his own person; and not
only so, but that in such a sacrifice God the Father
would smell a sweet savor.

He begins with the prophets but at length
comes down to the lowest rank and embraces all
his disciples. In this manner he commends all
without exception who truly worship God and love
the gospel. To receive a person in the name of a
prophet or in the name of a righteous person
means to do them good for the "sake of honoring
their doctrine, or of paying respect to piety."
Though God enjoins us to perform offices of
kindness to all humankind, yet he justly elevates
his people to a higher rank, that they may be the
objects of peculiar regard and esteem. . . .

"Shall receive a prophet's reward." This clause
is variously interpreted by commentators. Some
think that it denotes a mutual compensation, or,
in other words, that spiritual benefits are
bestowed on the prophets of God instead of
temporal benefits. But if this exposition is
admitted, what shall we say is meant by the
righteous person's reward? Others understand it
to mean that those who shall be kind to them
will partake of the same reward which is laid up
for prophets and the righteous. Some refer it to
the intercourse of saints and suppose it to mean
that as by our kind actions we give evidence that
we are one body with the servants of Christ, so
in this way we become partakers of all the
blessings which Christ imparts to the members
of his body.

I consider it simply as denoting the reward
which corresponds to the rank of the person to
whom kindness has been exercised; for Christ
means that this will be a remarkable proof of the
high estimation in which he holds his prophets and
indeed all his disciples. The greatness of the reward

African schismatic Christian group in the early church. They
were persecuted aggressively by imperial forces, with a number
turning themselves in to the authorities and thereby volunteering
for martyrdom.
[19]Hammond, *Paraphrase and Annotations upon All the Books of the
New Testament*, 1:45.

will make it evident that not one kind office which was ever rendered to them has been forgotten. By way of amplification, he promises a "reward" to the very meanest offices of kindness, such as giving them a cup of cold water. He gives the name of "little ones" not only to those who occupy the lowest place, or are held in least estimation in the church, but to all his disciples, whom the pride of the world tramples under foot. COMMENTARY ON A HARMONY OF THE EVANGELISTS.[20]

---

[20]CTS 1:475-77 (CO 45:296-97); citing Gen 8:21.

11:1-30 "COME TO ME"

When Jesus had finished instructing his twelve disciples, he went on from there to teach and preach in their cities.

[2]Now when John heard in prison about the deeds of the Christ, he sent word by his disciples [3]and said to him, "Are you the one who is to come, or shall we look for another?" [4]And Jesus answered them, "Go and tell John what you hear and see: [5]the blind receive their sight and the lame walk, lepers[a] are cleansed and the deaf hear, and the dead are raised up, and the poor have good news preached to them. [6]And blessed is the one who is not offended by me."

[7]As they went away, Jesus began to speak to the crowds concerning John: "What did you go out into the wilderness to see? A reed shaken by the wind? [8]What then did you go out to see? A man[b] dressed in soft clothing? Behold, those who wear soft clothing are in kings' houses. [9]What then did you go out to see? A prophet?[c] Yes, I tell you, and more than a prophet. [10]This is he of whom it is written,

"'Behold, I send my messenger before your face,
who will prepare your way before you.'

[11]Truly, I say to you, among those born of women there has arisen no one greater than John the Baptist. Yet the one who is least in the kingdom of heaven is greater than he. [12]From the days of John the Baptist until now the kingdom of heaven has suffered violence,[d] and the violent take it by force. [13]For all the Prophets and the Law prophesied until John, [14]and if you are willing to accept it, he is Elijah who is to come. [15]He who has ears to hear,[e] let him hear.

[16]"But to what shall I compare this generation? It is like children sitting in the marketplaces and calling to their playmates,

[17]"'We played the flute for you, and you did not dance;
we sang a dirge, and you did not mourn.'

[18]For John came neither eating nor drinking, and they say, 'He has a demon.' [19]The Son of Man came eating and drinking, and they say, 'Look at him! A glutton and a drunkard, a friend of tax collectors and sinners!' Yet wisdom is justified by her deeds."[f]

[20]Then he began to denounce the cities where most of his mighty works had been done, because they did not repent. [21]"Woe to you, Chorazin! Woe to you, Bethsaida! For if the mighty works done in you had been done in Tyre and Sidon, they would have repented long ago in sackcloth and ashes. [22]But I tell you, it will be more bearable on the day of judgment for Tyre and Sidon than for you. [23]And you, Capernaum, will you be exalted to heaven? You will be brought down to Hades. For if the mighty works done in you had been done in Sodom, it would have remained until this day. [24]But I tell you that it will be more tolerable on the day of judgment for the land of Sodom than for you."

[25]At that time Jesus declared, "I thank you, Father, Lord of heaven and earth, that you have hidden these things from the wise and understanding and revealed them to little children; [26]yes, Father, for such was your gracious will.[g] [27]All things have been handed over to me by my Father, and no one knows the Son except the Father, and no one knows the Father except the Son and anyone to whom the Son chooses to reveal him. [28]Come to me, all who labor and are heavy laden, and I will give you rest. [29]Take my yoke upon you, and learn from me, for I am gentle and lowly in heart, and you will find rest for your souls. [30]For my yoke is easy, and my burden is light."

a *Leprosy* was a term for several skin diseases; see Leviticus 13 b Or *Why then did you go out? To see a man...* c Some manuscripts *Why then did you go out? To see a prophet?* d Or *has been coming violently* e Some manuscripts omit *to hear* f Some manuscripts *children* (compare Luke 7:35) g Or *for so it pleased you well*

OVERVIEW: For the Reformation exegetes, John's christological question allows Jesus to provide a reminder that one's conception of the Messiah should make proper use of Old Testament texts and should be cautioned against self-constructed ideals. Many agree that John the Baptist did not question Jesus' identity for his own sake but for his disciples. Various forms of unbelief hinder identifying Jesus as the promised Messiah. Philipp Melanchthon, for example, explains how Jesus resolves the misunderstandings of the type of Messiah he is by pointing to his preaching the gospel to the poor and his miraculous works that they can verify by seeing them with their own eyes.

Zwingli notes that Jesus points to John's greatness by highlighting his humility. Indeed, it is John's humility, more than his unique role, that Jesus calls "great." Other commentators focus on the uniqueness of John's role as one who supersedes the role of a prophet and initiates a new sacrament. John is the "messenger" or "Elijah" (see Ex 23:20 and Mal 3:1; 4:5) who pronounces and immediately precedes the Lord's coming. As the distant proclamations of the prophets moved to the more immediate heralding of John the Baptist, violent rejections increased (see Mt 12:18-21; 26:13-4). Erasmus points to the contrast between the styles of John and Jesus in Matthew 11:16-19, which illustrates the fickle nature of the generation and their unwillingness to receive the message of repentance no matter the messenger. In spite of the resistance of unbelief, the content of the message, "wisdom," will prove to be true to the chagrin of Jesus' generation of leaders.

Though there has been "amazement" at Jesus' teaching and displays of authority in Galilee, as a whole the crowds were not accepting his message of kingdom repentance. The collective examples of Chorazin, Bethsaida, and Capernaum provide a poignant reminder of the need for inward change or repentance. As Calvin notes, God's capacity to exact final, total, and perfect judgment, even to enforce different nuances of judgment, is much greater than humans can fathom.

There were at least two main Reformation approaches to dealing with the hypothetical situation Jesus raises by commenting on what repentance among these foreign cities might have portended. One view explains that Jesus is not discussing saving grace and internal repentance, but simply that outward, civil repentance (i.e., reforms) would have saved the cities from ruin. Others take the approach that Jesus is simply describing a hypothetical condition that points to the repentance that should have happened in these cities.

Jesus declares that the ones who have been granted access to the mysteries of God through the preaching of the gospel are the unlikely ones. Furthermore, all those who pursue God, the kingdom, or righteousness through human wisdom or other prideful, self-righteous endeavors are thwarted. It is through the mercy of the Father that the Son is acknowledged by sinful humans. The intratrinitarian relationship is the basis of the exclusive salvation offered in Jesus. In terms of his gospel message, Jesus having "all things" means that the Son's life and preaching is the only true revelation of the Father, as Calvin describes.

Compared to those who have known the "iron yoke" of God's judgment (see Deut 28:47-48), the unachievable standard of the law, and the heavy burden of their sins, coming to Jesus offers them tremendous relief. Even though they are now yoked for him and they carry the "burden" of his teaching, there is rest for their souls. As Luther contends, Christ's law is light because he has taken away the whole law, including its curse.

11:1-19 *John's Messianic Questions*

QUESTIONS ABOUT THE IDENTITY OF JESUS. HENRY HALL: John the Baptist, he had indeed awakened the people as with the sound of a trumpet and stirred them up to a general expectation of the Messiah's coming, but yet many of them remained in suspense and were not so well satisfied about the person of the Messiah, whether John himself or Jesus was he, as appears in Luke 3:15. This scruple was necessary to be cleared, and therefore John being cast into prison, and now near to his martyrdom, he dispatches out two of his disciples in an embassy unto Christ, to know of him whether he was . . . that grand redeemer of Israel, so much desired and so long expected, or whether they should look for some other.

It was not out of any doubt that John himself had (as some ancients have thought) that he sent to Christ this message, for the oracle from heaven had satisfied him in this, and he others. But it was out of a pious desire to inform and settle his disciples who were not yet so well resolved in that matter, as Chrysostom[†] and other interpreters ancient and modern have observed. Our Savior therefore having at that time, as appears by another parallel place, wrought many miracles in healing the sick, cleansing the lepers, raising the dead, he returns this answer. . . . Go and show to John what things you have heard and seen, implying fairly that such divine words and works carried light and conviction enough along with them to reveal their author, and that anyone who could not be moved by such great wonders and miracles was nothing more than a miracle of unbelief, whom such great wonders and miracles could not move. HEAVEN RAVISHED.[1]

WHY JOHN SENDS HIS DISCIPLES TO JESUS. HUGH LATIMER: Now John, intending to correct and amend their false opinion which they had of Christ and of him—for they regarded him too much, and Christ, who was to be most regarded, they esteemed for nothing in comparison of John—therefore John, that good and faithful man, seeing the ignorance of his disciples, acted a wise part. For hearing them talk of the wonderful works which Christ, our Savior, did, he sent them to Christ with this question, "Are you he that should come, or shall we look for another?"

When we look only upon the outward show of these words, a man might think that John himself was doubtful whether Christ were the Savior of the

world or not because he sent his disciples to ask such a question of him. But you must understand that it was not done for John's sake to ask such a question, but rather for his disciples' sake. For John thought that this would be the way to bring them to a good trade, namely, to send them to Christ. For, as for John himself, he doubted not; he knew that Christ was the Savior of the world; he knew it, I say, while he was yet in his mother's womb. For we read in the Gospel of Luke that after the angel came to Mary and brought her such tidings, she arose, and went through the mountains, and came to Jerusalem to Elizabeth her cousin, and as she saluted her, John being unborn, yet knew Christ, who should be born of the Virgin Mary. After that we read in the third chapter of Matthew that when John should baptize Christ, he said to Christ, "I have more need to be baptized of you than you of me." So that it manifestly appears that John doubted not of Christ but knew most certainly that he was the eternal Son of God and the Redeemer which was promised to the fathers to come into the world. JESUS THE TRUE MESSIAH.[2]

JOHN'S DISCIPLES NEED TO HEAR FROM THE CHRIST HIMSELF. PHILIPP MELANCHTHON: John sends his own disciples to inquire, not because he himself was doubting, but so that the disciples might hear from Christ's own mouth that they should expect no other Messiah, and so that they might be led to believe by seeing the miracles with their own eyes. This is the basic point of this envoy.

Second, the reason that the disciples had doubts, moreover, was because the average person was of the belief that the Messiah would restore a political kingdom and would have armies, and after defeating the Gentiles they would occupy provinces, just as the monarchs Cyrus, Alexander, and others did. Therefore, when they were seeing that this Jesus was only a poor preacher, they were influenced by his humble appearance to doubt whether he is the Messiah.

---

[1]Hall, *Heaven Ravished or A Glorious Prize* (1644), 1-2*; citing Jn 1:32-33. [†]Chrysostom, *Homilies on Matthew*, NPNF[1] 10:238-45.

[2]Latimer, *Select Sermons and Letters*, 277-78*.

Third, Christ directs his response to their grounds for doubting, however, and teaches of what sort the future kingdom of the Messiah will be, when he says, "The poor have the gospel preached to them." Likewise, "Blessed is the one who is not made to stumble because of me." In other words, the kingdom of the Messiah will not be political, built up with riches, an army, and similar to the powers of the world, but it will be as you see it, the Messiah accomplishing his end through the preaching of the gospel, and he will gather the eternal church from all the nations by the message of the gospel, and through the gospel he will give the remission of sins, and the Son himself will restore those who believe and repent, and will endow them with the Spirit and eternal life. For these reasons the Messiah was promised, not so that he could establish a worldly power. ANNOTATIONS ON THE GOSPELS.[3]

THE VALUE OF JESUS' ANSWER TO JOHN'S QUESTION. THOMAS JACKSON: How this answer of our Savior could possibly either confirm or ratify John's former belief of Christ's person, office, or actions, or add any increase to his knowledge or comfort; or lastly give any part of satisfaction to the distrust or diffidence of his disciples; seeing there is nothing more contained in this answer, than John and his disciples undoubtedly knew before. For so it is said in the second verse of this chapter, when John being in prison had heard the works of Christ, he sent two of his disciples, and said unto him, "Are you he that should come, or do we look for another?" Now what works done by Christ could John hear of in prison which were not truly miraculous, which were not the very same with those that our Savior in my text informs John to have been wrought by him, as restoring of the blind to their sight, the lame to their limbs, the sick to health, the dumb to speech, the dead to life, and so on? . . .

So that our Savior's answer, though it seemed doubtful in the premises, is in conclusion as perfect

as if he had directly and expressly said: Go, tell John that I am he that was to come, and that you are not to expect another, seeing whatsoever you can expect or desire in any one or more, whom you may imagine yet to come, that you may have in me alone; for true blessedness is all that you or any man can desire, and "blessed is he whosoever shall not be offended in me." But though John and his disciples could desire no more of him that was to come than to be truly blessed in him, yet might they desire some further proof than his bare assertion or authority, that they might be truly blessed in him. . . . All this is true, yet notwithstanding all this, the things which they did hear and see were undoubted pledges and visible assurances of this invisible blessedness, which here he promises, and of which every person might have undoubted experience in themselves, so they would not be offended in him. CHRIST'S ANSWER UNTO JOHN'S QUESTION.[4]

THE GREATNESS OF JOHN'S HUMILITY. HULD-RYCH ZWINGLI: Christ intends to show here the prominence of John by the greatness of his humility. But he did not in this saying circumscribe the extent of humility, as if no one could be more humble than John was. Rather, could someone be more insignificant or humble even than John was, he would be greater. I am not taken off the track in this because there is no one before me who shares this interpretation. You know well what is meant by "kingdom of heaven" in many places in the New Testament, namely, nothing other than "believing people." Thus Christ would have wanted to indicate here that God does not measure prominence by pomp or great glory or name, but by humility; in that no one as yet born has surpassed John. But whoever should seek to surpass him would have to do it through humility. That some of the earlier interpreters have interpreted this passage to refer to Christ or the angels seems to me to be out of place here. AN EXPOSITION OF THE ARTICLES.[5]

---

[3]MO 14:839-40.

[4]Jackson, *Christ's Answer unto John's Question* (1625), 470-74; citing Mt 11:6.
[5]Zwingli, *The Defense of the Reformed Faith*, 1:244.

Violence and the Kingdom of Heaven.

Philipp Melanchthon: "The law and the prophets up to the time of John," that is, "You are foolish to imagine that now the law of Moses will reign among the Gentiles, and the whole world will be a Jewish state." Cast away this error; now is the end of this state, and another kingdom is coming, a kingdom of the heavens, and it comes by force. But do not take these words to mean that Christ will seize power by force, as Alexander did, but that divine power bursts forth against the raging madness of the devils and tyrants, and it advances even though the devils and tyrants do not wish it. "And the violent seize it"—that is to say, those who are not timid, who do not flee dangers, but stand fast and place the glory and confession of God before their own life and all pleasures.

Here let's give an explanation for that phrase "The law up to John" and point out that while many seek subtle interpretations, we prefer to be content with this simpler one, that here Christ is speaking about the end of the state. Therefore, here he is speaking about the law to the extent that it is political, that is, about ceremonies and legal matters . . . and also about the moral law, to the extent that it is external discipline, exerting civil control. And let the distinction of the three parts of the law be recited to the people in a plain and simple way. . . .

Christ testifies for John that he is a faithful teacher and a witness concerning the Messiah. And he says that he is not like a courtier who plays the sycophant to lords. . . . Afterward he dwells on the description of the office itself. What was a prophet among the people? A person who foretells about the Messiah, gives guidance in some political decisions, and preserves the law of Moses. Therefore, John says, "I am not a prophet." And Christ says, "You are more than a prophet."

Why? Because he points out that the Messiah is at hand and lays the foundation for the new church, he baptizes, he receives Gentiles and Jews; to the other prophets it was not granted to establish the new sacrament. Therefore, he says, "A greater has not arisen," namely, a greater in that office, because no one's office is greater than that of John after Christ. Therefore, Christ excepts himself when he says, "The one who is least in the kingdom of heaven is greater"—that is, Christ, who was far more humble than all people, is greater than John. He baptizes in the Holy Spirit, is the Redeemer and Savior, just as John says. From his fullness we receive all things. Annotations on the Gospels.[6]

Seeking the Kingdom of Heaven with Zeal.

Stephen Marshall: Is the kingdom of heaven a business of that nature that all who are rightly informed about it will seek it violently, eagerly, with all their strength? . . . I desire that for the time to come we might make it our only work for ourselves, to "work out our salvation with fear and trembling." I wish I knew what to say to inflame your hearts about it, wish the Lord did please to open your eyes and show you how little the world is worth, and how little good is to be found in it, and how far below your souls and how much your immoral souls are worth, and how excellent a thing the kingdom of heaven is, that you might be contented with Paul for time to come, to make it your work to pursue after it, to account all loss to win Jesus Christ, do anything, or be anything, so it be in the pursuit of the kingdom of heaven. . . . I would have you all seriously to think upon, to provoke you to be vigorous, and violent in advancing the kingdom of Christ. . . .

The second part you have in the next words, the success of their violence, "they take it by force." It is a metaphor taken from a castle taken by storm, by the violence of those who will take it or lose their blood, so the violent take the kingdom of heaven; and these words are both restrictive and they are promissory; they are restrictive, they are the violent and no other that get it; if any work in the world it be true that the "sluggard is clothed with rags," it is true here; those who only cry, "Lord, Lord," shall never come into the kingdom of heaven; this is a peculiar mercy in store for these violent spirits, that

---

[6]MO 14:840-41.

the violent and no other shall get into heaven; and then as it is restrictive, so it is promissory, though careless endeavors and slight labors may prove abortive, vigorous prosecution of it shall not miscarry. Those who "seek shall find, to those who knock it shall be opened, to those who ask it shall be granted, those who seek wisdom, as people seek silver and gold," the Lord will give it them. He has laid it up in store; let those who have violent hearts offer violence to it, and the Lord has promised they shall not miss of it. A Sermon Preached.[7]

The Role of John and Receiving Faith.

John Calvin: The word "prophesied" is emphatic; for the Law and the Prophets did not present God before the eyes of human beings but represented him under figures and shadows as absent. The comparison, we now perceive, is intended to show that it is highly criminal in people to remain indifferent, when they have obtained a manifestation of the presence of God, who held his ancient people in suspense by predictions. Christ does not class John with the ministers of the gospel, though he formerly assigned to him an intermediate station between them and the prophets. But there is no inconsistency here: for although John's preaching was a part of the gospel, it was little more than a first lesson. . . .

He now explains more clearly in what manner John began to preach the kingdom of God. It was in the character of Elijah, who was to be sent before the face of God. Our Lord's meaning therefore is that the great and dreadful Day of the Lord, which Malachi described, is now seen by the Jews, when Elijah, who was there promised, discharges his office as a herald. Again, by this exception, if you are willing to receive it, he glances at their hardened obstinacy, in maliciously shutting their eyes against the clearest light. But will he cease to be Elijah if he shall not be received? Christ does not mean that John's official status depends on their approbation. But having declared that he is Elijah, he charges them with carelessness and ingratitude, if he does not obtain that respect to which he is entitled. . . .

We know that it is customary with Christ to introduce this sentence, whenever he treats of subjects which are highly important, and which deserve no ordinary attention. He reminds us, at the same time, of the reason why the mysteries of which he speaks are not received by all. It is because many of his hearers are deaf, or at least have their ears closed. But now, as every person is hindered not only by their own unbelief but by the mutual influence that people exercise on each other, Christ here exhorts the elect of God, whose ears have been pierced,[†] to consider attentively this remarkable secret of God, and not to remain deaf with unbelievers. Commentary on a Harmony of the Evangelists.[8]

Unbelief Rejects Harsh and Gentle Messages.

Desiderius Erasmus: Neither way had been profitable for unbelievers. . . . John meaning to stir up this nation to penance, as it were with a sorrowful song came forth with great austerity and hardness of life, fasting and abstaining from all delicacies and wine, drinking water. And some said that he was possessed with the devil, being that far from following him. The Son of Man came forth meaning to stir up this nation to the love of heavenly doctrine, as it were with a merry song of the pipes, and that he might allure them the more with his gentleness, he hid not in desert places, nor wearing no notable rough garment . . . but framing himself to all people, and not despising the company of anyone, eats all manner of meats, and drinks whatsoever is set before him. Again, they pick quarrels, to falsely call him a great eater and drunkard, the friend of publicans and sinners. Those who are not moved with austerity and roughness will not be won by fair speaking and gentleness. But this nation by

[7]Marshall, *A Sermon Preached to the Honorable House of Commons* (1647), 30-31, 32-33, 39-40*.

[8]CTS 2:16-17* (CO 45:304-5); citing Mal 4:5. †Ex 21 describes the ear-piercing ceremony in which a slave, who loves and wishes to stay with his master, has his ear pierced publicly and becomes a servant for life.

every occasion is made worse and turns every remedy and medicine into a matter of greater disease and sickness. As by more ways they are provoked to health and salvation, the more evident it shall be to all people that they perish through their own malice. And by the wisdom of God, by whose counsel all these things be done, shall have the praise of the righteousness among her children, when they shall see those who appeared as great and just before the world, to be repelled from the kingdom of heaven for their unbelief. Contrariwise, when they shall see sinners, publicans, harlots, heathen people, humble and abject, to be received into everlasting salvation for the readiness of their faith. Paraphrases.[9]

11:20-24 *Woe to the Unrepentant Cities*

Outward Miracles and Inward Movement. Juan de Valdés: From these words we may infer as a consequence that at the day of judgment, they will be more chastised who, having had more opportunities for departing from evil and for applying themselves to good and thus to live modestly and purely in the present life, shall have led profane and worldly lives. And here that is much to the purpose, which I often repeat, that the wicked always come off badly when associated with the good. Had Christ not preached in Chorazin, in Bethsaida, and in Capernaum, they would not have come to be punished, at the day of judgment, worse than Tyre, Sidon, and Sodom. Here two doubts present themselves. The one is whether outward miracles are adequate without inward movement to work penitence, sorrow for sin, or repentance; while the other is, How can these two things be made to harmonize, that there be predestination and that these cities, against which Christ here declaims, should deserve to be so rebuked and so chastised, as Christ threatens them?

As to the first doubt, I say thus from what I have attained, that outward miracles are adequate without inward movement to induce outward penitence, grief for sin, and repentance, with which men and women depart from outward evil and apply themselves to that which is good outwardly. . . . That such is the fact appears from this that many saw Christ's miracles and externally repented; but as that repentance was human it did not penetrate inwardly; it changed the exterior, but it did not change the interior; and I understand Christ rebuked these cities in relation to this external change, because they had not made it which they could have made, moved by the miracles which they saw, as Tyre, Sidon, and Sodom would have done.

And if anyone suggests why should these cities have made this change or demonstration and not those, I should reply that I think that these would have done so because their vices were more apparent and because they had no external works wherewith to justify themselves, covering their inward impiety and exculpating their outward bad mode of living as had those which not regarding themselves as greatly inculpated with external vices and regarding themselves as holy by their external works could not come to the knowledge of their inward impiety nor could they judge themselves to be very guilty by their external life. . . .

That which is here rendered "many of his miracles" is, in the Greek, the majority of his mighty acts, but he means miracles, works wrought by supernatural virtue and power. In saying "they would have repented," or, they would have shown themselves penitent "in sackcloth and ashes," he touches upon a Jewish practice. This was that they who recognized that they had offended against God, dressed themselves in sackcloth, and sat in dust or in ashes; of which there is ample mention in holy Scripture. When he says, "They would have remained" . . . he means the successors of those who dwelt in that city, not being consumed as were both they and it. He says, "for the land," instead of the inhabitants of the land. Commentary upon the Gospel of St. Matthew.[10]

---

[9]EP 50v*.

[10]Valdés, *Commentary upon the Gospel of St. Matthew*, 205-6.

SALVATION OF PERSONS VERSUS PRESERVA-TION OF CITIES. JOHN LIGHTFOOT: Besides Matthew's continuing this portion to that which went before, the upbraiding of chief cities is so answerable to the matter contained in the end of the former section, that it easily shows it to be spoken at the same time. . . . When Christ says that if the things done in these cities had been done in Tyre and Sidon, and Sodom, and Gomorrah, they would have repented and would have remained till now; he understands not saving grace and saving repentance in them, but such an external humiliation as would have preserved them from ruin. As the case was with Nineveh, they repented and were delivered from the threatened destruction; their repentance was not to salvation of the persons, but to the preservation of their city; as Ahab's humbling prevented the present judgment, and not his final condemnation. THE HARMONY, CHRONICLE, AND ORDER OF THE NEW TESTAMENT.[11]

THE UNBELIEF OF CHORAZIN AND BETH-SAIDA. BENJAMIN COXE: Manifest scope of our Savior in this place is to show the open inexcusableness of the impenitence and unbelief of Chorazin and Bethsaida. The last words of the verse, from which your doubt arises, may be understood to be figurative speech, like that in Luke 19:40: "If these should hold their peace, the stones would immediately cry out." Otherwise, the words may be thus rendered, "They had possibly repented," or, "They would possibly have repented." This translation would be found well to agree to the signification of the potential particle which is here used in the Greek. And then this will be the true and easy interpretation of this passage, namely, "A man would think they should have repented." Beyond this, this place must not be stretched. For no interpretation must be given of any place of Scripture that shall indeed make it to contradict the Scripture itself

in other places. SOME MISTAKEN SCRIPTURES SINCERELY EXPLAINED.[12]

CAPERNAUM IS ESPECIALLY GUILTY. JOHN CALVIN: He expressly addresses the city of Capernaum, in which he had resided so constantly that many supposed it to be his native place. It was indeed an inestimable honor that the Son of God, when about to commence his reign and priesthood, had chosen Capernaum for the seat of his palace and sanctuary. And yet it was as deeply plunged in its filth as if there had never been poured upon it a drop of divine grace. On this account, Christ declares that the punishment awaiting it will be the more dreadful, in proportion to the higher favors which it had received from God. It deserves our earnest attention in this passage, that the profaning of the gifts of God, as it involves sacrilege, will never pass unpunished; and that the more eminent any one is, they will be punished with the greater severity, if they shall basely pollute the gifts which God has bestowed upon them. And, above all, an awful vengeance awaits us if, after having received the spiritual gifts of Christ, we treat him and his gospel with contempt. COMMENTARY ON A HARMONY OF THE EVANGELISTS.[13]

11:25-30 Come to the Son, Know the Father

JESUS REJOICES IN THE HUMBLE. MARTIN CHEMNITZ: He is saying the same thing that Peter says in 1 Peter 5:5: "God resists the proud but gives grace to the humble." From those who are unwilling "to take their reason captive in obedience to God" is hidden the wisdom of the gospel, because of their own fault and wickedness. For it is the divine order that those who wish to be exalted should humble themselves under the mighty hand of God. Therefore, Christ gives thanks to the Father when he hides the mystery of the gospel from those who trust in their own wisdom and righteousness—that is, those who are the wise of

---

[11]Lightfoot, *The Harmony, Chronicle and Order of the New Testament* (1655), 27-28.

[12]Coxe, *Some Mistaken Scriptures Sincerely Explained* (1646), 7.
[13]CTS 2:29-30* (CO 45:313).

the world—and reveals it to babes, that is, the humblest and lowliest and most insignificant people in the world. And this "good pleasure" is without respect to merits or honor. Thus, Christ does not say it is a "good pleasure" before God that some follow the doctrine of the gospel, but he takes great pleasure in receiving poor, condemned sinners who flee to Christ without any merit or worthiness, while he justly and properly rejects the important people who trust in their own virtues. Loci Theologici.[14]

How the Father Hides Himself. David Bramley: How is God here said to hide the things of himself and his Christ from women and men? Answer: Not by darkening of them, but by not enlightening of them; not by taking away their sight, but by not giving them sight; by denying them the eye salve, without which none can see spiritual things. From this observe that God blinds and hardens the wicked, not by changing them from better to worse, but only by not changing them from worse to better. He does not harden them by infusing or inferring any wicked quality into them which before was not in them; but by not infusing nor inferring better qualities into them, than by nature they have in them; thus, people are said to blind one another. Christ's Result of His Father's Pleasure.[15]

The Father Is Revealed by the Son. John Calvin: This is a different kind of knowledge from the former; for the Son is said to know the Father, not because he reveals him by his Spirit, but because, being the lively image of him, he represents him visibly in his own person. At the same time, I do not exclude the Spirit, but explain the revelation here mentioned as referring to the manner of communicating information. This agrees most completely with the context; for Christ confirms what he had formerly said that all

things had been delivered to him by his Father, by informing us that the fullness of the godhead dwells in him. The passage may be thus summed up: First, it is the gift of the Father that the Son is known, because by his Spirit he opens the eyes of our mind to discern the glory of Christ, which otherwise would have been hidden from us. Second, the Father, who dwells in inaccessible light and is in himself incomprehensible is revealed to us by the Son, because he is the lively image of him so that it is in vain to seek for him elsewhere. Commentary on a Harmony of the Evangelists.[16]

Come to Me. Wolfgang Musculus: He does not say, "If anyone comes to me, I will give him life." But, just the opposite, he calls to himself those who are slow to act, saying, "Come to me." And here one can see the image of the heavenly Father expressed, so far as relates to his immense goodness, which both the prophets describe and commend, as at Isaiah 55: "All you who thirst come to the waters" . . . and that often-repeated phrase "Turn to me and you will be saved."

In the second passage, notice whom he calls to himself. He does not say, "Come to me all you who are righteous," but "All you who labor and are burdened." Truly, whom else would he call to himself than those for whose sake he came into the world, yes, for the sake of those whom he received that measure of power from the Father? "The Spirit of the Lord is upon me, because he anointed me and sent me to the poor to proclaim the gospel, to cleanse those contrite in heart, to preach forgiveness to captives, to give sight to the blind, to set free those who are downtrodden." From this and from the passage at hand one can see that the power, which Christ received from the Father when he was sent into this world, he received not so much for his own sake as for the afflicted, so that he might bring ready aid to those who were laboring. For this reason, he sent his Son, and gave him power over everything, so that he might be the

---

[14]Chemnitz, *Loci Theologici*, 1:199-200; citing 2 Cor 10:5; Lk 14:11; 18:14; Mt 11:25-26.
[15]Bramley, *Christ's Result of His Father's Pleasure* (1647), 4; citing Rev 3:18.

[16]CTS 2:41-42 (CO 45:319-20); citing Col 2:9.

one who can bring help to the suffering of human beings.

Whom, then, should we understand the "laboring" and "burdened" to be? Chrysostom[†] understands them to be those who are weighed down with the burdens of the law, and secondarily from Pharisaic traditions, under which heavy burdens, so to speak, the pious at that time were struggling for the attainment of righteousness, but in vain. For the law was not given for the purpose of justifying. But we understand it in general terms to refer to all those who, having been crushed under the weight of sins and by the wickedness of a corrupt nature, of which they are aware, struggle to cast off depravity and to attain to righteousness. But since that righteousness cannot be attained any more than depravity can be cast out without the grace of the Holy Spirit, nothing else does this struggle amount to than labor and the affliction of the spirit.

Therefore, sinners are called to Christ who are pressed down with a sense of sin and who struggle to calm their conscience. And those are alone the ones who come to Christ with benefit. There is no place with Christ for the self-righteous and hypocrites, on the one hand, and for those sinners, on the other, who experience no sense of their sin. Great is the number of those today who in their sins are made openly foolish and insensible.

"And I will give you life" is the third thing that he promises to the afflicted and laboring, whom he calls to himself. Truly he promises that which is so greatly sought by those people, and is sought in vain, and sought with anxiety of the mind, which to the afflicted is the sweetest of all things: namely, rest for their mind, a peacefulness of conscience. "And I, he says," as if he says, "Why do you seek it elsewhere where it cannot be found?" To this point also relates that statement "Come to me." He means, "Hasten to me, I say, you who seek in vain elsewhere." "I will give you life." Note the certitude of the promised help. A doctor, although he is good, promises nothing else to the sick person, nor is he able, than his diligence and effort, to the best of his ability, but

he certainly does not promise health. But Christ here does not say, "I will try, I will see, I will attempt, I will put forth the effort to see if I can restore life to you." But instead, he says the most certain thing of all, "I will restore life to you." COMMENTARY ON MATTHEW.[17]

TAKE MY YOKE UPON YOU. JOHN CALVIN: Many persons, we perceive, abuse the grace of Christ by turning it into an indulgence of the flesh; and therefore Christ, after promising joyful rest to wretchedly distressed consciences, reminds them, at the same time, that he is their deliverer on condition of their submitting to his yoke. He does not, he tells us, absolve people from their sins in such a manner that, restored to the favor of God, they may sin with greater freedom, but that, raised up by his grace, they may also take his yoke upon them, and that, being free in spirit, they may restrain the licentiousness of their flesh. And hence we obtain a definition of that rest of which he had spoken. It is not at all intended to exempt the disciples of Christ from the warfare of the flesh, that they may enjoy themselves at their ease, but to train them under the burden of discipline, and keep them under the yoke.

"Learn of me." It is a mistake, I think, to suppose that Christ here assures us of his meekness, lest his disciples, under the influence of that fear which is usually experienced in approaching persons of distinction, should remain at a distance from him on account of his divine glory. It is rather his design to form us to the imitation of himself, because the obstinacy of the flesh leads us to shrink from his yoke as harsh and uneasy. Shortly afterward, he adds . . . "My yoke is easy." But how shall anyone be brought willingly and gently to bend their neck unless, by putting on meekness, they are conformed to Christ? That this is the meaning of the words is plain; for Christ, after exhorting his disciples to bear his yoke, and desirous to prevent

---

[17]Musculus, *In Evangelistam Matthaeum Commentarii* (1556), 366-67; citing Lk 4. [†]Chrysostom, *Homilies on Matthew*, NPNF[1] 10:247-48.

them from being deterred by its difficulty, immediately adds, "Learn of me," thus declaring that when his example shall have accustomed us to meekness and humility, we shall no longer feel his yoke to be troublesome. Commentary on a Harmony of the Evangelists.[18]

Why the Yoke of Christ Is Easy. Martin Luther: Now sin is a grievous burden of which no one is eased but the one whom Christ, the Son of God, delivers, and that by the Holy Ghost, whom he has merited for us of the Father, which makes our hearts cheerful and ready to do all things which God requires of us. But what is this that he says? "Take my yoke on you." Is this to refresh, if I take one burden from one, and lay upon him another? This is that of which we have often spoken, the gospel does first make astonished and discourage, and is grievous to the flesh, for it tells us that all our own things are nothing, that our own holiness and righteousness are of no importance, that all things which are in us are damned, that we are the children of wrath and indignation. This is very hard, and is an intolerable burden to the flesh, and therefore he calls it a burden or yoke. . . . As if he would say, the yoke of the law, under which you lived before was grievous to be borne, but my burden is not so grievous, it is light and tolerable, you may easily bear it. Our wise say now that the yoke of Christ is more grievous than the yoke of the law was; and they allege the fifth chapter of Matthew, but Christ does there interpret the law, how it ought to be understood, he does not make laws but says that murders and adulteries proceed from an evil and unclean heart. And so, he does only expound the law of Moses and prescribes not any laws there. But the yoke of Christ is therefore easy, and his burden light, because he takes away not only ceremonial and human laws, but even the whole law, the curse, sin, death, and whatsoever may come to us from the law, all this Christ takes away from me and endues me with his Spirit, by the motion and instinct thereof I do gladly, willingly, and with pleasure perform all the duties of the law. It is therefore also called easy, sweet, and light, for that he himself helps us and takes part of the burden, if we are not of sufficient strength. It appears indeed grievous and intolerable to the world, but it is otherwise when there is one ready to ease the burden. The Thirty-Third Sermon of Dr. Martin Luther.[19]

---

[18]CTS 2:44-45 (CO 45:321-22).

[19]Luther, *Complete Sermons*, 5:352-54*.

12:1-50 JESUS IS LORD OVER ALL

At that time Jesus went through the grainfields on the Sabbath. His disciples were hungry, and they began to pluck heads of grain and to eat. ²But when the Pharisees saw it, they said to him, "Look, your disciples are doing what is not lawful to do on the Sabbath." ³He said to them, "Have you not read what David did when he was hungry, and those who were with him: ⁴how he entered the house of God and ate the bread of the Presence, which it was not lawful for him to eat nor for those who were with him, but only for the priests? ⁵Or have you not read in the Law how on the Sabbath the priests in the temple profane the Sabbath and are guiltless? ⁶I tell you, something greater than the temple is here. ⁷And if you had known what this means, 'I desire mercy, and not sacrifice,' you would not have condemned the guiltless. ⁸For the Son of Man is lord of the Sabbath."

⁹He went on from there and entered their synagogue. ¹⁰And a man was there with a withered hand. And they asked him, "Is it lawful to heal on the Sabbath?"—so that they might accuse him. ¹¹He said to them, "Which one of you who has a sheep, if it falls into a pit on the Sabbath, will not take hold of it and lift it out? ¹²Of how much more value is a man than a sheep! So it is lawful to do good on the Sabbath." ¹³Then he said to the man, "Stretch out your hand." And the man stretched it out, and it was restored, healthy like the other. ¹⁴But the Pharisees went out and conspired against him, how to destroy him.

¹⁵Jesus, aware of this, withdrew from there. And many followed him, and he healed them all ¹⁶and ordered them not to make him known. ¹⁷This was to fulfill what was spoken by the prophet Isaiah:

¹⁸"Behold, my servant whom I have chosen,
    my beloved with whom my soul is well
        pleased.
I will put my Spirit upon him,
    and he will proclaim justice to the Gentiles.
¹⁹He will not quarrel or cry aloud,
    nor will anyone hear his voice in the streets;

²⁰a bruised reed he will not break,
    and a smoldering wick he will not quench,
until he brings justice to victory;
    ²¹and in his name the Gentiles will hope."

²²Then a demon-oppressed man who was blind and mute was brought to him, and he healed him, so that the man spoke and saw. ²³And all the people were amazed, and said, "Can this be the Son of David?" ²⁴But when the Pharisees heard it, they said, "It is only by Beelzebul, the prince of demons, that this man casts out demons." ²⁵Knowing their thoughts, he said to them, "Every kingdom divided against itself is laid waste, and no city or house divided against itself will stand. ²⁶And if Satan casts out Satan, he is divided against himself. How then will his kingdom stand? ²⁷And if I cast out demons by Beelzebul, by whom do your sons cast them out? Therefore they will be your judges. ²⁸But if it is by the Spirit of God that I cast out demons, then the kingdom of God has come upon you. ²⁹Or how can someone enter a strong man's house and plunder his goods, unless he first binds the strong man? Then indeed he may plunder his house. ³⁰Whoever is not with me is against me, and whoever does not gather with me scatters. ³¹Therefore I tell you, every sin and blasphemy will be forgiven people, but the blasphemy against the Spirit will not be forgiven. ³²And whoever speaks a word against the Son of Man will be forgiven, but whoever speaks against the Holy Spirit will not be forgiven, either in this age or in the age to come.

³³"Either make the tree good and its fruit good, or make the tree bad and its fruit bad, for the tree is known by its fruit. ³⁴You brood of vipers! How can you speak good, when you are evil? For out of the abundance of the heart the mouth speaks. ³⁵The good person out of his good treasure brings forth good, and the evil person out of his evil treasure brings forth evil. ³⁶I tell you, on the day of judgment people will give account for every careless word they speak, ³⁷for by your words you will be justified, and by your words you will be condemned."

³⁸*Then some of the scribes and Pharisees answered him, saying, "Teacher, we wish to see a sign from you."* ³⁹*But he answered them, "An evil and adulterous generation seeks for a sign, but no sign will be given to it except the sign of the prophet Jonah.* ⁴⁰*For just as Jonah was three days and three nights in the belly of the great fish, so will the Son of Man be three days and three nights in the heart of the earth.* ⁴¹*The men of Nineveh will rise up at the judgment with this generation and condemn it, for they repented at the preaching of Jonah, and behold, something greater than Jonah is here.* ⁴²*The queen of the South will rise up at the judgment with this generation and condemn it, for she came from the ends of the earth to hear the wisdom of Solomon, and behold, something greater than Solomon is here.*

⁴³*"When the unclean spirit has gone out of a person, it passes through waterless places seeking rest, but finds none.* ⁴⁴*Then it says, 'I will return to my house from which I came.' And when it comes, it finds the house empty, swept, and put in order.* ⁴⁵*Then it goes and brings with it seven other spirits more evil than itself, and they enter and dwell there, and the last state of that person is worse than the first. So also will it be with this evil generation."*

⁴⁶*While he was still speaking to the people, behold, his mother and his brothers*ᵃ *stood outside, asking to speak to him.*ᵇ ⁴⁸*But he replied to the man who told him, "Who is my mother, and who are my brothers?"* ⁴⁹*And stretching out his hand toward his disciples, he said, "Here are my mother and my brothers!* ⁵⁰*For whoever does the will of my Father in heaven is my brother and sister and mother."*

a Or *brothers and sisters*; also verses 48, 49   b Some manuscripts insert verse 47: *Someone told him, "Your mother and your brothers are standing outside, asking to speak to you"*

Overview: In two instances, Jesus' interaction with the Pharisees results in greater antagonism from the leaders. In the first case, Jesus declares the disciples innocent in the face of the leaders' accusations. In his reply, Jesus chastises them for their lack of understanding of the Law (Mt 12:5) and the Prophets (Mt 12:7) and declares that he is greater than the temple. The Reformation commentators maintain Jesus' innocence by indicating that Old Testament characters have prioritized the Sabbath rightly, unlike the contemporary Pharisees. Furthermore, they affirm that Jesus exerts his authority over the Sabbath as the one, true God ("the Lord of the Sabbath") and that he also demonstrates the errors of the Pharisees' prideful self-righteousness. The reformers argue that Jesus' use of Hosea intensifies God's disapproval, now rejection, of the insufficient sacrifices of disobedient humans.

In the second episode, Jesus heals the man with a withered hand as a display of the good that the Pharisees should be doing on the Sabbath. Jesus' words condemn merely external attempts at righteousness because these deeds often lack any brotherly love, which is a clear command. Calvin exhorts that keeping the Sabbath should have included showing kindness to a neighbor, regardless of which day of the week it is.

As an indication of the animosity that Jesus' ministry and the crowds' reaction provoke with the religious leaders, Matthew provides the story of a blind and mute man who is demon-possessed. The man's dual maladies are not a result of natural causes and provide the perfect context for a display of Christ's divine power over satanic forces. The stubborn unbelief of the religious leaders is also on display as they attribute Jesus' power to what Calvin labels a magical enchantment, enabled by the demons' prince.

Jesus also warns of the seriousness of opposing God's purposes by pointing out the eternal consequences of blaspheming the Holy Spirit. The identification of the unpardonable sin—or "blasphemy of the Spirit"—is a concern for the reformers. Some contend that a person who resists the Holy Spirit has also rejected the Father and the

Son. For example, Heinrich Bullinger asserts that to blaspheme the Holy Spirit requires a direct and personal rejection of his saving work.

As the accusation of the religious leaders reflects their hearts, Jesus exhorts that these revealing words will be sufficient evidence for final condemnation. The "overflow" of the words indicate not just the presence of evil but also the preponderance of evil in a person's heart. The reformers comment on Jesus' masterful use of metaphors to illustrate the power of words and their ability to expose the true motives of the heart. Through these verbal analogies, Jesus is able to make the poignant connection between words and just judgment.

After discussing the sign of Jonah, Jesus returns to his exorcising of the evil spirit and comments that if the evil is allowed to return the new circumstance will be worse than the former. Aegidius Hunnius explains that Jesus is warning against those who have heard the gospel preached, recognized its truth, but then later have wavered on their surrender to it.

Mary was reproved for being impetuous in interrupting Jesus' teaching. Calvin explains how Jesus uses the encounter to teach the value of relationships formed in the gospel community. Jesus had challenged his disciples on a few occasions of the need for the radical reorienting of human relationships as a result of following him. Family relationships will be strained and in some cases reconfigured on the basis of the new relationships found in Christ (see Mt 10:21, 35-37; 18:5; 19:8-12). Those who do the will of the heavenly Father are placed in a new family with Christ.

12:1-21 *Jesus Is Lord of the Sabbath*

CHRIST DID NOT TRANSGRESS THE LAW.
JOHN MAYER: It is certain that Christ being a perfect pattern of obedience in all things did not transgress or maintain any transgression against any law of God. For he says that he came "not to destroy the law, but to fulfill it." Wherefore it is to be held that all his speech here tends to nothing

else but to convince the Pharisees of blindness and ignorance touching the right keeping of the Sabbath, according to the commandment, it being never enjoined to rest so strictly as they thought; yea their best and most understanding men, David, Abiathar, and the priests by their practice did plainly show that the law was not so to be understood. And to show that he needed not to allege examples, but that his allowance was sufficient to justify his disciples, he says, "One greater than the temple is here, and the Son of Man is Lord of the Sabbath." He is God that first appointed the Sabbath, and therefore knows best what may be done upon it. And withal he makes way to the utter dissolving of the Sabbath after his resurrection, seeing he has power as a Lord over it to dispose thereof as it pleases him. A COMMENTARY UPON THE NEW TESTAMENT.[1]

CHRIST IS THE SOVEREIGN LORD OF THE SABBATH.
GIOVANNI DIODATI: Seeing God has not tied his ministers in his temple to the observation of the Sabbath rest, they doing their ministry that day, though it be very painful; my disciples likewise following and serving me may very well be exempted from it, seeing that I am true God with my Father and that my service sanctifies these actions, as the service of the temple sanctifies those. "Profane"—he applies himself to the capacity of the hearers, when he calls that to profane, what the priests in the exercise of their ministry did in the temple ("greater than the temple"). Namely, I myself, ever-living God, Lord of the temple, and the Messiah, who really and in truth am all that which was figured by the temple and the service belonging to it. Another reason, which has a relation to the Pharisees cruel hypocrisy, who through an ostentation of external discipline went against charity, not pitying the poor apostles' distress, who did eat ears of corn for mere necessity. . . . He yields a reason for the apostles' innocence; for if there were any offense in their act, he was to judge of it, being the sovereign Lord of all

---

[1] Mayer, *A Commentarie upon the New Testament* (1631), 1:172.

God's exterior service, and of the due observance of it. And therefore, since he did not find fault with it, it belonged not to them to undertake the censuring of it. He shows also that he has power to exempt his own from the observation of the Sabbath, when necessity or charity to their neighbor, which is the end of the law, requires it. Pious Annotations.[2]

God Desires Mercy Rather Than Sacrifice. Martin Luther: With purpose and zeal he seems to be deviating from Sabbath and temple, even to veneration of sacrifices, so that he might silence all of them. For with Sabbath, temple, proud sacrifices, what remains for them? And thus, on the occasion of the Sabbath, he destroys their whole religion and lifts himself up. . . .

Therefore, the place treated here is taken from Hosea 6: "I desire mercy, not sacrifice, and knowledge of God more than burnt offerings." Christ relates this directly against the cult of the Jews, upon which they were exceedingly presumptuous. For by it they were exalting nothing other than sacrifice, as in Matthew 23, where they gave preference to sacrifices to the temple itself and the altar, but not to honoring parents. Therefore, it was a dreadful heresy to set sacrifices before mercy. Therefore, he said, "You are merely priests and glory about sacrifices to which God does not pay attention, nor does he have need of them. Meanwhile, jealousies, cruelties, and indeed without mercy and affection, so that also while fasting you do not want my few disciples to eat grains from the corn, to whom it is yet proper to give to eat by a favorable law of love and compassion."

It is the same way from the beginning of the world, so that blinded by the opinions of the hypocrite, false judge, and religion, they might always be most unmerciful, and disapproving to every good work, always leading nothing other than disparaging, judging, damning, and looking down on sinners, infirm, paupers, derelicts, admiring only themselves, and declaring that they are saints and sons of God. Just as the priests and Levites passed by the one almost dead, but the Samaritan paid attention to him; that is, he showed mercy, which is pleasing to God above all sacrifices.

Yes, expanding on this, Christ said, "And he does not only prefer mercy to sacrifice, but simply annuls sacrifice from Hosea, saying, 'I do not desire sacrifice.'" Because they forsake mercy and choose sacrifices, therefore in contrast, God chooses mercy and rejects sacrifices, not so much by a change of work as of holiness, but on account of what is effectual, just as it is written, "Sacrifices of the wicked are detestable." "They do not know how much evil they did." For who does not detest the one who rejects and despises the precepts of God about mercy and is avaricious, cruel, negligent, contemptuous, withholding, damning, and so on against a neighbor. And in the place of his teaching, he comes with his own sacrifices, by a special passion of an offering?

Whence Jeremiah. I did not instruct you about sacrifices. But this is what I commanded: "Hear my voice." Not which you choose, even which is pleasing to you, but what I choose and what is pleasing to me, I desire to be observed. But this you neither know nor care, therefore you do not understand what the prophet Hosea said. On the contrary, you do not know how great an evil you have done, while you seem to make the most for yourself, because you tread down the precepts of love and mercy through manifold acts of disobedience and desire to satisfy God by your sacrifices selected by you. This is just like a fool ridiculing God, evidently as if he ought to test and to crown your disobedience on account of your sacrifices. And in this way, you impious ones offer for yourselves and your precepts, as if you with ready sacrifices are made whole and all, but God with his precepts is nothing and someone who is a laughable jester. Notes on Select Chapters of Matthew.[3]

The Form and Substance of the Law. John Calvin: This narrative and that which immediately precedes it have the same object; which is to

---

[2]Diodati, *Pious Annotations* (1643), D3v*.

[3]Luther, *Annotationes in Aliquot Capita Matthei*, 32-33; citing Hos 6:6; Mt 23:18; 15:5-6; Prov 15:8; Eccl 5:1; Jer 7:22.

show that the scribes watched with a malicious eye for the purpose of turning into slander everything that Christ did, and consequently that we need not wonder if men whose minds were so depraved were his implacable enemies. We see also that it is usual with hypocrites to pursue what is nothing more than a shadow of the righteousness of the law, and as the common saying is, to stickle more about the form than about the substance. . . . No man who was free from malice would have refused to acknowledge that it was a divine work, which those good teachers do not scruple to condemn. Whence comes such fury, but because all their senses are affected by a wicked hatred of Christ, so that they are blind amid the full brightness of the sun? . . .

Christ again points out what is the true way of keeping the Sabbath and, at the same time, reproves them for slander, in bringing as a charge against him what was a universal custom. For if any person's sheep had fallen into a ditch, no person would have hindered it from being taken out; but in proportion as a human being is of more value than a sheep, so much the more are we at liberty to assist them. It is plain, therefore, that if anyone should relieve the necessity of brethren, he did not, in any degree, violate the rest which the Lord has enjoined. . . .

He who takes away the life of a human being is held to be a criminal; and there is little difference between manslaughter and the conduct of those who do not concern themselves about relieving a person in distress. So then Christ indirectly charges them with endeavoring, under the pretense of a holy act, to compel them to do evil; for sin is committed, as we have already said, not only by those who do anything contrary to the law, but also by those who neglect their duty. COMMENTARY ON A HARMONY OF THE EVANGELISTS.[4]

THE SPIRIT AND THE CALLING OF CHRIST.
RICHARD SIBBES: In the words you have a description of Christ, his nearness to God: "Behold my servant whom I have chosen, my beloved in

whom my soul is well pleased." And then his calling and qualification: "I will put my Spirit upon him." And the execution of that calling: "He shall show judgment to the Gentiles." Then the quiet and peaceable manner of the execution of his calling: "He shall not strive nor cry, neither shall any man hear his voice in the streets." . . .

God put his Spirit upon him, to set him apart, to ordain him, and to qualify him with abundance of grace for the work; for there are these three things especially meant by putting the Spirit upon him, separation or setting apart, and ordaining, and enriching with the gifts of the Spirit. When any one is called to great place, there is a setting apart from others and an ordaining to that particular and a qualifying. If it be a calling of God, he qualifies where he ordains always. But Christ had the Spirit before. What does he mean, then, when he says he will put the Spirit upon him now?

I answer, he had the Spirit before, answerable to that condition he was in. Now he received the Spirit answerable to that condition he was to undertake. He was perfect then for that condition. Now he was to be made perfect for that office he was to set upon. He was always perfect. He had abundance of Spirit for that estate he was in, but now he was to enter upon another condition, to preach the gospel, to be a prophet, and after to be a priest. Therefore, he says now especially, I will put my Spirit upon him. A DESCRIPTION OF CHRIST.[5]

THE EVANGELICAL MEEKNESS OF JESUS.
DESIDERIUS ERASMUS: They (the Pharisees) had now a will toward murder, and nothing lacked but a suitable occasion. But Jesus, not ignorant of what they intended, withdrew himself from that place, lest he might seem to have given some occasion of extreme delaying to the raging and furious men. He might have spitefully repressed them, he might have overwhelmed them with miracles, he might have destroyed them also, but minding to show the evangelical meekness, gave place to their rage and fury, if perhaps they would relent and repent. And

---

[4] CTS 2:52-54 (CO 45:327-28).

[5] WRS 1:4, 15*.

thus far he gave place to them, that nevertheless in other places he distributed his heavenly doctrine unto the multitude, which followed him thick and threefold, and as many sick men, or otherwise miserable as were brought to him, he healed them. For his time was not yet come; the gospel was not yet sufficiently spread abroad. Wherefore he gave place to them not to provide for himself, but to take from them the occasion of a wicked deed and to teach withal, the wisdom of the gospel ought not to be defended against the disobedient with threats, with checks, or with contentions but with mildness and meekness. Therefore, he commanded the multitude that followed him that they should not disclose him, lest the rumor spreading abroad, the Pharisees might be stirred more and more. PARAPHRASES.[6]

A BRUISED REED AND A SMOKING FLAX.
RICHARD SIBBES: This bruised reed is a person who, for the most part, is in some misery, as those were who came to Christ for help, and by misery is brought to see sin the cause of it; for whatsoever pretenses sin makes, yet bruising or breaking is the end of it; they are sensible of sin and misery, even unto bruising; and, seeing no help in themselves, are carried with restless desire to have supply from another with some hope which a little raises him out of themselves to Christ, though they dare not claim any present interest of mercy. This spark of hope being opposed by doublings, and fears rising from corruption, makes them as smoking flax; so that both these together, a bruised reed and smoking flax, make up the state of a poor distressed person. Such a one as our Savior Christ terms poor in spirit, who sees a want, and withal sees himself indebted to divine justice, and no means of supply from himself or the creature, and thereupon mourns, and upon some hope of mercy from the promise and examples of those who have obtained mercy are stirred up to hunger and thirst after it.

This bruising is required before conversion, so that the Spirit may make way for itself into the heart by leveling all proud, high thoughts, and that we may understand ourselves to be what indeed we are by nature. . . . Again, this bruising makes us set a high price upon Christ. The gospel is the gospel indeed then; then the fig leaves of morality will do us no good. . . . Nay, after conversion we need bruising, that reeds may know themselves to be reeds, and not oaks; even reeds need bruising, by reason of the remainder of pride in our nature, and to let us see that we live by mercy. THE BRUISED REED AND SMOKING FLAX.[7]

12:22-32 Blasphemy Against the Holy Spirit

A DISPLAY OF DIVINE, NOT DEVILISH POWER.
JOHN CALVIN: Matthew says that a twofold plague had been inflicted on the man. Many persons, no doubt, are blind and deaf on account of natural defects; but it is evident that this man had become blind and had been deprived of the use of speech though there was no defect in his optical nerves, or in the proportion of his tongue. We need not wonder that so much liberty should be allowed to Satan in injuring the bodily senses, when God justly permits him to corrupt or pervert all the faculties of the soul.

Hence, we infer that there was a visible display of the power of God, which drew upon him the admiration of the great body of the people, who were not at all actuated by any wicked disposition. For how came it that all admired, but because the fact compelled them to do so? . . . Moved with admiration, those who saw it ask each other, "Is not Jesus the Christ?" Acknowledging the power of God, they are led, as it were by the hand, to faith. Not that they suddenly profited as much as they ought to have done (for they speak doubtfully), but yet it is no small proficiency to be aroused to consider more attentively the glory of Christ. Some look upon this as a full affirmation, but the words convey no such meaning; and the fact itself shows that an un-expected occurrence had struck them forcibly, and

---

[6]EP 53v.

[7]WRS 1:43-44*; citing Mt 5:3.

that they did not form a decided opinion, but only that it occurred to them that he might be the Christ.

The scribes cannot withhold the acknowledgment of a fact so open and manifest, and yet they maliciously carp at what Christ did by divine power. Not only do they obscure the praise of the miracle, but endeavor to turn it into a reproach, as if it were performed by magical enchantment; and that work, which could not be ascribed to a man, is alleged by them to have the devil for its author. . . . The opinion expressed by the scribes, that there is a prince among wicked spirits, did not arise from a mistake of the common people or from supposition, but from a conviction entertained among the godly, that the reprobate have a head, in the same manner as Christ is the head of the church. COMMENTARY ON A HARMONY OF THE EVANGELISTS.[8]

ENDEAVORING TO CAST OUT DEVILS. WALTER BRIDGES: First, our Lord argues against his blasphemers, here from the absurdity, thus a kingdom, city, or house to be divided against itself is absurd. If Satan's should so be, it would be destructive thereto. Second, our Savior argues from example, I cast out devils by the same power that your sons (which can so do) cast them out, but ask them and they will tell you that they cast them out by the finger of God, therefore by that power I cast them out. Third, another argument our Savior draws from his office, as if he should say, you would hardly stumble at my casting out devils, did you but know this, that Jesus Christ came to destroy the works of the devil. DIVISION DIVIDED.[9]

CHRIST, THE GREATER POWER. JUAN DE MALDONADO: Many moderns think that these exorcists were those Jews who had some kind of magic art handed down by King Solomon, as Josephus[†] writes, and of whom St. Luke makes mention. They are called sons of the Pharisees because they were Jews, and some of them were their sons. Why do you say that I, rather than your sons, cast out devils by Beelzebub, since we both cast them out? Why do you judge badly of me and well of them, when we both perform the same act?

I should very willingly concur, did I not think that Christ intended to convey more than they say; for the apostles cast out devils in the name of Christ. Our Lord's argument then is, "Your sons." That is, the apostles who are of your nation, in whom do they cast them out? Is it not in my name? If, then, they cast out devils, not in the name of Beelzebub, but in mine, how do you say that I cast them out in the name of Beelzebub? For, if they cast them out in my name, I am greater than the devils; for they are cast out in my name and by my power. I do not cast them out, therefore, in the name of Beelzebub; for, if the apostles cast them out by my power, which you cannot deny, much more so do I whose the power is. Therefore, they shall be your judges, because they shall sit upon twelve seats judging the twelve tribes of Israel (Mt 19:28; St. Jerome[‡]). I, however, think the subject to be of another judgment, which divines call the judgment of comparison; for the apostles would be the judges of the Pharisees, because it will be seen in that last judgment that the apostles cast out devils in the name of Christ, which, when the Pharisees had seen and believed, yet they said that Christ himself—whom they ought much more to have believed to have cast them out by his own power—cast them out by Beelzebub, as he said. . . .

Christ terms himself and his advent "the kingdom of God," because it was the beginning of it and it opened our way to it (St. Jerome, St. Chrysostom, Theophylact).[§] Christ's meaning is "If I, by the Spirit of God, as I have before shown, cast out devils, then is that true which I myself, my apostles, and you have preached, that the kingdom of God is come unto you; for the Holy Ghost, who works miracles by us, bears witness that our testimony is true." A COMMENTARY ON THE HOLY GOSPELS.[10]

---

[8]CTS 2:64-66 (CO 45:334-35).
[9]Bridges, *Division Divided* (1646), 11-12, 34; 1 Jn 3:8.

[10]JMG 398-400; citing Acts 19:13; Lk 10:17. [†]Josephus, *Antiquities of the Jews* 8.2. [‡]Jerome, *Commentary on Matthew*, FC 117:143. [§]Jerome, *Commentary on Matthew*, FC 117:143. Chrysostom, *Homilies on Matthew*, NPNF[1] 10:258-62. Theophylact, *Commentary on Matthew*, 20r.

The Blasphemy of Unbelief. Huldrych Zwingli: Concerning the sins which are to be forgiven or retained, we may learn from the very words of Christ, who says in Matthew 12:31, "Every sin or blasphemy may be forgiven a person, but blasphemy of the Spirit cannot be forgiven." These words Jesus himself explains: "Whoever says a word against the Son of Man may be forgiven, but whoever speaks against the Holy Spirit cannot be forgiven either in this time or in the age to come." In these words of Christ, we learn that all sins and blasphemy may be forgiven a person, except for the sin and blasphemy against the Holy Spirit. Now theologians ask quite seriously what the sin against the Holy Spirit is, but they speak of it as blind person speak of colors—in ignorance, if you please. The sin that cannot be forgiven is unbelief. This is the one sin God shall not forgive as we may actually determine from Luke 12:9. . . . You see clearly from this that to deny God or not to believe is the sin which God does not forgive; for Luke supports the meaning of the earlier phrase "Whoever shall deny me" by what follows, namely, "that the one who slanders the Holy Spirit shall not be forgiven." An Exposition of the Articles.[11]

Blasphemy Against the Trinity. John Donne: Consider that God the Father, whom, as the root of all, we consider principally in the creation, created men and women in a possibility and ability to persist in that goodness in which he created them. And consider that God the Son came and wrought a reconciliation for humankind to God and so brought a treasure in his human nature: a sufficient ransom for all the world. But someone may not know this or may not believe this, other than historically, morally, or civilly, and so rejects and shakes off God the Son. And then consider that the Holy Ghost comes and presents means of applying all this, and makes the general satisfaction of Christ reach and spread itself upon my soul, in particular, in the preaching of the Word,

in the seals of the sacraments, in the absolution of the church. Yet I might preclude its ways and shut up myself against the Holy Ghost, and so reject him and shake him off. When I have resisted Father, Son, and Holy Ghost, is there a fourth person in the Godhead to work upon me? If I blaspheme, that is, deliberately pronounce against the Holy Ghost, my sin is irremissible therefore, because there is nobody left to forgive it, nor way left, wherein forgiveness should work upon me. So far it is irremissible on God's part and on mine too. Sermon 35: On Whit Sunday.[12]

The Filthiest Sin. Heinrich Bullinger: Blasphemy against the Son of Man is committed of the ignorant, who are not yet enlightened; and tends against Christ, whom the blasphemer thinks to be a seducer because he knows him not. Such blasphemers the word of the Lord manifestly testifies what . . . a great part of the Jews were; for upon the cross the Lord prayed, crying, "Father, forgive them; for they know not what they do" and the apostle Paul says, "If they had known the Lord of glory, they would not have crucified him." Whereupon Peter in the Acts, speaking to the Jews, says, "I know that you did it through ignorance; now therefore turn you and repent that your sins may be wiped out." But the blasphemy against the Holy Ghost is said to be a continual fault-finding or reproach against the Holy Spirit of God; that is, against the inspiration, illumination, and works of the Spirit. For when he does so evidently work in the minds of men and women that they can neither gainsay it nor yet pretend ignorance, and that for all this they do resist, mock, despise, and continually snap at the truth, which they in their consciences do know to be most wholesome and true. In so doing they blaspheme the Holy Spirit and power of God. As for example, the Pharisees, being by most evident reasons and unreprovable miracles convinced in their own minds, could not deny but that the doctrine and works of our Lord Jesus Christ were the truth and miracles of the very God;

---

[11]Zwingli, *The Defense of the Reformed Faith*, 1:329-30; citing Mt 12:32.

[12]Donne, *Eighty Sermons* (1640), 347-48, 350.

and yet, against the testimony of their own consciences, they did of mere envy, rebellious doggedness, and false apostasy, continually cavil that Christ did all by the means and inspiration of Beelzebub, the devil. . . .

For it is impossible without faith to please God; without faith there is no remission of sins; without faith there is no entrance into the kingdom of God. But the sin against the Holy Ghost is mere apostasy and flat rebellion against the true faith which the Holy Ghost by his illumination pours into our hearts; which illumination these untoward apostates incessantly call darkness; they name it a mere seduction and with taunts blaspheme it openly. OF SIN, AND THE KINDS THEREOF.[13]

12:33-37 Out of the Heart the Mouth Speaks

WORDS REVEAL THE HEART. THEODORE BEZA: "Make," that is, "determine" or "establish," that is, "in your words about me." For, Jesus is arguing (or so it seems to me) from the effect to the cause. For, although they were not able to find fault with his work, namely, the casting out of the demons, nevertheless they were charging him with being a magician. But truly, Christ says, the work reveals the author of it. Therefore, either admit that one is good from whom a good work proceeds or demonstrate that both are evil. At the same time, Christ exposes their hypocrisy.

The Vulgate and Erasmus render the Greek phrase . . . with *ex abundatia* (from the abundance), but I have chosen *ex redundantia* (from the overflow). Their translation does not sufficiently express the meaning of the Greek. For, this should not be taken in a general sense, since quite often on the inside there is not much of the thing about which someone converses, nor do the heart and mouth always agree. But it is spoken specifically by Christ against the hopeless wickedness of those addressing him, as if it were written, "Because it is overflowing in your heart, your mouth vomits out

that blasphemy." The term "treasure" likewise looks to this in the verse that follows, where in general terms it is said that people gladly draw forth from their heart, as it were, the cache that is especially pleasing to them.

"You will be justified." The sense is, "you will be absolved," since it stands in opposition to the phrase "you shall be condemned." Therefore, they are foolish who from this passage and ones like it try to establish the righteousness of works—that is, the quality whereby in ourselves we are just before God—since in this passage "to be justified" does not mean the same thing as "to be made just," rather "to be declared just." That from which we are just is different from the testimony of that justness. And Paul in particular from all of Scripture bears witness that we, although we are not just in ourselves, nevertheless are justified in Christ (who is our righteousness), when he is received by faith. In other words, we are reckoned for just and accordingly absolved. But this faith is reckoned from its fruits (that is, from the works), namely, so that true faith may be distinguished from false and adulterous faith, as James teaches. Moreover, Christ makes mention of speech, not so as to exclude the other works of a person, but to relate it to the matter at hand. And certainly speech, since it is an indicator of thoughts and character, is one of the chief actions of a person, and indeed in compared to the others it is the most important, as James 3 abundantly teaches. ANNOTATIONS ON MATTHEW 12:33-37.[14]

THOSE WHO SEEK TO HURT GOD'S WORD WILL NOT PREVAIL. ARGULA VON GRUMBACH:

How can you hope to say anything good
When your heart on such evil broods?
In Matthew's Gospel it's written,
In chapter twelve, just try to listen.
I feel no bitterness whatever
If for the sake of God I suffer;
Had you merely insulted me

---

[13]DHB 2:422-24.

[14]Beza, *Annotationes Majores in Novum Dn. Nostri Jesu Christi Testamentum* (1594), 79.

I'd not have answered, but let it be,
Shown myself a Christian meek
And turned to you the other cheek;
But since God's word you seek to hurt
Strongly I will resist your work
None of which is of any avail.
The gates of hell will not prevail.

"JOHANNES OF LANZHUT": ATTACK
AND RESPONSE.[15]

**JESUS ILLUSTRATES THE LINK BETWEEN
WORDS AND JUDGMENT.** JOHANNES PISCATOR:
After showing them the magnitude of the sin of
the Pharisees, he continues on to point out the
source or root cause, specifically, the malice of their
hearts, which he proves from the effects, drawing
various similes. First he compares the tree and its
fruit . . . and second the nature of vipers . . . and
then a gushing and overflowing spring in the same
verse, and finally a treasury or storehouse from
which something is drawn out. Moreover he
straightforwardly states his point, in no uncertain
terms, in verse 34 where he says, "How are you able
to speak good things when you are evil?" . . . And
so, in this second part of the passage he is accusing
the Pharisees of malice. The third part of the
passage follows and arises as an effect from the
previous two: the threat of God's punishment.
Truly, on the basis of that blasphemy and that
malice, he threatens the Pharisees with eternal
damnation. He shows the certainty of that
punishment, first from a simpler statement and
then a proverbial one. He uses the simpler one in
verse 36, where he intimates that people—specifically here those whose sins would not be forgiven—
are going to be damned for some careless word,
that is, a word of no use to the glory of God and
edification of a neighbor, and from this it is left to
be understood that people will be condemned
much more because of their blasphemies of the
Holy Spirit, which certainly are words derogatory
to the glory of God and ruinous of a neighbor. The

proverbial maxim in verse 37 is illustrated with a
side-by-side comparison of contrasting statements.
For, just as a person will be justified—that is, will
be pronounced pious and innocent—from pious
speech, or, more specifically, speech that pertains to
the glory of God and the building up of a neighbor,
so will a person be pronounced impious—that is,
condemned—from impious speech and blasphemy.
LOGICAL ANALYSIS OF MATTHEW.[16]

12:38-45 The Demand for a Sign

**NO REPENTANCE AND THE REJECTION OF
WISDOM.** MARTIN BUCER: "The signs that are
produced through me and will be produced in the
future, just as they will become evidence against
you, so for others who are savable they happen and
will happen. To you a sign will be given, the sort
that was seen in Jonah. I will be greatly hated by
you and finally delivered up to your hands, and you
will kill me, and you will confine me in the tomb
for three days. But soon I will rise again with great
strength, I will bring on the kingdom of God, I will
administer it with the utmost power, using the
most humble and downcast ministers of all, against
whom, with all your wisdom and power you will
accomplish nothing, however much you try. From
that sign the rest of my power will be revealed to
you, and it will be plain to see, and it will render
you without excuse." And clearly they experienced
this sign when, against their commands and with
the punishments disregarded with which they were
threatened, the apostles with great confidence were
bearing witness to the resurrection of our Lord
Jesus Christ, demonstrating it also with signs and
wonders. And they were astonished because of it
and were cut to their heart, but they could not
figure out how to stop them. Concerning this sign
also see above, chapter 1. The whole sign of which
he speaks, furthermore, came to pass against him.
On the three-day period in which Christ was in
the tomb, see below in its relevant place.

---

[15]Grumbach, *Argula von Grumbach*, 189-90 (AvG 146); citing
Mt 5:39; 16:18.

[16]Piscator, *Analysis Logica Evangelii Secundum Matthaeum* (1594),
195-96.

Because he made mention of the sign of Jonah, he thought also of the Ninevites, to whom that preacher had been sent, and whom they heard after repenting. And so, from their example and from that of the queen of the South, that is, Sheba, whose kingdom was further to the south of Judea, he admonishes those obstinate Pharisees for their impiety and foretells that they, regardless of how respectable they seem to themselves, will be judged by those sinners and Gentiles. For, those Ninevites quickly repented when Jonah preached to them, while the queen, stirred only by the reputation of Solomon, came from the ends of the earth—for the region of Sheba borders the ocean, which nowadays they call fertile Arabia—to hear his wisdom. But the Pharisees in contrast not only hold in contempt Jesus, but also kill him, whom they have in the present, who is infinitely better than Jonah and Solomon, assuredly the very righteousness and wisdom of God, the Christ. Here the power of the Spirit of God revealed itself marvelously; it terrified those wicked people so that they dared not contradict that magnificent message of Christ concerning himself; for, he professed unequivocally here that he is the Christ when he affirmed that he is better than Jonah and Solomon. As for that phrase, "They will stand up with this generation. . . ." He is speaking in human terms concerning the judgment, as he did a little above, when he said, "Consequently, they themselves will pass judgment on you." For, the repentance of the Ninevites will completely condemn the lack of repentance on the part of the Jews, and the zeal for wisdom, with which the queen of Sheba was burning, will condemn the contempt for the true celestial wisdom whereby the scribes and Pharisees were scorning Christ and his teaching. For these, gathered together with them, will condemn them, although, while the pious are of one mind and will with Christ and are members of him, they will pass judgment together with Christ on the impious, not so much by example and deeds, as by the Word of God. Finally, notice from this passage that God always had his own among the Gentiles as well, because "He is not only the God of the Jews, but also of the Gentiles." COMMENTARY ON MATTHEW.[17]

WHY THE SIGN OF JONAH IS THE ONLY SIGN GIVEN.

LANCELOT ANDREWES: So have you, as in a sign, set forth Christ's death by Jonah's drowning, Christ's burial by Jonah's abode there, and Christ's resurrection by Jonah's emersion again. . . . None but that? Why afterward, between this and his passion, he showed diverse others, and how then says he, none but it? Signs indeed he showed, yet not any of them so pregnant for the purpose they sought as was this. They sought a sign of the season, as by the sixteenth chapter is plain, that this was the time the Messiah was to come. To put them out of doubt of that; to that point none so forcible as his death and rising again figured in that of Jonah. That, and none but that. All he did else, the prophets had done the like; given signs from heaven, which they here sought, yea even raised the dead. But raise himself being dead, get forth of the heart of the earth when once he was in, that passed their skill. Never a patriarch or prophet of them all could do that . . . none but he. So as therein he showed himself indeed to be the true and undoubted Messiah, and never so else in any sign of them all.

For signs being compounded of power and goodness, not power alone but power and goodness, that is, the benefit or good of them they be done for; never so general, so universal, so great a good, as by Christ's death, as it might be Jonah's casting in; nor ever so great, so incomparably great a power, as by raising himself from death to life, set forth in Jonah's casting up again; those two, by these two, more manifest than by any another. The sign of the greatest love and power—love to die, power to rise—that ever was wrought. A SERMON PREACHED BEFORE THE KING'S MAJESTY.[18]

THE TERROR OF NEW SINS.

GIOVANNI DIODATI: After Christ had confuted his

---

[17]Bucer, *In Sacra Quatuor Evangelia, Enarrationes Perpetuae* (1536), 315; citing Rom 3:29.
[18]Andrewes, *Ninety-Six Sermons*, 2:391, 395-96*.

malignant adversaries, upon the occasion of the possessed man's deliverance, he now instructs the people, wishing them to beware that the devil has not any place to return by God's just judgment upon any new sins, for in that case the precedent benefit will aggravate the new ingratitude. And under this figure he teaches all them who have been delivered from the devil's spiritual tyranny to beware lest they fall into it again, for that he, being driven as out of his old habitation, will every way endeavor to come into it again with greater fury and ruin. Now this threatening is set forth to terrify all people, but takes effect in none, but only in such whose faith is but only for a time, not lively, nor soundly rooted, as the elect's is, in whom Christ dwells, and never departs from them. PIOUS ANNOTATIONS.[19]

GOSPEL PROCLAMATION AND SPIRITUAL WARFARE. AEGIDIUS HUNNIUS: The Lord goes on to threaten the unbelieving Jews, those blasphemous and obstinate contemptors of his words and actions, with the judgment of God. He does this using figurative language, the point of which is this: that since he himself thus far, by the proclamation of the gospel, has labored to cast out the devil from their hearts by dispersing those deadly shadows of unbelief through the power and gleam of the gospel, and since by his miracles he brought it about that their consciences were held bound by the power of the truth and their house began to be cleansed in some way, but nonetheless again they gave a place to the demon that had been driven out, therefore their situation will suddenly collapse and grow worse, and they themselves will be bound by Satan with tighter chains and locks, from which they will never, or certainly only with much more difficulty, be able to extricate themselves and be free. And he draws an analogy from the present miracle of the demon that was driven away and cast out from the poor man, transferring language commonly used for describing the corporeal

casting out of demons to make note of the spiritual benefit, and saying, "when an unclean spirit departed. . . ." The devil is said to go out from the man in this passage in that, by virtue of the proclamation of the Word of God, the man is released from his bonds and freed from the tyranny and power of Satan. Therefore, since Satan was driven away by this spiritual reason from the heart of some man, "he walks through waterless places," he finds himself cast out into a desert, at which time he is induced to reflect on his old host. Moreover, since there is no rest for him anywhere unless he is troubling the human race, he thinks he should make every effort to enter into people so that they are under his sway and to enslave them to the power below. But short of assailing some other person, at least he could seek out his old host to see if he might be able to recover and possess him again. And to make the assault stronger, he enlists new soldiers, as it were, and he seeks reinforcements, by taking on and joining with "seven spirits more wicked than himself," so that, supported by their help and strength, he might gain possession of his old palace. COMMENTARY ON MATTHEW.[20]

12:46-50 Jesus' True Family

THE MINISTRY OF THE WORD SHOULD BE HONORED ABOVE ALL. MARTIN LUTHER: Finally, his mother came, wishing to speak to him. . . . No doubt it was on account of some great matter. But he, being now caught up by the feeling of wrath against the blasphemers and with zeal for his Father's glory, listens to nothing, not even his mother. And thereby he teaches that servants of the Word should not care for even the honor of their parents over the ministry of the Word. And therefore he says, "What is a mother? The Word of God is to be far preferred to mother, brothers, and everything. Whoever hears it is my mother, brother, sister, and everything." He demonstrates that he possesses an ineffable love toward God above all

---

[19]Diodati, *Pious Annotations* (1643), D4r; citing Mt 24:24; 2 Thess 2:13; 2 Tim 2:19; 1 Jn 3:9; 5:18.

[20]Hunnius, *Commentarius in Evangelium Secundum Matthaeum* (1594), 767-68.

things—and that everyone should possess such a love—and that nothing is to be cared for above or equally with God. ANNOTATIONS ON MATTHEW.[21]

THE CLOSEST OF RELATIONSHIPS. JOHN CALVIN: These words were unquestionably intended to reprove Mary's eagerness, and she certainly acted improperly in attempting to interrupt the progress of his discourse. At the same time, by disparaging the relationship of flesh and blood, our Lord teaches a very useful doctrine; for he admits all his disciples and all believers to the same honorable rank, as if they were his nearest relatives, or rather he places them in the room of his mother and brethren. Now this statement is closely connected with the office of Christ; for he tells us that he has been given, not to a small number of individuals, but to all the godly, who are united in one body with him by faith. He tells us also that there is no tie of relationship more sacred than spiritual relationship, because we ought not to think of him according to the flesh, but according to the power of his Spirit, which he has received from the Father to renew women and men, so that those who are by nature the polluted and accursed seed of Abraham begin to be by grace the holy and heavenly sons of God. . . . To sum up the whole, this passage, first, teaches us to behold Christ with the eyes of faith; and, second, it informs us that all who are regenerated by the Spirit and give them-selves up entirely to God for true justification are thus admitted to the closest union with Christ and become one with him.

When he says that they do the will of his Father, he does not mean that they fulfill, in a perfect manner, the whole righteousness of the law; for in that sense the name brother, which is here given by him to his disciples, would not apply to any person. But his design is to bestow the highest commendation on faith, which is the source and origin of holy obedience and at the same time covers the defects and sins of the flesh, that they may not be imputed. . . .

Although these words seem to imply that Christ has no regard to the ties of blood, yet we know that in reality he paid the strictest attention to human order and discharged his lawful duties toward relatives; but he points out that, in comparison of spiritual relationship, no regard, or very little, is due to the relationship of the flesh. Let us, therefore, attend to this comparison so as to perform all that nature can justly claim and, at the same time, not to be too strongly attached to flesh and blood. Again, as Christ bestows on the disciples of his gospel the inestimable honor of being reckoned as his brethren, we must be held guilty of the basest ingratitude if we do not disregard all the desires of the flesh and direct every effort toward this object. COMMENTARY ON A HARMONY OF THE EVANGELISTS.[22]

---

[21]LW 67:184-85 (WA 38:553).

[22]CTS 2:90-92 (CO 45:350-51).

13:1-33 JESUS TEACHES IN PARABLES

That same day Jesus went out of the house and sat beside the sea. ²And great crowds gathered about him, so that he got into a boat and sat down. And the whole crowd stood on the beach. ³And he told them many things in parables, saying: "A sower went out to sow. ⁴And as he sowed, some seeds fell along the path, and the birds came and devoured them. ⁵Other seeds fell on rocky ground, where they did not have much soil, and immediately they sprang up, since they had no depth of soil, ⁶but when the sun rose they were scorched. And since they had no root, they withered away. ⁷Other seeds fell among thorns, and the thorns grew up and choked them. ⁸Other seeds fell on good soil and produced grain, some a hundredfold, some sixty, some thirty. ⁹He who has ears,ᵃ let him hear."

¹⁰Then the disciples came and said to him, "Why do you speak to them in parables?" ¹¹And he answered them, "To you it has been given to know the secrets of the kingdom of heaven, but to them it has not been given. ¹²For to the one who has, more will be given, and he will have an abundance, but from the one who has not, even what he has will be taken away. ¹³This is why I speak to them in parables, because seeing they do not see, and hearing they do not hear, nor do they understand. ¹⁴Indeed, in their case the prophecy of Isaiah is fulfilled that says:

""You will indeed hear but never understand,
    and you will indeed see but never perceive."
¹⁵For this people's heart has grown dull,
    and with their ears they can barely hear,
    and their eyes they have closed,
lest they should see with their eyes
    and hear with their ears
and understand with their heart
    and turn, and I would heal them.'

¹⁶But blessed are your eyes, for they see, and your ears, for they hear. ¹⁷For truly, I say to you, many prophets and righteous people longed to see what you see, and did not see it, and to hear what you hear, and did not hear it.

¹⁸"Hear then the parable of the sower: ¹⁹When anyone hears the word of the kingdom and does not understand it, the evil one comes and snatches away what has been sown in his heart. This is what was sown along the path. ²⁰As for what was sown on rocky ground, this is the one who hears the word and immediately receives it with joy, ²¹yet he has no root in himself, but endures for a while, and when tribulation or persecution arises on account of the word, immediately he falls away.ᵇ ²²As for what was sown among thorns, this is the one who hears the word, but the cares of the world and the deceitfulness of riches choke the word, and it proves unfruitful. ²³As for what was sown on good soil, this is the one who hears the word and understands it. He indeed bears fruit and yields, in one case a hundredfold, in another sixty, and in another thirty."

²⁴He put another parable before them, saying, "The kingdom of heaven may be compared to a man who sowed good seed in his field, ²⁵but while his men were sleeping, his enemy came and sowed weedsᶜ among the wheat and went away. ²⁶So when the plants came up and bore grain, then the weeds appeared also. ²⁷And the servantsᵈ of the master of the house came and said to him, 'Master, did you not sow good seed in your field? How then does it have weeds?' ²⁸He said to them, 'An enemy has done this.' So the servants said to him, 'Then do you want us to go and gather them?' ²⁹But he said, 'No, lest in gathering the weeds you root up the wheat along with them. ³⁰Let both grow together until the harvest, and at harvest time I will tell the reapers, "Gather the weeds first and bind them in bundles to be burned, but gather the wheat into my barn."'"

³¹He put another parable before them, saying, "The kingdom of heaven is like a grain of mustard seed that a man took and sowed in his field. ³²It is the smallest of all seeds, but when it has grown it is

larger than all the garden plants and becomes a tree, so that the birds of the air come and make nests in its branches."

[33] He told them another parable. "The kingdom of heaven is like leaven that a woman took and hid in three measures of flour, till it was all leavened."

a Some manuscripts add here and in verse 43 *to hear*   b Or *stumbles*   c Probably *darnel*, a wheat-like weed   d Or *bondservants*; also verse 28

OVERVIEW: Matthew introduces this section by saying that Jesus taught them "many things in parables." With that comment, the theme of needing to hear the words of Jesus is illustrated through a cluster of parables. The connection between hearing the parables and the need for interpreting them truthfully can be seen in that Jesus himself provides the interpretation for two of his parables. The Reformation commentators describe the spiritual effects of hearing the parables and their function as literary devices in the Gospel.

Using Isaiah 6, Jesus indicates that the inability to "hear" about the kingdom in the parables is due to the nation of Israel's long history of rejecting God's Word and his message about the Messiah. Jesus' disciples (the ones who would hear) were blessed because the prophets and "righteous people" (a remnant) from Israel's past had longed for the days of the coming of the Messiah. Those who have heard the Word truly preached but are not fruitful can only blame their prideful and unbelieving hearts, not the Word itself.

The second parable provided by Matthew gives some indication of the mixed multitude of Jesus' audience. The Reformation commentators contend for varying positions as to whether the "field" in the parable represents the church or the entire human population. Though Matthew separates the parable from its interpretation (Mt 13:36-43), the commentators connect the two parables by indicating that both depict that some people will reject the Word of God and that others will receive it by hearing.

Matthew pairs these two parables with similar imagery in which the kingdom of heaven is compared to something that starts small and then grows, a theme that Juan de Valdés notes. Like the mustard seed, the kingdom's humble beginnings contrast with the superiority of its final state. The Reformation commentators contend that these parables serve to encourage disciples so that they are not discouraged by the few that initially respond to the gospel.

THE EXCELLENCY OF THE GOSPEL IN THE PARABLES. THOMAS MOCKET: The Evangelist goes on in describing the prophetical office of Christ, recites seven parables concerning the nature, efficacy, worth, and excellency of the gospel, Christ, and his church. The first parable is of the seed sown, verse 3 expounded verse 18, which is the gospel preached, which does not thrive in some hearers so well as in others, either because they do not receive it or do not carefully keep and cherish it, that it might bring forth fruit unto everlasting life. The scope is to comfort the godly against the unprofitableness of some hearers and to admonish his hearers, and in them all others, so to hear, as to be careful to keep the word and profit by it.

The second is the parable of the tares, verse 24, expounded verse 37. Tares, an unusual and hurtful weed unknown in our parts, much like our fine tare, signifies heretics, schismatics, hypocrites, and profane livers, who by the devil's wily working creep into the church among the wheat or good men and women, to undermine and hurt the church. The scope of this—and the seventh parable of the draw-net cast into the sea, gathering together both good and bad, verse 47—is to show that the church will ever have good and bad people in it, and to comfort the godly against the scandal of pestilent errors and profane livers in the visible church. The third is of the mustard seed, verse 31, and the fourth is of the leaven, verse 33, both signifying the same thing, namely, the gospel and work of grace in the soul, and church of Christ, which grow up from small beginning to a great height, beyond expectation. See Ezekiel 47:1, 5, and Daniel 2:34-35, and this to set forth his mighty power in his church, word, and ordinances. And the scope is to comfort the godly against the offense that might be taken at the small beginning of grace in themselves or any of the church, that sometimes in some places is very little low and contemptible.

The fifth is of the hidden treasure, verse 44. And the sixth is of the pearl of a great price, verses 45-46; both signify Christ and gospel grace—of more worth than any treasure or pearl though never so rich and rare—revealed and conveyed by the gospel. As the scope of the four foregoing parables is to set forth the gospel, Christ, and his saving graces and gifts by their nature, force, and efficacy, so here by their worth and excellency resembled to an hidden treasure, verse 44, and to a rich pearl, verses 45-46. The scope of both is to set out the worth and excellency of the gospel, or rather Christ and his saving graces and gifts revealed, set forth and conveyed by the gospel and how much; therefore, Christians ought to esteem Christ and the gospel for Christ's sake and grace's sake, seeing it is the instrument and means of the revelation and participation of Jesus Christ and his saving graces and a means to prepare them for eternal life. GOSPEL DUTY AND DIGNITY.[1]

13:1-9 *The Parable of the Sower*

THE SEED ONLY GROWS IN FAITHFUL HEARTS. THE ENGLISH ANNOTATIONS: This is the first of the seven parables in this chapter, wherein it is intimated that the seed of eternal life, which is sown in the preaching of the gospel, thrives not so well in one as in another. The reason is that people, for the most part, either do not receive it, or lose it, or suffer it not to ripen. Therefore, he admonishes his hearers that their flocking after him would not profit them except that they kept it in faithful hearts and brought forth the fruits thereof in newness of life, which in

likelihood only a fourth part of them would do. ANNOTATIONS ON MATTHEW 13:1.[2]

HOW DO WE COME TO CHRIST? JOHN CALVIN: It is not without good reason that the Evangelists begin with informing us that a vast multitude had assembled and that when Christ beheld them, he was led to compare his doctrine to seed. That multitude had been collected from various places: all were held in suspense; all were alike eager to hear, but not equally desirous to receive instruction. The design of the parable was to inform them that the seed of doctrine, which is scattered far and wide, is not everywhere productive because it does not always find a fertile and well cultivated soil. Christ declared that he was there in the capacity of a farmer, who was going out to sow seed, but that many of his hearers resembled an uncultivated and parched soil, while others resembled a thorny soil so that the labor and the very seed were thrown away. I forbear to make any further inquiry into the meaning of the parable till we come to the explanation of it, which, as we shall find, is shortly afterward given by our Lord. It may only be necessary, for the present, to remind the reader that if those who ran from distant places to Christ, like hungry persons, are compared to an unproductive and barren soil, we need not wonder if, in our own day, the gospel does not yield fruit in many, of whom some are lazy and sluggish, others hear with indifference, and others are scarcely drawn even to hear. COMMENTARY ON A HARMONY OF THE EVANGELISTS.[3]

WHY THE WORD DOES NOT TAKE ROOT. THOMAS LAMB: Christ, expounding the parable of the sower, says, "When anyone hears the Word of the kingdom and understands it not, then comes the wicked one and catches away that which was sown in their heart; this is the one who received seed by the wayside."

And here it is to be noted that the Word is said to be caught away out of the heart of those who

---

[1]Mocket, *Gospell Duty and Dignity* (1648), 3-4*.

[2]Downame, ed., *Annotations*, HH3v*.
[3]CTS 2:100-101* (CO 45:356-57).

never understood it. In like manner, it may be said by the apostle of an apostate that they tread underfoot the Son of God and counted the blood of the covenant an unholy thing by which they were sanctified; although they never had the benefit of the blood of Christ applied to their heart and soul by faith and the Holy Spirit. The reason of both is because human sin cannot make void the power of God's grace; the Word of God's gospel always retains the nature of fruitful seed, and in preaching to the person respects the heart as its proper residence, although all who hear it do not in heart receive with meekness that which is grafted in them. . . . I answer, that when Christ in the parable of the stony ground gives the reason why such as received the Word with joy, and believed for a while, and in the time of tribulation and persecution are offended, and go away to be only because they have no root in themselves, namely, the Word had no root in their hearts; as yet the scope of Christ herein was not to extenuate but to aggravate the sin of these temporizing apostates. And the reason appears, because the deficiency was not in the means of grace, but in the persons themselves, who pretending and professing to abound in the reception of grace from the means of grace, which as it always retains the nature of fruitful seed in itself, so the whole reason why it was not fruitful in them was from the pride and self-conceited excellency that was in them, which was as stones in the ground which hindered the Word from taking root in their hearts and from being fruitful in their lives and conversations, if Christ may be believed in the parable, and the exposition thereof made by himself. ABSOLUTE FREEDOM FROM SIN.[4]

THE FAILURE OF THE SEED IS NOT THE FAULT OF THE SEED. MARTIN LUTHER: [A point should be noted] against the fanatical spirits[†] who think that the spoken word is useless because it does not bear fruit in most people. They are fools—as if

they themselves were bearing fruit when, precisely because they despise God's word, they are the worst of men!

This is a widespread and especially common heresy since human beings are such that everyone is eager to judge others while paying no heed to themselves. . . . This same thing happens in the church. People of this kind condemn the saints because of certain things that they do on account of the Word of God, and they look for a church, or saints, without sin, though that is impossible to find. And so, they reach the conclusion either that they [the other churches or saints] do not possess the true word or that the external word is useless.

But here you see that it is the seed upon the good ground that bears fruit, or, rather, that if there were no seed, no fruit would follow upon the earth. Thus, if the spoken word were not in the church, there would be no fruit in it.

And so, the height of wisdom is not to be offended by the throng of those who despise the Word. It is unbelievable what great people are coming to ruin even today through this scandal, thinking that nothing should be seen in the church unless it has the highest appearance of holiness. . . .

Is it not, therefore, obvious madness to assign to the Word the blame that belongs to the hearers? "A person has no concern for the Word they have heard, therefore that word is not the true Word." "The devil does not love God, therefore God is not the true God." "The son does not honor the father, therefore the father is not his true father." "A bandit does not obey the prince, therefore the prince is not a true prince." Ungrateful and proud people must be stricken with this same insanity, so that they say and do nothing but what is perverse. And yet, as I said, this disease is a common one: that people make judgments about the word based on particular fruits and they string together a most fallacious argument, as follows: "Wherever everything found in the Word does not come to pass, there the true Word is absent. Not all the things found in the Word come to pass among these people or those people. Therefore, they do not have the true Word."

---

[4]Lamb, *Absolute Freedom from Sin by Christ's Death for the World* (1656), 154-56.

The gospel before us refutes the major premise, saying that many of the things that are found in the Word do not come to pass—among the thorns, on the rocky ground, and on the road. Therefore, their conclusion is false. Annotations on Matthew 13:1-9.[5]

13:10-17 *The Function of the Parables*

The Heavenly Disposed in Earthly Matters. Richard Sibbes: In the next place observe, Christ teaches by parables, helping the soul by the body, the understanding by the sense; teaching us, out of objects of our sense, to raise up our souls to divine meditations, so as the soul is beholden to the body as well as the body to the soul, though not in so eminent a measure. But it may be questioned: Are not parables hard to be understood? I answer: It is true, if they are not unfolded they are hard; but if they are once manifested, they are of excellent use; and like the cloud, lightsome toward the Israelites, to give to them light, but toward the Egyptians a cloud of darkness. And carnal people are earthly in heavenly matters; and, on the contrary, those who are spiritually minded are heavenly disposed in earthly matters. The Rich Pearl.[6]

The Nature of Parables. Giovanni Diodati: This was a kind of teaching used among the Jews and followed by our Savior as very useful to make the truth known and to cause the apprehension to enter into the spirit of the hearers by a well appropriated similitude of some framed narration. Wherein a parable differs from an allegory, which takes the figure of a true history, but in a various sense, to represent moral or spiritual things; and from an enigma which has more obscurity and brevity than a parable; and from a plain similitude

inserted in the natural and proper extent of the discourse, and is therefore clear and plain to be understood. Pious Annotations.[7]

Seeing and Hearing Christ. Martin Luther: To see and hear is to be understood here simply of the outward seeing and hearing, to wit, that they saw Christ come in the flesh, heard his sermons, and were present at those miracles which he did among the Jews. The Jews saw the same according to the flesh, yea and felt them also; yet did they not truly acknowledge him for Christ, as the apostles did, and especially Peter in the name of all the rest did confess him, saying, "You are Christ, the Son of the living God." We grant indeed that there were some among the Jews, which acknowledged him, as the apostles did, but the number of them was very small, wherefore he takes his apostles here severally unto himself. Many prophets and kings have seen Christ, although in the spirit, as the Lord himself says to the Jews of Abraham, "Your father Abraham rejoiced to see my day, and he saw it and was glad." The Jews thought then that he had spoken of the bodily seeing, but he spoke of the spiritual seeing, whereby all Christian hearts did behold him, before he was born. For if Abraham saw him, undoubtedly many other of the prophets, in whom the Holy Ghost was, saw him also. And although this feeling saved the holy fathers and prophets, yet did they always with most inward and heartfelt affection desire to see Christ in the flesh also, as is commonly shown in the Prophets. Wherefore the Lord says here to his disciples, who saw him both in the flesh and in the Spirit, blessed are the eyes that see those things you see. As if he said, Now is the acceptable year and time of grace; the matter which is now in hand is so weighty and precious, that the eyes are worthily said to be blessed, which see it. For now was the gospel preached openly and manifestly both by Christ himself and also by his apostles, whereupon he here calls them all blessed,

---

[5]LW 67:187-89* (WA 38:553-54). †Luther referred to many of his radical opponents, including the Anabaptists and Spiritualists, as fanatical spirits (*Schwärmer*), criticizing many aspects of their thought, including the neglect of the external Word for supposed special revelations of the Holy Spirit.
[6]WRS 7:255*; citing Ex 14:19-20.

[7]Diodati, *Pious Annotations* (1643), D4v.

which see and hear such grace. THE TWENTY-EIGHTH SERMON OF DR. MARTIN LUTHER OF THE LAW AND GOSPEL.[8]

13:18-23 Interpreting the Parable of the Sower

SPREADING THE GOOD SEED OF THE GOSPEL. JOHANNES BRENZ: It is interpreted by Christ. The farmer stands for Christ; the field is the world. For Christ refers this to himself; he scatters better seed in the field of the world, and there is nothing about divided households in this with respect to the Father. For first Christ expounded the law of God exactly in order that some might be able to know intelligently that it was charged to him by an act of God, as is written in Matthew and Luke. Then he spoke the gospel clearly, because according to that alone we have peace with the Father and eternal life. To this might not be a stretched teaching, but even by those things he attended to our salvation. For he exposed himself to various afflictions, and he offered himself so to the cross, which is death's, in order that he might reckon satisfaction for our sins, and by his own passion he might reconcile us with God the Father himself. Finally, after he was raised from the dead, he sent the Holy Spirit into the apostles, who by a wonderful mission confirmed their gospel, so that it might be made known in the whole world of the earth. Whence also the apostles scatter most diligently and faithfully that good seed of the gospel, or the teaching of Christ, into the whole world. And whoever holds to this teaching preached through Christ and the faith scattered through the apostles is certainly just and blessed. PERICOPAE EVANGELIORUM.[9]

THE MINGLING OF TWO KINGDOMS. JOHN COSIN: Here is a parable propounded, which is afterward explained by Christ himself to be intended of his church; the state and condition of which, as it is now at this present, besides the beginning and the progress and the ending of it, as it has been heretofore, and as it shall be in time to come, are all set forth to us under their several similitudes. And first, it is compared to a field; a field as large as the world, sowed by him with good seed and by his enemy over-sowed with bad. . . . For by the kingdom of heaven here is not meant the kingdom of glory that we are to live in hereafter, but the kingdom of grace that we live in now, which is the true and the visible church of Christ here upon the earth. . . . So that in reference to this appellation we are not to attend so much what this kingdom appears to be now, as what it will be when Christ shall appear hereafter, to translate those who have lived well in his kingdom of grace here to his kingdom of glory there. And it is a great comfort to us this, that our Savior thus mingles his kingdoms; that he makes the kingdom of grace and the kingdom of glory all one, the church and heaven itself all one; assuring us that if we see him as he looks . . . in this his glass, as Paul terms it, the glass of his ordinances and statutes in this kingdom of his word and sacraments, we have already begun to see him as he looks in heaven, and as he is in his majesty in that kingdom of eternal glory. APPENDIX 7.[10]

WORKING TOWARD A PURE CHURCH. NIELS HEMMINGSEN: First, it is here to be known, Christ entreats neither of the duties of pastors nor of the magistrates, but only takes away the stumbling block, with which the weak are troubled, when they see there are many impure folk in the church. For to the pastors is committed the spiritual sword, with which they separate the impure from the church by excommunicating them so that being stricken with shame, they may at length amend and the good people not be defiled with their infection. To the magistrate also is a sword committed, but it is a secular sword as they term it, with which he punishes and casts out the troublers

---

[8]Luther, *Complete Sermons*, 5:299-300; citing Jn 8:56.
[9]Brenz, *Pericopae Evangeliorum* (1556), 109.

[10]WJC 1:351-53.

of human fellowship. But albeit that pastors and magistrates did their duty never so diligently; yet shall they never be able to purge the church so clean, but that some dregs of impure doctrine and wicked life will remain which when we see, we must not be offended but taking warning by this parable, we must purge it as much as we can, committing the rest unto God.

For Christ does not, by this saying, bear with the maintenance of filthiness in the church, but only exhorts his faithful servants not to be discomforted when they are fain to suffer the evil to live with them. Of this place, therefore, we may gather: First, how great God's mercy is, which so patiently suffers the evil in his church so that they may repent. Second, that by these things we may comfort ourselves against the stumbling block of the fewness of those who obey the gospel. And third, that the Anabaptists are confuted, who deny any congregation (wherein are many wicked folks) to be the church. . . . In the sentence given upon the godly is set forth a double reward, namely, the blessing of his Father and the inheritance of God's kingdom. The one is set as contrary against cursing and the other is set against eternal punishment. We may, therefore, gather a double argument hereof. One of the punishment of the ungodly, and the other of the reward of the godly. And either of them both—if it be thought upon as it ought to be—is effectual to work in us the fear of God and true and continual repentance.

By this means, therefore, all the whole parable aims at this mark: that the ungodly should leave their own way, whereby they sin; that the unrighteous should leave their thought whereby they despair of the forgiveness of their sins and— according to the saying of the prophet—be converted to the Lord because they are ready to forgive. In this readiness nothing wants; but there is in it almighty mercifulness and merciful almightiness, to whom be glory forever. Amen. A POSTIL, OR EXPOSITION OF THE GOSPELS.[11]

---

[11]Hemmingsen, *A Postill, or Exposition of the Gospels* (1569), 64-65*.

13:24-30 *The Parable of the Weeds*

THE DAMAGING EFFECT OF TARES. HEINRICH BULLINGER: The kingdom of heaven in the present does not mean life and blessed happiness, which is something that we will enjoy in the future age, but the whole mystery or activity of the gospel and the kingdom of God. Therefore, it encompasses the teaching of the gospel, which is called the language of the kingdom; it includes the pious themselves, who are called the children of the kingdom, as well as the church in which our Lord reigns and which is called his domain, as well as the works that are done in the church.

Accordingly, the activity of the Word of God, the Lord says, and of the church, and especially of salvation, is like to a man sowing good seed. . . . And this is the sense of the parable: The seed of the Word of God is ruined and choked, not only for the reasons and means here laid out, by thick vines or by the laziness of those who take up the seed of the Word into their souls, but also because corrupted seed is spread, by which I mean a false image of the true Word, which some mix and sow in with the gospel truth like tares with wheat. That happens when Satan approaches and works to corrupt those whom, up to this point, he has not been able to turn aside from the purity of the gospel by vain speculations or the blows of persecutions or the lure of pleasures.

And so, vice and corruption are not just in the field or in the hearer; they also exist in the seed and the sower. Thus, corrupt and heretical doctrine is rightly compared to tares, which the Greeks call *aira* or *thyaros*, and Latin speakers call *lolium*, as it is in Dioscurides.[†] For Pliny[‡] sometimes labels tares a disease of grains, sometimes a plague, since it chokes wheat, and Virgil[§] called it "fruitless tares." In the same way the church has nothing more ruinous than corrupt and heretical teaching. For it corrupts those natures sometimes that are excellent, and those whom it does not corrupt, it nevertheless troubles until they grow weak. By perverse doctrine is assembled a crowd of contentious people, who hold to what is false with no less zeal and vigilance than church leaders do the truth. Yes, even erroneous doctrine has a marvelous force; just as also they produce from tares that which, gathered up and made into bread, induces the deepest sleep, likewise vertigo and vomiting, and it fills the body with foul ulcers. It also does great damage to the eyes, clouding them over. And it's from this, surely, that the old joke is derived, that "they live on tares," usually referring to those who are dim-sighted and are nearly blind. And clearly corrupt doctrine causes blindness and produces a vertigo and ulcers of the soul, and undermines completely the health of the mind, and in the end kills it. COMMENTARY ON MATTHEW.[12]

GOOD AND BAD WILL MINGLE IN THE CHURCH. JOHN CALVIN: In order to reap the advantage of this parable, it is necessary to ascertain the object which Christ had in view. Some think that, to guard a mixed multitude against satisfying themselves with an outward profession of the gospel, he told them that in his own field bad seed is often mixed with the good, but that a day is coming when the tares shall be separated from the wheat. They accordingly connect this parable with the one immediately preceding, as if the design of both had been the same. For my own part, I take a different view. He speaks of a separation in order to prevent the minds of the godly from giving way to uneasiness or despondency when they perceive a confused mixture of the good along with the bad. Although Christ has cleansed the church with his own blood, that it may be without spot or blemish, yet hitherto he suffers it to be polluted by many stains. I speak not of the remaining infirmities of the flesh, to which every believer is liable, even after that he has been renewed by the Holy Spirit. But as soon as Christ has gathered a small flock for himself, many hypocrites mingle with it, persons of immoral lives creep in, nay, many wicked people insinuate

themselves; in consequence of which, numerous stains pollute that holy assembly, which Christ has separated for himself. Many persons, too, look upon it as exceedingly absurd that ungodly or profane or unprincipled people should be cherished within the bosom of the church. Add to this that very many, under the pretense of zeal, are excessively displeased when everything is not conducted to their wish, and, because absolute purity is nowhere to be found, withdraw from the church in a disorderly manner or subvert and destroy it by unreasonable severity.

In my opinion, the design of the parable is simply this: So long as the pilgrimage of the church in this world continues, bad people and hypocrites will mingle in it with those who are good and upright, that the children of God may be armed with patience and, in the midst of offenses which are fitted to disturb them, may preserve unbroken steadfastness of faith. It is an appropriate comparison, when the Lord calls the church his field, for believers are the seed of it; and though Christ afterward adds that the field is the world, yet he undoubtedly intended to apply this designation, in a peculiar manner to the church, about which he had commenced the discourse. But as he was about to drive his plough through every country of the world, so as to cultivate fields and scatter the seed of life throughout the whole world, he has employed a synecdoche[†] to make the world denote what more strictly belonged only to a part of it. COMMENTARY ON A HARMONY OF THE EVANGELISTS.[13]

13:31-33 The Mustard Seed and the Leaven

THE STEADY GROWTH OF THE KINGDOM. JUAN DE VALDÉS: Christ means that just as the grain of mustard seed, which is the least of all that are sown, being sown goes on to increase in size until it becomes a large tree, so the kingdom of heaven, being in this present life the meanest and the most

---

[12]Bullinger, In . . . Evangelium secundum Matthaeum commentariorum (1546), 6:135r-135v. †Dioscorides, De Materia Medica 2.122. ‡Pliny, Natural History 18.44. §Virgil, Georgics 1.154.

[13]CTS 2:118-20* (CO 45:367-68). †Synecdoche is a figure of speech in which a part is taken to represent the whole, or vice versa.

despised of all things that are taught, it, when preached, goes on to increase in size, in numbering more persons, and in character, giving greater perfection to those who are comprehended in it; until that, manifesting its importance in the life eternal, it will be seen that it transcends all the kingdoms of the world, which in this present life are great and illustrious. This is the proper application of the parable, where there is no occasion to insist upon the birds building their nests, since it appears that Christ only mentions it as an incident, indicative of the greatness of the tree; and as I have stated, our attention should only be directed to Christ's principal intention in them. Christ suggests by this parable that there comes to pass in the kingdom of heaven that which occurs to leaven and dough; for that just as a little leaven has such power that it suffices to leaven a great mass of dough, so the preaching of the kingdom of heaven, which, in the eyes of the world is insignificant and vile, is of such power that it suffices to justify, to mortify, to vivify, and to glorify all who are the people of God predestinated to life eternal; so that Christ's purpose in this parable is to show the power of preaching the kingdom of heaven, the power of the kingdom itself. In saying "three measures," he means a great mass of dough. COMMENTARY UPON THE GOSPEL OF ST. MATTHEW.[14]

THE KINGDOM STARTS SMALL. JOHN CALVIN: "The kingdom of God" is compared to a "grain of

mustard, which is the smallest among the seeds" but grows to such a height that it becomes a shrub, "in which the birds build their nests." It is likewise compared to leaven, which, though it may be small in amount, spreads its influence in such a manner as to impart its bitterness to a large quantity of meal. If the aspect of Christ's kingdom be despicable in the eyes of the flesh, let us learn to raise our minds to the boundless and incalculable power of God, which at once created all things out of nothing and every day raises up things that are not, in a manner which exceeds the capacity of the human senses. Let us leave to the proud their disdainful laugh till the Lord, at an unexpected hour, shall strike them with amazement. Meanwhile, let us not despond, but rise by faith against the pride of the world till the Lord give us that astonishing display of his power, of which he speaks in this passage.

The word *leaven* is sometimes taken in a bad sense, as when Christ warns them to "beware of the leaven of the Pharisees and of the Sadducees," and when Paul says, that "a little leaven leavens the whole lump." But here the term must be understood simply as applying to the present subject. As to the meaning of the phrase, the kingdom of God, and the kingdom of heaven, we have spoken on former occasions. COMMENTARY ON A HARMONY OF THE EVANGELISTS.[15]

---

[14]Valdés, *Commentary upon the Gospel of St. Matthew*, 246.

[15]CTS 32:127-28* (CO 45:372-73); citing 1 Cor 1:28; Mt 16:11; 1 Cor 5:6.

13:34-58 PARABLES OF THE KINGDOM

[34]All these things Jesus said to the crowds in parables; indeed, he said nothing to them without a parable. [35]This was to fulfill what was spoken by the prophet:[a]

"I will open my mouth in parables;
I will utter what has been hidden since the foundation of the world."

[36]Then he left the crowds and went into the house. And his disciples came to him, saying, "Explain to us the parable of the weeds of the field." [37]He answered, "The one who sows the good seed is the Son of Man. [38]The field is the world, and the good seed is the sons of the kingdom. The weeds are the sons of the evil one, [39]and the enemy who sowed them is the devil. The harvest is the end of the age, and the reapers are angels. [40]Just as the weeds are gathered and burned with fire, so will it be at the end of the age. [41]The Son of Man will send his angels, and they will gather out of his kingdom all causes of sin and all law-breakers, [42]and throw them into the fiery furnace. In that place there will be weeping and gnashing of teeth. [43]Then the righteous will shine like the sun in the kingdom of their Father. He who has ears, let him hear.

[44]"The kingdom of heaven is like treasure hidden in a field, which a man found and covered up. Then in his joy he goes and sells all that he has and buys that field.

[45]"Again, the kingdom of heaven is like a merchant in search of fine pearls, [46]who, on finding one pearl of great value, went and sold all that he had and bought it.

[47]"Again, the kingdom of heaven is like a net that was thrown into the sea and gathered fish of every kind. [48]When it was full, men drew it ashore and sat down and sorted the good into containers but threw away the bad. [49]So it will be at the end of the age. The angels will come out and separate the evil from the righteous [50]and throw them into the fiery furnace. In that place there will be weeping and gnashing of teeth.

[51]"Have you understood all these things?" They said to him, "Yes." [52]And he said to them, "Therefore every scribe who has been trained for the kingdom of heaven is like a master of a house, who brings out of his treasure what is new and what is old."

[53]And when Jesus had finished these parables, he went away from there, [54]and coming to his hometown he taught them in their synagogue, so that they were astonished, and said, "Where did this man get this wisdom and these mighty works? [55]Is not this the carpenter's son? Is not his mother called Mary? And are not his brothers James and Joseph and Simon and Judas? [56]And are not all his sisters with us? Where then did this man get all these things?" [57]And they took offense at him. But Jesus said to them, "A prophet is not without honor except in his hometown and in his own household." [58]And he did not do many mighty works there, because of their unbelief.

a Some manuscripts Isaiah the prophet

OVERVIEW: Through the use of Psalm 78, Matthew shows Jesus' teaching in parables to be another sign of his messianic identity. Calvin reflects Reformation commentary by wrestling with the concept of how Jesus' teaching fulfills the psalm. He concludes that Jesus' figurative language is the best way to deliver divine mysteries.

Matthew's second pairing of Jesus' parables emphasizes the great value of the kingdom. The similar parables picture the abandonment of other treasures due to the discovery of the kingdom. The reformers draw attention to the "spiritual meaning" intended by the parables: the complete surrender prompted by the gospel. Unless one abandons all other pursuits, the wealth of the gospel is missed.

The final parables of this section are unequal in length. The Reformation commentators note how the judgment theme establishes a clear connection with the conclusion of the earlier parable (cf. Mt 13:49-50 with Mt 13:41-42).

Jesus' probing question to the disciples about understanding returns to the emphasis earlier in the discourse concerning the need to "hear" and "understand." The brief parable about the master who brings out new and old treasures raises the questions about what is the "old" and the "new." The Reformation writers comment that the patristic interpretation understood Jesus to be encouraging his disciples to be like a scribe who knows the "old" (Law and Prophets) and connects it to the "new" (the gospel of the kingdom).

Matthew concludes this section with a brief narrative about Jesus' reception in Nazareth. Interestingly, the community recognizes both his wisdom and his mighty works (see Mt 11:19-20), yet they fail to connect those "signs" with his messianic identity. Erasmus notes how the judgment of the Nazarenes is based on external qualities instead of Christ's virtues and how that misjudgment of unbelief would be to their own shame.

13:34-43 The Parable of the Wheat and Tares Explained

Why Jesus Spoke in Parables. Martin Bucer: Jesus spoke all these things in parables. Mark adds that with many such parables Christ taught the crowds according as they were able to hear but separately to expose all things to his own disciples. When what I taught above is confirmed, that the Lord's use of parables was not on account of the lost only, but he was seeking, with the capability of the people, even then the will of the Father, which he was wanting the gospel to be revealed to people not suddenly, nor equally to all, but with respect to its own order. Hence, ours being fulfilled, he writes that it was written through the prophet who said, "I will open my mouth in parables." . . . Because it is just as if he said, "Christ was speaking all things in parables," in order that he might apply that of the prophet correctly, "I will open." . . . For not otherwise was the prophet's word fulfilled than that the Lord had thus himself spoken that psalm about himself, four single times regarding this way of using parables. About that fulfillment of the oracles of Scripture see at length above in chapter 2. But because the prophet said, opening his mouth to them in parables and enigmatic utterances from the beginning, which the Evangelist calls the things hidden from the foundation of the world, when yet he sang in this psalm of the most able benefit exhibited to the Israelite people by a divine work, and at the same time the penalties of infidelity that they gave, here it seems to be seen that truly remote places, even as parables in them, which they joined by a divine work to the fathers, he concealed with respect to the wise and also educated. **Commentary on Matthew.**[1]

How Jesus Fulfills the Psalm. John Calvin: Matthew does not mean that the psalm, which he quotes, is a prediction that relates peculiarly to Christ, but that, as the majesty of the Spirit was displayed in the discourse of the prophet, in the same manner was his power manifested in the discourse of Christ. The prophet, when he is about to speak of God's covenant, by which he adopted the seed of Abraham, of the benefits he continued to bestow upon his people, and of the whole government of the church, introduces his subject in lofty terms: "I will open my mouth in parables"—that is, "I will not speak of trifling matters, but will handle with becoming gravity subjects of the highest importance." When he adds, "I will utter dark sayings," the meaning is the same; such repetitions being very frequent in the Psalms. The Hebrew word *meshalim* signifies comparisons; and it came afterward to be applied to "weighty sentences," because comparisons generally impart beauty and energy to a discourse. The word *chidoth*

---

[1]Bucer, *In Sacra Quatuor Evangelia, Enarrationes Perpetuae* (1536), 324-25.

sometimes denotes "riddles" and at other times "short sayings."

Now though Matthew seems to allude to the word *parable*, he undoubtedly means that Christ spoke figuratively in order that his very style, being more brilliant than ordinary discourse, might carry more weight and dignity. In short, he says that what is contained in the psalm was fulfilled; because the use of allegories and figures tended to show that Christ was treating of the hidden mysteries of God, and to prevent his doctrine from being despised. Hence, too, we infer that there was no inconsistency in the various objects Christ had in view when he spoke to the people in a dark manner. Though he intended to conceal from the reprobate what he was saying, yet he labored to make them feel, even in the midst of their amazement, that there was something heavenly and divine in his language. COMMENTARY ON A HARMONY OF THE EVANGELISTS.[2]

BURNING AND UNQUENCHABLE JUDGMENT.

HUGH LATIMER: Now when our Savior heard the request of his disciples, he performs their desire and begins to expound unto them the parable, saying, "I am he that sows good seed: the adversary, the devil, is he who sows evil seed." Here our Savior, good people, makes known that he goes about to do us good; but the devil does quite the contrary, and he seeks to spoil and destroy us with his filthy and naughty seed of false doctrine. The field here is the whole world. The harvest is the end of the world. The reapers are the angels of God, who are his servants; for as every lord or master has his servants to wait upon him, and to do his commandments, so the angels of God wait upon him to do his commandments. The angels at the time of the harvest shall gather first all such as have been evil and have given occasion of wickedness and go forward in the same without repentance or amendment of their lives. All such, I say, shall be gathered together and cast into the furnace of fire, "where shall be weeping and gnashing of teeth." For

in the end of this wicked world all such as have lived in the delights and pleasures of the same, and have not fought with the lusts and pleasures of their flesh, but are proud and stubborn, or bear hatred and malice to their neighbors, or are covetous persons; also all naughty servants that do not their duties, and all those that use falsehood in buying and selling, and care not for their neighbors, but sell to them false wares, or otherwise deceive them; all these are called "the offenders of this world," and all such shall be cast into the furnace where shall be weeping, and wailing, and gnashing of teeth. . . . Therefore, our Savior, desirous to set out the pains of hell to us and to make us afraid thereof, calls it fire, yea, a burning and unquenchable fire. For as there is no pain so grievous as fire is, so the pains of hell pass all the pains that may be imagined by anyone. There shall be sobbing and sighing, weeping and wailing, and gnashing of teeth, which are the tokens of unspeakable pains and griefs that shall come upon those who die in the state of damnation. For you must understand that there are but two places appointed by Almighty God, for all humankind, that is, heaven and hell. And in whatever state a person dies, in the same they shall rise again, for there shall be no alteration or change. THE PARABLE OF THE TARES.[3]

IDENTIFYING THE WHEAT AND TARES. MENNO

SIMONS: This first parable is explained by Christ himself saying, he who sows the good seed is the Son of Man; the field is the world (understand it rightly, Christ says, it is the world, and not the church, as Gellius claims); the good seed are the children of the kingdom; but the tares are the children of the evil; the enemy that sowed them is the devil; the harvest is the end of the world; and the reapers are the angels. Reader, understand it rightly. Christ, the Son of Man, sows his seed, God's word, by means of his Spirit, in the world. All who hear it, believe, and obey are called the children of the kingdom. In the same manner, the opponent sows his tares, false doctrine, in the

---

[2]CTS 2:129* (CO 45:373-74); citing Ps 78:2.

[3]Latimer, *Select Sermons and Letters*, 358-59.

world, and all that hear and follow him are called the children of evil. Both wheat and tares grow together in the same field, namely, in the world. The farmer does not want the tares to be plucked up before their time, that is, they do not want them destroyed by putting them to death, but want them left until the harvest, lest the wheat be pulled up for tares. REPLY TO GELLIUS FABER.[4]

13:44-52 Parables About the Kingdom of Heaven

THE JOY OF THE TREASURE. JOHN STALHAM: In general is that in the text and observation, "for joy thereof," the joy of finding the treasure and of the "treasure" found, and "the joy of the pearl of great price," once truly found, this brings the man and merchant to consent to the selling of all and this brings his consent into act. "For joy," he parts with his sins, one and another, one as another in an absolute hatred of them never to have to do with them again. "For the joy of the treasure," he parts with his parts and gifts, so as they shall be new molded and cast and have a new stamp out of the mint and treasury of Christ's holiness. "For joy" of the riches of Christ's righteousness he lets go his own; and "for joy" of greater profits, sweeter pleasures, higher honors, and better friends, which come in by the gospel pearl, he fits loose from all worldly advantages and creature engagements; and "for joy" of inward spiritual privileges, he lets go confidence in outward. "For joy" of Christ, the root of all spiritual life, strength, and activeness, he renounces his own supposed sufficiency; "For joy" of the glory of free grace, he hates his own ends, and "for joy" of an eternal life—which its begun in the right knowledge of God in Christ—he gives up this temporal life. VINDICATION OF REDEMPTION.[5]

THE GREAT POWER OF GOD'S WORD. HEIN-RICH BULLINGER: After this by two other

similitudes, taken from the grain of mustard seed and from leaven, he shows how great the power of the word of God is and how evidently it works in them by whom it is received, although it seems to the world vile and contemned. In the fourth place, by two other similitudes, proposed touching a treasure hid in the field and a most precious pearl, he signifies that the price of God his word is so great that in comparison hereof we ought to condemn all things in the world although they be never so precious, yea that we ought, with the very loss of all our goods, to provide us the word of God. THE SUM OF THE FOUR EVANGELISTS.[6]

THE CHRISTIAN LIFE OF LABORING AND TRADING. RICHARD SIBBES: The Christian, like a good merchant, trades for pearls. A Christian life, therefore, is a life of trading, a venturing life; and therefore, a life of danger, being ever as it were in danger of death, as the merchant is at sea, yet ever sure that his God will not forsake them, but assist and defend them off from the rocks of Satan's temptations, and accusations, and terror of conscience, and despair on the one side, and from the alluring waves of the world, that they fall not into that dangerous whirlpool on the other side. Their life is also a life of labor, laboring in his particular calling with faithfulness, having ever an eye on their other calling; and thus by a holy use of the things here below, their mind is ever climbing up the hill to see the end of all their labor and to aim at it in all their thoughts, words, and deeds. And as it is a life of labor, so it is not fruitless. . . .

To proceed: this merchant seeks, then finds, then sells all to get the pearl that he thus found, wherein we will show what this pearl is. First, therefore, by this pearl is meant Christ Jesus, with all his graces and prerogatives derived to us, by the means of his ordinances. Christ is the great pearl; all the rest are pearls, but no otherwise than as they lead us to Christ, the peerless pearl. THE RICH PEARL.[7]

---

[4]Simons, Complete Writings, 750.
[5]Stalham, Vindiciae Redemptionis in the Fanning and Sifting of Samuel Oates (1647), 158.

[6]Bullinger, The Summe of the Foure Evangelists (1582), B6.
[7]WRS 7:256-57*.

THE PRECIOUS PEARL OF CHRIST. JACQUES LEFÈVRE D'ÉTAPLES: Let us draw out the spiritual meaning of this parable. The kingdom of heaven is the kingdom of Christ. The hidden treasure is Christ the Lord. To him the Father gave all things, and for us all things are in him, and in whom (as Paul says) all the treasures of wisdom and knowledge are hidden. The field is the field of the holy Scriptures, the gospel of the kingdom. The person who finds it is any person of faith. This person goes away and sells all their possessions when they leave behind the world for the sake of the gospel, strip off the affections of the flesh and exchange earthly things for heavenly ones. The "rejoicing" indicates that the denial of all things for Christ's sake should be pleasant and voluntary. They buy that field, meaning that they give up all possessions freely and willingly for the gospel, and so they possess the treasure, that is, Christ, and grace in Christ which is better than all life and more precious than all treasure. Nor can it be obtained, unless one gives up all their possessions for that treasure hidden in the holy gospel, and unless they denounce all the things that they have. For, if they retain the affections of the flesh for themselves, if anything of this earth, they will never have that treasure. Instead, they will lack that eternal treasure. The spiritual meaning of the parable that comes right after is pretty much the same: The kingdom of heaven is the kingdom of Christ. The temporal merchant is one who buys temporal things. The temporal stands for a spiritual merchant who by pious works of faith obtains spiritual things. The good pearls, which are also large pearls, are gifts of God looking and aiming at only one object, and they represent all good things. The precious pearl that was found represents Christ, his trustworthiness, and his law, about which it is said, "The law of the Lord is an undefiled law, converting souls; the testimony of the Lord is sure, offering wisdom to the simple." And again: "I have loved your commands more than gold and topaz." And what is the price for the single large pearl? The renunciation of all earthly things. For, the one who finds it, goes away and sells all that he has and buys it. Also, this precious pearl is described as desirable; it is the most precious of all desirables, and is a single object, to make its lover one with the beloved, that is, Christ. COMMENTARY ON THE FOUR GOSPELS.[8]

THE PRESENT MIXTURE OF GOOD AND BAD. JOHN CALVIN: No new instruction is here given by Christ but what he formerly taught is confirmed by another parable, that the church of God, so long as it exists in the world, is a mixture of the good with the bad, and is never free from stains and pollutions. And yet the design of this parable is perhaps different. It may be that Christ intends not only to remove the offense which perplexes many weak minds because they do not find in the world all the purity that might be desired, but likewise to employ the influence of fear and modesty in restraining his disciples from delighting themselves with the empty title or mere profession of faith. For my own part, I cheerfully adopt both views. Christ informs us that a mixture of the good and the bad must be patiently endured till the end of the world; because, till that time, a true and perfect restoration of the church will not take place. Again, he warns us that it is not enough—and what is more that it is of little consequence to us—to be gathered into the fold unless we are his true and chosen sheep. . . . The preaching of the gospel is justly compared to a net sunk beneath the water to inform us that the present state of the church is confused. . . . So far as lies in our power, let us endeavor to correct vices and let us exercise severity in removing pollutions; but the church will not be free from every spot and blemish, until Christ shall have separated the sheep from the goats. COMMENTARY ON A HARMONY OF THE EVANGELISTS.[9]

THE PREACHER MUST KNOW BOTH TESTAMENTS WELL. ERASMUS SARCERIUS: All the circumstances in the family must be diligently

---

[8]Lefèvre, *Commentarii Initiatorii In Qvatvor Evangelia* (1523), 62v; citing Ps 19:7; 119:127 (Vg 118:127). [9]CTS 2:132-33 (CO 45:376); citing Mt 25:32.

considered, [that we may see] how careful, how diligent the family is to bring forth things both new and old. There is the father. As father of the family, he is the steward and possesses the provisioned store, in which are things new and old. All this applies exceedingly well to preachers of the word, whom I believe to be understood properly by the "learned scribe." These should teach others after the example of the disciples. They have need of being thoroughly instructed in the doctrine of the both the Old and New Testaments so that they may strengthen both themselves and the others whom they teach. The passage in 1 Corinthians 4 concerning stewards and the authority given stewards is pertinent here. "Bring forth" [in the passage] means "to dispense." The "treasure house" is the richly provisioned store of things old and new, that is, the doctrine of the Old and New Testaments. His speech is a "treasure house," not a quick or light knowledge that has only a passing acquaintance with the Old and New Testaments, but the solid and firm knowledge of the Word that the apostle requires of an overseer in Titus 1: "An overseer must be blameless . . . embracing that faithful speech that accords with doctrine, so that he also may be able to exhort through sound doctrine and to persuade through refutation." Finally, so that the overseer is a ready preacher, it is necessary that he have an uncommon knowledge of the Old and New Testaments. This one the parable calls a "learned scribe," that is, one who has a solid grasp of the Word and who aptly teaches it. For this reason, Paul wishes an overseer to be *didaktikon*, that he may teach aptly, divide the word aptly, and preserve a sure and methodical way of teaching. On the Gospel of Matthew.[10]

Understanding and Drawing on Biblical Wisdom. John Calvin: We must keep in recollection what we have formerly seen, that all the parables of Christ were explained in private.

And now the Lord, after having taught them in this kind and familiar manner, warns them at the same time that his object, in taking such great pains to instruct them, was not merely that they might be well informed but that they might communicate to others what they had received. In this way he whets and excites their minds more and more to desire instruction. He says that teachers are like householders, who are not only careful about their own food, but have a store laid up for the nourishment of others; and who do not live at ease as to the passing day but make provision for a future and distant period. The meaning, therefore, is that the teachers of the church ought to be prepared by long study for giving to the people, as out of a storehouse, a variety of instruction concerning the word of God, as the necessity of the case may require. Many of the ancient expositors understand by things new and old the law and the gospel; but this appears to me to be forced. I understand them simply to mean a varied and manifold distribution, wisely and properly adapted to the capacity of every individual. Commentary on a Harmony of the Evangelists.[11]

13:53-58 *Jesus Rejected at Nazareth*

The Dignity of the Gospel. Jeremy Taylor: After which discourses, he retired from the seaside and went to his own city of Nazareth, where he preached so excellently upon certain words of the prophet Isaiah, that all the people wondered at the wisdom which he expressed in his divine discourses. But the people of Nazareth did not do honor to the prophet, who was their countryman, because they knew him in all the disadvantages of youth and kindred and trade and poverty; still retaining in their minds the infirmities and humilities of his first years, and keeping the same apprehensions of him, a man, a glorious prophet, which they had to him a child in the shop of a carpenter. The Great Exemplar.[12]

---

[10]Sarcerius, *In Matthaeum Evangelistam* (1538), 193v-94r; citing 1 Cor 4:1-2; 1 Tim 3:2.

[11]CTS 2:133-34 (CO 45:376-77).
[12]Taylor, *Works*, 2:514*.

REJECTING THE PHYSICIAN'S MEDICINE.
DESIDERIUS ERASMUS: But Jesus, rebuking their
gross and over rude judgment, esteeming a person
not for their virtues but for fortune and nobility of
birth, says to them, "A prophet is nowhere less set
by than in his own country, and in his own family,
and among his own kinfolks." And where in other
places he was readily believed and showed many
miracles, here he worked none, but that with
laying on his hands, he healed a few who were sick.
Not because his power was redirected or diminished, or his will changed, but because their
unbelief did not allow the opportune time. For
like as a physician cannot profit the sick if he
rejects his medicine; not because the art of the
physician is not effectual, but because the sick man
is in fault. PARAPHRASES.[13]

THE SOURCES OF CONTEMPT FOR JESUS.
ERASMUS SARCERIUS: "In his home country"
Bethlehem. "He was teaching." To teach is the office
of Christ the king. "So that they were amazed."
Amazement is the effect of the word's power.
"Where did this one get these things?" They say
this out of contempt, that you may know that the
Bethlehemites and how it follows that they take
offense at the lowliness of Christ's person, and yet
for all that were unable to discredit his teaching.
This passage is a *mimesis*[†] that expresses the
natural stance of all people toward the word who
consider how it comes to them rather than its
nature. For they say, "Is this not the carpenter's son?"

"Wisdom" is a true and powerful understanding
of God's word. By "powers" understand miracles
both external and internal in the conscience. For
the amazement of the Bethlehemites shows what
was in their consciences. "Is this not his mother?" A
confirmation as to his origin. "Brothers and sisters."
Terms of kinship and relation, which in Hebrew
signify any kinsperson or relative, not as in Latin.
"Where did this man get all these things?" These
words testify that the Bethlehemites had been
conquered in their conscience by the truth of

[Christ's] teaching. Whence Christ had it and
whether he might be something more than a
simple man, they do not see because of the
arguments of their reason and the humbleness of
his person. Learn here, then, that humble persons
who are held in contempt, even if they should
teach the truth, are nonetheless the cause of offense.
Their word is not believed since those who are
offended by the humility of their person condemn
it. Nothing is more frequent than this sort of
offense today. Observe this offense in the particular
case of the Jews. Why did they not receive Christ?
Because they were offended by the humbleness of
his person. See 1 Corinthians 1 on the cause of the
Jews' stumbling.

"As for this one." This points to the person not
the teaching, though the latter is not able to be free
from suspicion long when the persons are held in
contempt. Countless examples of this are available
today, which confirm that divisions immediately
follow the contempt of persons. The first and most
efficacious step to destroying the pure word is to
hold the person of preachers in contempt. Here we
have noted the cause of scandals, which proceed
from the judgments of reason and not from the
doctrine of Christ. They do not estimate the word
in its own nature or power, but from their
self-conceived judgments.

"There is not a prophet." This is an opinion
common to human nature, whereby we always
make more of and hold in greater esteem those
who are strangers and sojourners as opposed to
locals and natives, even if the latter are often more
learned and prudent. Because the Bethlehemites
were so greatly offended by Christ's person,
Christ in turn answers concerning his person.
"And he did not do powerful works there." Christ
adds the reason: because of their lack of faith.
Miracles occur in order to strengthen those who
ought to believe and do believe. ON THE GOSPEL
OF MATTHEW.[14]

---

[13]EP 62r*.

[14]Sarcerius, *In Matthaeum Evangelistam* (1538), 194r-95r. [†]Mimesis
is a rhetorical strategy in which the author imitates the gestures,
pronunciation, or utterances of someone else.

14:1-21 THE FEEDING OF THE FIVE THOUSAND

At that time Herod the tetrarch heard about the fame of Jesus, ²and he said to his servants, "This is John the Baptist. He has been raised from the dead; that is why these miraculous powers are at work in him." ³For Herod had seized John and bound him and put him in prison for the sake of Herodias, his brother Philip's wife,ᵃ ⁴because John had been saying to him, "It is not lawful for you to have her." ⁵And though he wanted to put him to death, he feared the people, because they held him to be a prophet. ⁶But when Herod's birthday came, the daughter of Herodias danced before the company and pleased Herod, ⁷so that he promised with an oath to give her whatever she might ask. ⁸Prompted by her mother, she said, "Give me the head of John the Baptist here on a platter." ⁹And the king was sorry, but because of his oaths and his guests he commanded it to be given. ¹⁰He sent and had John beheaded in the prison, ¹¹and his head was brought on a platter and given to the girl, and she brought it to her mother. ¹²And his disciples came and took the body and buried it, and they went and told Jesus.

¹³Now when Jesus heard this, he withdrew from there in a boat to a desolate place by himself. But when the crowds heard it, they followed him on foot from the towns. ¹⁴When he went ashore he saw a great crowd, and he had compassion on them and healed their sick. ¹⁵Now when it was evening, the disciples came to him and said, "This is a desolate place, and the day is now over; send the crowds away to go into the villages and buy food for themselves." ¹⁶But Jesus said, "They need not go away; you give them something to eat." ¹⁷They said to him, "We have only five loaves here and two fish." ¹⁸And he said, "Bring them here to me." ¹⁹Then he ordered the crowds to sit down on the grass, and taking the five loaves and the two fish, he looked up to heaven and said a blessing. Then he broke the loaves and gave them to the disciples, and the disciples gave them to the crowds. ²⁰And they all ate and were satisfied. And they took up twelve baskets full of the broken pieces left over. ²¹And those who ate were about five thousand men, besides women and children.

a Some manuscripts *his brother's wife*

OVERVIEW: To begin this chapter, Matthew uses a narrative flashback to recount the vengeful demise of John the Baptist. Once again, a leader in Israel (Herod in this case) has mistakenly identified Jesus. Somewhat like the Nazarenes who had recognized Jesus' miraculous power but had still not granted him his due (Mt 13:54-58), Herod associates Jesus' miraculous power with John the Baptist.

The Reformation commentators often discuss Herod's complex political environment and his disdain for John for personal reasons. Many of them discuss the possible instigations behind Herod's actions, especially his oath and its result. Herod was not grieved over John's death, but his grief was motivated by a fear of repercussions from the crowd. Calvin poses a contrast between the political calculations of Herod and the personal vendetta of Herodias against the humble piety of John's disciples who cared for the prophet's body after his execution. Luther probes the deeper providences of God in letting a godly man like John the Baptist suffer such a cruel death.

As Jesus' day of ministry (preaching and healing; see Mk 6:34, Lk 9:11) stretches on until evening, the isolated location provides an opportunity for a spectacular miracle, which is recorded in all four canonical Gospels. In Matthew's account of the feeding of the five thousand, the role of the disciples is emphasized. Perhaps as a continuation of their ministry to the cities throughout Israel (Mt 11:1; cf. Mk 6:30-32, Lk 9:10-12), Jesus charges the disciples with providing the food for the crowd. Calvin contends that the gracious provision of food by Jesus illustrates his earlier point of first seeking the kingdom (Mt 6:33) before seeing the necessary things of daily life provided by God. When the disciples point out the impossibility of the task, Jesus then multiplies the provisions and uses the disciples to distribute the food. The reformers comment that this strategic display of Jesus' power played an important role in strengthening the disciples' faith and bringing glory to God.

14:1-12 Herod's Execution of John the Baptist

THE BACKGROUND OF HEROD AND JOHN THE BAPTIST. CARDINAL CAJETAN: "In that time"— after Christ had accomplished many miracles, after the crowds had gathered to hear Christ's teaching. For this period, when Christ's fame had spread, was after the decapitation of John, as Herod's own words clearly testify. It is accepted that John was beheaded around the Passover, when the Lord also satisfied five thousand men with five loaves. Between those events and Christ's baptism by John more than two years had flowed, as the parallels in the Gospel of John make plain when one computes the number of paschal solemnities that John mentions. These matters will be shown more clearly in the commentary on John. "Herod the Tetrarch heard." ["Tetrarch" is added] to distinguish this man from his father, King Herod, whom Matthew mentioned above when narrating Christ's nativity. The latter was the king and father of Archelaus and this Herod, who was called a "Tetrarch" and not a king. And so he was! For without a kingly title he was merely prince of a part of his father's kingdom. It was he who afterward clothed Jesus in a splendid garment to mock him and sent him back to Pilate. "[Heard] of the fame of Jesus, and he said to his servants." This term (pueri, lit. "boys") refers not to an age but a condition of life. That is, they are his servants.

"This is John the Baptist; he has risen from the dead!" Herod supposed that the soul of John had entered into Jesus. He calls this "entering" a rising from the dead instead of taking again the same body, supposing that John's spirit had entered this life anew in another body. For this reason, he says that "this man" [i.e., Jesus] is John, not with regard to the body, but to the spirit—from the principal part "the spirit" thereby denominating the whole John. "And therefore these powers are at work in him." Before being beheaded, John the Baptist had performed no miracle, as one reads in the eleventh chapter of the [Gospel of] John. Yet one who is supposed to have returned to life after a decapitation is believed also to have greater power! As if, on the basis of his former merits, he had borne from the other life the power of working miracles that he did not possess previously. GOSPEL WITH COMMENTARY.[1]

HEROD'S HISTORICAL BACKGROUND. GIOVANNI DIODATI: "Herod." Surnamed Antipas, who was the son of the great Herod, by some surnamed Ascalonites, who caused the children to be slain. "Tetrarch." This name signifies a lord or prince of the fourth part of a country. By this it seems that under Alexander's successors began this division of all Palestine, called also Judea, into four parts of which ancient Judea, namely, the land of the tribe of Judah, made the one. Now after the death of Herod the Great, Anthony, and after him the emperor Augustus, divided also this kingdom of Herod's into four parts among his children, taking ancient Judea away from them and the title of kings, though by abuse they yet retained it among themselves and to this Herod's lot fell Perea and Galilee under the name of tetrarchy, whether the ancient partitions were yet observed or whether there were some alteration. "He is risen." This was a common error that they thought the souls of such as were deceased were transmigrated into some other body. Pythagoras and his disciples were of this opinion. "Show forth," that is, to confirm his

---

[1]Cajetan, Evangelia cum Commentariis, 43v-44r.

resurrection, and to invest him in the greater authority. "Mighty works . . . the powers work in him," the Jews call the angels so. The meaning is, he is a man wholly divine and celestial and has angels to assist him, working in him and by him. "Had laid hold," namely, having found him within his territories, whither it is likely John went by divine inspiration to divert Herod from his incest; for otherwise Herod had no jurisdiction in Judea, of which John Baptist was, and where he made his ordinary abode, nor had not received any such power from the Romans, as afterward his son Herod Agrippa did. Pious Annotations.[2]

Political and Marital Mistakes. Wolf-gang Musculus: Josephus[†] in the same book [18], chapter 9, writes how this Herod Antipater was captivated with love for the wife of his brother Philip, and when he was taken in as a guest at his house while on his way to Rome, promised an incestual marriage with the woman if he could return from Rome safely and put away his legal wife. His sins were threefold: (1) He divorced his legitimate wife and married another; (2) he married the wife of his brother while his brother was still living; (3) his brother had three children with her, and so those nuptials were not permissible, even if the brother were already dead.

John, therefore, when he learned of those things, very bravely called out the king after the example of Elijah, and as Chrysostom[‡] in his homily about the words of the apostle [Timothy], "use modest wine," wrote, "in the middle of the form and a crowd of people, openly, he was saying, 'You cannot have the wife of your brother.'" Here we should take note of the deftness and frankness of admonishment that the person of God employs: (1) that he castigates such a great tyrant; (2) that he does it to his face; (3) that he does it openly, in public; (4) that he does it with eloquent force, not saying, "Whoever marries the wife of his brother is unrighteous," or, "Whoever marries the wife of a brother who is still living, sins, since he is doing something that is not lawful." Rather, "It is not lawful for you to have the wife of your brother."

Therefore, on the urging of his wife, Herod threw John into the prison of Machaerus. Clearly, she was afraid that if Herod should obey John, he would divorce her as he did his first wife. For, who trusts a husband who has divorced a wife already who did nothing wrong just because he conceived an incestuous love?

So what Josephus writes about the fear of sedition is believable, that the woman used it to pressure Herod to murder the holy man, so that both causes, that ascribed by the Gospels, and that ascribed by Josephus, are true.

I ask you, why did he want to kill him? Obviously because he was called out by him so freely. Herod was possessed by a double desire, that of ruling and that of a wife that was not his own. Herodias feared divorce, since she was conscious of her own guilt. Hence each of them was seeking the murder of the one who reprimanded them. Commentary on Matthew.[3]

The Source of Herod's Grief. Johann George Dorsche: Here is the story of how Herod bound himself by an oath to his daughter. It is told with the same words with which Ahasuerus bound himself to Esther. We should say a few things about the oath. Generally speaking, an oath is of two types, either extrajudicial or judicial. This oath of Herod is extrajudicial because, again, it is of two types, either assertory or promissory. An assertory oath is one whereby someone, based on a request or not, asserts something out of necessity. About the promissory oath there are various approaches in moral theology. It is said (1) not to be able to bind, if concerning the matter it turns

---

[2]Diodati, *Pious Annotations* (1643), E1r; citing Lk 3:1; 1 Macc 10:38; 11:28; Lk 23:7; Acts 12:1.

[3]Musculus, *In Evangelistam Matthaeum Commentarii* (1556), 418-19. [†]Josephus, *Antiquities of the Jews* 18.5.1. Musculus refers to chapter 9, but Josephus discusses this in chapter 5. [‡]Musculus does not appear to be quoting Chrysostom's sermon directly. In his homily on 1 Timothy 5:21-23, Chrysostom does mention the need to address public sins, even those of leaders, without partiality.

out not to lie in our power. They relate to this the vow of perpetual chastity. For, although a man knows that in present circumstances that he can control himself, still he does not know whether he can remain in that disposition perpetually, whence such an oath is void. Nevertheless, the one who puts forward an oath of this sort, even if he is not bound to keep it, still is not altogether without blame, because he swore it without thinking clearly and with a certain carelessness, because oaths involve the witness of God's name threefold. (2) An oath is not binding if it is unjust, as was the case with the promise of Herod. For, an oath ought not to be a bond of injustice. (3) It is not obligatory if it is against the rights of a superior, if an inferior by oath promises something whereby there is a diminution of the rights of a superior. (4) They say that an oath of this sort is not valid if someone swears contrary to the improvement of a situation, for example, if someone swears that he does not wish to hold a magistracy and yet out of necessity he is needed, then he is not obliged by this oath. (5) He is not held to an oath if he swears an oath whose outcome is worse than he expected, something that even Herod clearly understands.

Here it is usually asked whether Herod became sad in truth or only hypocritically. Some think that he did so only hypocritically. They gather that from verse 5. I think that we cannot really say that his sadness was all hypocritical, for, although he certainly wished to kill him, nevertheless he could have changed his mind and possibly that sadness stemmed from another cause other than from a love a John, such as a fear of some danger. Therefore, it is probable that he was in fact afraid rather than that his attitude had changed; nevertheless, that sadness was temporary. COMMENTARY ON THE FOUR EVANGELISTS.[4]

HEROD'S RASH VOW. JEREMY TAYLOR: For now that the Baptist had fulfilled his office of bearing witness to Jesus, God was pleased to give him his

writ of ease and bring him to his reward. Upon this occasion, John, who had so learned to despise the world and all its exterior vanities and impertinent relations, did his duty justly and so without respect of persons that as he reproved the people for their prevarications so he spared not Herod for his but, abstaining from all expresses of the spirit of scorn and asperity, mingling no discontents, interests, nor mutinous intimations with his sermons, he told Herod it was not lawful for him to have his brother's wife. For this sermon, he felt the furies and malice of a woman's spleen, was cast into prison, and about a year after was sacrificed to the scorn and pride of a lustful woman and her immodest daughter, being, at the end of the second year of Christ's preaching, beheaded by Herod's command. Herod would not retract his promise, because of his honor and a rash vow he made in the gaiety of his lust and complacencies of his riotous dancing. His head was brought up in a dish and made a festival-present to the young girl (who gave it to her mother). A cruelty that was not known among the barbarisms of the worst of people, to mingle banqueting with blood and sights of death. THE GREAT EXEMPLAR.[5]

HEROD'S INWARD REJOICING AT THE REQUEST. RICHARD WARD: First, Jerome[†] and some others think that Herod and Herodian agreed together that he should make a feast and her daughter should dance at it; with which he seeming to be extraordinarily pleased should make this promise to give her whatsoever she should ask and then she should ask John's head; at which request (although in heart he rejoiced, yet) outwardly he should seem to be sorry, so that those who were with him might excuse him, as being unwilling to have done this bloody fact. Now the reasons that are given for the confirming of this opinion are these; to wit, because, except he had wished John's death, he would not have beheaded him for his oath's sake; for in such oaths and promises, it is always understood that the thing be honest and lawful

[4]Dorsche, *In Quator Evangelistas Commentarius* (1706), 238-39; citing Mk 6:23; Esther 5:3.

[5]Taylor, *Works:* 2:309*.

which is desired. And therefore, her request not being such, he need not have granted it, if he would. Because it is not probable that he could be so strangely overtaken and delighted with a dance that in recompense thereof he should make such a large promise, as to give her whatsoever she should ask. . . . Because, if he had not been consenting hereunto, he could easily have corrected the request of the maid and have directed her to ask some other thing, which was more profitable for he than was John's head. Because there was no need to fear the offending of those who sat at meat with him, if he had not beheaded John; for we do not read of any hatred they bare him, or desire, or delight, they had in his death. Because the text says plainly, "When he would have put him to death, he feared the multitude, because they counted him as a prophet." THEOLOGICAL QUESTIONS.[6]

OATHS AND FOLLY. JOHN CALVIN: "On account of the oath, and of those who sat at table with him." . . . Though he had sworn a hundred times, yet if there had been no witness, he would not have held by his oath. No inward feelings of religion constrained Herod to do this, but the mere love of power drove him headlong; for he reckoned that he would sink in the estimation of those who were present if he did not fulfill his engagement. Thus, it frequently happens that ungodly people fail to perform their duty because they do not look to God, but are only intent on this object, that they may not incur the reproaches of others . . . he committed a more heinous offense in fulfilling a foolish promise than if he had violated his oath. First, he was deeply in fault for such haste in swearing; for the design of an oath is to confirm a promise in a doubtful matter. Next, when it appeared that he could not be relieved from his engagement without involving himself in an aggravated crime, he had no right to implicate the sacred name of God in such wickedness; for what could be more at variance

with the nature of God than to lend his countenance to a shocking murder? . . . Let the one who has made a rash oath suffer the punishment of their folly; but, when a person has taken the name of God in vain, let them beware of doubling their guilt by employing this as pretense for committing some enormous crime. . . .

It was an additional aggravation of this detestable crime that the head of the holy man was made, after his death, a matter of sport. But in this way the Lord sometimes gives up his people to the pride of the wicked, till he at length makes it evident that their blood is precious in his sight. . . .

One thing only remained to complete the woman's cruelty. It was to leave the corpse of the holy man unburied; for there is reason to believe that, when his disciples performed this duty, the attendants of the tyrant had thrown out the corpse . . . God was pleased with the carefulness which was manifested by the disciples when they came to commit to the tomb the body of their master. Moreover, it was an attestation of their piety; for in this way they declared that the doctrine of their master continued to have a firm hold of their hearts after his death. This confession was therefore worthy of praise, more especially as it was not without danger; for they could not do honor to a man who had been put to death by the executioner without exciting against themselves the rage of the tyrant. COMMENTARY ON A HARMONY OF THE EVANGELISTS.[7]

HEROD'S HONOR. MARTIN LUTHER: He is happy because he is able to put aside this vulpine sadness completely and he rejoices that his will is compelled by the oath to kill the innocent John. Meanwhile, the "saintly" man thinks that his foxlike craftiness has been made splendid and praiseworthy, because he honors the name of God through what he had sworn. And so he is compelled on account of obedience to the second commandment to do something against obedience to the fifth commandment, because the lower law gives way to

---

[6]Ward, *Theological Questions upon . . . St. Matthew* (1640), 153*.
†Jerome, *Commentary on Matthew*, FC 117:167.

[7]CTS 2:227-29 (CO 45:433-34).

the higher, just as the whole second tablet yields to the first. O theologian of the deepest depth!

The one who killed John did it immediately, without a care in the world and without debating the matter. Surely he first asked whether it was necessary to kill an innocent person because of that oath, right? No, he asked nothing of the sort. But forthwith without any due process or legal debate, he pronounced the sentence and executed it. Compare now that crafty fox with Darius the king of the Persians, who worked the whole day to rescue Daniel—after he had been deceived by a decree and unwisely had condemned him—from the hands of his nobles and afterward he punished them brutally. But that accursed fox is not worthy to be compared with the best king, except that a side-by-side comparison elucidates our point more clearly.

After these events he is buried by his disciples. Who can say what they thought? They see such a wonderful teacher so cruelly and evilly killed, and they wonder if there is not a God who sees such unworthy deeds, and certainly it was troubling, not just for the weak in faith, but even for the strong. For, who would not murmur against the providence of God, his righteousness and goodness, who sees so holy a man so pitifully neglected by God? It takes great faith to bear and understand these things. This is what it means to make the world foolish in its wisdom. This is the wisdom of God clouded in mystery, to know that God especially loved his dearest John then when, by human wisdom, he seemed especially to neglect and hate him. NOTES ON SELECT CHAPTERS OF MATTHEW.[8]

14:13-21 Jesus Feeds Five Thousand

WHY DID JESUS WAIT SO LONG? THE ENGLISH ANNOTATIONS: Dinnertime, or the usual hour to provide it, is past. There may be many reasons why Christ, who could have done this miracle at any hour, would thus long defer it: as first, because of this delay, he might raise the disciples' minds to a

more serious attention and making so clear and express a remonstrance of his power. Second, that it might appear that he did not rashly, but upon urgent necessity, put forth his power for doing miracles, for indeed he was not at all desirous of gain or ambitious of human applause. Third, that the hungry multitude might more deeply apprehend the greatness of the miracle by their own sense of the necessity in which they now were. Fourth, that this miracle might appear so much more illustrious, by how much greater the supply must be to satisfy so many so hungry stomachs. Last, that he might plainly demonstrate to them and to us that he has power ever ready and providence ever watching to relieve those that depend on him, which he will do when he knows it is most opportune and best. ANNOTATIONS ON MATTHEW 14:15.[9]

CHRIST'S AFFECTION FOR THE CROWDS. DAVID PAREUS: Christ's wholly divine affection toward the crowds follows. First is spoken about a departure; before their coming he proceeded on the way, providing for their desires by grace. Luke adds that he welcomed them—namely, of the most human of words—praising their zeal. Matthew and Mark add third that . . . moved by mercy, he was joined to them, then that most ardently he saw that they had a lack of affection for his teaching; then that he saw more of them to be sick, weak, ill, who with trouble and difficulty had come such a long way by foot. Whereby, as Luke has, "and he was speaking to them about the kingdom of God," that is, he was preaching to them the gospel of grace. And as many of them wanted healing, he restored them to health, and all day he expended himself to this work. Then evening fell. Therefore, it both attested abundantly to himself and confirmed his own benevolence for the devotion of the crowds, that in this way he was gratifying their needs and necessary things, who sought in earnest his grace and glory and preferred it to all things. COMMENTARY ON THE GOSPEL OF MATTHEW.[10]

---

[8]Luther, *Annotationes in Aliquot Capita Matthei*, 50r-50v.

[9]Downame, *Annotations*, JJ2r*.

[10]Pareus, *Theologi Archipalatini in S. Matthae Evangelium Commentarius* (1631), 380.

Christ Feeds Both Souls and Bodies.
John Calvin: Hitherto Christ had bestowed his whole attention on feeding souls, but now he includes within his duties as a shepherd the care even of their bodies. And in this way, he confirms his own saying, that to those who seek the kingdom of God, and his righteousness, all other things will be added. We have no right, indeed, to expect that Christ will always follow this method of supplying the hungry and thirsty with food; but it is certain that he will never permit his own people to want the necessaries of life, but will stretch out his hand from heaven, whenever he shall see it to be necessary, to relieve their necessities. Those who wish to have Christ for their provider must first learn not to long for refined luxuries but to be satisfied with barley bread.

Christ commanded that the people should sit down in companies; and he did so, first, that by this arrangement of the ranks the miracle might be more manifest; second, that the number of the men might be more easily ascertained, and that, while they looked at each other, they might in their turn bear testimony to this heavenly favor. Third, perceiving that his disciples were anxious, he intended to make trial of their obedience by giving them an injunction which at first sight appeared to be absurd; for, as no provisions were at hand, there was reason to wonder why Christ was making arrangements that resembled a feast. To the same purpose is what follows, that he gave them the loaves, in order that in their hands the astonishing increase might take place, and that they might thus be the ministers of Christ's divine power; for as if it had been of small importance that they should be eyewitnesses, Christ determined that his power should be handled by them. Commentary on a Harmony of the Evangelists.[11]

Christ Is the Master of the Feast. Joseph Hall: The virtue is not in the means, but in the agent: "Bring them here to me." How much more easy had it been for our Savior to fetch the loaves

to him than to multiply them! The hands of the disciples shall bring them, that they might more fully witness both the author and manner of the instant miracle. Had the loaves and fishes been multiplied without this bringing, perhaps they might have seemed to have come by the secret provision of the guests; now there can be no question either of the act or of the agent. As God takes pleasure in doing wonders for men and women, so he loves to be acknowledged in the great works that he does. He has no reason to part with his own glory; that is too precious for him to lose or for his creature to embezzle. And how justly did you, O Savior, in this, mean to teach your disciples that it was you only who feeds the world, and upon whom both themselves and all their fellow creatures must depend for their nourishment and provision; and that, if it came not through your hands, it could not come to theirs! . . .

He who is the master of the feast marshals the guests: "He commanded the multitude to sit down on the grass." They obey and expect. O marvelous faith! So many thousands sit down, and address themselves to a meal, when they saw nothing but five poor barley loaves and two small fishes! None of them say, Sit down to what? Here are the mouths, but where is the meat? We can soon be set, but when shall we be served? . . . But they meekly and obediently dispose themselves to their places and look up to Christ for a miraculous purveyance. It is for all who would be Christ's followers to lead the life of faith; and even where means appear not, to wait upon that merciful hand. Nothing is more easy than to trust God when our barns and coffers are full, and to say, "Give to us our daily bread," when we have it in our cupboard. But when we have nothing, when we know not how or whence to get anything, then to depend upon an invisible bounty, this is a true and noble act of faith. Contemplations.[12]

How This Miracle May Be Understood.
Johannes Brenz: This has not been accomplished†

---

[11]CTS 2:233-34* (CO 45:438); citing Mt 6:33.

[12]Hall, *Contemplations on the Historical Passages of the Old and New Testaments*, 4:484-85*.

for the sake of those five thousand men alone, but also for the universal church of God. Christ himself signifies this when, in Matthew 16, he reprimands his disciples' weakness of faith using the example of this miracle: "Why do you think within yourselves that you have brought no bread, O you of little faith? Do you not yet understand or do you not have in memory those five loaves?" . . .

Let us therefore see what the use of this miracle may be. Its general use is to prove the truth of Christ's gospel. However, this miracle's special use is as a cure for care and anxiety about how to procure enough to eat. For the crowd is devoted to this pursuit more than any other, that they might obtain nourishment for themselves. And if they are not able to gain this by just and legitimate means, they procure it by iniquity and injustice. "If God will not help," they say, "let Satan be our helper; only let us have food!" Christ, therefore, performs this miracle in order to teach by what just and

pious means we might be able to provide food. First, therefore, the crowd follows Christ into the desert so as to hear his preaching. Only then is bread provided to them, without any effort on their part.

Let us, then, follow Christ into the desert—not indeed after the manner of the monks or hermits, but as Christians. That is, let us devote ourselves to this end: whether we are in the city, or the countryside, or wherever the voice of Christ's gospel may be, to hear and grasp it as we are able. This being done piously and diligently, it cannot be that God will not provide for our nourishment, according to the saying: "Seek first the kingdom of God and his righteousness, and all these things will be added to you." MATTHEW 14:13-21.[13]

---

[13]Brenz, *In Scriptum Apostoli et Evangelistae Matthaei*, 532.
†Reading *editum* for *aeditum* here; the latter does not appear in any dictionary. In addition, a 1567 edition of the same text reads *editum*.

14:22-36 JESUS WALKS ON WATER
AND HEALS THE SICK

²²*Immediately he made the disciples get into the boat and go before him to the other side, while he dismissed the crowds.* ²³*And after he had dismissed the crowds, he went up on the mountain by himself to pray. When evening came, he was there alone,* ²⁴*but the boat by this time was a long way*ᵃ *from the land,*ᵇ *beaten by the waves, for the wind was against them.* ²⁵*And in the fourth watch of the night*ᶜ *he came to them, walking on the sea.* ²⁶*But when the disciples saw him walking on the sea, they were terrified, and said, "It is a ghost!" and they cried out in fear.* ²⁷*But immediately Jesus spoke to them, saying, "Take heart; it is I. Do not be afraid."*

²⁸*And Peter answered him, "Lord, if it is you, command me to come to you on the water."* ²⁹*He said,* "Come." *So Peter got out of the boat and walked on the water and came to Jesus.* ³⁰*But when he saw the wind,*ᵈ *he was afraid, and beginning to sink he cried out, "Lord, save me."* ³¹*Jesus immediately reached out his hand and took hold of him, saying to him, "O you of little faith, why did you doubt?"* ³²*And when they got into the boat, the wind ceased.* ³³*And those in the boat worshiped him, saying, "Truly you are the Son of God."*

³⁴*And when they had crossed over, they came to land at Gennesaret.* ³⁵*And when the men of that place recognized him, they sent around to all that region and brought to him all who were sick* ³⁶*and implored him that they might only touch the fringe of his garment. And as many as touched it were made well.*

a Greek *many stadia,* a *stadion* was about 607 feet or 185 meters   b Some manuscripts *was out on the sea*   c That is, between 3 a.m. and 6 a.m.   d Some manuscripts *strong wind*

OVERVIEW: This scene in the Gospel picks up where the previous one ended. After the miracle of feeding the five thousand, Jesus dismisses the crowd and secludes himself for a time of extended prayer, in a manner consistent with his earlier teaching on prayer (Mt 6:5-6). The disciples, who departed from Jesus earlier, find themselves in another treacherous storm on the sea.

The testing of the disciples' faith, including Peter's, intrigues the reformers. Luther describes how Peter forgot the word with which Jesus beckoned him and therefore lost faith. Erasmus commends Peter's initial faith but warns about how quickly faith fades when the exigencies of the context are the point of focus. Reminiscent of the disciples' cry in Matthew 8:25, Peter pleads for the Lord to save him and as in the earlier episode receives a rebuke for his little faith (see Mt 8:26).

Upon his arrival on shore, Jesus again begins to minister through healing by people simply touching his garment, a sign of faith paralleling the woman with the hemorrhage (Mt 9:21-22). Juan de Valdés points out that the men of Gennesaret demonstrate faith before the miracle, in contrast to the disciples in the boat, who had faith in retrospect.

14:22-33 *Walking on Water*

CHRIST WAS PRAYING FOR THEM. JOHN TRAPP: Christ compelled them, which is no more than commanded them (say some) to get into a ship: (1) Lest they should take part with the rash many-headed multitude, who would have made him a king, thus he many times prevents sin in this by removing occasions. (2) To inure them to the cross, and to teach them, as good soldiers, to suffer hardship, which the flesh takes heavily. (3) To give them proof of his power, now perfected in their weakness, when they were ready to be shipwrecked, and (4) to teach them to pray to him absent, whom present they had not prized to the worth, as appears. When we cast our precious things at our heels, as children, our heavenly Father lays them out of the way another while, that we may know the worth by the want, and so grow wiser.

"He sent the multitudes away" that he might shun even the suspicion of sedition. Secret prayer fattens the soul, as secret morsels feed the body. Therefore, it is said to be the banquet of grace, where the soul may solace herself with God. Only . . . get into such a corner, as where we may be most free to call upon God without distraction, remembering our own fickleness and Satan's restlessness. Retire we must sometimes, and into fit places to meet God . . . Christ here upon the mountain. While the disciples were periling and well nigh perishing, Christ was praying for them; so he is still for us, at the right hand of the majesty on high. A COMMENTARY OR EXPOSITION UPON THE FOUR EVANGELISTS.[1]

CHRIST IS THE HIGH ADMIRAL OF THE SEAS.
THOMAS CARTWRIGHT: It is apparent and confessed that our Savior Christ would here declare himself to be the Lord, and as it were, the high admiral of the seas, which has power to alter the proper nature and native property thereof; which as in times past he declared by causing the water to stand stiff like a wall barred with iron bars, which (as Aristotle says) will never be stayed, unless it rest upon another element; and (to use his words) in another's bounds: even so he declared it now, in causing them, which (through weakness) naturally give place to all heavier bodies, contrary to their nature, to be as solid and as firm underfoot, as if they had been paved with marble stone. Whereupon it follows that the alteration was in the sea and not in any change of either our Savior Christ or of Peter's body. . . . For if this miracle stood in any miraculous change of their bodies, then is not our Savior Christ's empire of

the sea established out of this place. Besides, that by this interpretation of theirs, the corrupt opinion of the apostles is strengthened, which judged of our Savior Christ that he was a ghost and no true body, which indeed he had been, if he had not had the natural property of a body, which is to press down, and to weigh heavy upon the waters; except that our Savior Christ, by the power of his Godhead, bore up himself and Peter too; whereby remains the property of the bodies still, giving them no more advantage than if the miracle were in the waters; considering that the weight of the bodies is not taken away, but borne up and sustained by the power of Christ, remaining in his person, and not communicated with the sea, which is his creature; for as it is an idol and no God that has not the essential properties of God; so is it a phantom and no true body that wants the natural properties of a body. A CONFUTATION OF THE RHEMISTS TRANSLATION.[2]

THE DISCIPLES' FEAR AND FAITH.
AEGIDIUS HUNNIUS: We see Peter consoled by the Lord Jesus as he takes hold of the plank of faith and little by little emerges from the sea of doubts and grasps fully the undoubted hope of the Lord's aid that was to follow. In the meantime, he acts prudently, in that he does not commit himself to the sea's billows before he is bidden by the Lord. Yet perhaps to some this might seem rash, that on the word of the one who was walking over the waters, Peter should commit himself to the waves. For if it had not been the Lord, but a ghost as he supposed, and it had said to Peter, "come"—would he not have been horribly deceived absent a prodigious degree of discernment? But to respond to this objection is easy, if we remind ourselves that the things which Peter says and does here have proceeded from a certain heroic impulse of the Holy Spirit. For having been strengthened by his trust in God, Peter has no doubt that it is the Lord and not a ghost, for God would in no way permit

[1]Trapp, *A Commentary or Exposition upon the Four Evangelists* (1647), 414-15; citing Jn 6:15.

[2]Cartwright, *A Confutation of the Rhemists Translation . . . on the New Testament* (1618), 64.

that a ghost should bid him, "Come." And thus when Peter hears the Lord Jesus saying "Come," at this word he springs from the boat into the waters and walks about on the sea as if it were nothing but solid earth, after the example of his master. Of course, he did not do this from his own power, as Christ did, but another's power—doubtless the same that had called him from the boat. But though he had descended from the ship through extraordinary trust and up to a point had been walking about wonderfully without any miraculous sign, when a rougher wave crashed over him, he at once shrank back in fear of being drowned. And as the faith within his heart was drowning somewhat during this moment of testing, so too he began to sink outwardly. Therefore, he cries out for Christ's help, saying "Lord, save me!" Christ takes him by the hand as he thus struggles and begins to sink and rebukes his hesitation: "O you of little faith, why did you hesitate?" For it was due to his faith, as I said, that he did not fear to commit himself to the sea at the command and bidding of God. On the other hand, it was due to doubt that he was trembling and crying out like a coward. For this reason the Lord castigates him with these words, so that he may both revive and save him and by his aid create anew one who was all but dead. . . .

Christ then enters the boat together with Peter, and immediately the winds are silent at his command, the sea is checked, the waves subside, and suddenly a calm replaces that horrible tempest that had nearly impelled the souls of the disciples to complete and deadly despair—so vehement and extraordinary was their fear, according to Mark's testimony (for there were some others there besides the twelve disciples). For though on the evening of the preceding day they had witnessed an illustrious miracle before their very eyes, this present miracle nonetheless surpassed the estimation they had formed by far. Struck by its incredible majesty, they recognized that he plainly ruled and commanded the winds, sea, waves, and storms by divine power. And thus they approached and worshiped him, not by performing any public act of reverence, but with religious adoration and humble devotion, as to the only-begotten Son of God. These things are declared well enough indeed by their confession, "Truly, you are the Son of God." By the gaze of faith, which looked beyond the human nature that was presenting itself to their eyes and senses, they recognized within him a more sublime nature, a divine nature, according to which he was the natural Son of God made manifest in the flesh or human nature that he had assumed. This divine nature was declared, as it were, to human eyes by the power of such great signs and miracles. COMMENTARY ON MATTHEW.[3]

LEARN FROM PETER'S FAITH. MARTIN LUTHER: We have similar examples in the New Testament. Peter was strong and confident in faith. When he saw Jesus walking on the water, he said, impelled by his strong faith, "Lord call me to come to you," and stepped out of the ship into the water. He was confident that the water would bear him. Peter had a remarkable faith and a bold spirit, so that he ventured upon the water and danger, and even death, making the venture boldly and daringly by reason of his faith in Christ. But when he thought he was most secure, the wind and storm arose and he forgot the Word and lost faith; he fell, sank into the water, and permitted Satan to tear faith out of his heart. Where was his great faith then? Faith is a tender, subtle thing, and we so easily make a mistake and are liable to stumble; but the devil is watchful, and unless men exercise watchfulness, he quickly gains his point. TWENTY-FIRST SUNDAY AFTER TRINITY, SECOND SERMON.[4]

PETER'S NEED OF CONTINUAL FAITH. DESIDE-RIUS ERASMUS: They were so afraid that, being almost beside themselves, they cried out for fear. But Jesus suffered them not to be in danger any longer, but by and by spoke to them that they might know him by his speech, whom in the dark they could not see. "Be of good cheer, it is I, fear

---

[3]Hunnius, *Commentarius in Evangelium Secundum Matthaeum* (1594), 488-90*.
[4]Luther, *Precious and Sacred Writings*, 14:265.

not." At this word by and by their mind was comforted. But Peter, who always had a singular love toward Jesus, thinking nothing at all hard that he would command, said, "Lord, if it is you, command me to come unto you upon the water." For he marveled not that Jesus walked upon the water, but he thought that he himself might do so likewise, if Jesus would. But Jesus, framing and fashioning his weakness by all means to the strength of perfect faith, had him come. At that word, Peter nothing lingering, leaped down out of the boat and began to haste to Jesus, walking upon the water. And as long as his faith nothing wavered, the moist element served him. But when he cast his eyes a little from Jesus, and began to look about him, and to consider the boisterousness of the wind, the hurling of the waves, and his own feebleness, he was afraid again and began to sink down and be in danger of drowning. Fear came of the boisterousness of the winds, peril came of fear, and fear of distrust. And again, the greatness of peril raised up the spark of faith, and now being almost overwhelmed with waves cried out, "Lord, save me; I perish." But Jesus, putting his disciple in remembrance that the peril which he feared came not of the waves or winds, which before served his turn, but of the weakness of faith. Reaching out his hand caught him and lifted him up saying, O you that yet have little trusted me, why did you waver? For it is not enough to have a strong faith for the time, but it must be continual and constant, nor must you not look how great the peril is, or what your strength is able to bear, but what I am able to do to him that does trust and believe in me. PARAPHRASES[5]

DOUBT AND FEAR IN PETER. CORNELIUS À LAPIDE: "Lord save me." From hence it is clear that Peter did not doubt that he who appeared was Christ. For otherwise he would not have called upon him in his great peril, but upon God, as shipwrecked sailors are wont to do. His only doubt was whether Christ would allow him to be buried in the waves. Well says St. Augustine,[†] "That shaking, brethren, was as it were the death of faith. But when he cried out, faith rose again. He could not have walked unless he had believed, neither could he have begun to sink unless he had doubted. In Peter, therefore, we must regard the common condition of us all, that if in any temptation the wind is about to sink us in the waves, we should cry aloud to Christ."

"And straightway—wherefore didst thou doubt!" Greek, *eis ti edistasas*, that is, "why did you divide your mind in two?" For two things were here presented to Peter, that is to say, the strength of the wind making him afraid of being drowned and the voice of Christ instilling confidence and security. But the strength of the wind was more obvious and therefore more powerful than the voice of Christ. Thus, its effect was in this instance to cause Peter's faith to fail; but he rose again after his lapse.

Almost every temptation arises from distrust of God, because people either trust to themselves, or to human aid, and do not immediately betake themselves to God by prayer. Hence then let those who are tempted learn to turn away their minds from the thing which suggests the temptation, and turn it wholly to God, and fix it upon him, and humbly implore his help. Very beautifully says St. Chrysostom,[‡] "Like as a young bird which, before it is able to fly, falls out of its nest upon the ground, whose mother quickly restores it to the nest so also at this time did Christ to Peter." Therefore, let those who are tempted invoke Christ; so shall they resist the temptation, and overcome it. For if Peter had believed the word of Christ, he would not have doubted, nor have begun to sink. COMMENTARY ON THE FOUR GOSPELS.[6]

JESUS IS A KING TO BE ADORED. JOHANNES PISCATOR: At this reference is pledged to Christ that he is the Son of God, namely, he is the only-born son of God, and indeed the true God,

---

[5]EP 64v- 65r.

[6]Lapide, *Commentary on the Four Gospels* (1639), 298-99; citing Mt 14:27-33. [†]Augustine, Sermon 14, *De Verbis Domini Secundum Matthaeum*. [‡]Chrysostom, *Homiles on Matthew*, NPNF[1] 10:311.

one with the Father and the Holy Spirit. Therefore, they relate something false who contend that the flesh of Christ is to be adored. Because undoubtedly they contend on that account so that they might maintain in part by way of reason that it is everywhere. Because if one particularity of the divine nature is assigned to the flesh of Christ, all the rest also is necessary to be assigned; because particularities of the divine nature are not able to be separated from each other when they might be the exact same unmixed essence of God. But the quality of the divine nature is worthy of adoration; when it is a special consequence of omnipotence, omniscience, and omnipresence. For on that account, God is worthy of adoration, and indeed he alone; because he alone is omnipotent, omniscient, omnipresent, and then infinite in majesty and endowed with glory. But in the flesh of Christ there is not omnipotence, nor omniscience, nor omnipresence or being everywhere; and then the flesh of Christ is not God. Therefore, it is not worthy of adoration. Meanwhile, it is true; God in manifest flesh—or the Son of God incarnate—is to be adored. Just as it is true, a king wielding a crown and scepter ought to be adored as becomes a civilian, granted that he is not adored before he carries the crown and scepter. But afterward, because he is king, he is adored even when he is not carrying the crown and scepter. But it would be a foolish thing to adore the crown and scepter, even when they were carried by the king. LOGICAL ANALYSIS OF MATTHEW.[7]

FROM UNBELIEF TO BELIEF. JOHN CALVIN: While our Lord kindly preserves Peter, he does not connive at Peter's fault. Such is the object of the chastisement administered, when Peter is blamed for the weakness of his faith. But a question arises, "Does every kind of fear give evidence of a weakness of faith? For Christ's words seem to imply that, where faith reigns, there is no room for doubt." I reply that Christ reproves here that kind of doubt

that was directly opposed to faith. A person may sometimes doubt without any fault on their part; and that is, when the word of the Lord does not speak with certainty on the matter. But the case was quite different with Peter, who had received an express command from Christ and had already experienced his power, and yet leaves that twofold support and falls into foolish and wicked fear.

I understand these words to refer not only to the disciples, but to the sailors and other passengers. So, then those who had not yet declared that he was their master instantly acknowledge that he is the Son of God, and by this term render to him the honor of the Messiah. Though at that time this lofty mystery was not generally known, how God was to be manifested in the flesh, yet as they had learned from the prophets, that he who was to be the Redeemer would be called the Son of God, those who under this designation proclaim the glory of Christ, declare their belief that he is the Christ. COMMENTARY ON A HARMONY OF THE EVANGELISTS.[8]

14:34-36 *Healing the Sick*

THE NATURE OF THE DISCIPLES' CONFESSION. JUAN DE VALDÉS: Although the godless recognize God by outward miracles, they do not follow God, which happened to the men who were in this boat who knew that Christ was the Son of God by outward miracle, but they did not follow Christ. So that we know by the result that there is this difference between the confession of these men, who affirm that Christ is the Son of God, and the confession of Peter, which we shall see in chapter 16; that theirs was of flesh and blood, of human discourse and judgment; which judged by that which it saw, of that which it did not see; while that of Peter was by divine inspiration and revelation; and for that reason Christ did not pronounce these persons blessed, as he did Peter, nor did these persons follow Christ, as did Peter. And here we understand that miracles, although

---

[7]Piscator, *Analysis Logica Evangelii Secundum Matthaeum* (1594), 233-34.

[8]CTS 2:242-43 (CO 45:443-44); citing 1 Tim 3:16.

they apparently work some impression upon people; effectively it is very slight and is soon dissipated; and thus, it remains that miracles only avail to confirm the faith of those who believe by revelation and divine inspiration. [Also] that faith is of such efficacy that it obtains from God all that it desires, although those who believe to attain that which they wish or desire are not righteous, not having that inspired and revealed faith, which

embraces the remission of sins and reconciliation with God; as was the case with these men of Gennesaret, who believed that in touching the hem of Christ's garment, there would be such efficacy that it would heal them of their infirmities; by touching it, they were healed. Commentary upon the Gospel of St. Matthew.[9]

---

[9]Valdés, *Commentary upon the Gospel of St. Matthew*, 264-65.

15:1-39 TRADITIONS AND FAITH

Then Pharisees and scribes came to Jesus from Jerusalem and said, [2]"Why do your disciples break the tradition of the elders? For they do not wash their hands when they eat." [3]He answered them, "And why do you break the commandment of God for the sake of your tradition? [4]For God commanded, 'Honor your father and your mother,' and, 'Whoever reviles father or mother must surely die.' [5]But you say, 'If anyone tells his father or his mother, "What you would have gained from me is given to God,"[a] [6]he need not honor his father.' So for the sake of your tradition you have made void the word[b] of God. [7]You hypocrites! Well did Isaiah prophesy of you, when he said:

[8]"'This people honors me with their lips,
　　but their heart is far from me;
[9]in vain do they worship me,
　　teaching as doctrines the commandments
　　　　of men.'"

[10]And he called the people to him and said to them, "Hear and understand: [11]it is not what goes into the mouth that defiles a person, but what comes out of the mouth; this defiles a person." [12]Then the disciples came and said to him, "Do you know that the Pharisees were offended when they heard this saying?" [13]He answered, "Every plant that my heavenly Father has not planted will be rooted up. [14]Let them alone; they are blind guides.[c] And if the blind lead the blind, both will fall into a pit." [15]But Peter said to him, "Explain the parable to us." [16]And he said, "Are you also still without understanding? [17]Do you not see that whatever goes into the mouth passes into the stomach and is expelled?[d] [18]But what comes out of the mouth proceeds from the heart, and this defiles a person. [19]For out of the heart come evil thoughts, murder, adultery, sexual immorality, theft, false witness, slander. [20]These are what defile a person. But to eat with unwashed hands does not defile anyone."

[21]And Jesus went away from there and withdrew to the district of Tyre and Sidon. [22]And behold, a Canaanite woman from that region came out and was crying, "Have mercy on me, O Lord, Son of David; my daughter is severely oppressed by a demon." [23]But he did not answer her a word. And his disciples came and begged him, saying, "Send her away, for she is crying out after us." [24]He answered, "I was sent only to the lost sheep of the house of Israel." [25]But she came and knelt before him, saying, "Lord, help me." [26]And he answered, "It is not right to take the children's bread and throw it to the dogs." [27]She said, "Yes, Lord, yet even the dogs eat the crumbs that fall from their masters' table." [28]Then Jesus answered her, "O woman, great is your faith! Be it done for you as you desire." And her daughter was healed instantly.[e]

[29]Jesus went on from there and walked beside the Sea of Galilee. And he went up on the mountain and sat down there. [30]And great crowds came to him, bringing with them the lame, the blind, the crippled, the mute, and many others, and they put them at his feet, and he healed them, [31]so that the crowd wondered, when they saw the mute speaking, the crippled healthy, the lame walking, and the blind seeing. And they glorified the God of Israel.

[32]Then Jesus called his disciples to him and said, "I have compassion on the crowd because they have been with me now three days and have nothing to eat. And I am unwilling to send them away hungry, lest they faint on the way." [33]And the disciples said to him, "Where are we to get enough bread in such a desolate place to feed so great a crowd?" [34]And Jesus said to them, "How many loaves do you have?" They said, "Seven, and a few small fish." [35]And directing the crowd to sit down on the ground, [36]he took the seven loaves and the fish, and having given thanks he broke them and gave them to the disciples, and the disciples gave them to the crowds. [37]And they all ate and were satisfied. And they took up seven baskets full of the

broken pieces left over. ³⁸Those who ate were four thousand men, besides women and children. ³⁹And

after sending away the crowds, he got into the boat and went to the region of Magadan.

a *Or is an offering* b *Some manuscripts law* c *Some manuscripts add of the blind* d *Greek is expelled into the latrine* e *Greek from that hour*

OVERVIEW: Jesus replies to the critical question of the Pharisees and scribes with a harsh rebuke of their self-righteousness. Among our Reformation commentators, Philipp Melanchthon notes that Jesus' reproach of self-righteousness replacing true obedience echoes previous warnings delivered by the Old Testament prophets. Other reformers indicate that external motivations will not suffice for true obedience and that the desire to "honor" parents must be reflected in a desire to help them.

As he did earlier (Mt 13:57), Jesus' reminder of Israel's longstanding unbelief evokes his plea for the crowd to hear and understand. Cajetan notes that their traditions caused them to make unwise decisions about true piety. Jesus' brief parable points to the need for a believing heart over religious ritual. Jacques Lefèvre d'Étaples remarks that the disciples should be able to discern this straightforward, figurative speech by this point in Jesus' ministry. Instead, Jesus has to warn his disciples not to follow the teaching of the Pharisees because they will be uprooted in judgment (cf. Mt 5:20).

While the leaders of Israel resist Jesus' being referred to as the Son of David (Mt 12:23; 21:15), the Canaanite woman appeals to him by that title. Fittingly, the primary interest of the reformers in commenting on this narrative is to learn from the pattern of Christian faith exemplified by her. Her humble persistence in the midst of seeming rebuff reflects the depth or greatness of her faith. Niels Hemmingsen describes how this encounter with the woman draws the focus to her faith as a witness to unbelieving Jews and as an example to the disciples who would eventually be sent as a witness to all nations (Mt 28:19-20).

The chapter ends with two narratives that are similar to previous ones in Matthew. In what has now become a familiar scene for Matthew's readers, Jesus is seen healing all sorts of diseases and the

crowd marvels at Jesus' authority (cf. Mt 7:28; 9:8, 33; 13:54). Wolfgang Musculus observes that Jesus' compassionate ministry among the crowds is having a profound effect in that the crowds are moving from amazement at Jesus' miracles to glorifying God in response. The second narrative parallels one from the previous chapter with the common elements of a large, hungry crowd, a secluded location, meager provisions, insipid disciples, and Jesus glorifying God through the miraculous feeding.

15:1-14 *Traditions and Commandments*

KEEPING THE COMMANDMENTS AND A GOOD CONSCIENCE. PHILIPP MELANCHTHON: Respect is necessary, by a good conscience, to the second commandment of God, that is, so that a person may have a good conscience next to every commandment. May they not be an adulterer, not a fornicator, not a thief, nor a liar, nor a murderer, not great in heart knowing and desiring unjust hatred against a neighbor. . . . The following works commanded by God are true respect for God with faith.

Ezekiel 20: You ought not to walk in the precepts of your father, but walk in my precepts. This clearly draws us back to the commandments of God, and he prescribes that we do that which he teaches. And this teaching is often repeated and is great comfort to the godly, to know that acts of worship to God are these: those works necessary for public life, honorable marriage life, and other honorable works of one's calling. In the same way, our endurance in the cross, as the psalm says, "The sacrifices of God are a contrite spirit." **ANNOTATIONS ON THE GOSPELS.**[1]

---

[1]MO 14:878.

TRADITION AND PIETY. CARDINAL CAJETAN: Here they are not asking a question but are making an accusation, and not just against the disciples; they apply their actions to Jesus and charge him with a transgression. Matthew, like Mark, has insinuated that in their charges they are not concerned that they stain themselves through uncleanliness, but that they transgress the traditions of their elders. In his response, he blunts the nail with a nail. If the scribes had asked about the reason for their behavior, he would have explained it. But since they are not seeking to know why, but are making charges and attacking the innocent teacher, he skips over the reason why the disciples do not keep to that tradition, and responds directly to the charge, by showing them that this is where they go astray greatly in their efforts to keep to the traditions of the elders. And he shows them this by accusing them in the same way, but not with the same spirit, in which they had accused him. "Your great zeal for the traditions of the elders is so great that it redounds to the transgression of the precepts of God, and so how can it be excused?" It is as if he said plainly, "You arose to this charge not from a zeal for righteousness, but from a love of your own authority, since you place your mandates before those of God. If the love of a more complete righteousness were motivating you, you would be zealous first to observe God's commands and then worry about human precepts. But when you burn with zeal for frivolous human matters, treating God's mandates as secondary, it appears that the love of your own authority motivates you." But if there is regard for the use of the material in connection with necessary piety, the opposite is found to be true: that is, that the material necessary to piety ought to be applied only to piety rather than to religion, but also, if it is dedicated to God by a vow, it ought to be transferred into the material of piety. And this arises from the part of the material which in such a case is made material owed to piety. Here are some examples that I can offer: A son is bound to help an indigent father, and for this reason the possessions of the son are constituted as owed to necessary piety, and therefore if the son is unable to give his possessions and help his father at the same time, that is, to offer a gift to God and to help his father, then the offering should be omitted and help be given to the father, because an offering to God must not be made from things owed, from things necessary to piety. The Pharisees, therefore, were going astray, not knowing and not willing to discern that which belongs to religion from that which arises from the part of the material related to human necessities. And therefore, they were teaching that sons should say to their parents that the gift which would have been advantageous to you I have given to God and you have been excluded, that it is given to God, the common Father, and that God receives his gift for you. COMMENTARY ON MATTHEW.[2]

HONORING AND HELPING ONE'S PARENTS. HULDRYCH ZWINGLI: Christ says in clear words that the clerics or Pharisees who render fathers and mothers helpless before their children by their prattle transgress the law of God. They teach that when a son gives them something which their father or mother may ask for or need afterward, he should say to them, "Father, I have put this into the treasury of the church, for your sake." But they actually dishonor father and mother by this. In this context "to honor" means not only "to give respect," but also "to help." AN EXPOSITION OF THE ARTICLES.[3]

GOD'S ORDINANCES MUST REMAIN. DIRK PHILIPS: God does not will, yes, it is an abomination before him that one should break or change his ordinance for any fleshly purpose. And that is what God meant when he said through Moses and in many other places that one shall not add to his Word nor subtract therefrom, but one shall maintain everything he has commanded so that one be not punished nor found a liar.

Therefore, it is very necessary that by an ordinance of the Lord these following points are noted and encouraged: First, who the author and

---

[2]Cajetan, *Evangelia cum Commentariis*, 45r-45v.
[3]Zwingli, *The Defense of the Reformed Faith*, 1:239; citing Mt 15:4-6; Mk 7:10-12.

institution of the ordinance is; thereafter, what the ordinance in itself is; finally, why God has made the ordinance. Thereby it must remain, and there may be no change in it, for it is a real, Pharisaical nature to change God's institution, ordinance, and command, and to set them upon a wrong basis. Nothing but evil can come from that. For through such changes, the good is changed into bad, light into darkness, divine into human, and the spiritual into carnal, and thus misused. And misuse destroys everything that is good. Notice to what other ordinances of the Lord have come through misuse, yes, what abominable idolatry has been motivated therewith and is still [being] motivated. ABOUT THE MARRIAGE OF CHRISTIANS.[4]

15:15-20 *Proper Understanding of Scriptural Teaching*

THE REASONABLENESS OF CHRIST'S HARSH REPLY. JOHN CALVIN: As the scribes were presumptuous and rebellious, Christ did not take great pains to pacify them, but satisfied himself with repelling their hypocrisy and pride. The offense which they had formerly taken up was doubled when they perceived that not through oversight, but seemingly on purpose Christ despised their washings as trifles. Now when Christ did not hesitate to inflame still more by keen provocation, wicked and malicious persons, let us learn from his example, that we ought not to be exceedingly solicitous to please everyone by what we say and do. His disciples, however, as is usually the case with ignorant and unlearned people, no sooner perceive the result to be unfavorable than they conclude that Christ's reply had been unseasonable and improper. For the object of their advice was to persuade Christ to soothe the rage of the Pharisees by softening the harsh expression which he had employed.

It almost always happens with weak persons that they form an unfavorable judgment about a doctrine as soon as they find that it is regarded with doubt or meets with opposition. And certainly it were to be wished, that it should give no offense, but receive the calm approbation of all; but, as the minds of many are blinded, and even their hearts are kindled into rage by Satan, and as many souls are held under the benumbing influence of brutal stupidity, it is impossible that all should relish the true doctrine of salvation. Above all, we ought not to be surprised to behold the rage of those who inwardly nourish the venom of malice and obstinacy. Yet we ought to take care that, so far as may be in our power, our manner of teaching shall give no offense; but it would be the height of madness to think of exercising greater moderation than we have been taught to do by our heavenly master. We see how his discourse was made an occasion of offense by wicked and obstinate people; and we see at the same time, how that kind of offense which arose from malignity was treated by him with contempt. COMMENTARY ON A HARMONY OF THE EVANGELISTS.[5]

JESUS' USE OF ISAIAH. JOHN TOMBES: A passage cited out of the prophesy of Isaiah 29:13 wherein our Savior makes use of the Septuagint's translation, which is somewhat different in words, though not in sense, from the Hebrew, for whereas in the Hebrew the words are, "And their fear toward me is taught from," or "by the precepts of men," the Septuagint reads, "But in vain do they worship me, teaching for doctrines the commandments of men," in which there is a sin charged upon these Pharisees, to wit, the teaching as doctrines the commandments of men. Such doctrines are as nothing else but men's commandments which being taught by those that were to be teachers of the law, and seemed to be such instead of God's precepts were therefore accounted as God's worship or his fear. There is a censure passed on this practice, "In vain do they worship me," which words are not in the Hebrew, yet may be collected from the woe threatened to such teachers, whereby God disclaims

---

[4]CRR 6:557-58; citing Mt 15:1-9; Deut 4:2; 12:32; Prov 30:6; Mt 15:11.

[5]CTS 2:255-57 (CO 45:451-52).

such teaching and practice as being no service of his, though the teachers and practitioners of such commands of men imagined they honored God thereby. So the plain truth that this enunciation of our Lord Christ affords is this: That however they think of their actions, they do in vain worship God, who teach for doctrines men's precepts. . . .

It is plain that these Pharisees and scribes did many ways teach contrary to the law of God, to wit, in expounding the laws of God as if they did only prohibit the gross external act, they urged the smaller matters of the law, as tithing of mint, and neglected the greater. But in this place that which our Savior objects to them is that they sought to establish the traditions of men, though God's commands were thereby rejected or neglected. Particularly that a man was not to regard the honoring of his father and mother, if he had taken on him the rash and impious vows of Corban, which was directly *contra legem*, against the law, to allow men for an unjust oath's sake to break God's plain precept. But chiefly that they taught men to observe things *prater legem*, besides the law, instead of God's law, as the washing hands afore meals, the washing of cups and pots, brazen vessels and tables, with many such like traditions invented by men. These things they strictly urged on the people, excepting much at the omission of them, conniving at, yea countenancing the transgression of God's precepts; they ascribed so much authority to the traditions of the elders that they made it a great crime to transgress them; they conceived and taught that the [practice of] not observing them made men unholy and unclean, else they would not have been offended with Christ . . . they conceived their observation of them did please God as if he were thereby honored. THE LEAVEN OF PHARISAICAL WILL-WORSHIP.[6]

THE DISCIPLES' FAITH AND UNDERSTANDING.
JACQUES LEFÈVRE D'ÉTAPLES: When Peter said, "Explain to us this parable," he was looking back to that which the Lord had said, "What enters into

the mouth does not defile a person," which did not include a parable but was just straightforward talk. Therefore, the Lord accuses him and the rest of the apostles with a lack of understanding, since by now they should have a consummate understanding and a trained sense from constantly hearing him. But what they were asking he explained to them fully, and the explanation is clear. But you will object, "Is it not true that those things which enter into the body sometimes defile a person?" No, since the Lord did not refer to everything, but only that which is necessary, that is, food that enters into the body for the sake of sustaining its nature, while the hands are unwashed. For, if you break the fast, if you drink too much wine, if you become inebriated, it is not what enters that is a sin for you, but what comes out from your heart, in other words, your willing consent to break the fast, to drink too much wine, and to become drunk. The same with your will to commit adultery, to fornicate, steal, or whatever other thing of this sort that you do. All these things come out from the heart and manifest themselves in exterior action. "Out of the heart," he says, "come evil thoughts, homicide, adultery, fornications, thefts, and all other things like them." Furthermore, after leaving from that place to which the scribes and Pharisees had come in order to accuse him of transgressing the traditions of men, he went out into parts of Tyre and Sidon. COMMENTARY ON THE FOUR GOSPELS.[7]

THE IMPORTANCE OF A CLEAN HEART. DESIDE-RIUS ERASMUS: Jesus, intending to sharpen the desire of his disciples with a little chiding, who should have been now more cunning in understanding of parables, and out of one to have divined and guessed another, said, "Are you also still without understanding. . . . " These are bodily things, and affect and touch nothing but the body. . . . But the things which go out of the mouth are the things which human beings speak. Talking comes not from the stomach but from the heart. And what is in the human heart, that indeed is

---

[6]Tombes, *The Leaven of Pharisaical Will-Worship* (1643), 2-3; citing Is 29:14; Mt 5:21, 27, 33, 38, 43; 23:23.

[7]Lefèvre, *Commentarii Initiatorii in Quatuor Evangelia* (1523), 68r.

pure and clean, or else impure and unclean. For from that fountain spring noisome thoughts, wherewith people go about to lie in wait to hurt their brother, from thence spring murder, adultery. . . . Therefore whereas the Pharisees teach and observe superficially these foolish trifles, yet they do not abhor those things, whereby the mind is defiled in deed. They lie in wait for the one who does them good, they suborn and prepare false witness, they backbite the reputation of their neighbor, and so seek for their own glory, then they envy the glory of God, falsely reproving the works which are done by his Spirit. . . . But what awkward kind of holiness is this, to have washed and clean hands, and to have both mind and tongue defiled with so many mischievous vices. PARAPHRASES.[8]

LEAVE THE BLIND BEHIND. ARGULA VON GRUMBACH:

> In chapter fifteen you can see
> Matthew clearly telling us,
> That God commands to leave behind
> The hard of heart, whose eyes are blind.
> Let the Father draw you near
> And do not flee to human fare,
> To Aristotle, and Decretal,
> God leaves no scope at all
> For fantasies and new additions,
> Which wound his word, obscure its mission.
> What you so long have plied
> God will no more abide;
> Deceiving rich and poor alike
> No one can possibly be your life:
> You wheel and deal, you strut around
> Affluence in your life abounds
> Yet dare to claim a spiritual name
> When all we see is greed and shame.
> And hypocritically market
> God's word like some cheap trinket.

"JOHANNES OF LANZHUT": ATTACK AND RESPONSE.[9]

15:21-31 *The Canaanite Woman's Faith*

CHRIST'S SPECIAL RELATION TO KING DAVID. SAMUEL RUTHERFORD: In this compilation, consider why Christ is called the Son of David, never the son of Adam; never the son of Abraham? It is true, he is called frequently the Son of Man, but never when any prays to him, and he is reckoned in his genealogy, David's son, Abraham's son, the son of Adam; but the son of David is his ordinary style when prayers are directed to him in the days of his flesh. The reason is that Christ had a special relation to Abraham being his seed, but more special to David, because the covenant was in a special manner established with David as a king, and the first king in whose hand the church, the feeding thereof as God's own flock was as God's deposition and pawn laid down; the Lord established the covenant of grace with David and his son Solomon, who was to build him a house, and promised to him an eternal kingdom, and grace and perseverance in grace, and that by a sure covenant. "The sure mercies of David." THE TRIAL AND TRIUMPH OF FAITH.[10]

THE UNWAVERING FAITH OF THE CANAANITE WOMAN. HENRICH BULLINGER: But why do I heap together many examples? Does not the only faith of the Canaanite or Syrophoenician woman declare more plainly than that it can be denied, how that faith is a most assured persuasion of things believed? For being overlooked, and, as it were, slighted by the Lord, she wavered not in faith; but following him, and hearing also that the Lord was sent to the lost sheep of the house of Israel, she goes on to worship him. Moreover, being put back and, as it were, touched with the foul reproach of a dog, she goes forward yet humbly to cast herself prostrate before the Lord, requesting to obtain the thing that she desired. She would not have persevered so stiffly if faith had not been a certification in her believing mind and heart.

---

[8]EP 66v-67r*.
[9]Grumbach, *Argula von Grumbach*, 181 (AvG 140).

[10]Rutherfurd, *The Trial and Triumph of Faith* (1645), 44; citing Is 55:3; 2 Sam 7.

Wherefore the Lord, moved with that faith of hers, cried, "Woman, great is your faith; be it done to you even as you will." Of True Faith.[11]

The Canaanite Woman Overcomes Temptations. David Chytraeus: In this second history, there are two principal topics: The first is an example of great and burning faith, which overcomes two grievous temptations (*tentationes*).[†] The first concerns her [the Canaanite woman] election (*particularitate*),[‡] since she is not from Israel and therefore not enrolled among those who must be saved. The second concerns her unworthiness, seeing as she is a "dog," polluted and abject. She opposes the first temptation concerning election with the universal promise of grace as well as God's severest mandate that all who believe themselves to be from Israel—that is, to be righteous—are pleasing to God because of Christ. Although in his ministry of preaching Christ only taught among the people of Israel, the benefits nonetheless extend to all nations, as it has been written: "In your offspring all people will be blessed." Here the Canaanite woman says, "Even dogs eat from the crumbs falling from their masters' table"—that is, the nations partake of the benefits of the Messiah who was promised to the people of Israel and are the "wild olive" engrafted into the cultivated tree.

To the second temptation concerning her unworthiness she opposes the doctrine of the gospel, the free forgiveness of sins and the welcome of men and women for the sake of Christ. These things can be learned more accurately from the more expansive comments [elsewhere] in the Evangelists, daily exercises of faith, and prayer.

[The second topic in this passage] is a perfect example of true prayer that invokes the true God or Jehovah, the Messiah promised to David, that strives for the mercy of Christ that is set forth in [God's] promises, and that seeks a particular good—the liberation of her daughter from a demon. This prayer does not grow faint, nor is broken by the delay or tarrying of divine aid. Commentary on Matthew.[12]

The Pattern of Sincere Faith. Menno Simons: Here you have another fine example and pattern of sincere, Christian faith, for when this woman perceived how powerfully Jesus preached grace, and hearing besides that he could do what he desired, that he manifested love and mercy, that he sent none away comfortless; she approached him without hesitation, and despaired not of his grace, mercy, love, and power, although she was not heard at the first or second request. Unshaken in her faith and prayer, her desire was such that she might be as one of the dogs which partake of the spiritual crumbs of his mercy, and obtain relief for her poor daughter who was so sadly vexed by a devil. Yes, she manifested such a faith, constancy, humility, and piety that the Lord said to her, O woman, great is your faith; be it unto you even as you will.

If with spiritual eyes we consider this woman's faith and fruits we will be taught of her, especially in two particulars. For as soon as she heard that the Lord taught mercy, grace, repentance, and reformation, that he preached the kingdom of God, raised the dead, made the blind to see, the deaf to hear, the crippled to walk, the lepers to be cleansed, the sick to be healed, and that he cast out unclean spirits; that he reproved the scribes, Pharisees, and the common people for their unbelief, perverseness, blind hypocrisy, and carnal lives, and testified that he was the prophet and Messiah who was promised in the Law and the Prophets—things whereby all Judea and the adjacent area were greatly moved—her womanly heart and mind were so turned to him through such testimonies, miracles, doctrines, and deeds of love, that she did not doubt his mercy, power, goodness, and grace. She,

---

[11]DHB 1:924.

[12]Chytraeus, *Commentarius in Matthaeum Evangelistam* (1558), 269-70; citing Gen 22:18; Rom 11:17. [†]There is likely a connection to Luther's concept of *Anfechtungen* here, especially as Luther published a sermon on the same text that bears some striking similarities to this commentary: LW 76:378-82. [‡]For a similar use of the term *particularitate*, see Lutheran theologian Aegidius Hunnius's commentary on Heb 9:8.

therefore, went to him with a sincere desire, in sure and true faith, trusting with all her heart that he would not deny her humble prayer, but that he would graciously hear and grant it. She also obtained what she desired. She heard and believed; she saw and confessed. . . .

In the second place, she admonishes all pious parents that they should have a Christian solicitude for the salvation of their children, because she so faithfully entreated for her demon-possessed daughter, not desisting till she was heard. . . . If now I seek the praises of the Lord with all my heart, and if I love the salvation of my neighbors, many of whom I have never seen, how much more should I have at heart the salvation of my dear children whom God has given me; who are out of my loins, and are my natural flesh and blood; so that the mighty Lord may be praised by them and be eternally honored in them. THE TRUE CHRISTIAN FAITH.[13]

WHAT MAKES FAITH GREAT OR SMALL. JOHN BOYS: Christ here showed his justice in leaving . . . ungrateful Jews and coming into Tyre and Sidon, countries of the Gentiles; and this should terrify us, in that our unthankfulness has worthily deserved, that Christ should depart from our coasts into some newfound land, taking his word from us and bestowing it upon a people that will bring forth better fruit thereof.

Christ's mercy does appear, first generally toward all the Gentiles in making them his people who were no people, a favor in other ages unknown unto the sons of men, as it is now revealed unto his holy apostles and preachers by the Spirit, that the Gentiles also should be inheritors, and of the same body, and partakers of Gods promise in Christ by the gospel; more particularly toward this Canaanite woman, in hearing her prayers and helping her child; and this may comfort us, in that the Lord over all is rich unto all that call upon him.

The two chief virtues of a Christian are faith and love, both are most eminent in this woman;

her faith is such as that our Evangelist reports it with, "behold, a woman of Canaan." It is strange that a woman, and that not a Jew but a Gentile, and among all the Gentiles of the most accursed and wicked nation, a Canaanite, should have such a measure of faith as to conquer not only the world, but also the lord of the world. This woman overcame Christ, not by force, but by faith.

In comparison, as the disciples' faith is elsewhere called little; the disciples' faith was little, considering their great master; and this woman's faith was great, considering her little means of instruction. A little faith, so little as a grain of mustard, and that implicit, confused and enfolded, is sufficient for some at some time, to wit, in the beginning of their conversion, and in the house of some grievous temptation; but where God does give greater means, he looks for a greater measure; when he bestows a greater portion of grace, then he does expect a greater proportion of goodness. Little faith in this untaught woman was great. AN EXPOSITION OF THE DOMINICAL EPISTLES AND GOSPELS.[14]

THE REASON FOR CHRIST'S ACTIONS. NIELS HEMMINGSEN: It is written in this gospel that Christ dismissed this woman. Why did he so? Why did he say that he was sent not only to the lost sheep of the house of Israel? Is not he the same Lord who says, "Come to me all you that labor and are heavy laden?" I answer, the Lord did not do this without great cause. First, he did it so that the woman's faith might by this delay be exercised and increased. Second, that she might be an example of godliness, against the stiff-necked Jews, who despised Christ. Third, that the Lord might show how he would be overcome by the persistence of our prayers. Fourth, that by this example he might teach the present beholders a true experiment of godliness.

But the Lord assigns another cause why he put back this woman. For he says, I was sent only to the lost sheep of the house of Israel. I answer,

---

[13]Simons, *Complete Writings*, 384, 386.

[14]Boys, *An Exposition of the Dominicall Epistles and Gospels* (1610), 52-53, 61.

Christ says this not as though he denied the Gentiles access to his grace; for that same woman was a Gentile; but there are other causes. First, he means here to note the obstinate malice and unthankfulness of the Jews, who do not acknowledge Christ, who was sent peculiarly to them. The second is, for that the selfsame Christ should preach God's word to the Jews before his death, who after his death should give commandment to preach it to the Gentiles. For the Lord had forbidden his gospel to be preached to the Gentiles before his death. But afterward when he was risen from death, he gave this commandment to the apostles: Go into the whole world and preach the gospel to all people. This commandment manifestly declares that Christ's benefits belong both to the Jews and Gentiles; that is to say, that all, whether Jew or Gentile, who receive Christ, and truly repent, are partakers of Christ's benefits, so that by his blood all their sins are washed away . . . whether we be kings, nobles, citizens, or country folk. A POSTIL, OR EXPOSITION OF THE GOSPELS.[15]

THE WOMAN YIELDS TO THE LORD'S JUDGMENT.

MARTIN LUTHER: She removes out of her sight and mind that Christ shows himself so ungentle and hard to be entreated, she being constant and nothing moved at this, perseveres in the trust of his goodness, whereof she had heard and which she had conceived in her mind, suffering herself in no wise to be turned from it. . . . But this is the hardest to nature and reason, to be so utterly destitute, and to depend on the word of God without any feeling of comfort, even when a man feels and tries all things to be contrary. God give to us such a mind and faith that we may so do, especially at the point of death and in extreme necessities. . . .

But what does this woman? She does not so fall from hope, she still sticks to the words which she had heard of Christ, albeit he went about by this other repulse as with a certain force to wrest them out of her heart, she suffers not herself to be strayed away neither with that ungentle silence, neither with this hard answer, she continues steadfastly in a sure confidence, believing that under this difficulty which Christ did pretend, that grace was as yet hidden and laid up for her, which she had heard reported of him, she cannot be brought as yet to judge Christ not to be bountiful and gracious, and that he can deny the help which she desires. This was to persevere strongly in faith. . . .

This woman is not yet discouraged and past hope, but yields to this judgment of the Lord, she confesses of her own accord that she is a dog, she neither desires anything but that which is wont to be given to dogs, namely, the crumbs which falls from their master's table. Does she not seem to have used marvelous cunning? She takes Christ at his own words. He had made her like a dog, which acknowledges it and desires that he will only suffer her to be a dog according to his own saying; what should he do here? How should he escape? He was now as it were even taken. For the crumbs under the table are granted to the dog, for to dogs they are said to be due. Here therefore Christ, being as it were overcome, opens himself wholly and grants the desires of the woman, and says that she is not now a dog, "but a true Israelite." These things are written for the instruction and comfort of all us, whereby we ought to learn how deeply sometimes Christ hides his grace from us and how we must not judge God according to our own sense and opinion, but only according to his words. For we see here that albeit Christ showed himself very hard to this woman, yet he did not plainly deny to help her but whatsoever he answered, however it seemed to pretend a denial, yet was it not a denial, but did hang in doubt, and left an entrance for faith, although but small. THE TENTH SERMON OF DR. MARTIN LUTHER OF THE WOMAN OF CANAAN.[16]

CHRIST RESTORES THE GLORY OF GOD.

WOLFGANG MUSCULUS: Behold, the affability and

---

[15]Hemmingsen, *A Postill, or Exposition of the Gospels* (1569), 88*.

[16]Luther, *Complete Sermons*, 5:96-98*.

humanity of Christ. Although he desired to be hidden, yet he was not burdened by the crowds running violently to him, but he immediately healed their sick. We are very much by another nature—oh the sorrow—nothing less than bringing Christ's gentleness and kindness to those who are distressed. But how was it not so difficult in relation to them, and also in relation to the Canaanite, when yet she was long provided with greater faith? Those who have greater faith are also trained more, so that they may be an example to others of excellent faith. Therefore, those who have less faith, as weak, are cured by God soon thereafter. In the same manner, those who were long since injured and not cured immediately are not reckoned to God as ungrateful. . . .

Wonder is on account of the strangeness of such a pious man, because he goes beyond mortals. When the deaf hear, the blind see, the lame walk, the mute are restored their speaking, this is unusual and beyond mortals. Therefore, when the crowds see this, they are astonished. And also by his grace those miracles in Christ's divine dispensation are preordained or destined in order that they move mortal souls to amazement and faith. But I ask, who is that one today that we are not astonished by their seeing, walking, hearing, speaking, who were not only previously deaf, blind, mute, and lame, but were not that entirely? These things are worthless that are common. . . .

Because they were ignorant of the goodness of the God who visits his people, the Pharisees were ascribing these things not to God, but to the virtue of Satan. Behold, the wisdom of the wise is destroyed and is conquered by foolish people. Therefore, to the glory of God he made the ability to see, to hear, to speak, to walk, and also to be healthy. For these are signs of life that God alone is able to give. On that account they are reviled in the likenesses of the psalm, for having ears, they do not hear, having eyes, they do not see, having feet, they do not walk. . . . Therefore, just as Satan darkened the glory of God in his image by divine allowance, so he renders humans blind, mute, lame, deaf, and infirm. Thus Christ, the restorer of the glory of God, makes from the mute, speakers, from the deaf hearers, from the blind, those who see, from the sick, those who are healthy. Therefore, may we also glorify God, not only on account of this body, but also on account of spiritual health, sight, hearing, speaking, which is given by a kind God, so that from a sick spirit they may be made healthy: from a deaf heart, hearing: from a blind heart, seeing: from being mute, to speaking and singing praise of God. COMMENTARY ON MATTHEW.[17]

15:32-39 Jesus Feeds Four Thousand

THE DOUBLE IMAGE OF FEAR AND GRACE.

MARTIN LUTHER: I hope dearly beloved, that you do well understand the meaning of this text. For your understanding is sufficiently well grounded in these mysteries, so that you do easily perceive what good is to be looked for in the gospel, and what is prescribed to us therein, namely, the true nature and quality of faith. And this is the cause why Christ is of all the Evangelists set forth to be so loving and gentle; for although the doings and works described of them often vary, nevertheless the simplicity of faith remains always alike. Moreover, this text does so lively set forth Christ to us in his colors that it may be manifest and well known to every one of us, what we ought to promise ourselves concerning him, to wit, that he is merciful, bountiful, gentle, who succors all that fly unto him for help. And such ought to be the image of faith. For the Scripture sets before us a double image; one of fear, which represents to our eyes the horrible wrath of God, before which no one is able to stand, but rather we are all forced to be cast down in mind when we see it, unless we be strengthened by faith. Although, against this is set the other image, namely, of grace, which faith does attentively behold, and takes from hence principles of comfort, and conceives trust and confidence in the favor of God, having this hope, that man

---

[17]Musculus, *In Evangelistam Matthaeum Commenarii* (1556), 445; citing a combination of quotations from Ps 115:6-7; 135:17 (Vg. 113:14, 15; 134:17).

cannot promise to himself from God so many good things, but that he has infinite more treasures in a readiness for him. You have now often heard that there are two sorts of good things, spiritual and corporeal. The gospel by these temporal and corporeal good things teaches us the faith of children, and they are to the weak as a certain mean or help, whereby they may learn the goodness of God, how bountiful he is in bestowing his riches upon us, and that we ought in spiritual things also to put our hope and trust in him. For if we be now instructed by the gospel, that God will give food to our belly, we may thereupon account with ourselves that he will nourish and clothe our souls with spiritual good things. If I cannot commit my body to him that he may feed it, much less can I commit my soul to him that he may always preserve it. The Twenty-Fifth Sermon of Dr. Martin Luther of God's Providences and Care of His Children.[18]

Christ's Power Shown Through Ordinary Means. David Dickson: Follows the miracle and the orderly disposing of it, as the Lord's power may be best seen; hence learn that ere the Lord work, he will have it seen how little ground he has to work upon; therefore, by asking his disciples, he draws forth how few loaves and fishes for such a work were to be had. He will not despise his own appointed ordinary means, for so far as they can reach; nor will he do anything extraordinary, further than is necessary; for he could have fed them without these seven loaves, but he will take them and make use of them seeing they may be had. Christ uses them to shame the unbelief of his servants by making them actors in the work, which they could not believe to see; for "he gave to the disciples, and they to the multitude." There is no scant when the Lord gives the banquet, for all are filled when he invites his guests, as here. His manifold wisdom will glorify himself as he pleases, but ever in a way sufficient to manifest his divine power; for there are here more loaves and fewer people, and fewer fragments, than when by five loaves five thousand were fed, but one basket proves the miracles as well as a hundred, and the fewer the ordinary means be, he will show his power the more. A Brief Exposition.[19]

---

[18]Luther, *Complete Sermons*, 5:285*.

[19]Dickson, *Brief Exposition* (1651), 189.

16:1-28 JESUS IS THE MESSIAH

And the Pharisees and Sadducees came, and to test him they asked him to show them a sign from heaven. [2]He answered them,[a] "When it is evening, you say, 'It will be fair weather, for the sky is red.' [3]And in the morning, 'It will be stormy today, for the sky is red and threatening.' You know how to interpret the appearance of the sky, but you cannot interpret the signs of the times. [4]An evil and adulterous generation seeks for a sign, but no sign will be given to it except the sign of Jonah." So he left them and departed.

[5]When the disciples reached the other side, they had forgotten to bring any bread. [6]Jesus said to them, "Watch and beware of the leaven of the Pharisees and Sadducees." [7]And they began discussing it among themselves, saying, "We brought no bread." [8]But Jesus, aware of this, said, "O you of little faith, why are you discussing among yourselves the fact that you have no bread? [9]Do you not yet perceive? Do you not remember the five loaves for the five thousand, and how many baskets you gathered? [10]Or the seven loaves for the four thousand, and how many baskets you gathered? [11]How is it that you fail to understand that I did not speak about bread? Beware of the leaven of the Pharisees and Sadducees." [12]Then they understood that he did not tell them to beware of the leaven of bread, but of the teaching of the Pharisees and Sadducees.

[13]Now when Jesus came into the district of Caesarea Philippi, he asked his disciples, "Who do people say that the Son of Man is?" [14]And they said, "Some say John the Baptist, others say Elijah, and others Jeremiah or one of the prophets." [15]He said to them, "But who do you say that I am?" [16]Simon Peter replied, "You are the Christ, the Son of the living God." [17]And Jesus answered him, "Blessed are you, Simon Bar-Jonah! For flesh and blood has not revealed this to you, but my Father who is in heaven. [18]And I tell you, you are Peter, and on this rock[b] I will build my church, and the gates of hell[c] shall not prevail against it. [19]I will give you the keys of the kingdom of heaven, and whatever you bind on earth shall be bound in heaven, and whatever you loose on earth shall be loosed[d] in heaven." [20]Then he strictly charged the disciples to tell no one that he was the Christ.

[21]From that time Jesus began to show his disciples that he must go to Jerusalem and suffer many things from the elders and chief priests and scribes, and be killed, and on the third day be raised. [22]And Peter took him aside and began to rebuke him, saying, "Far be it from you, Lord![e] This shall never happen to you." [23]But he turned and said to Peter, "Get behind me, Satan! You are a hindrance[f] to me. For you are not setting your mind on the things of God, but on the things of man."

[24]Then Jesus told his disciples, "If anyone would come after me, let him deny himself and take up his cross and follow me. [25]For whoever would save his life[g] will lose it, but whoever loses his life for my sake will find it. [26]For what will it profit a man if he gains the whole world and forfeits his soul? Or what shall a man give in return for his soul? [27]For the Son of Man is going to come with his angels in the glory of his Father, and then he will repay each person according to what he has done. [28]Truly, I say to you, there are some standing here who will not taste death until they see the Son of Man coming in his kingdom."

a Some manuscripts omit the following words to the end of verse 3   b The Greek words for *Peter* and *rock* sound similar   c Greek *the gates of Hades*   d Or *shall have been bound . . . shall have been loosed*   e Or "[May God be] *merciful to you, Lord!*"   f Greek *stumbling block*   g The same Greek word can mean either *soul* or *life*, depending on the context; twice in this verse and twice in verse 26

OVERVIEW: In a near replay of a narrative from earlier in the Gospel (Mt 12:38-40), Jesus is confronted by an allied group of Pharisees and Sadducees in search of a sign. The Reformation commentators indicate that the times were ripe with signs, if the interested parties would simply discern them. Johannes Piscator notes how Jesus critiques the religious leaders for discerning the signs for the weather but being unwilling and unable to discern the signs of the Messiah.

Erasmus summarizes Jesus' rebuke of the disciples and posits that it produced its desired effect in them, understanding. By referencing the earlier feedings of the multitudes, Jesus gives some indication that one motivation of those earlier occurrences was to nurture the disciples' faith.

Throughout Matthew, the identity of Jesus as the Christ, the Son of David, the Son of Man, and the Son of God has been a prevailing theme. The interweaving of Jesus' two questions and Peter's reply provide a clear interconnection between a variety of christological titles (Son of Man, Jesus, Christ, Son of the living God). The Reformation commentators recognize the crucial importance of Peter's confession and Jesus' response. William Tyndale, like many of the reformers, declares that Peter's statement is the common confession of all Christians. Such a rich, theological text has drawn a variety of interpretations on its particulars. Some of the reformers hold that the "rock" is the confession, others contend that the rock was Christ himself, while Roman Catholic interpreters favor Peter as the rock to which Jesus refers.

Three interconnected themes of Christology, ecclesiology, and soteriology provide not only some direction for the ongoing work of Christ but also a fundamental relationship between Christ, the church, and the church's mission. Martin Chemnitz and others explain that the analogy of the keys is used because only through the preaching of the gospel is entrance into the kingdom granted. The declaration of Jesus' identity as the Christ provides the context for a reminder of Jesus' incarnational purpose.

Peter expresses his displeasure at the seeming conflict of Jesus' christological identity and his purposes of death and resurrection. Jesus' rebuke of Peter as "Satan" gives some insight into the spiritual dimension of human decisions and will, which may contrast with the purposes of God. Calvin indicates that Peter is preferring earthly comforts, but that Peter is not alone in this dread of the cross. Everyone who has forsaken all to follow Christ will be rewarded with eternal life. Those who have cherished their earthly pursuits more than Christ will receive eternal death. The full rewards of discipleship only appear when the Son of Man comes in glory, a reference to Christ's coming at the end of the age (Mt 13:39-43, 49-50).

16:1-12 *The Sign of Jonah*

THE CHALLENGE FOR A SIGN. MARTIN LUTHER: See how they approach—not to be taught (for they wish to be the teachers, not the students), but to make Christ into an iterant entertainer and jester for themselves, to perform signs at their behest— which would serve rather to confirm them in their own teaching as the sort of people who have such a great performer at their beck and call. Moreover, as if those miracles done by him to this point were nothing at all—nothing, that is, but deeds done on earth—they ask for a heavenly miracle. . . . That is why the Evangelist observantly reports that they were asking for this sign "testing him," that is, with malice, trickery, and cunning, like the desperate scoundrels they were. And they want him to be reduced in the sight of the people so long as he is not doing the signs that they choose and command themselves. In contrast, they care nothing for the signs that the Father has given and willed to be done through him. . . .

"You adulterers, you foreigners—you are no longer sons of Abraham and the fathers; you will not have any sign, except the sign of Jonah the prophet. This is a scandalous sign, by which you will not be built up—since you do not want to be built up, but you ridicule and blaspheme the Builder. Rather, you will be offended; you will stumble, fall, and perish. This, I say, is the sign that will be given to you, so that you who are not moved to believe by signs of glory and power will be offended at me because of the scandals of the cross and weakness. And you will understand neither my suffering nor my resurrection. For from the signs of glory and power you could have been drawn to believe me, that I am from God—since no one has done such things before—and, thus having become my disciples, to hear the mysteries of my suffering and cross. But since you do not believe the signs of glory, it will come to pass that, once they have come to an end, I shall be set before you weak, crucified, and dead; then you will be all the less able to believe in me, since you will be offended at the enormity of the scandal of the cross. After I rise, you will most especially not believe, and thus you will perish by a righteous judgment, since you have spurned the signs of the present time glorious as they are." ANNOTATIONS.[1]

THIS GENERATION'S LACK OF DISCERNMENT.
JOHN TILLINGHAST: There were three remarkable signs set upon this time by either of which this generation might have known or discerned Jesus Christ to be the true Messiah. First, there was at this time the departure of the scepter from Judah, prophesied of by Jacob, as you may find in Genesis 49:10: "The scepter shall not depart from Judah, nor a lawgiver from between his feet, until Shiloh come." That is, until Christ come; so that whensoever the scepter was taken away from Judah, they might then conclude, now will the Messiah come, now is he in the world, whether we see him or not, yet he is come, for the scepter was not to depart till he was come; now it is observable that at this very time the scepter was taken away, for this Herod that was now king in Judea, he was a stranger, and not of the blood of the Jews. . . .

Second, there was another remarkable sign of the time, and that was the expiring or ending of Daniel's seventy weeks. It is foretold to Daniel that seventy weeks should be the term of time unto the Messiah's appearance in Daniel 9:24: "Seventy weeks are determined upon your people, and upon your holy City, to finish the transgression, and to make an end of sins, and to make reconciliation for iniquity, and to bring in everlasting righteousness. . . ." Seventy weeks was the determined time of Christ's coming; that is, from the time the angel

here speaks these words, seventy weeks, or 490 years, reckoning so many days as there are in so many weeks, for that indeed is the Holy Ghost's way of account; now it was clear enough that the seventy weeks must be either expired, or very near expiring about that time; and therefore that was another great sign of the time, that the Lord Jesus came and declared himself to be the Messiah, about that time that Daniel had foretold the Messiah was to come forth.

Third, there was another evident sign of this time, and that was, Christ's doing of those things that were foretold should be accomplished by the Messiah, and that in the day of his appearance; as Christ's opening the eyes of the blind, the ears of the deaf, causing the lame to walk; in Matthew 11: "The lame walk, the dumb speak, the dead are raised, the lepers are cleansed, and the poor receive the gospel." Here were the signs of the times. It was foretold by the prophets that when the Messiah came, these things should be done, now they saw these things done; Jesus Christ comes and does these very works and miracles that they expected should be done by the Messiah, therefore this was a very convincing sign of the time, that Jesus Christ was the Messiah. SIGNS OF THE TIMES, TWO SERMONS ON MATTHEW 16:3.[2]

DISCERNING THE SIGN OF JONAH. JOHANNES PISCATOR: But to show that they are ignorant, he shows by an example. You are able, he says, to judge the signs of the storm. Yet you are not able, even if you want, to judge the signs of the time. That is, you would be able to learn from the Word of God that the time of the presenting of the Christ is already present, and what was predicted about the Christ through the prophets is already beginning to be fulfilled in me. In that you either neglect learning of these things or conceal its power, it appears that you are hypocrites. The same objection is increased by heavy indignation or reproof of their malice, where he says, an evil and adulterous generation requires a sign. The voluntary showing

---

[1]LW 67:263-64, 266* (WA 38:601-2, 604-5).

[2]Tillinghast, *Eight Last Sermons*, 47-49.

of a sign is the fulfillment of the type of Jonah; that this is touched on by a single word, yet it is explained fully above in chapter 12. The meaning is that Jonah lay in the belly of the sea monster for three days, just as buried, and afterward then being ejected and expulsed into free air, he was returned to life; this was a type of the things that would happen to the Christ. Whereby in that they will be fulfilled, they will be a sign, that that one would be the Christ. But in me they will be fulfilled; for I will lay buried for three days in the belly of the earth and on the third day then I will rise again. Therefore, that thing will be a sign that I am the Christ. Finally, the event is added of him and of the discourse; indeed, that Jesus departed, leaving them behind. LOGICAL ANALYSIS OF MATTHEW.[3]

THE RIDDLE OF JESUS' REBUKE. DESIDERIUS ERASMUS: Now you should of yourselves have conjectured what my riddle meant when I said, beware of the leaven of the Pharisees and Sadducees. I had now taught you that it little mattered what kind of meat we eat. I had now diversely declared and beaten upon it, that those who have in hand the matter of the gospel should utterly cast away such vile cares. The disciples being more attentive and diligent by this little chiding understood that Jesus meant that they should take heed diligently and beware of the doctrine of the Pharisees, which had nothing that was sincere and clean but was corrupt with ambition, avarice, envy, and other vices, whereas the doctrine of the gospel tasted of no such thing. For their doctrine does infect people rather than feed them; and therefore it must be taken heed of diligently, because they want to deceive unaware and simple people by the false cloak of godliness, which is the very poison of true godliness. PARAPHRASES.[4]

TRUTH FROM THE WORD OF GOD PROMPTS FAITH. JOHN CALVIN: The word *leaven* is very

evidently used by Christ as contrasted with the pure and uncorrupted Word of God. In a former passage, Christ had used the word in a good sense, when he said that the gospel resembled leaven, but for the most part this word is employed in Scripture to denote some foreign substance, by which the native purity of any thing is impaired. In this passage, the naked truth of God, and the inventions which people contrive out of their own brain, are unquestionably the two things that are contrasted. The sophist must not hope to escape by saying that this ought not to be understood as applicable to every kind of doctrine; for it will be impossible to find any doctrine but what has come from God that deserves the name of pure and unleavened. Hence it follows that leaven is the name given to every foreign admixture; as Paul also tells us that faith is rendered spurious, as soon as we are "drawn aside from the simplicity of Christ."

It must now be apparent who are the persons of whose doctrine our Lord charges us to beware. The ordinary government of the church was at that time in the hands of the scribes and priests, among whom the Pharisees held the highest rank. As Christ expressly charges his followers to beware of their doctrine, it follows that all who mingle their own inventions with the word of God or who advance anything that does not belong to it must be rejected, how honorable whatsoever may be their rank or whatever proud titles they may wear. COMMENTARY ON A HARMONY OF THE EVANGELISTS.[5]

16:13-23 Peter's Confession of Jesus as the Christ

THE IDENTITY AND TEACHING OF CHRIST. GEORGE CLOSE: Our Savior Christ, having first drawn from his disciples a confession of the peoples' fantastical and erroneous misconceptions, presses them to lay down what he had truly taught and they had learned of him what he was; which

---

[3]Piscator, *Analysis Logica Evangelii Secundum Matthaeum* (1594), 245-46.
[4]EP 69v.

[5]CTS 2:284 (CO 45:469); citing Mt 13:33; 2 Cor 11:3.

proceeded neither of ignorance, to learn of them what opinions were held, nor of ambitious humor (as vain people commonly do) to make inquiry, after vulgar rumors, either to glory in the people's praises or to revenge their calumniations; but that hearing their opinions, he might instruct them aright, or otherwise to draw from them a confession of the truth. THE ROCK OF RELIGION: CHRIST, NOT PETER.[6]

A TRUE CONFESSION. JOHN CALVIN: The confession is short, but it embraces all that is contained in our salvation; for the designation Christ, or Anointed, includes both an everlasting kingdom and an everlasting priesthood to reconcile us to God and, by expiating our sins through his sacrifice, to obtain for us a perfect righteousness, and, having received us under his protection, to uphold and supply and enrich us with every description of blessings. . . . For the redemption, which God manifested by the hand of his Son, was clearly divine; and therefore it was necessary that he who was to be the Redeemer should come from heaven, bearing the impress of the anointing of God. Matthew expresses it still more clearly: "You are the Son of the living God," for, though Peter did not yet understand distinctly in what way Christ was the begotten of God, he was so fully persuaded of the dignity of Christ that he believed him to come from God, not like other men, but by the inhabitation of the true and living Godhead in his flesh. When the attribute "living" is ascribed to God, it is for the purpose of distinguishing between him and dead idols. COMMENTARY ON A HARMONY OF THE EVANGELISTS.[7]

THE CONFESSION COMMON TO ALL CHRISTIANS. WILLIAM TYNDALE: Peter in the Greek signifies a stone in English. This confession is the *rock*. Now is Simon Bar-Jonah, or Simon Jonas's son, called Peter because of his confession.

Whosoever then of this wise confesses Christ is called Peter. Now is this confession common to all that are true Christians. Then is every Christian man and woman a "Peter." Read Bede, Augustine, and Jerome of the manner of loosing and binding; and note how Jerome checks the presumption of the Pharisees in his time, which yet had not so monstrous interpretations as our new gods have feigned. . . . It was not for naught that Christ bade "beware of the leaven of the Pharisees." Nothing is so sweet that they make not sour with their traditions. The gospel, that joyful tidings, is now bitterer than the old law. Christ's burden is heavier than the yoke of Moses. Our condition and estate are ten times heavier than was ever the Jews', the Pharisees have so leavened Christ's sweet bread. MARGINAL NOTES ON THE FIRST TWENTY-ONE CHAPTERS OF ST. MATTHEW'S GOSPEL.[8]

THE ROCK OF PETER'S CONFESSION. RICHARD TAVERNER: Jesus hearing this, so that he would wring out yet a more certain and higher confession of his disciples, who ought best to have known him, asked them, saying, "But who say you that I am?" Then Peter made answer for him and his fellows (for of all them was the question asked) and said, "You are Christ the Son of the living God." Jesus answered, "Blessed are you Simon the son of Jonah, for flesh and blood has not opened this to you, but my heavenly Father. And I say again to you, you are Peter (or Cephas in the Hebrew that is to say a rock) and upon this rock shall I build my church," that is to say, upon this rock of your confession I shall build my church. For this confession contains the sum of the Christian faith, according to the apostle Paul, saying, "If you confess with your mouth our Lord Jesus and with your heart believe, that God raised him from death to life, you shall be saved." So the Christian church is built, not upon the person of Peter, but upon the faith, as Chrysostom says.[†] And this is the confession of faith: "You are Christ, the Son of the living God."

---

[6]Close, *The Rock of Religion: Christ, Not Peter* (1624), 23-25*.
[7]CTS 2:289 (CO 45:472-73).

[8]Tyndale, *Expositions and Notes*, 234.

Wherefore Peter (as Augustine affirms[†]) does here represent the holy church to whom the keys were delivered. THE GOSPELS WITH BRIEF SERMONS.[9]

THE MASTER BUILDER OF GOD'S HOUSE.

HEINRICH BULLINGER: The true master builder of this house of God says in the Gospel, "Upon this rock I will build my church." For the same Son of God is he who makes us worthy of his kingdom; he gives us faith, by which we are made true members of the church of God. But albeit the Lord himself be the only and principal builder of his church, yet he refuses not the labors of men and women in the building; yea, rather he joins them with him in building of the church, whom also he vouchsafes to call master builders. . . . And if so be it that they object, that many interpreters, both Greek and Latin, have understood by the rock Peter himself; we refuse human authority, and do affirm and bring forth heavenly authority. Christ said not, I will build my church upon you, but upon a rock; and that selfsame rock that you have confessed. Yea, and Peter takes his name of *petra*, which signifies a rock, even as a Christian of Christ. And Peter also himself by the rock understood Christ. OF THE UNITY OF THE CHURCH.[10]

PROCLAIMING THE KEYS OF THE KINGDOM.

MARTIN CHEMNITZ: Why does Christ attach to the ministry the name "keys" of the kingdom of heaven? To indicate that the preaching of the Word is not a vain and useless babbling of words, but that the Holy Spirit is present in this ministry, is efficacious through it, and wants, by this means as with a kind of keys, the kingdom of heaven to be unlocked and many to be brought into it. Therefore ministers of the Word should, by this term, since they hear that the keys of the kingdom of heaven have been given and entrusted to them, bestir themselves to speak the doctrine of sin,

repentance, faith, forgiveness of sins, new obedience . . . not coldly and lightly, nor only in general or superficially, as a story, but set it forth and apply it to their hearers faithfully and diligently, sure that the Holy Spirit wants to kindle, increase, strengthen, and preserve repentance, faith and new obedience in the hearts of the hearers through this their ministry. This name also encourages their spirits, that their labor is not in vain in the Lord. But if ever in the ministry they bind and retain sins to the impenitent, according to the Word of God, with threat of divine wrath and curse, they should know that this is regarded as valid and certain also in heaven. In the same way, if they loose and forgive sins by proclaiming the grace of God to the penitent and believing, they should be sure that it is not only good words (as is commonly said), but that the same is also certain and confirmed in heaven.

Similarly, the name "keys" should admonish the hearers not to despise the Word and ministry and regard it as a vain sound of words by which only the ears are struck, but that they might know and be firmly persuaded that if they want to enter the kingdom of heaven, the approach and entrance is not given and granted to them except through these keys. . . . When they hear the promise of the gospel set forth for believers on the basis of the Word of God, let them not think that they are only words, and that of a human being; but let them consider and firmly believe that it is the voice of the Holy Spirit himself, bringing comfort to our hearts through this means, and that whatever is loosed on earth in that way is loosed and forgiven in heaven by God himself, because it is done through the keys of the kingdom of heaven. . . . Christ wanted to speak in this way about the ministry: "I will give unto you the keys of the kingdom of heaven." MINISTRY, WORD, AND SACRAMENTS.[11]

PETER IS GIVEN THE KEYS. JUAN DE MALDO-

NADO: The power of opening and shutting the

---

[9]Taverner, *On Saynt Andrewes Day: The Gospels with Brief Sermons* (1542), xxii; citing Rom 10:9. [†]Chrysostom, *Homilies on Matthew*, NPNF[1] 10:319-20. [†]Augustine, *Sermons on Selected Lessons*, NPNF[1] 6:337.
[10]DHB 4:79-81.

[11]Chemnitz, *Enchiridion*, 132-33; citing 1 Cor 15:58; Mt 16:19.

kingdom of heaven is called the keys by metaphor. The same power is immediately expressed by the other metaphor of binding and loosing. The question is, in what this power consists? The followers of Luther and Calvin say that it means (merely) the teaching that their sins have already been forgiven, or that they will be if we believe the gospel. But if so, Christ, in giving Peter the keys, gives him nothing more than that which the scribes and Pharisees had before: "Woe to you lawyers, for you have taken away the key of knowledge; you yourselves have not entered in, and those that were entering in you have hindered." It has been proved, however, that Christ not only gave more to Peter than to the scribes and Pharisees, but more even than to the other apostles. Something, then, is meant by the power of the keys more than the power of teaching. Besides, Christ gave this power not only to the twelve apostles, but also to the seventy-two disciples. But the keys and the power of binding and loosing he gave to the apostles alone. Thus, the power of binding and loosing and the power of teaching are not one and the same power. Besides, Christ had already given the power of teaching to the apostles; but that of the keys he had not given.

It has been shown that the apostles had had given to them a general power of teaching; but the use of it was restricted for a time, that they should not go among the Gentiles, because it was not fitting that the gospel should be preached to the Gentiles before it had been preached to the Jews. Supposing a special power only to have been given to them, what would it have to do with the present question? Certainly, if to teach and to remit sins be one and the same thing, wherever they could teach they could also forgive sins. But we see that the power of teaching had been given them, but the power of the remission of sins had not been given. Therefore, they are not the same power.

We see, also, that in this place where the keys are given, and with them the power of binding and loosing, no mention is made of teaching. On the other hand, where the apostles are commanded to preach the gospel to every creature, no mention is

made of the keys, or of binding and loosing. A COMMENTARY ON THE HOLY GOSPELS.[12]

TRUE VERSUS BORROWED CONFESSION OF CHRIST. PILGRAM MARPECK: For Christ Jesus built his church upon a different foundation, namely, upon the present confession, which, under the covenant of circumcision, God promised for the future to the ancients. That future was realized by the confession of Peter, and by all believers who confess Christ to be the Lord and the Son of the living God. Whoever, along with Peter, confesses him, by revelation of the Father with his own confession, he is worthy to receive baptism. The Lord asked his disciples, "Who do people think that I am," so that the disciples could say for themselves; neither the Lord, nor those who belonged to him took satisfaction from the fact that they were simply confessing him for the sake of others. Therefore, he says, "But who do you think that I am?" Then Peter said, "You are the Son of the living God." Upon this basis and upon one's own confession, and not upon a borrowed confession or the confession of someone else, Christ built his church. Even today, a believer may say those words on behalf of the church, especially if, prior to uttering them, each one has confessed their own faith before the assembly or the congregation. But before such individual and true confession has been made, no one may truly be called a member of the community of the church of Christ, a member of the church, for upon this foundation, upon the confession of the faith of Peter, the Lord built his church. THE ADMONITION OF 1542.[13]

IDENTIFYING THE ROCK FROM THE TEXT. [ANONYMOUS ENGLISH AUTHOR]: I said we had to consider what the foundation and rock is, whereupon the church of God is built, for that is expressed in verse 18. You are Peter, and upon this rock I will build my church, and the gates of hell

---

[12]JMG 2:42-43; citing Lk 11:52; Mt 23:2; Lk 11:52; Mt 23:2; Lk 11:52; Mt 10:7; 28:19; Mk 16:15.
[13]CRR 2:226-27*.

shall not overcome it. Concerning the true meaning and sense of these words, what it is that Christ appoints to be that rock, whereupon he will build his church, there is no small variance between us and the Church of Rome. We, according to the tenor of the rest of the Scriptures and circumstance of the place, affirm that Christ by this word *petra*, a Rock, means that which Peter confessed, which was Christ himself. . . . First, that even the very words of the text do argue that when Christ says upon this *rock* I will build my church, by this word *petra*, a rock, he means not the person of Peter the apostle, but that which Peter confessed, which was Christ. It may appear by this that it pleased the Holy Ghost that the Evangelist should alter and change the name *petros* into *petra* when as he might have used the self same word to express that their meaning was to make Peter the rock whereupon he would build his church. For, although the word *petros* and *petra* do agree in signification in that both of them by interpretation doth signify a stone or rock, yet the alteration and change of that word in propriety of speech and termination in gender, and in construction of person does import that the Holy Ghost by these diverse words would mean a diverse thing. A Godly Sermon.[14]

Christ Is the Only Foundation of His Church. Huldrych Zwingli: It follows further, "And I say to you, that you are a man of the rock and upon the rock I shall build my church." Christ says in the first instance, "And I say to you that you are a man of the rock," as if to say, "You say of me, in the name of all the others," as John 6:69 indicates clearly, "that I am the Son of God. And I say to you, in turn, that you, the son of Jonah, shall henceforth be called Peter, as I have promised you, which means 'man of the rock' because of the firm and solid confession." This promise Christ made when Andrew, Simon's brother, introduced him to Christ for the first time and when Christ said, "You are Simon son of Jonah, you shall be called Cephas,

which means a man of the rock." Note in this connection, Matthew 16:18, where he gives the promised name to Simon.

With regard to this name, the pope errs in two ways. First of all, he says that the phrase, "and upon this rock I shall build my church," refers to Peter and all subsequent popes. Yet, Christ did not say, "upon this man of the rock I shall build my church." He said, "upon the rock after which I named you, I shall build my church." He did not stay with the man of the rock, but turned again to the very rock from which he derived the name and upon which he, along with all other believers, is grounded. For, had the church been built upon Peter, it would have tumbled at the very moment when he denied Christ by an oath. . . . It follows then that Peter cannot be the foundation or ground of the church; for there can be no other [foundation] than Christ. If then Christ is the true rock and foundation of all believers who assures that the house, built upon him, cannot be moved, it must follow also that everyone who confesses him—as Peter and all the disciples had done—will be named after the rock, "a man of the rock." . . . In short, those who believe, as the disciples and Peter believed, that Christ is the Son of the living God, are built upon the rock and are therefore called "men of the rock." An Exposition of the Articles.[15]

16:24-28 *Taking Up the Cross to Follow the Son of Man*

The Character of a Disciple of Christ. Edward Reynolds: Now from this time of Peter's confession, Christ to take off all mistakes touching his kingdom, began to acquaint his disciples with his sufferings. At which Peter is presently offended and takes upon him to advise his master and rebuke him, "Be it far from you, this shall not be unto you." Hereupon Christ sharply reprehends him, "It is not now, You are Peter, but you are Satan, a tempter, and adversary to the work of Christ's mediation"—for so much the word

---

[14]*A Godlye Sermon*, 31-33.   [15]Zwingli, *The Defense of the Reformed Faith*, 1:301-2; citing Jn 1:43.

elsewhere implies—not now a stone for building, but a stone of offense: "You savor not the things of God, but the things which are of human beings." That is, you have a carnal and corrupt judgment of me and of my kingdom, conceiving of it according to the common apprehensions and expectations of human beings, and not according to the counsel and will of God.

In this reprehension, there is a personal correction and doctrinal instruction, teaching his disciples and the people that all they who would (as Peter had done) own him for the Messiah and king of the church must not promise themselves great things under him in the world, but must resolve to walk in the steps which he would tread out before them, namely, to deny themselves, as he did and "to bear a cross," as he also did, and so to follow him. And to take off all prejudice and scandal, he assures them that whatever their fears and suspicions might be of so hard a service, yet thus to deny themselves was the only way to save themselves, and thus to bear a cross was the only way to a crown and glorious reward, which, lest it should seem an empty promise without evidence and assurance, he undertakes to confirm shortly after by an ocular and sensible demonstration, which we may understand either of his glorious transfiguration the week after, or of his glorious ascension in their sight, or of his pouring forth the Holy Spirit upon them in fiery tongues, or of his more full manifestation of his kingdom and glory unto his servant John by the ministry of angels in his glorious revelation, unto all which, though the context seems to relate principally unto the first, may that promise of our Savior be understood to refer.

The words then are a character of a disciple of Christ. They must deny themselves, and that not in some more easy matters, but thoroughly, and in all things, so far as suffering, and suffering to the uttermost; pain, death, shame, for those three things are contained in the cross. SELF-DENIAL.[16]

[16]Reynolds, *Self-Denial: Opened and Applied in a Sermon* (1657), 4-5*; citing Num 22:22; 2 Sam 19:22; Mt 26:42; Jn 19:17; Mt 27:1-2; Acts 1:9; 2:2-3; Rev 1:1.

THE DREAD OF THE CROSS. JOHN CALVIN: Christ therefore throws his disciple to a distance from him because, in his inconsiderate zeal, he acted the part of Satan; for he does not simply call him "adversary," but gives him the name of the devil, as an expression of the greatest abhorrence.

You are an offense to me; for you relish not those things which are of God, but those which are of human beings. We must attend to this as the reason assigned by our Lord for sending Peter away from him. Peter was an offense to Christ, so long as he opposed his calling; for, when Peter attempted to stop the course of his master, it was not owing to him that he did not deprive himself and all humankind of eternal salvation. This single word, therefore, shows with what care we ought to avoid everything that withdraws us from obedience to God. And Christ opens up the original source of the whole evil, when he says that Peter relishes those things which are of human beings. . . .

As Christ saw that Peter had a dread of the cross, and that all the rest were affected in the same way, he enters into a general discourse about bearing the cross, and does not limit his address to the twelve apostles, but lays down the same law for all the godly. We have already met with a statement nearly similar. But in that passage, the apostles were only reminded of the persecution which awaited them, as soon as they should begin to discharge their office; while a general instruction is here conveyed, and the initiatory lessons, so to speak, inculcated on all who profess to believe the gospel. . . .

Presenting himself to everyone as an example of self-denial and of patience, he first shows that it was necessary for him to endure what Peter reckoned to be inconsistent with his character, and next invites every member of his body to imitate him. The words must be explained in this manner: "If anyone would be my disciple, let them follow me by denying themselves and taking up their cross, or, let them conform themselves to my example." The meaning is that none can be reckoned to be the disciples of Christ unless they are true imitators of him and are willing to pursue the same course. COMMENTARY ON A HARMONY OF THE EVANGELISTS.[17]

THE DIVINE SON OF MAN. JOHANN GERHARD: [John] Cameron, in his *Myrothecium Evangelicum*,[†] in regard to the phrase "Son of Man" in this passage and elsewhere, states expressly that it is not the human nature of Christ that is meant here by the title "Son of Man," but the person to whom is granted the office of mediator, and it does not mean that the human nature of Christ is endowed with infinite power, but only that the person granted that office has been given infinite power to judge all people. It is to Christ the mediator, who is neither simply man nor simply God, but the God-man, that infinite power is given. Now, although easily we grant that the person who will administer judgment is not a mere man, but a God-man, still our assertion is not lessened from the fact that, since that power of administering judgment is infinite, assuredly including omniscience and omnipotence, in truth it is given to Christ . . . John 5.27 has, "because he is the Son of Man," that is to say, according to his human nature, since nothing can be given to the divine person in the temporal realm, and also, since the Son of Man is going to administer judgment in the glory of the Father, which glory is completely divine and infinite, truly divine and infinite power is given Christ the man, that is to say, to the human nature of Christ. Christ added the reason why he said that that life and the power of judgment has been given to him from the Father, because he is the Son of Man, so that we may understand that all things have been given to him as a man. But the only-born Son is not a sharer of life, but is by nature life. Meanwhile, through that assertion that that infinite glory is communicated to Christ the man, it does not follow that the argument is weakened that the old theologians drew from this for the true deity of Christ. For, unless the divine majesty belongs to Christ essentially according to his deity, it would not be able to be communicated to the assumed human nature personally. Whence we embrace completely that which Chrysostom[‡] says in homily 56 on these words in Matthew: the Son of Man will come in the glory of the Father. ANNOTATIONS ON MATTHEW.[18]

WHY JESUS PREFERS THE TITLE SON OF MAN. THOMAS TAYLOR: Nay, by this title our text must needs understand the whole Christ, God and man, the Son of God and the Son of Man, for though his speech express him the Son of Man, yet the action here referred unto him—to be the just judge of all the world—proclaims him to be the Son of God; and he is indeed the Son of Man, but coming in the glory of his Father. But why does Christ ordinarily, speaking of himself, call himself the Son of Man? He might have said, the Son of God shall come in the glory of his Father, which might seem to have added more weight to his words.

Answer: Yet he uses the other title, first, in respect of himself. To note that he was a true man; being not only a man, but "the son of man," that born man, having flesh and blood nowhere else but from man. And herein this second Adam was opposed to the first, who was a man, but not the son of man; for he was "the Son of God" by creation. The first Adam was framed of the earth, and so was made a man, but not the Son of Man; the second Adam took flesh of the virgin, and so was not man, but the Son of Man also. Again, it implies that he was a weak and frail man; as the Hebrew phrase founds: "Lord, what is man, or the son of man, that you should respect him?" Being so base and vile, "Who are you that fear a mortal man?" Or the Son of Man, that is a weak and frail creature. . . .

Second, in respect of his hearers and human judgment, who commonly esteemed him no other, and rose no higher in their judgment of him than of a mere man, though perhaps a great and holy man. He would tender the weakness of his hearers;

---

[17]CTS 2:302 (CO 45:480-81); citing Mt 10:38.

[18]Gerhard, *Annotationes Posthumae in Evangelium D. Matthaei* (1663), 739-40. [†]John Cameron, *Myrothecium Evangelicum* (Saumur, France: Isaac and Henri Desbordes, 1677), 37. [‡]Chrysostom, *Homilies on Matthew*, NPNF[1] 10:331.

for scarely the disciples themselves after a great while could come to acknowledge the majesty of the Son of God, in this Son of Man; and therefore, he speaks of himself as they are able to conceive him, more intending their instruction than his own reputation.

Third, in respect of the argument. For the manner of Scripture in speaking of the last judgment is to use this phrase above other: Because this was appropriated to the Messiah by Daniel, to which Christ undoubtedly had reference: "I beheld, and there came as a Son of Man in the clouds of heaven." To show that as he showed himself in the nature of man to be judge on earth, so he would show himself in a visible manner a judge in heaven. The Works of That Faithful Servant of Christ.[19]

QUESTIONS ABOUT THE COMING OF THE SON OF MAN. Juan de Valdés: Christ, purposing to declare when this life eternal shall fully and completely commence, says, "For the Son of Man shall come." . . . meaning that it shall commence from the day of judgment; on which day he says, God shall "give every person according to their work," meaning that he will give eternal life to those who shall have lost the present life for his sake; and that he will give eternal death to those who shall not have been willing to lose the present life for his sake.

I do not understand what Christ subjoins, saying, "I tell you of a truth that there be some of them" . . . and I state that I do not understand it, for it does not agree with what some say, that they saw Christ in his kingdom, who saw him transfigured upon Mount Tabor; for I do not understand that to have been the kingdom of Christ, neither would it be to the purpose in relation to what precedes; neither do I agree with what others say, that the disciples did not taste of death, because they did not feel the agony of death, like others; for I know that according to the idiom of the Hebrew tongue, "to taste of death" is the same as to die; neither do I agree with what others say that they saw Christ in his kingdom, who saw Christ glorified after the coming of the Holy Spirit, his gospel having been accepted by the majority of the nations; because I see that Christ here speaks of the day of judgment, on which day, he will discover his glory and his majesty to the whole world.

True it is that Mark's words "till they have seen the kingdom of God come with power" might be applied to the coming of the Holy Spirit; and there is no doubt but that the disciples saw it come as such, at the time they received the Holy Spirit; from which time we understand the kingdom of heaven commenced, that which was preached in the time of Christ. And if it could be said that some of those who were present at the time Christ spoke these words are reserved unto the day of judgment, never having died, there would be nothing to doubt. In point of fact, we attain to know but little of the mysteries of God, however much we presume upon our attainment of them; and, therefore, it is a safe thing to confess our blindness in relation to them. COMMENTARY UPON THE GOSPEL OF ST. MATTHEW.[20]

---

[19]Taylor, *Works*, 48; citing Lk 3:38; Ps 8:5; Is 51:12; Dan 7:13.

[20]Valdés, *Commentary upon the Gospel of St. Matthew*, 294-95; citing Mk 9:1.

17:1-13 THE TRANSFIGURATION

And after six days Jesus took with him Peter and James, and John his brother, and led them up a high mountain by themselves. ²And he was transfigured before them, and his face shone like the sun, and his clothes became white as light. ³And behold, there appeared to them Moses and Elijah, talking with him. ⁴And Peter said to Jesus, "Lord, it is good that we are here. If you wish, I will make three tents here, one for you and one for Moses and one for Elijah." ⁵He was still speaking when, behold, a bright cloud overshadowed them, and a voice from the cloud said, "This is my beloved Son,ᵃ with whom I am well pleased; listen to him." ⁶When the disciples heard this, they fell on their faces and were terrified. ⁷But Jesus came and touched them, saying, "Rise, and have no fear." ⁸And when they lifted up their eyes, they saw no one but Jesus only.

⁹And as they were coming down the mountain, Jesus commanded them, "Tell no one the vision, until the Son of Man is raised from the dead." ¹⁰And the disciples asked him, "Then why do the scribes say that first Elijah must come?" ¹¹He answered, "Elijah does come, and he will restore all things. ¹²But I tell you that Elijah has already come, and they did not recognize him, but did to him whatever they pleased. So also the Son of Man will certainly suffer at their hands." ¹³Then the disciples understood that he was speaking to them of John the Baptist.

a Or my Son, my (or the) Beloved

OVERVIEW: Once on the mountain, Jesus transforms before the disciples' eyes into a glorious figure accompanied by two central figures from the Old Testament. Though Matthew makes no effort to provide a rationale for why these two figures appear, the heavenly voice asserts, in no uncertain terms, Jesus' supremacy over them and whatever representation they carry. The reformers have two main theological interests in the transfiguration text: Christology and unity of the testaments. Matthew's description of the transfigured Christ prompts Martin Chemnitz to defend his affirmation of the hypostatic union in Christ. Heinrich Bullinger asserts his position that the transfigured state gives Christ's followers some idea of what Christ's glorified body will be like.

In declaring Jesus' divine sonship, the heavenly voice revisits an address from Jesus' baptism with the added exhortation to heed his words (a recurring theme throughout the Gospel [e.g., Mt 7:24-27; 13:10-23]). Juan de Valdés states that the heavenly voice confirms that Christ is accomplishing the will of the Father. Other reformers comment on the relationship of the testaments, reflecting on the Son's relationship to the Old Testament characters. As Zwingli points out, Christ is an accessible revelation from the Father. In the descent down the mountain, the discussion establishes a connection between the transfiguration and the postresurrection witness of the disciples and the immediate intention of Christ's suffering. The interplay of Christ's glorious identity followed by a pronouncement of his sufferings echoes a similar compositional strategy in the previous chapter (Mt 16:13-23).

17:1-8 Jesus Is Gloriously Transfigured

NOTES ON THE TRANSFIGURATION ACCOUNT.
GIOVANNI DIODATI: "Transfigured." Not by any change in his natural shape, form, and stature of body, but by a new and miraculous splendor with which he was clothed as for a pattern of his celestial glorification, doing this to assure his disciples that he died not for want of power to

avoid it, but willingly. "Moses." To signify the consent and concordance of the Law and the Prophets to Christ. Now it was known to the apostles who these were, either by inward revelation or by Christ's words, or some words of their own. . . .

"Overshadowed." Namely, those representations of Moses and Elijah, which certainly was but in vision and vanished away, this cloud involving and covering them. And Jesus remained alone, being there present in his true body and real substance. "Well pleased." Christ then is the mediator through whom God reconciles the world to himself and outside of him, loves no man in it. "Hear him." God appoints here his Son, Jesus Christ, to be the only doctor of his church, and allows his doctrine only—which speaks the same things with Moses and the Prophets—rejecting all other doctrines which proceed not from his mouth. PIOUS ANNOTATIONS.[1]

DETAILED EXAMINATION OF THE TRANSFIGURATION. DAVID CHYTRAEUS: This is a testimony of Christ's calling and power, as well as the truth of his teaching. As it is said in 2 Peter 1: "Not by following cleverly composed fables have we preached the power and coming of our Lord Jesus Christ to you, but we ourselves were eyewitnesses of his majesty on the mountain, when the word was declared to him by the divine magnificence: 'This is my Son in whom I delight, listen to him!'"

This is also a shining testimony of the immortality of the soul and the restitution and glorification of our bodies, of the better and eternal life that will follow after this one. For Moses, who died and was buried 1,500 years before this, nonetheless still lives and is speaking with Christ!

[This passage] teaches of what sort the bodies will be that are raised in that eternal life—namely, illustrious, shining, clear, and free from all filth of the mortal body, for "the just will shine as the sun" and "star differs from star in brightness."

This is a testimony that in eternal life the blessed will mutually recognize and see one another, as in this history Moses and Elijah are clearly recognized.

[This passage] admonishes us that after they have departed this life the souls of the saints in no way pass their time in inert and lazy idleness or slumber like Epimenides.[†] Rather, they enjoy the vision and words of God and speak together concerning the marvelous creation of humanity and its redemption through Christ. They are also dedicated to the care of the church and pray for it, just as Moses and Elijah are described in Luke 9 as having spoken with Christ about his passion and death, which he was about to undergo in Jerusalem.[‡]

Peter, gazing on the glory of Christ and the conversation taking place between the saints, desired with all his heart to be a sharer in that blessed fellowship and joy. And beside himself with ecstasy because of that immense joy, he rushed forward and desired to build tabernacles for Christ and the saints so that he might enjoy the vision of them longer. In this way, we should also crackle with flaming desire for the blessed fellowship of all the saints in heaven.

Moses and Elijah were speaking with Christ concerning his passion and death. This means that the sacrifices of the Mosaic law and "Elijah"—the latter standing for the declarations of all the prophets—demonstrate with concordant testimonies that it was necessary for Christ to suffer and thus to enter into his glory.

The word of the eternal Father—"This is my beloved Son, in whom I delight, listen to him!"—was already explained above, in chapter 3, under seven topics.

[This] concerns the revelation of God, namely that the eternal Father wishes to be recognized and worshiped as he reveals himself through the Son.

[This verse teaches] the right way of recognizing and invoking God, namely, through the Son and his faithfulness.

This is a testimony concerning the two distinct persons of the eternal Father and of the Son in the same divine essence.

---

[1] Diodati, *Pious Annotations* (1643), E2v*.

It is a summation of the gospel, that the eternal Father for the sake of his beloved Son desires to love and to adopt us also as his children, as it is said in Ephesians 1: "He has loved us in the Beloved."

[This verse] concerns the true and highest ways to worship God, which are to hear the Son of God, to embrace by faith his teaching, and to call upon the eternal Father through the faithfulness of his beloved Son.

These words—"This is my beloved Son, in whom I am well pleased. Listen to him!"—are taken from three places in Scripture. Psalm 2: "The Lord said to me, 'You are my son.'" Isaiah 40: "Behold my servant, who is well pleasing to my soul." Deuteronomy 18: "I will raise up a prophet for you from among your brothers. You will listen to him." COMMENTARY ON MATTHEW.[2]

THE BODY'S TRUE NATURE IN GLORIFICATION.

HEINRICH BULLINGER: He makes clear what kind of future [body] will be in glory, and what kind [he will have] when he comes to judge the living and the dead. Truly, indeed, the condition has been circumscribed in which the body in glory will remain: It will not be cast aside, nor will it be destroyed, nor will it be deified, that is, the body will [not] be absorbed or consumed by the divine nature. The human substance will remain. Yet corruption will be removed from it (as the apostle said in 1 Cor 15), and the splendor of glory will be added. For the Lord said most clearly that the apostles would see him as such coming in glory. Therefore, I say, though by the resurrection at the end will be removed—by the flesh of the Lord—corruption, death, disease, and the rest of the body's infirmities, yet here he desires to make known the body's and flesh's true nature in glorification or to be illuminated, not to be destroyed. Yes, the angels say after the

resurrection, "He is risen; he is not here. Behold the place where they laid him." In the same manner the body of Christ was not glorified everywhere . . . by the work of the resurrection.

Then at last, when in the work of Luke the disciples reckoned the rejuvenated body of the Lord to be a ghost, the Lord himself, offering the members of his body for them to touch and behold, said, "Touch and see, for a ghost does not have flesh and bone as you see I have." The same thing is said in the Scriptures of the Evangelists and also apostles regarding his coming back in judgment just as he ascended into heaven. But he ascended, truly, by circumscription and collocation with respect to the body into the heavens, as the Acts of the Apostles testifies to us. Therefore, he retains a real body in heaven; truly with a body he will return to judge. Even Zechariah testified, "They will look upon the one whom they pierced." With regard to glorification or glory, for that reason, he does not lay aside the reality of his body. On that account, against Scripture and character of faith and against the catholic and orthodox faith of all the church, they think those who contend that the body of Christ is in the heavens to be proud, now to be scattered through all, to be bound in no place, but by glorification to be done in that manner; whoever, I say, thinks the flesh of Christ to be deified in glory, that is, to be absorbed by divinity, and also for that reason we name the Creator by new or shameful names, because we confess Christ in glory seated till now as a creature, that is, to be a real man, although at the same time true God. COMMENTARY ON MATTHEW.[3]

THE UNION OF CHRIST'S DIVINE AND HUMAN NATURES.

MARTIN CHEMNITZ: That mode of the hypostatic union of the divine and human natures in Christ, which the Damascenes call *perichoresis*,[†] is finely illustrated from the opening of the metaphors of the union of the light and body of the sun, of fire and iron, of body and

---

[2]Chytraeus, *Commentarius in Matthaeum Evangelistam* (1558), 288-91*; citing 2 Pet 1:16; Dan 12:3; Mt 13:43; 1 Cor 15:41; Mt 3:17; Eph 1:6; Ps 2:7; Is 40:1; Deut 18:18. †According to legend, Greek philosopher Epimenides of Knossos (c. seventh century BC) fell asleep in a cave sacred to Zeus for seven years. ‡Lk 9:31 actually says that the three speak of Jesus'"departure" (*exodus*), making this a rather loose paraphrase.

[3]Bullinger, *In . . . Evangelium secundum Matthaeum commentariorum* (1546), 7:164-65; citing Lk 24:39; Zech 12:10.

spirit. . . . So for another reason Moses' face shown, or by participation. Another reason Christ's face shown, according to Matthew 17 is that it was inhabited by the person of divine glory, shining from the face of Christ. Truly the same he even set forth in the union of spirit and body in a man. For not by a spirit so united to the body through helping or touching, in the same way when two solid bodies join together so as it becomes one or contiguous, nothing is between those joined solid bodies or mutual participation comes between; but his own spirit by union permeates the whole body everywhere, as—just as Augustine says[‡]—the whole would be in the whole body, and in every member would be everything, and also the body in that union of spirit might have its own immanence, so as this spirit alone sharing its own powers, strength, and faculties, shares with every member, that is, in those and through those it would work and be effective. Origen[§] fittingly explains *perichoresis* by a metaphor of fired iron, as if some lump of iron would always be put in the fire, receiving the fire in all its pores and in all its veins, even receiving all the effects of fire, if neither the fire ceases from it at some time, nor it is separated from the fire, we speak of the effect of the whole fire, just as we see in furnaces often made, since neither is separated in it, nor of the fire, but also if anyone attempts to join and to touch, they feel the strength not of the iron but of the fire. And indeed, to the saints that remain, some heat of the word of God was set to be reached. Truly in that spirit (rather in the whole human nature of Christ) this divine fire was believed to rest essentially, from which some heat came to the rest. On these things, see Origen. ON THE TWO NATURES IN CHRIST.[4]

THE NATURE OF THE TRANSFIGURATION.

THOMAS ADAMS: The manner is set down. He was transfigured before them, and his face did shine as the sun, and his raiment was white as the light. Some are of the opinion that this clarity was in the air about him, not in the body of Christ. But that is false, for he himself was transfigured, not the air about him. Some have said that his very substance was changed from mortality to immortality for the time. But that is false, for transfiguration is properly from one figure to another, not from one nature to another. Some say this transition was not by any change into that which was not before, but by a manifestation of that which was (not revealed) before. These affirm that Christ took from his mother an immortal and impassible body, but this is a most impossible opinion. How then could this be? If Christ reserved mortality, how was he capable of glory? If he took immortality, then was there a change of his substance. Neither, but only a change of his form. . . . The fashion of his countenance was altered. There is a change, not of his person, but of his look, not his countenance, but the fashion of his countenance. This was done by the clarity that was in his body, as in the very subject. This splendor was after one manner in his body, after another in his garment. In his body inherently, in his garment by an external whiteness poured upon it. . . .

But here it is questioned, why did Moses and Elijah appear, rather than David and Abraham, from whose loins Christ Jesus came and who were so famous among the people? First, to manifest a difference between the Lord and the servants. Moses and Elijah were of high esteem with the Jews, Christ was not regarded a man of no repute among them; therefore he would now show that he was the Lord, and they but the servants to wait upon him. That he was not Elijah, but the God of Elijah. . . .

Second, if it be granted that Moses was dead, and that Elijah died not, this declares that Christ is the Savior of both quick and dead. . . .

Third, to come nearer home, Moses was called the lawgiver, and Elijah was (after a sort) the law restorer; now the Jews slandered Christ for a lawbreaker. Their common imputation against him was that he transgressed the law and was contrary

[4]Chemnitz, *De Duabus Naturis in Christo de Hypostatica Earum Unione* (1589), 40-42; citing Ex 34:29-35. [†]John of Damascus, *Exposition of the Orthodox Faith* 1.14. [‡]Augustine, *De Trinitate* 6.10, NPNF[1] 3:103. [§]Origen, *On First Principles* 2.6.6.

to the Prophets. Therefore, he was content to be put to his purgation and to justify himself. Think not that I am come to destroy the Law or the Prophets; I am not come to destroy, but to fulfill. . . .

Fourth, they meet that brought the law, with Christ that brought the gospel to show that law and gospel must be joined together. But we are freed by Christ from the law? I answer, there is a double obligation of the law: the obligation of penalty, and the obligation of duty. We are freed from the obligation of penalty, but not from the obligation of duty. . . .

Fifth, to show that this was the true Messiah, to whom both Law and Prophets bear witness. Moses in the Law, as it is cited by Peter: "A prophet shall the Lord your God raise up unto you among your brethren, like unto me; him shall you hear in all things." And Elijah instead of all the prophets, who was the clearest of all the prophets. . . . Therefore, as Christ had three witnesses from the earth, Peter, James, and John, so he had three from heaven: the voice of the Father, Moses, and Elijah. That now he who fulfilled both the testaments might enjoy both the testimonies. A COMMENTARY ON 2 PETER.[5]

CHRIST ACCOMPLISHES THE WILL OF THE FATHER. JUAN DE VALDÉS: The terms in which the eternal Father gives us testimony of Christ are worthy of profound consideration, since it is so that by them we understand that Christ is the Son of God; and because he calls him "his beloved," we understand that Christ is the Son of God, wholly otherwise than are they so, whom holy Scripture calls children of God, since Christ is the beloved, the dear and favored one, and he is the first born and only begotten, his generation being divine, and, as might be said, "Whose goings forth have been of old, from everlasting," being one and the same, and of the same substance with God, the same as the Father. And, therefore, with Christ alone has God been and still is well pleased, for, as says Isaiah, "In him the pleasure of the Lord has prospered," meaning that in Christ,

God's purpose has been accomplished; for that, by laying the sins of us all upon Christ, and chastising us all in Christ, Christ bore the chastisement without deviating a point from the will of God. . . . That (command) "Hear him," is much more to be noted by us Christians, in order that we may know that it concerns us to stop our ears wholly against human prudence and reason, and to all natural light, and to open them to Christ only; to follow what he shall tell us, however much human prudence with natural light shall roar and shout the contrary.

In that which Matthew narrates, "When they lifted up their eyes" may be understood, what Christ himself has stated in chapter 11, that the Law and the Prophets served until John came. Nay, I understand that it ever is so, that although every one, while he does not hear the Father's voice, while he has not inward inspiration, sees Moses and Elijah with Christ, using the Law and the Prophets to see Christ; but when hearkening, he hears the voice of the Father, being inwardly inspired and drawn to Christ, Moses and Elijah disappear, no longer availing himself either of the Law and of the Prophets, in order to see Christ, to accept his righteousness, and to cleave only to that. Where I will say this, that Moses and the prophets are so polite, that as soon as Christ enters, they walk out, giving way to Christ; and, therefore, the best expedient of all to liberate a man from Moses and the prophets is to introduce him to Christ, to Christian faith, and afterward to Christian life. COMMENTARY UPON THE GOSPEL OF ST. MATTHEW.[6]

THE TEMPORARY GLORY OF THE LAW AND PROPHETS. JOSEPH HALL: He graciously touches and comforts them: "Arise, fear not." That voice, which shall once raise them up out of the earth, might well raise them up from it; that hand, which by the least touch restored sight, limbs, and life, might well restore the spirits of the dismayed. . . .

"They looking up saw no man save Jesus alone," and that, doubtless, in his wonted form; all was

---

[5]Adams, *An Exposition upon the Second Epistle General of St. Peter* (1633), 329-32*; Mt 5:17; Acts 3:22.

[6]Valdés, *Commentary upon the Gospel of St. Matthew*, 299-301; citing Mic 5:2; Is 53:10.

now gone—Moses, Elijah, the cloud, the voice, the glory. Tabor itself cannot be long blessed with that divine light, and those shining guests; heaven will not allow to the earth any long continuance of glory; only above is constant happiness to be looked for and enjoyed, where we shall ever see our Savior in his unchangeable brightness, where the light shall never be either clouded or varied. Moses and Elijah are gone; only Christ is left; the glory of the Law and the Prophets was but temporary, yea, momentary, that only Christ may remain to us entire and conspicuous; they came but to give testimony to Christ; when that is done, they are vanished. CONTEMPLATIONS ON THE HISTORICAL PASSAGES.[7]

JESUS IS THE LIGHT. HULDRYCH ZWINGLI: Christ Jesus is light, which makes itself common to everyone and does not refuse its splendor to any creature. Artists who excel in some art and are acquainted with some honor, they hide and refuse others from this [honor], which is a human weakness. Truly God neither hides nor refuses his good works from anyone but sets them out openly for everyone so that they may use and enjoy them. Therefore, the light of God is brightest; it is not hidden from anyone since it is set forth in an open place for the whole world. But if it is hidden until now, it is not a fault of the light, but our weakness. But who will say, "Why then does God train us in this way?" It appears to him this way so that we may at last then fully seize the brightness of this light since it is coming into our domain. Here we are to walk by faith on the journey to this point, in which the target is set before us so that we may walk piously, with sanctity, and innocently, in which, if we fix our eye on the target and follow the light of Christ, then we will not be able to go astray. And this is the purpose for which he forbids the apostles to carry out, for it was not yet time. ANNOTATIONS ON MATTHEW'S GOSPEL.[8]

JESUS MAINTAINED DIVINE POWER HIS ENTIRE LIFE. JOHN CALVIN: We have said that the time for making known the vision was not yet fully come; and, indeed, the disciples would not have believed it if Christ had not given a more striking proof of his glory in his resurrection. But after that, his divine power had been openly displayed, that temporary exhibition of his glory began to be admitted, so as to make it fully evident that, even during the time that he emptied himself, he continued to retain his divinity entire, though it was concealed under the veil of the flesh. There are good reasons, therefore, why he enjoins his disciples to keep silence, till he be risen from the dead. . . .

No sooner is the resurrection mentioned than the disciples imagine that the reign of Christ is commenced; for they explain this word to mean that the world would acknowledge him to be the Messiah. That they imagined the resurrection to be something totally different from what Christ meant is evident from what is stated by Mark, that they disputed with each other what was the meaning of that expression which he had used, to rise from the dead. Perhaps, too, they were already under the influence of that dream, which is now held as an undoubted oracle among the rabbis, that there would be a first and a second coming of the Messiah; that in the first he would be mean and despised, but that this would be shortly afterward followed by his royal dignity. And, indeed, there is some plausibility in that error, for it springs from a true principle. The Scripture, too, speaks of a first and a second coming of the Messiah; for it promises that he will be a redeemer to expiate by his sacrifice the sins of the world. And such is the import of the following prophecies: "Rejoice, daughter of Zion, behold, your King comes, poor, sitting on a donkey." "We beheld him, and he had no form or beauty, and he resembled a leper, so that we had no esteem for him." Again, Scripture represents him as victorious over death, and as subjecting all things to his dominion. COMMENTARY ON A HARMONY OF THE EVANGELISTS.[9]

[7]Hall, *Contemplations on the Historical Passages of the Old and New Testaments*, 4:523*.

[8]Zwingli, *Annotationes*, 6.1:328.

[9]CTS 2:317-18 (CO 45:490); citing Phil 2:7; Zech 9:9; Is 53:3-4.

17:9-13 *Elijah and John the Baptist*

The Coming Day of Judgment. Henry Hammond: These two then being the parts of that great and dreadful day, the destruction of the unbelieving Jews that stood out and persecuted and crucified Christ and Christians, and the rescue of a remnant, the persevering believers, and John the Baptist being the prophet, sent into the wilderness, like Elijah, to foretell this destruction, and to preach repentance for the averting of it, there is little reason of doubting, but that that prophecy of Malachi was exactly thus fulfilled, and that consequently this was the matter of the discourse of Elijah and Moses with Christ, though as in a vision somewhat obscurely and darkly delivered, upon which the disciples discerning this to be the day spoken of by Malachi, but not discerning that Elijah was yet come—and so that that precedent part was yet fulfilled—ask Christ this question, why then is it resolved on by all that Elijah must first come? First, that is, before this great and terrible day of the Lord, which they now heard was approaching, and had nothing to say against it, but the known Scripture prediction that Elijah was first to come. That which has been thus explained from this advantage of the disciples' question is indeed the very same with what Luke—the only one of the four Evangelists that mentions anything of this discourse of Elijah and Moses with Christ—relates of it. . . . They related his exodus, or going out which he should accomplish at Jerusalem, which that it agrees perfectly with what has here been said. Paraphrase and Annotations.[10]

Christ Also as Elijah, Not Only John the Baptist. Pilgram Marpeck: I fear that those false prophets who wait for a second commission will experience what the Jews experienced because they did not want, in their view, to have the son of a carpenter for a Messiah.

They completely overlooked the time, for they saw and desired in Christ only the scandalous and not the true, and thus they must perish even to this day. May God grant them the recognition of their error. Although, according to these prophets, an Elijah will come who will reveal and punish all hypocrites and liars, yet he will certainly not work against the command and Word of Christ (which has its effect in faith); rather, he will bring them to justice and reveal them, just as, to their own shame, the hypocrites and liars must be exposed. Christ himself announces that Elijah must indeed come, and he (Christ) presents himself as Elijah when he says, "Elijah has already come." Although the texts refer to John the Baptist alone, it cannot really be understood to refer only to him, but also to Christ. It is not John but Christ alone to whom power and glory belong, who has set all things right. John was only the evangel, and he himself said, "I am not Elijah." But whoever wishes to understand John as being Elijah, who had corrected all things, which is impossible, has Matthew 11:9-11 against him: "If you want to suppose that he is Elijah." . . . Thus, it is proved and demonstrated that our acceptance of the Word of Christ and our faith in him is more authoritative than God's commission and requirement of John. For Christ is not sent to the unbelieving, not because Christ lacks anything, but because he who rejects him is found to be lacking. This Elijah-Christ who has been sent to us from the Father has, during the time of his humanity, drawn to himself and saved the obedient ones who gave heed to and reverenced the commands of the Father. A Clear and Useful Instruction.[11]

John the Baptist as Elijah. Martin Luther: Otherwise, the simplicity and truth of the literal sense will be destroyed, and the authority of the entire Scripture will be put in danger, and there will be as many Elijahs and Christs as there are new prophets who will arise, for anyone

---

[10]Hammond, *Paraphrase and Annotations upon All the Books of the New Testament*, 87-88.

[11]CRR 2:74-75; citing Mt 13:55; Jn 7:40-44; Mt 17:12; Mk 9:12; Rom 5:18, 19; Jn 1:21; Mt 9:2, 22, 28; 15:28; Lk 5:31-35.

will be allowed to say, using the allegorical sense: "Behold, here is Elijah! Behold, here he is!" And so there will never be another Elijah who can be certain, if it is assumed that John is not he.

It remains for us to understand correctly the words of Christ in which he says, "Elijah indeed will come, and he will restore all things." Of course, these words in the simplest interpretation appear to prophesy of someone other than John. But to this the response can or, rather, ought to be made that Christ himself immediately in the same context corrects what he says—or, rather, [he corrects] the understanding of those who would understand his words as if concerning Elijah the Tishbite—saying, "Nevertheless, I tell you Elijah has already come." Why do we not weigh this word "I tell you, Elijah has already come" as being equal to the one "Elijah indeed will come"—especially since the Evangelists testify that on this basis the apostles understood that he had spoken concerning John, that is, that John was the Elijah about whom they had inquired out of Malachi, having been taught by the Pharisees. If, therefore, Christ himself says that the Elijah about whom the apostles asked out of Malachi has already come

and performed his office and suffered, why should we await another?

Now, it is also certain that Malachi is not foretelling the coming of the ancient Elijah whom Scripture names by the well-known surname "the Tishbite." But here it is not Elijah the Tishbite who is being prophesied, but simply some prophet Elijah. And so, from Malachi nothing definitive can be asserted about Elijah the Tishbite in support of the old opinion. Who are we, I ask, to add "Tishbite" when Scripture does not add it? We thus deceive ourselves by making that addition. Therefore, we should believe Christ and Gabriel that Malachi prophesied about John. That is firm and certain, whereas the opinion is an opinion.

Christ's word should therefore be understood in the "Elijah indeed will come," that is, "You heard the truth; the Pharisees spoke the truth: 'Elijah will come,' because the Scripture must be fulfilled. And so, Elijah must come and restore all things, for not one jot will pass from the law. . . . But what had to be done and fulfilled has, I tell you, already been done and fulfilled." ANNOTATIONS.[12]

---

[12]LW 67:314-15 (WA 38:660-61); citing Mt 5:18.

17:14-27 JESUS' AUTHORITY

¹⁴And when they came to the crowd, a man came up to him and, kneeling before him, ¹⁵said, "Lord, have mercy on my son, for he has seizures and he suffers terribly. For often he falls into the fire, and often into the water. ¹⁶And I brought him to your disciples, and they could not heal him." ¹⁷And Jesus answered, "O faithless and twisted generation, how long am I to be with you? How long am I to bear with you? Bring him here to me." ¹⁸And Jesus rebuked the demon,ᵃ and itᵇ came out of him, and the boy was healed instantly.ᶜ ¹⁹Then the disciples came to Jesus privately and said, "Why could we not cast it out?" ²⁰He said to them, "Because of your little faith. For truly, I say to you, if you have faith like a grain of mustard seed, you will say to this mountain, 'Move from here to there,' and it will move, and nothing will be impossible for you."ᵈ

²²As they were gatheringᵉ in Galilee, Jesus said to them, "The Son of Man is about to be delivered into the hands of men, ²³and they will kill him, and he will be raised on the third day." And they were greatly distressed.

²⁴When they came to Capernaum, the collectors of the two-drachma tax went up to Peter and said, "Does your teacher not pay the tax?" ²⁵He said, "Yes." And when he came into the house, Jesus spoke to him first, saying, "What do you think, Simon? From whom do kings of the earth take toll or tax? From their sons or from others?" ²⁶And when he said, "From others," Jesus said to him, "Then the sons are free. ²⁷However, not to give offense to them, go to the sea and cast a hook and take the first fish that comes up, and when you open its mouth you will find a shekel.ᶠ Take that and give it to them for me and for yourself."

a Greek *it*   b Greek *the demon*   c Greek *from that hour*   d Some manuscripts insert verse 21: *But this kind never comes out except by prayer and fasting*
e Some manuscripts *remained*   f Greek *stater*, a silver coin worth four drachmas or approximately one shekel

OVERVIEW: Jesus highlights the need for faith in the episode of the man and his demon-possessed son. Most of the narrative highlights the lack of faith that still remains among the disciples in spite of previous rebukes (e.g., Mt 6:30; 8:26; 14:31; 16:8). Wolfgang Musculus distinguishes among various types of Christian faith, which allows believers in Christ to be described as lacking faith. Other reformers use this narrative as an opportunity to reflect on the relationship of prayer and fasting to faith.

When Jesus returns to Capernaum, tax collectors seek him to question whether he will pay the temple tax. In his reply, Jesus establishes his divine sonship again through his statement and subsequent miracle. The Reformation commentators note the humility and power that Christ displays in this narrative. Jesus humbly submits himself to the temple tax, and yet by receiving the coin from the fish's mouth, Jesus could have usurped earthly establishments with his divine authority. Jesus says that he will pay the tax so that he does not cause others to stumble, a lesson he will drive home with his disciples in the next chapter (Mt 18:6, 7, 9). Calvin notes that Jesus' use of divine power helps the disciples to see that his kingdom and authority exist though he is cloaked in humility.

17:14-23 The Demoniac and the Need for Faith

SATAN ATTACKS IN MANY WAYS. JOHN CALVIN: Matthew describes a different sort of disease from what is described by Mark, for he says that the man was lunatic. But both agree as to these two points, that he was dumb, and that at certain intervals he became furious. The term *lunatic* is applied to those who, about the waning of the moon, are seized with epilepsy or afflicted with giddiness. I do not admit the fanciful notion of Chrysostom, that the word lunatic was invented by a trick of Satan in order to throw disgrace on the good creatures of God;[†] for we learn from undoubted experience that the course of the moon affects the increase or decline of these diseases. Yet this does not prevent Satan from mixing up his attacks with natural means. I am of opinion, therefore, that the man was not naturally deaf and dumb, but that Satan had taken possession of his tongue and ears; and that, as the weakness of his brain and nerves made him liable to epilepsy, Satan availed himself of this for aggravating the disease. The consequence was that he was exposed to danger on every hand and was thrown into violent convulsions, which left him lying on the ground in a fainting state and like a dead man.

Let us learn from this how many ways Satan has of injuring us, were it not that he is restrained by the hand of God. Our infirmities both of soul and body, which we feel to be innumerable, are so many darts with which Satan is supplied for wounding us. We are worse than stupid if a condition so wretched does not arouse us to prayer. But in this we see also an amazing display of the goodness of God that, though we are liable to such a variety of dangers, he surrounds us with his protection; particularly if we consider with what eagerness our enemy is bent on our destruction. We ought also to call to remembrance the consoling truth that Christ has come to bridle his rage and that we are safe in the midst of so many dangers, because our diseases are effectually counteracted by heavenly medicine.

We must attend also to the circumstance of the time. The father replies that his son had been subject to this grievous disease from his infancy. If Satan was permitted to exert his power to such an extent on a person of that tender age, what reason have not we to fear, who are continually exposing ourselves by our crimes to deadly strokes, who even supply our enemy with darts, and on whom he might justly be permitted to spend his rage, if it

were not kept under restraint by the astonishing goodness of God? COMMENTARY ON A HARMONY OF THE EVANGELISTS.[1]

THE EXCEEDING VALUE OF FAITH. MARTIN BUCER: In that he made the sick that were everywhere with him well, who is able to be led not by reason nor by allurements, nor threats, so that he allows them to heal for themselves? Truly, evil, depravity, perverseness, iniquity, moroseness, captiousness, sternness, obstinacy, all these are the fruit of infidelity, which binds wretched people to the control of Satan, such are restored from it. Just as in contrast, faith, as it renders children of God, so it produces those who are pure, virtuous, kind, gentle, courteous, obedient, followers of all good, that is, as I will say by a single word, those expressing the image of God.

After indeed he had so reproved them, as to repentance, if those among them who were able to be healed, he called out, he commanded that all those having weakness be brought to himself. And before he cured him, he exhorted the father to believe, affirming that all things are possible to those who believe. The one who was being admonished for a lack of faith also was he who was asking that his faith would be increased by him, although he confesses to believe in him. For he was saying, as Mark has, help my unbelief. Such a prayer is necessary for us all. For if faith is wholly sufficient, nothing will be lost for our good. But concerning the nature of faith, see above at length on chapter 8. . . .

That certainly it ought to heighten our diligence, so that from his strength and skills, now most powerfully when also Christ came to us through the Gospel itself, also came in this one [demon] so that he might drive it out, that we would be diligent. For he tests all things, so that he might be compelled to walk with Christ. But that Christ was allowing the poor one to be twisted before the eyes of the father and to be mangled for a while, so that

---

[1]CTS 2:322-23* (CO 45 493-94); citing Mk 9:17. [†]Chrysostom, *Homily 57 on Matthew*, NPNF[1] 10:340.

he might drive on the faith of the father, he made and might also teach those present that sometimes demons are permitted in someone, that is, in them also with respect to whom he fixed power to be brought; actually finally, if they sustain faith, of what sort by its work of all strength, adversaries to be children. COMMENTARY ON MATTHEW.[2]

WHAT CHRIST'S SHARP REBUKE TEACHES.

DAVID DICKSON: This sharp rebuking, both of the misbelieving Jews and also of the apostles, for depriving themselves of the use of the gift of miracles by their unbelief, teaches that nothing grieves our Lord more than peoples' unbelief, for this obstructs all the blessings which are appointed to come by faith; therefore, he upbraids the multitude and his disciples among the rest with this sharp rebuke, "O faithless generation." The longer that Christ has offered himself to a people or person and the more patience he has shown toward them, the more he is provoked by their misbelief to reject them, and departs from them and therefore says, "How long shall I be with you? How long shall I suffer you?" . . .

From Christ's answer, learn that unbelief may be lurking till it be brought forth in trial and, not being observed timeously by ourselves nor repented of in secret, may be brought forth before others to our shame openly, and so we are chastised for it, as the disciples were to whom Christ answers, "Because of your unbelief." Unbelief, and other unrepented sins, may mar the exercise of most excellent gifts; for the apostles could not cure this child, "Because of their unbelief." The least measure of the faith of miracles being put to work, upon the warrant of God's Word, if it be purged from unbelief, and from secure and carnal confidence, and be put forth in the own vigor—as the least grain of mustard seed does put forth the sharpness, taste, and smell of its own kind—it is able to effectuate the greatest works and to overcome the greatest difficulties and put the case

they seemed as impossible as the removing of mountains. Therefore says he, "If you have faith." A BRIEF EXPOSITION.[3]

THE NATURE OF FAITH CHRIST REQUIRES.

WOLFGANG MUSCULUS: In the first place, no one is inclined to doubt about the words of Christ, which are all most true; yet it is contemplated, about which kind of faith Christ is here speaking. For there is not just one kind of faith, but various kinds, also not of this opinion and excellence. But there are three kinds of faith assigned in the Scriptures, which differ much among themselves, although any one of them is represented by the designation "faith."

The first is this faith that such things as are set out in the Scripture are believed to be a certain thing; so that we hear in the Scriptures that God is, and that he is omnipotent, the Creator of all things, from whom all things suspend. And thus, also the rest of the things shown that Scripture mentions. This faith is called historical. The second kind is this faith that is credited by the promises of God, and is seized by mercy, even the grace of God in Christ Jesus. And this is called justifying faith. . . . The third is this that believes strongly that with God nothing is impossible, and the spirit is struck by a blowing of the Spirit for accomplishing an astonishing thing. And this is called miraculous faith. . . .

The third is not for all Christians but certain ones, and this is not for all time, but it has its own time, just as also its own reason. This is a single gift of the Holy Spirit, as is seen in 1 Corinthians 2. To another is given faith in the same Spirit. Because certainly this is not intended to speak about justifying faith, which is given not just to certain ones but to all the elect. This faith saves no one, does not alter hearts, does not necessarily have love joined, and therefore is such that it is also given to the impious. Concerning this, Christ stated this, when he said, "If you have faith like a mustard seed." . . . This is that which Chrysostom

---

[2]Bucer, *In Sacra Quatuor Evangelia, Enarrationes Perpetuae* (1536), 370.

[3]Dickson, *Brief Exposition* (1651), 204-6*.

also notes, and the material itself, about which Christ's sermon is declared. Therefore, it is also true that Christ said this, and at the same time is true, for us to be able to be believing, also if we do not do an astonishing thing, and only much greater, which if we move mountains through miraculous faith. But it is our perverse curiosity, as we prefer this faith, which he makes miraculous, that of which he justifies and saves us. Greater gifts are described. See 1 Corinthians 13. COMMENTARY ON MATTHEW.[4]

THE RELATIONSHIP BETWEEN FASTING AND PRAYER. JOHANN GERHARD: Christ truly asks for faith, prayer, and fasting for casting out demons, yet it was felt less, as if fasting deserves the fleeing of demons from him; the demon was afflicted and it fled. . . . Indeed, fasting stands out by them as equal, and estimated little by the devil; yet it is required by Christ because by it, man restores dependence to prayers. Therefore, through it nothing is done to fallen demons, nor deserves it.[†] . . . Therefore, Christ delivers such steps that fasting arouses prayer, prayer sharpens faith, and faith casts out demons by virtue of Christ. So that it has the same given place like 1 John 5:4. If truly faith casts out demons not by you, but by virtue or merit of Christ, by how much smaller by fasting such merit was ascribed, as that it even loses its value among the hypocrites. ANNOTATIONS ON MATTHEW.[5]

FAITH IS OBTAINED BY PRAYER AND FASTING. THOMAS CARTWRIGHT: Herein, being contrary to themselves, they are also in this directly contrary to our Savior Christ when they say, Besides faith, prayer and fasting are necessary to the throwing out of the devil; whereas our Savior says that if they had but so much faith as a grain of mustard seed, they should have done the cure, where therefore it was said that prayer and fasting

was needful, he means that by prayer, they should have asked faith wherewith to have gotten the upper hand, of their infidelity or staggering in that point of casting forth the devil. Which prayer, that it might have been more forcible, ought to have been accompanied with fasting; so that by this latter sentence, he requires faith, even the same which he did in the former. Only here he further tells them, how wanting this faith they might have obtained it, namely, if they had sought it by prayer and fasting. A CONFUTATION OF THE RHEMISTS TRANSLATION.[6]

WHY JESUS DISCUSSED HIS PASSION BEFOREHAND. JOHANNES BRENZ: "And when they had returned to Galilee. . . ." Christ often tells his disciples about his passion beforehand. He does this, first, so that they might learn that his kingdom will not be worldly, on this earth, for they were expecting that Christ would exercise his dominion over the world in visible majesty, and they were promising themselves kingdoms and principalities by means of Christ. That is why Christ preaches to them about his passion: to warn them that his kingdom will be spiritual, not worldly. Second, he teaches about his passion so that when it happens, they will not be made to stumble but rather retained in their [apostolic] office. And though Christ's diligence did not prevent his disciples from stumbling, flight, and denial—still, it was of great benefit to them after his resurrection for confirming their faith. This example has a warning for us as well. Even if it seems likely that our own admonitions are accomplishing nothing, we must all the same not give up and indulge in lazy napping. Instead, we must perform the office that has been mandated to us from heaven. There will be a time when its usefulness will be revealed. We will speak concerning Christ's passion itself elsewhere. MATTHEW 17:22-23.[7]

---

[4]Musculus, *In Evangelistam Matthaeum Commenarii* (1556), 485.
[5]Gerhard, *Annotationes Posthumae in Evangelium D. Matthaei* (1663), 764*; citing Is 58:3. [†]Gerhard here cites Chemnitz, *Harmoniae Evangelicae*, 1295-1304.

[6]Cartwright, *A Confutation of the Rhemists Translation . . . on the New Testament* (1618), 88.
[7]Brenz, *In Scriptum Apostoli et Evangelistae Matthaei*, 692.

17:24-27 The Son of Man Pays the Temple Tax

Christ's Power and Poverty Demonstrated. John Lightfoot: Christ is demanded the half shekel that every Israelite was bound by the law annually to pay for the redemption of his life. . . . Now the proper time of collecting that began a little before the Passover, as we have observed before out of the treatise Shekalim. And though it were now almost half a year past the Passover, yet is this the first time that Jesus had been at his own house in Capernaum, since the time of gathering that money had come in. This half shekel that every Israelite paid yearly went to the repair of the temple, and to the buying of things needful for the service there; Christ pays his church duties, therefore here, though, as his own words argue, he being the son of the great king, for whom that tribute was demanded, might have pleaded immunity; for kings take tribute of strangers, not of their own children. His paying it by a miraculous compassing of it out of a fish's mouth shows at once his divine power that could make all things serve his ends and his great care to discharge his due payments and to avoid offense; and withal, his poverty, when he is put to a miracle for such a little sum of money, for he would not work miracles where there was not need. His paying for Peter with him, was because he was of the same town, and so was under the same demand of payment, and he knew that he was in the same want of money. The other disciples were to pay in the place of their several houses. The Harmony, Chronicle, and Order of the New Testament.[8]

Lest We Offend the Magistrate. Martin Luther: Of his own accord he stoops down to the magistrate and says, "Lest we give offense to them." It is as if he were saying, "Since we are travelers in this kingdom and are compelled to live by their law, lest we appear to be seditious in their own house, let us obey them and give them what is owed. Nevertheless, in order to show that I am the Lord of all things, even of this kingdom, go and mint money in the fish's mouth and offer the shekel from his mouth." O marvelous coiner without gold or silver! He goes begging as a pauper and shows himself able to make mounts of gold from the mouth of any fish, if he should wish. Therefore, this subjection to the magistrate is something freely rendered. It is as if the greatest king in the world willingly entered a leper house and gave a small coin in accord with the regulations of the hospital, while the hospitaller meanwhile remained unaware how great a king he had within his own realm. Annotations on Matthew.[9]

Christ Pays the Tax as a Servant. John Calvin: "Does not your master pay?" Some think that the collectors of the tribute intended to throw blame on Christ, as if he were claiming exemption from the common law. For my own part, as men of that class are insolent and abusive, I interpret these words as having been spoken by way of reproach. It was customary for every man to be enrolled in his own city; but we know that Christ had no fixed habitation in one place. Those people therefore inquire if he be exempted from the law on the ground of his frequent removals from place to place.

"He says, Yes." Peter's reply contains a modest excuse to satisfy them, "he will pay," says he; from which we infer that Christ had formerly been accustomed to pay, for Peter promises it as a thing about which there was no doubt. That they address him rather than the other disciples was, as I conjecture, because Christ lived with him; for if all had occupied the same habitation, the demand would have been made on all alike. . . .

"What do you think, Simon?" In this Christ gave a proof of his divinity, by showing that nothing was unknown to him. But what is the object of his discourse? Is it to exempt himself

---

[8]Lightfoot, *The Harmony, Chronicle and Order of the New Testament* (1655), 42; citing Ex 30:13.

[9]LW 67:321 (WA 38:667).

and his followers from subjection to the laws? Some explain it thus, that Christians have a right to be exempted, but that they voluntarily subject themselves to the ordinary government because otherwise human society cannot be maintained. To me, however, the meaning appears to be more simple: for there was danger lest the disciples might think that Christ had come in vain, because, by paying tribute, he cut off the hope of deliverance; and therefore he simply affirms that he pays tribute, solely because he voluntarily refrains from exercising his right and power. Hence it is inferred that this takes nothing from his reign. But why does he not openly claim his right? It is because his kingly power was unknown to the collectors of the tribute. For, though his kingdom be spiritual, still we must maintain that as he is the only Son of God, he is also the heir of the whole world, so that all things ought to be subject to him, and to acknowledge his authority. The meaning, therefore, is that God has not appointed kings and established governments over mankind in such a manner as to place him, who is the Son, in the same rank indiscriminately with others, but yet that, of his own accord, he will be a servant along with others, till the glory of his kingdom be displayed. COMMENTARY ON A HARMONY OF THE EVANGELISTS.[10]

---

[10]CTS 2:369-70 (CO 45:522).

CHRISTIAN OBLIGATIONS AND LIBERTY.

DAVID CHYTRAEUS: Christ, numbering the money owed by the temple to the Roman magistrate, teaches both that the church must fulfill all worldly obligations and that the right of the "temple" must be defended. The latter pertains to the principal goods, namely true doctrine and true worship.

Let the doctrine concerning Christian liberty be repeated here, and let the distinction between civil and Christian liberty be held in mind.

Christian liberty is liberty from sin, from God's wrath, from the curse of the law, from the ceremonies and civil laws of Moses, and from ceremonies that are adiaphora, except in the case of scandal. "He who commits sin is a slave of sin, but if the Son should set you free, you will be truly free." "Therefore, stand in the liberty in which Christ has called you."

Political liberty is the ability to manage one's own affairs and to perform works of the body according to one's own will, and not be compelled to do anything against decent laws. On the other hand, political servitude means one's body and affairs are outside one's use and will. In this way, Joseph was a slave of Potiphar and nonetheless was supremely free in terms of Christian liberty. COMMENTARY ON MATTHEW.[11]

---

[11]Chytraeus, *Commentarius in Matthaeum Evangelistam* (1558), 294; Jn 8:36; Gal 5:1.

18:1-35 TRUE GREATNESS, TRUE FORGIVENESS

At that time the disciples came to Jesus, saying, "Who is the greatest in the kingdom of heaven?" [2]And calling to him a child, he put him in the midst of them [3]and said, "Truly, I say to you, unless you turn and become like children, you will never enter the kingdom of heaven. [4]Whoever humbles himself like this child is the greatest in the kingdom of heaven.

[5]"Whoever receives one such child in my name receives me, [6]but whoever causes one of these little ones who believe in me to sin,[a] it would be better for him to have a great millstone fastened around his neck and to be drowned in the depth of the sea.

[7]"Woe to the world for temptations to sin![b] For it is necessary that temptations come, but woe to the one by whom the temptation comes! [8]And if your hand or your foot causes you to sin, cut it off and throw it away. It is better for you to enter life crippled or lame than with two hands or two feet to be thrown into the eternal fire. [9]And if your eye causes you to sin, tear it out and throw it away. It is better for you to enter life with one eye than with two eyes to be thrown into the hell[c] of fire.

[10]"See that you do not despise one of these little ones. For I tell you that in heaven their angels always see the face of my Father who is in heaven.[d] [12]What do you think? If a man has a hundred sheep, and one of them has gone astray, does he not leave the ninety-nine on the mountains and go in search of the one that went astray? [13]And if he finds it, truly, I say to you, he rejoices over it more than over the ninety-nine that never went astray. [14]So it is not the will of my[e] Father who is in heaven that one of these little ones should perish.

[15]"If your brother sins against you, go and tell him his fault, between you and him alone. If he listens to you, you have gained your brother. [16]But if he does not listen, take one or two others along with you, that every charge may be established by the evidence of two or three witnesses. [17]If he refuses to listen to them, tell it to the church. And if he refuses to listen even to the church, let him be to you as a Gentile and a tax collector. [18]Truly, I say to you, whatever you bind on earth shall be bound in heaven, and whatever you loose on earth shall be loosed[f] in heaven. [19]Again I say to you, if two of you agree on earth about anything they ask, it will be done for them by my Father in heaven. [20]For where two or three are gathered in my name, there am I among them."

[21]Then Peter came up and said to him, "Lord, how often will my brother sin against me, and I forgive him? As many as seven times?" [22]Jesus said to him, "I do not say to you seven times, but seventy-seven times.

[23]"Therefore the kingdom of heaven may be compared to a king who wished to settle accounts with his servants.[g] [24]When he began to settle, one was brought to him who owed him ten thousand talents.[h] [25]And since he could not pay, his master ordered him to be sold, with his wife and children and all that he had, and payment to be made. [26]So the servant[i] fell on his knees, imploring him, 'Have patience with me, and I will pay you everything.' [27]And out of pity for him, the master of that servant released him and forgave him the debt. [28]But when that same servant went out, he found one of his fellow servants who owed him a hundred denarii,[j] and seizing him, he began to choke him, saying, 'Pay what you owe.' [29]So his fellow servant fell down and pleaded with him, 'Have patience with me, and I will pay you.' [30]He refused and went and put him in prison until he should pay the debt. [31]When his fellow servants saw what had taken place, they were greatly distressed, and they went and reported to their master all that had taken place. [32]Then his master summoned him and said to him, 'You wicked servant! I forgave you all that debt because you pleaded with me. [33]And should not you have had mercy on your fellow servant, as I had mercy on you?' [34]And in anger his master

delivered him to the jailers,ᵏ until he should pay all his debt. ³⁵So also my heavenly Father will do to *every one of you, if you do not forgive your brother from your heart."*

a Greek *causes . . . to stumble;* also verses 8, 9   b Greek *stumbling blocks*   c Greek *Gehenna*   d Some manuscripts add verse 11: *For the Son of Man came to save the lost*   e Some manuscripts *your*   f Or *shall have been bound . . . shall have been loosed*   g Or *bondservants;* also verses 28, 31   h A *talent* was a monetary unit worth about twenty years' wages for a laborer   i Or *bondservant;* also verses 27, 28, 29, 32, 33   j A *denarius* was a day's wage for a laborer   k Greek *torturers*

OVERVIEW: Jesus responds to the disciples' inquiry into the greatest in the kingdom by providing an extending lesson on humility and mutual love for each other. Instead of using himself as an example as he does later (cf. Mt 20:20-28), Jesus here refers to a child.

A company of disciples can aid one another or serve as a stumbling block to each other. Jesus' response highlights the need for those in the kingdom to avoid giving offense and instead to further the glory of God and to act out of sincere love for neighbor. Martin Bucer explains that to give offense is to have attitudes or actions that can stymie someone else's spiritual growth. Calvin concurs and adds that disciples should go to great lengths to avoid causing an offense among fellow believers.

The reformers often discuss aspects of God's providential care for his children. Though Jesus' disciples face various hardships because of their humble position, the heavenly Father cares for them and will preserve them.

Jesus' address moves from those who would offend his "little ones" to the disciples themselves. For the reformers, Jesus' teaching lays out principles about how reconciliation should be sought and forgiveness granted. Menno Simons warns against obstinacy in seeking reconciliation or in granting forgiveness. In a move from the smallest audience ("in private") to discuss the grievance to the largest appropriate context ("tell it to the church"), Jesus instructs his followers how to seek restoration.

The Protestant reformers vary in their interpretation of what kinds of sinful behaviors fit this church-discipline process. For example, some limit the offenses to be dealt with corporately to offenses that offend the whole church body, not just individuals. Other interpreters include personal offenses as well. There is also variance on the administration of this churchly discipline. Some commentators contend that the elders, not the entire church, should be responsible for the rebuke of the erring party. Others hold that the final court of appeals for brotherly offenses is the whole assembly, though communication may come through the bishop. Additionally, some comments stress the role of individual Christians in correcting offenses in connection with the authority of the corporate body. As Wolfgang Musculus emphasizes, the whole process is to be a loving display of the care for each other's souls.

Peter's question on the extent of forgiveness sets the context for a parable on forgiveness. Luther contends that Jesus' parable portrays the forgiveness of sins that is an axiom in the kingdom of God. Niels Hemmingsen draws similarly on the parable to show how sins like debts demand payment and that debt can accrue to an insurmountable level. The high standard set by the parable is that those who have been forgiven much must be gracious in extending forgiveness to others.

18:1-14 Jesus, the Faithful Shepherd of His Sheep

THE WEAKNESS OF A CHILD. MARTIN LUTHER: [Christ] not only bears with this foolishness of theirs in kindness, but he even takes it up as an opportunity to speak and teach about his kingdom. For there was among this people the very deeply rooted opinion that the kingdom of the Messiah would be temporal and worldly, to such an extent that it was impossible for it to be removed from all of their hearts. He therefore opposes this opinion, powerfully and at length, in order to uproot this carnal idea from the hearts of his disciples. And, calling a child to him, he engages in personification, so that by means of this demonstration what he is about to say would stick the more firmly to [their minds]. It is as if he were saying, "I see that your carnal notion [will] not be sufficiently changed by mere words. I am therefore setting this child before you so that you will remember him hereafter and always. Behold, here is a child. Tell me, is he fit for the worldly, or temporal, kingdom of which you are (no doubt) dreaming? It would be a poor kingdom—or, rather, it would be no kingdom at all—if it had to be ruled by this child. But just as much as this child is fit to rule over a worldly kingdom, even so it is inappropriate to think that my kingdom is of this world. For the kingdom that I am establishing is of such a kind that all the wise of the world understand much less about it than this child understands about a kingdom of the world. Therefore, your opinion and speculation about a kingdom of the world must be laid aside when you wish to speak about my kingdom. For my kingdom will be of such a kind that in it you must be children who are ruled and do not rule, just as in the kingdom of the world this child does not rule but is ruled."

"In sum: The kingdom I am originating is different from a worldly kingdom. In it, I shall not make you kings or wise or righteous people in this world, but foolish subjects, sinners in the sight of the world, just as this child is ruled, foolish, and subject to the rod. Your way of thinking about my kingdom must, therefore, be different from the common thinking. For I am making you not kings, but children; not wise, but fools; not righteous, but heretics and fit for the fire." Annotations.[1]

What Aspects of Children We Should Imitate. Cornelius Jansen: "And he said, 'Truly, I say to you, unless you should be converted'"— converted from this ambitious intention and desire

for primacy and honor. "And become," with firm purpose of mind, "as little children are"—in stature, age, and nature, that is to say, in simplicity, innocence, and humility of mind. For thus Christ himself explains his statement in verse 4. He does not, therefore, wish us to imitate children in all things, since they also possess great foolishness and other vices. But we are to imitate them insofar as they are admirably modest, simple, and candid, unacquainted with all ambition, haughtiness, and jealousy. They put themselves before none; they yield to all. They think great things of others, little of themselves. Hilary[†] adds more: "Children follow their father, love their mother, do not know how to desire evil, care nothing for wealth, are not insolent, do not hate, do not lie, believe what is told them, and suppose whatever they hear is true." These things are indeed true, yet most do not seem to be Christ's aim here. "You will not enter into the kingdom of heaven"—in it, you will not be the first, but will instead be nothing, "since no unclean thing will enter into it."[‡] Christ does not mean that they are constrained by a particular mortal sin, but rather that they must be wholly reformed from the jealous desire for primacy as from a stain.

"Whoever therefore may humble"—not their head, knees, words, or garments, for hypocrites can make a show of these things too—but humble "themselves." This means to have such a heart and mind that one truly must be considered to be "like this little child," the smallest and most humble in both body and soul, utterly free from all haughtiness, pride, and desire for privilege. Such a person is perfectly humble, like little children; such a person is an exemplar of perfect humility and "littleness" in the whole makeup of body and soul. "This one is great in the kingdom of heaven." "Great" here in fact means "greatest," for whoever is the least here will be the greatest there.

"And whoever should receive," namely, with hospitality. By this one office of humility every kind of beneficence is signified. "One such little one," meaning whoever should humble himself as a child. For by "children" Christ speaks about those who are metaphorically represented rather than

---

[1]LW 67:323-24 (WA 60:66-67).

about the metaphors or children themselves, as is clear from the parallel verse that follows. "In my name"—for my sake, because he is mine, having emptied himself for my sake. "He receives me"—I reckon it just as highly as if he had received me myself, and I will reward him accordingly, since these [little ones] are so like me. COMMENTARY ON THE GOSPEL OF MATTHEW.[2]

JUDGING THE KINGDOM BY WORLDLY STANDARDS. RICHARD TAVERNER: First therefore you shall understand that an example of the natural ignorance, blindness, and infirmity of humankind is here set forth in the disciples of Christ, which as yet measured the kingdom of heaven after the fashion of the kingdom of the world. The disciples come therefore to Christ and ask him, Who is the greater man in the kingdom of heaven? Surely, according to the mind of ancient doctors, this was a certain human affection, which crept into the apostles' minds and as it were a prick of envy and of ambition. They had heard of the kingdom of heaven, they had seen three apostles led apart with Christ into the mountain that is to wit, Peter, James and John, they had heard how the keys of the kingdom of heaven were given to Peter, and how it was said to him, Blessed are you Simon the son of Jonah. . . . For these and such other things which as yet they did not perfectly understand, they had a little privy grudge and envy at Peter, says to him as they thought the principality of the kingdom of heaven was appointed where nevertheless they perceived he was younger in years then they. They came therefore, as I said, to Jesus and asked him who shall have the chief authority in the kingdom of heaven? For it could not be yet driven out of their heads, but that there should be such like dignities and powers in the heavenly and spiritual kingdom as they saw in prince's courts of this world. Our Savior Christ, therefore, so that he would clean banish this carnal affection and utterly

expel the same out of their minds, calls a certain child unto him, whom he sets in the minds of his disciples, the child being yet very tender of age and but a babe, void of all affections either of ambition or of envy, simple, pure, innocent, and living by the only guide and conduct of nature. This child being thus set among them, our Savior says in this wise unto them. Verily, only be converted and be made as children; it is not possible for you to come into the kingdom of heaven. For declaration of this text, you shall understand, that Christ did not here command the apostles, that they should have the age of children but the innocence, and the thing that the children do possess because of their childhood, they should possess by their industry, so that in malice they might be children, but not in wisdom. THE GOSPELS WITH BRIEF SERMONS.[3]

JESUS' LESSON OF HUMILITY. JOHN BOYS: The sum whereof is briefly this, he that in Christ's church is most servant is the greatest, and he that is most lordly, the least; or he that is least in his own conceit is the greatest in God's eye; the least in this kingdom of heaven which is present, shall be the greatest in that kingdom of heaven which is to come. It is certain that there arose a disputation among which of them should be greatest, and is yet to cloak their ambitious pride, they do not ask who shall be greatest among us, but indefinitely "who is the greatest in the kingdom of heaven," understanding by "the kingdom of heaven" the kingdom of Christ in this world, for they carnally conceived that Christ after his resurrection would restore the kingdom of Israel and so reign as a monarch upon earth, and therefore they request to sit next to him at his right hand and on his left in his kingdom. . . . Doubtless he knew who they were which ambitiously contended to be greatest in his kingdom, yet he called all his apostles, as being assured that his lesson of humility was exceedingly necessary for them all. It is reported in the chapter 20 of this Gospel how James and John only desired to sit on

---

[2]Jansen, *Commentarius in Evangelium secundum Matthaeum*, 326-28; citing Rev 21:27. †Hilary of Poitiers, *Commentary on Matthew*, FC 125:193. †The original text reads Rev 12 rather than Rev 21, but this is clearly a typo.

[3]Taverner, *On Saynt Andrewes Day: The Gospels with Brief Sermons* (1542), xxxvii-xxxviii.

his right hand and on his left in his kingdom; yet Christ admonished them all, and said, "You know that the princes of the nations have dominion over them, and they that are great exercise authority upon them; it shall not be so with you, but whosoever will be chief among you, let him be your servant." THE THIRD PART FROM ST. JOHN BAPTIST'S NATIVITY.[4]

STRIVING FOR REWARD WITHOUT PAIN.

THEODORE BEZA: They strive for the reward before they have taken any pain; and whereas they should have helped and reverenced one another, they were ambitious and despisers of their brothers. See Matthew 19:14 and 1 Corinthians 14:20. . . . [Jesus said,] "Verily I say to you, except you be converted and become as little children, you shall not enter into the kingdom of heaven." Not in lack of discretion, but that they be not vainglorious, seeking to advance themselves to worldly honors. He calls them little children now which humble themselves with all humility and subjection. THE BIBLE AND HOLY SCRIPTURES CONTAINED.[5]

THE OFFENSE OF HINDERING SOMEONE'S FAITH.

MARTIN BUCER: Here Christ speaks not of such offenses as the good are wont to give unto the evil, but of such as the evil give unto the good, or to those that endeavor to become good and godly. These offenses—as may be gathered by the places of Scripture which make mention thereof—are what things soever be spoken or done, that give any occasion of sin, either because they are evil of themselves or else because they are not discretely done and according to Christian charity. . . . That is to say, when we so behave ourselves in all things which we either speak or do, that they may make to edification and appear to be done in the spirit of Christ. Whereupon we may take that to be an offense, whatsoever we say or do that makes not to the furtherance of God's

glory and the salvation of our brethren, proceeding of a sound and unfeigned faith and ordered according to sincere and true love. . . .

For as much therefore as Christ so sorely detests offenses and cries woe unto the world because of offenses, woe unto the one by whom offense comes; we must, with all diligence, take heed both in these things and in all other, that we be offensive to no one, but especially the little ones; I mean not in age only, but in faith and understanding also. The perfect knowledge of God and of Christ is life everlasting. Whatsoever therefore may either hinder or obscure it by any means, let it neither be spoke nor done of us. But let us remove all such things to the uttermost of our powers. And let us provoke them both by exhortations and examples, that they express and declare those things in their life, giving no place herein either to their own affections or others', fain that it is better to be drowned in the sea than to give offense. MIND AND EXPOSITION.[6]

AVOID SPIRITUAL OFFENSES.

JOHN CALVIN: Now as there are various kinds of offenses, it will be proper to explain generally what is meant by offending. If anyone through our fault either stumbles or is drawn aside from the right course or hindered in it, we are said to offend him. Whoever then desires to escape that fearful punishment which Christ denounces, let them stretch out their hand to the little ones who are despised by the world and let them kindly assist them in keeping the path of duty. . . .

This passage may be explained in two ways. It may be taken actively, as meaning that Christ pronounces a curse on the authors of offenses; and then by the term "world" we must understand all unbelievers. Or it may be taken passively, as meaning that Christ deplores the evils which he perceives to be rapidly coming on "the world on account of offenses"; as if he had said, that no plague will be more destructive or attended by more fearful calamities than the alarm or desertion

---

[4]Boys, *The Third Part from St. John Baptist's Nativity to the Last Holy Day* (1610), 105-9.
[5]Beza, *La Bible, qui est Toute La Saincte Escriture*, 9.

[6]Bucer, *The Mind and Exposition* (1566), 49-50, 65-66.

of many on account of offenses. The latter meaning is more appropriate. . . .

To awaken more powerfully their care and anxiety, our Lord reminds his disciples that there is no possibility of walking but in the midst of various offenses. . . . It must be held by us as a fixed principle that it is the will of God to leave his people exposed to offenses, in order to exercise their faith and to separate believers, as the refuse and the chaff, from the pure wheat. . . .

After having exhorted his disciples to beware of offenses, he again breaks out against those who occasion them. . . . He adds that neither a right eye nor a right hand ought to be spared if they occasion offense to us; for I explain these words as added for the purpose of amplification. Their meaning is that we ought to be so constant and so zealous in opposing offenses that we would rather choose to pluck out our eyes, or cut off our hands, than give encouragement to offenses. COMMENTARY ON A HARMONY OF THE EVANGELISTS.[7]

THE ANGELIC MINISTERS OF GOD'S PROVIDENTIAL CARE. HUGO GROTIUS: Since Christ was accustomed to speak such that his speaking was to be understood best by the Jews, and Jews old and young believed that individuals, at least those of the pious, were given by God to the care of an angel. This belief also remained for Christians, as is clear from Acts 12:15 and many older Scriptures. Approval of this opinion by Christ is completely probable. It is certainly sure that ministering angels are of divine providence. Whence it seems credible through steps of providence for duties of angels to be distinguished. By universal providence, it is in some way common that God preserves and also directs civil societies of humankind, which we call the republic. But these things, by a great consensus both of Jews and Christians of old, connected the same attributes to be the angels from Daniel, and this just as beyond all controversy Clement of Alexandria[†] shows. But just as the matter of kingdoms is universal to the state, so the matter of individuals God ordains for the state of kingdoms in most cases. But states of this sort are taken away, these which in true faith consecrate it to God, and in the same manner estimate their property as for themselves. Just as God supports those with a special providence, so he appears to present individuals with ministering angels, who evidently help the steps and efforts of their own, either continually or certainly until they have arrived at the clearest possession of their own divine Spirit. ANNOTATIONS ON MATTHEW.[8]

CHRIST SEEKS AND SHEPHERDS HIS CHILDREN. JUAN DE VALDÉS: Christ proceeds to show, in relation to his children, that he values and esteems them, however insignificant they may be; and in these words tells three things. First, that the main design of his coming into the world was "to save that which is lost." He means to give eternal life to those who lost it in Adam. And here it is right to say that just as through Adam's disobedience we all died, so through Christ's obedience we all rise again; though the resurrection will only be glorious for those who believe that they have died in Adam and that they have risen again in Christ, they will study to live in the present life as dead and as risen again, imitating that life which has to be lived in the life eternal, the pattern of which, as to purity, goodness, sincerity, truth, and fidelity, and so on, we see in Christ.

Second, that it is the joy of Christ's heart that every one of those whom he leads to believe that they have died in Christ and that they are risen in Christ do study to live as dead and as risen again. Christ compares this his joy to that of the shepherd, who, going in search of a sheep that he had lost, finds it, so that the comparison of the shepherd may agree in this, that just as the shepherd goes diligently in search of the lost sheep, and when he finds it, rejoices over it, so Christ came diligently in search of those who are his sheep,

---

[7]CTS 2:336-38 (CO 45:502-3).

[8]Grotius, *Annotationes in Novum Testamentum . . . ad Matth. I–XIII*, 1:83-84. [†]Clement of Alexandria, *Eclogae ex Scripturis propheticis* XLI, PG 9:717-18.

predestinated to life eternal, who were lost, wandering among people of the world, condemned to eternal death, and it rejoiced his heart when he found them, having died for them, and having risen again for them; and he rejoices continuously with every one of them who accept his death and his resurrection for their own.

Third, that it is the will of God that these children, whom Christ sought and found and whom he seeks and finds, should in no wise perish; understanding that they would be in danger of perishing were they to be despised, scandalized, and maltreated by others; especially by those who are preeminent in Christian life; to whom I understand that Christ here principally addresses himself; admonishing them that they should not despise or scandalize his children when they shall be infirm and weak in faith. COMMENTARY UPON THE GOSPEL OF ST. MATTHEW.[9]

18:15-20 *If Your Brother or Sister Sins Against You*

MAINTAINING GENUINE CHRISTIAN FAITHFULNESS. MENNO SIMONS: These words of Christ teach, in the first place, that if anyone sins against his brother through negligence, infirmity, thoughtlessness, inexperience, or any mistake, that the latter should not hate him in his heart for it, nor copy his transgression. But out of genuinely brotherly faithfulness he should admonish and in love reprove him, lest his dear brother fall into greater error and perish but in this way be restored; and he, as Moses says, be not guilty for his sake. It is the nature and anointing of all true Christians not to hate any for wrong done but to seek with all their hearts how they may teach the wrongdoer and lead him on the straight path of love. Therefore, a true Christian is a stranger to hatred.

In the second place, these words teach us that he who has transgressed should receive the admonition of his brother in love and be reconciled. . . . Yes; no less is it the nature and disposition of true believers that those who are born of the holy seed of divine faith, when they trespass against a brother, have neither peace nor rest in their hearts as long as they are not reconciled by a sincere reconciliation with him in Christ Jesus. . . . Although the first transgression may not of itself be so fatal, yet it causes the transgressor, if he regard not love, to become estranged and carnal, so that he must bear severe punishment on account of his contrariness. For it is evident that he wrongs his brother, rejects the admonition of love, acts contrary to Christian charity, despises the church of God, rejects the Word of the Lord, and that he would rather continue unreproved in his transgression through his stubbornness, would rather walk in the crooked paths of wrong; yes, forsake the kingdom and people of Christ, than to humble his stubborn, proud flesh and be reconciled in love, according to the Word of the Lord, with his brother against whom he has transgressed. . . .

In the third place, these words teach us if the transgressing brother will receive in love the brotherly admonition of his wronged brother, be humbly reconciled, and so repudiate his wrongdoing, then he must no more remember, but sincerely forgive him; even if he has sinned against him more grievously than is the case. Even as God, for Jesus' sake, forgives all of our sins; so must we also in Christ forgive our neighbor all his transgressions which he has committed against us, small and great. And we should not, under any circumstance, indulge in hatred or vengeance against him, even though he should never reform. . . . From all of which it is more than clear that these three several admonitions of which Christ speaks (first, between him and you alone; second, before witnesses, and third, before the church) must not be understood of all the offensive, carnal sinners, upon whom the eternal sentence of death is already pronounced, but of the transgression of brother against brother. THE COMPLETE WRITINGS.[10]

---

[9]Valdés, *Commentary upon the Gospel of St. Matthew*, 315-16.

[10]Simons, *Complete Writings*, 980-81.

OFFENSES AGAINST THE COMMUNITY. HULD-RYCH ZWINGLI: Immediately preceding these words, he spoke of an offense and that no member (i.e., no brother), be it our eye, hand, or foot, ought to be so precious to us that we would allow it to remain next to us to offend us. Rather, should it not stop offending us, we are to cut it off just like a foul, rotten member which is cut off so as not to infect and spoil the entire body. Thus, Christ says, first, "If your brother sins against you." "Against you" means "against you, O church or community." For this is the manner in which God speaks, namely, he addresses the multitudes in the singular, Deuteronomy 32:7 and Psalm 81:9-10 and in many other instances: "Israel, if you hear me, no new god shall arise in you." "In you" means as much as, "among you, O children of Israel." Similarly, "against you" here means "against the church."

He says second, "Whoever sins." From this we deduce that the ban is only to be imposed upon one who sins. Now you heard shortly before which sin is to be understood here, namely, the one which offends and infects like a hereditary disease. But of other sins, which do not offend openly, Christ spoke to Peter and through him to all of us, "You ought to forgive your brother seventy times seven." Indeed, we ought to forgive one who oppresses and one who is banned, should he repent and change his ways. AN EXPOSITION OF THE ARTICLES.[11]

THE ROLE OF ELDERS IN CHURCH CONFLICT. FRANCIS JOHNSON: To which end also consider both the phrases there used and the party spoken unto. Touching the phrases, first, those words, "Tell the church, and if he hear not the church" . . . from which a reason may be gathered thus: they are to be told that are to be heard. And they are to be heard and they are to admonish the offenders so brought. But the elders are to admonish them; therefore the elders are to be told and to be heard. Now that the elders are to admonish such, see 2 Chronicles 19:8-10 with 1 Thessalonians 5:12-14.

That the elders are to be heard, see also, 1 Thessalonians 5:12 with Deuteronomy 17:11-13, Luke 10:16, and Hebrews 13:17. And that the elders were told in Israel, see Deuteronomy 19:16-17, 21:19-20; 22:15-17; and Deuteronomy 25:7-8 with Matthew 5:22, Acts 6:11-12. . . .

Then also for the other phrases, where it is said, "Let him be to you as a heathen and publican," it may be understood thus: You may now (having used the former means) deal with him, as you may bring him before the Roman magistrates, to have your right by their means against him. For now the Jews lived under the Romans, who though they left the Jews to their own laws for religion, yet admitted them in dealing one with another for right in their matters, to come to their judgment seat, as may be seen by that which is written Acts 18:12-15 and by diverse particular records in other histories. A SHORT TREATISE.[12]

THE IMPORTANT ROLE OF THE CHURCH IN DISCIPLINE. THOMAS CARTWRIGHT: [Some] tie this key of excommunication unto the bishop's girdle alone; which is against the mind of our Savior Christ and circumstance of the place; but if they will say so, and speak so strangely, they must warrant it with some other places of Scriptures, where the church is taken for one, which is as much to say, one man is many, one member is a body, one alone is a company. And beside this strangeness of speech, it destroys the sovereignty of the medicine which our Savior Christ prepared for such a festered sore, as would neither be healed by private admonition, neither with admonition before one or two witnesses. For as the fault grows, so our Savior Christ would have the number of those before whom he should be checked and rebuked likewise grow. Therefore, from a private admonition he rises unto the admonition before two or three, and from them to the church, which if we should say, it is but one, so that a single bandage should be laid upon a dangerous wound.

---

[11]Zwingli, *The Defense of the Reformed Faith*, 1:226-27; citing Mt 18:7-9, 22.

[12]Johnson, *A Short Treatise Concerning the Exposition of Those Words of Christ* (1611), B2*.

And therefore, our Savior does not rise from two to one—for that were not to rise but to fall, nor to proceed, but to go backward—but to many. But Paul is the best interpreter, who in a case of excommunication declares that the same is to be done in the presence and with consent of the assembly, whereof the party which is to be excommunicated, is a member. . . . I conclude, therefore, that to tell the church is not to tell the bishop or minister of the word only, but a company which has oversight of the church; by whom, or by whose mouth, which is the minister of the word, the rest of the body of the church is to be advertised; to the end that the sword of excommunication cut not without their counsel and consent. Whereupon it is evident that the places of these fathers, which give power to the bishops to bind and to loose, do not restrain it unto them, shutting out the rest of the church, which might be showed by many testimonies out of them, if the same were needful. A CONFUTATION OF THE RHEMISTS TRANSLATION.[13]

THE PRIESTHOOD AND KINGDOM OF CHRIST.

ROBERT BROWNE: First, Christ has given power to every Christian to retain the sins of every brother who he knows to trespass against him and not to forgive him, except he sees him repent. So that if any person wants this power, he is not to be counted a Christian. And this power reaches so far, not only for open but even for private offenses, to judge and take anyone for a heathen and a publican, if he will not be reformed. Now this liberty and power, every Christian must hold, or else he is the servant of human beings and not of Christ. If then a particular Christian cannot want it, how shall the whole church be without it and yet be named the church of Christ? Every particular Christian is a king and a priest unto God, a king because he holds the scepter of God's Word to judge the offenders, a priest because in every place he offers incense and a pure offering to the name of the

Lord as it is Malachi. So then he is utterly without the kingdom and priesthood of Christ that liberty be denied him, I mean of judging and rebuking the particular offender and forsaking their fellowship if they will not be reformed. How much more shall the church be without this kingdom and priesthood of Christ and so without Christ himself, if it want this liberty and power. Likewise we showed before every Christian has power severely to forsake wicked fellowship and not to company together with wicked brethren. . . .

For they have not the keys of the kingdom of heaven to bind and loose, to retain or remit people's sins, and therefore what right can they have in the kingdom of Christ? If they cannot openly and particularly rebuke, how shall they openly and particularly bind? For being full retained as brethren in the church, how shall they pronounce them to be bound in heaven? How shall they shut the gates of heaven against those whom still they keep in the bosom of the church? AN ANSWER TO MASTER CARTWRIGHT.[14]

DISCIPLINE AND THE CARE FOR SOULS.

WOLFGANG MUSCULUS: These words are added as a confirmation and emphasis, no, even a kind of augmentation of what went before. The emphasis lies in the fact that he says, "Again I say to you, if two of you. . . ." These words seem to relate to confirming that phrase where he said, "Go and reprove him in private; and if he will hear you, you will have won your brother." For we find that statement more striking than his assertion that the person who holds in contempt the church in a stubborn way will be condemned in the heavens also. Hence for the sake of confirming and emphasizing it, he says, "Again I say to you, if two of you will agree. . . ." Obviously, the agreement of two people in a matter pertaining to the salvation of a brother is of such great importance to God. And the fact that he says, "On anything that they will ask," augments it. It is as if he were saying, "Not

---

[13]Cartwright, *A Confutation of the Rhemists Translation . . . on the New Testament* (1618), 92.

[14]Browne, *An Answere to Master Cartwright* (1585), 38-39; citing Mal 1:11.

only in that case about which I just now spoke, but in anything. . . ."

Here the love and concord of believers is commended to us, since it is so valuable to the Father in heaven. Without it our request is not efficacious. There is a clarification in the fact that he does not simply say, "Where two or three of you are gathered," but adds, "in my name." There is an explanation given in the fact that he says, "There I am in their midst." For, he himself is our mediator, through whom we obtain all things. Our faith is so weak that we can barely believe that what things a few of us ask for can be obtained from the Father. But it must be recognized that Christ alone counts more to the Father than all the countless hordes of mortals. COMMENTARY ON MATTHEW.[15]

18:21-35 Jesus Teaches About Forgiveness

THE FORGIVENESS OF SINS IN THE KINGDOM. MARTIN LUTHER: We have often taught that the kingdom of God wherein he reigns by the gospel is nothing else but such a state or government, wherein is mere forgiveness of sins; so that where such a government is not, wherein sin is pardoned, neither is there the gospel nor kingdom. Wherefore those two kingdoms are to be separated one, wherein sins are punished, and another wherein they are forgiven, or wherein the law is exacted, and wherein that which is due by the law, is remitted. In the kingdom of God, where he reigns by the gospel, there is no exacting of the law, neither any dealing by the law, but only remission and forgiveness, neither wrath or punishing, but brotherly service and well doing one to another. Notwithstanding the civil law or magistrate is not taken away, for this parable speaks not anything of worldly government, but of the kingdom of God only. Wherefore the one who is yet governed only by the regiment of the world is yet far off from the kingdom of heaven, for worldly government pertains wholly to inferior things. As if a prince governs his people so that he suffers injury

to be done to none, punishing offenders, he does well, and is therefore commended. For in that government, this sentence flourishes: Pay what you owe, which if you do not, you shall be cast into prison. Such government we must have, howbeit we come not to heaven by it, neither is the world therefore saved, but this government is therefore necessary, that the world do not become worse. THE TWENTY-NINTH SERMON OF DR. MARTIN LUTHER OF THE EXERCISE AND INCREASING OF FAITH.[16]

CHRIST PAYS THE DEBT OF OUR SINS. NIELS HEMMINGSEN: When does the creditor demand the debt? Although he does continually put us in mind of this debt, yet he is to be thought then chiefly to call for a reckoning of it, first as often as our own conscience charges us with sin, and as it were cites us to the judgment seat of God. Second, when the Holy Ghost comes in the ministry of the law, reproves sin, and cites us unto punishment, if payment be not made. Again, when the signs of God's wrath are seen, either in heaven or on earth. And moreover, when we are vexed with cross or sickness, which are as it were God's ministers that call upon us for the payment of the debt.

But why are sins called debts? Because that as ordinary debts do bind men to payment, so do sins bind people to satisfaction of the penalty, unless there be made a discharge. Wherefore do we owe? This is told already. For we owe so much as he put into the hands of our forefather, Adam, all the which we have lost, and moreover have burdened ourselves with new debts, provoking God's wrath against us by our daily transgressing of his most holy law.

How great is the sum of the debt? The creditor answers that you owe ten thousand talents, and that you have not one halfpenny toward it; so far are you off from ever being able to discharge so great a debt. The Ten Commandments contain the parcels of the debt. There is demanded of you the fear of God, love, faith, and

---

[15]Musculus, *In Evangelistam Matthaeum Commentarii* (1556), 500-501.

[16]Luther, *Complete Sermons*, 5:319.

patience in the first commandment. Inasmuch as you have not performed this obedience and discharged yourself of it, you have run up unpaid debts. After this manner is the debt to be examined in every several commandment of the first and second table; and thereupon the greatness of the debt is to be gathered.

But what is to be done in this case? We must follow the example of this debtor who falls down before his creditor, humbling himself and desiring release, which he also obtains. That is to wit, we must acknowledge the greatness of our sin; we must be sorry from our heart that we have not paid what we ought; and upon trust of Christ, we must flee unto our heavenly Father, desiring forgiveness and release of the debt. A Postil, or Exposition of the Gospels.[17]

Receiving Forgiveness and Provoking Wrath. John Hoskin: Now a word or two how he was dealt withal for his barbarous cruelty toward his fellow servant. First, his other fellow servants were greatly moved at his unmerciful dealings, insomuch that they accuse him to their master, for indeed human beings (who are the principal work of nature), crowned with glory and worship, and for whose sake the very angels are sent to minister, especially for such as shall receive the inheritance of salvation, by nature loves mercy; knowing there is no one but shall have need of mercy. . . . Now his fellow servants bring in their verdict against him for his discourtesy and monstrous inhumanity. Then comes in the second point, namely, that the king is altered and his mind clean changed, for whereas before there was no sign of anger at all in him, but extended his great favor toward him, in forgiving him the debt, verse 27, now his mercy is turned into mere and severe

justice, and his goodwill into extreme wrath. Third, whereas before he used no hard speeches, nor any unkind words unto him, now he calls him lewd and evil servant, verse 32, wherein we are to take heed how we incur the Lord's displeasure, by any hard and cruel dealings toward our debtors or poor brethren. For even as mercy covers a multitude of sins, even so cruelty in not hearing their complaints and not showing mercy incurs the wrath of God. For he shall cry himself and not be heard, for the Lord is the avenger of all such things. A Sermon upon the Parable of the King.[18]

The Danger of Seeking Revenge. Martin Luther: It is a thing most abhorring from Christianity, and even blasphemous, when it is said, "I cannot, neither will I forgive him that which he has committed against me. I will be revenged. . . ." Surely those blind people are ignorant, that they do take from God his glory, to whom alone vengeance belongs, and channel it to themselves, and so they give up to the devil their own souls, which they have received of God, and ought to render them unto him again, whereunto they are perhaps provoked even with some small or trifling matter. . . . Neither is it sufficient, if in gestures, signs, mouth, or tongue, that you show yourself a friend unto them and forgive them, but you must do it from your heart, otherwise God will not forgive you, yea you shall be driven out of the kingdom of grace. Wherefore if at any time we have tried the mercy of God toward us, we must also readily pardon our fellow brethren, which have offended us. For in that respect the merciful Father forgives us our sins, that we also should forgive our brethren, and show mercy toward them, even as he is merciful toward us and remits sin, death, the fault, and the punishment. The Eleventh Sermon of Dr. Martin Luther of the Kingdom of God.[19]

---

[17]Hemmingsen, *A Postill, or Exposition of the Gospels* (1569), 301. Hemmingsen continues by providing examples such as the "sinful" woman in Lk 7, David as penitent, and the publican in Lk 18. The word *arrerages* has been amended to "unpaid debts."

[18]Hoskin, *A Sermon upon the Parable of the King* (1609), C7-C8.
[19]Luther, *Complete Sermons*, 5:123-24.

19:1-30 MARRIAGE, CHILDREN, AND RICHES

Now when Jesus had finished these sayings, he went away from Galilee and entered the region of Judea beyond the Jordan. [2]And large crowds followed him, and he healed them there.

[3]And Pharisees came up to him and tested him by asking, "Is it lawful to divorce one's wife for any cause?" [4]He answered, "Have you not read that he who created them from the beginning made them male and female, [5]and said, 'Therefore a man shall leave his father and his mother and hold fast to his wife, and the two shall become one flesh'? [6]So they are no longer two but one flesh. What therefore God has joined together, let not man separate." [7]They said to him, "Why then did Moses command one to give a certificate of divorce and to send her away?" [8]He said to them, "Because of your hardness of heart Moses allowed you to divorce your wives, but from the beginning it was not so. [9]And I say to you: whoever divorces his wife, except for sexual immorality, and marries another, commits adultery."[a]

[10]The disciples said to him, "If such is the case of a man with his wife, it is better not to marry." [11]But he said to them, "Not everyone can receive this saying, but only those to whom it is given. [12]For there are eunuchs who have been so from birth, and there are eunuchs who have been made eunuchs by men, and there are eunuchs who have made themselves eunuchs for the sake of the kingdom of heaven. Let the one who is able to receive this receive it."

[13]Then children were brought to him that he might lay his hands on them and pray. The disciples rebuked the people, [14]but Jesus said, "Let the little children come to me and do not hinder them, for to such belongs the kingdom of heaven." [15]And he laid his hands on them and went away.

[16]And behold, a man came up to him, saying, "Teacher, what good deed must I do to have eternal life?" [17]And he said to him, "Why do you ask me about what is good? There is only one who is good. If you would enter life, keep the commandments." [18]He said to him, "Which ones?" And Jesus said, "You shall not murder, You shall not commit adultery, You shall not steal, You shall not bear false witness, [19]Honor your father and mother, and, You shall love your neighbor as yourself." [20]The young man said to him, "All these I have kept. What do I still lack?" [21]Jesus said to him, "If you would be perfect, go, sell what you possess and give to the poor, and you will have treasure in heaven; and come, follow me." [22]When the young man heard this he went away sorrowful, for he had great possessions.

[23]And Jesus said to his disciples, "Truly, I say to you, only with difficulty will a rich person enter the kingdom of heaven. [24]Again I tell you, it is easier for a camel to go through the eye of a needle than for a rich person to enter the kingdom of God." [25]When the disciples heard this, they were greatly astonished, saying, "Who then can be saved?" [26]But Jesus looked at them and said, "With man this is impossible, but with God all things are possible." [27]Then Peter said in reply, "See, we have left everything and followed you. What then will we have?" [28]Jesus said to them, "Truly, I say to you, in the new world,[b] when the Son of Man will sit on his glorious throne, you who have followed me will also sit on twelve thrones, judging the twelve tribes of Israel. [29]And everyone who has left houses or brothers or sisters or father or mother or children or lands, for my name's sake, will receive a hundredfold[c] and will inherit eternal life. [30]But many who are first will be last, and the last first."

a Some manuscripts add and whoever marries a divorced woman commits adultery; other manuscripts except for sexual immorality, makes her commit adultery, and whoever marries a divorced woman commits adultery   b Greek in the regeneration   c Some manuscripts manifold

OVERVIEW: As Jesus continues to minister to large crowds, the opposition of the religious leaders continues with a question about the legitimacy and legality of divorce. During the Reformation, marriage was a matter of some dispute. While the Roman Catholic Church continued to regard it as a sacrament, the Protestant reformers rejected that designation, but they upheld its value, even for members of the clergy.

In the Reformation commentary on this passage, Jesus' teaching highlights the sanctity of marriage and the stubborn unbelief that is drawn to a casual view of divorce. Jesus' correction of the Pharisees' question on divorce draws on God's original, creative intent for marriage as expressed in Genesis 1 and 2.

Jesus' high view of marriage causes the disciple to wonder if anyone can match this high esteem for marriage. Many reformers held that Jesus' use of an "exception clause" does not intend to compensate for the hardened hearts in his teaching on marriage but allows for divorce in the case of adultery because the marriage vow is already broken. Jesus established celibacy as a viable option to marriage, but only if that singleness is ordained for that individual by God. Zwingli argues that Jesus releases his disciples from being bound to remain single (or to marry) by not imposing a punishment on those who cannot receive the disciples' comment on remaining single.

Having affirmed the need for childlike humility among the disciples in the previous chapter (Mt 18:3-4), Matthew provides another encounter involving Jesus and children. The reformers utilized this text in their polemics for or against infant baptism, and their comments on the text often reflect their bent on this theological issue.

During the sixteenth century, the vast majority of Christians were baptized as infants, continuing the medieval practice. However, the variation in belief and practice among groups such as the Anabaptists set them apart and contributed to their persecution. Among those who support baptizing infants, the comments typically contend that the children brought to Christ were children of his disciples. From the contrary view, the Anabaptist leader Dirk Philips remarks that Jesus includes the children among those receiving the kingdom, but he does not baptize them. Calvin opposes the Anabaptist position by stating that this text establishes a different standard for infants than for adults, who are adopted by God through faith.

In a gripping narrative, Matthew tells his readers of a young man who approaches Jesus with a question about eternal life. The impossibility of a "rich man" entering into the kingdom connects with previous warnings from Jesus that he did not come to help the "healthy" or the "righteous" (Mt 9:12-13). Like others, Peter Walpot identifies selfishness as the young man's great barrier to faith. Juan de Valdés explains that though it is impossible for humans to meet the perfect standard of holiness required by Jesus (Mt 5:20, 48), God can save and grant access to the kingdom by the work of the Spirit. Jesus' instruction about abandoning everything to follow him sets the context for Peter's question about rewards for Jesus' disciples. Calvin explains that the promise to Peter (and other apostles) to judge over Israel and the other "many" things that will come as part of the greater promise of eternal life.

19:1-12 *Marriage and Divorce*

MARRIAGE AS A DIVINE INSTITUTION.

JACQUES LEFÈVRE D'ÉTAPLES: Although the Lord knew that the Pharisees had come to him, not out of a desire to learn but to tempt and reprehend him, still he did not refuse them kindness, and instead with all modesty he gave satisfaction to their inquiry, using the example of Genesis 1–2, where it is read thus in chapter 1: "And God created man in his image and likeness; in the image of God he created him, he created them male and female." And in chapter 2 like this: "And the Lord God fashioned the rib, which he had taken from Adam, into a woman, and he brought her to Adam, and Adam said, 'This now is bone from my bones, and flesh from my flesh; she will be called woman, since she was taken from a man. Wherefore a man will leave his father and mother and will cling to his wife and the two will be one flesh.'" These words, "Wherefore a man will leave his father," and those that follow, the Gospel seems to attribute to God. And rightly so, for, even if in the story of Genesis Adam appears to speak these things, nevertheless he was speaking in the Spirit, and the Spirit of God was saying these things. For, when the mystery of which he spoke happened, he was sleeping. Rightly then these are understood to be words of God, who was proclaiming both what was done and what will happen in the future. From these things the Lord truly gathers that a man and a woman are one flesh, and that the Lord said it and did the joining, and since that is the case, since God joined together the man and woman, it follows that no one should separate them, nor is it permitted to divorce one's wife for any reason. Christ drew this teaching of his from the words of God and from his work. Against that no rationale coming from a human being can prevail. Nevertheless, the Pharisees offer a human rationale, as if Moses counts more than God. Matthew insinuates that by that which he adds. COMMENTARY ON THE FOUR GOSPELS.[1]

DIVORCE IS NOT SANCTIONED BY THE LAW.

RICHARD TAVERNER: Here the Pharisees, thinking that they had now got a good quarrel against our Savior, Christ Jesus, to snatch him up, said unto him, "If it be thus as you say that God would have wedlock so inviolably kept, why then did Moses make it lawful to the husband, for any manner cause, to put from him his wife, so that he give her a libel of divorcement as who should say, how does Moses dare be so bold to license that thing which God would not have done?" To this objection our Savior answered, Moses did not permit nor license this thing unto you because the thing of the own nature was honest and rightful, but forasmuch as he knew the stubbornness and

hardness of your hearts; therefore, he granted unto you the letter and lighter inconvenience that you should not commit the more grievous offense. For assuredly Moses did not allow all kinds of divorces, in that he had rather that the same were suffered or rather winked at than murder should ensue and be committed. Neither did the libel of divorcement among the crooked Jews, which Moses their lawmaker enacted that it should be given to the woman, make the divorce good and lawful, but rather that same libel was a witness and testimony of the hard heart of the Jews, which for every light cause and trifle would put away their wives, and for this cause the law of Moses gave the commandment, that such stubborn and hard husbands which would needs for such light occasions put away their wives or else do worse and commit further inconvenience, to give them the said libel of divorcement for a certain record and witness that she is now free from his yoke and at her liberty. THE GOSPELS WITH BRIEF SERMONS.[2]

DIVORCE WITNESSES TO THE HARDNESS OF YOUR HEART.

DESIDERIUS ERASMUS: Jesus answered that he did not permit you this because it was right and good of nature, but knowing the hardness of your heart, he suffered the lesser ill, that you should not commit the greater. . . . And the book of divorce does not make that the divorce is right and good, but it witnesses your hardness, which will cast off your wife for every light cause and provide her of a new husband taking away liberty from you that you shall not call her again once cast off. But from the beginning, whereas the malice of humankind was not yet increased nor the nature of men and women was not yet infected with so many vices, because there was not so cruel hatred that poisoning or murder should be feared, there was no license of divorce, and the same law shall not now be loosed and set at liberty, after that the doctrine of the gospel does renew and make perfect the sincerity of the nature. Moses wished

---

[1]Lefèvre, *Commentarii Initiatorii in Quatuor Evangelia* (1523), 84r.

[2]Taverner, *On Saynt Andrewes Day: The Gospels with Brief Sermons* (1542), liiii-lv.

the same that I do teach, but your manners bent over much unto murder, put him in fear that he does not require this of you. I, who do not abolish the law but make it more perfect, plainly say to you that it is unlawful and against the mind of God and against the will of Moses which you do commonly, refusing your wives for every cause. Paraphrases.[3]

Except in the Case of Adultery. Michael Sattler: Here (like Christ) we do not permit that one divorce his wife unless it be for fornication, that is, because of adultery. For when Christ says, "but I say to you . . ." as he also does often in Matthew 5, he abrogates the law, insofar as it is conceived literally and not spiritually, as he is also the perfecting of the law. Therefore, he is the mediator of a better testament which is founded upon better promises. Therefore, he abrogates the former divorcing and no longer makes concessions to hardness of heart, but rather renews the ordinance of his Father, saying, "From the beginning it was not so." Since then, God so created, that there should be one husband and one wife, and what God has united, that let human beings not separate. Therefore, any minor cause—anger, which is hardness of heart; displeasure, contrariety, faith or unbelief—may not separate, but only fornication. He who divorces without fornication, the only reason, and remarries, commits adultery; and he who takes a divorced woman causes her to commit adultery; for Christ says, "These two are one flesh." On Divorce.[4]

Maintaining the Perpetual Union of Marriage. Martin Bucer: It is agreed by all who determine of the kingdom and offices of Christ by the holy Scriptures, as all godly people ought to do, that our Savior upon earth took not on him either to give new laws in civil affairs or to change the old. But it is certain that matrimony and divorce are civil things. While the Christian

emperors knowing, gave conjugal laws and referred the administration of them to their own courts, which no true ancient bishop ever condemned, our Savior came to preach repentance and remission. Seeing, therefore, those who put away their wives, without any just cause, were not touched in their conscience by the sin, through a misunderstanding of the law, he recalled them to a right interpretation, and taught that the woman in the beginning was so joined to the man that there should be a perpetual union both in body and spirit; where this is not, the matrimony is already broke, before there be yet any divorce made or second marriage. Judgement of Martin Bucer Concerning Divorce.[5]

Not Everyone Can Receive This Teaching. Huldrych Zwingli: What else is it, by the everlasting God! than absolute folly, nay even, shamelessness, to arrogate to one's self what belongs to God alone? To think one's self able to do that than which there is nothing one is less able to do? But after that loathing of ourselves through which we recognized at once our rashness and our weakness, the hope of a remedy began to show itself, though from afar. For weighing more carefully Christ's words and the custom of our predecessors in this matter, we found that the whole question was far easier than we had thought. For when he says, "All people cannot receive this saying," and again, "The one who is able to receive it, let them receive it," he prescribes no punishment for those who cannot receive it. Nay, either because of the vastness of the thing which he did not wish enjoined up each and all, or on account of our weakness, which he know better than we ourselves, he did not want this thing laid up against us, and so left it free. Therefore, our souls which had been nigh unto despair were mightily refreshed when we learned those who were unable to receive the saying were threatened with no punishment by him who can send both body and soul into hell. Petition Concerning the Marriage of Priests.[6]

---

[3]EP 78v*.
[4]CRR 1:102-3; citing Deut 24; Eph 2; Rom 10; Heb 8; Gen 1–2.

[5]Bucer, *Judgement of Martin Bucer Concerning Divorce* (1644), 11.
[6]Zwingli, *The Latin Works and the Correspondence*, 1:157.

HUSBAND AND WIFE AS ONE. JOHANNES BUGENHAGEN: Marriage is rent apart and severed when two spouses separated with such shame and wantonness. The adulterer is stuck in fatal judgment before God and is not in marriage (as the pope dreams) but outside of marriage (as God and Christ say). "What God has joined, let no human being separate," as Christ says in Matthew 19. However, what has God joined? Is it two spirits or two dreams? Is it not two in one flesh? Read properly what it is written there. If you properly understand the joining you must, without doubt, also understand properly the separating, the severing, or the rending of marriage. Christ says there that a man should not divorce or withdraw from his wife but remain with her, forsake father and mother, and cling to his wife so that the two are thus not two but one flesh. (Note this well also against the shameful deserting about which we intend to speak later.) Do you not see what joining means when Christ says, "What God has joined together?" They are two fleshly beings, that is, two people, man and woman, ordered by God so that they remain together and are one flesh. They must not cast each other aside, not in this way or in another way that one might do or devise in order to get rid of the wife, indeed, also not with the law which some heathen had and which Moses had also conceded to the Jews, namely, with a letter of divorce. They should remain together, and they are not separated, even if they had one hundred thousand letters of divorce. Whoever gives such letters of divorce, whether it is the temporal authority or someone else, acts unjustly and is worth noting in this matter. If they marry again on account of such a letter of divorce, this is no marriage but a punishable adultery, as Christ says. This is the matter which Christ discusses. Note this so that you do not misuse some of the words because of a lack of understanding (as has happened to some of the doctors) in order to ruin miserable, forsaken spouses (concerning whom we are speaking here) in body and soul. . . .

If one partner wants to remain absent for the sake of the letter of divorce or the letter of dung, the other partner should complain about this and seek help from the authorities, for a human being should not separate what God has joined. However, if the two bodies are separated if one commits adultery or secretly deserts the other, then this commandment, "A human being shall not separate . . ." has been broken among us. A person should preserve his marriage, but now he breaks it. The person should not desert, not leave his spouse, not separate in this way what God has joined. However, now he does it. Therefore, he must be punished. However, the innocent partner, who has been violated, should be protected, defended, and cared for with good advice. MARRIAGE MATTERS.[7]

GOD GIVES THE ABILITY TO REMAIN CHASTE. HULDRYCH ZWINGLI: Here he makes it free, since he says, whoever can keep it, let him keep it. Thus, if he can keep it, let him keep it; if he cannot keep it, then let him marry. But now the keeping of it depends not upon our ability, but upon God; else why does he say, he who can keep it, let him keep it? Not that we should understand "ability," as if it came from ourselves, but as given by God. The meaning is, "To whom God has given the power to keep it, let him keep it; to whom ability is not given, he is not bound to keep it." How then have men ventured to forbid it since God did not wish to forbid it on account of its difficulty? But he gave it to whom he would. And those to whom he gave it became bound to keep it. He to whom it is given, feels it very well, needs no such subtle question as, "How can I know whether it is given to me or not?" Now the sum of this article or words of Christ is, "To whom is given by God the ability to keep it, let him keep it; and those to whom it is not given are not bound by any divine law to keep it." PRIESTS TO PREACH AND TO MARRY.[8]

19:13-15 To Such Children Belongs the Kingdom of Heaven

THE IDENTITY OF THE CHILDREN WHO COME. JOHN LIGHTFOOT: Whose children were these

---

[7]JBSW 2:1116-17, 1138; citing Deut 24:1-4.
[8]Zwingli, *The Latin Works and the Correspondence*, 1:179.

that were brought to Christ? Not unbelievers doubtless, but the children of some who professed Christ. Why did they bring them? Not to be healed of any disease doubtless, for then the disciples would not have been angry at their coming; for why at theirs, more than at all others, that had come for that end? Their bringing, therefore, must needs be concluded to be in the name of disciples, and that Christ would so receive them and bless them; and so he does and asserts them for disciples, and "to whom the kingdom of heaven belonged," taking the kingdom of heaven in the common acceptation of the gospel. THE HARMONY, CHRONICLE, AND ORDER OF THE NEW TESTAMENT.[9]

WHY CHILDREN ARE PLEASING TO GOD. DIRK PHILIPS: Christ also gave us to understand sufficiently why children are pleasing to God, since he set children before us as an example and in addition admonished us that we should become like them. For thus he spoke to his disciples, "Truly, I say to you, unless you turn and become like children, you will never enter the kingdom of heaven. Whoever humbles himself as this child, he is the greatest in the kingdom of heaven."

Since Christ has now set the children as an example for us and said that we should become as children and humble ourselves, it follows from this without any contradiction, first, that children (so long as they are in their simplicity) are guiltless and reckoned as without sin by God; second, that if there is still something good in children (though they have, indeed, become participants of the trespass and sinful nature of Adam), namely, the simple and unassuming and humble nature in which they please God (yet all out of pure grace through Jesus Christ) so long as they remain in it. For this reason, Christ also set the children as an example for us that we, in this regard, must become like them.

But now many arrogant persons dispute about the salvation of children and become fools before

the Lord over such disputations, no matter how wise and intelligent they are regarded by the world. For they dispute and chatter much about the salvation of children, but where this concern is of the greatest necessity for themselves, that is, to learn true simplicity and humility from the children, as Christ admonishes us, that they do not even think of a single time.

Since then infants are saved and included in the hand and grace of God, and the kingdom of heaven belongs to them, therefore, it is a great lack of understanding that one should baptize children so that through this they might be kept and saved, and besides this condemn children who die without baptism. . . . So we wish now to return to the previously mentioned words of the Lord, "Let the children come to me, for to such belongs the kingdom of heaven." Let these words remain unfalsified in their true meaning, namely, that children are saved and that the kingdom of heaven belongs to them. THE BAPTISM OF OUR LORD.[10]

CHILDREN AND BAPTISM. JOHN CALVIN: This narrative is highly useful; for it shows that Christ receives not only those who, moved by holy desire and faith, freely approach to him, but those who are not yet of age to know how much they need his grace. Those little children have not yet any understanding to desire his blessing; but when they are presented to him, he gently and kindly receives them, and dedicates them to the Father by a solemn act of blessing. We must observe the intention of those who present the children; for if there had not been a deep-rooted conviction in their minds that the power of the Spirit was at his disposal, that he might pour it out on the people of God, it would have been unreasonable to present their children. . . .

He declares that he wishes to receive children; and at length, taking them in his arms, he not only embraces, but blesses them by the laying on of hands; from which we infer that his grace is extended even to those who are of that age. And no

---

[9]Lightfoot, *The Harmony, Chronicle and Order of the New Testament* (1655), 51.

[10]CRR 6:91-92, 94; citing Mt 18:3-4; 19:14.

wonder; for since the whole race of Adam is shut up under the sentence of death, all from the least even to the greatest must perish, except those who are rescued by the only redeemer. To exclude from the grace of redemption those who are of that age would be too cruel; and therefore, it is not without reason that we employ this passage as a shield against the Anabaptists. They refuse baptism to infants because infants are incapable of understanding that mystery which is denoted by it. We, on the other hand, maintain that since baptism is the pledge and figure of the forgiveness of sins, and likewise of adoption by God, it ought not to be denied to infants, whom God adopts and washes with the blood of his son. Their objection, that repentance and newness of life are also denoted by it, is easily answered. Infants are renewed by the Spirit of God, according to the capacity of their age, till that power which was concealed within them grows by degrees, and becomes fully manifest at the proper time. Again, when they argue that there is no other way in which we are reconciled to God, and become heirs of adoption than by faith, we admit this as to adults, but, with respect to infants, this passage demonstrates it to be false. Certainly, the laying on of hands was not a trifling or empty sign, and the prayers of Christ were not idly wasted in air. . . . In short, by embracing them, he testified that they were reckoned by Christ among his flock. And if they were partakers of the spiritual gifts, which are represented by baptism, it is unreasonable that they should be deprived of the outward sign. But it is presumption and sacrilege to drive far from the fold of Christ those whom he cherishes in his bosom, and to shut the door and exclude as strangers those whom he does not wish to be forbidden to come to him. COMMENTARY ON A HARMONY OF THE EVANGELISTS.[11]

TWO DUTIES WITH CHILDREN. PHILIPP MELANCHTHON: We will discuss the two groups of children, about those of an early age who should be brought to baptism, although they are not capable of being taught, and about children, who now are capable of being taught. Concerning both groups I say that it is the duty of parents to commit each to Christ, just as the age of each permits.

They should bring the very young children to baptism and see to it that they become members of the church of God, since here they learn that such young children are received truly and assuredly by God, and that God wishes such to become members of the church through ministry and to be brought to the ministry, that is to say, to baptism.

And let it be a great consolation to parents that this age is an heir to eternal life and that, weak as it is, it is pleasing to God and protected by God, and that citizens of the kingdom of God are childlike. Therefore, let them know that it is God's command that parents themselves should see to it that children are brought to baptism.

Then after they come to the point where they can be taught, parents should educate them, just as Paul bid in Ephesians 6: "Bring them up in discipline and the instruction of the Lord." Parents also should commend their children to God in constant prayers. All these things are included in the phrase, "Bring the children to Christ."

Just as I said before, that parents should train children when they reach an age when they are capable of being taught, so now again I say, that not only should you see to it that infants are baptized, but afterward it is necessary to education children about God and the Son of God, and little by little to instill in them the whole teaching of the gospel, and to accustom them to prayer and the acceptance of the Son of God. This phrase "Permit the little children to come unto me" embraces all these things. You are not only parents who take care of their bodies, but you ought also to lead their minds to God. You, father, mother, ought to be, as it were, shepherds of your children, and to educate them and to accustom them to prayer. If you do not do it, God will punish this negligence, just as he punished Eli for not chastising his sons. ANNOTATIONS ON THE GOSPELS.[12]

---

[11]CTS 2:389-91 (CO 45:534-35).

[12]MO 14:924-27.

19:16-30 *The Rich Young Man*

THE SUPREME GOODNESS OF GOD. AEGIDIUS HUNNIUS: He asks about good works, specifically which kind have the power and merit to acquire eternal life with God. Wherefore, the response of Christ must be directed to the question of the young man in this sense: If the power to be saved lies completely in doing good things, the ready explanation is prescribed in the law as to what must be done and not done, and the promise is added that if anyone keeps and fulfills it fully, then that person can obtain eternal life. But, alas, you cannot just keep the Ten Commandments in some casual way, if you wish to reach your goal through obedience; no, perfect, absolute, and in all respects full obedience that deviates not even a little bit from the norm and standard of the commands of the Lord is what is needed.

When the Lord asks, "Why do you call me good, when there is only one who is good, that is, God," he is not removing from himself the title of God or due praise for his goodness, but this phrase looks to the salvation of the young man and his preconceived opinion about Jesus, whom he thinks is just a man, plain and simple. Therefore, the sense of Christ's response is this: Because besides God no one is good, and you deny in your heart that I am God, are you not contradicting yourself by calling me good at the same time that you disparage my divinity? And someone will ask how it can be true that he pronounces Christ and God as the only ones who are good? Are not the angels also good and holy, and people good and holy, although with an imperfect and incomplete goodness, while the angels have a perfected goodness? I respond that God alone is good in his essential and uncreated goodness, which is simply and without complexity united with his nature, and therefore unchanging. But the goodness of the angels is something created together with them and is not united with the angelic essence, but can be lost while the substance of the angels remains, though horribly corrupt, as one can see in the case of fallen angels. Therefore, the goodness of angels

is of a separate essence from them and, as I said, can be changed into the opposite state of sin. COMMENTARY ON MATTHEW.[13]

GOD'S LAW LEADS TO LIFE. THOMAS CRANMER: Jesus answered, "If you will come to the eternal life, keep the commandments." But the prince, not satisfied herewith, asked further which commandments. The scribes and Pharisees had made so many of their own laws and traditions to bring heaven to heaven besides God's commandments, that this man was in doubt whether he would come to heaven by those laws and traditions or by the laws of God, and therefore he asked Christ which commandments he meant. Whereunto Christ made him a plain answer, rehearsing the commandments of God, saying, You shall not kill, you shall not bear false witness, honor your father and mother, and love your neighbor as yourself. By which words Christ declared that the laws of God be the very way that does lead to eternal life, and not the traditions and laws of human beings. So that this is to be taken for a most true lesson taught by Christ's own mouth, that the works of the moral commandments of God be the very true works of faith which lead to the blessed life to come. But the blindness and malice of humanity, even from the beginning, has ever been ready to fall from God's commandments. As Adam the first man, having but one commandment, that he should not eat of the fruit forbidden, notwithstanding God's commandments, he gave credit unto the woman, seduced by the subtle persuasion of the serpent, and so followed his own will and left God's commandment. And ever since that time, all his succession has been so blinded through original sin that they have been ever ready to fall from God and his law and to invent a new way unto salvation by works of their own device so much, that almost all the world forsaking the true honor of the only eternal

---

[13]Hunnius, *Commentarius in Evangelium Secundum Matthaeum* (1594), 1187-89.

living God, wandered about their own fantasies. THE SECOND PART OF THE SERMON OF GOOD WORKS.[14]

A HARD SAYING HEARD BY HARD HEARTS. PETER WALPOT: That he should give up his wealth was certainly a narrow gate for the rich young ruler, and he left very sad. Therefore, Christ said, Oh, how hard it is for the rich to enter into the kingdom of God! I say to you, it is easier for a camel to go through the eye of a needle than for a rich man to enter the kingdom of God. For just as it is impossible for a camel to go through the eye of a needle, so is it impossible for a rich man to become small enough to enter into the kingdom of heaven. For if we must become as children, who have nothing, to enter the kingdom of heaven, then a rich man must give up much before he is like an animal small enough to go through the eye of a needle. That is a hard saying. But even harder still are the hearts of those who hear this and will not empty themselves but would rather hang onto their wealth and greed. Here is where we get the phrase—the Word of God would not be so difficult if not for human selfishness. TRUE YIELDEDNESS AND THE CHRISTIAN COMMUNITY OF GOODS.[15]

IDENTIFYING THE RICH MAN. JUAN DE VALDÉS: Reverting to Christ's words, I understand that he, purposing the more to enhance the difficulty of which he had spoken, added, "And again I say unto you, it is easier" . . . and effectively it is so, for the reasons we have above noticed, when a person alone, not being aided by Christ's Spirit, presumes to enter and to remain in the kingdom of God, to live like a Christian; while it is not so, when human beings accept the grace of the gospel and receive therewith the Christian spirit, they go on gradually to adopt Christian life, and they live as one should live in the kingdom of God; for it is thus, that in such a person, the Spirit of God renders that

possible which is naturally impossible. And for this reason, meeting the disciples' amazement, Christ said, "With human beings this is impossible" . . . while all things being possible to God; all things are possible to those who have the Spirit of God, as had Paul, when he said, "I can do all things through Christ that strengthens me," while Christ says, "all things are possible to the one who believes."

It seems to me that I may rest satisfied with the commentary upon these words, and, if it shall appear extraordinary to anybody that Christ should have invited this person to be his associate, knowing that he would not consent; while Christ had rejected the society of others who desired to follow him, let such a one know that Christ never purposed that this youth should be a follower of his, save to quell his arrogance, by giving him self-knowledge. And if, to another, it shall appear hard that Christ should put such difficulty in the way of a rich man's entrance into the kingdom of heaven, and then have to solve it, by saying that what is impossible to human beings is possible to God; since it appears that the same difficulty may be put in the way to everything else to which we humans as humans are attached; let them know that, because riches are those which most tyrannize over us, and those which keep the other affections of this present life alive within us, Christ, willing that we, who accept his gospel, should lose all the affection that we have to everything of the present life in order that we make room for the affection that we ought to have for things of the life eternal, he puts all this difficulty in the way of the rich man's entrance into the kingdom of heaven. Now the rich man is he who is affectionately devoted to his property, be it little or much; while on the contrary, he is poor, who has lost all affection for all that he possesses. COMMENTARY UPON THE GOSPEL OF ST. MATTHEW.[16]

THE GLORIES OF THE COMING KINGDOM. JOHN CALVIN: That the disciples may not think

[14]Cranmer, *Miscellaneous Writings and Letters* (1846), 144.
[15]Liechty, ed., *Early Anabaptist Spirituality*, 151.
[16]Valdés, *Commentary upon the Gospel of St. Matthew*, 342-43; citing Phil 4:13; Mk 9:22.

that they have lost their pains and repent of having begun the course, Christ warns them that the glory of his kingdom, which at that time was still hidden, was about to be revealed. . . . And what does he then promise to them? That they shall be partakers of the same glory. . . . By assigning to them thrones, from which they may judge the twelve tribes of Israel, he compares them to assessors, or first councilors and judges, who occupy the highest seats in the royal council. . . . This was a very high rank, but hitherto was concealed; and therefore, Christ holds their wishes in suspense till the latest revelation of his kingdom, when they will fully receive the fruit of their election. And though the kingdom of Christ is, in some respects, manifested by the preaching of the gospel, there is no doubt that Christ here speaks of the last day. . . .

I explain regeneration as referring to the first coming of Christ; for then the world began to be renewed and arose out of the darkness of death into the light of life. And this way of speaking occurs frequently in the Prophets, and is exceedingly adapted to the connection of this passage. For the renovation of the church, which had been so frequently promised, had raised an expectation of wonderful happiness, as soon as the Messiah should appear; and therefore, in order to guard against that error, Christ distinguishes between the beginning and the completion of his reign. COMMENTARY ON A HARMONY OF THE EVANGELISTS.[17]

THE REWARD OF LEAVING ALL TO FOLLOW CHRIST. HUGH LATIMER: So Peter, in forsaking his old boat and net, was allowed as much before God, as if he had forsaken all the riches in the world. Therefore he shall have a great reward for his old boat; for Christ says that he shall be one of those who shall sit and judge the twelve tribes of Israel. And to signify them to be more than others, he gives them the name of judges; meaning that they shall condemn the world; like as God speaks of the queen of Sheba, that in the last day she shall arise and condemn the Jews who would not hear

Christ, and she came so great a journey to hear the wisdom of Solomon. Then he answered and said, "Whosoever leaves father, or mother, or brethren, for my sake, shall receive a hundredfold, and shall inherit everlasting life." Now what is this, to leave father and mother? When my father or mother would hinder me in any goodness, or would persuade me from the honoring of God and faith in Christ, then I must forsake and rather lose the favor and goodwill of my father and mother, than forsake God and his holy word.

And now Christ says, "The first shall be last, and the last shall be first," alluding to Peter's saying, which sounded as though Peter looked for a reward for his deeds; and that is it which is the greatest hindrance if a man come to the gospel and hears the same and afterward looks for a reward, such a man shall be "the last." If these sayings were well considered by us, surely we should not have such a number of vain gospelers as we now have, who seek nothing but their own advantage under the name and color of the gospel. Moreover, he teaches us to be meek and lowly, and not to think much of ourselves. THE PARABLE OF THE HOUSEHOLDER.[18]

THE LAST WHO SHALL BE FIRST. FRANCISCUS GOMARUS: "Many who are first will be last and the last first"; that is, indeed all these who are faithful concerning those in question are heirs of eternal life. But at the same time not all are worthy; for many of them, who are first with respect to calling (or who serve Christ a long time) in the inheritance of eternal life, are last. Indeed, this is not with relationship to time, because all of those are given eternal life at the same time. But this is with regard to honor or degree of glory. And vice versa, many who excel for a long time with respect to their calling and service and yet are last (they are such who are called at the end of their life) are first among the heirs of eternal life. Else they excel with respect to degrees of the glory of heaven. The occasion of this division is this:

---

[17]CTS 2:405-6 (CO 45:544-45).

[18]Latimer, *Select Sermons and Letters*, 369.

Because granted that first works are lesser with respect to duration, yet greater with respect to a poor spirit, or if as they call, they were established with respect to humility. Because also by a parable it is signaled not obscurely in Matthew 20:10. Truly for this reason God is Lord of all, and they are indebted to no one. Grace to set free, by which he gives eternal life to all truly believing, equal in duration, indeed unequal in glory. And greater glory to those who serve out of consideration of their infirmity and of the grace of God, endowed by a continuously poor spirit, by works of faith, hope, love, to God and the church, by a good example. For even if their humility be imperfect without connection of flesh opposed to the spirit, yet that surrendered by imperfection on account

of Christ has acceptance. And in heaven he crowns with grace; and you are endowed with less of a poor spirit, granted that you call for a long time and by a work of suffering he carries along. For as God is accustomed to give grace to the humble, in the same way for those of greater humility. But if anyone objects to the joining of the good works of the apostles to be something arrogant, as we approved at first, yet nevertheless it is promised with respect to honor in eternal life, anticipating the rest of Christianity. ILLUSTRIOUS SELECTIONS FROM THE GOSPEL OF MATTHEW.[19]

---

[19]Gomarus, *Illustrium ac Selectorum ex Evangelio Mattaei* (1644), 95-96; citing Mt 25:34, 46; 1 Thess 4:14, 15, 17; Rom 11:34; 1 Cor 15:41-43; 1 Pet 5:5; Mt 19:28.

20:1-34 PROPHECIES AND REQUESTS

"For the kingdom of heaven is like a master of a house who went out early in the morning to hire laborers for his vineyard. ²After agreeing with the laborers for a denarius[a] a day, he sent them into his vineyard. ³And going out about the third hour he saw others standing idle in the marketplace, ⁴and to them he said, 'You go into the vineyard too, and whatever is right I will give you.' ⁵So they went. Going out again about the sixth hour and the ninth hour, he did the same. ⁶And about the eleventh hour he went out and found others standing. And he said to them, 'Why do you stand here idle all day?' ⁷They said to him, 'Because no one has hired us.' He said to them, 'You go into the vineyard too.' ⁸And when evening came, the owner of the vineyard said to his foreman, 'Call the laborers and pay them their wages, beginning with the last, up to the first.' ⁹And when those hired about the eleventh hour came, each of them received a denarius. ¹⁰Now when those hired first came, they thought they would receive more, but each of them also received a denarius. ¹¹And on receiving it they grumbled at the master of the house, ¹²saying, 'These last worked only one hour, and you have made them equal to us who have borne the burden of the day and the scorching heat.' ¹³But he replied to one of them, 'Friend, I am doing you no wrong. Did you not agree with me for a denarius? ¹⁴Take what belongs to you and go. I choose to give to this last worker as I give to you. ¹⁵Am I not allowed to do what I choose with what belongs to me? Or do you begrudge my generosity?'[b] ¹⁶So the last will be first, and the first last."

¹⁷And as Jesus was going up to Jerusalem, he took the twelve disciples aside, and on the way he said to them, ¹⁸"See, we are going up to Jerusalem. And the Son of Man will be delivered over to the chief priests and scribes, and they will condemn him to death ¹⁹and deliver him over to the Gentiles to be mocked and flogged and crucified, and he will be raised on the third day."

²⁰Then the mother of the sons of Zebedee came up to him with her sons, and kneeling before him she asked him for something. ²¹And he said to her, "What do you want?" She said to him, "Say that these two sons of mine are to sit, one at your right hand and one at your left, in your kingdom." ²²Jesus answered, "You do not know what you are asking. Are you able to drink the cup that I am to drink?" They said to him, "We are able." ²³He said to them, "You will drink my cup, but to sit at my right hand and at my left is not mine to grant, but it is for those for whom it has been prepared by my Father." ²⁴And when the ten heard it, they were indignant at the two brothers. ²⁵But Jesus called them to him and said, "You know that the rulers of the Gentiles lord it over them, and their great ones exercise authority over them. ²⁶It shall not be so among you. But whoever would be great among you must be your servant,[c] ²⁷and whoever would be first among you must be your slave,[d] ²⁸even as the Son of Man came not to be served but to serve, and to give his life as a ransom for many."

²⁹And as they went out of Jericho, a great crowd followed him. ³⁰And behold, there were two blind men sitting by the roadside, and when they heard that Jesus was passing by, they cried out, "Lord,[e] have mercy on us, Son of David!" ³¹The crowd rebuked them, telling them to be silent, but they cried out all the more, "Lord, have mercy on us, Son of David!" ³²And stopping, Jesus called them and said, "What do you want me to do for you?" ³³They said to him, "Lord, let our eyes be opened." ³⁴And Jesus in pity touched their eyes, and immediately they recovered their sight and followed him.

a A *denarius* was a day's wage for a laborer   b Or *is your eye bad because I am good?*   c Greek *diakonos*   d Or *bondservant*, or *servant* (Greek *doulos*)
e Some manuscripts omit *Lord*

OVERVIEW: The parable of the vineyard shows the abounding grace of God (the vineyard owner), which is strikingly balanced in the generosity of his rewards. The reformers provide diverging interpretations of this parable. Some read it as encouraging pious, diligent, and faithful work among Christ's followers. Many others focus on an interpretation of self-righteousness seen in the parable's conclusion.

The next, brief narrative interlude prepares readers for a series of narratives (Mt 20:20–21:16) that focus on Jesus as king and the true nature of his kingdom. In commenting on Christ's prediction of his own death, the reformers note how Jesus' multiple predictions of his death serve as a means of building up the faith of his disciples and prepare them for what follows.

As the reformers comment on the encounter with the mother of John and James, they attempt to explain the connection between Jesus' predictions of his death and the future reign in the kingdom. Some assert that the mother's request shows some measure of faith since she assumes that Jesus is the king and that he will establish his kingdom with the disciples serving as vice regents. However, the petition also shows a lack of faith and understanding on the nature of the kingdom on the part of the mother and her present, though silent, sons. Some reformers suggest that his disciples misunderstand Jesus' prediction altogether.

Jesus' reference to sharing his cup provides a perpetual symbol of his sacrificial death (see Mt 26:27-29). As the other disciples express their anger over the ambition of the two brothers, Jesus reminds them all of the servant leadership required in the kingdom. Philipp Melanchthon emphasizes how Christ ends the lesson in humility by pointing to his own death for the sins of others. The true depth of humble service is seen in the sacrificial death of the king himself.

The regal references to Jesus continue in this narrative with the cries of the two blind men, addressing him as the kingly "son of David." Connecting Jesus with a promised figure from the Old Testament, they do not request specific blessings but plea for mercy. Juan de Valdés asserts that the men's blindness helped them to be aware of their need for mercy and stirred them to be diligent in their request.

20:1-16 *Laborers in the Vineyard*

HUMBLE LABORERS. NIELS HEMMINGSEN: Whether your labor be profitable and commanded to you by the householder, you may know by two things, namely by the commandment, and by your calling. Every labor that makes to the planting, watering, cherishing, and preserving of this vineyard, has a commandment: that is to wit, the labor that serves to the glory of God, the edifying of the church . . . is commanded by God in the first table and in the fourth commandment. Besides this, it is not enough that you are commanded to labor, unless you be enabled to labor by lawful vocation. For he that takes upon him to labor in the vineyard without calling, is rash and brings forth no fruit.

In laboring you must beware, first, that you be not proud if you seem to yourself to labor more or also better than another. Second, that you have not an eye to the reward of your labor performed, but to the commandment of the householder, who has set you in his vineyard, to the intent you should work. Third, that you despise not such as work less than yourself. And fourth, that you grudge not against the master of the house, though he appears generous to those who seem to have wrought less than you.

What is to be looked unto, and continually to be thought upon while you are working: First it behooves everyone to think they are brought into the Lord's vineyard, not to be idle, but to work. For in the Lord's vineyard there is no room for sloth and sluggishness. No one can—without displeasing the master of the house—put over their talk to another person. Therefore, whosoever is brought into this vineyard, let them labor diligently without deceit. For cursed is the one who does the Lord's work deceitfully. Second, in laboring, let them think they stand in their master's fight, who not only beholds the outward doings but also sees the secrets of the heart, and esteems the work by the meaning of the heart, rather than by the effect of the work. Third, this looking on of the master shall stir up the laborer to work heedfully, that they may with a cheerful mind bear out the heat and burden of the day. Fourth, an eye is to be had to nothing else than to the goodness of the householder, God, which commands to labor; and that one thing alone will encourage a person to go through with their task lustily. Fifth, when you have done all that you can do, you shall say you are an unprofitable servant. For if you either be proud because you came sooner into the Lord's vineyard or despise others that may seem to have wrought less than you, or murmur against the good man of the house who is a like liberal to others as to you.... Three things are here found fault within the murmurers. First, that they presume upon the worthiness of their work. Second, that they do not commend and set forth the liberality of the householder, but rather blame him for it. Third, that they envy others for the bountifulness of the liberal householder toward them. Such are all they that seek to justify themselves by works, being utterly void of faith. A POSTIL, OR EXPOSITION OF THE GOSPELS.[1]

SELF-RIGHTEOUS SELF-ASSESSMENT. WOLF-GANG MUSCULUS: Here we get a depiction of the kind of laborers that God finds most pleasing: He prefers those in whom he can manifest his own goodness. They are those who work for no fixed reward, but, motivated by a faith in God's goodness, submitted and went to work. They are happy with whatever they receive, since they know that they deserve nothing. To make this clear, Christ constructed a parable where payment begins with the most recent, as a way of admonishing the disciples that God does not value so much work and effort as a grateful spirit, humility, and dependency on his goodness. For, how much did those latest workers accomplish in the vineyard in the span of one hour?

"And they thought that they would receive more." Why so? Was it because they had derived that

assurance for themselves from the goodness of the owner of the vineyard? No, not at all, but from an estimation of their own labor. For, they were comparing their own work with the modest labor of the more recent workers, and they were concluding that if those people receive so much, we deserve a lot more. This is clear from the fact that they begin to grumble, saying, "Those more recent workers worked only for an hour, and you made them equal to us who bore the weight of the day and the heat."

We should take note of the nature of the self-righteous in this passage, how perverse and depraved they are, and as such, cannot please God, and they exhibit three great vices. The first is that they think that, even contrary to the agreement made, they will receive pay as merited by their works. In this way the self-righteous usually value their own works highly. The second is that they envy the merciful kindness of God to newcomers, about which they should be rejoicing and praising his goodness along with his grace. But see, they exhibit envy toward their brothers and they devalue their work and hold it in contempt.

The third is that which follows from those depraved emotions, namely, that they murmur against the landowner's fairness, charging him with being wicked.... Then, when they [i.e., the self-righteous] hear that the preaching of the grace of the gospel is so great that prostitutes and sinners will enter into the kingdom of heaven, they audaciously say that if God does this he will not be righteous. Then they too will envy those who are saved by the grace of the Lord and will murmur against the goodness of the Lord, when one day they see sinners and the last placed before themselves. And likewise, will it be declared to them then how no harm is being done and how God in his goodness can save whom he wishes, and how salvation does not rest upon human merits, but on the kindness of God's grace. COMMENTARY ON MATTHEW.[2]

---

[1]Hemmingsen, *A Postill, or Exposition of the Gospels* (1569), 67-68*.

[2]Musculus, *In Evangelistam Matthaeum Commentarii* (1556), 519-20.

THE FIRST WILL BE LAST. MARTIN LUTHER: We will let such fables pass and abide by the simple teaching and meaning of Christ, who wishes to show by this parable how it actually is in the kingdom of heaven or in Christendom upon the earth; that God here directs and works wonderfully by making the first last and the last first. And all is spoken to humble those who are great that they should trust in nothing but the goodness and mercy of God. And on the other hand, that those who are nothing should not despair, but trust in the goodness of God just as the others do. Therefore we must not consider this parable in every detail, but confine ourselves to the leading thought, that which Christ designs to teach by it. We should not consider what the coin means, not what the first or the last hour signifies; but what the householder had in mind and what he aims to teach, how he desires to have his goodness esteemed higher than all human works and merit, even that his mercy alone must have all the praise. . . .

Therefore, if one were to interpret it critically, the coin would have to signify temporal good, and the favor of the householder, eternal life. But the day and the heat we transfer from temporal things to the conscience, so that work-righteous persons do labor long and hard, that is, they do all with a heavy conscience and an unwilling heart, forced and coerced by the law; but the short time or last hours are the light consciences that live blessed lives, led by grace, and that willingly and without being driven by the law. Thus they have now each a coin, that is, a temporal reward is given to both. But the last did not seek it; it was added to them because they sought first the kingdom of heaven and consequently they have the grace to everlasting life and are happy. The first however seek the temporal reward, bargain for it and serve for it; and hence they fail to secure grace and by means of a hard life they merit perdition. For the last do not think of earning the coin, nor do they thus blunder, but they receive all. When the first saw this, by a miscalculation they thought they would receive more, and lost all. Therefore, we clearly see, if we look into their hearts, that the last had no regard for their own merit but enjoyed the goodness of the householder. The first however did not esteem the goodness of the householder, but looked to their own merits, and thought it was theirs by right and murmured about it. SERMON FOR SEPTUAGESIMA SUNDAY.[3]

THE INWARD CALLING OF A TRUE LABORER. JUAN DE VALDÉS: From the words, whence it seems that Christ took occasion to utter this parable, and from the words with which it concludes . . . it is readily inferred that it is his intention to show how the first shall be last and the last first. Where it is to be understood that the householder is God; the vineyard is the church; which, as Christ has showed in other parables, comprises good and bad; the laborers, who go to dig the vineyard, are we all; and the householder's steward is Christ. And it is so, that all who enter into the church, enter, being called of God, but some are so with only the outward calling, which is the preaching of the gospel, while others are so, both outwardly and inwardly.

They who enter with only the outward call, believing by report, they never understand the righteousness of Christ, and pretending to attain eternal life by their works, laboring and wearying themselves by day and by night, they find themselves to be so rich in outward works, that they hold themselves to be the first in the kingdom of God. While those who enter with the outward and with the inward call, believing by revelation, they embrace the righteousness of Christ, and as they do not work in order to be righteous, but because they are righteous, however much they may work, it always appears to them that they work but little, and thus they hold themselves to be last in the kingdom of God. But when Christ shall come to judgment, he will admit those who hold themselves to be last, and he will cast out from the kingdom those who hold themselves to be first; disregarding the amount of works done by both, but regarding

---

[3]Luther, *Precious and Sacred Writings*, 11:106-9; citing Mt 6:33.

the faith and the intention with which they will have worked. Whence will result the murmurs of those who will be excluded from the kingdom, who will plead their good works; but their pleas will profit them but little. . . .

Here I will add two things. The one, that this is ever thus, that they, who, according to human judgment, are first, for that they are very rich in outward works are according to divine judgment, last, for they work without faith; and just as faith, without works of faith, is worth nothing, so works without faith are worth nothing. While, on the other hand, they who, according to human judgment, are last, as being poor in outward works are first according to the divine judgment. COMMENTARY UPON THE GOSPEL OF ST. MATTHEW.[4]

20:17-19 *Jesus Predicts His Crucifixion and Resurrection*

PREDICTING DEATH, PROCLAIMING RESURRECTION. AUGUSTIN MARLORAT: Now our Savior Christ does more plainly preach and speak of his death and passion to his disciples. For now the time of his passion was at hand, the time of darkness and offense; and this was the last journey that he made to Jerusalem. But the disciples which followed him were astonished and afraid; for he ascending to Jerusalem went before them. Therefore, although they were admonished and told before what the end of the Lord should be, yet notwithstanding because that which he had often spoken did profit them nothing at all, he now repeats the whole sum again from the beginning to the ending and exhorts them to constancy, lest they should fall so soon as they were tempted. But he confirms them by two manner of ways: for he, foreshowing that which should come, not only does guard and fortify them, lest a sudden mischief should cause them to faint; but also by the offense of the cross he sets before them a show of his deity, lest a sudden

onset should discourage them, they being persuaded that he is the Son of God, and therefore the conqueror of death. The second way by which he does confirm them is of the resurrection which should mostly follow. And truly, this exhortation was very necessary for them. For because they saw by experience before that he had grievous adversaries at Jerusalem, they go with Christ, not only afraid, but also greatly astonished. They therefore rather wished that he would seek to be quiet in some byway or corner without danger than willingly to put himself into the bands of such cruel enemies. But although this fear might by many means be reprehended as ungodly, yet notwithstanding in that they followed Christ, they show a sign of great obedience and piety. They cheerfully and without sorrow considered it truly far better to run and make haste to whatsoever the Son of God would have led them; and so their reverence deserves great praise, in that they rather seek to endanger themselves than to forsake him. EXPOSITION OF THE HOLY GOSPEL OF MATTHEW.[5]

NO FEAR OF DEATH. MARTIN CHEMNITZ: So far our Savior Jesus Christ has predicted his coming passion and death several times to his disciples. He first did it in Matthew 16:21, when Peter reproved him, but on account of which he was called Satan. Then on the mountain in Luke 9:31. Moses and Elijah also spoke with him about his leaving, which was fulfilled in Jerusalem. Also in Matthew 17:12, in going down from the mountain he spoke again about the things that he would suffer by the scribes. But in the first place in Mark 9:31, he secretly crossed over to Galilee and was instructing his disciples about the passion. Now afterward when the time was at hand with respect to which the favorable decreed passion of the Father approached, of his own free will he went down to Jerusalem, as if to the celebration of the now imminent Passover. But indeed, on this

---

[4]Valdés, *Commentary upon the Gospel of St. Matthew*, 352-54.

[5]Marlorat, ed., *A Catholike and Ecclesiasticall Exposition of the Holy Gospell After S. Mathewe*, 443-44.

account, he went so that this new pascal lamb might be sacrificed, and in this way the work of redemption of the human race might be accomplished. And since he was seeing that his disciples were for this closer departure, but were afraid both for themselves and for Christ, he was preceding them; along with others, either disciples or the rest from the people to precede so they might be anointed. In this way indeed, also by this gesture he often gives that they should by no means be afraid for his own death, but to be prepared and cheerful, to the all-knowing will of his heavenly Father. And at the same time, he also desired to provoke the disciples by his own example, so that they would test the pure and would follow him without fear. A HARMONY OF THE FOUR GOSPELS.[6]

20:20-28 A Mother's Request About the Kingdom

LOOKING FOR A KINGDOM. RICHARD TAVERNER: She comes therefore to Christ with her two sons. They had heard Christ say a little before that they which would follow him in the new birth, when he should sit in the seat of his majesty should also sit upon twelve seats judging the twelve tribes of Israel. And that all they which had left house or brothers and sisters, father or mother, wife or children or their lands for his name sake, should receive a hundred times as much and should enjoy everlasting life. They therefore, being as yet imperfect and having little understanding of the spiritual kingdom but thinking rather that Christ's kingdom should be a worldly and temporal reign, came with their mother, requesting of him that the one of them might sit on the right hand of him in his kingdom and the other on the left, meaning that they might be in some high authority with him. . . .

Truly (as says Chrysostom[†]) our Lord knew that they could follow his passion, but he asks them this, to the intent all we might hear and know,

that none can reign with Christ, unless he follows in his passion. For a precious thing is not gotten but with a precious price. We call the passion of the Lord not only the persecuting of the heathen but also all violence which we suffer striving against sin. This passion and cross we be all bound to abide, if we will be counted to be of Christ's flock. Yes, and when the glory of Christ requires we must also not refuse to suffer corporal death for his sake. THE GOSPELS WITH BRIEF SERMONS.[7]

MISUNDERSTOOD RESURRECTION AND THE KINGDOM. JOHN LIGHTFOOT: The order is plain of itself, and yet the connection is somewhat strange, for in the last words before, Christ had foretold of his death, yet the sons of Zebedee here desire to sit on his right hand and left in his kingdom. . . . The disciples sometimes were mistaken, conceiving that Christ presently after his resurrection should obtain the scepter of an earthly kingdom, whereupon some of them ambitious of priority above the rest desired to sit on his right hand and left. . . . It is true indeed that the Jewish nation, and the disciples with them, erred in judging about the Messiah in his kingdom, but they erred as far also about the Messiah in his resurrection, till experience had informed them better. Therefore, it cannot well be imagined that the wife and sons of Zebedee thought of Christ's resurrection in this their request, but conceived of his temporal kingdom according to the notions of the rest of the nation about it. What therefore our Savior had spoken instantly before of his being scourged, crucified, killed, and rising again, they understood it not in the sense that he spoke it. It may be his naming these two the Sons of Thunder gave them some blind encouragement to such a request. Christ foretells his own death and their suffering martyrdom under the title of baptism. THE HARMONY OF THE FOUR EVANGELISTS.[8]

---

[6]Chemnitz, *Harmoniae Evangelicae*, 1849.

[7]Taverner, *On Saynt Andrewes Day: The Gospels with Brief Sermons* (1542), xxvi. [†]Chrysostom, *Homilies on Matthew*, NPNF[1] 10:380.
[8]Lightfoot, *The Harmony of the Four Evangelists* (1644), 52*; citing Acts 1.

BAPTISM AND THE CUP. GIOVANNI DIODATI:
To arrive to the glory of my kingdom, you must
pass through many combats and troubles, following my example. Therefore, before you seek after
the reward, you should examine yourselves how
you are disposed toward the combat. "To drink," an
ordinary term in Scripture to signify the afflictions
and calamities distributed to each one as it were for
their portions. "Baptized," this kind of figure is
taken from the ancient manner of baptizing,
plunging the whole body in water above the head.
So Christ has been wholly plunged in anguish and
torments. And it should seem that Christ had a
relation to the two sacraments of the Christian
church, which are signs and tokens of grace on
God's side, and on the human side binds him to
imitate Christ, as 1 Corinthians 12:13. "We are . . ."
[is] an ignorant and presumptuous answer.

"You shall drink," not truly by your own
strength and power, as you presume at this
present, but by the help and special grace of my
Spirit. "Is not mine," namely, in the quality of
mediator in which I do converse here in the world,
I have no charge to give degrees of the glory to
come, but only to gain my church's salvation. "It is
prepared" the honor to sit in God's kingdom with
Christ is not given for kindred's sake, or any other
by respect, but out of pure grace and favor,
according to the purpose of choosing those whom
the Father approved from the beginning of the
world. PIOUS ANNOTATIONS.[9]

AN IMPROPER REQUEST. JOSEPH HALL: It was a
sore check: "You know not what you ask." In our
ordinary communication, to speak idly is sin; but,
in our requests to Christ, to be so inconsiderate as
not to understand our own petitions must be a
foul offense. As faith is the ground of our prayers,
so knowledge is the ground of our faith. If we
come with indigested requests, we profane that
name we invoke.

To convince [of] their unfitness for glory, they
are sent to their impotency in suffering: "Are you
able to drink of the cup whereof I shall drink, and
to be baptized with the baptism wherewith I am
baptized?" O Savior, even you, who were one with
your Father, had a cup of your own: never was a
potion so bitter as that which was mixed for you.
Yes, even your draught is stinted: it is not enough
for you to sip of this cup; you must drink it up to
the very dregs. When the vinegar and gall were
offered to you by men, you did but kiss the cup;
but when your Father gave into your hands a
potion infinitely more distasteful, you, for our
health, did drink deep of it, even to the bottom,
and said, "It is finished." And can we repine at
those unpleasing draughts of affliction that are
tempered for us sinful people, when we see you. . . .
When they talk of your kingdom, you speak of
your bitter cup, of your bloody baptism. Suffering
is the way to reigning. "Through many tribulations
must we enter into the kingdom of heaven."
CONTEMPLATIONS.[10]

THE HUMILITY OF A CHRISTIAN LEADER.
JOHN MAYER: The scope of Christ here is to pacify
the men who had indignation at the two, desiring
superiority; and how does he pacify them? Truly
by showing, as Chrysostom[†] has noted, that they
who desire superiority are the more debased,
becoming servants to all, so that there was no cause,
why they should envy them this their desire. And
as it was necessary upon this occasion, he teaches
them, and all Christians, not to desire preeminence
as an honor, but to account of it as a burden, the
greatest is he, be as he ought to be, being a common servant to all, as he himself was, howsoever
among the rulers of the Gentiles it was otherwise.
So that, as I take it, this saying does not pertain to
ecclesiastical persons only, but to all Christians, it
being not their part to affect worldly honors, as the
heathen do, but if any be promoted to use their
preferment to the benefit of others, and not to
magnify themselves by ruling tyrannically and
exacting upon those over whom they are set. . . .

---

[9]Diodati, *Pious Annotations* (1643), E4r*; citing Ps 69:2; Eph 1:4.

[10]Hall, *Contemplations on the Historical Passages of the Old and New Testaments*, 4:547*.

The princes of the Gentiles rule over them, and by all means seek their own honor and not the good of their subjects; but I would not have you like unto the Gentiles, but contrary unto them. Therefore, set not your minds upon honors and dignities, striving to be one above another, but upon my example, the greater any of you be, the more intending to serve, though with great labor and danger of life for the common good of others. TREASURY OF ECCLESIASTICAL EXPOSITIONS.[11]

KINGDOM GREATNESS. DIRK PHILIPS: In addition, [in Matthew 18] the Lord Jesus reprimanded his disciples who argued and disputed with one another about who should be greatest in the kingdom of heaven and said: Truly, truly, I say to you, except you turn around and become as children, you will not come into the kingdom of heaven. Whoever humbles himself as this child—which he had set in the midst of his disciples—that one is the greatest in the kingdom of heaven. And whoever accepts such a child in my name, that one accepts me. For if anyone confuses one of the least of these who believe in me, it would be better for him that a millstone be bound on his neck and he would be drowned in the deepest of the sea. . . . Read this with understanding of what the Lord's meaning is. When the mother of the children of Zebedee desired from the Lord that her two sons might sit beside him in his kingdom, the one on the right and the other on the left hand, and as the ten disciples heard that, they became indignant at her. Then Jesus called them to himself and spoke, you know that the worldly princes rule and the authorities have power, but it shall not be so among you; rather if someone wants to be the greatest among you, that one will be your servant. And whoever will be the chief, that one is your servant. Just as the Son of Man did not come to be served but to serve, and he gave his life as a deliverance for many. THE FRISIAN-FLEMISH DIVISION.[12]

THE PERFECT RANSOM. PHILIPP MELANCHTHON: This is a remarkable thought that is considered carefully as we think, how great a thing our sin is, in turn how great the severity of God's justice is, and then how great his mercy is. Therefore, first we say this, "We acknowledge ourselves to be infirm and hard, that we are not greatly terrified by thinking of our sins, nor do we see how great a thing our sin is and the anger of God." . . .

But we lament this, our hardness, and rightly we are exceedingly terrified, and we think God to be angry by all the sins of the saints and ungodly. For God is just and we do not think him to remit sins from levity, as if he is not truly angry. But they are the same, truly he is angered by sins, and yet he spares his own creatures, and he does not want him to die. At the same time, he is both just and merciful. And this wonderful mixture of justice and mercy, no one is able to express enough, but we will learn in eternal life. And yet this is the beginning of doctrine. For the Scripture so often says that the Son is the ransom and compensation for us. When such a ransom is paid, it was necessary for the anger to be great against sin. These things are often considered much.

Then is considered, "By what means was the work by a ransom and so great a sacrifice?" To this is responded, "God has these two virtues: justice and mercy." And a wonderful thing retains only both. And it is justice to be angry about sin and to punish it. Therefore, when God wanted to spare the human race and yet not to omit justice, he resolved that as a son who was an intercessor for us he might carry the penalty for the whole human race. And truly he wanted his Son to take on the nature of humankind, because with the human race he would be an accused. It was proper for someone in the human race to carry the penalty, and it was needful for this one to be innocent. And as such a one carries the penalty, he might be worthy, sufficient, and equal, and as he was able to conquer death, it was needful for this one carrying such a load, to be God, because by human nature alone, he neither would be sufficient for a ransom, not able to carry the penalty, nor to conquer death. . . .

---

[11]Mayer, *A Treasury of Ecclesiastical Expositions . . . upon the Scriptures* (1622), 242. [†]Chrysostom, *Homilies on Matthew*, NPNF[1] 10:383.
[12]CRR 6:482.

But after God's justice was satisfied through punishment of an innocent one, he exercised mercy toward the human race, and he saved the remaining. Truly Christ said this, to make himself the ransom (*lytron*). Annotations on the Gospels.[13]

20:29-34 The Merciful Son of David Heals Two Blind Men

The Faithful Request for Mercy. Richard Ward: "The Son of David"—We see here how the blind men acknowledge Christ to be the promised Messiah, who was promised under a double name. First, sometimes under the name of David. . . . Second, sometimes under the name of the Son of David. . . . "Have mercy upon us."—We see here that these blind men desire mercy in general, but they name nothing in particular, to teach us, that all our prayers are to be referred to the will of God. . . .

In this history observe these three things: First, the blind men cry unto Christ, but he seems not to hear them at all. Second, they persevere and continue crying, but yet they gain nothing thereby. Third, afterward—as though they had done some evil thing—they are reproved and blamed by the multitude for their prayers. Yet notwithstanding all this they do not desist, but are so much the more fervent in their prayers, as is here plainly expressed, and "they cried so much the more" . . . they give not over, but continue praying to teach us that we must be perseverant in prayer and continue therein until we have obtained that which we want or else until God's will be otherwise revealed. Theological Questions.[14]

Visible Faith. John Calvin: "Have mercy on me, O Lord." I stated, a little ago that there was at first but one who cried out, but the other was induced by a similar necessity to join him. They confer on Christ no ordinary honor when they request him to have mercy and relieve them; for they must have been convinced that he had in his power the assistance or remedy which they needed. But their faith is still more clearly exhibited by their acknowledgment of him as Messiah, to whom we know that the Jews gave this designation, Son of David. They, therefore, apply to Christ, not only as some prophet, but as that person whom God had promised to be the only author of salvation. The cry proved the ardor of the desire; for, though they knew that what they said exposed them to the hatred of many, who were highly displeased with the honor done to Christ, their fear was overcome by the ardor of desire, so that they did not refrain on this account from raising their voice aloud. . . .

If Satan endeavored to throw obstacles in the way of two blind men by means of pious and simple persons, who were induced by some sentiments of religion to follow Christ, how much more will he succeed in accomplishing it by means of hypocrites and traitors, if we be not strictly on our guard? Perseverance is therefore necessary to overcome every difficulty, and the more numerous the obstacles are which Satan throws in the way, the more powerfully ought we to be excited to earnestness in prayer, as we see that the blind men redoubled their cry.

"What do you wish that I should do to you?" He gently and kindly asks what they desire; for he had determined to grant their requests. . . . They implored the mercy of Christ, that he might relieve their wretchedness; but now the Evangelist expresses that Christ was induced to cure them, not only by undeserved goodness, but because he pitied their distress. For the metaphor is taken from the bowels (*splanchna*), in which dwells that kindness and mutual compassion which prompts us to assist our neighbors. Commentary on a Harmony of the Evangelists.[15]

Blindness Brings Sight. Juan De Valdés: Had these two blind men not known their blindness, they would not have asked soundness

[13]MO 14:937-39.
[14]Ward, *Theological Questions upon . . . St. Matthew* (1640), 267-68*; citing Jer 30:9; Ezek 34:23; Hos 3:5; Is 9:6; 16:5; Jer 23:5, 15.

[15]CTS 2:430-32 (CO 45:561-62).

(of vision), and had they not very greatly desired soundness, they would not have been thus importunate in asking it; and at the least, having been rebuked, they would have been silent, and thus they would not have recovered the sight of their eyes. Precisely thus does it happen to men and women; and thus it is that those who do not know themselves to be blind do not ask God to open their inward eyes; while those who know themselves to be blind, if they do not very strongly desire to see, they are not importunate in prayer, and thus neither these nor those recover sight; while they only do recover sight who, by the gift of God, know themselves to be blind and, imitating these two blind men, ask of Christ importunately that he cure them; and they never desist from asking, however much men of the world or hellish fiends rebuke them and interrupt them; nay, they are so much the more impetuous and the more importunate in asking, in proportion as they are the more rebuked and interrupted. Christ opens the inward eyes of such, and they, recognizing Christ by them, follow Christ, imitating Christ. And here I understand that none follow Christ, save those, who, having, by the benefit of Christ, recovered their inward sight, begin to know Christ. COMMENTARY UPON THE GOSPEL OF ST. MATTHEW.[16]

---

[16]Valdés, *Commentary upon the Gospel of St. Matthew*, 362.

21:1-17 THE TRIUMPHAL ENTRY

Now when they drew near to Jerusalem and came to Bethphage, to the Mount of Olives, then Jesus sent two disciples, ²*saying to them, "Go into the village in front of you, and immediately you will find a donkey tied, and a colt with her. Untie them and bring them to me.* ³*If anyone says anything to you, you shall say, 'The Lord needs them,' and he will send them at once." * ⁴*This took place to fulfill what was spoken by the prophet, saying,*

> ⁵*"Say to the daughter of Zion,*
> *'Behold, your king is coming to you,*
> *humble, and mounted on a donkey,*
> *on a colt,ᵃ the foal of a beast of burden.'"*

⁶*The disciples went and did as Jesus had directed them.* ⁷*They brought the donkey and the colt and put on them their cloaks, and he sat on them.* ⁸*Most of the crowd spread their cloaks on the road, and others cut branches from the trees and spread them on the road.* ⁹*And the crowds that went before him and that followed him were shouting, "Hosanna to the Son of David! Blessed is he who comes in the name of the Lord! Hosanna in the highest!" * ¹⁰*And when he entered Jerusalem, the whole city was stirred up, saying, "Who is this?" * ¹¹*And the crowds said, "This is the prophet Jesus, from Nazareth of Galilee."*

¹²*And Jesus entered the templeᵇ and drove out all who sold and bought in the temple, and he overturned the tables of the money-changers and the seats of those who sold pigeons.* ¹³*He said to them, "It is written, 'My house shall be called a house of prayer,' but you make it a den of robbers."*

¹⁴*And the blind and the lame came to him in the temple, and he healed them.* ¹⁵*But when the chief priests and the scribes saw the wonderful things that he did, and the children crying out in the temple, "Hosanna to the Son of David!" they were indignant,* ¹⁶*and they said to him, "Do you hear what these are saying?" And Jesus said to them, "Yes; have you never read,*

> *"'Out of the mouth of infants and nursing babies you have prepared praise'?"*

¹⁷*And leaving them, he went out of the city to Bethany and lodged there.*

a Or *donkey, and on a colt*   **b** Some manuscripts add *of God*

OVERVIEW: The divine orchestration of Jesus' entry into Jerusalem is made clear in Matthew's citation of Zechariah 9:9. The Old Testament quotation reasserts the kingly image, and therefore is of significant interest to the Reformation exegetes. Many commentators compare or harmonize the various accounts of Jesus' arrival into Jerusalem. Another common effort is to explain the use of the Zechariah text.

The royal welcome and proclamation by the crowds in Jerusalem heralds Jesus' arrival as the saving king. Intermingled with the excitement of the crowds, the widespread misunderstanding of his identity (Mt 21:10-11) and his saving purposes sets the stage for the crowds to turn against Jesus when he does not meet their expectations. This irony prompts the reformers to encourage their readers to understand Jesus in light of the Old Testament prophecies and the New Testament narratives about him.

Jesus' entrance into the temple creates two scenes of conflict. First, Jesus cleanses the temple from the traders who had turned the area into a marketplace. As seen in his reference to two Old Testament texts (Is 56:7; Jer 7:11), the illicit trading had hindered the fundamental role of the temple as a place of prayer. Many reformers attempt to explain in greater detail the Old Testament texts as a legitimate rationale for Jesus' actions.

Second, as Jesus heals those around him, the angry religious leaders challenge him because of his miracles and the acclamation of the crowds. Jesus answers the leaders' question with a provocative quotation from Psalm 8, an allusion to his identity as the Son of Man and their role of opposing the work of God and the rule of the Son (Ps 8:2-8). Johannes Piscator emphasizes the significance of the Old Testament texts selected to demonstrate Jesus' messianic identity to the religious leaders, the crowds, and later disciples.

21:1-11 The Triumphal Entry into Jerusalem

HARMONIZING THE GOSPELS AND ZECHARIAH. THOMAS JACKSON: If we compare the evangelical relations concerning the manner of our Savior's coming to Jerusalem with the prophet's predictions, they agree so well that Zechariah in this particular may share well with Isaiah in that title of the evangelical prophet. Yet in the manner of the evangelical stories concerning this point, there is some variation in words, but no contradiction or contrariety in sense. . . . "Go unto the village," St. Matthew says, "over against you. And straight you shall find a donkey tied and a colt with her: loose them and bring them unto me." St. Mark relates the same story thusly, "You shall find a colt tied, whereon never man sat, loose him and bring him." See Luke 19:30. This variation of words has raised a doubt among interpreters as well of the prophet as of the Evangelists, whether our Savior did ride part of the way upon the donkey, and part upon the colt, or all the way upon the colt alone. Such as think our Savior did ride only upon the colt labor to save the truth of the prophetical prediction and St. Matthew's portrayal, how it was fulfilled by a synecdoche usual, as they allege, in the Hebrew dialect. To say the king of Zion should come riding upon a donkey, and upon the foal of a donkey, is a speech as justifiable in grammatical sense, as that Jonas should be sleeping in the sides of the ship (so are the words of the prophecy) whereas he could not sleep but in one side of the

ship at one time. But as for synecdoches, metonymies, or other like words of art, grammar, or rhetoric, unless they be reduced to some logical or rational maxim, they edify no better in divinity than an allegory or mystical interpretation, which is not grounded upon some historical relation of matter of fact, according to the plain literal or grammatical sense. . . .

The Evangelists use the like speech when they say: The malefactors which were crucified with our Savior did revile him; whereas in such distinct apprehension as St. Luke had of this circumstance, one of the two only did revile him, or at least continue in this wicked mind; but the party reviling being not so distinctly known by name or by other circumstances (as Barabbas was) to the other Evangelists as unto St. Luke, they make their expressions in the plural. It is a general rule worthy of every commentator's actual consideration, that albeit every Evangelist relate nothing but the truth, yet no one of them relates the whole truth concerning our Savior's life and actions, his death and passion; nor do they always observe the order and method of all circumstances, or occurrences, as will appear hereafter. The manner of our Savior's coming to Jerusalem might be, and no doubt was, more distinctly represented to the disciples' senses than it had been to the prophet Zechariah's spirit. For . . . the light of prophecy was not always distinctly evident, but indefinitely. And this might be the reason why the prophet foretells that our Savior should come riding both upon the donkey, and the colt, when as three Evangelists mention only the colt. And albeit St. Matthew mentions both, yet it may be replied that he historically in that passage declares nothing of his own observation but only relates the prophet's words, which he saw now fulfilled, although our Savior had rid only upon the donkey, or upon the colt. THE HUMILIATION OF THE SON OF GOD.[1]

THE HUMILITY OF CHRIST. MARTIN LUTHER: In the story of this Gospel, we will first direct our

---

[1] Jackson, *Works*, 2:848-49*; citing Mk 11:2; Lk 19:30.

attention to the reason why the Evangelist quotes the words of the prophet, in which was described long ago and in clear, beautiful, and wonderful words, the bodily, public entrance and advent of our Lord Jesus Christ to the people of Zion or Jerusalem, as the text says. In this the prophet wanted to show and explain to his people and to all the world who the Messiah is and how and in what manner he would come and manifest himself, and offers a plain and visible sign in this that he says, "Behold, thy king cometh unto thee, meek, and riding upon an ass" . . . so that we would be certain of it, and not dispute about the promised Messiah or Christ, nor wait for another.

He therewith anticipates the mistaken idea of the Jews, who thought, because there were such glorious things said and written of Christ and his kingdom, he would manifest himself in great worldly pomp and glory, as a king against their enemies. . . . The Evangelist therefore quotes this saying of the prophet to punish the blindness and false notions of those who seek bodily and temporal blessings in Christ and his gospel, and to convince them by the testimony of the prophet, who shows clearly what kind of a king Christ was and what they should seek in him, in that he calls him just and having salvation and yet adds this sign of his coming by which they are to know him: "He comes to thee meek, and riding upon a colt, the foal of an ass." As if to say, poor, miserable, almost beggarly horseman upon a borrowed ass who is kept by the side of its mother not for ostentation but for service. With this he desires to lead them away from gazing and waiting for a glorious entrance of a worldly king. And he offers such signs that they might not doubt the Christ, nor take offense at his beggarly appearance. All pomp and splendor are to be left out of sight, and the heart and the eyes directed to the poor rider, who became poor and miserable and made himself of no kingly reputation that they might not seek the things of this world in him but the eternal, as is indicated by the words, "just and having salvation." SERMON ON FIRST SUNDAY IN ADVENT.[2]

---

[2]Luther, *Precious and Sacred Writings*, 10:41-43.

A ROYAL ENTRANCE. JUAN DE VALDÉS: As to the ceremony of the boughs, I have already said that they referred to the feast (of Tabernacles) which they held in the seventh month; and it is truly something divine that those multitudes, without knowing what they did, should have done in honor of Christ what they did in honor of God, adding thereto the casting of their garments on the road; a ceremony taken I know not where; but it pleases me to consider Christ, who, as to himself, humbled himself by riding upon a donkey, while as to the multitudes, he was exalted by all those ceremonies to the best of their ability; by the boughs, by their garments, and by the exclamations, which they shouted; "Hosanna," which is tantamount to "help us now"; and, by adding, "Son of David," they confessed Christ to be the Messiah, as we have previously seen. And by saying, "Blessed be he that cometh" . . . they confirmed the opinion they held, that he was the Messiah, sent by God to redeem Israel; but not as they thought, from the tyranny of men in the present life; but from the tyranny of the flesh, of the devil, of hell, and of death, to life eternal; which liberation they begin to feel in the present life, who have to enjoy it in the life eternal. Repeating their Hosanna with that "in the highest," I think that they meant that their voices should ascend on high, so that they should be heard of God.

And it is to be understood that to shout Hosanna is the same as though they had cried out "God save the king," which we are in the habit of doing when the king enters any place. And also that these words with which the multitudes honored Christ are taken from Psalm 118:25-26, where there is a verse that says, "I beseech you, O Lord, save now: I beseech you, O Lord, prosper now: Blessed is he who comes in the name of the Lord." Where remitting myself to my commentary upon this psalm, I will say this: that it would have been the greatest happiness of those multitudes had they known what they did and what they said; knowing that they were inspired by God to do it and to say it; as it will be our greatest happiness, when, being inspired by God, as were they, we shall know that that is inspiration of God, and we shall embrace it; our happiness consisting in that we shall know both the omnipotence of God and of Christ; the power of their inspirations within us; and we shall thus be the more certified of our justification, resurrection, and glorification. Commentary upon the Gospel of St. Matthew.[3]

On Christ, the King, and His Kingdom.

Niels Hemmingsen: The second place, which the text of the Gospel contains, imposes the description of Christ our king and of his kingdom. Which description is confirmed by the testimony of Zechariah, which the Evangelist alleges that we may understand, how this pomp was not instituted rashly, but foreshowed long before, according to the will of God and the secret counsel of the Trinity. For this pomp teaches us many things of the state of Christ our king and of his kingdom. First this pomp of Christ's riding into Jerusalem makes a difference between Christ our king and the kings of the world, and shows the diversity of their kingdoms. For this base pomp does sufficiently argue neither that Christ is a worldly king nor that the administration of his kingdom is worldly. . . . Second, this story teaches that under this base pomp lies hid a certain almightiness and Godhead. For when he says, "you loose it and bring it unto me," and again, "the Lord has need of them," and also, "he shall by and by let them go." Christ our King gives us to understand that by his heavenly power he is able to bring to pass what he likes; and even that he has the hearts and wills of human beings in his hand.

Therefore, although the kingdom of Christ seemed disposable in this world; yet not withstanding if a person look upon the power and divinity of this king, nothing is more stately; nothing is more mighty; nothing finally is more glorious than it. Moreover, the prophecy of the prophet contains three things. First an exhortation to the church, at that time cast down and utterly

under foot. Be glad (he says) and leap for joy, daughter of Zion. Hereby we are taught that the gospel pertains to those who are cast down and underfoot, and altogether broken in spirit. Second, this prophecy contains a commandment from God that we should do homage to this king, like as the second Psalm exhorts where it says, "kiss the son." Third, this prophecy contains a description of the person of Christ, namely, that he is the king that was promised to the church. "Behold," it says, "your king comes." As if he should have said, here is at length that king that was promised to you, of whom are written so many testimonies, which shall restore the kingdom of God that the devil has invaded and destroyed through sin. The one who says that this king is gentle and meek, to the intent we should not shun him as a cruel tyrant, but rather come unto him with full confidence, and demand of him the salvation promised. A Postil, or Exposition of the Gospels.[4]

The Lord Saves.

John Calvin: This prayer is taken from Psalm 118:25. Matthew relates expressly the Hebrew words in order to inform us that these applauses were not rashly bestowed on Christ, and that the disciples did not utter without consideration the prayers which came to their lips, but that they followed with reverence the form of prayer, which the Holy Spirit had prescribed to the whole church by the mouth of the prophet. For, though he speaks there of his own kingdom, yet there is no reason to doubt that he principally looks, and intends others to look, to the eternal succession, which the Lord had promised to him. He drew up a perpetual form of prayer, which would be observed, even when the wealth of the kingdom was decayed; and therefore, it was a prevailing custom that prayers for the promised redemption were generally presented in these words. And the design of Matthew was, as we have just hinted, to quote in Hebrew a well-known psalm, for the purpose of showing that Christ was acknowledged by the multitude as a Redeemer. The

---

[3]Valdés, *Commentary upon the Gospel of St. Matthew*, 367-68.

[4]Hemmingsen, *A Postill, or Exposition of the Gospels* (1569), 3-4*.

pronunciation of the words, indeed, is somewhat changed; for it ought rather to have been written, *Hoshiana* (הושיע נא), "Save now, we beseech you"; but we know that it is scarcely possible to take a word from one language into another without making some alteration in the sound. Nor was it only the ancient people whom God enjoined to pray daily for the kingdom of Christ, but the same rule is now laid down for us. And certainly, as it is the will of God to reign only in the person of his Son, when we say, "May your kingdom come," under this petition is conveyed the same thing which is expressed more clearly in the psalm. Besides, when we pray to God to maintain his Son as our King, we acknowledge that this kingdom was not erected by human beings and is not upheld by the power of human beings, but remains invincible through heavenly protection. He is said to come "in the name of God," who not only conducts himself, but receives the kingdom, by the command and appointment of God. COMMENTARY ON A HARMONY OF THE EVANGELISTS.[5]

PROOF OF THE MESSIANIC KING. CHRISTOPH CORNER: The third proof stems from the title of king that he claims for himself and from the witness of the people of his church about his kingdom and majesty. And included in this is the accompaniment of the crowd that acknowledges and celebrates this king. Second is the decoration or covering of the donkey and colt; they are covered with the togas or garments of the attendants, a cheap decoration that reminds us of his humility and directs our minds to a consideration of the spiritual kingdom. Third, the decoration and coverings of the roads, which are clothes laid out so that the king might proceed gently and be received in honor. Fourth, the joyous crowd, which had gathered together for the festival, carries and scatters about palm and olive branches, signifying that he will be victorious and the author of peace, just as the Israelites were ordered to take up branches of palms and boughs of leafy trees and

rejoice before the Lord in the feast of the Tabernacles. Fifth is the public thanksgiving, prayer, and celebration. With great excitement and passion, the crowd hails him, shouting, "Hosanna! Save, Help," so that the omnipotent and highest God might support the king promised to David and give blessings in the kingdom and victory against enemies and peace to the people of his church. The crowd celebrates also that he is a king blessed and praised, and because through him all nations will be blessed and evil removed, and because he comes as a king sent and anointed by the Lord, and by his bidding and decree will take up the governance of such a great kingdom. Moreover, a remarkable image of the church of God is represented here, which is the coming together of people who acknowledge and truly worship Christ the blessed and eternal king, a just one, a Savior, who dispenses righteousness and salvation; and the members of that church are marvelously moved by his humility and delight in it, as opposed to being offended by it, as the Pharisees, and hold him in contempt and indict him.

Other proofs arising from this story also help to confirm this proposition [that Christ is the messianic king], among which are these: the disturbance in the city, for such a spectacle that reveals Christ's singular majesty creates admiration in the citizens, and the enemies are terrified to try anything against Christ; the testimony of the crowd professing him to be the promised prophet, about whom it was foretold in Deuteronomy 18; his assumption of the responsibilities of a true king, for, he after being greeted as king when he enters into the temple, he first gives his attention to cleansing the worship and removing the abuses of the temple, and then he bestows blessings on many; the indignation and murmuring of the priests whom it irritates that he is hailed, honored, and received as the Christ. But Christ defends his own deeds and the deeds of the people against them. THE ECONOMY OF THE GOSPELS.[6]

---

[5]CTS 2:451-52* (CO 45:574-75).

[6]Corner, *Oikonomia Evangeliorum* (1567), A4r-A5r; citing Lev 23; Gen 22.

UNDERSTANDING THE CROWD'S HOSANNA.

JACQUES LEFÈVRE D'ÉTAPLES: Not only did the disciples do as the Lord commanded, but [as we see] from Mark 11 and Luke 19, they found matters just as the Lord had told them beforehand, for it was his to know the outcome of events before they were even conceived on a human level (*ab homine concepta*). This was a property of God. And through the things that transpired at that time, a mystery was made plain, namely the "untying" [*solution*] of the two peoples.[†]

The Jewish people are represented by the donkey that was under the yoke, since they were under the yoke of the law. The foal, which was not under the yoke, [represents] the Gentiles who were bound by no law of God—but by idolatry. Now both are untied [*soluitur*]: the former from the yoke of the law through grace, and the latter from the shackle of idolatry through true knowledge of God. But this "Son" [of David][†] belongs to the donkey that is untied through doctrine, and indeed is a spiritual Son. The earthly Jerusalem represents the heavenly Jerusalem. To this [heavenly city] Christ our king leads both peoples when he "mounts" them through the obedience of their faith. First, however, he outfits the people with apostolic gear, which are the virtues and graces of apostolic doctrine. Those vestments that are strewn in the road and the [palm] branches that they cut from the trees signify divine honors. Thus, also the crowds that go before him and the crowds that follow, crying out, signify the crowds of the blessed who are perennially praising God.

And what do those crowds cry out that go before and are following? *Hosiah na*—that is, "save, I pray!" To whom were they saying this? To whom were they crying out? To the "Son of David," who is Christ, the ever-blessed Lord. What sort of salvation were they seeking? An earthly one? Not at all! This is understood through what is added: "Blessed is he who comes in the name of the Lord, *Hosiah na!*" That is, "save I pray, in the highest." Now, to save "in the highest" belongs to God alone. This cry was uttered through the motion of the Holy Spirit. If it was directed toward Christ, then

he is indicated to be true God. I say "if" this cry, *Hosiah na*, was directed to Christ, since there is another sense, which I judge to be truer, in which the cry is not directed to Christ—except insofar as he is God—but to the Father. If therefore this word, *Hosannah*—that is, "save, I pray!"—was directed to the Father, then this is the voice of one who wishes well and beseeches. And the phrase "to the Son of David" is understood from the verb *Hosiah* to mean "[Save] the king!" For in Hebrew, one joins the verb to the dative case or that which certainly corresponds to it. We see this in Ezekiel 34: "I will save my flock." Or Psalm 43: "And their right arm will not save them." Or Psalm 97: "His right arm will save him." In these passages, the verb is joined to the dative or that which corresponds to the dative. Among us [in Latin], however, the verbs "save!" (*salua*) or "make safe" (*saluum fac*)—as with the Greek *sōzō*, which can be considered an equivalent—always require an object in the accusative case. This is why in Psalm 97 in Greek reads *esōsen auton hē dexia autou* ("His right hand saved him").[§] In Latin one would need to say, *saluauit ipsum dextera eius* ("his right hand saved him"). When, therefore, the crowds were saying *Hosiah na filio Dauid*, it is as if they said, "Save the Son of David, I pray! Save him, I say, you who are Most High!" When Matthew's translation, and ours, left the object [Son of David] in the dative—*hōsan na tō huiō Dauid* (Matthew), *Osannah filio Dauid* (ours)—they have not erred. For they have also retained the [Hebrew] verb that requires the dative case, or at least that which performs the dative function. If instead they had not kept the Hebrew word [*Hosannah* untranslated], but had said [in Latin], "save" [*salua*] or "make safe [*saluum fac*], I pray," then indeed it would have been necessary to change the dative object into an accusative and say *Saluum fac obsecro filium Dauid* ("Save, I pray the Son of David"). This expression of praise and favorable invocation appears to be taken from Psalm 117 [118:25-26], "O Lord, save us! Make us to prosper, oh Lord! Blessed is he who comes in the name of the Lord!" The Holy Spirit poured out these words in the crowds and children so that they could hear the spirit of David speaking in them. Thus, they truly understood that he [Christ] was the Son of David, or truly the Messiah. And we further understand the meaning of this praise from Luke, who says "all the crowds of those descending rejoiced and began to praise God." This cry was therefore an expression of joy in the Holy Spirit, of praise, and of favorable invocation—of praise to Father and to Christ, insofar as he was God, and of favorable invocation for the same Christ, insofar as he was man. None of the other kings of the Hebrews were given such praise at any time, but it was peculiar to Christ alone and owed to the prophetic Spirit [in the crowds], who was the Holy Spirit. What at length Jesus did upon entering the earthly Jerusalem, Matthew indicates when he adds . . . COMMENTARY ON THE FOUR GOSPELS.[7]

21:12-17 *Jesus Cleanses the Temple*

CHRIST'S FORCEFUL CLEANSING. JOHN HOWSON: Whereas in all other places and against all other sins he uses words and reproofs and reprehensions, and those also tempered with humility, mildness, and gentleness, here he uses force, and execution, and external discipline, and present correction, by casting them out of the temple, by making a whip of small cords, and so whipping them out; by overthrowing the tables of the money-changers, and the seats and chairs of those who sold doves: and whereas he says of himself that he "was sent into the world, not to judge the world, but that the world might be saved by him"; yet in this case, in this sin, in this abuse, and profanation of the temple, as it were forgetting his accustomed gentleness, and the end of his coming, he exercises

punishment, strikes with a whip, overthrows the tables, casts abroad the money, and to conclude, casts them out of the temple; and that by himself alone and with his own hands.

Here our Savior, the prince of peace and fountain of mercy, comes to Jerusalem and with his own hands does punish and abuse, and the profanations of the temple of God. Adam sinned, and he sent his angels or cherubim to cast him out of paradise. The wicked Sodomites sinned, and he sent his angels, and it rained fire from heaven and consumed them. . . . Only this sin of profaning and abusing his temple, he corrects and chastens with his hands, he sends not his angels, he sends not fire, he sends not water, he sends not his prophets, but he comes himself and executes punishment on them. . . .

I amplify this point, and urge all these circumstances of our Savior's force, and extraordinary violence used in this place, and the miraculous performing of it; to show unto you how odious this sin is of profaning the church of God with buying and selling. A SERMON PREACHED AT PAUL'S CROSS.[8]

CHRIST EXPRESSES HIS AUTHORITY TO REFORM HIS TEMPLE. AEGIDIUS HUNNIUS: "And Jesus entered into the temple." These things indeed which are recorded here happened in the city. It is worthwhile to consider what took place in the temple. Since he wished to establish himself as the King of Israel, sung and promised by the prophets, it was proper that the same works might provide both an illustrious testimony and fulfill the clear prediction of the prophets that "the Christ would come into his temple" and that "the latter house built after the return from the captivity would outshine the temple of Solomon." Because this temple was sacred to the Christ (namely, the God of the Hebrews) and because it, together with the whole ritual worship conducted within it, pertained solely to Christ, being set apart in its gatherings and its works for the Messiah—for this

---

[7]Lefèvre, *Commentarii Initiatorii in Quatuor Evangelia* (1523), 90r-90v; citing Ps 118:25-26; Lk 19:37. †A more basic translation would have been "solution" or "meaning," but there seems to be deliberate wordplay here with the "untying" of the donkey that serves Lefèvre's allegory. ‡Lefèvre seems to have in mind the title "Son of David," which is applied to Christ in this passage. §His Greek text appears to read *auton* here. But in modern editions of the Septuagint (Greek translation of the Old Testament), the verse reads: *esōsen autō hē dexia autou*, *autō* being a dative object of "save."

[8]Howson, *A Sermon Preached at Paul's Cross*, 18-19, 21.

reason, the Lord entered as one who had full authority to reform it. Discerning abuse in the holy place, namely the traffic of those who were buying and selling, he decreed that the temple must be wholly purged and reformed. Perhaps if the Jews had conducted their business, which was required for the sacrifices of the present festival, in Jerusalem outside the holy place, they could not have been reprimanded. That would have been the appropriate and legal time and place for it. But for this traffic to be set up in the temple itself—that was utterly intolerable. Therefore the Lord, moved and inflamed in a rush of divine zeal, "cast out at once those who were buying and selling, and having made a whip of cords, overturned the tables of the moneychangers greedy for profit, scattering them, and overthrew and drove out the stalls and chairs of those who were selling doves and other beasts." Those in the temple, though they were many, were scrambling to flee from Christ, though he was approaching them alone. This was because they could not help but recognize the divine authority in his marvelous work, which made them cast themselves down at his feet in fear. In the meantime, he proclaims the reason for his action from the prophets Isaiah and Jeremiah, saying, "It has been written that my house shall be called a house of prayer, but you have made it a den of robbers." The prior clause cited by Christ comes from Isaiah, where these words appear: "My house will be called a house of prayer for all peoples." The latter clause appears in Jeremiah: "You have made the house which is called by my name into a den of robbers." By this accusation, the Savior indicates that those Jewish buyers and sellers had profaned the temple no less than the priests and the people had done in the time of the ancient prophets. And he shows that this profanation was not at all to be taken lightly, seeing as the house of God was for the holiest worship and prayers not only of the Jews but also of the proselytes who had come to Jerusalem to worship the Lord. This they turned not only into a house of trade, but a horrid den where souls were robbed, since the teachers and priests of the people permitted them to profane the temple. In this way,

they slew the people's souls for eternity and led them headlong into damnation and Gehenna.

Having caried out this reformation, Christ is now said "to have taught in the temple" on the same day and the following (as Luke reports). He called back and restored the Jerusalem temple to its true purpose by his salutary teachings. At the same time he rendered that purpose clear by miracles, by which the doctrine he was putting forth was miraculously confirmed. Blind men approached him whose sight he restored. The lame came to him whose bodies he rendered whole. The leaders of the priests were seeing the miracles that he was performing and also hearing children acclaim him in the temple: "Hosanna to the Son of David!" Still, they were not allowing themselves to be persuaded by any arguments so that they themselves might recognize him as the Son of David or Messiah. On the contrary, the children's acclaim so inflamed them to jealousy that they said to him, not without chagrin, "Do you hear what these are saying?" That is, "do you not understand that the children and people are expressing praise for you that is inappropriate to your person? It is appropriate rather that you impose silence on them and stop their mouths." Yet Christ's response approves the children's praise and confirms it by a testimony by the testimony of prophetic scripture: "Did you never read, 'from the mouth of infants and nursing babies you have prepared for yourself praise?'" These words are taken from the Psalm of David 8, which elsewhere, namely, 1 Corinthians 15, Ephesians 1, and Hebrews 2, are interpreted with reference to the Messiah. By putting forth the present testimony, Christ teaches that this prophetic word along with the "Hosanna" in Psalm 118 pertain to himself. For by divine inspiration it was predicted that, at some point in the future, he would be acclaimed in this way. And the text adds that the Lord Jesus left behind the ungrateful priests, scribes, and Pharisees and departed outside the city, returning to Bethany, where he had raised Lazarus from the dead. COMMENTARY ON MATTHEW.[9]

[9]Hunnius, *Commentarius in Evangelium Secundum Matthaeum* (1594), 694-96; citing Is 56:7; Jer 7:11; Ps 8:2.

A HOUSE OF PRAYER. EDWIN SANDYS: In the house of God, they had the law both read and expounded, they offered sacrifice, and they prayed. But because the service for which the temple was ordained, though not only yet principally, is prayer, therefore he has said, "My house shall be called the house of prayer." In Deuteronomy, it is called the place which God chose to cause his name to dwell there. It is true indeed, says Solomon, that God will dwell on the earth. . . .

The request which Solomon made unto God, in the first dedication of the temple, was that if his people Israel should at any time for their sins be overthrown before the enemy, or heaven be so shut up that they should be in distress for want of rain, or if there should be famine in the land, or pestilence, or blasting, or mildew, or grasshopper, or caterpillar, if the enemy should besiege them, if they should fall into any adversity, whether it were of body, or of mind, his ears might always be open to the prayers which they should make before the Lord, in the house of prayer. Hear the supplications of your people Israel, which pray in this place.

Nor only their supplications, but moreover, Solomon adds, as touching the stranger that is not of your people Israel, who shall come out of a far country for thy name's sake and shall come and pray in this house, hear in heaven your dwelling place, and do according to all that the stranger calls for unto you, that all the people of the earth may know your name and fear you as your people Israel do. Agreeable whereunto are the words of the prophet Isaiah, "It shall be in the last days that the mountain of the house of the Lord shall be prepared in the top of the mountains and shall be exalted above the hills, and all nations shall flow unto it." And again, the strangers that cleave unto the Lord to serve him, and to love the name of the Lord, and to be his servants, every one that keeps the Sabbath and pollutes it not and embraces my covenant, them will I bring also to my holy mountain, and make them joyful in my house of prayer: their burnt offerings, and their sacrifices shall be accepted upon mine altar. For my house

shall be called a house of prayer for all nations. A SERMON PREACHED IN YORK.[10]

A PROPER APPLICATION OF PROPHECY. JOHN CALVIN: Christ quotes two passages taken out of two prophets; the one from Isaiah 56:7, and the other from Jeremiah 7:11. What was written by Isaiah agreed with the circumstances of the time; for that passage predicts the calling of the Gentiles. Isaiah therefore promises that God will grant, not only that the temple shall recover its original splendor, but likewise that all nations shall flow to it and that the whole world shall agree in true and sincere piety. He speaks, no doubt, metaphorically, for the spiritual worship of God, which was to exist under the reign of Christ, is shadowed out by the prophets under the figures of the law. Certainly, it was never fulfilled that all nations went up to Jerusalem to worship God; and therefore, when he declares that the temple will be a place of prayer for all nations, this mode of expression is equivalent to saying that the nations must be gathered into the church of God and that with one voice they may worship the true God, along with the children of Abraham. But since he mentions the temple, so far as it then was the visible abode of religion, Christ justly reproaches the Jews with having applied it to totally different purposes from those to which it had been dedicated. The meaning therefore is: God intended that this temple should exist until now as a sign on which all his worshipers should fix their eyes; and how base and wicked is it to profane it by turning it into a market?

Besides, in the time of Christ, that temple was actually a house of prayer. That is, so long as the law with its shadows remained in force. But it began to be a house of prayer for all nations when the doctrine of the gospel resounded out of it, by which the whole world was to be united in one common faith. And though shortly afterward it was totally overthrown, yet even in the present day the fulfillment of this prophecy is manifest; for

---

[10]Sandys, *Sermons of the Most Reverend Father in God* (1616), 109-11*; citing Is 2:2; 56:6-7.

"since out of Zion went forth the law," those who wish to pray aright must look to that beginning. I do acknowledge that there is no distinction of places, for it is the will of the Lord that men and women should call upon him everywhere; but as believers who profess to worship the God of Israel are said to "speak in the language of Canaan," so they are also said to come into the temple, because out of it flowed the true religion. It is likewise the fountain of the waters, which, enlarged to an astonishing degree within a short period, flow in great abundance, and give life to those that drink them, as Ezekiel mentions, which, going out from the temple, spread, as Zechariah says, from the rising to the setting sun. Though in the present day we make use of temples (or churches) for holding the holy assemblies, yet it is for a different reason; for, since Christ was manifested, no outward representation of him under shadows is held out to us, such as the fathers anciently had under the law.

It must also be observed that by the word *prayer* the prophet expresses the whole worship of God; for, though there was at that time a great variety and abundance of religious rites, yet God intended briefly to show what was the object of all those rites; namely, that they might worship him spiritually, as is more clearly expressed in the fiftieth psalm, where also God comprehends under prayer all the exercises of religion.

"But you have made it a den of robbers." Christ means that the complaint of Jeremiah applied equally well to his own time, in which the temple was not less corrupted. The prophet directs his reproof against hypocrites, who, through confidence in the temple, allowed themselves greater liberty in sinning. For, as it was the design of God to employ outward symbols as a sort of rudiments for instructing the Jews in true religion, so they satisfied themselves with the empty pretense of the temple, as if it were enough to give their attention to outward ceremonies; just as it is customary with hypocrites to "change the truth of God into a lie."

But the prophet exclaims that God is not bound to the temple nor tied to ceremonies, and therefore that they falsely boast of the name of the temple, which they had made a den of robbers. For as robbers in their dens sin with greater hardihood because they trust that they will escape punishment, so by means of a false covering of godliness hypocrites grow more bold so that they almost hope to deceive God. Now as the metaphor of a den includes all corruptions, Christ properly applies the passage of the prophet to the present occasion. COMMENTARY ON A HARMONY OF THE EVANGELISTS.[11]

JESUS DISPLAYS HIS AUTHORITY. JOHANNES PISCATOR: In describing the regal entrance of Christ into the city, the Evangelist first describes the actions that came before where the Lord prepared himself for that entry, up to verse 8, and then the actions that made up the actual entry itself. Then he narrates the effect among the citizens, and then the Lord's activities that ensued, that is, those for which he came into the city. Last, the effect of those actions on the priests and the scribes.

In the fourth and last part, two actions of the Lord, which took place immediately after he entered into the city—whereby, to be sure, he demonstrated his kingly power—are talked about in broad terms: the cleansing of the temple and the healing of the sick in the temple. The cleansing of the temple is shown partly from deeds and partly from the words that give an explanation for the deeds. The deeds were two: the casting out of those who were selling and buying in the temple and the overturning of the furniture being used for that exchange. The words were likewise two: one, the statement of God concerning the right use of his temple, namely, that it is a house of prayer, from Isaiah 56:7. The second is a reproach of the abuse of the temple for greed, expressed in the words of God which are at Jeremiah 7:11, with which God once similarly made his charge of hypocrisy against the Jews. The second action, that is, the healing of the

---

[11]CTS 3:12-14* (CO 45:581-82); citing Is 2:2; Mic 4:2; Is 19:18; Ezek 47:9; Zech 14:8; Jer 7:11; Rom 1:25.

sick, is highlighted by drawing attention to the blind and the lame. That all relates to the fourth section of this text. In the fifth and last section a twofold effect of those actions on the priests and the scribes is described: indignation at and chiding of Jesus for calmly putting up with the honorific acclamation of children . . . and his approval of it through his silence. Against this chiding Jesus defends himself by asserting his deity, meaning that he deserved the joyous honor of the boys by which they were offended, inas-much as he is the one "who prepared praise for himself from the mouths of infants and nursing babies," just as David already once recognized. By these words he is intimating by reasoning from the lesser that he has obtained much more praise for himself from the mouth of more fully grown children who have the ability to use reason and speech. LOGICAL ANALYSIS OF MATTHEW.[12]

[12]Piscator, *Analysis Logica Evangelii Secundum Matthaeum* (1594), 323-24.

21:18–22:14 REJECTING JESUS' AUTHORITY

[18]*In the morning, as he was returning to the city, he became hungry.* [19]*And seeing a fig tree by the wayside, he went to it and found nothing on it but only leaves. And he said to it, "May no fruit ever come from you again!" And the fig tree withered at once.*

[20]*When the disciples saw it, they marveled, saying, "How did the fig tree wither at once?"* [21]*And Jesus answered them, "Truly, I say to you, if you have faith and do not doubt, you will not only do what has been done to the fig tree, but even if you say to this mountain, 'Be taken up and thrown into the sea,' it will happen.* [22]*And whatever you ask in prayer, you will receive, if you have faith."*

[23]*And when he entered the temple, the chief priests and the elders of the people came up to him as he was teaching, and said, "By what authority are you doing these things, and who gave you this authority?"* [24]*Jesus answered them, "I also will ask you one question, and if you tell me the answer, then I also will tell you by what authority I do these things.* [25]*The baptism of John, from where did it come? From heaven or from man?" And they discussed it among themselves, saying, "If we say, 'From heaven,' he will say to us, 'Why then did you not believe him?'* [26]*But if we say, 'From man,' we are afraid of the crowd, for they all hold that John was a prophet."* [27]*So they answered Jesus, "We do not know." And he said to them, "Neither will I tell you by what authority I do these things.*

[28]*"What do you think? A man had two sons. And he went to the first and said, 'Son, go and work in the vineyard today.'* [29]*And he answered, 'I will not,' but afterward he changed his mind and went.* [30]*And he went to the other son and said the same. And he answered, 'I go, sir,' but did not go.* [31]*Which of the two did the will of his father?" They said, "The first." Jesus said to them, "Truly, I say to you, the tax collectors and the prostitutes go into the kingdom of God before you.* [32]*For John came to you in the way of righteousness, and you did not believe him, but the tax collectors and the prostitutes believed him. And*

even when you saw it, you did not afterward change your minds and believe him.

[33]*"Hear another parable. There was a master of a house who planted a vineyard and put a fence around it and dug a winepress in it and built a tower and leased it to tenants, and went into another country.* [34]*When the season for fruit drew near, he sent his servants[a] to the tenants to get his fruit.* [35]*And the tenants took his servants and beat one, killed another, and stoned another.* [36]*Again he sent other servants, more than the first. And they did the same to them.* [37]*Finally he sent his son to them, saying, 'They will respect my son.'* [38]*But when the tenants saw the son, they said to themselves, 'This is the heir. Come, let us kill him and have his inheritance.'* [39]*And they took him and threw him out of the vineyard and killed him.* [40]*When therefore the owner of the vineyard comes, what will he do to those tenants?"* [41]*They said to him, "He will put those wretches to a miserable death and let out the vineyard to other tenants who will give him the fruits in their seasons."*

[42]*Jesus said to them, "Have you never read in the Scriptures:*

"'The stone that the builders rejected
    has become the cornerstone;[b]
this was the Lord's doing,
    and it is marvelous in our eyes'?

[43]*Therefore I tell you, the kingdom of God will be taken away from you and given to a people producing its fruits.* [44]*And the one who falls on this stone will be broken to pieces; and when it falls on anyone, it will crush him."[c]*

[45]*When the chief priests and the Pharisees heard his parables, they perceived that he was speaking about them.* [46]*And although they were seeking to arrest him, they feared the crowds, because they held him to be a prophet.*

22 *And again Jesus spoke to them in parables, saying,* [2]*"The kingdom of heaven may be compared to a king who gave a wedding feast for his* *son, ³and sent his servants[d] to call those who were invited to the wedding feast, but they would not come. ⁴Again he sent other servants, saying, 'Tell those who are invited, "See, I have prepared my dinner, my oxen and my fat calves have been slaughtered, and everything is ready. Come to the wedding feast."' ⁵But they paid no attention and went off, one to his farm, another to his business, ⁶while the rest seized his servants, treated them shamefully, and killed them. ⁷The king was angry, and he sent his troops and destroyed those murderers and burned their city. ⁸Then he said to his servants, 'The wedding feast is ready, but those invited were not worthy. ⁹Go*

therefore to the main roads and invite to the wedding feast as many as you find.' ¹⁰And those servants went out into the roads and gathered all whom they found, both bad and good. So the wedding hall was filled with guests.

¹¹"But when the king came in to look at the guests, he saw there a man who had no wedding garment. ¹²And he said to him, 'Friend, how did you get in here without a wedding garment?' And he was speechless. ¹³Then the king said to the attendants, 'Bind him hand and foot and cast him into the outer darkness. In that place there will be weeping and gnashing of teeth.' ¹⁴For many are called, but few are chosen."

a Or *bondservants*; also verses 35, 36 b Greek *the head of the corner* c Some manuscripts omit verse 44 d Or *bondservants*; also verses 4, 6, 8, 10

OVERVIEW: The various encounters and parables in this section point to Jesus' authority—and challenges to it. Though Mark provides varying details of Jesus' encounter with the fig tree (see Mk 11:12-25), Matthew's focus is on the display of Jesus' authority as the fig tree withers at once. Among the reformers, Martin Bucer indicates that Jesus is clearly trying to emphasize the power of faith to the disciples along with the need to produce the "fruit" of faith. Heinrich Bullinger also remarks that Jesus' words then drive home the lesson on the nature of true faith and serve as an encouragement for his disciples to be characterized by this fruitful faith.

When Jesus is confronted by the religious leaders, he answers their question with one of his own, which draws on the consistent practice of Israel's leaders in rejecting the prophets. Calvin states that Jesus' reply actually answers the question and exposes the doubting hearts of the leaders.

The Reformation commentators connect the parables of the two sons and the tenants as being follow-up rebukes to the religious leaders' question and unbelief. In Jesus' parable of the two sons, the penetrating question is which son's actions result in obedience, not just verbal compliance.

Drawing on the Old Testament's rich imagery of Israel as the Lord's vineyard (Ps 80:8-9; Is 5:1-7), Jesus' parable of the tenants characterizes the

sustained, violent, rebellious unbelief of Israel's leaders. Erasmus comments that the Jewish leaders' rejection of Jesus comes from the malice in their hearts.

Jesus uses Psalm 118 to present one of his strongest condemnations of unbelieving Israel (cf. Mt 23:37-39). Philipp Melanchthon describes how that foundation stone then serves as a stone of judgment where unbelievers will be judged for their repeated rejections and will be crushed to dust as the just end of the enemies of the Lord (see Ps 2:9; 89:19-23).

Jesus' rebuke of Israel's leaders—and by extension the nation as a whole—at the end of Matthew 21 sets the context for the parable of the wedding feast in Matthew 22. Due to this context, the reformers interpret the "invited" ones as the nation of Israel who have been called by God. Niels Hemmingsen focuses on the intriguing twist of the guest who lacks the proper clothes and therefore is removed from the banquet. The guest's surprise at his unpreparedness appears similar to other places in Matthew where judgment is meted out on those who think they are secure (Mt 7:22-23; 25:41-46). Moreover, those who come to the banquet through grace are not to boast over those who are rejected, because not everyone who is invited will eventually come.

21:18-27 *Jesus' Authority Challenged*

THE POWER AND FRUIT OF FAITH. MARTIN BUCER: In that moment, he explained nothing else of the mystery to them, rather merely by this act, he exhorted them to steadfast trust in God, promising that all things are possible for them, even to move mountains, in fact, nothing at all would be [impossible], were they not to ask, if only they would believe when they ask. Then, as they were praying, they would remit, "What if you have something against another?" On this subject, there is enough above in the sixth [chapter], where it is on prayer. Also in the eighth [chapter], where faith was discussed, and above in [chapter] 17, after the account of the lunatic, as in the forgiveness of a brother's offense. . . . Doubtless, therefore, the Lord cursed the fig tree because he wanted to declare to them the efficacy of faith. Furthermore, we see the barrenness of the Jewish people to have been foreshadowed, who during his time, in order to bear the fruit of goodness, never had what he wanted, which led finally to the curse of God, to drying up to the roots, and by this time, even to the fruit. It had been without fruit, nor could its ceremonial leaves boast except in vain. Let us consider this truth and ourselves lest we have a multitude of words and external displays of worship without the solid fruit of piety, which we have only by the Lord's engrafting. It is exceedingly worthless to be a good tree without good fruit. COMMENTARY ON MATTHEW.[1]

UNBELIEF JUDGED, TRUE FAITH ENCOURAGED. HEINRICH BULLINGER: We have heard of ingratitude, rebellion, hypocrisy, and the harshest incredulities of the city of Jerusalem and the nation of the Jews: therefore, now are joined incredulities, hypocrisies, and the penalty of falsehood, destruction and devastation of the nation and city. For the unfruitful fig, though nevertheless adorned with foliage, and as if bearing in mind the fruit, he sketches in words the condition and state of the city and nation. Certainly, the people had a kind of faith, but they were want of true fruit—faith, love, obedience, and justice. Therefore, the Lord rebuked them, and they dried up. That is, they were completely destroyed. Whoever are like the Jews in respect to customs and rebellion should expect the same from the most just Lord. Since, by true faith and obedience, one may evade the anger of God, on that account the Lord recommends faith to them, and he indicates this has such great power. For when the disciples were marveling that the fig tree withered suddenly and were asking, "How did the fig tree wither at once?" he responded, "If you have the faith. . . ." Therefore, by the opportunity of the tree, he recommends faith to all. As if he said, "They are subject to reviling on account of the need of faith, and they are completely laid waste: therefore, you should take care that you have faith." For also Paul, in Romans 11, says, "Through unbelief they were broken off, you stand fast in true faith. So that you are not arrogant in spirit, you should fear."

Soon also he shows the distinction of true faith, saying, "And you do not doubt." For true faith is the substance and firmest certainty without discerned conviction: just as we show elsewhere. And how great the character of faith is signified through a hyperbole, he says, "If you say to this mount. . . ." for through the mountains, a thing in the world that is considered the largest, which we put altogether to be immobile, invincible, and perpetual. Therefore, the mountain is the character of the devil and sin. The mountain is the union and power of the king. The mountain is the wisdom of philosophy and oratory, erudition and eloquence. . . . And rightly faithful prayers are committed to us, for these increases of faith are yielded by divine grace. But also, the apostles are consistently asking, "Increase our faith, Lord." COMMENTARY ON MATTHEW.[2]

THE CURSE THAT AWAITS HYPOCRITES. JOHN CALVIN: I take for granted that Christ did not

---

[1]Bucer, *In Sacra Quatuor Evangelia, Enarrationes Perpetuae* (1536), 422; citing Mt 17; 5; 18.

[2]Bullinger, *In . . . Evangelium secundum Matthaeum commentariorum* (1546), 9:192-93; citing Rom 11:20.

pretend hunger but was actually hungry; for we know that he voluntarily became subject to the infirmities of the flesh, though by nature he was free and exempt from them.

But here lies the difficulty. How was he mistaken in seeking fruit on a tree that had none; more especially, when the season of fruit had not yet arrived? And again, why was he so fiercely enraged against a harmless tree? But there would be no absurdity in saying that as man he did not know the kind of tree; though it is possible that he approached it on purpose, with full knowledge of the result. Certainly it was not the fury of passion that led him to curse the tree—for that would not only have been an unjust, but even a childish and ridiculous revenge; but as hunger was troublesome to him according to the feeling of the flesh, he determined to overcome it by an opposite affection; that is, by a desire to promote the glory of the Father, as he elsewhere says, "My meat is to do the will of my Father," for at that time he was contending both with fatigue and with hunger. I am the more inclined to this conjecture because hunger gave him an opportunity of performing a miracle and of teaching his disciples. So, when he was pressed by hunger and there was no food at hand, he finds a repast in another way; that is, by promoting the glory of God. He intended, however, to present in this tree an outward sign of the end which awaits hypocrites, and at the same time to expose the emptiness and folly of their ostentation. Commentary on a Harmony of the Evangelists.[3]

The Prayer Offered by Faith. Aegidius Hunnius: "And seeing that the fig tree was immediately. . . ." Mark, who has pursued the details of this history more fully, mentions that the disciples had heard the Lord Jesus speak when he had cursed the fig tree on the way to Jerusalem. Because Christ was seeing that the traffic that he had abolished in the temple court just the day before was resuming, once more he ejected those who were buying and selling. This being done, he

departed in the evening of that day with his disciples, namely, to Bethany, where he enjoyed the hospitality with Lazarus, who recently had been raised from the dead. When it was morning (on Tuesday, that is), the Lord returned to the city. It was on this second journey that the apostles observed that the fig tree was withered from the root. Peter, having recollected the previous day's curse, spoke individually: "Rabbi, behold the fig tree that you cursed has withered!" That which Peter spoke individually, Matthew attributes to others as well, who were marveling that the fig tree had withered so quickly and were no less inquisitive than Peter. In fact, through Peter they did ask the Lord, "How has the fig tree immediately withered?" And Jesus answered, "Amen, I say to you. . . ." Those words about "moving mountains" were then spoken and promised. They are interpreted with regard to a similar speech described in Matthew 17; the summary is there. At first glance, this discourse appears to be given for the apostles, who were endowed with the gift of performing miracles. And insofar as it looks to the external performance of miracles, it has nothing to do with us. We possess neither the command, nor the calling, nor the promise to perform miracles or to "move mountains." . . . And if we attempt it without a special calling, the business will not succeed. As a matter of fact, the Lord appears to speak proverbially even with respect to the apostles and to intimate that, by faith, they would be able to perform difficult tasks in the future. Either that, or the *species* of "miracle" is given here for the genus, as in the discourse of the apostle [Paul]. Furthermore, Christ is not speaking of an uncertain faith that someone might conceive by natural human ability without any reliance on the foundation of the revealed word. Rather, he speaks of the faith that depends on the sure word. His meaning, therefore, is that if the apostles are bid by a particular and certain word of God to move a mountain, they ought to believe that it will come to pass and ought not to doubt of the endeavor's success in the slightest. Yet for this reason the Savior's discourse is not accommodated to us except spiritually, so

---

[3]CTS 3:18* (CO 45:584-85); citing Jn 4:34.

that we might command "mountains to move" whenever we by faith overcome the peak of diabolical temptations. By faith we also empty the gates of hell of their power and humble them, so that they no longer hinder us or snatch away the palm of salvation. We must observe here how Christ opposes faith and doubt as contraries, saying "If you may have faith and not doubt." . . .

"And everything that you ask." . . . He adds a general promise, vowing that they will receive everything that they ask—that is, whatever they ask from God as believers or from faith. By the term "believers" the soul, as it were, or form of prayer is expressed, which is faith. Then their hands grasp the good things for which they ask. At the same time, they are taught that this sort of prayer, to which so splendid a promise is attached, must lean on God's word. Otherwise, the prayer will not flow from faith, which depends on God's word. That is why the requests that he [God] promises to accept from the faithful occur whenever we pray for all those things that God himself defines in his word. John expresses this limitation elegantly: "This is the confidence that we have before God, that if we should ask according to his will, he hears us." COMMENTARY ON MATTHEW.[4]

CHRIST'S CALLING AND CREDENTIALS. JOHN CALVIN: "By what authority do you do these things?" As the other schemes and open attempts to attack Christ had not succeeded, the priests and scribes now attempt, by indirect methods, if they may possibly cause him to desist from the practice of teaching. They do not debate with him as to the doctrine itself, whether it was true or not, for already had they often enough attacked him in vain on that question, but they raise a dispute as to his calling and commission. And, indeed, there were plausible grounds; for since a man ought not, of his own accord, to intermeddle either with the honor of priesthood or with the prophetical office, but ought to wait for the calling of God, much less

would any man be at liberty to claim for himself the title of Messiah, unless it were evident that he had been chosen by God; for he must have been appointed, not only by the voice of God, but likewise by an oath, as it is written.

But when the divine majesty of Christ had been attested by so many miracles, they act maliciously and wickedly in inquiring whence he came, as if they had been ignorant of all that he had done. For what could be more unreasonable than that, after seeing the hand of God openly displayed in curing the lame and blind, they should doubt if he were a private individual who had rashly assumed this authority? Besides, more than enough of evidence had been already laid before them that Christ was sent from heaven so that nothing was farther from their wish than to approve of the performances of Christ, after having learned that God was the author of them. They therefore insist on this, that he is not a lawful minister of God because he had not been chosen by their votes, as if the power had dwelt solely with them. But though they had been the lawful guardians of the church, still it was monstrous to rise up against God. We now understand why Christ did not make a direct reply to them. It was because they wickedly and shamelessly interrogated him about a matter which was well known.

"Whence was the baptism of John?" Christ interrogates them about the baptism of John, not only to show that they were unworthy of any authority, because they had despised a holy prophet of God, but also to convict them by their own reply of having impudently pretended ignorance of a matter with which they were well acquainted. For we must bear in mind why John was sent, what was his commission, and on what subject he most of all insisted. He had been sent as Christ's herald. He was not deficient in his duty. . . . In short, he had pointed out Christ with the finger, and had declared him to be the only Son of God. From what source then do the scribes mean that the new authority of Christ should be proved, since it had been fully attested by the preaching of John?

We now see that Christ employed no cunning stratagem in order to escape, but fully and perfectly

[4]Hunnius, *Commentarius in Evangelium Secundum Matthaeum* (1594), 700-702; citing 1 Cor 13; 1 Jn 5:14.

answered the question which had been proposed; for it was impossible to acknowledge that John was a servant of God, without acknowledging that he was himself the Lord. Commentary on a Harmony of the Evangelists.[5]

The Whole Testimony of John. Juan de Maldonado: Christ did not answer the question of the priests, lest he should excite them more against him by the truth; but he proposed another question for them to answer. For they could not answer that the baptism of John was from heaven, because they would have been compelled to admit by the testimony of all people that Christ performed all his acts, not by human, but by divine, authority; for John had said of him, "Behold the Lamb of God, behold him who takes away the sins of the world." By the baptism of John, Christ means not his mere baptism alone of people by water, but his whole profession, teaching, preaching, and doctrine, as the whole law of Moses is expressed by the word "circumcision." . . .

He does not answer as they did, "I know not," for he could not with truth. He said, "but neither," and therefore the particle *nec*, which usually expresses similitude, does do so here, not to that which was said, namely, *nescimus*, but to that which was understood or which follows; that is, because they did not answer Christ as to whence was the baptism of John, so neither did Christ tell them by what authority he performed his works. A Commentary on Matthew's Gospel.[6]

21:28-46 Parables of the Two Sons and the Landowner

Portraits of Repentance and Unbelief. David Dickson: They have done with Christ; their plot is disappointed, but Christ does pursue them, convincing them of disobedience and denouncing deserved judgment upon them in two parables. The scope of the first is to show that

sundry of publicans and open sinners, of whom they esteemed least, were more righteous and blessed than they were, because the publicans, like the penitent son, repented their backwardness unto God's commandments, and were led in by faith to the Messiah, and were made subjects of the kingdom of grace, and so heirs of the kingdom of glory; but they, notwithstanding a fair profession of obedience to God, were like the other disobedient and counterfeit son, biding still in their impenitency and unbelief, and in the way to be debarred from the kingdom of grace and glory. Hence learn, first, that people will more readily acknowledge the fault in another person than in themselves; therefore, does Christ draw forth these men's judgment by a parable. Second, he will have the conscience of the wicked, subscribing to the righteousness of God's judgment against themselves, as will appear by, "What do you think?" compared with their answer. Third, the most odious and despised sinners, repenting and believing in Jesus, do find grace and a place both in the church and in heaven above, but such as confide in their own righteousness are debarred; for, "harlots," says Christ, "go into the kingdom of heaven before you." . . .

Christ gives reasons for condemning these wicked men. First, the more blameless and holy that the preacher of repentance and righteousness by Christ be found, the greater is the sin of those who do not receive the message; for so Christ agreed that these men sinned, saying, "John came in the way of righteousness, and you did not believe him." Second, albeit self-conceited righteous people do not believe the doctrine of righteousness by Christ, yet God will manifest the power of his truth in the conversion of despised sinners; for the harlots believed John, albeit the Pharisees did not. Third, the sight and example of other folks believing and repenting in Christ, if it does not move us unto acknowledging of our sins also and fleeing unto Christ, it shall stand as a witness against us, to exacerbate our sin and condemnation. Therefore, says he, "And you when you had seen it you repented not." Fourth, remorse for not believing God's word in

---

[5]CTS 3:21-23 (CO 45:587-88); citing Ps 110:4; Heb 7:21.
[6]JMG 2:208; citing Jn 1:29; Gal 5:3.

his servant's mouth, in time bygone, is a special spur and preparative to believe it the more solidly for time to come; therefore says he, "You repented not, that you might believe him," that is, when you saw that the publicans had outstripped you in the way of righteousness by believing John's testimony of me, you did not lament your unbelief that you might give him so much the more credit for time to come, and so recover your loss by faith in me. A BRIEF EXPOSITION.[7]

WHO WILL ENTER THE KINGDOM. ERASMUS SARCERIUS: "Amen, I say to you." Applying the parable to them, Christ takes an oath as in a true and serious matter. The sum of the application is this: the sinful nations will be converted, while in the meantime the Jews will be condemned and rejected, for they judged themselves righteous and despised the promises of Christ. The cause of this rejection must be diligently noted: it is unbelief itself, which Christ in the following was forcefully illustrating for them along with the consequences that follow from unbelief, namely, to hate, persecute, and kill the preachers of the word. The punishments are also added, both temporal (in Mt 24) and eternal (in Mt 25).

"Because even the tax collectors and prostitutes. Sinners of either sex who are guilty of obvious faults. "Will go before you into the kingdom." They will come to a knowledge of the gospel more swiftly than you who believe yourselves righteous because of your works. The reason that the former go before is that they recognize their sins and so are urged to embrace the gospel, while the latter are impeded by their own "righteousness."

"For [John] came to you." The explanation why the tax collectors and prostitutes will go before the scribes and teachers of the law and thus all Israel into the kingdom of God is that they believed John, who was a preacher of true righteousness, that is, of faith. Likewise, the reason why the Jews will not come into the kingdom of heaven is that they did not believe that John was a preacher of the true

righteousness that is free. As the apostle says in Romans 10, "For being ignorant of the righteousness of God and seeking to establish their own righteousness, they did not submit to God's righteousness."

This explanation is formed from diverse causes, from which some lead to the kingdom of God, while others impede access to it. The first causes are: to embrace the gospel, to believe him [John],[†] and to receive the free gift of righteousness. The latter causes are contrary to the first. Christ takes the opportunity from the preceding question that was posed by the chief priests about John's baptism to urge on them John's preaching about true righteousness. That is, "If you had believed John, whom even the tax collectors and prostitutes believe, you would easily understand that I am the Messiah as well as the power by which I teach among you." Through "John," Christ also understands all the other prophets, all of whom by implication he shows to have prophesied about the true righteousness that he himself now teaches.

"In the way of righteousness." Teaching true righteousness and by his preaching removing all obstacles to the righteousness that is true and free. "And you did not believe him." This is the cause that delays Israel from the kingdom of God, just as faith is the cause that has opened the kingdom of God to the tax collectors and prostitutes.

"But you, seeing." To be impressed by the righteousness of works. "To see" is used as a figure of speech for "understand," as if Christ had said, "Your consciences were conquered by John's preaching, yet you still did not wish to believe him." "Neither did you repent afterward." [Repentance] is to relinquish the unbelief in one's heart toward the free righteousness of faith. This passage makes clear that *to repent* means not only to desist from external vices and to change one's external for the better. Rather, *to repent* is to put away the impiety and unbelief from one's mind so that, as Christ says, "you may believe in him." ON THE GOSPEL OF MATTHEW.[8]

---

[7]Dickson, *Brief Exposition* (1651), 244-45*.

[8]Sarcerius, *In Matthaeum Evangelistam* (1538), 289r-290v; citing Rom 10:3. [†]The pronoun here, *illi*, could refer to either John or Jesus, but the overall context implies believing in John as a preacher of righteousness.

Speak the Truth. Desiderius Erasmus: Because a simple and plain question could not wring out the confession of truth, Jesus put forth another question by a riddle, that unawares they shall give sentence against themselves: what do you think of that I will propose now? A certain man had two sons. He came to the one and said: Son, go and work this day in my vineyard. He answered forwardly, I will not. But straight afterward repenting himself, he went into the vineyard. The father likewise came to the other son and said: go, and labor in my vineyard this day. He answered readily, lo I go, sir, and yet he went not. Therefore, of these two, whether think you fulfilled his father's will. They not understanding to what end these went, answered: The first son, which repenting forthwith, went into the vineyard. Then Jesus, turning the parable upon them, said: "Certainly, I tell you truth, that the publicans and common women shall go before you in the kingdom of heaven." They, being rebels against God before with their wicked life yet by and by touched and moved by penance, obeyed the doctrine of the gospel. You, who be the people of God by title and profession and you who said in times past and this day say, we will do all things whatsoever the Lord says to us, which also have ever in your mouth the precepts of God, and the Lord's temple, the Lord's temple, the Lord's temple, being so many ways provoked, cannot be moved to penance. For John came showing you the way of righteousness, and that the wrath of God was at hand, and the ax set at the tree roots, unless immediately you would repent. You saw the publicans and common women (desperate folks after your judgment) obedient unto him. You could not be moved unto penance neither by the great holiness of John, neither by his wholesome doctrine, neither by his threatening, neither by the example of the publicans and common women. So, it comes to pass that they through faith, take from you the kingdom of God: you, vainly professing God with your mouth, be shut out for the unbelief of your mind. Paraphrases.[9]

[9]EP 82v-83v.

Rebellion in the Vineyard. Martin Luther: With this parable Christ attacks the Pharisees and scribes who blasphemed him and wanted to sacrifice him on the chopping block, for he knew well what they had in mind. Therefore, he provokes them against his own neck, so that they will not hold back from their plans. And they even understand that Christ has directed this at them, since at the end of the chapter they defend themselves nicely. How good it has made them is also evident in that they seek to seize him; they would gladly have killed him if they had not feared the people. That is how good they became and what they learned. They received the sermon by wanting neither to suffer nor to listen to the truth. And so it came to pass as he had said, "They cast the Son out of the vineyard," for they crucified Christ. They understood this parable of the vineyard well, since the prophets often mention that Jerusalem and the people of God are called a vineyard, as in Psalm 80. . . .

They well know this parable of the vineyard from the prophets. They indeed perceived that he meant them when he spoke not of the vines but of the workers who dug and cultivated in the vineyard. For the high priests, Pharisees and scribes, priests and Levites were the regents who were supposed to teach the people. . . .

But what happened? He often looked into whether the workers worked faithfully, fertilized well, planted and pruned the vines. When the time came for him to enjoy the fruit, he sent for wine from the berries. And the servants also would have gladly harvested the vineyard, but the righteous vine-growers and hirelings come along and kill the servants, the prophets, such as Hosea, Amos, Jeremiah, and Isaiah. None of them preached without being killed for it. . . . This is what he means when he says, "He sent out his servants, and they beat them to death." For if he had sent a hundred servants, they would not have been converted, but would have killed them all. He does even more, however, and says, "The third time, I will send my own Son," who is the heir and Lord of the vineyard. And he thinks that because they know he is the Lord, that will spare him and say: "This is the heir, not a servant. Those who came before were [only] servants." [He thinks:] "Now I will give them a better preacher than the prophets were, so that they convert." But what happened? They dealt with him the same as they did the prophets. For when they saw him and he wanted to ask about how things were in the people of Israel, they became embittered and said: "Hold on! This is the heir. All we have to do is beat him to death and will be the lords of the vineyard." ANNOTATIONS.[10]

CHRIST, THE CORNERSTONE AND STUMBLING STONE. DESIDERIUS ERASMUS:

He put them another parable even as dark, wherewith he does recite secretly and lays before their eyes their notable unkindness, which being provoked by so many benefits of God did not only not amend but also cruelly killed the prophets one after another, who were sent, that at their preaching they might not repent. And not content herewith finally they would kill the Son of God himself, and that after that he was cast out of the vineyard, showing as it were the place where he should be crucified, by which he declares both that their invincible malice is unworthy of pardon—seeing that nothing was omitted that might call them back to a better mind—and that he should suffer nothing of them, which he knew not of before. . . .

After these things, Jesus shows that through their resistance, he being condemned and rejected should die a spiritual death, but by his resurrection through the power of the Father, he should be made noble throughout all the world and should be so sound and strong that whoever stumbled against him, should be his own destruction. And that in declaring of this, he might less offend them, he brings a prophecy out of the Psalms. "Have you never read in the Scriptures," he asks, "the stone which the builders did refuse and cast away, the same is made the head of the corner?" This is done of the Lord, and it is wonderful in our eyes;

signifying that they built the synagogue, but casting out Christ, without whom no building was sure, but yet that stone rejected of them, should be in great estimation and price in the church of the Gentiles. And therefore Jesus did add, therefore I say unto you, the kingdom of God shall be given to other people which shall bring forth fruits fitting for the gospel. And as this stone shall bring health to those who obey the gospel, so it shall bring destruction unto those who be disobedient through unbelief. PARAPHRASES.[11]

REPEATED REJECTION OF THE PROPHETS. PHILIPP MELANCHTHON:

A landowner planted a vineyard, that is, God chose the people of Israel. And encircled them with a wall, that is, the law. And he made there a winepress, that is, the ministry of teaching. And he built a tower, that is, he gave a kingdom and temple to them. And he rented it out to farmers, that is, to the seed of Jacob. And he went away, and he sent servants, that is, prophets at any given time, Elijah, Elisha, Isaiah, Zechariah, Jonah, Jeremiah, whom the people killed. And finally, he sent his son, and the people killed him as well. And to give an indication of their stubbornness and blasphemy, he expressly says to throw off their lord and establish their own kingdom: "We will seize the inheritance," they say, just as later in the passion they say, "We do not want this one to rule over us."

This blasphemy and this disease are the cause of all evils. The impious wish to establish religions and rules according to their own judgment, wisdom, and will, and they make religions that are convenient, and they do not want to put up with God's rule. They are always exclaiming in their heart, "We do not want this one to rule over us!" This is a horrific madness, to hold God in contempt and to want to establish religions and kingdoms that are useful to us, as if God is nothing, just as the kings of Israel erected an idol, just as Nebuchadnezzar did, just as Antiochus and many others saw fit to institute religions and cults by

---

[10]LW 68:113-16 (WA 47:412-15); citing Ps 80:8-10; Mt 21:41, 46.   [11]EP 83v-84v.

their own will, as if God is nothing, imagining that their own wisdom rules and not God. . . . Let us learn to understand and flee this sin, and let us pray to God not to let us rush into this blindness, but to always pray in our heart that the Son of God be our governor, so that he might rule over us, so that the inheritance of the kingdom might always remain with him.

These two things are contrasted: "This is my beloved Son, hear him," and, "We do not wish this one to rule." Let us give obedience to God when he bids us hear his Son, just as also it is said in the psalm: "Give a kiss to the Son." And penalties are applied to those who hold the Son in contempt: His anger will become enflamed. And this is the penalty mentioned: "He will bring those wretches to a wretched end." God destroyed such contemptuous people way back in the beginning, in the flood, and in his punishment of the people of Israel, and finally when Jerusalem was wiped out.

Next comes a quote from the Psalms: "The stone that the builders rejected became the chief cornerstone. This came about from the Lord, and it is marvelous in our eyes." This pleasant little verse you all ought to commit to memory, and those, who are able to read, should often read this whole psalm, which in fact the Jews back then were singing on each of the Sabbaths, and it is a wonder that the blindness was so great that they did not want to understand it. It foretells clearly that the Messiah will suffer, and yet afterward will rule and gather together the eternal church. Therefore, this short little verse teaches us many things, as you can see: that the Messiah will come and suffer, that the very synagogue will resist the Messiah, and that the Messiah will end up the victor and gather his church from among the Gentiles and Jews. ANNOTATIONS ON THE GOSPELS.[12]

BUILDERS REJECT THE STONE. MARTIN LUTHER: First, with the passage "the stone that the builders have rejected," Christ wants to show the Jews that the time is coming in which the gospel

and the kingdom of Christ shall be taken from them and given to the Gentiles, who will bring its fruit, as they themselves answer that the lord of the vineyard will kill the murderers and let out his vineyard to others.

Second, with this verse he wants to confirm the chief article of our Christian doctrine, that we are justified before God only through faith in Christ. But how does this verse harmonize with the view and judgment of the Jews and with what Christ says, that the kingdom will be taken from them? . . .

It is indeed amazing that all the worship that was given to the Jewish people should be taken away from them. Things will change. Oh, how the Jews will take offense and be astonished at this, for they are in the office the church! After all, they are not called wreckers or destroyers here, but builders, those who build, improve, and maintain the building. They are God's people. God commended his house to them. They are supposed to govern and build it. And it is really amazing that those who are supposed to be preachers and regents of the people do not perform and carry out that for which God has established them. . . . Nevertheless, this is what happened, and the Gentiles, who did not have it before, have been given the kingdom and worship. And those who did have it have lost it. Whose fault is this? Is God being unfair to them? No, they reject themselves, for they come along and do not want to have the stone that God has laid down as the cornerstone. He had given them the promise of the Messiah and made them into builders, but with the stipulation that they give heed to the stone and build themselves and other people upon it. Now that the precious stone comes and wants to satisfy and fulfill the Scriptures, for which reason he was chosen to be the stone, they do not want to accept the stone. Instead, they mock, spit upon, scourge, and crucify him. They do nothing that might contribute to the edification of the people of God, but rather do everything to destroy them. . . . They do not want to tolerate faith in the foundation, in Christ. Therefore, the text properly concludes that the kingdom should be taken from them, and they should be rejected, for they do not want to be with

---

[12]MO 14:947-49; citing Dan 3:1; 1 Macc 1:14-15; Ps 2:12; 118:22.

the stone. Our Lord God wants the stone to be built upon, not to be rejected. By rejecting it, however, they do themselves the greatest harm. And since God wants to retain the stone, he must forsake them. Therefore, Christ answers properly and makes perfect sense here. ANNOTATIONS.[13]

22:1-14 *The Parable of the Wedding Feast*

A RICH, ROYAL FEAST. JOHN MURCOT: So here, it is a king that makes this feast; kings usually have larger, more noble spirits, as they have larger purses, and therefore at their feasts they usually show the magnificence and glory of their kingdom. And so does God here, brethren; a king, yea the King of heaven, the King of glory, the King of kings, and King of saints, he will show the glory of his kingdom, and his magnificence, the excellency of his greatness in making this feast; therefore surely there must needs be fullness of love and joy. It is a feast, not an ordinary, but a marriage feast, and such used to be more than ordinary also, being a time of greatest rejoicing. . . .

It is a feast, a marriage feast, not only for a servant or friend being married, but for a son, the only son, a son and heir of all, a beloved son, most dearly beloved; all these surely will exceedingly heighten the considerations of the fullness of the feast brethren, the fullness of that love which shall there be manifested and of the believer's joy in that love; these things are heightened to us in that place of Matthew. Indeed, the very feast here in the Gospel is heightened by these considerations; but much more than this. Yea, consider yet further, it is a marriage feast, for which preparation has been making from eternity, God has been providing for it. SEVERAL WORKS OF MR. JOHN MURCOT.[14]

CHRIST'S MARRIAGE FEAST. CORNELIUS À LAPIDE: For "marriage," the Syriac version has throughout "feast," meaning marriage feast. The whole parable may be expounded and applied as follows: First, "The king" is God the Father; the "son of the king," the "bridegroom" is God's incarnate Son, Jesus Christ, whose spouse is the church, whose nuptials were begun in the incarnation of Christ, for in it Christ espoused human nature to himself, hypostatically, and the church, that is, all faithful people, mystically, to be his spouse by grace. But in heaven, these nuptials shall be consummated with glory. . . . Wherefore, tropologically, "by 'marriage,' understand," says Origen, "the union of Christ with the soul; and by 'offspring,' good works."

Second, God the Father made "a marriage feast" for Christ, since in Judea, and in the whole world, he has, through Christ, spread a table of evangelical doctrine and sacraments, especially the sacrament of the Eucharist.

Third, to this nuptial feast the Jews were invited by God, through Moses and the prophets, as the servants of God, both before and after the incarnation of Christ, that they might believe first that it was about to take place, and then that it had taken place; that so, believing in Christ, repenting and seeking grace from him, they might obtain justice and salvation.

Fourth, "bulls and fatlings" have only the general signification of rich provision for a banquet. They denote the grandeur of the doctrines of the gospel, says St. Jerome,[†] and of the sacraments. . . .

Fifth, the "field," the "farm," whither those who were invited went away, despising the invitation, signify temporal good things, which drew away the Jews from the faith of Christ and from heavenly good things; and which led them to slay the servants of God, yea, even Christ himself. Wherefore, God sent Titus,[‡] who slew the Jews as being murderers, and burned up their city, namely, their capital, Jerusalem. Christ in this parable has an allusion to Isaiah 25:6. COMMENTARY ON THE FOUR GOSPELS.[15]

---

[13] LW 68:120-22 (WA 47:418-21).
[14] Murcot, *Several Works*, 345-46*.

[15] Lapide, *Commentaria in Quatuor Evangeli* (1639), 409. †Jerome, *Commentary on Matthew*, FC 117:249. ‡Titus, who later became the Roman emperor (79–81 AD), was the Roman general who put down a Jewish rebellion that culminated in the siege and sacking of Jerusalem, including the complete destruction of the temple in 70 AD. Countless Jews were killed or enslaved.

GOD'S REDEMPTIVE PLAN. RICHARD BAXTER: God the Father that sent his son into the world to cleanse them from their sins and espouse them to himself. By his "Son" for whom the marriage is made is meant the Lord Jesus Christ the eternal Son of God, who took to his Godhead human nature, that he might be capable of being their Redeemer when they had lost themselves in sin. By the "marriage" is meant the conjunction of Christ to the soul of sinners, when he gives up himself to them to be their Savior, and they give up themselves to him as his redeemed ones, to be saved and ruled by him: The perfection of which marriage will be at the day of judgment, when the conjunction between the whole church and Christ shall be solemnized. The word here translated "marriage" rather signifies the marriage feast: and the meaning is that the world is invited by the gospel to come in and partake of Christ and salvation, which comprehends both pardon, justification, and right to salvation, and all other privileges of the members of Christ. The invitation is God's offer of Christ and salvation in the gospel. The servants that invite them are the preachers of the gospel who are sent forth by God to that end; the preparation for the feast there mentioned is the sacrifice of Jesus Christ and the enacting of a law of grace and opening a way for revolting sinners to return to God. There is mention of sending second messengers because God chooses not to take the first denial, but to exercise his patience till sinners are obstinate.

The first persons invited are the Jews; upon their obstinate refusal they are sentenced to punishment, and the Gentiles are invited, and not only invited, but by powerful preachings and miracles, and effectual grace compelled, that is, infallibly prevailed with to come in. The number of them is so great that the house is filled with the guests; many come sincerely, not only looking at the pleasure of the feast, that is, at the pardon of sin, and deliverance from the wrath of God, but also at the honor of the marriage, that is, of the Redeemer, and their profession by giving up themselves to a holy lifestyle. But some come in

only for the feast, that is, justification by Christ, having not the wedding garment of sound resolution for obedience in their life, and looking only at themselves in believing, and not to the glory of their Redeemer; and these are sentenced to everlasting misery, and fare as ill as those that came not in at all. MAKING LIGHT OF CHRIST AND SALVATION.[16]

THE PROPER WEDDING GARMENT. NIELS HEMMINGSEN: It follows that the king coming in saw a man without his wedding garment. What is this wedding garment? This is needful to be known, that we may enjoy the sweetness of Christ's marriage perpetually. At the last day, there shall stand in this king's sight two kinds of people, of whom the one refused to come to this wedding, as the Turks and the ungodly Jews and many heathen nations at this day. . . . And the other sort came to the marriage, that is to say, they conveyed themselves into the outward congregation of the church at the preaching of the gospel. Although these are not all of one hue. For some truest to their own works and think their shamefulness to be covered with the garment of their works. Is this the wedding garment? No, in truth, for they are thrust out from the marriage; but none are thrust out from the marriage that bring a wedding garment with them. Some others have not works but evil works; although they brag of faith and boast themselves to be faithful and they suppose that this their favorite boast is the wedding garment, but they are deceived. For of such hypocrites the Lord says, "Not everyone that says unto me, Lord, Lord, shall enter into the kingdom of heaven, but he that does the will of my Father which is in heaven." And some others believe aright and these mortify the flesh and live in the spirit and repent and set their minds to live blamelessly. These only have that wedding garment. Therefore, whether you call lively faith or holiness of life the wedding garment, you shall not take your mark amiss. For as the calling to

---

[16]Baxter, *Making Light of Christ and Salvation* (1691), 1-4.

this marriage requires faith, so it requires also true holiness. A POSTIL, OR EXPOSITION OF THE GOSPELS.[17]

REMOVED FROM THE FEAST. PILGRAM MARPECK: No greater punishment nor vengeance can be found than to fall from one transgression and sin into another and still assume that one participates in the table fellowship of Christ, although they are and remain only at their own table which has become a trap for them and from which they eat judgment to themselves, and not from the Lord's table. Although they have been invited or else appear at the wedding banquet with soiled garments, they will nevertheless not taste the Lord's Supper eternally, but rather they will eat their own meal from their table perverted into a trap and will be judged so that they will depart exiled and condemned. . . . The Lord commands such dishonest people to be bound hands and feet and to be thrown into outer darkness. Those are all terrible and hard sayings which cause consternation and fright when one seriously considers them. Happy are those who thus allow themselves to be alarmed by the Word of God and who are earnestly shocked because of it. Salvation draws near to them. For they are prepared for and led to the Lord Christ through the genuine fruits of repentance so that he bestows his grace upon them. FIVE FRUITS OF REPENTANCE.[18]

---

[17]Hemmingsen, *A Postill, or Exposition of the Gospels* (1569), 292; citing Mt 7:21. [18]CRR 2:488.

22:15-46 THE GREATEST COMMANDMENT

¹⁵*Then the Pharisees went and plotted how to entangle him in his words. *¹⁶*And they sent their disciples to him, along with the Herodians, saying, "Teacher, we know that you are true and teach the way of God truthfully, and you do not care about anyone's opinion, for you are not swayed by appearances.*ᵃ *¹⁷Tell us, then, what you think. Is it lawful to pay taxes to Caesar, or not?" *¹⁸*But Jesus, aware of their malice, said, "Why put me to the test, you hypocrites? *¹⁹Show me the coin for the tax." And they brought him a denarius.*ᵇ *²⁰And Jesus said to them, "Whose likeness and inscription is this?" *²¹*They said, "Caesar's." Then he said to them, "Therefore render to Caesar the things that are Caesar's, and to God the things that are God's." *²²*When they heard it, they marveled. And they left him and went away.*

²³*The same day Sadducees came to him, who say that there is no resurrection, and they asked him a question, *²⁴*saying, "Teacher, Moses said, 'If a man dies having no children, his brother must marry the widow and raise up offspring for his brother.' *²⁵Now there were seven brothers among us. The first married and died, and having no offspring left his wife to his brother. *²⁶So too the second and third, down to the seventh. *²⁷After them all, the woman died. *²⁸In the resurrection, therefore, of the seven, whose wife will she be? For they all had her." *²⁹*But Jesus answered them, "You are wrong, because you know neither the Scriptures nor the power of God. *³⁰For in the resurrection they neither marry nor are given in marriage, but are like angels in heaven. *³¹And as for the resurrection of the dead, have you not read what was said to you by God: *³²'I am the God of Abraham, and the God of Isaac, and the God of Jacob'? He is not God of the dead, but of the living." *³³And when the crowd heard it, they were astonished at his teaching.*

³⁴*But when the Pharisees heard that he had silenced the Sadducees, they gathered together. *³⁵*And one of them, a lawyer, asked him a question to test him. *³⁶"Teacher, which is the great commandment in the Law?" *³⁷And he said to him, "You shall love the Lord your God with all your heart and with all your soul and with all your mind. *³⁸This is the great and first commandment. *³⁹And a second is like it: You shall love your neighbor as yourself. *⁴⁰On these two commandments depend all the Law and the Prophets."*

⁴¹*Now while the Pharisees were gathered together, Jesus asked them a question, *⁴²*saying, "What do you think about the Christ? Whose son is he?" They said to him, "The son of David." *⁴³He said to them, "How is it then that David, in the Spirit, calls him Lord, saying,*

⁴⁴*"'The Lord said to my Lord,*
"Sit at my right hand,
until I put your enemies under your feet"'?

⁴⁵*If then David calls him Lord, how is he his son?" *⁴⁶And no one was able to answer him a word, nor from that day did anyone dare to ask him any more questions.*

---

a Greek *for you do not look at people's faces*   b A *denarius* was a day's wage for a laborer

---

OVERVIEW: The series of questions posed by Jesus' opponents in this section of Matthew's text leads to a simple yet profound statement. In the first case, the bitterness of the Pharisees causes them to form an unlikely alliance with the politically savvy Herodians. Jesus immediately recognizes the scheming behind their carefully worded question about paying taxes. His response about rendering to Caesar and to God what is their appropriate due prompts the question of what it is that is due to God. Calvin indicates that true worship of God is not hindered by the form of government or civil law. Luther encourages his audience not only in the content of Jesus' reply to such a sinister test but also in belief that God provides such wisdom to all who would testify to the truth of the Word of God.

Next, the skeptical Sadducees lay a trap for Jesus with a complicated, if not ridiculous, case study on marriage in the resurrected state. Jesus' pointed correction reveals their ignorance of God's original design for marriage (see Mt 19:1-12) and their deeper unbelief regarding resurrection. Among the reformers, Thomas Cranmer recognizes that Jesus' description of the Sadducees' error lays the fault on their ignorance of the Scriptures.

The Pharisees then collude to propose their own question to Jesus about the greatest commandment in the law. Jesus' response is both summative and insightful. Some reformers note that Jesus passes over the detailed commands (i.e., the Ten Commandments) of Deuteronomy 5 for the command of Deuteronomy 6:5, which appears as Moses' own summary to the commands of his previous chapter. Heinrich Bullinger asserts that humans are to concentrate all efforts in all aspects of life to love God.

To love a neighbor wholeheartedly excludes lying, murder, stealing, oppressing the poor, neglecting the widows, seeking revenge, and other actions or attitudes that put oneself before others. Of particular interest to the reformers is what Jesus means by the Law and the Prophets depending on these commands. Zwingli warns that one has not kept the "commands" of the Hebrew Scriptures if that person is not perfectly keeping these two chief standards.

Finally, Jesus reverses the questioning by asking a question of the Pharisees. Their reply that the Messiah is the Son of David creates Jesus' opportunity to use a biblical text (Ps 110:1) to expand their notion of the Messiah's identity and purpose. The reformers note that the lack of submission from Israel's leaders sets the context of the strong rebukes of the next chapter.

22:15-22 Pharisees Ask About Paying Taxes to Caesar

THE POLITICAL CONNIVING OF THE HERODIANS. LANCELOT ANDREWES: The twenty-second chapter of Matthew in effect is nothing other than a chapter of controversies: with the Sadducee, verse 23; with the Pharisee, verse 22; with the scribe, verse 34; and here with the Herodian. With the Pharisees, of the great commandment; with the scribes, of the Messiah. . . . The Herodian was a politician, and his question, accordingly, about a secular point. . . . The Pharisees and Sadducees had no further end but to set him on ground, and so to expose him to the contempt of the people. The Herodians had laid a more dangerous plot; they came with this mind, says Luke, "to catch him," by catching somewhat from him, whereby they might lay him fast and draw him within danger of the state. A SERMON PREACHED AT WHITEHALL.[1]

WORSHIP GOD AND HONOR HUMAN AUTHORITY. JOHN CALVIN: He appears also to glance at their hypocrisy, because, while they carelessly permitted the service of God to be corrupted in many respects, and even wickedly deprived God of his authority, they displayed such ardent zeal about a matter of no importance; as if he had said, "You are exceedingly afraid, lest, if tribute be paid to the Romans, the honor of God may be infringed; but you ought rather to take care to yield to God that service which he demands from you, and, at the same time to render to humans what is their due." We might be apt to think, no doubt, that the distinction does not apply; for, strictly speaking, when we perform our duty toward humans, we thereby render obedience to God. But Christ, accommodating his discourse to the common people, reckoned it enough to draw a distinction between the spiritual kingdom of God, on the one hand, and political order and the condition of the present life, on the other. We must therefore attend to this

---

[1]Andrewes, *Ninety-Six Sermons* 5:129*.

distinction, that, while the Lord wishes to be the only lawgiver for governing souls, the rule for worshiping him must not be sought from any other source than from his own word, and that we ought to abide by the only and pure worship which is there enjoined; but that the power of the sword, the laws, and the decisions of tribunals do not hinder the worship of God from remaining entire among us. COMMENTARY ON A HARMONY OF THE EVANGELISTS.[2]

THE WISDOM OF CHRIST. MARTIN LUTHER: Here you plainly see the wisdom and marvelous dexterity of Christ. He wills the tribute money to be showed unto him and asks of the image and superscription thereof. They answering that it is Caesar's, he very well and most freely infers that they are under Caesar, unto whom they were compelled to pay tribute. As if he said, If you have so let in Caesar, that his money is coined with you, surely he bears rule over you, as though he should say, It is come to pass through your own fault that Caesar rules over you. What should they say or do unto this question? They marveled and went their ways, they thought that they should notably have overcome him, but for all their subtlety and wisdom they were deceived.

This is written for our comfort, that we who are Christians may know that we have such wisdom, as exceeds all wisdom, such strength and righteousness, as whereunto no strength and righteousness of man is like. For against the Holy Ghost there is no counsel. . . . We must not, therefore, be afraid that our doctrine shall perish and be put to disgrace and shame. For let all the wise of the world rise against the word of God, yea and be never so circumspect and set themselves against it, yet shall they have the foil and be overcome. It may be that they bark and bite, so that it seems unto men as though they would destroy the gospel, but when they have set themselves against it to extinguish it, they shall in no way prevail, but in the snare that they have laid

for others they themselves shall at length be taken. THE SIXTEENTH SERMON . . . GIVING TRIBUTE TO CAESAR.[3]

CHRIST'S CLEVER REPLY. LANCELOT ANDREWES: They now come to Christ to receive his resolution, which part he will take to. It is, for them, a contentious debate.[†] If to retain the people's favor, to avoid their outcry, he speaks but doubtfully of Caesar's tribute, "they have what they would," it is that they came forth to bring him in disgrace with the state and in danger of his life. Thus, would they fain have had it; and therefore, when truly they could not, as by this answer it is too plain, untruly they suggested, "We found this man denying to pay tribute unto Caesar." But if this is not, if he be for the tribute, yet will it not be from the purpose; they shall set the people (as good as a wasp's nest) upon him; they shall subject him to their clamor and public disgrace. He that must be their Messiah must proclaim a jubilee, must cry, "No tribute!" Otherwise he is not for them. If he betray them to the servitude of tolls and taxes, away with him; not him, but Judas of Galilee. So have they him at a dangerous dilemma, imagining he must needs take one part.

But that was their error. For Christ took a way between both. For as neither part is simply true, so is there some truth in both. Therefore, he answers not absolutely, as they fondly conceived he needs must, but with a double query, as indeed he should, which was not the answer they looked for. But it was such as they missed their purpose and knew not how to reprove it.

The sum of this is that Christ is neither Gaulonite nor Herodian; nor are Christians any more Gaulonites to deny Caesar his request, nor Herodians to grant him God's, and leave God none at all. But rather they are ready to acknowledge what due is to either, both faith to God and allegiance to Caesar. NINETY-SIX SERMONS.[4]

---

[2]CTS 3:44-45 (CO 45:602).

[3]Luther, *Complete Sermons*, 5:165-66.
[4]Andrewes, *Ninety-Six Sermons*, 5:131-32*. [†]Literally, "a very quodlibet," which was a type of free-flowing academic debate where questions might be asked at random.

22:23-33 Sadducees Ask About the Resurrection

IGNORANCE OF GOD'S WORD. THOMAS CRAN-MER: As touching the first, ignorance of God's Word is the cause of all error, as Christ himself affirmed to the Sadducees, saying that they erred because they knew not the Scripture. How would they then eschew error that will be still ignorant? And how would they come out of ignorance that will not read nor hear that thing, which should give them knowledge. He that now has most knowledge, was at the first ignorant, yet he did not forbid them to read, for fear he should fall into error; but he diligently read, lest he should remain in ignorance, and through ignorance, in error. THE SECOND PART OF THE SERMON, OF THE HOLY SCRIPTURE.[5]

GOD OF THE LIVING. PHILIPP MELANCHTHON: Now I come to Christ's arguments about the afterlife. You see that severe darkness will be in that person. The Sadducees have openly denied the afterlife, and they have sought ridiculous arguments. People rage in this way when they depart from the word of God, and they themselves seek ironies through their opinions. Christ broke their argument, and he said in eternal life there is no such future union as might be in union in this life. Afterward, he made an excellent argument: God is the God of the living, not of the dead. God is the God of Abraham. Therefore, Abraham lives. This argument contains an excellent consolation, not only about future life, but also about this life, because of course God truly cares for us. To say that God is the God of the living is to say that he cares. Because he is good, he would keep those who call him God, just as in the first command is said: I am the Lord your God, that is, the one who cares for you, hears your prayers, helps you, keeps you. You should consider this well, and in your prayers, faith should always be aroused, prayers which you ask not of an idle God, but one who most certainly desires to care, to hear, to help, to save, if you

believe in his Son. Moreover, the Sadducees were well refuted by the resuscitation of Christ himself and many others who were resuscitated and beheld by many. ANNOTATIONS ON THE GOSPELS.[6]

22:34-46 The Two Greatest Commandments

JESUS' USE OF MOSES' SUMMARY OF THE LAW. CHRISTOPH CORNER: The chief proof of it is from the authority of Scripture. For, from the sixth chapter of Deuteronomy of Moses, Christ, a most skilled teacher of the law, recites the sum of the law with marvelous succinctness, and explicates it clearly lest he himself seem to introduce a new teaching of the law. And he makes two members of that command, one about completely loving God, and one about loving one's neighbor. And as the former includes the precepts of the first table of the Mosaic law, so the latter comprise the mandates of the second table in a few words. God, addressing the Israelites through Moses, professes that he is the Lord, one God, distinct from all idols, gathering to himself a people by whom he might truly be worshiped; and, in fact, he constituted chief worship in the complete love of himself. The one who has such a love fulfills all the worship which is owed to God. And truly he wants to be loved and worshiped alone before all creatures, and he wants the whole person, with all interior and exterior members and with the person's complete life to be devoted to this worship, which the words "all" appear to demand.

He also distributes this love through the members of a person: We ought to love God first, with our whole heart, in such a way that our whole heart is pure and truly enflamed with a love for God, and starting from that fount, as it were, all our thoughts, senses, and emotions serve God alone and are ascribed to his glory alone. Second, our whole soul ought to love God, that is, our whole life, in such a way that all the actions and functions of it, both interior and exterior, seek and look to nothing else than the true worship of God

---

[5]Cranmer, *Certayne Sermons* (1547), B2r-B2v.

[6]MO 14:961.

and the obedience owed to him. Third, the whole mind, with the result that all the powers of the mind are subservient to God, that we understand, think, desire, decide, follow, do, and approve nothing than that which is pleasing to God and celebrate his name, power, truth, and goodness truly and wholly, and that there is nothing in the whole person that does not devote itself to obedience and veneration of him and most readily and completely fulfills whatever is pleasing to him only. THE ECONOMY OF THE GOSPELS.[7]

LOVE FOR GOD. HEINRICH BULLINGER: By this we understand that the greatest love that may be is required at our hands to be God-ward; as that which challenges man wholly, however big he be, and all the parts of man, each peculiar unto itself. In the mind is human understanding. In the heart is the seat of affections and will. Human strength contains all human ability, as the very words, deeds, counsel, riches, and his whole substance. Finally, the soul is human life. And we verily are commanded to employ all these upon the love of God when we are bidden to love God with all our soul, with all our strength, with our whole mind, and our whole heart. Nothing is overlooked, but all is contained in this. We are God's wholly and altogether; let us altogether therefore and wholly love God. Let nothing in all the world be dearer to us than God: let us not spare for God's sake anything of all that which we possess, however dear to us or good it be; but let us forsake, spend, and give it for God's sake, and as the Lord by his word appoints; for in doing so we love God before and above all things.

We are also commanded to stick to God only, and to embrace him alone. For to whom we do wholly owe all that we have, to him is all the whole sincerely, simply, and fully to be given. Here are they condemned whosoever will at once love God and the world together. The Lord requires the whole heart, the whole mind, the whole soul, and all the strength; finally, he requires all whatsoever we are, or have in possession; he leaves nothing therefore for you to bestow on others. By what right then will you give to the flesh, the devil, to other gods, or to the world, the things that properly are God's own? And God verily alone is the chiefest, eternal, greatest, mightiest creator, deliverer, preserver, most gentle, most just, and best of all. He alone does give, has given, and is able to give to humankind all that is expedient for the safeguard of body and soul. God alone does minister to men's and women's ability to live well and blessedly; and therefore, God deserves to be loved alone, and that too before and above all other things. OF THE LOVE OF GOD AND OUR NEIGHBOR.[8]

LOVING GOD WITH OUR WHOLE MIND. JAKOB ANDREAE: He also wants us to love God with our whole mind, that is, that we don't elevate our own understanding above God and his Holy Word but rather that, when God has said something, we believe it and do it obediently. Or that, when he promises something, we do not first argue a great deal about it or judge[†] his Word according to our understanding and blind reason, but rather believe it with simplicity[‡] and, obediently follow him, give him alone the glory since he knows what he has ordained, and understand ourselves as responsible to submit to his Word and will.

This is the greatest commandment, and the one who keeps it does not only what God ordered in the first tablet but also what is contained in the second commandment, which reads thus: "love your neighbor as yourself," concerning which Christ says that it is like the first commandment. For it is enclosed and contained in the first commandment. Whoever loves God above all else cannot do otherwise but, for the sake of God and his commandments, to also love one's neighbor as oneself, to do to one's neighbor what one would wish others to do to them, and moreover to bear with one's neighbor as one wants one's neighbor to bear with them. And this is also the sum of all that

---

[7]Corner, *Oikonomia Evangeliorum* (1567), Ff8r-Ggr.

[8]DHB 1:183.

that Moses wrote concerning God's law, and that the prophets emphasized in their sermons when they explained the law of Moses to the people and earnestly emphasized this for them. A SERMON ON MATTHEW 22.[9]

LOVE FOR NEIGHBOR. ANDREAS BODENSTEIN VON KARLSTADT: Indeed, the second commandment and work regarding the love of neighbor depends on the commandment and work of the love of God. Love of neighbor must be abandoned whenever it obstructs God's love or when both cannot happen. It is possible to hate, persecute, or kill the neighbor out of love for God. But to hate and persecute God is prohibited for all eternity, and there is not a single instance which permits us to hate God. Whoever loves father or mother more than God is not worthy of God. We have been commanded to love God more than anyone else. . . . Therefore, love of God is a work on which love of neighbor depends. For this reason, Moses says, "You shall honor father and mother, as God commanded"—with the same will, understanding, and manner which God commanded you.

Love of neighbor (be they angel, human being, or Christ in his humanity) must be governed by love of God and must be in line with it, just as a carpenter must be in line with plumb line and square. It is totally impossible for one who does not love God to love the neighbor in a divine manner, for we must love the neighbor as God demands and because this pleases God—this is impossible without the love of God. For this reason, Moses proclaimed the Ten Commandments and then began to explain the first commandment through the love of God, and that God declares "those who love me and keep my commandments."

With this I have done justice to the second question as well, regarding the Law and the Prophets, which depend on two commandments which is ever so true. For all commandments and prohibitions deal with love of God and neighbor. It

is not sufficient not to hate; love is also required. You must love your neighbor and speak well of them, and not harm them or treat the neighbor as if there were no God who seeks (or might seek) those who belong to him. You must love your neighbor, if you wish to fast, pray, sing, and do good works, acceptable in the sight of God. Without love of neighbor, God abhors you and your alleged good works. Even then you cannot love your neighbor unless of course you love God—who has shown you how to love—with a love abounding in faith. REGARDING THE TWO GREATEST COMMANDMENTS.[10]

THE GREAT REVERSAL. PETER WALPOT: This little word "yourself" contains within it the idea of true community and all works of love and mercy which one person can show another person. Indeed, to love your neighbor as yourself is the measure of true community and all good things. Where God has poured out this kind of love in the heart of a person, true community is learned through the Holy Spirit and in the bonds of peace. There one seeks no advantage over the neighbor but rather mutuality and common concern for each other. It is not loving your neighbor as yourself when one seeks to hold and possess one's wealth out of selfishness. . . . For to love one's neighbor as oneself is not to have part, or even half, but the whole in common and to give all things for the common use. Anything less is a heathen and false love, not a Christian love. TRUE YIELDEDNESS AND THE CHRISTIAN COMMUNITY OF GOODS.[11]

LOVE FOR ENEMIES. MATTHIEU VIREL: True love for your neighbor is when we love our neighbor in God only and for the honor of God. For if your neighbor is loved, because he or she is your parent or your friend, without considering the love of God, this love is not Christian, but natural and common even to brute beasts. For this reason, Jesus Christ says in the Gospel, if you love those

[9]Andreae, *Ein Christliche Predigt* (1578), 9-10. †Or "adjust." ‡Or "give it our simple faith."

[10]CRR 8: 234; citing Lk 14:26; Mt 10:37; Deut 5:16, 6.
[11]Liechty, ed., *Early Anabaptist Spirituality*, 153; citing Rom 5.

who love you, what reward will you have? For even the lawbreakers do that. This is why he commanded love of the enemy, in which how we are to love our neighbor for the love of God is more manifestly demonstrated than in other places. For enemies cannot be loved for their own sake, instead they are hated. However, considering them in God, they are no longer an enemy, instead they are a neighbor. Just as the rivers come from the sea and return to it, so does genuine love toward your neighbor. This true love must flow from God and return to God, otherwise it is stagnant. THE SUMMARY OF THE LAW.[12]

THE ETERNAL COMMANDMENTS. HULDRYCH ZWINGLI: So far, the commandments of his will still stand firm unto eternity; for they are no less than an expression of his will. These commandments, a believer does out of love; the godless hates them. Believers do not do them in their own strength. Rather, God effects in them love, counsel, and works, as much as they do. In all things they know full well that their doing and their works are naught; but that whatever takes place is God's alone. And though they may not do the works and the will of God, or even work against God's commandments, they do not despair; for they know Christ Jesus to be their salvation. Now the simple person will say, "Which are the commandments of God that shall not ever pass away?" Answer: Those, on which all Laws and Prophets depend: "You shall love the Lord your God with all your heart, soul and mind. And you shall love your neighbor as yourself." Everything pertaining to these two commandments in holy Scripture, one is obliged to do unto eternity. You may say, "Under the first commandment, one might well include ceremonies, for one does these to the honor of God." I retort, "No." If it were to the honor of God, he would not have rejected these through Isaiah and Ezekiel. Show me though, when he has ever let up on or placed in a secondary position the commandments of the first order. Therefore, they

stand firm to all eternity together with everything that depends on them. AN EXPOSITION OF THE ARTICLES.[13]

THE LAW OF LOVE. MARTIN LUTHER: As if the Lord would say: The one who possesses love to God, and love to their neighbor, has all things, and therefore fulfills the law; for the whole Law and all the Prophets point to these two themes, namely, how God and our neighbor are to be loved. . . . Let us see in the first place how Christ explains the law, namely, that it must be kept with the heart. In other words, the law must be spiritually comprehended; for the one who does not lay hold of the law with the heart and with the Spirit will certainly not fulfill it. Therefore, the Lord here gives to the lawyer the ground and real substance of the law and says that these are the greatest commandments, to love God with the heart and our neighbor as ourselves. . . . Since works are of no profit to a person, why then did God give so many commandments to the Jews? To this I answer, these commandments were given to the end that we might become conscious whether we really love God with all our heart, and with all our soul, and with all our strength, and in addition our neighbor as ourselves. . . . That the Jews practiced circumcision, fasted much, prayed much, and performed other like services was not pleasing to God, for it did not come from the heart, as this commandment requires: You shall love God with all your heart. . . .

Now here Christ shows the Pharisees and the scribes a twofold kindness. In the first place, he dispels their blindness and teaches them what the law is. In the second place, he teaches them how impossible it is for them to keep the law. Their blindness he dispels, in that he teaches them what the law is, namely, that love is the law. . . . for if it had been possible for human reason to comprehend it, the Pharisees and scribes, who at that time were the best and wisest of the people, could have understood it; but they thought it consisted alone

---

[12]Virel, *La Religion Chrestienne*, 118-19.

[13]Zwingli, *The Defense of the Reformed Faith*, 1:189; citing Mt 22:37-40.

in performing the external works of the law; in giving to God, whether it be done willingly or unwillingly; but their inward blindness, their covetousness, and their hardened heart they could not see, and thought they thoroughly understood the law and were fine fellows, holy and pious people; but they stood in their own light. For no one is able to keep the law unless their nature is thoroughly renewed. SERMON ON THE EIGHTEENTH SUNDAY AFTER TRINITY.[14]

PSALM 110 AND THE IDENTITY OF CHRIST.

JUAN DE VALDÉS: To comprehend these words two things must be considered. One, that Christ was not disparaged in being called the Son of David, since it is evident that he was so called, by them, who desired to honor him, and that Matthew commences his gospel by calling him so, and that Paul says that he was made of the seed of David according to the flesh. And the other that, that passage, "The Lord said unto my Lord, 'Sit on my right hand,'" was commonly understood among the Jews as relating to the Messiah, to Christ; which even the Jews, who have lived since Christ, understand in the same sense, though they do not admit that it refers to our Christ, because they do not recognize him as the Messiah. These two things considered, we understand that Christ designed by these words to convince the Pharisees that they ought to have held a higher opinion of the Messiah than they did hold. They only held him to be a son of David, and therefore a mere human being, while Christ designs to show them that David held him to be more than a son, and therefore to be more than a mere human being; since, speaking by the Spirit, he calls him Lord, and he would not have called him Lord had he not recognized him to be more than son; David indeed knew him to be a son by human generation (birth), while he recognized him to be the Son of God by divine generation, and therefore he called him Lord.

I understand this to be the right apprehension of these words. And if anyone shall say that the Pharisees might well have answered Christ by saying that David calls the Messiah Lord although he is his son just as he worshiped Solomon . . . when he was elected king, although he was his son; I shall in reply say that they could not; for what David did with Solomon was not by the Spirit as when he called the Messiah Lord, but by the flesh; it was an external ceremony appropriate to temporal rule. And if another shall say to me that the Pharisees might well have answered Christ by saying that those words of David do not affect the Messiah, nay, that it appears that they are words spoken to David in the name of the Jewish nation, as I have shown in my exposition of the Psalms, I shall reply to him and say that they could not; for we have stated that those words were commonly understood of the Messiah before the time of Christ, of which apprehension it appears to have been Christ's design to avail himself (in argument).

And therefore, well does the Evangelist say that no one could answer him a word, for they knew nothing of the divine mystery of the divine generation of the Messiah. And when it is added, "Neither dared any man from that day forth" . . . the Evangelist shows that all the questions which they addressed to Christ were armed with malice, for they ceased to question when they knew that his answers were divine. Had they questioned with sincerity, the desire to ask would have increased, being delighted with the answers he gave them; but, as they questioned but to accuse him falsely, they would not ask, seeing that their aim failed. COMMENTARY UPON THE GOSPEL OF ST. MATTHEW.[15]

CHRIST'S OTHER QUESTION: WHOSE SON HE IS. JAKOB ANDREAE: For this reason, Christ the Lord also, after the question about the law's greatest commandment, soon brought up the other question he had kept in reserve for the Pharisees concerning the Christ and asked them whose Son the Christ was: to which the Pharisees

---

[14]Luther, *Precious and Sacred Writings*, 14:171-72, 176-77.

[15]Valdés, *Commentary upon the Gospel of St. Matthew*, 397-98; citing Rom 1:3; Ps 110:1.

answered "David's." Which was indeed answered rightly, but insufficiently. For the Christ, or Messiah, is the anointed Savior whom David was promised would be born into his line, and therefore be David's son, as it stands written. The Lord swore to David a true oath, from which he will not turn away. I will place on your throne the fruit of your body. And again: I swore one thing by my holiness and I will not lie to David, his seed will be eternal and his throne will be for me like the sun. Also: see the time is coming, says the Lord, when I will awaken for David a righteous shoot, and he will be a king who will rule well. A SERMON ON MATTHEW 22.[16]

CHRIST AS DAVID'S LORD. DIRK PHILIPS: With these words, Christ clearly testifies that he is not a natural son of David, otherwise he could not be and be called David's Lord, since the son is not lord of the father but the father is lord of the son. However, Christ is David's God and Lord; therefore, he is not his natural son as one conceived of his seed and become man, but born out of his seed according to the flesh and out of the genealogy of Judah, out of which genealogy David had descended. And no one who is understanding of Scripture should be astonished that Scripture calls Christ the seed of the woman and Abraham and the fruit of the loins of David and the body of Mary. For since the Scripture calls Christ sin, who knew of no sin, on account of the fact that he was sacrificed for our sins, what wonder is it that the same Scripture calls Christ the seed of the woman and Abraham, a fruit of the loins of David and the body of Mary on account of the reasons previously

touched upon, even though he neither actually is nor may be considered as such by any Christian. THE ENCHIRIDION.[17]

WHY CHRIST HAD TO BE MORE THAN A MAN. JAKOB ANDREAE: Because this king had to deliver us not from fleshly enemies but rather from spiritual enemies—from sin, death, the devil, hell, and damnation—he could not be only a human. For even if one were to melt all the power of humankind into one lump it would still be nothing against the might of one single demon.

So that we might actually know what kind of a man the Christ would be, the Lord further asks the Pharisees and says: how does David, speaking in the Spirit, call him a lord, when he says, "The Lord said to my lord: sit at my right hand until I lay under enemies under your feet as a footstool." If David now calls him a lord, how is he then his son? For God's law points out in the fourth commandment that no son is the lord of his father, but rather the father is and remains his son's lord for as long as they live on the earth. Even if a son were raised up to great might and honor, even so God's commandment stands forever and ever: you shall honor your father and mother, and so, though the son might well rule and reign over all that he has been granted power over, but he is responsible to honor his father and recognize him as his lord until he is in the grave. But since the Christ, or Messiah, is written about thus in the Psalms, that he is David's lord and David recognizes and honors him as his lord, we can glean that he must be more than a mere man, that is, the Almighty Son of God. A SERMON ON MATTHEW 22.[18]

---

[16]Andreae, *Ein Christliche Predigt* (1578), 12-13; citing Ps 132:11-12; 89:36; Jer 23:5-6.

[17]CRR 6:144*; citing Rom 1:3; 9:6; Heb 7:14; Rom 8:3; 2 Cor 5:21.
[18]Andreae, *Ein Christliche Predigt* (1578), 13-14; citing Ps 110:1.

23:1-39 CONDEMNATION AND MOURNING

Then Jesus said to the crowds and to his disciples, [2]"The scribes and the Pharisees sit on Moses' seat, [3]so do and observe whatever they tell you, but not the works they do. For they preach, but do not practice. [4]They tie up heavy burdens, hard to bear,[a] and lay them on people's shoulders, but they themselves are not willing to move them with their finger. [5]They do all their deeds to be seen by others. For they make their phylacteries broad and their fringes long, [6]and they love the place of honor at feasts and the best seats in the synagogues [7]and greetings in the marketplaces and being called rabbi[b] by others. [8]But you are not to be called rabbi, for you have one teacher, and you are all brothers.[c] [9]And call no man your father on earth, for you have one Father, who is in heaven. [10]Neither be called instructors, for you have one instructor, the Christ. [11]The greatest among you shall be your servant. [12]Whoever exalts himself will be humbled, and whoever humbles himself will be exalted.

[13]"But woe to you, scribes and Pharisees, hypocrites! For you shut the kingdom of heaven in people's faces. For you neither enter yourselves nor allow those who would enter to go in.[d] [15]Woe to you, scribes and Pharisees, hypocrites! For you travel across sea and land to make a single proselyte, and when he becomes a proselyte, you make him twice as much a child of hell[e] as yourselves.

[16]"Woe to you, blind guides, who say, 'If anyone swears by the temple, it is nothing, but if anyone swears by the gold of the temple, he is bound by his oath.' [17]You blind fools! For which is greater, the gold or the temple that has made the gold sacred? [18]And you say, 'If anyone swears by the altar, it is nothing, but if anyone swears by the gift that is on the altar, he is bound by his oath.' [19]You blind men! For which is greater, the gift or the altar that makes the gift sacred? [20]So whoever swears by the altar swears by it and by everything on it. [21]And whoever swears by the temple swears by it and by him who dwells in it. [22]And whoever swears by

heaven swears by the throne of God and by him who sits upon it.

[23]"Woe to you, scribes and Pharisees, hypocrites! For you tithe mint and dill and cumin, and have neglected the weightier matters of the law: justice and mercy and faithfulness. These you ought to have done, without neglecting the others. [24]You blind guides, straining out a gnat and swallowing a camel!

[25]"Woe to you, scribes and Pharisees, hypocrites! For you clean the outside of the cup and the plate, but inside they are full of greed and self-indulgence. [26]You blind Pharisee! First clean the inside of the cup and the plate, that the outside also may be clean.

[27]"Woe to you, scribes and Pharisees, hypocrites! For you are like whitewashed tombs, which outwardly appear beautiful, but within are full of dead people's bones and all uncleanness. [28]So you also outwardly appear righteous to others, but within you are full of hypocrisy and lawlessness.

[29]"Woe to you, scribes and Pharisees, hypocrites! For you build the tombs of the prophets and decorate the monuments of the righteous, [30]saying, 'If we had lived in the days of our fathers, we would not have taken part with them in shedding the blood of the prophets.' [31]Thus you witness against yourselves that you are sons of those who murdered the prophets. [32]Fill up, then, the measure of your fathers. [33]You serpents, you brood of vipers, how are you to escape being sentenced to hell? [34]Therefore I send you prophets and wise men and scribes, some of whom you will kill and crucify, and some you will flog in your synagogues and persecute from town to town, [35]so that on you may come all the righteous blood shed on earth, from the blood of righteous Abel to the blood of Zechariah the son of Barachiah,[f] whom you murdered between the sanctuary and the altar. [36]Truly, I say to you, all these things will come upon this generation.

[37]"O Jerusalem, Jerusalem, the city that kills the prophets and stones those who are sent to it! How

often would I have gathered your children together as a hen gathers her brood under her wings, and you were not willing! [38]*See, your house is left to you* *desolate.* [39]*For I tell you, you will not see me again, until you say, 'Blessed is he who comes in the name of the Lord.'"*

a Some manuscripts omit *hard to bear*   b *Rabbi* means *my teacher,* or *my master;* also verse 8   c Or *brothers and sisters*   d Some manuscripts add here (or after verse 12) verse 14: *Woe to you, scribes and Pharisees, hypocrites! For you devour widows' houses and for a pretense you make long prayers; therefore you will receive the greater condemnation*   e Greek *Gehenna;* also verse 33   f Some manuscripts omit *the son of Barachiah*

OVERVIEW: Before Jesus begins a list of specific judgments against the scribes and Pharisees, he announces to the crowds and his disciples a general warning against these leaders. Among the reformers, Juan de Valdés supposes that Jesus allows for his followers to observe the teachings of the Pharisees because much of the content of their teaching was drawn from the Bible. Though Jesus said that their teaching should be heeded (see Mt 5:17-19), he provides two warnings against following the lifestyle of the scribes and Pharisees. First, their efforts at piety are halfhearted and prone to minimalism or self-justification of lax standards. Second, the most notorious aspect of their deeds is that they do the deeds to be seen by others. The reformers sum up Jesus' assessment of the Pharisees by noting their practice of requiring complete obedience from their disciples while living in their own hypocrisy and hoping for their own glory.

The Reformation commentators also highlight various charges that Jesus makes against the religious leaders. For example, Calvin notes that Jesus focuses on the second table of the Ten Commandments not to overlook matters regarding the necessary honoring of God but instead to provide charity toward others as the litmus test of the person who is truly worshiping God. Wolfgang Musculus makes a connection between Christ's condemnation of the religious leaders' concern for an external show and the earlier similar critiques that Jesus gave in the Sermon on the Mount (see Mt 6:1-18).

Though the Lord has been gracious to Jerusalem (a prophetic use of the city's name that is representative of the nation as a whole, see Is 2:1-5; 62:1-12), the stubborn unbelief of the people and their leaders continues. Like an Old Testament prophet, Jesus pronounces an interim period of judgment when Israel will be left desolate of the widespread blessings of the Lord (e.g., Jer 16:10-15). Yet, as in Old Testament prophecies, hope remains that in the future the Coming One will be warmly received by the nation (e.g., Is 11). For the reformers, Jesus' lament provides a strong word of judgment but also a word of promise and encouragement for the Jews. Luther indicates that Jesus' statement about not seeing him until the Jews say, "Blessed is he who comes in the name of the Lord," is a promise to the Jews specifically and implies a future, general turning of Israel to the Messiah.

23:1-36 Woes to Scribes and Pharisees

A GUARDED FOLLOWING. JUAN DE VALDÉS: Christ, desiring to explain the reason why he willed that his disciples should not act as the scribes and Pharisees did, says, "For they talk and do not," meaning, for they do not observe that which they teach others to observe. And proceeding further with this explanation he says, "For they bind heavy burdens," meaning, that they burdened the people with strange and intolerable observances, taking care not to bear them themselves, not even so much as to move them with a finger. It may be gathered from these words of Christ, that although the life of the scribes and Pharisees was bad, for their minds were bad, their doctrine was not so bad as to render it injurious, at that time, to follow it. . . .

And if it shall appear to any one that this is contrary to what Christ stated in chapter 16, cautioning his disciples that they should beware of the doctrine of the scribes and Sadducees [sic], I will tell them that, as I understand it, Christ here spoke of the doctrine which consisted in doing that which pertained to the fulfillment of the law and of human constitutions; while there he spoke of the doctrine, which consists in believing, in accepting Christ as the Messiah promised in the law, which acceptance was impeded by the doctrine of those, who, in their dreamy imaginations, conceived a profane and worldly Messiah and wrested the holy Scriptures to make them speak of what they had dreamed.

From that passage, "But all their works they do" . . . we glean another thing worthy of consideration, for Christ, in laying down the characteristics of those scribes and Pharisees, opens our eyes to recognize all those to be scribes and Pharisees in whom we see the following features. First, delighting that their works, which they hold to be good, and which the vulgar persuaded by them hold to be good, be seen by human beings, in order that they may be prized by them and esteemed by them.

Second, the manifestation of sanctity by external indications, as by the Pharisees and scribes with their phylacteries, which bore certain sentences from the Bible, or from the commandments in the Decalogue, written on them; and with their borders or fringes, which they attached to four parts of their vestments, to indicate austerity of life. Third, the being ambitious, seeking to occupy the seat of honor in all the public places they visited, such as were the feasts held at that time, and in the synagogues. Fourth, the being proud and hollow, seeking to be saluted and reverenced in public, and to be called masters, as did the scribes and Pharisees, who insisted on being called "Rabbi," which signifies master, but, being derived from a word that signifies much, means master of many sciences.

From that, "But be not you called," we glean another thing worthy of consideration, enabling us to understand some things affecting the duty of the Christian. First, that Christians are in no way to pride themselves upon being called by a name that signifies greatness or authority, as was that of rabbi, and as is now that of master. Second, that they recognize no one as master but Christ. COMMENTARY UPON THE GOSPEL OF ST. MATTHEW.[1]

EXALTED TITLES AND EGOS. GIOVANNI DIODATI: "Be not you." This is not to be rashly understood for a total rejection of civil and respectful titles for public offices, which are marks of order, and documents of the mutual bond which is between superiors and inferiors; but the meaning is, "Avoid the vainglory which the false doctors annex unto these titles, and do not attribute to yourselves the authority of absolute masters of my church; but refer all the glory to me only, and touch nothing but that which you have learned of me."

"Call no one." As the preceding commandment was directed to the pastors, so this teaches the believers in general not to yield that absolute reverence nor power over their consciences to any living person, which belongs to God only, as ignorant people did use to do to the Pharisees. For laying these abuses aside, these titles of honor may be used in a good sense.

"Greatest." The highest dignity in the church is not in domination and lordship, but in ministry and service. PIOUS ANNOTATIONS.[2]

THE TRUE FATHER. HULDRYCH ZWINGLI: Christ did not intend to prohibit the calling of one's physical father by that name, but rather that we ought not set up any other forerunner, teacher, or guide, except the heavenly teacher, father, and guide. This is indicated by the preceding phrase "you ought not be called master," which in the same context concerns teaching as well. This is also indicated by the subsequent words, "you ought not be called leaders, for your sole leader is Christ." Now the Latin term for this word *leader* is *master*, but the Greek term is *kathegetes*, which

---

[1]Valdés, *Commentary upon the Gospel of St. Matthew*, 401-02*.
[2]Diodati, *Pious Annotations* (1643), F1v*; citing 2 Cor 1:24; 1 Pet 5:3; 1 Cor 4:15; Phil 2:22; 1 Thess 2:11.

means as much as "forerunner" or "guide." In short, Christ does not want any other teacher for us but God and no one to be elevated as father; for the heavenly Father alone is our Father and no one else ought to lead us but the one Christ. Heaven and earth will have to fall before this his word. He intends to have it thus eternally; for his testament is an eternal one; he has never nor shall he ever change it. From this it follows that all who have elevated themselves to be fathers, as well as all those who called them fathers and who banded together, acted against God and against the honor and order of Christ. AN EXPOSITION OF THE ARTICLES.[3]

WOES TO HYPOCRITES. MARTIN LUTHER: This is a great cry of woe and an unfriendly farewell that he utters over the great lords in the spiritual estate who are supposed to govern the people, such as preachers and bishops. He is not particularly addressing the commoner, though we want to make the application as well, but calls them here by name: "Pharisees and scribes." . . .

This chapter has eight cries of woe. First, he calls them "hypocrites," false saints, which is a disgraceful name, just as when someone is called a false or fraudulent person who deceives and lies. Going in, everything looks beautiful, but in fact it is all fake. They portray themselves as good and deceive the country and people. "You are supposed to be the pillars and cornerstones of the people by teaching God's Word purely and leading holy lives, but you are fake, teach lies, and live falsely. Why? You close the kingdom of heaven; you do not go in and you prevent others from entering."

This is a dreadful sermon and a hard rebuke. Those who are supposed to have the preaching office, authority, and right to teach, and are supposed to use it for our salvation, instead lead us into condemnation, to the devil, even though God established the preaching office so that people might be saved from hell. "Although you were entrusted with making the kingdom of

heaven available, you have done the opposite and closed it." . . .

And Christ gives them the authority to possess the office from Moses. They did not creep in or gain the office unjustly; therefore, it is also proper for them to use it. But now they come along and corrupt the people, though they are supposed to serve them for their salvation. And the people are obliged to listen to them, as stated in Deuteronomy. . . . Now if someone has the authority that people are supposed to give heed to them as to God himself and he does the opposite to condemnation, that is truly an abomination. The most harmful is a false preacher. He is the worst person on earth, and there is not thief, murderer, or scoundrel on earth whose wickedness can compare to the that of such a preacher who has the people's obedience in God's name but strikes them dead and leads them into the abyss of hell with false preaching. SERMONS.[4]

DEMANDS OF VAINGLORY. PETER STERRY: The Lord notes three things in these men: their practice, their principle, and their end. Their practice: This is twofold. First, their practice is impositions upon women and men. They require universal obedience. People must believe all that they say, though they believe it not. People must observe their rules, though they themselves neglect and break them. "They bind heavy burdens and grievous to be borne on others' shoulders, but they themselves will not move them with one of their fingers." Thus, it is for the most part: They are such as have too little in them who take too much upon them. Second, their practice is industry among people. "Woe unto you scribes, and Pharisees, hypocrites; for you compass sea and land to make one proselyte, and when he is made, you make him twofold more the child of hell than yourselves." They spare no care, cost, or pains to make a convert; but it is to themselves by a blind obedience, and implicit faith. While they promise to bring a person to heaven, they make their heart like hell; full of bitter zeal, a violent heat, without any light at all. This was their practice.

---

[3]Zwingli, *The Defense of the Reformed Faith*, 1:207-8*.

[4]LW 68:161-63 (WA 47:452-55); citing Deut 17:12.

Their principle is hypocrisy. "Woe unto you scribes, and Pharisees, hypocrites!" They pretended to come in the name of God, as sent forth from God: yet they had nothing of the divine presence resting on them, working in them, or going forth by them: but were, as other people. . . .

Their end: this is twofold: First, there is vainglory. "All their works they do to be seen by others." Second, there is covetousness. "You devour widows' houses, and for a pretense make long prayers." God and glory are the baits, which the devil lays for women and men. One has escaped the hook of the devil who cares not for these. The one who cares not to have any possession or to make any appearance in this world—that one is already in heaven and dwells with God. This is the way of these people, whom the Lord reproves and condemns. He warns his own disciples to take heed, that they follow not their examples. He gives them two cautions to this purpose. The first caution is in the verse before my text: "And call no man your father upon the earth; for one is your father, which is in heaven." The second caution is my text: "Neither be you called masters: for you have one master, which is Christ." You see the context. THE TEACHINGS OF CHRIST IN THE SOUL.[5]

MORE DISCIPLES, MORE JUDGMENT. GIOVANNI DIODATI: "You compass," that is: You bestow an extreme deal of study and labor, and use your utmost endeavor to make a Gentile become Jew. "Proselyte" is a Greek name signifying a man that comes home, or returns from without. And so were called the Gentiles that embraced the Jewish religion, and there were of them of diverse sorts and degrees, some turning to their religion and society, and inhabiting among the Jews, and being circumcised. Others turned to their religion, and dwelt among them, but were not circumcised. Others turned to their religion, but neither dwelt with them nor were circumcised. "You make him," teaching him to set his righteousness and ground

his salvation upon his works, and not upon me who am the only end of the law. And turning him from the true and spiritual meaning of the law by your false doctrines and from God's pure service by your traditions, infecting him by the example of your hypocrisy and other vices, you cause his conversion to Judaism to serve him for nothing but for his greater condemnation. "Twofold more," that is, far more superstitious and fervent in your sect than you are yourselves, as ordinarily the disciples of false doctors out vie their masters. "Child," that is, worse, more desperate, a lost child and deserving eternal death. PIOUS ANNOTATIONS.[6]

FALSE STANDARDS. DAVID DICKSON: Hence learn, first, corrupt churchmen do corrupt religion also, and mislead the people fearfully; they become blind guides, whose office requires that they should be wise and seeing guides, in which case woe to the people, but chiefly woe to the blind guides. Second, swearing by the creature is no new sin, for these corrupt hypocrites did foster swearing by the creatures, as by the temple, altar, gold, and gifts. Third, corrupt churchmen make things to be sin or no sin as it serves their purpose, as here they made an oath by the temple to be none and an oath by the gold of the temple to oblige. Fourth, to make light of any oath by the creature as not obligatory does open a door to superstition and perjury; for to swear by the temple, they said, it was nothing. . . .

The Lord rebukes them sharply for this their corrupt doctrine. First, when people depart from the rule of God's Word in determining of sin, they prove themselves foolish and blind. Therefore, Christ calls them, "You fools and blind." Second, as anything draws more near unto God in relation of service, so is it in a higher degree more holy, to wit, by way of consecration, and use. For the temple that signified Christ and his church is more holy than the gold which signified the gifts of Christ. Third, superstition and error blinds the mind and besots the heart, for he says, "You fools and blind. . . ."

[5]Sterry, *The Teachings of Christ in the Soul* (1648), 2-3*.

[6]Diodati, *Pious Annotations* (1643), F1v*.

Our Lord goes on to tell more of their corrupt doctrine. Hence, learn that he that swears by the creature, whether he intend to swear by God or not, swears indirectly by God the Creator also, because the creature has nothing but from God, and as it is his creature; for says Christ, "The one who swears by the temple or heaven swears by him that dwells therein." . . . Such oaths are not allowed anyway here, but a double fault is taxed in the Pharisees, first that they taught others to swear by the creatures, next that they made some of such oaths not obligatory, and some of them obligatory, as they thought fit. A BRIEF EXPOSITION.[7]

TRUE LOVE AND TRUE WORSHIP. JOHN CALVIN: Christ charges the scribes with a fault which is found in all hypocrites, that they are exceedingly diligent and careful in small matters but disregard the principal points of the law. . . . But as Christ makes the chief righteousness of the law to consist in mercy, judgment, and faith, we must first see what he means by these words; and, second, why he left out the commandments of the first table, which strictly relate to the worship of God, as if godliness were of less value than the duties of charity. Judgment is taken for equity, or uprightness, the effect of which is that we render to every person what belongs to them and that no one deceives or injures others. Mercy proceeds farther and leads a person to endeavor to assist their brethren with their property, to relieve the wretched by advice or by money, to protect those who are unjustly oppressed, and to employ liberally for the common good the means which God has put into their hands. Faith is nothing else than strict integrity; not to attempt anything by cunning, or malice, or deceit, but to cultivate toward all that mutual sincerity which all people wish to be pursued toward themselves. The sum of the law, therefore, relates to charity. . . .

If it be objected that in this way humans are preferred to God, because charity, which is performed toward them, is reckoned more valuable than religion, the answer is easy. Christ does not here contrast the second table of the law with the first, but, on the contrary, draws from the manner in which the second table is kept the proof whether or not God is truly and sincerely worshiped. As piety lies within the heart, and as God does not dwell among us in order to make trial of our love toward him and does not even need our services, it is easy for hypocrites to lie and falsely to pretend to love God. But the duties of brotherly love fall under the senses and are placed before the eyes of all, and therefore in them the impudence of hypocrites is better ascertained. . . . Not that it is enough to discharge our duties toward others if we do not first render to God what we owe to him, but because he who regulates his life according to God's commandment must be a sincere worshiper of God. . . . He therefore acknowledges that whatever God has enjoined ought to be performed, and that no part of it ought to be omitted, but maintains that zeal for the whole law is no reason why we ought not to insist chiefly on the principal points. . . .

Nothing, therefore, could be more ridiculous than to strain out the wine or the water, so as not to hurt the jaws by swallowing a gnat, and yet carelessly to gulp down a camel? But it is evident that hypocrites amuse themselves with such distinctions; for while they pass by "judgment, mercy, and faith" and even tear in pieces the whole law, they are excessively rigid and severe in matters that are of no great importance; and while in this way they pretend to kiss the feet of God, they proudly spit in his face. COMMENTARY ON A HARMONY OF THE EVANGELISTS.[8]

CLEAN HEARTS AND GOOD WORKS. AUGUSTIN MARLORAT: The Lord does prosecute the same matter still; and figuratively he reproaches the scribes . . . that they only seek for this one thing carefully, that they may shine and seem excellent before others. For by the outward side of the platter, he understands metaphorically an external

---

[7] Dickson, *Brief Exposition* (1651), 266-67*.

[8] CTS 3:89-93 (CO 45:631-33).

show; as if he should say: he has no care of cleanness, but only of that which appears to the face of human beings; even as if a person should wipe away the spots upon the outward side of the cup but should leave it all foul and filthy within.

Therefore, he reproves their hypocrisy, because they only sought to reform their lives according to the outward appearance and sight of human beings, and they might get unto themselves a vain fame of holiness, so that he reduces them in the verse following to the pure and sincere affection of living well. . . .

Out of a pure mind, clean thoughts, words, and deeds all do come; but to an impure mind those things that are outside bring no cleanness at all. This is a figurative kind of speech. For the right order of cleaning is to begin at the inward part first, that afterward an external cleanness may follow which is nothing else than the effect of the internal cleanness.

We must, therefore, first of all purge that which is within; because indeed it were a ridiculous thing to feed the eyes with cleanness and to drink of an unclean and poisoned cup. . . . Here is another similitude but appertaining to the same end that the other did which went before. For he compares them to sepulchers, which people of this world ambitiously build after a fine and trim fashion for themselves. Even as therefore in sepulchers the picture or carving draws the eyes of people unto it, when as within them the putrefied and corrupted carcasses are laid up; even so Christ says that hypocrites do deceive by the external show, because they are filled with fraud and iniquity. . . . He always pierces even to the inward parts and teaches to purge the conscience. For it is a most easy matter to change and alter the outward person. EXPOSITION OF THE HOLY GOSPEL OF MATTHEW.[9]

PERILS OF EXTERNAL PIETY. WOLFGANG MUSCULUS: This place condemns them especially on account of hypocrisies that are appraised thus

far also in those whom this chapter reproves. For he does not say, "Woe to you, because you are full of iniquity," as this may be seen to damn so many, because they are iniquitous. Rather he says, "Because you have the appearance of justice to others, while within you are full of pretense and iniquity." And as he reveals their despicable hypocrisy, he uses metaphors most suitable to all of graves, evidently whitewashed, which appear beautiful on the outside, yet inside they are full of the bones of the dead, as well as all filth, undoubtedly putrid, foul smells, and worms. There were certain whitewashed ones, which this chapter reproaches: since they were multiplying phylacteries because they were extending borders; they were praying long prayers; they were surrounding sea and dry ground of one proselyte by power; they were tithing mint and dill; they were cleansing dishes and cups; they were adorning the tombs of the prophets; they were showing sadness with respect to fasting and liberality of giving. About these things see above on chapter 6. Certainly on account of these things, they are given in the sight of others, just as justice. Truly the bones of the dead and the inside of tombs were unclean, which this chapter joins with their hypocrisy, clearly works void of glory, which first were brought in filth reclining at the table, first an assembly in the synagogues, first greetings in the open space, and the title of rabbis.

In like manner since from the entrance of the kingdom of heaven they will not enter, they were impeding others. Because as plunderers and greedy, they were devouring the homes of widows; because they were giving more harm to the work of the proselyte; because they were seducing people with false doctrine, by favor of gain; because they were loaded down by laws, they were neglecting justice and mercy by iniquity and lack of mercy; because of eagerness for pleasure, they were intemperate. And as he added, they were unmerciful, true enemies, and persecutors. Of course, that uncleanness, putridity, and foul smell, by which they were filled at the same time by hypocrisy, they were concealing as an incrusted

[9]Marlorat, ed., *A Catholike and Ecclesiasticall Exposition of the Holy Gospell After S. Mathewe*, 538-39*.

tomb. Because this same thing Christ declared to be extremely detestable, as we know them on that account to be worthy above all, by whom he is slandered. For whoever does wickedly may be worthy to be condemned; yet by a twofold name he condemns those who join pretense of justice to wickedness. For in the eyes of the God of all, the same hypocrisy in them, being contrary to honesty and truth, is most unclean and extremely detested. COMMENTARY ON MATTHEW.[10]

ACCEPTING PROPHETS, REJECTING THEIR MESSAGE. DESIDERIUS ERASMUS: Because through false boasting of holiness, you build up honorably the tombs of the prophets and garnish the graves of just people, whom your forefathers had slain, and making as though you favored the virtue of those who were slain and detest the cruelty of them by whom they were slain. . . . For as much as you be of this mind, truly you declare that you be the very natural children of them which killed the prophets, of whom they were admonished frankly and freely; and you would have been no better than they, if it had chanced you to live in their time. Go to be like your elders, and you fulfill what is lacking in their extreme cruelty so that nothing may be lacking. They killed the prophets; you kill him, whom the prophets prophesied. O serpents, the offspring of vipers, O murderers, the children of murders. Since your malice is so invincible, since you can be amended by no benefits, by no miracles, by no gentle or rough communication, by no promises nor threats; in case you may escape in the mean season the judgment of humans, how will you escape the judgment of hell? The which you heap the more upon you, because you be not afraid from the desire of killing by the wicked example of your elders. So many prophets were sent of whom you have slain many. At last, I came myself, against whom, you know what you have endeavored. PARAPHRASES.[11]

KILLING THE PROPHETS. HEINRICH BULLINGER: It seems simply that these are an exposition that the words of the Lord know about Zechariah, son of Berechiah, with respect to whom it is said that he is one numbered among the twelve prophets. For this unfortunate thing is seen between the temple and altar, that is, on account of a time which the altar indeed was destroyed, but the temple was not yet built or complete. For the words of the Lord, "Between the temple and the altar," seem to be explained not about a place but a time. And Zechariah the prophet certainly spoke in the second year of Darius the king, but the temple was completed in the sixth year of the same king. In the meantime, however, Zechariah vehemently rebuked the customs, both of the priests and the people, who by chance of name was killed by unpleasant ones. The Scriptures certainly nowhere mention his death. In fact, they, to which we have brought consent both the Lord's words and to the history of their time, are seen also of the prophet Zechariah. The Lord adds these: "Truly I say to you, all these things will come upon (this) generation," which is a violent assertion. As if he said, "There is not a turning away of the justices of God as anyone expects it." For certainly all evil falls from heaven into that lineage of the serpent who was indulging in the most impious things himself in paradise threatening the truthful and powerful Lord. But these also put words or themselves, by which a religious one seems today to pursue the true gospel, and also to destroy severely his faithful confessors. COMMENTARY ON MATTHEW.[12]

AVOID ASSOCIATING WITH PERSECUTORS. PHILIPP MELANCHTHON: The accusation is twofold, that they themselves now kill the prophets and teachers sent by God, and that many hypocrites in all times will always persecute the church. And he shows how great is the magnitude of this sin. Since the intent is the same in all persecutors, and all are incited by the devil, and they wish the

---

[10]Musculus, *In Evangelistam Matthaeum Commenarii* (1556), 567.
[11]EP 90r-90v*.

[12]Bullinger, *In . . . Evangelium secundum Matthaeum commentariorum*, 9:207.

same thing, that is, that God be blasphemed, along with the Son, and that the truth be crushed, and that they give encouragement to each other, each individual is guilty of many persecutions. Therefore, all are horribly punished. So he says, "All the righteous blood falls on you, poured out from Abel all the way up to Zechariah . . ."

Here the story of Zechariah is recited, and Basil tells that there was a report handed down from the elders, that Zechariah, the father of John the Baptist, when he was testifying about the youth born from the Virgin Mary, that he was the Messiah, was killed by the priests. And because this story was recent, Christ, then, including all times, names first Abel, and then the last in the line, and the latest, Zechariah. I am content with this story, nor do I wish to seek another interpretation, but let us give thought to how great an evil it is to be a member of that group who persecutes the church, who heaps up blasphemies, idolatry, and murders in the world and is ruled by the devil, who is a liar and a murderer. Let us consider these great evils and let us flee any association with persecutors, and let us pray to God that he himself strengthen us in the knowledge of his word and in the true faith. ANNOTATIONS ON THE GOSPELS.[13]

23:37-39 Jesus' Lament over Jerusalem

CHRIST'S MATERNAL LOVE CONTRASTS AND DISGRACES THE ISRAELITES. JOHN CALVIN: We now perceive the reason why Christ, speaking in the person of God, compares himself to a hen. It is to inflict deeper disgrace on this wicked nation, which had treated with disdain invitations so gentle, and proceeding from more than maternal kindness. It is an amazing and unparalleled instance of love, that he did not disdain to stoop to those blandishments, by which he might tame rebels into subjection. A reproof nearly similar is employed by Moses that God, like an eagle with outspread wings, embraced that people. And though in more than one way God spread out his

wings to cherish that people, yet this form of expression is applied by Christ, in a peculiar manner, to one class, namely, that prophets were sent to gather together the wandering and dispersed into the bosom of God. By this he means that, whenever the Word of God is exhibited to us, he opens his bosom to us with maternal kindness, and, not satisfied with this, condescends to the humble affection of a hen watching over her chickens. Hence it follows, that our obstinacy is truly monstrous if we do not permit him to gather us together. And, indeed, if we consider, on the one hand, the dreadful majesty of God and, on the other, our mean and low condition, we cannot but be ashamed and astonished at such amazing goodness. For what object can God have in view in abasing himself so low on our account? When he compares himself to a mother, he descends very far below his glory; how much more when he takes the form of a hen and deigns to treat us as his chickens?

Besides, if this charge was justly brought against the ancient people, who lived under the law, it is far more applicable to us. For though the statement—which I quoted a little ago from Moses—was always true, and though the complaints which we find in Isaiah are just, that in vain did God spread out his hands every day to embrace a hard-hearted and rebellious people," that, though he rose up early, he gained nothing by his incessant care of them; yet now, with far greater familiarity and kindness, he invites us to himself by his Son. And, therefore, whenever he exhibits to us the doctrine of the gospel, dreadful vengeance awaits us if we do not quietly hide ourselves under his wings, by which he is ready to receive and shelter us. Christ teaches us, at the same time, that all enjoy safety and rest who, by the obedience of faith, are gathered together to God because under his wings they have an impregnable refuge.

We must likewise attend to the other part of this accusation, that God, notwithstanding the obstinate rebellion of his ancient people, was not all at once so much offended by it as to lay aside a father's love and a mother's anxiety, since he did

---

[13]MO 14:979-80.

not cease to send prophets after prophets in uninterrupted succession; as in our own day, though he has experienced a marvelous depravity in the world, he still continues to dispense his grace. But these words contain still deeper instruction, namely, that the Jews, as soon as the Lord gathered them together, immediately left him. Hence came dispersions so frequent that they scarcely remained at rest for a single moment under the wings of God, as we see in the present day a certain wildness in the world, which has indeed existed in all ages; and, therefore, it is necessary that God should recall to himself those who are wandering and going astray. But this is the crowning point of desperate and final depravity, when people obstinately reject the goodness of God and refuse to come under his wings.

I said formerly that Christ speaks here in the person of God, and my meaning is that this discourse belongs properly to his eternal Godhead; for he does not now speak of what he began to do since he was manifested in the flesh, but of the care which he exercised about the salvation of his people from the beginning. Now we know that the church was governed by God in such a manner that Christ, as the eternal Wisdom of God, presided over it. In this sense Paul says, not that God the Father was tempted in the wilderness, but that Christ himself was tempted.

Again, when the sophists seize on this passage, to prove free will, and to set aside the secret predestination of God, the answer is easy. "God wills to gather all people," say they; "and therefore all are at liberty to come, and their will does not depend on the election of God." I reply: The will of God, which is here mentioned, must be judged from the result. For since by his word he calls all people indiscriminately to salvation, and since the end of preaching is that all should betake themselves to his guardianship and protection, it may justly be said that he wills to gather all to himself. It is not, therefore, the secret purpose of God but his will, which is manifested by the nature of the word, that is here described; for, undoubtedly, whomsoever he efficaciously wills to gather, he

inwardly draws by his Spirit and does not merely invite by the outward voice of humankind.

If it be objected that it is absurd to suppose the existence of two wills in God, I reply, we fully believe that his will is simple and one; but as our minds do not fathom the deep abyss of secret election, in accommodation to the capacity of our weakness, the will of God is exhibited to us in two ways. And I am astonished at the obstinacy of some people, who, when in many passages of Scripture they meet with that figure of speech *anthropopatheia*, which attributes to God human feelings, take no offense, but in this case alone refuse to admit it. But as I have elsewhere treated this subject fully, that I may not be unnecessarily tedious, I only state briefly that, whenever the doctrine, which is the standard of union, is brought forward, God wills to gather all, that all who do not come may be inexcusable. COMMENTARY ON A HARMONY OF THE EVANGELISTS.[14]

GOD'S LOVING DESIRE FOR REPENTANCE.
NIELS HEMMINGSEN: These words of Christ calling upon Jerusalem by name contain first an upbraiding. Second, they declare Christ's affection toward them. Third, they help us to understand that they perish through their own default; and last they threaten punishment.

For when he says, how often would I have gathered you together, he upbraids them with ingratitude, for that they would neither receive the benefit that was offered them, nor had any regard of their own welfare and much less would acknowledge the liberality of these benefactors or be thankful to him for it. Would God that a number of those who hear the gospel at this day were not like them, which thing verily they show by their fruits.

The Lord declares his affection toward them when he compares himself to a hen, which loves her chickens most entirely, and does all that he is able to do, to the intent he may keep them from

---

[14]CTS 3:107-9* (CO 45:642-43); citing Deut 32:11; Is 65:2; Jer 7:13; 1 Tim 3:16; 1 Cor 10:9.

the souls that are enemies to them. God forbid that it should enter into any godly heart to think that Christ determined otherwise with himself concerning the Jews by some secret will, than he pretended by his tears and by his speech. For it is a horrible thing to think that there are contrary wills in Christ, who himself condemns a double heart. Therefore, he willed their salvation indeed, according to the saying of the prophet; I will not the death of a sinner; but that they should convert and live.

In the third place, when the Lord says, "And you would not," he openly testifies that the Jews perished through their own default and that of their own malice they strived against Christ, who offered them salvation. He says not, "And God would not receive you into favor, but you would not." Wherefore we may learn two things hereby: One is, that being made wary by the harm of the Jews, we give care to God's word, and yield ourselves obedient to Christ when he allures us and that we strive not against the Holy Ghost, who stirs up the wits of all people that hear the gospel. Another is that whosoever hear the word and obey it not, do perish through their own fault. Their destruction and damnation are not to be ascribed to any destiny or secret will of God, as though there were some whom he would not have saved.

Fourth, when he adds, "And your house shall be left desolate unto you," although this threat of punishment pertains especially to the Jews that were persecutors, to whom he threatens the utter overthrow of their religion, commonwealth, and private state. Yet in general, it pertains to all persecutors of the gospel. And he threatens them, that at least wise some of them should amend. For all the threats of the prophets have a covert condition, namely, unless you repent; like as we see in the Ninevites, and as we hear Christ witnessing in these words, "Unless you repent, you shall perish altogether." A POSTIL, OR EXPOSITION OF THE GOSPELS.[15]

---

[15]Hemmingsen, *A Postill, or Exposition of the Gospels* (1569), 25-26*; citing Lk 13:3-5.

A FUTURE HOPE FOR THE JEWS. MARTIN LUTHER: "Behold, your house is left unto you desolate." Oh! a terrible visitation, which is also illustrated in the instance of the Jews. They killed the prophets so long that God sent them no more. He suffered them to be without any preaching, without any prophets 1,500 years, he took his Word from them and his wings he drew to himself. And thus their house is left desolate and no one builds up their souls, God no longer dwells among them. It has happened to them as they wished. As Psalm 109:17 says concerning them: "Yea, he loved cursing, and it came unto him; and he delighted not in blessing, and it was far from him." Here all the righteous bloodshed upon the earth is come upon them, and this gospel is fulfilled in them. . . .

Finally comfort is spoken here to the Jews, when the Evangelist adds, "Truly I say unto you, you shall not see me henceforth, until you shall say, 'Blessed is he who comes in the name of the Lord.'" Christ spoke these words on Tuesday, after Palm Sunday, and they form the conclusion and the last words of his preaching upon earth; hence they are not yet fulfilled but they must be fulfilled. True they did once receive him on Palm Sunday, but these words were not fulfilled on that occasion. "You shall not see me henceforth" is not to be understood in the sense that they never saw him afterward in the body, because they did, in that they afterward crucified him. He means, they shall not see him again as a preacher and as Christ, to which end he was sent. His office and he in his office were never seen again by them. In this he gave them his last, his farewell, sermon, and his office, for which he came, was now closed.

Thus, it is certain that the Jews must yet say to Christ, "Blessed is he that cometh in the name of the Lord." This very truth Moses proclaimed in Deuteronomy 4:30-31: "In the latter days you shall return to Jehovah your God and hearken unto his voice; for Jehovah your God is a merciful God; he will not fail you, neither destroy you, nor forget the covenant of your fathers which he swore unto them." It was also preached in Hosea 3:4-5: "The children of Israel shall abide many days without king, and without prince, and without sacrifice, and without pillar, and without ephod or teraphim; afterward shall the children of Israel return, and seek Jehovah their God, and David their king, and shall come with fear unto Jehovah and to his goodness in the latter days." Likewise, Azariah declared this truth in 2 Chronicles 15:2-5 thus: "If you forsake Jehovah, he will forsake you. Now for a long season Israel was without the true God, and

without a teaching priest, and without law; but when in their distress they turned unto Jehovah, the God of Israel, and sought him, he was found of them." This passage cannot be understood as referring to the Jews of that present time for they were never before without princes, without prophets, without priests, and without teachers and the law. SERMON ON ST. STEPHEN'S DAY.[16]

---

[16]Luther, *Precious and Sacred Writings*, 10:235-38*.

24:1-51 TEACHINGS ABOUT THE END OF THE AGE

Jesus left the temple and was going away, when his disciples came to point out to him the buildings of the temple. ²But he answered them, "You see all these, do you not? Truly, I say to you, there will not be left here one stone upon another that will not be thrown down."

³As he sat on the Mount of Olives, the disciples came to him privately, saying, "Tell us, when will these things be, and what will be the sign of your coming and of the end of the age?" ⁴And Jesus answered them, "See that no one leads you astray. ⁵For many will come in my name, saying, 'I am the Christ,' and they will lead many astray. ⁶And you will hear of wars and rumors of wars. See that you are not alarmed, for this must take place, but the end is not yet. ⁷For nation will rise against nation, and kingdom against kingdom, and there will be famines and earthquakes in various places. ⁸All these are but the beginning of the birth pains.

⁹"Then they will deliver you up to tribulation and put you to death, and you will be hated by all nations for my name's sake. ¹⁰And then many will fall away[a] and betray one another and hate one another. ¹¹And many false prophets will arise and lead many astray. ¹²And because lawlessness will be increased, the love of many will grow cold. ¹³But the one who endures to the end will be saved. ¹⁴And this gospel of the kingdom will be proclaimed throughout the whole world as a testimony to all nations, and then the end will come.

¹⁵"So when you see the abomination of desolation spoken of by the prophet Daniel, standing in the holy place (let the reader understand), ¹⁶then let those who are in Judea flee to the mountains. ¹⁷Let the one who is on the housetop not go down to take what is in his house, ¹⁸and let the one who is in the field not turn back to take his cloak. ¹⁹And alas for women who are pregnant and for those who are nursing infants in those days! ²⁰Pray that your flight may not be in winter or on a Sabbath. ²¹For then there will be great tribulation, such as has not been from the beginning of the world until now, no, and never will be. ²²And if those days had not been cut short, no human being

would be saved. But for the sake of the elect those days will be cut short. ²³Then if anyone says to you, 'Look, here is the Christ!' or 'There he is!' do not believe it. ²⁴For false christs and false prophets will arise and perform great signs and wonders, so as to lead astray, if possible, even the elect. ²⁵See, I have told you beforehand. ²⁶So, if they say to you, 'Look, he is in the wilderness,' do not go out. If they say, 'Look, he is in the inner rooms,' do not believe it. ²⁷For as the lightning comes from the east and shines as far as the west, so will be the coming of the Son of Man. ²⁸Wherever the corpse is, there the vultures will gather.

²⁹"Immediately after the tribulation of those days the sun will be darkened, and the moon will not give its light, and the stars will fall from heaven, and the powers of the heavens will be shaken. ³⁰Then will appear in heaven the sign of the Son of Man, and then all the tribes of the earth will mourn, and they will see the Son of Man coming on the clouds of heaven with power and great glory. ³¹And he will send out his angels with a loud trumpet call, and they will gather his elect from the four winds, from one end of heaven to the other.

³²"From the fig tree learn its lesson: as soon as its branch becomes tender and puts out its leaves, you know that summer is near. ³³So also, when you see all these things, you know that he is near, at the very gates. ³⁴Truly, I say to you, this generation will not pass away until all these things take place. ³⁵Heaven and earth will pass away, but my words will not pass away.

³⁶"But concerning that day and hour no one knows, not even the angels of heaven, nor the Son,[b] but the Father only. ³⁷For as were the days of Noah, so will be the coming of the Son of Man. ³⁸For as in those days before the flood they were eating and drinking, marrying and giving in marriage, until the day when Noah entered the ark, ³⁹and they were unaware until the flood came and swept them all away, so will be the coming of the Son of Man. ⁴⁰Then two men will be in the field; one will be taken and one left.

⁴¹*Two women will be grinding at the mill; one will be taken and one left.* ⁴²*Therefore, stay awake, for you do not know on what day your Lord is coming.* ⁴³*But know this, that if the master of the house had known in what part of the night the thief was coming, he would have stayed awake and would not have let his house be broken into.* ⁴⁴*Therefore you also must be ready, for the Son of Man is coming at an hour you do not expect.*

⁴⁵*"Who then is the faithful and wise servant,ᶜ whom his master has set over his household, to give* them their food at the proper time? ⁴⁶*Blessed is that servant whom his master will find so doing when he comes.* ⁴⁷*Truly, I say to you, he will set him over all his possessions.* ⁴⁸*But if that wicked servant says to himself, 'My master is delayed,'* ⁴⁹*and begins to beat his fellow servantsᵈ and eats and drinks with drunkards,* ⁵⁰*the master of that servant will come on a day when he does not expect him and at an hour he does not know* ⁵¹*and will cut him in pieces and put him with the hypocrites. In that place there will be weeping and gnashing of teeth."*

a Or *stumble*   b Some manuscripts omit *nor the Son*   c Or *bondservant*; also verses 46, 48, 50   d Or *bondservants*

OVERVIEW: Jesus' apocalyptic forecast of the destruction of the temple prompts a cluster of questions from the disciples concerning future things. Their intertwined questions have three aspects: the timing of the temple's destruction, a sign of Jesus' coming, and a sign of the end of the age. The Reformation commentators attempt to clarify each element of Jesus' reply and connect it to other biblical texts. The reformers also note that the "last days" in Jesus' teaching are marked with cataclysmic battles with evil and the devil. The commentators hold that Jesus' message, though it contains a prediction of many hardships, is still gospel (i.e., good news) because it ends with the declaration of salvation for the righteous (Mt 25:46).

The horrific scenes of tribulation presented by Jesus draw attention to the suddenness, the difficulty, the uniqueness, and the pervasive human deception all present in the last days. The culmination of these cataclysmic events will be the coming of the Son of Man, one of a few Daniel references that the reformers attempt to explain. One particular element of judgment that captures the reformers' attention is the destruction of Jerusalem, which they take to be symbolic of future, universal judgments as well.

After a brief depiction of the events surrounding the end of the age, Jesus returns to his earlier themes of the disciples' need for readiness and the swiftness of the end. The reformers note that the general signs that Jesus provides do not indicate a specific time period but do encourage requisite readiness. Calvin draws from Christ's imagery of the contrast of the fates of a servant who is faithful and diligently awaiting the master's return versus that of the slothful servant who doubts that the master will come any time soon. The image of the dreadful, suddenness of Christ's coming and the awful judgment that awaits the unprepared should arouse the sleepy Christian to faithful service.

24:1-14 *Signs of the End*

ONE PROPHECY WITH MULTIPLE PARTS. JUAN DE VALDÉS: To the curious questions of the disciples who desired to know the time of the ruin of Jerusalem and of the day of judgment, Christ so answered that from his reply they could neither gather the one nor the other; because as to the ruin of Jerusalem, it seems that he does not tell them, but that they should understand Daniel's prophecy. And, as to the day of judgment, he does not tell them, but of many signs that shall previously be seen, advising how they should regulate themselves at that time, and bring them down to the exhaustion of all their curiosity in a continuous waiting, daily and hourly, for his coming to judgment; I here learn that I ought to mortify and to slay all manner of curiosity in myself. . . . The other thing is that all this chapter being a prophecy of the ruin of

Jerusalem and of the day of judgment, it is no marvel that Christ should proceed throughout it, mixing the one with the other, in the way that some prophets, nay the leading ones, proceed in their prophecies. They mix some things with others, as is seen in Isaiah and Jeremiah, who do so when prophesying about the liberation of the Jewish nation from the Babylonian captivity, their return to Jerusalem, the rebuilding of the city, and of the temple, with the two advents. The first advent is the humble one which we have seen, and which we see in those who are his members. And the second is the glorious one, which we shall see in him, and in those who are his members; and thus the happiness of the kingdom of Christ in the present life, as to the communication of the Holy Spirit which is communicated to those who believe, with the glory of the kingdom of God in the life eternal, as to the seeing God face-to-face, the knowing of him as he knows us. So do they go on mixing up one thing with another, that all human prudence combined does not suffice to enable anyone to distinguish the one from the other.

Where I understand that just as the spirit of prophecy is necessary to make a distinction in what the prophets state, so likewise is the spirit of prophecy necessary to make distinction in what Christ here states, by the spirit of prophecy.

I likewise understand that just as the happy return of the Jewish nation to Jerusalem was as a shadow of the most happy return of the Christian people, after the resurrection, to the kingdom of God and life eternal, which is the heavenly Jerusalem, so also the special ruin of Jerusalem, with the persecutions, with the hardships, and with the miseries that went before it, was as a shadow of the general ruin of the whole world, with the persecutions, with the hardships, and with the miseries which will anticipate it. COMMENTARY UPON THE GOSPEL OF ST. MATTHEW.[1]

THE TEMPTATIONS OF THE LAST DAYS.

DAVID DICKSON: The Lord's words serve not to satisfy his people's curiosity, but for their instruction and utility. . . . It is better for us to guard against the hazard wherein we may be, before the world's end, than to be curious about the time when it shall end. . . .

To the end his disciples not only then living, but in all ages following, should guard themselves against all sorts of temptations unto the end of the world, he warns them . . . the Lord will suffer blasphemies and heresies to arise in the visible church, for the punishing of some, and trial of others for he says, "Many shall come in my name" . . . pretending themselves to be Christ. When the only one true Christ is not received, it is justice that many false, pretend Christs should come, and deceive them who will not receive the truth in love. Therefore he forewarns, "that they shall deceive many." . . .

Another temptation of the church is the terror of wars. . . . If wars fall out about religion and the gospel, it is no small trial; therefore, he tells us, "You shall hear of wars." We must in such times keep fast the faith, and thereby study to keep our hearts in peace . . . "that you are not troubled." . . . When we have digested one trouble, we must not think to pass so, but must expect greater troubles, and pray for constant patience for "the end is not yet." . . . It is decreed in heaven to punish the wickedness of the world, and specially the contempt of the gospel, by provoking kingdoms and nations one against another, and to plague all by famine, and pestilence and earthquakes . . . it is but a deposit and a beginning of the sorrows which God will bring at length upon this wicked world. . . .

The third sort of the exercise of Christ's disciples is persecution, imprisonment, and slaughter. Christians must resolve for the gospel to lose their lives. . . . Christ's disciples need not to look for love from this world, but rather must expect to be hated wherever they shall come, albeit there were no other cause but the profession of Christ's name and his truths. The fourth temptation or fourth sort of exercise of Christ's disciples is the apostasy of professors, when persecution arises for the gospel. A BRIEF EXPOSITION.[2]

---

[1] Valdés, *Commentary upon the Gospel of St. Matthew*, 433-35*.

[2] Dickson, *Brief Exposition* (1651), 274-76*.

PERSEVERING IN TRUTH AND OBEDIENCE.
JOHN CALVIN: This warning differs from the former, in which Christ foretold that many would come in his name. For there he spoke only of impostors, who, shortly after the commencement of the gospel, gave out that they were the Christ; but now he threatens that in all ages false teachers will arise, to corrupt sound doctrine. . . . There is therefore no reason why error and certain impostures of the devil and corruptions of piety should strike pious minds with dismay; since no one is properly founded on Christ who has not learned that we must stand firm against such attacks; for this is the undoubted trial of our faith, when it is in no degree shaken by the false doctrines which arise. Nor does he only say that false prophets will come, but likewise that they will be so crafty as to deceive and draw away sects after them. . . .

How far and wide this evil extends every person ought to know, but there are very few who observe it. For in consequence of the superior clearness with which the light of the gospel discovers human malice, even good and properly regulated minds grow cool and almost lose the desire to exercise benevolence. Each of them reasons thus with himself, that the duties which they perform to one person or to another are thrown away, because experience and daily practice show that almost all are ungrateful, or treacherous, or wicked. This is unquestionably a weighty and dangerous temptation; for what could be more unreasonable than to approve of a doctrine, by which the desire of doing good and the vigor of charity, appear to be diminished? And yet when the gospel makes its appearance, charity, which ought to kindle the hearts of all people with its warmth, rather grows cool. But we must observe the source of this evil, which Christ points out, namely, that many lose courage because through their weakness they are unable to stem the flood of iniquity which flows on every hand. Christ requires from his followers, on the other hand, such courage as to persist in striving against it. . . . Although, then, the charity of many, overwhelmed by the mass of iniquities, should give way, Christ

warns believers that they must surmount this obstacle, lest, overcome by bad examples, they apostatize. And therefore, he repeats the statement, that no one can be saved, unless they strive lawfully, so as to persevere to the end. COMMENTARY ON A HARMONY OF THE EVANGELISTS.[3]

A HAPPY ENDING. JAKOB ANDREAE: This beloved word (*euangelium* or *gospel*) of the Lord Christ is a sweet and comforting word, which in good German we would call "good news."[†] But since in these words we do not hear of cheerful things, but rather of great terrifying miseries and distressing dangers, someone might, not unreasonably, be surprised how this text and word is truly called a gospel, and can be a gospel, that is a joyful message to the community of God. . . . But then again, if we regard the end of Christ's sermon and reconsider it with diligence, we will find that this word is not a common one but rather an exemplary one in all the Gospels, with which Christ the Lord comforts his poor Christian community. A SERMON ON MATTHEW 24.[4]

24:15-28 *Interpreting Daniel*

INTERPRETATION OF DANIEL'S PROPHECY.
HEINRICH BULLINGER: The Lord cites this text so that the prophecy may have even greater validity, and he sends readers back to the passage from Daniel so that they may be more fully instructed there. "For let the reader understand," he says.[†] That is, let them read *so that* they understand— namely, with diligence. Or [the Lord's sense could be] that everything the Romans will accomplish against the Jews will be so congruent to this divine prediction of the prophet [i.e., Daniel] that no reader in the future could fail to understand the prophet's meaning. The passage is found in Daniel, the ninth chapter, and has been interpreted by us in [our commentary on] the first chapter of 1 Peter.

---

[3]CTS 3:127-28 (CO 45:655-56); citing 2 Tim 2:5.
[4]Andreae, *Ein Christliche uber das Euangelium . . . Matthei am 24* (1578), B1r-B2r. [†]Or a "joyful message."

A few comments repeated from there will meet the needs of this passage: "And after the seven weeks," says Daniel, "Christ shall be cut off for sixty-two weeks, and he shall have nothing. And the imperial people[†] who are to come shall destroy the city or sanctuary (or temple), and its end shall be as the flood, and the appointed desolation shall last until the end of the war." He identifies the chief cause of the nation and city's destruction as the death of the Son of God. "They shall kill," he says, "their Messiah, and they shall be nothing to him."[§] . . . For though they had crucified him, he nonetheless rose on the third day, ascended into heaven, and now sits at the right hand of the Father, thence to come again as the judge of both living and dead. Or "they shall be nothing to him" [could mean that] they were unable to make any charge or crime stick to him, as even the Roman judge Pilate testified by saying "I find no cause of guilt in this man." Therefore the "imperial people," namely, the supremely formidable soldiers of the Roman Empire who crossed the sea from Italy, as even Balaam long ago had predicted, were dispatched by God to exact vengeance for [Christ's] innocent blood. These by the will and bidding of God will overturn the holy city itself as well as the temple. This overturning will be similar to the flood, which with the greatest force destroyed all things at once, leaving nothing left. We have heard that the city along with the temple and Galilee along with Samaria and Judea will be torn up from the roots. In addition, "the appointed Desolation shall last until the end of the war." This means that, when the Messiah is cut off there will be continuous war, and he will devastate his own nation and will hand it over to the hand of the Romans, who must harass it most cruelly and bring it to an end. For after the Lord had ascended into heaven, straightaway the seeds were cast by Pilate and soon by other leaders as well, from which sedition sprouted. Day by day, moment by moment new disturbances, new calamities and disturbances were arising, until at length they were torn up from the roots in a just war. [The text] in Daniel follows: "And he will confirm the covenant with many for one week, and

in the middle of the week he will make sacrifice and offering to cease, and the Desolation of Abomination—or "devastator"—will be over the pinnacle or gate [of the temple]." And he goes on to speak more fully about the Messiah and that final week. That "covenant" that "he will confirm with many" is the new covenant or remission of sins for all, Jew as well as Gentile, which was procured through Christ's death and blood and promised to them if they should have faith. And that "one week" comprises the age of Christ and chiefly his proclamation and redemption. ON THE GOSPEL OF ST. MATTHEW, THE APOSTLE AND HIS WORK.[5]

THE END OF TWO KINGDOMS. MARTIN LUTHER: In this chapter there is a description of the end of two kingdoms; of the kingdom of the Jews, and also of the kingdom of the world. . . . Notice therefore that Matthew unites the two and at the same time conceives the end, both of the Jewish nation and of the world. He therefore cooks both into one soup. But if you want to understand it, you must separate and put each by itself, that which really treats of the Jews, and that which relates to the whole world. This we wish to do now.

Notice, first, how Christ prophesies in this chapter concerning the final destruction of the Jewish nation, which the Jews did not at all believe, even though they had been clearly told through great signs and words, the promises of God, which he made to the fathers, like unto which had happened to no other people upon the earth. For this reason they strongly insisted and depended

---

[5]Bullinger, In . . . Evangelium secundum Matthaeum commentariorum (1546), 211v-212r; citing Dan 9:26-27; Num 24:24.
[†]Bullinger appears to interpret "let the reader understand," which in many modern Bibles and commentaries is treated as an editorial aside by the Gospel writer, as Jesus' own recommendation to go back and read Dan 9 more carefully. [‡]Unlike translations of the Hebrew, which have some variation of "people of the [singular] prince who is to come," principalis here identifies the people themselves as "princely" or "imperial [Roman]." [§]The background and the tenor of Bullinger's commentary supports the sense that it is the Jewish people who are identified here as Christ's murderers and who will be reduced to "nothing" after the Roman campaign.

upon it and thought it will continue forever. . . . For this reason, God announced besides his miracles with clear and plain prophesies that their kingdom shall have an end and that God had abolished the external reign of the law, meats, offerings, and so on, and would establish another which shall endure forever, as the angel announced to the virgin concerning Christ, as recorded in Luke 1:33. "And he shall reign over the house of Jacob forever; and of his kingdom there shall be no end." Among the various passages which treat of the end of Judaism, there is especially one that is introduced by Christ, namely: the prophet Daniel 9:25-27 speaks of the terrible abomination. SERMON ON THE TWENTY-FIFTH SUNDAY AFTER TRINITY.[6]

FALSE CLAIMS OF CHRIST'S PRESENCE.
PILGRAM MARPECK: To such people the false prophets usually come and say: Come, I will show you Christ in our gathering, company, or church, and you will find Christ. You will see there the true life in Spirit and grace, and God dwelling in our hearts as chamber and temple. . . . Therefore, such people hear the falsely acclaimed [Christians] rather than those who truly know Christ and are led into strange hearts unknown to Christ, away from their own hearts in which alone they can and should find Christ. . . .

May the Lord protect and preserve us from such prophets about whom he himself warned us, as well as from all other evil and errors, that we seek the goodness of Christ in his word and truth in no other place than our own hearts. There he reveals himself to us and with the Father dwells in us if we truly love and keep his commandments which are not difficult. Those are the true signs by which each may judge whether Christ dwells in him. Such a heart will soon find the true gathering and fellowship of Christ's saints. For where the carcass is, the eagles will gather. There also the gathering and true fellowship of the saints will soon be found. MEN IN JUDGMENT.[7]

ONE END PORTENDS ANOTHER.
MARTIN LUTHER: This refers to both parts, and the meaning is that the distress shall not endure long, for the sake of the godly; for the war against the Jews did not last quite two years, when peace was declared. But since all this has reference also to the end of the world, we wish to apply these passages concerning the Jews also to ourselves, so that we do justice to the Evangelist.

That a war shall come again as came upon the Jews, I do not expect, because the text says: There shall be such tribulation as shall never be again, as we also read and see; but another punishment shall come upon us; as that was a temporal war, so at the end of the world will a spiritual war come over the ungodly, who will be in the same condition as the Jews. Thus they will agree with one another: as that calamity came upon Jerusalem according to God's ordering and everything was ground to powder; so abominable and even worse, shall it be before the last day, when he shall come and make an end of the whole world. . . .

Therefore, this passage in Daniel concerning the abomination applies also to us. For we also have indeed a real abomination or desolation sitting in a holy place, namely: in Christendom and in the consciences of men and women, where God alone should sit and reign, of which Daniel speaks in very clear words in the eighth and ninth chapters. SERMON ON THE TWENTY-FIFTH SUNDAY AFTER TRINITY.[8]

NEARNESS OF THE END.
PHILIPP MELANCHTHON: There is a future resurrection of the dead and a universal judgment. Let us learn also from the prophets and the words of Christ that this day is not far off, as many imagine, saying that, although there may be a future resurrection and judgment, nevertheless they are thousands of years in the future, and therefore are free from care and laugh at the whole mention of a judgment. Christ says in this chapter, "Concerning that day and hour not even the angels know, but only the Father

---

[6]Luther, *Precious and Sacred Writings*, 14:364-65.
[7]CRR 2:482-83.
[8]Luther, *Precious and Sacred Writings*, 14:370-71.

alone." He did not wish to reveal the day, but still he indicated that the span of time is near to the end, so that we might be afraid. For a lack of concern is increasing in the world.

Daniel clearly says that in the end of the fourth monarchy the judgment will come. And God distributed the ages of the world after the flood into monarchies, so that we might know that the end is approaching, and when time is reaching its end. But all people ought to know the word that is said to have been handed down from Elias, and it is believable that many such words have been handed down from the prophets and the fathers, along these lines: The age of the earth will be six thousand years, and afterward, destruction. Two thousand years, emptiness. Two thousand years, law. Two thousand, the days of the Messiah. And if anything is missing, it is missing because of our sins, which are many. And it is indisputable from a reckoning of the years of the world, which God wanted us to know from a book handed down through the fathers and prophets, that already five thousand five hundred plus years have passed.

Since these things are so, it is more than certain that the end of the world is not far off, because God will cut off the time around the end, just as it is written: "Unless those days are shortened, no flesh will be saved."...

Why are these things foretold? I respond: Primarily for two reasons. The first is so that those who are living carefree lives might be admonished and repent and not become excessively barbarous and profane. The second is so that pious people who fear the magnitude of the punishments and of the public and private miseries, might nevertheless have consolation, because God has mixed in consolations into these threats; he says that he will protect his church and that repentance and prayer will help to mitigate the punishments. Pray that you might be able to escape these evils, lest they come upon you. ANNOTATIONS ON THE GOSPELS.[9]

[9]MO 14:983-85.

24:29-51 *The Unknown Day and Hour*

THE DAY OF THE LORD. MARTIN BUCER: From these things I think it is clear that those things which the Evangelists relate that the Lord foretold concerning signs in the sun and the moon, as Luke wrote, or darkening the sun and the moon, as Mark and Matthew have it, which are without a doubt the same things, concerning falling stars, the shaken powers of the heavens, the roaring of the sea, the confusion and lamentation of the people, all these things will happen on that last day, and that through these things the Lord wanted to describe that day. Thus, Peter in his second epistle, in the third chapter, has it like this: "The day of the Lord will come as a thief in the night, in which the heavens will pass away like a blast...." If someone wishes to consider the words of the Lord more closely and to compare the individual narrations of the Evangelists more carefully, that person will see that the things which the Lord foretold have broader implications than all those ordinary things that were foretold for the same time, and also the things that will happen on the day of judgment itself, which Peter plainly corroborates. Therefore, what Luke says, that "there will be signs in the sun and moon," should not be understood as if the signs have to precede the day of the Lord, but the signs here are understood as unusual and miraculous things, which, not so much portend, but rather show as present, not the very day of the Lord, but his anger against the wicked, just as also the sign of Christ that will appear in heaven, about which we find in Matthew. Furthermore, although once the elect are made immortal, all things truly will be changed, and there will stand a new heaven and a new earth, which change now the anxious creation awaits, having been subjected to vanity against its will, according to Romans 8, nevertheless, it is the custom of the Scriptures, through the darkening of the sun and moon, similar events of the stars, which are foretold here, to signify an intense stirring up of divine vengeance. Thus Joshua 3 and 24, Jeremiah 15, Ezekiel 32, Joel 2 and 3, Amos 8, Micah 3, and in other passages where we read about the vengeance of God foretold against both the Jews and other nations. Commentary on Matthew.[10]

Judgment and the Coming of the Son of Man. Wolfgang Musculus: Some people want this sign to be the body of Christ itself, exhibiting the tokens of his passion, the wounds of his hands, feet and side, as Chrysostom[†] supposes in his second explanation of the passage. But some understand it to be the sign of the cross, which is similar. Among these is also Chrysostom in his first explanation, who interprets it as a symbol of the justification of Christ, since he is bringing judgment on his enemies. It's as if someone who had been struck by a stone would bring the stone with him to trial against the one who struck him. To me it seems that this sign of the cross will be triumphal against all the impious and the prince of this world, and signal the freeing of the elect. Thus, what is a scandal to the Jews and foolishness to the Gentiles, will appear with the utmost honor to bring about the never-ending trepidation and sadness of the impious. The kings and princes of this world have their own symbols which, attached to the gates of the cities, indicate the dominion and power of the rulers. So the cross, a sign of Christ when it appears in the clouds to the eyes of all, will signify that this crucified Jesus is the lord of heaven and earth, so that those who do not want to believe now, then will see it with their very own eyes and cower with great fear.

The emphasis here is not simply on the fact that the Son of Man will come in the clouds, but that they will see they Son of Man. In other words, the one whom they contempt and persecute, at that time they will see with great power and glory coming to judge them. And so also below in chapter 26, while forced to stand in the Sanhedrin, he will say, "Hereafter you will see the Son of Man coming in the clouds with great power." Likewise, in John 19 he quotes from the prophet: "And they will see the One whom they pierced." For, his advent is in every way a threat to his adversaries; he will be such that they cannot help but be downcast, and this time they will not be able to hold him in contempt as being weak and inferior. This is what it means when he says that he will come with great power and glory. For, he does not say, "And you will see me coming," but, "And they will see the Son of Man (whom they held in contempt) coming with great power and glory." Commentary on Matthew.[11]

Signs Create Readiness. John Trapp: "You know that summer is nigh," which is so much the sweeter, because brought in, and led out by winter; so will eternal life be to the saints, here tossed and troubled with a variety of sufferings. Many sharp showers they must here pass through, light is sown for the righteous . . . sown only; and seedtime we know is usually wet and showery. Although it is fair weather often with God's children, when it is foulest with the wicked; as the sun rose upon Zoar, when the fire fell upon Sodom. But, if they should have never a good day in this world, yet heaven will make amends for all. And what is it for one to have a rainy day, who is going to take possession of a kingdom?

"Know that it is near." Some space then there shall be, it seems, between the foregoing signs and the coming of Christ. But though space be granted, yet grace is uncertain. Make sure work therefore quickly, lest you come late, and be left outdoors for your lingering.

"This generation shall not pass." That generation that immediately precedes the end of the world. That this is the sense appears by the antithesis. But of that day and hour knows no one. . . . The generation and age wherein Christ shall come, you may know by the signs that foreshow it, but the day and hour you must not look to know, be you never so intelligent.

---

[10]Bucer, *In Sacra Quatuor Evangelia, Enarrationes Perpetuae* (1536), 466.

[11]Musculus, *In Evangelistam Matthaeum Commentarii* (1556), 575-76. [†]Chrysostom, *Homilies on Matthew*, NPNF[1] 10:441.

"Heaven and earth shall pass." What God has written, he has written. His word is established in heaven, says David. It endures forever, says Peter; it remains firm as Mount Zion, and shall stand inviolable, when heaven shall pass away with a great noise, and the earth with its works shall be burnt up. A COMMENTARY OR EXPOSITION UPON THE FOUR EVANGELISTS.[12]

HEED THE SON OF MAN. ROBERT GELL: The Lord Jesus very often styles himself the Son of Man. . . . And the reason is given by some that thereby he might signify his human nature, which he took upon him for humanity's sake. For what is the Son of Man, but a human being, as David explains one by the other. Or, when he calls himself the Son of Man, he intimates that he lives in mean repute, and a contemptible estate among human beings. Or he gave himself that name, by which he would be more familiarly known and called. And this is all interpreters make of this, when our Lord calls himself the Son of Man. But I believe our Lord had greater reason than these, why he called himself the Son of Man. Nor do I doubt but he had reference unto Daniel, who was most punctual in his observation touching the Messiah, and the time of his appearing in the flesh, and his coming to judgment, he is called the Son of Man. . . .

Of this last coming, I understand our Lord here to speak. And this is parallel to the days of Noah; in what respects we shall understand from the more full and large explication of it. Wherein may be observed many parallels between the days before the flood, and the coming of the Son of Man. I shall content myself with these following. First, in the days before the flood they were eating and drinking, marrying, and giving in marriage. And in these days, before the coming of the Son of Man, there is the like eating, and drinking, marrying, and giving in marriage. Second, they were so doing, until Noah entered into the ark. And these will be doing the same until the coming of the Son of Man to take them away. Third, there was a flood prepared in the days of Noah to take those away who were eating and drinking and so on. And there is a like flood of calamities, a new deluge, an overflowing scourge prepared in the days of the coming of the Son of Man, to take these away. Fourth, those of the old world knew not, until the flood came and took them all away. And these of this later world so doing, will not know (until the coming of the Son of Man) a like flood of calamities and judgments which shall take them all away. NOAH'S FLOOD RETURNING.[13]

BE READY FOR JUDGMENT. JUAN DE VALDÉS: Christ here touches upon three remarkable topics, by all of which he designs to keep us alert, daily and hourly, in expectation of his coming to judgment. The first, that his coming to judgment will be like the coming of the deluge, for that, just as in the deluge almost all perished because they were heedless as though it were not about to come, they only saving themselves, who were heedful, expecting, knowing, and believing that it was about to come. So at his coming to judgment almost all will perish, because they will be heedless, as though he were not about to come; they only saving themselves, who shall be heedful, expecting, knowing, and believing that he is about to come, while it will make people of the world [feel] secure. . . .

The second, that at Christ's coming, the good and the bad, the just and the unjust, will be mixed up together; that the good and the just will be taken up and borne away to immortality and eternal life, while the bad and the unjust will be left in affliction and misery. . . . And I call those good and just who, by their Christian life, imitating Christ, bear testimony to their Christian faith, of their incorporation into Christ.

The third, that it is the duty of every Christian to keep Christ's coming always before their eyes, daily and hourly expecting him, without ever lapsing for a moment, were it possible, into

---

[12]Trapp, *A Commentary or Exposition upon the Four Evangelists* (1647), 555*; citing 2 Pet 3:10.

[13]Gell, *Noah's Flood Returning*, 2-3*; citing Mt 8:20; 9:6; 16:20; Heb 2:14-17; Ps 8:4; Dan 7:13.

heedlessness; and how useful and profitable this continuous heedfulness is to Christians, to maintain them in Christian duty, in order to make them live in the present life as dead, leading a life very similar to that which is about to be lived in the life eternal, they know by personal experience, who, being true Christians, strive to live Christianly.

As to the comparison wherein the day of judgment is compared to the burglar . . . Christ's meaning is that just as the master of the house, being aware that a burglar is about to come to break into it, is alert to defend it, so every one of us, being aware that this day of judgment is about to come and that it will involve those in perpetual misery whom it shall find unprepared, ought to be alert and prepared to defend themselves on that day, as did Noah against the deluge. COMMENTARY UPON THE GOSPEL OF ST. MATTHEW.[14]

MANY REMINDERS FOR CONSTANT READI-NESS. EDMUND GRINDALL: [This text sets] forth before our eyes the severity of God's terrible judgment at the last day, when the Lord himself shall come, with the voice and summoning of the archangel, with the sound of the trumpet from heaven in judgment, to render to every one according to that they have done in the flesh, be it good or evil, and therewith also the suddenness of the same judgment, which shall come as a thief in the night, without giving any forewarning, as a snare that catches the bird, and as the lightning which most suddenly in one moment flashes from east to the west over all heaven. . . . The text [is] . . . the very conclusion of a sermon, made by Christ himself, sitting on Mount Olivet, upon occasion that his disciples asked him of the signs of his coming and of the end of the world. . . . Therefore be you also ready, for the Lord will come at the hour which you think not on, which sentence as most notable and worthy to be regarded, our Savior in that sermon does sundry times repeat. . . . It is the conclusion of a similitude going before, which is this: If the good man of the house had known

what hour the thief would have come, he would surely have watched and not have suffered his house to have been robbed. And therefore, be ready. As if he should say [that] the good man of a house would be diligent to save and preserve his house and worldly goods, being things corruptible, how much more ought you to be continually vigilant, lest the day of judgment which comes suddenly, as a thief in the night, find you fleeing in sin and wickedness, and so you lose a far more excellent treasure, redeemed not with gold and silver, but with the precious blood of the immaculate Lamb, Christ our Savior. A SERMON AT THE FUNERAL.[15]

FEAR OF JUDGMENT STIMULATES FAITHFUL-NESS. JOHN CALVIN: As Christ had formerly exhorted the whole family in general to watch for his coming, so now he demands extraordinary care from the principal servants, who had been appointed over others for the purpose of pointing out, by their example, the path of sobriety, watchfulness, and strict temperance. By these words he reminds them that they were not elevated to high rank for the purpose of indulging in ease, indolence, and pleasure; but that, the higher the rank of honor which they had obtained, the heavier was the burden which was laid on them; and therefore, he declares that it is especially demanded from such persons that they exercise fidelity and wisdom. . . .

By these words, Christ briefly points out the source of that carelessness which creeps upon wicked servants. It is because they trust to a longer delay, and thus of their own accord involve themselves in darkness. They imagine that the day when they must render an account will never come; and, under the pretext of Christ s absence, they promise themselves that they will remain unpunished. For it is impossible but that the expectation of him, when it does occur to our minds, shall shake off sleep, and still more, that it shall restrain us from being carried away by wicked sensuality. No excitement of exhortation,

---

[14]Valdés, *Commentary upon the Gospel of St. Matthew,* 430-31.

[15]Grindall, *A Sermon at the Funeral . . . Prince Ferdinandus* (1564), A3*.

therefore, can be more powerful or efficacious than to represent to us that rigid tribunal which no one will be able to escape. That each of us may be careful to discharge his duty earnestly and keep himself strictly and modestly within our own limits, let us constantly make our minds familiar with the thought of that last and sudden coming of the Lord, the neglect of which leads the reprobate to indulge in wickedness. COMMENTARY ON A HARMONY OF THE EVANGELISTS.[16]

---

[16]CTS 3:165-66 (CO 45:679-80).

25:1-46 ON BEING READY
FOR THE COMING JUDGMENT

"Then the kingdom of heaven will be like ten virgins who took their lamps[a] and went to meet the bridegroom.[b] [2]Five of them were foolish, and five were wise. [3]For when the foolish took their lamps, they took no oil with them, [4]but the wise took flasks of oil with their lamps. [5]As the bridegroom was delayed, they all became drowsy and slept. [6]But at midnight there was a cry, 'Here is the bridegroom! Come out to meet him.' [7]Then all those virgins rose and trimmed their lamps. [8]And the foolish said to the wise, 'Give us some of your oil, for our lamps are going out.' [9]But the wise answered, saying, 'Since there will not be enough for us and for you, go rather to the dealers and buy for yourselves.' [10]And while they were going to buy, the bridegroom came, and those who were ready went in with him to the marriage feast, and the door was shut. [11]Afterward the other virgins came also, saying, 'Lord, lord, open to us.' [12]But he answered, 'Truly, I say to you, I do not know you.' [13]Watch therefore, for you know neither the day nor the hour.

[14]"For it will be like a man going on a journey, who called his servants[c] and entrusted to them his property. [15]To one he gave five talents,[d] to another two, to another one, to each according to his ability. Then he went away. [16]He who had received the five talents went at once and traded with them, and he made five talents more. [17]So also he who had the two talents made two talents more. [18]But he who had received the one talent went and dug in the ground and hid his master's money. [19]Now after a long time the master of those servants came and settled accounts with them. [20]And he who had received the five talents came forward, bringing five talents more, saying, 'Master, you delivered to me five talents; here, I have made five talents more.' [21]His master said to him, 'Well done, good and faithful servant.[e] You have been faithful over a little; I will set you over much. Enter into the joy of your master.' [22]And he also who had the two talents came forward, saying, 'Master, you delivered to me two talents; here, I have made two

talents more.' [23]His master said to him, 'Well done, good and faithful servant. You have been faithful over a little; I will set you over much. Enter into the joy of your master.' [24]He also who had received the one talent came forward, saying, 'Master, I knew you to be a hard man, reaping where you did not sow, and gathering where you scattered no seed, [25]so I was afraid, and I went and hid your talent in the ground. Here, you have what is yours.' [26]But his master answered him, 'You wicked and slothful servant! You knew that I reap where I have not sown and gather where I scattered no seed? [27]Then you ought to have invested my money with the bankers, and at my coming I should have received what was my own with interest. [28]So take the talent from him and give it to him who has the ten talents. [29]For to everyone who has will more be given, and he will have an abundance. But from the one who has not, even what he has will be taken away. [30]And cast the worthless servant into the outer darkness. In that place there will be weeping and gnashing of teeth.'

[31]"When the Son of Man comes in his glory, and all the angels with him, then he will sit on his glorious throne. [32]Before him will be gathered all the nations, and he will separate people one from another as a shepherd separates the sheep from the goats. [33]And he will place the sheep on his right, but the goats on the left. [34]Then the King will say to those on his right, 'Come, you who are blessed by my Father, inherit the kingdom prepared for you from the foundation of the world. [35]For I was hungry and you gave me food, I was thirsty and you gave me drink, I was a stranger and you welcomed me, [36]I was naked and you clothed me, I was sick and you visited me, I was in prison and you came to me.' [37]Then the righteous will answer him, saying, 'Lord, when did we see you hungry and feed you, or thirsty and give you drink? [38]And when did we see you a stranger and welcome you, or naked and clothe you? [39]And when did we see you sick or in prison and visit you?' [40]And the King will answer

them, 'Truly, I say to you, as you did it to one of the least of these my brothers,ᶠ you did it to me.'

⁴¹"Then he will say to those on his left, 'Depart from me, you cursed, into the eternal fire prepared for the devil and his angels. ⁴²For I was hungry and you gave me no food, I was thirsty and you gave me no drink, ⁴³I was a stranger and you did not welcome me, naked and you did not clothe me, sick and in prison

and you did not visit me.' ⁴⁴Then they also will answer, saying, 'Lord, when did we see you hungry or thirsty or a stranger or naked or sick or in prison, and did not minister to you?' ⁴⁵Then he will answer them, saying, 'Truly, I say to you, as you did not do it to one of the least of these, you did not do it to me.' ⁴⁶And these will go away into eternal punishment, but the righteous into eternal life."

a Or torches b Some manuscripts add *and the bride* c Or *bondservants*; also verse 19 d A *talent* was a monetary unit worth about twenty years' wages for a laborer e Or *bondservant*; also verses 23, 26, 30 f Or *brothers and sisters*

OVERVIEW: To punctuate his themes of the need for readiness for his coming and the judgment to follow, Jesus provides two related parables. In the Reformation commentaries, the details of the ten virgins receive varied levels of attention. Where some reformers see implications with each detail of the story, others focus on a primary point: Christian vigilance until Christ returns. Martin Bucer discourages a complex investigation of the elements of the parable because the thrust of the parable is perceived easily. Other reformers see needed faith as being represented by either the readiness of the wise virgins or their oil specifically.

In the second parable, Jesus provides further insight into the type of behavior that results from genuine readiness. All three of the servants entrusted with talents in the parable expect the master to return and to have to give account for the master's gifts. However, the commentators note that the ways in which they act in anticipation of the master's return show the true nature of their readiness.

The humble Son of Man, who has been a main feature of Matthew's narratives, provides a spectacular contrast with the royal figure who now pronounces judgment over all the nations. Moreover, even in this regal setting, the Son of Man associates himself with his humble past by referring to those who were hungry, thirsty, outcast, sick, and in prison. Drawing again on Daniel, Jesus concludes by delineating that his judgment is final in that the outcome is eternal punishment or eternal life. The

Reformation commentators explain that the judgment scene at the end of the sermon prompts fear that can lead to faith in the Son of Man.

25:1-13 *Parable of the Ten Virgins*

VAIN PROFESSIONS. WILLIAM BRIDGE: Sometimes the doctrine and grace of the gospel is called the kingdom of heaven: The kingdom of heaven is like to a grain of mustard seed. . . . This cannot be meant here, because in the gospel there are not ten virgins. Sometimes the state of glory above is called the kingdom of heaven; that is not meant here, because there are no foolish virgins. Sometimes the church of Christ under the new covenant is called the kingdom of heaven, for there God appears, manifests himself, and it is heaven on earth; and this is that which is here called the kingdom of heaven. This kingdom is described by the governor, king, and head thereof and by the subjects of that kingdom. The subjects are described by their agreement and disagreement. First, they agree in this, that they are all virgins; though some foolish, yet virgins, not defiled with men nor the pollutions of the world. It is possible a foolish and unfound heart may go thus far in religion, to be free from the pollutions of the world, yea, through the knowledge of Christ, says the apostle Peter. Second, they agree in this, that they have all their lamps, good and bad, wise and foolish under ordinances, which are the lamps, whereby the golden oil of the sanctuary is emptied into our hearts. Third, they agree in this, that they are all expectants, wise and foolish await the bridegroom's coming. They all think to receive good and have a good day by the coming of Jesus Christ; this is far, yet thus far may a foolish virgin go. Fourth, they all agree in this that they had oil in their lamps, so that oil they had once, but they had not enough, and so none; parts and gifts, and common graces a man may have, not only his lamp, but some oil in it for a time, yet be a foolish virgin. Fifth, they agree in this, that they keep company, have communion, and fellowship together in the church; yea, so far that the foolish are not known until Christ's coming. So smoothly may a foolish virgin carry it yet remain foolish. Sixth, they all agree in this also; that they hold out their profession, with lamps, and waiting till the bridegroom comes. So that possibly, a person may be a professor of the gospel, and bear up their profession among the best, even to the last, yet be unfound at heart, and a foolish virgin. Thus far they agree. But second, though these virgins agree in many things, yet they disagree in the point of wisdom; for the wise got so much oil as did last until the end; the foolish not so. CHRIST'S COMING OPENED IN A SERMON.[1]

FAITH AND WORKS. JUAN DE MALDONADO: It would rather appear that this number was chosen to show a great number of persons, and that universality was meant. . . . Thus, the kingdom of heaven is said to be like ten, that is, for many. By ten virgins, St. Chrysostom, Theophylact, Euthymius, St. Augustine, St. Gregory,[†] as cited above, think that all who were truly virgins are meant, but this is too forced a sense. . . . Origen and St. Jerome,[‡] and, as appears, St. Ambrose, neither of all people, nor of virgins alone, but of all the faithful, and of these alone. Their opinion seems good—first, because it is plain that Christ speaks only of those who had received lamps, which only the faithful have: for the lamp is faith; second, because Christ teaches that faith without good works does not satisfy for salvation.

Another part of the question is the meaning of the five wise and the five foolish. St. Hilary[§] says that the five wise include all the faithful, and the five foolish all the contrary. . . . Origen and St. Jerome[◊] . . . say that the wise virgins are all people who have good works with faith, and that the foolish are such as have faith indeed, but not works. This seems not merely the best, but the only good explanation, because the great subject of the parable is that faith without works is of no avail for salvation. Again, because the same is taught both by previous parables and subsequent ones, that it is not enough to believe unless we also watch to good works, because we know not at what hour the Lord will come. The same is again inculcated in another parable, in which, as here are the virgins, so there is the guest who entered in at the wedding feast by faith, but who, because he had no wedding garment, that is, works, was cast out. A COMMENTARY ON MATTHEW'S GOSPEL.[2]

THE WISDOM OF FAITH. JOHANNES BUGENHAGEN: Concerning the virgins who took their lamps and went out to meet the bridegroom, that is, Christ, we say that these must either be Christians or they must then have been considered to be Christians. From among them some go in with the bridegroom to the wedding. Some who were locked out must hear: "I do not know you." Now, since they are called virgins but are locked out and it does them no good that they are virgins, it follows surely that the others who were allowed to enter the wedding were not allowed to enter on account of their virginity. I am speaking here of virginity in the flesh with which our opponents also deal, and they are also accustomed to read this text of the Gospel concerning the virgins in the

---

[1]Bridge, *Christ's Coming Opened in a Sermon* (1648), 1-2*.

[2]JMG 2:297-99; citing Gen 31:7, 41; Lev 26:26; Num 14:22; Ps 119:105; Mt 24:45; 24:14; 22:12. [†]Chrysostom, *Homilies on Matthew*, NPNF[1] 10:383. Theophylact, *Commentary on Matthew*, 42v. Euthymius Zigabenus, *Expositio in Matthaeum*, PG 129:629-30. Augustine, *Sermons on Selected Lessons*, NPNF[1] 6:401-2. Gregory the Great, *Homiliae in in Evangelia*, PL 76:1118-23. [‡]Jerome, *Commentary on Matthew*, FC 117:281-82. [§]Hilary of Poitiers, *Commentary on Matthew*, FC 125:260-62. [◊]Jerome, *Commentary on Matthew*, FC 117:282.

churches, although the parable has something more worthy in it. Why, then, are some virgins accepted? Because they were wise. Why, then, are the others rejected? Because they were foolish.

Thus, you see that virginity is not accepted so that it might fill paradise but wisdom is. In the same way, virginity is also not rejected but foolishness is. Absolutely no attention is paid here to virginity. However, faith in Christ the bridegroom is cleverness and wisdom. . . . However, foolishness and ignorance are unbelief which, though it also desires to be viewed as Christian among our virgins, can nevertheless not be viewed in such a way, for it does not steer itself with trust to the bridegroom Christ but to its virginity. It trusts only in its works and godliness, not in the bridegroom or the bridegroom's goods. Faith sends oil into their vessels inwardly. However, unbelief is satisfied when the lamps are adorned, that is, that it only appears to be pretty and glistens outwardly for the sake of hypocrisy. Therefore, faith is also accepted, and unbelief is rejected. CONCERNING THE MARRIAGE OF BISHOPS AND DEACONS.[3]

BE READY ALWAYS. GIOVANNI DIODATI: "The kingdom," namely, the state of the church, wherein God reigns in the person of the Messiah. Marlorat has it thus: This similitude shows us that it is not sufficient for us to be once prepared and disposed to follow Jesus Christ, except we also persevere in it. "Ten virgins," a similitude taken from the fashion used at weddings, at which anciently the maidens, who were the bride's kinswomen and acquaintances, went forth with lamps and lights in great troops to meet the bridegroom, when he came to the bride's house, to have her away to his own house, which was commonly done in the nighttime. Now the bridegroom is Christ, the time of the wedding is at his last coming; the night is the church's estate in the world. The virgins are they that make profession of the purity of the gospel. The wise virgins are the true believers that are provided in their hearts with instructions in

faith and piety, and with the gift of the Spirit, which is the oil that burns, howsoever not always in actual exercise. The foolish ones are they in the church who have neglected to gain or preserve the foresaid gift of the Spirit. The lamps are the hearts; the slumber is the slackening or ceasing from continual exercises of piety and expecting of Christ, caused by the infirmity of the flesh through his long staying. "Give us," many shall seek after that which they have despised, but then it will be too late. PIOUS ANNOTATIONS.[4]

THE READINESS OF FAITH. HUGH LATIMER: Take heed and be not proud, and be humble and low, and trust not too much in yourselves; but put your only trust in Christ our Savior. And yet you may not utterly set aside the doing of good works, but especially look that you have always oil in readiness for your lamps, or else you may not come to the wedding, but shall be shut out, and thrust into everlasting darkness. This oil is faith in Christ, which if you lack, then all things are unsavory before the face of God; but a great many people are much deceived, for they think themselves to have faith when indeed they have it not. Some peradventure will say, How shall I know whether I have faith or not? Truly you shall find this in you, if you have no mind to leave sin; then sin grieves you not, but you are content to go forward in the same, and you delight in it, and hate it not, neither do you feel what sin is; when you are in such a case, then you have no faith, and therefore are likely to perish everlastingly. For that person who is sore sick, and yet feels not their sickness, they are in great danger, for they have lost all their senses; so those persons who have gone so far in sin, that they feel their sin no more, are like to be damned, for they are without faith. THE PARABLE OF THE TARES.[5]

DAILY READINESS. JOHN CALVIN: Some interpret this slumbering in a bad sense, as if believers, along with others, abandoned themselves

---

[3]JBSW 2:868-69.
[4]Diodati, *Pious Annotations* (1643), F3r.
[5]Latimer, *Select Sermons and Letters*, 362*.

to sloth, and were asleep amid the vanities of the world; but this is altogether inconsistent with the intention of Christ, and with the structure of the parable. There would be greater probability in explaining it to denote death, which overtakes believers before the coming of Christ. . . . But I take it more simply as denoting earthly occupations, in which believers must be engaged so long as they dwell in the body; and, though forgetfulness of the kingdom of God ought never to steal upon them, yet the distracting influence of the occupations of this world is not inappropriately compared to sleep. For they cannot be so constantly occupied with the thought of meeting Christ as not to be distracted, or retarded, or entangled by a variety of cares, in consequence of which, while they watch, they are partly asleep.

With respect to the cry, I view it as taken metaphorically for his sudden arrival . . . indeed, our Lord cries daily, that he will come quickly, but at that time, the whole frame of the world will resound with the cry, and his dreadful majesty will fill heaven and earth in such a manner, as not only to awaken those who are asleep, but to bring the dead out of their graves.

This is a reproof of the late repentance of those who never think of what they are in want of until the door is shut against every remedy. For those who do not make provision for a long period are charged with folly, because they are careless, and flatter themselves amid their poverty, and allow the season of mutual intercourse to pass in such a way as to despise the aids which were offered to them. As they do not, in proper time, bethink themselves about procuring oil, Christ, mocking the knowledge which they have acquired when it is too late, shows how their stupidity will be punished when they shall see themselves to be empty and unprovisioned, while there is no remedy. . . . Christ here points out the time when he shall summon all people to his tribunal, each carrying their bundle, that they may bring with them according as they have done in their body. That portion of grace received, which every person has laid up for himself, is, therefore, justly compared to a stock of

provisions for a journey, which would not be enough for a greater number of persons. COMMENTARY ON A HARMONY OF THE EVANGELISTS.[6]

ENCOURAGING FAITH. PHILIPP MELANCHTHON: The metaphor about the virgins is an image of the church in whatever time but especially for the last time, and it binds together teaching, reproof, and consolation. The teaching is this, in the church in this life, there are, have been, and always will be good and evil, prudent and foolish virgins. And those virgins who in kind and title are similar to those truly named virgins are also called hypocrites. And this teaching gives opportunity to remember that we should not think that, on account of the multitude of evils in the church, every kind of despicable human is from God, and the church is ruined, just as saints are often damaged by this grief, looking around at such a great multitude of evil and feeling badly everywhere. . . .

Regarding reproof, and now he said there would be many foolish virgins. What separates prudent virgins from foolish? Both are called virgins. The title is the same, the outward appearance of both the hypocrites and those rightly named is the same. Who are the prudent virgins? We endeavor to define them briefly and clearly. The prudent virgins are those who hold fast a foundation and call upon God in true repentance and true faith. But the foundation means necessary teaching in all articles of the faith, among which also it is necessary to embrace true knowledge of justifying faith. . . .

Regarding consolation, it is consolation because he calls it a covenant. And in the same way it is declared to be a great and glowing thing to be prized, that holds fast the church, yes him, as a covenant never willing to forsake us. There is also this great consolation, because he says that there will always be some true church and prudent virgins who long for him with true faith and hope.

We considered all these things in these few words, about which much more may be said, but

---

[6]CTS 3:171-73 (CO 45:683-84); Rev 22:20; Jn 5:28.

no one is able to exhaust the wisdom of God thoroughly. May we attend to, as we observe repentance, and may we advance, as we have been prepared. May we have oil in our vases . . . that is, in our hearts. ANNOTATIONS ON THE GOSPELS.[7]

VIGILANCE AND FAITH. MARTIN BUCER: There is no one among the pious who is unaware how feebly we keep watch in the work of the Lord and how negligently we await him. For the flesh distracts us constantly to the cares and pleasures of life, and causes us to sleep, and it is for that reason that the Lord in so many ways exhorts us to vigilance. Clearly these two parables, which Matthew relates in this chapter, pertain to the same thing. Therefore, putting aside the nonsense of allegorizing and considering that which the Lord wanted to teach by this first parable, let us take from it what he himself plainly said we should take from this parable, namely, that we should be vigilant at all times, since we do not know in what hour the Son of Man is coming.

This is clearly the only thing he wanted to teach here. Therefore, all the discussion about virginity, the lamps, the oil, those selling the oil, have nothing to do with the meaning of this parable. This one thing is relevant, that the virgins who had prepared themselves entered into their wedding ceremony with the groom, while the unprepared were excluded and ignored; it warns us that we should always stay vigilant and prepared, so that wherever we are, when the groom comes, we also may meet him, that is, to go to him with a willing and eager mind, instructed in the full faith. And we should be even more careful, since we are going to a wedding of eternal blessedness, from which those wretches are excluded who did not faithfully and vigilant await the Lord in love. Some make the oil out to be good works, but the poor fellows do not consider that a person is still ill-equipped to come to the tribunal of Christ even if that person does all good works, that is, does all the things that are asked of him. For, a servant like this would still be

useless, but faith relies on the merits of Christ, and from him there is nothing that cannot be promised to a person from the divine goodness, which also most fully perceives all things, because the one who trusts in God cannot be confounded. Therefore, it is only by this means that the elect are prepared for the advent of Christ, and that is the only thing that shines a light on good works. And the same renders them vigilant, since it surely transports the whole mind and soul to God, in whom alone it is persuaded that all good works are stored up for themselves. Would that we be able to perceive and hold these things rightly, and this parable be pondered enough to produce great fruit for us. COMMENTARY ON MATTHEW.[8]

25:14-30 *Parable of the Talents*

SELFLESS SERVANTS. PETER WALPOT: We may understand by the talents or pounds that each should give according to what they can or should do, whether it be in admonition and preaching, or in giving money or temporal possessions as they have received (for this is also lent by the Lord), or if you can in some other way be of service to your neighbor. Nothing is more pleasing to God than that you live your life in service of the common Christian good. Those who do this give joy to their Lord. But those who hide their money in a cloth are those who serve their neighbors neither with words nor their temporal possessions. They do not desire community because they have a piece of Belial in their hearts. They want to keep everything for themselves, which benefits nobody. Such selfish and deceptive servants will be thrown to ruination. TRUE YIELDEDNESS AND THE CHRISTIAN COMMUNITY OF GOODS.[9]

WASTING TALENTS. JOHN MAYER: For the servant receiving five talents and the servant receiving two talents, I think with Bede,[†] that two

---

[7]MO 14:990-94.

[8]Bucer, *In Sacra Quatuor Evangelia, Enarrationes Perpetuae* (1536), 471-72.

[9]Liechty, ed., *Early Anabaptist Spirituality*, 154-55.

orders are hereby set forth, the first, of doctors, the second, of common professors. The doctor has five talents, faith, love, the knowledge of tongues, the gift of prophecy, and of working miracles; the professor has two talents, faith, and love, all which are comprehended in one by Luke, because they flow from one and the same spirit. Both orders are said to double their talents, because they study to improve their diverse gifts to the good of others, according to their power, so that glory redounds to God from every good gift in them, and grace to their neighbor. These are said to be but two, because there be but a few such, according to Ambrose. The evil servant with one talent, according to the common consent, is that sort of Christian, whether doctors or common people, who through negligence, do not study to improve their gifts to God's glory, for this is enough to condemn a person, though they be no notorious wicked person. The talent taken from him and given to him with ten talents is very rightly applied by Calvin, to the greater glory of the most laborious in the work of the Lord, arising from the gross negligence of others. A Treasury of Ecclesiastical Expositions.[10]

Gifted for His Glory. David Dickson: As in the parable, the faithful servant, whether his talents were fewer or more, was accepted of his master and made partaker of his joy, so every person—who in the discharge of his calling, does seek faithfully the glory of Christ, and increase of his kingdom—shall be accepted in the day of judgment and put in full possession of eternal life. As before the master in the parable, so also before Christ in the day of judgment, no excuse shall serve to save the slothful and unfaithful servant— let people deceive themselves now as they will, and please themselves with pretenses as they will—all excuses shall be retorted and made matter of their condemnation, and the unfaithful

servant shall be cast into hell. As in the parable, he who had one talent but had it not for his master's use is counted as if he had none and is deprived of the possession of what he possessed, but not for his master's use. So, whosoever has gifts whereby others are not profited or Christ's kingdom is not promoted, what they have is counted as if they had it not; or as if they had lost it, or put it away, and as others were not profited by this gift, so neither shall they themselves be profited by it. But those who use their gifts well for the glory of Christ shall be amply rewarded, the reason whereof he gives. For, unto every person who has gifts, so as they have them for their master's use (which is in effect to have them) it shall be given, they shall have increase of gifts, and graces, and rewards. But such as have not what they have for the Lord's service, shall be deprived of all good, which they themselves might have of such gifts, and shall be utterly deprived of whatsoever good they seem to have, and they themselves also shall perish. A Brief Exposition.[11]

Admonition Against Laziness. Heinrich Bullinger: Just as he praised the industrious servants for their goodness and fidelity, so he scolded and found fault with the lazy and bad servant, calling him evil and slothful. He is evil, because he tries to trick his master, and he rejects the spirit of God and does what the devil prods him to do. He is slothful because he was not willing to increase the talent. Therefore, slothfulness and laziness are characteristic of the impious and hypocrites, for which they use the pretext of election and some other things. To these a punishment is added. For the master says to those standing around him, "Take the talent away from him and give it to him who has ten talents." And it is a punishment far graver to be stripped of the gifts of God and for one's heart to be left empty of God and all piety. And that judgment of God is extended straightaway to all people lazily doing the works of God, according to God's most just

---

[10]Mayer, *A Treasury of Ecclesiastical Expositions . . . upon the Scriptures* (1622), 294-95*. †Bede, *Expositio in Evangelium S Matthaei*, PL 92:108-9.

[11]Dickson, *Brief Exposition* (1651), 294-95.

judgment. For, "to all who have . . ." as if he were saying, "Not only will the talent be taken away from this servant, but from all the idle and sluggish, whatever good thing God has given them, it will be taken away if they do not increase it but lessen it instead." . . . "What does this indicate?" Chrysostom[†] says, that "those who receive the gift of teaching for the benefit of others but do not use it will lose that gift as well. But those who use these gifts zealously and industriously will thus receive a greater gift, just as the servants did for their success." More can be learned by comparing chapter 13. Therefore, let us rouse ourselves to keep vigilant about these things, and let our industriousness be stirred up lest we receive the gift of God in vain, or lest with an empty pretext of words we find an excuse for our laziness. But the punishment for the lazy slave did not stop here, but unbearable torture and a terrible sentence is added. For, the judge says, "Cast out the useless servant into the outer darkness. . . ." To this end the master, by punishment and reward, has incited all people to vigilance, and especially ministers of the Word. COMMENTARY ON MATTHEW.[12]

25:31-46 The Judgment of All Nations

SUFFERING UNTIL THE SEPARATION. WILLIAM PERKINS: When all the kindred of the earth and all unclean spirits shall stand before Christ, sitting in the throne of his glory, then as a good shepherd he shall separate them one from another, the righteous from the wicked and the elect from the reprobate. He, who knows the hearts of all people knows also how to do this and he will do it. This full and final separation is reserved to Christ and shall not be accomplished until the last day. For so it is in the parable, that the tares must grow with the wheat until harvest, and the reapers must separate them and gather the wheat into the barn, but the tares must be burned with unquenchable fire.

Second, whereas this separation must not be before the end of the world, hence we learn the estate of God's church in this life. It is like a flock of sheep mingled with goats, and therefore the condition of God's people in this world is to be troubled many ways by those with whom they live. For goats will strike at the sheep, will disturb their pasture, and will make their water muddy, so much that they cannot drink of it. And therefore we must prepare ourselves to bear all annoyances, crosses, and calamities that shall befall us in this world by the wicked ones, among whom we live.

Third, we are taught that goats and the sheep be very like and feed in one pasture and lie both in one fold all their lifetime. Yet Christ can and will sever them asunder at the last day. Therefore, considering as we are born of Adam, we have the nature of the goat, even of the wild beast, and not of the sheep; it stands us in hand to lay aside our goatish conditions, and to take unto us the properties of the sheep of Christ, which he expresses in these words, "My sheep hear my voice, I know them, and they follow me." And the properties are three: to know him, to be known of him, and to follow him, namely, in obedience. And he that finds them all in himself wears the brand and mark of the true sheep of Christ. But contrariwise, they that make profession of Christ, and yet therewithal join not obedience, howsoever the world may account of them, they are but goats and no sheep. Let us therefore with the knowledge of Christ join obedience to his word, that when the day shall come that the goats must be separated from the sheep, we may be found to be in the number of the true sheep of Christ. We may deceive men both in life and death, and bear them in hand that we are sheep, but when the judgment shall come, we cannot deceive Christ. It is he that formed us, he knows our hearts, and therefore can easily discern what we are. AN EXPOSITION OF THE APOSTLE'S CREED.[13]

---

[12]Bullinger, In . . . Evangelium secundum Matthaeum commentariorum, 10:221r. [†]Chrysostom, Homilies on Matthew, NPNF[1] 10:454.

[13]Perkins, An Exposition of the Symbole or Creede of the Apostles (1616), 263*; citing Ezek 34:18; Jn 10:27.

Hypocrisy Exposed. Giovanni Diodati: "All nations." At the general judgment which he will hold of all the world, that which he will make of his own house (which is his church) shall be chiefly remarkable. As under the same shepherd and the same sheepfold, there are foul and stinking goats, and pure, simple, and sweet sheep; so there shall be hypocrites, destitute of the Spirit of sanctification, and true believers, regenerated to the image of Christ, who is the true Lamb without blemish. And indeed, that which is next spoken of the works of the true spiritual charity, neglected, or shown toward Christ's spiritual members, cannot properly belong to those who have been without the communion of the church. And in this judgment of God's church, the default of good works is the ground of the condemnation of hypocrites, because that thereby is shown the falsity of their faith and profession. And contrariwise the practice of them is the true proof of a lively faith, and the accomplishment of the duties of the evangelical covenant, on the believers' behalf; and the beginning of the spiritual life, which shall never be perfected in heaven, unless it be begun in this world. See concerning this judgment, Psalm 50:4, Ezekiel 34:17, Hebrews 10:30, and James 2:24. And as the life everlasting is altogether holiness and charity, so Christ represents the disposition which is necessary unto it, by the pureness of the sheep, and by spiritual charity practiced toward his as toward himself. Pious Annotations.[14]

Judging Faith by Works. Heinrich Bullinger: We must think that the kingdom of heaven and the other special gifts of God are not as the hire that is due to servants but as the inheritance of the children of God. For although in the last day of judgment the judge shall reckon up many works, for which he shall seem as it were to recompense the elect with eternal life; yet, before that recital of good works, he shall say "Come, you blessed of my Father, possess the kingdom prepared for you since the beginning of the world." Now if you demand, why he shall in the day of judgment make mention rather of works than of faith; my answer is that it is a point or usual custom in the law for judgment not only to be just, but also by the judge's pronunciation to have the cause made manifest to all people wherefore it is just. And God does deal with us after the order of humankind. Wherefore he does not only give just judgment but will also be known of all people to be a just and upright judge. But we are not able to look into the faith of other people, which does consist in the mind; and therefore, we judge by their words and deeds. Honest words and works bear witness of a faithful heart, whereas dishonest pranks and speeches do betray a kind of unbelief. The works of charity and humanity declare that we have faith in our deeds: whereas the lack of them argues the contrary. And therefore the Scripture admonishes us that the judgment shall be according to our works. Of Christian Liberty, Works and Merits.[15]

Faith Creates Works for Christ's Sake. Martin Luther: The second reason why Christ especially mentions these works of mercy and their omission from the fifth commandment is that he wishes to remind us, who have been called to be Christians, have received mercy through our Lord, have been redeemed from the wrath of God and the guilt of the fifth commandment and from eternal death, and on the contrary have a gracious God, who is good to us in time and in eternity, to remind us, I say, to look upon all this and regard it as having been done not only for our salvation but also for an example. For, since he has shown us such mercy as to save us, we are also to act toward our neighbor in a manner as not to transgress against the fifth commandment, which especially demands love and mercy.

And we are not to do these things simply because of the commandment and of the threat

---

[14]Diodati, *Pious Annotations* (1643), F3r*.

[15]DHB 2:346*.

of judgment, but for the sake of the example of the excellent and great goodness God has shown. For this example cannot be without blessed results, as God's work of redemption is not without power and good fruit. Although most people become worse from having heard the gospel, there must nevertheless be some who rightly understand it and remain faithful to it; for he says that he will separate them into two flocks; therefore, there must also be pious ones who have kept this commandment.

Therefore, see to it that you are among those who are kind and merciful here upon earth for Christ's sake, or who even suffer for his sake. Then you may joyfully await the last day, and need not be afraid of the judgment, for he has already selected you and placed you among those who shall stand at his right hand. . . . Notice, however, as I said, that he wishes to distinguish the good works of the Christians from the works of the Turks and the heathen. For he speaks of the works done unto him, of which both parties claim to be ignorant, the wicked excusing themselves because they had not seen him. . . . But herewith he has most beautifully explained the fifth commandment, that it means, he who fulfills it can be nothing else than a believing Christian, who did it unto Christ. TWENTY-SIXTH SUNDAY AFTER TRINITY.[16]

FEAR, THEN FAITH. DAVID JORIS: That is the will of the one who has perfected, created, and prepared all things well to his glory. So that everyone will carry out their work, service, and office reasonably and truly with trembling, obedience, and willingness, in order to become united with or like his only Son Jesus Christ, the living Word and the wisdom of the Father. He will eternally abide and dominate over, fulfill, and complete all things. The Father's pleasure is for us to be a mirror, student, judge, and as the white of a target. Weep, all who do not regulate or conduct their life after this, when what is to come arrives. O, then they will weep bitterly! For although it is a

word of mercy, of salvation and grace, it is also a word of righteousness and of severe judgment, each one adding according to what each has worked or said. . . . Pay attention. ON THE WONDERFUL WORKING OF GOD.[17]

SHEEP ENTER THROUGH THE RIGHT DOOR. ARGULA VON GRUMBACH:

> My Lord and God I love more dear
> Than saving my life in craven fear.
> At the judgment I'll not be scorned
> Not yet be placed at his left hand,
> Where goats and kids must take a stand.
> The right door I will surely see,
> For Christ says: "Those who believe in me
> From judgment will be fully free
> And pass from death to life with me."

"JOHANNES OF LANZHUT": ATTACK AND RESPONSE.[18]

ETERNAL PUNISHMENT AND YET A GOOD GOD. WOLFGANG MUSCULUS: Those who measure all things in rational terms, who do not consider anything reliable that cannot be comprehended by human reason, dispute how it can be that a body burn forever and not be consumed, since the very nature of bodies is not able to endure it. Second, they dispute how fire can burn up, not only bodies but also evil spirits, which are not corporeal in any way. Good people think that it is unnatural that it takes place within God's will, and they do not consider the nature of creation is that it is and has what it is and has, not from itself, but from the will of God. And they do not consider how it is possible that it not be obedient to the will and command of God, since he is the Creator. Others make their argument from the quality of fire, such that we are not talking about a corporeal fire, but a metaphorical one, and that it stands for the enormous pain and repentance of souls.

---

[16]Luther, *Precious and Sacred Writings*, 14:389, 391-92*.

[17]CRR 7:116.

[18]Grumbach, *Argula von Grumbach*, 193 (AvG 149); citing Mt 25:32; Lk 17:33.

Augustine[†] relates that there were those who tried to undermine the idea that punishment lasts forever, and he calls them the "compassionate ones," from the fact that they applied the argument of compassion to it, as if the compassion of God could not bear that any mortals and (according to some) demons be condemned and perish forever.

Some of those [thought] that it would come about through the intercession of the saints . . . and thus they thought that no one would be condemned, even if they had to suffer some punishment in proportion to their sins, but that would be temporary, and afterward even the impious themselves will be saved.

Against their errors this one single sentence of Christ pushes back: "Go, cursed ones, into the eternal fire, which has been prepared for the devil and his angels"; and, "They will go into eternal punishment," where it is foretold that there will be an eternal punishment in the form of an eternal fire, not just for the devil and his angels, but for all those who in truth do not belong to Christ, even if they were imbued with his sacrament. Nor can they escape by interpreting "eternity" to mean "a long time." For, by that logic, not only would the fire come to an end, but also eternal life, about which here it is added, "And the righteous will go into eternal life." Therefore, they are deservedly condemned who, possessed of an evil conscience and seeking some solace for their perverse life, contrives those things against so plain a statement of Christ.

They will go," he says, "into punishment." After the judge gives his sentence, there is not chance for appeal to a tribunal, nor can anyone intervene, but soon after follows the execution of the judgment. And even if they will not go of their own accord to their punishment, they will be sent, nonetheless, into this fire by the angels and the heavenly powers. We saw this above in the thirteenth chapter, in the parable of the tares. Commentary on Matthew.[19]

The Last Word. Richard Ward: The four last things are death, judgment, hell, and heaven, and they are thus differenced. Nothing is more horrible than death, nothing more terrible than judgment, nothing more intolerable than hell, nothing more delectable than heaven. And therefore blessed are they who by death are brought unto heaven, but wretched and infinitely miserable are all they who by judgment are sent unto hell. . . .

First, depart, get you gone, flee hence, out of my sight, and from the society of the elect, forever. Second, you cursed, which loved not blessing; and therefore are now justly excluded out of heaven and deprived of all felicity and happiness. Third, into the fire; not into the scorching flame, or parching heat, but into the burning fire. Fourth, into everlasting fire; not into a fire that will either burn and quite consume them, or, which will be consumed itself at the last; which will either cause them to die, or die and extinguish itself; but into everlasting fire, which shall never go out, but torment them world without end. Fifth, with the devil and his angels; as they said unto the Almighty, depart from us, we desire not the knowledge of you or your law, and wished that the righteous might be taken out of their sight; so they shall be excluded and driven out of the presence of God, and deprived of the society of saints and angels, their companions thenceforward being only devils, wicked angels, and damned spirits. . . .

How do the wicked enter into hell and the godly into heaven? By the powerful and commanding voice of Christ, which is of such force that neither the greatest rebel that ever was among humankind, nor all the devils in hell shall be able to withstand it. How can these words, "The wicked shall go into everlasting punishment," stand, or accord with those of the prophet, "The Lord is merciful, and will not be angry forever"? The prophet speaks of God's anger in regard of those who repented; for with such God will not be angry forever. He chastens indeed the faithful when they sin, but it is but

---

[19]Musculus, *In Evangelistam Matthaeum Commentarii* (1556), 598-99. [†]Augustine, *City of God*, NPNF[1] 2:452-78.

with temporal punishments (as is evident from Is 7 and Jer 18 and Ezek 18) and when they repent and turn unto him, then he repents of his punishments and corrections, and turns to them in love. Now Christ speaks here of perverse and obstinate sinners, who will not (by the longsuffering of God) be led unto repentance and unto whom God will be a swift and severe judge. THEOLOGICAL QUESTIONS.[20]

---

[20]Ward, *Theological Questions upon . . . St. Matthew* (1640), 335-36; citing Jer 3:12.

26:1-16 JESUS ANOINTED BEFORE HIS COMING SUFFERING

When Jesus had finished all these sayings, he said to his disciples, ²"You know that after two days the Passover is coming, and the Son of Man will be delivered up to be crucified."

³Then the chief priests and the elders of the people gathered in the palace of the high priest, whose name was Caiaphas, ⁴and plotted together in order to arrest Jesus by stealth and kill him. ⁵But they said, "Not during the feast, lest there be an uproar among the people."

⁶Now when Jesus was at Bethany in the house of Simon the leper,ᵃ ⁷a woman came up to him with an alabaster flask of very expensive ointment, and she poured it on his head as he reclined at table. ⁸And when the disciples saw it, they were indignant, saying, "Why this waste? ⁹For this could have been sold for a large sum and given to the poor." ¹⁰But Jesus, aware of this, said to them, "Why do you trouble the woman? For she has done a beautiful thing to me. ¹¹For you always have the poor with you, but you will not always have me. ¹²In pouring this ointment on my body, she has done it to prepare me for burial. ¹³Truly, I say to you, wherever this gospel is proclaimed in the whole world, what she has done will also be told in memory of her."

¹⁴Then one of the twelve, whose name was Judas Iscariot, went to the chief priests ¹⁵and said, "What will you give me if I deliver him over to you?" And they paid him thirty pieces of silver. ¹⁶And from that moment he sought an opportunity to betray him.

a *Leprosy* was a term for several skin diseases; see Leviticus 13

OVERVIEW: The reformers note that Matthew not only relates the passion events but also gives some deeper, theological motivations behind the events portrayed in the text. Jesus announces the timing of his suffering and crucifixion to his disciples, giving a clear indication of his readiness for what will happen (cf. Mt 16:21; 17:12, 22-23; 20:18-19). Meanwhile, the religious leaders are fearful and perplexed, and they declare their intentions to postpone their sinister plans. It is also apparent that while the leaders plan on disposing of Jesus in secret, Jesus describes his death as a public event.

Matthew's account of Jesus' anointing at Bethany contains some details that vary from other Gospel accounts. The reformers often harmonize some elements with other Gospels—including the identity of the woman, who is unnamed by Matthew, but identified by John as Mary, the sister of Martha and Lazarus (Jn 11:2; 12:3)—but they also note the variance as providing some indication of the author's unique intention in relaying the account.

The general resistance of the disciples to the woman's action follows in line with other opposition the disciples provide in their ignorance or reluctance toward Jesus' ultimate purposes. By comparison, the reformers point to the woman as a model of a faithful person who chooses the appropriate good deeds based on kingdom purposes.

The faithful woman sacrificing a valuable perfume to prepare Jesus' body for burial provides the backdrop for the shocking willingness of Judas to deliver Jesus to the chief priests for just thirty pieces of silver. Whether Judas's original motive was political or financial is not indicated in the text, but the reformers indict Judas of unbelief that has now led him to be susceptible to a payment for a betrayal.

26:1-5 The Plot to Kill Jesus

THE CLIMAX OF CHRIST'S LIFE. HEINRICH BULLINGER: After all these things there is placed, as the finishing and the most perfect accomplishing of all our salvation, the most holy and most profitable history of the passion and redemption of Christ the Lord; wherein he fully executes all the offices as well of a priest, as of a king, and in a brief sum does propose his greatest force to be beholden of all people. For he teaches diligently both by all his words and by all his deeds, he institutes his famous sacrament, he prays most fervently, he sacrifices for sin, he purges sinners, he delivers, he pities, he defends his servants, and he treads down and punishes the wicked, showing everywhere incredible humility, and declaring sometime no small glory, when as all the elements, being troubled at his death, showed most plain tokens as it were of their great sorrow. Matthew handles all these things in a goodly order and in a pure, plain, and lively style. For first he shows the time wherein he suffered, and proposes the sum of his passion. Then he describes some causes of the Lord's death, proceeding partly from the envy and malice of the priests against Christ, and partly from the covetousness and horrible treason of Judas, who sold his Lord to the senate of bishops. THE SUM OF THE FOUR EVANGELISTS.[1]

BLINDING HATRED. DESIDERIUS ERASMUS: For these chiefly conspired against Jesus because they feared lest (if he should be preserved) they should lose their lucre and authority. Therefore it was decreed there through wicked counsel that they should lay hands upon Jesus and kill him, not openly and violently, but by discrete and guile. Therefore when these great men agreed among themselves ungraciously of the murder, they consulted of the time. For although they thirsted deeply for the innocent blood, being mad with envy and hatred, yet they thought best to defer the death to another time, because the most holy Jewish feast was at hand. For they feared if they should set upon him on that day that the people might come together, lest any tumult or business should rise, because there were many among the people, which seeing his miracles, and hearing his

marvelous doctrine, and marking the great soberness and gentleness of his manners, had a great opinion of him. They feared the people, which feared not God; nor feared not to defile the holy day with murder, which did not eat leaven bread. Satan gave them this counsel, desiring to keep close that sacrifice which should bring health and salvation to the world. But it pleased otherwise to the divine counsel. For it was not seemly that the sacrifice should be privily cast away, which the father would to be offered not only for the salvation of the Jews, but for the salvation also of the whole world. PARAPHRASES.[2]

GOD'S PLAN FOR CHRIST'S DEATH. JOHN CALVIN: Matthew does not mean that they assembled during the two days, but introduces this narrative to show that Christ was not led by any opinion of humankind to fix the day of his death; for by what conjectures could he have been led to it, since his enemies themselves had resolved to delay for a time? The meaning therefore is that by the spirit of prophecy he spoke of his own death, which no one could have suspected to be so near at hand. John explains the reason why the scribes and priests held this meeting: it was because, from day to day, the people flocked to Christ in greater multitudes. And at that time, it was decided at the instigation of Caiaphas that he should be put to death because they could not succeed against him in any other way.

They did not think it a fit season, till the festival was past and the crowd was dispersed. Hence, we infer that, although those hungry dogs eagerly opened their mouths to devour Christ, or rather rushed furiously upon him, still God withheld them by a secret restraint, from doing anything by their deliberation or at their pleasure. So far as lies in their power, they delay till another time; but, contrary to their wish, God hastens the hour. And it is of great importance for us to hold that Christ was not unexpectedly dragged to death by the violence of his enemies but was led to it by the

---

[1] Bullinger, *The Summe of the Foure Evangelists* (1582), C5*.

[2] EP 97r*.

providence of God; for our confidence in the propitiation is founded on the conviction that he was offered to God as that sacrifice which God had appointed from the beginning. And therefore, he determined that; his Son should be sacrificed on the very day of the Passover, that the ancient figure might give place to the only sacrifice of eternal redemption. Those who had no other design in view than to ruin Christ thought that another time would be more appropriate; but God, who had appointed him to be a sacrifice for the expiation of sins, selected a suitable day for contrasting the body with its shadow, by placing them together. Hence also we obtain a brighter display of the fruit of Christ's suffering. COMMENTARY ON A HARMONY OF THE EVANGELISTS.[3]

26:6-13 *An Anointing for Burial*

ANOINTED BY A WOMAN. JOHN MAYER: I think that as Calvin intimated by leaving out Luke's history of the woman, a sinner, anointing Christ's feet in the house of one Simon, that she was another woman and not the woman here spoken of, or by any other Evangelist, which is plain to any that considers the history. . . . I herein rather assent to Chrysostom,[†] denying her to be Mary, of whom only excellent things are spoken, but this being noted a sinner, and likewise Jerome[‡] well observed, that the conscience of her sins made her stand behind at Jesus' feet, whereas this woman comes to his head. For the woman spoken of by the other three Evangelists, I cannot see how she should be one and the same. The anointing indeed was in Bethany, and by a divine instinct, as a presage of his burial, but seeing in two, the ointment was said to be poured upon his head out of a box, but two days before the Passover, all the disciples murmuring. In one it is said that she anointed his feet and wiped them with his hair of her head, six days before the Passover, Judas only murmuring. . . . Moreover, Mary being a woman well known to the disciples, it is not likely that they would murmur any act done

by her, but treacherous Judas only, who being blinded with covetousness, conspired against his own Lord and master. But another woman coming, who was not so well known unto them, they might peradventure speak against her seeming prodigality, till that hearing their master, to whom the heart is open, they are satisfied. A TREASURY OF ECCLESIASTICAL EXPOSITIONS.[4]

A GOOD OFFERING. JOHN CALVIN: But Christ plainly makes this exception, that what he wished to be done once would not be agreeable to him in future. For by saying that the poor will always be in the world, he distinguishes between the ordinary service, which ought to be maintained among believers, and that extraordinary service, which ceased after his ascension to heaven. . . . In short, this passage teaches us that, though the Lord commands us to dedicate to him ourselves and all our property, yet, with respect to himself, he demands no worship but that which is spiritual, and which is attended by no expense, but rather desires us to bestow on the poor what superstition foolishly expends on the worship of God.

By these words Christ confirms what we have said, that the precious ointment was not valued by him on account of its odor, but solely in reference to his burial. It was because he wished to testify by this symbol, that his grave would yield a sweet odor, as it breathed life and salvation through the whole world. . . .

He says that this action will do honor to Mary, because it will be praised by the doctrine of the gospel. Hence, we infer that we ought to estimate our works not by human opinion, but by the testimony of the word of God. When he says that she will be held in honorable remembrance throughout the whole world, by this comparison he indirectly censures his disciples; for among strangers, and in distant parts of the world, all nations with one consent will applaud this action,

---

[3]CTS 3:185-86 (CO 45:692-92); citing Jn 11:48.

[4]Mayer, *A Treasury of Ecclesiastical Expositions . . . upon the Scriptures* (1622), 304-05; citing Lk 7:37; Jn 12:1-3. [†]Chrysostom, *Homilies on Matthew*, NPNF[1] 10:461-65. [‡]Jerome, *Commentary on Matthew*, FC 117:291-307.

which the members of his own household condemned with such bitterness. Christ gently
reproves the disciples also for not entertaining
sufficiently honorable views of his future reign; but
at the same time, by this expression he bears
testimony to the calling of the Gentiles, on which
our salvation is founded. COMMENTARY ON A
HARMONY OF THE EVANGELISTS.[5]

**THE ANOINTING WAS REBUKED BY SOME BUT
APPROVED BY JESUS.** AEGIDIUS HUNNIUS:
Nonetheless, the prior opinion appears more
accurate. Furthermore, what we call "lavender" is
likely equivalent to the *pseudonardus* [lit., "pseudo-
ointment"] that is named in comparison to genuine
ointment (*probatam nardum*). This was the
unguent that she [Mary] poured over Jesus' head as
he was reclining. She desired to distinguish the
Lord with the highest honors possible, since she
had perceived him to be the Son of God from the
miracles that he had performed and chiefly from
the raising of her brother, Lazarus. So worthy was
this guest [i.e., Jesus], for whom no effort or service
was spared. As I mentioned, John recounts how
the Lord Jesus' feet were also anointed with part of
this ointment. These actions appeared unworthy to
Judas Iscariot, because the ointment was poured
out so "wastefully" (as he was reckoning), and the
ointment that was so rare and precious was lost.
[Those who were present][†] were unable to restrain
him from expressing his indignation of mind
openly. "Why this waste?" he said. He was saying
this not out of serious concern for the poor, but for
the sake of his own private gain. "For he bore the
money bag and was a thief," as John notes, and he
was in the habit of taking furtively whatever had
been contributed to the Lord and his companions
and putting it to private use. And thus, it was
grieving the man that this profit was being
"embezzled" from him. Furthermore, since he was
pretending to care for the poor, the other disciples
were moved by this hypocritical display and joined
in the protest, for they did not yet recognize his

hypocrisy, avarice, impiety of heart, and other
wicked deeds. Therefore, they said, "Why this loss?"
They call it loss because according to the judgment
of human reason this anointing appeared not at all
necessary for Christ and so was both useless and
detrimental to the poor. This opinion was
confirmed all the more as they watched part of the
ointment flow from Christ's body to the ground.
They judged that this ointment could have been
allocated more carefully and better by far if by its
sale the needs of the poor were alleviated. For they
said, "It could have been sold for much," and as
Mark has it, "for three hundred denarii, which
would have aided the poor." A denarius is so called
because it equaled ten copper coins.[†] . . .

The Lord sees and approves the woman's work
as good and holy, and then he says, "Why are you
harassing the woman?" From this it appears that
Mary was not a little disturbed by the unanimous
murmuring of the disciples. That is why Christ
accepts her deed and indicates openly and with the
greatest earnestness that he approves it. "She has
performed a good work for me," he says. He also
adds the evident reason for this assertion: "She has
poured this ointment over my body to prepare me
for burial." It was customary among Eastern
peoples to anoint the bodies of the deceased with
precious ointments and to bury them with
aromatics. Christ, therefore, being soon to die,
interprets the woman's deed as having been done
by the secret and unspoken impulse of God, so
that it became indeed a symbol of his imminent
passion and death. This death was anticipated by
the woman's anointing, since otherwise anointings
customarily took place after a death. Christ affirms
that so clear and memorable a work had set this
woman apart, declaring that "her memory will be
kept and celebrated in a holy and religious manner
until the end of the age wherever this gospel is
preached in all the world." The Lord sanctifies this
with an oath and indicates what will come to pass,
as outcome itself testifies, for the deed of this holy
woman is celebrated even today, memorialized for
all down the ages in the writings and records of the
blessed Evangelists. The Lord also responds to the

---

[5]CTS 3:189-91 (CO 45:695-96).

disciples' objection concerning the needs of the poor by saying "the poor you will always have with you." And—as is added in Mark's Gospel—"you will be able to benefit them whenever you wish," and thus nothing is lost to the poor by this anointing of my body. But that the addition—"you will not always have me"—is spoken by the Lord concerning his visible presence is clear from the context. It was by this visible presence that he had till that point lived with his disciples, and by it that they were able to devote themselves to and perform works for him such as the woman performed. Commentary on Matthew.[6]

26:14-16 A Bargain for Betrayal

A Premeditated Betrayal. John Boys: I need not here relate how the king of glory was envied by the Pharisees, accused by the priests, accused of the people, condemned by Pilate, buffeted by the soldiers, mocked of the captains, last of all, which was worst of all (an action which the sun did blush to see) crucified among thieves as a malefactor, even by his own countrymen, and all this said, and more than can be said, through a treacherous act of a miscreant apostle, who played the merchant with his master, as you hear in the text, "What will you give me, and I will deliver him unto you?"

First, as a peddler having no certain standing, he ran up and down the city, seeking traders, not traders seeking him, as if his ware had been so bad, that none would buy it, except he did expose it basely; for it is said, he went unto the chief priests. Second, whereas he should have said, "You shall give me this much, or else you shall go without him," he says only . . . "what will you give?" leaving it to the discretion of the buyers. Third, he did not take ready coin for his ware, for it appears in the text and Theophylact[†] observes it, that the chief priests at this time did only promise him money, not pay. Yet Judas, an unhappy merchant, after he

wrought journey work with the devil, sold his most loving master to strangers his most hateful enemies; even Jesus the world's Savior, in whom is all treasure, for a little silver, and that without any good assurance, for he says only, "What will you give?" An Exposition of the Dominical Epistles and Gospels.[7]

Judas's Descent to Betrayal. Aegidius Hunnius: Judas bore this response from the Lord with so twisted a mind—especially since he understood that he had been deprived of a portion of the money—that, polluted with impiety, he hurried to the camp and banner of his master's sworn enemies, namely, to the chief priests. To them he openly pledged his efforts to destroy and hand over his Lord. He did this in part to avenge himself for the rebuke that he had taken so ill and in part to compensate the wished-for profit and morsel that had been snatched from his jaws with reward he gained from his crime and the price of his betrayal. For since Satan had filled his dishonest heart with hatred and was holding him fast through the snares of avarice, Judas was in no time at all able to be incited to this monstrous crime and unheard-of parricide. The chief priests settled on thirty pieces of silver, one of which is equal to our half-thalers. This came about not by random chance, but that the prophetic scripture might be fulfilled that predicted in clear terms the criminal pact between Judas the betrayer and the chief priests. For it is written: "I said to them, 'If it is good in your eyes, bring forth my wages. But if not, be silent.' And they weighed out my wages, thirty pieces of silver. And the Lord said to me, 'Cast it into the Lord's house, so that it may be given to the potter—the lordly price at which I was valued by them.' And I bore thirty pieces of silver and cast them into the Lord's house, so that they might be given to the potter."[†]

"And from that time forth he was seeking an opportunity." After the hope of wealth was set

---

[6]Hunnius, *Commentarius in Evangelium Secundum Matthaeum* (1594), 820-21. [†]Text simply reads "they." [‡]An *as* (pl. *asses*) was the copper coin of least value in the Roman Empire.

[7]Boys, *An Exposition of the Dominicall Epistles and Gospels* (1610), 127-28*. [†]Theophylact, *Commentary on Matthew*, 45r.

aflame in the impious traitor, he would not think of letting the opportunity to perform the deed and gain the wealth to pass him by. In the meantime, the sin slept so deeply in his breast that he did not perceive the atrocity of so great, so horrible, and so abominable a crime; neither did he pull his foot back from the first step of that sin. Rather, he endeavored by every means to bring forth the crime that had been conceived in his mind—bring it forth as the saddest of all works. COMMENTARY ON MATTHEW.[8]

MISPLACED VALUES. JOSEPH HALL: How unequal is this rate! You that valued Mary's ointment, which she bestowed upon the feet of Christ, at three hundred pieces of silver, sells thy master, on whom that precious odor was spent, at thirty. Worldly hearts are penny-wise, and pound-foolish; they know how to set high prices upon the worthless trash of this world; but for heavenly things, or the God that owns them, these they shamefully undervalue.

"And I will deliver unto you." False and presumptuous Judas! It was more than you could do; your price was not more too low than the undertaking was too high. Had all the powers of hell combined with you, they could not have delivered your master into the hands of men. The act was none but his own; all that he did, all that he suffered, was perfectly voluntary. Had he been pleased to resist, how easily he could have with one breath blown you and your accomplices down into their hell! It is no thanks to you that he would be delivered. CONTEMPLATIONS.[9]

---

[8]Hunnius, *Commentarius in Evangelium Secundum Matthaeum* (1594), 822; citing Zech 11:12-13. †The text here seems to be a mixture of the Vulgate and a fresh translation from the Hebrew.

[9]Hall, *Contemplations on the Historical Passages of the Old and New Testaments*, 4:566*.

26:17-30 THE PASSOVER AND THE LORD'S SUPPER

Now on the first day of Unleavened Bread the disciples came to Jesus, saying, "Where will you have us prepare for you to eat the Passover?" [18]He said, "Go into the city to a certain man and say to him, 'The Teacher says, My time is at hand. I will keep the Passover at your house with my disciples.'" [19]And the disciples did as Jesus had directed them, and they prepared the Passover.

[20]When it was evening, he reclined at table with the twelve.[a] [21]And as they were eating, he said, "Truly, I say to you, one of you will betray me." [22]And they were very sorrowful and began to say to him one after another, "Is it I, Lord?" [23]He answered, "He who has dipped his hand in the dish with me will betray me. [24]The Son of Man goes as it is written of him, but woe to that man by whom the Son of Man is betrayed! It would have been better for that man if he had not been born." [25]Judas, who would betray him, answered, "Is it I, Rabbi?" He said to him, "You have said so."

[26]Now as they were eating, Jesus took bread, and after blessing it broke it and gave it to the disciples, and said, "Take, eat; this is my body." [27]And he took a cup, and when he had given thanks he gave it to them, saying, "Drink of it, all of you, [28]for this is my blood of the[b] covenant, which is poured out for many for the forgiveness of sins. [29]I tell you I will not drink again of this fruit of the vine until that day when I drink it new with you in my Father's kingdom."

[30]And when they had sung a hymn, they went out to the Mount of Olives.

a Some manuscripts add *disciples*   b Some manuscripts insert *new*

OVERVIEW: At the Passover meal, Jesus stuns the twelve disciples by announcing that he will be betrayed by one of them, continuing a theme from the previous narrative. Jesus also institutes a new commemorative meal. In the Reformation commentary on the Lord's Supper, significant attention is given to the institution of the meal and its meaning. Two main interests of the commentators are the poignancy of the symbols in the supper as signs of Christ's death and how to interpret Jesus' words "This is my body." The proper understanding of those words—in particular, whether they were literal or figurative—and the subsequent question of Christ's presence in the sacrament was a source of considerable debate during the early modern period. Various positions were held between Roman Catholics and Protestants as well as among Protestants, most notably between Luther and Zwingli, whose disagreement culminated at the Colloquy of Marburg (1529). The reformers also address the supper in their theologi-cal treatises, although those works sometimes prefer convincing argumentation over succinct textual insights. In their commentaries, the reformers are typically more constrained to dealing with the features provided in the text.

The reformers recognize the Gospel narrative as providing practical guidance for contemporary observances of the Lord's Supper. For example, Heinrich Bullinger considers Judas's presence at the supper and how that might instruct the church on who should participate in the Lord's Supper. In addition, Johannes Bugenhagen points to the Protestant interest in providing both the bread and the cup to the laity (communion in "two kinds") as opposed to the Roman Catholic practice of providing only the host (communion in "one kind"). On a slightly different note, Luther contrasts the simplicity and intentionality of Jesus' choice of the bread and the cup with the various stages of the Passover meal. The reformers acknowledge that Jesus' spilled blood enables a new covenant, which includes the forgiveness of sins. In addition to the proclamation of forgiveness, the supper points to the future feast of the kingdom (Mt 9:15; 22:1-13; 25:10) that Jesus will celebrate with his disciples.

26:17-25 Betrayal Predicted

Is It I, Rabbi? Juan de Maldonado: "One of you." Christ discovers the traitor without injury, by showing that he knew him, but not naming him. Many have inquired why Christ said this. . . . He did it to give Judas an opportunity of repenting, and to urge him to a change of purpose, when he saw that his designs could not be concealed. Christ also may be thought to have said it to show that he died, not against his will, nor as circumvented by craft, nor without his expectation: but knowingly, willingly, resolutely, and when, from his knowledge of the design of the traitor, he might have defeated it, and yet would not do so. But why did Christ not name him? We may reply that it was in accordance with the lovingkindness of Christ to spare the name and reputation even of his own betrayer, and to be content with showing that he was not ignorant of his betrayer; but would not name him, because it was not necessary to his object, which was to show that he died of his own knowledge and free-will. . . .

It seems strange why the apostles, who were innocent, should have been troubled, as if each thought the above words spoken of himself. Nor were they only so much grieved at the great wickedness that Christ should be betrayed by his own follower, whoever he were—though no doubt this did afflict them greatly—but, as St. Matthew shows, they were sorry because each thought the saying possibly spoken of himself, and was anxious, and said, "Is it I?" Origen, St. Chrysostom, Euthymius, and Theophylact[†] give as the cause, that even if they knew themselves innocent, yet they put more faith in the words of Christ than in their own consciences. . . . Judas did not say like the rest, "Is it I, Lord?" but "Is it I, Rabbi?" as if, even when he most especially wished to dissemble his treachery, he was compelled by his pride to

betray himself by addressing Christ with a less honorable title than the rest. Commentary on Matthew's Gospel.[1]

26:26-30 This Is My Body

We Cannot Confuse the Sign with the Thing Signified. Huldrych Zwingli: The sacraments we esteem and honor as signs and symbols of holy things, but not as though they themselves were the things of which they are the signs. For who is so ignorant as to try to maintain that the sign is the thing which it signifies? If that were the case, I would only need to write the word "ape" and your majesty would have before him a real ape. But the sacraments are signs of real things, things which once took place really, literally, and naturally, they now represent and recall and set before our eyes. Please do not misunderstand me, O king. Christ atoned for our sins by his death, and the Lord's Supper is a commemoration of this fact, as he himself said, "Do this in remembrance of me." By this commemoration all the benefits which God has displayed in his Son are called to mind. And by the signs themselves, the bread and wine, Christ himself is as it were set before our eyes, so that not merely with the ear, but with the eye and palate we see and taste that Christ whom the soul bears within itself and in whom it rejoices. . . . The supper signifies all the divine favor bestowed on us in Christ, and also that in thankfulness we are to embrace our brethren with the same love with which Christ has received and redeemed and saved us. An Exposition of the Faith.[2]

Rightly Understanding the Sign and Thing Signified in the Supper. John Calvin: There are three mistakes against which it is here necessary to be on our guard; first, not to confound the spiritual blessing with the sign; second, not to seek Christ on earth or under earthly elements; third, not to imagine any other kind of

---

[1]JMG 2:383-84, 390. [†]Chrysostom, *Homilies on Matthew*, NPNF[1] 10:467. Euthymius Zigabenus, *Expositio in Matthaeum*, PG 129:663-64. Theophylact, *Commentary on Matthew*, 45v. [2]LCC 24:247-49*.

eating than that which draws into us the life of Christ by the secret power of the Spirit, and which we obtain by faith alone. First, as I have said, let us always keep in view the distinction between the sign and the thing signified, if we do not wish to overturn everything; for otherwise we shall derive no advantage from the sacrament, if it does not, according to the measure of our small capacity, lead us from the contemplation of the earthly element to the heavenly mystery. And therefore, whoever will not distinguish the body of Christ from the bread and the blood from the wine will never understand what is meant by the Lord's Supper, or for what purpose believers use these symbols.

Second, we must attend to the proper method of seeking Christ; that is, our minds must not be fixed on the earth, but must ascend upwards to the heavenly glory in which he dwells. For the body of Christ did not, by clothing itself with an incorrupt-ible life, lay aside its own nature; and hence it follows that it is finite. But he has now ascended above the heavens, that no gross imagination may keep us occupied with earthly things. And certainly, if this mystery is heavenly, nothing could be more unrea-sonable than to draw down Christ to the earth, when, on the contrary, he calls us upwards to himself.

The last point which, I said, claimed our attention is the kind of eating. We must not dream that his substance passes, in a natural manner, into our souls; but we eat his flesh, when, by means of it, we receive life. For we must attend to the analogy or resemblance between bread and flesh, which teaches us that our souls feed on Christ's own flesh in precisely the same manner as bread imparts vigor to our bodies. The flesh of Christ, therefore, is spiritual nourishment, because it gives life to us. Now it gives life, because the Holy Spirit pours into us the life which dwells in it. And though the act of eating the flesh of Christ is different from believing on him, yet we ought to know that it is impossible to feed on Christ in any other way than by faith, because the eating itself is a consequence of faith. COMMENTARY ON A HARMONY OF THE EVANGELISTS.[3]

MORTAL OR IMMORTAL—WHICH BODY DO WE EAT? HULDRYCH ZWINGLI: We oppose the erroneous teaching of our adversaries that the natural body of Christ is presented to us in the symbols because this is the force and effect of the words: "This is my body." The argument is met by the words of Christ already adduced which deny the continued presence of his body in the world. And if that was the force of the words, the body presented would be his passible body, for when he spoke the words, he still had a mortal body, hence the disciples partook of his mortal body. For he did not possess two bodies, one immortal and impassible, the other mortal. And if the apostles ate his mortal body, which do we eat? Naturally, the mortal body. But the body that was once mortal is now immortal and incorruptible. Therefore, it follows that if we eat his mortal body, he necessarily has a body which is both mortal and immortal. Therefore, he must have two bodies, the one mortal, which both we and the apostles eat, and the other immortal, which remains at the right hand of God. Otherwise, we are forced to say that the apostles ate the mortal body and we ate the immortal one. And that is plainly ridiculous. AN EXPOSITION OF THE FAITH.[4]

SINNERS AND THE SUPPER. HEINRICH BULLINGER: The Lord himself, who is the searcher of hearts, severely, diligently, plainly, and in many words in his last supper, before he distributed the mysteries, admonished Judas, being a hypocrite, a thief, a traitor, a murderer, yea, a parricide, a blasphemer, and a forsaker of his master; but being admonished, when notwithstanding he departed not from the table, but tarried among the saints. The Lord did not violently put him away, nor bade him openly to depart, neither withheld he the Lord's bread from him, but gave it unto him as he did unto others, although he knew assuredly what he was, which thing the ministers of the church do not always so certainly know of those who sit down at the table. Neither did the Lord offend any whit at all in so doing, neither did he cast that which was

---

[3]CTS 3:209-10 (CO 45:708).

[4]LCC 24:261*.

holy to the dogs. For the Lord warned him diligently of all matters whereof he was to be warned; and he, hearing and understanding them all, remains notwithstanding among the saints, vaunts himself for one of the faithful, not for a hog, and as one of the faithful takes part of the bread and of the cup. By which hypocrisy, notwithstanding, he provoked the heavy judgment of God against him. . . .

This is a commemoration, memorial, or remembrance, sign or sacrament, of my body which is given for you. "This cup" (or rather the wine in the cup) "signifies or represents unto you my blood which was once shed for you." . . . As if he should say, "Now am I present with you, before your eyes; I shall die and ascend up into heaven, and then shall this holy bread and wine be a memorial or token of my body and blood given and shed for you. Then break the bread and eat it, distribute the cup and drink it; and do this in the remembrance of me, praising my benefits bestowed on you in redeeming you and giving you life." OF THE LORD'S HOLY SUPPER.[5]

FIGURATIVE SPEECH IN THE SUPPER. THOMAS CRANMER: Truth it is indeed that the words be as plain as may be spoken; but that the sense is not so plain, it is manifest to every person who weighs substantially the circumstances of the place. For when Christ gave bread to his disciples, and said, "This is my body," there is no one of any discretion who understands the English tongue, but they may well know by the order of the speech, that Christ spoke those words of the bread, calling it his body, as all the old authors also do affirm, although some of the papists deny the same. Wherefore this sentence cannot mean as the words seem and purport, but there must be some figure or mystery in this speech, more than appears in the plain words. For by this manner of speech plainly understand without any figure as the words lie, can be gathered none other sense, but that bread is Christ's body, and that Christ's body is bread, which all Christian ears do abhor to

hear. Wherefore in these words must be sought out another sense and meaning than the words of themselves do bear.

And although the true sense and understanding of these words be sufficiently declared before, when I spoke of transubstantiation; yet to make the matter so plain that no scruple or doubt shall remain, here is occasion given more fully to treat thereof. In which process shall be showed that these sentences of Christ, "This is my body," "This is my blood," be figurative speeches. And although it be manifest enough by the plain words of the gospel and proved before in the process of transubstantiation that Christ spoke of bread when he said, "This is my body," likewise that it was very wine which he called his blood. A DEFENCE.[6]

THE SYMBOLS OF THE SUPPER. GEORGE ESTEY: Matthew has "This is my blood," so that the thing signified is the blood of Christ, and by wine, first, to teach that we must have some sweet feeling of Christ, and second, that it is he who cheers our hearts. Now this is his blood shed and poured out for us whereby is signified his death and merits for us. Note by the way the leprosy of sin, which could not be cured, but by the blood of God.

"'Testament' in effect here is the same with "covenant," save that testament or will implies death and is nothing but God's agreement with humanity for their salvation. This to continue and be effectual, is but one. And is the pleasure of God to save men for Christ's sake, and according to diverse considerations is old, till Christ, for the Jews in ceremonies, and to vanish. New, not but that it was heretofore, but was by Christ so clearly published as it seemed new. . . . The benefits of this . . . are the same we have heard of before in Christ. All which, this wine is given as a seal to confirm, that they belong to the due receiver. This must we drink as eat the former, by commandment in remembrance. AN EXPOSITION UPON THE LORD'S SUPPER.[7]

---

[5]DHB 4:425-26, 439.

[6]Cranmer, *A Defence of the True and Catholike Doctrine of the Sacrament* (1550), 121-22.
[7]Estey, *Certain Godly and Learned Expositions upon Diverse Parts of Scripture*, 84*.

A Simple Meal. Martin Luther: Hence, with these gestures, he doubtless intended to distinguish his Supper conclusively from the old paschal supper. . . .

In summary, they had eaten the paschal lamb without his having commanded them to eat or drink, nor had he placed or laid it before anyone, but each one had eaten and drunk whatever he wished of that which stood before him, as Matthew and Mark say, "As they were eating, he took bread." . . . But now the meal proceeds in an entirely new manner. He takes and chooses a certain, particular loaf, pronounces thanks over it, breaks it, and divides it among them and offers it to them, and commands them to eat. Then he adds, "This is my body which is given for you." In the same way also he took the cup, choosing and giving a special draught for them all. Of other loaves he does not command them to eat, or drink out of other cups, nor does he place or lay anything before anyone as he does here. With all this he doubtless indicated that this bread and wine were not ordinary bread and wine as was customary with the Passover, but something quite different, special, nobler, namely, as he says in his own words, it is his body and his blood.

Thus we have seen that Matthew and Mark agree, both speaking with utmost simplicity and with practically the same words, except that Matthew adds this phrase at the end, "for the forgiveness of sins." . . .

It is much more useful to observe that since the Evangelists all so unanimously record these words in their perfect simplicity, "This is my body," one may conclude that there certainly can be no figure of speech or any trope in them. Had there been a trope there, one of them would certainly have touched on it with at least one letter, so that a different text or interpretation might have resulted. This they do on other occasions when one inserts what the other omits or expresses it in different words. Confession Concerning Christ's Supper.[8]

---

[8]LW 37:311-13 (WA 26:457-59); citing Mt 26:26; Mk 14:22; Mt 12:28 and Lk 11:20.

The Cup Is Commanded. Johannes Bugenhagen: Let us look at the little word *similiter* in context of the whole command of Christ. Christ took the bread and gave thanks during the supper. In the same way, he also took the cup and gave thanks after the supper. Christ broke the bread so that each one should eat from it in the supper. In the same way, he commanded each one to drink from the cup after the supper with these words, "Drink of it, all of you," so that each one might share in the cup here just as in the bread. Christ gave the bread to his disciples in the supper. In the same way or manner, he also gave the cup to the same disciples after the supper. Christ commanded his disciples to eat the bread in the supper. In the same way, he also commanded those same disciples of his to drink the cup after the supper. . . .

Let us now observe the words of the command of Christ regarding the cup from which we may also surely hear whether the laity also belong to the cup of the Lord. . . . He says, "It is my blood," as Matthew clearly attests. He does not say, "It is my body and blood together." Therefore, he also says clearly, "which is shed for you." Do you still not hear? What does this sacrament benefit you if you do not have the command of Christ? We believe what we hear from Christ. Afterward, make as many concomitances as you will with human thoughts. Just be sure to see to it that you do not take away anything from the command of Christ. The Divine Majesty does not wish to be despised. No one should build on your thoughts here but solely on the words and on the command of Christ. If it is to be a sacrament of faith, one cannot act differently. He also says, "Drink of it, all of you." He also commands the cup to the disciples, to whom he gave the bread, and tells them to do this and to drink often. I ask again on the basis of the words of the Lord about the cup: "Do the laity not also belong to the new testament, that is, to the forgiveness of sins? Do the laity not also belong to the blood of Christ? Is the blood of Christ not also shed for the laity for the forgiveness of sins? Should the laity not also remember the Lord and confess and proclaim his death, as much as they are commanded to do so, to their friends and acquaintances to the honor of God, to their own salvation, in opposition to the devil and the mad world, whatever the cost? How did we come to this point that the tyrants forbid us the cup?" AGAINST THIEVES OF THE CUP.[9]

CHRIST'S NATURAL BODY GIVEN ON THE CROSS, NOT IN THE BREAD. DIRK PHILIPS:

This is after all certain and true, in addition, also incontrovertible, that it was not the bread but the true body of Christ that sat with the apostles at the table and gave them bread and wine and spoke the words "This is my body." . . . This same body and no other is given and broken for us and sacrificed on the cross. How can we then believe otherwise than what Christ himself said? That is, that his body, yes, his natural body conceived of the Holy Spirit and born out from the virgin Mary, is delivered into death for us? But the apostles ate the bread and drank the wine; therewith they were assured with all believers of the redemption Christ has won for us with his body and blood. . . . Judas also ate of the bread and drank of the wine, but nevertheless he did not receive the flesh and blood of Christ. For all that God gives us in the use of the sacraments, that faith receives, and God works in his elect alone through his Spirit, what the sacraments signify externally. Therefore, it is impossible without faith to become partakers of Christ and his gifts. It is even more impossible that the unbelieving and evil ones (in whom Satan dwells) may receive the pure, unblemished, and holy flesh and the precious blood of Jesus Christ. THE SUPPER OF OUR LORD JESUS CHRIST.[10]

---

[9]JBSW 1:622-24; citing Mt 26:28; Mk 14:24.

[10]CRR 6:116-18; citing Mt 1:20; Lk 1:31.

26:31-75 JESUS PRAYS, JUDAS BETRAYS,
PETER DENIES

[31] Then Jesus said to them, "You will all fall away because of me this night. For it is written, 'I will strike the shepherd, and the sheep of the flock will be scattered.' [32] But after I am raised up, I will go before you to Galilee." [33] Peter answered him, "Though they all fall away because of you, I will never fall away." [34] Jesus said to him, "Truly, I tell you, this very night, before the rooster crows, you will deny me three times." [35] Peter said to him, "Even if I must die with you, I will not deny you!" And all the disciples said the same.

[36] Then Jesus went with them to a place called Gethsemane, and he said to his disciples, "Sit here, while I go over there and pray." [37] And taking with him Peter and the two sons of Zebedee, he began to be sorrowful and troubled. [38] Then he said to them, "My soul is very sorrowful, even to death; remain here, and watch[a] with me." [39] And going a little farther he fell on his face and prayed, saying, "My Father, if it be possible, let this cup pass from me; nevertheless, not as I will, but as you will." [40] And he came to the disciples and found them sleeping. And he said to Peter, "So, could you not watch with me one hour? [41] Watch and pray that you may not enter into temptation. The spirit indeed is willing, but the flesh is weak." [42] Again, for the second time, he went away and prayed, "My Father, if this cannot pass unless I drink it, your will be done." [43] And again he came and found them sleeping, for their eyes were heavy. [44] So, leaving them again, he went away and prayed for the third time, saying the same words again. [45] Then he came to the disciples and said to them, "Sleep and take your rest later on.[b] See, the hour is at hand, and the Son of Man is betrayed into the hands of sinners. [46] Rise, let us be going; see, my betrayer is at hand."

[47] While he was still speaking, Judas came, one of the twelve, and with him a great crowd with swords and clubs, from the chief priests and the elders of the people. [48] Now the betrayer had given them a sign, saying, "The one I will kiss is the man; seize him." [49] And he came up to Jesus at once and said,

"Greetings, Rabbi!" And he kissed him. [50] Jesus said to him, "Friend, do what you came to do."[c] Then they came up and laid hands on Jesus and seized him. [51] And behold, one of those who were with Jesus stretched out his hand and drew his sword and struck the servant[d] of the high priest and cut off his ear. [52] Then Jesus said to him, "Put your sword back into its place. For all who take the sword will perish by the sword. [53] Do you think that I cannot appeal to my Father, and he will at once send me more than twelve legions of angels? [54] But how then should the Scriptures be fulfilled, that it must be so?" [55] At that hour Jesus said to the crowds, "Have you come out as against a robber, with swords and clubs to capture me? Day after day I sat in the temple teaching, and you did not seize me. [56] But all this has taken place that the Scriptures of the prophets might be fulfilled." Then all the disciples left him and fled.

[57] Then those who had seized Jesus led him to Caiaphas the high priest, where the scribes and the elders had gathered. [58] And Peter was following him at a distance, as far as the courtyard of the high priest, and going inside he sat with the guards to see the end. [59] Now the chief priests and the whole council[e] were seeking false testimony against Jesus that they might put him to death, [60] but they found none, though many false witnesses came forward. At last two came forward [61] and said, "This man said, 'I am able to destroy the temple of God, and to rebuild it in three days.'" [62] And the high priest stood up and said, "Have you no answer to make? What is it that these men testify against you?"[f] [63] But Jesus remained silent. And the high priest said to him, "I adjure you by the living God, tell us if you are the Christ, the Son of God." [64] Jesus said to him, "You have said so. But I tell you, from now on you will see the Son of Man seated at the right hand of Power and coming on the clouds of heaven." [65] Then the high priest tore his robes and said, "He has uttered blasphemy. What further witnesses do we need? You have now heard his blasphemy.

⁶⁶"What is your judgment?" They answered, "He deserves death." ⁶⁷Then they spit in his face and struck him. And some slapped him, ⁶⁸saying, "Prophesy to us, you Christ! Who is it that struck you?"

⁶⁹Now Peter was sitting outside in the courtyard. And a servant girl came up to him and said, "You also were with Jesus the Galilean." ⁷⁰But he denied it before them all, saying, "I do not know what you mean." ⁷¹And when he went out to the entrance, another servant girl saw him, and she said to the bystanders, "This man was with Jesus of Nazareth." ⁷²And again he denied it with an oath: "I do not know the man." ⁷³After a little while the bystanders came up and said to Peter, "Certainly you too are one of them, for your accent betrays you." ⁷⁴Then he began to invoke a curse on himself and to swear, "I do not know the man." And immediately the rooster crowed. ⁷⁵And Peter remembered the saying of Jesus, "Before the rooster crows, you will deny me three times." And he went out and wept bitterly.

a Or keep awake; also verses 40, 41   b Or Are you still sleeping and taking your rest?   c Or Friend, why are you here?   d Or bondservant   e Greek Sanhedrin   f Or Have you no answer to what these men testify against you?

OVERVIEW: In this section, Matthew records several significant events in quick succession: Jesus' prediction of Peter's denial, his prayer in the garden, Judas's betrayal, Jesus' arrest, and Peter's denial of Christ. Once again on the Mount of Olives, the backdrop of the previous two chapters, Jesus returns to an analogy of his disciples as sheep (Mt 25:32). As Wolfgang Musculus notes, instead of a rebuke for the impending scattering of his disciples, Jesus' words are meant to prepare them for the regathering that would follow. The reformers point out that Peter's prideful declaration prompts the response of Jesus' prediction of his denial.

They also highlight the agony that Jesus suffered in his passion, particularly during his prayer in the garden. Just as Jesus had instructed his disciples to pray in submission to the will of the Father (Mt 6:10), in his own prayer he submits to the great purposes of God, though in great agony. The sleeping disciples reveal their weaknesses; though they professed to die for Jesus, they cannot even pray for him. Martin Chemnitz laments that some inappropriately downplay Jesus' words so that it does not appear that Jesus tries to avoid his death on the cross. Others indicate that the two wills of Christ (human and divine) are on display in the narrative.

In response to Judas's kiss and the arrest of Jesus, one of his disciples draws a sword and swings with deadly intent, hitting the ear of one of the arresting party. Jesus preempts a deadly melee and uses the moment to instruct, once again, about the radical nature of his kingdom compared to earthly ones and the meek restraint of power required by the current state of his kingdom. The reformers extolled the meekness that Jesus displayed as he was arrested.

The scene shifts from the garden to the court of the high priest and represents the most direct confrontation in Jesus' appearances before Jewish or Roman leaders. Matthew's account of the trial portrays the inability of the leaders to bring any worthwhile charge against Jesus. The reformers remark that, like in the garden, Jesus' silence while on trial reveals his control of the situation and his wisdom. When nothing substantial arises from the accusations, the high priest takes the lead in the questioning. His inquisition focuses on a question of Christ's identity, which has been a major theme in Matthew's narratives. Calvin dissects the high priest's question to propose that the Jews, who were contemporary with Jesus, understood the Messiah to be as much the Son of God as the Son of David.

Jesus affirms his identity as the Christ, but then also declares the culmination of his work, his glorious coming from heaven (see Mt 24:29-31). Zwingli notes that Jesus' demeanor and responses reflect the wisdom he had given his disciples as they were embarking on their preaching mission (Mt 10:16-20). Though Jesus presents his identity and works with truthful accuracy, the council sentences him to death based on the high priest's charge of blasphemy.

Matthew recounts Peter's denial in vivid detail. Peter's remembrance of Jesus' words dashes his pride and causes him to cry the tears of a broken man. His immediate grief leads Juan de Valdés to affirm that Peter's repentance was a different sort than that of Judas.

26:31-35 The Disciples Will Fall Away

A LOVING SHEPHERD. WOLFGANG MUSCULUS: Christ declared this to his disciples not in a reproaching or condemning spirit, but more than this, so that they might understand by divine providence all things that would be, not only for themselves but also for those in the future even before they appear. And even knowing and seeing this, he placed himself on the will of the Father, thus they themselves also did. Neither did they lose courage, even when they were scattered, since it would be endured only for a modest time, after which he would gather them again, whence also he mentions his resurrection. The same metaphor of a shepherd and sheep fully reveals this to be spoken by the Lord, linking together a pained and entirely friendly spirit. For who can look with disdain at sheep fleeing as the result of a stricken shepherd? Who does not know a shepherd to be a herder and preserver of sheep? If he were stricken, it would not be possible for another to obtain the sheep, inasmuch as they are dispersed and scattered. Because the shepherd knows this, that he is not able to drive out a hostile from the sheep, he is certainly not able to be enraged if he sees one or one in the future about to walk away. Then he did not say, "But after I am raised up, I will not know you anymore. I will give you up like fugitives," but, "I will go before you into Galilee." That is—I will advise you again—"I will gather you, and as a shepherd

going before his flock, thus I will go before and lead you." The place that Christ cites, namely Zechariah 13, reads in just as many words, except that there it is not, "I will strike," but, "Strike." However, in the same way it is the voice of God that is doing the commanding. But it is rightly said by Christ that the Father wanted to strike him, when he himself swore it. For the servant himself, being stricken, was indeed explaining the crucifixion of Christ. Indeed, by the striking of this shepherd, that very one was cut off by him who spoke it beforehand. And by saying this now, Christ rightly serves the faith of the disciples, in order that they may know that what would happen to them was first a work of the Father; then that it will happen to them just as to the sheep now to be perceived in the Father's providence. Whence also soon that word from the prophet is presented in the person of God: "And I will turn my hand against the little ones," certainly knowing the sheep of the flock who are dispersed by a stricken shepherd. COMMENTARY ON MATTHEW.[1]

PETER'S PRIDE. JOHN UDALL: The first cause of his fall was his presumption, and that is also in two things. The first is not leaning unto the words of his Lord and master. For Christ told him that he should deny him. But he, notwithstanding being either blinded with consideration of his own power (as hereafter shall appear) or else carried away with a preposterous zeal to follow him wither so ever he went, replied that though all people should forsake him, yet he would not. And surely this is most worthy the consideration. For if we begin at the first man that ever was, and continue throughout the whole Scriptures, we shall find that the little regard given unto the Word of God was the beginning of their fall. . . .

The second branch of Peter's presumption consists in this that he says, "I am ready to go

[1]Musculus, *In Evangelistam Matthaeum Commenarii* (1556), 622; citing Zech 13:7.

with you into prison and unto death." Peter thought he was strong enough to be a martyr, when indeed he had scarce learned the principles of his faith, nor that which is most necessary for all to know: namely, his own power and ability and how he must learn to stand before the Lord. Here you see Peter thinking himself a valiant soldier and yet is not so, out of which we note the pride of the human heart, and confidence that flesh and blood conceives of itself. For by nature, we are so blind that though we are naked, yet we vaunt ourselves as though we were gorgeously apparelled, though we are of no force to do anything. PETER'S FALL.[2]

26:36-46 Jesus Prays in the Garden of Gethsemane

THE REALITY OF CHRIST'S SUFFERING. MARTIN CHEMNITZ: The words which Christ prayed in his agony, "Let this cup pass from me," they do not want to interpret as flight from death, and they try to prove it by adding as arguments: (1) His willing and perfect obedience to the Father, (2) his measureless love toward the human race, (3) the fortitude which was in Christ which overcame the powers of all created things, (4) his good conscience. Therefore, the cup which he asks, "to be taken from him," they interpret as the perdition of Judas, the offense taken by the disciples, the rejection of the Jews, and the destruction of Jerusalem.

But I reply: The cup simply and properly signifies the suffering itself, as is clear from Matthew 20:22-23. . . . Furthermore, this discussion of the flight from death on the part of Christ is not some idle subtlety, but the correct explanation of it has great value. . . .

Furthermore, we must retain the passages which testify that in Christ there was not a simulated but a true and intense feeling of anguish. For that is why the Holy Spirit uses a word of such emphatic power to describe the suffering of

Christ, "He began," he says, "to be troubled"; this word expresses very great sorrow, so that a person flees the fellowship of other people, accepts no consolation, as the saying goes, "eating his own heart out, avoiding human companionship." Thus, the Savior says, "My soul is sorrowful, even to death." Likewise, the agonies were so great that the sweat distilled through little drops of blood and an angel came and comforted him. And that this sorrow was not simulated is confirmed by Isaiah 53:4: "Truly he has born our infirmities." And in Isaiah 49:4, the Son of God says, "I have spent my strength for nothing and in vain." And there is no stronger argument than that from Isaiah 53:6, 10. For the Father laid on him, together with our sins, all those terrors of divine wrath which were deserved by our sins, for it was his will to crush him in infirmity, says the text. And these penalties were not something simulated, as the rich epicure learns who, however, bears only the punishment for his own sin. Therefore, if Christ was a true ransom, if he redeemed us with a true satisfaction, we must not argue about simulated sufferings; for the sorrow was far greater than the limitation of our soul can comprehend . . . on him the sins of the whole world were laid, and on him the Father poured out his total wrath. THEOLOGICAL COMMONPLACES.[3]

A PAYMENT FOR SINS. HUGH LATIMER: Now to sustain and suffer the sorrow of death is not to sin, but he came into this world, with his passion to purge our sins. Now this that he suffered in the garden is one of the bitterest pieces of all his passion. This fear of death was the bitterest pain that ever he abode, due to sin which he never did, but became debtor for us. All this he suffered for us, this he did to satisfy for our sins. . . .

He suffered for you and me in such a degree, as is due to all the sins of the whole world. It was as if you would imagine that one man had committed all the sins since Adam, you may be sure he should be punished with the same horror of death

[2]Udall, Peter's Fall (1584), A3-C1.

[3]Chemnitz, Loci Theologici, 1:111-12; citing Lk 22:43-44; Lk 16:1-24.

in such a sort as all humans in the world should have suffered. Even if our Savior Christ had committed all the sins of the world, all that I for my part have done, all that you for your part have done, and that any man else has done, if he had done all this himself, his agony that he suffered should have been no greater nor grievous, than it was. This that he suffered in the garden was a portion, I say, of his passion and one of the bitterest parts of it. And this he suffered for our sins and not for any sins that he had committed himself for all we should have suffered every man according to his own deserts.

This he did of his goodness, partly to purge and cleanse our sins, partly because he would taste and feel our miseries . . . that he should rather help and relieve us, and partly he suffered to give us an example, to behave ourselves as he did. He did not suffer to discharge us clean from death, to keep us clean from it, not to taste of it. No, you must not take it so. We shall have the beholding of this dreadful face every one of us, we shall feel it ourselves. Yet our Savior, Christ, did suffer to the end, to signify to us that death can be overcome. . . . Oh, it was a grievous thing that Christ suffered here. Oh, the greatness of his sorrow that he suffered in the garden, partly to make amends for our sins and partly to deliver us from death, not so that we should not die bodily, but that this death should be a way to a better life, and to destroy and overcome hell. THE SEVENTH SERMON.[4]

AN EXAMPLE IN SUFFERING. MILES COVER-DALE: In the perfect example and the mirror of our life, Christ Jesus, we find an earnest servant love, a doctrine how we ought to behave ourselves in adversity. First, we see that Christ, of an exceeding great love, takes upon himself all infirmities of humanity and becomes like his brethren in all things, except sin. Being a very true man, he is therefore not ashamed before his disciples to acknowledge his infirmity, sorrow, heaviness, and fear, and to complain thereof unto his Father.

A fear by reason of the death and passion, he receives as a very man. For not to feel trouble is not human nature, and passion is no passion if it smart not, if it be not felt. Christ, therefore, both in his mind and body, feels the passion; he feels the conflict of death, albeit in wrestling withal, he overthrows it. Oh, the exceeding fervent love of our head and foregoer Jesus Christ, who, for our health, comes into so great an agony and trouble that above natural moisture, through the fearful conflict of the passion and death, he sheds his blood and sweats it. But with hearty desire, he runs to his heavenly Father; to him he complains of his weakness and distress; to him he gives over himself in all obedience and contentment of mind; of him also he receives comfort and strength. In the meantime, he forgets not his disciples, but comes to them, exhorts them to watch and pray, and has great compassion with their feebleness and sloth. FRUITFUL LESSONS.[5]

26:47-56 Judas's Betrayal and Jesus' Arrest

JUDAS BETRAYS JESUS. JOHN CALVIN: The Evangelists are careful to state that our Lord foresaw what happened; from which it might be inferred that he was not dragged to death by external violence, except so far as wicked men carried into execution the secret purpose of God. Although, therefore, a melancholy and frightful spectacle was exhibited to the disciples, yet they received, at the same time, grounds of confidence to confirm them, since the event itself showed that nothing occurred by chance . . . For what need was there for so great a force to take Christ, who, they were aware, was not provided with any defensive arms? The reason for such careful preparation was that the divine power of Christ, which they had been compelled to feel by numerous proofs, inwardly tormented them; but, on the other hand, it is a display of amazing rage that, relying on the power of arms, they do not hesitate to rise up against God. . . .

---

[4]Latimer, *Seven Sermons Before Edward VI*, 190-92*.

[5]Coverdale, *Fruitfull Lessons upon the Passion* (1593), fol. L*.

[Judas] felt assured that his treachery was concealed by a kiss and by soothing words. This salutation, or exclamation, therefore, was a pretense of compassion. I offer the same opinion about the kiss. . . . Thus he excels the rest in the appearance of affection, when he appears to be deeply grieved at being separated from his master; but how little he gained by his deception is evident from Christ's reply. . . . For Christ does not employ an ironical address when he calls him friend, but charges him with ingratitude, that, from being an intimate friend, who sat at his table, he had become a traitor, as had been predicted in the psalms. . . . This shows clearly what I hinted a little ago that, whatever may be the artifices by which hypocrites conceal themselves and whatever may be the pretenses which they hold out, when they come into the presence of the Lord, their crimes become manifest; and it even becomes the ground of a severer sentence against them, that, having been admitted into the bosom of Christ, they treacherously rise up against him. For the word *friend*, as we have stated, contains within itself a sharp sting. COMMENTARY ON A HARMONY OF THE EVANGELISTS.[6]

A CHRISTIAN MUST ENDURE INJUSTICE AND EVIL WITHOUT RESORTING TO VIOLENCE.

MARTIN LUTHER: Look at St. Peter in the garden. He wanted to defend his Lord Christ with the sword and cut off Malchus's ear. Tell me, did not Peter have great right on his side? Was it not an intolerable injustice that they were going to take from Christ not only his property but also his life? Indeed, they not only took his life and property, but in so doing they entirely suppressed the gospel by which they were to be saved and thus robbed heaven. You have not yet suffered such a wrong, dear friends. But see what Christ does and teaches in this case. However great the injustice was, he nevertheless stopped St. Peter, bade him put up his sword, and would not allow him to avenge or prevent this injustice. In addition, he passes a

sentence of death upon him, as though upon a murderer, and said, "He who takes the sword will perish by the sword." This should help us understand that we do not have the right to use the sword simply because someone has done us an injustice and because the law and justice are on our side. We must also have received power and authority from God to use the sword and to punish wrong. Furthermore, a Christian should also suffer it if anyone desires to keep the gospel away from them by force. . . .

Now, if you are genuine Christians, you must certainly act in this same way and follow this example. If you do not do this, then you give up the name of Christian and the claim that the Christian law is on your side, for then you are certainly not Christians but are opposing Christ and his law, his doctrine, and his example. But if you do follow the example of Christ, you will soon see God's miracles and he will help you as he helped Christ, whom he avenged after the completion of his passion in such a way that his gospel and his kingdom won a powerful victory and gained the upper hand, in spite of all his enemies. ADMONITION TO PEACE.[7]

THE IMPATIENCE OF THE SWORD. PILGRAM

MARPECK: Are these not truly the unspiritual Philistines who, together with their Goliath, trust only in human power? Such a trust is contrary to the true manner of the patience of Christ; it contradicts the genuine and true David. Armor and sword do not fit him. He kills all his enemies with their own sword. Under the new David, their own impatience consumes them. As the Lord says, "Whoever fights with the sword will be destroyed by it." Human coercion will destroy all who [support] a human, forcibly imposed faith, and all who claim the word of faith, but who trust and depend upon human protection and power; like Peter, they will be driven to a denial. Peter also thought that Christ would be a temporal and earthly redeemer who would save them with carnal weapons. Thus, Peter pledged that he was prepared

---

[6]CTS 3:240-42 (CO 45:728-29); citing Ps 41:9; 55:12-14.

[7]LW 46:29-30* (WA 18:311-12); citing Jn 18:10.

to give his life for the Lord. However, he received no help from the Lord in his carnal fighting; Jesus, for example, helped the one whose ear Peter had cut off. Then, Peter denied the Lord three times, and swore that he had never known the man. CONCERNING THE LOWLINESS OF CHRIST.[8]

FULFILLING THE SCRIPTURES. MARTIN LUTHER: That is why the Evangelists state that Christ suffered in order that the Scripture might be fulfilled. God wanted things done in the way it pleased him; he could very well have done otherwise but it was not his will to do so. . . . Accordingly, Christ now says here, "Thus it must be, in order that the Scriptures be fulfilled," as much as to say, "I would have been glad if it could have been otherwise, but don't inquire further, believe the Scripture; if you don't want to believe and follow the Scripture, so be it." . . . For ourselves, we will stand with the little remnant of the faithful, trusting the Scriptures. With twelve legions of angels, the Lord could have totally wiped out, not only the Jews, but the whole world, indeed a hundred thousand worlds, one upon the other. But he needed to suffer that the Scripture might be fulfilled; so, not because he was compelled or forced, but to fulfill the Scripture, that God might be found faithful and true to his Word. Human reason says, "Is God really so weak that he lets himself be crucified? Why does he humiliate himself this way?" But Christ replies, "Be gone with your sophistries! I could well have arranged things differently." THE HAPPENINGS IN GETHSEMANE.[9]

26:57-68 Jesus on Trial

THE WISDOM OF SILENCE. HULDRYCH ZWINGLI: In that Christ holds his peace at the false witnesses, it was not so much because of his meekness, as because of his wisdom. This example ought they to follow which are oppressed with false witnesses and chiefly before such a judge as esteems and gives credit to false witnesses. For then no answers or excuses are worth anything, it shall be most safeguarded to keep silence. I adjure thee that you tell me, whether you be the Son of God? By this question, it is manifested that the Jews confessed and knew right well that the Messiah should be the Son of God. But they ask him this captious question, to the intent that they might cavil and maliciously accuse him in his answer, that is, that they might take and trap him in his talk, that he, who had made himself the Son of God, should therefore be worthy to die, and that according to the law. . . .

This is a gentle and healthful admonition, as though he would say, "Indeed you see me now humble, and as it were the son of the carpenter, but be not offended with this my humility, for now is the time of humility; I do not now show forth my glory and power, but shortly you shall see what manner of one I am." He is guilty of death. The chief priest speaks this to his accomplices, which were like unto himself, namely, haters of Christ, "he has blasphemed," he says, "what need do we have of any more witnesses?" They feign themselves, as though they had a care for the glory of God, when as nevertheless their minds are ungodly and impure. A BRIEF REHEARSAL OF THE DEATH, RESURRECTION, AND ASCENSION OF CHRIST.[10]

JESUS FINALLY SPEAKS. WILLIAM PERKINS: Now follows the third point, which is the adjuring of Christ. For Caiaphas, the high priest, charged him to tell him whether he was the Christ, the Son of God or no. To adjure a man is to charge and command him in the name of God to declare a truth, not only because God is witness thereof, but also because he is a judge to revenge if he speaks not the truth. . . . And here is a thing at which to wonder: Caiaphas, the high priest, adjures him in the name of God, who is very God, even the Son of God. And this shows what a small account he made of the name of God; for he did it only to get advantage on Christ's words, and so do many

---

[8]CRR 2:448-49.
[9]Luther, *Complete Sermons*, 5:380-82.

[10]Zwingli, *A Briefe Rehersal*, 91-92*.

nowadays, who for a little profit or gain make a matter of nothing to abuse the name of God a thousand ways.

Christ being thus adjured, though silent before, yet now in reverence to God's majesty, answered and said, first, "You have said it." And in St. Mark, "I am he." In this answer, appears the wonderful providence of God. For though Caiaphas take hence the occasion of condemning Christ, yet has he drawn from him a most excellent confession, that he is the Son of God and our only Savior. And by this means, he proceeds to shut heaven against himself and to open the same for us. AN EXPOSI-TION OF THE APOSTLES' CREED.[11]

THE MESSIAH, THE SON OF GOD. JOHN CALVIN: From the words of Caiaphas we may infer that it was at that time common among the Jews to bestow on the Messiah the title of the Son of God; for this form of interrogation could not have originated in any other way than from the ordinary custom; and, indeed, they had learned from the predictions of Scripture that he was not less the Son of God than the Son of David. It appears, too, that Caiaphas employed this epithet, with the view either of terrifying Christ or of exciting a prejudice against him; as if he had said, "See where you are going; for you cannot call yourself the Christ, without claiming, at the same time, the appellation of Son of God, with which Scripture honors him." . . .

I have no doubt that the servants were embold-ened to spit on Christ, and to strike him with greater insolence, after they had seen that the council, so far as their decision had influence, condemned him to death. The object of all these expressions of contempt was to show that nothing was more unlikely than that he should be a prince of prophets, who, in consequence of being blind-folded, was not able even to ward off blows. But this insolence was turned by the providence of God to a very different purpose; for the face of Christ, dishonored by spitting and blows, has

restored to us that image which had been disfig-ured, and almost effaced, by sin. COMMENTARY ON A HARMONY OF THE EVANGELISTS.[12]

26:69-75 Peter Denies Jesus

HUMILITY COMES AFTER THE FALL. JUAN DE VALDÉS: Learning through all Christ's history that St. Peter was very lively and very proud, taking the lead in everything, and frequently without consideration—as he did when he rebuked Christ, because he spoke of his death, and as he did when he said that he should not be offended when Christ had told him that he would be offended, and as he did when he cut off another man's ear—I understand that Christ purposed (as I have before stated), to mortify vivacity in St. Peter by allowing him to fall into temptation in order that he might learn to know himself, and might be humbled; as, indeed, he did learn to know himself and was humbled.

And here, I understand the reason why God often allows those who are his to fall into tempta-tions: it is because the human mind is exceedingly vain and arrogant and, therefore, needs to be let down, beaten down, and humbled. Here likewise, I learn that it concerns the Christian to desire, as one might say, not to deny Christ for anything upon earth and not to presume, concerning himself, that he will be self-sufficient not to deny him; but, let him ask God to give him strength to enable him to resist the temptations, by which he will be solicited to deny him.

Here also, I understand the reason why, to Christians who propose and resolve upon many things that are holy and good, they frequently issue quite contrary to what they determined: it is because their resolution is taken without consider-ation of their own personal impotence. . . .

St. Peter's denial proceeded from weakness and frailty; although, in the first instance, he denied simply; in the second he denied with an oath; while in the third he denied, adding curses to the

---

[11]Perkins, *An Exposition of the Symbole or Creede of the Apostles*, 197-98*.

[12]CTS 3:256, 259 (CO 45:739, 740).

oath. Where I understand that, if St. Peter had denied, having resolved to deny, having made up his mind to do so, taking pleasure in doing so, he would not have wept bitterly, as he did immediately upon his repentance; nay, he would have done what Judas did upon his repentance, as St. Matthew presently relates, setting before us, after an example of frailty, wherewith the weak are comforted, another example of malignity, with which the malignant are made to quake. COMMENTARY UPON THE GOSPEL OF ST. MATTHEW.[13]

PETER'S WEAKNESS IS REFLECTED IN US. JOHN CALVIN: Peter's fall, which is here related, is a bright mirror of our weakness. In his repentance, also, a striking instance of the goodness and mercy of God is held out to us. This narrative, therefore, which relates to a single individual, contains a doctrine which may be applied to the whole church, and which indeed is highly useful, both to instruct those who are standing about anxiety and fear, and to encourage those who have fallen, by holding out to them the pledge of pardon. And first it ought to be observed that Peter acted inconsiderately when

he entered into the hall of the high priest. It was his duty, no doubt, to follow his master; but having been warned that he would revolt, he ought rather to have concealed himself in some corner, so as not to expose himself to an occasion of sinning. Thus, it frequently happens that believers, under an appearance of virtue, throw themselves within the reach of temptation.

It is therefore our duty to pray to the Lord to restrain and keep us by his Spirit, lest, going beyond our measure, we be immediately punished. We ought also to pray, whenever we commence any undertaking, that he may not permit us to fail in the midst of our efforts or at the beginning of the work, but may supply us with strength from heaven till the end. Conviction of our weakness ought not, indeed, to be a reason for indolence to prevent us from going wherever God calls us; but it ought to restrain our rashness so that we may not attempt anything beyond our calling; and it ought also to stimulate us to prayer that God, who has given us grace to begin well, may also continue to give us grace to persevere. COMMENTARY ON A HARMONY OF THE EVANGELISTS.[14]

---

[13]Valdés, *Commentary upon the Gospel of St. Matthew*, 472-74. [14]CTS 3:260* (CO 45:741-42).

27:1-31 THE SUFFERING OF THE CHRIST

When morning came, all the chief priests and the elders of the people took counsel against Jesus to put him to death. [2]And they bound him and led him away and delivered him over to Pilate the governor.

[3]Then when Judas, his betrayer, saw that Jesus[a] was condemned, he changed his mind and brought back the thirty pieces of silver to the chief priests and the elders, [4]saying, "I have sinned by betraying innocent blood." They said, "What is that to us? See to it yourself." [5]And throwing down the pieces of silver into the temple, he departed, and he went and hanged himself. [6]But the chief priests, taking the pieces of silver, said, "It is not lawful to put them into the treasury, since it is blood money." [7]So they took counsel and bought with them the potter's field as a burial place for strangers. [8]Therefore that field has been called the Field of Blood to this day. [9]Then was fulfilled what had been spoken by the prophet Jeremiah, saying, "And they took the thirty pieces of silver, the price of him on whom a price had been set by some of the sons of Israel, [10]and they gave them for the potter's field, as the Lord directed me."

[11]Now Jesus stood before the governor, and the governor asked him, "Are you the King of the Jews?" Jesus said, "You have said so." [12]But when he was accused by the chief priests and elders, he gave no answer. [13]Then Pilate said to him, "Do you not hear how many things they testify against you?" [14]But he gave him no answer, not even to a single charge, so that the governor was greatly amazed.

[15]Now at the feast the governor was accustomed to release for the crowd any one prisoner whom they wanted. [16]And they had then a notorious prisoner called Barabbas. [17]So when they had gathered, Pilate said to them, "Whom do you want me to release for you: Barabbas, or Jesus who is called Christ?" [18]For he knew that it was out of envy that they had delivered him up. [19]Besides, while he was sitting on the judgment seat, his wife sent word to him, "Have nothing to do with that righteous man, for I have suffered much because of him today in a dream." [20]Now the chief priests and the elders persuaded the crowd to ask for Barabbas and destroy Jesus. [21]The governor again said to them, "Which of the two do you want me to release for you?" And they said, "Barabbas." [22]Pilate said to them, "Then what shall I do with Jesus who is called Christ?" They all said, "Let him be crucified!" [23]And he said, "Why? What evil has he done?" But they shouted all the more, "Let him be crucified!"

[24]So when Pilate saw that he was gaining nothing, but rather that a riot was beginning, he took water and washed his hands before the crowd, saying, "I am innocent of this man's blood;[b] see to it yourselves." [25]And all the people answered, "His blood be on us and on our children!" [26]Then he released for them Barabbas, and having scourged[c] Jesus, delivered him to be crucified.

[27]Then the soldiers of the governor took Jesus into the governor's headquarters,[d] and they gathered the whole battalion[e] before him. [28]And they stripped him and put a scarlet robe on him, [29]and twisting together a crown of thorns, they put it on his head and put a reed in his right hand. And kneeling before him, they mocked him, saying, "Hail, King of the Jews!" [30]And they spit on him and took the reed and struck him on the head. [31]And when they had mocked him, they stripped him of the robe and put his own clothes on him and led him away to crucify him.

a Greek he   b Some manuscripts this righteous blood, or this righteous man's blood   c A Roman judicial penalty, consisting of a severe beating with a multi-lashed whip containing embedded pieces of bone and metal   d Greek the praetorium   e Greek cohort; a tenth of a Roman legion, usually about 600 men

OVERVIEW: Matthew reminds his readers of the collusion that lurks behind Jesus' trial, which the reformers note. As Luther indicates, the sinister conniving of the leaders provides a stark contrast with Jesus' innocence. The tragic episode of Judas' betrayal ends with his own guilt-ridden death.

Two elements of the biblical text draw the attention of most Reformation interpreters. First, the ordering of Matthew's narrative creates an interesting juxtaposition between the repentance of Peter and the despair of Judas. There are no immediate details given for Peter's repentance other than that he wept bitterly. However, much more detail is given to Judas' "repentance": his change of thinking, the declaration of Jesus' innocence, his admission of sin, along with returning the silver, all of which reflect Judas's sense of guilt. Zwingli suggests that Judas did not experience genuine, godly sorrow, which leads to repentance, but human guilt, which leads to despair (see 2 Cor 7:10). Second, Matthew attributes the prophecy, which is fulfilled, to Jeremiah, though the text's closest parallel is Zechariah 11:12-13. A variety of solutions, including a scribal error, were suggested by the reformers, though none completely remove the difficulties.

Jesus appears before Pilate, and although Matthew reports little of the dialogue, it is clear that Jesus' manner and responses amazed Pilate. The governor attempts a political maneuver to escape the pressure of the religious leaders while at the same time sparing Jesus' life. The reformers point out that Pilate's wife calls Jesus a righteous man and Pilate himself attests to Jesus' innocence by asking about the evil he had committed. The commentators contrast the innocence of Jesus with the guilt of the characters in the narrative: Judas, Pilate, and the Jewish leaders.

Matthew provides few details of Jesus' brutal treatment by the Roman guards. The guards' mocking attestation of Jesus as the King of the Jews provides an inner-textual link with a similar declaration by the pious magi earlier in the text (Mt 2:2). Whereas the discerning magi subvert the desires of Herod and preserve Jesus' life, the guards comply with Israel's leaders and take an active part in his crucifixion. The reformers often discuss the details of Jesus' passion as being given to provide insight into the depth of his suffering and to connect that suffering with messianic predictions, whether Jesus' own predictions or those of the Old Testament prophets.

27:1-10 *Judas's Despair*

GUILTY MEN CONDEMN INNOCENT JESUS.

MARTIN LUTHER: In the house of the high priest Caiaphas, it became obvious, also to the consciences of the witnesses themselves, that the Lord was innocent since the witnesses could not agree until the high priest asked him whether he was the Christ, the Son of God. But here before Pilate, his innocence becomes apparent before all the people, and his adversaries and accusers have the wind taken out of their sails, not only in the council, privately among themselves, but also publicly before the Roman court. . . . [Jesus] made an exemplary confession before the high priests and before Governor Pilate; thus not only before his own people, the Jews, who were agitating for his death, but also before the whole Roman Empire. . . .

The Evangelist Matthew reports two things here. The first is that the high priests and elders of the people have taken counsel concerning Jesus and delivered him to the governor, Pilate. The second point has to do with events as they developed for the betrayer, Judas. First, the record tells how the high priests and elders of the people plotted together to put Jesus to death. This deliberation among themselves was done without and apart from the testimony of witnesses. It was a secret, clandestine meeting where they connived to formulate what they would allege and present as evidence before the governor, Pilate. Because it is a secret consultation, the Evangelist does not want to announce it at this place. But later the gist of their counseling together is submitted in the accusation before the governor. They allege and accuse Christ of being a murderer and heretic. But now they debate how they want to formulate their accusation before Pilate, namely: We want to accuse him of being an insurrectionist and a murderer; if that will not do the trick, we shall then say that he is a blasphemer and seducer of the people. There they plot secretly, but later these thoughts erupt publicly. . . . Christ suffers at the hand of both authorities and yet his innocence comes to light and wickedness is exposed, for they are doing him an injustice. The high priests have already condemned him to death, and now Pilate condemns him as well. THIRD SERMON OF HOLY WEEK (1534).[1]

TRUE REPENTANCE VERSUS FALSE REPENTANCE. ROBERT ALLEN: Now the excellency of truth above hypocrisy, we may also easily perceive by comparing these examples of Judas and Peter together. For although the repentance of Judas might externally be thought greater than Peter's—insomuch as Judas confessed his sin openly and restored the money which he had received for the hire of his wickedness, but Peter wept not openly, he does not openly confess his sin, but only secretly to God when he had withdrawn himself from company—yet because that which Peter did was done in truth and he sought to God for mercy, in truth of his goodness; therefore was it accepted of God, when as the repentance of Judas being extorted and in despair of God's mercy through an evil conscience both it and Judas himself were rejected. This repentance growing from an evil cause, it rested in an evil issue. For he most unnaturally, cruelly, and violently threw down himself as it were from a high gallows, or windbeam, and so hanged himself, that with the vehemence of the fall, his bowels gushed out of his body. Thus (as the common saying is) he must needs go whom the devil drives. For like as he gave entertainment to the devil, to fill his heart to practice his wickedness; so no doubt, through the just judgment of God, the devil's fall was as great with him, to drive him to work his horrible mischief upon himself. . . . And if at any time we fall, let us pray earnestly to God that it may please him, to vouchsafe to give us Peter's repentance, which was a true and believing repentance; and not the confounding and despairing repentance of Judas. THE DOCTRINE OF THE GOSPEL.[2]

GOD'S JUDGMENT ON SIN. HULDRYCH ZWINGLI: In Judas is set forth a most horrible example of God's judgment of purposed malice and unfaithfulness upon those who sin, of which men the betrayer is a figure. God calls all men mercifully to his grace, but they whom the devil blinds and moves do despise him who calls them; or being allured to be in the number of the sons of God, do go backward, wrapping themselves in sins after such a sort, that they can by no means be pulled back again. Satan does so blind them that they cannot ponder the heinousness of their wickedness until he has thrown them down headlong into hell, and then, as the length be their eyes opened, that they may set the greatness of their wickedness and the sharpness of the punishment, but yet in such a sort that in the meantime they cannot consider the exceeding greatness of God's mercy, neither can they run to the same. They are sorry indeed, not because they have offended the chief God, but because they see their end prepared for them. And thereby comes desperation and tormenting of the conscience, in which they perish. Let us, therefore, take heed from shedding of innocent blood, from covetousness, and from willful stubbornness, for they who are possessed with these mischievous acts are similar to Judas and shall come to the similar end that he did. To this are they driven at the length, who would never obey the Lord admonishing them. It profited Judas nothing to be in the number of the twelve, nothing to be the disciple of Christ, nothing to be partaker of the holy table, nothing also to have preached the word of truth, but for all this at the length his hypocrisy was made manifest and also punished. So, these things shall profit us nothing if [it] so be that we shall be unfaithful and hypocrites. It is impossible for any man to please God without faith. A BRIEF REHEARSAL OF THE DEATH, RESURRECTION, AND ASCENSION OF CHRIST.[3]

MATTHEW AND THE PROPHETS. THOMAS JACKSON: For my part, if I could be fully persuaded (as I am not to the contrary) that the reason why St. Matthew did purposely ascribe these words in

---

[1]Luther, *Complete Sermons*, 5:404-6.
[2]Allen, *The Doctrine of the Gospel* (1606), 312-13.
[3]Zwingli, *A Briefe Rehersal*, 100-101*.

the prophet Zechariah, to Jeremiah, was because the prophet Zechariah had Jeremiah in this and many other prophecies for his instructor or guide. . . .

Maldonado, in his comments upon St. Matthew,[†] is very free and not afraid, as Junius and other good writers are, to admit of a misnomer, neither occasioned by the Evangelist's forgetfulness, nor from mistake of letters, or abbreviations by the transcribers, but rather by a voluntary insertion of the prophet Jeremiah his name by some bold transcriber or interpreter, when as the Evangelist had only said, "the prophet" (as his usual manner is) without any intimation what prophet it was, leaving that wholly to the diligent reader's search or observation. For so he does in that remarkable prophecy, "Behold a virgin shall conceive, and bear a son." . . . He says no more than all this was foretold by the prophet, without any mention or intimation of Isaiah's name: nor does he name the prophet Hosea, when he records the fulfilling of his prophecy, "Out of Egypt have I called my Son." And in verse 23 of the same chapter [Matthew 2], he shall be called a "Nazarene." He giving the reason why Joseph, by the disposition of the divine providence, did divert his intended return to Bethlehem, where Christ was born, and took up his dwelling in Nazareth, says this was done that it might be fulfilled which was spoken by the prophets, not so much as intimating the name of any one prophet, by whom this was foretold. And if the curious reader would observe his allegations of prophetical testimonies, throughout his whole gospel, he shall find the prophet's name (whose testimony he most faithfully records) concealed or omitted three times as often as it is expressed. And in those few places, wherein the prophet's name, whose authority he alleged, is expressed, it may without any danger be questioned whether they were so expressed or inserted by interpreters or transcribers. For the addition of names, or change of some vowels, does in no way vitiate the divine truth of prophecy; though the custom of latter interpreters or translators, be far more commendable to express the prophet's name, or the chapter and verse, to which the evangelical story refers,

in the margin, not in the body of the text. However, the misnomers of persons or places inserted to the body of the discourse does [in] no way corrupt the true sense, and meaning, either of historical or prophetical truth; the error is imputable only to the transcriber or interpreter, not to the author. THE HUMILIATION OF THE SON OF GOD.[4]

UNDERVALUING JESUS. JOHN CALVIN: How the name of Jeremiah crept in, I confess that I do not know nor do I give myself much trouble to inquire. The passage itself plainly shows that the name of Jeremiah has been put down by mistake, instead of Zechariah; for in Jeremiah we find nothing of this sort, nor any thing that even approaches to it. Now that other passage, if some degree of skill be not used in applying it, might seem to have been improperly distorted to a wrong meaning; but if we attend to the rule which the apostles followed in quoting Scripture, we shall easily perceive that what we find there is highly applicable to Christ. The Lord, after having complained that his labors were of no avail, so long as he discharged the office of a shepherd, says that he is compelled by the troublesome and unpleasant nature of the employment to relinquish it altogether, and, therefore, declares that he will break his crook, and will be a shepherd no longer. He afterward adds that when he asked his salary, they gave him thirty pieces of silver. The import of these words is that he was treated quite contemptuously as if he had been some mean and ordinary laborer.

. . . It became necessary that what had formerly been spoken figuratively should now be literally and visibly accomplished in his person. So, then, when he was compelled by their malice to take leave of them and to withdraw his labors from them as unworthy of such a privilege, they valued him at thirty pieces of silver. And this disdain of the Son of God was the crowning act of their extreme impiety: the price of him that was valued. Matthew does not quote the words of Zechariah; for he merely alludes to the metaphor, under which

---

[4]Jackson, *Works*, 2:895-96; citing Mt 2:15. [†]JMG 498-501.

the Lord then complains of the ingratitude of the people. But the meaning is the same, that while the Jews ought to have entirely devoted themselves, and all that they possessed, to the Lord, they contemptuously dismissed him. By this clause, Matthew confirms the statement that this was not done without the providence of God because, while they have a different object in view, they unconsciously fulfill an ancient prediction. COMMENTARY ON A HARMONY OF THE EVANGELISTS.[5]

27:11-26 Jesus Before Pilate

MEEKNESS OF JESUS. DESIDERIUS ERASMUS: When Jesus stood before the governor as guilty, they accused him of many things, speaking nothing of blasphemy, of the religion, of the temple defiled and broken, and of the coming of the Son of Man, with the things by which they knew that Pilate, thinking little of such superstition, would be little moved; they try in other feigned faults, which might stir the president's mind against Jesus, saying, "We have found this man going about to subvert our nation, and for hiding tributes to be given to Caesar, and saying that he is Christ the king." Pilate hearing mention of the king, because this seemed to touch Caesar, demanded of Jesus, "Are you the king of the Jews?" Jesus lest he should seem proud, if he should make no answer, says, "You have said it," not utterly denying that he was king, but yet adding that his kingdom is spiritual not worldly, that it pertains nothing to Caesar or Herod. Again, when his accusers called upon the matter, Pilate desiring to get out of him, whereby he might be delivered, "Do you not hear the great faults they lay against you?" But to these Jesus answered utterly nothing, insomuch as the president marveled greatly that an innocent man in danger of death did keep silence with so great meekness. PARAPHRASES.[6]

A DREADFUL CHOICE. JOHN CROMPE: Seeing you [Jesus] are balanced in the scales with

Barabbas, the greatest malefactor of your time, and a necessity laid upon the people of releasing either you or him, it cannot possibly be imagined but that you must be taken, and he cast; you saved, and he condemned. For whereas he has been a thief and taken away by violence the bread of the poor and needy, why, you have been a feeder of them and a supplier of their wants and necessities upon all occasions. Whereas he has been a cutter and robber on the highways, and by that means wounded and mangled the peaceable passengers, traveling as it were, between Jerusalem and Jericho; why, you as the good Samaritan, have healed them again, by binding up their wounds and pouring in wine and oil unto them. Whereas he has been a murderer and slain the living, why, you have been a reviver and restorer of life to those who have been dead. All these therefore, and thousands more, to which you have been helpful and beneficial in one kind or other, will call and cry out loud, set free and at liberty to us, not Barabbas our cruel enemy; but Christ our courteous friend; even, our kind and common benefactor.

For it is impossible, even in the judgment of Pilate himself, that any should be so ungrateful as to do the contrary, which occasioned him to make tender of the most notorious delinquent that was then in their custody, to be in competition with Christ; that so he might be sure—as he upon good ground and reason conceived and imagined—not to fail of the freedom and release of Jesus. And yet for all this, they cry out again, with one voice and unanimous consent, "Not this man but Barabbas," as you see in the text. . . .

An unhappy exchange for you Jews, thus to desire the wolf before the lamb; the noxious and violent, before the righteous and innocent; the impious and ungodly life-taker, before the peaceable and merciful life-giver; wretched men that you are, so to prefer death before life; sin before God; and Barabbas, no, the devil before Christ with whom you shall be sure, for your pains, to suffer eternal pains in hell fire; except you can and do repent and be heartily sorry for the same. . . . For Pilate, although before he had openly declared both

---

[5]CTS 3:272-73 (CO 45:749); citing Zech 11:13.
[6]EP 105r*.

that Christ was innocent and that he had authority to quit him; yet giving place either to the favor or fury of this multitude of the Jews rather than to justice, he pronounced sentence of death against him and delivered him to the pleasure of his enemies, to do with him even what they would. THE GREAT WEEK OF CHRIST'S PASSION.[7]

JESUS' INNOCENCE DECLARED. JOHN CALVIN: Although the thoughts which had passed through the mind of Pilate's wife during the day might be the cause of her dream, yet there can be no doubt that she suffered these torments, not in a natural way (such as happens to us every day), but by an extraordinary inspiration of God. It has been commonly supposed that the devil stirred up this woman in order to retard the redemption of mankind; which is in the highest degree improbable, since it was he who excited and inflamed, to such a degree, the priests and scribes to put Christ to death. We ought to conclude, on the contrary, that God the Father took many methods of attesting the innocence of Christ, that it might evidently appear that he suffered death in the place of others, that is, in our place. God intended that Pilate should so frequently acquit him with his own mouth before condemning him, that in his undeserved condemnation the true satisfaction for our sins might be the more brightly displayed. Matthew expressly mentions this, that none may wonder at the extreme solicitude of Pilate when he debates with the people in the midst of a tumult for the purpose of saving the life of a man whom he despised. And, indeed, by the terrors which his wife had suffered during the night, God compelled him to defend the innocence of his own Son; not to rescue him from death, but only to make it manifest that in the room of others he endured that punishment which he had not deserved. COMMENTARY ON A HARMONY OF THE EVANGELISTS.[8]

THE DEATH OF THE INNOCENT MAN. HEINRICH BULLINGER: With these words he very clearly shows that the judge passed his sentence on Christ, compelled not by the evidence of the case or by what is right and fair, but overcome by the malicious wickedness of the accusers, or rather, by their brutal savageness and from fear of a riot. And it is the nature of all wicked judges to have regard for the person in their judgment, and to judge from upset emotions, hate, fear, hope, love, or grief, and not from fairness and goodness. He appears in this case to fear the riot, but in far less important matters and facing a more dangerous, obstinate mob, he exhibited not even the slightest fear. No, he had already at this point slaughtered rioters in the harshest ways by sending soldiers upon them, and straightaway he suppressed them. Josephus[†] testifies that he did that more than once. But here he utilizes a new formula for condemning or passing sentence, one which you could scarcely find employed throughout all of human history. For, first he absolves the one whom he is condemning. Furthermore, he does not openly condemn him, but permits him to be like a condemned person for their pleasure. For, he plainly testifies that Jesus is blameless and innocent and one who in no way deserves death; meanwhile, he hands him over to the judgment of the accusers. By doing this, by giving him up, he was condemning a completely just man unjustly and against his own conscience, a man whom he knew without question should be set free and defended. But by standing up and making the assertion, he was casting all the blame back onto the Jews, invoking a defense for those things which were going to be done in regard to that innocent spilled blood. And so that this thing might be more manifest and that it might be less likely for people to forget, he consecrates himself with a well-known and visible symbol. For, he orders them to bring him water, and sitting there in the hall and in a conspicuous place before the tribunal, and while everyone is watching, he washes his hands, explaining his actions at the same time with these words: "I am innocent of the blood of this righteous man; you see to this matter. . . ."

---

[7] Crompe, *Hebdomada Magna: or the Great Week of Christ's Passion* (1641), 90-101*; citing Mk 15:7.
[8] CTS 3:283 (CO 45:756).

The words that Pilate added to the rite are plain and clear. For in the clearest possible way, he testifies that Jesus is righteous and innocent. Second, he wishes himself to seem innocent as well, since he makes it out that he is forced into this position by the Jews. For this reason, he adds, "You see to it," transferring all blame from himself onto the Jews, just as a little before we heard the priests saying to Judas as well, "You see to it." And I think that we should pay close attention to this passage concerning the innocence of Christ, for, from here the sure salvation of the faithful is certainly derived—the fact that the Lord is condemned and dies, but he does not die by his own fault or as someone who is guilty. For, the indisputable testimony of his innocence by a Gentile judge is witnessed by such a great throng. Moreover, he dies on account of our sins, and he is condemned because of what we have done. Because of this, a little above I reminded the reader that his condemnation is the liberation or absolution of the faithful, and that his death is our life, which is the most important and useful thing we can take from this passage. COMMENTARY ON MATTHEW.[9]

27:27-31 Mistreatment of Jesus

A CRUEL DEATH. HULDRYCH ZWINGLI: The wonderful great cruelty of the soldiers is described by the Evangelists, whether they were hired of the Jewish priests to do it or whether they did it of their own lust, so that they are rather to be counted beasts than men, which have so put away all humanity. Most cruel wolves exercise their fierceness upon a most meek lamb. Neither can they be satisfied with their outrageousness by any means, they beat him, they spit upon him, they mock him, only they devour him not. He who clothes all things is stripped out of his clothes. He who adorns all things is made deformed. The meekness of Christ is to be marked which receives all reproach in himself for us, bearing his own cross to deliver us from everlasting punishment. He took upon him all our sins, making satisfaction upon the tree for them that we might know to whom we should fly and on whom we should lay the burden of our sins. A BRIEF REHEARSAL OF THE DEATH, RESURRECTION, AND ASCENSION OF CHRIST.[10]

FROM PROPHET TO KING. KING JAMES I OF ENGLAND (VI OF SCOTLAND): This purple or scarlet dye may also admit a metaphorical allusion to the blood of Christ that was shed for us. For the robes of his flesh were dyed in that true purple and scarlet dye of his blood, whose blood must wash our sins that we may appear holy and unspotted before him in our white robes, washed in the blood of the Lamb. They first stripped him then, for it is thought, and not improbably, that his own clothes were after the ancient form of a prophet's garment; only his coat, without any seam in it, was to fulfill the prophecy of David, that they should cast lots for it; and did also signify the indivisible unity of the church, which I pray God the true church of Christ would now well remember. Now therefore, when they were to declare him a king, they took off his prophet's garment, and put a royal robe upon him. TWO MEDITATIONS.[11]

CHRIST'S MISTREATMENT FULFILLS PROPHECY. JUAN DE VALDÉS: I hold it to be certain that Christ was beyond all comparison more offended by the malignity with which he was accused by the Jews than by the brutality with which he was maltreated and derided by the Gentiles; who, because Christ was accused of having made himself a king, put him forward in derision and mockery in regal garb, in order to treat him afterward worse than a servant and slave.

It is said that the robe in which they mantled him was a soldier's cloak; I rather think it to have been a royal robe. When they compelled Simon, the

---

[9]Bullinger, In . . . Evangelium secundum Matthaeum commentariorum, II:252v-253r. †Bullinger is perhaps referring to Josephus's commentary on the Aqueduct Riots. Jewish War 2.175-77.

[10]Zwingli, A Briefe Rehersal, 122-23. [11]King James I (James Stuart), Two Meditations of the King's Majesty, 20-21.

Cyrene, to carry Christ's cross, I do not think that they purposed to relieve Christ of fatigue, but to get the more quickly to the place of crucifixion. . . .

Here I will say this, that the one who shall consider Christ standing among those soldiers, treated with such inhumanity and brutality, and shall ponder those words of Isaiah, where he says in 53:3, "He is despised and rejected of man, a man of sorrows, and experienced in grief from whom we hid, as it were, our facets; he was despised, and we esteemed him not," will be constrained to say that Isaiah, in vision, saw Christ precisely in that plight in which the Evangelist reports him to have been. Whence it may be gathered how profitable it is for those who are tempted to doubt in relation to Christian truth to compare with simplicity and humility the prophecies of Christ's passion and death with the narratives written by the Evangelists. COMMENTARY UPON THE GOSPEL OF ST. MATTHEW.[12]

---

[12]Valdés, *Commentary upon the Gospel of St. Matthew*, 482-83.

27:32-66 THE CRUCIFIXION, DEATH, AND BURIAL OF JESUS

[32] As they went out, they found a man of Cyrene, Simon by name. They compelled this man to carry his cross. [33] And when they came to a place called Golgotha (which means Place of a Skull), [34] they offered him wine to drink, mixed with gall, but when he tasted it, he would not drink it. [35] And when they had crucified him, they divided his garments among them by casting lots. [36] Then they sat down and kept watch over him there. [37] And over his head they put the charge against him, which read, "This is Jesus, the King of the Jews." [38] Then two robbers were crucified with him, one on the right and one on the left. [39] And those who passed by derided him, wagging their heads [40] and saying, "You who would destroy the temple and rebuild it in three days, save yourself! If you are the Son of God, come down from the cross." [41] So also the chief priests, with the scribes and elders, mocked him, saying, [42] "He saved others; he cannot save himself. He is the King of Israel; let him come down now from the cross, and we will believe in him. [43] He trusts in God; let God deliver him now, if he desires him. For he said, 'I am the Son of God.'" [44] And the robbers who were crucified with him also reviled him in the same way.

[45] Now from the sixth hour[a] there was darkness over all the land[b] until the ninth hour.[c] [46] And about the ninth hour Jesus cried out with a loud voice, saying, "Eli, Eli, lema sabachthani?" that is, "My God, my God, why have you forsaken me?" [47] And some of the bystanders, hearing it, said, "This man is calling Elijah." [48] And one of them at once ran and took a sponge, filled it with sour wine, and put it on a reed and gave it to him to drink. [49] But the others said, "Wait, let us see whether Elijah will come to save him." [50] And Jesus cried out again with a loud voice and yielded up his spirit.

[51] And behold, the curtain of the temple was torn in two, from top to bottom. And the earth shook, and the rocks were split. [52] The tombs also were opened. And many bodies of the saints who had fallen asleep were raised, [53] and coming out of the tombs after his resurrection they went into the holy city and appeared to many. [54] When the centurion and those who were with him, keeping watch over Jesus, saw the earthquake and what took place, they were filled with awe and said, "Truly this was the Son[d] of God!"

[55] There were also many women there, looking on from a distance, who had followed Jesus from Galilee, ministering to him, [56] among whom were Mary Magdalene and Mary the mother of James and Joseph and the mother of the sons of Zebedee.

[57] When it was evening, there came a rich man from Arimathea, named Joseph, who also was a disciple of Jesus. [58] He went to Pilate and asked for the body of Jesus. Then Pilate ordered it to be given to him. [59] And Joseph took the body and wrapped it in a clean linen shroud [60] and laid it in his own new tomb, which he had cut in the rock. And he rolled a great stone to the entrance of the tomb and went away. [61] Mary Magdalene and the other Mary were there, sitting opposite the tomb.

[62] The next day, that is, after the day of Preparation, the chief priests and the Pharisees gathered before Pilate [63] and said, "Sir, we remember how that impostor said, while he was still alive, 'After three days I will rise.' [64] Therefore order the tomb to be made secure until the third day, lest his disciples go and steal him away and tell the people, 'He has risen from the dead,' and the last fraud will be worse than the first." [65] Pilate said to them, "You have a guard[e] of soldiers. Go, make it as secure as you can." [66] So they went and made the tomb secure by sealing the stone and setting a guard.

a That is, noon b Or earth c That is, 3 p.m. d Or a son e Or Take a guard

OVERVIEW: In the movement from the scourging to the crucifixion, the attention shifts back to the Jewish crowds and religious leaders seen in the sign declaring that Jesus is the King of the Jews. Calvin explains how the scene at the cross hinges on the verbal ridicules or tests of Jesus. Reminiscent of the devil's temptation of Jesus, the passersby give him two tests to prove his divine Sonship, both requiring him to avoid death. The religious leaders join the mocking chorus with a test of promising to believe him if he comes down from the cross. Among the Reformation commentators, Wolfgang Musculus points out that the fact that they remain in their unbelief even after all of his miracles and even Lazarus's resurrection demonstrates the vanity of their words.

The reformers often connect the scene of the crucifixion with the poetic images of Psalm 22, thereby providing a fuller understanding of Christ's suffering and his cry of dereliction. From the psalm, the afflicted one appears to be forsaken by God as his enemies mock, demean, punish, and even kill him. However, Psalm 22:24 declares that the Lord has not despised or rejected him. Instead, when he cries to the Lord for help, God hears him. William Perkins explains that Jesus, as the Son of God, was not forsaken, which would be impossible in the intratrinitarian relationships.

Joseph of Arimathea is an intriguing character in the burial narrative, and he draws the reformers' attention. Calvin describes the importance of Jesus' burial in order to declare the reality of his death. He also notes that Joseph's willingness to identify with Jesus in his death takes an incredible act of courage and faith. Furthermore, the Reformation commentators note the fear that drives the religious leaders even in Jesus' death. Instead of reveling in their victory, they are terrified of an even greater defeat, which would indeed come.

27:32-44 *The Crucifixion*

RECOGNIZING THE KING. JOHN BOURCHIER: King of the Jews, not carnally, but spiritually; not by circumcision, but by faith; king of those who do believe with the heart and confess him with the mouth to be the true Messiah. Pilate was blind and could not see this. The Jews were obstinate and would not know this. But now it is revealed to infants and toddlers, by regeneration; for all that are born of God know that by nature they were sin's subjects . . . yet, for their redemption, they find him here, *Regem Judaeorum* (King of the Jews), king of all those that confess his name. . . .

With this title did the wise men seek him, "Where is he that is born king of the Jews?" With this title did the soldiers deride him, "Hail king of the Jews." And with this title did Pilate think to dishonor him, as it is in this text, "Jesus of Nazareth, king of the Jews." A king. Indeed he was, though Pilate knew it not, whose kingdom, though it be in this world, yet is it not of this world, having nothing in it that is temporal or terrestrial but all spiritual and celestial; depending not upon humans, but upon God, consisting not in riches, pomp, cities, castles, forts, armies, but in righteousness, peace, and joy in the Holy Ghost. He is the universal monarch, in whose hands are the hearts of kings, whose viceregents only they are here upon earth. JESUS OF NAZARETH.[1]

CHRIST AS THE PERFECT SAVIOR. JOHN CALVIN: These circumstances carry great weight; for they place before us the extreme abasement of the Son of God, that we may see more clearly how much our salvation cost him, and that, reflecting that we justly deserved all the punishments which he endured, we may be more and more excited to repentance. For in this exhibition, God has plainly showed to us how wretched our condition would have been if we had not a Redeemer. But all that Christ endured in himself ought to be applied for our consolation. This certainly was more cruel than all the other tortures that they upbraided and reviled and tormented him as one that had been cast off and forsaken by God. And, therefore, David, as the

---

[1]Bourchier, *Jesus Nazarenus, Rex Judaeorum* (1637), 26-28, 100-102*; citing Mt 2:2; Rom 14:17.

representative of Christ, complains chiefly of this among the distresses which he suffered. . . .

They charge Christ with teaching falsehood because, now that it is called for, he does not actually display the power to which he laid claim. But if their unbridled propensity to cursing had not deprived them of sense and reason, they would shortly afterward have perceived clearly the truth of his statement. Christ had said, "Destroy this temple, and after three days I will raise it up," but now they indulge in a premature triumph, and do not wait for the three days that would elapse from the commencement of its destruction. Such is the daring presumption of the wicked. . . .

"If you are the Son of God." Wicked people demand from Christ such a proof of his power that, by proving himself to be the Son of God, he may cease to be the Son of God. He had clothed himself with human flesh and had descended into the world on this condition, that, by the sacrifice of his death, he might reconcile men to God the Father. So then, in order to prove himself to be the Son of God, it was necessary that he should hang on the cross. And now those wicked men affirm that the Redeemer will not be recognized as the Son of God unless he come down from the cross, and thus disobey the command of his Father, and, leaving incomplete the expiation of sins, divest himself of the office which God had assigned to him. COMMENTARY ON A HARMONY OF THE EVANGELISTS.[2]

MALICE PAIRED WITH UNBELIEF. WOLFGANG MUSCULUS: Now they have an unfettered excuse for their disbelief. It's as if they were saying: "The fact that up to this point we did not believe him, nor did we accept him as the king of Israel, even though he did miracles, now it appears that we did it with good reason. And how foolish are they, who earlier greeted him as king of Israel! We are not ones to give our assent rashly, unless we are made certain, and lest we be seduced. But now, if he is king of Israel, let him descend from the cross and immediately we will believe him, so that he might see that we are blameless." In this way at the same time, they mock Christ, and they accuse those who believed on him of being foolish, but they pass themselves off as being wise and prudent. But in reality, their malice was such that, even if he had descended from the cross, they would still not have trusted him. And which was the greater miracle, to call forth a dead person from the sepulcher on the fourth day, and to restore him to life, or to descend from the cross while still alive? Therefore, why did they not believe? They were blinded by their own malice.

So let's consider here the insanity of the impious, that they blame Christ for putting his hope in God, since nothing is more praiseworthy than putting one's hope in God. Why did they not say, "Did a good man have hope in God, but now is deserted by him?" They are not willing to put the blame on God. And yet by this very statement they brand God with the greatest insult, because they laugh at one who placed his hope in him. If they were wise, they would be more inclined to conclude this: "He trusts in God, therefore he will free him, for this is his will." Does not the Scriptures say, "He hoped in me; I will free him." If they grant and confess that he has put his hope in God, why did they ignore that which most certainly follows from that?

They may retort: "This would be the case, if he were not the enemy of God." My response: "If he is the enemy of God, how does he trust in God?" Who is so crazy to place his hope in the enemy? You say, "He blasphemed." How is it possible for someone who has placed all his hope in God to blaspheme God? But this is the malice of the blindness of the Pharisees.

Concerning this mockery, the Holy Spirit expressly complains at Psalm 22:8. Moreover, who could help but marvel at the stupendous blindness of the priests, scribes, and Pharisees, who knew well that verse of Psalm 22. Yet, they did not hesitate to fulfill this prediction of the prophet concerning Christ, and to turn into disgrace that which supplies for us today the foundation of our

---

[2]CTS 3:303-5* (CO 45:769-70); Is 53:4; Ps 22:7; Jn 2:19.

faith. The phrase about the robbers mocking him serves to increase the disgrace that Christ is suffering on the cross. For, the prophecy of Psalm 22, that "all seeing me have mocked me," is so completely fulfilled that even the robbers who are being crucified did not feel compassion for Christ and they too joined in on the mocking.

And so Matthew says, "The robbers cast the same insult on him." It's as if he were saying, "It wasn't enough that the priests, the scribes and elders, and the rest of the people who passing by and were not a part of his suffering mocked him; but the very shared suffering on the cross ought to have moved their minds to pity." Meanwhile, there is no contradiction that Luke writes that this was only done by one of the robbers. COMMENTARY ON MATTHEW 27:42-44.[3]

GOD FORSAKEN. JOHN FOXE: While the Jews and the priests thus were scorning him, in the meantime the soldiers which crucified him drew lots for his coat, because it was seamless and could not well be divided, to fulfill the rest of the psalm that followed saying, "They parted my garments among them, and upon my coat they drew lots." . . .

The pains and torments which this innocent Lamb of God sustained upon the cross were great, the rebukes and scorns which he abided were greater; but especially that which he suffered in spirit and soul was greatest of all, when as he not only in body decaying for weakness and bleeding, but also in soul fainting with anguish and discomfort, began to cry with a loud voice, "My God, my God, why have you forsaken me?" Seeming by these words to be in such a case, as happens to God's child sometimes, thinking with themselves that God hath utterly left and forsaken them; not that God did ever forsake his Son, Christ, but this was the voice of his human nature,[†] teaching us not to think it strange, though our feeble heart do faint sometimes through despair, or lack of present comfort, as

happens many times even to the elect children of God. A SERMON OF CHRIST CRUCIFIED.[4]

A CRY FOR MERCY. WILLIAM PERKINS: In the opening of this complaint, many points must be scanned. The first is, what was the cause that moved Christ to complain? It was not any impatience or discontentment of mind, or any despair, or any dissembling, as some would have it: but it was an apprehension and a feeling of the whole wrath of God, which seized upon him both in body and soul. The second, what was the thing whereof he doth complain? That he is forsaken of God the Father. And from this point arises another question. How Christ, being God, can be forsaken of God? For the Father, the Son, and the Holy Ghost are all three but one and the same God. By God we must understand God the Father, the first person. According to the common rule, when God is compared with the Son or the Holy Ghost, then the Father is meant by this title, God; as in this place: not that the Father is more God than the Son, for in dignity all the three persons are equal: but they are distinguished in order only, and the Father is first. And again, whereas Christ complains that he was forsaken, it must be understood in regard of his human nature, not of his divinity. And Christ's humanity was forsaken, not that his divinity and humanity were severed, for they were ever joined together from the first moment of the incarnation; but the divinity of Christ, and so the divinity of the Father, did not show forth his power in the humanity, but did as it were lie asleep for a time, that the humanity might suffer. When a person sleeps, the soul is not severed from the body, but lies as it were dead, and exercises not itself: even so the divinity lay still and did not manifest his power in the humanity, and thus the humanity seemed to be forsaken. . . . ["My God, my God"] these words are words of faith, I say not of justifying faith whereof Christ stood not in need: but he had such a faith or hope, whereby he did put his

---

[3]Musculus, Wolfgang, *In Evangelistam Matthaeum Commentarii* (1556), 660-61.

[4]Foxe, *Writings of John Fox, Bale, and Coverdale*, 57-58*. [†]The 1570 edition has "humanity" instead of "human nature."

confidence in God. The last words, "Why have you forsaken me?" seem at the first to be words of distrust. How then (will some say) can these words stand with the former? For faith and distrust are flat contraries. Christ did not utter any speech of distrust, but only make his moan and complaint by reason of the greatness of his punishment, and yet still relied himself on the assistance of his Father. . . . Though Christ himself at his death did bear the wrath of God in such measure, as that in the sense and feeling of his human nature he was forsaken. Yet for all this he was the Son of God, and had the Spirit of his Father, crying, "My God, my God." AN EXPOSITION OF THE APOSTLES' CREED.[5]

27:45-56 The Death of Jesus

CHRIST'S CLOSING WORDS. AEGIDIUS HUN-NIUS: This eclipse lasted around three hours, from the sixth hour to the ninth, that is, from our noon to three o'clock. Upon the departure of that darkness, Jesus is written to have cried out, *Eli, Eli, lama asabtani*[†] meaning, "My God, my God, why have you forsaken me?" The sense of divine wrath against the sins of the world wrung this sad cry from him, all the sins that were laid on him, without exception, and that he was then bearing before God. And in that moment, he truly felt what it was to be abandoned by God and to be cast way from the enjoyment of his countenance and benefits. Here occurred Christ's profoundest "descent into hell" as the heavenly Father poured out his infinite wrath like a hurricane on him because of our sin. Christ would not have been strong enough to struggle against such terrors and temptations; neither could he have borne that hard force of God and sense of infinite justice, if he himself had not been God and strengthened his flesh with his omnipotent power, so as to bear that immense weight and mass that would have been intolerable to all other creatures.

Thus, this cry of lament was not out of despair, but was produced by the excruciating experience of those hellish terrors. For though he complains that

he has been deserted by God, yet he calls him *his* God all the same when he says, "My God." To the hands of this same God, he soon after commits his spirit. The fact that the Evangelists recorded these words of the Savior in the Hebrew idiom was done first of all so that it might be utterly clear that the first verse of Psalm 22 was fulfilled in him. That is why Matthew wished to preserve the very form of the psalmist's words as they were uttered by the Lord on the cross, as did the other Evangelists. The second reason [that the words are recorded in the Hebrew idiom] is in to show what occasioned his enemies' virulent mockery. From the repeated words, "Eli, Eli," they seized material with which to mock him as he did battle with the horrors of hell. For they said, "He is calling Elijah." And then some from among them—who were especially children of the devil—added with execrable contempt, "Come, let us see whether Elijah will come to deliver him." It would scarcely have been a wonder if a heavenly thunderbolt had been hurled down the mouth and throat of those whose voice so utterly abused the Lord of glory! "And at once one of them ran and got a sponge. Filling it with vinegar, he placed it on a branch so that [Jesus] might drink." Mark attributes the statement (full of diabolical mockery!) about "Elijah" to this scoundrel in particular who offers vinegar to the Lord Jesus. "But Jesus, when he had once again uttered a loud cry, gave up his spirit." His cry was: "Father, into your hands I commend my spirit," upon which death immediately overtook him.

The Evangelist reports as a miracle the fact that he breathed out his spirit with so great a shout, since the voice typically fails those who are moments away from death, so that they can speak nothing clearly or articulately. The centurion observed that Jesus expired with so strong a shout—and indeed not a shout of despair, but one full of trust, commending his soul to the heavenly Father. From this prodigious event, along with the other accompanying miracles (concerning which we will speak in their place), the centurion was led to repentance. COMMENTARY ON MATTHEW.[6]

---

[5]Perkins, *An Exposition of the Symbole or Creede of the Apostles*, 211-12*.

[6]Hunnius, *Commentarius in Evangelium Secundum Matthaeum* (1594), 868-70. [†]This is how Hunnius transcribes the text.

Wonders After Christ's Death. David Dickson: In this close of Christ's suffering learn, first, that the Son of God according to his humanity truly died, and his soul was separate from his body, "yielded up his spirit." Second, he died not by constraint, but willingly for of his own accord he "yielded up his spirit." Third, in dying, he was conqueror over death, for before death could come at him, as a weakling, which cannot live any longer, Christ being so strong as to cry out "with a loud voice," sets upon death and yields up his spirit. . . .

Our Lord, being dead as man, sets forth the glory of his divinity more than before in four wonders. The first wonder is "the veil of the temple" or the mid-wall of partition, which divided between the sanctuary and the body of the temple, "was torn in two from top to bottom," wherein Christ gave all people to understand (1) that his death was the fulfilling and the accomplishment of all the Levitical rites and figures of the temple, and of all the ceremonies annexed unto it, and that now they were to be esteemed as torn, and to be done away; (2) that now by the gospel sealed up in his death, the way unto heaven was made plain and open; (3) that the partition wall between Jew and Gentiles, to wit, the ceremonial law which divided them asunder, was torn and no more to stand in force.

The second wonder is the "earth shook," whereby the Lord gave people to understand (1) that as he is Lord of heaven, which had given testimony unto him by hiding its glory when he is suffering shame, so also he is Lord of the earth, which now trembles before her Lord. . . .

The third wonder is "the rocks were split," to show the power of Jesus, who could subdue the greatest difficulties and overcome the hardness of whatsoever obstinate hearts, upon whom he pleases to show his power.

The fourth wonder is "the tombs were opened," which was done to show that Christ died and was buried, not to remain under the great power of death and the grave, but to quicken the dead and to raise them out of their graves; and that he neither died nor rose for his own sake, but that he might redeem his own from death and give unto them resurrection and life. A Brief Exposition.[7]

Strange Signs Accompany Christ's Death. Theodore Beza: The context of the narration to this point leads us to understand that, after the rocks were split, the tombs opened, which obviously bears witness to the fact that death was conquered by the death of Christ. The events that are related afterward concerning the resurrection and appearance of certain saints, although told without interruption by the Evangelist lest they scatter into pieces, as it were, the story of one and the same deed, nevertheless, as is apparent from the very next verse, followed the resurrection of Christ. . . .

And this "appearance" indicates that they did not resurrect to again dwell among the human race, to die again later, as Lazarus and others did, but rather so that they might accompany Christ into eternal life, by whose power they resurrected; and also so that there might be sure testimonies of the quickening power of Christ, as is the opinion of Jerome[†] on this passage, and rightly so, though Augustine[‡] disagrees with him in Epistle 99 to Euodius. But if someone asks to whom they appeared, with whom they conversed, or even when they ascended into heaven, I would say that I am gladly ignorant of all these things that God did not reveal to us. But I think that the fable about the descent of the soul of Christ to the underworld also arose from here—yes, I call it a fable, as indeed this part of the Apostles' Creed has usually been treated; but, despite the fact that it is not included in the oldest versions of the Apostles' Creed, there is no other reason to think that it should be expunged, assuming it is rightly explained.

The lack of any additional information and the fact that this was a pagan centurion from Pilate's cohort, show that by this term he wished to indicate only how Christ, not only was innocent, but also obviously just, as can be inferred from his words as reported at Luke 23:47; and he reckons

---

[7]Dickson, *Brief Exposition* (1651), 342-43*.

him to be some sort of hero, as if the gods were bearing witness to this from heaven, as indicated by the word "was," as if he ceased to exist. But for the Jews, this phrase had a completely different and blasphemous meaning behind it. ANNOTATIONS ON MATTHEW 27:52-54.[8]

27:57-66 The Burial of Jesus

THE REALITY OF DEATH. JOHN CALVIN: The burial of Christ is now added as an intermediate transition from the ignominy of the cross to the glory of the resurrection. True, indeed, God determined, for another reason, that Christ should be buried, that it might be more fully attested that he suffered real death on our account. . . .

Now though this affection of Joseph deserved uncommon praise, still we ought first to consider the providence of God in subduing a man of high and honorable rank among his countrymen to wipe away the reproach of the cross by the honor of burial. And, indeed, as he exposed himself to the dislike and hatred of the whole nation and to great dangers, there can be no doubt that this singular courage arose from a secret movement of the Spirit. For though he had formerly been one of Christ's disciples, yet he had never ventured to make a frank and open profession of his faith. When the death of Christ now presents to him a spectacle full of despair and fitted to break the strongest minds, how comes he suddenly to acquire such noble courage that, amid the greatest terrors, he feels no dread and hesitates not to advance farther than he had ever done, when all was in peace? Let us know then that, when the Son of God was buried by the hand of Joseph, it was the work of God. . . .

For rich people, being naturally proud, find nothing more difficult than to expose themselves voluntarily to the contempt of the people. Now we know how mean and disgraceful an act it was to receive from the hand of the executioner the body of a crucified man. Besides, as people devoted to riches desire to avoid everything fitted to excite prejudice, the more eminent he was for wealth, the more cautious and timid he would have been, unless a holy boldness had been imparted to him from heaven. The dignity of his rank is likewise mentioned, that he was a counselor, or senator, that in this respect also the power of God may be displayed. For it was not one of the lowest of the people that was employed to bury the body of Christ in haste and in concealment, but from a high rank of honor he was raised up to discharge this office. For the less credible it was that such an office of kindness should be performed toward Christ, the more clearly did it appear that the whole of this transaction was regulated by the purpose and hand of God. . . . Matthew and Mark relate only that the women looked at what was done, and marked the place where the body was laid. But Luke states, at the same time, their resolution, which was that they returned to the city and prepared spices and ointments, that two days afterward they might render due honor to the burial. COMMENTARY ON A HARMONY OF THE EVANGELISTS.[9]

FEAR OF THE RESURRECTION. MARTIN LUTHER: The high priests, the Pharisees, and the elders have now accomplished what they wanted. Christ has been crucified, he is dead, his body has been taken down from the cross like they wanted—their purposes have been accomplished, but they still are not satisfied. They are nervous and fearful because of the crucified man who is dead and has been buried. Before Pilate they use the excuse that his disciples might steal the body and say that he is risen. However, in their hearts they have not forgotten the Lord Jesus' words which he had spoken while still alive, namely, that in three days he would arise. This was a sharp stinging thorn in their minds. What if it were true? What will happen to us if he arises from the dead? FIFTH SERMON OF HOLY WEEK.[10]

---

[8]Beza, *Annotationes Majores in Novum Dn. Nostri Jesu Christi Testamentum* (1594), 156. [†]Jerome, *Commentary on Matthew*, FC 117:308-23. [‡]Augustine, *To Evodius* 3.9, NPNF[1] 1:517-18.

[9]CTS 3:330-32, 335* (CO 45:787, 789-90). [10]Luther, *Complete Sermons*, 5:438.

SEALING HIS TOMB. DAVID DICKSON: Christ's enemies are vexed about him, how to suppress him, as here is to be seen; while he is alive, and while he is dead they can never be secure enough, for fear he shall overcome them; when they have him dead, they know not how to make the sepulcher sure. They make of his words, and of his servant's words, as best serves their purpose. For when he told them that though they destroyed the temple of his body, yet he would raise it again the third day, they passed by his meaning, and simply regarded it as his manner of speaking; and now they take up his meaning and make advantage of it against him. When Christ and his cause are brought low, every wicked person will speak as they please, as here they call the God of truth a deceiver. Hypocrites do respect religion, only for their own ends, and as it may serve their turn. They pretended to have great respect to the Sabbath, that they may have Christ shortly out of the way; and now they stand not to pollute the Sabbath, by making a business to secure his sepulcher. He that sets not God before his eyes, but is given to please men, will prove a slave to every man's affection; such a man is Pilate, who grants whatsoever Christ's enemies do require. Whatsoever power of craftiness can work for obscuring Christ's glory, his enemies will go about it carefully, albeit with ill success; as here, they seal the gravestone, and set a watch, thinking to keep Christ fast in the tomb. A BRIEF EXPOSITION.[11]

LIKE A SEED, WE ARE BURIED AND RAISED TO A GLORIOUS LIFE. DAVID CHYTRAEUS: The history of the Christ's burial admonishes us that Christ rested the whole seventh day in the tomb for this reason: that he might raise us who are dead and buried through death in the dust of the earth to the honor of the eternal Sabbath, that is, to true knowledge and celebration of God and to the perpetual life and joy that rests in God. For the seeds of fruits are cast into the earth and putrefy, afterward springing to life again and rising from the earth's bosom with wonderful beauty and richness. So too our bodies, liable as they are to ignominious corruption and weakness, are buried in the earth and putrefy. Nonetheless, those who lie in Christ's tomb will surely be called back to life by Christ. Those bodies will then be eternal and glorious, marvelous in beauty and arrayed in light. They will once more be the dwelling places of the soul and of the whole divinity.

This simile of Paul [i.e., concerning the seed] has been expressed in the choicest verses by that best of poets, Stigelius.[†] Let the studious learn them, and when they observe the crops spring to life in the fields this year let them reflect [on the poem] carefully:

> Truly, the wheatfields tell of the soul's
>   immortal glory,
> which bring forth the living bud from the
>   lifeless body.
> Dry seeds are buried beneath upturned earth,
> whose end, you would say, was nothing.
> Yet these, growing, rise by a secret power,
> and having grown by silent strength they bear
>   the hardy stalk.
> So too our corpses, buried in tilled graves,
> made glorious, will receive a living beauty.
> Dipped first in death, the true badges of life
> will live through ages of eternal light before God.

COMMENTARY ON MATTHEW.[12]

---

[11]Dickson, *Brief Exposition* (1651), 346-47.

[12]Chytraeus, *Commentarius in Matthaeum Evangelistam* (1558), 525-26. [†]Johann Stigel (1515–1562) was a German poet who studied and taught at the University of Wittenberg.

28:1-15 THE RESURRECTION

Now after the Sabbath, toward the dawn of the first day of the week, Mary Magdalene and the other Mary went to see the tomb. ²And behold, there was a great earthquake, for an angel of the Lord descended from heaven and came and rolled back the stone and sat on it. ³His appearance was like lightning, and his clothing white as snow. ⁴And for fear of him the guards trembled and became like dead men. ⁵But the angel said to the women, "Do not be afraid, for I know that you seek Jesus who was crucified. ⁶He is not here, for he has risen, as he said. Come, see the place where heᵃ lay. ⁷Then go quickly and tell his disciples that he has risen from the dead, and behold, he is going before you to Galilee; there you will see him. See, I have told you." ⁸So they departed quickly from the tomb with fear and great joy, and ran to tell his disciples. ⁹And behold, Jesus met them and said, "Greetings!" And they came up and took hold of his feet and worshiped him. ¹⁰Then Jesus said to them, "Do not be afraid; go and tell my brothers to go to Galilee, and there they will see me."

¹¹While they were going, behold, some of the guard went into the city and told the chief priests all that had taken place. ¹²And when they had assembled with the elders and taken counsel, they gave a sufficient sum of money to the soldiers ¹³and said, "Tell people, 'His disciples came by night and stole him away while we were asleep.' ¹⁴And if this comes to the governor's ears, we will satisfy him and keep you out of trouble." ¹⁵So they took the money and did as they were directed. And this story has been spread among the Jews to this day.

a Some manuscripts the Lord

Overview: Some of Jesus' faithful female disciples come to the tomb to attend to Jesus' body. However, their roles are instantaneously changed from ministers to Jesus' physical needs to witnesses to the resurrection. Among the Reformation commentators, Miles Coverdale notes how the appearance of the angel before the women stirred their fears and then allayed them. To engender faith and dispel fears, the angel reminds the women that Jesus, the crucified one, is now raised, just as he had predicted (Mt 26:31-32; cf. 16:21; 17:22-23; 20:17-19). The awe of the women creates an invigorating mixture of fear and joy as they hurry to the disciples to give their report. When they encounter the risen Jesus along the way, he charges them along the same lines as the angel. He states that they should have no fear as they give witness to his resurrection and that they will see him in Galilee as he had promised (Mt 26:31-32). Wolfgang Musculus remarks on the graciousness of Christ in appearing to the women in addition to their encounter with the angel. The certainty of his resurrection grows as he appears to them, increasing their faith.

The reformers reflect on the eternal significance of Jesus' death and resurrection, truths that will not be defeated by the erroneous report of the guards, but rather which themselves defeat sin and death, bringing hope to all those who believe. As John Donne puts it, "My bell tolls for death . . . for I live, even in death."

28:1-10 He Is Not Here; He Has Risen!

Heralding the Resurrection. Miles Coverdale: First, we hear again the great zeal and the fervent love and diligence of these devout women, in that they desire to show honor unto the Lord being dead; but the angel, a messenger of his resurrection, commands them to declare this joy to the disciples and to get them to the Lord now being alive. Heavenly is the messenger and proclaimer of the resurrection, for it passes far all natural reason and all flesh. Therefore, are the women also afraid of him and at the fair brightness of his countenance and apparel. For our feeble flesh is not able to sustain the glorious shine of the heavenly light and godly clearness, but is afraid at it and fears. Nevertheless, God by his angel does right soon comfort the women's weakness, takes from them their fear, speaks lovingly unto them, and makes them apostles, that is, messengers and proclaimers of the joyful resurrection. So little does God reject our weakness that he makes even women to be the declarers of his resurrection; for he ever delights of the last to make the first. Forasmuch then as they were the beginners of death in sin, they are here first before the apostles, chosen to be declarers of that immortal life, which even out of death is come forth to us in Christ.

As Christ with the earthquake died on the cross, so raises he with the earthquake, which also was heard in the sending of the Holy Ghost. This signified that through his death and resurrection, and by the power of the Holy Ghost—when the apostles declare the same in the world—the whole world should be moved and changed. And though the ungracious falsehood of the high priests undertook with their lies to hide and suppress the truth of Christ's resurrection, yet God did direct it another way. . . .

The angel is not ashamed to call Jesus the crucified, for the cross is the token of Christ's victory; through the cross began his honor and glory; through the cross was death overcome; the cross is the glorious token of all Christians. FRUITFUL LESSONS UPON THE PASSION.[1]

TWO REASONS THE GUARDS TREMBLED. THE ENGLISH ANNOTATIONS: At the sight of his glory and in conscience of their own guilt, having seen the earth tremble, the grave open, the heavy stone rolling away from the sepulcher, the dead body which they had in their charge to watch gone, and a person of such a dreadful presence and heavenly

glory and spoke of him as more than a man, they [the guards] could not but know that they were not now dealing with an infirm man but God. Therefore, all astonished, they tremble and become like dead men. Here were two main causes for fear: (1) Their own horror of conscience, who were actors in the death of Jesus. (2) Fear of their governor, whose anger they might well expect, if he should not credit their reports but construe all as incredible excuses of their own default and negligence in watching. Thus, God showed them how vain it was to take up arms against him and also made them witnesses against themselves and the malicious priests. ANNOTATIONS ON MATTHEW 28:4.[2]

FEAR AND THE RESURRECTION. PETER MARTYR VERMIGLI: The angel came down from heaven; there were no human witnesses; the angel is present to announce the resurrection. The condition of our future life is manifested by the same work in the same way. We shall be like angels of God, bright as the sun; thus, the angel was wonderfully resplendent. The earth trembled because the nature of things is turned upside down in the resurrection. The guards were rightly terrified. The women were frightened by the appearance of the angel because of the discord which stems from sin between our nature and the nature of angels, with which we nonetheless should be familiar since they are our guardians. This discord will endure until we put aside our bodies.

The guards became like dead men. They wanted to keep Christ in his tomb, even as today the princes want to keep the gospel buried by arms and councils. Let human prudence rise up—it counts for nothing against God. Indeed, everything turns out the opposite. They wanted to terrify people who approached; they themselves were terrified. They wanted to hinder Christ from coming forth; they themselves were hindered and made like dead men. The angel consoles the women, "Do not be afraid." After fear, godly people take comfort from

---

[1] Coverdale, *Fruitfull Lessons upon the Passion* (1593), X5-Y.

[2] Downame, ed., *Annotations*, OO1v*.

the angels because they speak the words of God, and the word of God consoles us. The guards were not consoled because they were enemies of God, and they continued in their hostility. ORATION ON CHRIST'S RESURRECTION.[3]

UNDERSTANDING THE ANGELS' MESSAGE.
AEGIDIUS HUNNIUS: "And the angel answered the women." The angel sees that the women are utterly terrified at his presence, so he comforts them, saying, "Do not be afraid." It is as if he should say, "Now is not the time for either fearing or indulging sadness, but rather for rejoicing and exultation." "I know that you seek Jesus, who was crucified. He is not here; he has risen!" He means this: "It does not at all escape me that you have come to seek the Lord Jesus in the tomb. But nobody should seek one who is living among the dead. For Jesus is no longer dead, but has risen from death, and now lives." But when he says, "He is not here," the context of his words argue that the statement is about the local presence [of Christ]. It was in this sense that the women were seeking him so as to anoint his body, and according to this mode of presence he was not in the tomb. By these words, nothing is derogated from Christ the Savior's nonlocal and invisible presence which he, insofar as he is human, possess as a consequence of the personal union and session at the right hand [of the Father]. I have already expounded on this at length in chapter 26 with regard to the saying, "The poor you will always have with you, but me not always." I refer the reader to *locus communis* treated in that passage. The angel challenged them to look with their own eyes at "the place where the Lord had been laid." By seeing the tomb was empty, they would conclude with all the more certainty that he had arisen. Next, he bids them to "go quickly and proclaim to the disciples" the resurrection of Jesus who was crucified. "Tell his disciples that he has risen from the dead and goes before you into Galilee. There you will see him. Behold, I have told this to you." Through the preaching of the women,

the angel wished the apostles to recall the Lord's own preaching to them when he had gone out to the garden with them and said, "You will all suffer offense because of me this night. For it has been written, 'I will strike the shepherd, and the sheep of the flock will be scattered.' But after I have arisen, I will go ahead of you into Galilee." Thus, the angel hints at the future, so that by comparing the prediction with its outcome, they might more easily believe that the Lord has truly risen from the dead.

"And they swiftly departed from the tomb." It is recorded that they went away "with fear and great joy." But how is it that these [feelings] are able to coexist in the same person—indeed coexist in the highest degree? I respond: Either [feeling] was perfectly able to have a place, though in different respects. The vision of the angels had excited *fear* in them, while this longed-for announcement concerning the Lord's resurrection had filled them with *joy*. They run therefore to announce this joyful gospel to the disciples: to those who had no hope of joy, they present this gospel, removing and washing away the grief and sorrow of spirit that had nearly consumed them till that third day. COMMENTARY ON MATTHEW.[4]

THE HOPE OF RESURRECTION. JOHN DONNE: There is our comfort collected from this *surrexit*, he is risen, equivalent to the discomfort of the *non est hic*, he is not here; that this his rising declares him to be the Son of God, who therefore can and will, and to be that Jesus, an actual Redeemer, and therefore has already raised us. . . . The grave (now, since Christ's Resurrection, and ours in him) does not bury the dead man, but death himself. My bell tolls for death, and my bell rings out for death, and not for me that die; for I live, even in death; but death dies in me, and has no more power over me. . . .

Christ was, and I am . . . free among the dead, not detained in the state of death. For, says

---

[3]Vermigli, *Life, Letters, and Sermons*, 224.

[4]Hunnius, *Commentarius in Evangelium Secundum Matthaeum* (1594), 885-88; citing Mt 26:11, 31.

St. Peter, "It was not possible he should be held by it." Not possible for Christ, because of the prediction of so many prophets, whose words had infallibility in them; not possible especially because of the union of the divine nature: Not possible for me neither, because God has afforded me the marks of his election, and thereby made me partaker of the divine nature too. But yet these things might, perchance, not fall into the consideration of these women. They did not; but they might, they should have done. For, as the angel tells them here, Christ had told them of this before: *Sicut dixit*, he is risen, as he said. SERMON 25: ON EASTER DAY.[5]

THE COMFORT OF CHRIST'S WORDS. ROBERT ROLLOCK: He is not content to tell them only "the Lord is risen"; no, one word will not suffice them, but he confirms it by Christ's prediction, "He said it before, the Lord was to suffer and to rise the third day." So he confirms them by the Lord's own testimony. These prophecies and predictions which are foretold of Christ are much worth, for they have this use. When you read them in that Old Testament, they seal up the word of the gospel, of the manifestation of Christ in the flesh, of his suffering and glorification, that that report of old is fulfilled. But before I leave this, I see the Lord will not let his own forget his word which he had once told them. Suppose they would forget it, yet the Lord will have it called to their remembrance. These women would have forgotten that which the chief priests remembered when they sought a guard of Pilate to watch the sepulcher. Sometimes it comes to pass that the godly remember not so much as the wicked, who hear the word to their destruction; but if you be one of his, he will have it called to your memory; but if you be none of his, he will not regard that, when you hear, you let it go in your one ear and out the other. . . . So then this is a great mercy, that he will bring that word that you have condemned to your remembrance, and before you remember it not, he will send down an angel from the heaven to call it to your remembrance. We have not angels now, as these women had then, but, I say to you, as many true and faithful ministers are as like many angels. Take away these men who preach the gospel . . . you shall forget the Word of God that is preached. LECTURES UPON THE HISTORY OF THE PASSION.[6]

THE MIRACLE OF RESURRECTION. JUAN DE VALDÉS: Although they showed their affection, they also showed how small was their faith, since they thought they should find him in the tomb; while he had promised that he would rise again on the third day. And hence may be gathered what I am in the habit of saying, that Christians are frequently moved by one intention of their own, and by another, to which they are moved by the Holy Spirit. The intention, by which these holy women were moved, was to anoint Christ; while the Holy Spirit's impulse was with the intention that they should see Christ risen from the dead. And here I understand it to be a good token when a person is moved by a good intention, but it issues in another, a better, I mean that it is a token that that better [intention] is from the Holy Spirit.

As to that, "There was a great earthquake," I am reminded of what I stated in my exposition of the psalms; that God was wont upon such occasions as the death and resurrection of Christ to move the earth by earthquakes, to certify us, that God himself, as one might say, consents sympathizingly in Christ's death, and raises Christ up. . . .

Here it has to be taken into consideration that the guard who watched the sepulcher were men, while they who came to see the sepulcher were women; now these were firm and constant, while the men feared, trembled, and became as dead men. God's works ever produce these same effects, they terrify and alarm people of the world to such an extent as to make them lose all self-control; while they comfort and cheer the children of God, even unto their transformation into God. That, "Behold he goes

---

[5]Donne, *Eighty Sermons* (1640), 249*; citing Acts 2:24.

[6]Rollock, *Lectures upon the History of the Passion . . . of Our Lord Jesus Christ* (1616), 362-63.

before you into Galilee . . ." has to be combined with what Christ promised his disciples when the supper was over, saying, "But after that I shall have risen again, I shall go before you into Galilee."

As to the reasons why Christ was pleased to allow himself to be seen by his disciples in Galilee, and not in Jerusalem, as he allowed himself to be seen by the holy women, I remit myself to what others say, since I dare not speak upon conjecture of things, in relation to which I cannot speak without some sort of evidence or experience. In those words of the angel, "Jesus, the crucified," it is very worthy of consideration, that that which is ignominious in the eyes of the world and of the children of Adam, who follow the judgment of human prudence, is glorious in the eyes of God and of the children of God, who follow the judgment of the Holy Spirit; and for that reason the angel of God, in speaking to the holy women, who were the daughters of God, calls Christ, "Jesus, the crucified," giving him the most honorable and glorious title that he could give him as man, for that Christ has conquered, not by resurrection, but by death. COMMENTARY UPON THE GOSPEL OF ST. MATTHEW.[7]

JESUS' APPEARANCE TO THE WOMEN. WOLF-GANG MUSCULUS: Now the Evangelist, after describing the scene with the angel, follows up with a description of the Lord's appearance. First, he describes how he revealed himself to the pious women soon after his resurrection. The first thing that he talks about is the obedience of the women, in other words, their willingness to carry out what the angel had bid them to do. He adds how they were overcome with joy by the words of the angel, but also to the same degree with fear. They experienced joy because of the resurrection of Christ, of which the angel had informed them; they had fear because of the unusualness of the vision and because of the magnitude of the miracle. The reality of the resurrection had not yet completely sunk in, and yet they were affected by a certain joy from the words of the angel. And since

they had received the angel's surprising announcement, the very cause of their joy, while in a state of utter grief, they clearly could not believe it. We read the same thing about the apostles, that because they were overcome with joy, that is, an overwhelming longing for their Lord and an unusual miracle, they could not believe it. Thus, the minds of the women wrestled between joy for the resurrection that the angel had announced to them, and fear, because of the unusualness of the miracle, until they were made certain of the resurrection when they saw the Lord on their journey. And the apostles themselves did not immediately believe those who announced that the Lord had risen until they had seen the Lord.

Let us consider here the care of the Lord which he has for his disciples, which is the reason why he offered himself to be seen by those women who loved him and were seeking him. He shows his regard for them in that he is not willing that his resurrection be announced to them by these women from the information of the angel only, but he shows himself to them to be seen, so that now they might have confidence in a message that they witnessed, not just with their ears, but also with their eyes. And so, for the sake of establishing the certainty of his resurrection, he wanted it not only to be announced by angels to women and by women to the disciples, but he offered himself both to the women and the disciples to be seen and handled.

In my judgment, it is simpler to say that the Evangelist wrote, not what was permitted by the Lord, but what was attempted by the women; not what the women accomplished, but what they tried to do. The fact that they wanted to embrace the feet of the Lord while prostrate on the ground was a gesture of those who are expressing adoration. For this reason, the Evangelist says, "And they adored him." We do not read that they said anything, but by their actions, they express the same thing that Thomas did in words: "My Lord and my God."

And rightly they fall at the feet of Jesus. First, he ought to be adored as God. Second, they fall at his feet in his role an envoy of peace, whose feet were

---

[7]Valdés, *Commentary upon the Gospel of St. Matthew*, 496-98.

beautiful like those announcing peace. He does not say, "Do not rejoice," but, "Do not fear." It is fear that he removes from them, not joy. And so, clearly Christ is not able to tolerate anyone wavering in fear because of his name. The resurrection of the Lord is not the source of fear for believers, but of true and eternal joy. These words console those with anxious consciences. He gives them the same command that the angel did, but here it must be noted that he calls the disciples his brothers. The angel did not say, "Go, announce to his brothers," but "to his disciples." Nor do any of the disciples call Christ his brother, but Lord and God. Let us learn, therefore, in what place Christ holds his disciples. He considers them brothers; and in what place the disciples hold the Lord, that is, in the place of their Lord and God. See Psalm 22: "I will tell your name to my brothers." COMMENTARY ON MATTHEW.[8]

28:11-15 The Lie of the Guard

AN UNLIKELY STORY. THOMAS LUSHINGTON: To say then they came by night makes it but the more unlikely. They could not watch one hour with him in Gethsemane when it concerned his life while there was yet hope to vindicate him from the cross; and can they now watch with him a whole night when he was dead and buried? If they were for a night's exploit, they would have done it the night before, when there was a fairer opportunity and greater security. They now had no more means this night, but more danger. When they went to Gethsemane, they had but two swords in all and were there disarmed of them; but one coat apiece, and some stripped of that; no weapon to assault, nor armor to defend. Fit furniture and fair voyage for poor fishermen to make to Mount Calvary in a dark night, to affront the Roman watch. And to what end? If their master could rise again, what need they come hither? If not, they did him no wrong to abandon him. THE RESURRECTION RESCUED.[9]

AN UNBELIEVABLE LIE. MARTIN LUTHER: It is astonishing to me that the Jews so obstinately opposed such faithful testimonies and manifest signs, even against their own consciences. For they knew well that Christ had been buried and, furthermore, that his tomb had been secured both with a seal and by guards appointed by the chief priests and the governor Pilate, so that no one could steal anything from the tomb, and they themselves must confess that the tomb is empty and he is gone. When they give the soldiers money and command them to say, "His disciples came by night and stole him away while we were asleep," they show that they themselves regard it as true. Neither does it sound credible to others, for not even Pilate believed it. Surely no one would believe it if someone said to us, "That thief hung on the gallows for two days and was carefully secured with guards; nevertheless, someone came and stole him from the gallows," especially if that person were in danger of meeting the same end as the hanged thief. The disciples were much too timid to chance so many guards in order to carry away the dead body. Their lie was not at all believable. The Romans were not children to let themselves be so easily fooled. ON THE PASSION, DEATH, AND RESURRECTION OF OUR LORD JESUS CHRIST.[10]

THE PRICE OF A LIE. HEINRICH BULLINGER: Or, "When the women had gone away"; this is just a way to make a connection in the story, as if we might say, "Meanwhile, while the angel and the Lord himself were speaking with the women, the soldiers went into the city, where they were discussing openly the glory of the one who had resurrected." To others it seemed that the soldiers still guarded the tomb when the women came, yes, and heard the conversation of the women with the angel. But how likely this is, let the reader decide. I think that the soldiers left the tomb shortly after the Lord's resurrection and went into the city, and then afterward the women approached.

---

[8]Musculus, *In Evangelistam Matthaeum Commentarii* (1556), 678-79.
[9]Lushington, *The Resurrection Rescued from the Soldiers' Calumnies* (1659), 24-25.
[10]LW 69:287 (WA 28:432).

Matthew now gets around to telling what was done by the soldiers when they were in the city. Some of them go to the priests and relate what they saw, that the angel descended from heaven, and that, when there was an earthquake, the stone from the mouth of the tomb rolled away, and that Christ rose again, while they themselves were half dead with fear because of the angel. And it was only right that the resurrection of the Lord have testimonies that are plain to see and indisputable, even brought forth by his enemies themselves.

But here again we have occasion to see the impiety and malice of the priests. For, although they ought to have been moved to repentance by these clear and manifest signs, they instead purchase a lie from the soldiers, just as before they purchased the work of a traitor, except that now they are more generous or profuse in their pay out. They prescribe the formula for making the lie, but composed in such a way that it proves what the prophet said, "Iniquity lies to itself." For, without remembering that proverb, that a "liar should have a good memory," they tell the soldiers, "Say that his disciples came in the night and stole him from us while we slept." For, if the soldiers slept, how did they know that the disciples carried off his body? Or do we see and hear while we are sleeping? Or if they did not sleep, why did they not do their duty and drive away the thieves? But mendacity and impiety usually contradict themselves in this way. Still, the greedy soldiers take the money, and like hired contractors they tell the lie just as they had been instructed. There are people like them today who are not ignorant of the true gospel, but, after taking money from the priests, they rehearse human fabrications and against their own consciences they tell a lie for a price. COMMENTARY ON MATTHEW.[11]

WANTING TO BELIEVE THE LIE. JOHN CALVIN: It was the finishing stroke of the vengeance of God to blind the Jews, that the resurrection of Christ was buried by the perjury of the soldiers, and that so gross a falsehood was believed. And hence it is evident that those who did not believe that Christ was risen were deceived by a voluntary error, as the world voluntarily gives itself up to be deceived by the snares of Satan. For if a man had but opened his eyes, it was unnecessary that he should make a long inquiry. Armed soldiers say that the body of Christ was stolen from them by a feeble, timid, small, and unarmed body of men. What plausible grounds have they for saying so? They add that this was done while they were asleep. How then do they come to know that it was stolen? And if they had any suspicion of the disciples, why did they not track their footsteps? Why did they not, at least, make a noise? It was therefore a childish subterfuge, which would not have screened them from punishment if they had had to deal with an honest and upright governor; but through the connivance of Pilate, that enormous wickedness was allowed to pass unnoticed. . . .

Though it may appear strange that God should permit this false report to gain currency to extinguish the glory of his son, we ought to render the honor which is due to his just vengeance. For we perceive that this nation deserved to have its light taken away by clouds, because it so eagerly seizes hold on an idle and childish falsehood; next, because almost all have struck on the stone of stumbling, it was proper that their eyes should be darkened, that they might not see that the cup of giddiness was presented to them; and, in short, that they were abandoned to every kind of madness, as Isaiah had foretold. For God would never have permitted them to be deceived by such a foolish credulity, but in order that those who had despised the redeemer might be shut out from the hope of salvation. . . . But though this falsehood obtained currency among the Jews, this did not prevent the truth of the gospel from flying at liberty to the very ends of the earth, as it always rises victorious over all the obstacles in the world. COMMENTARY ON A HARMONY OF THE EVANGELISTS.[12]

---

[11]Bullinger, In . . . Evangelium secundum Matthaeum Commentariorum (1546), 12:265v.

[12]CTS 3:351-52 (CO 45:801); citing Is 6:9.

28:16-20 THE GREAT COMMISSION

¹⁶*Now the eleven disciples went to Galilee, to the mountain to which Jesus had directed them. ¹⁷And when they saw him they worshiped him, but some doubted. ¹⁸And Jesus came and said to them, "All authority in heaven and on earth has been given to* me. ¹⁹*Go therefore and make disciples of all nations, baptizing them in*ᵃ *the name of the Father and of the Son and of the Holy Spirit, ²⁰teaching them to observe all that I have commanded you. And behold, I am with you always, to the end of the age."*

a Or *into*

OVERVIEW: When Jesus meets his disciples in Galilee, some disciples worship him (Mt 28:9). However, some are still doubtful, even after Jesus' appearance to them. Among the reformers, Aegidius Hunnius describes how Jesus sets the context for the commission to follow by declaring his universal authority in heaven and on earth. With his supremacy over all things and all people declared, Jesus commissions his disciples to extend the scope of their ministry to all nations. The central thrust of their ministry will be to make disciples through their proclamation of the gospel of the kingdom (Mt 10:7, 26-28). The new disciples are to be baptized, signifying their confession of Christ (Mt 10:32), in the name of the Father, Son, and Holy Spirit. Furthermore, the new disciples are to be taught the teachings of Christ so that they might obey his commands. At the conclusion of the commission (and the Gospel), Jesus reminds his disciples of his presence and authority until he ushers in the glorious stage of the kingdom.

The Reformation discussion hovers around three main areas. First, there is some discussion of Jesus' power over the nations and how that sets the scope of the commission. Heinrich Bullinger casts Christ's commission to make disciples of all nations in the light of his saving work for humanity. Second, the reformers express clear differences about the relationship between the command to make disciples and the related instructions for baptism in the name of the Trinity. Third, there is considerable discussion among the reformers about

how teaching new disciples to observe Jesus' teaching encourages holy living. Christ's commission to his disciples includes the holistic witness of life and word. Calvin notes that Matthew's Gospel concludes with the promise of Christ's presence and power through the Spirit, enabling disciples to obey the commission.

28:16-17 *Some Worshiped, Some Doubted*

EVEN NOW, MIXED RESPONSES. WOLFGANG MUSCULUS: The same thing was said before about the women. The Evangelists mention this adoration for good reason. For they are pointing out to the apostles and to the believers that the testimony in Christ of the resurrection was so great that they were moved to adore him as God and Lord. For from the power of the resurrection, he was revealed as the Son of God . . . as it says in Romans 1.

Why? Did some of the eleven apostles who had gathered in Galilee fall off from their certainty about the resurrection of Christ, which they had formed from his appearances on the day of the resurrection and on the eighth day afterward at Jerusalem? I don't think so. For, it seems that this doubt was not about whether Christ had truly resurrected, but whether this that was appearing to them on the mountain truly was that Christ whom they had seen at Jerusalem and knew for sure had resurrected. This doubt was not taking away their faith in the resurrection any more than that doubt diminished their belief in his humanity, when they saw him walking on the water and thought in their dismay that he was an apparition; their doubt in that instance was not about the true body of Christ, but whether this which they were seeing walking on the surface of the sea was truly Christ or instead just an apparition. It had already been confirmed to them so many times and so they knew that Christ indeed had resurrected from the dead. But whether that which was appearing on this mountain was Christ himself, some of them were not sure immediately, until he had come closer to them and revealed himself. Likewise, today as well we see many good people do not immediately give their assent at the hearing of the gospel. But for a while they hesitate, not because they have doubts about the doctrine and truth of Christ, but they are not able to decide immediately whether the information they are being given about Christ is true or not until they are able to know it for certain after examining the matter more closely. COMMENTARY ON MATTHEW.[1]

28:18-20 *Jesus Commissions His Disciples*

EMPOWERING THE COMMISSION. AEGIDIUS I IUNNIUS: As he is about to send the apostles into the world to preach the gospel to every creature, he first speaks beforehand about his own majesty, which he will receive at the appropriate time, so that then his own inviolable rank might correspond with his office. Moreover, he says that he has been given *exousia*. This word, since it indicates power that is efficacious, as is apparent from equivalent passages of Scripture, we have to detest that perfidy of Beza, who dared to translate this word as "authority" here, rendering this remarkable passage in his version of the New Testament like this: "All authority is given to me in heaven and earth." He attributes too much to Jesus the Nazarene, as a man, giving him all authority in heaven and earth, at a time when he does not have all power and efficacious capability or potency. But the very Gentiles themselves bear witness to the fact that capability or potency is far more than authority, which can

sometimes denote rank devoid of power. For example, Cicero[†] in his speech against Piso, speaking of Metellus, says this: "And that which was not yet in his power, he obtained by his authority." That's how Cicero sees it. And truly Beza's impudence is all the more intolerable because he translates the term *exousia* as "power" when it is used in regard to the apostles, such as at Matthew 10, Mark 6, and Luke 10, and for good reason. But when he uses it in regard to Christ, he disdains the majesty that he received according to the flesh and translates that term with the word "authority."

And Christ goes on to say that all power was given to him, and to such an extent that it is totally all power in heaven and earth that is given to him. Those who contend that it is a finite power, show by that very fact that they are declaring war on the most obvious truth from their premise. For all power in heaven and in earth is without a doubt the power that is unique to God alone by his nature, but to Christ, as the Son of Man, communicated according to the flesh personally. Christ in his confession before the leaders of the Jewish people calls this "the power of God." COMMENTARY ON MATTHEW.[2]

A MESSAGE FOR ALL HUMANITY. HEINRICH BULLINGER: The Lord Jesus offering himself to be beholden most manifestly of his disciples in Galilee confirms them in the truth of faith. And because all things which hitherto have been declared in this book concerning the doctrine, the deeds, the death, and the resurrection of Christ do pertain to the common salvation of all humanity, therefore he sends forth his disciples as messengers into all the world, commanding them to baptize and to preach the gospel to every creature, promising the meanwhile that he, although in body he goes up to heaven, will be with his, and with his holy church continually and unto the end of the world. THE SUM OF THE FOUR EVANGELISTS.[3]

---

[1]Musculus, *In Evangelistam Matthaeum Commentarii* (1556), 680.

[2]Hunnius, *Commentarius in Evangelium Secundum Matthaeum* (1594), 1653-55. [†]Cicero, *In Pisonem*, LCL 252:150-51.
[3]Bullinger, *The Summe of the Foure Evangelists* (1582), C8v.

A Lasting Commission. John Lightfoot: His appointing them into Galilee to such a mount—it is like to that mount near Capernaum where he had chosen the apostles and made his Sermon—was not barely to appear to the eleven, for that had he done before, and that could he have done at Jerusalem, but it was an intended meeting, not only with the eleven, but with the whole multitude of this Galilean and other disciples, and therefore he published this appointment so often, before and after his resurrection. And we cannot so properly understand his being seen of above five hundred brethren at once, of which the apostle speaks of any other time and place as of this. . . . Particularly [Jesus] gives command and commission to go and disciple all nations: For whereas hitherto he had confined them to preach only to Israel, now must they preach to every creature. . . .

[The nations] had been taught of the devil, his oracles and delusions and so on, but now they must all be taught of God by the preaching of the gospel. They had in some few numbers in this space been taught by Israel to know the Lord and proselyte into their religion, but now such proselyting should not need, for all must come to the knowledge of God, the gospel carrying the knowledge of him, and it being carried through all nations. Those of them who had come into the church of Israel and the true religion had been inducted and sealed into it, by being baptized. . . . And so that proselyte sacrament [as I may so call it] must be carried and continued among all nations, as a badge of homage and subjection to Christ to whom all power is given in heaven and earth; and of the profession of the true God, the Father, Son, and Holy Ghost, against all false gods and false worship. Infants born of Christian parents are to bear this badge, though when they undertake it, they understand not what they do, because none in Christian families should continue without the note of homage to Christ's sovereignty, and this distinctive mark against heathenism that worships false gods, as no male among Israel after eight days old must be without the badge of circumcision.

Discipling was not of persons already taught, but to that end that they should be taught, and if the disciples understood this word in Christ's command after any other sense, it was different from the sense of the word, which the nation had ever used and only used. For in their schools a person was made . . . a scholar or disciple, when he gave in himself to such a master to be taught and trained up by him; and in the discipling of proselytes to the Jew's religion, it was of their very like tenor. That sense therefore that many put upon these words, namely, that none are to be baptized but those that are thoroughly taught, is such a one as the apostles and all the Jewish nation had never known or heard of before.

That wretched and horrid opinion that denies the divinity of Christ, and the divinity of the Holy Ghost, little observes, or at least will not see why the administration of baptism among the Gentiles must be in the name of the Father, Son, and Holy Ghost, whereas among the Jews it was only in the name of Jesus—namely, for this reason, that as by that among the Jews, Jesus was to be professed for the true Messiah against all other, so by this among the Gentiles who had worshiped false gods, the Father, Son, and Holy Ghost should be professed the only true God. The Harmony, Chronicle, and Order of the New Testament.[4]

The Witness of Word and Life. Robert Browne: When Christ appointed the apostles to plant churches throughout the world, he appointed them not to talk of and profess the word from their mouths only, but he gave them charge in these three things, as being the chief marks of a planted church: namely, preaching the word, administration of the sacraments, and reformation of life, which is the chief thing of all to set forth his church and kingdom. For he commanded them to preach and baptize, and because preaching and baptizing are nothing without amendment of life,

---

[4]Lightfoot, *The Harmony, Chronicle and Order of the New Testament* (1655), 75-76; citing Mt 5; 1 Cor 15:6; Is 54:13; Heb 8:11; Acts 2:38.

he added these words, "teaching them to observe and do all things, whatsoever I have commanded you." AN ANSWER TO MASTER CARTWRIGHT.[5]

THE PRIORITY OF MAKING DISCIPLES. HANS DENCK: That infant baptism is wrong is amply testified by truth in that the first and foremost business of the messengers of Jesus Christ is to teach and make disciples for the Lord and to seek the kingdom, above all else. This we are to do also. Whoever baptizes anyone before he is a disciple, testifies by this deed that baptism is more essential than teaching and knowledge. . . . If, on the other hand, teaching is more important than baptism, one ought to leave baptism alone and pursue teaching. And if one should ever prefer baptism, one would then have to admit that it is more important [than teaching]; but this is anti-Christian teaching. Now, if anyone wants to say that he places teaching ahead for any of those who are willing to hear it, the same splits and tears asunder the commission of Christ as if he had been ordered to go to the Jews and preach, but to the heathen to baptize; this is as if one should baptize Isaac since his father Abraham has now become a disciple. Yet the commandment is as follows, "Go then and teach" or "make disciples of all nations, baptizing them (that is, those whom you have made disciples) in the name of the Father, who has drawn them, and the Son, under whose yoke they place themselves, and the Holy Spirit, in whose power they are to remain and fulfill the will of the Father." To sum up, just as Christ is Christ before anyone believes this, so the teaching is right teaching before anyone is baptized; but faith is not faith unless there is a Christ; consequently, baptism is not baptism, unless there is teaching. CONCERNING GENUINE LOVE.[6]

IN THE NAME OF THE TRINITY. MARTIN CHEMNITZ: What is the meaning of these words: I baptize you in the name of the Father, and of the Son, and of the Holy Spirit? First is signified that baptism is administered in the name, that is, on command, of God the Father, and of the Son, and of the Holy Spirit. Second is indicated that we are baptized in the name, that is, in, or with, invocation, of the true God, or as the Greek words say, into the name, that is, into the knowledge and invocation, of the true God, who is the Father, Son, and Holy Spirit.

Third, this above all is the thrust of those words, that in the administration of baptism a minister does not function in his own name, but that God the Father, Son, and Holy Spirit, himself present, deals through the outward ministry with the one to be baptized, so that God the Father, because of the merit of the Son, receives him into grace and sanctifies [him] by the Holy Spirit unto righteousness and life eternal, so that in the name is the same as in the stead and place of God the Father, Son, and Holy Spirit, as Paul says in that same passage regarding the preaching of the gospel and absolution. MINISTRY, WORD, AND SACRAMENTS.[7]

DISCIPLES MUST GO. WILLIAM BRIDGE: In regard of a nation, in regard of a kingdom in the world, "Go," says our Lord and Savior Christ unto his disciples, "and teach all nations." The nations did not come to Christ and say, "Lord, the Jews have refused the gospel, and therefore we beseech you that the gospel may be preached unto us, and we will receive it." No, but before ever they sent any such message to have the gospel come down to them, the gospel is sent to them, "Go," says our Savior. "Go preach to all nations." "But Lord," they might say, "suppose that in those nations we meet with such a man as Herod, such a man as Pilate. Shall we preach the gospel, and the free remission of sins then to such a one?" "Go," says Christ, "I make no exceptions; go, and preach to all nations." "But suppose that a Judas come in when we are preaching the gospel?" Christ says, "I make no exceptions. If a Judas will come and submit, go, preach to all. Go preach the gospel. Go preach to all nations." EVANGELICAL REPENTANCE.[8]

---

[5]Browne, *An Answere to Master Cartwright*, 10-11.
[6]Denck, *Selected Writings*, 279-80.

[7]Chemnitz, *Enchiridion*, 112-13; citing 2 Cor 2:10; 5:20.
[8]WWB 2:220.

Mission and Message. Desiderius Erasmus: Like as I died for the health of all people, so there is no nation which belongs not to my right. It shall be your part to get unto me, as much as lies in you, all kind of people. But you shall not get them by weapons of war, but by the same means that I got unto me this right, by wholesome doctrine, by a life worthy and suitable for the gospel, with free will doing with patient suffering of ills. Go you therefore as trusty ambassadors, and trusting me your author, teach first the Jews, then the next neighbors unto them, afterward all the nations of the whole world. Teach what they ought to believe of me, and what they ought to trust of me. First, to acknowledge the heavenly Father, the maker, the orderer, and the restorer of all things visible and invisible. . . . They must acknowledge also his son Jesus, by whom through his eternal and unsearchable counsel, he has purposed to deliver mankind from tyranny of sin and death, and by the doctrine of the gospel, to open the way unto everlasting felicity. . . . They must acknowledge also the Holy Ghost, whom I have now partly given unto you, and will give more fully, after that I come into heaven, whose secret inspiration shall comfort, teach, and strengthen the minds of those who trust in me. . . . After that you have taught these things if they believe the things that you have taught, if they repent them of their former life, if they be ready to embrace the doctrine of the gospel, then dip them in water, in the name of the Father, the Son, and the Holy Ghost, that by this holy sign, they may trust themselves to be delivered from the filthiness of all their sins, freely through the benefit of my death, and now to be chosen to the number of the children of God. . . . Let this token be sufficient for all people who come to the profession of the gospel, which is easy to be had in every place. But lest anyone might think it sufficient to salvation, once to be baptized, and to profess the faith of the gospel, they must be taught again by what means they may keep their innocence, by what means they may go forward to perfection of the evangelical godliness; I have omitted nothing which may make to the obtaining of everlasting health. And that heavenly spirit which you shall receive will not suffer you to forget that which you have learned of me. Therefore, whatsoever I have commanded you, deliver you the same to be kept of them. Paraphrases.[9]

Good News for the Nations. John Spilsbury: This blessed commission of Christ to his apostles was chiefly for us Gentiles, saying, "All power is given me in heaven, and in earth. Go you therefore and teach all nations, baptizing them in the name of the Father, Son, and Holy Ghost." As if Christ had said, "Go now into all nations, and preach the gospel freely, as well to one nation as to another; for the gospel shall not now be confined any more to one place or people, then to another. God is now a God of the Gentiles, as well as of the Jews; go therefore as well to the Gentiles as to the Jews, even unto all nations, and there preach the gospel, and so make disciples by teaching them; and such so taught, them baptize in the name of the Father, Son, and Holy Ghost, that is, into the true and orderly profession of that which they have been taught and believed." So that here teaching goes before baptizing and presupposes understanding and faith in that which is taught; this being the only place of Christ's instituting the ordinance of baptism. A Treatise Concerning the Lawful Subject of Baptism.[10]

Preach and Baptize. Menno Simons: I will place the words of Christ, according to Matthew and Mark, before the reader, so that he may see what rule and law he has made concerning the practice of baptism and what command he has given. Christ says, "All power is given unto me in heaven and in earth. Go you, therefore, and teach all nations, baptizing them [understand, those whom you have made or make disciples by your doctrine] in the name of the Father, and of the Son, and of the Holy Ghost, teaching them to observe all things whatsoever I have commanded you."

---

[9]EP 109r-109v.
[10]Spilsbury, *A Treatise Concerning the Lawful Subject of Baptism*, 28.

Behold, this is the word and ordinance of the Lord, how we are to baptize and when. I think these words are too plain to be twisted with glosses or changed with subtlety, namely, that we are to preach the gospel, and baptize those who believe it. . . . Yet through no other command nor ordinance than to preach the gospel, make disciples by means of the doctrine, baptize these same disciples, and so gather unto the truth, and obedience, as the regenerate children of God, and thank his great and glorious name forever. And with such a people that walks in his fear, love, word, ordinances, and commands, he will always be, even to the end of the world. REPLY TO GELLIUS FABER.[11]

BAPTISM PRECEDED AND FOLLOWED BY TEACHING. PILGRAM MARPECK: Christ, however, commanded his disciples, the apostles, to baptize in a different way than John, for he says, "Baptize them in the name of the Father, the Son, and the Holy Spirit." Accordingly, the apostles, who received the command and who in turn commanded others, proclaim the gospel that Christ had been sacrificed for the sins of the whole world, had assuaged the wrath of the Father, had repaid unrighteousness with his blood and saved men from eternal death. They proclaimed that, from now on, every believer could be reunited with God the Father, the Son, and the Holy Spirit; every believer could have a new and eternal life, and could lead a blameless life. Whoever accepted the teaching of the apostles was baptized in the name of God. Henceforth, in view of the fact that God had atoned for sin through Christ, who had reunited them with God the Father, Son, and Holy Spirit, they no longer needed to live according to the flesh, now, they could conduct themselves in a divine way of life. . . .

We must note further that instruction is mentioned both before and after baptism and, thus, baptism stands, in an orderly way, in the middle. Such an order has the following meaning. All people by nature are unacquainted with divine matters, so they must first be made aware of the teaching of the gospel, through which a person first comes to true faith, as is witnessed in Scripture. Before anything else is done with respect to divine matters, they have to be, through the word of teaching, taught and enlightened in the knowledge and the will of God. This is the first instruction, namely, that the gospel is openly proclaimed to all creatures and salvation is freely offered to everyone. This proclamation is included in the words that the Lord speaks: "Teach all nations." Wherever, then, the Holy Spirit touches the heart, so that person can truly believe the gospel, a child of God is born, and their birth is witnessed in baptism, openly revealed and carried out as we shall note later.

After baptism, a different kind of teaching follows, a teaching which is directed to the regenerate and baptized children of God; they are taught to observe all that Christ has commanded, as is fitting for obedient children, and at all times to seek to do the will of their Father. . . .

Thus, briefly concerning the order: First, to learn, we are instructed to know the will of God and to believe Christ. When we have been taught that we can know Christ and believe in him, then it is time to be baptized, to take off our old fleshly lusts and to put on Christ, a new spiritual life. After that, just as we have agreed, in being baptized, to complete the will of God, we learn, or are instructed, to be obedient in all things, and not again return to sin, as a dog does to its vomit or as a washed sow again to its dirt. . . .

In the third place, there are some who say that "in the name of God" means on God's behalf or in the place of God, just as, when a man says, "do that in my name," he means "do it for my sake." We grant this understanding its value for, if one looks correctly at the manner of speech and at the mystery of baptism, it turns out that to say, "In the name of the Father, the Son, and the Holy Spirit," is the same as to say God himself. It carries this meaning: we are baptized in the name of God, and then we actually confess by faith that God has been gracious to us through Christ, who has forgiven us

[11]Simons, *Complete Writings*, 701.

all our sins and has reconciled us to God so that, thereafter, we may also rely upon him and seek to fulfill his will. Consequently, we are baptized in the name of the Holy Trinity. When we are baptized, we fully commit ourselves to God and into him and, through baptism, we make the commitment to deny ourselves and to no longer carry on by ourselves but, rather, to let the self die. Then, similar to its meaning to other places, the little word "in" refers to the covenant. THE ADMONITION OF 1549.[12]

THE SPIRIT-ENABLED MISSION. JOHN CALVIN: "And lo, I am with you always." As Christ gave to the apostles a commission which they were unable to discharge by reliance on merely human power, he encourages them by the assurance of his heavenly protection. For before promising that he would be with them, he began with declaring that he is the king of heaven and earth, who governs all things by his power and authority. The pronoun "I" must be viewed as emphatic; as if he had said that the apostles, if they wished zealously to perform their duty, must not consider what they are able to do, but must rely on the invincible power of those

under whose banner they fight. The nature of that presence which the Lord promises to his followers ought to be understood spiritually; for it is not necessary that he should descend from heaven in order to assist us, since he can assist us by the grace of his Spirit, as if he stretched out his hand from heaven. For he who, in respect of his body, is at a great distance from us, not only diffuses the efficacy of his Spirit through the whole world, but even actually dwells in us.

Even to the end of the world. It ought likewise to be remarked that this was not spoken to the apostles alone; for the Lord promises his assistance not for a single age only, but even to the end of the world. It is as if he had said that though the ministers of the gospel be weak and suffer the want of all things, he will be their guardian, so that they will rise victorious over all the opposition of the world. In like manner, experience clearly shows in the present day that the operations of Christ are carried on wonderfully in a secret manner, so that the gospel surmounts innumerable obstacles. COMMENTARY ON A HARMONY OF THE EVANGELISTS.[13]

---

[12]CRR 2:175-76, 182-84; citing 2 Pet 2:22.

[13]CTS 3:390-91 (CO 45:826).

Map of Europe at the Time of the Reformation

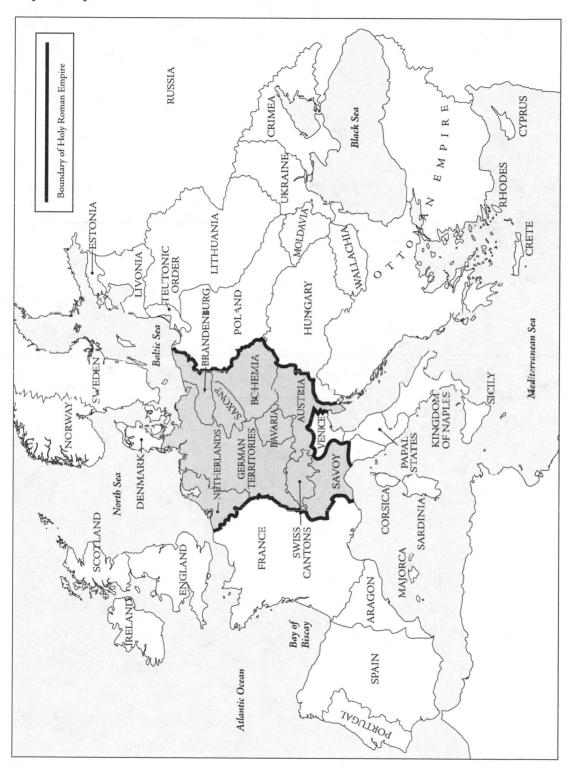

Timeline of the Reformation

	German Territories	France	Spain	Italy	Switzerland	Netherlands	British Isles
1309–1377		Babylonian Captivity of the Papacy					
1337–1453		d. Nicholas of Lyra Hundred Years' War	b. Paul of Burgos (Solomon ha-Levi)(d. 1435) Alonso Tostado (1400–1455)				Hundred Years' War
1378–1415		Western Schism (Avignon Papacy)		Western Schism			
1384							d. John Wycliffe
1414–1418					Council of Basel (1431–1437)		
1415				Council of Constance; d. Jan Hus; Martin V (r. 1417–1431); Council of Florence (1438–1445)			
1450	Invention of printing press						
1452				b. Leonardo da Vinci (d. 1519)			
1453				Fall of Constantinople			
1455–1485	b. Johannes Reuchlin (d. 1522)						War of Roses; rise of House of Tudor
1456	Gutenberg Bible						
1460				Pope Pius II issued *Execrabilis*			
1466		b. Jacques Lefèvre d'Étaples (d. 1536)					
1467						b. Desiderius Erasmus (d. 1536)	b. John Colet (d. 1519)
1469	b. Antoius Broickwy von Königstein (d. 541)						
1470				b. Santes Pagninus (d. 1541)			b. John (Mair) Major (d. 1550)
1475				b. Michelangelo (d. 1564)			
1478	b. Wolfgang Capito (d. 1541)		Ferdinand and Isabella	b. Jacopo Sadoleto (d. 1547)			b. Thomas More (d. 1535)

	German Territories	France	Spain	Italy	Switzerland	Netherlands	British Isles
1480	b. Balthasar Hubmaier (d. 1528); b. Andreas Bodenstein von Karlstadt (d. 1541)						
1481–1530			Spanish Inquisition				
1482					b. Johannes Oecolampadius (d. 1531)		
1483	b. Martin Luther (d. 1546)						
1484	b. Johann Spangenberg (d. 1550)				b. Huldrych Zwingli (d. 1531)		
1485	b. Johannes Bugenhagen (d. 1554)						b. Hugh Latimer (d. 1555)
1486	r. Frederick the Wise, Elector (d. 1525); b. Johann Eck (d. 1543)						
1488	b. Otto Brunfels (d. 1534)						b. Miles Coverdale (d. 1568)
1489	b. Thomas Müntzer (d. 1525); b. Kaspar von Schwenckfeld (d. 1561)						b. Thomas Cranmer (d. 1556)
1491	b. Martin Bucer (d. 1551)		b. Ignatius Loyola (d. 1556)				
1492			Defeat of Moors in Grenada; Columbus discovers America; expulsion of Jews from Spain	Alexander VI (r. 1492–1503)			
1493	b. Justus Jonas (d. 1555)						
1494							b. William Tyndale (d. 1536)
1496	b. Andreas Osiander (d. 1552)					b. Menno Simons (d. 1561)	
1497	b. Philipp Melanchthon (d. 1560); b. Wolfgang Musculus (d. 1563); b. Johannes (Ferus) Wild (d. 1554)						

	German Territories	France	Spain	Italy	Switzerland	Netherlands	British Isles
1498				d. Girolamo Savonarola	b. Conrad Grebel (d. 1526)		
1499	b. Johannes Brenz (d. 1570) b. Justus Menius (d. 1558)			b. Peter Martyr Vermigli (d. 1562)			
1500			b. Charles V (–1558)				
1501	b. Erasmus Sarcerius (d. 1559)						
1502	Founding of University of Wittenberg			Julius II (r. 1503–1513)		b. Frans Titelmans (d. 1537)	
1504					b. Heinrich Bullinger (d. 1575)		
1505	Luther joins Augustinian Order			b. Benedict Aretius (d. 1574)			
1506		b. Augustin Marlorat (d. 1562)		Restoration of St. Peter's begins			
1507				Sale of indulgences approved to fund building			
1508	b. Lucas Lossius (d. 1582)						
1509		b. John Calvin (d. 1564)					r. Henry VIII (–1547)
1510	Luther moves to Rome			b. Immanuel Tremellius (d. 1580)			b. Nicholas Ridley (d. 1555)
1511	Luther moves to Wittenberg						
1512				Sistine Chapel completed			
1512–1517				Fifth Lateran Council; rejection of conciliarism			
1513	Luther lectures on Psalms			r. Pope Leo X (–1521)			b. John Knox (d. 1572)
1515	Luther lectures on Romans	r. Francis I (–1547); b. Peter Ramus (d. 1572)					
1516		Est. French National Church (via Concordat of Bologna)		Concordat of Bologna		Publication of Erasmus's Greek New Testament	
1517	Tetzel sells indulgences in Saxony; Luther's Ninety-five Theses						

	German Territories	France	Spain	Italy	Switzerland	Netherlands	British Isles
1518	Heidelberg Disputation; Luther examined by Cajetan at Diet of Augsburg			Diet of Augsburg			
1519	Leipzig Disputation	b. Theodore Beza (d. 1605)	Cortés conquers Aztecs; Portuguese sailor Magellan circumnavigates the globe		Zwingli appointed pastor of Grossmünster in Zurich; b. Rudolf Gwalther (d. 1586)		
1520	Publication of Luther's "Three Treatises"; burning of papal bull in Wittenberg		Coronation of Charles V	Papal Bull v. Luther: *Exsurge Domine*			
1521	Luther excommunicated; Diet/Edict of Worms—Luther condemned; Luther in hiding; Melanchthon's *Loci communes*	French-Spanish War (–1526)	French-Spanish War; Loyola converts	Papal excommunication of Luther			Henry VIII publishes *Affirmation of the Seven Sacraments* against Luther; awarded title "Defender of the Faith" by Pope
1521–1522	Disorder in Wittenberg; Luther translates New Testament						
1521–1525		First and Second Habsburg–Valois War					
1522	Luther returns to Wittenberg; Luther's NT published; criticizes Zwickau prophets; b. Martin Chemnitz (d. 1586)		Publication of Complutensian Polyglot Bible under Cisneros		Sausage Affair and reform begins in Zurich under Zwingli		b. John Jewel (d. 1571)
1523	Knight's Revolt	Bucer begins ministry in Strasbourg	Loyola writes Spiritual Exercises	r. Pope Clement VII (–1534)	Iconoclasm in Zurich		
1524	Luther criticizes peasants; d. Johann von Staupitz				Erasmus's disputation on free will		
1524–1526	Peasants' War						
1525	Luther marries; execution of Thomas Müntzer; publication of Luther's *Bondage of the Will*				Abolition of mass in Zurich; disputation on baptism; first believers' baptism performed in Zurich		

	German Territories	France	Spain	Italy	Switzerland	Netherlands	British Isles
1526					Zurich council mandates capital punishment of Anabaptists	Publication of Tyndale's English translation of NT	
1527	d. Hans Denck (b. c. 1500) d. Hans Hut (b. 1490) b. Tilemann Hesshus (d. 1588)			Sack of Rome by mutinous troops of Charles V	First Anabaptist executed in Zurich; drafting of Schleitheim Confession		
1528	Execution of Hubmaier						
1529	Second Diet of Speyer; evangelical "protest"; publication of Luther's catechisms; Marburg Colloquy; siege of Vienna by Turkish forces	Abolition of mass in Strasbourg			d. Georg Blaurock (b. 1492)		Thomas More appointed chancellor to Henry VIII
1530	Diet of Augsburg; Confession of Augsburg	d. Francois Lambert (Lambert of Avignon) (b. 1487)	Charles V crowned Holy Roman Emperor				
1531	Formation of Schmalkaldic League				d. H. Zwingli; succeeded by H. Bullinger		
1532		Publication of Calvin's commentary on Seneca; conversion of Calvin	b. Francisco de Toledo (d. 1596)				
1533	b. Valentein Weigel (d. 1588)	Nicholas Cop addresses University of Paris; Cop and Calvin implicated as "Lutheran" sympathizers	b. Juan de Maldonado (d. 1583)				Thomas Cranmer appointed as Archbishop of Canterbury; Henry VIII divorces
1534	First edition of Luther's Bible published	Affair of the Placards; Calvin flees d. Guillame Briçonnet (b. 1470)		Jesuits founded; d. Cardinal Cajetan (Thomas de Vio) (b. 1469)			Act of Supremacy; English church breaks with Rome
1535	Bohemian Confession of 1535; Anabaptist theocracy at Münster collapses after eighteen months				b. Lambert Daneau (d. 1595)		d. Thomas More; d. John Fisher

	German Territories	France	Spain	Italy	Switzerland	Netherlands	British Isles
1536	Wittenberg Concord; b. Kaspar Olevianus (d. 1587)				First edition of Calvin's *Institutes* published; Calvin arrives in Geneva (–1538); First Helvetic Confession	Publication of Tyndale's translation of NT; d. W. Tyndale	d. A. Boleyn; Henry VIII dissolves monasteries (–1541)
1537					Calvin presents ecclesiastical ordinances to Genevan Council		
1538					Calvin exiled from Geneva; arrives in Strasbourg (–1541)		
1539		Calvin publishes second edition of *Institutes* in Strasbourg		d. Felix Pratensis			Statute of Six Articles; publication of Coverdale's Great Bible
1540				Papal approval of Jesuit order			d. Thomas Cromwell
1541	Colloquy of Regensburg	French translation of Calvin's *Institutes* published	d. Juan de Valdés (b. 1500/1510)		d. A. Karlstadt; Calvin returns to Geneva (–1564)		
1542	d. Sebastian Franck (b. 1499)			Institution of Roman Inquisition			War between England and Scotland; James V of Scotland defeated; Ireland declared sovereign kingdom
1543	Copernicus publishes *On the Revolutions of the Heavenly Spheres*; d. Johann Eck (Johann Maier of Eck) (b. 1486)						
1545–1547	Schmalkaldic Wars; d. Martin Luther			First session of Council of Trent			b. Richard Bancroft (d. 1610)
1546	b. Johannes Piscator (d. 1625)						
1547	Defeat of Protestants at Mühlberg	d. Francis I; r. Henri II (–1559)					d. Henry VIII; r. Edward VI (–1553)
1548	Augsburg Interim (–1552) d. Caspar Cruciger (b. 1504) b. David Pareus (d. 1622)						

	German Territories	France	Spain	Italy	Switzerland	Netherlands	British Isles
1549	d. Paul Fagius (b. 1504)	d. Marguerite d'Angoulême (b. 1492)			Consensus Tigurinus between Calvin and Bullinger		First Book of Common Prayer published
1550	b. Aegidius Hunnius (d. 1603)						
1551–1552				Second session of Council of Trent			
1552	d. Sebastian Münster (b. 1488) d. Friedrich Nausea (b. c. 1496)						Book of Common Prayer revised
1553	d. Johannes Aepinus (b. 1449)				Michael Servetus executed in Geneva		Cranmer's Forty-Two Articles; d. Edward VI; r. Mary I (d. 1558)
1554							Richard Hooker (d. 1600)
1555	Diet of Augsburg; Peace of Augsburg establishes legal territorial existence of Lutheranism and Catholicism b. Johann Arndt (d. 1621)	First mission of French pastors trained in Geneva				b. Sibbrandus Lubbertus (d. 1625)	b. Lancelot Andrewes (d. 1626) b. Robert Rollock (d. 1599); d. Hugh Latimer; d. Nicholas Ridley d. John Hooper
1556	d. Pilgram Marpeck (b. 1495) d. Konrad Pellikan (b. 1478) d. Peter Riedemann (b. 1506)		Charles V resigns			d. David Joris (b. c. 1501)	d. Thomas Cranmer
1557							Alliance with Spain in war against France
1558			d. Charles V				b. William Perkins (d. 1602); d. Mary I; r. Elizabeth I (–1603)
1559		d. Henry II; r. Francis II (–1560); first national synod of French reformed churches (1559) in Paris; Gallic Confession		First index of prohibited books issued	Final edition of Calvin's Institutes; founding of Genevan Academy	b. Jacobus Arminius (d. 1609)	Elizabethan Settlement

	German Territories	France	Spain	Italy	Switzerland	Netherlands	British Isles
1560	d. P. Melanchthon	d. Francis II; r. Charles IX (1574); Edict of Toleration created peace with Huguenots	d. Domingo de Soto (b. 1494)		Geneva Bible		Kirk of Scotland established; Scottish Confession
1561-1563				Third session of Council of Trent			
1561						Belgic Confession	
1562	d. Katharina Schütz Zell (b. 1497/98)	Massacre of Huguenots begins French Wars of Religion (–1598)					The Articles of Religion—in Elizabethan "final" form (1562/71); publication of Latin edition of Jewel's *Apology*
1563	Heidelberg Catechism						
1564				b. Galileo (d. 1642)	d. J. Calvin		b. William Shakespeare (d. 1616); publication of Lady Ann Bacon's English translation of Jewel's *Apology*
1566	d. Johann Agricola (b. 1494)			Roman Catechism	Second Helvetic Confession		
1567						Spanish occupation	Abdication of Scottish throne by Mary Stuart; r. James VI (1603–1625)
1568						d. Dirk Phillips (b. 1504) Dutch movement for liberation (–1645)	*Bishops' Bible*
1570		d. Johannes Mercerus (Jean Mercier)		Papal Bull *Regnans in Excelsis* excommunicates Elizabeth I			Elizabeth I excommunicated
1571	b. Johannes Kepler (d. 1630)		Spain defeats Ottoman navy at Battle of Lepanto				b. John Downame (d. 1652)
1572		Massacre of Huguenots on St. Bartholomew's Day		r. Pope Gregory XIII (1583–1585)		William of Orange invades	b. John Donne (d. 1631)
1574		d. Charles IX; r. Henri III (d. 1589)					

	German Territories	France	Spain	Italy	Switzerland	Netherlands	British Isles
1575	d. Georg Major (b. 1502); Bohemian Confession of 1575						
1576		Declaration of Toleration; formation of Catholic League		b. Giovanni Diodati (d. 1649)		Sack of Antwerp; Pacification of Ghent	
1577	Lutheran Formula of Concord						England allies with Netherlands against Spain
1578	Swiss Brethren Confession of Hesse d. Peter Walpot		Truce with Ottomans				Sir Francis Drake circumnavigates the globe
1579			Expeditions to Ireland			Division of Dutch provinces	
1580	Lutheran Book of Concord						
1581			d. Teresa of Avila				Anti-Catholic statutes passed
1582				Gregorian Reform of calendar			
1583							b. David Dickson (d. 1663)
1584		Treaty of Joinville with Spain	Treaty of Joinville; Spain inducted into Catholic League; defeats Dutch at Antwerp			Fall of Antwerp; d. William of Orange	
1585	d. Josua Opitz (b. c. 1542)	Henri of Navarre excommunicated		r. Pope Sixtus V (–1590)			
1586							Sir Francis Drake's expedition to West Indies; Sir Walter Raleigh in Roanoke
1587	d. Johann Wigand (b. 1523)	Henri of Navarre defeats royal army					d. Mary Stuart of Scotland
1588		Henri of Navarre drives Henri III from Paris; assassination of Catholic League Leaders	Armada destroyed				English Navy defeats Spanish Armada
1589		d. Henri III; r. Henri (of Navarre) IV (–1610)	Victory over England at Lisbon				Defeated by Spain in Lisbon
1590		Henri IV's siege of Paris		d. Girolamo Zanchi (b. 1516)			Alliance with Henri IV

	German Territories	France	Spain	Italy	Switzerland	Netherlands	British Isles
1592	d. Nikolaus Selnecker (b. 1530)						
1593		Henri IV converts to Catholicism					Books I-IV of Hooker's *Laws of Ecclesiastical Polity* published
1594		Henri grants toleration to Huguenots					
1595		Henri IV declares war on Spain; received into Catholic Church		Pope Sixtus accepts Henri IV into Church			Alliance with France
1596		b. René Descartes (d. 1650) b. Moïse Amyraut (d. 1664)					
1597							Book V of Hooker's *Laws of Ecclesiastical Polity* published
1598		Edict of Nantes; toleration of Huguenots; peace with Spain	Treaty of Vervins; peace with France				
1600	d. David Chytraeus (b. 1531)						
1601							b. John Trapp (d. 1669)
1602					d. Daniel Toussain (b. 1541)		
1603							d. Elizabeth I; r. James I (James VI of Scotland) (–1625)
1604	d. Cyriacus Spangenberg (b. 1528)						d. John Whitgift (b. 1530)
1605						b. Rembrandt (d. 1669)	Guy Fawkes and gunpowder plot
1606							Jamestown Settlement
1607							b. John Milton (d. 1674)
1608							
1610		d. Henri IV; r. Louis XIII (–1643)	d. Benedict Pererius (b. 1535)			The Remonstrance; Short Confession	

	German Territories	France	Spain	Italy	Switzerland	Netherlands	British Isles
1611							Publication of Authorized English Translation of Bible (AV/KJV); George Abbot becomes Archbishop of Canterbury (–1633)
1612							b. Richard Crashaw (d. 1649)
1616							b. John Owen (d. 1683)
1617							b. Ralph Cudworth (d. 1689)
1618–1619						Synod of Dordrecht	
1618–1648	Thirty Years' War						
1620							English Sepratists land in Plymouth, Massachusetts
1621							d. Andrew Willet (b. 1562)
1628							Puritans establish Massachusetts Bay colony
1633	d. Christoph Pelargus (b. 1565)						Laud becomes Archbishop of Canterbury
1637	d. Johann Gerhard (b. 1582)					*Statenvertaling*	
1638							d. Joseph Mede (b. 1638)
1640				Diodati's Italian translation of Bible published			
1642–1649							English civil wars; d. Charles I; r. Oliver Cromwell (1660)
1643		d. Louis XIII; r. Louis XIV (–1715)					
1643–1649							Westminster Assembly
1645							d. William Laud (b. 1573)

	German Territories	France	Spain	Italy	Switzerland	Netherlands	British Isles
1648		Treaty of Westphalia ends Thirty Years' War					Books VI and VIII of Hooker's *Laws of Ecclesiastical Polity* posthumously published
1656	d. Georg Calixtus (b. 1586)						
1658							d. Oliver Cromwell
1659							Richard Cromwell resigns
1660							English Restoration; r. Charles II (–1685)
1662							Act of Uniformity; Book VII of Hooker's *Laws of Ecclesiastical Polity* posthumously published
1664						d. Thieleman Jans van Braght (b. 1625)	d. John Mayer (b. 1583)
1671							d. William Greenhill (b. 1591)
1677							d. Thomas Manton (b. 1620)
1678						d. Anna Maria von Schurman (b. 1607)	
1688							Glorious Revolution; r. William and Mary (-1702); d. John Bunyan (b. 1628)
1691							d. Richard Baxter (b. 1615)

BIOGRAPHICAL SKETCHES OF
REFORMATION-ERA FIGURES AND WORKS

This list is cumulative, including all the authors cited in the Reformation Commentary on Scripture
to date as well as other people relevant to the Reformation and Reformation-era exegesis.
For works consulted, see "Sources for Biographical Sketches," p. 477.

Cornelius À Lapide (1567–1637). Flemish Catholic biblical exegete. A Jesuit, Lapide served as professor of Holy Scripture and Hebrew at Louvain for twenty years before taking a similar role in Rome, where he taught until his death. He is best known for his extensive commentaries on the Scriptures. Encompassing all books of the Bible except Job and the Psalms, his work employs a fourfold hermeneutic and draws heavily on the work of patristic and medieval exegetes.

Thomas Adams (1583–1653). Anglican minister and author. He attended the University of Cambridge where he received his BA in 1601 and his MA in 1606. Following his ordination in 1604, Adams served as curate at Northill in Bedfordshire. In 1611, he became vicar of Willmington. Three years later he served the parish of Wingrave, Buckinghamshire, where he remained until 1618. From 1618 to 1623 Adams was preacher at St. Gregory by St. Paul's. He also served as chaplain to Henry Montague, First Earl of Manchester, and Lord Chief Justice of England. Among his most important works are the *Happiness of the Church* (1618) and an extensive commentary on 2 Peter (1638).

Johannes Aepinus (1499–1553). German Lutheran preacher and theologian. Aepinus studied under Martin Luther,* Philipp Melanchthon* and Johannes Bugenhagen* in Wittenberg. Because of

his Lutheran beliefs, Aepinus lost his first teaching position in Brandenburg. He fled north to Stralsund and became a preacher and superintendent at Saint Peter's Church in Hamburg. In 1534, he made a diplomatic visit to England but could not convince Henry VIII* to embrace the Augsburg Confession.* His works include sermons and theological writings. Aepinus became best known as leader of the Infernalists, who believed that Christ underwent torment in hell after his crucifixion.

Johann Agricola (c. 1494–1566). German Lutheran pastor and theologian. An early student of Martin Luther,* Agricola eventually began a controversy over the role of the law, first with Melanchthon* and then with Luther himself. Agricola claimed to defend Luther's true position, asserting that only the gospel of the crucified Christ calls Christians to truly good works, not the fear of the law. After this first controversy, Agricola seems to have radicalized his views to the point that he eliminated Luther's *simul iustus et peccator* ("at the same time righteous and sinful") paradox of the Christian life, emphasizing instead that believers have no need for the law once they are united with Christ through faith. Luther responded by writing anonymous pamphlets against antinomianism. Agricola later published a recantation of his views, hoping to assuage relations with Luther, although they were never personally reconciled. He published a commentary on Luke, a series of sermons on Colossians, and a massive collection of German proverbs.

Henry Ainsworth (1571–1622/1623). English Puritan Hebraist. In 1593, under threat of persecution, Ainsworth relocated to Amsterdam, where he served as a teacher in an English congregation. He composed a confession of faith for the community and a number of polemical and exegetical works, including annotations on the Pentateuch, the Psalms and Song of Songs.

Henry Airay (c. 1560–1616). English Puritan professor and pastor. He was especially noted for his preaching, a blend of hostility toward Catholicism and articulate exposition of English Calvinism. He was promoted to provost of Queen's College Oxford (1598) and then to vice chancellor of the university in 1606. He disputed with William Laud* concerning Laud's putative Catholicization of the Church of England, particularly over the practice of genuflection, which Airay vehemently opposed. He also opposed fellow Puritans who wished to separate from the Church of England. His lectures on Philippians were his only work published during his lifetime.

Albert the Great (1201–1280). German theologian, philosopher, scientist, and ecclesiastic. Albert was born in Lauingen, located in the Bavarian-Swabian region. After completing his studies at Padua, Albert joined the Dominicans in 1220s. Upon finishing further theological studies at Cologne, Albert became a conventual lecturer during the 1230s at Hildesheim, Freiberg (Saxony), Regensburg, and Strasbourg. In the early 1240s, Albert was sent to Paris where he became a master of theology, and regent of the university in 1245. He served as regent until 1248. While at Paris, Albert commenced his paraphrases of Aristotle's works. Furthermore, Albert authored a systematic theology, and lectured on the four Gospels and nine books of the Old Testament. Albert is best known for having taught Thomas Aquinas,* who, as his assistant, transcribed his course on the works of Dionysius and Aristotle's *Nicomachean Ethics*.

Alexander (Ales) Alesius (1500–1565). Scottish Lutheran theologian. Following the martyrdom of his theological adversary Patrick Hamilton (c. 1504–1528), Alesius converted to the Reformation and fled to Germany. In 1535 Martin Luther* and Philipp Melanchthon* sent him as an emissary to Henry VIII* and Thomas Cranmer.* He taught briefly at Cambridge, but after the Act of Six Articles reasserted Catholic sacramental theology he returned to Germany, where he lectured at Frankfurt an der Oder and Leipzig. Alesius composed many exegetical, theological and polemical works, including commentaries on John, Romans, 1–2 Timothy, Titus and the Psalms.

Robert Allen (fl. 1596–1612). English Protestant clergyman and writer. Allen is known only by his writings, which reveal few biographical details except that he was a minister and he wrote from London and Suffolk. His works include a theological summary of Proverbs and Ecclesiastes, an exposition of the Gospel, and a catechism.

Andreas Althamer (c. 1500–1539). German Lutheran humanist and pastor. Forced from the chaplaincy at Schwäbisch-Gmünd for teaching evangelical ideas, Althamer studied theology at Wittenberg before serving as a pastor in Eltersdorf, Nuremberg, and Ansbach. A staunch Lutheran, he contended against Reformed theologians at the 1528 disputation at Bern and delivered numerous polemics against Anabaptism. He also composed an early Lutheran catechism, published at Nuremberg in 1528.

William Ames (1576–1633). English Puritan theologian. Heavily influenced by William Perkins* while at Cambridge, Ames was unable to find employment in the English church due to his Puritan commitments. Most of his life was spent in exile in the Netherlands, where he served as chaplain to English forces at The Hague and was the pastor of a small congregation. Best known as a controversialist during his early career, Ames was the theological advisor to the president of the Synod of Dort (1618–1619) and was later installed as chair of theology at the University of Franeker in

Friesland. *The Marrow of Theology* (1627) is viewed as a model of seventeenth-century Puritan theology.

Moïse Amyraut (1596–1664). French Reformed pastor and professor. Originally intending to be a lawyer, Amyraut turned to theology after an encounter with several Huguenot pastors and having read Calvin's* *Institutes*. After a brief stint as a parish pastor, Amyraut spent the majority of his career at the Saumur Academy. He was well known for his irenicism and ecumenicism (for example, in advocating intercommunion with Lutherans). Certain aspects of his writings on justification, faith, the covenants and especially predestination proved controversial among the Reformed. His doctrine of election is often called hypothetical universalism or Amyraldianism, stating that Christ's atoning work was intended by God for all human beings indiscriminately, although its effectiveness for salvation depends on faith, which is a free gift of God given only to those whom God has chosen from eternity. Amyraut was charged with grave doctrinal error three times before the National Synod but was acquitted each time. Aside from his theological treatises, Amyraut published paraphrases of almost the entire New Testament and the Psalms, as well as many sermons.

Anabaptists of Trieste (1539). Following a meeting between Swiss Brethren and the Hutterites at Steinabrunn on December 6, 1536, around 140 radicals were arrested and imprisoned in Falkenstein Castle. After six weeks in captivity, the ninety men of the group were forced to march to Trieste to be sold as galley slaves. Twelve days after arrival, all but twelve prisoners managed to escape and return to Moravia, where they published a confession of their beliefs.

Jakob Andreae (1528–1590). German Lutheran theologian. Andreae studied at the University of Tübingen before being called to the diaconate in Stuttgart in 1546. He was appointed ecclesiastical superintendent of Göppingen in 1553 and supported Johannes Brenz's* proposal to place the church under civil administrative control. An ecclesial diplomat for the duke of Württemberg, Andreae debated eucharistic theology, the use of images, and predestination with Theodore Beza* at the Colloquy of Montbéliard (1586) to determine whether French Reformed exiles would be required to submit to the Formula of Concord.* Andreae coauthored the Formula of Concord. He and his wife had eighteen children.

Lancelot Andrewes (1555–1626). Anglican bishop. A scholar, pastor and preacher, Andrews prominently shaped a distinctly Anglican identity between the poles of Puritanism and Catholicism. He oversaw the translation of Genesis to 2 Kings for the Authorized Version.* His eight-volume collected works—primarily devotional tracts and sermons—are marked by his fluency in Scripture, the Christian tradition and classical literature.

Thomas Aquinas (1225–1274). Dominican medieval theologian. Thomas Aquinas was born into a noble family in Rocasecca, Italy. In 1230 Thomas's father sent him to the abbey at Monte Casino as a child oblate. When, at age fourteen, Thomas was given the choice between taking his final vows and leaving, he chose to go to Naples to study at the school recently founded by the Holy Roman Emperor. While studying at Naples, Thomas came into contact with the Dominicans, and joined this order in 1244. Although his family objected to his decision at first, to the point of actually imprisoning Thomas, they came to accept his decision the following year. Afterwards, Aquinas traveled to Paris where he began his formal studies under Albert the Great (1200–1280). Aquinas followed his teacher to Cologne in 1248 where he was ordained a priest, and completed his course in theology. Four years later, he was appointed a bachelor in the Dominican convent in Paris where he lectured on Peter Lombard's (1096–1160)* *Sentences*. In 1256, Thomas was incepted as a master of the sacred page, and he taught in Paris until 1259. In 1261, he was appointed lecturer at a school in Orvieto. Four years later, Aquinas was transferred to Rome, and in 1268 returned to Paris. In 1272, the Dominican order appointed Aquinas to start a new school in Naples. A mystical experience reportedly caused Aquinas to abruptly cease his writing. Aquinas died at a monastery in Fossanova. In addition to his major works, *Summa Theologia* and *Summa Contra Gentiles*, Aquinas's voluminous corpus includes extensive commentaries on Jeremiah, Lamentations, Isaiah, Job, and an incomplete one on the Psalms. Aquinas also wrote commentaries on the Gospels of Matthew and John as well as the Pauline Epistles. Furthermore, at the request of the pope, Aquinas produced the *Catena Aurea*, a commentary on the four Gospels consisting of exegetical statements by the Latin and Greek fathers. One of the most significant features of Aquinas's biblical commentaries is his emphasis on the literal meaning of a Scriptural text. As a representation of medieval Catholic theology, Aquinas's theology was regularly challenged by the Protestant reformers.

Benedict Aretius (d. 1574). Swiss Reformed professor. Trained at the universities of Bern, Strasbourg and Marburg, Aretius taught logic and philosophy as well as the biblical languages and theology. He advocated for stronger unity and peace between the Lutheran and Reformed churches. Aretius joined others in denouncing the antitrinitarian Giovanni Valentino Gentile (d. 1566). He published commentaries on the New Testament, as well as various works on astronomy, botany and medicine.

Aristotle (388–322 BC). Ancient Greek philosopher and scientist. Aristotle was born in Stagira, Chalkdice, northern Greece. He is considered the "Father of Western Philosophy" along with his teacher, Plato, because his teaching produced the bases for almost every discipline studied in the Western world. After his father's death while he was still a child, Aristotle was raised by his guardian, Proxenus of Atarneus. At the age of about eighteen, Aristotle joined Plato's Academy in Athens, where he remained until his was thirty-seven. Aristotle's writings cover a wide range of subjects: physics, biology, zoology, metaphysics, logic, ethics, aesthetics, poetry, theater, music, rhetoric, psychology, linguistics, and politics. Shortly after Plato's death, King Philip II of Macedonia requested his services as a tutor to his son, Alexander the Great. Aristotle began tutoring the young prince in 343 BC. While teaching Alexander, Aristotle was able to acquire hundreds of books for the library of what would become his Lyceum. Aristotle's work profoundly shaped scholarship during the Middle Ages and early modern period as his logic was employed in the exegesis of Scripture and formation of theology. Among the major theologians who incorporated Aristotle's methods into their theological systems was Thomas Aquinas.* Aristotle's methods and categories would also be utilized by many Protestant theologians throughout the sixteenth and seventeenth centuries.

Jacobus Arminius (1559–1609). Dutch Remonstrant pastor and theologian. Arminius was a vocal critic of high Calvinist scholasticism, whose views were repudiated by the Synod of Dordrecht. Arminius was a student of Theodore Beza* at the academy of Geneva. He served as a pastor in Amsterdam and later joined the faculty of theology at the university in Leiden, where his lectures on predestination were popular and controversial. Predestination, as Arminius understood it, was the decree of God determined on the basis of divine foreknowledge of faith or rejection by humans who are the recipients of prevenient, but resistible, grace.

Johann Arndt (1555–1621). German Lutheran pastor and theologian. After a brief time teaching, Arndt pastored in Badeborn (Anhalt) until 1590, when Prince Johann Georg von Anhalt (1567–1618) began introducing Reformed ecclesial policies. Arndt ministered in Quedlinberg, Brunswick, Eisleben and Celle. Heavily influenced by medieval mysticism, Arndt centered his theology on Christ's mystical union with the believer, out of which flows love of God and neighbor. He is best known for his *True Christianity* (1605–1609), which greatly influenced Philipp Jakob Spener (1635–1705) and later Pietists.

John Arrowsmith (1602–1659). English Puritan theologian. Arrowsmith participated in the Westminster Assembly, and later taught at Cambridge. His works, all published posthumously, include three sermons preached to Parliament and an unfinished catechism.

Articles of Religion (1562; revised 1571). The Articles underwent a long editorial process that drew from the influence of Continental confessions in England, resulting in a uniquely Anglican blend of Protestantism and Catholicism. In their final form, they were reduced from Thomas Cranmer's* Forty-two Articles (1539) to the Elizabethan Thirty-Nine Articles (1571), excising polemical articles against the Anabaptists and Millenarians as well as adding articles on the Holy Spirit, good works and Communion. Originating in a 1535 meeting with Lutherans, the Articles retained a minor influence from the Augsburg Confession* and Württemberg Confession (1552), but showed significant revision in accordance with Genevan theology, as well as the Second Helvetic Confession.*

Anne Askew (1521–1546). English Protestant martyr. Askew was forced to marry her deceased sister's intended husband, who later expelled Askew from his house—after the birth of two children—on account of her religious views. After unsuccessfully seeking a divorce in Lincoln, Askew moved to London, where she met other Protestants and began to preach. In 1546, she was arrested, imprisoned and convicted of heresy for denying the doctrine of transubstantiation. Under torture in the Tower of London she refused to name any other Protestants. On July 16, 1546, she was burned at the stake. Askew is best known through her accounts of her arrests and examinations. John Bale (1495–1563), a bishop, historian and playwright, published these manuscripts. Later John Foxe (1516–1587) included them in his *Acts and Monuments*, presenting her as a role model for other pious Protestant women.

Mary Astell (1666–1731). English writer and philosopher. Astell received an informal education from her uncle, a clergyman. Left almost penniless after the death of her parents, she settled in London, where she made her career as a writer. She is best known for her proto-feminist works, including *A Serious Proposal to the Ladies* (1694,

1697), *Some Reflections on Marriage* (1700), and *The Christian Religion, as Professed by a Daughter of the Church of England* (1705). In these works she argues for the moral and intellectual equality of the sexes and the need for women to receive a similar education to men so that they can navigate the world by themselves. Retiring from writing, Astell spent her final decades organizing a charity school for girls in Chelsea backed by the Society for the Propagation of Christian Knowledge.

Augsburg Confession (1530). In the wake of Luther's* stand against ecclesial authorities at the Diet of Worms (1521), the Holy Roman Empire splintered along theological lines. Emperor Charles V sought to ameliorate this—while also hoping to secure a united European front against Turkish invasion—by calling together another imperial diet in Augsburg in 1530. The Evangelical party was cast in a strongly heretical light at the diet by Johann Eck.* For this reason, Philipp Melanchthon* and Justus Jonas* thought it best to strike a conciliatory tone (Luther, as an official outlaw, did not attend), submitting a confession rather than a defense. The resulting Augsburg Confession was approved by many of the rulers of the northeastern Empire; however, due to differences in eucharistic theology, Martin Bucer* and the representatives of Strasbourg, Constance, Lindau and Memmingen drafted a separate confession (the Tetrapolitan Confession). Charles V accepted neither confession, demanding that the Evangelicals accept the Catholic rebuttal instead. In 1531, along with the publication of the Augsburg Confession itself, Melanchthon released a defense of the confession that responded to the Catholic confutation and expanded on the original articles. Most subsequent Protestant confessions followed the general structure of the Augsburg Confession.

Augustine of Hippo (354–430 AD). North African bishop and theologian. Augustine was born in Thagaste (Ahras, Algeria), a small town in the Roman province to Numidia, the son of a Christian mother, Monica, and a non-Christian father, Patricius, a local official of modest means.

Enabled by local patronage, Augustine received a classical education, which afforded him the opportunity to pursue advanced training in rhetoric at Carthage. Upon completing his education at Carthage, Augustine taught rhetoric there as well as in Rome and Milan, where he was appointed official rhetorician of that city. Inspired by his reading of Cicero's *Hortensius*, Augustine embarked upon a quest for wisdom. While in Carthage, Augustine was repulsed by the seemingly simplistic Christianity he encountered, and therefore joined the Manicheans. Having become disillusioned by the Manichaeans' failure to lead him to the wisdom they promised, Augustine was eventually drawn to orthodox Christianity by the preaching of Ambrose (340–397) and his reading of the Neo-Platonist philosopher Plotinus (204–270). As a result of his conversion in 386, Augustine abandoned his secular ambitions in favor of a celibate life fully committed to intellectual and spiritual devotion to God. Towards this end, Augustine returned to north Africa to establish a semi–monastic community. However, in 391, while visiting Hippo Regius, he was forcibly ordained into the priesthood, and made bishop of that church in 396. In addition to his many duties as a bishop, Augustine engaged in controversies against the Manicheans, Donatists, and Pelagians, which took up the remainder of his life and career. He died in 430 while the Vandals besieged Hippo. Among his many works, Augustine devoted several to exegesis. He outlines exegetical principles in his *De Doctrina Christiana* ("On Christian Doctrine"), and he authored extensive series of homilies on most of the books of the New Testament as well as the Old Testament books of Psalms and Genesis (incomplete). During the Reformation era, both Catholic and Protestant theologians appealed to and engaged with Augustine's theology, especially his emphases upon original sin and humanity's need for God's grace.

Authorized Version (1611). In 1604 King James I* commissioned this new translation—popularly remembered as the King James Version—for uniform use in the public worship of the Church of England. The Bible and the Apocrypha was divided into six portions and assigned to six companies of nine scholars—both Anglicans and Puritans—centered at Cambridge, Oxford and Westminster. Richard Bancroft, the general editor of the Authorized Version, composed fifteen rules to guide the translators and to guard against overly partisan decisions. Rather than offer an entirely fresh English translation, the companies were to follow the Bishops' Bible* as closely as possible. "Truly (good Christian Reader)," the preface states, "we neuer thought from the beginning that we should need to make a new Translation, nor yet to make of a bad one a good one . . . but make a good one better, or out of many good ones, one principall good one, not iustly to be excepted against: that hath bene our endeauour, that our mark." Other rules standardized spelling, dictated traditional ecclesial terms (e.g., *church, baptize* and *bishop*), and allowed only for linguistic marginal notes and cross-references. Each book of the Bible went through a rigorous revision process: first, each person in a company made an initial draft, then the company put together a composite draft, then a supercommittee composed of representatives from each company reviewed these drafts, and finally two bishops and Bancroft scrutinized the final edits. The text and translation process of the Authorized Version have widely influenced biblical translations ever since.

Gervase Babington (1549/1550–1610). English Anglican bishop. Born into an influential family, Babington studied at Cambridge and spent time as a preacher at the university and as prebendary of Hereford Cathedral before serving, in turn, as bishop of Llandaff, Exeter, and Worcester. He published a number of sermons, expositions of the Ten Commandments and Lord's Prayer, and notes on Genesis, Exodus, and Leviticus.

Robert Bagnall (b. 1559 or 1560). English Protestant minister. Bagnall authored *The Steward's Last Account* (1622), a collection of five sermons on Luke 16.

Friedrich Balduin (1575–1627). German Lutheran theologian. After spending time in the pastorate at Freiberg and Oelsnitz, Balduin was appointed professor of theology at Wittenberg in 1604, where he remained until the end of his life. He also served as head of the theology faculty, superintendent of churches, and assessor of the consistory. Known for his commitment to Lutheran orthodoxy, Balduin's major works include a commentary on the Pauline letters and writings on exegesis, homiletics, and casuistry.

John Ball (1585–1640). English Puritan theologian. Ball was a respected educator. He briefly held a church office until he was removed on account of his Puritanism. He composed popular catechisms and tracts on faith, the church and the covenant of grace.

John Barlow (1580/1581?–1629/1630). English Protestant minister. Educated at Oxford, Barlow ministered in Plymouth, Halifax, and Chester. A number of his sermons have been preserved, including his teachings on 2 Timothy 1 and 1 Thessalonians 4:18.

Thomas Bastard (c. 1565–1618). English Protestant minister and poet. Educated at Winchester and New College, Oxford, Bastard published numerous works, including collections of poems and sermons; his most famous title is *Chrestoleros* (1598), a collection of epigrams. Bastard was alleged to be the author of an anonymous work, *An Admonition to the City of Oxford*, which revealed the carnal vices of many clergy and scholars in Oxford; despite denying authorship, he was dismissed from Oxford in 1591. Bastard was recognized as a skilled classical scholar and preacher. He died impoverished in a debtor's prison in Dorchester.

Jeremias Bastingius (1551–1595). Dutch Reformed theologian. Educated in Heidelberg and Geneva, Bastingius pastored the Reformed church in Antwerp for nearly a decade until the Spanish overran the city in 1585; he later settled in Dordrecht. He spent the last few years of his life in Leiden on the university's board of regents. He wrote an influential commentary on the Heidelberg Catechism that was translated into English, Dutch, German and Flemish.

Johann (Pomarius) Baumgart (1514–1578). Lutheran pastor and amateur playwright. Baumgart studied under Georg Major,* Martin Luther* and Philipp Melanchthon* at the University of Wittenberg. Before becoming pastor of the Church of the Holy Spirit in 1540, Baumgart taught secondary school. He authored catechetical and polemical works, a postil for the Gospel readings throughout the church year, numerous hymns and a didactic play (*Juditium Salomonis*).

Richard Baxter (1615–1691). English Puritan minister. Baxter was a leading Puritan pastor, evangelist and theologian, known throughout England for his landmark ministry in Kidderminster and a prodigious literary output, producing 135 books in just over forty years. Baxter came to faith through reading William Perkins,* Richard Sibbes* and other early Puritan writers and was the first cleric to decline the terms of ministry in the national English church imposed by the 1662 Act of Uniformity; Baxter wrote on behalf of the more than 1700 who shared ejection from the national church. He hoped for restoration to national church ministry, or toleration, that would allow lawful preaching and pastoring. Baxter sought unity in theological, ecclesiastical, sociopolitical and personal terms and is regarded as a forerunner of Noncomformist ecumenicity, though he was defeated in his efforts at the 1661 Savoy Conference to take seriously Puritan objections to the revision of the 1604 Prayer Book. Baxter's views on church ministry were considerably hybrid: he was a paedo-baptist, Nonconformist minister who approved of synodical Episcopal government and fixed liturgy. He is most known for his classic writings on the Christian life, such as *The Saints' Everlasting Rest* and *A Christian Directory*, and pastoral ministry, such as *The Reformed Pastor*. He also produced *Catholick Theology*, a large volume squaring current Reformed, Lutheran, Arminian and Roman Catholic systems with each other.

Thomas Becon (1511/1512–1567). English Puritan preacher. Becon was a friend of Hugh Latimer,* and for several years chaplain to Archbishop Thomas Cranmer.* Becon was sent to the Tower of London by Mary I and then exiled for his controversial preaching at the English royal court. He returned to England upon Elizabeth I's* accession. Becon was one of the most widely read popular preachers in England during the Reformation. He published many of his sermons, including a postil, or collection of sermon helps for undertrained or inexperienced preachers.

Belgic Confession (1561). Written by Guy de Brès (1523–1567), this statement of Dutch Reformed faith was heavily reliant on the Gallic Confession,* although more detailed, especially in how strongly it distances the Reformed from Roman Catholics and Anabaptists. The Confession first appeared in French in 1561 and was translated to Dutch in 1562. It was presented to Philip II (1527–1598) in the hope that he would grant toleration to the Reformed, to no avail. At the Synod of Dordrecht* the Confession was revised, clarifying and strengthening the article on election as well as sharpening the distinctives of Reformed theology against the Anabaptists, thus situating the Dutch Reformed more closely to the international Calvinist movement. The Belgic Confession in conjunction with the Heidelberg Catechism* and the Canons of Dordrecht were granted official status as the confessional standards (the Three Forms of Unity) of the Dutch Reformed Church.

Robert Bellarmine (1542–1621). Italian Catholic cardinal. A Jesuit, Bellarmine first taught at Louvain before being appointed chair of polemical theology at the Roman College. Much of Bellarmine's career was devoted to the refutation of Protestant teachings, and his three volume work, the *Controversies* (1586–93), was widely disseminated in the post-Tridentine era as the foremost refutation of the evangelical message. He was influential in the official revision of the Vulgate* text during the reign of Pope Clement VIII (1536–1605), with the resulting version, the Sixto-Clementine Vulgate, providing the basic biblical text for Catholics until Vatican II. Bellarmine is also a controversial figure in the history of science. Appointed to the Holy Office, also known as the Inquisition, by Pope Paul V (1550–1621), it was he who examined Galileo Galilei (1564–1642) and ordered him to treat heliocentrism as a hypothesis rather than a reality, believing the evidentiary threshold had not yet been met. Later in his career, Bellarmine's attention turned to works on devotion and piety, and include his extensive commentary on the Psalms (1611).

Bernard of Clairvaux (1090–1153). French abbot and theologian. Born the son of a Bugundian knight, Bernard became interested in the new reforming movement at Citeaux, and thus abandoned his preparation for a secular career in favor of monastic life there. Towards this end, Bernard persuaded thirty-one of his friends and relatives to follow him to Citeaux, and join the Cistercian order. Among this group were four of Bernard's brothers. In 1115, Bernard went with others of his order to found a Cistercian monastery at Claivaux. Bernard's austere approach to the monastic life attracted many followers to the point that by the time of his death there were sixty-eight Cistercian houses. Throughout his career, Bernard preached, mediated theological disputes, and advised. Bernard is best known for having preached the Second Crusade (1147–1150) as well as advising his former student, Pope Eugenius III (r. 1145–1153), and engaging in theological controversies with Peter Abelard (1079–1142) and Gilbert of Poitiers (1085–1154). One of the distinguishing characteristics of Bernard's theology is his Christocentric mysticism. Among Bernard's most important works are his treatises *On Consideration* and *On Loving God* along with his *Sermons on the Song of Songs* as well as many other sermons on the liturgical year and other subject. Many of the reformers in the sixteenth century cited Bernard extensively, especially Martin Luther* and John Calvin*.

Richard Bernard (1568–1641). English Puritan minister. A moderate Puritan, Bernard eschewed separation from the Church of England, spending the majority of his career in parish ministry at Batcombe, Somerset. Many of his works, including a handbook for pastors and a household catechism, were well received and printed numerous times during his lifetime.

Theodore Beza (1519–1605). French Reformed pastor and professor. Beza was compatriot and successor to John Calvin* as moderator of the Company of Pastors in Geneva during the second half of the sixteenth century. He was a noteworthy New Testament scholar whose *Codex Bezae* formed the basis of the New Testament section of later English translations. A leader in the academy and the church, Beza served as professor of Greek at the Lausanne Academy until 1558, at which time he moved to Geneva to become the rector of the newly founded Genevan Academy. He enjoyed an international reputation through his correspondence with key European leaders. Beza developed and extended Calvin's doctrinal thought on several important themes such as the nature of predestination and the real spiritual presence of Christ in the Eucharist.

Theodor Bibliander (1504?–1564). Swiss Reformed Hebraist and theologian. Professor of Old Testament at the Zurich Academy from 1531, Bibliander published two Hebrew grammars, a collection of letters by Zwingli* and Oecolampadius*, commentaries on Isaiah, Ezekiel, and Nahum, a Latin translation of the Qur'an, and a tract warning Christians against the threat of Islam. He taught a universalist view of predestination, arguing that God saved all people unless they rejected divine grace. Following a dispute with double-predestinarian Peter Martyr Vermigli*, he was forced into retirement in 1560.

Thomas Bilson (1546/1547?–1616). English Anglican Bishop and theologian. A celebrated preacher and theologian, Bilson served as canon of Winchester Cathedral and warden of Winchester College before becoming bishop of Worcester. He held this position for only one year, however, before his appointment to the wealthier see of Winchester. As an advisor to King James I,* he preached at his coronation, and he was involved with the publication of the 1611 Authorized Version,* being part of the Cambridge company responsible for translating the Apocrypha, the author of part of the front matter, and one of the text's final editors. His extant writings defend the episcopacy against Erastianism, condemn rebellion, and argue for a literal understanding of Christ's descent into hell.

Hugh Binning (1627–1653). Scottish Presbyterian theologian. At the age of eighteen, Binning became a professor of philosophy at the University of Glasgow. In his early twenties he left this post for parish ministry, and died of consumption a few years later. His commentary on the Westminster Confession and a selection of his sermons were published after his death.

Samuel Bird (d. 1604). Anglican minister and author. A native of Essex, Bird matriculated at Queen's College, Cambridge, where he received his BA in 1570 and his MA in 1573, at which time he was also elected a fellow of Corpus Christi College, Cambridge. For reasons unknown, Bird resigned his fellowship sometime in 1576. He spent nearly the entirety of his post-university career as rector of St. Peter's in Ipswich until his death in 1604. Among Bird's major works are *A Friendlie Communication or Dialogue Betweene Paule and Demas, wherein is Disputed How We are to Use the Pleasures of This Life* (1580), *Lectures upon the 11. Chapter of Hebrews and upon the 38. Psalme* (1598), and *Lectures upon the 8 and 9 Chapters of the Second Epistle to the Corinthians* (1598).

Bishops' Bible (1568). Anglicans were polarized by the two most recent English translations of the Bible: the Great Bible (1539) relied too heavily on the Vulgate* and was thus perceived as too Catholic, while the Geneva Bible's* marginal notes were too Calvinist for many Anglicans. So Archbishop Matthew Parker (1504–1575) commissioned a new translation of Scripture from the original languages with marginal annotations (many of which, ironically, were from the Geneva Bible). Published under royal warrant, the Bishops' Bible became the official translation for the Church of England. The 1602 edition provided the basis for the King James Bible (1611).

Christopher Blackwood (1607/1608–1670). English Baptist pastor. Initially an Anglican priest, Blackwood served at the parishes of Stockbury and Rye until Puritan sympathies led him to migrate to New England. Returning to England, he pastored briefly at Cranbrook until Baptist preaching caused him to leave the established church, be rebaptized, and serve as a pastor of a General Baptist congregation in Staplehurst. Joining the Parliamentary Army in their goal to evangelize Ireland, he helped plant a number of Baptist churches and pastored at Wexford, Kilkenny, and Dublin. His numerous writings include treatises on baptism and repentance, a catechism, and a commentary on the first ten chapters of Matthew.

Georg Blaurock (1492–1529). Swiss Anabaptist. Blaurock (a nickname meaning "blue coat," because of his preference for this garment) was one of the first leaders of Switzerland's radical reform movement. In the first public disputations on baptism in Zurich, he argued for believer's baptism and was the first person to receive adult believers' baptism there, having been baptized by Conrad Grebel* in 1525. Blaurock was arrested several times for performing mass adult baptisms and engaging in social disobedience by disrupting worship services. He was eventually expelled from Zurich but continued preaching and baptizing in various Swiss cantons until his execution.

Bohemian Confession (1535). Bohemian Christianity was subdivided between traditional Catholics, Utraquists (who demanded Communion in both kinds) and the *Unitas Fratrum*, who were not Protestants but whose theology bore strong affinities to the Waldensians and the Reformed. The 1535 Latin edition of this confession—an earlier Czech edition had already been drafted— was an attempt to clarify and redefine the beliefs of the *Unitas Fratrum*. This confession purged all earlier openness to rebaptism and inched toward Luther's* eucharistic theology. Jan Augusta (c. 1500–1572) and Jan Roh (also Johannes Horn; c. 1490–1547) presented the confession to King Ferdinand I (1503–1564) in Vienna, but the king would not print it. The *Unitas Fratrum* sought, and with slight amendments eventually obtained, Luther's advocacy of the confession. It generally follows the structure of the Augsburg Confession.*

Bohemian Confession (1575). This confession was an attempt to shield Bohemian Christian minorities—the Utraquists and the *Unitas*

Fratrum—from the Counter-Reformation and Habsburg insistence on uniformity. The hope was that this umbrella consensus would ensure peace in the midst of Christian diversity; anyone who affirmed the 1575 Confession, passed by the Bohemian legislature, would be tolerated. This confession was, like the Bohemian Confession of 1535, patterned after the Augsburg Confession.* It emphasizes both justification by faith alone and good works as the fruit of salvation. Baptism and the Eucharist are the focus of the sacramental section, although the five traditional Catholic sacraments are also listed for the Utraquists. Though it was eventually accepted in 1609 by Rudolf II (1552–1612), the Thirty Years' War (1618–1648) rendered the confession moot.

Samuel Bolton (1606–1654). English Anglican minister. Bolton served a number of parishes in London before being elected to the Westminster Assembly. He spent the remainder of his career as master of Christ's College, Cambridge. A number of his writings were published, including works on sin, the sacraments, and Christian freedom.

Book of Common Prayer (1549; 1552). After the Church of England's break with Rome, it needed a liturgical manual to distinguish its theology and practice from that of Catholicism. Thomas Cranmer* drafted the Book of Common Prayer based on the medieval Roman Missal, under the dual influence of the revised Lutheran Mass and the reforms of the Spanish Cardinal Quiñones. This manual details the eucharistic service, as well as services for rites such as baptism, confirmation, marriage and funerals. It includes a matrix of the epistle and Gospel readings and the appropriate collect for each Sunday and feast day of the church year. The 1548 Act of Uniformity established the Book of Common Prayer as *the* authoritative liturgical manual for the Church of England, to be implemented everywhere by Pentecost 1549. After its 1552 revision, Queen Mary I banned it; Elizabeth I* reestablished it in 1559, although it was rejected by Puritans and Catholics alike.

The Book of Homilies (1547; 1563; 1570). This collection of approved sermons, published in three parts during the reigns of Edward VI and Elizabeth I,* was intended to inculcate Anglican theological distinctives and mitigate the problems raised by the lack of educated preachers. Addressing doctrinal and practical topics, Thomas Cranmer* likely wrote the majority of the first twelve sermons, published in 1547; John Jewel* added another twenty sermons in 1563. A final sermon, *A Homily Against Disobedience*, was appended to the canon in 1570. Reprinted regularly, the *Book of Homilies* was an important resource in Anglican preaching until at least the end of the seventeenth century.

Martin (Cellarius) Borrhaus (1499–1564). German Reformed theologian. After a dispute with his mentor Johann Eck,* Borrhaus settled in Wittenberg, where he was influenced by the radical Zwickau Prophets. He travelled extensively, and finally settled in Basel to teach philosophy and Old Testament. Despite his objections, many accused Borrhaus of Anabaptism; he argued that baptism was a matter of conscience. On account of his association with Sebastian Castellio (1515–1563) and Michael Servetus (1511–1553), some scholars posit that Borrhaus was an antitrinitarian. His writings include a treatise on the Trinity and commentaries on the Torah, historical books, Ecclesiastes and Isaiah.

Sigmund Bosch (unknown). German Anabaptist hymn writer. An elder in the Swiss and South German Anabaptist churches, Bosch collaborated with Pilgram Marpeck* in his ministry. He is known to have composed three hymns and a letter on the end times, which he addressed to the congregation in Austerlitz.

John Bourchier (d. 1660). English Puritan parliamentarian. Bourchier served as a justice of the peace in Yorkshire until imprisoned at the outbreak of the English Civil War. After his release, he was elected as the member of parliament for Ripon, and in this capacity he served as a judge at the trial of Charles I and signed the king's death warrant. Deemed too ill for trial with the other regicides, he died soon after the Restoration of the monarchy under Charles II.

John Bowle (d. 1637). Anglican pastor. After matriculating from Cambridge, Bowle was household pastor to Sir Robert Cecil (1563–1612) and held a pastorate at Tilehurst in Berkshire. He was appointed dean of Salisbury in 1620 and bishop of Rochester in 1629.

John Boys (1571–1625). Anglican priest and theologian. Before doctoral work at Cambridge, Boys pastored several parishes in Kent; after completing his studies he was appointed to more prominent positions, culminating in his 1619 appointment as the Dean of Canterbury by James I.* Boys published a popular four-volume postil of the Gospel and epistle readings for the church year, as well as a companion volume for the Psalms.

John Bradford (1510-1555). English Reformer, prebendary of St. Paul's, and martyr. Bradford was born in Blackley, Manchester, to an affluent family. After grammar school, Bradford at first began legal studies at the Inner Temple in London. However, while there, he heard the preaching of a fellow student, and thus converted to an evangelical faith. This conversion caused Bradford to abandon his study of law and enroll at St. Catherine's Hall, Cambridge, to study theology. He completed his MA in 1549, and in the same year, received an appointment of fellow at Pembroke Hall, Cambridge. In August, 1550, Bishop Nicholas Ridley ordained Bradford a deacon, and appointed him his personal chaplain. Bradford's exceptional preaching moved King Edward VI to select him as his chaplain and prebendary at St. Paul's Cathedral. After Mary Tudor succeeded her half-brother to throne, Bradford was tried and convicted of heresy on January 31, 1555. He was executed at the stake on July 1 of the same year.

Anne Bradstreet (1612–1672). English-American Puritan poet. Born in Northampton, Bradstreet married at sixteen and emigrated to the Massachusetts Bay Colony, of which both her father and husband would serve as governors. Mother to eight children, Bradstreet also wrote poetry. Much of her verse reflects on marriage, children, and her Puritan faith. While her writing received a mixed reception from contemporaries, many of whom viewed poetry as outside a woman's purview, she is today celebrated as the most significant early English poet in North America.

Thieleman Jans van Braght (1625–1664). Dutch Radical preacher. After demonstrating great ability with languages, this cloth merchant was made preacher in his hometown of Dordrecht in 1648. He served in this office for the next sixteen years, until his death. This celebrated preacher had a reputation for engaging in debate wherever an opportunity presented itself, particularly concerning infant baptism. The publication of his book of martyrs, *Het Bloedigh Tooneel of Martelaersspiegel* (1660; *Martyrs' Mirror*), proved to be his lasting contribution to the Mennonite tradition. *Martyrs' Mirror* is heavily indebted to the earlier martyr book *Offer des Heeren* (1562), to which Braght added many early church martyrs who rejected infant baptism, as well as over 800 contemporary martyrs.

David Bramley (unknown). English lay preacher. Two works by Bramley survive, an exposition of Matthew 11:25 and a treatise arguing for the acceptance of lay preachers without university training like himself. On both tracts, he is identified simply as a "Preacher of the Gospel."

Johannes Brenz (1499–1570). German Lutheran theologian and pastor. Brenz was converted to the reformation cause after hearing Martin Luther* speak; later, Brenz became a student of Johannes Oecolampadius.* His central achievement lay in his talent for organization. As city preacher in Schwäbisch-Hall and afterward in Württemberg and Tübingen, he oversaw the introduction of reform measures and doctrines and new governing structures for ecclesial and educational communities. Brenz also helped establish Lutheran orthodoxy through treatises, commentaries and catechisms. He defended Luther's position on eucharistic presence against Huldrych Zwingli* and opposed the death penalty for religious dissenters.

Guillaume Briçonnet (1470–1534). French Catholic abbot and bishop. Briçonnet created a short-lived circle of reformist-minded humanists in his diocese under the sponsorship of Marguerite d'Angoulême. His desire for ecclesial reform developed throughout his prestigious career (including positions as royal chaplain to the queen, abbot at Saint-Germain-des-Prés and bishop of Meaux), influenced by Jacques Lefèvre d'Étaples.* Briçonnet encouraged reform through ministerial visitation, Scripture and preaching in the vernacular and active study of the Bible. When this triggered the ire of the theology faculty at the Sorbonne in Paris, Briçonnet quelled the activity and departed, envisioning an ecclesial reform that proceeded hierarchically.

William Bridge (1600?–1670). English Puritan minister. Bridge ministered in Norfolk and Essex until excommunicated as a Nonconformist and exiled, leading him to Rotterdam, where he copastored a church with Jeremiah Burroughs.* Returning to England, he was a member of the Westminster Assembly and pastored at Great Yarmouth until ejected from the ministry by the Act of Uniformity (1662). Many of Bridge's sermons were published during his life, and he also composed a number of works designed to encourage struggling believers.

Walter Bridges (unknown). English Anglican minister. Three works are attributed to Bridges. Two were published anonymously, a sermon on Joab before the House of Commons and a catechism for those taking the Eucharist, while a third, a sermon on unity given before the Lord Mayor and Aldermen of London, names him and his position as preacher at St. Dunstans-in-the-East, London.

Thomas Brightman (1562–1607). English Puritan pastor and exegete. Under alleged divine inspiration, Brightman wrote a well known commentary on Revelation, influenced by Joachim of Fiore (d. 1202). In contrast to the putatively true churches of Geneva and Scotland, he depicted the Church of England as a type of the lukewarm Laodicean church. He believed that the Reformation would result in the defeat of the Vatican and the Ottoman Empire and that all humanity would be regenerated through the spread of the gospel before Christ's final return and judgment.

Hugh Broughton (1549–1612). English Puritan Hebraist and theologian. Following his time as a student and fellow at Cambridge, Broughton established himself as a scholar and preacher in London. His first work, *A Concent of Scripture* (1588), an attempt to harmonize the chronology of Scripture, caused significant controversy and led him to spend much of the next two decades traveling throughout Europe. On the Continent, he built a reputation in disputes with numerous Jewish, Catholic, and Protestant scholars and helped to plant an English Reformed church in Amsterdam, a congregation he may also have pastored for a time. Broughton's extensive writings include comments on numerous aspects of the Old Testament and New Testaments, a genealogy of Christ, and an explication of Christ's descent into hell.

Robert Browne (c. 1550–1633). English Nonconformist minister. While drawn to Puritan teachings, Browne began his career within the Church of England, ministering in London and Cambridge. Convinced that more radical reformation was needed outside the constraints of the state, Browne is recognized as the first to found a separatist church, establishing a congregation in Norwich, with those who followed him becoming known as Brownists. After a brief imprisonment, he left for Middelburg in the Netherlands, gathering a church based on the principles he espoused in his two most important works, *A Treatise of Reformation Without Tarrying* (1582) and *The Life and Manners of All True Christians* (1582), which set forth the foundations of congregationalist church government. Browne did not remain a separatist, however, and after a few years returned to England and reentered the Church of England, serving as a school headmaster and pastoring in Northamptonshire.

Otto Brunfels (c. 1488–1534). German Lutheran botanist, teacher and physician. Brunfels joined the Carthusian order, where he developed interests in the natural sciences and became involved with a humanist circle associated with Ulrich von Hutten and Wolfgang Capito.* In 1521, after coming into contact with Luther's* teaching, Brunfels abandoned the monastic life, traveling and spending time in botanical research and pastoral care. He received a medical degree in Basel and was appointed city physician of Bern in 1534. Brunfels penned defenses of Luther and Hutten, devotional biographies of biblical figures, a prayer book, and annotations on the Gospels and the Acts of the Apostles. His most influential contribution, however, is as a Renaissance botanist.

Martin Bucer (1491–1551). German Reformed theologian and pastor. A Dominican friar, Bucer was influenced by Desiderius Erasmus* during his doctoral studies at the University of Heidelberg, where he began corresponding with Martin Luther.* After advocating reform in Alsace, Bucer was excommunicated and fled to Strasbourg, where he became a leader in the city's Reformed ecclesial and educational communities. Bucer sought concord between Lutherans and Zwinglians and Protestants and Catholics. He emigrated to England, becoming a professor at Cambridge. Bucer's greatest theological concern was the centrality of Christ's sacrificial death, which achieved justification and sanctification and orients Christian community.

Johannes Bugenhagen (1485–1558). German Lutheran pastor and professor. Bugenhagen, a priest and lecturer at a Premonstratensian monastery, became a city preacher in Wittenberg during the reform efforts of Martin Luther* and Philipp Melanchthon.* Initially influenced by his reading of Desiderius Erasmus,* Bugenhagen grew in evangelical orientation through Luther's works; later, he studied under Melanchthon at the University of Wittenberg, eventually serving as rector and faculty member there. Bugenhagen was a versatile commentator, exegete and lecturer on Scripture. Through these roles and his development of lectionary and devotional material, Bugenhagen facilitated rapid establishment of church order throughout many German provinces.

Henry Bull (d. 1575?). English Protestant theologian and martyrologist. Little is known about Bull's circumstances after he was expelled from Magdalen College, Oxford, for snatching the censer from the hand of a priest officiating Mass. A committed reformer, he edited, translated, compiled, and published a number of Protestant works, including a book of prayers and meditations and writings by John Hooper* and Martin Luther.* He also worked alongside John Foxe* in the compilation of *Acts and Monuments*, while Miles Coverdale's* *The Letters of the Martyrs* is largely Bull's work.

Heinrich Bullinger (1504–1575). Swiss Reformed pastor and theologian. Bullinger succeeded Huldrych Zwingli* as minister and leader in Zurich. The primary author of the First and Second Helvetic Confessions,* Bullinger was drawn toward reform through the works of Martin Luther* and Philipp Melanchthon.* After Zwingli died, Bullinger was vital in maintaining adherence to the cause of reform; he oversaw the expansion of the Zurich synodal system while preaching, teaching and writing extensively. One of Bullinger's lasting legacies was the development of a federal view of the divine covenant with humanity, making baptism and the Eucharist covenantal signs.

Heinrich Bünting (1545–1606). Lutheran theologian and pastor. Bünting was born in Hanover, Germany, and studied theology at the University of Wittenberg, where he graduated in 1569. Upon finishing his studies at Wittenberg, Bünting became a pastor at Lemgo, where he was dismissed in 1575. Afterward he moved to Gronau an der Leine, where he served until his appointment as superintendent in Goslar. However, due to controversy over some of his teachings, Bünting was relieved of his position in 1600, retiring thereafter to Hanover, where he lived the remainder of his life. Bünting's most notable work is his *Itinerarium Sacrae Scripturae* (1581), a summary of biblical geography. Throughout this treatise, Bünting follows the travels of various major biblical figures, highlighting their theological as well as exegetical importance. When published, the *Itinerarium Sacrae Scripturae* was the most complete summary of biblical geography. Among the work's distinctive features is its collection of maps.

John Bunyan (1628–1688). English Puritan preacher and writer. His *Pilgrim's Progress* is one of the best-selling English-language titles in history. Born to a working-class family, Bunyan was largely unschooled, gaining literacy (and entering the faith) through reading the Bible and such early Puritan devotional works as *The Plain Man's Pathway to Heaven* and *The Practice of Piety*. Following a short stint in Oliver Cromwell's parliamentary army, in which Bunyan narrowly escaped death in combat, he turned to a preaching ministry, succeeding John Gifford as pastor at the Congregational church in Bedford. A noted preacher, Bunyan drew large crowds in itinerant appearances and it was in the sermonic form that Bunyan developed his theological outlook, which was an Augustinian-inflected Calvinism. Bunyan's opposition to the Book of Common Prayer and refusal of official ecclesiastical licensure led to multiple imprisonments, where he wrote many of his famous allegorical works, including *Pilgrim's Progress*, *The Holy City*, *Prison Meditations* and *Holy War*.

Michelangelo Buonarroti (1475–1564). Italian Catholic artist and poet. Michelangelo was born in Florence but spent the majority of his career in Rome, completing artworks commissioned by the popes of the early sixteenth century. One of the most recognized artists of all time, his artworks include the *Pietà* (1499), *David* (1501–1504), the ceiling of the Sistine Chapel (1508–1512), *Moses* (1515), and the *Last Judgment* (1536–1541), which remain famous and have done much to shape Western aesthetics. Toward the end of his life, his interests shifted toward architecture, culminating with his contributions to the designs of St. Peter's Basilica in Rome. Michelangelo is thought to have been devoutly Catholic throughout his life, but recent scholarship has considered the complexity of his relationship with the Catholic Reformation and the Protestant movement.

Jeremiah Burroughs (c. 1600–1646). English Puritan pastor and delegate to the Westminster

Assembly. Burroughs left Cambridge, as well as a rectorate in Norfolk, because of his nonconformity. After returning to England from pastoring an English congregation in Rotterdam for several years (1637–1641), he became one of only a few dissenters from the official presbyterianism of the Assembly in favor of a congregationalist polity. Nevertheless, he was well known and respected by presbyterian colleagues such as Richard Baxter* for his irenic tone and conciliatory manner. The vast majority of Burroughs's corpus was published posthumously, although during his lifetime he published annotations on Hosea and several polemical works.

William Burton (d. 1616). English Puritan minister. Burton first ministered in Norwich, where he was present for the burning of Francis Kett (d. 1589) for Arianism. He later pastored in Bristol, Reading, and London. Throughout his life, he published a number of his sermons and treatises as well as a brief catechism.

Anthony Cade (d. 1641). Anglican pastor. Cade served as tutor and chaplain to George Villiers, First Duke of Buckingham (1592–1628), a close confidante of King James I* before holding a number of pastoral positions in Leicestershire and Northamptonshire.

Cardinal Cajetan (Thomas de Vio) (1469–1534). Italian Catholic cardinal, professor, theologian and biblical exegete. This Dominican monk was the leading Thomist theologian and one of the most important Catholic exegetes of the sixteenth century. Cajetan is best-known for his interview with Martin Luther* at the Diet of Augsburg (1518). Among his many works are polemical treatises, extensive biblical commentaries and most importantly a four-volume commentary (1508–1523) on the *Summa Theologiae* of Thomas Aquinas.*

Georg Calixtus (1586–1656). German Lutheran theologian. Calixtus studied at the University of Helmstedt where he developed regard for Philipp Melanchthon.* Between his time as a student and later as a professor at Helmstedt, Calixtus traveled through Europe seeking a way to unite and reconcile Lutherans, Calvinists and Catholics. He attempted to fuse these denominations through use

of the Scriptures, the Apostles' Creed, and the first five centuries, interpreted by the Vincentian canon. Calixtus's position was stamped as syncretist and yielded further debate even after his death.

John Calvin (1509–1564). French Reformed pastor and theologian. John Calvin was born in Noyon, France. After receiving his primary education in the aristocratic family of Charles de Hangest, he attended the University of Paris to prepare for further study of theology. However, after completing his BA degree, as per his father's instructions, Calvin proceeded to the study of the law at Orleans of Bourges. While at Orleans, Calvin's interests in Greek and Latin literature were reawakened. Upon his father's death, Calvin resumed his study of classical literature at the newly founded College of Royal Readers in Paris under the direction of Guillaume Bude. The product of these studies was his commentary on Seneca's *De Clementia* (1532). Sometime between 1533 and 1534 Calvin experienced a "sudden conversion" due largely to the influence to Martin Luther's 1520 treatises. Calvin's embracing of an evangelical faith forced him to flee France. From there he went to Basel, where he wrote the first edition of his *Institutes of the Christian Religion* in 1536. The *Institutes* became a theological dogmatics for the Reformed churches. Calvin spent most of his career in Geneva (excepting a three-year ministry in Strasbourg with Martin Bucer*). In Geneva, Calvin reorganized the structure and governance of the church and established an academy that became an international center for theological education. He was a tireless writer, revising his *Institutes* several times, and authoring theological treatises as well as biblical commentaries. Calvin is also known for his debates with his contemporaries, including Michael Servetus, whose anti-Trinitarian views led to his execution in Geneva in 1553. Calvin also maintained friendly correspondence with many reformers, including Melanchthon* and Bullinger*, the latter of whom he was able to come to an agreement with regarding the presence of Christ in the Lord's Supper with the signing of the *Consensus Tigurinus* in 1551, which brought a degree of unity between Geneva and Zurich and to the Reformed tradition. One of the foremost figures during the Reformation period, Calvin has an extensive exegetical and theological legacy.

Wolfgang Capito (1478?–1541). German Reformed humanist and theologian. Capito, a Hebrew scholar, produced a Hebrew grammar and published several Latin commentaries on books of the Hebrew Scriptures. He corresponded with Desiderius Erasmus* and fellow humanists. Capito translated Martin Luther's* early works into Latin for the printer Johann Froben. On meeting Luther, Capito was converted to Luther's vision, left Mainz and settled in Strasbourg, where he lectured on Luther's theology to the city clergy. With Martin Bucer,* Capito reformed liturgy, ecclesial life and teachings, education, welfare, and government. Capito worked for the theological unification of the Swiss cantons with Strasbourg.

Pietro Carnesecchi (1508–1567). Italian humanist. Carnesecchi rose in the papal bureaucracy under Medici patronage, but after the death of Clement VII* he began to deviate from Catholic orthodoxy, aligning himself with Juan de Valdés.* While he retained relations with the established church, he also read Protestant works by theologians such as Luther,* Calvin,* and Bucer,* and his only extant doctrinal writing defends Bucer's view of the Eucharist over that of Zwingli.* Carnesecchi was able to avoid arrest by the Inquisition for a time, and his condemnation to death in absentia was pardoned under Pope Pius IV (1499–1565). However, Pius V (1504–1572) was a longtime opponent of Carnesecchi, and upon his election to the papal office, reopened the case and those of a number of others suspected of Protestant leanings. While seeking refuge in Florence, Carnesecchi was betrayed to the Inquisition by Cosimo I de' Medici, and following trial he was beheaded.

François Carrière (d. 1665). French Catholic theologian. A Franciscan doctor of theology, Carrière composed a commentary on the whole Bible, a summary of Catholic doctrine, and a history of the papacy.

John Carter (1554–1635). English Puritan minister. After graduating from Cambridge, Carter served as vicar at Bramford, Suffolk, until disputes over his Puritanism within the congregation led him to be moved to the nearby parish of Belstead.

Thomas Cartwright (1535–1606). English Puritan preacher and professor. Cartwright was educated at St. John's College, Cambridge, although as an influential leader of the Presbyterian party in the Church of England he was continually at odds with the Anglican party, especially John Whitgift.* Cartwright spent some time as an exile in Geneva and Heidelberg as well as in Antwerp, where he pastored an English church. In 1585, Cartwright was arrested and eventually jailed for trying to return to England despite Elizabeth I's* refusal of his request. Many acknowledged him to be learned but also quite cantankerous. His publications include commentaries on Colossians, Ecclesiastes, Proverbs and the Gospels, as well as a dispute against Whitgift on church discipline.

Mathew Caylie (unknown). English Protestant minister. Caylie authored *The Cleansing of the Ten Lepers* (1623), an exposition of Luke 17:14-18.

Jan Cents (Unknown). Dutch Anabaptist. Believed to be a leader of the Anabaptist congregation in Amsterdam, Cents was the first signer and possibly author of a confession intended to unite Frisian and High German Mennonites.

John Chardon (d. 1601). Irish Anglican bishop. Chardon was educated at Oxford. He advocated Reformed doctrine in his preaching, yet opposed those Puritans who rejected Anglican church order. He published several sermons.

Christian Chemnitz (1615–1666). German Lutheran theologian. Grandnephew of Martin Chemnitz,* Christian Chemnitz was principal at the high school in Jena before serving the church as a deacon and archdeacon in Weimer and Braunschweig then as superintendent in Eisenach. Returning to Jena, he received his doctorate and replaced John Major as professor of theology, also serving as dean of the theology faculty and rector of the university. He wrote on numerous biblical, pastoral, and controversial topics, with his works including a defense of Lutheranism, instructions for young ministers, and a series of sermons on judgement.

Martin Chemnitz (1522–1586). German Lutheran theologian. A leading figure in establishing Lutheran orthodoxy, Chemnitz studied theology and patristics at the University of Wittenburg, later becoming a defender of Philipp Melanchthon's* interpretation of the doctrine of justification. Chemnitz drafted a compendium of doctrine and reorganized the structure of the church in Wolfenbüttel; later, he led efforts to reconcile divisions within Lutheranism, culminating in the Formula of Concord*. One of his chief theological accomplishments was a modification of the christological doctrine of the *communicatio idiomatium*, which provided a Lutheran platform for understanding the sacramental presence of Christ's humanity in the Eucharist.

David Chytraeus (1531–1600). German Lutheran professor, theologian and biblical exegete. At the age of eight Chytraeus was admitted to the University of Tübingen. There he studied law, philology, philosophy, and theology, finally receiving his master's degree in 1546. Chytraeus befriended Philipp Melanchthon* while sojourning in Wittenberg, where he taught the *Loci communes*. While teaching exegesis at the University of Rostock Chytraeus became acquainted with Tilemann Heshusius,* who strongly influenced Chytraeus away from Philippist theology. As a defender of Gnesio-Lutheran theology Chytraeus helped organize churches throughout Austria in accordance with the Augsburg Confession.* Chytraeus coauthored the Formula of Concord* with Martin Chemnitz,* Andreas Musculus (1514–1581), Nikolaus Selnecker* and Jakob Andreae.* He wrote commentaries on most of the Bible, as well as a devotional work titled *Regula vitae* (1555) that described the Christian virtues.

David Clarkson (1622–1686). English Puritan theologian. After his dismissal from the pastorate on account of the Act of Uniformity (1662), little

is known about Clarkson. At the end of his life he ministered with John Owen* in London.

Robert Cleaver (1571–1613). English Puritan pastor. Cleaver served as rector at Drayton in Oxfordshire until silenced by Archbishop Richard Bancroft for advocating Nonconformity. Despite opposition from ecclesiastical authorities, Cleaver enjoyed a reputation as an excellent preacher. His published works include sermons on Hebrews 4 and Song of Songs 2 as well as one on the last chapter of Proverbs. Cleaver also authored *The Parsimony of Christian Children*, which contained a defense of infant baptism against Baptist criticisms.

George Close (unknown). English Protestant preacher. A series of Close's sermons on Matthew 16 were copied and published while he served as a reader at St. Antholin, London.

Michael Cobabus (d. 1686). German Lutheran theologian and mathematician. Trained in philosophy, mathematics, and theology at the University of Rostock, Cobabus remained in the city, serving as rector of the city school until appointed professor of mathematics at the university. He later received a doctorate in theology from the University of Griefswald and exchanged his position in the Rostock mathematics faculty for a professorship in theology.

Johannes Cocceius (1603–1669). German Reformed theologian. Cocceius first served as professor of biblical philology in his hometown of Bremen before moving to Franeker, where he taught Hebrew and theology, and finally to Leiden, where he spent the majority of his career as professor of theology. Cocceius is perhaps best remembered for his exposition of Reformed federal theology, defining the relationship between humanity and God in terms of progressive covenants. His critics, chief among them Gisbertus Voetius (1589–1676), argued that Cocceius's view of salvation history ignored the unity of the Scriptures and spiritualized the Old Testament. His other writings are extensive, including commentaries on all the books of the Bible, an influential Hebrew and Aramaic lexicon, and numerous works on theology, ethics, and philology.

John Colet (1467–1519). English Catholic priest, preacher and educator. Colet, appointed dean of Saint Paul's Cathedral by Henry VII, was a friend of Desiderius Erasmus,* on whose classical ideals Colet reconstructed the curriculum of Saint Paul's school. Colet was convinced that the foundation of moral reform lay in the education of children. Though an ardent advocate of reform, Colet, like Erasmus, remained loyal to the Catholic Church throughout his life. Colet's agenda of reform was oriented around spiritual and ethical themes, demonstrated in his commentaries on select books of the New Testament and the writings of Pseudo-Dionysius the Areopagite.

Vittoria Colonna (1490–1547). Italian Renaissance poet. Born into a noble family, Colonna was betrothed at three years of age to Fernando d'Ávalos (1489–1525), and they married in 1509. D'Ávalos was largely absent on military campaigns during their marriage, while she exercised his governorship of Benvenuto and became involved in the literary circles of Rome and Naples. One of the most important writers of her age, her friends included Pietro Bembo (1470–1547), Marguerite de Navarre,* and Michelangelo Buonarroti.* Writing primarily in the Petrarchan style, Colonna's reputation as a poet grew after the death of her husband, and much of her poetry was dedicated to his memory. Spiritual concerns form a major element of Colonna's writings, promoting contemplation and the ascetic life. While denied her desire to take holy orders in widowhood, Colonna spent much of her life residing in religious communities, and she was actively involved in movements seeking their improvement, collaborating with reformers such as Reginald Pole,* Juan de Valdés,* and Bernardo Ochino.*

Gasparo Contarini (1483–1542). Italian statesman, theologian and reform-minded cardinal. Contarini was an able negotiator and graceful compromiser. Charles V requested Contarini as the papal legate for the Colloquy of Regensburg (1541), where Contarini reached agreement with Melanchthon* on the doctrine of justification (although neither the pope nor Luther* ratified the agreement). He had come to a similar belief in the priority of faith in the work of Christ rather than works as the basis for Christian life in 1511, though unlike Luther, he never left the papal church over the issue; instead he remainied within it to try to seek gentle reform, and he adhered to papal sacramental teaching. Contarini was an important voice for reform within the Catholic Church, always seeking reconciliation rather than confrontation with Protestant reformers. He wrote many works, including a treatise detailing the ideal bishop, a manual for lay church leaders, a political text on right governance and brief commentaries on the Pauline letters.

Christoph Corner (1518–1594). German Lutheran theologian. Professor of philosophy, rhetoric, and theology at the University of Frankfurt, Corner participated in the drafting of the Formula of Concord.* He also served as superintendent of churches in Mark Brandenberg.

Antonio del Corro (1527–1591). Spanish Reformed pastor and theologian. After encountering the ideas of Martin Luther* and other reformers, Corro abandoned the Hieronymite order. Leaving Spain to avoid charges of heresy, he traveled through Europe, spending time in Geneva and Lausanne before pastoring churches in France and the Low Countries. The arrival of Spanish armies in the Netherlands saw Corro and his family relocate to England, where he pastored a church of Spanish exiles in London and taught at Temple Church and Oxford. Corro courted controversy throughout his career, entering into debates with a wide array of Protestant theologians. In England, he was suspended from his pastorate for slander and examined a number of times for heresy, with some finding suggestions of Arianism in his Christology. Although these charges were never upheld, they clouded his later career and legacy.

Antonius Corvinus (1501–1553). German Lutheran theologian and administrator. After meeting Luther* and Melanchthon,* Corvinus left the humanist circle of Erasmus* to serve as a pastor in cities including Goslar, Witzenhausen, and Pattensen. A signatory of the Schmalkald Articles,* much of his career was devoted to constructing the organizational apparatus of the Lutheran church, and he established disciplinary procedures and church orders for numerous cities in northern Germany. His expository postils on the Gospels, Epistles, Psalms, and Genesis were also distributed widely in order to aid preachers of the region.

John Cosin (1594–1672). Anglican preacher and bishop. Early in his career Cosin was the vice chancellor of Cambridge and canon at the Durham cathedral. But as a friend of William Laud* and an advocate for "Laudian" changes, he was suspected of being a crypto-Catholic. In 1640 during the Long Parliament a Puritan lodged a complaint with the House of Commons concerning Cosin's "popish innovations." Cosin was promptly removed from office. During the turmoil of the English Civil Wars, Cosin sojourned in Paris among English nobility but struggled financially. Cosin returned to England after the Restoration in 1660 to be consecrated as the bishop of Durham. He published annotations on the Book of Common Prayer* and a history of the canon.

John Cotton (1584–1652). New England Puritan minister. Cotton was born to Puritan parents in Derby, England. He entered Trinity College, Cambridge, graduating with his bachelor's degree in 1603. Afterward, Cotton became a fellow at Emmanuel College, Cambridge, which at the time was heavily influenced by Puritanism. There, Cotton finished his master's degree in 1606. Cotton then served as head lecturer, dean, and catechist for the college. It was in this period that he heard the preaching of Richard Sibbes,* which proved instrumental in Cotton's personal conversion. Cotton received a bachelor of divinity in 1610 from Cambridge and was shortly thereafter ordained into the priesthood of the Church of England. However, Cotton's increasing nonconformity brought him into conflict with episcopal authorities, which prompted him to move to the colony of Massachusetts in July 1633. Upon his arrival, he immediately assumed a position of

leadership as the teacher of the First Church of Boston. Throughout his tenure, Cotton exerted significant influence in the civic and ecclesiastical affairs of the colony. He continued in his ministry at First Church until his death on December 23, 1652. Over the course of his ministry, Cotton wrote nearly forty works. Among these were the *Keys of the Kingdom of Heaven, and the Power Thereof* (1644) and *Exposition upon the Thirteenth Chapter of Revelation* (1655).

Council of Constance (1414–1418). Convened to resolve the Western Schism, root out heresy and reform the church in head and members, the council asserted in *Sacrosancta* (1415) the immediate authority of ecumenical councils assembled in the Holy Spirit under Christ—even over the pope. Martin V was elected pope in 1417 after the three papal claimants were deposed; thus, the council ended the schism. The council condemned Jan Hus,* Jerome of Prague (c. 1365–1416) and, posthumously, John Wycliffe. Hus and Jerome, despite letters of safe conduct, were burned at the stake. Their deaths ignited the Hussite Wars, which ended as a result of the Council of Basel's concessions to the Bohemian church. The council fathers sought to reform the church through the regular convocation of councils (*Frequens*; 1417). Martin V begrudgingly complied by calling the required councils, then immediately disbanding them. Pius II (r. 1458–1464) reasserted papal dominance through *Execrabilis* (1460), which condemned any appeal to a future council apart from the pope's authority.

Council of Trent (1545–1563) Convoked by Pope Paul III (r. 1534–1549) with the support of Charles V*, the nineteenth ecumenical council was convened in the northern Italian city of Trent. Attended primarily by Italian clerics, it met in three distinct phases. Beginning in December 1545, during its first eight sessions, the council issued doctrinal decrees, asserting the authority of tradition alongside Scripture, the authenticity of the Vulgate, the prerogative of the church in interpretation, and the necessity of human cooperation in the work of salvation. Ecclesial abuses were also addressed, as attempts were made to eliminate absenteeism and pluralism and devolve power from Rome to bishoprics and parishes. The council was suspended following the outbreak of the plague in Trent in March 1547. A number of Protestant delegates were present during the second phase of the council, which met between May 1551 and April 1552 under the supervision of Pope Julius III (r. 1550–1555). The primary achievement of this period of the council was the clarification of teachings on the seven sacraments, with transubstantiation, the objective efficacy of the Eucharist, and the necessity of auricular confession confirmed as dogma. Reconvened by Pope Pius IV (r. 1559–1565) in 1561, the third phase of the council addressed the relationship between bishops and Rome, resulting in affirmations of the divine appointment of the church hierarchy and the obligation of bishops to reside in their dioceses. Clerical education, the regulation of marriage, and teachings on purgatory, indulgences, the use of images, and the saints were also addressed.

Miles Coverdale (1488–1568). Anglican bishop. Coverdale is known for his translations of the Bible into English, completing William Tyndale's* efforts and later producing the Great Bible commissioned by Henry VIII* (1539). A former friar, Coverdale was among the Cambridge scholars who met at the White Horse Tavern to discuss Martin Luther's* ideas. During Coverdale's three terms of exile in Europe, he undertook various translations, including the Geneva Bible*. He was appointed bishop of Exeter by Thomas Cranmer* and served as chaplain to Edward VI. Coverdale contributed to Cranmer's first edition of the Book of Common Prayer.*

William Cowper (Couper) (1568–1619). Scottish Puritan bishop. After graduating from the University of St. Andrews, Cowper worked in parish ministry for twenty-five years before becoming bishop. As a zealous Puritan and advocate of regular preaching and rigorous discipline, Cowper championed Presbyterian polity and lay participation in church government.

Cowper published devotional works, sermon collections and a commentary on Revelation.

Benjamin Coxe (fl. 1646). English Baptist minister. Coxe began his career in the Church of England, ministering at parishes in Devonshire, Bedford, and Coventry. After preaching against infant baptism, he was challenged to a public debate by Richard Baxter.* Coxe lost and was briefly arrested after refusing to leave the city. Following his release, he joined a congregation of Anabaptists in London.

Walter Cradock (1606–1659). Welsh Anglican minister. Cradock was born in Llangwm, Monmouthshire, Wales. After completing his education at the University of Oxford, Cradock assumed his first position as curate at Peterson-super-Ely, Glamorgan. In 1633, Cradock, along with some other Welsh ministers, was reported to Archbishop William Laud* and the Court of High Commission for preaching nonconformity and for refusing the *Book of Sports*. In 1634 Cradock traveled throughout Wexham and Herefordshire encouraging the establishment of Welsh Nonconformist congregations. Cradock later became pastor of an Independent congregation at Llanfair Waterdine in 1639. When the English Civil War began, Cradock and his conventicle moved to Bristol, but when Royalist forces came to occupy the city, he and some of his group departed for All-Hallows-the-Great, where he preached regularly with Henry Jessey (1603–1663). In 1641, Cradock was among the group of preachers for Wales commissioned by the Long Parliament. Later, he served as regular preacher for the Barebones Parliament. Throughout this period, Cradock was an ardent supporter of Oliver Cromwell. Cradock lived the remainder of his life quietly while ministering to a congregation at Llangwm. Throughout his career, Cradock authored a number of devotional works, among which were *Gospel Liberty* (1648) and *Gospel Holiness* (1655).

Thomas Cranmer (1489–1556). Anglican archbishop and theologian. Cranmer supervised church reform and produced the first two editions of the Book of Common Prayer.* As a doctoral student at Cambridge, he was involved in the discussions at the White Horse Tavern. Cranmer contributed to a religious defense of Henry VIII's* divorce; Henry then appointed him Archbishop of Canterbury. Cranmer cautiously steered the course of reform, accelerating under Edward VI. After supporting the attempted coup to prevent Mary's assuming the throne, Cranmer was convicted of treason and burned at the stake. Cranmer's legacy is the splendid English of his liturgy and prayer books.

Richard Crashaw (1612–1649). English Catholic poet. Educated at Cambridge, Crashaw was fluent in Hebrew, Greek and Latin. His first volume of poetry was *Epigrammatum sacrorum liber* (1634). Despite being born into a Puritan family, Crashaw was attracted to Catholicism, finally converting in 1644 after he was forced to resign his fellowship for not signing the Solemn League and Covenant (1643). In 1649, he was made a subcanon of Our Lady of Loretto by Cardinal Palotta.

Herbert Croft (1603–1691). Anglican bishop. As a boy Croft converted to Catholicism; he returned to the Church of England during his studies at Oxford. Before the English Civil Wars, he served as chaplain to Charles I. After the Restoration, Charles II appointed him as bishop. Croft ardently opposed Catholicism in his later years.

John Crompe (d. 1661). Anglican priest. Educated at Cambridge, Crompe published a commentary on the Apostles' Creed, a sermon on Psalm 21:3 and an exposition of Christ's passion.

Oliver Cromwell (1599–1658). Commander of the Parliamentary forces during the English Civil War. Lord Protector of the Commonwealth of England, Scotland, and Ireland. Cromwell was born in Huntingdon, East Anglia, the only surviving son of Robert Cromwell. In 1616, he enrolled at the University of Cambridge as a fellow commoner. However, he withdrew from the university the following year due to his father's death. He represented Huntingdon in Parliament in 1628, and later Cambridge in the Short and Long Parliaments. During the Civil

War, he commanded the Parliamentary forces, which he led to victory at the Battles of Marston Moor (1644) and Naseby (1645). After the execution of King Charles I in 1649, he became a member of the Council of State. It was at this time that the monarchy was abolished. In 1653, he was elevated to the position of Lord Protector of the Commonwealth. He declined the crown, though it was offered him in 1657. As Lord Protector, he endeavored to lead the postwar recovery, suppress military resistance, and advance British influence throughout Europe and the world. Moreover, he promoted a limited religious toleration in the kingdoms of England, Scotland, and Ireland. After his death in 1658, his son Richard (1626–1712) succeeded him as Lord Protector. However, due to incompetence, Richard was forced to resign, which paved the way for the Restoration of the monarchy in 1660 with the ascension of Charles II (1630–1685) to the throne. One year after the Restoration, Oliver Cromwell's body was disinterred from Westminster Abbey, hung on the gallows at Tyburn, and cast into an unmarked grave.

Caspar Cruciger (1504–1548). German Lutheran theologian. Recognized for his alignment with the theological views of Philipp Melanchthon,* Cruciger was a scholar respected among both Protestants and Catholics. In 1521, Cruciger came Wittenberg to study Hebrew and remained there most of his life. He became a valuable partner for Martin Luther* in translating the Old Testament and served as teacher, delegate to major theological colloquies and rector. Cruciger was an agent of reform in his birthplace of Leipzig, where at the age of fifteen he had observed the disputation between Luther and Johann Eck.*

Elisabeth Cruciger (c. 1500–1535). German Lutheran hymnist. Following her conversion to Lutheranism, Cruciger left the Praemonstraten-sian order and relocated to Wittenberg, where she married Caspar Cruciger.* While her authorship has been contested, recent scholarship has assigned Cruciger the place of the first female Lutheran hymnist for her composition of "Lord

Christ is the Only Son of God" (Herr Christ der einig Gotts Sohn) (1524).

Ralph Cudworth (d. 1624) English Protestant minister. Father of noted Cambridge Platonist Ralph Cudworth (1617–1688), the elder Cudworth was a fellow of Emanuel College, Cambridge and rector of Aller in Somersetshire.

Marguerite d'Angoulême (1492–1549). French Catholic noblewoman. The elder sister of King Francis I of France, Marguerite was the Queen of Navarre and Duchess of Alençon and Berry. She was a poet and author of the French Renaissance. She composed *The Mirror of a Sinful Soul* (1531)—condemned by the theologians of the Sorbonne for containing Lutheran ideas—and an unfinished collection of short stories, the Heptaméron (1558). A leading figure in the French Reformation, Marguerite was at the center of a network of reform-minded individuals that included Guillame Briçonnet,* Jacques Lefèvre d'Etaples,* Gérard Roussel (1500–1550) and Guillaume Farel (1489–1565).

Jakob Dachser (1486–1567). German Anabaptist theologian and hymnist. Dachser served as a Catholic priest in Vienna until he was imprisoned and then exiled for defending the Lutheran understanding of the Mass and fasting. Hans Hut* rebaptized him in Augsburg, where Dachser was appointed as a leader of the Anabaptist congregation. Lutheran authorities imprisoned him for nearly four years. In 1531 he recanted his Radical beliefs and began to catechize children with the permission of the city council. Dachser was expelled from Augsburg as a possible insurrectionist in 1552 and relocated to Pfalz-Neuberg. He published a number of poems, hymns and mystical works, and he versified several psalms.

Jean Daillé (1594–1670). French Reformed pastor. Born into a devout Reformed family, Daillé studied theology and philosophy at Saumur under the most influential contemporary lay leader in French Protestantism, Philippe Duplessis-Mornay (1549–1623). Daillé held to Amyraldianism—the belief that Christ died for all humanity inclusively, not particularly for the elect

who would inherit salvation (though only the elect are in fact saved). He wrote a controversial treatise on the church fathers that aggravated many Catholic and Anglican scholars because of Daillé's apparent demotion of patristic authority in matters of faith.

Lambert Daneau (1530?–1595). French Reformed pastor and theologian. After a decade of pastoring in France, following the St. Bartholomew's Day Massacre, Daneau fled to Geneva to teach theology at the Academy. He later taught in the Low Countries, finishing his career in southern France. Daneau's diverse works include tracts on science, ethics and morality as well as numerous theological and exegetical works.

John Davenant (1576–1641). Anglican bishop and professor. Davenant attended Queen's College, Cambridge, where he received his doctorate and was appointed professor of divinity. During the Remonstrant controversy, James I* sent Davenant as one of the four representatives for the Church of England to the Synod of Dordrecht.* Following James's instructions, Davenant advocated a *via media* between the Calvinists and the Remonstrants, although in later years he defended against the rise of Arminianism in England. In 1621, Davenant was promoted to the bishopric of Salisbury, where he was generally receptive to Laudian reforms. Davenant's lectures on Colossians are his best-known work.

William Day (1605–1684). Anglican theologian. Born and raised in Windsor, Berkshire, Day received his early education from Eton College. Afterward, he matriculated at King's College, Cambridge, where he was elected a fellow in 1624. Day received his BA in 1629, and MA in 1632. In 1635, Day was incorporated MA at Oxford and in 1637 became vicar of Mapledurham, Oxfordshire. Throughout his long career, Day conformed to all the ecclesiastical changes dictated by the government through the Restoration, during which he retained his vicarage. Finally, Day was made divinity reader at the King's Chapel, Windsor Chapel. He published two commentaries, *An Exposition of the Book of the Prophet Isaiah* (1654) and *A Paraphrase and Commentary upon the Epistle of St. Paul to the Romans* (1666).

Defense of the Augsburg Confession (1531). See *Augsburg Confession.*

Hans Denck (c. 1500–1527). German Radical theologian. Denck, a crucial early figure of the German Anabaptist movement, combined medieval German mysticism with the radical sacramental theology of Andreas Bodenstein von Karlstadt* and Thomas Müntzer.* Denck argued that the exterior forms of Scripture and sacrament are symbolic witnesses secondary to the internally revealed truth of the Sprit in the human soul. This view led to his expulsion from Nuremberg in 1525; he spent the next two years in various centers of reform in the German territories. At the time of his death, violent persecution against Anabaptists was on the rise throughout northern Europe.

Stephen Denison (unknown). English Puritan pastor. Denison received the post of curate at St. Katherine Cree in London sometime in the 1610s, where he ministered until his ejection from office in 1635. During his career at St. Katherine Cree, Denison waded into controversy with both Puritans (over the doctrine of predestination) and Anglicans (over concerns about liturgical ceremonies). He approached both altercations with rancor and rigidity, although he seems to have been quite popular and beloved by most of his congregation. In 1631, William Laud* consecrated the newly renovated St. Katherine Cree, and as part of the festivities Denison offered a sermon on Luke 19:27 in which he publicly rebuked Laud for fashioning the Lord's house into a "den of robbers." Aside from the record of his quarrels, very little is known about Denison. In addition to *The White Wolf* (a 1627 sermon against another opponent), he published a catechism for children (1621), a treatise on the sacraments (1621) and a commentary on 2 Peter 1 (1622).

Arthur Dent (d. 1607). English Puritan preacher. Ordained in the Church of England, Dent ministered in Essex, where he made his Puritan sympathies clear and was disciplined for refusing to wear a surplice and make the sign of the cross. He published a number of works, including an

exposition of the Articles of Faith and an exposition of Revelation targeted against the Roman Catholic Church.

Marie Dentière (1495–1561). Belgian Reformed theologian. Dentière relinquished her monastic vows and married Simon Robert (d.1533), a former priest, in Strasbourg. After Robert died, she married Antoine Froment (1508–1581), a reformer in Geneva, and became involved in the reform of that city. Her best-known writings are a tract addressed to Marguerite d'Angoulême,* the *Very Useful Epistle* (1539), in which she espoused the evangelical faith and the right of women to interpret and teach scripture, and a preface to Calvin's sermon on 1 Timothy 2:8-12. Dentière is the only woman to have her name inscribed on the International Monument to the Reformation in Geneva.

Edward Dering (c.1540–1576). English Puritan preacher. An early Puritan, Dering's prospects of advancement in the Elizabethan church were effectively ended after a sermon in front of the Queen in which he described her as an "untamed and unruly heifer" while criticizing the state of the church and clergy. While continuing with intemperate and critical attacks throughout his career, Dering established himself as a preacher at St. Paul's Cathedral in London, where he became known for his pastoral concern and desire to teach the assurance of salvation.

Jean D'Espagne (1591–1659). French Independent pastor. After leading churches at Orange and the Hague, D'Espagne departed under accusations of immorality and settled in London, where he pastored a French congregation. A fractious figure, he led a group that separated from the established French congregation and entered into numerous controversies. Many of his extant writings are targeted toward errors he perceived in the theology and practice of others.

David Dickson (1583?–1663). Scottish Reformed pastor, preacher, professor and theologian. Dickson defended the Presbyterian form of ecclesial reformation in Scotland and was recognized for his iteration of Calvinist federal theology and expository biblical commentaries. Dickson served for over twenty years as professor of philosophy at the University of Glasgow before being appointed professor of divinity. He opposed the imposition of Episcopalian measures on the church in Scotland and was active in political and ecclesial venues to protest and prohibit such influences. Dickson was removed from his academic post following his refusal of the oath of supremacy during the Restoration era.

Veit Dietrich (1506–1549). German Lutheran preacher and theologian. Dietrich intended to study medicine at the University of Wittenberg, but Martin Luther* and Philipp Melanchthon* convinced him to study theology instead. Dietrich developed a strong relationship with Luther, accompanying him to the Marburg Colloquy (1529) and to Coburg Castle during the Diet of Augsburg (1530). After graduating, Dietrich taught on the arts faculty, eventually becoming dean. In 1535 he returned to his hometown, Nuremberg, to pastor. Later in life, Dietrich worked with Melanchthon to reform the church in Regensburg. In 1547, when Charles V arrived in Nuremberg, Dietrich was suspended from the pastorate; he resisted the imposition of the Augsburg Interim to no avail. In addition to transcribing some of Luther's lectures, portions of the Table Talk and the very popular *Hauspostille* (1544), Dietrich published his own sermons for children, a manual for pastors and a summary of the Bible.

Louis de Dieu (1590–1642). Dutch Reformed pastor and linguist. Committed to his pastoral and teaching ministry in Leiden, Dieu turned down the opportunity to teach theology and Old Testament at the University of Utrecht. He published grammars of Hebrew (1626) and Persian (1639); a comparative grammar of Hebrew, Aramaic, and Syriac (1628); and a collection of writings on the New Testament text.

Giovanni Diodati (1576–1649). Italian Reformed theologian. Diodati was from an Italian banking family who fled for religious reasons to Geneva. There he trained under Theodore Beza;* on completion of his doctoral degree, Diodati became professor of Hebrew at the academy. He

was an ecclesiastical representative of the church in Geneva (for whom he was a delegate at the Synod of Dordrecht*) and an advocate for reform in Venice. Diodati's chief contribution to the Italian reform movement was a translation of the Bible into Italian (1640–1641), which remains the standard translation in Italian Protestantism.

John Dod (c. 1549–1645). English Puritan pastor. Over the course of his lengthy pastoral career (spanning roughly sixty years), Dod was twice suspended for nonconformity and twice reinstated. A popular preacher, he published many sermons as well as commentaries on the Ten Commandments and the Lord's Prayer; collections of his sayings and anecdotes were compiled after his death.

John Donne (1572–1631). Anglican poet and preacher. Donne was born into a strong Catholic family. However, sometime between his brother's death from the plague while in prison in 1593 and the publication of his *Pseudo-Martyr* in 1610, Donne joined the Church of England. Ordained to the Anglican priesthood in 1615 and already widely recognized for his verse, Donne quickly rose to prominence as a preacher—some have deemed him the best of his era. His textual corpus is an amalgam of erotic *and* divine poetry (e.g., "Batter My Heart"), as well as a great number of sermons.

Dordrecht Confession (1632). Dutch Mennonite confession. Adriaan Cornelisz (1581–1632) wrote the Dordrecht Confession to unify Dutch Mennonites. This basic statement of Mennonite belief and practice affirms distinctive doctrines such as nonresistance, shunning, footwashing, and the refusal to swear oaths. Most continental Mennonites subscribed to this confession during the second half of the seventeenth century.

Johann George Dorsche (1597–1659). German Lutheran theologian. Dorsche pastored briefly at Entzheim before being called to Strasbourg, where he earned his doctorate, was appointed professor of theology, and served as a preacher at the cathedral. He spent the last five years of his life as professor of theology at the University of Rostock. Dorsche published a number of theological works as well as commentaries on the Gospels and Hebrews.

John Downame (c. 1571–1652). English Puritan pastor and theologian. See *English Annotations*.

Charles Drelincourt (1595–1669). French Reformed pastor, theologian and controversialist. After studying at Saumur Academy, Drelincourt pastored the Reformed Church in Paris for nearly fifty years. He was well known for his ministry to the sick. In addition to polemical works against Catholicism, he published numerous pastoral resources: catechisms, three volumes of sermons and a five-volume series on consolation for the suffering.

The Dutch Annotations (1657). See *Statenvertaling*.

Daniel Dyke (d. 1614). English Puritan preacher. Born of nonconformist stock, Dyke championed a more thorough reformation of church practice in England. After the promulgation of John Whitgift's* articles in 1583, Dyke refused to accept what he saw as remnants of Catholicism, bringing him into conflict with the bishop of London. Despite the petitions of his congregation and some politicians, the bishop of London suspended Dyke from his ministry for refusing priestly ordination and conformity to the Book of Common Prayer.* All of his work was published posthumously; it is mostly focused on biblical interpretation.

John Eachard (unknown). English Anglican minister. After graduating with his master of arts from Trinity College, Cambridge, Eachard was the vicar at Darsham in Suffolk. At least two of his sermons, one on Matthew 3:10 and another on Revelation 12:11, were published in his lifetime.

Johann Eck (Johann Maier of Eck) (1486–1543). German Catholic theologian. Though Eck was not an antagonist of Martin Luther* until the dispute over indulgences, Luther's Ninety-five Theses (1517) sealed the two as adversaries. After their debate at the Leipzig Disputation (1519), Eck participated in the writing of the papal bull that led to Luther's excommunication. Much of Eck's work was written to oppose Protestantism or to defend Catholic doctrine and the papacy; his *Enchiridion* was a manual written to counter Protestant doctrine. However, Eck was also deeply invested in the status of parish preaching, publishing a five-volume set of postils. He participated in the assemblies at Regensburg and Augsburg and led the Catholics in their rejection of the Augsburg Confession.

Edward VI of England (1537–1553). English monarch. Son of Henry VIII* and Jane Seymour (1508–1537), Edward ascended to the throne as a minor, leaving the practical power of the monarchy in the hands of those appointed by the Regency council as Lord Protector of the Realm, first, his uncle, Edward Seymour, duke of Somerset (1500–1552), and afterwards, John Dudley, duke of Northumberland (1504–1553). Under Somerset and Northumberland, and with Thomas Cranmer* installed as Archbishop of Canterbury, the eclectic reforms made during the reign of Henry VIII were drawn into the service of a thoroughly Protestant transformation. During the reign of Edward, communion in two kinds was instituted, all services were held in the vernacular, and a series of ecclesiastical visitations oversaw the suppression of Catholic religion. Alongside the flood of Protestant refugees from the continent that sheltered in the kingdom, the publication of the revised Book of Common Prayer*, the Book of Homilies* and the Forty-Two Articles (1553) helped establish the future direction of Anglicanism.

Elizabeth I of England (1533–1603) English monarch. The daughter of Henry VIII* (r. 1509–1547) and Anne Boleyn (c. 1501–1536), Elizabeth outwardly conformed to Catholicism during the reign of her sister Mary I (r. 1553–1558), but her Protestant upbringing encouraged the hopes of many reformers upon her accession in 1558. With the 1559 Elizabethan Settlement, Elizabeth redefined England as a Protestant country, with the Act of Supremacy asserting the monarch as the head of the English church, and the Act of Uniformity establishing the 1559 *Book of Common Prayer* as the valid order of service within the realm. However, Elizabeth resisted the aggressive persecution of Catholics for political reasons, while also allowing some traditional vestments, furniture and ceremonies to be retained. Her moderate and pragmatic reforms frustrated many who wished for more thorough change and led to the emergence of the Puritan movement. Elizabeth faced numerous threats during her reign, including the machinations of Scottish Catholics and claims to the throne of Mary Stuart (1542–1547), leading to her rival's imprisonment and execution in 1587; the attempted invasion of England by Spain, which culminated in the celebrated defeat of the Spanish Armada in 1588; and a Catholic rebellion in Ireland that was suppressed during the Nine Years War (1594–1603). Elizabeth never married, and was succeeded on the throne by James I* following her death in 1603.

Edward Elton (1569–1624). Puritan minister. Elton served as pastor of St. Mary Magdalen's Church in Bermondsey, Surrey. Richard Baxter* praised him for his exegetical works, among which were *Three Excellent Pious Treatises in Sundry Sermons upon the Whole Seventh, Eighth, and Ninth Chapters of the Epistle to the Romans* and *An Exposition of the Epistle of St. Paul to the Colossians.*

English Annotations (1645; 1651; 1657). Under a commission from the Westminster Assembly, the editors of the English Annotations—John Downame* along with unnamed colleagues—translated, collated and digested in a compact and accessible format several significant Continental biblical resources, including Calvin's* commentaries, Beza's* *Annotationes majores* and Diodati's* *Annotations.*

Desiderius Erasmus (1466–1536). Dutch Catholic humanist and pedagogue. Erasmus, a celebrated humanist scholar, was recognized for translations of ancient texts, reform of education according to classical studies, moral and spiritual writings and the first printed edition of the Greek New Testament. A former Augustinian who never left the Catholic Church, Erasmus addressed deficiencies he saw in the church and society, challenging numerous prevailing doctrines but advocating reform. He envisioned a simple, spiritual Christian life shaped by the teachings of Jesus and ancient wisdom. He was often accused of collusion with Martin Luther* on account of some resonance of their ideas but hotly debated Luther on human will.

George Estey (c. 1560–1601). English Anglican priest. After graduating from Cambridge, Estey was ordained in the Church of England and served as vicar of St. Mary in Bury St. Edmunds, Suffolk.

Paul Fagius (1504–1549). German Reformed Hebraist and pastor. After studying at the University of Heidelberg, Fagius went to Strasbourg where he perfected his Hebrew under Wolfgang Capito.* In Isny im Allgäu (Baden-Württemberg) he met the great Jewish grammarian Elias Levita (1469–1549), with whom he established a Hebrew printing press. In 1544 Fagius returned to Strasbourg, succeeding Capito as preacher and Old Testament lecturer. During the Augsburg Interim, Fagius (with Martin Bucer*) accepted Thomas Cranmer's* invitation to translate and interpret the Bible at Cambridge. However, Fagius died before he could begin any of the work. Fagius wrote commentaries on the first four chapters of Genesis and the deutero-canonical books of Sirach and Tobit.

Guillaume Farel (1489–1565) French Reformed preacher and theologian. At the vanguard of the French Reformation, Farel was a student of Jacques Lefèvre d'Étaples* and member of Archbishop Briçonnet's* circle in Meaux until his desire for more rapid change saw him depart in 1523 to preach the Protestant message in Basel, Montbéliard, Strasbourg, Bern, and Aigle. During this period of his ministry, he composed the first French Protestant book, an evangelical commentary on the Lord's Prayer and the Apostle's Creed, as well as the first French Confession of Faith. A catalyst in Geneva's acceptance of the Reformation in 1536, it was Farel who persuaded Calvin* to settle in the city. After he and Calvin were banished from Geneva in 1538, Farel accepted the pastorate in Neuchâtel, a position he held until his death while continuing to travel and support the Reformation in the French-speaking lands.

John Fary (unknown). English Puritan pastor. Fary authored *God's Severity on Man's Sterility* (1645), a sermon on the fruitless fig tree in Luke 13:6-9.

Margaret Fell (1614–1702). English Quaker. Known as the "Mother of Quakerism," Fell was born at Dalton-in-Furness in northern England. The daughter of a local judge, she married Thomas Fell, who was a judge as well as a member of Parliament, representing Lancashire. In 1652, under the preaching of George Fox (1624–1691), Fell and her daughters became members of the Society of Friends (the Quakers). From that time onward, she became a pivotal figure in the subsequent development of the Quaker movement. Throughout her extensive correspondence to powerful members of the nobility, including King Charles II (r. 1660–1685), she pleaded for the release of imprisoned Quakers. Fell was arrested in 1664 for leading Quaker meetings and for her refusal to swear the Oath of Obedience, and she was sentenced to four and a half years imprisonment. After her release, she married George Fox in 1669, her first husband having died eleven years earlier. In addition to her advocacy for incarcerated Quakers, Fell enhanced the work of the Quaker Women's Meeting, which consisted of caring for the sick and elderly as well as orphans and prisoners. Her exegetical works include *For Mannaseth Ben Israel* and *A Loving Salutation to the Seed of Abraham*, both published in 1656, and translated into Hebrew (the latter believed to have been translated by the Jewish philosopher Benedict Spinoza). Moreover during her imprisonment, she authored her most famous treatise, *Women's Speaking Justified, Proved and Allowed of by the Scriptures*.

William Fenner (1600–1640). English Puritan pastor. After studying at Cambridge and Oxford, Fenner ministered at Sedgley and Rochford. Fenner's extant writings, which primarily deal with practical and devotional topics, demonstrate a zealous Puritan piety and a keen interest in Scripture and theology.

Charles Ferme (1566–1617). Scottish Reformed pastor and educator. After studying and teaching at the University of Edinburgh, Ferme pastored in Philorth, where he later served as the principal of a newly chartered university. The reconstitution of the episcopacy brought challenges for Ferme, and his resistance saw him imprisoned a number of times, including a three-year incarceration on the Isle of Bute. His only extant writing is a logical analysis of Romans.

Henry Ferne (1602–1662). English Protestant minister. Ferne ministered at a number of parishes in the north of England before serving as an extraordinary chaplain to Charles I* after earning his doctorate of divinity. A committed Royalist, he left official ministry during the Civil War (1642–1651), though he often preached, wrote a number of theological treatises against the Roman Catholics, and accompanied the king on a number of occasions. After the Restoration, Ferne served as master at Trinity College, Cambridge, and dean of Ely Cathedral before becoming bishop of Chester.

Richard Ferrers (Unknown). English poet. Ferrers is remembered for his poem *The Worth of Woman* (1622), defending the equality and value of women.

First Helvetic Confession (1536). Anticipating the planned church council at Mantua (1537, but delayed until 1545 at Trent), Reformed theologians of the Swiss cantons drafted a confession to distinguish themselves from both Catholics and the churches of the Augsburg Confession.* Heinrich Bullinger* led the discussion and wrote the confession itself; Leo Jud, Oswald Myconius, Simon Grynaeus and others were part of the assembly. Martin Bucer* and Wolfgang Capito* had desired to draw the Lutheran and Reformed communions closer together through this document, but Luther* proved unwilling after Bullinger refused to accept the Wittenberg Concord (1536). This confession was largely eclipsed by Bullinger's Second Helvetic Confession.*

John Fisher (1469–1535). English Catholic bishop and theologian. This reputed preacher defended Catholic orthodoxy and strove to reform abuses in the church. In 1521 Henry VIII* honored Fisher with the title *Fidei Defensor* ("defender of the faith"). Nevertheless, Fisher opposed the king's divorce of Catherine of Aragon (1485–1536) and the independent establishment of the Church of England; he was convicted for treason and executed. Most of Fisher's works are polemical and occasional (e.g., on transubstantiation, against Martin Luther*); however, he also published a series of sermons on the seven penitential psalms. In addition to his episcopal duties, Fisher was the chancellor of Cambridge from 1504 until his death.

Matthias Flacius (1520–1575). Lutheran theologian. A native of Croatia, Matthias Flacius commenced his studies at the University of Tubingen, and completed them at Wittenberg, where through Luther's influence, he embraced the university's evangelical theology. Flacius began his career as instructor of Hebrew at the University of Wittenberg in 1544, and remained in this post until 1549. As a devoted follower of Luther's teachings, Flacius sought to defend them in their purity which drove him and Nikolaus von Amsdorf as leaders of the Gnesio-Lutherans to oppose the more moderate positions of Philipp Melanchthon and his sympathizers, the Philippists, in several controversies concerning the role of free will and good works in justification as well as relations with Calvinism. After serving as a professor at the University of Jena (1557–1561), Flacius spent the remainder of his life as an independent scholar, frequently moving from one city to another to escape persecution. Flacius died in Frankfurt am Main in 1575. His important exegetical works are *De vocabula Dei* (1549), *Clavis Scripturae Sacrae* (1567), and *Glossa Novi Testamenti* (1570). Flacius also published two historical works, *Catalogus Testium Veritatis* (1556) and the *Magdeburg Centuries*.

Marcantonio Flaminio (1498–1550). Italian humanist and poet. Flaminio was dependent on patronage, and he spent much of his life in the houses of noble benefactors in Bologna, Genoa, and Verona. While he never left the Roman church, he was drawn to intellectual currents that sought reform. In Naples, he participated in an intellectual circle that included Juan de Valdés* and Pietro Carnesecchi* before joining the house of Cardinal Pole* in Viterbo. Alongside his poetry and humanistic writings, Flaminio also edited one of the most significant Italian texts of the Reformation, Benedetto de Mantova's* *The Benefit of Christ* (1543).

John Flavel (c. 1630–1691). English Puritan pastor. Trained at Oxford, Flavel ministered in southwest England from 1650 until the Act of Uniformity in 1662, which reaffirmed the compulsory use of the Book of Common Prayer. Flavel preached unofficially for many years, until his congregation was eventually allowed to build a meeting place in 1687. His works were numerous, varied and popular.

Giovanni Battista Folengo (1490–1559). Italian Catholic exegete. In 1528 Folengo left the Benedictine order, questioning the validity of monastic vows; he returned to the monastic life in 1534. During this hiatus Folengo came into contact with the Neapolitan reform-minded circle founded by Juan de Valdés.* Folengo published commentaries on the Psalms, John, 1–2 Peter and James. Augustin Marlorat* included Folengo's comment in his anthology of exegesis on the Psalms. In 1580 Folengo's Psalms commentary was added to the Index of Prohibited Books.

John Forbes (1568?–1634). Scottish Reformed pastor. While minister at Alford in Aberdeenshire, Forbes was appointed moderator of the Presbyterian Aberdeen Assembly, which met against the orders of King James I.* Refusing to accept the monarch's jurisdiction, he was exiled to the Continent and settled in the Netherlands, where he pastored English congregations at Middleburg and Delft until forced out under the reforms of Archbishop Laud.*

Formula of Concord (1577). After Luther's* death, intra-Lutheran controversies between the Gnesio-Lutherans (partisans of Luther) and the Philippists (partisans of Melanchthon*) threatened to cause a split among those who had subscribed to the Augsburg Confession.* In 1576, Jakob Andreae,* Martin Chemnitz,* Nikolaus

Selnecker,* David Chytraeus* and Andreas Musculus (1514–1581) met with the intent of resolving the controversies, which mainly regarded the relationship between good works and salvation, the third use of the law, and the role of the human will in accepting God's grace. In 1580, celebrating the fiftieth anniversary of the presentation of the Augsburg Confession to Charles V (1500–1558), the *Book of Concord* was printed as the authoritative interpretation of the Augsburg Confession; it included the three ancient creeds, the Augsburg Confession, its Apology (1531), the Schmalkald Articles," Luther's *Treatise on the Power and Primacy of the Pope* (1537) and both his Small and Large Catechisms (1529).

John Foxe (1516–1587). English Protestant martyrologist, historian. John Foxe was born in Boston, Lincolnshire. After completing his early education, Foxe became a fellow at Magdalen College, Oxford, where he completed his BA degree in 1537, and MA in 1543. Also he was lecturer in logic from 1539 to 1540. However, in 1545, Foxe was forced to resign from Magdalen because he had adopted Protestant beliefs. After leaving Oxford, Foxe became tutor to the children of the Earl of Surrey. During this time Foxe made the acquaintance of John Bale (1495–1562) who fostered his interest in history. When Mary Tudor ascended the throne of England in 1553, Foxe fled to the continent. While there, Foxe traveled to Frankfurt, where in 1555 he met Edmund Grindal (1519–1583), who had been composing accounts of Protestant martyrs. Foxe later joined Grindal in Basel, where he translated his narratives into Latin. Foxe published the book resulting from his labors in Basel in 1559. After Elizabeth I* succeeded to the throne in the same year, Foxe returned to England. Upon his return he began working with the printer, John Day, who published the first English edition of Foxe's work. This voluminous work, *The Acts and Monuments*, underwent four editions during the remainder of the author's lifetime. *The Acts and Monuments* contributed significantly to the development of the

national identity and piety of Elizabethan England. Shorter versions of this work are known simply as *Foxe's Book of Martyrs*.

Francis I of France (1494–1547). French monarch. Francis ascended to the French throne following the death of Louis XII (1462–1515), who was both his cousin and father-in-law. Much of Francis's reign was dominated by warfare. In Italy, victory over the Swiss allowed him to assert his dynastic claim to the Duchy of Milan, and extract liberties for the French church from Pope Leo X* through the Concordat of Bologna. His campaign against Charles V* was less successful, however, as Milan was lost and following defeat at the Battle of Pavia, Francis was taken prisoner. His release was negotiated by his sister, Marguerite d'Angouleme*, though he reneged in its terms once reaching safety, ensuring continued conflict with the Holy Roman Emperor throughout his reign. Francis fostered humanistic learning within his kingdom, and while he resisted Lutheran and other evangelical thought, he gave some space for its expression, giving protection to scholars such as those gathered around his sister and Bishop Guillaume Briçonnet* at Meaux. His desire for social order saw him take increasingly strident steps against the Reformation, however, particularly after his bedchamber was pamphleted during the Affair of the Placards, and the final years of his reign saw a significant increase in attempts to reassert Catholic doctrine and stamp out Protestantism with persecution.

Sebastian Franck (1499–1542). German Radical theologian. Franck became a Lutheran in 1525, but by 1529 he began to develop ideas that distanced him from Protestants and Catholics. Expelled from Strasbourg and later Ulm due to his controversial writings, Franck spent the end of his life in Basel. Franck emphasized God's word as a divine internal spark that cannot be adequately expressed in outward forms. Thus he criticized religious institutions and dogmas. His work consists mostly of commentaries, compilations and translations. In his sweeping historical *Chronica* (1531), Franck supported numerous heretics condemned by the Catholic Church and criticized political and church authorities.

Leonhard Frick (d. 1528). Austrian Radical martyr. See *Kunstbuch.*

John Frith (1503–1533). English reformer, author, and martyr. Frith was born in Westerham, Kent. He was the son of Richard Frith, the innkeeper of the White Horse Inn. After receiving his earlier education at Sevenoaks Grammar School and Eton College, Frith matriculated at Queen's College, Cambridge, where Stephen Gardiner (1497–1555), future bishop of Winchester, and opponent of the English Reformation, was his tutor. Frith graduated with his BA degree in 1525, having obtained proficiency in Latin and mathematics. While still a student, Frith met Thomas Bilney (1495–1531), who most likely introduced him to evangelical faith. After graduating, Frith became a junior canon at Christ Church, Oxford. However, while at Oxford, Frith along with nine others was imprisoned in a fish cellar for possessing what ecclesiastical authorities considered "heretical books." Upon his release, Frith traveled to the Continent, where he assisted William Tyndale* with his translation work. Also while on the Continent, Frith translated some antipapal polemical works, and authored *A Disputation of Purgatory.* Upon Frith's return to England in 1532, he was arrested and imprisoned several times for publicly preaching against transubstantiation and purgatory. Eventually, Frith was imprisoned in the Tower of London, and later transferred to Newgate Prison. He was burned at the stake on July 4, 1533.

Libert Froidmont (1587–1653). Belgian philosopher, scientist, and theologian. A childhood friend of Cornelius Jansen (1585–1638), Froidmont entered the Society of Jesus and his early career was focused on philosophy and the sciences, teaching at Antwerp, Saint-Michel, and Louvain. Drawn to the rigorous but controversial Augustinianism of Jansen, Froidmont earned his doctorate in theology in 1628 and succeeded Jansen as chair of theology at Louvain. While publishing a number of theological and exegetical works,

including a commentary on Paul's letters, Froidmont was also active in the scientific and philosophical debates of his era. He published against Nicolas Copernicus (1473–1543) and Galileo Galilei (1564–1642), whom he argued were wrong but not heretical, and was one of the first to engage with the thought of René Descartes (1596–1650).

William Fulke (1538–1589). English Protestant theologian. Responsible for preaching and lecturing on Old Testament and other subjects, William Fulke courted controversy during his tenure as fellow at Cambridge. He was briefly expelled for his advocacy of Vestarians and later resigned until acquitted of being in an incestuous marriage. He left Cambridge to serve as chaplain to Robert Dudley, Earl of Leicester (1532–1588), returning almost a decade later as master of Pembroke College. He is best remembered as a controversialist and was the author of numerous anti-Catholic tracts.

Thomas Fuller (1608–1661). English Protestant minister. Fuller, the son of a minister, graduated from Cambridge, and his early career was overseen by his uncle John Davenant,* who secured his nephew a number of pastoral positions. Known for his wit and moderation, Fuller was a chaplain in the Royal army during the Civil War (1642–1651), and he served as an extraordinary chaplain to King Charles II (1630–1685) after the Restoration. He composed a number of exegetical and pastoral works, but he is primarily remembered for his historical writings. These include histories of the Crusades and the church in England as well as a biographical dictionary, the *History of the Worthies of England* (1622).

Gallic Confession (1559). This confession was accepted at the first National Synod of the Reformed Churches of France (1559). It was intended to be a touchstone of Reformed faith but also to show to the people of France that the Huguenots—who faced persecution—were not seditious. The French Reformed Church presented this confession to Francis II (1544–1560) in 1560, and to his successor, Charles IX (1550–1574), in 1561. The later Genevan draft, likely written by

Calvin,* Beza* and Pierre Viret (1511–1571), was received as the true Reformed confession at the seventh National Synod in La Rochelle (1571).

Geneva Bible (originally printed 1560). During Mary I's reign many English Protestants sought safety abroad in Reformed territories of the Empire and the Swiss Cantons, especially in Calvin's* Geneva. A team of English exiles in Geneva led by William Whittingham (c. 1524–1579) brought this complete translation to press in the course of two years. Notable for several innovations—Roman type, verse numbers, italics indicating English idiom and not literal phrasing of the original languages, even variant readings in the Gospels and Acts—this translation is most well known for its marginal notes, which reflect a strongly Calvinist theology. The notes explained Scripture in an accessible way for the laity, also giving unlearned clergy a new sermon resource. Although controversial because of its implicit critique of royal power, this translation was wildly popular; even after the publication of the Authorized Version (1611) and James I's* 1616 ban on its printing, the Geneva Bible continued to be the most popular English translation until after the English Civil Wars.

Johann Gerhard (1582–1637). German Lutheran theologian, professor and superintendent. Gerhard is considered one of the most eminent Lutheran theologians, after Martin Luther* and Martin Chemnitz.* After studying patristics and Hebrew at Wittenberg, Jena and Marburg, Gerhard was appointed superintendent at the age of twenty-four. In 1616 he was appointed to a post at the University of Jena, where he reintroduced Aristotelian metaphysics to theology and gained widespread fame. His most important work was the nine-volume *Loci Theologici* (1610–1625). He also expanded Chemnitz's harmony of the Gospels (*Harmonia Evangelicae*), which was finally published by Polykarp Leyser (1552–1610) in 1593. Gerhard was well-known for an irenic spirit and an ability to communicate clearly.

George Gifford (c. 1548–1600). English Puritan pastor. Gifford was suspended for nonconformity in 1584. With private support, however, he was able to continue his ministry. Through his published works he wanted to help develop lay piety and biblical literacy.

George Gifford (d. 1620). English Puritan minister. A celebrated preacher in Maldon, Essex, Gifford was removed from the pulpit when he refused to subscribe to Articles of Conformity drawn up by Archbishop John Whitgift.* Allowed to continue ministry in the office of lecturer, he also served as a representative for Essex at Puritan synods. He published numerous works, including a primer for common Christians, a dialogue between a Catholic and a Protestant, and two works on witchcraft.

Anthony Gilby (c. 1510–1585). English Puritan translator. During Mary I's reign, Gilby fled to Geneva, where he assisted William Whittingham (c. 1524–1579) with the Geneva Bible.* He returned to England to pastor after Elizabeth I's* accession. In addition to translating numerous continental Reformed works into English—especially those of John Calvin* and Theodore Beza*—Gilby also wrote commentaries on Micah and Malachi.

Bernard Gilpin (1517–1583). Anglican theologian and priest. In public disputations, Gilpin defended Roman Catholic theology against John Hooper (c. 1495-1555) and Peter Martyr Vermigli.* These debates caused Gilpin to reexamine his faith. Upon Mary I's accession, Gilpin resigned his benefice. He sojourned in Belgium and France, returning to pastoral ministry in England in 1556. Gilpin dedicated himself to a preaching circuit in northern England, thus earning the moniker "the Apostle to the North." His zealous preaching and almsgiving roused royal opposition and a warrant for his arrest. On his way to the queen's commission, Gilpin fractured his leg, delaying his arrival in London until after Mary's death and thus likely saving his life. His only extant writing is a sermon on Luke 2 confronting clerical abuses.

Paul Glock (c. 1530–1585). German Radical preacher. A teenage convert to Hutterite Anabaptism, Glock spent nineteen years imprisoned at

Hohenwittlingen, unwilling to recant. While incarcerated, he wrote hymns, a confession and defense of his beliefs, and numerous letters that proved influential in the development of Anabaptist thought. After helping extinguish a fire at the prison in 1576, Glock was freed and settled with the Brethren in Moravia.

Glossa ordinaria. This standard collection of biblical commentaries consists of interlinear and marginal notes drawn from patristic and Carolingian exegesis appended to the Vulgate*; later editions also include Nicholas of Lyra's* *Postilla.* The *Glossa ordinaria* and the *Sentences* of Peter Lombard (c. 1100–1160) were essential resources for all late medieval and early modern commentators.

Franciscus Gomarus (1563–1641). Dutch Reformed theologian and pastor. A religious refugee at an early age, Gomarus's family was forced to leave Bruges for the Palatinate, with Gomarus receiving a Reformed education at Strasbourg, Neustadt, Oxford, Cambridge, and Heidelberg. He pastored at Frankfurt am Main until becoming professor of theology at the University of Leiden, where he came into extended conflict with colleague Jacobus Arminius* over predestination. Gomarus left Leiden in protest when Conradus Vorstius,* a follower of Arminius with Socinian tendencies, was appointed over his objections. Gomarus then pastored briefly at Middelburg before teaching at the Reformed academy at Saumur and the University of Groningen. Representing the university at the Synod of Dordrecht,* Gomarus was a leading opponent of Remonstrant theology and a key figure in ensuring their censure.

Robert Gomersall (1602–1646?). English Protestant minister and dramatist. Little is known of Gomersall's life beyond his graduation from Oxford and entrance into the ministry. He published a number of poetic and dramatic works, including a tragedy on the life of Italian prince Ludovicio Sforza (1452–1508) and a poetic meditation on Judges 19–20.

Thomas Goodwin (1600–1679). Puritan minister. Goodwin was born October 5, 1600, in Norfolk.

After receiving his early education from local schools, Goodwin matriculated at Christ College, Cambridge, which was a prime center of Puritan influence. He graduated with the BA degree in 1616 and MA in 1620. Upon receiving his MA, Goodwin became a fellow and lecturer at the university. In October 1620, Goodwin experienced a profound conversion on his twentieth birthday. After his conversion, Goodwin joined the Puritan party at Cambridge. He was licensed to preach in the Church of England in 1625. Three years later, Goodwin became lecturer at Trinity Church. He served as vicar of this church from 1632 to 1634. Unwilling to comply with Archbishop William Laud's* directives for conformity, Goodwin was forced to resign all of his ecclesiastical and academic positions, and leave Cambridge. During the remainder of the 1630s, due to John Cotton's* influence, Goodwin came to adopt the principles of Independency. In 1639, in order to escape the increasing restrictions of unauthorized preachers, Goodwin fled to the Netherlands, where he worked with other English Independent exiles. In 1641, Goodwin returned to England per Parliament's request, and preached before it on April 27, 1642. Goodwin was later appointed a delegate to the Westminster Assembly. In the Assembly, Goodwin proved himself to be one of the foremost advocates of Independency. After the Westminster Assembly adjourned, Goodwin was appointed a lecturer at Oxford, and a year later became president of Magdalen College. Furthermore, Goodwin served as an advisor to Oliver Cromwell (1599–1658) and as the Lord Protector's Oxford commissioner. Goodwin also tended to Cromwell on his deathbed. In addition to his university and advisory duties, Goodwin pastored an Independent church at Oxford. Notably, Goodwin was one of the primary authors of the Savoy Declaration of Faith (1658), which served as the confession of faith for the Independent/Congregational churches. When Charles II ascended to the throne of England in 1660, Goodwin withdrew from Oxford to London, where he pastored an Independent congregation until his death at the age of eighty. Throughout his career, Goodwin produced an enormous literary corpus, which includes many exegetical works. Best known among these are his expositions of Ephesians and Revelation.

Marie le Jars de Gournay (1565–1645). French Catholic writer and editor. Born into the minor nobility, the early death of Gournay's father led her family to relocate to their estate in Picardy, where she taught herself Latin and Greek. After reading the *Essais* (1580) of Michel de Montaigne (1533–1592), she committed herself to a life of literature and became active in the intellectual circles of Paris. While she translated many classical writings, she is best known for her editorial work on Montaigne's essays and her advocacy for the rights of women, laid out in a number of writings including *The Equality of Men and Women* (1622) and *The Ladies' Grievance* (1626).

Simon Goulart (1543–1628) French Reformed pastor, translator, and theologian. Goulart spent most of his career as a pastor in Geneva and its surrounds, particularly at the city parish of St. Gervais, and was the leader of the Company of Pastors during the last decades of his life. A prolific translator, he published numerous French editions of classical, patristic, and contemporary works from diverse authors including Plutarch, Seneca, Chrysostom, Cyprian, Tertullian, Beza*, Perkins* and Vermigli*. He also composed numerous devotional writings, important histories of early French Protestantism, and polemical treatises supporting the Huguenot cause.

Conrad Grebel (c. 1498–1526). Swiss Radical theologian. Grebel, considered the father of the Anabaptist movement, was one of the first defenders and performers of believers' baptism, for which he was eventually imprisoned in Zurich. One of Huldrych Zwingli's* early compatriots, Grebel advocated rapid, radical reform, clashing publicly with the civil authorities and Zwingli. Grebel's views, particularly on baptism, were influenced by Andreas Bodenstein von Karlstadt* and Thomas Müntzer.* Grebel advocated elimination of magisterial involvement in governing the church; instead, he envisioned the church as lay Christians determining their own affairs with strict adherence to the biblical text, and unified in volitional baptism.

William Greenhill (1591–1671). English Puritan pastor. Greenhill attended and worked at Magdalen College. He ministered in the diocese of Norwich but soon left for London, where he preached at Stepney. Greenhill was a member of the Westminster Assembly of Divines and was appointed the parliament chaplain by the children of Charles I. Oliver Cromwell included him among the preachers who helped draw up the Savoy Declaration. Greenhill was evicted from his post following the Restoration, after which he pastored independently. Among Greenhill's most significant contributions to church history was his *Exposition of the Prophet of Ezekiel.*

Catharina Regina von Greiffenberg (1633–1694). Austrian Lutheran poet. Upon her adulthood her guardian (and half uncle) sought to marry her; despite her protests of their consanguinity and her desire to remain celibate, she relented in 1664. After the deaths of her mother and husband, Greiffenberg abandoned her home to debtors and joined her friends Susanne Popp (d. 1683) and Sigmund von Birken (1626–1681) in Nuremberg. During her final years she dedicated herself to studying the biblical languages and to writing meditations on Jesus' death and resurrection, which she never completed. One of the most important and learned Austrian poets of the Baroque period, Greiffenberg published a collection of sonnets, songs and poems (1662) as well as three sets of mystical meditations on Jesus' life, suffering and death (1672; 1683; 1693). She participated in a society of poets called the Ister Gesellschaft.

Lady Jane Grey (1537–1554). English Protestant monarch, sometimes known as "the Nine Days Queen." The eldest daughter of Henry Grey and Frances Brandon, the daughter of Henry VIII's* younger sister Mary, Jane received an extensive Protestant and humanist education. She married Lord Guildford Dudley (c. 1535–1554), son of

Edward VI's* chief minister John Dudley, Duke of Northumberland (1504–1553). Seeking to avoid succession by Edward's Catholic half-sister Mary I, Edward and Northumberland conspired to alter the order of succession, naming Jane as heir in the king's will. Following Edward's death, Jane reluctantly took the crown on July 9, 1553, but Northumberland and other Protestants were unable to raise adequate support for her claim and the Privy Council proclaimed Mary queen on July 19. Upon Mary's accession, Jane was imprisoned in the Tower of London and after trial was executed alongside her husband for treason. A handful of her writings exist demonstrating her religious affections, while the story of her martyrdom is prominent in John Foxe's Acts and Monuments.

Edmund Grindal (c. 1519–1583). English Anglican archbishop. Grindal began his career in the church as chaplain to Nicholas Ridley* and King Edward VI* until forced to exile in Strasbourg during the reign of Mary I.* Returning to England upon the accession of Elizabeth I,* Grindal helped set the direction for the Church of England, participating in the 1559 Westminster Conference and serving as a member of the committee revising the liturgy. A moderate reformer, he reluctantly became bishop of London despite concerns over continuing Roman practices such as the wearing of vestments and the use of wafer bread for communion. His tenure as archbishop of York was marked by disputes with Presbyterians who wished to abolish the episcopacy and prayer book. Grindal was appointed Archbishop of Canterbury in 1575, but a conflict with Queen Elizabeth I hampered his ability to make change. He refused her request to suppress the "prophesyings" of Puritan clergy and meetings for theological discussion and sermon preparation. After addressing a remonstrance to the queen, he refused to resign, and he was stripped of the administrative power of his position until his death.

Hugo Grotius (1583–1645). Dutch lawyer, statesman, and humanist. Grotius began practicing law at The Hague in 1599, was appointed Advocate-General of the Fisc for the provinces of Holland, Zeeland, and West Friesland in 1607 and in 1613 became pensionary of Rotterdam. As debates between Calvinists and Arminians came to national significance, Grotius sided with the Remonstrants, especially in his rejection of Reformed arguments for the independence of the church, defending the right of the state to appoint ministers and adjudicate over matters of doctrine. Following the victory of Maurice of Orange (1567–1635) over Grotius's patron Johan van Oldenbarnevelt (1547–1619) and the condemnation of Arminianism at the Synod of Dordrecht* (1618–1619), Grotius was imprisoned, though only briefly, as he escaped in a book chest and fled to Paris. Unable to secure return from exile, Grotius became a Swedish ambassador to France while seeking religious toleration and the establishment of a Christian republic. A number of his works from this period, in particular *De Jure Belli ac Pacis* (On the law of war and peace, 1625) made a significant contribution to the establishment of international law.

Argula von Grumbach (c. 1490–c. 1564) German Lutheran noblewoman. Grumbach, an attendant of Queen Kunigunde of Austria (1465–1520), was one of the first women to publish in support of the Reformation. She is best known for letters from 1523 and 1524 written in defense of Arsacius Seehofer (1503–1545), a lecturer at the university of Ingolstadt accused of Lutheranism. For unknown reasons, Grumberg ceased to publish after 1524, although her private correspondence after this time demonstrates a continued effort to support evangelical reform.

Johann Jacob Grynaeus (1540–1617). Swiss Reformed theologian. Raised Lutheran, Grynaeus replaced his father as pastor at Rotelen. After becoming professor of Old Testament at Basel, however, Grynaeus caused conflict by embracing Reformed theology. He avoided controversy by spending two years at the University of Heidelberg. Upon his return to Basel, his opponents had largely died, and he was made superintendent of the church in the city and professor of New Testament. Grynaeus aligned the Basel church with his Reformed convictions and reorganized the city's educational system while preaching regularly and composing numerous theological, exegetical, and practical works.

William Guild (1586–1657). Scottish Reformed minister and theologian. Guild was born in Aberdeen and educated at Marischal College. He was licensed to preach in 1605 and ordained to serve as minister of the parish of King Edward in 1608. In 1617, Guild joined the protest for the liberties of the Scottish national church. While in Edinburgh, Guild met the acquaintance of Bishop Lancelot Andrewes,* who was accompanying King James VI/I* on his royal visit to the city. Moreover, Guild dedicated his best-known work, *Moses Unveiled* (1620), to both Andrewes and the king. He was later appointed chaplain to Charles I, and shortly thereafter received the degree of doctor of divinity. In 1631, Guild was given his second charge in Aberdeen. When he assumed this charge, Guild expressed his support for episcopacy. He signed the National Covenant in 1638 with some conditions. However, when in 1640 an army came to Aberdeen to enforce full subscription to the Covenant, Guild fled to the Netherlands. After returning to Scotland later that year, he was appointed Guild Principal for King's College Aberdeen, but was deprived of this post by Oliver Cromwell's (1599–1658) military commissioners in 1651. Following his deprivation, Guild lived in retirement until his death in Aberdeen.

Rudolf Gwalther (1519–1586). Swiss Reformed preacher. Gwalther was a consummate servant of the Reformed church in Zurich, its chief religious officer and preacher, a responsibility fulfilled previously by Huldrych Zwingli* and Heinrich Bullinger.* Gwalther provided sermons and commentaries and translated the works of Zwingli into Latin. He worked for many years alongside Bullinger in structuring and governing the church in Zurich. Gwalther also strove to strengthen the connections to the Reformed churches on the Continent and England: he was a participant in the Colloquy of Regensburg (1541) and an opponent of the Formula of Concord.*

Matthias Hafenreffer (1561–1619). German Lutheran theologian. After holding pastoral positions in Herenberg, Ehingen, and Stuttgart, Hafenreffer was appointed professor of theology at Tübingen, a position he held for more than twenty-five years. He composed exegetical works on Nahum, Habakkuk, and Ezekiel, a number of polemical works, and a theological *loci communes* that served as a common textbook within the Lutheran churches for much of the seventeenth century.

Henry Hall (unknown). English Protestant preacher. A fellow of Trinity College, Cambridge, Hall preached and published a sermon given before the House of Commons in 1644 on Matthew 11:12.

Joseph Hall (1574–1656). English Anglican bishop and controversialist. After studying at Cambridge, Hall courted controversy with a series of satires before entering the ministry of the Church of England. As a pastor, Hall served parishes in Suffolk and Essex and was chosen by James I* as an English delegate at the Synod of Dordrecht.* Upon his return, Hall was appointed bishop of Exeter and later transferred to the see of Norwich, where, despite his low-church preferences, his defense of the episcopacy saw him convicted of praemunire by the Puritan parliament and imprisoned in the Tower of London for a short time with a number of other bishops. Hall's literary output was extensive and included controversial tracts against the Brownists and Arminians, treatises on virtue and union with Christ, and numerous devotional works.

Hans Has von Hallstatt (d. 1527). Austrian Reformed pastor. See *Kunstbuch*.

Henry Hammond (1605–1660). Anglican priest. After completing his studies at Oxford, Hammond was ordained in 1629. A Royalist, Hammond helped recruit soldiers for the king; he was chaplain to Charles I. During the king's captivity, Hammond was imprisoned for not submitting to Parliament. Later he was allowed to pastor again, until his death. Hammond published a catechism, numerous polemical sermons and treatises as well as his *Paraphrase and Annotations on the New Testament* (1653).

Jörg Haug (Unknown) German Anabaptist leader. Haug was a radical preacher during the 1525 Peasant's Revolt and composed a tract entitled *A Christian Order of a True Christian* (1524) enumerating seven degrees of faith reached by Christians.

Peter Hausted (d. 1645). Anglican priest and playwright. Educated at Cambridge and Oxford, Hausted ministered in a number of parishes and preached adamantly and vehemently against Puritanism. He is best known for his play *The Rival Friends*, which is filled with invective against the Puritans; during a performance before the king and queen, a riot nearly broke out. Haustead died during the siege of Banbury Castle.

Erhart Hegenwald (Unknown). Swiss Protestant teacher and doctor. A teacher at the Pfäffen Monastery in St. Gallen and at the Schola Carolina in Zurich, Hegenwald recorded the minutes of Zwingli's* First Zurich Disputation in 1523. Correspondence demonstrates he remained in contact with the Zurich reformers while he studied medicine at Wittenberg, and after graduating in 1526, he may have practiced as a physician in Frankfurt.

Heidelberg Catechism (1563). This German Reformed catechism was commissioned by the elector of the Palatinate, Frederick III (1515–1576) for pastors and teachers in his territories to use in instructing children and new believers in the faith. It was written by theologian Zacharias Ursinus (1534–1583) in consultation with Frederick's court preacher Kaspar Olevianus* and the entire theology faculty at the University of Heidelberg. The Heidelberg Catechism was accepted as one of the Dutch Reformed Church's Three Forms of Unity— along with the Belgic Confession* and the Canons of Dordrecht—at the Synod of Dordrecht,* and became widely popular among other Reformed confessional traditions throughout Europe.

Ursula Hellrigel (b. c. 1521). Austrian Anabaptist. Imprisoned for her heterodox beliefs at 17, authorities sought Hellrigel's recantation, but she refused to acquiesce. After five years she was released from prison and exiled from the Tyrol. The thirty-sixth hymn in the first known Anabaptist hymnal, the *Ausbund* (1654), is commonly attributed to her.

Niels Hemmingsen (1513–1600). Danish Lutheran theologian. Hemmingsen studied at the University of Wittenberg, where he befriended Philipp Melanchthon.* In 1542, Hemmingsen returned to Denmark to pastor and to teach Greek, dialectics and theology at the University of Copenhagen. Foremost of the Danish theologians, Hemmingsen oversaw the preparation and publication of the first Danish Bible (1550). Later in his career he became embroiled in controversies because of his Philippist theology, especially regarding the Eucharist. Due to rising tensions with Lutheran nobles outside of Denmark, King Frederick II (1534–1588) dismissed Hemmingsen from his university post in 1579, transferring him to a prominent but less internationally visible Cathedral outside of Copenhagen. Hemmingsen was a prolific author, writing commentaries on the New Testament and Psalms, sermon collections and several methodological, theological and pastoral handbooks.

Henry IV of France (1553–1610). French monarch. Son of Jeanne of Navarre* and Antoine de Bourbon (1518–1562), Henry's religious loyalties wavered throughout his life. Raised Protestant at the behest of his mother, he practiced Catholicism while attending the Valois court. After his mother's death in 1572, Henry succeeded her as King of Navarre and soon afterwards married Margaret of Valois (1553–1615), the daughter of Henry II of France (1519–1559) and Catherine de' Medici (1519–1589). Their wedding provided the occasion for the St. Bartholomew's Day Massacre, when Catholic forces seized the opportunity to decimate the Huguenot leadership gathered to celebrate the nuptials in Paris, leading to an outbreak of mob violence that devastated the Huguenot movement. A great proportion of the Protestants in France were killed in the weeks that followed the wedding, while many others, including Henry, reconverted to Catholicism. In 1576, Henry escaped the influence of the Valois court, returned his allegiance to Protestantism and took a leadership role amongst the Huguenots. Following the assassination of Henry III of France (1551–1589), Henry was the presumptive heir, but French Catholics were unwilling to accept his rule and Henry was unable to assert his prerogative outside Huguenot strongholds. In 1593, therefore, Henry converted again to Catholicism, with legend claiming he justified his decision with the phrase "Paris is worth a mass." Over the following years, Henry established his authority throughout his kingdom, and while remaining Catholic, provided some relief to Protestants, particularly through the Edict of Nantes (1598), essentially ending the Religious Wars. Henry's pragmatic reign ended with his assassination by a Radical Catholic in 1610.

King Henry VIII of England (1491–1547). English monarch. The second son of Henry VII (r. 1485–1509) and Elizabeth of York (1466–1503), Henry VIII succeeded his father to the English throne, his elder brother Edward having died in 1502. Soon after accession, he married his brother's widow, Catherine of Aragon (1485–1536). Following several stillbirths and the birth of a daughter, Mary, Henry, who was desperate for a male heir to head off dynastic challenges, wished separation from Catherine in order to marry Anne Boleyn (c. 1501–1536). Believing his marriage cursed as it transgressed the commands in Leviticus against marrying a brother's widow, Henry sought dispensation from the church for his annulment and remarriage. While the case was first heard by a papal legate in England, it was transferred to Rome upon the order of Pope Clement VII,* who wished to placate Charles V, Catherine's nephew, whose troops had recently sacked Rome and held the pope under house arrest. Henry asserted praemunire, arguing that as king, he was supreme in his own kingdom. With the formation of the Reformation Parliament in 1529, the legislative process to disentangle the English Church from the Roman was begun. The issue of Henry's divorce was finalized in 1533, after Thomas Cranmer* became Archbishop of Canterbury and declared his marriage to Catherine invalid. While Henry's divorce, assertion of royal supremacy, and subversion of Catholic institutions gave impetus to English Protestantism, Henry's beliefs remained essentially Catholic, and these continued to be enforced by law. He ultimately married six times, and was succeeded by Edward VI,* his son by his third wife, Jane Seymour (1508–1537). Elizabeth I,* Henry's daughter by Anne Boleyn, later became Queen and with the Elizabethan Settlement in 1559, redefined England as a Protestant country.

George Herbert (1593–1633). Anglican minister, theologian, and poet. Herbert was born in Montgomery Powys, Wales, on April 3, 1593, to a noble family. After completing his early education at Westminster School, Herbert matriculated at Trinity College, Cambridge, in 1609. He graduated with both his bachelor's and master's degrees. Shortly thereafter Herbert was elected a fellow of the college, and then became Reader of Rhetoric. From 1620 to 1627, Herbert was Public Orator for the University of Cambridge. In 1624, Herbert was elected to Parliament. However, after the death of King James I,* and of his other major patrons, Herbert withdrew from politics to pursue a career in the church. Toward this end, Herbert was ordained to the priesthood of the Church of England in 1630, and appointed rector of Fugglestone St. Peter and later Bemerton St. Andrews in Wiltshire near Salisbury. While at St. Andrews, Herbert composed his collection of poems titled *The Temple* and his guide for rural ministers, *A Priest to the Temple, or The Country Parson: His Character and Rule of Holy Life*. Twice a week Herbert traveled to Salisbury, where he attended services at Salisbury Cathedral. Following the services, Herbert would compose music with the cathedral musicians. Herbert died of consumption in 1633.

Tilemann Hesshus (1527–1588). German Lutheran theologian and pastor. Hesshus studied under Philipp Melanchthon* but was a staunch Gnesio-Lutheran. With great hesitation—and later regret—he affirmed the Formula of Concord.*

Heshuss ardently advocated for church discipline, considering obedience a mark of the church. Unwilling to compromise his strong convictions, especially regarding matters of discipline, Hesshus was regularly embroiled in controversy. He was expelled or pressed to leave Goslar, Rostock, Heidelberg, Bremen, Magdeburg, Wesel, Königsberg and Samland before settling in Helmstedt, where he remained until his death. He wrote numerous polemical tracts concerning ecclesiology, justification, the sacraments and original sin, as well as commentaries on Psalms, Romans, 1–2 Corinthians, Galatians, Colossians and 1–2 Timothy, and a postil collection.

Edo Hilderich (1533–1599). German Lutheran historian and theologian. Hilderich (also named Hildericus) was born to a noble family in Frisia. After attending a local school, Hilderich went on to the University of Wittenberg, where he received the degree of master of philosophy in 1556. Among his teachers was Philip Melanchthon.* In 1559, Hilderich was appointed to the Faculty of Arts at Wittenberg. He also served as professor of mathematics at the University of Jena from 1564 until 1567, when he resigned the post in order to return to the arts faculty at Wittenberg, of which he became dean in 1570. Three years later he became rector of the academy in Magdeburg, and went from there to the University of Frankfurt in 1575. In 1577, Hilderich became professor of history and Hebrew at Frankfurt. Following the expulsion of the Reformed theologians from the University of Heidelberg in 1578, he went there to be the second professor of theology and Hebrew language. He received his doctorate at Heidelberg a year later. However, Hilderich's refusal to sign the Formula of Concord resulted in removal from his post. On June 3, 1581, he accepted the professorship of theology at the University of Altdorf, where he later became rector in 1582, and professor of Hebrew in 1584. Hilderich's most important exegetical work is his *Oratio de politia et hierarchia populi Iudaici*, published in 1570, in which he traces the history of ancient Israel's government.

Samuel Hieron (1576?–1617). English Puritan minister. After graduating from Cambridge, Hieron became a minister in the Church of England and gained a reputation as a popular preacher in London before becoming the vicar at Modbury in Devonshire. Many of his sermons were published during his lifetime, and he also composed treatises on prayer and the value of Scripture.

Cornelis Hoen (c. 1460–1524). Dutch humanist, jurist, and theologian. A lawyer at the Court of Holland at the Hague, Hoen was prosecuted in 1523 over his sympathy for the evangelical message. He proposed a symbolic interpretation of Christ's presence in the Eucharist justified with reference to Matthew 24:23 in an influential, posthumously-published treatise.

Melchior Hoffman (1495?–1543). German Anabaptist preacher. First appearing as a Lutheran lay preacher in Livonia in 1523, Hoffman's claim to direct revelation, his perfectionist teachings and his announcements that the end of the world would occur in 1533 saw him alienated from both Lutheran and Reformed circles. After converting to Anabaptism in Strasbourg in 1530, a city he claimed would rise as the spiritual Jerusalem, Hoffman escaped brief arrest and fled to the Netherlands, where his preaching made him the first to bring the radical faith to the Low Countries. Believing himself to be Elijah, Hoffman gathered numerous followers, including future Anabaptist leaders Obbe Philips* and Jan Mathijs (d. 1534), until his arrest in Strasbourg in 1533, whereupon he was imprisoned for the final decade of his life. A tendency toward mystical allegory and apocalyptic exegesis supported by direct revelation is found in his writings, which include commentaries on Romans, Revelation, and Daniel 12 alongside numerous tracts, pamphlets, and letters.

Nathaniel Holmes (1599–1678). English Puritan theologian. Educated at Oxford, Holmes was a preacher in the Anglican Church until his millenarian views led him to establish an independent congregation. His publications include defenses of infant baptism and exclusive psalmody;

treatises against witchcraft, usury, and astrology; and a commentary on the Song of Solomon.

Christopher Hooke (unknown). English Puritan physician and pastor. Hooke published a treatise promoting the joys and blessings of childbirth (1590) and a sermon on Hebrews 12:11-12. To support the poor, Hooke proposed a bank funded by voluntary investment of wealthy households.

Richard Hooker (c. 1553–1600). Anglican priest. Shortly after graduating from Corpus Christi College Oxford, Hooker took holy orders as a priest in 1581. After his marriage, he struggled to find work and temporarily tended sheep until Archbishop John Whitgift* appointed him to the Temple Church in London. Hooker's primary work is *The Laws of Ecclesiastical Polity* (1593), in which he sought to establish a philosophical and logical foundation for the highly controversial Elizabethan Religious Settlement (1559). The Elizabethan Settlement, through the Act of Supremacy, reasserted the Church of England's independence from the Church of Rome, and, through the Act of Uniformity, constructed a common church structure based on the reinstitution of the Book of Common Prayer.* Hooker's argumentation strongly emphasizes natural law and anticipates the social contract theory of John Locke (1632–1704).

Thomas Hooker (1586–1647) English-American Puritan Preacher. Hooker ministered at churches in Surrey and Essex and established a school to teach pastors until threatened with arrest as Archbishop Laud* worked to suppress Puritanism. Fleeing to Holland and then New England, he pastored a church in New Town (later Cambridge), Massachusetts before playing an important role in the foundation of Hartford, Connecticut and assisting with the composition of the state constitution.

John Hooper (d. 1555). English Protestant bishop and martyr. Impressed by the works of Huldrych Zwingli* and Heinrich Bullinger,* Hooper joined the Protestant movement in England. However, after the Act of Six Articles was passed, he fled to Zurich, where he spent ten years. He returned to England in 1549 and was appointed as a bishop. He stoutly advocated a Zwinglian reform agenda, arguing against the use of vestments and for a less "popish" Book of Common Prayer.* Condemned as a heretic for denying transubstantiation, Hooper was burned at the stake during Mary I's reign.

John Hoskin (unknown). English Protestant preacher. Hoskin published a sermon on Matthew 18:23 in 1610 in which he is identified as a minister of God's Word and student of divinity.

Rudolf Hospinian (Wirth) (1547–1626). Swiss Reformed theologian and minister. After studying theology at Marburg and Heidelberg, Hospinian pastored in rural parishes around Zurich and taught secondary school. In 1588, he transferred to Zurich, ministering at Grossmünster and Fraumünster. A keen student of church history, Hospinian wanted to show the differences between early church doctrine and contemporary Catholic teaching, particularly with regard to sacramental theology. He also criticized Lutheran dogma and the Formula of Concord*. Most of Hospinian's corpus consists of polemical treatises; he also published a series of sermons on the Magnificat.

Hans Hotz (dates unknown). Swiss Anabaptist leader. Born in Grüningen, near Zurich, Hotz was an associate of Georg Blaurock.* He defended Anabaptism as spokesman for the Swiss Brethren at disputations in Zofingen (1532) and Bern (1538).

John Howson (1557?–1632). English Anglican bishop. Howson held a number of pastoral positions in Oxfordshire before becoming vice chancellor of Oxford University. An opponent of Puritanism, he was appointed bishop of Oxford in 1619, and then to the bishopric of Durham in 1628, where he was an advocate for the reform program of Archbishop Laud.*

Caspar Huberinus (1500–1553). German Lutheran theologian and pastor. After studying theology at Wittenberg, Huberinus moved to Augsburg to serve as Urbanus Rhegius's* assistant. Huberinus represented Augsburg at the Bern Disputation (1528) on the Eucharist and images.

In 1551, along with the nobility, Huberinus supported the Augsburg Interim, so long as communion of both kinds and regular preaching were allowed. Nevertheless the people viewed him as a traitor because of his official participation in the Interim, nicknaming him "Buberinus" (i.e., scoundrel). He wrote a number of popular devotional works as well as tracts defending Lutheran eucharistic theology against Zwinglian and Anabaptist detractions.

Balthasar Hubmaier (1480/5–1528). German Radical theologian. Hubmaier, a former priest who studied under Johann Eck,* is identified with his leadership in the peasants' uprising at Waldshut. Hubmaier served as the cathedral preacher in Regensberg, where he became involved in a series of anti-Semitic attacks. He was drawn to reform through the early works of Martin Luther*; his contact with Huldrych Zwingli* made Hubmaier a defender of more radical reform, including believers' baptism and a memorialist account of the Eucharist. His involvement in the Peasants' War led to his extradition and execution by the Austrians.

Aegidius Hunnius (1550–1603). German Lutheran theologian and preacher. Educated at Tübingen by Jakob Andreae (1528–1590) and Johannes Brenz,* Hunnius bolstered and advanced early Lutheran orthodoxy. After his crusade to root out all "crypto-Calvinism" divided Hesse into Lutheran and Reformed regions, Hunnius joined the Wittenberg theological faculty, where with Polykarp Leyser (1552–1610) he helped shape the university into an orthodox stronghold. Passionately confessional, Hunnius developed and nuanced the orthodox doctrines of predestination, Scripture, the church and Christology (more explicitly Chalcedonian), reflecting their codification in the Formula of Concord.* He was unafraid to engage in confessional polemics from the pulpit. In addition to his many treatises (most notably *De persona Christi*, in which he defended Christ's ubiquity), Hunnius published commentaries on Matthew, John, Ephesians and Colossians; his notes on Galatians, Philemon and 1 Corinthians were published posthumously.

Jan Hus (d. 1415). Bohemian reformer and martyr. This popular preacher strove for reform in the church, moral improvement in society, and an end to clerical abuses and popular religious superstition. He was branded a heretic for his alleged affinity for John Wycliffe's writings; however, while he agreed that a priest in mortal sin rendered the sacraments inefficacious, he affirmed the doctrine of transubstantiation. The Council of Constance* convicted Hus of heresy, banned his books and teaching, and, despite a letter of safe conduct, burned him at the stake.

Hans Hut (1490–1527). German Radical leader. Hut was an early leader of a mystical, apocalyptic strand of Anabaptist radical reform. His theological views were shaped by Andreas Bodenstein von Karlstadt,* Thomas Müntzer* and Hans Denck,* by whom Hut had been baptized. Hut rejected society and the established church and heralded the imminent end of days, which he perceived in the Peasants' War. Eventually arrested for practicing believers' baptism and participating in the Peasants' War, Hut was tortured and died accidentally in a fire in the Augsburg prison. The next day, the authorities sentenced his corpse to death and burned him.

George Hutcheson (1615–1674). Scottish Puritan pastor. Hutcheson, a pastor in Edinburgh, published commentaries on Job, John and the Minor Prophets, as well as sermons on Psalm 130.

Roger Hutchinson (d. 1555). English reformer. Little is known about Hutchinson except for his controversies. He disputed against the Mass while at Cambridge and debated with Joan Bocher (d. 1550), who affirmed the doctrine of the celestial flesh. During the Marian Restoration he was deprived of his fellowship at Eton because he was married.

Andreas Hyperius (1511–1564). Dutch Protestant theologian. After a peripatetic humanist education that encompassed studies in theology, canon law, and medicine, Hyperius became professor of theology at Marburg in 1541 and held this position until his death. Often viewed as mediating between Lutheran and Reformed thought, Hyperius was particularly concerned with the practical application of theology, demonstrated in his composition of the first Protestant text on homiletic method.

Abraham Ibn Ezra (1089–c. 1167). Spanish Jewish rabbi, exegete and poet. In 1140 Ibn Ezra fled his native Spain to escape persecution by the Almohad Caliphate. He spent the rest of his life as an exile, traveling through Europe, North Africa and the Middle East. His corpus consists of works on poetry, exegesis, grammar, philosophy, mathematics and astrology. In his commentaries on the Old Testament, Ibn Ezra restricts himself to *peshat* (see *quadriga*).

Valentin Ickelshamer (c. 1500–1547). German Radical teacher. After time at Erfurt, he studied under Luther,* Melanchthon,* Bugenhagen* and Karlstadt* in Wittenberg. He sided with Karlstadt against Luther, writing a treatise in Karlstadt's defense. Ickelshamer also represented the Wittenberg guilds in opposition to the city council. This guild committee allied with the peasants in 1525, leading to Ickelshamer's eventual exile. His poem in the Marpeck Circle's *Kunstbuch* is an expansion of a similar poem by Sebastian Franck.*

Arthur Jackson (1593?–1666). English Presbyterian minister. Known for his pastoral concern, Jackson served at a number of parishes in London. Imprisoned briefly for his support of the Royalist cause, after the Restoration, he was ejected from ministry following the 1662 Act of Uniformity. Jackson's primary works are a series of annotations of many books of the Old Testament.

Thomas Jackson (1579–1640). Anglican theologian and priest. Before serving as the president of Corpus Christi College at Oxford for the final decade of his life, Jackson was a parish priest and chaplain to the king. His best known work is a twelve-volume commentary on the Apostles' Creed.

King James I of England (VI of Scotland) (1566–1625). English monarch. The son of Mary, Queen of Scots, James ascended to the Scottish throne in 1567 following his mother's abdication. In the Union of the Crowns (1603), he took the English and Irish thrones after the death of his cousin, Elizabeth I.* James's reign was tumultuous and tense: Parliament and the nobility often opposed him, church factions squabbled over worship forms and ecclesiology, climaxing in the Gunpowder Plot. James wrote treatises on the divine right of kings, law, the evils of smoking tobacco and demonology. His religious writings include a versification of the Psalms, a paraphrase of Revelation and meditations on the Lord's Prayer and passages from Chronicles, Matthew and Revelation. He also sponsored the translation of the Authorized Version*—popularly remembered as the King James Version.

Cornelius Jansen (1585–1638). Dutch Catholic bishop and theologian. Jansen studied and taught in France and Holland, joining the theological faculty of the University of Leuven after receiving his doctorate. He later became bishop of Ypres. An ardent Augustinian, his posthumously published work *Augustinus* (1640) caused great controversy by advocating for the utterly gratuitous character of God's grace in opposition to the teachings of Jesuit Luis de Molina (1536–1609), which put greater emphasis on human choice. Due to its perceived Protestant leanings, *Augustinus* was judged heretical, and Jansen's followers, known as Jansenists, took up his cause in a series of conflicts that carried on into the eighteenth century.

Jeanne of Navarre (1528–1572) French Reformed noblewoman. Daughter of Henry II, King of Navarre (1503–1555) and Marguerite d'Angoulême*, Jeanne was forced into a strategic marriage at age 12 by her uncle, Francis I* to William, Duke of Cleves (1516–1592). Shifting political alignments allowed her an annulment after four years and in 1548 she wed the first Prince of the Blood, Antoine de Bourbon (1518–1562). Jeanne took the throne of her father, and after making a public announcement of her conversion to the evangelical faith, established a Reformed community at Béarn. A regular correspondent of reformers such as Calvin* and Beza* and an advocate for the reformation of her lands, Jeanne nevertheless remained largely neutral and advocated tolerance during the first years of religious war. At the outbreak of the Third War of Religion (1569–1570), however, she recognized her moderate position was untenable, and from the Protestant stronghold of La Rochelle served as political head for the Huguenot cause alongside Gaspard de Coligny (1519–1572), commander of the Huguenot armed forces.

John Jewel (1522–1571). Anglican theologian and bishop. Jewel studied at Oxford where he met Peter Martyr Vermigli.* After graduating in 1552, Jewel was appointed to his first vicarage and became the orator for the university. Upon Mary I's accession, Jewel lost his post as orator because of his Protestant views. After the trials of Thomas Cranmer* and Nicholas Ridley,* Jewel affirmed Catholic teaching to avoid their fate. Still he had to flee to the continent. Confronted by John Knox,* Jewel publicly repented of his cowardice before the English congregation in Frankfurt, then reunited with Vermigli in Strasbourg. After Mary I's death, Jewel returned to England and was consecrated bishop in 1560. He advocated low-church ecclesiology, but supported the Elizabethan Settlement against Catholics and Puritans. In response to the Council of Trent, he published the *Apoligia ecclesiae Anglicanae* (1562), which established him as the apostle for Anglicanism and incited numerous controversies.

St. John of the Cross (Juan de Yepes y Álvarez) (1542–1591). Spanish Catholic mystic. Born into poverty, Álvarez entered the Carmelite order in Medina del Campo, where, after studying theology at Salamanca, he met the famed mystic Teresa of Ávila (1515–1582). Drawn to her vision of the contemplative life, with two others, he established the first house of Discalced (barefoot) Carmelite Friars and became a leader in the Catholic reform movement. An exceptional administrator and spiritual leader, for more than twenty years, John of the Cross sought to return his order to its original vision of asceticism and prayer while establishing many new reformed Carmelite houses. He encountered significant resistance in his work for renewal, however, and spent nine months imprisoned and tortured by his

Carmelite superiors. Considered among the foremost poets in Spanish literary history, his poems, including *The Spiritual Canticle*, *Ascent of Mount Carmel*, and *The Dark Night of the Soul* demonstrate his overriding desire for spiritual growth and closeness to God.

Francis Johnson (1562–1618). English Brownist pastor. A popular Puritan preacher at Cambridge, Johnson was arrested for slander and factitiousness after a sermon criticizing the ecclesiastical hierarchy and the comfortable lives of the ministers at the school. Retracting some of his statements, he was released and expelled from Cambridge. While pastoring an English church in the Netherlands, he came across writings from followers of Robert Browne* and became convinced of the need to separate from the established church and commit to congregational church polity, but his attempts to institute these changes in the church led to his firing. Returning to England, Johnson became pastor of the Brownist church in London, for which he was arrested numerous times until he convinced the Privy Council to allow him to found a Brownist church in Newfoundland. The expedition was canceled, however, and he returned to the Netherlands, where he pastored separatist churches, some alongside Henry Ainsworth* and John Smyth,* until his death.

Justus Jonas (1493–1555). German Lutheran theologian, pastor and administrator. Jonas studied law at Erfurt, where he befriended the poet Eobanus Hessus (1488–1540), whom Luther* dubbed "king of the poets"; later, under the influence of the humanist Konrad Muth, Jonas focused on theology. In 1516 he was ordained as a priest, and in 1518 he became a doctor of theology and law. After witnessing the Leipzig Disputation, Jonas was converted to Luther's* cause. While traveling with Luther to the Diet of Worms, Jonas was appointed professor of canon law at Wittenberg. Later he became its dean of theology, lecturing on Romans, Acts and the Psalms. Jonas was also instrumental for reform in Halle. He preached Luther's funeral sermon but had a falling-out with Melanchthon* over the Leipzig Interim. Jonas's most influential contribution was translating Luther's *The Bondage of the Will* and Melanchthon's *Loci communes* into German.

Robert Jones. A pseudonym; see Thomas Lushington.

William Jones (1561–1636). Anglican minister and theologian. After teaching at Cambridge, Jones ministered at East Bergholt in Suffolk for forty-four years, publishing a commentary on Philemon and Hebrews and tracts on suffering, the nativity, and arrangements to be made before one's death.

David Joris (c. 1501–1556). Dutch Radical pastor and hymnist. This former glass painter was one of the leading Dutch Anabaptist leaders after the fall of Münster (1535), although due to his increasingly radical ideas his influence waned in the early 1540s. Joris came to see himself as a "third David," a Spirit-anointed prophet ordained to proclaim the coming third kingdom of God, which would be established in the Netherlands with Dutch as its *lingua franca*. Joris's interpretation of Scripture, with his heavy emphasis on personal mystical experience, led to a very public dispute with Menno Simons* whom Joris considered a teacher of the "dead letter." In 1544 Joris and about one hundred followers moved to Basel, conforming outwardly to the teaching of the Reformed church there. Today 240 of Joris's books are extant, the most important of which is his *Twonder Boek* (1542/43).

Jörg Haugk von Jüchsen (unknown). German Radical preacher. Nothing is known of Haugk's life except that during the 1524–1525 Peasants' War in Thuringia, he was elected as a preacher by the insurrectionists in his district. He composed one extant tract, titled *A Christian Order of a True Christian: Giving an Account of the Origin of His Faith*, published in 1526 but likely written before the Peasants' War. While lacking reference to most distinctive Anabaptist doctrines, this pamphlet became popular among radicals as it set out the stages of Christian growth toward perfection.

Andreas Bodenstein von Karlstadt (Carlstadt) (1486–1541). German Radical theologian. Karlstadt, an early associate of Martin Luther* and Philipp Melanchthon* at the University of Wittenberg, participated alongside Luther in the dispute at Leipzig with Johann Eck.* He also influenced the configuration of the Old Testament canon in Protestantism. During Luther's captivity in Wartburg Castle in Eisenach, Karlstadt oversaw reform in Wittenberg. His acceleration of the pace of reform brought conflict with Luther, so Karlstadt left Wittenberg, eventually settling at the University of Basel as professor of Old Testament (after a sojourn in Zurich with Huldrych Zwingli*). During his time in Switzerland, Karlstadt opposed infant baptism and repudiated Luther's doctrine of Christ's real presence in the Eucharist.

Edward Kellett (d. 1641). Anglican theologian and priest. Kellett published a sermon concerning the reconversion of an Englishman from Islam, a tract on the soul, and a discourse on the Lord's Supper in connection with Passover.

David Kimchi (**Radak**) (1160–1235). French Jewish rabbi, exegete and philosopher. Kimchi wrote an important Hebrew grammar and dictionary, as well as commentaries on Genesis, 1–2 Chronicles, the Psalms and the Prophets. He focused on *peshat* (see *quadriga*). In his Psalms commentary he attacks Christian interpretation as forced, irrational and inadmissible. While Sebastian Münster* censors and condemns these arguments in his *Miqdaš YHWH* (1534–1535), he and many other Christian commentators valued Kimchi's work as a grammatical resource.

Moses Kimchi (**Remak**) (1127–1190). French Jewish rabbi and exegete. He was David Kimchi's* brother. He wrote commentaries on Proverbs and Ezra-Nehemiah. Sebastian Münster* translated Kimchi's concise Hebrew grammar into Latin; many sixteenth-century Christian exegetes used this resource.

Andreas Knöpken (c. 1468–1539). German Lutheran pastor. Knöpken worked in Pomerania as assistant to Johannes Bugenhagen* before relocating to Riga. Here he served as pastor of

St. Peter's, and after a brief setback that saw him return to his previous position, he returned and won a disputation before the authorities, which allowed him to undertake the evangelical reform of the city. Knöpken oversaw the reorganization of the churches and schools, composed the church order, wrote a commentary on Romans, and arranged a number of hymns based on the Psalms.

John Knox (1513–1572). Scottish Reformed preacher. Knox, a fiery preacher to monarchs and zealous defender of high Calvinism, was a leading figure of reform in Scotland. Following imprisonment in the French galleys, Knox went to England, where he became a royal chaplain to Edward VI. At the accession of Mary, Knox fled to Geneva, studying under John Calvin* and serving as a pastor. Knox returned to Scotland after Mary's death and became a chief architect of the reform of the Scottish church (Presbyterian), serving as one of the authors of the Book of Discipline and writing many pamphlets and sermons.

Antonius Broickwy von Königstein (1470–1541). German Catholic preacher. Very little is known about this important cathedral preacher in Cologne. Strongly opposed to evangelicals, he sought to develop robust resources for Catholic homilies. His postils were bestsellers, and his biblical concordance helped Catholic preachers to construct doctrinal loci from Scripture itself.

Kunstbuch. In 1956, two German students rediscovered this unique collection of Anabaptist works. Four hundred years earlier, a friend of the recently deceased Pilgram Marpeck*—the painter Jörg Probst—had entrusted this collection of letters, tracts and poetry to a Zurich bindery; today only half of it remains. Probst's redaction arranges various compositions from the Marpeck Circle into a devotional anthology focused on the theme of the church as Christ incarnate (cf. Gal 2:20).

Osmund Lake (c. 1543–1621). English Pastor who ministered at Ringwood in Hampshire.

Thomas Lamb (d. 1686). English Nonconformist minister. Lamb earned a living as a soap boiler while serving as a teaching elder and occasional preacher at a congregational church in London. Convicted of the necessity of adult baptism and the invalidity of infant baptism, he formed a Particular Baptist congregation and led this church for four years before rejoining the Church of England as a layman, retracting his former teachings and becoming a vocal opponent of separatism. Toward the end of his life, he turned to philanthropy, seeking to improve the lives of the poor and prisoners and to further the religious education of children.

François Lambert (Lambert of Avignon) (1487–1530). French Reformed theologian. In 1522, after becoming drawn to the writings of Martin Luther* and meeting Huldrych Zwingli,* Lambert left the Franciscan order. He spent time in Wittenberg, Strasbourg, and Hesse, where Lambert took a leading role at the Homberg Synod (1526) and in creating a biblically based plan for church reform. He served as professor of theology at Marburg University from 1527 to his death. After the Marburg Colloquy (1529), Lambert accepted Zwingli's symbolic view of the Eucharist. Lambert produced nineteen books, mostly biblical commentaries that favored spiritual interpretations; his unfinished work of comprehensive theology was published posthumously.

Eitelhans Langenmantel (d. 1528). German Radical writer. The son of the mayor of Augsburg, Langenmantel was converted to Anabaptism and was rebaptized by Hans Hut* in 1527. Arrested for his heterodox views later that year, he was freed after accepting the validity of infant baptism during a debate, but after renouncing his recantation in 1528, he was rearrested and beheaded. Seven tracts he composed during 1526 and 1527 survive, focusing on the Lord's Supper and the moral life.

Emilia Lanier (1569–1645). English poet. The daughter of a musician at the court of Elizabeth I,* she received a humanist education at the home of Susan Bertie, Countess of Kent (b. 1554). Following a long affair with Henry Carey (1526–1596), Lord Chamberlain to the queen, and after conceiving a child, she married a distant cousin,

Alfonso Lanier (unknown). She is best known for a book of poetry written in the hope of securing a patron, *Salve Deus Rex Judaeorum* (1611), which contains a number of protofeminist themes. Modern scholars have also suggested she may be the "Dark Lady" who appears in a number of William Shakespeare's (1564–1616) sonnets.

Hugh Latimer (c. 1485–1555). Anglican bishop and preacher. Latimer was celebrated for his sermons critiquing the idolatrous nature of Catholic practices and the social injustices visited on the underclass by the aristocracy and the individualism of Protestant government. After his support for Henry's petition of divorce he served as a court preacher under Henry VIII* and Edward VI. Latimer became a proponent of reform following his education at Cambridge University and received license as a preacher. Following Edward's death, Latimer was tried for heresy, perishing at the stake with Nicholas Ridley* and Thomas Cranmer.*

William Laud (1573–1645). Anglican archbishop, one of the most pivotal and controversial figures in Anglican church history. Early in his career, Laud offended many with his highly traditional, anti-Puritan approach to ecclesial policies. After his election as Archbishop of Canterbury in 1633, Laud continued to strive against the Puritans, demanding the eastward placement of the Communion altar (affirming the religious centrality of the Eucharist), the use of clerical garments, the reintroduction of stained-glass windows, and the uniform use of the Book of Common Prayer.* Laud was accused of being a crypto-Catholic—an ominous accusation during the protracted threat of invasion by the Spanish Armada. In 1640 the Long Parliament met, quickly impeached Laud on charges of treason, and placed him in jail for several years before his execution.

Ludwig Lavater (1527–1586). Swiss Reformed pastor and theologian. Under his father-in-law Heinrich Bullinger,* Lavater became an archdeacon in Zurich. In 1585 he succeeded Rudolf Gwalther* as the city's Antistes. He authored a widely disseminated book on demonology, commentaries on Chronicles, Proverbs, Ecclesiastes, Nehemiah and Ezekiel, theological works, and biographies of Bullinger and Konrad Pellikan.*

Laws and Liberties of the Inhabitants of Massachusetts (1647). North American colonial constitution. The first printed set of laws in the American colonies, the 1647 *Laws and Liberties of the Inhabitants of Massachusetts* was a revision of the *Massachusetts Body of Liberties* (1641), a legal code collected by Puritan minister Nathaniel Ward (1578–1652). The *Laws and Liberties* codified Puritan expectations of doctrine and morality, and included provision for the punishment for heresy, stipulating banishment for Anabaptism. The majority of the document consists of practical clauses addressing general and specific aspects of communal and commercial life.

John Lawson (unknown). Seventeenth-century English Puritan. Lawson wrote *Gleanings and Expositions of Some of Scripture* (1646) and a treatise on the sabbath in the New Testament.

Jacques Lefèvre d'Étaples (Faber Stapulensis) (1460?–1536). French Catholic humanist, publisher and translator. Lefèvre d'Étaples studied classical literature and philosophy, as well as patristic and medieval mysticism. He advocated the principle of *ad fontes*, issuing a full-scale annotation on the corpus of Aristotle, publishing the writings of key Christian mystics, and contributing to efforts at biblical translation and commentary. Although he never broke with the Catholic Church, his views prefigured those of Martin Luther,* for which he was condemned by the University of Sorbonne in Paris. He then found refuge in the court of Marguerite d'Angoulême, where he met John Calvin* and Martin Bucer.*

Edward Leigh (1602–1671). English Puritan biblical critic, historian and politician. Educated at Oxford, Leigh's public career included appointments as a Justice of the Peace, an officer in the parliamentary army during the English Civil Wars and a member of Parliament. Although never ordained, Leigh devoted himself to the study of theology and Scripture; he participated in the

Westminster Assembly. Leigh published a diverse corpus, including lexicons of Greek, Hebrew and juristic terms, and histories of Roman, Greek and English rulers. His most important theological work is *A Systeme or Body of Divinity* (1662).

John Lightfoot (1602–1675). Anglican priest and biblical scholar. After graduating from Cambridge, Lightfoot was ordained and pastored at several small parishes. He continued to study classics under the support of the politician Rowland Cotton (1581–1634). Siding with the Parliamentarians during the English Civil Wars, Lightfoot relocated to London in 1643. He was one of the original members of the Westminster Assembly, where he defended a moderate Presbyterianism. His best-known work is the six-volume *Horae Hebraicae et Talmudicae* (1658–1677), a verse-by-verse commentary illumined by Hebrew customs, language and the Jewish interpretive tradition.

Wenceslaus Linck (1482–1547). German Lutheran theologian and preacher. As dean of the theology faculty at the University of Wittenberg and successor to Johannes von Staupitz* as the prior of the Augustinian Monastery, Linck worked closely with Martin Luther* and attended the Heidelberg Disputation with him. He replaced Staupitz as vicar-general of the Augustinian order in 1520 in Germany, a capacity in which he pronounced all members free from their vows before renouncing the order himself. After periods of ministry in Munich and Altenburg, Linck settled in Nuremberg, where he became known as an exemplary preacher and an advisor to cities undertaking Protestant reform. He published a significant number of sermons and practical tracts as well as a paraphrase and annotations on the Old Testament.

Peter Lombard (1095–1160). Scholastic theologian, bishop of Paris. Though little is known about his life, some records indicate that Lombard came from the region of Novara in Lombardy. Bernard of Clairvaux* patronized his studies at Reims, and later recommended him for further study at St. Victor in Paris. In 1144,

Lombard participated in an examination of the writings of Gilbert of Poitiers for heresy. Lombard became a canon at Notre Dame in 1145, and an archdeacon there in 1156. Meanwhile he spent a year and a half in Rome as an assistant to Theobald, bishop of Paris. Lombard was elected bishop of Paris in 1159. He died less than a year later. Lombard's most important work was the *Four Books of the Sentences*, which served as the standard textbook for theology throughout the remainder of the Middle Ages, and at the beginning of the early modern period. Additionally, Lombard produced commentaries on the Psalms and Pauline epistles.

Johannes Lonicer (1499–1569). German Lutheran theologian and linguist. After studying in Erfurt and Wittenberg, Lonicer renounced his Augustinian vows. He briefly taught Hebrew at the University of Freiburg, but controversy saw him flee to Strasburg, where he worked with a printer, translating some early Lutheran vernacular works into Latin. At the opening of the University of Marburg, Lonicer was appointed to teach Greek and Hebrew, and he later also served as professor of theology.

Lucas Lossius (1508–1582). German Lutheran teacher and musician. While a student at Leipzig and Wittenberg, Lossius was deeply influenced by Melanchthon* and Luther,* who found work for him as Urbanus Rhegius's* secretary. Soon after going to work for Rhegius, Lossius began teaching at a local gymnasium (or secondary school), *Das Johanneum*, eventually becoming its headmaster. Lossius remained at *Das Johanneum* until his death, even turning down appointments to university professorships. A man of varied interests, he wrote on dialectics, music and church history, as well as publishing a postil and a five-volume set of annotations on the New Testament.

Sibrandus Lubbertus (c. 1555–1625). Dutch Reformed theologian. Lubbertis, a key figure in the establishment of orthodox Calvinism in Frisia, studied theology at Wittenburg and Geneva (under Theodore Beza*) before his appointment as professor of theology at the University of Franeker.

Throughout his career, Lubbertis advocated for high Calvinist theology, defending it in disputes with representatives of Socinianism, Arminianism and Roman Catholicism. Lubbertis criticized the Catholic theologian Robert Bellarmine and fellow Dutch reformer Jacobus Arminius*; the views of the latter he opposed as a prominent participant in the Synod of Dordrecht.*

Thomas Lushington (1590–1661). English Anglican minister. Best known as the tutor of polymath Sir Thomas Browne (1605–1682), Lushington also served as a chaplain to Richard Corbet, bishop of Oxford. Committed to the program of Archbishop Laud,* he lost his position during the English Civil Wars and retired to write. Most of his works were published anonymously or pseudonymously, including a translation of a commentary on Hebrews by Polish theologian Johannes Crellius (1590–1633) as G. W. and a series of sermons given at Oxford as Robert Jones.

Martin Luther (1483–1546). German Lutheran priest, professor, and theologian. Martin Luther was born in Eisleben, Saxony, to an entrepreneurial minor. Upon completing his earlier education at Eisenach, Luther matriculated at the University of Erfurt where he completed his BA in 1502, and MA in 1505. While at Erfurt, Luther studied the philosophy of William of Ockham (1285–1347), and his disciple, Gabriel Biel (1420–1495). After receiving his MA, Luther proceeded to the study of law. However, a number of events culminating in his promise to St. Anne (the patron saint of minors) to become a monk compelled Luther to withdraw from law school and join the Augustinian monastery at Erfurt in 1505. At this monastery, Luther was ordained a priest. Later, the Augustinians sent Luther to the University of Wittenberg to study theology. In 1512, Luther received his doctorate, and took up the post of lecturer in Bible at Wittenberg, a position he would hold the rest of his life. While a professor at this university, Luther reinterpreted the doctrine of justification. Convinced that righteousness comes only from God's grace, he disputed the sale of indulgences with his *Ninety–Five Theses*, which

he reportedly posted to the door of All Saints' Church in Wittenberg on October 31, 1517. Luther's positions brought conflict with Rome. He challenged the Mass, transubstantiation, and communion in one kind, and his denial of papal authority led to excommunication. Though Luther was condemned by the Diet of Worms, Frederick III, the Elector of Saxony, provided him safe haven. Luther later returned to Wittenberg with public order collapsing under Andreas Bodenstein von Karlstadt* and steered a more cautious path of reform. Among his most influential works are three treatises published in 1520: *To the Christian Nobility of the German Nation, On the Babylonian Captivity of the Church,* and *On the Freedom of a Christian.* His rendering of the Bible and liturgy in the vernacular, as well as his hymns and sermons, proved extensively influential.

Georg Major (1502–1574). German Lutheran theologian. Major was on the theological faculty of the University of Wittenberg, succeeding as dean Johannes Bugenhagen* and Philipp Melanchthon.* One of the chief editors on the Wittenberg edition of Luther's works, Major is most identified with the controversy bearing his name, in which he stated that good works are necessary to salvation. Major qualified his statement, which was in reference to the totality of the Christian life. The Formula of Concord* rejected the statement, ending the controversy. As a theologian, Major further refined Lutheran views of the inspiration of Scripture and the doctrine of the Trinity.

John (Mair) Major (1467–1550). Scottish Catholic philosopher. Major taught logic and theology at the universities of Paris (his alma mater), Glasgow and St Andrews. His broad interests and impressive work drew students from all over Europe. While disapproving of evangelicals (though he did teach John Knox*), Major advocated reform programs for Rome. He supported collegial episcopacy and even challenged the curia's teaching on sexuality. Still he was a nominalist who was critical of humanist approaches to biblical exegesis. His best-known publication is *A History of Greater Britain, Both England and Scotland* (1521), which promoted the union of the kingdoms. He also published a commentary on Peter Lombard's *Sentences* and the Gospel of John.

Juan de Maldonado (1533–1583). Spanish Catholic biblical scholar. A student of Francisco de Toledo,* Maldonado taught philosophy and theology at the universities of Paris and Salamanca. Ordained to the priesthood in Rome, he revised the Septuagint under papal appointment. While Maldonado vehemently criticized Protestants, he asserted that Reformed baptism was valid and that mixed confessional marriages were acceptable. His views on Mary's immaculate conception proved controversial among many Catholics who conflated his statement that it was not an article of faith with its denial. He was intrigued by demonology (blaming demonic influence for the Reformation). All his work was published posthumously; his Gospel commentaries were highly valued and important.

Thomas Manton (1620–1677). English Puritan minister. Manton, educated at Oxford, served for a time as lecturer at Westminster Abbey and rector of St. Paul's, Covent Garden, and was a strong advocate of Presbyterianism. He was known as a rigorous evangelical Calvinist who preached long expository sermons. At different times in his ecclesial career he worked side-by-side with Richard Baxter* and John Owen.* In his later life, Manton's Nonconformist position led to his ejection as a clergyman from the Church of England (1662) and eventual imprisonment (1670). Although a voluminous writer, Manton was best known for his preaching. At his funeral in 1677, he was dubbed "the king of preachers."

Benedetto da Mantova (c. 1495–c. 1556). Italian Catholic monk. Benedetto entered the Benedictine order in Mantua and served as dean at San Giorgio Maggiore in Venice. At San Nicolò l'Arena on Mt. Etna, he became acquainted with Waldensian and Protestant thought, which influenced his composition of *The Benefit of Christ*, one of the most significant Italian writings of the Reformation. Marcantonio Flaminio* was asked to rewrite the text in more elegant prose before its anonymous

publication in 1543, and although the work drew the ire of the Inquisition, Benedetto's authorship was not uncovered during his lifetime. His increasingly radical spiritualism saw him arrested in Padua, though nothing of his later life is known.

Felix Mantz (d. 1527). Swiss Anabaptist Leader. An early supporter of Zwingli* in Zurich, Mantz's frustration with the pace of the magisterial Reformation led him to found an independent congregation, the Swiss Brethren, with Conrad Grebel,* Georg Blaurock,* and others. Mantz and Grebel represented the Brethren in two disputations with Zwingli over infant baptism in 1525. Defeated, the Brethren refused to cease meeting and rebaptizing adults, which they considered a first baptism, leading to suppression by the Zurich authorities. Mantz was able to spread his message for a time, traveling through a number of Swiss regions despite several arrests. Imprisoned by the Zurich authorities in March 1526 with Grebel and Blaurock, he briefly escaped, but having returned to his practice of believers' baptism, he was executed by drowning, the punishment for Anabaptism, in January 1527.

Lucrezia Marinella (1571–1653). Venetian poet and writer. While famous for her writings, very little is known of Marinella's personal life. As was expected of a women of her class, she spent most of her life in seclusion, and she did not participate in public life. She married a physician, but the fact that she had two children is only known from her will. Marinella's writings spanned a number of subjects, including, philosophy, religious poetry, and proto-feminist texts on the abilities of women and their place in society. Perhaps her best-known work is *The Nobility and Excellence of Women and the Defects and Vices of Men* (1600), in which she argues for the moral and intellectual superiority of women.

Augustin Marlorat (c. 1506–1562). French Reformed pastor. Committed by his family to a monastery at the age of eight, Marlorat was also ordained into the priesthood at an early age in 1524. He fled to Geneva in 1535, where he pastored until the Genevan Company of Pastors sent him to

France to shepherd the nascent evangelical congregations. His petition to the young Charles IX (1550–1574) for the right to public evangelical worship was denied. In response to a massacre of evangelicals in Vassy (over sixty dead, many more wounded), Marlorat's congregation planned to overtake Rouen. After the crown captured Rouen, Marlorat was arrested and executed three days later for treason. His principle published work was an anthology of New Testament comment modeled after Thomas Aquinas's* *Catena aurea in quatuor Evangelia.* Marlorat harmonized Reformed and Lutheran comment with the church fathers, interspersed with his own brief comments. He also wrote such anthologies for Genesis, Job, the Psalms, Song of Songs and Isaiah.

Pilgram Marpeck (c. 1495–1556). Austrian Radical elder and theologian. During a brief sojourn in Strasbourg, Marpeck debated with Martin Bucer* before the city council; Bucer was declared the winner, and Marpeck was asked to leave Strasbourg for his views concerning paedo-baptism (which he compared to a sacrifice to Moloch). After his time in Strasbourg, Marpeck traveled throughout southern Germany and western Austria, planting Anabaptist congregations. Marpeck criticized the strict use of the ban, however, particularly among the Swiss brethren. He also engaged in a christological controversy with Kaspar von Schwenckfeld.*

Stephen Marshall (c. 1594–1655). English Presbyterian minister. Known for his Nonconformist preaching, Marshall pastored in Essex before appearing on the national stage prior to the Civil War (1642–1651). An advocate of armed rebellion against a lawful sovereign over religious matters, he preached before Parliament a number of times, was a member of the Westminster Assembly, and served as lecturer at St. Margaret's, Westminster. He also ministered to Archbishop Laud* and Charles I* before their executions.

Gregory Martin (1542?–1582). English Catholic priest and translator. After studying at Oxford, Martin tutored the sons of the Duke of Norfolk until leaving for the college of Douai, where he received his doctorate. He taught for two years at the English college in Rome before returning to the college of Douai, which was temporarily based at Rheims. While he composed a number of polemical writings, he is best known as the primary translator of the Douai-Rheims Bible, an English translation of the Vulgate with commentary and notes intended to provide a Catholic alternative to the influx of Protestant annotated English Bibles. The New Testament was published at Douai in 1582 and the Old Testament at Rheims in 1609–1610.

Mary I of England (1516–1558). English monarch. Daughter of Henry VIII* and his first wife Catherine of Aragon (1509–1553), Mary was raised in the strict Catholicism of her mother. Her succession of Edward VI, her half-brother, was briefly contested by Lady Jane Grey*, daughter of Henry VIII's younger sister, in whom Protestants placed their hopes, but unable to raise adequate support, this challenge was quickly dismissed. Upon her ascent, Mary set about the task of restoring the Catholic religion, a reversal of royal policy that was positively received by much of the populace. While able to reestablish relations with the Pope and reassert the mass and other aspects of Catholicism, the impoverishment of the church following the dissolution of the monasteries and the closure of the chantries was difficult to overcome. Other aspects of popular piety, including the cult of the saints, pilgrimages, and the doctrine of purgatory, were not restored during her reign. Mary looms large in the Protestant imagination, and her persecution of evangelicals led to the moniker "Bloody Mary." The accounts of martyrs such as Thomas Cranmer*, Hugh Latimer*, and Nicholas Ridley* were immortalized in John Foxe's (1516–1587) *Acts and Monuments** and became a mainstay of Protestant propaganda.

Johannes Mathesius (1504–1565). German Lutheran theologian and pastor. After reading Martin Luther's* *On Good Works,* Mathesius left his teaching post in Ingolstadt and traveled to Wittenberg to study theology. Mathesius was an important agent of reform in the Bohemian town of Jáchymov, where he pastored, preached and taught. Over one thousand of Mathesius's sermons are extant, including numerous wedding and funeral sermons as well as a series on Luther's life. Mathesius also transcribed portions of Luther's Table Talk.

Anthony Maxey (d. 1618). Anglican minister. Maxey was born in Essex and educated at Westminster School. After completing his early education at Westminster, Maxey matriculated at Trinity College, Cambridge, in 1578. Maxey graduated Cambridge with the BA (1581), MA (1585), BD (1594), and DD (1608) degrees. However, he was unable to obtain a fellowship at Trinity. King James I* appointed Maxey as his chaplain and dean of Windsor on June 21, 1612. Maxey was also inducted into the Order of the Garter. He died on May 3, 1618. Maxey's published works consist of three sermons: *The Churches Sleep*; *The Golden Chain of Man's Salvation*; and *The Fearful Point of Hardening*.

John Mayer (1583–1664). Anglican priest and biblical exegete. Mayer dedicated much of his life to biblical exegesis, writing a seven-volume commentary on the entire Bible (1627–1653). Styled after Philipp Melanchthon's* *locus* method, Mayer's work avoided running commentary, focusing instead on textual and theological problems. He was a parish priest for fifty-five years. In the office of priest Mayer also wrote a popular catechism, *The English Catechisme, or a Commentarie on the Short Catechisme* (1621), which went through twelve editions in his lifetime.

Joseph Mede (1586–1638). Anglican biblical scholar, Hebraist and Greek lecturer. A man of encyclopedic knowledge, Mede was interested in numerous fields, varying from philology and history to mathematics and physics, although millennial thought and apocalyptic prophesy were clearly his chief interests. Mede's most important work was his *Clavis Apocalyptica* (1627, later translated into English as *The Key of the Revelation*). This work examined the structure of Revelation as the key to its interpretation. Mede saw the visions as a connected and chronological

sequence hinging around Revelation 17:18. He is remembered as an important figure in the history of millenarian theology. He was respected as a mild-mannered and generous scholar who avoided controversy and debate, but who had many original thoughts.

Philipp Melanchthon (1497–1560). German Lutheran educator, reformer, and theologian. Philipp Melanchthon was born in the Palatinate, the son of an armorer. He attended the Latin school in Pforzheim, where he lived with the sister of Johannes Reuchlin* to whom he was related by marriage. Having completed his early education, Melanchthon went on to attend the University of Heidelberg, where he received his BA in 1511. Afterwards, he earned his MA from the University of Tubingen in 1514. In 1518, Reuchlin recommended Melanchthon for the new professorship of Greek at the University of Wittenberg, where he remained for the rest of his life. There, Melanchthon taught Greek, rhetoric, and logic. Melanchthon is known as the partner and successor to Martin Luther* in reform in Germany and for his pioneering *Loci Communes*, which served as a theological textbook. Melanchthon participated with Luther in the Leipzig disputation, helped implement reform in Wittenberg, and was a chief architect of the Augsburg Confession.* Later, Melanchthon and Martin Bucer* worked for union between reformed and Catholic churches. On account of Melanchthon's ecumenical disposition and his modification of several of Luther's doctrines, he was held in suspicion by some.

Andrew Melville (1545–1622). Scottish Reformed theologian. Melville was born at Baldovie on August 1, 1545, to an evangelical family. After finishing his early education at Montrose Grammar School, he matriculated at St. Mary's College, St. Andrews, in 1559. Melville graduated St. Andrews in 1564, after which he traveled to Paris, where he studied Greek, Hebrew, mathematics, and other languages. While in Paris, Melville came under the influence of Petrus Ramus,* whose pedagogical methods he would later utilize in Scotland. From there, he proceeded to Poitiers to study law. There, he became regent of the College of St. Marceon. However, when Poitiers came under siege, Melville departed the city for Geneva, where Theodore Beza* warmly received him. Shortly after Melville's arrival in Geneva, he assumed the chair of humanities at the academy. Melville remained in this position at the academy until 1573, when he returned to Scotland. In 1574, Melville was appointed principal of the College of Glasgow. While in this post, Melville led in the reform of the college's curriculum, and engaged in ecclesiastical controversy. He served on the committee that drafted the Second Book of Discipline, and was elected moderator of the General Assembly in 1578. In 1580, Melville became principal of St. Mary's College, St. Andrews, where he initiated the same types of reform as he did at Glasgow. Throughout his career, Melville denounced royal ecclesiastical supremacy, arguing strongly for the autonomy of the national church. For this he was summoned to the Privy Council in Edinburgh in 1584 on the possible charge of treason for his resistance to royal ecclesiastical authority. Though they could not charge Melville with sedition, the Privy Council still determined to consign him to trial, but Melville managed to escape to England. While in England, he visited Puritan leaders at Oxford and Cambridge. He also lectured on Genesis in London. Melville returned to Scotland in 1585, and became rector of the University of St. Andrews in 1590. He was eventually deprived of this rectorship in 1587 for his opposition to episcopacy. In 1606, along with several ministers, he was summoned to appear before Hampton Court, where he gave some uncompromising speeches. These speeches resulted in Melville's imprisonment in several places, including the Tower of London. Melville was released from the Tower on April 19, 1611, and from there traveled to France. Having arrived in France, Melville proceeded through Paris and Rouen to Sedan, where he assumed the chair of theology. He remained in Sedan until his death in 1622.

Melville authored an extensive literary corpus, which includes a commentary on Romans.

Justus Menius (1499–1558). German Lutheran pastor and theologian. Menius was a prominent reformer in Thuringia. He participated in the Marburg Colloquy and, with others, helped Martin Luther* compose the Schmalkald Articles.* Throughout his career Menius entered into numerous controversies with Anabaptists and even fellow Lutherans. He rejected Andreas Osiander's (d. 1552) doctrine of justification—that the indwelling of Christ's divine nature justifies, rather than the imputed alien righteousness of Christ's person, declared through God's mercy. Against Nikolaus von Amsdorf (1483–1565) and Matthias Flacius (1520–1575), Menius agreed with Georg Major* that good works are necessary to salvation. Osiander's view of justification was censored in Article 3 of the Formula of Concord*; Menius's understanding of the relationship between good works and salvation was rejected in Article 4. Menius translated many of Luther's Latin works into German. He also composed a handbook for Christian households and an influential commentary on 1 Samuel.

Johannes Mercerus (Jean Mercier) (d. 1570). French Hebraist. Mercerus studied under the first Hebrew chair at the Collège Royal de Paris, François Vatable (d. 1547), whom he succeeded in 1546. John Calvin* tried to recruit Mercerus to the Genevan Academy as professor of Hebrew, once in 1558 and again in 1563; he refused both times. During his lifetime Mercerus published grammatical helps for Hebrew and Chaldean, an aid to the Masoretic symbols in the Hebrew text, and translated the commentaries and grammars of several medieval rabbis. He himself wrote commentaries on Genesis, the wisdom books, and most of the Minor Prophets. These commentaries—most of them only published after his death—were philologically focused and interacted with the work of Jerome, Nicholas of Lyra,* notable rabbis and Johannes Oecolampadius.*

Thomas Mocket (1602–1670?). British Puritan minister. Mocket ministered in Wales and

England, publishing numerous works, including a catechism, a tract on the duties of Christians, and an excursus on the celebration of Christmas.

Peter Moffett (d. 1617). English Protestant clergyman. Rector at Fobbing, Essex, Moffett published a commentary on the Song of Solomon and a sermon on 1 Timothy 1:16.

Ambrose Moibanus (1494–1554). German Lutheran bishop and theologian. Moibanus helped reform the church of Breslau (modern Wroclaw, Poland). He revised the Mass, bolstered pastoral care and welfare for the poor, and wrote a new evangelical catechism.

Olympia Morata (1526/27–1555). Italian Protestant humanist and theologian. Daughter of a humanist scholar, her father taught in the court of Ferrara, and she was raised alongside Anna d'Este (1531–1607), daughter of Protestant Renée of France (1510–1574) and later wife of Francis, Duke of Guise (1519–1563), a central antagonist in the St. Bartholomew's Day Massacre. A precocious scholar, Morata's classical, humanist, and biblical studies drew her toward the evangelical currents of the court, but these Protestant leanings also raised the constant suspicion of the Inquisition. In 1550, Morata married Andreas Grundler (unknown), a German Protestant doctor, and moved to his native Schweinfurt, where, facing limited opportunities due to her gender, she continued her studies and privately tutored in Greek and the classics. She developed an extensive correspondence with friends, especially noblewomen she had met at court, and Protestant leaders including Luther*, Melanchthon* and Matthias Flacius (1520–1575), whom she asked to translate some of Luther's work into Italian. Most of Morata's writings were destroyed during the siege of Schweinfurt in 1553–1554, and while she was able to resettle in Frankfurt, she died of tuberculosis soon afterwards. In her writings that survived the siege, her scholarly erudition is clear, and her letters demonstrate a ministerial care for her correspondents and desire for the spread of the Reformation message.

Thomas More (1478–1535). English Catholic lawyer, politician, humanist and martyr. More briefly studied at Oxford, but completed his legal studies in London. After contemplating the priesthood for four years, he opted for politics and was elected a member of Parliament in 1504. A devout Catholic, More worked with church leaders in England to root out heresy while he also confronted Lutheran teachings in writing. After four years as Lord Chancellor, More resigned due to heightened tensions with Henry VIII* over papal supremacy (which More supported and Henry did not). Tensions did not abate. More's steadfast refusal to accept the Act of Supremacy (1534)—which declared the King of England to be the supreme ecclesial primate not the pope—resulted in his arrest and trial for high treason. He was found guilty and beheaded with John Fisher (1469–1535). Friends with John Colet* and Desiderius Erasmus,* More was a widely respected humanist in England as well as on the continent. Well-known for his novel *Utopia* (1516), More also penned several religious treatises on Christ's passion and suffering during his imprisonment in the Tower of London, which were published posthumously.

Henry Morley (d. 1616). English Protestant preacher. Morley published a sermon of the cleansing of the leper given at St. Paul's Cathedral in London during an outbreak of the plague in 1603.

Sebastian Münster (1488–1552). German Reformed Hebraist, exegete, printer, and geographer. After converting to the Reformation in 1524, Münster taught Hebrew at the universities of Heidelberg and Basel. During his lengthy tenure in Basel he published more than seventy books, including Hebrew dictionaries and rabbinic commentaries. He also produced an evangelistic work for Jews titled *Vikuach* (1539). Münster's *Torat ha-Maschiach* (1537), the Gospel of Matthew, was the first published Hebrew translation of any portion of the New Testament. Despite his massive contribution to contemporary understanding of the Hebrew language, Münster was criticized by many of the reformers as a Judaizer.

Thomas Müntzer (c. 1489–1525). German Radical preacher. As a preacher in the town of

Zwickau, Müntzer was influenced by German mysticism and, growing convinced that Martin Luther* had not carried through reform properly, sought to restore the pure apostolic church of the New Testament. Müntzer's radical ideas led to expulsions from various cities; he developed a highly apocalyptic theology, in which he heralded the last days that would establish the pure community out of suffering, prompting Müntzer's proactive role in the Peasants' War, which he perceived as a crucial apocalyptic event. Six thousand of Müntzer's followers were annihilated by magisterial troops; Müntzer was executed.

John Murcot (1625–1654). English Puritan pastor. After completing his bachelor's at Oxford in 1647, Murcot was ordained as a pastor, transferring to several parishes until in 1651 he moved to Dublin. All his works were published posthumously.

Simon Musaeus (1521–1582). German Lutheran theologian. After studying at the universities of Frankfurt an der Oder and Wittenberg, Musaeus began teaching Greek at the Cathedral school in Nuremberg and was ordained. Having returned to Wittenberg to complete a doctoral degree, Musaeus spent the rest of his career in numerous ecclesial and academic administrative posts. He opposed Matthias Flacius's (1505–1575) view of original sin—that the formal essence of human beings is marred by original sin—even calling the pro-Flacian faculty at Wittenberg "the devil's latrine." Musaeus published a disputation on original sin and a postil.

Wolfgang Musculus (1497–1563). German Reformed pastor and theologian. Musculus produced translations, biblical commentaries and an influential theological text, *Loci communes Sacrae Theologiae* (*Commonplaces of Sacred Theology*), outlining a Zwinglian theology. Musculus began to study theology while at a Benedictine monastery; he departed in 1527 and became secretary to Martin Bucer* in Strasbourg. He was later installed as a pastor in Augsburg, eventually performing the first evangelical liturgy in the city's cathedral. Displaced by the Augsburg Interim, Musculus ended his career as professor of

theology at Bern. Though Musculus was active in the pursuit of the reform agenda, he was also concerned for ecumenism, participating in the Wittenberg Concord (1536) and discussions between Lutherans and Catholics.

Georg Mylius (1548–1607). German Lutheran pastor and theologian. Mylius began his career as a preacher in Augsburg, rising to superintendent of the churches in the city after receiving his doctorate in theology. He was arrested and ejected from the city by the Catholic-dominated council for his opposition to the Gregorian calendar, returning briefly to learn of the death of his pregnant wife and child. After grieving in Ulm, Mylius spend the remainder of his career as a preacher and professor of theology at Wittenberg, with a brief hiatus teaching at Jena.

Hans Nadler (unknown). German Radical layperson. An uneducated and illiterate needle salesman, after receiving baptism from Hans Hut* in 1527, Nadler sought to share the faith with those he met during his extensive travels. He is remembered through the records of his arrest and examination, recorded by a court reporter, which give insight into his beliefs and activities as a committed Anabaptist layperson, whereby he affirmed believer's baptism, the spiritual reception of the Eucharist, and nonresistance.

Friedrich Nausea (c. 1496–1552). German Catholic bishop and preacher. After completing his studies at Leipzig, this famed preacher was appointed priest in Frankfurt but was run out of town by his congregants during his first sermon. He transferred to Mainz as cathedral preacher. Nausea was well connected through the German papal hierarchy and traveled widely to preach to influential ecclesial and secular courts. Court preacher for Ferdinand I (1503–1564), his reform tendencies fit well with royal Austrian theological leanings, and he was enthroned as the bishop of Vienna. Nausea thought that rather than endless colloquies only a council could settle reform. Unfortunately he could not participate in the first session of Trent due to insufficient funding, but he arrived for the second session. Nausea defended the laity's reception of the cup and stressed the importance of promulgating official Catholic teaching in the vernacular.

Melchior Neukirch (1540–1597). German Lutheran pastor and playwright. Neukirch's pastoral career spanned more than thirty years in several northern German parishes. Neukirch published a history of the Braunschweig church since the Reformation and a dramatization of Acts 4–7. He died of the plague.

Nicholas of Lyra (1270–1349). French Catholic biblical exegete. Very little is known about this influential medieval theologian of the Sorbonne aside from the works he published, particularly the *Postilla litteralis super totam Bibliam* (1322–1333). With the advent of the printing press this work was regularly published alongside the Latin Vulgate and the *Glossa ordinaria*. In this running commentary on the Bible Nicholas promoted literal interpretation as the basis for theology. Despite his preference for literal interpretation, Nicholas also published a companion volume, the *Postilla moralis super totam Bibliam* (1339), a commentary on the spiritual meaning of the biblical text. Nicholas was a major conversation partner for many reformers though many of them rejected his exegesis as too literal and too "Jewish" (not concerned enough with the Bible's fulfillment in Jesus Christ).

John Norden (1547–1625). English devotional writer. Norden was born at Somerset, and in 1564 entered Hart Hall, Oxford where he graduated with his BA in 1568, and MA in 1573. Norden spent most of his life Middlesex, moving later to St. Giles in the Fields in 1619, where he remained until his death in 1625. Throughout his life, Norden distinguished himself also as a cartographer, chorographer, and antiquarian. His best known devotional work was his Progress of Piety (1596).

Alexander Nowell (1517–1602). Anglican theologian. Born in Lancashire, Nowell was educated at Brasenose College, Oxford where he shared a room with the future martyrologist John Foxe. Nowell was elected a fellow at the same college, where he spent thirteen years. In 1543, he was appointed master of Westminster School,

and in December, 1551, a prebendary of Westminster Abbey. Though elected to the House of Commons in 1553, Nowell was permitted to assume his seat because as a prebendary, he had a seat in Convocation. Because of his evangelical convictions, Nowell lost prebendary in 1554, after which he fled to the Continent, traveling first to Strasbourg, and then to Frankfurt. When Elizabeth I ascended the throne, Nowell returned to England where he afterwards served as chaplain to Edmund Grindal. In 1561 Nowell became Dean of St. Paul's Cathedral, a post which he held until his death. Nowell's best known work was his Catechism originally written in Latin (1563), and translated into English by Thomas Norton in 1570.

Bernardino Ochino (1487–1564). Italian Reformed theologian. After serving as vicar general of the Franciscan order, Ochino left the foundation of the Capuchins, where he assisted in the composition of their constitution and served as vicar general. A famed preacher, his teaching came to the attention of the Inquisition as it began to reflect the thought of Juan de Valdés. Summoned to Rome in 1542, he fled to Geneva with Peter Martyr Vermigli* where his Reformed orthodoxy, tinged with Franciscan mysticism, was brought into the open. Following his flight, Ochino led an unstable life, with brief stays in Basel, Strasbourg, and Augsburg before moving to England with Vermigli in 1548 where he was able to compose a significant treatise against the Roman church. His doctrinal orthodoxy was questioned by the pastor of the Italian congregation in London, but his case left unresolved when he departed for Geneva, then Basel and Zurich, at the accession of Mary*. As pastor of a congregation of Italian refugees in Zurich, Ochino courted considerable controversy. He refused to have his works approved by the city magistrates before publication, and his opponents alleged that his Dialogi XXX (1563) included questionable teachings on the Trinity and divorce while seeming to advocate polygamy. Expelled from Zurich in 1563, he died in Moravia the following year.

Charles Odingsells (d. 1637). English Protestant preacher. Odingsells published two sermons on prophesying and miracles from Matthew 7 given at Langar in Nottinghamshire.

Johannes Oecolampadius (Johannes Huszgen) (1482–1531). Swiss-German Reformed humanist, reformer and theologian. Oecolampadius (an assumed name meaning "house light") assisted with Desiderius Erasmus's* Greek New Testament, lectured on biblical languages and exegesis and completed an influential Greek grammar. After joining the evangelical cause through studying patristics and the work of Martin Luther,* Oecolampadius went to Basel, where he lectured on biblical exegesis and participated in ecclesial reform. On account of Oecolampadius's effort, the city council passed legislation restricting preaching to the gospel and releasing the city from compulsory Mass. Oecolampadius was a chief ally of Huldrych Zwingli,* whom he supported at the Marburg Colloquy (1529).

Kaspar Olevianus (1536–1587). German Reformed theologian. Olevianus is celebrated for composing the Heidelberg Catechism and producing a critical edition of Calvin's *Institutes* in German. Olevianus studied theology with many, including John Calvin,* Theodore Beza,* Heinrich Bullinger* and Peter Martyr Vermigli.* As an advocate of Reformed doctrine, Olevianus oversaw the shift from Lutheranism to Calvinism throughout Heidelberg, organizing the city's churches after Calvin's Geneva. The Calvinist ecclesial vision of Olevianus entangled him in a dispute with another Heidelberg reformer over the rights of ecclesiastical discipline, which Olevianus felt belonged to the council of clergy and elders rather than civil magistrates.

Josua Opitz (c. 1542–1585). German Lutheran pastor. After a brief stint as superintendent in Regensburg, Opitz, a longtime preacher, was dismissed for his support of Matthias Flacius's (1520–1575) view of original sin. (Using Aristotelian categories, Flacius argued that the formal essence of human beings is marred by original sin, forming sinners into the image of Satan; his views

were officially rejected in Article 1 of the Formula of Concord.*) Hans Wilhelm Roggendorf (1533–1591) invited Opitz to lower Austria as part of his Lutheranizing program. Unfortunately Roggendorf and Opitz never succeed in getting Lutheranism legal recognition, perhaps in large part due to Opitz's staunch criticism of Catholics, which resulted in his exile. He died of plague.

Lucas Osiander (1534–1604). German Lutheran pastor. For three decades, Osiander— son of the controversial Nuremberg reformer Andreas Osiander (d. 1552)—served as pastor and court preacher in Stuttgart, until he fell out of favor with the duke in 1598. Osiander produced numerous theological and exegetical works, as well as an influential hymnal.

John Owen (1616–1683). English Puritan theologian. Owen trained at Oxford University, where he was later appointed dean of Christ Church and vice chancellor of the university, following his service as chaplain to Oliver Cromwell. Although Owen began his career as a Presbyterian minister, he eventually departed to the party of Independents. Owen composed many sermons, biblical commentaries (including seven volumes on the book of Hebrews), theological treatises and controversial monographs (including disputations with Arminians, Anglicans, Catholics and Socinians).

Ephraim Pagitt (1575–1647). English Protestant minister. Pagitt ministered at St. Edmunds in London until forced into retirement for his Royalist tendencies during the Civil War (1642–1646). Some of his later writings demonstrate sympathy for Presbyterian theology, and he became an opponent of Baptists and other sectarians. His most popular writing was *Heresiography* (1662), in which he set out to catalog the heretics he identified within the church.

Santes Pagninus (c. 1470–1541). Italian Catholic biblical scholar. Pagninus studied under Girolamo Savonarola* and later taught in Rome, Avignon and Lyons. He translated the Old Testament into Latin according to a tight, almost wooden, adherence to the Hebrew. This translation and his Hebrew lexicon

Thesaurus linguae sanctae (1529) were important resources for translators and commentators.

Johann Pappus (1549–1610). German Lutheran theologian. After a decade as a teacher of Hebrew and professor of theology at the Strasbourg academy, Pappus was appointed president of the city's company of pastors. Despite resistance from the Reformed theologian Johann Sturm (1507–1589), he led the city away from its Swiss Reformed alliances and toward subscription to the Lutheran Formula of Concord. A talented humanist, Pappus published more than thirty works on controversial, theological, historical, and exegetical subjects.

David (Wängler) Pareus (1548–1622). German Reformed pastor and theologian. Born at Frankenstein in Lower Silesia, Pareus studied theology at Heidelberg under Zacharias Ursinus (1534–1583), the principal author of the Heidelberg Catechism.* After reforming several churches, Pareus returned to Heidelberg to teach at the Reformed seminary. He then joined the theological faculty at the University of Heidelberg, first as a professor of Old Testament and later as a professor of New Testament. Pareus edited the *Neustadter Bibel* (1587), a publication of Martin Luther's* German translation with Reformed annotations—which was strongly denounced by Lutherans, especially Jakob Andreae* and Johann Georg Sigwart (1554–1618). In an extended debate, Pareus defended the orthodoxy of Calvin's exegesis against Aegidius Hunnius,* who accused Calvin of "judaizing" by rejecting many traditional Christological interpretations of Old Testament passages. Towards the end of his career, Pareus wrote commentaries on Genesis, Hosea, Matthew, Romans, 1 Corinthians, Galatians, Hebrews and Revelation.

Catherine Parr (1512–1548). The last of King Henry VIII's* six wives, Catherine Parr was Queen Consort to Henry from 1543 until his death in 1547. She enjoyed a close relationship with two of her step children, Elizabeth and Edward (the future Queen Elizabeth I* and King Edward VI), involving herself extensively in their education. Having married three more times after

the death of Henry VIII, Catherine died in 1548. Her published works are *Psalms or Prayers* (1543) and a *Lamentation of a Sinner* (1548).

Paul of Burgos (**Solomon ha-Levi**) (c. 1351–1435). Spanish Catholic archbishop. In 1391 Solomon ha-Levi, a rabbi and Talmudic scholar, converted to Christianity, receiving baptism with his entire family (except for his wife). He changed his name to Paul de Santa Maria. Some have suggested that he converted to avoid persecution; he himself stated that Thomas Aquinas's* work persuaded him of the truth of Christian faith. After studying theology in Paris, he was ordained bishop in 1403. He actively and ardently persecuted Jews, trying to compel them to convert. In order to convince Jews that Christians correctly interpret the Hebrew Scriptures, Paul wrote *Dialogus Pauli et Sauli contra Judaeos, sive Scrutinium Scripturarum* (1434), a book filled with vile language toward the Jews. He also wrote a series of controversial marginal notes and comments on Nicholas of Lyra's* *Postilla*, many of which criticized Nicholas's use of Jewish scholarship.

Christoph Pelargus (1565–1633). German Lutheran pastor, theologian, professor and superintendent. Pelargus studied philosophy and theology at the University of Frankfurt an der Oder, in Brandenburg. This irenic Philippist was appointed as the superintendent of Brandenburg and later became a pastor in Frankfurt, although the local authorities first required him to condemn Calvinist theology, because several years earlier he had been called before the consistory in Berlin under suspicion of being a crypto-Calvinist. Among his most important works were a four-volume commentary on *De orthodoxa fide* by John of Damascus (d. 749), a treatise defending the breaking of the bread during communion, and a volume of funeral sermons. He also published commentaries on the Pentateuch, the Psalms, Matthew, John and Acts.

Konrad Pellikan (1478–1556). German Reformed Hebraist and theologian. Pellikan attended the University of Heidelberg, where he mastered Hebrew under Johannes Reuchlin. In 1504 Pellikan published one of the first Hebrew grammars that was not merely a translation of the work of medieval rabbis. While living in Basel, Pellikan assisted the printer Johannes Amerbach, with whom he published some of Luther's* early writings. He also worked with Sebastian Münster* and Wolfgang Capito* on a Hebrew Psalter (1516). In 1526, after teaching theology for three years at the University of Basel, Huldrych Zwingli* brought Pellikan to Zurich to chair the faculty of Old Testament. Pellikan's magnum opus is a seven-volume commentary on the entire Bible (except Revelation) and the Apocrypha; it is often heavily dependent upon the work of others (esp. Desiderius Erasmus* and Johannes Oecolampadius*).

William Pemble (1591–1623). Puritan theologian and author. Pemble was born in Egerton, Kent. He was educated at Magdalen College, Oxford, where he graduated with his BA degree in 1614. Afterward he moved to Magdalen Hall, where he became a reader and tutor in divinity. He received his MA in 1618. Primarily a Hebrew scholar, Pemble authored commentaries on Ecclesiastes (1629), the first nine chapters of Zechariah (1629), and portions of Ezra, Nehemiah, and Daniel. Pemble also wrote *An Introduction to the Worthy Receiving the Sacrament* (1628), as well as treatises on predestination and justification. He died of a fever on April 14, 1623.

Benedict Pererius (1535–1610). Spanish Catholic theologian, philosopher and exegete. Pererius entered the Society of Jesus in 1552. He taught philosophy, theology, and exegesis at the Roman College of the Jesuits. Early in his career he warned against neo-Platonism and astrology in his *De principiis* (1576). Pererius wrote a lengthy commentary on Daniel, and five volumes of exegetical theses on Exodus, Romans, Revelation and part of the Gospel of John (chs. 1–14). His four-volume commentary on Genesis (1591–1599) was lauded by Protestants and Catholics alike.

William Perkins (1558–1602). English Puritan preacher and theologian. Perkins was a highly regarded Puritan Presbyterian preacher and biblical commentator in the Elizabethan era. He studied at Cambridge University and later became a fellow of Christ's Church college as a preacher

and professor, receiving acclaim for his sermons and lectures. Even more, Perkins gained an esteemed reputation for his ardent exposition of Calvinist reformed doctrine in the style of Petrus Ramus,* becoming one of the first English reformed theologians to achieve international recognition. Perkins influenced the federal Calvinist shape of Puritan theology and the vision of logical, practical expository preaching.

François Perrault (1577–1657). French Reformed pastor for over fifty years. His book on demonology was prominent, perhaps because of the intrigue at his home in 1612. According to his account, a poltergeist made a commotion and argued points of theology; a few months later Perrault's parishioners slew a large snake slithering out of his house.

Dirk Philips (1504–1568). Dutch Radical elder and theologian. This former Franciscan monk, known for being severe and obstinate, was a leading theologian of the sixteenth-century Anabaptist movement. Despite the fame of Menno Simons* and his own older brother Obbe, Philips wielded great influence over Anabaptists in the Netherlands and northern Germany where he ministered. As a result of Philips's understanding of the apostolic church as radically separated from the children of the world, he advocated a very strict interpretation of the ban, including formal shunning. His writings were collected and published near the end of his life as *Enchiridion oft Hantboecxken van de Christelijcke Leere* (1564).

Obbe Philips (1500–1568) Dutch radical leader. Trained as a physician, Philips was drawn to mystical Anabaptism, as taught by Melchior Hoffman (1495–1543) in his hometown of Leewarden. After adult rebaptism and ordination, he preached in Amsterdam, Delft, Appingedam, and Grongen, and he ordained other leaders including his brother Dirk Philips*, David Joris*, and Menno Simmons*. Disillusioned with the growth of revolutionary, enthusiastic, and apocalyptic elements within Anabaptism and unable to reconcile any visible church with the church of God, Philips withdrew from the radical movement in 1540, after which nothing is known of his life. His only extant writing, entitled *The Confession of Obbe Philips*, was published after his death and recounts elements of the history of the Anabaptist movement and defends his departure from the movement.

James Pilkington (1520-1576). Protestant bishop of Durham and Elizabethan author. Born in Lancashire, Pilkington received his early education at Manchester Grammar School. Afterwards, he entered Pembroke College, Cambridge, and later transferred to St. John's College, Cambridge, from where he graduated with his BA degree in 1539, and MA in 1542. Pilkington was appointed vicar of Kendal in 1545, but resigned this position shortly thereafter in order to return to Cambridge. While there, Pilkington was granted a license to preach, and was awarded the degree of Bachelor of Theology in 1551. In this same year, Pilkington became president of the college. When Mary Tudor succeeded her half-brother, Edward VI, in 1553, Pilkington fled to the Continent where he traveled to Zurich, Geneva, Frankfurt, and Strasbourg. He returned to England in 1559 when Elizabeth I ascended the throne of England. After returning to England, Pilkington became Regius Professor of Divinity at Cambridge and after, bishop of Durham in 1560. Pilkington's major work was his voluminous commentary on the Prophet Haggai.

Charles Pinner (Unknown). English Protestant pastor. Pinner studied at New College, Oxford, and served as rector at Wootton Bassett in Wiltshire. His extant writings include two sermons on 1 Timothy and two on 1 Peter.

Hector Pinto (c. 1528–1584). Portuguese Catholic theologian and exegete. A member of the order of Saint Jerome, Pinto taught theology and Scripture at the Universities of Sigüenza and Coimbra. A respected theologian and exegete, he published commentaries on Daniel, Nahum, Jeremiah, and Isaiah and an influential devotional work, *The Image of the Christian Life*.

Caritas Pirckheimer (1466–1532). German Catholic nun. Sister of famed humanist Wilibald Pirckheimer (1470–1530), Caritas received a humanistic education before entering the Franciscan convent at Nuremberg. Extolled by Erasmus* as one of the most learned women in Europe, Pirckheimer served as abbess at the advent of the Reformation, and her experiences are recorded in a journal covering the pivotal years of 1524–1528. While Nuremberg accepted Lutheran theology under the leadership of the city council and preachers such as Andreas Osiander (1498–1552), Pirckheimer defended the right of her order to continue in their vocation. She ultimately won a concession after a visit from Philip Melanchthon* in 1525, who recommended that the council allow those who wished to remain in the cloister to live out their vows in peace.

Johannes Piscator (1546–1625). German Reformed theologian. Educated at Tübingen (though he wanted to study at Wittenberg), Piscator taught at the universities of Strasbourg and Heidelberg, as well as academies in Neustadt and Herborn. His commentaries on both the Old and New Testaments involve a tripartite analysis of a given passage's argument, of scholia on the text and of doctrinal loci. Some consider Piscator's method to be a full flowering of Beza's* "logical" scriptural analysis, focused on the text's meaning and its relationship to the pericopes around it.

Amandus Polanus von Polansdorf (1561–1610). German Reformed educator and theologian. Polanus spent his career as an educator, serving as a tutor for noble families and a teacher at the Bohemian Brethren school in Moravia before earning his doctorate and becoming professor of Old Testament and later dean of the theological faculty at the University of Basel. His best-known work is the *Syntagma theologiae christianae* (1609), a compendium of Reformed dogmatics.

Constantino Ponce de la Fuente (1502–1559). Spanish Protestant theologian and preacher. A priest in Seville, Ponce de la Fuente was a critic of the established church and associated with the evangelical circle in the city. A popular preacher, he authored a catechism and a number of books on doctrine and the Christian life that focused on the work of Christ. Charged with heresy by the Inquisition, he admitted to the authorship of a number of heretical writings and died in prison awaiting trial while his works were added to the Index of Prohibited Books.

Matthew Poole (1624–1679). English Non-conformist minister. Having made known his preference for simplicity in worship, Matthew Poole was rector of St Michael-le-Querne until the passing of the 1662 Act of Uniformity led him to resign. Living off his inheritance, he preached occasionally and composed some brief tracts but devoted much of his effort to the compilation of Latin biblical commentary in the *Synopsis criticorum* (1669) and the composition of his own annotations on Scripture. He died in Amsterdam, having fled London during the Popish Plot (1678–1681). He believed his life was in danger for his anti-Catholic writings as part of a Catholic conspiracy to kill Charles II, which was ultimately revealed as a fiction concocted by Titus Oates (1649–1705).

Thomas Porter (d. 1667). English Anglican minister. A graduate of Christ's College, Cambridge, Porter ministered in Flintshire in Cheshire and at Whitchurch in Shropshire. Among his published works are a sermon on Matthew 5:13 and a response to antitrinitarian John Knowles (fl. 1646–1668).

Gabriel Powell (1575–1611). Puritan minister. Powell was born at Ruabon in Denbigshire in 1575. Having completed his studies at Jesus College, Oxford, Powell became master of the free-school in Ruthen. During his tenure at Ruthen, Powell closely studied the writings of the church fathers as well as philosophy, and afterward endeavored to publish several works based on this research. Finding his present location to be a hinderance to his literary objectives, Powell relocated to Oxford, entering St. Mary's Hall, where he finished his anticipated projects. Powell is chiefly known for his literary debate with Thomas Bilson (1547–1619) concerning Christ's descent into hell. Later, Richard Vaughan (1550–1607), bishop of London, appointed Powell his domestic chaplain. Powell died on December 31, 1611. In addition to many controversial and polemical works, Powell wrote a commentary on Romans 1.

Vavasor Powell (1617–1670). Welsh Puritan minister and author. Powell was born at Knucklas, Radnorshire, Wales. After completing his education at Jesus College, Oxford, Powell returned to Wales to assume the position of a local schoolmaster. During this time, Powell came under the influence of Walter Cradock's* preaching as well as the writings of Richard Sibbes* and William Perkins,* resulting in his conversion to Puritanism. Soon thereafter he became an itinerant preacher, traveling throughout Wales. He was arrested twice for nonconformity. During the Civil War, Powell first preached in London, and shortly thereafter pastored an Independent congregation in Wales. On December 26, 1641, Royalist forces arrested and imprisoned Powell. In 1646, as victory for the Puritans appeared inevitable, Powell was released, and allowed to return to Wales, having received a letter of endorsement from the Westminster Assembly. Back in Wales, Powell played a prominent role in the Westminster Assembly's 1650 commission for the better propagation of the gospel throughout Wales. In 1653, Powell returned to London, where he preached at St. Ann Blackfriars. It was at this time that Powell denounced Oliver Cromwell (1599–1658) for assuming the position of Lord Protector. For this reason, he was arrested and imprisoned. At the Restoration in 1660, Powell was again arrested and imprisoned for unauthorized preaching for seven years. Though released in 1667, Powell was once more arrested and incarcerated. He remained in custody until his death on October 27, 1660. Powell authored many poems and a concordance to the Bible.

Felix Pratensis (d. 1539). Italian Catholic Hebraist. Pratensis, the son of a rabbi, converted to Christianity and entered the Augustinian Hermits around the turn of the sixteenth century. In 1515, with papal permission, Pratensis published a new translation of the Psalms based on the Hebrew text. His *Biblia Rabbinica* (1517–1518), printed in Jewish and Christian editions, included text-critical notes in the margins as well as the Targum and rabbinic commentaries on each book (e.g., Rashi* on the Pentateuch and David Kimchi* on the Prophets). Many of the reformers consulted this valuable resource as they labored on their own translations and expositions of the Old Testament.

John Preston (1587–1628). Puritan minister and author. Preston was born at Upper Heyford, Northamptonshire, on October 27, 1587. He studied philosophy at King's College and Queen's College, Cambridge, earning his bachelor's degree in 1607. He became a fellow at Queen's in 1609, and a prebendary at Lincoln Cathedral a year later. During this period, Preston studied medicine and astronomy. In 1611, he received the MA degree. Sometime afterward, he experienced a conversion under the preaching of John Cotton.* After his conversion, Preston went on to study theology, concentrating mainly on Thomas Aquinas,* Duns Scotus, and William of Ockham. From there, he proceeded to the reformers, especially John Calvin.* Preston was appointed court chaplain in 1615. In this position he was influential in the promotion of Puritans to high civil office. Preston later assumed the positions of dean and catechist at Queen's College, Cambridge, where he distinguished himself by preaching a series of sermons that formed the basis of his body of divinity. In 1622, he received the degree of bachelor of divinity, becoming thereafter master of Emmanuel College, Cambridge. While at Emmanuel, Preston participated in the conflict between Calvinism and Arminianism. Moreover, in the same year, Preston succeeded John Donne* as preacher at Lincoln's Inn. Two years later, Preston accepted the lectureship at Trinity Church. He died at the age of forty in 1628. Throughout his prodigious career, Preston authored a sizable corpus, which includes published sermons on Romans.

Quadriga. The *quadriga,* or four senses of Scripture, grew out of the exegetical legacy of Paul's dichotomy of letter and spirit (2 Cor 3:6), as well as church fathers like Origen (c. 185–254), Jerome (c. 347–420) and Augustine* (354–430).

Advocates for this method—the primary framework for biblical exegesis during the medieval era—assumed the necessity of the gift of faith under the guidance of the Holy Spirit. The literal-historical meaning of the text served as the foundation for the fuller perception of Scripture's meaning in the three spiritual senses, accessible only through faith: the allegorical sense taught what should be believed, the tropological or moral sense taught what should be done, and the anagogical or eschatological sense taught what should be hoped for. Medieval Jewish exegesis also had a fourfold interpretive method—not necessarily related to the *quadriga*—called *pardes* ("grove"): *peshat,* the simple, literal sense of the text according to grammar; *remez,* the allegorical sense; *derash,* the moral sense; and *sod,* the mystic sense related to Kabbalah. Scholars hotly dispute the precise use and meaning of these terms.

Edward Rainbow[e] (1608–1684). Anglican minister, scholar, and bishop. Rainbow was born at Lincolnshire on April 20, 1608. After completing his education, Rainbow matriculated at Corpus Christi College, and later transferred to Magdalene College, Cambridge, where he graduated with the BA (1627), MA (1630), BD (1637), and DD (1643). He was elected a fellow at Magdalene in 1633 and a master there in 1642. In 1630, Rainbow accepted the mastership of the Kirton-in-Lindsey but shortly afterward moved to London. In 1632, Rainbow took holy orders and preached his first sermon in April of that year. His first appointment was that of curate of Savoy Hospital. Rainbow was recalled to Cambridge in 1633 and elected a fellow. Four years later he became dean of Magdalene and master of the same college in 1642. Though dismissed from his mastership by Parliament in 1650, Rainbow was restored to it in the year of the Restoration (1660). At the same time, he was appointed chaplain to the king. In 1661, Rainbow became dean of Peterborough, and appointed vice chancellor of Cambridge a year later. Rainbow was elected bishop of Carlisle in 1664. As bishop, Rainbow led in the systemic reform of his diocese. Rainbow died March 26, 1684. His published works consist of three published sermons and an incomplete treatise, *Verba Christi*.

Petrus Ramus (1515–1572). French Reformed humanist philosopher. Ramus was an influential professor of philosophy and logic at the French royal college in Paris; he converted to Protestantism and left France for Germany, where he came under the influence of Calvinist thought. Ramus was a trenchant critic of Aristotle and noted for his method of classification based on a deductive movement from universals to particulars, the latter becoming branching divisions that provided a visual chart of the parts to the whole. His system profoundly influenced Puritan theology and preaching. After returning to Paris, Ramus died in the Saint Bartholomew's Day Massacre.

Rashi (Shlomo Yitzchaki) (1040–1105). French Jewish rabbi and exegete. After completing his studies, Rashi founded a yeshiva in Troyes. He composed the first comprehensive commentary on the Talmud, as well as commentaries on the entire Old Testament except for 1–2 Chronicles. These works remain influential within orthodox Judaism. Late medieval and early modern Christian scholars valued his exegesis, characterized by his preference for peshat (see quadriga).

Reformatio Legum Ecclesiasticarum (1552). Under the leadership of Archbishop of Canterbury Thomas Cranmer,* Edward VI* established a committee of thirty-two bishops, theologians, and lawyers including Nicholas Ridley,* John Hooper,* Peter Martyr Vermigli,* Matthew Parker (1504–1575), and William Cecil (1520–1598) to align the laws of the English church with Reformed theology and English civil law. Completed in 1552, it touched on diverse topics, including church organization, doctrine and heresy, qualifications for ministry, and marriage and divorce. It was brought before Parliament in 1553, where it was blocked by John Dudley, Duke of Northumberland (1504–1553), who wished to decrease church powers, and then dropped upon the accession of Mary I. A manuscript of the proposal revised by John Foxe (1516/1517–1587)

was published in 1671, and while some elements of the Reformatio Legum Ecclesiasticarum were adopted under Elizabeth I, thoroughgoing reform of ecclesiastical law was not brought about until the *Book of Canons* (1604).

Remonstrance (1610). See *Synod of Dordrecht*.

Johannes Reuchlin (1455–1522). German Catholic lawyer, humanist and Hebraist. Reuchlin held judicial appointments for the dukes of Württemberg, the Supreme Court in Speyer and the imperial court of the Swabian League. He pioneered the study of Hebrew among Christians in Germany, standing against those who, like Johannes Pfefferkorn (1469–1523), wanted to destroy Jewish literature. Among his many works he published a Latin dictionary, an introductory Greek grammar, the most important early modern Hebrew grammar and dictionary (*De rudimentis hebraicis*; 1506), and a commentary on the penitential psalms.

Edward Reynolds (1599–1676). Anglican bishop. Reynolds succeeded John Donne* as the preacher at Lincoln's Inn before entering parish ministry in Northamptonshire. During the English Civil Wars, he supported the Puritans because of his sympathy toward their simplicity and piety—despite believing that Scripture demanded no particular form of government; later he refused to support the abolition of the monarchy. Until the Restoration he ministered in London; afterward he became the bishop of Norwich. He wrote the general thanksgiving prayer which is part of the morning office in the *Book of Common Prayer*.*

Urbanus Rhegius (1489–1541). German Lutheran pastor. Rhegius, who was likely the son of a priest, studied under the humanists at Freiburg and Ingolstadt. After a brief stint as a foot soldier, he received ordination in 1519 and was made cathedral preacher in Augsburg. During his time in Augsburg he closely read Luther's* works, becoming an enthusiastic follower. Despite his close friendship with Zwingli* and Oecolampadius,* Rhegius supported Luther in the eucharistic debates, later playing a major role in the Wittenberg Concord (1536). He advocated for peace during the Peasants' War and had extended interactions with the Anabaptists in Augsburg. Later in his career he concerned himself with the training of pastors, writing a pastoral guide and two catechisms. About one hundred of his writings were published posthumously.

Lancelot Ridley (d. 1576). Anglican preacher. Ridley was the first cousin of Nicholas Ridley,* the bishop of London who was martyred during the Marian persecutions. By Cranmer's* recommendation, Ridley became one of the six Canterbury Cathedral preachers. Upon Mary I's accession in 1553, Ridley was defrocked (as a married priest). Ridley returned to Canterbury Cathedral after Mary's death. He wrote commentaries on Jude, Ephesians, Philippians and Colossians.

Nicholas Ridley (c. 1502–1555). Anglican bishop. Ridley was a student and fellow at Cambridge University who was appointed chaplain to Archbishop Thomas Cranmer* and is thought to be partially responsible for Cranmer's shift to a symbolic view of the Eucharist. Cranmer promoted Ridley twice: as bishop of Rochester, where he openly advocated Reformed theological views, and, later, as bishop of London. Ridley assisted Cranmer in the revisions of the Book of Common Prayer.* Ridley's support of Lady Jane Grey against the claims of Mary to the throne led to his arrest; he was tried for heresy and burned at the stake with Hugh Latimer.*

Peter Riedemann (1506–1556). German Radical elder, theologian and hymnist. While traveling as a Silesian cobbler, Riedemann came into contact with Anabaptist teachings and joined a congregation in Linz. In 1529 he was called to be a minister, only to be imprisoned soon after as part of Archduke Ferdinand's efforts to suppress heterodoxy in his realm. Once he was released, he moved to Moravia in 1532 where he was elected as a minister and missionary of the Hutterite community there. His *Account of Our Religion, Doctrine and Faith* (1542), with its more than two thousand biblical references, is Riedemann's most important work and is still used by Hutterites today.

John Robinson (1576–1625). English Puritan pastor. After his suspension for nonconformity, Robinson fled to the Netherlands with his congregation, eventually settling in Leiden in 1609. Robinson entered into controversies over Arminianism, separation and congregationalism. Most of his healthy congregants immigrated to Plymouth in 1620; Robinson remained in Leiden with those unable to travel.

John Rogers (1505–1555). English Protestant Bible translator. Rogers was born in Deritend, Birmingham. After receiving his early education at the Guild School of St. John the Baptist, Rogers matriculated at Pembroke Hall, Cambridge, where he graduated with the BA degree in 1526. He served as rector of Holy Trinity the Less in London from 1532 to 1534, when he left for the Continent to serve as chaplain to the English merchants of the Company of the Merchant Adventurers. It was at this time that he met William Tyndale,* under whose influence he came to embrace an evangelical faith. After Tyndale's death, Rogers completed his late colleague's translation of the Old Testament, which had ended with 2 Chronicles, by adding Miles Coverdale's translation of the remainder, including the Apocrypha. The resulting work, known as the "Matthew Bible" (Rogers published it under the pseudonym "Thomas Matthew") was published in 1537. It has the distinction of being the first complete English Bible translated essentially from the original languages to be printed. "Matthew's Bible" served as the basis for the Great Bible (1540), which in turn was used by those who prepared the Bishops' Bible (1568), on which later the King James Version (1611) was produced. In 1540, Rogers enrolled at the University of Wittenberg, where he became close friends with Philipp Melanchthon.* During his three years at Wittenberg, Rogers was a superintendent of the Lutheran Church in northern Germany. When Rogers returned to England in 1548, he published a translation of Melanchthon's *Considerations of the Augsburg Interim*, and later served in a variety of ecclesiastical roles. Rogers was burned at the stake for heresy during the reign of Mary Tudor on February 4, 1555.

Nehemiah Rogers (1593–1660). Anglican priest. After studying at Cambridge, Rogers ministered at numerous parishes during his more than forty-year career. In 1643, he seems to have been forced out of a parish on account of being a Royalist and friend of William Laud.* Rogers published a number of sermons and tracts, including a series of expositions on Jesus' parables in the Gospels.

Richard Rogers (1550?–1618). English Presbyterian minister. Rogers spent much of his career as lecturer at Wethersfield, Essex, where he was well-known as a Nonconformist. His writings, which include an introduction to the Christian life and a commentary on the book of Judges, demonstrate his Puritan leanings.

Thomas Rogers (d. 1616). Anglican theologian and translator. Rogers attended Christ Church, Oxford, where he completed his BA degree in 1573 and MA in 1576. Later he served as rector of Horrigner in Suffolk, and chaplain to Archbishop of Canterbury, Richard Bancroft. He died at Horringer and was buried in his church. Among his many works were an exposition of the Thirty-Nine Articles as well as a paraphrase of the Psalms and a translation of Niels Hemmingsen's commentary on Psalm 84.

Robert Rollock (c. 1555–1599). Scottish Reformed pastor, educator and theologian. Rollock was deeply influenced by Petrus Ramus's* system of logic, which he implemented as a tutor and (later) principal of Edinburgh University and in his expositions of the Bible. Rollock, as a divinity professor and theologian, was instrumental in diffusing a federalist Calvinism in the Scottish church; he lectured on theology using the texts of Theodore Beza* and articulated a highly covenantal interpretation of the biblical narratives. He was a prolific writer of sermons, expositions, commentaries, lectures and occasional treatises.

David Runge (1564–1604). German Lutheran theologian. First appointed professor of Hebrew at the University of Greifswald, Runge supported and later replaced his father in teaching philosophy and theology. After receiving his doctorate, he was named to the theological faculty at Wittenberg, where he also served as dean and rector of the university.

Johann Rurer (1480–1542) German Lutheran pastor. Rurer was court chaplain to Margrave Casimir of Brandenberg–Kulmbach (1481–1527), and the first Protestant pastor in Ansbach. Conflict over church order and his desire for reform led to his expulsion, but he was recalled after Casimir's death by his successor, George (1484–1543), who sought a throughgoing Lutheran reformation of the town and appointed Rurer preacher at the collegiate church.

Samuel Rutherford (1600–1661). Scottish Reformed theologian. Rutherford was born in Nisbet, Roxburghshire. After completing his early education at Jedborough, Rutherford enrolled at the University of Edinburgh, where he received his MA degree in 1621. In 1623, Rutherford was appointed professor of humanities at Edinburgh. Two years later, he was dismissed from his position on account of misbehavior with the woman who would later be his wife. Sometime after this incident, he underwent a spiritual conversion. In 1625, Rutherford commenced the study of theology at Edinburgh. Upon finishing his studies, Rutherford was called to pastor a church in Antwoth by Solway in Kirkcudbrightshire. Throughout his ministry, Rutherford proved to be an ardent opponent to episcopacy. For this, he was summoned to appear before the Court of High Commission in 1630. Despite the court's warnings to cease and desist, Rutherford continued his nonconformity. Rutherford also participated extensively in the Arminian controversy, writing treatises against Arminius as well as the Jesuits. Since Rutherford's virulent opposition to Arminianism placed him in direct opposition with the English episcopacy, he was once again summoned by the Court of High Commission in 1636. After a three-day trial, Rutherford was deprived of his ministerial office and ordered not to preach anywhere in Scotland. Meanwhile he was confined to Aberdeen. In 1638, when the National Covenant was signed and Presbyterianism restored in Scotland, Rutherford left Aberdeen and assumed the post of professor of theology at St. Mary's College, St. Andrews. Later, Rutherford served as a commissioner to the Westminster Assembly, where he contributed to the discussions related to the Shorter Catechism. In 1647, Rutherford returned to Scotland, where he was appointed principal of St. Mary's College, and rector of the university in 1651. After the monarchy was restored, Rutherford was charged with treason, and deprived of all his ecclesiastical and university positions. He died on March 30, 1661. Throughout his career, Rutherford published many sermons and theological works, most famous of which is *Lex Rex* (The law is king), a treatise arguing against the divine right of kings.

Jacopo Sadoleto (1477–1547). Italian Catholic Cardinal. Sadoleto, attaché to Leo X's court, was appointed bishop in 1517, cardinal in 1536. He participated in the reform commission led by Gasparo Contarini.* However, he tried to reconcile with Protestants apart from the commission, sending several letters to Protestant leaders in addition to his famous letter to the city of Geneva, which John Calvin* pointedly answered. Sadoleto published a commentary on Romans that was censored as semi-Pelagian. His insufficient treatment of prevenient grace left him vulnerable to this charge. Sadoleto emphasized grammar as the rule and norm of exegesis.

Alfonso Salmerón (1515–1585). Spanish Catholic exegete and theologian. While studying at the Sorbonne, Salmerón met Ignatius Loyola (1491–1556) and, with five others, took a vow of poverty and service to church and pope. After ministering in France, the group traveled to Rome, where they were given papal approval to form the Society of Jesus. Salmerón helped write the constitutions of the order, and following the priorities of the Jesuits, spent much of his career focused on education. He lectured throughout Italy, served

briefly on the faculty of the University of Ingolstadt, and, in Naples, founded one of the first Jesuit colleges. He also undertook a number of missions as a papal emissary and served as a papal theologian at all three meetings of the Council of Trent. His primary works are his commentaries on the New Testament, which cover the Gospels, Acts, and Paul's letters.

Heinrich Salmuth (1522–1576). German Lutheran theologian. After earning his doctorate from the University of Leipzig, Salmuth served in several coterminous pastoral and academic positions. He was integral to the reorganization of the University of Jena. Except for a few disputations, all of Salmuth's works—mostly sermons— were published posthumously by his son.

Robert Sanderson (1587–1663). Anglican bishop and philosopher. Before his appointment as professor of divinity at Oxford in 1642, Sanderson pastored in several parishes. Because of his loyalty to the Crown during the English Civil Wars, the Parliamentarians stripped Sanderson of his post at Oxford. After the Restoration he was reinstated at Oxford and consecrated bishop. He wrote an influential textbook on logic.

Edwin Sandys (1519–1588). Anglican bishop. During his doctoral studies at Cambridge, Sandys befriended Martin Bucer.* Having supported the Protestant Lady Jane Grey's claim to the throne, Sandys resigned his post at Cambridge upon Mary I's accession. He was then arrested and imprisoned in the Tower of London. Released in 1554, he sojourned on the continent until Mary's death. On his return to England he was appointed to revise the liturgy and was consecrated bishop. Many of his sermons were published, but his most significant literary legacy is his work as a translator of the Bishop's Bible (1568), which served as the foundational English text for the translators of the King James Bible (1611).

Erasmus Sarcerius (1501–1559). German Lutheran superintendent, educator and pastor. Sarcerius served as educational superintendent, court preacher and pastor in Nassau and, later, in Leipzig. The hallmark of Sarcerius's reputation was his ethical emphasis as exercised through ecclesial oversight and family structure; he also drafted disciplinary codes for regional churches in Germany. Sarcerius served with Philipp Melanchthon* as Protestant delegates at the Council of Trent, though both withdrew prior to the dismissal of the session; he eventually became an opponent of Melanchthon, contesting the latter's understanding of the Eucharist at a colloquy in Worms in 1557.

Michael Sattler (c. 1490–1527). Swiss Radical leader. Sattler was a Benedictine monk who abandoned the monastic life during the upheavals of the Peasants' War. He took up the trade of weaving under the guidance of an outspoken Anabaptist. It seems that Sattler did not openly join the Anabaptist movement until after the suppression of the Peasants' War in 1526. Sattler interceded with Martin Bucer* and Wolfgang Capito* for imprisoned Anabaptists in Strasbourg. Shortly before he was convicted of heresy and executed, he wrote the definitive expression of Anabaptist theology, the Schleitheim Articles.*

Girolamo Savonarola (1452–1498). Italian Catholic preacher and martyr. Outraged by clerical corruption and the neglect of the poor, Savonarola traveled to preach against these abuses and to prophesy impending judgment—a mighty king would scourge and reform the church. Savonarola thought that the French invasion of Italy in 1494 confirmed his apocalyptic visions. Thus he pressed to purge Florence of vice and institute public welfare, in order to usher in a new age of Christianity. Florence's refusal to join papal resistance against the French enraged Alexander VI (r. 1492–1503). He blamed Savonarola, promptly excommunicating him and threatening Florence with an interdict. After an ordeal by fire turned into a riot, Savonarola was arrested. Under torture he admitted to charges of conspiracy and false prophecy; he was hanged and burned. In addition to numerous sermons and letters, he wrote meditations on Psalms 31 and 51 as well as *The Triumph of the Cross* (1497).

Leupold Scharnschlager (d. 1563). Austrian Radical elder. See *Kunstbuch*.

Leonhard Schiemer (d. 1528) Austrian radical martyr. Troubled by the hypocrisies he experienced, Scheimer left the Franciscan order and spent a period of time wandering. Attracted to the teachings of Hans Hut* after hearing him debate Balthasar Hubmaier* in Moravia, he was rebaptized and traveled widely throughout Austria and Southern Germany, spreading the Anabaptist message until he was arrested in Rattenberg, where he was condemned to death and beheaded. A number of his essays and hymns survive, dispersed among the *Kunstbuch** and other collections of radical writings.

Hans Schlaffer (c. 1490–1528). Austrian Radical martyr. Drawn by Luther's theology, Schlaffer resigned his priesthood in 1526 only to turn to Anabaptism soon afterward. While contemporaries recognized his ability as a preacher, he never settled in a ministry position. He spent time among Radical congregations in Freistadt, Nicholsburg, Augsburg, Nuremberg, and Regensburg before his arrest in Schatz, where he was executed. Nine writings by Schlaffer remain, most of which were composed during his imprisonment. They include confessions of his beliefs and devotional works, which have been preserved among Hutterite churches.

Schleitheim Articles (1527). After the death of Conrad Grebel* in 1526 and the execution of Felix Manz (born c. 1498) in early 1527, the young Swiss Anabaptist movement was in need of unity and direction. A synod convened at Schleitheim under the chairmanship of Michael Sattler,* which passed seven articles of Anabaptist distinctives—likely defined against both magisterial reformers and other Anabaptists with less orthodox and more militant views (e.g., Balthasar Hubmaier*). Unlike most confessions, these articles do not explicitly address traditional creedal interests; they explicate instead the Anabaptist view of the sacraments, church discipline, separatism, the role of ministers, pacifism and oaths. Throughout the document there is a resolute focus on Christ's example. Also referred to as the Schleitheim Confession and the Schleitheim Brotherly Union, the Schleitheim Articles are considered the definitive statement of Anabaptist theology, particularly regarding separatism.

Schmalkald Articles (1537). In response to Pope Paul III's (1468–1549) 1536 decree ordering a general church council to solve the Protestant crisis, Elector John Frederick (1503–1554) commissioned Martin Luther* to draft the sum of his teaching. Intended by Luther as a last will and testament—and composed with advice from well-known colleagues Justus Jonas,* Johann Bugenhagen,* Caspar Cruciger,* Nikolaus von Amsdorf (1483–1565), Georg Spalatin (1484–1545), Philipp Melanchthon* and Johann Agricola*—these articles provide perhaps the briefest and most systematic summary of Luther's teaching. The document was not adopted formally by the Lutheran Schmalkald League, as was hoped, and the general church council was postponed for several years (until convening at Trent in 1545). Only in 1580 were the articles officially received, by being incorporated into the *Book of Concord* defining orthodox Lutheranism.

Sebastian Schmidt (1617–1696). German Lutheran theologian. After serving as pastor in Entzheim and rector of the high school in Lindau, Schmidt became professor of theology at Strasbourg. His body of writings is extensive and includes commentaries on many of the Pauline letters, Hebrews, John, and Jeremiah.

Dietrich Schnepff (1525–1586). German Lutheran pastor and theologian. Schnepff taught briefly at the city school in Tübingen while working toward his theological doctorate before taking pastorates in Derendingen and Nürtingen. Returning to Tübingen as professor of theology, Schnepff also took on additional roles as rector of the university and pastor of the Collegiate Church.

Anna Maria van Schurman (1607–1678). Dutch Reformed polymath. Van Schurman cultivated talents in art, poetry, botany, linguistics and theology. She mastered most contemporary European languages, in addition to Latin, Greek, Hebrew, Arabic, Farsi and Ethiopian. With the encouragement of leading Reformed theologian

Gisbertus Voetius (1589–1676), van Schurman attended lectures at the University of Utrecht—although she was required to sit behind a wooden screen so that the male students could not see her. In 1638 van Schurman published her famous treatise advocating female scholarship, *Amica dissertatio . . . de capacitate ingenii muliebris ad scientias*. In addition to these more polemical works, van Schurman also wrote hymns and poems, including a paraphrase of Genesis 1–3. Later in life she became a devotee of Jean de Labadie (1610–1674), a former Jesuit who was also expelled from the Reformed church for his separatist leanings. Her *Eucleria* (1673) is the most well known defense of Labadie's theology.

Kaspar von Schwenckfeld (1489–1561). German Radical reformer. Schwenckfeld was a Silesian nobleman who encountered Luther's* works in 1521. He traveled to Wittenberg twice: first to meet Luther and Karlstadt,* and a second time to convince Luther of his doctrine of the "internal word"—emphasizing inner revelation so strongly that he did not see church meetings or the sacraments as necessary—after which Luther considered him heterodox. Schwenckfeld won his native territory to the Reformation in 1524 and later lived in Strasbourg for five years until Bucer* sought to purify the city of less traditional theologies. Schwenckfeld wrote numerous polemical and exegetical tracts.

Scots Confession (1560). In 1560, the Scottish Parliament undertook to reform the Church of Scotland and to commission a Reformed confession of faith. In the course of four days, a committee—which included John Knox*—wrote this confession, largely based on Calvin's* work, the Confession of the English Congregation in Geneva (1556) and the Gallic Confession.* The articles were not ratified until 1567 and were displaced by the Westminster Confession (1646), adopted by the Scottish in 1647.

Abraham Scultetus (1566–1625). Silesian Reformed theologian. Scultetus spent the majority of his career in service of the Palatinate, holding a number of pastoral roles before becoming court preacher to Elector Frederic V (1596–1632). Appointed professor of theology at Heidelberg in 1618, he represented the Palatinate at the Synod of Dordrecht* (1618–1619), where he opposed the theology of the Remonstrants. Scultetus is often vilified for encouraging Reformed Frederic V to take the crown of Lutheran Bohemia, an act that led to war and the defeat of Frederic V, but his exegetical, historical, and pastoral teachings nevertheless garnered significant respect from his contemporaries.

Second Helvetic Confession (1566). Believing he would soon die, Heinrich Bullinger* penned a personal statement of his Reformed faith in 1561 as a theological will. In 1563, Bullinger sent a copy of this confession, which blended Zwingli's and Calvin's theology, to the elector of the Palatinate, Frederick III (1515–1576), who had asked for a complete explication of the Reformed faith in order to defend himself against aggressive Lutheran attacks after printing the Heidelberg Confession.* Although not published until 1566, the Second Helvetic Confession became the definitive sixteenth-century Reformed statement of faith. Theodore Beza* used it as the organizing confession for his *Harmonia Confessionum* (1581), which sought to emphasize the unity of the Reformed churches. Bullinger's personal confession was adopted by the Reformed churches of Scotland (1566), Hungary (1567), France (1571) and Poland (1571).

Obadiah Sedgwick (c. 1600–1658). English Puritan minister. Educated at Oxford, Sedgwick pastored in London and participated in the Westminster Assembly. An ardent Puritan, Sedgwick was appointed by Oliver Cromwell (1599–1658) to examine clerical candidates. Sedgwick published a catechism, several sermons and a treatise on how to deal with doubt.

Nikolaus Selnecker (1530–1592). German Lutheran theologian, preacher, pastor and hymnist. Selnecker taught in Wittenberg, Jena and Leipzig, preached in Dresden and Wolfenbüttel, and pastored in Leipzig. He was forced out of his post at Jena because of suspicions that he was a crypto-Calvinist. He sought refuge in Wolfenbüttel, where he met Martin Chemnitz* and Jakob Andreae.* Under their influence Selnecker was drawn away from Philippist theology. Selnecker's shift in theology can be seen in his *Institutio religionis christianae* (1573). Selnecker coauthored the Formula of Concord* with Chemnitz, Andreae, Andreas Musculus (1514–1581), and David Chytraeus.* Selnecker also published lectures on Genesis, the Psalms, and the New Testament epistles, as well as composing over a hundred hymn tunes and texts.

Short Confession (1610). In response to some of William Laud's* reforms in the Church of England—particularly a law stating that ministers who refused to comply with the Book of Common Prayer* would lose their ordination—a group of English Puritans immigrated to the Netherlands in protest, where they eventually embraced the practice of believer's baptism. The resulting Short Confession was an attempt at union between these Puritans and local Dutch Anabaptists ("Waterlanders"). The document highlights the importance of love in the church and reflects optimism regarding the freedom of the will while explicitly rejecting double predestination.

Richard Sibbes (1577–1635). English Puritan preacher. Sibbes was educated at St. John's College, Cambridge, where he was converted to reforming views and became a popular preacher. As a moderate Puritan emphasizing interior piety and brotherly love, Sibbes always remained within the established Church of England, though opposed to some of its liturgical ceremonies. His collected sermons constitute his main literary legacy.

Menno Simons (c. 1496–1561). Dutch Radical leader. Simons led a separatist Anabaptist group in the Netherlands that would later be called Mennonites, known for nonviolence and renunciation of the world. A former priest, Simons rejected Catholicism through the influence of Anabaptist disciples of Melchior Hoffmann and based on his study of Scripture, in which he found no support for transubstantiation or infant baptism. Following the sack of Anabaptists at Münster, Simons committed to a nonviolent way of life. Simons proclaimed a message of radical discipleship of obedience and inner purity, marked by voluntary adult baptism and communal discipline.

Henry Smith (c. 1550–1591). English Puritan minister. Smith stridently opposed the Book of Common Prayer* and refused to subscribe to the Articles of Religion,* thus limiting his pastoral opportunities. Nevertheless he gained a reputation as an eloquent preacher in London. He published sermon collections as well as several treatises.

John Smyth (d. 1612). English Baptist minister. Ordained as an Anglican clergyman, Smyth served as a lecturer in Lincoln, but left the established church for a separatist congregation in Gainsborough. Moving to Amsterdam, he began to follow the teachings of Jacobus Arminius* and led a group to break away from the English Reformed congregation, undertake rebaptism, and form their own church. He soon decided he did not have the authority to establish a church and baptize, but trying to lead his congregation on another course saw him excommunicated with a number of his close followers. This smaller group was rejected when they attempted to join a Mennonite congregation, and so were forced to form another congregation, which dissolved after Smyth's death. Smyth wrote a number of the earliest English treatises expressing Baptist principles including *The Differences of the Churches of the Separation* (1608) and *The Character of the Beast* (1609). He also wrote a reflection on the Lord's Prayer, *A Paterne of True Prayer* (1605).

Domingo de Soto (1494–1560). Spanish Catholic theologian. Soto taught philosophy for four years at the University in Alcalá before entering the Dominican order. In 1532 he became chair of theology at the University of Salamanca; Soto sought to reintroduce Aristotle in the curriculum. He served as confessor and spiritual advisor to Charles V, who enlisted Soto as imperial theologian for the Council of Trent. Alongside commentaries on the works of Aristotle and Peter Lombard (c. 1100–1160), Soto commented on Romans and wrote an influential treatise on nature and grace.

Fausto Sozzini (1539–1604). Italian theologian. Without a formal education, Sozzini used his inherited wealth to travel widely throughout Europe after his family came under the suspicion of the Inquisition for Lutheranism. Spending time in Lyons, Zurich, and Geneva, he published his first work, an explanation of the prologue to John's Gospel, claiming Christ was not divine, but a human worthy of respect due his divinely appointed office. Returning to Italy, Sozzini served at the Florentine court of Isabella de Medici (1542–1576) for more than a decade, departing for Basel, then Transylvania and Poland after her death. His thoroughgoing rationalism saw him elevate human reason over divine revelation and traditional doctrine. He rejected the doctrine of the Trinity and Nicene orthodoxy, instead arguing that Christ was not divine and did not make atonement for humanity, but rather served as a model of victory over death for all people.

Cyriacus Spangenberg (1528–1604). German Lutheran pastor, preacher and theologian. Spangenberg was a staunch, often acerbic, Gnesio-Lutheran. He rejected the Formula of Concord* because of concerns about the princely control of the church, as well as its rejection of Flacian language of original sin (as constituting the "substance" of human nature after the fall). He published many commentaries and sermons, most famously seventy wedding sermons (*Ehespiegel* [1561]), his sermons on Luther* (*Theander Luther* [1562–1571]) and Luther's hymns (*Cithara Lutheri* [1569–1570]). He also published an analysis of the Old Testament (though he only got as far as Job), based on a methodology that anticipated the logical bifurcations of Peter Ramus.*

Johann Spangenberg (1484–1550). German Lutheran pastor and catechist. Spangenberg studied at the University of Erfurt, where he was welcomed into a group of humanists associated with Konrad Muth (1470–1526). There he met the reformer Justus Jonas,* and Eobanus Hessius (1488–1540), whom Luther* dubbed "king of the poets." Spangenberg served at parishes in Stolberg (1520–1524),

Nordhausen (1524–1546) and, by Luther's recommendation, Eisleben (1546–1550). Spangenberg published one of the best-selling postils of the sixteenth century, the *Postilla Teütsch*, a six-volume work meant to prepare children to understand the lectionary readings. It borrowed the question-answer form of Luther's *Small Catechism* and was so popular that a monk, Johannes Craendonch, purged overt anti-Catholic statements from it and republished it under his own name. Among Spangenberg's other pastoral works are *ars moriendi* ("the art of dying") booklets, a postil for the Acts of the Apostles and a question-answer version of Luther's *Large Catechism*. In addition to preaching and pastoring, Spangenberg wrote pamphlets on controversial topics such as purgatory, as well as textbooks on music, mathematics and grammar.

John Spilsbury (1593–1668). English Baptist pastor. A cobbler by trade, Spilsbury left congregationalism to found the first Particular Baptist church in London, teaching a theology that attempted to fuse Reformed teachings on the covenant and particular atonement with the Anabaptist demand for adult baptism upon confession of faith. He composed a number of works on baptism and may have been an author of the 1644 London Baptist Confession of Faith.

Georg Spindler (1525–1605). German Reformed theologian and pastor. After studying theology under Caspar Cruciger* and Philipp Melanchthon,* Spindler accepted a pastorate in Bohemia. A well-respected preacher, Spindler published postils in 1576 which some of his peers viewed as crypto-Calvinist. To investigate this allegation Spindler read John Calvin's* *Institutes*, and subsequently converted to the Reformed faith. After years of travel, he settled in the Palatinate and pastored there until his death. In addition to his Lutheran postils, Spindler also published Reformed postils in 1594 as well as several treatises on the Lord's Supper and predestination.

Statenvertaling (1637). The Synod of Dordrecht* commissioned this new Dutch translation of the Bible ("State's Translation"). The six theologians who undertook this translation also wrote prefaces for each biblical book, annotated obscure words and difficult passages, and provided cross-references; they even explained certain significant translation decisions. At the request of the Westminster Assembly, Theodore Haak (1605–1690) translated the *Statenvertaling* into English as *The Dutch Annotations Upon the Whole Bible* (1657).

John Stalham (d. 1681). English Puritan minister. Stalham likely ministered in Edinburgh before becoming vicar of Terling in Essex. An opponent of Quakerism who sought to remove disreputable ministers from their pulpits, Stalham himself lost his position with the 1662 Act of Uniformity, leading him to found a congregational church in the same village.

Johann von Staupitz (d. 1524). German Catholic theologian, professor and preacher. Frederick the Wise summoned this Augustinian monk to serve as professor of Bible and first dean of the theology faculty at the University of Wittenberg. As Vicar-General of the Reformed Augustinian Hermits in Germany, Staupitz sought to reform the order and attempted unsuccessfully to reunite with the conventional Augustinians. While in Wittenberg, Staupitz was Martin Luther's* teacher, confessor and spiritual father. He supported Luther in the early controversies over indulgences, but after releasing Luther from his monastic vows (to protect him), he distanced himself from the conflict. He relocated to Salzburg, where he was court preacher to Cardinal Matthäus Lang von Wellenburg (d. 1540) and abbot of the Benedictine monastery. Staupitz wrote treatises on predestination, faith and the love of God. Many of his sermons were collected and published during his lifetime.

Peter Sterry (d. 1672). English Puritan theologian. Associated with the Cambridge Platonists, Sterry was closely aligned with the Parliamentarians during the English Civil War, serving as chaplain to Robert Greville (1607–1643) and Oliver Cromwell.* After the execution of Charles I, he was appointed preacher to the Council of State and asked to examine its ministers. Cast out from influence after Cromwell's death, Sperry spent the last years of his career writing and tutoring private students.

Petrus Stevartius (1549–1624). German Catholic theologian. A Jesuit, Stevartius spent most of his career as professor of exegesis at the University of Ingolstadt, also serving as rector and procurator. He also established a library for the school and an orphanage in the city. His writings include commentaries on most Pauline letters and James and a defense of the Jesuits.

Michael Stifel (1486–1567). German Lutheran mathematician, theologian and pastor. An Augustinian monk, Stifel's interest in mysticism, apocalypticism and numerology led him to identify Pope Leo X as the antichrist. Stifel soon joined the reform movement, writing a 1522 pamphlet in support of Martin Luther's* theology. After Luther quelled the fallout of Stifel's failed prediction of the Apocalypse—October 19, 1533 at 8 a.m.—Stifel focused more on mathematics and his pastoral duties. He was the first professor of mathematics at the University of Jena. He published several numerological interpretations of texts from the Gospels, Daniel and Revelation. However, Stifel's most important work is his *Arithmetica Integra* (1544), in which he standardized the approach to quadratic equations. He also developed notations for exponents and radicals.

John Stoughton (1593?–1639). English Puritan minister. Stoughton pastored at Aller in Somerset and St. Mary Aldermanbury in the city of London. A Puritan, he was briefly arrested by Archbishop Laud, accused of financially supporting the Puritan cause. A collection of his sermons and other writings was published after his death.

Viktorin Strigel (1524–1569). German Lutheran theologian. Strigel taught at Wittenberg, Erfurt, Jena, Leipzig and Heidelberg. During his time in Jena he disputed with Matthias Flacius (1520–1575) over the human will's autonomy. Following Philipp Melanchthon,* Strigel asserted that in conversion the human will obediently cooperates with the divine will through the Holy Spirit and the Word of God. In the Weimar Disputation (1560), Strigel elicited Flacius's opinion that sin is a substance that mars the formal essence of human beings. Flacius's views were officially rejected in Article 1 of the Formula of Concord*; Strigel's, in Article 2. In 1567 the University of Leipzig suspended Strigel from teaching on account of suspicions that he affirmed Reformed Eucharistic theology; he acknowledged that he did and joined the Reformed confession on the faculty of the University of Heidelberg. In addition to controversial tracts, Strigel published commentaries on the entire Bible (except Lamentations) and the Apocrypha.

William Strode (1602–1645). English Anglican minister, dramatist, and poet. A Royalist and an opponent of Puritanism, Strode spent most of his life around Oxford, where he studied and then served as a public orator and canon of Christ Church. A popular poet, he also preached a number of times before the king and had a number of his plays performed at court.

William Strong (d. 1654). English Independent minister. Forced to leave his ministry in Dorset by Royalists during the Civil War, Strong built a reputation as a preacher in London, ministering to an independent congregation at St. Dunstan's-in-the-West. Many of his sermons were published, as well as treatises on communion with God and the covenants.

Johann Sutell (1504–1575). German Lutheran pastor. After studying at the University of Wittenberg, Sutell received a call to a pastorate in Göttingen, where he eventually became superintendent. He wrote new church orders for Göttingen (1531) and Schweinfurt (1543), and expanded two sermons for publication, *The Dreadful Destruction of Jerusalem* (1539) and *History of Lazarus* (1543).

Swiss Brethren Confession of Hesse (1578). Anabaptist leader Hans Pauly Kuchenbecker penned this confession after a 1577 interrogation by Lutheran authorities. This confession was unusually amenable to Lutheran views—there is no mention of pacifism or rejection of oath taking.

Synod of Dordrecht (1618–1619). This large Dutch Reformed Church council—also attended by English, German and Swiss delegates—met to settle the theological issues raised by the followers of Jacobus Arminius.* Arminius's theological disagreements with mainstream Reformed teaching erupted into open conflict with the publication of the *Remonstrance* (1610). This "protest" was based on five points: that election is based on foreseen faith or unbelief; that Christ died indiscriminately for all people (although only believers receive salvation); that people are thoroughly sinful by nature apart from the prevenient grace of God that enables their free will to embrace or reject the gospel; that humans are able to resist the working of God's grace; and that it is possible for true believers to fall away from faith completely. The Synod ruled in favor of the Contra-Remonstrants, its Canons often remembered with a TULIP acrostic—total depravity, unconditional election, limited atonement, irresistible grace, perseverance of the saints—each letter countering one of the five Remonstrant articles. The Synod also officially accepted the Belgic Confession,* Heidelberg Catechism* and the Canons of Dordrecht as standards of the Dutch Reformed Church.

Arcangela Tarabotti (1604–1652) Italian Catholic nun. At the age of eleven, Tarabotti entered a Benedictine convent as a student-boarder; three years later her father forced her to take monastic vows. The dignity of women and their treatment in the male-controlled institutions of early modern Venice concerned Tarabotti deeply. She protested forced cloistering, the denial of education to women, the exclusion of women from public life and the double standards by which men and women were judged. Tarabotti authored numerous polemical works and an extensive correspondence.

Johannes Tauler (c. 1300–1361) German mystical theologian. A Dominican friar and disciple of Meister Eckhart (c. 1260–c. 1328), Tauler spent most of his career as a mendicant preacher in Strasburg and Basel. Known through a collection of about eighty German sermons, Tauler taught a practical spirituality, accessible to those outside the cloister and intended to draw his audience to deeper contemplation of the divine nature.

Richard Taverner (1505–1575). English Puritan humanist and translator. After graduating from Oxford, Taverner briefly studied abroad. When he returned to England, he joined Thomas Cromwell's (1485–1540) circle. After Cromwell's beheading, Taverner escaped severe punishment and retired from public life during Mary I's reign. Under Elizabeth I,* Taverner served as justice of the peace, sheriff and a licensed lay preacher. Taverner translated many important continental Reformation works into English, most notably the Augsburg Confession* and several of Desiderius Erasmus's* works. Some of these translations—John Calvin's* 1536 catechism, Wolfgang Capito's* work on the Psalms and probably Erasmus Sarcerius's* postils— he presented as his own work. Underwritten by Cromwell, Taverner also published an edited version of the Matthew Bible (1537).

Jeremy Taylor (1613–1667) Anglican theologian, preacher, and author. Son of a barber, Taylor studied at Cambridge before the patronage of Archbishop Laud* drew him into the work of the English church. After serving as chaplain to Laud and King Charles I (1600–1649), he entered parish ministry. Following the outbreak of the Civil War (1642–51), his commitment to the Royalist cause saw him imprisoned at least three times. Withdrawing to Wales, he ran a school preparing students for university while serving as chaplain to the earl of Carbery. Known for his skill as a writer, it was here that Taylor composed many of his best known works, including his popular devotional manuals, *The Rules and Exercises of Holy Living* (1650), and *The Rules and Exercises of Holy Dying* (1651). After the Restoration, Taylor was made Bishop of Down and Connor in Ireland and served as vice-chancellor of the University of Dublin.

Thomas Taylor (1576–1633). English Puritan pastor. Taylor ministered in Watford and Reading before becoming minister at St. Mary Aldermanbury in the city of London. He wrote more than fifty works on diverse topics, including a commentary on

Titus, a response to the Gunpowder Plot, and an explanation of the role of the law under the gospel. **Thomas Taylor** (1576–1632). Puritan minister and commentator. Taylor was born in Richmond, Yorkshire. He was educated at Christ's College, Cambridge, where he earned the degrees of Bachelor of Arts (1595) and Master of Arts (1598). Prior to entering pastoral ministry, Taylor served as a fellow and lecturer in Hebrew at the university. Throughout his academic career, Taylor was significantly influenced by the writings of William Perkins.* At the age of twenty-five, Taylor preached a virulent sermon against the papacy before Queen Elizabeth I.* As a Puritan, Taylor denounced the ecclesiastical policies of Archbishop Richard Bancroft.* In 1612, Taylor became minister of a church in Watford, Hertfordshire. While serving this charge, Taylor preached regularly in Berkshire and Reading. Moreover, Taylor formed and led a Puritan seminary, where he personally trained Nonconformist preachers. In the early 1620s, Taylor served as a chaplain to Edward Conway (1564–1631), secretary of state under James VI/I* (1566–1625). In 1625, Taylor was called to be curate and lecturer at St. Aldermanbury, London. While there, he organized and ran another Puritan seminary. Two years later, Taylor joined several other Puritans' efforts to send relief to oppressed Reformed ministers on the Continent. Taylor retired from his labors in 1630 due to ill health. He died of pleurisy in 1632. His main works include *Christ Revealed; or The Old Testament Explained* and *An Exposition of Titus.*

Teresa of Ávila (1515–1582). Spanish monastic reformer and mystical theologian. Born into a wealthy merchant family, Teresa entered the Carmelite order at Ávila in 1535. While Teresa initially enjoyed the lax practices of the convent, reading devotional literature caused her to deepen her spirituality, and in 1555 she began to have visions of God and claimed to have mystical union with him. Convinced the monastic life required complete withdrawal, Teresa could no longer tolerate the practices of her Carmelite cloister and founded the Discalced Carmelites with John of the Cross* (1542–1591) in 1562, which was committed to enclosure and strict asceticism. By her death, she had personally founded fourteen houses for her new order despite significant resistance from Carmelite leaders. She also wrote extensively. Her best-known works are *The Way of Perfection* (1577), a method for the contemplative life, and *The Interior Castle* (1577), a manual for spiritual growth.

Thirty-Nine Articles. See *Articles of Religion.*

Thomas Thorowgood (1595–1669). English Puritan pastor. Thorowgood was a Puritan minister in Norfolk and the chief financier of John Eliot (1604–1690), a Puritan missionary among the Native American tribes in Massachusetts. In 1650, under the title *Jews in America, or, Probabilities that Americans be of that Race*, Thorowgood became one of the first to put forward the thesis that Native Americans were actually the ten lost tribes of Israel.

John Tillinghast (1604–1655). English Puritan minister. Tillinghast began his ministry in the Church of England, pastoring two congregations in Sussex until he moved to London and became an independent, leading him to pastor Puritan congregations in Suffolk and Norfolk. He was a member of the Fifth Monarchists, a millenarian Puritan sect that believed the political upheaval of their time was ushering in the kingdom of Christ.

Frans Titelmans (1502–1537). Belgian Catholic philosopher. Titelmans studied at the University of Leuven, where he was influenced by Petrus Ramus.* After first joining a Franciscan monastery, Titelmans realigned with the stricter Capuchins and moved to Italy. He is best known for his advocacy for the Vulgate and his debates with Desiderius Erasmus* over Pauline theology (1527–1530)—he was deeply suspicious of the fruits of humanism, especially regarding biblical studies. His work was published posthumously by his brother, Pieter Titelmans (1501–1572).

Francisco de Toledo (1532–1596). Spanish Catholic theologian. This important Jesuit taught philosophy at the universities of Salamanca and Rome. He published works on Aristotelian philosophy and a commentary on Thomas Aquinas's* work, as well as biblical commentaries on John, Romans and the first half of Luke. He was also the general editor for the Clementine Vulgate (1598).

John Tombes (1603–1676). English Baptist pastor. After leaving Oxford, Tombes held many pastoral positions in Anglican churches throughout the Midlands until founding a Baptist church in Bewdley, Worcestershire. He left this congregation following a debate with Richard Baxter,* leading him to take on a number of pastoral positions in Herefordshire while continuing to seek public debates and writing against Quakerism and Roman Catholicism.

Laurence Tomson (1539–1608). English Reformed politician and translator. Tomson was born in Northhamptonshire and educated at Magdalen College, Oxford. He graduated with his BA degree (1559) and MA degree (1564). Tomson was a fellow at Magdalen until he resigned in 1569. Prior to this resignation, Tomson was part of a diplomatic delegation to France. From 1575 to 1587, Tomson served in the House of Commons and attended the royal court at Windsor in 1582. He went on further embassies throughout Europe, where he occasionally lectured on Hebrew. Tomson died on March 29, 1608. Tomson's chief exegetical contribution was his revised text and annotations of the New Testament of the Geneva Bible.

Edward Topsell (d. 1638?). English Protestant minister. Topsell held a number of pastoral posts in Sussex, Dorset, and the Midlands before being appointed perpetual curate of St. Botolph's, Aldersgate, in the city of London. While he composed a number of religious works, including his lectures on Ruth, which were so popular they appeared in three editions, he is primarily remembered for his two illustrated works on natural history, which cataloged four-footed animals and serpents.

Alonso Tostado (1400–1455). Spanish Catholic bishop and exegete. Tostado lectured on theology, law and philosophy at the University of Salamanca, in addition to ministering in a local parish. Tostado entered into disputes over papal supremacy and the date of Christ's birth. Tostado's thirteen-volume collected works include commentaries on the historical books of the Old Testament and the Gospel of Matthew.

Daniel Toussain (1541–1602). Swiss Reformed pastor and professor. Toussain became pastor at Orléans after attending college in Basel. After the third War of Religion, Toussain was exiled, eventually returning to Montbéliard, his birthplace. In 1571, he faced opposition there from the strict Lutheran rulers and was eventually exiled due to his influence over the clergy. He returned to Orléans but fled following the Saint Bartholomew's Day Massacre (1572), eventually becoming pastor in Basel. He relocated to Heidelberg in 1583 as pastor to the new regent, becoming professor of theology at the university, and he remained there until his death.

John Trapp (1601–1669). Anglican biblical exegete. After studying at Oxford, Trapp entered the pastorate in 1636. During the English Civil Wars he sided with Parliament, which later made it difficult for him to collect tithes from a congregation whose royalist pastor had been evicted. Trapp published commentaries on all the books of the Bible from 1646 to 1656.

Immanuel Tremellius (1510–1580). Italian Reformed Hebraist. Around 1540, Tremellius received baptism by Cardinal Reginald Pole (1500–1558) and converted from Judaism to Christianity; he affiliated with evangelicals the next year. On account of the political and religious upheaval, Tremellius relocated often, teaching Hebrew in Lucca; Strasbourg, fleeing the Inquisition; Cambridge, displaced by the Schmalkaldic War; Heidelberg, escaping Mary I's persecutions; and Sedan, expelled by the new Lutheran Elector of the Palatine. Many considered Tremellius's translation of the Old Testament as the most accurate available. He also published a Hebrew grammar and translated John Calvin's* catechism into Hebrew.

Richard Turnbull (d. 1593). English minister. A preacher in London, Richard Turnbull published sermons on James, Jude, and Psalm 15.

William Tyndale (Hychyns) (1494–1536).
English reformer, theologian and translator.
Tyndale was educated at Oxford University, where
he was influenced by the writings of humanist
thinkers. Believing that piety is fostered through
personal encounter with the Bible, he asked to
translate the Bible into English; denied permission, Tyndale left for the Continent to complete
the task. His New Testament was the equivalent
of a modern-day bestseller in England but was
banned and ordered burned. Tyndale's theology
was oriented around justification, the authority of
Scripture and Christian obedience; Tyndale
emphasized the ethical as a concomitant reality of
justification. He was martyred in Brussels before
completing his English translation of the Old
Testament, which Miles Coverdale* finished.

John Udall (1560?–1592). English Puritan pastor.
Udall began his pastoral career in the Anglican
parish of Kingston-upon-Thames, becoming
known for his preaching and Puritan convictions,
particularly his rejection of the episcopacy. While
facing discipline for his views, he published
anonymous and pseudonymous pamphlets critical
of the established church alone and with friends,
leading to his losing his position in London and
relocating to Newcastle, where he continued in
ministry and criticism. Udall was arrested under
suspicion of complicity in publishing the critical
tracts and, unwilling to deny that he wrote them,
was convicted and sentenced to death. The death
sentence was not carried out, however, and he
remained in prison almost two years until
pardoned, but died soon after release.

Guillaume du Vair (1556–1621). French Catholic
priest, lawyer, and writer. While du Vair took holy
orders in his youth, much of his life was spent
serving the state as a counselor of the parliament
of Paris, a representative of King Henry IV both
in France and abroad, and as Keeper of the Seals,
the highest legal office in the country. The last
four years of his life were spent as the bishop of
Lisieux. His studies on Epictetus and the Stoics,
and attempts to relate Stoicism to the Christian
faith, were influential in the dissemination of this
philosophy during the seventeenth and eighteenth
centuries. He also wrote significant works on
politics, the moral life, prayer, and the use and
abuse of the French language.

Juan de Valdés (1500/10–1541). Spanish
Catholic theologian and writer. Although Valdés
adopted an evangelical doctrine, had Erasmian
affiliations and published works that were listed
on the Index of Prohibited Books, Valdés rebuked
the reformers for creating disunity and never left
the Catholic Church. His writings included
translations of the Hebrew Psalter and various
biblical books, a work on the Spanish language
and several commentaries. Valdés fled to Rome in
1531 to escape the Spanish Inquisition and worked
in the court of Clement VII in Bologna until the
pope's death in 1534. Valdés subsequently
returned to Naples, where he led the reform- and
revival-minded Valdesian circle.

Henry Vaughan (1617/1618–1661). English
Protestant preacher. Possibly a student at Christ's
College, Cambridge, Vaughan published a sermon
on Matthew 5:20 given to the House
of Commons.

Thomas Venatorius (c. 1490–1551). German
Lutheran theologian, mathematician, and
humanist. Following a humanistic education,
Venatorius spent the majority of his career in
Nuremberg, where he advocated for reform as the
head of the city's school system and as a preacher
and pastor in the city's churches. His theological
and pastoral works include one of the first
Protestant works on ethics, a short catechism, and
a commentary on 1 Timothy. He also edited the
first Greek edition of Archimedes's writings and
translated Aristophanes's *Plutus*.

Peter Martyr Vermigli (1499–1562). Italian
Reformed humanist and theologian. Vermigli
was one of the most influential theologians of the
era, held in common regard with such figures as
Martin Luther* and John Calvin.* In Italy,
Vermigli was a distinguished theologian, preacher
and advocate for moral reform; however, during
the reinstitution of the Roman Inquisition
Vermigli fled to Protestant regions in northern

Europe. He was eventually appointed professor of divinity at Oxford University, where Vermigli delivered acclaimed disputations on the Eucharist. Vermigli was widely noted for his deeply integrated biblical commentaries and theological treatises.

Matthieu Virel (fl. 1561–1595). French Reformed pastor and theologian. Only two episodes from Virel's life are known: he preached the reformation message at Namur in 1561, and sixteen years later he pastored a French congregation in Basel. He published two known works: an excursus on the calendar and a brief summary of the Christian religion.

Pierre Viret (1511–1571). Swiss Reformed pastor and teacher. Converted to Protestantism at the University of Paris, Viret returned to his hometown, Orbe, where Guillaume Farel* brought him into ministry. Preaching also at Payerne and Neuchâtel, Viret's success in spreading the Reformed faith led to an assassination attempt before he and Farel sought to reform Geneva. Soon after the Genevan Assembly voted to accept the Reformation, Viret relocated to Lausanne, where he established the Reformed faith, served as chief pastor, and founded a Reformed academy. After almost twenty-five years, he was exiled from the city, spending a short time pastoring and teaching in Geneva until establishing himself in southern France, where he brought the evangelical faith to Lyons, pastored, and served as an advisor to Jeanne d'Albret, the queen of Navarre (1528–1572).

Juan Luis Vives (1492?–1540). Spanish Catholic humanist. Born into a Jewish family but baptized Catholic, Vives spent most of his life outside Spain following the persecution of his family by the Inquisition. After studying in Paris, he lived in Bruges, where he became part of the intellectual circle around Erasmus,* and taught at Oxford toward the end of his life. Vives largely avoided entering into religious controversies, and his works received a mixed reception from both Catholics and Protestants. He is best known for his educational and social writings, including an influential Latin primer, works on pedagogy and

women's education, and arguments for pacifism and poor relief.

Gisbertus Voetius (1589–1676). Dutch Reformed theologian. Voetius pastored at Vlijmen and Heusden and served as the youngest delegate at the Synod of Dordrecht* before becoming professor of theology and Oriental languages at the University of Utrecht. While Voetius's writings demonstrate concern for missions, practical piety, and personal purity, he also entered into numerous theological controversies during his career. His Reformed commitments led to ongoing conflicts with Arminians and Catholics, and he sought to uphold the importance of the Old Testament against Johannes Cocceius's (1603–1669) formulation of the covenants. He also entered into debate with René Descartes (1596–1650) and his followers, arguing from an Aristotelian perspective that to accept Cartesian skepticism was to reject biblical truth and the Christian tradition.

Conradus Vorstius (1569–1622). Dutch Arminian-Socinian theologian. A student of David Paraeus* and Johannes Piscator,* Vorstius's Socinian tendencies emerged during his tenure as professor of theology at Steinfurt. After an apology and examination, he was allowed to replace Arminius* as professor of theology at Leiden though never permitted to teach, as his questioning of the doctrine of atonement and the eternity, foreknowledge, and omnipresence of God drew wide censure, ultimately from King James I of England.* Exiled to Gouda and deposed at the Synod of Dordrecht,* Vorstius published numerous theological works and a commentary on the Pauline letters.

Vulgate. In 382 Pope Damasus I (c. 300–384) commissioned Jerome (c. 347–420) to translate the four Gospels into Latin based on Old Latin and Greek manuscripts. Jerome completed the translation of the Gospels and the Old Testament around 405. It is widely debated how much of the rest of the New Testament was translated by Jerome. During the Middle Ages, the Vulgate became the Catholic Church's standard Latin translation. The Council of Trent recognized it as the official text of Scripture.

George Walker (1581–1651). Puritan minister. Walker was born at Hawkshead, Lancashire, and educated at St. John's College, Cambridge. After graduating Cambridge, Walker moved to London, where he became rector of St. John the Evangelist on Watling Street in 1614. He served this parish for nearly forty years. Throughout his ministry, Walker showed himself to be an ardent opponent of the papacy and practices within the Church of England that he deemed not sufficiently reformed. Toward this end, Walker engaged numerous disputations and literary debates with both conformists and Catholics. For his sermons that were critical of the Church of England, he was summoned to appear before Archbishop Laud in 1635 and the Star Chamber in 1638, which fined and imprisoned him for twelve weeks. On another occasion, Walker was incarcerated for as long as two years for his nonconformity until released by the Long Parliament. In 1643, Walker was selected to serve in the Westminster Assembly and to participate in the trial of Laud. Walker died in London. Among his many published sermons and polemical works is a treatise on justification.

Thomas Walkington (d. 1621). Anglican minister and author. Born in Lincoln, he was educated at Cambridge, graduating with his BA in 1597 and his MA in 1600. Walkington was elected a fellow at St. John's College, Cambridge, in 1602. Later, he received a BD from Oxford and a DD from Cambridge. He served as rector of parishes in Northamptonshire, Lincolnshire, and Middlesex. A prolific author, Walkington published works on diverse subjects. Among his biblical works are *An Exposition of the First Two Verses of the Sixth Chapter to the Hebrews in form of a Dialogue* (1609) and *Theologicall Rules to Guide Us in the Understanding and Practice of Holy Scripture* (1615).

Peter Walpot (d. 1578). Moravian Radical pastor and bishop. Walpot was a bishop of the Hutterite community after Jakob Hutter, Peter Riedemann* and Leonhard Lanzenstiel. Riedemann's *Confes-sion of Faith* (1545; 1565) became a vital authority for Hutterite exegesis, theology and morals. Walpot added his own *Great Article Book* (1577), which collates primary biblical passages on baptism, communion, the community of goods, the sword and divorce. In keeping with Hutterite theology, Walpot defended the community of goods as a mark of the true church.

Richard Ward (c. 1601–1684). English Anglican pastor. Educated at Cambridge and St. Andrews, Ward pastored in London and Essex. His published writings include a commentary on Matthew and an explanation of the Solemn League and Covenant (1643), which allied Scottish Covenanters and English Parliamentarians during the First English Civil War (1642–1646).

Thomas Watson (d. 1686). English Puritan pastor. After graduating from Cambridge, Watson became pastor of St. Stephen Walbrook in the city of London, a pulpit he served for twenty years, though he was imprisoned for a year for his part in the plot of Christopher Love (1618–1651) to restore Charles II to the throne. A well-respected preacher, Watson was expelled from official ministry by the 1662 Act of Uniformity, though he continued to preach in private until his retirement. While Watson published many sermons and devotional works, he is perhaps best known for *A Body of Divinity* (1692), a series of sermon on the Westminster Catechism.

Valentin Weigel (1533–1588). German Lutheran pastor. Weigel studied at Leipzig and Wittenberg, entering the pastorate in 1567. Despite a strong anti-institutional bias, he was recognized by the church hierarchy as a talented preacher and compassionate minister of mercy to the poor. Although he signed the Formula of Concord,* Weigel's orthodoxy was questioned so openly that he had to publish a defense. He appears to have tried to synthesize several medieval mystics with the ideas of Sebastian Franck,* Thomas Müntzer* and others. His posthumously published works have led some recent scholars to suggest that Weigel's works may have deeply influenced later Pietism.

Hieronymus Weller von Molsdorf (1499–1572). German Lutheran theologian. Originally intending to study law, Weller devoted himself to theology after hearing one of Martin Luther's* sermons on the catechism. He boarded with Luther and tutored Luther's son. In 1539 he moved to Freiburg, where he lectured on the Bible and held theological disputations at the Latin school. In addition to hymns, works of practical theology and a postil set, Weller published commentaries on Genesis, 1–2 Samuel, 1–2 Kings, Job, the Psalms, Christ's passion, Ephesians, Philippians, 1–2 Thessalonians and 1–2 Peter.

Westminster Assembly (1643–1652). English church council. Called by English Parliament to advise on church reform, the Westminster Assembly was made up of more than 120 clergymen, thirty parliamentary observers, and a delegation from the Church of Scotland. Beginning with a review of the Articles of Religion,* the most heated debates were undertaken over ecclesiology, as factions argued for presbyterianism, congregationalism, Erastianism, and episcopalianism, with the council ultimately recommending presbyterianism to the parliament. Much of the legacy of the assembly is held in the major documents it produced, the *Directory for Public Worship* (1644), *The Form of Presbyterial Church Government* (1645), the *Westminster Confession of Faith* (1646), the *Shorter Catechism* (1647), and the *Larger Catechism* (1648), which became foundational for the English and Scottish churches and many of the Reformed denominations.

John Whitgift (1530–1604). Anglican archbishop. Though Whitgift shared much theological common ground with Puritans, after his election as Archbishop of Canterbury (1583) he moved decisively to squelch the political and ecclesiastical threat they posed during Elizabeth I's* reign. Whitgift enforced strict compliance to the Book of Common Prayer,* the Act of Uniformity (1559) and the Articles of Religion.* Whitgift's policies led to a large migration of Puritans to Holland. The bulk of Whitgift's published corpus is the fruit of a lengthy public disputation with Thomas Cartwright,* in which Whitgift defines Anglican doctrine against Cartwright's staunch Puritanism.

Johann Wigand (1523–1587). German Lutheran theologian. Wigand is most noted as one of the compilers of the *Magdeburg Centuries*, a German ecclesiastical history of the first thirteen centuries of the church. He was a student of Philipp Melanchthon* at the University of Wittenburg and became a significant figure in the controversies dividing Lutheranism. Strongly opposed to Roman Catholicism, Wigand lobbied against innovations in Lutheran theology that appeared sympathetic to Catholic thought. In the later debates, Wigand's support for Gnesio-Lutheranism established his role in the development of confessional Lutheranism. Wigand was appointed bishop of Pomerania after serving academic posts at the universities in Jena and Königsburg.

Thomas Wilcox (c. 1549–1608). English Puritan theologian. In 1572, Wilcox objected to Parliament against the episcopacy and the Book of Common Prayer,* advocating for presbyterian church governance. He was imprisoned for sedition. After his release, he preached itinerantly. He was brought before the courts twice more for his continued protest against the Church of England's episcopal structure. He translated some of Theodore Beza* and John Calvin's* sermons into English, and he wrote polemical and occasional works as well as commentaries on the Psalms and Song of Songs.

Johann (Ferus) Wild (1495–1554). German Catholic pastor. After studying at Heidelberg and teaching at Tübingen, this Franciscan was appointed as lector in the Mainz cathedral, eventually being promoted to cathedral preacher—a post for which he became widely popular but also controversial. Wild strongly identified as Catholic but was not unwilling to criticize the curia. Known for an irenic spirit—criticized in fact as *too* kind—he was troubled by the polemics between all parties of the

Reformation. He preached with great lucidity, integrating the liturgy, Scripture and doctrine to exposit Catholic worship and teaching for common people. His sermons on John were pirated for publication without his knowledge; the Sorbonne banned them as heretical. Despite his popularity among clergy, the majority of his works were on the Roman Index until 1900.

Andrew Willet (1562–1621). Anglican priest, professor, and biblical expositor. Willet was a gifted biblical expositor and powerful preacher. He walked away from a promising university career in 1588 when he was ordained a priest in the Church of England. For the next thirty-three years he served as a parish priest. Willet's commentaries summarized the present state of discussion while also offering practical applications for preachers. They have been cited as some of the most technical commentaries of the early seventeenth century. His most important publication was *Synopsis Papismi, or a General View of Papistrie* (1594), in which he responded to many of Robert Bellarmine's critiques. After years of royal favor, Willet was imprisoned in 1618 for a month after presenting to King James I* his opposition to the "Spanish Match" of Prince Charles to the Infanta Maria. While serving as a parish priest, he wrote forty-two works, most of which were either commentaries on books of the Bible or controversial works against Catholics.

Thomas Wilson (d. 1586). English Anglican priest. A fellow of St John's, Cambridge, Wilson fled to Frankfurt to escape the Marian Persecution. After his return to England, he served as a canon and Dean of Worcester.

George Wither (1588–1667). English poet, satirist, and hymn writer. Wither was born in Bentworth, Hampshire. After finishing his early education under the tutelage of a local minister, Wither continued his studies at Magdalen College, Oxford. Afterward, he studied law at the Inns of Chancery. Wither commenced his literary career with the publication of an elegy on the occasion of the death of Henry Frederick, Prince of Wales (1594–1612). Most of Wither's literary works

consist of satirical pamphlets for which he was regularly arrested, imprisoned, and released. He fought in the Parliamentary Army during the Civil War. A conforming Anglican, Wither composed numerous hymns as well as translations of the Psalms. Two of Wither's major works are *Preparation to the Psalter* (1619), in which he explores various literary aspects of the Bible, and *Hymns and Songs of the Church* (1622/1623). He died in London.

John Woolton (c. 1535–1594). Anglican bishop. After graduating from Oxford, Woolton lived in Germany until the accession of Elizabeth I.* He was ordained as a priest in 1560 and as a bishop in 1578. Woolton published many theological, devotional and practical works, including a treatise on the immortality of the soul, a discourse on conscience and a manual for Christian living.

John Wycliffe (c. 1330–1384). English theologian, philosopher, and reformer known as "the Morning Star of the Reformation." While holding benefices from a number of parishes, Wycliffe spent the majority of his career at Oxford, where he studied, taught, and served as head of Balliol College. His early work focused on logic and metaphysics, but after entering into the service of John of Gaunt, Duke of Lancaster (1340–1399) and serving as a royal envoy to discuss taxes with papal representatives, Wycliffe turned his attention to more practical concerns. His criticism of papal power and wealth drew initially civil and ecclesiastical approval, but application of his principle that any headship profiting the governor rather than the governed is illegitimate to the English church brought controversy and censure. This criticism increased as he rejected transubstantiation, criticized monasticism, argued along Augustinian lines that only the invisible body of the elect constituted the true church, that Scripture belongs to the body of the elect rather than the institutional church, and that as many leaders of the visible church were likely reprobate, their offices and sacraments were invalid. While dismissed from Oxford in 1381, powerful defenders protected Wycliffe from further consequences during his lifetime, but he was condemned as a heretic at the Council of Constance (1515), whence he was exhumed and his remains burned. While largely condemned by contemporaries, Wycliffe, and his followers, the Lollards, are often viewed as forerunners of the Reformation who prepared the way for the tumult of the sixteenth century.

Girolamo Zanchi (1516–1590). Italian Reformed theologian and pastor. Zanchi joined an Augustinian monastery at the age of fifteen, where he studied Greek and Latin, the church fathers and the works of Aristotle and Thomas Aquinas.* Under the influence of his prior, Peter Martyr Vermigli,* Zanchi also imbibed the writings of the Swiss and German reformers. To avoid the Inquisition, Zanchi fled to Geneva where he was strongly attracted to the preaching and teaching of John Calvin.* Zanchi taught biblical theology and the *locus* method at academies in Strasbourg, Heidelberg, and Neustadt. He also served as pastor of an Italian refugee congregation. Zanchi's theological works, *De tribus Elohim* (1572) and *De natura Dei* (1577), have received more attention than his commentaries. His commentaries comprise about a quarter of his literary output, however, and display a strong typological and christological interpretation in conversation with the church fathers, medieval exegetes, and other reformers.

Katharina Schütz Zell (1497/98–1562). German Reformed writer. Zell became infamous in Strasbourg and the Empire when in 1523 she married the priest Matthias Zell, and then published an apology defending her husband against charges of impiety and libertinism. Longing for a united church, she called for toleration of Catholics and Anabaptists, famously writing to Martin Luther* after the failed Marburg Colloquy of 1529 to exhort him to check his hostility and to be ruled instead by Christian charity. Much to the chagrin of her contemporar-

ies, Zell published diverse works, ranging from polemical treatises on marriage to letters of consolation, as well as editing a hymnal and penning an exposition of Psalm 51.

Martha Elizabeth Zitter (Unknown). German Catholic nun. Zitter entered the Ursuline convent in Erfurt during her teenage years. Most of what is known about her is drawn from a letter she composed to her mother, explaining her decision to leave the order and become Lutheran, which focuses on aspects of her vows and Roman Catholic piety she believes to be unbiblical. Despite this public departure from the Roman church, however, Zitter returned toward the end of her life.

Ulrich Zwingli (1484–1531). Swiss Reformed humanist, preacher and theologian. Zwingli studied at the University of Vienna, and afterwards the University of Basel, where he received his BA and MA in 1504 and 1506. Ordained in September 1506, Zwingli became priest of the church in Glarus where he taught himself Greek, and read deeply in the church fathers. During this period, Zwingli was also greatly impacted by the writings of Desiderius Erasmus*. In 1516, Zwingli accepted the position of priest at the Benedictine Abbey at Einsiedeln in Schwyz, where he intently studied the Greek New Testament, and learned Hebrew. When he became a preacher in the city cathedral at Zurich, Zwingli enacted reform through sermons, public disputations, and conciliation with the town council, abolishing the Mass and images in the church. Zwingli broke with the lectionary preaching tradition, instead preaching serial expository biblical sermons. He later was embroiled in controversy with Anabaptists over infant baptism and with Martin Luther* at the Marburg Colloquy (1529) over their differing views of the Eucharist. Zwingli, serving as chaplain to Zurich's military, was killed in the Second Battle of Kappel.

SOURCES FOR
BIOGRAPHICAL SKETCHES

General Reference Works

Allgemeine Deutsche Biographie. 56 vols. Leipzig: Duncker & Humblot, 1875–1912; reprint, 1967–1971. Accessible online via deutsche-biographie.de/index.html.

Baskin, Judith R., ed. *The Cambridge Dictionary of Judaism and Jewish Culture.* New York: Cambridge University Press, 2011.

Benedetto, Robert, ed. *The New Westminster Dictionary of Church History.* Vol. 1. Louisville: Westminster John Knox Press, 2008.

Bettenson, Henry and Chris Maunder, eds. *Documents of the Christian Church.* 3rd ed. Oxford: Oxford University Press, 1999.

Betz, Hans Dieter, Don Browning, Bernd Janowski and Eberhard Jüngel, eds. *Religion Past & Present: Encyclopedia of Theology and Relgion.* 13 vols. Leiden: Brill, 2007–2013.

Bremer, Francis J. and Tom Webster, eds. *Puritans and Puritanism in Europe and America: A Comprehensive Encyclopedia.* 2 vols. Santa Barbara, CA: ABC-CLIO, 2006.

Gritsch, Eric W. *A History of Lutheranism.* Minneapolis: Fortress Press, 2002.

Haag, Eugene and Émile Haag. *La France protestante ou vies des protestants français.* 2nd ed. 6 vols. Paris: Sandoz & Fischbacher, 1877–1888.

Hillerbrand, Hans J., ed. *Oxford Encyclopedia of the Reformation.* 4 vols. New York: Oxford University Press, 1996.

Kolb, Robert, and Timothy J. Wengert, eds. *The Book of Concord: The Confessions of the Evangelical Lutheran Church.* Translated by Charles Arand et al. Minneapolis: Fortress, 2000.

McKim, Donald K., ed. *Dictionary of Major Biblical Interpreters.* Downers Grove, IL: InterVarsity Press, 2007.

Müller, Gerhard, et al., ed. *Theologische Realenzyklopädie.* Berlin: Walter de Gruyter, 1994.

Neue Deutsche Biographie. 28 vols. projected. Berlin: Duncker & Humblot, 1953–. Accessible online via deutsche-biographie.de/index.html.

New Catholic Encyclopedia. 15 vols. New York: McGraw-Hill, 1967; 2nd ed., Detroit: Thomson-Gale, 2002.

Oxford Dictionary of National Biography. 60 vols. Oxford: Oxford University Press, 2004.

Pelikan, Jaroslav. *The Christian Tradition.* 5 vols. Chicago: University of Chicago Press, 1971–1989.

Stephen, Leslie, and Sidney Lee, eds. *Dictionary of National Biography.* 63 vols. London: Smith, Elder and Co., 1885–1900.

Terry, Michael, ed. *Reader's Guide to Judaism.* New York: Routledge, 2000.

Wordsworth, Christopher, ed. *Lives of Eminent Men connected with the History of Religion in England.* 4 vols. London: J. G. & F. Rivington, 1839.

Additional Works for Individual Sketches

Akin, Daniel L. "An Expositional Analysis of the Schleitheim Confession." *Criswell Theological Review* 2 (1988): 345–70.

Astell, Mary. *The Christian Religion, as Professed by a Daughter of the Church of England.* Edited by Jacqueline Broad. Toronto: Iter Inc and the Center for Reformation and Renaissance Studies, 2013.

Bald, R. C. *John Donne: A Life.* Oxford: Oxford University Press, 1970.

Beeke, Joel, and Randall J. Pederson. *Meet the Puritans.* Grand Rapids: Reformation Heritage Books, 2006.

Bireley, Robert, *The Refashioning of Catholicism, 1450–1700,* Washington, DC: Catholic University of America Press, 1999.

Blok, P. J., and P. C. Molhuysen, eds. *Nieuw Nederlandsch Biografisch Woordenboek.* 10 vols.

Brackney, William H. *A Genetic History of Baptist Thought: With Special Reference to Baptists in Britain and North America.* Atlanta: Mercer University Press, 2004.

———. *Historical Dictionary of the Baptists.* 2nd ed. Lanham, MD: Scarecrow, 2009.

Brook, Benjamin. *The Lives of the Puritans*. 3 vols. London: James Black, 1813. Reprint, Pittsburgh, PA: Soli Deo Gloria, 1994.

Brown, Peter. *Augustine of Hippo: A Biography*. Berkeley & Los Angeles, CA: University of California Press, 1967.

Burke, David G. "The Enduring Significance of the KJV." *Word and World* 31, no. 3 (2011): 229-44.

Campbell, Gordon. *Bible: The Story of the King James Version, 1611–2011*. Oxford: Oxford University Press, 2010.

Cathcart, William. *The Baptist Encyclopaedia*. 3 vols. Philadelphia: Louis H. Everts, 1881.

Charles, Amy. *A Life of George Herbert*. Ithaca, NY: Cornell University Press, 1977.

Christian, Jacob. *The Sovereign Map: Theoretical Approaches to Cartography Throughout History*. Chicago: University of Chicago Press, 2006.

Coffey, John. *Politics, Religion, and the British Revolutions: The Thought of Samuel Rutherford*. Cambridge: Cambridge University Press, 1997.

Colish, Marcia. *Peter Lombard*, 2 vols. Leiden, Netherlands: Brill, 1993.

Culpepper, Scott. *Francis Johnson and the English Separatist Influence: The Bishop of Brownism's Life, Writings, and Controversies*. Macon, GA: Mercer University Press, 2011.

Doornkaat Koolman, J ten. "The First Edition of Peter Riedemann's 'Rechenschaft.'" *Mennonite Quarterly Review* 36, no. 2 (1962): 169-70.

Emerson, Everett H. *John Cotton*. New York: Twayne, 1990.

Fischlin, Daniel and Mark Fortier, eds. *Royal Subjects: Essays on the Writings of James VI and I*. Detroit: Wayne State University Press, 2002.

Fishbane, Michael A. "Teacher and the Hermeneutical Task: A Reinterpretation of Medieval Exegesis." *Journal of the American Academy of Religion 43*, no. 4 (1975): 709-21.

Friedmann, Robert. "Second Generation Anabaptism as Illustrated by the Walpot Era of the Hutterites." *Mennonite Quarterly* 44, no. 4 (1970): 390-93.

Frymire, John M. *The Primacy of the Postils: Catholics, Protestants, and the Dissemination of Ideas in Early Modern Germany*. Leiden: Brill, 2010.

Furcha, Edward J. "Key Concepts in Caspar von Schwenckfeld's Thought, Regeneration and the New Life." *Church History* 37, no. 2 (1968): 160-73.

Gordon, Bruce, *The Swiss Reformation*. Manchester: Manchester University Press, 2002.

Greaves, Richard L. *Society and Religion in Elizabethan England*. Minneapolis: University of Minnesota, 1981.

Greiffenberg, Catharina Regina von. *Meditations on the Incarnation, Passion, and Death of Jesus Christ*. Edited and translated by Lynne Tatlock. The Other Voice in Early Modern Europe. Chicago: University of Chicago Press, 2009.

Grendler, Paul. "Italian biblical humanism and the papacy, 1515-1535." In *Biblical Humanism and Scholasticism in the Age of Erasmus*. Edited by Erika Rummel, 225-76. Leiden: Brill, 2008.

Haemig, Mary Jane. "Elisabeth Cruciger (1500?–1535): The Case of the Disappearing Hymn Writer." *Sixteenth Century Journal* 32, no. 1 (2001): 21-44.

Harpley, W., ed. *Report and Transactions of the Devonshire Association for the Advancement of Science, Literature and Art* 24 (July 1882). Plymouth: William Brendon and Son, 1892.

Heiden, Albert van der. "Pardes: Methodological Reflections on the Theory of the Four Senses." *Journal of Jewish Studies* 34, no. 2 (1983): 147-59.

Hendrix, Scott H., ed. and trans. *Early Protestant Spirituality*. New York: Paulist Press, 2009.

Hvolbek, Russell H. "Being and Knowing: Spiritualist Epistelmology and Anthropology from Schwenckfeld to Böhme." *Sixteenth Century Journal* 22, no. 1 (1991): 97-110.

Kahle, Paul. "Felix Pratensis—a Prato, Felix. Der Herausgeber der Ersten Rabbinerbibel, Venedig 1516/7." *Die Welt des Orients* 1, no. 1 (1947): 32-36.

Kelly, Joseph Francis. *The Ecumenical Councils of the Catholic Church: A History*. Collegeville, MN: Liturgical Press, 2009.

Koop, Karl, ed. *Confessions of Faith in the Anabaptist Tradition 1527–1660*. Translated by Cornelius J. Dyck et al. CRR 11. Kitchener, ON: Pandora Press, 2006.

Lake, Peter. *The Boxmaker's Revenge: "Orthodoxy", "Heterodox" and the Politics of the Parish in Early Stuart London*. Stanford, CA: Stanford University Press, 2001.

Lane, Anthony N. S. *Calvin and Bernard of Clairvaux*. Princeton, NJ: Princeton Theological Seminary, 1996.

Lane, Belden C. *Ravished by Beauty: The Surprising Legacy of Reformed Spirituality*. Oxford: Oxford University Press, 2011.

Lee, Jason K. *The Theology of John Smyth* (Macon, GA: Mercer University Press, 2003).

Lockhart, Paul Douglas. *Frederick II and the Protestant Cause: Denmark's Role in the Wars of Religion, 1559–1596*. Leiden: Brill, 2004.

Lubac, Henri de. *Medieval Exegesis: The Four Senses of Scripture.* 3 vols. Translated by Mark Sebanc and E. M. Macierowski. Grand Rapids: Eerdmans, 1998–2009.

Manetsch, Scott, *Calvin's Company of Pastors: Pastoral Care and the Emerging Reformed Church, 1536–1609.* Oxford: Oxford University Press, 2013.

Manschreck, Clyde Leonard. *Melanchthon, the Quiet Reformer.* New York: Abingdon, 1958.

Marinella, Lucrezia. *The Nobility and Excellence of Women and the Defects and Vices of Men.* Edited and translated by Anne Dunhill. Chicago: University of Chicago Press, 1999.

Matheson, Peter, *Argula von Grumbach: A Woman's Voice in the Reformation.* Edinburgh: T&T Clark, 1995.

McGuire, Daniel Patrick. *The Difficult Saint: Bernard of Clairvaux and his Tradition.* Collegeville, MN: Cistercian Publication, 1991.

McKinley, Mary B. "Volume Editor's Introduction." In *Epistle to Marguerite of Navarre and Preface to a Sermon by John Calvin,* edited and translated by Mary B. McKiney. Chicago: University of Chicago Press, 2004.

M'Crie, Thomas. *The Life of Andrew Melville.* 2 vols. Edinburgh: William Blackwood, 1819.

Norton, David. *A Textual History of the King James Bible.* New York: Cambridge University Press, 2005

Nuttall, Geoffrey. *The Welsh Saints, 1640–1660: Walter Cradock, Vavasor Powell, Morgan Llwyd.* Cardiff: University of Wales Press, 1957.

Oberman, Heiko A. *Luther: Man Between God and the Devil.* New York, NY: Doubleday, 1989.

O'Meara, Thomas F. *Albert the Great: Theologian and Scientist.* Chicago: New Priory Press, 2013.

Packull, Werner O. "The Origins of Peter Riedemann's Account of Our Faith." *Sixteenth Century Journal* 30, no. 1 (1999): 61-69.

Papazian, Mary Arshagouni, ed. *John Donne and the Protestant Reformation: New Perspectives.* Detroit: Wayne State University Press, 2003.

Paulicelli, Eugenia. "Sister Arcangela Tarabotti: Hair, Wigs and Other Vices." In *Writing Fashion in Early Modern Italy: From Sprezzatura to Satire,* by idem, 177-204. Farnham, Surrey, UK: Ashgate, 2014.

Pragman, James H. "The Augsburg Confession in the English Reformation: Richard Taverner's Contribution." *Sixteenth Century Journal* 11, no. 3 (1980): 75-85.

Rashi. *Rashi's Commentary on Psalms.* Translated by Mayer I. Gruber. Atlanta: Scholars Press, 1998.

Raynor, Brian. *John Frith: Scholar and Martyr.* Kent, UK: Pond View Books, 2000.

Reid, Jonathan A. *King's Sister—Queen of Dissent: Marguerite of Navarre (1492–1549) and her Evangelical Network.* Leiden: Brill, 2009.

Schmidt, Josef, "Introduction" in Johannes Tauler, *Sermons.* New York: Paulist Press, 1985, 1-34.

Smith, Hannah. "Mary Astell, *A Serious Proposal to the Ladies* (1694), and the Anglican Reformation of Manners in Late-Seventeenth-Century England." In *Mary Astell: Reason, Gender, Faith,* edited by William Kolbrenner and Michal Michelson, 31-48. New York: Routledge, 2007.

Spinka, Matthew. *John Hus: A Biography.* Princeton, NJ: Princeton University Press, 1968.

———. *John Hus at the Council of Constance.* New York: Columbia University Press, 1968.

———. *John Hus and the Czech Reform.* Hamden, CT: Archon Books, 1966.

Steinmetz, David C. *Reformers in the Wings: From Geiler von Kayserberg to Theodore Beza.* Oxford: Oxford University Press, 2000.

———. "The Superiority of Pre-Critical Exegesis." *Theology Today* 37, no. 1 (1980): 27-38.

Stjerna, Kirsi. *Women of the Reformation.* Malden, MA: Blackwell Publishing, 2009.

Synder, C. Arnold. "The Confession of the Swiss Brethren in Hesse, 1578." In *Anabaptism Revisited: Essays on Anabaptist/Mennonite Studies in Honor of C. J. Dyck.* Edited by Walter Klaassen, 29-49. Waterloo, ON; Scottdale, PA: Herald Press, 1992.

———. "The Schleitheim Articles in Light of the Revolution of the Common Man: Continuation or Departure?" *Sixteenth Century Journal* 16, no. 4 (1985): 419-30.

Thornton, Wallace. *John Foxe and His Monument: A Theological-Historical Perspective.* Birmingham, AL: Aldersgate Heritage Press, 2013.

Todd, Margo. "Bishops in the Kirk: William Cowper of Galloway and the Puritan Episcopacy of Scotland." *Scottish Journal of Theology,* 57 (2004): 300-312.

Tschackert, Paul. "Varel, Edo Hilderich of." In *General German Biography* (ADB). Volume 39. Leipzig: Duncker & Humblot, 1895.

Van Liere, Frans. *An Introduction to the Medieval Bible.* New York: Cambridge University Press, 2014.

Voogt, Gerrit. "Remonstrant-Counter-Remonstrant Debates: Crafting a Principled Defense of Toleration after the Synod of Dordrecht (1619–1650)." *Church History and Religious Culture* 89, no. 4 (2009): 489-524.

Wabuda, Susan. "Henry Bull, Miles Coverdale, and the Making of Foxe's Book of Martyrs." In *Martyrs and Martyrologies: Papers Read at the 1992 Summer Meeting and the 1993 Winter Meeting of the Ecclesiastical History Society*, edited by Diana Wood, 245-58. Oxford: Blackwell, 1993.

Wallace, Dewey D. Jr. "George Gifford, Puritan Propaganda and Popular Religion in Elizabethan England." *Sixteenth Century Journal* 9, no. 1 (1978): 27-49.

Wawrykow, Joseph P. *The Westminster Handbook to Thomas Aquinas*. Louisville, KY: Westminster John Knox, 2005.

Wendel, Francois. *Calvin: The Origins and Development of His Religious Thought*. New York: Harper & Row, 1963.

Wengert, Timothy J. "'Fear and Love' in the Ten Commandments." *Concordia Journal* 21, no. 1 (1995): 14-27.

Wiesner-Hanks, Merry, ed. *Convents Confront the Reformation: Catholic and Protestant Nuns in Germany*. Translated by Joan Skocir and Merry Wiesner-Hanks. Milwaukee: Marquette University Press, 1996.

———. "Philip Melanchthon and John Calvin against Andreas Osiander: Coming to Terms with Forensic Justification." In *Calvin and Luther: The Continuing Relationship*, edited by R. Ward Holder, 63-87. Göttingen: Vandenhoeck & Ruprecht, 2013.

Wilkinson, Robert J. *Tetragrammaton: Western Christians and the Hebrew Name of God*. Leiden: Brill, 2015.

Yarnell, Malcolm. "Christopher Blackwood: Exemplar of the Seventeenth-Century Particular Baptists." *Southwestern Journal of Theology* 57, no 2 (Spring 2015): 181-205.

BIBLIOGRAPHY

Adams, Thomas. *An Exposition upon the Second Epistle General of St. Peter*. London: R. Badger for J. Bloome, 1633. Digital copy online at hathitrust.org.

Allen, Robert. *The Doctrine of the Gospel by a Plaine and Familiar Interpretation*. London: Thomas Creede, 1606. Digital copy online at EEBO.

Andreae, Jakob. *Ein christliche Predig uber das Evangelion Matthei am 22. Cap. von Gesetz und der Person Christi*. Tübingen: Georgen Gruppenbach, 1578. Digital copy online at prdl.org.

———. *Ein christliche Predigt uber das Euangelium auff den xxv. Sontag nach Trinitatis Matthei am 24*. Leipzig: Hanß Steinman, 1578. Digital copy online at prdl.org.

Andrewes, Lancelot. *Ninety-Six Sermons by the Right Honourable and Reverend Father in God, Lancelot Andrewes*. 5 vols. Oxford and London: James Parker, 1841–1843. Digital copy online at books .google.com.

———. *The Wonderfull Combate (for God's Glory and Man's Salvation) Betweene Christ and Satan*. London: Iohn Charlwood for Richard Smith, 1592. Digital copy online at EEBO.

Babington, Gervase. *A Briefe Conference Betwixt Man's Frailtie and Faith Wherein Is Declared the True Vse, and Comfort of Those Blessings Pronounced by Christ in the Fifth of Matthew*. London: H. Middleton for T. Charde, 1584. Digital copy online at EEBO.

Baxter, Richard. *Making Light of Christ and Salvation, Too Oft the Issue of Gospel Invitations*. 2nd ed. London: R. White for Nevil Simmons, 1691. Digital copy online at EEBO.

Bernard, Richard. *The Good Man's Grace. Or His Stay in All Distresse*. London: F. Kingston, 1621. Digital copy online at EEBO.

Beza, Theodore. *The Bible and Holy Scriptures Contained* [an English translation of the Bible with marginal notes]. London: Christopher Barker, 1576.

———. *La Bible, qui est Toute La Saincte Escriture: Contenant le Vieil et le Nouveau Testament*. Geneva: Zacharie Durant, 1566.

———. *A Discourse of the True and Visible Markes of the Catholique Churche*. Translated by T. Wilcox. Third printing. London: For J. Deane, 1623.

———. *Theodori Bezae Annotationes majores in Novum Dn. Nostri Jesu Christi Testamentum. In duas distinctae partes, quarum prior explicationem in quatuor Evangelistas et Acta Apostolorum: Posterior vero in Epistolas et Apocalypsin continet. Quibus etiam adjuncti sunt indices rerum ac verborum locupletissimi*. Geneva: Jeremie des Planches, 1594. Digital copy online at prdl.org.

Blackwood, Christopher. *Expositions and Sermons upon the First Ten Chapters of the Gospel of Matthew*. London: Henry Hills for Francis Tyton and John Field, 1659. Digital copy online at EEBO.

———. *A Treatise Concerning Deniall of Christ: A Subject of Most High Concernment for All Those Who Intend to Follow Christ*. London: For Edward Blackmore, 1648. Digital copy online at EEBO.

Bolton, Samuel. *ΑΜΑΡΤΩΛΟΣ ΑΜΑΡΤΙΑ: Or, The Sinfulness of Sin*. London: G. M. for Andrew Kemb, 1646.

Bourchier, John. *Jesus Nazarenus, Rex Judaeorum. Or, a Tract Concerning the Inscription Fastened by Pilate's Command.* London: N. Okes, 1637. Digital copy online at EEBO.

Boys, John. *An Exposition of the Dominicall Epistles and Gospels Used in Our English Liturgie Throughout the Whole Yeare Together with a Reason Why the Church Did Chuse the Same.* London: F. Kingston for W. Aspley, 1610. Digital copy online at EEBO.

———. *The Third Part from St. John Baptist's Nativitie to the Last Holy Day in the Whole Yeere.* London: For William Aspley, 1615. Digital copy online at EEBO.

Bradford, John. *Godlie Meditations upon the Lordes Prayer, the Beleefe, and Ten Commaundementes with Other Comfortable Meditations, Praiers and Exercises.* London: R. Hall, 1562. Digital copy online at EEBO.

Bramley, David. *Christ's Result of His Father's Pleasure. Or His Assent to His Father's Sentence.* London, 1647. Digital copy online at EEBO.

Brenz, Johannes. *In Scriptum Apostolie et Evangelistae Matthaei de Rebus Gestis Domini Nostri Jesu Christi Commentarius.* Tübingen: Morhard, 1566. Digital copy online at prdl.org.

———. *Pericopae Evangeliorum, quae Singulis Diebus Dominicis Publicè in Ecclesia Recitari Solent.* Frankfurt am Main: Peter Braubach, 1556. Digital copy online at prdl.org.

Bridge, William. *Christ's Coming Opened in a Sermon.* London: For Peter Cole, 1648.

———. *The Works of William Bridge.* 3 vols. London: For Peter Cole, Printing Press in Cornhill, 1654. Digital copy online at EEBO.

Bridges, Walter. *Division Divided. Or, Ruines Fore-runner Discovered and Decyphered in a Sermon.* London: For Andrew Crooke, 1646. Digital copy online at EEBO.

Bromiley, G. W., ed. *Zwingli and Bullinger.* Edited by Geoffrey W. Bromiley. LCC 24. Louisville, KY: Westminster John Knox, 1953.

Broughton, Hugh. *The Holy Genealogie of Jesus Christ, Both His Naturall Line of Fathers, Which S. Luke Followeth, chap. 3, and His Kingly Line, Which S. Matthew Followeth, chap. 1, with Fit Notation of Their Names.* London: W. White, 1612. Digital copy online at EEBO.

Browne, Robert. *An Answere to Master Cartwright His Letter for Ioyning with the English Churche.* London, 1585. Digital copy online at EEBO.

Bucer, Martin. *In Sacra Quatuor Evangelia, Enarrationes Perpetuae.* Basel: Johann Herwagen, 1536. Digital copy online at prdl.org.

———. *The Judgement of Martin Bucer Concerning Divorce Written to Edward the Sixth, in His Second Book of the Kingdom of Christ, and Now English.* London: Matthew Simmons, 1644. Digital copy online at EEBO.

———. *The Mind and Exposition of That Excellent Learned Man Martin Bucer upon These Words of St. Matthew.* Emden, 1566. Digital copy online at EEBO.

Bugenhagen, Johannes. *In IIII. Priora Capita Euangelii Secundum Matthaeum.* Wittenberg: Joseph Klug, 1543.

———. *Selected Writings.* 2 vols. Edited by Kurt K. Hendel. Minneapolis: Fortress, 2015.

Bull, Henry. *Christian Praiers and Holie Meditations wel for Priuate as Publique Exercise.* London: H. Middleton, 1578. Digital copy online at EEBO.

Bullinger, Heinrich. *The Decades of Henry Bullinger.* Translated by H. I. Edited for the Parker Society by Thomas Harding. 4 vols. Cambridge: Cambridge University Press, 1849–1852. Digital copy online at books.google.com.

———. *In Sacrosanctum Iesu Christi Domini Nostri Evangelium Secundum Matthaeum Commentariorum Libri XII.* Zurich: Christoph Froschauer, 1546. Digital copy online at prdl.org.

———. *The Summe of the Foure Evangelists*. Translated by J. Tomkys. London: For W. Ponsonby, 1582.

Burroughs, Jeremiah. *A Sermon Preached Before the Honorable House of Commons Assembled in Parliament . . . August 26, 1646*. London: Matthew Simmons for Hanna Allen, 1646. Digital copy online at books.google.com.

Burton, William. *Ten Sermons upon the First, Second, Third and Fourth Verses of the Sixth of Matthew Containing Diverse, Necessary, and Profitable Treatises*. London: Richard Field for T. Man, 1602. Digital copy online at EEBO.

Cajetan, Cardinal (Thomas de Vio). *Evangelia cum Commentariis*. Paris: Roigny, 1532. Digital copy online at prdl.org.

Calvin, John. *Commentarius in Harmoniam Evangelicam*. CO 45. Edited by G. Baum, E. Cunitz and E. Reuss. Brunswick: C. A. Schwetschke, 1891. Digital copies online at archive-ouverte.unige.ch /unige:650.

———. *Commentary on a Harmony of the Evangelists: Matthew, Mark, and Luke*. 3 vols. CTS 31–33. Translated by William Pringle. Edinburgh: Calvin Translation Society, 1845–1846. Digital copies online at archive.org.

Capito, Wolfgang. *In Hoseam Prophetam V. F. Capitonis Commentarius*. Strasbourg: J. Hervagius, 1528. Digital copy online at prdl.org.

Carter, John. *A Plaine and Compendious Exposition of Christ's Sermon in the Mount Contayned in the 5, 6, and 7 chapters of Saint Matthew*. London: W. Sransby for S. Man, 1627. Digital copy online at books.google.com.

Cartwright, Thomas. *A Confutation of the Rhemists Translation, Glosses and Annotations on the New Testament*. Leiden: W. Brewster, 1618. Digital copy online at prdl.org.

Chemnitz, Martin. *De Duabus Naturis in Christo de Hypostatica Earum Unione: De Communicatione Idiomatum, et Aliis Quaestionibus inde Dependentibus*. Rev. ed. Jena: Typis Tobiae Steinmanni, 1589. Digital copy online at prdl.org.

———. *Harmoniae Evangelicae, a praestantiss . . . in Harmoniam Hist. Evangelicæ de Passione, Crvcifixione, Mort et, Sepvltvra Christi Salvatoris Nostri, ex Quatuor Euangelistis Contextam Commentarius Conscriptus*. Geneva: Sumptibus haeredum Iacobi Berjon, 1628.

———. *Loci theologici*. 2 vols. Translated by J. A. O. Preus. St. Louis: Concordia Publishing House, 1989.

———. *Ministry, Word, and Sacraments: An Enchiridion*. Edited and translated by Luther Poellot. St. Louis: Concordia Publishing House, 1981.

———. *A Substantial and Godly Exposition of the Praier Commonly Called the Lord's Praier*. Translated by John Legate. Cambridge: Cambridge University Press, 1598. Digital copy online at EEBO.

Chytraeus, David. *Commentarius in Matthaeum Evangelistam*. Wittenberg: Printed by Johannes Crato, 1558. Digital copy online at prdl.org.

Close, George. *The Rock of Religion: Christ, Not Peter, as It Was Delivered in Certaine Sermons upon Math. 16*. London: A. Mathewes for Mathew Law, 1624. Digital copy online at EEBO.

Corner, Christoph. *Oikonomia Evangeliorum*. Frankfurt an der Oder: Eichornus, 1567. Digital copy online at prdl.org.

Cosin, John. *The Works of the Right Reverend Father in God John Cosin, Lord Bishop of Durham*. 5 vols. Oxford: John Henry Parker, 1843–1855. Digital copy online at books.google.com.

Coverdale, Miles. *Fruitfull Lessons upon the Passion, Buriall, Resurrection, Ascension, and of the Sending of the Holy Ghost Gathered Out of the Foure Euangelists: With a Plaine Exposition of the Same*. London: T. Scarleth, 1593. Digital copy online at EEBO.

Coxe, Benjamin. *Some Mistaken Scriptures Sincerely Explained in Answer to One Infected with Some Pelagian Errours.* London: Thomas Paine, 1646. Digital copy online at books.google.com.

Cranmer, Thomas. *Certayne Sermons, or, Homilies, Appoynted by the Kynges Majestie.* London: Edwarde Whitchurche, 1547. Digital copy online at EEBO.

———. *A Defence of the True and Catholike Doctrine of the Sacrament of the Body and Bloud of our Saviour Christ.* London: Reynold Wolfe, 1550. Digital copy online at EEBO.

———. *Miscellaneous Writings and Letters of Thomas Cranmer.* Edited by John Edmund Cox for the Parker Society. Cambridge: Cambridge University Press, 1846. Digital copy online at books.google.com.

Crompe, John. *Hebdomada Magna, or, The Great Week of Christ's Passion. Handled by Way of Exposition upon the Fourth Article of the Apostles' Creed: He Suffered Under Pontius Pilate; Was Crucified, Dead, Buried.* London: Stephen Bulkley for Henry Twyford, 1641. Digital copy online at EEBO.

Denck, Hans. *Selected Writings of Hans Denck, 1500–1527.* Edited by Edward J. Furcha with Ford Lewis Battles. Lewiston, NY: Edwin Mellen Press, 1989.

Denison, Stephen. *The White Wolfe, or, A Sermon Preached at Paul's Crosse.* London: G. Miller for R. Milbourne, 1627. Digital copy online at EEBO.

Dent, Arthur. *A Learned and Fruitful Exposition upon the Lord's Prayer.* London: For N. Bourne, 1613. Digital copy online at EEBO.

D'Espagne, John. *The Use of the Lord's Prayer, Vindicated and Asserted Against the Objections of Innovators, and Enthusiasts.* Translated by C. M. D. M. London: Ruth Raworth for Richard Whitaker, 1646.

Dickson, David. *A Brief Exposition of the Evangel of Jesus Christ According to Matthew.* London: For R. Smith, 1651. Digital copy online at EEBO.

Diodati, Giovanni. *Pious and Learned Annotations upon the Holy Bible Expounding the Difficult Places Thereof Learnedly, and Plainly: With Other Things of Great Importance.* London: T.B. for Nicolas Fussell, 1643. Digital copy online at EEBO.

Donne, John. *Eighty Sermons Preached by That Learned and Reverend Divine John Donne.* London: For R. Royston and R. Marriot, 1640. Digital copy online at EEBO.

———. *Twenty-Six Sermons Preached by That Learned and Reverend Divine John Donne.* London: Thomas Newcomb, 1661. Digital copy online at EEBO.

Dorsche, Johann Georg. *In Quator Evangelistas Commentarius: per Solidam Apodixin, Analsin, Exegesin, Harmoniamitem, ac Parallelismum, verum sensum exhibens, falsum refutans.* Hamburgi: Sumptibus G. Liebernickelii, Typis N. Spiringii haeredum, 1706. Digital copy online at prdl.org.

Eachard, John. *The Axe Against Sin and Error; and the Truth Conquering. A Sermon on Matthew 3.10.* London: Matthew Simmons, 1646. Digital copy online at EEBO.

Erasmus, Desiderius. *Desderii Erasmi Roterodami Opera Omnia.* Edited by Jean LeClerc. Leiden: Van der Aa, 1704–1706. 10 vols. Reprint, Hildesheim: Georg Olms, 1961–1962.

———. *The New Testament Scholarship of Erasmus: An Introduction with Erasmus' Prefaces and Ancillary Writings.* Edited by Robert D. Sider. CWE 41. Toronto: University of Toronto Press, 2019.

———. *Paraphrase on Matthew.* Translated and annotated by Dean Simpson. Contributing editor Robert D. Sider. CWE 45. Toronto: University of Toronto Press, 2008.

Estey, George. *Certaine Godly and Learned Expositions upon Divers Parts of Scripture.* London: J. Roberts for Richard Banckworth, 1603. Digital copy online at EEBO.

Foxe, John. *Writings of John Foxe, Bale, and Coverdale.* London: W. Clowes and Sons for the Religious Tract Society, 1831. Digital copy online at books.google.com.

Fuller, Thomas. *A Fast Sermon Preached on Innocents' Day*. London: L. N. and R. C. for John Williams, 1642. Digital copy online at EEBO.

Gell, Robert. *Noah's Flood Returning: Or, A Sermon Preached August the 7th, 1655*. London: J. L. to be sold by Giles Calvert, 1655. Digital copy online at EEBO.

Gerhard, Johann. *Annotationes Posthumae in Evangelium D. Matthaei, Apostoli & Evangelistae*. Jena: Georgi Sengenwaldi, 1663. Digital copy online at prdl.org.

A Godlye Sermon Preached Before the Queens Most Excellent Majestie upon the 17, 18, 19 Verses of the 16 Chapter of S. Mathew. London: John Windet for John Perin, 1585.

Gomarus, Franciscus. *Examen Controversiarum De Genealogia Christi* (1627). In *Opera Theologica Omnia, Maximam Partem Posthuma: Suprema Autoris Voluntate à Discipulis Edita. Cum Indicibus Necessariis*. Edited by Johannes Vereem Adolphus Sibelius Martinus Ubbenius. Amsterdam: Joannis Janssonii, 1644.

———. *Illustrium ac Selectorum ex Evangelio Mattaei, Locorum Explicatio*. In *Opera Theologica Omnia, Maximam Partem Posthuma: Suprema Autoris Voluntate à Discipulis Edita. cum Indicibus Necessariis*. Edited by Johannes Vereem Adolphus Sibelius Martinus Ubbenius. Amsterdam: Joannis Janssonii, 1644.

Greiffenberg, Catharina Regina von. *Meditations on the Incarnation, Passion, and Death of Jesus Christ*. Edited and translated by Lynne Tatlock. The Other Voice in Early Modern Europe. Chicago: University of Chicago Press, 2009.

Grindal, Edmund. *A Sermon at the Funeral Solemnitie of the Most High and Mighty Prince Ferdinandus*. London: John Day, 1564. Digital copy online at EEBO.

Grotius, Hugo. *Annotationes in Novum Testamentum. Volumen I. Continens Annotationes ad Matth. I–XIII*. Gronigen: W. Zuidema, 1826. Digital copy online at prdl.org.

Grumbach, Argula von. *Argula von Grumbach: A Woman's Voice in the Reformation*. Edited by Peter Matheson. Edinburgh: T&T Clark, 1995.

———. *Schriften*. Edited by Peter Matheson. Quellen und Forshungen zur Reformationgeschichte 83. Heidelberg: Gütersloher Verlagshaus, 2010.

Hall, Henry. *Heaven Ravished: Or, A Glorious Prize, Achieved by an Heroicall Enterprize*. London: J. Raworth for Samuel Gellibrand, 1644. Digital copy online at EEBO.

Hall, Joseph. *Contemplations on the Historical Passages of the Old and New Testaments*. 8 vols. London: T. Nelson and Sons, 1860.

Hammond, Henry. *A Paraphrase and Annotations upon All the Books of the New Testament, Briefly Explaining All the Difficult Places Thereof*. New ed. in 4 vols. Oxford: Oxford University Press, 1845. Digital copies online at archive.org.

Hemmingsen, Niels. *A Postill, or, Exposition of the Gospels That Are Usually Red in the Churches of God*. Translated by A. Golding. London: H. Bynneman for L. Harrison and G. Byshop, 1569. Digital copy online at EEBO.

Hieron, Samuel. *The Discoverie of Hypocrisie in Two Sermons upon Matthew 3. Verse 10. And Three Other, Called the Perfect Patterne of True Conversion, upon Matth. 13. Ver. 44*. London: T. Creed for T. Man, 1609. Digital copy online at books.google.com.

Hooper, John. *Later Writings of Bishop Hooper*. Edited for the Parker Society by Charles Nevinson. Cambridge: University Press, 1852. Digital copy online at hathitrust.org.

Hoskin, John. *A Sermon upon the Parable of the King That Taketh an Accompt of His Servants*. London: G. Eld for J. Wright, 1609.

Howson, John. *A Sermon Preached at Paules Crosse the 4 of December 1597*. London: A. Hatfield for Thomas Adams, 1597. Digital copy online at EEBO.

Hubmaier, Balthasar. *Balthasar Hubmaier: Theologian of Anabaptism*. Translated and edited by H. Wayne Pipkin and John H. Yoder. Classics of the Radical Reformation 5. Scottdale, PA: Herald Press, 1989.

Hunnius, Aegidius. *Commentarius in Evangelium secundum Matthaeum*. Frankfurt: Johannes Spieffi, 1595. Digital copy online at prdl.org.

Jackson, Thomas. *Christ's Answer unto John's Question: Or, An Introduction to the Knowledge of Jesus Christ, and Him Crucified*. London: G. Purslow for J. Clarke, 1625. Digital copy online at EEBO.

———. *The Knowledge of Christ Jesus. Or The Seventh Book of Commentaries upon the Apostles Creed: Containing the First and General Principles of Christian Theologie; With the More Immediate Principles Concerning the True Knowledge of Christ. Divided into Foure Sections*. London: M. Flesher for J. Clarke, 1634. Digital copy online at EEBO.

———. *The Works of the Reverend and Learned Divine, Thomas Jackson*. 3 vols. Edited by Barnabas Oley. London: J. Macock for John Martyn, Richard Chiswell, and Joseph Clark, 1673.

Jansen, Cornelius. *Tetrateuchus sive Commentarius in Sancta Jesu Christi Evangelia*. 2 vols. Avenione: Typis Francisci Seguin, via Bouquerie, 13, 1853. Digital copy online at prdl.org.

Johnson, Francis. *A Short Treatise Concerning the Exposition of Those Words of Christ, Tell the Church, &c. Mat. 19. 17*. Amsterdam, 1611. Digital copy online at EEBO.

Joris, David. *The Anabaptist Writings of David Joris*. Translated and edited by Gary K. Waite. CRR 7. Scottdale, PA: Herald Press, 1994.

Karlstadt, Andreas Bodenstein von. *The Essential Carlstadt*. Translated and edited by E. J. Furcha. CRR 8. Scottdale, PA: Herald Press, 1995.

Knox, John. *The Works of John Knox*. Collected and edited by David Laing. 6 vols. Edinburgh: For the Bannatyne Club, 1855. Digital copy online at books.google.com.

Kolb, Robert, and Timothy J. Wengert, eds. *The Book of Concord: The Confessions of the Evangelical Lutheran Church*. Minneapolis: Fortress, 2000.

Lamb, Thomas. *Absolute Freedom from Sin by Christ's Death for the World*. London: H. H. for Larnar, Calvert, Moon and Brewster, 1656. Digital copy online at books.google.com.

Lapide, Cornelius à. *Commentaria in Vetus et Novum Testamentum: Commentaria in Quatuor Evangelia*. 2 vols. Antwerp: Nutium, 1639. Digital copy online at prdl.org.

Latimer, Hugh. *Master Hugh Latimer, Seven Sermons Before Edward VI* [English Reprints edition]. Edited by Edward Arber. London: A. Constable, 1895. Digital copy online at books.google.com.

———. *Select Sermons and Letters of Dr. Hugh Latimer*. London: The Religious Tract Society, 1830. Digital copy online at books.google.com.

Lefèvre d'Étaples, Jacques. *Commentarii Initiatorii in Quatuor Evangelia*. Basil: Cratandri, 1523. Digital copy online at prdl.org.

Liechty, Daniel, ed. *Early Anabaptist Spirituality: Selected Writings*. Classics of Western Spirituality. Mahwah, NJ: Paulist Press, 1994.

Lightfoot, John. *The Harmony, Chronicle, and Order of the New Testament*. London: A.M. for Simon Miller, 1655. Digital copy online at EEBO.

———. *The Harmony of the Four Evangelists, Among Themselves, and with the Old Testament*. London: R. Cotes for Andrew Crooke, 1644. Digital copy online at EEBO.

Lushington, Thomas [Jones, Robert, pseud.]. *The Resurrection Rescued from the Souldiers Calumnies*. London: For Richard Lownds, 1659. Digital copy online at EEBO.

Luther, Martin. *Annotationes in Aliquot Capita Matthei (1538)*. In *Opera Omnia Domini Martini Lutheri*. Wittenberg: Per Iohannem Lufft, 1554.

———. *The Complete Sermons of Martin Luther: Sermons on Gospel Texts.* 7 vols. Edited by Eugene F. A. Klug. Grand Rapids: Baker Books, 2000.

———. *D. Martin Luthers Werke, Kritische Gesamtausgabe: Deutsche Bibel.* 12 vols. Weimar: Hermann Böhlaus Nachfolger, 1906–1961. Digital copies online at archive.org.

———. *D. Martin Luthers Werke, Kritische Gesamtausgabe: [Schriften].* 73 vols. Weimar: Hermann Böhlaus Nachfolger, 1883–2009. Digital copies online at archive.org.

———. *Luther's Works* [= "American Edition"]. 82 vols. planned. St. Louis: Concordia; Philadelphia: Fortress, 1955–1986; 2009–.

———. *The Precious and Sacred Writings of Martin Luther.* 14 vols. Edited by John Nicholas Lenker. Minneapolis: Lutherans in All Lands, 1904–1907.

———. *Thirty Foure Special and Chosen Sermons of Dr. Martin Luther.* Translated by William Gace. London: Thomas Paine for Francis Tyton, 1649.

Maldonado, Juan de. *A Commentary on the Holy Gospels: S. Matthew's Gospel.* 2 vols. Translated and edited by George J. Davie. London: John Hodges, 1888. Digital copy online at prdl.org.

Marlorat, Augustin, ed. *A Catholike and Ecclesiasticall Exposition of the Holy Gospell After S. Mathewe: Gathered Out of All the Singular and Aproved Deuines (Which the Lorde Hath Geven to Hys Church).* Translated by Thomas Timme. London: Thomas Marshe, 1570. Digital copy online at EEBO.

Marpeck, Pilgram. *The Writings of Pilgram Marpeck.* Edited by William Klassen and Walter Klaassen. CRR 2. Scottdale, PA: Herald Press, 1978.

Marshall, Stephen. *A Sermon Preached to the Honorable House of Commons Assembled in Parliament.* London: Richard Cotes for Steven Botwell, 1647. Digital copy online at EEBO.

Mayer, John. *A Commentarie upon the New Testament.* 7 vols. London: Thomas Cotes for John Bellamie, 1631.

———. *A Treasury of Ecclesiastical Expositions, upon the Difficult and Doubtful Places of the Scriptures.* London, 1622.

Melanchthon, Philipp. *Philippi Melanthonis Opera Quae Supersunt Omnia.* 28 vols. Corpus Reformatorum 1–28. Edited by C. G. Bretschneider. Halle: C. A. Schwetschke, 1834–1860. Digital copy online at archive.org.

Mocket, Thomas. *Gospell Duty and Dignity. A Discourse of the Duty of a Christians, and Their Priviledges by Christ, Grounded on Matthew 13.46.* London: A. M. for Christopher Meredith, 1648. Digital copy online at books.google.com.

Morley, Henry. *The Cleansing of the Leper.* London: H. Lownes for C. Knight, 1609. Digital copy online at EEBO.

Müntzer, Thomas. *The Collected Works of Thomas Müntzer.* Edited by Peter Matheson. Edinburgh: T&T Clark, 1988.

Murcot, John. *Several Works of Mr. John Murcot.* London: R. White for Francis Tyton, 1657. Digital copy online at EEBO.

Musculus, Wolfgang. *In Evangelistam Matthaeum Commentarii tribus tomis digesti.* Basel: Johannes Herwagen, 1556. Digital copy online at prdl.org.

Odingsells, Charles. *Two Sermons, Lately Preached at Langar in the Valley of Belvoir.* London: W. Stansby, sold by J. Parker, 1620. Digital copy online at EEBO.

Oecolampadius, Johannes. *Enarratio in Evangelium Matthaei.* Edited by Oswald Mykonius. Basel: Andreas Cratander, 1536. Digital copy online at prdl.org.

Pagitt, Ephraim. *The Mysticall Wolfe: Set Forth in a Sermon Preached in the Church of Edmond the King, in Lombard-Street.* London: Marie Okes to be sold by Robert Trot, 1645. Digital copy online at EEBO.

Pareus, David. *Theologi Archipalatini in S. Matthae Evangelium Commentarius.* Oxford: J. Lichfield, 1631.

Perkins, William. *An Exposition of the Lord's Praier in the Way of Cateschisme.* Edinburgh: R. Walde-graue, 1593. Digital copy online at EEBO.

———. *An Exposition of the Symbole or Creede of the Apostles According to the Tenour of the Scriptures, and the Consent of Orthodoxe Fathers of the Church.* Reviewed and corrected ed. Cambridge: John Legatt at the University Press, 1616.

Philips, Dirk. *The Writings of Dirk Philips, 1504–1568.* Translated and edited by Cornelius J. Dyck, William E. Keeney, and Alvin J. Beachy. CRR 6. Scottdale, PA: Herald Press, 1992.

Piscator, Johannes. *Analysis Logica Evangelii Secundum Matthaeum.* London: R. Field for B. Nortoni, 1594.

Polansdorf, Amandus Polanus von. *The Substance of Christian Religion.* Translated by E. Wilcocks. London: R. Field for J. Oxenbridge, 1595. Digital copy online at EEBO.

Porter, Thomas. *Spiritual Salt: Or, A Sermon on Matt 5:13.* London: T. R. and E. M. for Ralph Smith, 1651. Digital copy online at EEBO.

Rhegius, Urbanus. "A Homily or Sermon of the Famous Doctour Urbanus Rhegius of Fayth and Resurrection, upon the Gospell of Mathew, in the 9th Chapter. . . ." In Martin Luther, *A Fruitful and Godly Exposition and Declaration of the Kingdom of Christ.* London: For Gwalter Lynne, 1548.

Reynolds, Edward. *Self-Deniall: Opened and Applied in a Sermon Before the Reverend Assembly of Divines.* London: For Robert Bostock, 1646.

Rollock, Robert. *Lectures, upon the History of the Passion, Resurrection, and Ascension of Our Lord Jesus Christ.* Edinburgh: A. Hart, 1616. Digital copy online at EEBO.

Rutherfurd, Samuel. *A Sermon Preached Before the Right Honorable House of Lords, in the Abbey Church at Westminster, Wednesday, 25th Day of June 1645.* London: R.C. for Andrew Crook, 1645. Digital copy online at EEBO.

———. *The Trial and Triumph of Faith: Or, an Exposition of the History of Christ's Dispossessing of the Daughter of the Woman of Canaan.* London: John Field to be sold by Ralph Smith, 1645.

Sandys, Edwin. *Sermons of the Most Reverend Father in God.* London: John Beale for Thomas Chard, 1616.

Sarcerius, Erasmus. *In Matthaeum Evangelistam, Iusta Scholia, per omnes circumstantias ad methodi formam fere tractata.* Frankfurt: Christian Egenolff, 1538. Digital copy online at prdl.org.

Sattler, Michael. *The Legacy of Michael Sattler.* Edited by John Howard Yoder. CRR 1. Scottdale, PA: Herald Press, 1973.

Sibbes, Richard. *The Complete Works of Richard Sibbes.* 7 vols. Edited by Alexander Balloch Grosart. Edinburgh: James Nichol, 1862–1864.

Simons, Menno. *The Complete Writings of Menno Simons.* Edited by Leonard Verduin, J. C. Wenger, and Harold Stauffer Bender. Scottdale, PA: Herald Press, 1966.

Smyth, John. *A Paterne of True Prayer: A Learned and Comfortable Exposition or Commentarie upon the Lord's Prayer.* London: Felix Kyngston for Thomas Man, 1605. Digital copy online at EEBO.

Spilsbury, John. *A Treatise Concerning the Lawful Subject of Baptism.* London, 1643.

Stalham, John. *Vindiciae Redemptionis, in the Fanning and Sifting of Samuel Oates.* London: A. M. for Christopher Meredith, 1647. Digital copy online at EEBO.

Sterry, Peter. *The Teachings of Christ in the Soule.* London: R. Dawlman, 1648. Digital copy online at EEBO.

Stuart, James (King James I of England and James VI of Scotland). *Two Meditations of the King's Majesty*. London: J. Billium, 1620.

Strode, William. *A Sermon Concerning Swearing, Preached Before the King's Majesty*. Oxford: Leonard Lichfield, 1644. Digital copy online at EEBO.

Strong, William. *The Certainty of Heavenly, and the Uncertainty of Earthly Treasures*. 5th ed. London: J. R. for Benjamin Billingsley, 1656.

Taverner, Richard. *On Saynt Andrewes Day: The Gospels with Brief Sermons upon Them for All the Holy Dayes in the Yere*. London: Rycharde Bankes, 1542. Digital copy online at EEBO.

Taylor, Jeremy. *The Great Exemplar or Sanctity and Holy Life According to the Christian Institution; Described in the History of the Life and Death of the Ever-Blessed Jesus Christ, the Saviour of the Word*. In *The Whole Works of the Right Reverend Jeremy Taylor*. 10 vols. Edited by Charles Page Eden. London: Longman, Brown, Green and Longmans, 1850. Digital copy online at books.google.com.

Taylor, Thomas. *The Works of That Faithful Servant of Jesus Christ*. London: T. R. and E. M. for John Barlet the elder and John Barlet the younger, 1653. Digital copy online at books.google.com.

Theophylact of Ochrid. *In quatuor Euangelia enarrationes, denuo recognitae*. Translated by Johannes Oecolampadius. [Basel]: Andreas Cratander, 1525. Digital copy online at books.google.com.

Tillinghast, John. *Mr. Tillinghast's Eight Last Sermons*. London: M. S. for Livewell Chapman, 1655. Digital copy online at EEBO.

Tombes, John. *The Leaven of Pharisaical Will-Worship: Declared in a Sermon [Fermentum Pharisaeorum]*. 2nd ed. London: Richard Cotes for Andrew Crooke, 1643.

Trapp, John. *A Commentary or Exposition upon the Four Evangelists, and the Acts of the Apostles*. London: A. M. for John Bellamie, 1647. Digital copy online at EEBO.

Tyndale, William. *Expositions and Notes on Sundry Portions of the Holy Scriptures Together with The Practice of Prelates*. Edited by H. Walter for the Parker Society. Cambridge: Cambridge University Press, 1849. Digital copy online at books.google.com.

Udall, John. *Peter's Fall: Two Sermons upon the History of Peter's Denying Christ*. London: J. Windes and T. Judson for N. Ling, 1584. Digital copy online at EEBO.

Valdés, Juan de. *Commentary upon the Gospel of St. Matthew*. Translated by John T. Betts. London: Trübner, Ludgate Hill, 1882. Digital copy online at books.google.com.

Vaughan, Henry. *A Sermon Preached at the Public Fast, March the Eight in the Afternoon at St. Maries Oxford*. Oxford: Leonard Lichfield, 1644. Digital copy online at EEBO.

Vermigli, Peter Martyr. *Life, Letters, and Sermons*. Edited by John Patrick Donnelly. Kirksville, MO: Thomas Jefferson University Press, 1999.

———. *Loci communes*. London: J. Kyngston, 1576. Digital copy online at prdl.org.

Virel, Matthieu. "Le Sommaier de la Loy, Matthew 22:37." In *La Religion Chrestienne* (1582). Reprint ed. Geneva: Chez Eustace Vignon, 1586.

Viret, Pierre. *Exposition Familiere de L'oraison de Nostre Seigneur Jesus Christ, et des choses dignes de consyderer sur icelle, faite en forme de Dialogue*. Geneva: Jean Girard, 1551.

Ward, Richard. *Theologicall Questions, Dogmaticall Observations, and Evangelicall Essays upon the Gospel of Jesus Christ, According to St. Matthew*. London: Peter Cole, 1640. Digital copy online at EEBO.

Watson, Thomas. *The Beatitudes, or, A Discourse upon Part of Christ's Famous Sermon on the Mount*. London: Ralph Smith, 1660. Digital copy online at EEBO.

———. *A Body of Practical Divinity*. London: For Thomas Parkhurst, 1692. Digital copy online at EEBO.

Zell, Katharina Schütz. *Church Mother: The Writings of a Protestant Reformer in Sixteenth-Century Germany*. Edited and translated by Elsie McKee. The Other Voice in Early Modern Europe. Chicago: University of Chicago Press, 2006.

———. *The Writings: A Critical Edition*. Edited by Elsie McKee. Studies in Medieval and Reformation Thought. Leiden: Brill, 1999.

Zwingli, Huldrych. *Annotationes Huldrici Zwinglii in Evangelium Matthaei*. In *Huldreich Zwingli's Werke*, Erste vollstandige Ausgabe durch Melchior Schuler und Joh. Schulthess, volume 6.1. Zurich: Turici ex Officina Schulthessian, 1836. Digital copy online at books.google.com.

———. *A Briefe Rehersal of the Death, Resurrection, and Ascension of Christ, Gathered Together Oute of the Foure Euangelistes and Actes of the Apostles*. London: John Daye, 1560. Digital copy online at EEBO.

———. *The Defense of the Reformed Faith: Selected Writings of Huldrych Zwingli*. Translated by E. J. Furcha. Pittsburgh Theological Monographs. Allison Park, PA: Pickwick Publications, 1984.

———. *The Latin Works and the Correspondence of Huldreich Zwingli: Together with Selections from His German Works*. Vol. 1, *1510–1522*. Edited by Samuel Macauley Jackson. Translations by Henry Preble, Walter Lichtenstein, and Lawrence A. McLouth. New York: G. P. Putnam's Sons, 1912. Digital copy online at books.google.com.

Other Works Consulted

Bauer, David. *The Gospel of the Son of God*. Downers Grove, IL: IVP Academic, 2019.

Beckwith, Carl L., ed. *Ezekiel, Daniel*. RCS OT 13. Downers Grove, IL: IVP Academic, 2012.

Casey, Maurice. "The Jackals and the Son of Man (Matt. 8.20//Luke 9.58)." *Journal for the Study of the New Testament* 7, no. 23 (1985): 3-22.

Cummings, Brian. *The Literary Culture of the Reformation: Grammar and Grace*. Oxford: Oxford University Press, 2002.

De Jonge, Henk Jan. "Erasmus' Method of Translation in His Version of the New Testament." *Bible Translator* 37, no. 1 (1986): 135-38.

———. "*Novum Testamentum a Nobis Versum*: The Essence of Erasmus' Edition of the New Testament." *Journal of Theological Studies* 35, no. 2 (1984): 394-413.

Edwards, Mark U., Jr. *Printing, Propaganda, and Martin Luther*. Minneapolis: Fortress, 2005.

Farmer, Craig S., ed. *John 1–12*. RCS NT 3. Downers Grove, IL: IVP Academic, 2014.

Fowl, Stephen E. *Theological Interpretation of the Bible*. Cascade Companions. Eugene, OR: Cascade, 2009.

Frei, Hans W. *The Eclipse of Biblical Narrative: A Study in Eighteenth and Nineteenth Century Hermeneutics*. New Haven, CT: Yale University Press, 1974.

Krans, Jan. *Beyond What Is Written: Erasmus and Beza as Conjectural Critics of the New Testament*. New Testament Tools and Studies. Leiden: Brill, 2006.

Kreitzer, Beth, ed. *Luke*. RCS NT 3. Downers Grove, IL: IVP Academic, 2015.

Luz, Ulrich. *Matthew in History: Interpretation, Influence, and Effects*. Minneapolis: Fortress Press, 1994.

———. "The Son of Man in Matthew: Heavenly Judge or Human Christ." *Journal for the Study of the New Testament* 15, no. 48 (1992): 3-21.

Maier, Gerhard. *Biblical Hermeneutics*. Translated by Robert W. Yarbrough. Wheaton, IL: Crossway, 1994.

Marsh, William M. *Martin Luther on Reading the Bible as Christian Scripture: The Messiah in Luther's Biblical Theology and Hermeneutics*. Princeton Theological Monographs. Eugene, OR: Pickwick, 2017.

Mattox, Mickey L. "Martin Luther." In *Christian Theologies of Scripture: A Comparative Introduction*, edited by Justin S. Holcomb, 94-113. New York: New York University Press, 2006.

Minnis, Alastair. *Medieval Theory of Authorship: Scholastic Literary Attitudes in the Later Middle Ages*. 2nd ed. Philadelphia: University of Pennsylvania Press, 2010.

Muller, Richard A., and John L. Thompson, eds. *Biblical Interpretation in the Era of the Reformation: Essays Presented to David C. Steinmetz in Honor of His Sixtieth Birthday*. Grand Rapids: Eerdmans, 1996.

Ocker, Christopher. *Biblical Poetics Before Humanism and Reformation*. Cambridge: Cambridge University Press, 2002.

Pettegree, Andrew. *The Book in the Renaissance*. New Haven, CT: Yale University Press, 2010.

———. *Brand Luther: 1517, Printing, and the Making of the Reformation*. New York: Penguin, 2015.

Provan, Iain. *The Reformation and the Right Reading of Scripture*. Waco, TX: Baylor University Press, 2017.

Sarisky, Darren. *Reading the Bible Theologically*. Current Issues in Theology. Cambridge: Cambridge University Press, 2019.

Simonetti, Manlio, ed. *Matthew 1–13*. ACCS NT 1a. Downers Grove, IL: InterVarsity Press, 2001.

Stephens, W. P. "The Interpretation of the Bible in Bullinger's Early Works." *Reformation & Renaissance Review* 11, no. 3 (2009): 311-33.

Vessey, Mark. "The Tongue and the Book: Erasmus' *Paraphrases on the New Testament* and the Arts of Scripture." In *Holy Scripture Speaks: The Production and Reception of Erasmus' "Paraphrases on the New Testament,"* edited by Hilmar M. Pabel and Mark Vessey, 29-58. Toronto: University of Toronto Press, 2002.

Author and Writings Index

Subject Index

Scripture Index